The SAGE Handbook of

Intellectual Property

The SAGE Handbook of Intellectual Property

Edited by
Matthew David
and Debora Halbert

SAGE reference

Los Angeles | London | New Delhi
Singapore | Washington DC

SAGE

Los Angeles | London | New Delhi
Singapore | Washington DC

SAGE Publications Ltd
1 Oliver's Yard
55 City Road
London EC1Y 1SP

SAGE Publications Inc.
2455 Teller Road
Thousand Oaks, California 91320

SAGE Publications India Pvt Ltd
B 1/I 1 Mohan Cooperative Industrial Area
Mathura Road
New Delhi 110 044

SAGE Publications Asia-Pacific Pte Ltd
3 Church Street
#10–04 Samsung Hub
Singapore 049483

Editor: Chris Rojek
Assistant editor: Gemma Shields
Production editor: Shikha Jain
Copyeditor: Rosemary Campbell
Proofreader: Katie Forsythe
Indexer: Matthew David and Debora Halbert
Marketing manager: Michael Ainsley
Cover design: Wendy Scott
Typeset by: Ceveo Publisher Services
Printed and bound by CPI Group (UK) Ltd,
Croydon, CR0 4YY [for Antony Rowe]

MIX
Paper from responsible sources
FSC www.fsc.org FSC® C013604

At SAGE we take sustainability seriously. Most of our products are printed in the UK using FSC papers and boards. When we print overseas we ensure sustainable papers are used as measured by the Egmont grading system. We undertake an annual audit to monitor our sustainability.

Library of Congress Control Number: 2014940531

British Library Cataloguing in Publication data

A catalogue record for this book is available from the British Library

ISBN 978-1-4462-6634-2

Contents

Figures and Tables

FIGURES

TABLES

Notes on the Editors and Contributors

THE EDITORS

Matthew David teaches sociology at Durham University. His interests are in sharing and digital media. He is the author of *Peer to Peer and the Music Industry: The Criminalization of Sharing* (SAGE, 2010), *Social Research: An Introduction* (2nd Edition, with Carole D. Sutton, SAGE, 2011), *Science in Society* (Palgrave, 2005), and *Knowledge Lost in Information* (with David Zeitlyn and Jane Bex, Office of Humanities Press, 1998). He has also recently completed editing (with Peter Millward, SAGE, 2014) a four-volume collection on *Researching Society Online*. His most recent work in the area of file-sharing, live-streaming and new media has been published in *The British Journal of Sociology*, *The European Journal of Social Theory*, *Sport in Society* and *Crime, Media, Culture*, as well as in the *Oxford Handbook of Internet Studies* (Dutton ed., 2013). His research on other aspects of science and technology in society has been published recently in *Current Sociology*, *International Sociology* and *Sociology Compass*.

Debora Halbert is an Associate Professor of Political Science at the University of Hawai'i at Manoa where she teaches futures studies, public policy, and courses in law and society. In addition to being Department Chair for the political science department, Halbert is a faculty affiliate with the Hawaii Research Center for Futures Studies.

The bulk of her academic publications deal with intellectual property in the digital world, with an even more targeted focus on copyright law. Her most recent book, *The State of Copyright: The Complex Relationships of Culture Creation in a Globalized World* was published with Routledge in 2014. Her previous books include *Intellectual Property in the Information Age: The Politics of Expanding Ownership Rights* (Quorum, 1999) and *Resisting Intellectual Property* (Routledge, 2005). She has also published numerous articles on intellectual property as it relates to politics, culture, technology and the law. Her work on intellectual property is situated more broadly within a concern and interest in digital politics, the impact of information technology, and the future impacts of technology on social structures including politics, law and education. Thus, issues of file-sharing, privacy, digital politics, digital democracy, technology futures, and the concept of neuropolitics define additional research interests.

Halbert was recently a visiting scholar with Lund University's Pufendorf Institute working with members of the Lund Internet Institute on privacy, security and Internet issues. She continues to collaborate with LUii on these issues.

THE CONTRIBUTORS

Lillian Álvarez graduated in Law from the University of Havana in 1985. She has worked as a legal advisor in areas of foreign trade and investment and has 20 years' experience in the sphere of culture. She has worked as an advisor in the Cuban Ministry of Culture, in the National Center of Author's Rights and as a professor in the National Center of Higher Education for Culture in which she has given postgraduate courses in different aspects of Rights in Culture. She writes on author's rights as well as cultural rights, cultural diversity, trade treaties and other issues. Her articles have been published in journals and alternative websites. Her book, *Author? Rights: The Debate Today* was published in *Ciencias Sociales* (Social Sciences, 2006), Havana. This book engages an anti-hegemonic view on the issues. She won the Prize of Criticism of Social Sciences in her country. She has collaborated as a professor in the Latin American Program of Education at a Distance in Social Sciences (PLED). She has also participated in the Copy South Project. Currently she works in a network of intellectuals, artists and social fighters, 'In Defense of Humanity', collaborating on the subjects of access to knowledge, culture and the environment. As a poet she has published the books: *Ni el aire ni el espejo* (Neither the air nor the mirror; Editorial Extramuros, 2002); *Ya los reyes no existen* (The kings no longer exist; Editorial Abril, 2011), and *Como un cristal temblando* (Like a shimmering crystal; a personal anthology currently in press).

Anne Barron is an Associate Professor (Reader) in the Law Department at the London School of Economics, UK. Her current work centres on the relationships between public spheres, information capitalism and intellectual property rights.

Ian Brown is Associate Director of Oxford University's Cyber Security Centre and Professor of Information Security and Privacy at the Oxford Internet Institute. His research is focused on information security, privacy-enhancing technologies, and Internet regulation. He is an ACM Distinguished Scientist and BCS Chartered Fellow, and a member of the Information Commissioner's Technology Reference Panel. Since 1998 Dr Brown has variously been a trustee of Privacy International, the Open Rights Group, the Open Knowledge Foundation and the Foundation for Information Policy Research, and an adviser to Greenpeace, the Refugee Children's Consortium, Amnesty International and Creative Commons UK. He has consulted for the United Nations, Council of Europe, OECD, US Department of Homeland Security, JP Morgan, Credit Suisse, Allianz, McAfee, BT, the BBC, the European Commission, the Cabinet Office, Ofcom, and the National Audit Office.

Professor Brown's work has been covered by the BBC, CNN, CBC, Al Jazeera, and numerous newspapers and magazines. He has written for *The Financial Times*, *Daily Telegraph*, *New Statesman* and *Guardian*. In 2004 he was voted one of the 100 most influential people in the development of the Internet in the UK over the previous decade.

Hugo Cadenas is Assistant Professor in the Department of Anthropology at the University of Chile, has a PhD in Sociology at the University Ludwig Maximilian of Munich, Germany, a Master degree in Anthropology and Development at the University of Chile and a Bachelor in Social Anthropology at the same University. His areas of research include sociology of law, theory of social systems, anthropological theory, culture theory and socio-environmental issues. He is currently the editor of the journal of social sciences *Revista Mad – Universidad de Chile*.

Margaret Chon has been an active scholar and teacher of intellectual property and critical theory since joining the Seattle University School of Law faculty in 1996. She is currently the Donald & Lynda Horowitz Professor for the Pursuit of Justice, and was formerly Associate Dean for Research. She is the author of over 50 articles, book chapters and review essays on both intellectual property and on race. Professor Chon explores the global governance dimensions of intellectual property, especially their distributional consequences and social justice implications. Her immediate research projects include examining the role of certification marks in ensuring quality through global value networks, and exploring the role of public-private partnerships in providing access to IP-protected goods. Additional biographical information can be found at: www.law.seattleu.edu/faculty/faculty-profiles/margaret-chon.

Rosemary J. Coombe is the Tier One Canada Research Chair in Law, Communication and Culture at York University in Toronto, where she teaches in the Communication and Culture Joint PhD/MA Programme, the Sociolegal Studies Graduate Programme and the graduate program in Anthropology. She holds a joint PhD. in law and anthropology from Stanford University and publishes widely in anthropology, law and sociolegal studies. . Her work addresses the social and cultural implications of intellectual property, the protection of traditional knowledge and traditional cultural expressions, the politics of cultural heritage and cultural property protections and the intersection of these with international human rights practices. Her forthcoming book, *The Knowledge Economy and its Cultures*, explores the political work that cultural inscriptions are accomplishing under conditions of neoliberalism. Her scholarship may be found at www.yorku.ca/rcoombe

Colin Darch is presently a researcher in the Democratic Governance and Rights Unit in the Faculty of Law at the University of Cape Town. In a career spanning over 40 years he has worked in universities and research centres in Ethiopia, Tanzania, Mozambique, Zimbabwe and Brazil. He holds a doctorate in social and economic analysis from the University of Bradford in the United Kingdom. Apart from his interest in intellectual property issues, Darch has written extensively on access to information, and is the co-author, with Peter G. Underwood, of *Freedom of Information in the Developing World: The Citizen, the State and Models of Openness* (Oxford: Chandos, 2010).

Lisa Dobbin holds an MA in Communication and Culture, an interdisciplinary program run jointly by York and Ryerson Universities in Toronto. Her writing has been published in a number of outlets and she is an editor of the forthcoming volume, *Archives in Visual Art and Theory: Estonia and Beyond* (Estonian Academy of Arts, 2015).

Jake Dunagan is Global Foresight Lead at verynice design studio, a social enterprise based in LA and Austin. TX. He is a founder, and remains an affiliate, of the Governance Futures Lab at the Institute for the Future. Jake's work has been centred on the concept of social invention and especially how institutions, organizations and societies are adapting to the Neurocentric Age, a time of unprecedented capacity to view and modify the mind. He has helped create new political systems design tools and structures of citizen participation, as well as led research in comprehensive cognitive design, judicial foresight, kids' technologies, and the future of work. Jake also creates visual media, interactive experiences, and public projects that inject alternative visions of the future into the mental ecology of the present.

Graham Dutfield is a law professor at the University of Leeds, where he is Director of the LLM in Intellectual Property Law. His research on intellectual property crosses several disciplines, including law, history, politics and philosophy. More general scholarly interests include the law, the science and business of creativity and technical innovation from the enlightenment to the present, especially in the life sciences. Other research areas include intellectual property and access to knowledge, human rights, sustainable development, health, agriculture, genetics, biotechnology, traditional knowledge and bioprospecting. His most recent books are *Knowledge Management and Intellectual Property* (with S. Arapostathis, Edward Elgar, 2013), *Intellectual Property and Human Development: Current Trends and Future Scenarios* (with T. Wong, Cambridge University Press, 2010), and *Intellectual Property Rights and the Life Science Industries: Past, Present and Future*, 2nd edition (World Scientific Publishing, 2009).

Lee Edwards is Associate Professor in Communication and PR in the School of Media and Communication, University of Leeds. She is author of *Power, Diversity and Public Relations* (Routledge, 2014), co-author of *Understanding Copyright: Intellectual Property in the Digital Age* (SAGE, 2015), and co-editor of *Public Relations, Society and Culture: Theoretical and Empirical Explorations* (Routledge, 2011). She has published widely on public relations and the operation of power.

Andrew J. Eisenberg received his PhD in ethnomusicology from Columbia University in 2009, and is currently Visiting Assistant Professor of Music at NYU Abu Dhabi. He has carried out extensive research on sound and social relations in Mombasa, Kenya, with the support of Fulbright Hays and the Social Science Research Council; and on the music recording industry in Nairobi, Kenya, under the auspices of the European Research Council-funded 'Music, Digitisation, Mediation' research programme. Among his recent publications is the article 'Hip Hop and Cultural Citizenship on Kenya's "Swahili Coast"' (*Africa* 82:4), which won the 2013 Richard Waterman prize from the Popular Music Section of the Society for Ethnomusicology. He is now completing a monograph based on his research in Mombasa, Kenya, entitled *Sound and Citizenship: Islam, Aurality, and Social Belonging on the Kenyan Coast*.

Daniel Gervais is a Professor of Law at Vanderbilt Law School where he focuses on international intellectual property law and is the Director of the Vanderbilt Intellectual Property Program. He spent 10 years researching and addressing policy issues on behalf of the World Trade Organization (WTO), the World Intellectual Property Organization (WIPO), the International Confederation of Societies of Authors and Composers (CISAC) and Copyright Clearance Center, Inc. (CCC). He is the author of *The TRIPS Agreement: Drafting History and Analysis* (Sweet & Maxwell, 2010), a leading guide to the treaty that governs international intellectual property rights. Before joining Vanderbilt Law School in 2008, Professor Gervais was acting dean of the Common Law Section at the University of Ottawa, where he also served as vice-dean for research and received funding for his research from the Social Sciences and Humanities Research Council of Canada and from the Ontario Ministry of Research and Innovation. Before entering the academy, he practised law with Clark Woods and as a partner with the technology law firm BCF in Montreal. He also served as a consultant and legal officer at the WTO, as Head of the Copyright Projects section of the WIPO, and as vice-president of international relations at CCC. In addition, he chaired the sectoral work on culture, communications and information at the Canadian Commission for UNESCO, and was a consultant with the Paris-based Organisation for Economic Cooperation and Development. Professor Gervais is a panellist (domain name) at the WIPO Arbitration and Mediation Centre. He has been a visiting professor at numerous international universities, a visiting scholar at Stanford Law School, and is a visiting lecturer at the University of Amsterdam. In 2012 he was the Gide

Loyrette Nouel Visiting Chair at Sciences Po Law School in Paris. He is editor-in-chief of the peer-reviewed *Journal of World Intellectual Property* and editor of www.tripsagreement.net/.

Shubha Ghosh is the Vials Research Fellow and George Young Bascom Professor of Business Law and Elvehjem-Bascom Professor of Law at the University of Wisconsin. He has authored numerous scholarly articles and book chapters as well as several books in the fields of intellectual property, competition law and policy, international law and legal theory. At UW, Professor Ghosh currently teaches Intellectual Property, the Transactional Intellectual Property Seminar, and rotates among Patent, Copyright, and International Intellectual Property. Professor Ghosh has also worked with the World Intellectual Property Organization on the relationship between traditional knowledge and legal systems. Professor Ghosh's book *Identity and Invention* (focusing on human genome patenting and personalized medicine) was published by Cambridge University Press in 2012. He is researching a second book project comparing copyright and patent law in colonial India with developments in copyright and patent law since Independence in 1947. The book project is being considered for publication by Oxford University Press. Professor Ghosh is an author of numerous casebooks and teaching materials, including *Transactional Intellectual Property* (Lexis-Nexis 2012), now in its second edition.

Daniel Huizenga is a doctoral student in Socio-Legal Studies at York University. His research focuses on indigenous and customary land rights in South Africa, with a particular interest in how discourses of 'indigenous' and 'customary' are used by advocates, non-governmental organizations and legal practitioners. He received his BA in International Development Studies from Trent University in 2008 and his MA in Socio-Legal Studies from York University in 2010.

Sarah Ives addresses the connections between race, indigeneity, and natural resources in South Africa in her research. Based on 14 months of ethnographic fieldwork in the rural Western Cape between 2009 and 2013, her dissertation, 'Tea Stories: Cultivating Indigeneity in South Africa's Western Cape', explored the political, social and ecological relations in the farming of rooibos tea. Her current project examines race theory, politics and activism in a time of climate change. This research complements her previous work on ethnicity, television and development in South Africa. She received her doctorate in Anthropology from Stanford in 2014 and her Masters degree in Geography from the University of Washington in 2006. In 2014 Sarah will serve as a Postdoctoral Fellow in Stanford's 'Thinking Matters' program in liberal education.

Andrew Kirton is a Lecturer in the Department of Sociology, Social Policy & Criminology at the University of Liverpool. His analyses of the development of 'anti-file-sharing legislation' and of conflicts surrounding the circulation of intellectual property online reflect a broad interest in the relationship between culture, media and economy.

Bethany Klein is Senior Lecturer in Media and Communication in the School of Media and Communication, University of Leeds. She is author of *As Heard on TV: Popular Music in Advertising* (Ashgate, 2009) and co-author of *Understanding Copyright: Intellectual Property in the Digital Age* (SAGE, 2015).

William R. Kramer has a BS in wildlife biology, an MA in Environmental Policy and a PhD in Political Science (Futures Studies). He has worked as a wildlife biologist for the Smithsonian

Institution and the US Fish and Wildlife Service as Chief of the Branch of Endangered Species Recovery and Consultation. He subsequently taught biology and bioethics. His interests in astrobiology brought him to the University of Hawaii where he completed his dissertation regarding the relationship between bioethics and concepts of the ownership of life in the context of space exploration. As part of that work, he spent two weeks in a Mars simulation habitat in the high desert of Utah, provided mission support for NASA's Hawaii Space Exploration Analog and Simulation, and lectures at the International Space University in Strasbourg, France and elsewhere on a range of astrobiology and bioethics topics. He lives in Kailua, Hawaii.

Greg Lastowka is a Professor of Law at Rutgers School of Law-Camden and co-director of the Rutgers Institute for Information Policy & Law. He teaches and researches in the areas of intellectual property and Internet law. He is the author of *Virtual Justice* (Yale University Press, 2010).

David Lee is Lecturer in Cultural Industries and Communication in the School of Media and Communication, University of Leeds. He has published articles on creative labour and cultural policy in such journals as *Media, Culture and Society*, *International Journal of Cultural Policy* and *Television and New Media.*

Jyh-An Lee teaches Copyright, Patent, Intellectual Property Law, and Internet Law in the Faculty of Law at The Chinese University of Hong Kong. He holds a JSD from Stanford Law School and an LLM from Harvard Law School. Dr Lee is currently an advisory committee member for Copyright Amendment in the Taiwan Intellectual Property Office (TIPO) at the Ministry of Economic Affairs, and a member of the advisory board of the European Center for E-Commerce and Internet Law in Vienna. Before starting his academic career, he was a practising lawyer in Taiwan specializing in technology and business transactions.

Susanna H.S. Leong is an Associate Professor at the NUS Business School, National University of Singapore. Susanna received her LLB (Hons) from the National University of Singapore and her LLM (with Merit) from University College London, University of London. She teaches business-related law courses to undergraduate and graduate business students. Her research interests are in intellectual property and technology-related laws. She has published in several international and local academic journals. She is also the author of *Intellectual Property Law of Singapore* (Academy Publishing, 2013). Susanna is the Vice-Dean, Graduate Studies Office, NUS Business School. She is a Senior Fellow at the Intellectual Property Academy of Singapore. She is a member of the WIPO Domain Name Panel and a member of The Regional Centre for Arbitration, Kuala Lumpur (RCAKL) Panel. She is also a member of the Singapore Copyright Tribunal.

Raizel Liebler is the Head of Faculty Scholarship Initiatives at The John Marshall Law School and is a Berkman Center for Internet & Society at Harvard University Affiliate starting in Fall 2015. Raizel frequently presents and writes about the interaction between new, disruptive technologies and the law, including focusing on intellectual property, copyright, and rights of publicity. Her work has been cited by the California Supreme Court and in the New York Times. She is the founding editor of a well-regarded blog about technology and popular culture at The Learned Fangirl (www.thelearnedfangirl.com/).

Salvador Millaleo is Assistant Professor at the Center of Studies on Informatic Law at the University of Chile. He is a lawyer and possesses a doctorate (DPhil) in Sociology from the

University of Bielefeld, Germany. He was a research fellow at the University of Bielefeld and at the Max Planck Institute for Foreign and International Criminal Law in Freiburg. His research topics currently include sociology of law, Internet regulation and society, cyberpolitics, digital activism, intellectual property and traditional knowledge.

Peter Millward is Senior Lecturer in Sociology at Liverpool John Moores University. He has published widely in the field of the sociology of sport, with particular interests in broadcasting rights, transnational business patterns and fan movements in association football. His most recent monograph is *The Global Football League: Transnational Networks, Social Movements and Sport in the New Media Age* (Palgrave, 2011).

Giles Moss is Lecturer in Media Policy in the School of Media and Communication, University of Leeds. His research focuses on media policy and the relationship between media and politics. He is co-author of *Understanding Copyright: Intellectual Property in the Digital Age* (SAGE, 2015) and has published articles in a range of journals including *New Media & Society*, *The Journal of Information Technology & Politics* and *Political Studies*.

Dave O'Brien is a lecturer in Cultural and Creative Industries at City University London. He specializes in cultural value and urban cultural policy issues and has a PhD in Sociology from the University of Liverpool. His most recent book, *Cultural Policy*, was published by Routledge in 2014. His next book. *How Government Works*, will be published by Palgrave in 2015.

Chidi Oguamanam obtained his legal training in Ife and Lagos in South Western Nigeria, before completing advanced degrees in law at the University of British Columbia. He is called to the Bar in Nigeria and Canada. With strong legal practice experience, he consults extensively with firms, NGOs, States, and intergovernmental and subnational bodies. He is a professor at the Centre for Law, Technology and Society in the Faculty of Law, University of Ottawa. His interdisciplinary research interests focus on various legal and policy issue linkages to intellectual property law, especially in the areas of biotechnology, biodiversity, genetic resources, pharmaceuticals, agricultural knowledge systems, food security and food systems; public health law and policy; indigenous peoples and indigenous knowledge; and human rights and the global governance of knowledge in development contexts. Widely published in law and interdisciplinary platforms, he is the author of *International Law and Indigenous Knowledge* (University of Toronto, 2006), *Intellectual Property in Global Governance* (Routledge, 2012), and co-editor of *Innovation and Intellectual Property: Collaborative Dynamics in Africa* (University of Cape Town, 2013), and *Knowledge* and *Innovation in Africa: Scenario for the Future* (University of Cape Town, 2013).

Claudy Op den Kamp is a PhD candidate at Transtechnology Research, Plymouth University, UK, finalizing a research project investigating the relationship between copyright ownership, digitization of archival film and the construction of film history. She is a graduate of the University of Amsterdam (Film and Television Studies) and the University of East Anglia (Film Archiving). She has worked as Haghefilm Conservation's Account Manager in Amsterdam and prior to that as a Film Restoration Project Leader at the Nederlands Filmmuseum. Currently, she works as a research assistant at the University of Zurich on a research project for the digitization and restoration of archival film.

Alex Perullo is an Associate Professor of Anthropology and African studies at Bryant University (USA). He has published two books on Tanzanian music: *Live from Dar es Salaam:*

Popular Music and Tanzania's Music Economy (2011) and *Artistic Rights: Copyright Law for East African Musicians, Artists, Writers, and Other Authors* (2012). He has also published articles in academic journals and edited volumes on migration, youth cultures, ageing and popular music in Africa. He is currently working on a book that examines ownership, rights and music in Tanzania, Ghana and the African diaspora.

Fiona Philip is currently a Research Fellow on the AHRC-funded project Pararchive: Open Access Community Storytelling and the Digital Archive in the School of Media and Communication, University of Leeds. She was previously Postdoctoral Research Assistant for the ESRC-funded project Communicating Copyright: An Exploration of Copyright Discourses in the Digital Age.

Sarah Louisa Phythian-Adams researches and lectures in economics at the University of Liverpool. Her research interests are particularly focused on Arts & Cultural Economics and the impact of the creative industries sector, as well as behavioural economics and other applications of economic theory in 'non-standard' markets.

Matthew Rimmer is an Australian Research Council Future Fellow, an Associate Professor and Associate Director of Research at the ANU College of Law, and an Associate Director of the Australian Centre for Intellectual Property in Agriculture. He holds a BA (Hons) and a University Medal in literature, and a LLB (Hons) from the Australian National University. Rimmer received a PhD in law from the University of New South Wales for his dissertation on 'The Pirate Bazaar: The Social Life of Copyright Law'. He is a member of the ANU Climate Change Institute and a director of the Australian Digital Alliance. Dr Rimmer has published widely on copyright law and information technology, patent law and biotechnology, access to medicines, the plain packaging of tobacco products, clean technologies and traditional knowledge.

Dr Rimmer is the author of *Digital Copyright and the Consumer Revolution: Hands off my iPod* (Edward Elgar, 2007), *Intellectual Property and Biotechnology: Biological Inventions* (Edward Elgar, 2008) and *Intellectual Property and Climate Change: Inventing Clean Technologies* (Edward Elgar, 2011). He edited the collection, *Patent Law and Biological Inventions* (Federation Press, 2006), and co-edited the collections, *Incentives for Global Public Health: Patent Law and Access to Essential Medicines* (Cambridge University Press, 2010) and *Intellectual Property and Emerging Technologies: The New Biology* (Edward Elgar, 2012). Dr Rimmer was also a chief investigator in an Australian Research Council Discovery Project, 'Gene Patents In Australia: Options For Reform' (2003–2005), an Australian Research Council Linkage Grant, 'The Protection of Botanical Inventions'(2003), and an Australian Research Council Discovery Project, 'Promoting Plant Innovation in Australia' (2009–2011). He is currently the holder of an Australian Research Council Future Fellowship, 'Intellectual Property and Climate Change: Inventing Clean Technologies' (2011–2015).

Chris Rojek is Professor of Sociology at City University, London. He is the author of many books, the most recent of which are *Pop Music, Pop Culture* (Polity, 2011), *Fame Attack: The Inflation of Celebrity and its Consequences* (Bloomsbury, 2012) and *Event Power* (SAGE, 2013).

Jessica Silbey is a Law Professor at Suffolk University Law School in Boston, teaching in the areas of intellectual property and constitutional law. Professor Silbey's scholarly interests and expertise is in the cultural analysis of law, exploring the law beyond its doctrine to the contexts and processes in which legal relations develop and become significant for everyday actors. Professor Silbey has published widely in the field of law and film, exploring how film is used as a legal tool and how it becomes an object of legal analysis in light of its history as a cultural object and art form. Her books include *The Eureka Myth: Creators, Innovators and Everyday Intellectual Property* (Stanford University Press, 2015) and *Law and Justice on the Small Screen* (Hart Publishing, 2012). Professor Silbey received her BA from Stanford University and her JD and PhD (Comparative Literature) from the University of Michigan. After clerking for Judge Robert E. Keeton in the United States District Court for the District of Massachusetts and Judge Levin Campbell in the United States Court of Appeals for the First Circuit, she practised law in the disputes department of the Boston office of Foley Hoag LLP, focusing on intellectual property, bankruptcy and reproductive rights.

Uma Suthersanen holds a Chair in International Intellectual Property Law at Queen Mary, University of London. She is a Co-Director of Queen Mary Intellectual Property Research Institute, an Executive Committee Member of the British Literary and Artistic Copyright Association (having been the Chairman and Vice-Chairman from 2006–2013); an Executive Committee Member of the Association Littéraire et Artistique International; and a Visiting Fellow of the Intellectual Property Academy of Singapore. She holds an LL.B (Hons) from the National University of Singapore, and an LL.M and Ph.D from Queen Mary, University of London. She edits the *European Copyright and Design Reports* (Sweet & Maxwell), and is a Founding Editor of the *Queen Mary Perspectives in Intellectual Property* series (Edward Elgar). She has written extensively on copyright and design laws, and her books include *Design Law in the European Union and United States* (Sweet & Maxwell, 2010), and *Global Intellectual Property Law* (Edward Elgar, 2008, with G. Dutfield). She is currently working on the 2nd edition of *Global Intellectual Property Law*, as well as on a monograph on cultural heritage and intellectual property rights (based on a UK Arts and Humanities Research Council grant, 2010–2012). She is the director of teaching modules in *International and Comparative Copyright and Design Laws*, and in *Global Intellectual Property Law*, both in the London and Paris LL.M programmes.

John Tehranian is an academic, attorney and author. He is the Irwin R. Buchalter Professor of Law at Southwestern Law School and has previously served as a tenured Professor of Law at the University of Utah, S.J. Quinney College of Law, and as a Visiting Professor of Law at Loyola Law School. A graduate of Harvard University and Yale Law School, he is the author of dozens of articles and two books, *Whitewashed* (NYU Press, 2009) and *Infringement Nation* (Oxford University Press, 2011). He is also a founding partner of One LLP, an intellectual property and entertainment law firm where he has litigated numerous high-profile intellectual property lawsuits, including those involving Madonna, Don Henley, B.B. King, Bettie Page, Jimi Hendrix and Perez Hilton, among others. In 2013, *Variety*'s 'Legal Impact Report' recognized John as one of the world's top 50 entertainment lawyers. A frequent commentator for the broadcast and print media, he has spoken at numerous international conferences and his work has been widely cited, from testimony before Congress and decisions of the Israeli courts to amicus briefs before the United States Supreme Court and in such leading publications as the *Yale Law Journal* and *Harvard Law Review*.

Pradip Ninan Thomas is currently the Acting Head of School, School of Journalism & Communication, University of Queensland, Brisbane. He has written extensively on the political economy of communication, including a three-volume series on the media in India published by SAGE between 2010 and 2012. His latest publication is 'Public Sector Software and the Revolution: Digital Literacy in Communist Kerala', *Media, Culture & Society* 36(2): 258 (2014).

David S. Wall is Professor of Criminology at Durham University where he researches and teaches cybercrime, identity crime, policing and intellectual property crime. He has a sustained track record of funded research in these areas from the EU FP6 and FP7, ESRC, EPSRC, AHRC and other funders, he has also published a wide range of 40+ articles and 10+ books on these subjects which include: *Cybercrime and the Culture of Fear: Policing the Reassurance Gap in Cybersecurity* (Springer, forthcoming), *Policing Cybercrime* (Palgrave, 2014), *Cybercrime: The Transformation of Crime in the Information Age* (Polity, 2007, 2nd edn, 2015), *Crime and Deviance in Cyberspace* (ed., Ashgate, 2009), *Cyberspace Crime* (ed., Ashgate, 2003) and *Crime and the Internet* (ed., Routledge, 2001). He is an Academician of the Academy of Social Sciences (AcSS), a Fellow of the Royal Society of Arts (FRSA) and was a member of the ESRC Grants Assessment Panel 2009–2012. He is the Head of the School of Applied Social Sciences at Durham University and was formerly Head of the School of Law (2005–2007) and Director of the Centre for Criminal Justice (2000–2005) at the University of Leeds.

Natasha Whiteman is Lecturer in Media and Communication at the University of Leicester. She received her PhD from the Institute of Education, University of London. Her research interests include the study of media fandoms and videogame cultures on the Internet and the ethics of contemporary media audiences. She is the author of *Undoing Ethics: Rethinking Practice in Online Research* (Springer, 2012).

Peter K. Yu holds the Kern Family Chair in Intellectual Property Law and is the founding director of the Intellectual Property Law Center at Drake University Law School. He has served as Wenlan Scholar Chair Professor at Zhongnan University of Economics and Law in Wuhan, China, and as a visiting professor of law at the University of Haifa, the University of Hong Kong, the University of Strasbourg, and Washington and Lee University. Born and raised in Hong Kong, Professor Yu is a leading expert in international intellectual property and communications law. A prolific scholar and an award-winning teacher, he is the author or editor of five books and more than 100 law review articles and book chapters. He serves as the general editor of *The WIPO Journal* published by the World Intellectual Property Organization (WIPO). Professor Yu has spoken at events organized by WIPO, the International Telecommunication Union, the UN Conference on Trade and Development (UNCTAD), the UN Educational, Scientific and Cultural Organization (UNESCO), the Chinese, US and EU governments and at leading research institutions from around the world. His lectures and presentations have spanned more than 25 countries on six continents, and his publications have appeared in Chinese and English and have been translated into Arabic, French, Hausa, Japanese, Persian, Portuguese, Spanish and Vietnamese.

Martin J. Zeilinger is a media scholar and practitioner whose work focuses on digital remix culture and practices of appropriation. He holds a PhD in Comparative Literature from the University of Toronto, and was the SSHRC Banting Postdoctoral Fellow in Law & Culture at York University from 2011–2013. Currently, he teaches at the University of Toronto and at the Ontario College for Art & Design (OCAD) University, and is a faculty member at the International Summer Institute for the Cultural Study of Law held annually at Osnabrück University, Germany. He is co-editor of *Dynamic Fair Dealing* (University of Toronto Press,

2014), an interdisciplinary volume on the IP challenges faced by digital practitioners. His work on the interplay between intellectual property law and contemporary cultural practices has also been published in MIT's *Journal for Computer Music* (2014), in the *Journal of the International Assocation for the Study of Popular Music* (2012), and in the books *Sampling Media* (Oxford University Press, 2014), *The Perils of Pedagogy* (McGill-Queen's UP, 2013), and *Eyes Everywhere* (Routledge, 2012). As part of his curatorial practice in digital media, he is co-director and co-curator of the annual *Vector Game+Art Convergence Festival.*

Preface

Editing a collection of original works on intellectual property by authors from across the world, and from a wide range of academic disciplines, cannot help but to touch upon the practicalities of intellectual property rights, globalization and its limits, as well as upon the tensions that exist between different intellectual points of view regarding supposedly identical content. In bringing this collection to completion, the editors and authors were confronted with a range of issues relating to contracts, continents and content.

A Question of Contracts. Editing a collection of this magnitude creates a number of logistical difficulties, and we are not the first to have experienced them. In this regard, we were pleased to learn that SAGE, the publishers, had created an automated author/editor online 'portal' to help us manage the flow of information. Invitations to contribute, replies and acceptances, drafts, reviews, editors comments, new drafts, and final versions would all pass through and be held on this platform, promising to make the editors', and the authors', lives much easier. However, there was a problem. It is common knowledge, firstly, that many unfavourable things get buried in the 'small print' of contracts, and, secondly, that online 'click through' contracts between users and suppliers or online services are particularly notorious for gaining 'consent' even whilst the person clicking is very rarely fully 'informed'. Our portal was configured in such a fashion that we, the editors, were required to invite prospective authors to contribute chapters to the collection on themes we, the editors, were initially required to suggest, but which the authors would be fully able to alter later. Once invited to contribute the author was able to sign up via the portal by clicking the requisite button on the portal. Being a group of the world's most IP savvy intellectuals it was not surprising that our prospective authors in fact read the terms and conditions of the contracts they were required to assent to in order to 'click through' their agreement to participate via the portal. As the portal was structured in such a fashion as to require the editors to invite each author to contribute a chapter on a topic suggested by the editors, the contract was worded to make the author's contribution a 'work for hire', rather than the author's own copyrightable work. We, the authors and editors, were informed that the wording of the portal's click through contract could not be altered. This was deemed unacceptable by so many of our prospective contributors that the overall work would have ground to a halt if we had stuck with the portal. This attempted 'law as code' was however not the end of the line as we simply abandoned the portal and renegotiated the contract between publisher and authors, giving authors a clearer freedom to re-use their own work and retain control over that work in other formats.

While we as editors had initially sought to alter the contract language that would be issued to the authors, our initial efforts had been met with resistance on the part of SAGE. In fact, without the widespread revolt of so many of our authors, it is unlikely that altering the contract would have been accomplished. SAGE had indicated that it would negotiate with authors on a one-on-one basis, but such a process would have resulted in a wide and unfair distribution of rights. Only through coordinated negotiation were we able to alter the contract fairly for the group as a whole.

For those working in the arena of copyright law and its future implications, the lessons behind these contractual fights are illuminating. SAGE seeks to publish an exclusive Handbook that will cost a substantial amount of money, more money than any individual is likely to pay. The audience for such a work is, by definition, limited to University libraries. SAGE of course seeks to recoup the cost of editing and producing the volume, which it does in part by receiving all the contents of the Handbook for free from the authors. The editors in this case waived any advance because it was feared that those costs of production that could be set against any royalties due to the editors (such as in securing rights on images and graphics used, compiling the index etc.) would be more than the advance. We did not wish to end up owing SAGE for the privilege of collaborating on this Handbook. In the end the editors decided to compile the index themselves as the cost (to be deducted by SAGE from any royalties due to the editors) of having this done by someone else would have been most likely greater than the sum of all royalties due to them. As editors, we are entitled to a very small percentage of *net* sales. An indexer is paid an hourly rate. Needless to say, the political economy of academic publishing and the future of this endeavour where academics produce content for free and are not even extended the opportunity to re-produce their content in other venues where citations and visibility may be enhanced, help to illustrate the complexities and problems with contemporary copyright and contracts.

A Question of Continents. The extension of IPRs in time and space since the end of the Cold War and the rise of the World Trade Organization etc. has meant that the world is an increasingly interconnected and interdependent place (though it was already deeply so anyway). Nonetheless, this global world where everything is connected is not one where everyone is connected equally. Power and voice are distributed unevenly, and perhaps even more so now than when things were less integrated. In the creation of this collection we, the editors, made efforts to ensure that the collection brought together contributors from every continent, and we have been successful in that ambition. The editor's limitations in terms of accessing content outside the English language meant that there remains much to be said about intellectual property from a number of different perspectives. Though we made certain that translation services were available to authors whose work would require it, there are many scholars whom we simply would not have known to invite because of the language barriers that continue to exist.

We also secured funds to assist prospective contributors who wished to attend the symposium on IP held at the Durham University Institute for Advanced Study/Durham Castle in June/July 2013. Nonetheless, the spread of contributions remains biased towards North America and Western Europe; towards the English language, and from those in relatively affluent academic positions relative to less secure practitioner/activist positions. Nonetheless, this work has brought together contributors from North America, South America, The Caribbean, Europe, Africa, South Asia, East Asia and Australasia, so whilst attentive to biases in reality that are reflected in the composition of this work we also feel that we have been relatively successful in drawing upon the positive potentials of a globalized world to address, at least in part, the limits and problems associated with it.

In many ways, producing a Handbook like this was a lesson in withstanding attrition as we sought to balance publication deadlines and exacting standards of quality, with the busy lives and schedules of contributors. More time may have enabled more contributions and we regret these losses. However, our strict attitude to reviewing and of requiring authors to maintain the highest standards of depth and clarity in the work that we were willing to accept also meant that some interesting work was lost along the way. This is also the source of some regret, though the dilution of quality for quantity would have been far more regrettable. We remain grateful for the many authors who were willing and able to meet our deadlines and remain with the project to its completion.

A Question of Content. As every social scientist and humanities scholar knows organizing their colleagues is like herding cats. The idea of organizing a collection made up of as many such different disciplines as possible is therefore a task not for the faint hearted. Luckily for us we are not required to adjudicate when two lawyers and an economist take different views on the significance of the same appropriation artist; nor when political scientists and lawyers diverge on the question of traditional knowledge and bio-piracy. Ethnographers and sociologists can come to different conclusions as to the benefits of copyright for musicians in different parts of the world, whilst lawyers can disagree amongst themselves over the distinction between invention and discovery in the field of human and plant genetics. These are only some of the tensions that the keen eyed reader will note in this collection and to which we, the editors, have sought to draw some further attention to within our general introduction and section introductions. We are 'intensely relaxed' as the saying goes about such diversity in a collection such as this, and positively commend it to our readers. Whether these disciplinary tensions, as well as those that arise out of different geographies and economies, and between the different domains of IP covered in this collection, can be 'resolved' within a singular 'perspective' on IP in a global world is not something we can seek to answer in a work of this kind. However, we, the editors, are grateful to the contributions of all the authors in this collection, as their insights, complementary and in tension as they might be, have provided us with the inspiration for just such an ambitious next project – one that may try to bring some level of synthesis to the global debate about intellectual property and its future. Watch 'that' space.

Acknowledgements

Bringing together a work of this size the editors could not help but to have incurred a very great number of debts of gratitude. We might best start by thanking Chris Rojek from SAGE for initially working with us on the idea for this work, and in fact for first putting us in contact with one another in 2011. Martine Jonsrud for the early stages of practical editing, then Judi Berger and Gemma Shields for taking on this mountain of logistical headaches, technical and contractual tangles and for getting the whole thing rounded up into something close to a reasonable timescale. Then, thanks also to Shikha Jain and Sushant Nailwal from the SAGE production team and to Michael Ainsley in marketing and the copyeditor too. We would also like to extend a particular thanks to Johanna Schenner and to Ana Portela for their help with translation. Of course the contributors themselves, whose names appear throughout, deserve a special thanks as this work is fundamentally a collection of their talents and efforts. Thank you for the ideas collected here and for those 'behind the scenes' that also made things possible. Academic advice and other helpful input came from beyond the contributors alone, and we would particularly like to thank: Ann Bartow, Richard Bruce, Julie Dent, William Gallagher, Chris May, Matthew Petrasek, Laurie Onuizka, Caroline Ncube, Tobias Schonwetter, Martha Woodmansee, Siva Vaidhyanathan and Majid Yar. In 2013 we hosted an IP symposium at Durham University where contributors were invited to present their work in progress. We must thank Durham University's Institute of Advanced Study for the use of their excellent conference facilities during our 2013 IP symposium, David Held (for lending us a very nice bit of Durham Castle), Durham University's School of Applied Social Sciences for their financial assistance; and the financial support of the University of Hawaii Department of Political Science for co-sponsoring the symposium. We learned as much about the respective administrative bureaucracies from hosting this symposium as we did about intellectual property itself.

List of Acronyms

A&R	Artists and Repertoire
AAIPT	Alliance Against Intellectual Property Theft (UK) – now Alliance for IP
ABS	Access and Benefit Sharing
A2K	Access to Knowledge
ACA2K	African Copyright and Access to Knowledge
ACB	African Centre for Biosafety
ACE	Association des Cinémathèques Européennes
ACTA	Anti-Counterfeiting Trade Agreement
ACTI	Association of Science and Technology Companies – Chile
ADR	Alternative Dispute Resolutions
AGOA	African Growth and Opportunity Act
AIA	(Leahy-Smith) America Invests Act
ALCS	Authors Licensing and Collecting Service – UK
ARIPO	African Regional Intellectual Property Organization
ARV	Anti Retro Viral
ASCAP	American Society of Composers, Authors, and Publishers
ASEAN	Association of Southeast Asian Nations
ASF	Apache Software Foundation
ASILFA	Association Industrial de laboratorios Farmaceuticos - Chile
AT	Antarctic Treaty
AUTM	Association of University Technology Managers
AYUSH	Department of Ayurveda, Yoga, Unani, Siddha and Homeopathy – India
AZT	Azidothymidine
BASATA	National Arts Council – Tanzania
BBC	British Broadcasting Corporation
BCP	Biocultural Community Protocol – South Africa
BIRPI	United International Bureau for the Protection of Intellectual Property
BMI	Broadcast Music, Inc.
BPI	British Recorded Music Industry (formally the British Phonographic Industry)
BPO	Business Process Outsourcing
BRCA	Breast Cancer
BRELA	Business Registration and Licensing Agency – Tanzania
BRICS	Brazil, Russia, India, China, South Africa
BSD	Berkeley System Distribution
BSF	Benefit Sharing Fund
BSA	Business Software Alliance
C2C	Consumers to other Consumers
CAFC	United States Court of Appeals for the Federal Circuit
CAN	Climate Action Network
CBD	Convention on Biological Diversity

CC	Creative Commons
CD	Compact Disc
C-DAC	Centre for the Development of Advanced Computing
CDR	Community Design Regulation – EU
CDU	Christian Democratic Union – Germany
CDPA	Counterfeit Drug Prevention Act – USA
CEAC	Copyright Enforcement Advisory Council – India
CENDA	National Center of Author's Rights – Cuba
CEO	Chief Executive Officer
CESCR	United Nations Committee on Economic, Social and Cultural Rights
CGIAR	Consultative Group on International Agriculture Research Consortium
CHAMUDATA	Tanzanian Music Dance Association
CHM	Common Heritage of Mankind
CIF	Chamber of the Pharmaceutical Industry
CIPC	Companies and Intellectual Property Commission – South Africa
CIPRO	Companies and IP Registration Office – South Africa
CIS	Centre for Internet and Society – India
CISAC	International Confederation of Societies of Authors and Composers
CJEU	Court of Justice of the European Union (also known as ECJ – see below)
CMO	Collective Management Organization – Tanzania
CMT	Cut, Make Trim Factories
COP	Conference of the Parties to the UNFCCC (see below)
COSOTA	Copyright Society of Tanzania
CRC	Copyright Review Commission – South Africa
CSIR	Council for Scientific and Industrial Research – South Africa
CSO	Civil Society Organization
CSS	Content Scramble Systems
CTEA	Sonny Bono Copyright Term Extension Act – USA
CVS	Concurrent Versions System
DAT	Digital Audio Tape
DALRO	Dramatic, Artistic and Literary Rights Organization – South Africa
DCMS	Department for Culture, Media and Sport – UK
DDOS	Digital Denial of Service
DMCA	Digital Millennium Copyright Act – USA
DOC	Controlled Denomination of Origin – Italy
DRM	Digital Rights Management
DST	Department of Science and Technology - South Africa
DTI	Department of Trade and Industry – South Africa
DVD	Digital Versatile Disc
EAC	East African Community
ECHR	European Convention on Human Rights
ECJ	European Court of Justice (also known as CJEU – see above)
EFF	Electronic Frontier Foundation
EMG	Environmental Monitoring Group – South Africa
EPC	European Patent Convention, 1973
EPL	English Premier League
ETC Group	Action Group on Erosion, Technology and Concentration (formerly RAFT – see below)

EU	European Union
EULA	End User License Agreements
FA	Football Association
FAA	Federal Aviation Administration – USA
FACT	Federation Against Copyright Theft – UK
FAO	Food and Agricultural Organization
FBI	Federal Bureau of Investigation – USA
FCA	Federal Court of Australia
FDA	Federal Drug Administration – USA
FDA	Foreign Direct Investment
FERA	Federation of European Film Directors
FIAPF	Fédération Internationale des Associations de Producteurs Films
FIFA	Federation of International Football Associations
FOSS	Free and Open Source Software
FSF	Free Software Foundation
FTA	Free Trade Agreement
FTC	Federal Trade Commission – USA
GAO	Government Accountability Office – USA
GATT	General Agreement on Tariffs and Trade
GDP	Gross Domestic Product
GFHR	Global Forum for Health Research
GI	Geographical Indication
GII	Global Information Infrastructure
GLAM	Galleries, Libraries, Archives and Museums –UK
GNOME	GNU Object Model Environment
GNU	GNU is Not Unix
GPL	General Public License
GPS	Global Positioning System
GVA	Gross Value Added
GWR	Great Western Railway – UK
HADOPI	Haute Autorité pour la Diffusion des Œuvres et la Protection des droits d'auteur sur Internet – France
HD-DVD	High Definition Digital Versatile Disc
ICCPR	International Covenant on Civil and Political Rights
ICESCR	International Covenant on Economic, Social and Cultural Rights
ICT	Information and communication technologies
IDA	International Depositary Authorities
IFPI	International Federation of the Phonographic Industry
IGO	International Governmental Organisation
IIPA	International Intellectual Property Alliance
IK	Indigenous Knowledge
ILC	Indigenous and Local Communities
IMF	International Monetary Fund
IOC	International Olympic Committee
IP	Intellectual Property
IPECEA	Intellectual Property Enhanced Criminal Enforcement Act 2007 – South Africa
IPL	Internet Public Library
IPO	Intellectual Property Office – UK

IPR	Intellectual Property Rights
IPR-PFRD	Intellectual Property Rights from Publicly Financed Research and Development Act – South Africa
IPRS	Indian Performing Rights Society Limited
ISP	Internet Service Provider
IT	Information Technology
ITO	International Trademark Association
IUCN	International Union for the Conservation of Nature
IUPGRFA	International Undertaking on Plant Genetic Resources for Food and Agriculture
JIPA	Japan Intellectual Property Association
KAMP	Kenya Association of Music Producers
KBE	Knowledge Based Economy
KECOBO	Kenya Copyright Board
KEI	Knowledge Ecology International
LDC	Least-Developed Countries
LOCOG	London Organising Committee of the Olympic and Paralympic Games
LOS	United Nations Convention on the Law of the Sea
MAA	Manufacturers Aircraft Association – USA
MCPS	Mechanical-Copyright Protection Society – UK
MCSK	Music Copyright Society of Kenya
MICO	Mark Indicating Conditions of Origin
MIT	Massachusetts Institute of Technology
MLS	Multilateral System
MPAA	Motion Picture Association of America
MPEG	Moving Picture Expert Group
MSF	Médecins Sans Frontières
MTCT	Mother to Child Transmission
NASA	National Space and Aeronautics Administration – USA
NDA	Non-Disclosure Agreement
NESTA	National Endowment for Science Technology and the Arts – UK
NIPMO	National IP Management Office – South Africa
NII	National Information Infrastructure
NISCAIR	National Institute of Science Communication and Information Resources – India
NIH	National Institutes of Health – USA
NGO	Non Governmental Organization
NPO	Nonprofit Organization
OAPI	Organisation Africaine de la propriété intellectuelle
OAS	Organization of American States
OCIPE	Office of Companies and IP Enforcement – South Africa
OCW	OpenCourseWare
OECD	Organization of Economic Cooperation and Development
OER	Open Educational Resources
OMPI	Organisation Mondiale de la propriété intellectuelle (in English WIPO)
OSD	Open Source Definition
OSDL	Open Source Development Labs
OSI	Open Source Initiative
OSP	Online Service Provider

OST	1967 Treaty on the Principles Governing the Activities of States in the Exploration and Use of Outer Space, Including the Moon and Other Celestial Bodies
OSYU	Open Source Yoga Unity
P2P	Peer-to-Peer
PAIPO	Pan-African IP Organization
PBR	Plant Breeders' Rights
PC	Personal Computer
PCT	Patent Cooperation Treaty
PDO	Protected Denomination of Origin – EU
PGO/I	Protected Geographical Indication – EU
PGR	Plant Genetic Resources
PGRFA	Plant Genetic Resources for Food and Agriculture
PIC	Prior Informed Consent
PIPA	Protect Intellectual Property Act – US
PK	Public Knowledge
PLoS	Public Library of Science
PMA	Pharmaceutical Manufacturers' Association
PMC	PubMed Central
PPI	Pirate Parties International
PPL	Phonographic Performance Limited - India
PPUK	Pirate Party UK
PRiSK	Performers Rights Society of Kenya
PRS	Performing Rights Society – UK
PSS	Public Sector Software
R&D	Research and Development
RAFI	Rural Advancement Foundation International (now ETC Group – see above)
RCEP	Regional Comprehensive Economic Partnership – East Asia and the Australasia
RIAA	Recording Industry Association of America
SAARC	South Asian Association for Regional Cooperation
SAB	South African Breweries
SABAM	Société d'Auteurs Belge – Belgische Auteurs Maatschappij – Belgium
SACU	Southern African Customs Union
SAFACT	South African Federation Against Copyright Theft
SAI	Social Accountability International
SAIIPL	South African Institute of Intellectual Property Law
SAMRO	Southern African Music Rights Organization
SARC	South African Rooibos Council
SCD	Chilean Copyright Society
SCO Group	Santa Cruz Operation Group
SCRIPT	Society for Copyright Regulations of Indian Producers of Films and Television
SCMS	Serial Copy Management System
SDMI	Secure Digital Music Initiative
SETI	Search for extraterrestrial intelligence
SFLC	Software Freedom Law Center
SOPA	Stop On-line Piracy Act – USA

SPACE	Society for Promotion of Alternative Computing and Employment
SRA	Solicitors Regulation Authority – England and Wales
SSCR	WIPO Standing Committee on Copyright and Related Rights
SSRC	Social Science Research Council
TAC	Treatment Action Campaign
TERI	The Energy and Resource Institute
TIA	Technology Innovation Agency – South Africa
TIFA	Trade and Investment Framework Agreement – South Africa
TK	Traditional Knowledge
TKDL	Traditional Knowledge Digital Library – India
TOS	Terms of Service
TPB	The Pirate Bay
TPM	Technological Protection Measures
TPP	Trans-Pacific Partnership
TRIPS	Trade Related Aspects of Intellectual Property Agreement
TTIP	Transatlantic Trade and Investment Partnership
TTO	Technology Transfer Office
TWN	Third World Network
UCC	Universal Copyright Convention/Code
UCT	University of Cape Town
UDHR	Universal Declaration of Human Rights
UGC	User Generated Content
UN	United Nations
UNCTAD	United Nations Convention on Technology and Development
UNDP	United Nations Development Programme
UNEP	United Nations Environmental Programme
UNESCO	United Nations Educational, Scientific and Cultural Organization
UNFCCC	United Nations Framework Convention on Climate Change
UNIDO	United Nations Industrial Development Organization
UNISA	University of South Africa
UPOV	Act of the International Union for the Protection of New Varieties of Plants
USC	United States Court (of Appeal)
USCO	United States Copyright Office
USOC	United States Olympic Committee
USPTO	United States Patent and Trademark Office
USTR	United States Trade Representative
VARA	Visual Artists Rights Act – USA
VCR	Video Cassette Recorder
VfX	Visual Effects
WCT	WIPO Copyright Treaty
WIPO	World Intellectual Property Organization (in French OMPI)
WPPT	WIPO Performances and Phonograms Treaty
WTO	World Trade Organization
WWW	World Wide Web

Transatlantic Consumer Dialogue

Introduction

Matthew David and Debora Halbert

The term 'intellectual property rights' is used to refer to forms of legal protection offered to rights holders across a variety of legal regimes. It governs the application and/or exploitation of certain kinds of ideas, or at least the expression or tangible articulation of such ideas. Intellectual property rights exist as a curious balance between the idea of 'ownership' and a reluctance to accord such absolute rights in the domain of ideas. Intellectual property rights evolved as limited monopolies granted over innovative ideas and inventions and were designed to strike a balance between private remuneration and the public good. The emergence of an 'informational' economy and society that is increasingly global, has brought to the fore the importance of intellectual property rights, even as it has also highlighted the contradictions and tensions within such a set of socio-legal conventions. In this context it is important to note that IP is not 'real property', just as 'real property' is a social convention, not a natural (physical) attribute (in the way that being warm blooded is a 'property' of being a mammal).

Despite significant differences in what is covered by the legal regimes that are generally known as intellectual property and our understanding of real property, the term is designed to draw a direct parallel with those rights accorded to owners of physical forms of property. In other words, using the term intellectual property rights is intended to evoke the commonly understood and at this point virtually 'natural' concept of 'ownership', at least within capitalist societies. The underlying inherent nature of social relations has evolved over time. For example, it was (is) deemed heretical to question the divine right of rulers in feudal/theocratic societies whose rule was said to be natural, and was said to be a crime against 'nature' (and a crime against law) to question gendered roles and identities in patriarchal societies.

By definition, a capitalist society is one where owning property (capital) is, at a fundamental level, taken to be a natural and self-evident right. The end of the cold-war has seen the expansion of capitalism as an ideological and material system. To use Francis Fukuyama's much commented upon Hegelian thesis, the end of the Cold-War marks the end of 'History' (Fukuyama 2006). That capitalism is the final destination of human progress may be less than certain. However, the idea that it is so is certainly largely 'taken-for-granted' today. While intellectual property has always been controversial, it is only within the last days of the Cold-War and in the post-Cold War era of totalizing global capitalist reconstruction that the various regimes falling under the general umbrella term of intellectual property have become central to political discussion and have become widely known to the general public. Thus, within the contemporary capitalist frame, the primacy of property rights, and by extension the primacy of intellectual property rights, has expanded both geographically and conceptually. In particular, we have witnessed efforts at extending the global scope, temporal duration and range/depth of what it is that can be covered by intellectual property rights. The purpose of this collection is to describe, map and question the imperial ambitions and the natural self-evidence of such expansion.

WHAT IS INTELLECTUAL PROPERTY?

For most of its history, copyrights, patents, trademarks and trade secrets have been a fairly esoteric dimension of law and policy. Types of intellectual property protection were of use to businesses seeking to defend intangible assets from misappropriation by other businesses (legal or otherwise). Widespread appropriation and copying, however, required access to technologies and levels of development that limited the ability to copy to those who had access to the appropriate reproductive technologies. So, for example, to print unlicensed or unauthorized books, early copyright infringers would need their own printing press. Thus, the relevance of copyright infringement or patent infringement to everyday life was indirect. Whilst monopoly rights may have limited supply and hence increased prices for certain goods to consumers, regulation of the authority to produce a copy was something to be determined between suppliers. The general population may have experienced the effect of IP law (in terms of higher prices and/or new and innovative products produced in response to the incentive of such IP-based monopoly prices or access to cheaper pirated goods), but it was not members of the general public who were ever likely to have legal action taken against them. Not so today in relation to digital content. With virtually every person in the developed world and increasingly in the developing world having access to the means of reproducing a digital copy and using technology to reproduce inventions, the scope of possible infringement for laws designed for a different age increases immensely. Knowledge, of what these laws entail, however, remains less generally known.

Before delving into the conceptual, political and historical dimensions of intellectual property, it is worth identifying and briefly describing the key legal regimes that together are called intellectual property. These include copyright, patents, trademarks, trade secrets, the much newer geographical indications, and a variety of what are called sui generis legal regimes that protect plant genetic resources and some types of data. The following descriptions are general and cannot bring in all the nuances of local protections that may deviate from the international norms that have been established.

Copyright is often claimed to have originated with the 1710 Statute of Anne in England (Rose [1993] and variously discussed in this collection). Much debate (in this volume and elsewhere) addresses the distinctiveness and potential convergence between the Anglo-Saxon conception of copyright and Latin-based legal frameworks that assert the 'moral rights' of authors. In part, this emerged as a debate between authors, book publishers and the crown over the length of copyright – should it be perpetual or limited – and to protect publishers from piracy. The law today has expanded considerably from its earliest manifestation as a publisher's right to copy. Today, copyright is a limited monopoly right that lasts for a minimum of 50 years after the life of the author. However, in many countries, like the United States, the term of protection is the life of the author plus 70 years. Copyright protects expressions, not ideas, and these expressions must be 'fixed in a tangible form', meaning that the work must be written down or affixed in some manner (such as a computer's memory). The owner of the copyright, which can be distinct from the author, acquires the rights over the copy, meaning that they control who can and cannot make authorized copies of the original work. The copyright owner also controls what are called derivative works, works inspired by the initial creative act. They also control the public performance of the work. In some jurisdictions, the author retains what are called 'moral rights' in the work, meaning that even after the first sale, their work must continue to have the artistic integrity with which it began.

Copyright is not an absolute monopoly, others can utilize a copyrighted work under the constraints of what in the US is called 'fair use' and in the UK is called 'fair dealing', but which ultimately provides a small amount of flexibility for others to comment on, criticize or cite the original work. Each definition, concept and approach written into copyright law has been tested and challenged and it is safe to say that the boundaries of what constitute a fair use or a public performance changes over time. While you do not need to officially register a copyright for it to come into force (it does the moment something is fixed), registration makes it possible to pursue possible copyright infringement. Copyright infringement is the unauthorized production of a copyrighted work. Infringing behaviour can be either deliberate or unknowing, but in either case is associated with very expensive fines and the possibility of criminal sanctions.

Patents have an earlier starting point – some would argue with the guild system in Italy in the fifteenth century (May & Sell 2006). As patents have evolved today, they protect inventions and offer a more limited timeframe of protection than copyright but with more absolute monopoly control. Where the copyright regime recognizes that future creativity may build upon, reference or interact with other creative work, the underlying assumption behind patentable inventions is that by extending an absolute protection over a new design or invention, the inventor will have the incentive to share that idea with the public. In exchange, the inventor acquires the right to exclude all others from manufacturing, building, or in any other way using or producing the invention without explicit authorization. The term for patent protection is 20 years from the date the patent is filed. Virtually all jurisdictions now use a 'first to file' system when determining who is to be assigned the patent, instead of the 'first to invent' system that had remained active in the United States until 2011.

A patent protects inventions, business methods and designs, but, more broadly, patents also now protect different aspects of computer programs (they can also receive copyright protection), living organisms, seeds, ways of doing business, and much more. Acquiring a patent is much more rigorous than acquiring a copyright. A patent must be filed with the relevant national office and prior to being awarded it must be assessed to ensure that it meets the criteria of usefulness, novelty and non-obviousness. Each of these key terms has been thoroughly discussed by the courts. Furthermore, while the definition of what constitutes prior art differs across jurisdictions, the invention must not already exist – generally meaning it cannot have been in the public domain and/or already published. Thus, patents are intended to protect new, innovative, and useful items that will, it is hoped, further push science and technological development.

Trademarks are assigned to a company to protect a variety of words, colours, symbols, and even sounds that can be associated with that company's brand. In its most visible and popular forms, trademarks are internationally recognized brands for major multinational companies and are aggressively protected from all possible dilution of the brand. A trademark is a perpetual form of intellectual property so long as a company is actively using the mark. Trademarks are in part justified as a form of consumer protection – it is argued by most companies with valuable trademarks that the mark identifies a quality of good as well as the health and safety of the product being sold. Producing goods under a trademark without authorization is called counterfeiting and companies spend an enormous amount of time and energy seeking to stop counterfeit goods from entering the market as legitimate products. While there may only be profit margins at stake in the fights over counterfeit handbags, watches, or shoes, the implications for counterfeit pharmaceuticals is more significant, especially if consumers unknowingly purchase counterfeits that have not received the appropriate regulatory approval.

To make things more complex, some consumer goods will have different aspects protected by patents, trademarks and copyrights. Thus, it is safe to say that modern consumer items are a network of intangible property rights that remain associated with the item long after its sale to a prospective customer. In all cases, the laws prohibit the unauthorized production of copies of the original work. In all cases, modern technologies make such unauthorized copying far easier than at any time in the past.

Newer forms of intellectual property have also been developed with commercial protection in mind. Geographical indicators, for example, protect not an individual product, but provide products from a specific region with protection from confusion. The most popular examples include sparkling wine, or Champagne, which can only be called Champagne if it comes from the appropriate region in France. The same is true for a host of other products aligned closely with a region. Such a designation, which is often indicated by a certification by the relevant governing authority, is understood to establish authenticity in the product and ascertain that quality control measures have been met.

Other forms of intellectual property rights, as mentioned earlier, protect specific products or things. The types of intellectual property mentioned here are among the most prominent internationally. While it is difficult to sometimes divide them, each form does offer a different type of protection and lasts for different lengths of time. All that being said, the following section will seek to provide a general overview of the history of intellectual property.

BALANCING RIGHTS: A BRIEF HISTORY OF INTELLECTUAL PROPERTY AND ITS DIGITAL PRESENT

As numerous scholars have pointed out, even as regimes of intellectual property sought to nail down property rights in intangible ideas and expressions, the innovation and cultural exchange which violated these rights (and which was often called 'piracy') were in actuality the keystone to progress. Thus, a balance between ownership and exchange of ideas has always been the key to debates over intellectual property. These debates rage today as the idea of intellectual property becomes one of the driving economic principles of an information age economy and states reconfigure their national laws to better protect not simply the flow of tangible products, but also to ascertain ownership of property rights in the intangibles protected traditionally by intellectual property laws.

Controversies over the appropriate scope and balance of intellectual property have existed since the inception of these property laws. These tensions have always had an international dimension as well, given that nation-states sought to police the transfer of knowledge and technology protected by intellectual property across state lines to those in other countries who had or wanted the relevant technology and know-how. Whether it is looking at the debates surrounding the Statute of Anne, which dates to the early eighteenth century, or to the 1886 Berne and 1883 Paris Conventions which established national treatment rules and international protection of copyrights and patents respectively, there has always been a struggle between those who would like to see broader availability of ideas versus those who want to see ideas more controlled through property regimes; a struggle that has involved multiple actors from states to companies to individuals.

The development of intellectual property regimes in the nineteenth century reflected both philosophical and material differences in opinion. The United States, as a newly liberated colony, sought to evade both the strictures of former royal censors and to escape relative economic backwardness by adopting a 'relaxed' attitude to the intellectual property rights of other countries. In fact, early America is notorious as one of the world's biggest pirates. France, taking an enlightenment attitude to the general advantage of knowledge, similarly took a harder line in deciding when an inventor's claim warranted monopoly rights. The United Kingdom generally approved of relatively strong IP protection at home, but when faced with a free market abroad was more circumspect. The Dutch and Swiss suspended patent law just at the time when Germany and the United States introduced new forms of corporate legal ownership rights in ideas.

Whilst international conventions sought to balance competing interests (May 2007a), it was differences between nations, as well as between older and emerging sectors (such as between books and film) that meant only a relatively weak global IP regime prevailed up until the late twentieth century (Vaidhyanathan 2001). The post-1945 perception in the United States in particular, was that Japanese and German militarism in the 1930s had been fuelled by overly protectionist IP monopoly holding corporations and cartels (May & Sell 2006: 139). The Cold War also made rapid industrial development/reconstruction (such as in mainland China, Taiwan, Japan and South Korea in particular) a political and military priority. This industrial development was itself based on relatively unchecked access to patented technologies and the reproduction of what might have been copyright and trademark protected goods. Only after the Cold War could the economic demands of IPR (intellectual property rights) holders be brought to the fore (May 2007a). It was only then that a newly global network capitalist society pushed intellectual property to a central position in the regulation of economic and social life.

The same relationship to older European states that led the emergent United States to limit foreign IP rights in the interests of its own economic and cultural development is replicated today in relations between developing countries and wealthier nations. Yet with the change in the global balance of power, the United States, forgetting its own developmental history, is now the most vocal power in asserting the need for all countries to adopt a singular global IP regime under its leadership. The United States is a former poacher most avidly turned gamekeeper in this regard, and the contrast between its historical action and its contemporary advice is paralleled in relations between emerging and established players in a number of domains (such as between economic sectors and even fields within sectors).

As Manuel Castells (2010) observed, the current transformation of society cannot best be characterized as a 'post-industrial society' (Bell 1976). The notion that society has moved from the pre-industrial, through the industrial and now to the 'post' industrial age is a mistake. That an increasingly small percentage of the world's population now works in the production of food is due to the sheer intensity of innovation in the agricultural sector, not to the notion that agricultural production has been consigned to the back-room of historical development. That farming employs so few is because it is at the cutting edge of knowledge-intensive (and patent-protected) innovation. Ironically, the service sector is, in part at least, so large an employer because it is so far behind farming in terms of its replacement of people by information-rich (and hence IP-regulated) technologies. Nonetheless, in both these supposedly pre- and post-industrial domains, just as in the ongoing field of industrial manufacture, the global network society manifests the drive to replace knowing people with information-rich property (whether that be a digital recording, a manufacturing process or a genetically modified seed).

Nonetheless, the very network infrastructure, the digital network of networks that has been driven by and which itself promotes the development of today's global network capitalism; also offers the decommodified copy to be shared, as well as the invitation to come together to resist seed monopolies and prohibitions on generic pharmaceuticals. The rising significance of IPRs in the network society cannot simply be attributed to the rise of immaterial goods, such as digital content, whose sole market value relies upon legal scarcity rather than any 'natural' scarcity. This is the domain where conflict has been most open – linked as it is most directly to conflicts between traditional and new media communication. However, the increasing significance of informational content in the 'value chain'/ 'profitability' of industrial, service, agricultural and extractive industries (from iPhones and soya beans to branded coffee and mining operations) is intricately bound up with global trade and labour markets which have weakened the relative value of such assets that are not protected by monopoly controls.

Prior to the digitalization of everything, 'pirate' products had to be manufactured, distributed and sold much like the originals – and one still sees this process in place for pirated trademarked 'knock offs'. Law was, *as a general rule*, designed to provide protection against these commercial efforts. Book publishers without the appropriate rights could be punished for violating the copyright of the publisher who was authorized to produce a work. Companies without the patent to reproduce a specific invention could be stopped from doing so. Knock-off products could be confiscated and destroyed. The illegal use of intellectual property was unauthorized commercial use. Arguments deployed by the rightful owners of intellectual properties suggested that unless protection of these intangibles existed, no one would be willing to put the hard work into innovation only to see others profit from their hard work without having to do any actual work themselves. The debates were about the commercial exploitation of the work.

What has not changed in the last 30 years are the arguments assorted players make, because the tensions between assertions of absolute ownership and efforts to more freely exchange technologies, ideas, inventions and creative work remain the same. However, the pace, scope and type of issues that are at stake have indeed changed. Since the popularization of the personal computer and a method of sharing information based upon copying, there has been a fundamental shift in how one must police the boundaries of intellectual property laws. Instead of seeing possible 'pirate' businesses as the primary culprit in terms of intellectual property law, the focus has now shifted to the everyday user as an intellectual property 'pirate'. This transition in focus is most clear when it comes to copyright and entertainment products. The ease of copying associated with computer programs has meant that people sought to share these products without purchasing them. Under traditional copyright rules, once the first sale has occurred, the person purchasing the product is free to give it away or re-sell it without permission from the copyright owner. Digital technology, however, makes it possible for the individual consumer to become a node in the distribution of copyrighted works, often without commercial intent, that can go well beyond the gift of a book or DVD to a friend. In other words, digital sharing can make anybody into a 'pirate', or at least it can make anyone offering access to copies online as much if not more of a threat to copyright holders as were/are the traditional physical copy making counterfeiters which the term 'pirate' was once restricted to. Thus, the threat posed by copyright infringement in the information age is not a new industry seeking to create and sell fake copies of products, but individuals who share their copy with everyone for free. Laws like the 1998 No Electronic Theft (NET) Act passed in the United States sought (unsuccessfully) to remedy this situation – the non-commercial sharing of copyrighted products. Since the late 1990s, file-sharing has continued to be a motivating factor behind draconian Internet policy such as the three-strikes and you are out laws now in place in France, South Korea, New Zealand, Taiwan, Ireland and the UK, though there isn't much evidence that this approach works (Taylor 2013).

The same is true for music, movies, video games and any other product that can be shared via digital means. It is the individual consumer who becomes the most serious threat from an industry perspective, replacing the bootleg producers of old (see Marshall 2005), and 'traditional' industrial 'pirates' (Johns 2009) trafficking in the hard copy of such products. Certainly, counterfeiters still play a role in helping states construct a discourse of threat and of the need for enhanced laws. This is because tangible goods protected by trademark law, meaning knock-off designer handbags or clothing, auto-parts and medicines, remain tied to physical markets, at least until 3D printing becomes more sophisticated. However, the significance of the digital revolution is that it made everyone into a copyright infringer and has led copyright holders to accuse everyone of therefore being a 'pirate'. The law has also changed to reflect the interests of business against their worst enemies – their own fans and consumers. Whether such a war against their own former and potential customers does serve those businesses' best interests is less clear-cut if it alienates rather than contains those that may or may not be willing to pay.

It is the abolition of this distinction between producer and consumer that has allowed the term 'piracy' to migrate from its original legal meaning, at least in relation to IP, as a term to describe someone engaging in the production of IP infringing copies as a commercial enterprise, to a term loosely attached to anyone engaged in personal copying for private use. There has been a corresponding migration from primarily enforcing IP violations through civil penalties to shifting the focus to criminal penalties for both commercial and non-commercial infringement, though generally speaking criminalizing copyright and trademark theft has occurred whereas patent infringement is still deal with through the civil courts (Manta 2011). Extending criminal sanctions associated with commercial piracy to non-commercial sharing has been a marked feature of the intensification of IP regimes in recent years, even if it also reflects the increased difficulties IP defenders find themselves in when confronted with the ubiquitous free distribution of the very content they wish to sell. Ongoing extension and intensification of IP laws are as much *de jure* attempts to compensate for the *de facto* collapse of physical and technical control over the commercial application of ideas as they are manifestations of the increased power of IP-rich corporations and states in the world today.

The history of digital sharing media is one of cat and mouse struggle in the identification of liability and evasion (David 2010, 2013). Napster was closed down because it was said to have engaged in contributory infringement. Its central server was required as the conduit for the transfer of files between users, and when these files were copyright infringing, Napster could not evade responsibility for its direct involvement in the unlawful actions of its users. This led to the development of more distributed forms of software that did not require exchange to pass through the software provider's own server. Attempts to attribute liability on grounds of actively promoting infringement led to services removing any such promotional claims, or (in some cases) sharing software was itself 'pirated' and circulated beyond the control of its own developers. This promoted a targeting of uploaders, and such targeting promoted the development of 'torrent' based services where no one uploader can be identified as the liable supplier. Torrent service providers were then targeted. They then relocated servers to less regulated jurisdictions. Subsequent targeting of downloaders has now seen the rise in popularity of streaming – where users stream rather than copy content.

It should also be noted that the term 'piracy' is a contested term, both in its application to a range of activities from commercial copying to personal sharing, but also in the way the term has been accepted by those that would reject the whole notion of IP, and yet who see the IP 'pirate' label as a legitimate badge of rebel cool. So, for example, the immense international popularity of The Pirate Bay, the radicalization of Kim DotCom from storage locker entrepreneur into anti-IP activist, and the emergence of the Pirate Party in reaction to the overreach of intellectual property laws all suggest an effort to reclaim and rebrand the notion of 'piracy' itself.

Trademark and patent law have faced slightly different but equally radical shifts in terms of control versus sharing. The 'information age' offers a fundamental shift in consciousness from valuing the material production of a thing to valuing the idea expressed by, or which transcends, the material object. So, for example, the Nike shoe may be fundamentally similar to other athletic shoes but the value is attached to the idea of wearing a Nike shoe. The branding of a product and successfully getting people to form an allegiance with a brand is essential to how the modern economy functions. One does not only buy a product, but the lifestyle and emotional connection to a brand that companies work very hard to create. Corporations have responded to the understanding that it is knowledge within a knowledge economy that is important by seeking to place their employees under restrictive contracts regarding innovation and post-employment opportunities. It becomes difficult to capture the ideas a person might have in their head, but the new regimes of corporate contract law seek to do so.

The rise of global production and distribution chains, combined with the rise of global IPR protection, creates an interesting, and perhaps contradictory, dynamic. Increased freedom to move production to the most cost-effective locations, at the same time as having the freedom to then move the finished product throughout the globe, means that the costs of production are reduced. This is most true of goods that can be mass produced, and IPR-rich goods combine precisely this mix of abstracted information that can be combined with mechanical reproduction (whether that be in recordings, designs or chemical formulations, etc.). In conditions of globalized markets, the highest prices will remain only in those goods where production cost reductions (due to global outsourcing) are offset by the ability to maintain control over distribution by means of IPRs. Cheap and unprotected goods can be mass produced in low-cost locations, but can only then be sold at relatively low prices, in competition with other similar suppliers. Cheaply manufactured goods that are IP protected (whether these are medicinal drugs, handbags, pirated DVDs, or any number of other such things), become all the more attractive as they combine the advantage that they can be cheaply made using the logic of competitive global labour markets, whilst at the same time retaining prices that reflect monopoly control over distribution. However, such an attractive scenario also creates the incentives for non-IPRs holders to engage in forms of counterfeiting, piracy and patent infringement. Whilst IPR holders argue that global markets require globalized enforcement mechanisms to protect their monopoly-based incentives to create, it should also be pointed out that it is precisely this globalized enforcement of monopoly protection of one set of rights, in conditions where other forms of protection, such as over labour conditions and national markets, are being reduced, that makes IP protected goods such attractive (and profitable) targets for infringement. Any extension in duration, geographical reach and/or scope of what can be covered by IPRs must always simultaneously increase the value of such rights and the attractiveness of violating them.

Another curious paradox of global IPRs lies in the dynamic between local and global identities and identifications. The globalization of trade has led to a corresponding demand for protection of trademarks and brands now being made in one place and sold in another, even whilst their ownership may be located somewhere else entirely. A number of chapters in this collection touch on disputes that have arisen concerning local conlicts over global marks and brands. Others touch upon the consequence of worldwide IPRs being claimed by global economic actors on innovations and products with their origins in the traditions and practices of particular communities in more limited geographical areas. Yet, just as global brands and marks reach out to embrace the world in both sales and claims to protection; so it is that marks of distinctive location come to the fore precisely in order to distinguish themselves from what, until recently would not have shared a global space. It is only in a world of ubiquitous global brands that distinctive geographical indicators (GIs) become both relevant and valuable. However, a number of contributors to this collection seek to tease out the contradictions and difficulties of using the global IPR system to protect local and often indigenous communities from forms of predation by more powerful economic actors that also use and have been instrumental in creating that very system of international IPRs. Similarly, when seeking to promote 'farmers' rights' against 'breeders' rights' in sharing seed, it is important to note that 'farmers' rights' are not best equated fully with IPRs, even whilst the claims of indigenous and traditional farmers to being the 'custodians' of biodiversity skirts the parallel between custody and property rights. Global movements seeking to protect the rights of local communities are very aware of the contradictions involved in challenging global frameworks with universal rights claims in the name of particular groups and products. Academics and IP researchers need to be equally mindful of the paradoxes and pitfalls, limits and possibilities made plain by the contributors to this collection.

Where once a patent would have lasted only 14 years, the length of two seven-year apprenticeships, that term has been extended to 20 years in most countries. The period of copyright was originally not much longer. Now ongoing IP extensions allow protections to last a good many decades longer. As the value of ideas relative to physical costs of production increase, hence increasing the importance of IP, so extensions of IP further elevate the relative value of informational content. This creates a self-reinforcing spiral, even if it also makes any attempt to evade such IP monopolies all the more economically attractive.

Now more than ever, intellectual property is the subject of global regulation. With little to no public debate, the post-Cold-War reformulation of the General Agreement on Tariffs and Trade (GATT) became the instrument for the neo-liberalization of international trade, culminating in the creation of the World Trade Organization (WTO) in 1994/5. Central to the negotiations surrounding the replacement of GATT by the WTO was the formulation and implementation of the Trade Related Aspects of Intellectual Property Agreement (TRIPS) to govern IP as a trade-related issue. TRIPS, as a founding element of the WTO, required all signatories to the new organization to sign protection of foreign IP into their domestic legislation. Where the bulk of neo-liberal rules for international trade sought to decrease trade barriers, eliminate tariffs and open markets to foreign trade, TRIPS intended to impose a uniform standard of monopoly protection over intellectual-property-related goods and used the threat of trade sanctions to discourage recalcitrant nations from infringing the intellectual property of other nations.

TRIPS required all signatory countries to adapt their domestic law to its minimum standards. Some argue that TRIPS includes sufficient flexibilities for developing countries, and of course developing countries and the least developed countries were given additional time to conform with the law (Gervais 2008; Musungu 2006; Richards 2004). The initial concerns over TRIPS from a development perspective have been widely discussed (Drahos 2003; Gervais 2007). Furthermore, concerns about forum shopping between the WIPO (the World Intellectual Property Organization that currently manages the Berne and Paris treaties amongst many others, as well as negotiating new multilateral agreements) and the WTO that initially appeared have given way to an understanding of how these two organizations work together to enforce contemporary law. The advent of the development agenda at WIPO can be seen as a multilateral effort to rethink the implications of TRIPS and align the goals of WIPO with the development goals of the UN, or at least reframe the global enforcement of intellectual property rights within the needs for technology transfer and economic development recognized as essential by much of the Global South (De Beer 2009; May 2007b; Netanel 2009; Sell 2011; Suthersanen 2008; Yu 2009).

Despite efforts to reconfigure the global debate along lines more sympathetic to development and perhaps more open to flexibility, more contemporary bilateral TRIPs-plus agreements as well as plurilateral efforts to enhance intellectual property protection suggest that ongoing enhancement of intellectual property will remain a significant part of the political process (El-Said 2005; Yu this volume). The position of the chapters in this volume take into consideration this history and the contemporary state of negotiations regarding TRIPS, as well as the emerging negotiations over ACTA (the Anti-Counterfeiting Trade Agreement) and the TPP (the Trans-Pacific Partnership Agreement) (see Carrier 2013).

This general overview should highlight that while the debates surrounding issues of intellectual property are not new, the political, social and technological context within which these debates are made remain very relevant and continue to evolve. Issues of human rights, social justice, development and the future of innovation are part of the discussion that must be had. It is to these subjects that this Handbook will turn. Many chapters in the collection hinge around the question of 'balancing' rights. The language of intellectual property rights brings together the concepts of property and rights in a fashion that has led to many divergent interpretations. At least within a capitalist society the notion of property tends to be viewed as a primary, and perhaps even a natural right; the very foundation stone upon which 'liberty' depends. Yet, of course, the very notion of personal property rights as a foundation of freedom against tyranny, in particular the tyranny of the state, is paradoxical, as property is only ever a right granted in law, and traditionally law was made by the state. However, the rise of international multilateral and bilateral IPR treaties in recent years has led to the suggestion that IPRs (along with property rights more generally) have become rights 'beyond' the traditional state, and rights that transcend other rights typically (or traditionally) upheld at the level of the nation-state. The question then arises as to whether global IPRs can be, are and/or should be balanced against other rights, and where such balancing should take place. Chapters in this collection address this question on a number of fronts and at a number of levels. Should, is and how can the right to freedom of speech and expression be balanced against copyright in the case of music fans sharing 'their' favourite music? What then of the balance between rights to privacy and the right to know what Internet users are sharing if that content might infringe copyright? How can patent rights be balanced against development rights, the right to access life-saving medicines and rights in relation to climate change and climate change inhibiting technology transfer? Can these rights be traded, and if so should such 'trading' be left to the rights holders themselves, to national legislators, or to global forums?

SCOPE OF THE PROJECT

Compiling a Handbook on intellectual property today is a significantly different task than it would have been even 15 years ago. Today there is a global, widespread, interdisciplinary and complex debate about the issues emerging from intellectual property protection. Where an earlier volume would have focused primarily upon the conceptualization of intellectual property from a law and economics perspective, the scope of analysis available for understanding intellectual property today is far more vast and wide ranging.

Given the changing dimensions of the problems and practices associated with global intellectual property law, a Handbook on IP serves several key purposes at this time. First, it provides original contributions on the contemporary debates surrounding issues of intellectual property law. Second, it helps the reader understand the complexities and nuances of the interaction between forms of intellectual property and its applications that have gone beyond the conventional dimensions of copyright, patents and trademarks. Thus, contributors to this volume also focus on geographical indicators, farmer's rights, licensing for web-streaming, digital norms for file-sharing, and the expansion of rights into new areas of coverage, from patents for environmental technologies to discussions of the role intellectual property might play in space exploration and in governing brain science and innovation. Third, the Handbook makes clear that issues of intellectual property remain central to concerns over technology transfer, economic development and efforts to achieve the United Nations Millennium Development goals. Fourth, these chapters build upon the vast literature that has set the stage for our understanding of intellectual property in the information age. Thus, we see the contributions in this volume as not only helping to summarize the historical evolution of the intellectual property debate but also as pointing out the new areas of interest regarding intellectual property as well as highlighting the changes in policy that need to be made in order to balance competing interests in this area of law.

Whilst most treatments of issues associated with intellectual property are primarily legal and are thus limited by the frameworks imposed by a legal paradigm, this Handbook expands outside the law to understand issues of intellectual property from a variety of diverse disciplinary perspectives, including political science, sociology, philosophy, economics, archival, media and film studies, international relations, history, anthropology and public policy. What is appealing about taking a multidisciplinary approach to the subject matter is that intellectual property can be interrogated using a variety of conventional and emerging/alternative methods of analysis. Additionally, while doctrinal legal analysis is a critical element of our understanding of the evolution of copyright, patent, trademark, and other forms of law, research investigating user attitudes, technical affordances as well as political and economic relations require other methodological approaches as well.

We also see these contributions as addressing a broad range of concerns about the impact of contemporary and future intellectual property laws across a wide range of geographic regions, levels of development and potential new formulations of intellectual property. The shift in focus from the Cold War narrative of East versus West dominated by the US/Soviet struggle for ideological dominance has given way to a far more complex dialogue that articulates the multiple voices of the Global South. North–South issues emerge from the metanarrative of capitalism versus communism, to debate appropriate methods and types of development, the importance of technology transfer, and a sophisticated and comprehensive critique of global intellectual property rules as promulgated by the nations of the developed world.

That being said, the chapters in this volume demonstrate that even a narrative of North–South rebalancing cannot fully encapsulate the complexity of approaches and attitudes to international intellectual property law. What we have learned in the years since the passage of TRIPS is that far more nuanced and often regionally specific approaches must be taken. The chapters in this volume, many from the Global South, represent a range of views (some critical, others accepting) of the role intellectual property can (and should) play for countries seeking further economic development.

The chapters in this collection span the globe. Contributors are included from Europe, North America, the Caribbean, South America, Australia, Africa, South Asia and East Asia. Whilst a number of contributions take a global approach to particular aspects of IP, others address general or specific aspects of IP in relation to particular geographical areas and countries. Some chapters adopt a comparative approach to mapping particular IP disputes, whilst others combine historical archival research with contemporary data collection in particular countries. Nonetheless, and despite our efforts to include voices from all across the world, we recognize the limitations of a volume such as this.

The balance of contributions is not equal. Western Europe and North America are disproportionately represented in the collection. Chapters from Chile and Cuba were to be joined by others from Brazil and elsewhere in Latin America, but issues of language and time deterred these contributors. It should however be noted that a great many other chapters do address South American IP specifics within chapters discussing wider and parallel particulars. Similarly, the one excellent and wide-ranging chapter concerning IP in India was to have been joined by others, but this did not come to fruition. Likewise, the presence of excellent chapters by authors from Taiwan and Singapore, as well as coverage in another chapter about IP issues in Japan, does not overcome the largest single omission in the collection, that whilst a number of chapters do address China's position in the world today, there is no chapter devoted solely to intellectual property rights issues in the world's most populous country. Regarding Africa, whilst three chapters are devoted solely to specific countries, and a significant number of other chapters address in detail African case studies and examples, it is certainly also true that more could have been said.

It is difficult to underestimate the significance of the requirement that all contributions be in English in the ultimate construction of this volume. The global scope of the Handbook was limited to those who could write in English (even if only to the level sufficient to engage with the editors about getting their work translated, which was available and used). In an ideal world non-English speakers would not experience any disadvantage. Despite our best efforts this was not fully achieved. The final production of the work in English may explain why a number of non-English first language speakers were not persuaded to contribute. There are of course numerous areas that we would like to cover but are absent. Emerging issues such as the implications of 3D printing on copyright and patent law, the implications of nanotechnology, and patent trolling are among these.

We see this volume as moving the debate forward regarding issues of intellectual property. It should be noted that the intellectual property policy space is full – meaning that laws and policies have been promulgated worldwide and thus policy recommendations must by necessity focus on increasingly technical and detailed areas. Furthermore, a wide and ongoing debate about the depth, scope and impact of these laws means that the framework for understanding intellectual property has been well established, meaning that the contributors in this volume have all made an effort not to repeat what has already been discussed, but rather to push forward the dialogue on IP.

The debate has moved forward considerably since early critiques of intellectual property in an information age were made. Where the foundational literature by such important scholars as Jessica Litman (2006), Susan Sell (1998, 2003), Siva Vaidhyanathan (2001), Lawrence Lessig (2002, 2005, 2006), Christopher May (2000), Debora Halbert (1999) and others critiqued the expanding role copyright was playing and warned of the future implications for creativity, there are now more case studies, empirical evidence, and of course more opinions in general, than there were 20 years ago. Furthermore, in the aftermath of TRIPS, with the emergence of the counter-globalization movement and the efforts on the part of content industries to personalize the enforcement of intellectual property laws, a growing resistance to the expansion of intellectual property has emerged (David 2010; Halbert 2005). Finally, as many of the chapters in this volume will suggest, it is not possible to understand the application of copyright as universally problematic for the Global South and universally beneficial for the Global North (though of course this allocation of costs and benefits does prevail).

The study of intellectual property, as it has evolved outside of doctrinal legal analysis into the many disciplines discussed here, remains critical or at the least suspicious of the underlying justifications for strong protection. These chapters demonstrate that scholars approaching this topic remain sensitive to who benefits and who loses within the contemporary political economy structuring the law. In fact, a significant theme that runs through the entire collection is the effort to offer a critique of the status quo and avenues for improvement, whether these are minor repairs or substantive overhauls of the policy space. We see this volume as providing an opportunity for voices that may not get a hearing in the Congressional debates or international forums tasked with formulating the law – since many of the authors writing here represent the unorganized public, file-sharers, creative entities not acting within the copyright industry, indigenous peoples, or others marginalized in the contemporary political economy.

VOLUME OUTLINE

The volume is thematically divided into 11 parts, each with an introduction that situates its chapters within the larger themes of the section. That being said, there were many thematic configurations that could have been used. In many cases chapters could have been fitted together in alternative topical configurations. We chose not to divide all the chapters solely by type of legal regime, though some sections do so, in part because many of the issues raised by contributors cut across a range of types of intellectual property. The same can be said for an effort to organize the collection along geographical lines. Rather, we have chosen a topical approach that, at times, cuts across geographical and IP regimes, because underlying much of the scholarship here is a broader global approach, even whilst the politics at issue lies in the fact that 'one size fits all' global policies don't 'fit' and/or have radically divergent effects in difference places.

Part I introduces four chapters that use different political and economic frameworks to discuss the concept of intellectual property as an economic and political tool. These chapters take up the economic history, philosophical linkages, theoretical positions, and political contexts of intellectual property from a variety of perspectives. Part I does not claim ideological consistency. It embraces a multitude of views that speak to the multiple ways intellectual property can be ideologically situated. For example, where Chapter 1 introduces the reader to the political economy of intellectual property, Chapter 2 provides an economic analysis of the subject from the position of mainstream economic theory. Chapter 3 offers a historical contextualization of intellectual property within the classical liberal traditions of Locke, Hegel and Rawls, and the way these thinkers allow IP to be established as an international regime as understood through international relations theory, alongside Chapter 4 which offers an argument depicting the increasing globalization of the concept of IP that is distinct from its understanding as a tool of country-based international relations. The themes that emerge in these chapters are reflected throughout the volume; themes of social justice, the expansion of intellectual property as a political assertion of property rights in the information age, the tension between different positions on how much IP should exist, who benefits from its application, and how we strike a balance between too much and too little protection. Authors throughout the volume begin from different starting points on the legitimacy and future value of a system of intellectual property protection. The chapters in this first part introduce key and classical perspectives, both supportive and critical of intellectual property, as it has been conceived historically and how it is used today.

Part II deals with one of the most central issues facing the application of intellectual property in the world today – its relationship to future economic development, especially for countries in the Global South. Given how substantially the debate on issues of international intellectual property protection and development has evolved since its first iterations in the 1990s, the chapters in this part seek to make a far more nuanced and complex set of arguments about the role of intellectual property for economic development. Despite decades of criticism, the Trade Related Aspects of Intellectual Property Agreement (TRIPS) administered by the WTO has proven to be both a cost and a benefit to the Global South. The TRIPS regime as one that is multilateral in scope, instead of targeted bilateral agreements or the more recent country-club-type agreements, leaves room for developing countries to assert their rights, but remains a regime that serves the interests of some stakeholders (like the pharmaceutical industry) far more than others (such as many countries throughout the Global South). That being said, the authors in this section argue that TRIPS (and WIPO as well), can be used to support development and the creation of country-specific development projects.

That being said, Part II also provides insight from the perspective of the Global South by raising the controversies and complexities of TRIPS's application to Chile, Kenya and Tanzania. While dealing with different local industries and levels of analysis, these chapters help clarify the costs and benefits of TRIPS from the perspective of countries in the Global South. The final analysis is of course far more complex than a sweeping generalization of the net advantages or disadvantages of TRIPS. Other factors must be weighed, as the authors in this section clarify. These factors include the level of development, the political structure in place, the economic interests, either local or transnational, that have a stake in the application of the law, and the methods through which TRIPS is introduced and applied in the country under consideration.

As with the first part, the theme of development and its relationship to IP recur beyond the chapters in Part II and are taken up by other authors throughout this volume.

Part III, 'Branding the World', provides additional insight into how intellectual property interacts with economic development. This part, however, takes up different regimes of intellectual property and thus broadens the conversation to include trademarks, counterfeiting, geographical indicators and farmer's rights. While the bulk of intellectual property scholarship on the Global South and development focuses on patents and copyrights, the chapters in this part examine new intellectual property regimes and innovative uses of intellectual property within the context of the Global South and indigenous economic development. These chapters also take up the question of authenticity as it plays out in establishing brands, whether indigenous or those of popular commodities, and protecting the authentic against those who might seek to offer parallel goods at a cheaper price. While notions of the authentic must be interrogated in the context of indigenous communities, these same ideas of authenticity are essential to the existence of top branded products targeted by counterfeiters for sale and appropriation. Thus, the chapters in this part grapple with a range of themes from the creative use of intellectual property regimes to assert forms of indigenous ownership through geographic indications or brands to the notion of authenticity itself. No IP regime offers a panacea for dealing with the significant structural issues facing indigenous communities and poor farmers in the Global South, but the creative use of intellectual property may also help establish a foundation for future economic development.

Part IV, 'Between Economy and Culture', raises yet another issue that recurs throughout many chapters of this volume – how culture interacts with economic considerations and public policy. These chapters span a range of countries, from Cuba to South Africa, and levels of analysis, from the individual to the country specific. That being said, the chapters in this part grapple with the difficult intersection of intellectual property with cultural creativity. The chapters raise the question of what happens when creativity and culture become a commodity and they grapple with the ways the state can frame public policy to develop meaningful cultural policy. While the UK and the US tend to embrace culture as a commodity and frame intellectual property to benefit the individual property owner, Cuba has balanced author's rights, cultural rights and property rights differently. There is a critique to be made of such commodification, a critique seen in Darch's chapter on South Africa, a developing country that has followed the US path towards the commodification of culture. Finally, the emphasis on cultural commodification raises the question of the user and/or cultural producer. Within the sphere of commodity culture, people are framed as consumers of culture and as such cannot participate in culture absent their purchase power.

Part V, on the commons, introduces an important approach to what exists outside the law of intellectual property. A vibrant intellectual commons, or public domain, is understood to be a necessity for future innovation. The approaches taken to articulating the value of the commons in this part are many. They include understanding the emergence of a non-profit infrastructure for protecting and enhancing the public domain, describing the efforts by India to promote access to the commons either through protection of traditional knowledge (a concept that recurs throughout this work) or education and applying open source technologies throughout the subcontinent, as well as the emerging political movement for better and more rigorous open access as manifested through the international Pirate Party.

Part VI, 'Creative Copying', addresses the increased significance of intellectual property law for regulating the relationship between producers and consumers, rather than just relations between producers, a theme noted already in this introduction, and which recurs throughout this collection. This is most acutely observed in the changing relationship between creative authors and fans of their work. Whilst 'fans' (by any number of other names) have always engaged in forms of replication, imitation and modification, the digital age has made such practices more visible to other fans, wider audiences and to the authors of 'original' works (and their publishers, distributors and broadcasters). What can, with one hand, threaten the position of the author in relation to their work, may also, with the other hand, offer new scope to expand and deepen audience attachment to 'the work'.

Coming from the exact opposite direction is the problem of orphan works. Here, extensions of copyright duration have only added to the problems associated with works where (due to age) it is uncertain whether any remaining copyright holders exist. This uncertainty means that creative uses of older works are deterred as long as potential new users remain unwilling to use orphan works for fear of future infringement claims they cannot anticipate the magnitude of. Recent court cases over alleged 'appropriation'/'parody' by one author/artist relative to another again highlight the problematic relationship between creativity and copying, as well as between property rights and culture. Part VI of this collection brings together three authors, whose accounts of fanfiction, orphan works and appropriation/parody, show how creative copying is central to innovation. As such, IP law must be as much about protecting the scope to re-work content as it is about protecting author rights to control existing content.

Part VII, 'Audiences and Sharing', follows on directly from the themes addressed in Part VI. Just as fans of literary and other fictional works have always felt some sense of 'ownership' over the narratives and characters they enjoy, so music and sports fans have a deep identification (and sense of 'ownership') in relation to artists and athletes. The rise of file-sharing in relation to the music industry has given music fans new scope to circulate content beyond the control of traditional copyright holding record companies. Music file-sharing has transformed since 1999 through ever more distributed forms of network sharing, from central-server-based models, through peer-to-peer sharing, to torrent-based (peers-to-peer) sharing and more recently to streaming-based forms. These shifts have been in large part a direct response to legal efforts to target specific actors – from the central server of the software provider, to the uploader and then to the downloader. Every attempt to target one legal bottleneck in the network has led to that nexus being technically bypassed.

File-sharing really became significant from 1999 in music, whilst in sport things were delayed by a decade. What is most valuable in sport is live, fast and visual – three things that required a massively greater level of compression and broadband Internet capacity than was available at the turn of the millennium. Today copyright infringing sports streaming extends the problems experienced in the music industry as 'timeless time' means live events, recurrently streamed, are hard to close down relative to downloadable recordings; yet, in contrast, legal digital sports broadcasters have not yet suffered anything like the collapse in sales experienced by record companies. Technical and cultural networks do not always pull in the same direction. Attention to how audiences construct their ethical stances therefore becomes important. It is not sufficient simply to describe fans that infringe copyright as ethically deficient. They hold alternative moral frameworks, that neither law, nor technology, has been successful in either containing or reforming.

The boundary between 'creative' works protected by copyright, and 'functional' innovations protected by patent is itself not clear cut, and this is addressed in Part VIII, 'Creative Origins and Limitations'. Trade-related IPRs, in particular trademarks and trade secrets, occupy a separate space (discussed in earlier parts), but there is also a domain of crossover between utility and aesthetic valuation. Within this domain, design patents and copyright over functional codes co-exist within a field where the very notion of 'innovation' is itself contested. The history of IP in relation to video games is instructive here. At its inception the generic character of geometric shapes, actions, genres and narratives meant there was nothing in computer games that was open to IP protection. There was also no financial reward to protect either. The combination of greater graphical and narrative sophistication as well as expanding commercial markets changed that; but the shift from arcade machines to the home PC saw one commercial model collapse. Then came an ongoing battle over control, by both law and format. A significant contradiction has been that as games became more sophisticated, and hence warranted claims to IP protection, so this sophistication of 'play' has opened up the possibility of user generated content giving rise to IPR claims by users themselves, even in relation to the creators of the games they play.

Whilst narrative elements may warrant IP claims, rules do not. Whilst it is debatable who should be allowed to claim property rights in innovative products, another question is whether ownership incentivizes differently between the arts and the sciences, and whether such incentives are financial or moral in nature. Whilst the current ideological climate favours the view that money is the prime motivator for innovations of every kind, and whilst this is said to warrant a particular framing of IP law in relation to useful and creative arts, research suggests an interesting similarity between artists and scientists in that IPRs function mainly as a means of securing recognition rather than riches. Whilst earning an income by some means or another is important, IPRs are rarely the best means of securing income for creative workers. The creation of a separate domain of IP law to relate to industrial designs is a peculiar state of affairs. Some states don't make the distinction between art and design, whilst other, even neighbouring, states make a great deal of it. The legal and philosophical foundations used for making the distinction, where it is made, are also highly divergent and even contradictory.

Part IX focuses on themes of regulating innovative technology. Elevating IPRs to the status of human rights may confer upon them a status of rights that cannot be traded against other rights. Simply asserting that intellectual property rights are property rights like any other (which is a problematic suggestion in itself) does not set such property rights above other rights, at least in principle. As such, the assertion that a copyright or patent claim is a right on a par with rights conferred by ownership of physical objects would not then invalidate any other rights that might interfere with the full exercise and/or protection of such ownership and control. A range of other rights impinge upon and limit the exercise of intellectual property rights, as is also true of any other property rights, but this is even more true of IPRs, which have, since their inception been time limited and otherwise contained in order to achieve a balance between the rights and interests of holders and the rights and interests of the wider society.

Rights to life, health, welfare and development may come into conflict with the enforcement of patent rights, and these themes have been touched upon in earlier sections and are addressed more again in Parts X and XI. In Part IX it is rights to freedom of expression and rights to privacy that are explored relative to intellectual property rights. Attempts to regulate the infringement of copyrighted content, such as music, have expressly targeted individual users, and attempts to identify infringement has involved en masse surveillance of user behaviour, often in breach of Internet users' rights to privacy. The extent to which such practices have been deemed lawful or unlawful has ebbed and flowed and is different in different jurisdictions. Whilst the chapters in this part highlight the relentless pressure to extend the law in favour of IPRs relative to users' other rights, these chapters also show the relative failure of such lobby tactics in creating a unified and/or effective enforcement of IP relative to other rights.

While questions of patent law have threaded through the collection, Part X, 'Parameters of Patent', focuses in more specific detail on this significant area of law. On the one hand, a very large number of the most significant technical and scientific advances of the last 200 years were never subject to intellectual property claims or protection. On the other hand, some of the most profitable innovations of the same period have been patented, but could be said to have drawn upon a prior body of knowledge that was not controlled by IPRs. In addition, many argue that the less advanced states and economies have always had to infringe the IPRs or more powerful countries in order to develop.

The chapters in Part X adopt a number of different approaches to the position of patent within the global economy, and in relation to both economic and scientific development. How far can and does the patent system adapt to/fail in addressing the needs of developing societies in relation to accessing medicines and other patented products? How far have Western pharmaceutical and other companies engaged in 'biopiracy' (a term that inverts the 'piracy' label often aimed by IP holders at less advantaged actors) when using the IPR-free flora and culture of other parts of the world as foundations upon which to develop their then patented products? How can the very distinction between discovery and invention be defined in the first place? The question of what can be patented, what should be defined as a common heritage of humankind, and who should be allowed to own or prevent ownership by others are the common themes addressed by the chapters in this part.

The final part, 'Patenting the Future?', is based upon the understanding that intellectual property rights are always future oriented. The claim that innovation, and hence the future benefit of all members of society, requires that creators be given the right to profit from their innovation so as to motivate them to innovate, may only be accepted on a time-limited basis, but this again makes IPRs a form of property rights that is particularly time and hence future oriented. The chapters in the final part of this collection bring new perspectives on the future – the future of intellectual property and the future that may come into existence if we continue to extend IPRs in the fashion that we have up until now.

As IPRs extend in both time and depth of application, so it is that innovations along a number of frontiers of science and technology will confront human beings with paradoxical outcomes of their own 'success'. As neuroscience increasingly unearths the ways and means by which our brains work, how will we come to terms with the patent claims that will arise out of technologies that enhance human creative activities formally 'black-boxed' (at least over the last 200 years) under the obscure umbrella of 'romantic genius'? How might advances in space exploration lead us to question the very conceptions of 'life' and 'discovery/invention' that have until now been deployed to regulate our earth-bound frameworks over IPRs and who should be allowed to claim them? Given the role played by IPRs in promoting many of the technologies that have contributed to man-made climate change, how should IPRs be managed in relation to promoting sustainable development and climate-change-limiting technology transfer in the future?

CONCLUSION

While issues of copyright, patent and trademark have long and illustrious histories, fraught with legal battles that often span the many continents, it has only been with the information age and the challenge of digital reproduction that intellectual property has come to be a household term. While the foundational writings of the digital age established the scope of the problem – a heightened tension between practices of ownership and practices of sharing – the last 50 or so years have not seen any resolution to the myriad controversies that the various concepts of intellectual property create. Global networks of trade and communication combine and contradict. Global trade has led to and been further facilitated by the construction of global IP regimes, whilst global communication networks have facilitated and been facilitated by the creation of a 'global commons' within the 'global village' (McLuhan 1964) – a universal space in which it is taken for granted that all knowledge and information should be freely shared. Yet 'global culture', circulated across and beyond the control of any national borders and/or legal regulations, is the very oxygen that carries and promotes the self-same brands, patented technologies and creative works that, in the whirlwind of global flows, are said to be under threat.

Global flows are what, on the one hand, threaten to suspend the writ of IP law, yet, on the other, see it reaching the zenith of its significance and force. If anything, the scope, depth, disciplinary diversity and international dimensions of the scholarship on intellectual property only continue to expand. As such, this collection is but one node in a constantly evolving debate that marks an area of significant study, an area that will have an impact on how innovation, creativity and technology are owned and operated into the future.

REFERENCES

Bell, D. (1976) *The Coming of Post-industrial Society: A Venture in Social Forecasting*. New York: Basic Books.

Carrier, M.A. (2013) SOPA, PIPA, ACTA, TPP: An Alphabet Soup of Innovation-Stifling Copyright Legislation and Agreements. *Nw. J. Tech. & Intell. Prop.*, 11, pp. 21–163.

Castells, M. (2010) *The Rise of the Network Society: The Information Age: Economy, Society and Culture*, 2nd edn. Oxford, England: Wiley-Blackwell.

David, M. (2010) *Peer to Peer and the Music Industry: The Criminalization of Sharing*. London: SAGE.

David, M. (2013) Cultural, Legal, Technical, and Economic Perspectives on Copyright Online: The Case of the Music Industry. In W. Dutton, ed. *The Oxford Handbook of Internet Studies*. Oxford University Press, pp. 464–485.

De Beer, J. (2009) Defining WIPO's Development Agenda. In *Implementing the World Intellectual Property Organization's Development Agenda*. Ottawa: Wilfrid Laurier University Press, pp. 1–23.

Drahos, P. (2003) *Information Feudalism: Who Owns the Knowledge Economy?* New York: New Press.

El-Said, M. (2005) The Road from TRIPS-Minus, to TRIPS, to TRIPS-Plus. *The Journal of World Intellectual Property*, 8(1), pp. 53–65.

Fukuyama, F. (2006) *The End of History and the Last Man*. New York: Free Press.

Gervais, D. (2007) *Intellectual Property, Trade and Development: Strategies to Optimize Economic Development in a TRIPS-Plus Era*. Oxford: Oxford University Press. Available at: http://econpapers.repec.org/bookchap/oxpobooks/9780199216758.htm [accessed 3 December 2012].

Gervais, D. (2008) *The TRIPS Agreement: Drafting History and Analysis*. London: Sweet & Maxwell.

Halbert, D. (1999) *Intellectual Property in the Information Age: The Politics of Expanding Ownership Rights*. New York: Quorum Books.

Halbert, D. (2005) *Resisting Intellectual Property*. London and New York: Routledge.

Johns, A. (2009) *Piracy: The Intellectual Property Wars from Gutenberg to Gates*. Chicago: University of Chicago Press.

Lessig, L. (2002) *The Future of Ideas: The Fate of the Commons in a Connected* World. New York: Vintage.

Lessig, L. (2005) *Free Culture: The Nature and Future of Creativity*. New York: Penguin (Non-Classics).

Lessig, L. (2006) *Code: And Other Laws of Cyberspace, Version 2.0*. New York: Basic Books.

Litman, J. (2006) *Digital Copyright*. New York: Prometheus Books.

Manta, I.D. (2011) The Puzzle of Criminal Sanctions for Intellectual Property Infringement. *Harvard Journal of Law & Technology*, 24(2), pp. 469–517.

Marshall, L. (2005) *Bootlegging: Romanticism and Copyright in the Music Industry*. London: SAGE.

May, C. (2000) *A Global Political Economy of Intellectual Property Rights: The New Enclosures?* London: Routledge.

May, C. (2007a) *The World Intellectual Property Organization Resurgence and the Development Agenda*. London and New York: Routledge.

May, C. (2007b) World Intellectual Property Organization and the Development Agenda. *Global Governance*, 13, p. 161.

May, C. & Sell, S.K. (2006) *Intellectual Property Rights: A Critical History*. Boulder: Lynne Rienner Publishers.

McLuhan, M. (1964) *Understanding Media: The Extensions of Man*. London: Routledge.

Musungu, S. (2006) *The Use of Flexibilities in TRIPS by Developing Countries: Can They Promote Access to Medicines?* Geneva: South Centre.

Netanel, N. (2009) *The Development Agenda: Global Intellectual Property and Developing Countries*. Oxford and New York: Oxford University Press.

Richards, D. (2004) *Intellectual Property Rights and Global Capitalism: The Political Economy of the TRIPS Agreement.* Armonk, NY: M.E. Sharpe.

Rose, M. (1993) *Authors and Owners: The Invention of Copyright*, Cambridge, MA: Harvard University Press.

Sell, S.K. (1998) *Power and Ideas: North-South Politics of Intellectual Property and Antitrust.* Albany: State University of New York Press.

Sell, S.K. (2003) *Private Power, Public Law: The Globalization of Intellectual Property Rights.* Cambridge: Cambridge University Press.

Sell, S.K. (2011) Everything Old is New Again: The Development Agenda Then and Now. *The WIPO Journal*, 3(1), pp. 17–23.

Suthersanen, U. (2008) A2K and the WIPO Development Agenda: Time to List the 'Public Domain'. *UNCTAD-ICTSD Projects on IPRs and Sustainable Development.*

Taylor, J. (2013) *Three Strikes Doesn't Deter Copyright Infringement.* ZDNet. Available at: www.zdnet.com/three-strikes-doesnt-deter-copyright-infringement-7000020447/ [accessed 20 March 2014].

Vaidhyanathan, S. (2001) *Copyrights and Copywrongs: The Rise of Intellectual Property and How it Threatens Creativity.* New York: New York University Press.

Yu, P.K. (2009) A Tale of Two Development Agendas. *Northern University Law Review*, 35(2), pp. 466–529.

PART I

Foundations and Philosophies: Intellectual Property in a Global World

Matthew David and Debora Halbert

It could be said that intellectual property law has always been global, in the sense that the primary role of the nation-state has been to protect 'our' innovation and cultural creation from 'theirs'. From the earliest copyright statute, the Statute of Anne, in part designed to protect the London booksellers from the pirates in Scotland, protection of intellectual property has implied a transnational perspective. Intellectual property has long been protected via international agreements, with the Berne and Paris Conventions being perhaps the most prominent. Its integration into the World Trade Organization (WTO) via the Trade-Related Aspects of Intellectual Property (TRIPS) Agreement firmly established intellectual property as an important international issue and this first Part seeks to situate contemporary intellectual property law within the larger international and philosophical context.

Anne Barron's chapter begins by providing an important analysis of the contemporary global political economy of intellectual property. Barron's theoretical framework illuminates how global capital has engaged in the destruction of a knowledge commons at the international level, a theme reflected in many chapters in the handbook. Barron uses the General Public License (GPL) and the emergence of the Creative Commons as examples of legal resistance to the enclosure tactics of major IP-driven industries. She characterizes this resistance as a 'commons-ist' movement for freedom from the stranglehold wielded by the owners of strong IPRs. Yet for Barron, although commons-ism poses as a 'revolutionary' struggle, the revolution it envisages is primarily a technological one that leaves capitalism transformed but not overcome. Barron highlights the extent to which forms of free and open source software and Creative Commons licensing have used the rules of copyright law itself to create only limited suspensions of control within a system that ultimately maintains private property and market exchange. Thus, the libertarian ethos that motivates such innovations has remained, to date, contradicted by the 'unfreedom' associated with 'informational capitalism'. Barron's position is that the hopes accompanying these experiments exceed what can be realised through new arrangements for organizing information production alone (p. 9).

Barron's chapter is an excellent introduction to the concepts shaping contemporary IP debates and the key actors establishing the agenda. Lawrence Lessig, Yochai Benckler and Richard Stallman, have all played integral roles in the conceptualization of an alternative to the enclosure movement in information. Barron suggests that the creative commons movement and the hacker ethic that underlies these technologically driven projects might be capable of hacking capitalism itself, even if current manifestations have been largely incorporated by the market. Barron's chapter establishes the key themes grounding a global critique of intellectual property, as well as current efforts to offer an alternative and more open path, and an introduction to its key advocates.

From political economy to classical economics, Sarah Louisa Phythian-Adams brings the viewpoint of an economic historian to the study of intellectual property, especially copyright. She offers an economic history of intellectual property grounded in a description of the principles of neo-classical economics. Her goal is to understand and describe copyright law through the lens of economic philosophy, especially the role of the monopoly within a free-market tradition. Much like the other authors in this section, Phythian-Adams takes both a philosophical and economic approach to the understanding of intellectual property. She reminds the reader of the literature that has linked the evolution of intellectual property philosophically with the classical European philosophers that inform our contemporary understanding of intellectual property law. Any thorough understanding of the history of intellectual property needs to take into consideration the way it is grounded in the philosophies of Adam Smith, J.S. Mill, John Locke, and G.W.F. Hegel. Her chapter helps make those connections clear.

Economically, Phythian-Adams seeks to work through the tensions between market failures, monopolies, and the role of intellectual property. Using the lens of economics this chapter provides an important overview of the underlying economic rationale for intellectual property generally, and copyright specifically. In doing so, Phythian-Adams helps clarify how one might think about the balance between IPRs and individual use in the digital age when the cost of sharing has been reduced to zero. She discusses a variety of methods to offset the problems of free riders and distorted transaction costs that range from business-centred commercial options to government buyouts of important technologies that can then be placed in the public domain to spur further and future innovation. She also works systematically through the economic benefits of being copied. Ultimately, her review of the economic dimensions of copyright help make visible the underlying logics and possible advantages of thinking through a new balance to the copyright system.

Where Barron's chapter looks at the scope of intellectual property through the lens of global political economy, and Pythian-Adams takes up the economic theory behind intellectual property, Shubha Ghosh interrogates the relationship between the concept of international intellectual property and the nation-state. He begins by challenging the terminology 'international intellectual property' to better see the politics and ideological assumptions behind that concept. Ghosh is interested in interrogating the international philosophical dimensions of IP and develops a three-step process to do so, one that begins with the philosophy of international trade, moves on to theories of international relations, and finally ends with the step of critique. The underlying philosophical thinkers most often aligned with the study of intellectual property – Locke, Hegel, and Rawls – while often seemingly Western in focus, can be better understood as thinkers that help establish international intellectual property.

Ghosh begins by taking up the issue of international trade as grounded in domestic law. At a very literal level, intellectual property law exists to deal with what can be seen as cross-border externalities. There is a clear pragmatic, not philosophical impetus to such laws. However, he warns against situating the nation-state too near the centre of the analysis given that the flow of people, ideas and innovations across state boundaries has been central to the development of intellectual property laws since their inception.

International relations (IR) theory is also relevant because international flows move beyond trade where intellectual property is concerned. Like the area of international trade, traditional IR theory centres the nation-state as the unit of analysis. The privileging of the nation-state is especially visible in the theoretical contributions of realist international relations thinkers. However, the interaction between intellectual property and international relations theory suggests that things are more complex than centring analysis on the nation-state, especially when one introduces the Internet to modern debates over IP and IR.

The central argument offered by Ghosh regarding international intellectual property is in the analysis of how the philosophical traditions of Locke, Hegel and Rawls, which may seem to emerge from a predominant Western approach to thinking can be adapted to the global stage because these thinkers themselves were not removed from the global flow of ideas and products. Each of these theorists was already writing within an international context that transcended the nation-state and thus, to follow Ghosh's argument, their larger philosophical contributions are relevant to the study of international intellectual property. In the end, Ghosh makes visible that the intellectual property was always international intellectual property.

Halbert's chapter also takes up the issue of intellectual property beyond the nation-state. Her chapter shifts the view from the international to the global. Scholars of globalization have argued for a different understanding of the world that displaces the nation-state as a unit of analysis by highlighting the global flows of people, culture, power and economic goods. A globalized view can be applied to intellectual property. Like Ghosh, Halbert seeks to offer a new way of viewing the issue of intellectual property as something that transcends the domestic state. Drawing on an approach to political economy like that developed by Barron, Halbert argues that the global sphere of intellectual property is not one easily partitioned into debates between the traditional categories of analysis – rich/poor; north/south; capitalist/communist. Rather, there are multiple layers and linkages across state boundaries that converge to form different types of alliances when one looks at things globally instead of looking at things from the starting point of the nation-state within a 'community of nations'. How global rules to protect and expand intellectual property are constructed, then, can also be viewed politically as a contested space of economic interests that transcend a given nation-state. So too, it is argued, does the space of resistance flow globally. Thus, by decentring the nation-state as the unit of analysis, the argument of a globalized intellectual property view is that the lines of resistance and advocacy can be more clearly drawn to better reflect the politics of IP.

1

Intellectual Property and the 'Open' (Information) Society

Anne Barron

INTRODUCTION

Two apparently opposed forces are shaping global copyright law and practice at the present time. The first exemplifies the internalization to capitalism of a drive to 'accumulation by dispossession' (Harvey, 2003: Ch. 4), as previously public or common resources (in this context, cultural and knowledge resources) are enclosed and subjected to private control. Whether by lobbying legislative bodies at national, regional or international levels, or through private initiatives of one kind or another, the so-called 'creative industries' push ceaselessly now for a global copyright system that can continue to expand their dominion over – and ability to extract value from – ever more of the world's information assets. As well as enforcing their existing copyrights to the hilt in every significant market, the major firms in the sector (led by a handful of global corporations in the entertainment and software industries) have campaigned vigorously and successfully for expanded copyrights – and not only within particular nation states. Their goal has been to achieve a global harmonization of copyright norms such that all states are effectively obliged to enact higher standards of copyright protection, regardless of whether this serves domestic economic, social and cultural priorities. Meanwhile, these powerful corporate actors have also subjected the intangible assets under their control to regimes of private governance: designing digital rights management (DRM) systems to limit access to and use of software and cultural 'content' (digitized creations other than software), enforcing their terms of access and use via self-executing end-user licensing agreements, and enlisting Internet intermediaries in the project of shaping the networked environment itself so that traffic to and from suspect sites and users can be summarily disrupted, or blocked altogether. These regimes, which themselves have a global reach, are designed to supplement or supplant domestic and international copyright law with even more advantageous self-help arrangements, yet legislators have so far facilitated the emergence of these arrangements, thereby closing down the possibility of public oversight of the private power they serve. All of this is producing a privatization of previously public goods that some commentators have compared to the forced enclosure of common lands with the transition from feudal to post-feudal forms of landholding (Boyle, 2003, 2008).

Predictably, concern about the implications of copyright expansionism for fundamental rights and freedoms – to expression, the integrity of communications, data protection, privacy and due process – has prompted various proposals to constitutionalize the private relations between copyright owners, users of copyright material, and the intermediaries that enable content to flow from the former to the latter (see for example Article 19, 2013). The present chapter focuses on a different and more radical strategy: the mobilization of a countervailing force that aims to resist 'from below' the copyright industries' propertization drive. Best exemplified in the free software movement, it is the antithesis of that drive because in its purest form it stands for the collective (as opposed to individual or corporate) production of knowledge and cultural artefacts, and for making these artefacts accessible to and re-usable by the global public rather than keeping them under a right-holder's exclusive control.

At the heart of the free software movement, in turn, is the 'hacker' ethos – an ethos constituted of twin commitments to creative freedom and solidarity with other creators (manifested in activities of sharing and collaboration), a rejection of the division between producers and consumers of software (arising from a recognition of all users' creative potential), a passion for both the craft and the artistry of coding work, and a conviction that innovation is best served by liberating coding creativity – especially collective coding creativity. This ethos has given rise to a distinctive approach to the organization of software development projects and a set of maxims to guide programming conduct: always make accessible the source code of any program one creates so that the program's underlying structure can be readily understood and the program itself easily modified and improved by others; always allow the program and others' modified versions to circulate freely; endeavour to work with others to improve programs; and avoid causing divisions within programming communities unless the pursuit of technical excellence demands it (Barron, 2013).

Yet one of the key reasons why this ostensibly anti-proprietary approach to software development has risen to such prominence all over the globe is that its proponents have found in copyright itself – the very proprietary mechanism that renders code excludable – an instrument for instituting key aspects of the hacker ethos, notably the principle of universal access to source code. The technique is by now familiar. In general, free software developers eschew the option of placing their code in the public domain, thereby disclaiming their copyrights in it. Instead, they retain their copyrights, but license them with a view to subverting the exclusionary norms that copyright law institutionalizes and the approach to innovation that it underpins.

Free software licences are chiefly characterized by the fact that they guarantee a more extensive set of user freedoms than those provided for by copyright law or by conventional ('proprietary') copyright licences. Their proliferation is not merely the coincidental result of the spontaneous choices of thousands of individual developers: on the contrary, 'anti-proprietary' software licensing – better described as 'open' licensing[1] – has become the focus of a worldwide social movement. The movement first took shape through the free software community's broad acceptance of the model licence devised by Richard Stallman in the late 1980s (the General Public License, or GPL) as the desirable, if not obligatory, template for licensing code produced by members of the community. Licences based on the GPL are non-exclusive, perpetual (subsisting for the duration of the copyright in the licensed work unless breached by the licensee), applicable worldwide and royalty-free. They allow any user to run, copy and modify the licensed software without restriction (GPL v.3, cl. 2) and therefore grant the essential freedoms that define free software according to the FSF (Free Software Foundation, 2014). GPL-based licences also permit literal copies and modified versions of the licensed software to be 'conveyed'[2] subject to certain conditions. Literal copies may be conveyed as long as the conveyor makes it clear that the code is under copyright and licensed under the GPL, gives notice of the absence of any warranty and makes the source code available as well (GPL v.3, cl. 4 and 6). Additional conditions attach to the act of conveying modified versions (GPL, v.3, cl. 5). The most frequently discussed is the GPL's 'copyleft' clause (cl. 5(c)), which stipulates that if modified versions of the licensed software are conveyed to others, or if the licensed software is integrated with other software to form a new whole, these downstream products must also be licensed under the same (GPL) terms: the point of this term is to prevent the re-propertization of code released as free software through its incorporation into a work of the licensee's own which the latter chooses to treat as proprietary software. Effectively, then, the GPL is a legal mechanism for ensuring that any software which is acquired as, derived from, or intermingled with free software can only itself be distributed to other parties as free software: it operates to spread a regime of reciprocal sharing 'virally'.

By the late 1990s, the idea of using orchestrated open licensing strategies to effect a global transformation of the legal conditions under which cultural content is made publicly available had taken hold amongst many opponents of intellectual enclosure outside Stallman's world of hackers and geeks. A few experiments with open content licensing were conducted at this time, but it was not until the launch in May 2001 of the Creative Commons (CC) initiative that the idea began to be taken forward in a systematic way. CC was founded by a group mainly comprising US-based legal scholars (notably Lawrence Lessig and James Boyle) as a charitable corporation under US law, headquartered in the US. It remains a non-profit organization dedicated to 'develop[ing], support[ing], and steward[ing] legal and technical infrastructure that maximizes digital creativity, sharing, and innovation' (Creative Commons, 2014a). This infrastructure comprises a suite of standardized public copyright licences, together with software for encoding the licence terms into digitized content.[3]

Taking its cue explicitly from Stallman's GPL initiative, CC encourages creators to use its model licences to give users more freedom in relation to their content than publicly legislated copyright norms allow: making the templates available to all, free of charge and in both 'human-readable' and 'lawyer-readable' forms, is calculated to enhance their usability. All CC licences grant to the licensee at least the freedoms to copy and circulate the licensed work for non-commercial purposes; and they prohibit licensees from imposing technological measures on the licensed work that would restrict a recipient's ability to exercise the freedoms granted by the licence. The six licence templates are more divergent than Free and Open Source Software (FOSS) licences: this difference is significant and is explored further below. Nonetheless, they are tools that individuals can use to change the copyright norms around access and re-use that apply to their own works. Like FOSS licences, all CC-based licences are non-exclusive, royalty-free, subsist for the duration of the copyright in the licensed work, irrevocable unless breached by the licensee, and applicable worldwide.

While CC's stated goal is to build a 'global commons', it is not immediately clear what this means. On one level, the organization has set itself the ostensibly technical legal task of assisting creators in licensing their works so that 'a pool of pre-cleared content that can be mixed and shared' (Maracke, 2010: 10) grows over time. Yet Creative Commons is also a political project, and from the mid-2000s on, its growth – and, in particular, its expansion into a multinational organization with affiliates in over 70 jurisdictions – has brought a 'limited epistemic community of liberal US copyright lawyers' into increasingly agonistic conversations with civil society groups from all over the world, themselves 'rooted in a broader social movement … that aimed to create and preserve a "commons"' (Dobusch and

Quack, 2008: 6). These conversations have raised many questions about how Creative Commons relates to this wider movement: questions, in particular, about what it understands the politics of commoning to be.

In what follows, I seek answers to these questions through an exploration of Lawrence Lessig's early (1996–2004) writings on the dangers of the 'permission culture' he feared would emerge online as the result of the enclosures being endorsed in the official fora of global copyright policy-making, and the virtues of the 'free culture' that he hoped CC would bring about. I argue that these writings in turn are best understood as a subset of a much larger literature – including works by figures as diverse as Peter Drucker, Richard Florida, Robert Reich and Alvin Toffler – that insists on the centrality of information to contemporary societies due to an ongoing information technology 'revolution' that is powering the advance of a new age. Digital Information and Communication Technologies (ICTs), this literature tells us, are enormously enhancing the powers of human intelligence and the reach of human communication, just as the machines that drove the industrial revolution enhanced human physical capacities. In the 'Information Age' that has now dawned, so it is claimed, the intrinsic potential of information to catalyse a whole range of societal improvements – a more dynamic economy, transformed experiences of work, a more equal distribution of wealth and opportunity, a more vibrant civil society, restored or reconstituted communities, global integration, a richer and more diverse culture, and greater scope for personal freedom – stands ready to be unlocked.

As Nick Dyer-Witheford (1999) has noted, the utopian aspirations mobilized by talk of an information (technology) revolution in some ways echo those that have accompanied another tradition of revolutionary thinking – the Marxist tradition – whose political and intellectual fall from grace after the 1970s exactly paralleled the former's rise to ascendancy. The two discourses also share several themes: a belief in historical progress, an approach to history as organized into epochs or stages, an emphasis on technological change as a (if not the) trigger of shifts from one epoch to the next, the notion that an unfolding process of human emancipation accompanies these transformations, and of course the idea of revolution itself (Dyer-Witheford, 1999: 16). Yet a variant of information-revolutionary thinking has been embraced by the major copyright industry corporations and by political power-holders at national, regional and international levels. It has informed the communications, IT and Internet policies that now shape copyright law all over the globe – policies clearly more tailored to an aggressive form of information capitalism than to anything remotely resembling a recipe for a communist future. As a matter of official policy, the Information Age is an era in which copyright law and practice – comprising an ever-widening array of exclusionary copyright norms, technological means for protecting copyright material and monitoring its use, restrictive commercial copyright licences and enforcement mechanisms – fosters an expansion of private property in the means of intellectual production, not at all its supersession.

However, there are other variants of information revolutionary theory – and Lessig's is one – that seem on the face of it to share both Marx's vision of the future (what is a commons, after all, if not the outcome of a kind of communism?) and his account of the crises that would pave the way towards it. These variants claim that the (intellectual) property relations that first assumed their modern form in the eighteenth century are products of the Industrial Age that have now, as it were, become 'fetters' on the 'forces' of (information) production (echoing Marx, 1971: 20). Premised as they are on an asymmetry between the holders of monopoly rights in information and everyone else, intellectual property relations restrain the very processes of using, sharing and re-using information that in turn generate more information. Happily, the physical constraints that had previously slowed or channelled this generativity – the tangible vehicles that were necessary to carry informational content, together with the physical channels and organizational infrastructures that had to be built to enable their circulation – are now dissolving as a consequence of technological change. At the same time, thanks again to new ICTs, legal mechanisms for subjecting information to the rule of intellectual property are in the process of being overtaken by unfolding possibilities for sharing and exchanging it, and a worldwide movement is taking shape that is bringing these possibilities to fruition by building new relations of information production on the ruins of the old: reversing copyright's exclusionary logic to produce its opposite, a 'global [legal] infrastructure for sharing' (Creative Commons, 2014b). This 'commons-ism', it might even be said, is 'the real movement which abolishes the present state of things' precisely because its conditions 'result from the premises now in existence' (Marx and Engels, 1970: 57). It is being advanced by a vanguard whose interest – in free creativity – coincides with that of all humanity, and whose claims represent universal human needs. Unfortunately, the ruling class of the information society – which includes the corporate giants that dominate the copyright industries – can be counted upon to defend the privileges on which their profits depend: the expansionary agenda that defines official copyright policies at present is the fruit of their attempt to stem the tide of human destiny in this way. If the new possibilities for commons-ist information production are to be actualized, a revolutionary struggle will have to be waged against these forces of reaction, and radically new arrangements for organizing intellectual production will have to be devised.

Apart from Lessig, the most prominent legal scholars to have articulated versions of this position are Yochai Benkler (2006) and Eben Moglen (2003). Yet in marked contrast to the communism of Marx's vision, the various commons-isms professed by these authors in no way entail bringing capitalism to an end. In fact, as Dyer-Witheford has compellingly argued of information revolutionary theory generally, they derive much of their persuasive force from appropriating and rewriting Marxism in highly selective ways that subvert the central message of Marxism while at the same time harnessing the fervour that Marxist writings and social movements have long been able to inspire. Crucially, technological advance replaces class conflict as the driving force in the epochal shifts that mark the progress of history in these theories, and the new world they envision is one in which communism is unnecessary *because capitalism has revolutionized itself* (Dyer-Witheford, 1999: 26–37). Their appeal resides in their resonance with a widely shared conviction that something is wrong with capitalist society as it is currently organized, but they channel that conviction, not against capitalism as such, but against what are said to be its residual Industrial Age legal institutions, notably the copyright system in its current form.

INFORMATION SOCIETIES, INFORMATION REVOLUTIONS

Information Age theorizing can be dated to the 1970s, a crucial decade because it was a period in which a set of previously discrete innovations became aligned, then coalesced, and finally took shape as something resembling a 'force of nature' (Negroponte, 1995: 229), with its own internal dynamic and developmental trajectory. Discussion in the 1970s of how the 'mighty microchip' was revolutionizing modes of information storage and processing gave way in the 1980s to a discourse about the 'IT' revolution and – as fascination grew with how new technologies are also transforming communications media – talk of an 'ICT' revolution from the 1990s onwards. But it was the advent of the World Wide Web as a publicly available Internet application in 1991 that propelled copyright law to the front and centre of information policy in the world's advanced economies, including especially the US. The copyright system, it seemed to many, would be a major casualty of the upheavals unleashed by the Internet. Almost anything that qualified for copyright protection would be amenable to digitization and transmission through its networks. Once in circulation online, copyright works could be downloaded and stored by any user anywhere in the world with access to the necessary equipment and connections; once stored in digital form, they could be easily manipulated and/or re-transmitted through the network at lightning speed and minimal cost. Extant copyright norms seemed unenforceable in practice against unauthorized uses of this nature. The Internet seemed wholly inhospitable to the copyright industries as then structured: legitimate online commerce in copyright works seemed impossible to imagine here, much less arrange; at worst, it would become a lawless zone of rampant copyright piracy.

Against this backdrop, two broad visions of the nature of the 'information society', and copyright law's role in relation to it, gained currency in the early 1990s. One of these emerged from the libertarian subcultures already mushrooming across the Internet, though largely rooted in the US. The other took shape in the policy-making circles of the world's most technologically advanced nations, notably also the US. Both envisaged a new world opening up in 'cyberspace': a world constituted of information in electronic form. At times analogizing this world to the early American West or to outer space, both visions represented it as calling urgently for exploration and development: nothing less than the continuing evolution of human civilization depended on this (see, for example, Dyson, 1997; Gates, 1996). The two visions diverged, however, in their conceptions of how behaviour in cyberspace should be regulated, and in particular in their conceptions of how markets in information would operate online and the role property would play in relation to these markets. The official policies that emerged in the 1990s assumed that property rights in information would be insecure, and that information markets would fail, without substantial state intervention. Digi-libertarians, on the other hand, saw the state's proper role as that of unleashing 'natural' human liberties to compete and cooperate online, and perceived state-legislated IPRs as artificial and unwarranted impositions on these liberties. Freed from the constraints of the old order of matter and territory, cyberspatial interactions would generate their own norms and regularities – including new market structures and new forms of property – out of themselves.

Digi-libertarian philosophy was articulated most visibly and consistently by activist organizations such as the Electronic Frontier Foundation (EFF), set up in 1990, and publications such as *Wired*, a magazine/online periodical launched in 1993 (for an early survey, see Brockman, 1996). The EFF's position on copyright law's fate on the new 'electronic frontier' was most famously set out by one of its founders, John Perry Barlow, in an essay entitled 'Selling Wine Without Bottles: The Economy of Mind on the Global Net', first published in *Wired* in July 1993 (Barlow, 1993). Barlow's premise here was that the institution of copyright had been designed for a technological context in which intellectual products could only be made publicly available (durably, at least) through the medium of tangible things: hence texts were necessarily sold as books, just as wine is sold in bottles. Consequently, although ostensibly a form of property tailored to the specificities of intellectual objects, copyright is in fact tethered to the physical plane and oriented towards protecting the capital invested in the industrial production of standardized receptacles for informational content: it is, Barlow asserted (citing fellow libertarian Alvin Toffler [1991])[4] an archetypal 'Second Wave' institution. But '[n]ow, as information enters Cyberspace, the native home of Mind, these bottles are vanishing' and information is free to move within the boundless virtual spaces of the global Net. As a result, the 'natural behaviors' of pure information are beginning to reveal themselves. 'Freed of its containers', Barlow declared, 'information is obviously not a thing'. Rather, it is an activity or process that occurs in interactions 'between minds or objects or other pieces of information' and so has a temporal rather than a spatial existence. Information is 'experienced, not possessed', and it is experienced each time it is de-coded in these interactions to produce meanings. The more information is experienced, the more it generates ideas that live on in human belief systems and cultures; otherwise, it perishes. So to survive, information has to move; and for Barlow (quoting Stewart Brand's well-known hacker slogan) it 'wants to be free' (Brand, 1987: 202) to evolve through these flows.

Both technology and positive law, Barlow argued, have in the past hindered information's natural evolutionary impulse: technology, by fixing ideas in stable media (stone carvings, inked paper, celluloid recordings and so on) and 'exalting as a consequence the author's ability to determine the finished product'; and law, by stemming their flows in ways 'precisely contrary to the nature of information', that is, by restricting its sharing and re-use and controlling the channels through which it could move. But *digital* technology, in freeing information of its physical fetters, now promised to usher in Toffler's Third Wave and, with it, the post-industrial society. Digital technology undermines the controls placed by positive law on information's mobility: unauthorized copying and dissemination of digitized information is inevitable and unstoppable on the global Net.

Barlow acknowledged that the same technology would also inevitably be used to forge new 'bottles' adapted to cyberspace, and that these could be even more obstructive of information freedom than those they replaced. Content providers would seek to encrypt copyright works so that access (e.g. to read or to listen) required the provider's permission: these digital barricades would be designed to enclose ideas themselves, not merely their expressions, as the fixed works presupposed by copyright law had. Such endeavours would, however, be counter-productive: far from cultivating respect for the integrity of intellectual products, they would simply challenge the technically skilled to uncork the bottles and free their contents. The new enclosures would also inevitably fail: information freedom was encoded into the Net's very architecture, which treats blockages to information flows as damage and 'routes around' them.

At exactly the same time as Barlow was promoting this vision of the information society and copyright's (doomed) role within it, a quite opposed picture was in the process of being advanced by policy-makers at the heart of the world's most powerful states. A central place in this picture was occupied by copyright – supplemented by 'para-copyright' regimes of legal protection for technological fencing mechanisms – on the basis that without exclusionary techniques enabling the creative industries to charge for use of their information assets, these would be withheld from the Net completely. This alternative conception of the information society gained currency at a time when the continued advance of globalization was fuelling debates over how to develop national resources of information and intellectual capital so that domestic economies could compete successfully in world markets. In the US, concern about a rising trade deficit and a loss of technological edge (see for example Dertouzos et al., 1989; Porter, 1990) had generated a push to secure the conditions that could restore US success in global markets, especially in services and knowledge-intensive goods. One side-effect had been a campaign to expand the remit of the GATT to reach services and IPRs: this had ultimately borne fruit by the time the Uruguay Round of GATT talks opened in 1986 (for detailed explorations of this campaign, particularly with regard to IPRs, see Drahos and Braithwaite [2002] and May and Sell [2005]). Another was the launch of the first comprehensive national 'information society' policy by the Clinton-Gore administration on the crest of a wave of public and media interest in the World Wide Web.

In 1993, the US Government's Department of Commerce announced an agenda for action on a 'national information infrastructure' (NII). The agenda document declared that '[i]nformation is one of the nation's most critical economic resources' (Information Infrastructure Taskforce, 1993: 7) and that in an era of global markets and global competition, an 'information superhighway' would be of strategic importance in helping US businesses gain competitive advantage and in fuelling economic growth. (Echoing the apocalyptic tone characteristic of the breathless Internet hype of the time, the document makes the further claim that the NII would 'transform the lives of the American people' [1993: 6] by helping to 'unleash an information revolution that will change forever the way people live, work, and interact with each other' [1993: 5].) The initiatives needed to accelerate its development would include 'strengthen[ing] domestic copyright laws and international intellectual property treaties to prevent piracy' (1993: 13) of information and entertainment products – essential, it was said, if the market opportunities created by the NII for America's 'world-preeminent media and information industries' (1993: 12) were to be fully exploited.

In September 1995, the Working Group on IPRs that had been established pursuant to the agenda issued a White Paper – widely referred to as the Lehman report (after Bruce Lehman, then Assistant Secretary of Commerce) – that focused mainly on the copyright implications of the NII (Working Group on Intellectual Property Rights, 1995). The vision animating the Lehman report was of a future in which all uses of protected works online would be regulated by means of licences (1995: 52–3, 58). The transaction costs associated with licensing would be eased, if not eliminated, by new techniques for digitally 'tattooing' works with copyright management information (concerning authorship, ownership and terms of use) which would follow digital content wherever it went; and automated licensing systems could be linked with these techniques (1995: 191–4). More generally, with infringement online being easy and detection and enforcement difficult, copyright owners would use technological means such as encryption to protect their works. Technological tools for preventing or restricting access to works, limiting their use, monitoring permitted uses and enforcing licence terms (and payments) would proliferate (1995: 183–90). Technological protection would only be effective, however, if the integrity of these processes and systems was in turn underpinned both by social norms and by law. To these ends, the rising digital generation would need to be educated about the importance of respecting intellectual property online and the inevitability of pay-per-use business models for online content (1995: 201–10). Law would back up these efforts, supplementing copyright in digitized works with para-copyright regimes prohibiting the circumvention of technological protection measures applied to these works and the unauthorized removal or alteration of copyright management information (1995: 230–36). These legally protected DRM systems would make it possible and cost-effective for content providers to enforce copyrights in their content, while also empowering them to define rights broader than those provided for by copyright law – and all without incurring the burden of litigating or pursuing legislative reform. For recalcitrant lock-breakers and copyright pirates, technological means of detection and punishment would be accompanied by severe criminal penalties. In addition, Internet Service Providers would be drawn into the net of civil liability (see for example 1995: 114–24),[5] a move that would incentivize them to deploy their technological and informational capacities to police their subscribers' Internet usage and act against infringers – again at a distance from courts and legislators. At the same time, the deployment of technologies that could be used for infringing copyrights or breaking DRM locks would be outlawed. Yet despite the formidable array of locks, tags, tracking devices, automated payments and private police forces that would thereby be added to copyright law's arsenal, information would flow freely through (heavily patrolled) digital networks, because online transactions would be more or less 'frictionless'. True, private content-control regimes would also make the tracking of Internet users' reading, viewing and listening habits frictionless, with problematic implications for privacy; their pay-per-use logic would have distributional consequences;[6] and their self-enforcing character would exclude judicial oversight of contract terms and remedies.[7] However, licensing would be simple and swift, and it would lead to more and better quality information becoming available at a lower total social cost, because competition between providers would force prices down.

The NII initiative was mirrored shortly afterwards in Europe. Echoing the US Government's 1993 agenda for action on the NII, the 1994 report of Martin Bangemann's High-Level Group on the Information Society 'urg[ed] the European Union to put its faith in market mechanisms as the motive power to carry us into the Information Age' (European Commission, 1994: 4). Shortly thereafter, the themes of the Lehman Report were replicated in the 1995 European Commission Green Paper on copyright 'in the information society' (European Commission, 1995) and in a follow-up Communication from the Commission in 1996 (European Commission, 1996a). Meanwhile, in February 1995, a US-led 'agenda for a global information infrastructure' (GII), organized around similar principles and premised on the same expectations for the Information Age as the US national agenda,[8] became the focus of a G7 Ministerial Conference (European Commission, 1996b). By the end of 1996, the copyright aspects of this agenda had borne fruit in the form of two new international copyright treaties: the WIPO Copyright Treaty and the WIPO Performances and Phonograms Treaty.[9] The process of implementing the standards set out in these instruments by Contracting Parties has since yielded two measures that remain landmarks of US and EU copyright law to this day: the Digital Millennium Copyright Act (DMCA)[10] of 1998 and the Information Society Directive of 2001[11] respectively.

Although these global policies were justified by reference to utopian hopes for the information (technology) revolution not dissimilar to those entertained by John Perry Barlow, the official vision of the law-technology relation that they reflected contrasted markedly with Barlovian digi-libertarianism. Rather than giving technology free rein to co-evolve with the natural behaviours of information and the social norms and practices emerging spontaneously from interactions in cyberspace – for Lehman, 'such a legal free-for-all would transform the [information infrastructure] into a veritable copyright Dodge City' (Working Group on Intellectual Property Rights, 1995: 15) – law would regulate technology in two related ways. First, in proscribing circumvention technologies, law would endow technical systems for propertizing, monitoring and managing information with the *de facto* authority of legal systems. Consequently, law would endow the private actors operating and overseeing the design of these systems with the *de facto* authority of the state. The 'code'[12] thereby indirectly endorsed would shape what Lawrence Lessig – writing in 1996b – called the 'architecture' of cyberspace in a particular way. Cyberspace, Lessig noted then, was set to become a place where intellectual objects were owned absolutely, not because the copyright system enabled this, but because 'the designs of lawmakers [would have been] replaced by the designs of [software] codewriters' (Lessig, 1996b: 638), and a privatized law enabling absolute control of digitized content would have trumped the balanced arrangements set out in a copyright code that had been publicly enacted, enforced and applied. Further, this privatized law would be such as to give cyberspace a new 'nature', in that, though a human artefact, it would confront its subjects as underpinned by something equivalent to a law of nature: for the technically inept at least, there would be no choice but to obey the rules inscribed in DRM systems. 'Because one only enters cyberspace mediated by software, the code of software becomes the perfect panopticon of control' (1996a: 900).

LESSIGISM

Subsequent developments – the organized subversion of DRM systems, the advent of peer-to-peer file-sharing as a mass phenomenon, and the growing pervasiveness of (re)user-generated content – were to reveal this hoped-for technologization of control over intellectual property to be an impossible dream. Creative Commons, however, offered something other than a simple refusal of this project. The CC strategy was not to reject the official vision of technologically-enabled 'private ordering' as such, but to turn it to different ends: to *transform* the copyright licence from a tool of ever more finely tuned control over access to and use of cultural material into a charter of freedoms of access to, and (re)use of, information (Elkin-Koren: 2005; Dusollier: 2007). At the same time, it aimed to intervene in the technical 'architecture' of online rights management by building software tools that enabled these freedoms to 'run with' digitized content as it moved through digital networks.[13] Where a licensed work exists in digitized form, CC's machine-readable licence terms can be encoded in the digitized object itself so that they literally move with the content as it circulates through digital networks: when a user encounters the work online, the embedded code automatically indicates to the user the applicable terms.[14] The hoped-for upshot of these licensing and software tools (the 'legal and technical infrastructure' referred to above), when combined with the content to which these were applied by individual creators, was to be a 'vast digital commons' (Creative Commons, 2014a) – a pool of content that could be copied, edited, re-mixed, built upon and distributed by users more or less freely. Creative Commons was to be a 'steward' – not of this pool of content itself but the infrastructure that ensured its creation.

The vision animating this stewarding activity was once again indebted to Information Age thinking, and to this extent was continuous with Barlovian informationalism and official Information Society policy alike. The vision was 'nothing less than realizing the full potential of the Internet — universal access to research, education, full participation in culture, and driving a new era of development, growth and productivity' (Creative Commons, 2014a). The disagreement was only over the means of the vision's realization. For the founders of Creative Commons, the copyright industries' propertization strategies – variously described by Lessig as 'extremist', 'fundamentalist' and 'feudal' (Lessig, 2004a: 173, 261, 267) – were likely only to stifle the opportunities for digital technologies to be used widely to encourage creativity (Lessig, 2007) by impeding activities that were taken for granted in the networked environment: copying, pasting, posting to the Web, working collaboratively (to create resources such as Wikipedia, the free online encyclopedia, for example), creating remixes, mash-ups and so on. However, in contrast to the digi-libertarians' equally 'extremist' affirmation of the unregulated Internet's anarchy (Lessig, 1999: Ch. 3), and their outright rejection of copyright and para-copyright controls, the aim of Creative Commons was 'to build a layer of *reasonable* copyright on top of the extremes that now reign' (Lessig, 2004a: 282, emphasis in original) by devising alternative mechanisms – standardized, but nonetheless chosen by individual creators – to those endorsed by public legislation. These, it was hoped, would create 'a balance between the reality of the Internet and the reality of copyright laws' (Creative Commons, 2014a) by making it easier to share and build upon creative works. The intention of CC's founders was never that the organization would itself issue licences of creators' content, or maintain a database of licensed content; rather, the idea was that creators would choose from among the licence templates that the organization made available, and (oriented by these templates) determine for themselves how they wished to regulate the use of their works. CreativeCommons.org was to be 'a legal self-help site' (Creative Commons, 2014c) offering free legal documents for general use. 'We build infrastructure at Creative Commons. Our users build the commons itself' (Creative Commons, 2014a).

Lessig evidently saw in this infrastructure, and the licensing practices it would foster, a kind of DIY-democratization of IP lawmaking – which at the level of public legislation seemed by the end of the 1990s to have been irredeemably captured by corporate lobbies – oriented towards (re)creating the legal conditions for what he called a 'free culture.' He elaborated at length on this vision in a book published in 2004 under that title: *Free Culture*. The word 'free' here, first of all, designates a situation in which at least *some* cultural content is 'free for the taking' (Lessig, 2004a: 29) – by which Lessig meant 'free to re-use without anyone's permission'. Copyright law itself, Lessig pointed out, was initially designed with built-in safeguards for a cultural commons of intellectual things free for the taking, and for most of its history these safeguards had been maintained: its inherent limits (e.g. of duration and scope) had in the past guaranteed that absolute control of each and every use of cultural materials was impossible. However, copyright's rapid expansion since the 1970s, coupled with the rise of DRM/para-copyright law and growing copyright industry concentration, had led to its becoming 'the single most important regulator of creativity' (Lessig, 2004a: 162) by the turn of the century. This, Lessig suggested, had blocked alternative trajectories for online commerce in cultural goods:

> Digital technologies, tied to the Internet, could produce a vastly more competitive and vibrant market for building and cultivating culture; that market could include a much wider and more diverse range of creators; those creators could produce and distribute a much more vibrant range of creativity; and … earn more on average from this system than creators do today. … [if only the copyright industries would cease] using their power to get the law to protect them against this new, more efficient, more vibrant technology for building culture. (2004a: 8)

Law was serving 'more and more to protect [the copyright] industries against competition' (2004a: 19), stultifying in the process the very enterprise and initiative on which high-tech innovation depended. In a clever twist on the pro-market triumphalism that had greeted the ignominious fall of the Soviet bloc at the end of the 1980s, Lessig even managed to suggest an analogy between the IP-addicted corporate behemoths that were throttling cultural production in the US, and the rigid government-controlled bureaucratic behemoths that had already throttled industrial production in state-communist regimes:

> In a free society, with a free market, supported by free enterprise and free trade, the government's role is not to support one way of doing business against others. Its role is not to pick winners and protect them against loss. If the government did this generally, then we would never have any progress. … A world in which competitors with new ideas must fight not only the market but also the government is a world in which competitors with new ideas will not succeed. It is a world of stasis and increasingly concentrated stagnation. It is the Soviet Union under Brezhnev. (2004a: 127–8)

So much for freedom, but what was Lessig's understanding of a free *culture*? Here again, the centrality of the market to Lessig's way of thinking was evident. 'A free culture, like a free market, is filled … with rules of property and contract that get enforced by the state' (2004a: xvi). No less than innovation and markets, culture and markets were intimately linked, presumably because markets in intellectual property rights sustain markets in authors' works, which in turn sustain the marketplace of ideas constituting culture as such. Culture, in short, could be understood on the model of competitive exchange, even when no actual market transaction was involved. The objects of cultural exchange were narratives, ideas, music, images (often, though not necessarily, the commodified products of the cultural industries); the forms of cultural exchange were transactions between creators, consumers, sharers, re-users, modifiers and critics of cultural materials. Copying was the crucial lubricant of cultural exchange in all of its forms. For Lessig there could be no creativity without copying, since creators always already inhabit a culture and can only express themselves through it: hence culture had to be understood as both an environment for, and an artefact of, creativity (2004a: 129–30). 'Creators here and everywhere are always and at all times building upon the creativity that went before and that surrounds them now' (2004a: 28). Equally, sharing and 'tinkering' with received cultural forms – in a word, 're-mixing' (Lessig, 2004b) – 'is what humans have done since the dawn of man. It is how we learn and communicate' (2004a: 184, 46–7).

Culture/creativity, Lessig suggested, had always been regulated by the available technologies for copying and exchanging immaterial artefacts, and by the institutions (Lessig instanced laws, informal social norms and markets) structuring its production and reception at any given time. In the contemporary US (Lessig's writings of the mid-1990s to the mid-2000s clearly had an American readership in mind),[15] culture/creativity thus included the products of the creative industries, as well as the products of non-commercial activities such as 'telling stories, reenacting scenes from plays or TV, participating in fan clubs, sharing music, making tapes' (2004a: 8). Uniquely among cultural technologies of any era, though, digital technology promised to do away with the frictions that had impeded the natural dynamics of culture/creativity in the past – 'explod[ing] the boundaries' (2004a: 184) they imposed – while at the same time extending the cultural environment and widening the audience for creative products in previously unimaginable ways:

> The technology of digital 'capturing and sharing' promises a world of extraordinarily diverse creativity that can be easily and broadly shared. ... Technology has thus given us an opportunity to do something with culture that has only ever been possible for individuals in small groups, isolated from others. Think about an old man telling a story to a collection of neighbors in a small town. Now imagine that same storytelling extended across the globe. (2004a: 184–5)

For Lessig, though, the crucial barrier to instituting this global storytelling was that every cultural exchange online involves an act of copying that copyright law regulates. Consequently, '[e]very use of copyrighted content [online] at least presumptively triggers a requirement of permission' (Lessig, 2005a). Lessig's central message was that the law and practice of intellectual property impeded the potential of digital technology to usher in a new age of free culture, a culture unbound by the constraints that previously limited its generativity. The real threat to a free culture was neither property in culture nor markets in culture, but the interaction of corrupted forms of both: *feudal* intellectual property relations and *monopolistic* market practices. Over-expansive state-backed digital (copy)rights wielded in a context of industry concentration were producing a kind of information feudalism in which a 'cultural nobility' (Lessig, 2004a: 9) – the copyright-industrial dinosaur class – held sway over the cultural domain. The result was a 'permission culture' which fatally chilled creative expression, since permission 'is not often granted to the critical or independent' (2004a: 10). The digi-libertarian stance, Lessig insisted, offered no real antidote to this threat, because the danger would be equally present in the unregulated cyberspace whose virtues the Barlovians misguidedly extolled.

Yet despite these differences, Lessig shared a great deal with the 'extremists' he positioned at each end of the spectrum whose middle ground he claimed, not least a belief in the inevitable coming of an information society and an unshakeable faith in friction-free digital capitalism. 'We will have an information society. That much is certain. Our only choice now is whether that information society will be free or feudal' (2004a: 267). The positioning of the regressively feudal as the antithesis of the progressively free was of course significant, because what comes after feudalism in any epochal historical schema, as everybody knows, is capitalism. Lessig's argument was that the organization of copyright law and the copyright industries at the turn of the millennium was the result of a harmful mutation that had effectively reversed the proper course of history: a once-beneficial regime of law was now out of step with the evolutionary trends that had caused other feudal institutions to be overtaken by socially progressive capitalist ones.

FREE CULTURE; FREE SOFTWARE

I return to those themes in the concluding section. First, I aim to use Lessig's account of what a free culture is to illuminate one of the key conundrums thrown up by the Creative Commons phenomenon: why it has never in fact set out to promote a 'free as in free software' approach to building a free culture, even though it acknowledges the free software movement as a key inspiration. This difference is evident in the design of CC's licensing infrastructure. Four of the six CC licence templates deny one or more of the freedoms that the free software philosophy defines as essential: these templates negate the freedom to share for *any* purpose (including commercial purposes), or the freedom to modify the work (to make and circulate derivatives of it), or both.[16] CC's policy of endorsing 'no commercial use' and 'no derivatives' clauses prompted charges in the mid-2000s that while the free software movement adopts a firm ethical position and observes non-negotiable principles, CC deploys:

> no defined criteria by which *any* clauses can be categorically blocked … [and] there is no base level of freedom that every Creative Commons license must provide … [Consequently] CC has replaced what could have been a call for a world where 'essential rights are unreservable' with the relatively hollow call for 'some rights reserved'. (Mako Hill, 2005)

With a swipe at what he called the 'autism' of the free software world, Lessig shortly afterwards declared that reducing the six templates to one would amount to 'bullying the world into using a single license' (Lessig, 2005b). Yet the accusation of hollowness evidently rankled. In the same communiqué, Lessig stated that 'the fundamental value of every significant advance in the digital age [is] interoperability' and announced the launch of a project to establish a procedure through which CC 'share-alike' licences could be deemed compatible (and therefore interoperable) with non-CC copyleft licences. The gesture turned out to be hollow: although the procedure was introduced in 2007 (Garlick, 2013), no non-CC licence has to date been certified for compatibility (Creative Commons, 2014d). The attempt to re-characterize freedom in terms of interoperability only revealed Lessig's underlying commitment to a form of technological determinism, while at the same time drawing attention to a more fundamental interoperability problem: that which subsists between different CC licence types (a work licensed under a CC no-derivatives licence cannot for example be mixed with a work licensed under a CC share-alike licence).

The justification Lessig offered for the persistence of this intra-CC incompatibility – a serious limit on the 'freedom' of remix culture – is telling. '*That* incompatibility … is intended by the creator' (Lessig, 2005b, emphasis added). The freedom of the author to control what is done with his or her work ultimately prevails over the freedom of others to re-use it. It has been shown that Lessig's conception of 'free as in *Free Culture*' designates a situation in which *some* cultural content is free to re-use without anyone's permission. Only some, because at the heart of Lessig's vision of a free culture is not in fact the re-mixer but the author – and, in particular, the proprietary author. (For an insightful exploration of some possible consequences of CC's support for proprietary authorship, see Elkin-Koren, 2005: 398–402.) The essential freedoms celebrated by his, and CC's, free culture philosophy are the freedoms to hold copyrights – property rights – in eligible works of authorship *and to decide how far* to allow others freedom to do the acts that the copyright reserves exclusively to the authors of these works. CC sends a clear message that authors should alter the 'all rights reserved' default setting by releasing their works using one of its licence templates, and it makes it easier for authors to do so by offering the legal and technical infrastructure gratis to anyone who wants to use it. But CC does not send a clear message that copyright's exclusionary effect should be undone entirely: some rights can be reserved if the author wants to reserve them.

The essential freedoms celebrated by the free software philosophy, by contrast, make no distinction between authors and others. *Everyone* should be able to do *all* of the acts in relation to a work that copyright law reserves to the author alone, and *none* of the rights comprised in a copyright should be reserved. Whereas Stallman's project has been to hack copyright (on the basis that it is an alien imposition on the process of software innovation and should therefore be used only in a way that overturns it), Lessig's project has been to maintain copyright (on the basis that culture has always been 'proprietary' because authors 'need to eat' [Lessig, 2005a]).[17] It is no surprise, then, that the idea Lessig credited the free software movement with bequeathing to CC was not that of freedom as such but simply that of 'giv[ing] away free copyright licences' (2005a).

A further implication of Creative Commons' plurality of approved licence templates – which in turn reflects its rugged author-centric individualism – is that the organization does not in fact promote a commons. The idea of 'a commons' at play in contemporary debates about proprietary approaches to innovation is admittedly vague: indeed this is a key reason why a movement to build 'it' has been able to grow so fast. Yochai Benkler has offered the most sophisticated specification of the idea to date, but even this only reveals its elasticity:

> The salient characteristic of commons, as opposed to [private] property, is that no single person has exclusive control over the use and disposition of any particular resource in the commons. Instead, resources governed by commons may be used or disposed of by anyone among some (more or less well-defined) number of persons, under rules that may range from 'anything goes' to quite crisply articulated formal rules that are effectively enforced. (Benkler, 2006: 61)

Benkler proceeds to distinguish commons arrangements along two axes. The first registers the number of persons to whom resources subject to such arrangements are open: an 'open commons' is open to anyone; a 'limited-access commons' is open only to members of a defined group (and where that group collectively owns the resources which are subject to commons arrangements, these 'behave as property vis-à-vis the entire world except members of the group' [2006: 61]). The second axis registers the extent to which uses of resources (by those entitled to use them) are regulated.

The public domain is, in Benkler's terms, an open commons which is unregulated: anyone can use out-of-copyright works, for example, at will and without payment. But – although Benkler's characterization obscures this – works protected by copyright are also in a form of commons in his sense, because ownership of a copyright in a work does not amount to ownership of the work. Copyright law is a hybrid system in which rules defining rights of private property in works interact with rules providing for greater or lesser degrees of public access and use, on more or less restrictive terms. Copyright law in the UK, for example, defines a number of distinct regimes of rules for different categories of protected work.[18] Each regime combines exclusive property rights for copyright owners with freedoms of access and use for all others: by law, different categories of work attract different bundles of rights, each bundle defining the zone of the copyright owner's dominion over any work in that category; but these zones are limited (by exceptions, in duration and so forth) in different ways so that spaces of freedom are carved out for everyone else. If on Benkler's definition an intellectual commons exists 'where no single person has exclusive control over the use and disposition of any particular [intellectual] resource', then (assuming that the relevant resources here are works of authorship), copyright law itself defines a kind of intellectual commons: an open commons which is (formally and relatively heavily) regulated.

Every copyright licence, as between the parties to it, alters the statutory regime that would otherwise apply universally. By its nature, any copyright licence grants the licensee permission to make a use of the licensed work that the general law reserves to the copyright owner exclusively. A CC licence is more than usually permissive and applies to anyone, anywhere in the world, and for the entire duration of the copyright in the licensed work. In effect, it relaxes the rules that copyright law imposes on users of that work everywhere – but it doesn't remove them completely: material licensed under CC licences is not thereby placed in the public domain.[19] It follows that the status of a CC-licensed work is not fundamentally different from that of an unlicensed copyright work: each subsists in an open but regulated commons, albeit that the regulation affecting a CC-licensed work is lighter than that applicable to a work which is not so licensed. Moreover there is no *single* commons arrangement for CC-licensed works, because CC licence templates have in effect given rise to six distinct regimes of CC-rules governing the use of licensed material: not one 'pool of pre-cleared content that can be mixed and shared' (Maracke, 2010: 10), then, but six pools of content, each 'pre-cleared' for different categories of use, as follows:

(a) A licensee under a CC attribution-only licence (CC-BY) can use the licensed material in all the ways reserved exclusively to the copyright holder by the general law of copyright, but the author must be credited for any re-use.
(b) A licensee under a CC attribution/share-alike licence (CC-BY-SA) can use the licensed material in all the ways reserved exclusively to the copyright holder by the general law of copyright, but the author must be credited for any re-use, and the licensee, if re-circulating any material which is derived from the licensed work, must re-license it on the same terms.
(c) A licensee under a CC attribution/no commercial use licence (CC-BY-NC) has similar freedoms as under CC-BY except that these may not be exercised in any manner that is primarily intended for or directed toward commercial advantage or private monetary compensation.
(d) A licensee under a CC attribution/no commercial use/share-alike licence (CC-BY-NC-SA) has similar freedoms as under CC-BY-NC except that the licensee, if re-circulating any derivatives, must re-license them on the same terms.
(e) A licensee under a CC attribution/no commercial use/no derivatives licence (CC-BY-ND) can use the licensed material in some of the ways reserved exclusively to the copyright holder by the general law of copyright – i.e. by copying, distributing exact copies of, and publicly performing and communicating, the licensed works – but not in ways that involve the making of derivatives of the licensed work, and the author must be credited for any re-use.
(f) A licensee under a CC attribution/no commercial use/no derivatives licence (CC-BY-NC-ND) can use the licensed material in some of the ways reserved exclusively to the copyright holder by the general law of copyright – i.e. by copying, distributing copies of, and publicly performing and communicating, the licensed works – but not in any manner that is primarily intended for or directed toward commercial advantage or private monetary compensation and not in ways that involve the making of derivatives of the licensed work; and the author must be credited for any re-use.

Little wonder that CC-licensed works have been characterized as 'a privatised, individuated and dispersed collection of objects and resources that subsist in a technical-legal space of confusing and differential legal restrictions, ownership rights and permissions' (Berry and Moss, 2005).

It is worth noting in this context that works licensed in any of these ways are generally not licensed to, or by, collectives of creators. Unlike Stallman's Free Software Foundation, CC has never actively promoted the idea that authors should participate with others in producing integrated artefacts, and collaborative 'free culture' projects are unusual (for reflections on this, see Webber [2012]). Wikipedia is the biggest and best-known example, but although the Wikimedia Foundation Board of Trustees (the non-profit organization that operates Wikipedia) adopted CC-BY-SA as its main licence type in 2009,[20] Wikipedia preceded the launch of Creative Commons and was originally licensed under the FSF's GNU Free Documentation Licence template (a template intended for software documentation). Arguably, then, Wikipedia is best regarded as an outgrowth of the free software movement.

AFTER INFORMATION FEUDALISM?

Despite its departures from the free software model, CC licensing is spreading like wildfire. The latest estimates suggest that some 500 million copyright works have been made available online subject to a Creative Commons licence of one kind or another, and the UK Government's recent endorsement of the CC-BY licence template for publishing many outputs of publicly-funded academic research (Department of Business, Innovation and Skills, 2012; Research Councils UK, 2013) is just the latest sign of the current hegemony of this form of 'commons-ism' (for other prominent users of the templates, see Creative Commons [2014e]). But what exactly does it mean to be a Creative Commoner? Several commentators have puzzled over this question. Already in 2005, when CC was only three years old, David Berry and Giles Moss (2005) were characterizing it as committed to a 'commons without commonalty', while Benjamin Mako Hill (2005) was complaining of the 'hollowness' of this commitment and Niva Elkin-Koren was noting the 'ideological fuzziness' associated with its lack of 'a comprehensive vision of the information society' (2005: 390). What I hope to have revealed here are the roots of the limitations identified by these critics. In brief, CC's denial of commonalty proceeds from its implicit adoption of liberal legalism: a perspective on the social world that privileges the rights of individuals over the claims of any social group. Its incoherence proceeds from the inconsistency between its commitment to individual property rights and its simultaneous commitment to a version of what has been called 'information exceptionalism' (Schiller, 1996: 161–72; Söderberg 2008: 170–72). I elaborate on these points in this concluding section.

Liberal legalism is a term without a fixed referent (Brown and Halley, 2002: 5), and to say that freedom, equality and justice are its guiding ideals illuminates little. But a degree of precision is possible. Fundamentally, to be committed to liberal legalism is to assume that freedom can be equated with the individual capacity for choice, equality with equal freedom to pursue the objects of one's choices, and justice with the existence of a system of rights, guaranteed by law, in which these formally equal liberties are enshrined and mutually reconciled. Rights of property and contract are at the heart of this system of rights, because these are the central mechanisms by which individuals can realize their capacity for agency. Ideally, on this view, the state specifies, interprets and enforces the elements of the system so that the equal liberty of all is indeed ensured; in practice, it is prone to abuse its monopoly of coercive power and intrude too far into areas which should be zones of individual freedom. Those wedded to liberal legalism disagree about what constitutes an illegitimate intrusion: as Brown and Halley point out, there is a range of perspectives on how the state should go about its task of securing individual rights, and left-liberalism, free market conservatism, authoritarian conservatism and libertarianism are the main variants in the US. However, none of the perspectives accommodated by liberal legalism questions the ontological priority of the individual, the normative primacy of individual agency, the necessity of rights to institutionalize the possibility of agency, or the role of the state as the guarantor of these rights.

Both the free software movement and Creative Commons are equally wedded to liberal legalism. They also tend to reflect a libertarian outlook. Libertarianism in turn tends to be associated with strong beliefs in the market as a (if not the) crucial arena for the realization of freedom, and in competition as the primary mechanism for reconciling the rival projects of free individuals; and the architects of both movements manifest an appreciation of the centrality of property and contract to the legal institutionalization of competitive exchange. But both movements are also wedded to information exceptionalism – the doctrine that information has inherent natural characteristics that make it different from other resources – and both recognize that this has implications for the viability and justifiability of property rights in information.

Information is said to be different from tangible things because it is inexhaustible, infinitely shareable, leaky (relatively non-excludable) and liable to increase in value and generativity the more widely it is shared. As shown above, digi-libertarians of the Barlovian school have long argued that these special characteristics make copyright wholly redundant in the Information Age that digitization has ushered in. The philosophers of free software essentially agree, but have elaborated a way of living with the copyright system that uses it only to abuse it: uses it, that is to say, in a way that entirely undoes its functionality as a mechanism for excluding everyone apart from the right-holder from the resources that it protects. By contrast, Creative Commons does not reject this mechanism entirely. Yet it too is rhetorically wedded to information exceptionalism; and it too characterizes the digital revolution as capable of unleashing the potential of information freedom to transform society if only the 'feudal' intellectual monopolies that the state's Industrial Age captors have forced it to maintain are undone. There resides the obvious inconsistency in CC's position. These monopolies *can* be undone – the free software movement has shown the way – and yet CC itself has stopped short of urging authors to undo them completely. Why?

The analysis offered here points towards an explanation that has two related aspects. The first is CC's assumption that an individual's freedom of choice trumps any ethical obligations that s/he may incur through membership of a community, including a community of 'copy-fighters'. We have seen that for CC to approve only one licence template – as the FSF has done with the GPL and the Wikimedia Foundation with CC-BY-SA – would in Lessig's view be excessively prescriptive. It matters not that the point of this move would be to ensure that copyrights are licensed so that equivalent freedoms are available to all individuals. The GPL, after all, imposes its share-alike obligations *in the name of* individual freedom, and the FSF devised the GPL because of its conviction that since coding is a process of creating information, and information wants to be free, universal information freedom overrides the demands of particular code-writers. Lessig's rejection of this position is rooted, second, in his commitment to individual authorial property: his belief in the latter's naturalness ultimately prevails over his belief in the exceptional nature of information. In his view, culture has *always* been proprietary even though it is constituted of flows of information, and the natural necessity of authorial property has not been swept away by the digital revolution.

It is true that cultural progress has had a different trajectory to that of software (and, generally, technical) innovation. But this is not because culture is naturally proprietary. Far from being a natural invariant, the relationship between authorship and property was forged in the modern West in close association with the rise of print capitalism, and authorial property rights have primarily served to secure the cultural industries' profitability, not to meet authors' material needs. For this and other reasons, simple analogies between the space of culture and the space of the market are questionable, as is the assumption that property rights in authors' works are necessary conditions of authorship itself (Barron, 2012).

On one level, the encouragement CC gives to individual authors to control their own copyrights problematizes the authorial subordination that accompanies the power of copyright-wielding corporate actors in the creative industries (Elkin-Koren, 2005: 385–6). Yet the movement is premised on a disregard for (or even an uncritical embrace of) the implications for authors' lives and livelihoods of the licensing strategy it promotes. The working lives of those who seek to support themselves by deploying their creative or communicative skills are marked, as Gill and Pratt point out, by 'a preponderance of temporary, intermittent and precarious jobs; long hours and bulimic patterns of working; the collapse or erasure of the boundaries between work and play; poor pay; high levels of mobility; [but also] passionate attachment to the work and to the identity of the creative labourer' (Gill and Pratt, 2008: 14; and see further, for example, McRobbie, 2002; Beck, 2003; McKercher and Mosco, 2008; McKinlay and Smith, 2009; de Peuter, 2011). When the increasing recourse to CC licensing is viewed against this backdrop, it looks less like the triumph of authorial sovereignty and more like its opposite: licensors' surrender to 'users' (who could once again be corporate actors in the creative industries) of the power to extract value from their creations appears as little more than a reflection of a precariousness that makes creative workers exceptionally vulnerable to exploitation – all the more so because of the 'passionate attachments' that cathect them to their creative work. (For an interesting analysis of the nature of exploitation in the cultural industries, see Cohen [2012].) Where products of authorship are released under CC licences lacking a 'no commercial use' clause, they duly become (in Lessig's own [2007] words) 'open for business': fully available to be harvested for profit.

Speaking in 2010, Lessig himself endorsed the monetization of the information wealth contained in ostensibly non-market activities of sharing online:

> [Amazon] sells books, but it sells books in the particular way in which it does by building on a community that shares reviews and ratings of the products that are being sold; it *depends* on that community to make more money. ... [Microsoft's] user groups are monitored and managed ... [in a way that] guides these groups to facilitate them to produce the best kind of input *for free* ... thus leveraging these sharing communities into providing more profit for Microsoft. (Lessig, 2010, emphasis in original)

Practices of online sharing could be construed as contesting capitalism: indeed neo-Marxist writers such as Michael Hardt and Antonio Negri seem to see them as oriented towards reclaiming the means and outputs of collectively-produced knowledge and culture (what they call 'commonwealth') *from* capitalism (Hardt and Negri, 2009: 281–2, 308). Yet Lessig is interested in how capitalism can renew itself by 'leveraging these practices into providing more profit for' ... Microsoft? Evidently, accumulation by dispossession continues apace in a commons-ist world.

It is odd, to say the least, that Lessig should align himself with any aspect of Microsoft's business model: after all, the latter's invention of the proprietary approach to software innovation sparked the very antagonism that led to the free software movement from which Creative Commons took its inspiration (Gates, 1976). More generally, the ideological path Lessig has plotted for 🅭 is barely distinguishable from that of ©, and there is an ongoing debate within the organization as to whether it would be better advised to hew to the line that the free software movement has adopted since its inception (Creative Commons, 2014f). From the perspective of a social critic seeking to make sense of copyright law today, there is something to be said for a more thorough-going adoption of the philosophy and strategy of 'free'. Stallman's project of hacking copyright arguably represents an unwittingly dialectical reading of this proprietary institution as containing the seeds of its own overcoming, and the collaborative habits that the hacker ethos has cultivated give substance to the notion of 'creative commoning' that CC licensing alone palpably lacks. For these and other reasons, radical observers of the free software phenomenon have been able to find in it a potential for hacking capitalism itself. Johan Söderberg's (2008) analysis along these lines is particularly rich and suggestive.

Crucially, though, the assumption embedded in the hacker ethos that information is exceptional, coupled with its libertarian bias, equip the hacker perspective on freedom with blinkers of its own. Hackers do not in general place private property itself in question. While eschewing copyrights and patents on code, they embrace the notion that the reputations (whether individual or collective) garnered for a programmer's (or a program's, or a project's) technical merits can be objects of exclusive proprietary control, and they have no objection to private ownership of the means of producing the commercial software services that are sustained by the outputs of free software ecosystems: 'no commercial use' clauses are antithetical to the philosophy of free. It is clear that new forms of exploitation and domination attend the economic 'success' of Free and Open Source Software – a success built on these alternative property forms (Barron, 2013) – and a growing literature is emerging from the ongoing effort to understand 'the ways in which individual creative input, ostensibly "freely" given, is, at best, ambivalently positioned within [digital] capitalism …' (Burston et al., 2010: 219; and see also, for example, Boutang, 2012; Arvidsson and Peitersen, 2013; Scholz, 2013).

The libertarian perspective that orients the hacker worldview blinds it to the dark side of the new economy that hackers have been instrumental in bringing about. This perspective has produced a tendency to see the inequality and unfreedom involved with the new economy as inevitable necessities of information capitalism, and since information capitalism – no less than its industrial predecessor – relies upon property and its exchange, liberal legalism too remains firmly embedded within the hacker imaginary (see for example Coleman, 2013): like all visions of the information society, this one rests on dreams of transforming only the relations of *intellectual* property and its exchange. Nonetheless, the aspirations that propelled the experiments in information-commoning that began to proliferate around the turn of the millennium seem unlikely to disappear through being disappointed. They are already re-emerging as aspirations for the non-exploitative, solidaristic organization of the means of life itself.

NOTES

1 I eschew the term 'anti-proprietary' in what follows. Although the term 'open licensing' is an admittedly reductive shorthand for a wide variety of strategies, it is more accurate than 'anti-proprietary licensing' as a descriptor for the practices under discussion, if only because licensing presupposes the existence of a property right in respect of the uses that are licensed.

2 'Conveying' is defined to mean 'any kind of propagation that enables other parties to make or receive copies'.

3 The key terms of the core suite of Creative Commons licences are Attribution, NonCommercial, NoDerivatives and ShareAlike (the suite comprises different combinations of these key terms).

4 Toffler reciprocated in a subsequent essay of his own (co-written with others under the auspices of Newt Gingrich's Progress and Freedom Foundation), which situated Barlow's reflections on IPRs in relation to what were argued to be wider implications of cyberspace for the nature of markets, freedom, community and government (see Dyson et al.,1994).

5 This proposal sparked vigorous academic debate at the time. Some argued against the imposition of accessory liability on ISPs (e.g. Elkin-Koren, 1993); some argued for strict ISP liability (e.g. Hardy, 1994: 1042–6); and some supported the application to ISPs of traditional notions of contributory and/or vicarious liability (e.g. Ginsburg, 1995: 1492–5). A limited liability regime was in the end adopted in US law thanks to the lobbying efforts of ISPs themselves, who argued that imposing duties on them to monitor their users' activities for copyright infringements would make their services prohibitively expensive or drive them out of business completely, thereby limiting, or negating altogether, the promise of the information 'superhighway'. In 1998, the Digital Millennium Copyright Act added §512 to Title 17 of the United States Code, which established defined 'safe harbors' for ISPs engaging in hosting, caching, information location and transmission activities.

6 Many more online than offline uses would not only have to be licensed, but also paid for (indeed many uses previously excused as 'fair' would become 'fared' (Bell, 1998; Working Group on Intellectual Property Rights, 1995: 82).

7 These issues were highlighted at the time by Julie E. Cohen in several prescient articles (e.g. 1996, 1998a, 1998b, 2000).

8 US Vice President Al Gore introduced America's vision for the GII at the first World Telecommunication Development Conference in March 1994. In February 1995 this was amplified by the Information Infrastructure Task Force – in terms very similar to those of its earlier paper *NII: Agenda for Action* – in a paper entitled *Global Information Infrastructure: Agenda for Cooperation* (Information Infrastructure Taskforce, 1995). This document enunciated the US Government's intent to 'join with other governments' in fora such as WIPO to 'achieve high levels of intellectual property and technical protection in order to guarantee to right-holders the technical and legal means to control the use of their property over the GII', eliminate compulsory licensing (in favour of individualized transactional licensing), and provide effective enforcement against copyright infringements.

9 WIPO Copyright Treaty, adopted December 20, 1996 (WIPO Doc. CRNR/DC/94); Agreed Statements Concerning the WIPO Copyright Treaty, adopted December 20, 1996 (WIPO Doc. CRNR/DC/96); WIPO Performances and Phonograms Treaty, adopted December 20, 1996 (WIPO Doc. CRNR/DC/95); Agreed Statements Concerning the WIPO Performances and Phonograms Treaty, adopted December 20, 1996 (WIPO Doc. CRNR/DC/97).

10 Digital Millennium Copyright Act 1998 (Pub.L. 105–304, 112 Stat. 2860, 28 October 1998), amending the US Copyright Act 1976 (Pub. L. 94–553, 90 Stat. 2541, 19 October 1976) (17 U.S.C.).

11 Directive 2001/29/EC of the European Parliament and of the Council of 22 May, 2001 on the harmonization of certain aspects of copyright and related rights in the information society.

12 'Code' here signifies software in general, but more particularly the rules inscribed in it: 'Rules, for example, that require a password upon entry into a system' (Lessig, 1996a: 896). A lengthier exploration of code as a 'modality' of regulation in cyberspace was subsequently offered in Lessig (1999).

13 'Creative Commons' licences and tools were designed specifically to work with the web, which makes content that is offered under their terms easy to search for, discover and use' (Creative Commons, 2014c).

14 Having chosen a licence template, the licensor typically elects to include machine-readable code in the work that 'marks' it with the licence regulating its use (together with other details, such as attribution information), and enables the work to be found online using appropriate search engines (e.g. Google's advanced search option).

15 *Free Culture* frequently invokes an American past when culture was truly free, contrasting this with an alien present in which long-held domestic values have been compromised. Thus, 'American culture was born free, and for almost 180 years our country consistently protected a vibrant and rich free culture. We achieved that free culture because our law respected important limits on the scope of the interests protected by 'property' (Lessig, 2004a: 172).

16 Only two CC licences qualify as 'free culture' licences (i.e. licences that apply the principles of free software to content) (Linksvayer, 2008).

17 CC specifically denies that it is working to undermine copyright (see Steuer, 2010).

18 Thus, the regime of rules regulating the use of, say, musical works is different from that regulating the use of computer programs, and both differ from the regime affecting photographs.

19 CC does, however, offer a tool for dedicating works to the public domain. For the background to its launch by CC in 2009 (see Peters, 2009).

20 The justification for the change was to ensure that 'Wikimedia project content will be more interoperable with existing CC-BY-SA content and easier to re-use' (Wikimedia Foundation, 2009).

REFERENCES

Article 19 (2013) *The Right to Share: Principles on Freedom of Expression and Copyright in the Digital Age* (http://www.article19.org/resources.php/resource/3716/en/the-right-to-share:-principles-on-freedom-of-expression-and-copyright-in-the-digital-age).

Arvidsson, Adam and Peitersen, Nicolai (2013) *The Ethical Economy: Rebuilding Value After the Crisis.* New York: Columbia University Press.

Barlow, John Perry (1993) 'Selling Wine Without Bottles: The Economy of Mind on the Global Net' (a.k.a. The Economy of Ideas), *Wired* 2.03 (http://archive.wired.com/wired/archive/2.03/economy.ideas_pr.html).

Barron, Anne (2012) 'Kant, Copyright and Communicative Freedom', *Law and Philosophy*, 31: 1–48.

Barron, Anne (2013) 'Free Software as Critical Social Practice', *Economy and Society*, 42(4): 597–625.

Beck, Andrew (ed.) (2003) *Cultural Work: Understanding the Cultural Industries.* London: Routledge.

Bell, Tom W. (1998) 'Fair Use vs. Fared Use: The Impact of Automated Rights Management on Copyright's Fair Use Doctrine', *N. Carolina Law Review*, 76: 557–620.

Benkler, Yochai (2006) *The Wealth of Networks*. New Haven: Yale University Press.

Berry, David and Moss, Giles (2005) 'On the 'Creative Commons': A Critique of the Commons Without Commonalty', *Free Software Magazine*, 5 (http://www.freesoftwaremagazine.com/articles/commons_without_commonality).

Boyle, James (2003) 'The Second Enclosure Movement and the Construction of the Public Domain', *Law & Contemporary Problems*, 66(1): 33–74.

Boyle, James (2008) *The Public Domain*. New Haven: Yale University Press.

Boutang, Yann Moulier (2012) *Cognitive Capitalism*. Tr. E. Emery. Cambridge: Polity Press.

Brand, Stewart (1987) *The Media Lab: Inventing the Future at MIT*. London: Viking Penguin.

Brockman, John (1996) *Digerati: Encounters with the Cyber Elite*. New York: Hardwired.

Brown, W. and Halley, J. (eds) (2002) *Left Legalism/Left Critique*. Durham and London: Duke University Press.

Burston, J., Dyer-Witheford, N. and Hearn, A. (2010) 'Digital Labour: Workers, Authors, Citizens', *ephemera*, 10(3/4): 214–21.

Cohen, Julie E. (1996) 'A Right to Read Anonymously: A Closer Look at 'Copyright Management' in Cyberspace', *Connecticut Law Review*, 28: 981–1039.

Cohen, Julie E. (1998a) '*Lochner* in Cyberspace: The New Economic Orthodoxy of 'Rights Management'', *Michigan Law Review*, 97: 462–563.

Cohen, Julie E. (1998b) 'Copyright and the Jurisprudence of Self-Help', 13 *Berkeley Technology Law Journal*, 13(3): 1089–143.

Cohen, Julie E. (2000) 'Examined Lives: Informational Privacy and the Subject as Object', *Stanford Law Review* 52: 1373–438.

Cohen, Nicole S. (2012) 'Cultural Work as a Site of Struggle: Freelancers and Exploitation', *tripleC*, 10(2): 141–55.

Coleman, E. Gabriella (2013) *Coding Freedom: The Ethics and Aesthetics of Hacking*. Princeton: Princeton University Press.

Creative Commons (2014a) 'About [Creative Commons]' (http://creativecommons.org/about).

Creative Commons (2014b) 'History [of Creative Commons]' (http://creativecommons.org/about/history).

Creative Commons (2014c) 'Frequently Asked Questions' (https://wiki.creativecommons.org/FAQ#What_is_Creative_Commons_and_what_do_you_do.3F).

Creative Commons (2014d) 'Compatible Licenses' (http://creativecommons.org/compatiblelicenses).

Creative Commons (2014e) 'Who Uses CC?' (http://creativecommons.org/who-uses-cc).

Creative Commons (2014f) 'Understanding Free Cultural Works' (http://creativecommons.org/freeworks).

Department of Business, Innovation and Skills (2012) 'Letter to Dame Janet Finch on the Government Response to the Finch Group Report' (http://www.bis.gov.uk/assets/biscore/science/docs/l/12-975-letter-government-response-to-finch-report-research-publications.pdf).

de Peuter, Greig (2011) 'Creative Economy and Labor Precarity: A Contested Convergence', *Journal of Communication Inquiry*, 35(4): 417–25.

Dertouzos, Michael L., Lester, Richard K. and Solow, Robert M. (1989) *Made in America: Regaining the Productive Edge*. Cambridge, MA: MIT Press.

Dobusch, Leonhard and Quack, Sigrid (2008) 'Epistemic Communities and Social Movements: Transnational Dynamics in the Case of Creative Commons', Max Planck Institute for the Study of Societies Discussion Paper 08/8 (http://www.mpifg.de/pu/mpifg_dp/dp08-8.pdf).

Drahos, Peter with Braithwaite, John (2002) *Information Feudalism*. London: Earthscan.

Dusollier, Séverine (2007) 'Sharing Access through Private Ordering', *Chicago-Kent Law Review*, 82(3): 1391–435.

Dyer-Witheford, Nick (1999) *Cyber-Marx*. Chicago: University of Illinois Press.

Dyson, Esther (1997) *Release 2.0: A Design for Living in the Digital Age*. New York: Broadway.

Dyson, E., Gilder, G., Keyworth, G. and Toffler, A. (1994) 'A Magna Carta for the Knowledge Age: Cyberspace and the American Dream', *New Perspective Quarterly*, 11(4): 26–37.

Elkin-Koren, Niva (1993) 'Copyright Law and Social Dialogue on the Information Superhighway: The Case against Copyright Liability of Bulletin Board Operators', *Cardozo Arts and Entertainment Law Journal*, 13: 345.

Elkin-Koren, Niva (2005) 'What Contracts Cannot Do: The Limits of Private Ordering in Facilitating a Creative Commons', *Fordham Law Review* 74(2): 375–422.

European Commission (1994) *Europe and the Global Information Society: Recommendations of the High-level Group on the Information Society to the Corfu European Council*. Luxembourg: Office for Official Publications of the European Communities.

European Commission (1995) Green Paper on Copyright and Related Rights in the Information Society. Brussels: COM (95) 382 final.

European Commission (1996a) Follow-up to the Green Paper on Copyright and Related Rights in the Information Society. Brussels: COM (96) 568 final.

European Commission, (1996b) G7 Ministerial Conference on the Global Information Society: Ministerial Conference Summary. Brussels: European Commission.

Free Software Foundation (2014) 'What is Free Software?' (http://www.gnu.org/philosophy/free-sw.html).
Garlick, Mia (2013) 'Creative Commons Version 3.0 Licenses – A Brief Explanation' (http://wiki.creativecommons.org/Version_3#BY-SA_.E2.80.94_Compatibility_Structure_Introduced)
Gates, William Henry III (1976) 'An Open Letter to Hobbyists' (http://www.blinkenlights.com/classiccmp/gateswhine.html).
Gates, Bill (1996) *The Road Ahead.* Revised edn. New York: Penguin.
Gill, Rosalind and Pratt, Andy (2008) 'In the Social Factory? Immaterial Labour, Precariousness and Cultural Work', *Theory, Culture & Society*, 25(7–8): 1–30.
Ginsburg, Jane C. (1995) 'Putting Cars on the 'Information Superhighway': Authors, Exploiters, and Copyright in Cyberspace', *Columbia Law Review*, 95(6): 1466–99.
Hardt, Michael and Negri, Antonio (2009) *Commonwealth.* Cambridge, MA: Harvard University Press.
Hardy, I. Trotter (1994) 'The Proper Legal Regime for 'Cyberspace'', *University of Pittsburgh Law Review*, 993–1055.
Harvey, David (2003) *The New Imperialism.* Oxford: Oxford University Press.
Information Infrastructure Taskforce (1993) *National Information Infrastructure: Agenda for Action.* Washington, DC: IITF/National Telecommunications and Information Administration.
Information Infrastructure Taskforce (1995) *Global Information Infrastructure: Agenda for Cooperation* (http://www.ntia.doc.gov/report/1995/global-information-infrastructure-agenda-cooperation).
Lessig, Lawrence (1996a) 'Reading the Constitution in Cyberspace', *Emory Law Journal*, 45: 869–910.
Lessig, Lawrence (1996b) 'Intellectual Property and Code', *Saint John's Journal of Legal Commentary*, 11: 635–9.
Lessig, Lawrence (1999) *Code and Other Laws of Cyberspace.* New York: Basic Books.
Lessig, Lawrence (2004a) *Free Culture: How Big Media Uses Technology and the Law to Lock Down Culture and Control Creativity.* New York: Penguin.
Lessig, Lawrence (2004b) 'Free(ing) Culture for Remix', *Utah Law Review*, 961–75.
Lessig, Lawrence (2005a) 'On How it All Began' (http://creativecommons.org/weblog/entry/5668).
Lessig, Lawrence (2005b) 'On Compatibility' (http://creativecommons.org/weblog/entry/5709).
Lessig, Lawrence (2007) 'Laws that Choke Creativity' (http://www.ted.com/talks/larry_lessig_says_the_law_is_strangling_creativity).
Lessig, Lawrence (2010) 'Open' (http://blip.tv/lessig/episode-3749213).
Linksvayer, Mike (2008) 'Approved for Free Cultural Works' (http://creativecommons.org/weblog/entry/8051).
Mako Hill, Benjamin (2005) 'Towards a Standard of Freedom: Creative Commons and the Free Software Movement' (http://mako.cc/writing/toward_a_standard_of_freedom.html).
Maracke, Catharina (2010) 'Creative Commons International: The International License Porting Project – Origins, Experiences, and Challenges', *Journal of Intellectual Property, Information Technology and E-Commerce Law*, 1(4): 1–18.
Marx, Karl (1971) Preface to *A Contribution to the Critique of Political Economy.* Tr. S.W. Ryanzanskaya, M. Dobb (ed.). London: Lawrence & Wishart.
Marx, Karl and Engels, Friedrich (1970) *The German Ideology.* London: Lawrence & Wishart.
May, Christopher and Sell, Susan K. (2005) *Intellectual Property Rights: A Critical History.* Boulder, CO: Lynne Rienner Publishers.
McKercher, Catherine and Mosco, Vincent (eds) (2008) *Knowledge Workers in the Information Society.* Lanham, MD: Lexington.
McKinlay, Alan and Smith, Chris (eds) (2009) *Creative Labour: Working in the Creative Industries.* London: Palgrave Macmillan.
McRobbie, Angela (2002) 'From Holloway to Hollywood: Happiness at Work in the New Cultural Economy?' in Paul du Gay and Michael Pryke (eds) *Cultural Economy: Cultural Analysis and Commercial Life.* London: Sage. pp. 97–114.
Moglen, Eben (2003) 'The Dot.Communist Manifesto' (http://emoglen.law.columbia.edu/publications/dcm.html).
Moglen, Eben (2013) 'Why the FSF Gets Copyright Assignments from Contributors' (http://www.gnu.org/licenses/why-assign.html).
Negroponte, Nicholas (1995) *Being Digital.* London: Hodder and Stoughton.
Peters, Diane (2009) 'Expanding the Public Domain: Part Zero' (http://creativecommons.org/weblog/entry/13304).
Porter, Michael E. (1990) *The Competitive Advantage of Nations.* Cambridge, MA: Harvard University Press.
Research Councils UK (2013) 'RCUK Policy on Open Access and Supporting Guidance' (http://www.rcuk.ac.uk/RCUK-prod/assets/documents/documents/RCUKOpenAccessPolicy.pdf).
Schiller, Dan (1996) *Theorizing Communication: A History.* Oxford: Oxford University Press.

Scholz, Trebor (ed.) (2013) *Digital Labor.* New York: Routledge.

Söderberg, Johan (2008) *Hacking Capitalism: The Free and Open Source Software Movement.* London: Routledge.

Steuer, Eric (2010) 'Response to ASCAP's Deceptive Claims' (http://creativecommons.org/weblog/entry/22643).

Toffler, Alvin (1991) *The Third Wave.* New York: Bantam Books.

Webber, Chris (2012) 'Liberated Pixel Cup and Distributed Free Culture Projects' (http://labs.creativecommons.org/2012/07/11/liberated-pixel-cup-and-distributed-free-culture-projects/).

Wikimedia Foundation (2009) 'Wikimedia Foundation Announces Important Licensing Change for Wikipedia and its Sister Projects' (http://wikimedia-foundation.org/wiki/Press_releases/Dual_license_vote_May_2009).

Working Group on Intellectual Property Rights, Information Infrastructure Task Force (1995) *Intellectual Property and the National Information Infrastructure.* Washington, DC: US Department of Commerce.

2

'The Economic Foundations of Intellectual Property': An Arts and Cultural Economist's Perspective

Sarah Louisa Phythian-Adams

INTRODUCTION

Contemporary intellectual property (IP) law and practices are a complex area, but one arguably whose roots lie in a more basic application of economic theory as practised from 16th-century royal grants of 'monopoly privileges', through industrialization and the encouragement of scientific and mechanical invention, to post-20th-century considerations of the efficient operations of markets. The underlying principles of the development of such protections have at each stage focused on the encouragement of economic activity or the correction of perceived market failures. This chapter explores the issues of IP from the perspective of Arts and Cultural (or creative sector) economics and considers economic theory, both in terms of the principles behind basic IP protection mechanisms and evaluation in light of opposing theories. This chapter is not aimed at economic specialists, but aims to show the foundation and relevance of economic theory in IP matters.

A cursory look at the history of IP law will show its development from copyright and patent law, mainstays of industry, and comprising part of the infrastructure of modern economic systems since early industrialization. For many economic historians the act of rendering legal rights over the creative and novel is seen as a defining moment of transition of the UK economic system from feudal to capitalist (Bloxam, 1957), and so it is not completely unexpected that the later refinement of 'Intellectual Property Rights' laws would be met with intense scrutiny, debate and speculation and that they would continue to do so. Recent decades, with the growth of sectors dependent on IP, such as creative and technology industries, have seen an increase in IP-based litigation and concurrently a strengthening of frameworks of interpretation.

It is the intention of this chapter to demonstrate that the theoretical underpinning of IP regulation, particularly copyright, is shaped by the balance between two, sometimes opposing, economic instruments: those of market incentives and those of correcting for market failure. The most efficient means of understanding the economic rationale for the current development of IP regulation therefore begins with understanding its evolution.

ESTABLISHING THE ECONOMIC DOMAIN OF IP (A VERY BRIEF HISTORY)

The answer to the question 'What is IP?' will differ from an economist to a lawyer to a sociologist and even to that of a business consultant. Most simply put, to an economist, intellectual property is property. Such property is quite literally a fundamental of the capitalist market system where individuals in a society are able to own 'capital', to own the means to production. These 'factors of production' are then combined to create output (the many products ... the 'stuff' of modern markets from kumquats to iPads) and that output, as well as the factors of production, are all able to be traded freely by each individual in pursuit of their own individual maximal gains (more about this deceptively simple concept later). This, according to the founding classical economics of Adam Smith, enables free markets to equilibrate at optimum outputs across all markets, acting like an 'invisible hand' ensuring efficiency (the maximal gains) for the whole market.

> As every individual, therefore, endeavours as much as he can both to employ his capital ... in such a manner as its produce may be of the greatest value, he intends only his own gain, and he is in this, as in many other cases, led by an invisible hand to promote an end which was no part of his intention. Nor is it always the worse for the society that it was no part of it. By pursuing his own interest he frequently promotes that of the society more effectually than when he really intends to promote it. (Smith, 1981 [1776] book 4, chapter 2, p. 488)

In shaping this market equilibrium Smith also determined that there would be a 'natural' and 'market' price of commodities. The price of any product reflects the sum of: wages of labour, rent of land and 'profit of stock' (compensation of the capitalist for risking his resources). Moreover, he remarks that the difference between this natural price and market price comes about through the effect of demand exceeding supply and is determined according to supply and the willingness to pay. The ability of the merchant to withhold supply to garner these higher market prices is essentially the notion of a monopoly:

> A monopoly granted either to an individual or to a trading company has the same effect as a secret in trade or manufactures. The monopolists, by keeping the market constantly understocked, by never fully supplying the effectual demand, sell their commodities much above the natural price, and raise their emoluments, whether they consist in wages or profit, greatly above their natural rate. The price of monopoly is upon every occasion the highest which can be got. The natural price, or the price of free competition, on the contrary, is the lowest which can be taken, not upon every occasion, indeed, but for any considerable time together. The one is upon every occasion the highest which can be squeezed out of the buyers, or which, it is supposed, they will consent to give: the other is the lowest which the sellers can commonly afford to take, and at the same time continue their business.[1] (Smith, 1981 [1776] book 1, chapter 7, paragraph 26)

IP protection developed from both an Anglo-Saxon common law legal tradition and European civil law. From an economist's perspective it is of interest that some of the earliest IP laws – copyright privilege for the copy of books – were understood to be just this and were referred to as 'monopoly privileges'. Granting of such privileges spread across Europe with the development of the printing press, i.e. the means of copying.

These early privileges were granted in Europe by royal charter throughout the 15th to the 17th century (pre-dating Smith's seminal work on the wealth of nations). The first granted was in Venice in 1486[2] (Armstrong, 1990, p. 3), becoming commonplace from around 1492 onwards (1990, p. 6). By 1501, early privileges were documented in Germany and 1503 in France. The first copyright privilege was not granted in the UK (in England) until 1518 to the King's printer, of two years – a distinctly shorter term than those in Venice – and by 1557 the 'Worshipful Company of Stationers and Newspaper Makers' ('the Stationers' Company') had received a royal charter.[3] This charter made them a central English register – and once a member had asserted ownership of a text (or 'copy') by entering it in the 'entry book of copies' (the Stationers' Company Register), no other member was entitled to publish it. This essentially created a monopoly publishing right licensed under them. Although providing copy protection, the charter's purpose was in its essence to enable control of book production by the religious monarchy (Queen Mary I and King Philip).

These copyright privileges had developed alongside a sibling form of early IP protection – that of letters patent (decree of protection by the crown) pertaining to the work of foreign skilled craftsmen and inventors to allow them to settle in England and practice their trade – particularly to pass on their individual skill and new techniques to English apprentices (Klitzke, 1959, p. 624).[4] Over the next 100 years these patents became widely applied to novel skills and industry. However, throughout the reign of Queen Elizabeth (1558–1603) letters patent granting monopoly privileges were increasingly not limited to skilled individuals and new techniques but applied to ordinary commodities as diverse as coal and soap, for which the patent holder paid a handsome levy. This resulted in the monarch answering to parliament in 1601 for the abuses of the monopolies by royal charter to enrich herself and her courtiers at the expense of the English people. This led to the administration of patents being overturned to the common law courts, and by 1624 (under the monarchy of James I), the 'Statute of Monopolies' was passed. The statute repealed all prior patents including monopolies granted in the future, excepting those created over completely novel inventions, and requiring approval under the statute. Over the next 100 years 'patent' law developed with the industrial revolution and the limits and particulars of what could be registered as proprietary developed from this.

By 1694 amidst a backdrop of institutional change (that saw the 'glorious revolution' bring William of Orange to the English throne), parliament refused to renew the Stationers' Company's registration power. Instead, by 1710 parliament enacted the first piece of copyright legislation – the Copyright Act of 1709 (also known as the Statute of Anne). Its full title described its purpose as 'An Act for the Encouragement of Learning, by vesting the Copies of Printed Books in the Authors or purchasers of such Copies, during the Times therein mentioned'. The new statute did two things – it removed the Stationers' Company's monopoly power and restrictions of the book market and secondly it created a limit to the monopoly period for books (14 years for new books with a potential renewal term and 21 years for books already in print).

Patent law continued to develop internationally while internationalization of copyright protection occurred in the late 19th century at the Berne Convention in 1886. This convention represented the next significant step in the evolution of copyright in protecting works across national boundaries (Hatch, 1989). This went on to be updated eight times and the 1961 Rome Convention saw an extension of copyright protection to so-called 'related rights' such as publication and reproduction rights, public performance rights, broadcasting rights and the right to control derivative works (such as translations, adaptations, etc.).

This very brief history of the establishment of copyright and patents, evidences the strands of economic argument underpinning IP regulation – that of incentive and that of correction for market failure. In the case of books – the invention and rapid technological development of the printing press made them reliably copyable, transferring the physical property of a book to any publisher who printed it[5] (more about why this is a 'market failure' later). Secondly, letters patent protecting new skills and innovations were the answer to the problem of the development of English industry. The protection encouraged the inflow of new skills and techniques in order to stimulate growth. In both instances the initial 'spirit' of the market intervention was progressively disputed by an evolutionary attrition of implementation leading to an eventual redaction in favour of new regulation refocusing on the perceived central market issues. Since these times, IP regulation has evolved with market changes in a process of adaptation rather than redaction (I will revisit this later).

THE PROBLEM OF PROPERTY

An initial requirement when considering the case for intellectual property in economic theory is to deal with some demarcation issues regarding the reference to 'intellectual property' in contemporary economic and management theory. Firstly, the domain of 'intellectual' property versus that which is protected by IP law should be established. This is encapsulated by the difference between 'intellectual capital', 'intellectual assets' and 'intellectual property'. 'Intellectual capital' requires an extension of the notion of 'capital' as more than the kind of machinery that the word conjures. Capital can be not only physical – the nuts and bolts machinery of mass production – but also refer to the machinery of the mind. 'Human capital' is the capital stock of knowledge – that which creates the next Nobel prize for literature but also the mundane information an enterprise might hold, the knowledge and abilities of admin processes or the ability of Mike from procurement to get a discount on paper from a local supplier. According to Poltorak and Lerner (2011, p. xxvi) 'Intellectual capital is what is left of an enterprise after it has been stripped of all its tangible assets, such as land, buildings, machines, inventory and cash'.

From intellectual capital you can obtain intellectual assets – for example by tasking Mike to create a procurement procedure. This work product then becomes an 'intellectual asset'. Finally that small proportion of intellectual assets that become protected by law form 'Intellectual Property' and mainly comprise the 'holy-trinity' of patents, copyright and trade-marks (but includes industrial design rights; trade dress and trade secrets). Although IP encompasses this umbrella of rights protection, this chapter will focus mainly on 'copyright' due to its key relevance to the arts and cultural economy (or 'creative sector').

From the chapter's brief introductory history of IP law in England and Europe, it is easily verified that the early use of attribution of monopoly privileges based on royally assigned property rights solved practical problems: firstly, the recognition that some individuals had more knowledge than others – knowledge that had a higher potential for the generation of more output meant that those individuals needed to be induced to make that higher potential output work for the benefit of England; and secondly, in the ability, for example, to reproduce books, and that such knowledge was a precarious form of property.

Despite most neoclassical economic models requiring assumptions of 'perfect information' (costless information with instantaneous universal access), the problem of knowledge or 'information' is well considered in the field of economics. Indeed, the problem of knowledge specific to individual industries was considered by Jeremy Bentham in his (1795[6], p. 43) 'Manual of Political Economy' and later used in support of IP by John Stuart Mill in 1873 as a facilitator of innovation and creativity which benefits all of society (Mill, 1848, p. 933).

Economists' notions of information have developed rapidly in the last century, from the work of Hayek (1945) to the subsequent work of Stiglitz, Spence, Akerlof and other notable economists who found that information has an economic value since it allows those in possession to make economic choices yielding higher payoffs than they would obtain in the absence of information and that information asymmetries are shown to skew market outcomes and cause market failure. This has led to a greater understanding of the characteristics of certain goods which are based in information. Such 'information goods' are goods whose main value comes from the information they contain, like books, CDs, DVDs, computer software and files, i.e. essentially the goods of (but not restricted to) the creative industries and those goods for whom IP law is most relevant and which will be expounded in the next section.

INTERPRETATION OF PURPOSE – AN ECONOMIC PERSPECTIVE

The question must then be asked: What is the purpose of intellectual property regulation in contemporary markets? What market problems is it solving? Is it still solving the problem of incentive, is it correcting for any market failure? Paul Goldstein provides an interesting insight into the varying views of what copyright actually is:

> A policymaker in the United States will tell you that copyright is an instrument of consumer welfare, stimulating the production of the widest possible array of literary and artistic works at the lowest possible price. Ask the question of a practitioner on the European continent, and he will tell you that copyright is at best a watered-down version of author's right – that grand civil law tradition that places the author, not the consumer, at the centre of protection. A low protectionist will tell you that copyright is a monopoly that undesirably drives up the price of goods in the market place. A high protectionist will tell you that copyright is a property right – no more, no less – and one without which we would have very few creative works in the marketplace. (Goldstein, 1992, p. 79)

Let us consider these. The enhancement of innovation and creativity are still spurs to economic growth and job creation. Data from the Office for Harmonization in the Internal Market (2013) shows that in the European Union, Intellectual Property Rights intensive industries make up 26% of employment and 39% of GDP, and US data from 2010 suggests IP intensive industries accounted for 34.8% of GDP and 18.8% of US employment (Economics & Statistics Administration; US Patent and Trademark Office, 2012, vi–vii). More specifically, the adoption of IP regulation has been attributed to the profound growth effect in the Korean music market. The recorded music market there grew by 6% in value in the first six months of 2011, following a 12% increase in 2010. Pre-operational adoption of IP regulation, in 2005, it was ranked as the 33rd music market in the world, after government updating of copyright law in 2007, by 2012 it ranked as the 11th largest market (IFPI, 2012).[7]

So how does IP law stimulate production and innovation? It does so by providing what classical economists referred to as a 'bounty' (super-normal profit) from the granting of a temporary monopoly in the work created. As Smith established – monopoly power allows the monopolist to control supply and to restrict it to the point where the market raises the price to the optimum which the market can bear to give the producer the maximum profit. In Figure 2.1 I provide an illustration of the neoclassical model of the monopoly problem.

Figure 2.1 shows on the left side a perfectly competitive market. The area above the supply curve, below the market price represents a surplus for the producer, since they got a higher price than they were willing to sell for at each quantity. The area above the market price, below the demand curve, represents a surplus for the consumer since they were willing to pay a higher price than they had to. The market price is at its 'natural price' – which is 'the lowest that can be taken', i.e. at all outputs covering the marginal costs of production (the supply curve), this means an output of Q_{MC}, at a price of P_{MC}. On the right side of the diagram, a monopoly market is shown, where the demand curve in a market (for example, a book), also represents the average revenue curve for the firm. The perfectly competitive market price (P_{MC}) and quantity (Q_{MC}) are shown; however, the most profitable point of production (i.e. that which gives the highest profit) is at the point where marginal cost equals marginal revenue, which is the output Q_M. Looking at the demand equation an output of Q_M derives a market price of P_M.

A high market price (over and above the natural price) provides a 'bounty' for the producer.[8] Unfortunately the elicitation of such a bounty has repercussions in the market. On the

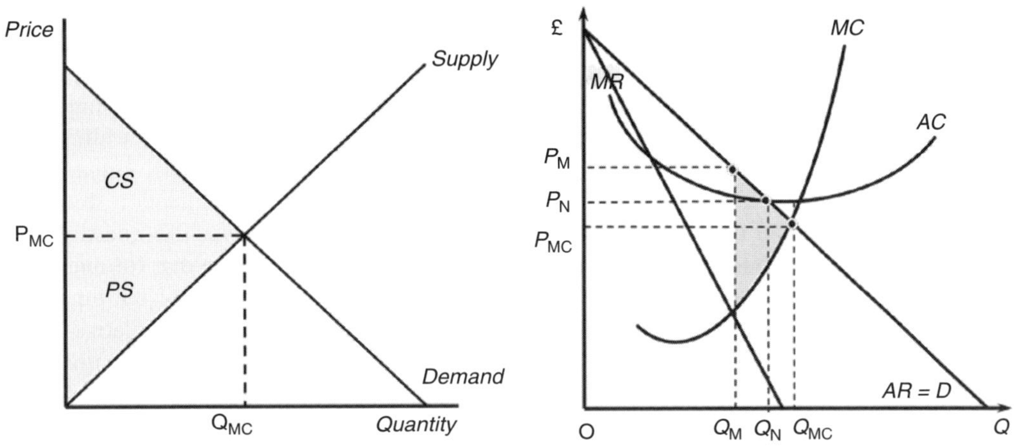

Figure 2.1 The monopoly problem
Note: Graphs generated by author.

left hand side, market welfare is maximized – i.e. the combination of consumer and producer surplus – but on the right side, the shaded area represents a deadweight loss in this welfare. This is the monopoly problem. When Adam Smith conjured the image of the invisible hand he also invoked the notion of maximal welfare of the market – that each pursuing their own interests creates the most welfare (utility extracted by agents – both buyers and sellers) in the market. The neoclassical model of the monopoly problem shows in the shaded area, a deadweight loss of welfare from the market caused by withholding supply to affect a larger market price. So we must consider in which circumstances it is efficient to permit (encourage) a monopoly.

Creative goods are much like information goods – the fixed cost of producing them is high relative to the marginal cost of reproducing them. Think of the case of a book – a writer invests time and effort in creating a plot, researching, laboriously typing up her manuscript, editing and reworking until a completed novel is created. The costs of these must be borne whether she sells one copy of the book or one million. They are essentially fixed costs. Now she incurs more costs (or rather the publisher does on her behalf) in printing copies of the book and distributing them varying with the amount produced. Now the price to the consumer must cover both the variable and fixed costs in order for the production of more books in future to be viable (i.e. a price exceeding P_N). If there was no copyright, then essentially another firm with the means to publish, can copy the work, incurring only the variable costs of production and sell the books at a lower price. In other words they can 'free-ride' on the intangible, information part of the good which represented the high fixed cost element of production.

Information goods represent a market problem in economies similar to that of a 'public good'. A public good is defined as a good whose consumption characteristics are (1) non-excludable and (2) non-rival. Non-excludability means that in providing the good, one cannot distinguish who benefits from it – for example, building a lighthouse will benefit all ships who pass by and it is impossible to exclude the benefits from any shipping company that has not contributed towards it. Non-rivalrousness means that once the good is provided it is not depleted by one individual's consumption, unlike for example a chocolate bar which can be consumed solely by its purchaser, the lighthouse continues to emit its guiding lights for the shipping company who bought it and any additional passers-by. Naturally, if all agents are acting in their own best interests, the optimum solution would be to not build the lighthouse yourself, but to let someone else incur the cost and simply 'free-ride'. Unfortunately, if free-riding is the dominant strategy for all of the agents in the economy no-one will produce the lighthouse and the market loses all of the welfare which would have been generated from the good being produced.

The solution to the public goods problem is government intervention in the form of direct provision of the lighthouse. However, to requisition the production of all information goods under government control would demand a level of government bureaucracy akin to the dystopian satire Brazil.[9] The more practicable solution therefore lies in the 'correction' of the properties of the good to remove the potential for free-riding. This solution lies in the granting of property rights; where no physical barriers restrain other individuals from taking this property they are replaced with legal ones. Unfortunately, the granting of property rights to an individual ineluctably confers monopoly power, so essentially, becomes a welfare trade-off – what economists call a 'second best solution'.[10] How second best the solution is depends on the calculation of the welfare losses against welfare gains in the market of each form of market failure. To be most efficient, the term of the monopoly will affect this trade-off, where the shorter the term of the monopoly, the lower the possibility of earning supernormal profit over and above covering the high fixed costs. There is therefore an optimal term for copyright. Pollock (2009) has estimated this: 'Using existing data on recordings and books we obtain a point estimate of around 15 years for optimal copyright term with a 99% confidence interval extending up to 38 years' (Pollock, 2009, p. 1). In other words at 15 years, the expected value of revenue is sufficient to have recouped high fixed costs of production (thus spurring future works), netted against the 'deadweight loss' welfare costs of the monopoly up to that point. However, some economists (e.g. Hasper, 2005) also consider an international element of market failure, that IP rights (IPRs) are a second-best solution for which different countries, particularly developing countries, suffer a disproportionate welfare loss (see Rimmer, Darch, Gervais, Oguamanam and Dutfield in this collection for non-economists' approaches to this question).

Now it is also arguable that for many creative goods, the fixed cost of the intangible 'knowledge' element is high relative to the marginal costs of production and in this sense the production of such goods are already akin to a 'natural monopoly'. A 'natural monopoly' exists in a situation where fixed costs are so high relative to variable costs that the most efficient market solution comes from having just one producer who is then able to exploit economies of scale from production. Indeed, for some arts and cultural goods this has historically been seen as the case. The advent of the broadcasting industry in the UK for example, had relatively very high fixed costs (making content and broadcasting it) and almost 'zero' marginal cost (the costs of an extra consumer). It having both natural monopoly characteristics and public goods characteristics (of being non-excludable and non-rival) suggested direct provision by government – which indeed was the early outcome of the market.

Baumol (2003) argues that the 'natural monopoly' issue hinges on the difference between the neoclassical idea of 'sunk costs' (costs that are not recoverable and are not of relevance in current decision making) and the reality of repeated 'sunk costs' such as in artistic production. Specifically – future sunk costs are not sunk in the present – they are still variable and, if future investors are to be persuaded to fund future fixed costs (which in the future may become sunk costs), past history must show recoupment! Interestingly, Baumol also posits that this is applicable to many areas of the 'new economy' in which innovation has become the prime weapon of competition in much of industry.

However, the extent to which a monopoly is created by IP assignment is different depending on the substitutability of the goods. Returning to the copyright of books, an author creates a work of fiction about a great detective, copyright protects his work of fiction, however, it does not protect the 'idea' of a work of fiction about a great detective – only *his* work. In other words there is in this sense only a weak monopoly, since the consumer is free to choose between writers of detective fiction. Not only this, but the consumer is also able to choose between detective fiction, romance novels or spy thrillers. There is an element of substitutability in the market, consumers are able to choose from many similar but not homogeneous products. Effectively, no barriers to entry are sustained. This is the definition of a monopolistically competitive market – and not a monopoly.

A monopolistically competitive market is one where a large number of firms compete (in selling 'similar' products but for which each holds a monopoly) so that the possibility of any one firm's decisions provoking any adjustment in other firms' behaviour are negligible. In the long run we also assume free entry and exit from the industry because there are no or low barriers to entry. In these respects, the industry resembles perfect competition, but because each firm sells a slightly different product, they face a downward-sloping demand curve (an ability to restrict supply to gain a higher price). The welfare inefficiency of a monopolistic market is different from that of a monopoly, in that the low barriers to entry mean that supernormal profit from high market prices can only be sustained in the short run, as in the long run, more firms will simply enter the market with similar (though not identical) products, pushing the price down.

A monopolistically competitive market cannot sustain super-normal profits in the long run and the length of time it can depends on the strength of the monopoly – i.e. the least imitable characteristics of the good. However, a monopoly can also be limited directly by term. Copyright does not provide infinite protection. In most economies (after the 1994 WTO Trade Related Aspects of Intellectual Property Rights Agreement, hereafter TRIPS [see Gervais in this collection]) copyright is held for the lifetime of the creator plus 50 years after their death. This differs to the system of patents which gives creators a monopoly for a much more limited period of time, but which is renewable by registration at a cost. A patent offers inventors the exclusive right to benefit from their inventions for the lifetime of the patent, which is usually about 20 years (TRIPS, 1994). Within this term it is expected that firms can recoup the costs of their investment in research and development. This is a crucial difference in the operational form of IP measures. Patent protection, as with trademarks, must be registered and registration maintained, whereas copyright arises automatically when a creative work is made, endowing the creator with all of the copyright and related rights associated.

Inherent in both patent and copyright monopoly terms is also a need to cover the cost of uncertainty. Research and development undertaken by a firm is not guaranteed to result in a profitable product or innovation, indeed, this process only ends in success a proportion of the time (how much depends on the industry and the skills of the individual organization). Likewise, every new book, record or game may not be a hit – and can therefore fail to recoup its fixed costs of production due to a lack of demand.[11]

This leaves the economist questioning – under what circumstances is a monopoly beneficial? What degree of monopoly is appropriate and for what term? The answer to these questions may be influenced by our economic philosophies.

ECONOMIC PHILOSOPHY – THEORETICAL STANDPOINTS

Economists may tend towards theoretical standpoints on the issue of IP. Any regulation is an intervention into the market which has efficiency (hence welfare) implications for that market. The Benathamite[12] or utilitarian philosophical standpoint holds that ultimately 'pleasure' (or 'utility', 'happiness') is the only good (i.e. all other goods purchased and economic activity is ultimately in pursuit of this) and that the greatest happiness for the greatest number should be the ultimate goal of humans. Notable utilitarians such as John Stuart Mill (1848), considered patents to be the corollary to an enlightened economy, a standpoint already stressed by Adam Smith almost a century before (Smith, 1759, p. 83); Mill advocated that it facilitates innovation and creativity which in turn benefits all of society (Mill, 1848, p. 933). Such Enlightenment thinkers argued that market forces and free enterprise (as opposed to government or academic committees) determining prices (and hence utility payoffs) led to preferable outcomes, but that within this framework patents encouraged innovation – and that innovation was the key element in economic growth, both by encouraging more research and development activity and by inducing venture capital investment into risky projects. Indeed, Johann Wolfgang von Goethe (1825) postulated regarding the British dominance of industry, 'One may well ask why are they in every respect in advance of us?' (cited by Klemm 1964, p.173) and reasoned that the British patents system transformed inventions into real assets and that this was the reason for the success experienced during the industrial revolution.

Mokyr (2009, p. 350) considers that, pragmatically, utilitarians were saying that 'patents were the price society paid for disclosure and that disclosure was essential for the unfettered dissemination of useful knowledge', i.e. the existence of the patent system ultimately made the technical details available to others. Such an argument can be extended to copyright, if the copyright is the price paid for disclosure of the information (e.g. the creative work itself), it still ultimately makes the work (and all information which has the potential for stimulating future work) available.

While the utilitarian approach to IP does give weight to individual sovereignty, the libertarian approach, characterized by John Locke,[13] puts individual rights at the forefront of the argument. Locke held that individuals have natural rights to property (as well as life and liberty), and that it is the obligation of the government to protect these rights. This extends to the belief that people have 'natural' rights over any product of their labour, and hence the protection of IP law. Locke's labour-mixing theory extends such ownership to anything he has applied his labour to,[14] in other words it becomes their property. However, such philosophy is problematic in modern creative media, as there are commonly multiple contributors to artistic creations, for example a song featuring numerous artists (Resnik, 2003). Moreover, the prevalence of 'works for hire' (discussed later) in some artistic production – such as movies involving a chain of creation – is a dark canvas on which to paint such a labour theory of value.

Hegelian[15] or 'personhood' theories provide yet another perspective, which is based on self-expression. Personhood deems creative works as an extension of the author's personality (Fromer, 2012) and requires IP regulation to define property in order for individuals to be able to express themselves as distinct to others. However, again this becomes difficult when a work is the product of multiple creators or indeed if a work requires little distinct creativity to produce it. Resnick (2003) cites the example of a photograph that could be taken by anyone, but an individual artist who takes it deems it a form of their expression.

NOT THE SPIRIT OF THE LAW BUT THE LETTER OF THE LAW

WIPO states on its website the aims of IP regulation:

> An efficient and equitable intellectual property system can help all countries realize intellectual property's potential as a catalyst for economic development and social and cultural well-being. The intellectual property system helps strike a

balance between the interests of innovators and the public interest, providing an environment in which creativity and invention can flourish, for the benefit of all. (WIPO, 2009)

What WIPO seems to be acknowledging is the trade-off between welfare gains and losses – i.e. to promote innovation in a situation where the free-rider problem would prevail. In view of this apparent trade-off, Towse (2003, p. 233) proposes a need for a policy 'balance' in creating market conditions that will be favourable for encouraging economic growth. This accords somewhat with our welfare maximizing economic theory and the utilitarian perspective. However, what must always be considered in the analysis of economic theory is the distance between economic theory and business practice. As with the historical practice of IP regulation (discussed above), attrition of core values can occur in the practice and we can assess these by identifying and considering instances when IP regulation does not appear to fulfil its brief, some instances will be highlighted in the following sections.

One such area is the phenomenon known as 'litigation through the margins'. This is a legal practice in which large corporations with substantial resources can literally litigate through the financial margins of smaller opponents, operationally exempting them from the full legal process of substantiating legal Intellectual Property Rights. On 31 October 2011, Modern Dog Design filed a complaint against Target and Disney for copyright infringement on a T-shirt produced by 'Target' for Disney's 'High School Musical' spinoff 'Sharpay's fabulous adventure', which featured a heart-shaped mural of dog sketches within which they alleged all 26 individual dog sketches had come from their compendium of dog sketches published in 2008. By December 2013 Modern Dog Design had been forced to sell its studio to fund the lawsuit and even started a charitable fund 'friends of Modern Dog' to enable them to survive the protracted litigation with Robynne Ray, co-founder of the company, stating 'it is very difficult for an individual or small company to litigate, due to the costs and time associated with a lawsuit'.[16] Such asymmetrical practice of IP law represents a market failure and a threat to the market welfare outcomes expected, if the practical regulation applies asymmetrically to large corporations, then it arguably only reinforces inefficient monopoly outcomes in the market, usurping utility from other individuals, therefore also reducing incentive. The lawsuit garnered a lot of attention internationally, since Disney was a main precipitant of the lobbying for greater IP protection which resulted in the Sonny Bono Copyright Term Extension Act of 1998 (also mockingly referred to as thc 'Mickey Mouse protection act') which extended copyright term in the USA.[17] However, on 2 January 2014 Modern Dog announced on their Facebook page that 'we ended our copyright infringement battle that began in 2011 by agreeing to a settlement between Modern Dog and the defendants ... We believe we helped pave the way for other small companies and individuals to do the same … '.[18]

Part of the issue above is the time and cost of litigation, but this cannot be simply blamed on large corporations purposefully pursuing a 'litigation through the margins' strategy. It is certainly apparent that ambiguity in the law (like ambiguity in any contracts) leads to greater transaction costs (discussed further later). Landes and Posner (1989) highlight the difficulties in deciding what is, and what is not, copyright infringement. One important issue they raise is in distinguishing between ideas and expression. For example, if an author of spy novels copies sections of Ian Fleming's James Bond works, that is infringing. However, if after reading James Bond, the individual is inspired to become a spy novel author and creates a character that shares similarities to James Bond, he does not infringe upon Fleming's work (Landes & Posner, 1989, p. 349). As discussed above, the outcomes of this distinction leads to two discrete market environments – i.e. the monopolistically competitive market of spy novels versus the monopoly market for *The Spy Who Loved Me* by Ian Fleming.

A second example is the 1879 case of *Baker v Selden*. In 1859 Selden created a book describing a proprietary bookkeeping system and illustrated it with blank bookkeeping forms. In 1867 Baker created a much more successful book in which he copied the forms but made minor 'improvements' such as rearranging columns and changing headings. He then sold these to people who wanted to use Seldon's system. Selden's widow sued, but Baker was found not guilty of infringement of copyright as he did not copy the expository portions of Selden's book, only the accounting tables – which were not covered by copyright (*Baker v Selden*, 1879).

A slight variant of this issue occurred in 2003 when a fake Jamie Oliver cookery book called *The Naked Chef 2* went viral. The 121-page book was the product of a disgruntled employee of Oliver's publishers (Penguin) and was compiled from genuine recipes from previous books, television shows and magazine articles. The individual then emailed the manuscript to a friend, and the book spread rapidly across the Internet.[19] Penguin expressed concern that because the book was full of genuine Jamie Oliver recipes, it could harm potential sales of future books. However, in terms of breach of copyright law, the individual responsible could not be found guilty of criminal copyright infringement because s/he did not distribute the book for financial profit (Alderson & Bisset, 2003).

A further area of inefficiency of the regulation is an information issue. We have established not only the uniqueness (and difficulties associated with information goods) and goods created with a large requisite of information (e.g. artistic product), but also that information incurs costs. In perfectly competitive markets information is assumed to be freely available, which means any regulation applied is also assumed to be informationally costless. However, in reality information is rarely costless or ubiquitous and ignorance of the law represents a market failure and a resulting welfare cost in the market. Mary Wallace Davidson's 2000 article 'Copyright' uses the case of librarians' knowledge of United States copyright law as an example. She contests that although most have a working knowledge of US copyright law in their domain, cross media elements pose more of a problem (e.g. the use of musical works captured on paper, recordings and film), essentially because they have not had to deal with legal issues of 'licensing electronic reference sources, storing and streaming digitally formatted sound to computer workstations, or providing library materials legally for distance-learning classes' (Davidson, 2000, p. 598). She further asserts that 'Fewer still know whether they are Online Service Providers (OSPs), as defined by the Digital Millennium Copyright Act of 1998 (DMCA), and if they are, what rights and responsibilities that definition imposes' (2000, p. 598).

Digital issues are particularly pertinent to the contemporary consideration of IP. Raymond Shih Ray Ku (2002, p. 264) succinctly presents the 'digital dilemma' of IP and the Internet:

> digital technology makes it possible to make an unlimited number of perfect copies of music, books, or videos in digital form, and through the internet individuals may distribute those digital works around at the speed of light … thus depriving copyright holders of revenue that they might otherwise have received if those individuals purchased those works in tangible form.

Fine's (2000) study investigating the influence of online downloading on physical music CD sales looked at sales of CDs in physical stores within a sample of US universities. It was found that students at that time were the demographic most willing to engage in downloading, so the study compared point-of-sale data of music CDs in physical stores at US universities before and after the establishment of Napster. It found that from the years 1997 to 2000 sales of CDs around universities decreased by more than 7%, when within the same period sales within the whole country increased by 18%, and thus concluded that downloading negatively influenced the sales of music CDs (Fine, 2000, p. 1).

Conversely, the same Internet technology also provides a way to control information if coupled with legal sanctions or digital tools such as encryption, trusted systems and digital watermarking technology (the practicability of digital rights management technology is considered later).

Varian (2005) asserts that in an increasingly technological world enforcing copyright will become almost impossible. This may be supported by the empirical evidence of online piracy. Songs, albums, films, TV shows and even books are illegally downloaded, copied and shared every day and it is estimated that piracy comprised 23.8% of the total bandwidth used by all Internet users in North America, Europe and Asia in January 2013 (NetNames, 2013). Internet-related technologies are constantly improving methods of dissemination, making management of IP increasingly difficult (World Economic Forum, 2013). It is akin to an evolutionary battle, but one in which a new form of piracy emerges before a means to combat it can be developed and the continuing advance of technology means that the impact of this lag will increase at an ever increasing rate.

A final issue of note in this section is that brought forward by Arnold Plant in his formative 1934 article 'The Economic Aspects of Copyright in Books', who argued that copyright leads to a 'principal agent' problem (Plant, 1934, p. 184). A principal agent problem occurs whenever a principle must use an agent to acquire some ends. In doing so he can never be sure that the agent is pursuing his (the principal's) aims or their own. Arts and cultural markets depend heavily on intermediaries who act as gate-keepers and market makers (e.g. A&R personnel, agents, etc.). Moreover, such industries operate in market environments which are prone to vertical and horizontal integration. Indeed, in the majority of creative industries, the economic environment could largely be described as oligopolistic with what is often described as a 'turbulent fringe', for example, the music industry is dominated by three large multinational firms that comprise around 85% of the market[20] (essentially an oligopoly) plus a 'turbulent' fringe of small independent firms (essentially monopolistic competition). Similar market environments exist in books, movies and broadcasting industries. As a result, for the majority of artists across these industries they must contract to distribute their work and likely with a large oligopoly power. This results in artists 'selling' a large proportion of their return on their intellectual property (the copyright, in return for royalties) to these firms. For example, artists signed to record labels receive only around 10–15% of net earnings on sales in royalties (from which significant costs of production, promotion and management may then be deducted). In doing so they will inevitably invoke a principal agent problem – as conflict of interests arise in what maximizes artists' benefit with their agent, moreover an agent with superior bargaining power. This asymmetry of power – and hence reward – leads to the disproportionate heaping of gains from IP into the hands of oligopolistic agents, rather than artists. David (2010) claims that due to this form of contracting most recordings leave artists owing their labels money – even in those cases where the record label breaks even.

THE PROBLEM OF MARKET POWER AND THE RELATIVE COSTS OF CREATION

We have already touched on the issues of large firms, but the existence of monopoly power (either as monopolist or oligopolist markets) complicates IP debates further.

The phenomenon of multiple artist projects was touched upon above in the aptness of economic philosophical stances. However, specifically the increasing preponderance of 'works for hire' can be considered in terms of its welfare distribution impact in the market. Works for hire (or corporate authorship) is a solution to a problem of organizing production in arts and cultural markets. Creative industries (for example making a movie) requires the organization of a multitude of creative specialists under flexible working patterns (Storper, 1989). Caves (2000) suggests that in the absence of ability to vertically and horizontally integrate the coordination of artists and the uncertainties of the product, firms will pursue organization of the most efficient contracts to reduce the very high transactions costs of contracts. 'Works for hire' contracts represent a low transaction cost solution to coordination issues (Caves, 2003) by employing artists specifically for their work product as an employee and therefore directly co-opting the intellectual property arising from it. This does two things: it removes the burden of fixed costs from the creating artist, but at the same time confers the intellectual property and potential for economic rent to the employer. This transference can be seen as welfare neutral only if the copyright period is just sufficient to cover the fixed costs of production, any excess leads to increased monopoly profit in the hands of a large, powerful monopoly agent.

Ronald Coase determined that transaction costs are not only a consideration of firms to organize production in the most efficient manor (Coase, 1937), but are of importance to all markets. In his seminal paper considering 'The Problem of Social Cost' (1960) he theorized that traditional ideas of market failure were not the issue, the real market failure was the failure to adequately define property rights or the inability to effectively trade these due to transaction costs. He used the case of pollution to illustrate this. The neoclassical 'Pigovian' view of pollution was that it was a market failure of production or consumption failing to internalize all of the associated costs. Coase showed that if property rights (i.e. the right to pollute or the right to not be polluted) were well defined and there were no transaction costs, the free market mechanism would find an optimum (maximal welfare) outcome. The problem arose because of transaction costs, if the right not to be polluted was given to many and there was one polluter, it is difficult to coordinate a trade for the market to compensate (and hence account for the costs of) pollution.

When we consider creative industries we also have a situation with high transaction costs, with many buyers of say a music CD or a movie essentially contracting with the producer. The existence of IP law essentially creates a generalized contract that purchase is not the absolute rights to that good (to copy, resell, broadcast, etc.), but to the *use* of that good, for one's own consumption. Inherent in IP law is therefore the notion that the individual is actually purchasing a 'fair use' of the good. Landes and Posner (1989) support this, arguing that in most creative goods markets, efficiency dictates that rights be attributed to the creators ('copyright') and that users purchase a 'fair use' of this good – for consumption.

The limits of fair use represent an area of ambiguity of the law – including some interesting caveats – such as some exemptions for educational purposes, transformative works (works that transform the original) and for 'parody'. The issue of what constitutes 'transformative work' is analysed in other chapters (see Terhanian, Liebler and Suthersanen in this collection). From an economic perspective, over and above the discussions in the earlier section regarding economic philosophy of ownership where a 'work-mixing' argument could apply, Towse (2002) notes that fair use[21] can be characterized as a legal equivalent to Pigovian welfare economics with its balance of social benefits and costs, which should permit limited use of copyrighted work without obtaining consent from the holder in the aim of advancing academic, political or social purposes. In other words, the limitations and exceptions to copyright are economically justified if it grants access to works which can then be used as inspiration or otherwise to create new works, thus maximizing creative output and social welfare.

However, the ambiguity in the extent to which 'fair use' should be a part of copyright (as with any ambiguity in contracting) can lead to extraneous transaction costs in the market. For example, in 2013 GoldieBlox, an American toymaker, released an online advertisement that used the melody from a Beastie Boys song 'Girls', with newly recorded music and amended lyrics. The band complained and GoldieBlox pre-emptively filed suit in November 2013 for a declaratory judgement of fair use claiming the song as a parody, Beastie Boys then counter-sued in December 2013 for copyright infringement. According to *The Economist*, lawyers remain at odds over whether the song was a parody or not, and the music on the advert has since been changed (*The Economist*, 2013). This is just one example of the costs that can be associated with copyright in the application of the ambiguous 'fair use' clause. Gordon (1982) considers the potential for transaction costs to exceed the value of copies to individual users, leading to market failure.

These disputes are often settled by a judge whose determination is directed to be based on fairly subjective factors, for example in the USA these are: (1) the purpose and character of the use; (2) the nature of the copyrighted work; (3) the amount/portion used; and (4) the effect on the potential market.[22] This is of particular relevance to transactions costs when the subjective nature of the ruling may result in the determinations being reversed in appeal. The recent case of *Cariou v Prince* (2011) is illustrative here. Cariou originally won his case for IP infringement against Prince's use of his photograph in his 2008 'Canal Zone' collection, as the changes made by Prince to Cariou's photographs weren't considered by the judge to be significant enough to constitute a change in meaning (i.e. 'fair use'). However, this was overturned on appeal. Prince's 'motivation' for the Canal Zone series was to comment on mass produced art. The series applied a similar set of small graffiti-like treatments to a number of popular photographs and for this reason the appeal judge determined that Prince's work 'transformed' the original work in a way that meant it was aesthetically different, and thus acceptable under the argument of 'fair use' (see Terhanian in this collection). Given the subjective nature of interpretation of the four factors and the large amount of judicial discretion, it seems likely that as intellectual property becomes ever more prominent economically, so too will the impacts of judicial 'flip-flopping' in creating extraneous transactions costs in markets.

Legally the exception for 'parody' may also seem to be on a similarly subjective footing. However, non-copyright infringement of 'parody' represents a clear area where an economic perspective is useful, since it confirms that the value of a parody lies in the parody, not in the original work; the parody is not displacing any market transaction or transfer of welfare, as no transaction would have occurred without the original and the parody does not displace trade in the original – it is essentially, purely an addition of welfare value in the market.

While discussing transaction costs in markets it is important to note that IP such as copyright can actually also create a disincentive to create new works by raising transactions costs. Such costs include copyright payment to previous creators as well as transaction costs of searching and tracing for payment (see Op den Kamp in this collection). An excellent example of the impact of prior works on costs of production is one of the surprise hits of the Cannes Film Festival of 2003 – a partially autobiographical documentary by director Jonathan Caouette. The film is reputed to have cost only $218 to make as it was comprised mostly of stock footage out of copyright. However, in preparation for cinematic release, the total spent rose to about $400,000 on sound, print, score and music/clip clearances added to illustrate mood and/or era (Boldrin & Levine, 2008). This movie was made possible by print which was out of copyright, but further would have had a much lower cost without paying for copyright licences.

As has also been discussed, upholding IP can be expensive. Boldrin and Levine (2002) expound on the costs involved in enforcing laws which include both the costs of writing these laws and of catching and prosecuting those who break them. William Landes (2003) also mentions the administrative costs involved in the copyright system. For instance, Disney was one of the most vociferous proponents lobbying for copyright extension, leading to the Sonny Bono Act (Decherney, 2012), and as such incurred substantial costs (more than $6.3 million between 1997 and 1998 [Responsive Politics, 2002]) to prevent Mickey Mouse and other Disney characters entering the public domain.

However, having considered transaction costs, it is interesting to note that remuneration practices in secondary markets[23] which would otherwise suffer prohibitive (i.e. market failure level) transaction costs have evolved to circumvent such failure. The use of blanket licensing is prevalent in most creative industries with substantial secondary market use – such as the music industry. This blanket licensing means that blanket fees are collected for things such as radio airplay and use of music in shops, etc., and then distributed amongst members by collecting societies.[24] However, this is by no means an unambiguous solution to the issues of transaction costs since it comes at the price of a trade-off of economic efficiency in remuneration. Under blanket licensing artists are remunerated by some set waiver fee, so they actually receive the same unit payment when their marginal productivity may not be equal.[25] Moreover, it has been argued that the collecting societies represent monopoly power in themselves, which attracts all of the criticisms of monopoly power previously expounded.

Given that the arguments for the existence of IP (that of necessity in creating incentive and correction for market failure) are detracted by this collection of economic issues it is pertinent to next consider the economics of a world without it.

A WORLD WITHOUT COPYRIGHT

Static and Dynamic Analysis of Loss of Welfare (Efficiency) in the Market

We have already considered deadweight loss in welfare in a market from monopoly, but welfare issues are complicated when considered dynamically (rather than just statically). The analysis of welfare is an argument of two parts – a static analysis and dynamic analysis (Waldfogel, 2011). Let us consider the case of copying music. Assuming the marginal costs of digital products is equal to zero (this is not unreasonable for digital copying), a static analysis considers music that already exists in the market. Here, welfare actually increases as file sharing increases! In this scenario, consumers obtain music without the price they would otherwise have to pay. This creates a larger consumer surplus, as surplus that would have been acquired by producers at the market price is transferred to consumers. However, an additional effect occurs: for the consumers who had a marginal utility (a value) for the music that was greater than zero but below market price, when the market determined that price they would not make a consumption decision; however, file sharing permits these and therefore creates an amount that was never available to the producer as surplus because it was the deadweight loss associated with the producer charging a higher than marginal cost price. In other words, it increases the welfare of the market (i.e. a net benefit to society) by allowing trades (for zero) that otherwise wouldn't have occurred.

However, the static analysis is only apt under the assumption that the music already exists. Dynamic analysis considers the evolving market. New music production requires producers to invest substantial fixed costs – which they will invest only if they believe they can recoup these. Therefore in the next period, neither consumers nor producers earn a surplus as no market is made. This is essentially the argument of Baumol (2003) above and the requisite of incentive – and an issue often confused (perhaps deliberately) in terms of welfare analysis in the market.

Does No Copyright Necessarily Mean No Profit?

In the absence of copyright protection is there really no longer an incentive to produce these goods? Not necessarily, as there are some characteristics of the product that are not information based – and therefore not imitable, or not immediately imitable. There may be market structure issues that cause first mover advantages and there may even be some benefits to being copied.

For example, first mover advantage is well established in business economics, that for the production of any good there is a time-lag for copying – for example, the originator of the 1975 'pet-rocks' fad (essentially rocks with eyes and features stuck and drawn on), became a millionaire between December 1975 and February 1976 before copycats could cash-in (Olson, 1999, p. 284). In addition, those later copies may be inferior to the original and moreover there may be an inherent value in owning an 'original'. Arguably, prior to the digital revolution these three advantages were sufficient to make an initial profit even in the presence of copying (note: the music industry has been subject to substantive piracy since the 1970s with the bootlegging of cassettes); but the technology of the digital age may have eroded both the time lag of copies and superiority of quality, thus perhaps even more strongly supporting the need for IP regulation (see Kirton in this collection).

However, some scholars have considered alternate solutions to the market problem of information goods, such as Gallini and Scotchmer (2002) and notably Varian (2005). He particularly redresses the argument of market collapse without copyright by suggesting that there is no reason stronger business models could not be adapted to take advantage of other potential competitive advantages.

Most crucially he considers transaction costs. 'If copies have a transaction cost – a direct cost of copying, an inconvenience cost or the copy is inferior to the original in some way, then the seller can set the price low enough that copying is not attractive' (Varian, 2005, p. 134). Essentially there are two ways the original becomes cheaper than the copy. Firstly, if the originator makes the price cheaper than those of potential copies (i.e. a limit-pricing model) and secondly by making the copy more expensive than the original. The latter hinges on the transaction costs of copies. This transaction cost can be deliberate by enforcing a system of digital rights management that may make it difficult to play the song track or watch the movie outside of a particular environment which is controlled, or may simply be an inconvenience cost or a quality opportunity cost. Think, for example, about downloading a file from the Internet such as a movie or a TV serial. In most cases the kind of websites they are downloadable from are unreliable and may include a multitude of pop-ups or spyware and adware that can potentially harm your computer. There is therefore a cost to choosing a 'free' download and instead, in terms of reliability and minimizing harm, it may be marginally beneficial to purchase from a reliable vendor (iTunes, LOVEFiLM, Netflix, etc.). Whereas the latter factor has become increasingly important – i.e. the convenience of relatively low-cost vendors versus illegal downloading sites, the former strategy of digital rights management has been largely abandoned since around 2007 – as in many cases it can be seen to create an inferior quality product, i.e. one that is less portable (Herman, 2013, pp. 161).

Secondly, the seller could sell physical complements along with the original creation ('bundling'). For example, when buying a CD from a record shop, possible complements that could also be sold along with the CD or included as a special offer might include a poster, t-shirt or even lottery ticket to, say, meet the band, these tangible extras cannot be downloaded with an illicit copy of the CD.

Thirdly, Varian suggested that a form of pure public provision could exist. Artists and other creators of intellectual property might be paid by the state or financed out of tax or other revenues. This approach is not so different from public universities where research and publication are considered integral to the job expectations for faculty (Varian, 2005).

Actually Varian came up with a plethora of suggestions, based on his formidable understanding of the microeconomic environment and theory of the firm, as wide ranging as: turning the product into a stream of products (i.e. a kind of subscription) or having a site license, where the purchase of one thing create access to a bundle of others (for example, again looking at the high knowledge industry used to dealing with intangible information goods, in academic journals where this tactic is often used). He also suggests modifying the product to sell highly personalized versions of a good which are less attractive to copy; use the good to advertise yourself or to advertise other things; and other carrot and stick methods like prizes, awards and commissions, which we will consider further below.

More Carrot, Less Stick

A number of economists (and indeed economic theory itself) suggests other methods for creating incentive in markets. Most commonly cited are grants and awards (subsidies) and prizes. Prizes can replicate the 'bounty' received by the right of monopoly, but as with the granting of a monopoly its efficiency (in maximizing overall market welfare) depends on whether it just recoups the variable plus fixed costs (and prior sunk costs) or not. Moreover, prizes are ex-post rewards, given afterwards, and like the goods themselves subject to uncertainty. Ex-ante incentives such as grants and subsidies can encourage the production of goods by removing the uncertainty. However, it also introduces uncertainty in terms of the quality and aptness of the work produced (given payment is already received) and also requires an awarding body to decide who receives the grant, which takes away the choice of the consumer in favour of 'the academy'.

As such, a joint problem with grants and prizes is the need to set up an administrative body to allocate and award. Both grants and prizes are further removed from the market system which means less efficiency (or more likely more areas for inefficiency). Moreover, it introduces a principal agent problem in acquiring the ends, with the principal offering a financial reward to an agent to produce a good, there is the possibility of political skew, rent-seeking behaviour and in general greater chances of corruption. As Macaulay said in 1841: 'I can conceive no system more fatal to the integrity and independence of literary men, than one under which they should be taught to look for their daily bread to the favour of ministers and nobles' (Macaulay, 1841).

Some economists advocate a widening of the copyright levy similar to that of the blank media levy operational in the US, Canada and some EU countries, whereby a levy is payable on any recordable media (cassettes, CDs, etc.) and distributed amongst artists (via collection societies) in mitigation of the costs of copyright infringement. An equivalent of a 'blank media' levy could be placed on hardware or Internet connection. Oksanen and Valimaki (2005) econometrically estimated an optimum levy of €5 per year for each Finnish broadband connection based on estimates of the costs of piracy. However, such a levy is subject to much debate, the existing blank media levy has been legally challenged in some countries (such as Australia) and not adopted by others (such as the UK) in that it is a tax distributed to private benefactors (not the state). Moreover, it is widely criticized for the same distributional issues as 'blanket licensing' discussed above.

Finally, Kremer (1988) highlights discussion by economists of an interesting alternate proposal – that of 'government buyout'. In 1839 the government of France bought out all patent rights to 'daguerreotype photography' (the first practicable photographic process invented by Louis Daguerre) and placed it in the public domain. What followed was a rapid world-wide adoption and numerous improvements. The process became public domain and the proliferation of the information and the freedom to copy caused rapid improvement upon it. This seems to offer the answer to the transactions costs problems and disincentive for future works that IP causes, whilst still retaining the incentive of production (the creator receives payment), i.e. it both rewards innovation, but removes monopoly and hindrance to further innovations. However, we must consider two things: firstly that it is still subject to the same issues as subsidising – where the money for the subsidy or buyout comes from. It must come from taxes which are not neutral of welfare issues. Secondly – like provision of copyright – determining an optimum buyout price requires knowledge of prior sunk costs.

It seems that no market alternative thus far suggested can offer an unambiguous improvement to that of IP law (of defining property rights). However, the ever-increasing move towards the 'weightless economy', with ever-increasing reliance on knowledge-based competitive advantages mean that it is a popular avenue of exploration for scholars and public policy think-tanks alike. In the 2002 Cato Policy Report, Tom W. Bell urges future regulation to 'encourage market-based alternatives to copyrights and patents'.

What have also not been considered thus far are the *benefits* of not pursuing copyright – the benefits of being copied.

Indeed, rather than just an infringement on property rights, reproduction of copyrighted works may well have some hidden benefits to the copyright holder. Liebowitz (1985) found this to be the case with the photocopying of academic journals, and showed, due to the concept of indirect appropriability, that there is an increased demand for them as copyable originals. Liebowitz suggests that the debate over copyright is therefore focusing too strongly on publisher's revenues, whilst ignoring important economic aspects such as indirect appropriability and price discrimination (Liebowitz, 1985, p. 956). As suggested by Gordon (1982), exceptions to IP can actually solve market failure. For example in cases where a copier cannot afford to purchase use of a good that is for socially beneficial activities such as education, teachers may be allowed to copy works under exceptions of fair use as they are not using the work for self-maximizing purposes, but to educate and improve social welfare. This therefore solves a case of market failure caused by high transaction costs between owner and user (Gordon, 2002).

Certainly, network effects for arts and cultural goods have been shown to be significant (Varian, 2005). Network economies are such that the more people who use a good the greater the demand becomes (for example, telephones, or social networking sites). The characteristics of arts and cultural goods are such that they are often 'experience goods' and experience goods are subject to uncertainty of reception and therefore heavily influenced by ex-ante information regarding the goods – which is heavily influenced by information networks (peers/experts/fashions).

Adler (1985) describes a learning process as key to understanding the superstar phenomenon amongst artists, due to art consumption being positively addictive (in that marginal utility from art consumption increases with ability to appreciate art, which increases with consumption), as 'consumption capital' is accumulated.[26] Such consumption capital arises from experience and becoming more knowledgeable of the art or artist and even discussing the art or artist with others. This last effect is amplified by positive 'network externalities', that even a slightly better known artist will be discussed more communally causing them to be discussed more, etc., in a snowball effect of consumption capital. This certainly suggests a strong economic rationale for inducing network effects to then help induce the snowball.

The fact that many creatives elect to either not litigate copyright infringement or avoid traditional IP via Creative Commons, FOSS, General Public License (GPL), and Berkley System Distribution (BSD) licences, etc. (discussed in other chapters) may evidence the benefits more permissible forms of intellectual protection discussed.

Schumpeter's Creative Destruction

An interesting argument against intellectual property is the application of the idea of 'creative destruction' (Schumpeter, 1942) which is generally applied to argue the case against intervention in industries dogged by monopolies. Schumpeter argues *for the existence of a 'perennial gale of creative destruction'*, in which dominance by one particular firm or individual offers an incentive for others to innovate an alternative, in doing so the new, creative solution trumps the slow moving leviathan-like responses of large monopolies destroying the market and remaking it as it does. This contrasts with the idea that there are no incentives for a creator to create without IP law and the establishment of temporary monopolies. Creative destruction captures the idea that one creator's success would spur on creators of the future and provide an incentive for further creation.

Non-monetary Remuneration

It must also be considered that incentive to create is not formed solely by the profit motive, particularly in arts and cultural sectors where intrinsic motivation is substantial (Frey, 1997). As far back as Adam Smith it was postulated that there may be satisfaction gained from more than just monetary remuneration, such as 'public admiration' (Smith, 1776). If we are to take the Benthamite or utilitarian view (that satisfaction is the only true currency), it is possible for a new work to cover its fixed costs from the intrinsic values associated with it, i.e. artistic satisfaction (Plant, 1934).

The intrinsic values associated with production of arts and creative works is also empirically supported by many of David Throsby's findings, that when wages rise in non-arts related fields, artists do not supply more labour to these fields, instead, when artists have earned a minimum income they would prefer to spend the rest of their time creating, so much so that a rise in non-arts wages causes a strong endowment effect which means less supply to the non-arts labour market and more to the arts markets (Throsby, 1994). So, if creating is preferred to leisure by artists, the need for copyright may be diminished.

This suggests that the moral rights elements of copyright (i.e. right of attribution), which does not necessarily need to diminish with copying may be of a more fundamental value to artists than the primary rights that are so often focused upon. Moral rights, which were originally part of the civil law tradition and later adopted into the Anglo-Saxon law tradition, focus on integrity, attribution, disclosure and the right of withdrawal. Each provides an incentive to create in encouraging artistic recognition of status and professionalism, as well as preserving reputation (Rushton, 1998). As a result, moral rights could well be a crucial feature of a pared-down copyright in sustaining future creation.

Conversely, as Boyle et al. (2010) point out, legislation sometimes introduces negative externalities (costs) to the very group it is intended to protect. Indeed, Landes (2001) analysed the Visual Artists Rights Act of 1990 which provided integrity and attribution rights for a limited group of visual arts, and showed that VARA adds transaction costs to the market, decreasing demand for art and reducing the remunerations of artists. This prediction was later confirmed by Boyle et al. (2010) who found artists in (US) states with moral rights protection lost between $3,840 and $4,065 per year, on average, as a result of these laws. Although moral rights are waivable in the US, it is notable this action would result in even further transaction costs, especially considering they have to be waived on an individual basis.

Finally, it is worth considering that until 1976 in the US, a copyright registration system existed. This is similar to the current system for patents and trademarks, whereby copyright would have to be registered (for a fee), then after a time re-registered (for a fee), and if not, they would drop into the public domain. Landes and Posner (2002) posit that this system could be reintroduced, which would, in theory, result in only valuable copyright being renewed and therefore no transaction costs existing for the majority of works, hence no disincentive for future creation. This is perhaps a corollary to the notion of an optimum period of protection and the arguments for shorter copyright terms in general.

SUMMARY THOUGHTS: ADAPTATION TO THE STATUS QUO?

What is most fundamental about markets is that they adapt. Whatever regulatory framework is put in place they adapt to extract the most welfare gains possible, the agents with the most market power being those who usurp the most gains. From the history of development and the case studies noted in this chapter it appears that current IP regulation is akin to a beast with brittle teeth. The spirit of the law attempts to aid efficiency in markets by clearly defining property rights, but those markets themselves fall short of perfect markets and so IP inevitably supports some aspects of market failure (i.e. monopoly rent). It also comes at a cost, in creating many avenues for increasing transactions costs in markets – which markets abhor. This abhorrence of extraneous transaction costs leads to solutions ranging from works-for-hire contracts to selective enforcement. IP is therefore imperfectly practised. But is the imperfect practice of enforcing property rights an argument for removing them? The author of this chapter would proffer that there is some merit in allowing an imperfect solution in the absence of an unambiguously better one.

There is also the potential for counterbalance under the current situation. The impact of piracy on the record industry is also an example. Piracy has been an often quoted concern of record industry moguls in the past decade. Particularly, in the United States, revenues from the record industry fell from $30 billion in 1999 to $16.5 billion in 2012 (World Economic Forum, 2013), attributed, as Liebowitz (2011) summarized in his study of the decline (and by the majority of reputable studies), to the advent of file sharing. However, Mortimer et al. (2012) found that the decline in album sales is much more pronounced for large artists than for small artists. This may be because for small artists, file sharing may have increased awareness of their music and therefore encouraged some additional album sales from a larger fan base even as it displaced album sales to others. File sharing has allowed for a much larger information network for smaller bands, which has outweighed the negative effects of file sharing. Mortimer et al. also conclude that the market for live music appears to have expanded after Napster, and the scope of existing recorded music contracts, which implies that although large artists lose market share in recording markets, concert revenues have been positively affected by file sharing.

Indeed, Lu and Poddar (2012) formulated an economic model of the deterrence of piracy much like the models of best response equilibria in duopoly markets, where the firm is faced with a decision either to deter piracy by aggressive litigation, which is costly but also increases the cost of piracy and hence deters it, or not, which imposes the cost of lost sales. In it they succinctly show that, like best response reactions in duopoly markets to price or quantity competition, this merely represents another strategic decision in markets dominated by large firms (which we have previously established are those with the greatest vested interest in preventing piracy).

While high public profile advocates, such as the much respected intellectual television personality Stephen Fry, strongly advocate a more Creative Commons approach to IP, upholding a regulatory framework which is sympathetic to the desired norms of the society which it serves; from an economic perspective the issues beg an obvious, yet interesting conclusion – that the regulation of monopoly power, rather than the act of clearly defining property rights that IP regulation brings, is the fulcrum of economic efficiency. This is of course notwithstanding the issues of transactions costs discussed earlier. In other words, much of the operational issues perceived as welfare negative may be more so because of the regulatory failure of monopoly power, than the underlying definition of Intellectual Property Rights.

CONCLUSION

This chapter has considered the issues of IP from an economic perspective, particularly regarding the highly IP dependent creative industry sector. It has considered the economic rationale for IP regulation in terms of incentive to create and in general corrections for market failure, whilst mitigated by the further market failure it can be said to generate. There is no universal economist consensus on a perfect IP regulatory framework – particularly over copyright with respect to creative industries – and opinions vary from complete abandonment to support of various modifications as well as continuance of the status quo. Given the immense lobbying power of large corporations in the USA and Europe, in the author's opinion it is unlikely that changes to the current system will occur without breach of some tipping point of sufficient detriment to spur action, and that markets will continue to adapt on an ad hoc basis to the changing environment. The work of new scholars like Pollock (discussed above) offer some interesting insight into more optimal terms for IP protection from an economic perspective. The growth and prevalence of alternate forms of licensing is a means for actual practitioners to meaningfully shape future practices of IP rights' implementation. The economic issues of IP in the future may not lie in reaffirming its conceptual basis but in adaptation of regulatory practices in an increasingly global economy, increasingly concentrated into oligopolistically dominated markets.

NOTES

1 Within the same work he accedes, in addition, that in this process the accumulation of capital also leads to 'the accumulation of wealth' (Smith, 1981 [1776]).
2 Granted to '*Rerum venetarum ab urbe condita opus*', a work by Marcus Antonius Coccius Sabellicus on the history of the great city, in the republic of Venice in 1486.
3 It was originally established in 1403 as the Guild of Stationers.
4 The first recorded letter of protection was given in 1331.
5 Prior to this they were only imitable by hand through scribes, subject to errors and with a substantial investment of labour in every copy.
6 Later published in 1843.
7 However, correlation isn't necessarily causation!
8 Later in neoclassical economics referred to as 'economic rent'.
9 *Brazil* (1985) is a British feature film directed and written by Terry Gilliam and written by Charles McKeown and Tom Stoppard (IMDB.com).
10 In welfare economics, a first best solution cannot be found when one or more optimality conditions cannot be satisfied. In such cases a second-best solution can be found.
11 Landes and Posner (1989) assert that because artists can never guarantee that revenues will exceed costs as demand is unknown, this uncertainty causes them to withdraw from creation in the first place.
12 Jeremy Bentham was an economic and social philosopher (1748–1832).
13 John Locke (1632–1704) was a classical liberalist philosopher widely regarded as one of the most influential 'enlightenment age' thinkers.
14 Originally Locke used the example of a farmer working land.
15 Hegel (1770–1831) was a German idealist philosopher.
16 www.printmag.com/interviews/modern-dog-copyright-and-the-burden-of-proof/.
17 Extended to life of author plus 70 years and for works of corporate authorship to 120 years after creation or 95 years after publication, whichever endpoint is earlier.
18 https://www.facebook.com/moderndog/posts/10153704548995193?stream_ref=10
19 The author notes personal receipt of this 'cookbook' by viral email!
20 Estimated from figures published in the Nielsen Company 2012 World Music Industry Report.
21 Within the UK, this is known as 'fair dealing'.
22 http://fairuse.stanford.edu/overview/fair-use/four-factors/
23 Secondary markets are markets for secondary uses of goods, for example, music primary markets are record sales and performance, but secondary markets include use in movies, radio-play or as background music in shops.
24 In the UK the main bodies dealing with music (largest secondary market) are PRS (Performing

Rights Society – who deal with performances of songs) and PPL (Phonographic Performance Ltd – who deal with writers' rights).

25 Economic efficiency in markets dictates that a labour unit be remunerated at the value of its marginal productivity.

26 Based on earlier work by Stigler and Becker (1977) and later developed into a theory of learning by consuming by Levy-Garboua and Montmarquette (1996).

REFERENCES

Adler, M. (1985) 'Stardom and Talent', *American Economic Review*, Vol.75, pp. 208–12.

Alderson, A. & Bisset, S. (2003) 'Bootleg Jamie Oliver Emailed Free to Millions Worldwide'. Available at: http://www.telegraph.co.uk/news/uknews/1437850/Bootleg-Jamie-Oliver-emailed-free-to-millions-worldwide.html (last accessed 4 November 2013).

Armstrong, Elizabeth (1990) *Before Copyright: The French Book-Privilege System 1498–1526*, Cambridge: Cambridge University Press.

Baker v Selden (1879) 101. U.S. 99 (1879).

Baumol, W. (2003) 'Applied Welfare Economics', in R. Towse (ed.) *Handbook of Cultural Economics*, Cheltenham, UK: Edward Elgar, pp. 20–31.

Bentham, J. (1795 [1843]) *Manual of Political Economy*, available from the online library of economics and liberty.

Bloxam, G.A. (1957) 'Letters Patent for Inventions: Their Use and Misuse', *The Journal of Industrial Economics*, Vol. 5(3), pp. 157–79.

Boldrin, M. & Levine, D.K. (2002) 'The Case Against Intellectual Property', *The American Economic Review*, Vol. 92, pp .209–12.

Boldrin, M. & Levine, D.K. (2008) 'The Devil in Disney', in *Against Intellectual Monopoly*, Cambridge: Cambridge University Press, pp. 99–107.

Boyle, M., Nazzaro, S., & O'Connor, D. (2010) 'Moral Rights Protection for the Visual Arts', *Journal of Cultural Economics*, Vol. 34(1), pp. 27–44.

Cariou V Prince (2011) Patrick Cariou V Richard Prince, US Court of Appeals, 11-1197-CV.

Cato Institute (2002) *The Great Debate on Intellectual Property*. Policy Report. Available at: http://object.cato.org/sites/cato.org/files/serials/files/policy-report/2002/1/property.pdf (last accessed 20 November 2013).

Caves, R.E. (2000) *Economies of the Creative Industries*, Cambridge, MA: Harvard University Press.

Caves, R.E. (2003) 'Contracts between Art and Commerce', *The Journal of Economic Perspectives*, Vol. 17(2), pp. 73–84.

Coase, R.H. (1937) 'The Nature of the Firm', *Economica*, Vol. 4(16), pp. 386–405.

Coase, R.H. (1960) 'The Problem of Social Cost', *Journal of Law and Economics*, Vol 3(1), pp. 1–44.

Creative Commons (2001) 'Creative Commons: About'. Available at: http://creativecommons.org/about/ (last accessed 1 January 2014).

David, M. (2010) *Peer to Peer and the Music Industry: The Criminalization of Sharing*, London: Sage.

Davidson, M.W. (2000) 'Copyright (Music Librarianship at the Turn of the Century)', *Music Library Association Quarterly Journal*: NOTES, Second Series', Vol. 56(3), pp. 598–604.

Decherney, P. (2012) *Hollywood's Copyright Wars: From Edison to the Internet*, New York: Columbia University Press.

Economics & Statistics Administration; US Patent and Trademark Office (2012) *Intellectual Property and the US Economy: Industries in Focus*, US Department of Commerce, March 2012.

Fine, M. (2000) 'Soundscan Study on Napster Use and Loss of Sales'. Available at: www.riaa.com (last accessed 1 January 2014).

Frey, B.S. (1997) *Not Just For The Money*, Cheltenham, UK: Edward Elgar Publishing.

Fromer, J.C. (2012) 'Expressive Incentives in Intellectual Property', *Virginia Law Review*, Vol. 98(8), pp.1745–824.

Gallini, N. & Scotchmer, S. (2002) 'Intellectual Property: When Is It the Best Incentive System?', in A. Jaffe, J. Lerner, & S. Stern (eds) *Innovation Policy and the Economy*, Vol. 2, Cambridge, MA: MIT Press.

Goldstein, Paul (1992) 'Copyright', *Law and Contemporary Problems*, Vol 55(2), pp. 79–91.

Gordon, W.J. (1982) 'Fair Use as Market Failure: A Structural and Economic Analysis of the *Betamax* [*Universal City Studios, Inc. v Sony Corp. of America*, 659 F.2d 963] Case and its Predecessors', *Journal of the Copyright Society of the U.S.A*, Vol. 30, pp. 253–326.

Gordon, W.J. (2002) 'Market Failure and Intellectual Property: A Response to Professor Lunney', *Boston University Law Review*, 4, p.1031.

Hasper, M. (2005) 'Intellectual Property Rights Protection in Developing Countries: The Effects of TRIPS on the Production and Dissemination of Cures Specific to Developing Country Diseases', Stanford University: Department of Economics.

Hatch, O.G. (1989) 'Better Late Than Never: Implementation of the 1886 Berne Convention', *Cornell International Law Journal*, Vol. 22, pp. 171–95.

Hayek, F.A. (1945) 'The Use of Knowledge in Society', *American Economic Review*, Vol. 35(4), pp. 519–30.

Herman, B.D. (2013) *The Fight Over Digital Rights: The Politics of Copyright and Technology*, Cambridge: Cambridge University Press.

IFPI (2012) 'Digital Music Report 2012: Focus on South Korea; Developing a Legitimate Business in China', International Federation of the Phonographic Industry (IFPI).

Klemm, Friedrich (1964) *A History of Western Technology*, Cambridge, MA: MIT Press.

Klitzke, Ramon A. (1959) 'Historical Background of the English Patent Law', *Journal of the Patent Office Society* (Patent and Trademark Office), Vol. 41(9), pp. 615–50.

Kremer, M. (1988) 'Patent Buyouts: A Mechanism for Encouraging Innovation', *Quarterly Journal of Economics*, November, pp. 1137–67.

Ku, Raymond S.R. (2002) 'The Creative Destruction of Copyright: Napster and the New Economics of Digital Technology', *The University of Chicago Law Review*, Vol. 69(1), pp. 263–324.

Landes, W.M. (2001) 'What Has the Visual Artist's Rights Act of 1990 Accomplished?', *Journal of Cultural Economics*, Vol. 25(4), pp. 283–306.

Landes, W.M. (2003) 'Copyright', in R. Towse *A Handbook of Cultural Economics*, Cheltenham: Edward Elgar, pp.132–42.

Landes, W.M. & Posner, R.A. (1989) 'An Economic Analysis of Copyright Law', *Journal of Legal Studies*, Vol. 18(2), pp. 325–63.

Landes, W.M. & Posner, R.A. (2002) 'Indefinitely Renewable Copyright', Olin Working Paper, No. 154. Chicago: University of Chicago Law School. Available at: http://www.law.uchicago.edu/files/files/154.wml-rap.copyright.new_.pdf (last accessed 1 January 2014).

Levy-Garboua, L. & Montmarquette, C. (1996) 'A Microeconomic Study of Theatre Demand', *Journal of Cultural Economics*, Vol. 20, pp. 25–50.

Liebowitz, S.J. (1985) 'Copying and Indirect Appropriability: Photocopying of Journals', *Journal of Political Economy*, Vol. 93(5) pp 945–57.

Liebowitz, S.J. (2011) 'The Metric is the Message: How much of the Decline in Sound Recording Sales is due to File-Sharing?' Available at: http://papers.ssrn.com/sol3/papers.cfm?abstract_id=1932518

Lu, Yuanzhu & Poddar, Sougata (2012) 'Accommodation or Deterrence in the Face of Commercial Piracy: The Impact of Intellectual Property Rights Protection', *Oxford Economic Papers*, Vol. 64, pp. 518–38.

Macaulay, T.B. (1841) 'Opposing Proposed Life + 60 Year Copyright Term', House of Commons speech.

Mill, J. Stuart (1848) *Principles of Political Economy with some of their Applications to Social Philosophy* (Ashley ed.), original text from the Online Library of Liberty.

Mokyr, J. (2009) 'Intellectual Property Rights, the Industrial Revolution, and the Beginnings of Modern Economic Growth', *American Economic Review: Papers & Proceedings*, Vol. 99(2), pp. 349–55.

Mortimer, J.H., Nosko, C., & Sorensen, A. (2012) 'Supply Responses to Digital Distribution: Recorded Music and Live Performances', *Information Economics and Policy*, Vol. 24(1), pp. 3–14.

NetNames (2013) 'Digital Piracy: Sizing the Piracy Universe', NetNames report, October. Available at: http://www.netnames.com/digital-piracy-sizing-piracy-universe

Nielsen Company (2012) *World Music Industry Report 2012*, Neilsen, USA, http://www.nielsen.com/

Office for Harmonization in the Internal Market (2013) 'IPR-Intensive Industries Contribution to Economic Performance and Employment in the European Union'. Available at: http://documents.epo.org/projects/babylon/eponet.nsf/0/8E1E34349D4546C3C1257BF300343D8B/$File/ip_intensive_industries_en.pdf

Oksanen, V. & Valimaki, M (2005) 'Copyright Levies as an Alternative Compensation Method for Recording Artists and Technological Development', *Review of Economic Research on Copyright*, Vol. 2(2), pp. 25–39.

Olson, J.S. (1999) *Historical Dictionary of the 1970s*, Westport, CT: Greenwood Publishing Group.

Plant, Arnold (1934) 'The Economic Aspect of Copyright in Books', *Economica*, Vol. 1(2), pp. 167–95.

Pollock, R. (2009) 'Forever Minus a Day? Calculating Optimal Copyright Term of Works', University of Cambridge Working Papers, O31 O34 L10, June 15.

Poltorak, A.I. & Lerner, P.J. (2011) *Essentials of Intellectual Property* (2nd edn), Hoboken, NJ: Wiley.

Resnik, D.B. (2003) 'A Pluralistic Account of Intellectual Property', *Journal of Business Ethics*, Vol. 46(4), pp. 319–35.

Responsive Politics (2002) 'Lobbying Spending database' - Walt Disney Co', via https://www.opensecrets.org/lobby/clientsum.php?id=D000000128&year=2002 (last accessed, 18 September 2014).

Rushton, M. (1998) 'The Moral Rights of Artists', *Journal of Cultural Economics*, Vol. 22, p. 29.

Schumpeter, Joseph (1942) *Capitalism, Socialism and Democracy*, New York: Harper.

Smith, Adam (1759) '*The Theory of moral Sentiments*', available from the online library of economics and liberty.

Smith, Adam (1981 [1776]) *An Inquiry into the Nature and Causes of the Wealth of Nations*, available from the online library of economics and liberty.

Stigler, George J. & Becker, Gary S. (1977) 'De gustibus non est disputandum', *American Economic Review*, Vol 67(2), pp. 76–90.

Storper, M. (1989) 'The Transition to Flexible Specialisation in the US Film Industry: External Economies, the Division of Labour and the Crossing of Industrial Divides', *Cambridge Journal of Economics*, Vol. 13, pp. 273–305.

The Economist (2013) 'Does Parody Trump Copyright?', *The Economist*,4 December.

Throsby, D. (1994) 'A Work Preference Model of Artist Behaviour', in Alan Peacock & Ilde Rizzo (eds) *Cultural Economics and Cultural Policies*, Boston: Springer, pp. 69–80.

Towse, R. (2002) *Copyright in the Cultural Industries*, Cheltenham, UK: Edward Elgar Publishing.

Towse, R. (2003) *A Handbook of Cultural Economics*, Cheltenham, UK: Edward Elgar Publishing.

TRIPS (1994) 'TRIPS Agreement: 1994', 1869 UNTS 299; 33 ILM 1197.

Varian, Hal R. (2005) 'Copying and Copyright', *Journal of Economic Perspectives*, Vol. 19(2), pp. 121–38.

Waldfogel, J (2011) '*Bye, Bye, Miss American Pie? The Supply of New Recorded Music Since Napster*', NBER Working Paper No. 16882, Issued in March 2011

WIPO (2009) 'Understanding Copyright and Related Rights'. Available at: http://www.wipo.int/freepublications/en/intproperty/909/wipo_pub_909.html#limitations (last accessed 12 December 2013).

World Economic Forum (2013) 'Intellectual Property Rights in the Global Creative Economy'. Available at: http://www3.weforum.org/docs/GAC/2013/WEF_GAC IntellectualPropertyRights_GlobalCreativeEconomy_Report_2013.pdf (last accessed 20 November 2013).

3

The Idea of International Intellectual Property

Shubha Ghosh

INTRODUCTION

'Intellectual property' is sometimes understood as a concept that transcends culture and history. International treaties such as the Berne and Paris Conventions and Trade Related Intellectual Property Rights (TRIPS) impose requirements on signatories about harmonization and substantive minima as if the principles around which signatories should harmonize were apparent and readily deducible. When recognized as a term that is of recent vintage, first used by a federal court in the United States only in the 1940s and made part of international agreements with the creation of the World Intellectual Property Organization in the 1970s, the historical and cultural contingency of intellectual property belies the perception of universalizability. Even those who adopt a strictly economic approach as a foundation for intellectual property have to concede that the relevant benefits and costs that define the scope of rights depend upon context, with perhaps different optimal rules for developed and developing countries.

This chapter makes the case for the contingency of intellectual property by examining another elusive concept, 'international intellectual property'. While of even more recent vintage than its close cousin, the term 'international intellectual property' has obtained salience with casebooks, treatises and law school courses transferring knowledge about this field. The International Intellectual Property Alliance submits briefs to courts advocating positions relevant to international trade and global principles of intellectual property ownership. An initial inclination is to define international intellectual property as some aggregate of intellectual property, a concept overarching the laws of individual nation states. In practice, one may conclude that international intellectual property is the projection of laws from particular nation states, the most obvious suspect being the United States. By critically examining the concept of international intellectual property, we can learn more about the interests and ideologies that inform intellectual property. A fortiori, the concept of international intellectual property may have more salience and relevance for legal analysis and policy making than what might seem on the surface to be the more general concept of intellectual property.

This chapter was originally titled 'A Philosophy of International Intellectual Property'. This initial title echoed the title

'Philosophy of Intellectual Property,' adopted by legal academics Justin Hughes and Peter Drahos for each author's respective article and book (Hughes, 1988; Drahos, 1996). Justin Hughes' important early piece on the philosophy of intellectual property grounds the concept in the work of Locke, Hegel and Rawls. Peter Drahos, in his book-length treatment of the subject, frames the debate in terms of Christian thought as well as more contemporary Marxist thinking to develop a non-propriatarian view of intellectual property rights. Little has been written about intellectual property in non-Western traditions, although there have been commentaries on the absence of copyright in Confucian China (Alford, 1997) and the grounding of intellectual property in Islamic notions of property (Malkawi, 2013). Inserting the word 'international' into the titles of Hughes' and Drahos' respective works raised the question of the applicability of a canonical philosophy of intellectual property across nation states. There are reasons, however, to question the existence of a philosophy of either intellectual property or international intellectual property. One way to support this point is by examining the idea of international intellectual property, the ultimate title of this chapter.

What is international intellectual property? Perhaps international intellectual property is like the unicorn or the minotaur. Like these beasts, international intellectual property is a metaphor, and any philosophy of such subjects bleeds into poetry. But looked at from another angle, international intellectual property has some valence. There is no supra-national entity that could grant international intellectual property rights (IPRs). IPRs would not constitute a res, or subject matter that would bear the hallmarks of property. On the other hand, if one takes the bundle of rights notion of property seriously, then international intellectual property would be the aggregate bundle of the national bundle of sticks granted by individual nation states. A philosophy of international intellectual property would be attuned to the national differences in these rights as they aggregate to form the global bundle of rights (Sykes, 2007).

At one level, such a conception of international intellectual property would be a species of comparative law. The conception would explain the variations across states that reflect historical, religious, cultural and other differences that would account for the various legal rights. But this approach is not very satisfactory as it is more descriptive than analytic. International intellectual property would be reduced to an analysis of cultural differences which would be useful but may not yield any more insight as to policy than an assessment of national politics. Perhaps, understanding individual states is the best we can do.

The problem with a purely comparative view of international intellectual property is that the narrative of dominant states will prevail, creating a potentially strained and narrow vision of the role of intellectual property. Arguably, this narrowing had occurred already with the implementation of the TRIPS Agreement through the Uruguay Rounds in 1994 (Menell & Scotchmer, 2007; Sykes, 2007). As conventional wisdom teaches, the developed countries, led by the United States, pushed a strong intellectual property agenda through the multilateral treaty mechanism on the rest of the world, meaning the large group of signatories from the developing world. This agenda was boosted by a philosophy of international property that was exclusively Western, the thinkers most often cited being Locke and Hegel. This reality from the 1990s reveals the problem of thinking of international intellectual property solely in comparative terms. By simply offering comparisons, such a poor philosophy allows the dominant narrative (and the interests they buttress) to win out in the arena of international relations. No normative counterweight allows for alternative systems.

But such an approach also ignores the realities of Doha and other counterforces that challenge the dominant narrative. Perhaps these counterforces are consistent with a realpolitik view of international intellectual property. But they also suggest that there might be a role for a more analytically careful and normatively meaty conception of international intellectual property. This chapter purports to provide such an approach, one that can account for reality but also offers avenues to change it.

My approach to a philosophy of international intellectual property is focused squarely on the adjective international. What obviously distinguishes a philosophy of intellectual property from that of international intellectual property is the international dimension. If counterfactually there were no states and one sovereign was the source of international intellectual property rights, then conventional theories of intellectual property, grounded in one's favourite philosopher, whether Locke or Hegel or Marx, would suffice. More generally, the philosophical traditions of that global entity would guide our understanding of intellectual property. What makes international intellectual property interesting, of course, is that intellectual property exists in a world of many states, each shaping its contours or, less frequently, ignoring it altogether. How, then, should we understand the idea of international intellectual property in a way that takes account of a world of many states?

This chapter presents this idea in three steps. The first two steps are an attempt to conceive of international intellectual property in terms of international trade and international relations. These steps take account of both economic and political relations among states as a way of defining international intellectual property. However, I conclude that these first two steps, while important and powerful, are also lacking in one way. How does one reconcile theories of international trade and law with conventional justifications of intellectual property grounded in the thought of Locke, Hegel and Rawls? The third step of this chapter addresses this question by re-examining how these thinkers engaged with questions of international trade and international relations. Combining the three steps provides a rich account of international intellectual property, an account that shows that there is more to our understanding of IPRs than can be found in any one philosophy.

STEP ONE: INTERNATIONAL TRADE

A theory of international trade invariably has to deal with the underlying economics that attempts to explain and guide trade among countries. In turn, any economic theory has to focus on the concept of 'comparative advantage' (Sykes, 2007). Traced back to David Ricardo in the eighteenth century, comparative advantage has been described as the least intuitive, but most compelling, concept in economic theory. The idea is that trade patterns between countries will be based on comparative advantage, in other words the relative advantage each trade partner has in producing various types of goods. Often, this advantage is measured in terms of the relative prices of the trading goods in a state of autarky, or no trade, where each country is self-sufficient. As countries move from a state of autarky to one of free trade, where goods move unimpeded across borders, a country will export the goods that are relatively cheaper in autarky and import the goods that are relatively more expensive. Through this process, prices will be equalized globally and arrive at a level at which all countries achieve gains from trade.

Within a stylized model, comparative advantage is a compelling concept through which to explain trade patterns. The challenge is to derive a complete and accurate analytical model that incorporates comparative advantage into a model of cross-border trade. Such models look at different variations such as number of countries, number of produced goods, preferences of consumers, production technologies and market structure – the stuff of economic analysis. I refer the interested reader to this extensive scholarly work (Dixit & Norman, 1980; Ghosh, 2010). My concern here is with the question of how comparative advantage arises and how this approach to international trade relates to intellectual property.

A central question to a theory of international trade based on comparative advantage is: What are the sources of comparative advantage? In other words, why do relative prices differ in a state of autarky. Price differences reflect differences in the economies of the trading countries. Basic explanations may point to differences in demand and differences in supply conditions across countries. The problem is such differences themselves would need explanation. A traditional theory of comparative advantage appeals to differences in relative factor endowments and the use of these factors in the production of goods. Under this view, called the Heckscher-Ohlin theory, relative prices in autarky reflect relative factor intensities in production. In a particular country, goods that are produced more intensively using the relatively more abundant factor will be cheaper in autarky. To take an example, if a country has relatively more forests than oil, the prices of goods that use relatively more timber in production will be relatively lower in autarky. Therefore, that country will have a comparative advantage in goods that use relatively more lumber in its production and export these goods.

The beauty of the Heckscher-Ohlin theory is that factor endowments are seen as exogenous. They are natural, so to speak, and do not need to be explained in order for the theory to work. The problem, however, is that the data does not line up with the theory. While factor endowments may explain some trade patterns, they do not explain them all. There are missing variables. Market structure may offer an alternative explanation for trade patterns. Countries with more competitive markets may have lower prices than countries in which markets are more concentrated. In addition, trade in some items, such as cars, clothing and agricultural goods, is in different varieties of products rather than in specialization among products. These alternative explanations suggest that comparative advantage may not be the real explanation for trade patterns. Instead, trade patterns among countries reflect expansions in domestic markets to meet non-domestic customers and fill unoccupied niches in overseas markets.

With this foundational notion of international trade, we can turn to the question of intellectual property. The existence of externalities explains intellectual property law. For any given nation, intellectual property provides a way for the rights holder to capture positive externalities generated by a new work. The theory is that if anyone can imitate the new work, then the incentives to create the work will be eviscerated. Therefore, some level of intellectual property rights are needed to resolve the problem of the positive externality generated for society through creation. I state the issue here as one of 'some level' because too broad a right can serve to limit the positive externalities that are generated through follow-on invention. Scholars have debated what the optimal level of intellectual property protection should be, and so I will not repeat that debate here (Menell & Scotchmer, 2007). For the sake of developing my argument, assume that the nation has implemented the optimal level of intellectual property rights, hence resolving the externality problem.

Once the nation has resolved the externality problem through domestic intellectual property protection, the next question is one of trade among states. In a world where each nation has resolved the positive externality problem through optimal intellectual property law, countries can trade through comparative advantage. Depending upon one's theory of comparative advantage and trade, the domestic intellectual property regime is arguably independent of international trade. However, there are two wrinkles that require examining how intellectual property law interacts with international trade.

The first wrinkle is the effect of intellectual property on comparative advantage. If comparative advantage reflects international differences in relative prices in autarky, one can see how intellectual property law might influence intellectual property. Suppose a nation grants patents and thereby stimulates invention in better ways of extracting natural resources, or in creating synthetic versions of natural resources that can augment the domestic natural endowment. Such a stimulus would affect relative prices in a state of autarky and would affect patterns of trade once the countries opened their borders to the movement of goods. The analysis here, however, is a dynamic one, connected to the relationship between trade, investment and growth. It can be reframed in terms of growth theory with predictions based on the parameters of technological change and population growth. Alternatively, the analysis can be understood in terms of strategic behaviour among countries, as each sets their optimal intellectual property policies in the light of potential advantages in trade. Whatever version one wants to tell, the bottom line is that the effect of intellectual property on comparative advantage and trade patterns is still a story of how trade develops and not necessarily one about international intellectual property. Rather, this first wrinkle shows how domestic intellectual property law affects global trade.

Domestic intellectual property can affect international trade in another way than through its influence on comparative advantage. If international trade is the result of differences in market structure or in the expansion of domestic markets into foreign states, then intellectual property can also influence international trade through its effects on markets. For example, trademark protection can lead to the creation of branded products that are recognized both domestically and overseas. These branded products provide the basis for an overseas market for goods produced domestically. Similarly, foreign brands might have domestic appeal. Trademark law provides a way to differentiate products that create markets globally. Copyright law and patent law can also serve to differentiate products on expressive dimensions, the domain of copyright, and on inventive dimensions, the domain of patent. To see the example for copyright, consider the market for different types of action adventure movies or detective novels. Copyright law promotes originality that would find expression in varieties of these types of works. Similarly, patent law can lead to variations in the functional aspects of automobiles or of smartphones, leading to product variety globally and trade in goods. But as with the case of comparative advantage, this market-based story is really one about domestic intellectual property and its relationship to international trade rather than about international intellectual property.

International intellectual property has greater salience in the second wrinkle to the intellectual property story. Optimal intellectual property was defined in terms of positive externalities within the nation. But externalities can arise across states. This cross-border externality, or spillover, can occur through leakage of the information and know-how protected by domestic intellectual property law. A resident of one country can read the patent granted in another and glean the knowledge. Cultural expressions can also pass across borders, if not in the form of the movies, books, or sound recordings themselves, but in written or oral reports about these forms of expression. International intellectual property serves to deal with these cross-border externalities (Ghosh, 2010).

The difficult question is how these cross-border effects operate. One way is through the transfer of knowledge and know-how as described in the previous paragraph. Ideas and information may move across borders through consumers and workers. Alternatively, goods containing intellectual property may move across borders allowing imitation, absent intellectual property protection overseas. Furthermore, grey markets may arise resulting in re-importation of goods from the foreign market back to the domestic market in response to differences in prices that result from differences in market structure and consumer demand as well as from exchange rate fluctuations. The existence of these types of spillovers suggests that trade among states driven by private decisions of traders and policy makers designing optimal intellectual property will not provide the optimal outcome, however defined, globally. International intellectual property law serves a role in reaching the best outcome among countries as a whole.

I have been careful in setting forth my arguments not to define too narrowly the normative basis for determining what constitutes optimal policy. Since the language has been one of economics, the normative criterion is welfarist. But there is no reason to limit the discussion to those terms. What the discussion so far shows is that international intellectual property is about the relationship among states. A philosophy of international intellectual property should centre on the relations among states. In developing this philosophy of international intellectual property, I focus on the following assumption. Individual states care only about the well-being of its own members and not about global well-being or the well-being of other states. Such a normative foundation serves as a realistic assumption on which to understand the philosophy of international intellectual property.

It should be stressed that this normative foundation does not countenance jingoistic or xenophobic values in assessing policy. The argument here is that the citizens of Country A need not consider the welfare of Country B in designing its legal system, and vice versa. To the extent that Country A adopts a legal system out of animus towards Country B, or out of an intent to harm Country B for racist or nativist reasons, such policies should be discounted. Legitimate arguments, however, for considering only the nation state in designing policy is that an individual country cannot and should not affect outcomes outside its borders. Therefore, the citizens of each country need only consider the implications of a course of policy within its own borders (Gilson, 1999; Hyde, 2003; Saxenian, 2006; Ghosh, 2013).

Concepts of sovereignty and comity are consistent with this normative criterion. Furthermore, adopting the nation state as the unit of analysis could be consistent with either a realist or idealist conception of international law. A realist would see the nation-state-centred approach as the basis for a rational actor model of international relations. An idealist, on the other hand, would see the state-centred approach as respecting aspects of individual autonomy and governance, either based on cultural values or the history of particular nation states.

Applying these criteria to intellectual property policy, a nation state is allowed to design intellectual property laws and institutions that maximize its own welfare without consideration of the benefits that accrue to other states. To the extent that individual state decision making results in either positive or negative spillovers to other countries, international institutions, such as treaties or organizations for global governance, may arise to assuage these external effects. Within this normative frame, a nation state would be allowed to limit mobility of labour across countries in order to contain information or knowledge within a country for the benefit of its own economy, even if there may be positive spillovers that result from the movement of people and information across borders. Therefore, the traditional arguments for high velocity labour markets do not necessarily generalize to the international level.

The nation-state-centred perspective is consistent with the current design of international intellectual property institutions. The World Trade Organization and its Trade Related Intellectual Property Rights (TRIPS) Agreement assumes that the nation state is the appropriate actor. The Agreement imposes substantive minima on how each nation state that is a signatory to the agreement must design its intellectual property laws in order to comply with the Agreement, or otherwise face the possibility of a dispute resolution process and attendant sanctions. Furthermore, the Agreement permits certain classes of nation states (e.g. developing countries) to establish timelines for meeting its treaty obligations. Underscoring the nation-state-centred perspective is the history leading up to the ratification of TRIPS, which rested on the concerns of the developed countries that developing countries were ‘free-riding’ on the intellectual property and innovation flowing from the developed countries. The Agreement was designed to make countries coordinate on a system of intellectual property rights that would facilitate the free flow of goods and services across borders without the fear of misappropriation of technology and information in countries with little or no intellectual property protection. When understood in this way, not only does the TRIPS Agreement support a nation-state-centred view of intellectual property policy and law making, but it also supports limitations on the movement of people that could facilitate the types of misappropriation of information that the original proponents of TRIPS were attempting to prevent.

Although the nation-state-centred argument is a prevalent one that needs to be taken seriously and does pose a potential impediment to supporting high velocity labour markets at the international level, there are several reasons to be sceptical of basing intellectual property policy solely on the welfare effects on the nation state.

First, a nation-state-centred approach runs the risk of policy myopia. Benefits that seem to be leaking from one nation state to another may in fact inure back to the source country. Therefore, ignoring spillover effects in designing national intellectual property law may lead to poor policy choices. For example, allowing skilled labour to leave a nation state may in fact impose benefits on the country to which the skilled labour emigrates. But the benefits may inure back to the originating country in the form of remittances or increased trade with the receiving country. South Asian émigrés to the United States have returned to South Asia, particularly India, to help develop Indian industry, which in turn benefits the United States culturally (food, movies, medical services, software, books). Conceptually, a spillover may have no recognizable boundaries, whether that of a firm, an industry, or a nation state. While it may be unrealistic for the policy makers of a nation state to be cosmopolitan in considering benefits to all other nation states in the design policy, a narrow focus solely on the interests of one's own nation state may often ignore the benefits of spillovers to the detriment of domestic policy making.

Second, a nation-state-centred focus on international intellectual property policy ignores history. It is well documented that the United States free-rode on industrial and cultural innovation in Europe during the nineteenth century. Manufacturing secrets made their way across the Atlantic in the acquired know-how of workers or even what would be described as industrial spies. Pirated editions of novels stocked the shelves of United States publishers, serving as disseminators of culture in the form of cheap books. Even within Europe, political and legal battles were waged over the scope and substance of patent and copyright laws, and industries and regions benefited from differential and lax intellectual property laws. The movement of people and the movement of information facilitated regional growth and fuelled economic prosperity more broadly. The current model of international intellectual property that is nation-state-centred and largely homogeneous neglects the boons from the movement of people and information across national borders.

Finally, global distributional concerns controvert a nation-state-centred system of international intellectual property. While international relations is not a zero-sum game by any means, too strong a set of intellectual property rights in the developed world may have adverse consequences on developing countries. Economic analyses of international trade and intellectual property (to which I will turn in the next section) suggest that uniform and strong intellectual property rights across countries benefit innovator countries at the expense of less innovative, developing countries. Strong intellectual property rights may in the long run spur innovation in developing states, but the short and medium run effects may be to worsen unequal wealth and income distribution globally. In many instances, it may be unrealistic for one or even several nation states to address global concerns through domestic intellectual property systems, as focusing solely on the benefits and costs to individual nation states may worsen the global trade environment in the long run. From a distributional perspective, the movement of persons and information may facilitate the creation of a global commons that could inure to the benefit of individual nation states.

STEP TWO: INTERNATIONAL RELATIONS THEORY

International trade theory would base international intellectual property on the existence of spillovers across nation states. But the meaning of spillovers is connected closely to how we understand relations among states. Trade theory would frame international relations in terms of economic exchange in goods and services that can move across borders. But international relations involve more than market transactions. Cultural transfer, diplomacy and political alliances also define how nation states relate to each other. The idea of international intellectual property also implicates international relations.

What is challenging is drawing the connections among international relations, international intellectual property, and law. If international intellectual property arose solely from the problem of spillovers between economically engaged nation states, a uniform system of national laws may to some extent solve the problem. But once a broader set of international relations is recognized, the question is what should law look like in order to govern international intellectual property. Since law requires a sovereign for the purposes of enforcement, the lack of a global sovereign makes the idea of international law meaningless. Instead, international relations entail a system of competing nation states each pursuing individual interests. The resulting world order is a product of the clash of these individual interests in various arenas: political, economic, technological and cultural. Under the realist view, international intellectual property would reflect the dominant set of interests as to desirable intellectual property rules and institutions. If the realist argument about international law is correct, then the idea of international intellectual property grounded in a theory of international relations is a simple one. International intellectual property is whatever the dominant nation states say it is (Booth and Smith, 1995).

Note that an economic theory of international trade would not lead to a realist position. According to economic theory, international trade would follow predictable patterns, perhaps based on comparative advantage, perhaps based on the expansion of markets to meet new consumer demand or in response to technological change. Economic exchange among nation states results in mutual benefit, and intellectual property rules serve to govern the spillovers that occur across borders. This genteel view is in some ways at the opposite extreme from the realist viewpoint. The economic view is based on mutuality while the realist view is based on the interplay of interests and dominance through economic and political power. But the theory of international trade may not provide a complete view of the way nation states interact. Therefore, economic theory alone is a poor account of international relations. The problem is that richer accounts may give way to a realist view of international relations.

Contemporary international law scholars address the criticism of international relations scholars that international law is irrelevant. What more recent scholars do is look to developments in international relations scholarship itself to discern approaches that might be useful for reconstructing international law. Professor Anne Marie Slaughter is the most prominent proponent of a theory of international law based on international relations theory (Slaughter, 2013). Her account is useful in construing international intellectual property grounded in international relations.

Professor Slaughter identifies five approaches to international relations theory: (1) realism; (2) liberalism; (3) institutionalism; (4) constructivism; and (5) critical theories. She shows how each separately has implications for understanding international law. The separate theories can also work in combination to analyse relationships across different areas of law. What has been less developed is how the different approaches to international relations can also inform the idea of international intellectual property.

Realism, as discussed above, posits that all international relations are the product of the interplay of national interests. While international relation theorists see this point as refuting the existence of international law, realism can inform the construction of international law. Lack of a global sovereign defeats some arguments for international law. But relationships among nation states occur through law-like institutions, such as multilateral treaties and international adjudication and arbitration. A realist can understand international law as a set of institutions which can define strategies for surviving in the global competition among nations. Negotiation, economic exchange and diplomacy are each informed by international law strategies garnered to pursue the interest of the represented nation state.

But realism is only one possibility. At the heart of realism is the fiction of national interest. But one is hard pressed to ground the existence of a national interest in any cognizable theory. Social choice theory, most famously through Arrow's Impossibility Theorem, denies the existence of national interests that mirror standard axioms of rational choice theory. According to Arrow's Theorem, the only possible preference relationship for a nation is that of a dictator (Arrow, 1951). But pragmatism advises against a 'l'état, c'est moi' conception of national interests. Instead, commitments are to individual freedom. Liberalism recognizes that the national interest is a fiction. What matters are the economic and political freedoms of individuals within a nation state. International relations build up from the interactions of individuals within and across borders. Consequently, international law grounded in liberalism would strive to protect individual rights and freedoms through the set of institutional mechanisms available in international relations.

While realism and liberalism each build on notions of private interest, institutionalism frames international relations in terms of institutions, which may provide some useful function or may be the product of historical accident. Customs unions, national banks, transnational courts and international governing bodies like the United Nations and the World Trade Organization are examples of institutions. They are the platform on which international relations occur. International law defines the rules and processes that guide these institutions. Using an analogy to digital devices, international law provides applications to run on a shared platform. There is no need to explain these institutions. But their existence is taken for granted and studied to guide international relations and international law.

Constructivism takes the point of contingency further by basing international relations on the construction of rules and institutions. A constitution would be an example of a constructivist view of international relations. Through the drafting of a constitution, nation states cooperate and negotiate to create an overarching set of principles to ground their interactions. International law is a construct arising from international relations (Cass, 2005). While institutionalism presumes the existence of institutions, constructivism guides how institutions are to be built. Both realism and liberalism presume the existence of interests, the first positioning them in the nation state and the second, in individuals. A constructivist would ask of these two theories where interests come from and how they are construed. While recognizing the contingency of institutions, constructivism would not see institutions as arbitrary. Instead, attention to the normative foundations of law and institutions is necessary. Construction is not solely technical, but also purposive.

Finally, critical theories take the constructivist approach a bit further by identifying systematic winners and losers in international relations. Colonial powers may continue to dominate the formerly colonized. Poor nations suffer at the hands of the rich. Economic power drives the relationships among states with the dominant nations as hegemon. Critical theories identify these sources of oppression and power and attempt to build points of resistance and counterforce. International law is guided by and can guide these values in shaping mechanisms and institutions for voice and vindication.

Some of the links to international intellectual property may be obvious for this brief summary of theories of international relations. The constructivist view, for example, would support developing institutions for the enforcement and definition of intellectual property rights. Liberalism, to take another example, might support international intellectual property as a set of individual entitlements in the fruits of one's creative and inventive labour. Although the specific contours of existing institutions would not be exactly determined, each theory provides a framework for conceptualizing the idea of international intellectual property. Reinforcing the connection between international relations and international intellectual property are the three areas that Professor Slaughter identifies as fruitful intersections of international relations and international law. These are: (1) humanity law, or the enforcement of international law by and against individual persons; (2) private–public partnerships, or the creation of institutions that combine public governance and private enterprise; and (3) the Internet, a technology that permits transnational interactions while remaining grounded in the nation state. Although Professor Slaughter does not present her three applications in terms of international intellectual property, they each have implications for that idea.

Humanity law demonstrates how transnational principles of law involve not only relationships among nation states, but also those between a nation state and a citizen. One example would be the litigation of a human rights violation by a citizen of one state against a foreign nation state. Another example would be criminal prosecution of a war criminal. In the domain of international intellectual property, global or multi-regional resolutions about the scope of protection for inventions, such as limits on biotechnology or software patenting, have implications locally in universities, research and development arms of companies, and laboratories of individual inventors. The transnational affects the local. A recent example is the multilateral treaty for limitations on copyright to allow access for the visually impaired. Global coalitions of interested citizens coalesced to impose limitations transnationally in order to benefit those who are hurt by too strong copyright laws. The enactment of this treaty regime demonstrates the construction of new institutions in the sphere of international intellectual property law.

Domestic intellectual property is an example of Professor Slaughter's second application to private–public partnership. Abraham Lincoln famously described a patent as providing the fuel of interest to the fire of invention. With intellectual property, private interest is stoked by publicly provided incentives. International intellectual property is defined by the coordination of various nation states in enhancing the incentives for private invention and commercialization. International coordination informs international legal institutions that govern international intellectual property.

Finally, Professor Slaughter's third example of the Internet highlights the connection between international relations and international intellectual property. Paradoxically, while the Internet allows the circumvention of traditional intellectual property rights, intellectual property is the foundation of the Internet. Individuals create code, develop technical systems and generate content with the support of copyright, patent, trademark and trade secret. However, the Internet can transcend national borders, allowing individuals to obtain works digitally that would be quarantined if brought across national borders. Users of the Internet seem to reside in a terra nullius. But the reality of the nation state descends through cease and desist letters for allegedly infringing online content or through the blockage of access to certain sites. For the idea of international intellectual property, the Internet offers a constructivist regime in which international relations take on new meanings, not purely a matter of state to state, but citizen to citizen across non-existent borders. What the Internet means for the idea of international intellectual property is a matter of what international relations theories might mean for the Internet.

STEP THREE: INTERNATIONAL INTELLECTUAL PROPERTY IN LOCKE, HEGEL AND RAWLS

What I have argued so far is that the idea of international intellectual property rests on a theory of the relationship among states. Such a conception, however, may seem to be in tension with a philosophy of intellectual property, which explains the relationship between creative activity and ownership. There, of course, is no reason why the two subjects should converge. At the same time, two logical questions are whether there is any relationship between the two and whether the two operate at cross-purposes. These last two questions are relevant for policy-making both at the domestic and international levels. What I examine in this part of the chapter is how the traditional philosophers who are often cited to justify intellectual property law, Locke, Hegel and Rawls, address the philosophy of international intellectual property law.

My goal is to show how the notions of property and rights in these three thinkers provided a foundation for unique systems of international relations. The question is whether accepting the respective philosophies of intellectual property would necessitate accepting the respective philosophies of international intellectual property. I am not suggesting a deterministic relationship. Instead, by presenting a wider frame for understanding these three thinkers, I hope to show possible relationships between a philosophy of intellectual property and a philosophy of international intellectual property. Based on these possible relationships, I suggest ways to think about intellectual property and international intellectual property together for analytical and policy purposes.

For each thinker, I present first an overview of his philosophy of intellectual property followed by a discussion of his philosophy of international trade. I conclude with the implications for the idea of international intellectual property.

John Locke, Commons and Mercantilism

Locke's appeal to a theory of intellectual property lies in his ideas of appropriation through labour and the commons. According to Locke, property rights are created through the mixture of human labour and nature (Merges, 2011; Ryan, 2012). The classic example of this method of acquiring property rights would be agriculture. An individual farmer demarcates a parcel of land through his toil and cultivation. This application of labour to land determines how property rights are defined. Labour provides legitimacy to the claim of ownership and, from an economic perspective, provides the incentive for individual management of the appropriated parcel.

As applied to intellectual property, the story of appropriation has intuitive appeal. A creator listens to sounds, studies nature, or acquires materials such as wood, clay or stone. Through this interaction with nature, the creative person proceeds to write a song, discover the bonding properties of materials, or produces a painting or a sculpture. Through the application of labour, a property right in the created work results, which can take the form of a copyright, a patent, or other type of intellectual property. Rights are grounded in the application of creative labour to nature to produce an original or new work.

Property rights, of course, can take many forms. Rights in land, for example, are often divided up temporally, spatially and across persons. Rights may also be delimited through contractual terms. Similarly, intellectual property rights can take the form of copyright, patent, trade secret or certain other forms, each of which can in turn be modified through contract. While the appropriation story informs how rights are obtained or justified, it does not by itself explain the scope of property rights. Tilling one half of a one acre parcel does not give rights to the entire acre. Creating a song does not give rights by itself to all variations of the musical tune. Scope of property rights are determined by something other than appropriation.

Property theorists who build on Locke point to his theory of the commons as providing the baseline for addressing the question of the proper scope of property rights (Shiffrin, 2001). According to Locke, prior to the creation of property rights, all resources were held in common by the entire population relevant to a particular resource. We shall return to this question of 'relevant to a particular resource' below, but let us for the sake of the current argument assume that the relevant population is well defined. They could be members of a particular village or a particularly geographically defined clan. Appropriation by particular individuals results in property rights as a matter of necessity, as individuals need to sustain their existence or accumulate wealth. But individual appropriation is limited by the baseline of the commons. An individual can take only as much as sufficient for individual needs, leaving the commons 'enough and as good' for others. Therefore, the scope of property rights is something much less than individual acquisition of all resources. Appropriation does not mean full appropriation.

Less than full appropriation, however, does not mean sharing what one individual has acquired. Sufficiency means that individual appropriation of the commons leaves enough for others to use. If thought of in terms of land and water, the commons cannot be polluted by individual appropriation and the acquisition cannot leave what remains in the commons inadequate for others to appropriate. With respect to intellectual property rights, the commons represents the realm of ideas and culture, meaning linguistic and expressive forms, basic scientific principles and know-how. Appropriation of property rights in a work of art or in a new machine does not mean full appropriation of all uses of that work of art or new machine. Others can still have access to ideas or basic scientific principles embodied in the respective works. Therefore, individual property rights are not unlimited.

Through the notion of the commons as a limit on individual property rights, Locke provides a foundation for a theory of civil society. While Locke's notion of property rights through appropriation provides a basis for market society, Locke's ideas do not support an unbounded form of capitalism through acquisition. Rather, property rights are a basis for organizing and governing society and not solely a tool for individual material acquisition. However, Locke did acknowledge material acquisition as the provenance of the state. Locke's theory of markets was in the mercantilist tradition (Vaughn, 1980). According to this tradition, individual states would strive to create markets for the purpose of maximizing the wealth of the nation state. In Locke's world, wealth would be measured by the accumulation of precious metals, such as gold, which were used as the basis for currency (Rees-Mogg, 1977; Kelly, 1991; Leigh, 1991).

As a theorist of international trade and relations, Locke does not articulate, or even have, a notion of a global commons. Civil society as built on the pre-appropriation commons is a local concept for Locke, perhaps existing at the level of the nation state but more likely existing more regionally. Nation states competed with each other for the accumulation of specie. Individual sovereigns design national rules in order to benefit the well-being of the nation state through the maximization of national wealth. Because of his conception of competition among nations, made both implicitly and explicitly, Locke develops a theory of international relations that is akin to the realist view, described in the previous section. National interest as defined by the accumulation of specie money structures international relations in a Lockean world, with the commons existing only locally, not globally.

Although Locke did not speak to international intellectual property, there are implications for the idea from his notions of property appropriation and international relations. Within a nation state, labour creates property rights that can serve as the basis for market exchange and the accumulation of specie. Through international trade, specie can be acquired from foreign nations, and the national sovereign can shape the terms of exchange to increase the movement of specie money into national borders. One strategy a national sovereign has to benefit its own nation is the legal scope of property rights, such as intellectual property. Combining Locke's theory of property rights and his views on mercantilism suggests that intellectual property rights should be defined to maximize national wealth.

The challenge is how to define the scope of intellectual property rights across nation states. Contemporary proponents of Locke advocate harmonization of intellectual property rights across nations. Specifically, developing countries should adopt the intellectual property systems of developed countries like the United States. The goal of harmonization is sometimes understood as bringing the benefits of Lockean civil society, namely property ownership, democratic participation and economic exchange, to the developing world. But when understood from Locke's view of mercantilism, the extension of Lockean property rights systems is equally consistent with maximizing the welfare of the developed world. Many patents in developing countries that have adopted stronger patent systems are owned by multinationals from developed countries. Intellectual property protections in developing countries create markets for entrepreneurs from developed countries. Although welfare is no longer measured by the acquisition of gold, harmonization to intellectual property rights as traditionally defined in developed countries results in the transfer of benefits to developed countries from developing countries. This point is not to say that there are no benefits for the conforming countries. But intellectual property harmonization may well be a form of modern-day mercantilism.

A more complete view of Locke's theory of property rights, one that takes account of his conception of international trade, has potentially stark implications for the idea of international intellectual property. These implications are not inevitable or deterministic. In my argument, the neo-mercantilist view of international intellectual property was based in part on the assumption that harmonization has occurred to the standard of strong intellectual property rights in developed countries. But intellectual property rights are also subject to revision, criticism and reform in developed countries. The European Union, the United States and Canada differ on key concepts such as fair use and patentable subject matter. My point here, however, is not to suggest that the idea of international intellectual property is hegemonic or that all proponents of Locke's ideas on property rights are neo-mercantilist. Rather, a complete understanding of Locke can show how his ideas can support a particular view of international intellectual property that is troubling. It is this more accurate and complete understanding that confronting the idea of international intellectual property can help identify.

Hegel, Global Civil Society and the Push of Markets

Justifications for intellectual property based on creative works embodying the personality of the creator are attributed to the German philosopher Georg Wilhelm Friedrich Hegel. Hegel's philosophy was grounded in human subjectivity acting upon the world. Individual creations are extensions of the human subject, and legal recognition of rights in these creations arose from protecting attributes of the human. While a Lockean view of appropriation would see the property acquired as fungible, providing a basis for transforming property into specie money, a Hegelian approach to property and intellectual property would find some dimension of inalienability in property acquired by an owner. This element of inalienability would place limits on the scope of property rights in its marketing and commodification (Radin, 1993; Muller, 2007).

Hegelian justifications for intellectual property are part of a broader continental approach to intellectual property law, with its emphasis on moral rights, which can be traced to Immanuel Kant's writings on copyright (Johns, 2009; Merges, 2011). Resonant in the continental tradition of intellectual property is the public sphere and the role of private rights in shaping one's engagement with others in public fora. Legal rights over one's writings through copyright permitted the owner to shape their voice and communicate through the written expression with others. A modicum of protection for the private sphere was needed to enhance the public. Hegelian approaches to intellectual property ground this private sphere in human personality that engages with other subjects in public discourse.

Hegel's view of civil society identifies the dimensions of public and private spheres. For Hegel, civil society consists of the state, the market and the family. Property relations were situated within civil society and implicated the organization of each of the elements of civil society. In this way, public and private were intertwined. The state defined a certain set of property relations that would shape exchange within the market. Commodities obtained within the market would in turn affect relations within the family. The intertwining of these arenas avoids a simple, unilinear relationship from state to family. State governance would be influenced by the internal dynamics of the family, which in turn would influence market transactions. Property shaped and was shaped by civil society.

Contemporary intellectual property reinforces Hegel's view of civil society. Through technologies for accessing and creating works, individuals within a family engage in activities that implicate the rights of creators. These disruptive activities have voice in the marketplace as competitive substitutes arise for existing modes of distributing commodities. In turn, actors turn to the state to realign the legal rights between creators and users. The dynamic interplay of the various sectors of civil society places intellectual property rights in a network of relationships that shape the public and private spheres. What would be ideal intellectual property rights depends on the ideals of civil society. Hegel's concern is with identifying the dialectic through which human history evolves. Policy makers and scholars might find in the dynamic interaction of the various sectors of civil society, a pathway for realizing some ideal arrangement of civil society.

Hegel presents a global view of universal history, one that might transcend specific cultural forms. In terms of the idea of international intellectual property, Hegel would be a globalist, seeing, through the push of history, common forms of intellectual property that would exist across nations. Unlike Locke, who saw civil society rooted in the local commons, Hegel does have a vision of global civil society, with the three sectors of state, market and family surviving in the global arena. Of these three, markets have the greatest influence on the global stage as merchants have the capacity to move goods and services across borders in search of opportunity and profit. History marches to the push and pull of markets. International intellectual property is the product of the push of global markets (Muller, 2007).

Locke and Hegel offer not only contrasting foundations for intellectual property, but also for the idea of international intellectual property. Under Locke's view of the commons, intellectual property rights are the product of a nation state that engages with other nation states for the maximization of national well-being, as measured by the accumulation of wealth in the form of specie. International intellectual property rights derive from the interaction of interests among the mercantilist nation states. Under Hegel's view, global civil society expands through the push of markets towards the progress of universal history. International intellectual property derives from the push of markets into global civil society. From a Lockean perspective, international intellectual property is instrumental to the pursuit of wealth. From a Hegelian perspective, international intellectual property derives from the protection of the individual in global civil society shaped by the push of markets globally. These two perspectives contrast with each other and with that of John Rawls, who offers an internationalist view of international intellectual property.

Rawls, Internationalism and Constitutional Limits on Intellectual Property

John Rawls provides a political theory of justice which influences many areas of law, including intellectual property. Rawls' theory of justice posits a natural state before society is formed. Individuals in the natural state seek to define a social contract which will govern relationships in the newly formed society. The challenge is identifying the criteria for the social contract. Disputes over justice stem from identifying this set of criteria. Since individuals will differ, and individuals will tend to advocate for criteria that protect their own interests, there is more than a plausible argument that no such criteria can exist (Pogge, 1989; Rawls, 1999; Merges, 2011).

What Rawls argued is that reflecting on the choice before society is formed, when one's position in society has not been determined, can support compelling principles of justice. If one does not know one's lot in society, members forming a society could agree that equality of liberty would be a necessary principle for the social contract. Rights should exist for all members of society and not just for a privileged few. Furthermore, in the to-be-formed society, the social contract should also include equality of opportunity as a criterion. Finally, Rawls demonstrated what is known as the difference principle, which states that the social objective is to maximize the well-being of the worst off in society. Also known as the maxi-min criterion, Rawls' difference principle would be agreeable to those in a state of nature, living under a veil of ignorance as to one's ultimate station in society. The maxi-min principle ensures that the social contract will protect the worst off, a guarantee for those who may in fact be in that situation once society is formed.

Robert Merges has developed a theory of intellectual property from Rawls' theory of justice. Professor Merges presents the following thought experiment (Merges, 2011). What if, in a state of nature, founders of the new society pondered the treatment of creative persons? Should the social contract permit the misappropriation of the works of these creative individuals? Since, under the veil of ignorance, each founder does not know whether she will be a creative person or not, the social contract should, under the difference principle, provide protection for the creative person. Therefore, there is an argument for intellectual property on Rawlsian grounds. I provide only a sketch of Professor Merges' more extensive argument that also rests on showing how misappropriation can lead to losses suffered by the worst off. The interested readers can pursue those details. The point, however, is that there is a basis for intellectual property on distributive justice grounds without appeal to either a Lockean theory of labour or a Hegelian theory of personality.

Professor Merges' argument develops Rawls to provide a justification for the existence of intellectual property. But the argument does not provide a basis for understanding the scope of intellectual property rights. While Lockeans would turn to the sufficiency principle and Hegelians would turn to global civil society as respective bases for defining intellectual property scope, the Rawlsian approach seems more open ended, presumably supporting unlimited intellectual property rights. Some attempt has been made to reformulate Professor Merges' argument in terms of a broader group than creative persons, such as a cumulative innovator or any other potential user of a creative work, for the purposes of the difference principle.

Elaborating Rawls' argument in terms of broader groups that are engaged with creativity and invention other than the originator of a work would justify intellectual property and help define limits (Ghosh, 2012).

Rawls has expanded his theory of justice to the global scale. These broader considerations have implications for international intellectual property. In his *The Law of Peoples*, Rawls frames his thought experiment about the veil of ignorance in terms of the choice of a global social contract, one that would be constructed to include the members of separate nation states (Rawls, 1999). His idea is that there are two original positions, one existing before the formation of a national social contract and the second existing as the created nation states coalesce to form an international community. The question is what would members of nation states that are themselves just and decent agree to as terms for a just international system. By referring to just and decent nation states, Rawls rules out authoritarian or totalitarian states that do not conform to norms of distributive justice. The global social contract that results would be an agreement, most likely in the form of a multilateral treaty, among just and decent nations on how to structure relations among nation states and their citizens.

From this thought experiment, Rawls derives eight foundational principles. These principles are: (1) respect for free and independent peoples; (2) the obligation to observe treaties and undertakings; (3) equality of peoples that are parties to the agreements that bind them; (4) the duty of non-intervention, except for human rights violations; (5) the right of a nation to defend itself; (6) the duty to honour human rights; (7) the obligation to follow specified restrictions in a time of war; and (8) the duty to assist other people living under unfavourable conditions that prevent just and decent society (Rawls, 1999).

As a list, these eight foundational principles may be disputed as being over inclusive or under inclusive. The language of each principle is sufficiently broad to allow for flexible interpretation and wide acceptance. If one accepts these eight for the sake of argument, what they provide is a basis for a transnational constitution governing the conduct of nation states. From the perspective of international relations theory (Cass, 2005), the principles provide a foundation for structuring and guiding existing international institutions in their mission and framing diplomatic relations among nations. The eight principles provide substance to the liberal paradigm of international relations by refining definitions of freedom that undergird the international order. For those who adopt a constructivist view of international relations, the principles are ones around which international organizations and institutions can be constructed. Specific ones, such as principles four and six pertaining to human rights and principle eight pertaining to 'people living under unfavourable conditions', provide rationales for a critical theory of international relations, one whose goal is to protect the truly disadvantaged with global application of Rawls' difference principle. In short, while there can be disagreement about the details of Rawls' proposed international social contract, the theory provides a rich framework for debates over international relations and the norms underlying international law.

Rawls' approach also has application to the idea of international intellectual property. Whilst Rawls' conditions for equality and difference principle can, per Merges, provide a basis for analysing and supporting intellectual property, the thought experiment of the international social contract and the eight foundational principles can inform our understanding of international intellectual property. Whilst Locke would help us understand international intellectual property as a national commons guided by mercantilism and Hegel as global civil society pushed by markets through the unwinding of universal history, Rawls supports a view that is internationalist, based on agreements among nations. Through these agreements, international intellectual property protects creative individuals, following Merges' argument, but subject to limitations grounded in Rawls' eight foundational principles. Locke grounds limitations on intellectual property in his notion of the local commons. Hegel would have us look to the sectors of civil society for limitations on intellectual property. Rawls, finally, would suggest that limitations on intellectual property can be found in the values of a just and decent society. His eight principles make these values concrete.

Limitations on international intellectual property follow from a number of Rawls' eight principles. For example, principles four and six speak to respect for human rights, with number four positing human rights as an exception to the duty of non-intervention and number six establishing the primacy of human rights. These principles suggest that protection of intellectual property rights arguably gives way to protection of human rights, such as providing access to medicines or to educational or cultural materials. If human rights are a trump to intellectual property, we can justify limits to patents on pharmaceuticals or on identification of genetic markers for proclivities to disease. We can also recognize limitations on copyrights on educational and instructional materials or the recently ratified treaty for access to copyrighted materials for visually impaired individuals. While some may counter these points by emphasizing the primacy of intellectual property rights, perhaps on Lockean or Hegelian grounds, Rawls' first principle of recognizing free and independent peoples under the international social contract would recognize the need for intellectual property rights. But the first principle would also justify limitations on these rights so as not to subordinate the rights of others who are users of intellectual property. The Rawlsian principles offer ways to balance the complex set of interests implicated by designing a social contract conducive to creation, invention and use (Pogge, 2002).

Since Rawls' principles are stated at such a high level, they serve to support broad claims such as the need for some intellectual property protection and the need for some identifiable limitations. Principle eight, however, presents a more specific articulation of how to construct the social construct. The duty to assist implies that a nation state has to take affirmative steps to help peoples living under unfavourable circumstances inconsistent with a just and decent society. Suppose members of a society are suffering under an epidemic of a fatal disease, with mortality at levels that would be inconsistent with a just and decent society. The eighth principle would require nation states to help those suffering through medical care. Even stronger, the argument would be that nation states should provide such assistance even if it would require placing limitations on patent rights. Such limitations might be in the form of compulsory licensing for export. Although principle eight does not prescribe any particular remedy, it provides a justification for many limitations on patent rights that nation states recognize.

With its prescription for an international social contract based on eight general, but carefully delineated, principles, a Rawlsian approach to international intellectual property may appear overly determined. But the arguments presented here should not be viewed as a doctrinal manifesto for international intellectual property. Instead, what we find when studying Rawls is a framework of analysis, a counterweight to Lockean and Hegelian justifications that can also add content to theories of the local commons and of global civil society. The final point is to appreciate the richness of the idea of international intellectual property, whether framed in mercantilist, globalist, or internationalist terms.

CONCLUSION

The idea of international intellectual property provides an avenue to assess and understand intellectual property. By critically examining the idea of international intellectual property, we can revisit traditional philosophers whose ideas are tapped to justify intellectual property and explore the full range of their views. A danger is that intellectual property as applied internationally is the extension of culturally specific and ideologically laden concepts to the rest of the world. By shifting the view to international intellectual property, we can not only highlight this point more emphatically but also provide alternative perspectives on international intellectual property. Such perspectives can be more inclusive of normative goals, other than wealth maximization, for structuring intellectual property institutions that are attuned to cultural differences across nations and issues of gender and racial inequality within nations.

Locke, Hegel and Rawls are some of the philosophers to whom advocates on different sides of the intellectual property debate appeal. Recognizing that these thinkers developed their ideas in global terms not only gives credence to the idea of international intellectual property, but also provides choices for those engaged in constructing and developing legal systems for intellectual property. Locke's mercantilism provides a different perspective on intellectual property and the commons. The latter is seen in national terms, rather than global ones. A strict application of Locke to intellectual property, when seen in light of his mercantilist views, posits the law as an instrument for national wealth maximization. Analogously, Hegel's view of universal history offers a global perspective on intellectual property. But international intellectual property, in the frame of universal history, serves as a homogenizing force, razing cultural differences with a Eurocentric view of markets, the state and the family. Ignoring the international dimensions of Locke's and Hegel's ideas provides a cautionary tale for those who use their respective ideas to design intellectual property institutions within a country. The broader global story reveals the underlying interests that drive intellectual property debates at the international level.

Perhaps Rawls provides a cure to the defects of Locke and Hegel. This point is the major lesson of this chapter. Rawls extended his theory of distributive justice to the international level. His ideas are truly international, in the sense that they consider the global sphere as a matter of relations between states. Through this international perspective, Rawls acknowledges differences across nation states, but also derives foundational principles that guide the relationships among states as they structure their laws and institutions. These principles can shape our understanding of international intellectual property that looks beyond the interests of any one state or set of states. What Rawls supports is a constitution for formulating international intellectual property, a constitution that establishes normative baselines for negotiation among states. What this chapter has done is examine the concept of international intellectual property and set forth a framework against which actual intellectual property institutions can be understood. It is the idea of international intellectual property that should in turn guide future explorations of intellectual properties and the adequacy of international institutions for making real the idea.

REFERENCES

Alford, William (1997) *To Steal a Book is an Elegant Offense: Intellectual Property Law in Chinese Civilization.* Stanford: Stanford University Press.

Arrow, Kenneth (1951) *Social Choice and Individual Values.* New York: Wiley.

Booth, Ken and Smith, Steve (eds) (1995) *International Relations Today.* Cambridge: Polity Press.

Cass, Deborah Z. (2005) *The Constitutionalization of the World Trade Organization.* Oxford: Oxford University Press.

Dixit, Avinash and Norman, Victor (1980) *Theory of International Trade.* Cambridge: Cambridge University Press.

Drahos, Peter (1996) *A Philosophy of Intellectual Property.* England: Dartmouth.

Ghosh, Shubha (2010) 'Open Borders, the US Economic Espionage Act of 1996, and the Global Movement of Knowledge and People', 21 King's L. J. 1–40.

Ghosh, Shubha (2012) 'Managing the Intellectual Property Sprawl', 49 San Diego L. R. 979-1031.

Ghosh, Shubha (2013) 'What the Treatment of Covenants not to Compete Teaches about Intellectual Property and Competition Norms', in Toshinko Takenaka (ed.), *Intellectual Property in Common Law and Civil Law.* Cheltenham, UK and Northampton, MA, USA: Edward Elgar. pp. 349–364.

Gilson, Ronald J. (1999) 'The Legal Infrastructure of High Technology Industrial Districts: Silicon Valley, Route 128, and Covenants Not to Compete', 74 N.Y.U.L. Rev. 575–622.

Hughes, Justin (1988) 'The Philosophy of Intellectual Property', 77 Georgetown L. J. 287–366.

Hyde, Alan (2003) *Working in Silicon Valley: Economic and Legal Analysis of a High-Velocity Labor Market.* London: M.E. Sharpe.

Johns, Adrian (2009) *Piracy: The Intellectual Property Wars from Guttenberg to Gates.* Chicago: University of Chicago Press.

Kelly, Patrick Hyde (1991) 'General Introduction: Locke on Money', in Patrick Hyde Kelly (ed.), *Clarendon Edition of the Works of John Locke: Locke on Money,* vol. 2. Oxford: Clarendon Press. pp. 1–105.

Leigh, Arthur H. (1991) 'John Locke and the Quantity Theory of Money', in Mark Blaug (ed.), *The Later Mercantilists.* Cheltenham, UK and Northampton, MA, USA: Edward Elgar. pp. 323–342.

Malkawi, Bashar H. (2013) 'The Alliance Between Islamic Law and Intellectual Property: Structure and Practice', 10(3) U. St. Thomas L.J. Available at: http://ir.stthomas.edu/ustlj/vol10/iss3/4

Menell, Peter S. and Scotchmer, Suzanne (2007) 'Intellectual Property', in A. Mitchell Polinksy & Steven Shavell (eds), *Handbook of Law and Economics.* Amsterdam: Elsevier. pp 1474–1570.

Merges, Robert P. (2011) *Justifying Intellectual Property.* Cambridge: Harvard University Press.

Muller, Jerry Z. (2007) *The Mind and the Market: Capitalism in Western Thought.* New York: Random House.

Pogge, Thomas W. (1989) *Realizing Rawls.* Ithaca: Cornell University Press.

Pogge, Thomas W. (2002) *World Poverty and Human Rights: Cosmopolitan Responsibilities and Reforms.* Cambridge: Polity Press.

Radin, Margaret Jane (1993) *Reinterpreting Property.* Chicago: University of Chicago Press.

Rawls, John (1999) *The Law of Peoples.* Cambridge, MA: Harvard University Press.

Rees-Mogg, William (1977) *Democracy and the Value of Money: The Theory of Money from Locke to Keynes.* London: The Institute of Economic Affairs.

Ryan, Alan (2012) *On Politics: A History of Political Thought. Hobbes to the Present.* New York: Norton.

Saxenian, AnnaLee (2006) *The New Argonauts: Regional Advantage in a Global Economy.* Cambridge, MA: Harvard University Press.

Shiffrin, Seana Valentin (2001) 'Lockean Arguments for Private Intellectual Property', in Stephen R. Munzer (ed.), *New Essays in the Legal and Political Theory of Property.* Cambridge: Cambridge University Press. pp. 138–167.

Slaughter, Anne-Marie (2013) 'International Law and International Relations Theory: Twenty Years Later', in Jeffrey L. Dunoff and Mark A. Pollak (eds.), *Interdisciplinary Perspectives on International Law and International Relations: The State of the Art.* Cambridge: Cambridge University Press. pp. 613–625.

Sykes, Alan O. (2007) 'International Law', in A. Mitchell Polinksy & Steven Shavell (eds.), *Handbook of Law and Economics.* Amsterdam: Elsevier. pp. 757–826.

Vaughn, Karen Iversen (1980) *John Locke: Economist and Social Scientist.* Chicago: The University of Chicago Press.

4

Globalization and Intellectual Property

Debora Halbert

INTRODUCTION

Despite the effort to control intellectual property (IP) globally, ideas, creative works, and inventions do not respect national borders and in many ways cannot respect them. While it is certainly possible to develop methods to stop a pirate book or video game publisher, how does one stop people from being inspired by seeing the works of others, or from viewing different types of innovations, and then wanting to emulate, copy, or produce these things themselves? And yet, in the face of such global inspiration, the history of international intellectual property and its protection is the history of expanding property rights and broadening efforts to curb and control the mechanisms for sharing at the global level (Halbert, 1999). The framing justification for international intellectual property protection has its roots in protecting what we call IP from being stolen by foreigners who 'take' the ideas, inventions, literature and technologies that have been developed in a nation-state not their own. Sovereign law stops at the border but because commercial goods and ideas travel beyond these borders, an international system to protect the 'property' of nationals quickly becomes relevant.

Despite the myriad international regulations promulgated to protect products of the mind over the last century, these efforts have not managed to halt the flow of ideas across borders. In an attempt to control the flow of ideas across borders, debates about the protection of IP internationally are wrapped into discourses of national competitiveness, cultural preservation and commercial exploitation. Those producing what they see as their IP have long sought to establish firm boundaries over how ideas, art, literature, and other creative and innovative works are used and circulated globally. The words used to justify international intellectual property protection – piracy, theft, ownership, and the concept of intellectual property itself – are not neutral, but already carry with them a set of assumptions about what is at stake on the global table. Intellectual property isn't tangible but the use of the word 'property' to describe these limited monopoly licences has made what was a metaphor into a reality.

While IP law is often categorized as an arcane body of law, better left to patent and copyright attorneys, these legal regimes are relevant to our everyday lives. Global IP laws, whether in the form of patents, trademarks, copyrights, geographical indications, or the many sui generis regimes that protect things like seeds, integrated circuits and software, are integrally linked to the possibilities of global economic development and social justice for the global south. As Madhavi Sunder states in her recent book on intellectual property:

> Intellectual property laws bear considerably on central features of human flourishing, from the developing world's access to food, textbooks, and essential medicines; to the ability of citizens everywhere to participate democratically in political and cultural discourse; to the capacity to earn a livelihood from one's intellectual contributions to our global culture. (Sunder, 2012: 4)

Intellectual property is the underlying legal scaffolding upon which creations are shared, technology is transferred, and art is inspired. Thus, the trajectory and scope of international intellectual property regulation should be clearly understood by any scholar interested in globalization.

In this chapter I want to build an analysis of how IP, and the many things it protects, moves from what we call international in scope to something we call global in scope. While the two concepts clearly overlap, the idea of globalization provides us with a conceptually different lens through which to study and understand issues of intellectual property. It allows us to ask different questions than those that are central to the concept of international law. At its most basic level, while international law and the process of negotiation remains centred in the nation-state, the concept of globalization seeks to transcend state-based analysis. Manfred Steger defines globalization as, 'a set of social processes that appear to transform our present social condition of weakening nationality into one of globality' (Steger, 2010: 10). The key to understanding globalization is to understand it as a constantly moving set of processes. Furthermore, as Steger notes, 'old geographical scales that distinguish sharply between *local*, *national*, *regional*, and *global* no longer work in a complex, networked world where these scales overlap and interpenetrate each other' (2010: 11).

The focus of this chapter is to elaborate on the complexities of how laws made by states to protect their domestic products internationally have become something more – a global system that transcends the state and reconfigures the way we understand the issue of IP in terms of spatiality, power and control. This chapter will first introduce the basic concepts relevant to the primary forms of intellectual property – copyright, patents and trademarks. The second part of the chapter will discuss the key treaties and agencies that establish the international norms for IP, while trying to avoid delving too deeply into the long history of international intellectual property law. There is a broad literature available on the history and scope of international intellectual property upon which this essay will draw (Bird, 2008; Gervais, 2003; May and Sell, 2006; Netanel, 2009: Oxfam GB, 2002; Ryan, 1998; Sell, 2003; Yu, 2004). The final section will look at IP through the frame of globalization and the tensions made visible in the intellectual property landscape when it is viewed through the lens of globalization.

THE BASICS OF INTELLECTUAL PROPERTY RIGHTS

As those with an interest in developing the international structures of IP recognize, creative and innovative work is intensely globalized because ideas have never respected the boundaries of the nation-state. The processes of cultural exchange may be voluntary, inadvertent or casual; they may be coercive and colonial or some combination. No matter the conditions through which contact occurs, humans through their interactions with each other spread ideas, innovations and art. Picasso's exposure to African art, for example, influenced his own art and by extension modern European art (Meldrum, 2006). Any number of foreign students coming to the United States to study will return to their home countries with new cultural influences and ideas. One cannot overestimate the power of American hip hop as it has transited the globe and adapted to numerous local cultures (Haupt, 2008; Kato, 2007). The colonial journeys of the past and the history of international trade more generally have created cultural intermingling that, while generally ignoring the contributions of those not from the West, have allowed for significant changes in the lives of everyone living on the planet (Coombe, 1998; Cowen, 2002; Smith, 1999).

Within the modern context, the flow of intangibles in the form of products based upon ideas and innovations has meant that at least two things must happen in order to make a profit. First, intangibles such as music, art or invention must be made into commercial products that can be bought and sold in some sort of physical form. Once in a tangible form – a CD, a piece of software in a box, an iPod, or a book – it is easy to apply traditional property rights. However, the key to owning IP is to create a property right in the intangibles captured by the tangible product. Extending ownership over something that can be copied and flows so easily has been the central challenge of the digital age and was recognized as such from very early in the process (Barlow, 1992). Thus, in the digital age, the copyright owner continues to 'own' the music on an iPod or CD, the software even after it has been downloaded, or the content of the book even after it has been purchased by the consumer. The consumer may own the package the item came in, but is not free to *reproduce* copies of the original work.

While you may sell the original copy of a book or a CD you have bought, you may not make additional copies of it, keep your initial purchase and sell or share the other copies. While you can listen to the music on your iPod, you cannot legally share additional copies of that music with others without the copyright owner's permission. Anyone who has read the licensing agreement attached to the digital download of virtually any copyrighted work knows that consumers today purchase a licence to use the property of a company under the rules they have provided, but they do not purchase the item itself.

A typical commercial property transaction conveys property from a seller to a buyer after the sale of the item. Intellectual property is, however, a type of property that remains with the IP owner, even after a purchase has been made. For many people, who assume when they buy something that it is theirs to do what they want with, wrapping their heads around how intellectual property is different from tangible property is difficult. As a law designed to restrict the production of more copies, copyright law extends its reach over a product well after the product has been sold. All other forms of intellectual property including patent law and trademark law offer extensive control to the IP owner, effectively prohibiting the use and reproduction of the item without authorization. While the cultural, technological and innovative products protected by copyright, patents or trademarks flow seemingly freely throughout the culture, their use and reproduction is legally protected and strictly enforced.

The politics of the digital age has been the politics of an expanding property rights discourse (Halbert, 1999). From the nineteenth century onwards, the trajectory of intellectual property has been towards a propertization and internationalization of culture (Löhr, 2011: 33–4). The emergence of a system of international intellectual property protection in the nineteenth century allowed states to regulate culture and knowledge under the terms of property (Löhr, 2011: 34). Once the creation of property rights in intangibles has been established, the second step is to create the legal architecture that can protect these products as they are exchanged. In fact, protecting IP can only be done through the law, given the nature of intangibles. However, there is no universal agreement on how to draw the lines of protection, what should be protected, and how long that protection should last. Thus, there is an ongoing struggle playing out at the global level over how much ownership should be exerted over intellectual property. This struggle will define how products of the mind will be exchanged well into the future.

International regulation of what is called intellectual property rights (IPRs) revolves around where to draw the line between what can be owned and what can be freely used without the permission of the copyright or patent owner. Drawing this line is not easy. It is a deeply political process that has significant implications for economic development, creativity and innovation. Draw the line too broadly around ideas and monopoly ownership stifles innovation and IP owners are given the legal ability to ignore the interconnectedness of all creative work and the source from which they acquired their own inspirations in favour of rigid property protections. Draw the line too loosely and one establishes a highly competitive landscape where the possibility of profit might be sacrificed to the quick pace of innovation and where many argue there will be no time to recoup the costs of innovation because the lead time and costs of original production for a new drug, piece of software, or movie far outweigh the ease with which it can be copied and enter the broader flow of ideas detached from its original innovator.

At the international level, copyrights and patents are limited and time-dependent. Copyright lasts for a minimum of the life of the author plus 50 years, according to international convention. Many countries, however, have longer terms, with the life of the author plus 70 years being most common. After that time, the copyrighted work enters what is called the 'public domain', and can be used without the permission of the original copyright owner. Works in the public domain can be modified, characters can be used for different creative storylines, and the work itself can be directly copied and produced without the permission of the copyright owner. One reason there are so many adaptations of Shakespeare is that his original works are free for anyone to use the way they see fit. Not so for works still under copyright, like Harry Potter or the Star Wars characters. Some creative workers would like to see the time for ownership increased or made perpetual (Helprin, 2007, 2010). Many would like to see contemporary copyright include more flexibility for use by those other than the copyright owner instead of enhanced and more absolute control (Aufderheide and Jaszi, 2011; Lessig, 2004). The struggle is over how much, when, and the level of generality to which, ideas are owned and controlled via copyright law.

Patent law offers a shorter, but includes a more absolute, period of protection than copyright. The international term of protection is 20 years for most inventions, from the date of filing. Patentable inventions must be original and offer an inventive step beyond the current state of art in a given area to receive protection (Adelman et al., 2010). Scientific and technological innovations covered by patents also become part of the public domain after the expiration of the patent term. At this time, anybody can then commercially exploit the idea. While there is no 'international patent', the World Intellectual Property Organization (WIPO) manages the Patent Cooperation Treaty (PCT) and thus serves as the international clearing house for patent filing by making it easier for inventors to file patents in multiple countries simultaneously.

Despite the language of balance often used to narrate the development of IPRs, it should be noted that the history of intellectual property has been a history of expanding rights. The primary global regulatory institutions dealing with issues of intellectual property have developed because there has been an interest in seeing more comprehensive global rules governing the protection of IP. These international agencies see their role as facilitating trade by protecting property rights and by expanding the scope and protection of intellectual property laws internationally. The evolution of intellectual property rights is bound up with the development of a global capitalist system (May and Sell, 2006). At the international level, treaties have been designed to preserve domestic economies from outside theft and provide protection for works that were sent into international trade (World Intellectual Property Organization, 2014b).

THE INTERNATIONAL LANDSCAPE OF INTELLECTUAL PROPERTY RIGHTS

With the underlying justification and basic tenets of copyright and patent law in mind, this section will now look at the regulatory structures of IP at the international level. The global ecology of intellectual property can only be briefly described here. The two primary organizations governing intellectual property rights at the global level are WIPO, a specialized agency of the United Nations (UN) and the World Trade Organization (WTO) via the Trade Related Aspects of Intellectual Property Agreement (TRIPS). The international scene has, as Ahmed Abdel Latif notes, undergone a turbulent decade:

> In the span of a few years, it has been confronted with a series of major challenges including the implementation of the World Trade Organization (WTO) Agreement on Trade-Related Aspects of Intellectual Property Rights (TRIPs), the exponential growth in the demand for intellectual property rights, the proliferation of international fora dealing with intellectual property matters, the conclusion of bilateral, regional and plurilateral agreements with far reaching intellectual property provisions and growing tensions between on one hand a potent drive for stronger enforcement of intellectual property rights and on the other hand a forceful push for greater access to medicines, technologies and knowledge. (Latif, 2011: 36)

These turbulent times are indicative of the present and future of international intellectual property.

Since the 1970s, the UN has been home to WIPO, which remains the central authority on IP and is responsible for overseeing and managing the vast majority of treaties pertaining to the subject, including the most famous – the Berne and Paris Conventions (May, 2007). Since becoming a UN specialized agency, WIPO has understood its role as promoting the expansion of IPRs globally, training people from the global south in the use of intellectual property laws, and claiming that strong protection of IP supports the larger mission of the United Nations regarding development. Economic development, it is argued by WIPO, occurs in the presence of strong intellectual property agreements and thus educating those in the global south about IP will lead to future development (Halbert, 2007).

As a state-based organization representing multiple different perspectives on the role of IP, WIPO has been somewhat responsive to the contemporary debates over the value of IP for development and the global south. For example, in response to controversies over the misappropriation of traditional knowledge and what has been called biopiracy, WIPO created the Intergovernmental Committee on Intellectual Property and Genetic Resources, Traditional Knowledge and Folklore. The committee has been part of the ongoing effort to understand traditional knowledge in the context of IP but has also highlighted the problems of working within an organization designed to negotiate with nation-states and not with indigenous groups. The creation of a structure to address issues of traditional knowledge has not yet convinced many indigenous peoples that their interests will be met under the auspices of the organization (Asia Indigenous Peoples Pact, 2012). Furthermore, IP as a modern commercial right, is an uneasy fit with traditional knowledge and cultural expressions produced and managed under very different regulatory regimes (Boateng, 2011; da Cunha, 2009).

WIPO has also recently taken up issues of development more substantively. The Development Agenda was initiated by civil society groups and states in the global south which sought clarification on how WIPO supported the UN's larger development goals. The result of these negotiations has been an effort to more clearly link WIPO's work with the UN's development goals (De Beer, 2009). Thus, despite being an agency that has often supported the efforts of the developed nations to protect their IP internationally, WIPO has also demonstrated its willingness to respond to and discuss perspectives on IP that are more critical of the status quo. However, the IP landscape remains very pro-IP, even as the politics of IP have changed. First, as Susan Sell notes, developing countries have become far more sophisticated in how they approach issues of intellectual property and development, especially around access to medicines, and thus have become more capable of negotiating around issues of IP. However, in response, developed countries have also changed their strategies, shifting to multilateral agreements to continue to increase IP protection (Sell, 2011: 20–1).

Other UN agencies have also played a role in the global protection of IP. First, despite its clearly secondary role, the Universal Copyright Convention (UCC) remains in place and is governed by the United Nations Educational, Scientific and Cultural Organization (UNESCO). Signatories to the UCC include only 18 member states to the Berne Convention's 166 signatory nations (United Nations Educational, Scientific and Cultural Organization, 2014; World Intellectual Property Organization, 2014a). However, while not as popular as the Berne Convention, during the Cold War and well into the 1980s, when neither the United States nor Russia had signed the Berne Convention, the UCC was the primary international mechanism covering copyrighted works for the US and the USSR. The significant difference between the UCC and the Berne Convention was the lack of a provision protecting an author's moral rights in the UCC, an issue important to the US which does not include such protection in domestic law. Furthermore, UNESCO with its focus on education and culture retains a slightly different perspective on the role of IP globally, which may be more prone to sharing to enhance development than privatizing rights.

Second, the UN Declaration on the Rights of Indigenous Peoples includes specific provisions regarding IPRs. This declaration was ratified by 144 nations, with only Australia, Canada, New Zealand and the United States voting against it (United Nations Permanent Forum on Indigenous Issues, 2013). The UN Declaration on the Rights of Indigenous Peoples extends to indigenous peoples the right to protect their cultural heritage and intellectual property in Article 31 (United Nations Permanent Forum on Indigenous Issues, 2013). While the declaration does not have the same force of law as the treaties governed by WIPO, it does highlight the concern felt by indigenous peoples regarding the methods and processes in place for preserving cultural heritage and traditional cultural expressions and knowledge.

Third, the Convention on Biological Diversity (CBD) also contains language related to intellectual property protection. Specifically, Article 16 on the Access to and Transfer of Technology indicates that any relevant technology transfers including those related to biotechnology must respect the existing international conventions on IP (Anon, 1993). Thus, throughout the UN, it is possible to see a general respect given to the concept of intellectual property and its relevance across all dimensions of international action.

Fourth, the Universal Declaration of Human Rights extends protection to 'the right freely to participate in the cultural life of the community, to enjoy the arts and to share in scientific advancement and its benefits', as well as the right to 'the protection of the moral and material interests resulting from any scientific, literary or artistic production of which he is the author' (United Nations, 2013). Such language offers assurance that a balance should be constructed between the individual rights to benefit from authorship and the cultural community of arts and sciences. It also places cultural and scientific creation within the context of international human rights discourses that could better ensure public access and 'fair use' (Hamelink, 2004: 47).

Outside the United Nations, the most significant international agreement dealing with IP is the TRIPS Agreement administered by the WTO. In order to join the WTO, member nations were required to sign up to the TRIPS and modify their domestic laws accordingly (Drahos, 2003). What was unique about the TRIPS method of IP protection was the claim that a lack of intellectual property protection was a barrier to trade (unlike the more conventional understanding that monopoly behaviour is a barrier to trade) and the specific inclusion of a dispute process that could enforce punitive sanctions against those that violated the agreement. Thus, TRIPS had teeth where WIPO did not. Daniel Gervais provides an excellent overview of the history and scope of the TRIPS agreement (Gervais, 2003).

The passage of TRIPS did not complete the efforts to regulate IP at the global level. The United States had pursued what many call TRIPS plus agreements bilaterally with many of its trading partners that enhanced the protection extended to intellectual property beyond that required by TRIPS (El-Said, 2005: 59; Gervais, 2007). TRIPS plus agreements tended to focus on strengthening patent provisions especially as they relate to public health and access to medicines and ensuring that copyright lengths extend beyond the 50-year minimum required in TRIPS (Gervais, 2007; Rossi, 2006).

Furthermore, the recent and controversial efforts to establish the Anti-Counterfeiting Trade Agreement (ACTA) have received significant attention, and as of this writing have met with massive public resistance around the world. Like its TRIPS predecessor, access to the negotiating table of ACTA was limited and followed what both Peter Yu and Daniel Gervais have called a country club model of membership (Yu, 2011: 2–3). However, public resistance around the world has at this point halted progress on formulating the agreement. Similar efforts to change United States law, in the form of the Stop On-line Piracy Act (SOPA), met with substantial resistance, including efforts by major web service companies such as Google who have an interest in preserving a freer flow of non-proprietary information to influence the debate (Constine, 2012).

While the UN's goals aspire to enhance the development of the global south, when it comes to IPRs, there is a specific interest in seeing that the law reflects the most restrictive protections available in the developed world even if these do not reflect the needs of the developing world. For example, at this point, all the former Eastern European countries have joined the WTO and the TRIPs agreement, requiring them to align their domestic laws with the international norms. Despite having acquiesced to the legal standards of the West, none of these countries have developed sufficiently vibrant indigenous cultural movements engaged in the international flow of cultural goods to require such strong protection. Instead, these rules work to protect American and European cultural products imported into the country and establish a system for fighting what the US considers to be massive piracy.

The resulting international legal regimes produced through state-based negotiations may contain flexibilities that can be pointed to as evidence that the current state of international law is not excessive and adequately reflects the needs of the developing world. However, these flexibilities were hard fought concessions and have been replaced in many cases by further bilateral negotiations. For example, the TRIPS agreement provided the developing world and least developed countries with a longer period in which to promulgate and adopt the relevant intellectual property laws. Such flexibility can be pointed to as evidence of the willingness of the developed world to facilitate development and ensure that these countries will benefit from the laws they are now party to. It can also be understood, however, as a flexibility that still requires all countries to ultimately have the same level of protection.

The continued differences between the rich and the poor, the continued commercial differences between culture industry producers and consumers, the continued ideological differences between those seeking more protection and those seeking to minimize protection mean that these international regulatory frameworks are the subject of contestation, political manoeuvrings, and efforts to push the law in opposing directions regarding the scale of protection. These struggles do not mean that developing countries cannot use IP to their benefit, and indeed, as Sell points out, some developing countries do see the law as being able to protect them from piracy from the West (Sell, 2011: 21). Rather, these divisions demonstrate that the global political economy of IP was not established with the interests of the global south in mind and thus to utilize this legal structure means reframing the production of intellectual property related goods in terms defined by a Western commercial market. In the next section, I will investigate the production of intellectual property regulation and the resistance to these laws in the context of globalization.

THE GLOBAL STRUGGLE OVER INTELLECTUAL PROPERTY AND THE FUTURE

Thinking about IP through global lenses means that one sees the processes of network formation across the traditional lines of analysis – states, ideologies, etc. These international struggles are fought asymmetrically with the sides in the debate not evenly matched in terms of financial backing or advocacy power. Additionally, the players on each 'side' are not always clear.

Take for example the complex position of the United States within global IP struggles. It is no secret that the US leads the charge in terms of an international intellectual property maximalist position at the behest of its commercial content producers – the publishing, movie, film, software and pharmaceutical industries. However, under the layer of corporate actors, who constitute the vast majority of copyright and patent ownership, is an additional layer of creative workers and content users who hope to benefit from a new digital world that is global in scope. Furthermore, activists would like to see the digital future be shaped by entirely new attitudes towards the copy that are quite visible within the US discourse on intellectual property. Thus, the US international policy position is at odds not only with the behaviour of the vast majority of people living on the planet but also with many of its own citizens. While the US government is at the forefront of international efforts to expand intellectual property protection, many US citizens are in direct opposition to these efforts. Thus, a traditional narrative that privileges the nation-state as the primary international actor loses the complexity of global struggles emanating from the same geographical territory.

One cannot reduce globalized debates over IP to primarily corporate battles versus anti-corporate forces either. For example, while a copyright maximalist position is clearly advocated by the US-based lobbying associations, including the Motion Picture Association of America (MPAA) and the Recording Industry Association of America (RIAA) and their international counterparts, the industry giant Google has favoured less restrictive copyright protection, in part because their business model requires access to information. The computer technology industry offers another examination of the complexities of the tension between how to protect copyrights and patents. The most visible corporate players such as Microsoft and Apple utilize copyright and patent laws to control innovation and development, but smaller firms and individual software designers often seek to enter the programming world using open source models. Furthermore, the rising popularity of Free and Open Source Software means that even the big technology giants offer products using open source programming as well.

One possible way of configuring the global context of the debate on intellectual property is to use the lens of digital futures and analogue pasts. Advocates for these two positions seek to shift the debate towards broader protection (analogue) or more flexible protection (digital). The struggle to expand intellectual property protection is central to the ongoing transformation of the world from an analogue to a digital environment. Thus, globalization of IP is linked to larger patterns of digitization and a networked future.

It is quite common in the IP literature, especially the literature written about copyright, to claim that the digital world has changed everything about copyright law. Copyright law was designed to protect the copy in a world where control over the means of copying was relatively centralized. Printing presses, recording studios and film production equipment, for example, were expensive and access to these services was centralized into industrial sectors. Reproduction of copyrighted works when the means of reproduction remained relatively difficult to access could be more easily controlled by law (Halbert, 2008). If one wanted to make a reproduction of a record, the equipment to reproduce it with the same quality as the original was simply not available to the average person. After the introduction of the tape recorder, copying became easier, but quality remained quite low. A cassette recording from the radio might have been adequate, but did not provide the same sound quality as a purchased recording. The same can be said for written materials. Until the photocopy machine, technologies of print reproduction made it quite difficult, though not impossible, to engage in copying or mass reproducing a text. However, even with the photocopy machine, the photocopied book was not the same quality as the original.

While illegal copying could be found, as the very existence of IP laws in the first place demonstrates, to develop a viable illegal commercial alternative for records, books or movies required a serious investment in equipment and the development of distribution networks for these goods. While such 'pirate' activity has long been part of the intellectual property debate, it has been the decentralization of the means of reproduction that has been most devastating to the concept of copyright as offering control over the copy. The decentralization of the means of reproduction in the digital present creates a fundamentally different relationship between people, ideas and technology. In a world where everyone has access to copying technologies for all forms of media, the circulation of goods without the control of the copyright owner becomes the norm and not the exception. Scholars focused on intellectual property law are quite aware that the issue of controlling digital copies is in need of reformulation (Benkler, 2006; Lessig, 2004; Zittrain, 2009).

In an attempt to grapple with the digital world through conventional practices, including domestic law making, many nations are changing their laws to protect digital works at a level far beyond that required by international agreements and at a level not seen in the analogue world. South Korea, New Zealand, Canada, Britain and Sweden, for example, have passed 'three strikes and you're out' laws that impose fines and criminal penalties on those who are caught file-sharing. These laws ban infringers from the Internet or impose other restrictive penalties after the third violation of the country's copyright laws (Winseck, 2011). The digital future we want to inhabit is at stake in the production of laws focused on how copyright will be regulated on the Internet. Who will control the cultural products that can now flow without any concern for the national boundaries of the state or the interests of property owners is one of the central points of struggle over the future of the Internet.

When efforts to maximize or minimize IP protection are mapped onto the framework of digital futures and analogue pasts, the underlying impulses motivating the different trajectories becomes more visible. The expansive growth of international intellectual property law is an effort by industry and country advocates for the analogue past to deal with the digital future by extending the laws in place for copying in a more controlled and centralized world. However, the digital future is a fundamentally different future where the means of reproduction have been so decentralized that controlling the copy means controlling individual behaviour in restrictive ways. Furthermore, what global individual behaviour demonstrates is that, more than anything, culture flows through sharing, inspiration and endless copying. Obviously, we continue to live in a less than perfect world where it is possible to talk of multiple Internets that do not connect, rather than a single global Internet (Knake, 2010: 26). However, the level of potential communication across national borders is more open than ever before. To seek to control, modify or halt this flow is to halt the potential of the Internet to connect people in ways that have never been possible before.

The digital future is also the future of the immaterial. The globalized reach of patents and trademarks, while not as affected by digitization as copyrights, are also indicative of the turn towards the immaterial. The extended protection provided to the underlying ideas as opposed to the products upon which these ideas are based shifts protection from the material object (which must be given up once sold) to the immaterial, which extends the rights of owners long after the material product has been relinquished. To extend control over intangibles, and indeed over time, space and territory, requires a different and more expansive level of property control. Thus, IP in the context of globalization and digitalization helps illustrate the difficulties of a legal regime tied to the nation-state in an era of globalized flows of culture, products, and knowledge and the possibility for perpetual control.

What becomes obvious in the trajectories between maximalism and minimalism is that the contemporary global economic system is built upon a recognition that the immaterial ideas in the form of innovation (protected by patents), expressions (protected by copyrights) and branding (protected by trademarks) are the most valuable part of a product. The raw material and the product itself are increasingly ancillary to the value created by branding and the underlying ideas (Klein, 2009). It is the 'intellectual property' of an item that adds value while its material existence can be produced in the globalized flow of cheap labour for only a minimal cost. Sweatshops throughout the global south producing cheap electronics and clothing for the globalized world can be sold at astronomically high prices not because labour costs are high, or workers valued, but because these material goods have been wrapped into an understanding of abstract value protected via intellectual property law.

The expansion of IP protection globally is aligned with a generation-long shift towards recognizing that it is the immaterial knowledge, the innovation, the branding, and the ideas behind a product that provide its primary value, rather than the material object itself. Valuing and protecting immaterial knowledge over the material product itself is most visible in the use of trademark law to create a global brand, as remarked upon by Naomi Klein in her work *No Logo* (Klein, 2009).

Nike, for example, is a global brand for a line of products not discernibly different from other sportswear. However, they are able to sell their brand for significantly more than the cost of production because of the added intellectual property value of the globally known swoosh. 'Knock-offs' of tangible products remain an important issue for many trademark owners as global branding also means the global circulation of unauthorized versions of a popular brand. These products enter the global flow of trade, cross borders indiscriminately, and challenge the concept of ownership of immaterial property as well as the underlying assumptions of the intellectual property system itself (Raustiala and Sprigman, 2012).

Branding Ethiopian coffee via trademark law is a case in point. Professor Madhavi Sunder tells the story of Getachew Mengistie, the director of Ethiopia's Intellectual Property Office, who realized that Ethiopian coffee farmers were paid only 3–6 per cent of the retail value of their internationally recognized coffee, coffee that Starbucks marketed and sold for up to US$26/pound. This story is not new, but instead exemplifies how the exploited raw materials of the global south are branded and sold to Western consumers with very little of the added value returning to the original producers. However, Mengistie sought to change this. He began working on a strategy to trademark Ethiopian coffee varieties and require companies such as Starbucks to pay a higher price for the initial raw material. Starbucks fought hard to keep the Ethiopian coffee free of trademark control, but, through international pressure, finally relented (Sunder, 2012: 40–2).

The story of Ethiopian coffee suggests that despite the overwhelming advantage created by intellectual property laws for corporate cultures, the laws themselves can be used and appropriated against those who have historically benefited. It is telling that one of the most significant global brands – Starbucks – which imposes its trademarked corporate world on everything it touches would resist the efforts of poor coffee growers in Ethiopia who attempted to utilize that same legal regime to protect their interests. The story of Ethiopian coffee is important not only because it illustrates the power of the brand in creating value for a material product but it is also important because it demonstrates that intellectual property laws can be used to address the disparities in wealth between the producers of the raw materials and the consumers of a branded product. That a country like Ethiopia may find value in global intellectual property laws and use them to defend its own efforts to funnel some of the commercial success of coffee back to its producers helps to highlight the complexities of a global system that does not align around clear cross-cutting ideologies. While many in Ethiopia may actively seek access to medicine without patent protection or download free versions of Microsoft because they cannot afford an official one, other Ethiopian actors may seek to use the law to defend commercial practices that could benefit the country. Thus, maximalist and minimalist trajectories may work in different regimes of IP quite differently depending on the situation of those impacted.

Having acknowledged the complexities of the trajectories of maximalism and minimalism and how these tendencies help us understand the processes of globalization as a moving set of strategies on the part of multiple actors across the globe, the remainder of this section will provide several examples from the domain of copyright law that highlight the divide between the analogue world grounded in a state-based legal system and the globalized world of digital culture. In each of these examples, the stark difference between the way the state reacts to the flow of digital goods and the very existence of these sites of globalization demonstrates the sea change we are undergoing in terms of grappling with the ways things will be shared in the digital future. These examples also illustrate the failure of state-based legal enforcement mechanisms to grapple with the cultural flows of the digital present and the impact this has on territoriality, sovereignty and the role of law, both domestically and internationally. These examples also point to the new trajectory in global intellectual property policing – where US domestic law becomes the global norm. I will discuss a few examples that illustrate the distinction between the analogue legal system and digital futures.

First, the recent shutdown of MegaUpload in conjunction with a raid on Kim DotCom's home in New Zealand highlights the approach to criminal copyright now understood as appropriate at the global level and represents a scorched earth approach to copyright infringement and international enforcement (Ernesto, 2012a). As part of the effort to destroy MegaUpload which, according to the indictment filed in a US federal court, was a haven for piracy, DotCom's New Zealand home was raided, his assets frozen, the website shut down, the servers seized, and all users, legitimate and illegitimate, deprived of their content without any opportunity to retrieve it. DotCom's extradition to the US was sought. In an action that required the collaboration of United States and New Zealand law enforcement to arrest a dual German/Finnish citizen living as a permanent resident of New Zealand and running a business that served a global customer base of millions, Kim DotCom and his criminal troubles are indicative of the globalized world of copyright within which we find ourselves.

As one of the world's most popular content sharing websites, the US shut down of MegaUpload was widely perceived to be an assertion of the supremacy of a copyright maximalist position in the wake of the failure of the ACTA legislation in the US (Bradley, 2012). While the case remains mired in legal technicalities, Kim DotCom has recently launched a new version of MegaUpload, called Mega that will be more difficult to police, as well as a new service called Megabox which will work with artists while responding technologically to the problems of piracy (Gallagher, 2012; Guarini, 2013). Kim DotCom's case exemplifies the nature of global copyright issues as they are filtered through the legal system of the analogue world. While he will ultimately be tried for breaking American law (while living in New Zealand), the 'product' he sold has no tangible form and is possibly located in every nation in the world. The global world of digital culture is almost impossible to manage under the analogue world of national and international law.

A second story that further clarifies the copyright maximalist position is the US government's efforts to extradite Richard O'Dwyer to the United States on charges of criminal copyright infringement. When he was arrested, O'Dwyer was a college student who ran a website called TV Shack. TV Shack allowed users to share links to online video content. As the *New York Times* article covering the case noted, O'Dwyer, 'has found himself in the middle of a fierce battle between two of America's great exports: Hollywood and the Internet' (Sengupta, 2012). At issue in this case is not the direct piracy of Hollywood material, but a website that linked to other sites that may have pirated Hollywood material. For creating this website, O'Dwyer was arrested by City of London police along with US Customs officials (Gabbatt, 2012). The US sought O'Dwyer's extradition to face criminal charges that could result in up to ten years in prison, a penalty well out of proportion with the 'crime'. While the case has not been widely reported in the United States, many in the UK find the US claims against a UK citizen threatening to their sovereignty and there have been popular efforts to halt the extradition. In 2012, O'Dwyer travelled to New York where he signed a 'deferred prosecution agreement' and was fined the equivalent of £20,000 (Gabbatt, 2012).

Extraditing possible criminals to face trial in a country where they committed crimes is not new, but is part of the legal structure in place that allows states to enforce their laws. However, O'Dwyer was never physically in the United States nor did his website have servers in the US, like DotCom did. Thus, unlike a crime against physical property that would have required O'Dwyer to have been physically in US territory to achieve the same results, O'Dwyer, according to this logic, can be arrested and tried in American courts for activities he undertook using his personal computer in a completely different country. While his extradition is pursued by the US government, the US government's agenda is that of Hollywood (Satran, 2012) and this case serves as a warning shot to those outside the US who would violate US law.

Similar efforts to shut down the widely popular file-sharing site, The Pirate Bay, in 2006 not only met with complete resistance on the part of the site's operators, but sparked a growing international political movement in the form of the Pirate Party to help reshape intellectual property laws worldwide (Erlingsson and Persson, 2011; Keating, 2008). Like MegaUpload, The Pirate Bay has a global user base and is popular amongst file-sharers. Until recently, The Pirate Bay controlled their servers in secret physical locations. However, discovery and a potential raid on the servers was always a threat, even with backup servers in place. In response to the fear of another raid, The Pirate Bay became truly global by moving its operations into the cloud in October 2012.

Cloud-based computing is a growing trend for all types of computer usages as technology savvy people seek to access their data instantaneously from wherever they may be. Mobile devices and the need to link multiple media devices to the same data encourage the notion of cloud-based management of data. Of course, 'the cloud' must also be located in a tangible place, but cloud hosting companies offer 'virtual machine' space where purchasers of space are not known, privacy is ensured via encryption technology, and if one server goes down it is easy to configure a different virtual server with total anonymity (Ernesto, 2012b). As The Pirate Bay operators told the online website, TorrentFreak, 'Moving to the cloud lets TPB move from country to country, crossing borders seamlessly without downtime. All the servers don't even have to be hosted with the same provider, or even on the same continent' (Ernesto, 2012b). While the cloud may have its own sets of problems, The Pirate Bay move highlights the way in which a global approach to file-sharing has become almost impossible to fight using the state-based law enforcement approach of the past.

While the nation-state remains the central unit of analysis in the creation of an international legal regime, these examples demonstrate that the flow of culture and the patterns of use by content users are changing. The corporate global model seeks regulatory control via the law and in the face of fundamentally different digital uses of creative work. These international actors include powerful trade organizations and industry players who are fully integrated into the negotiating arms of the most powerful states, those that have achieved full development – the United States, European countries, Japan and their trading partners. The views of the IP maximalists are enshrined in the language of property-based incentive structures. They continuously argue that without the protection of intellectual property, people would not create and their creations would not be publicly available. Their perspective on the use and application of international intellectual property is illustrated through the US positions in the examples above.

However, there is a global alternative to the maximalist position that has emerged as part of the resistance to the over emphasis on intellectual property (Halbert, 2005). The efforts to retain the space for a non-commercialized and free flow of culture, ideas, creative work and innovation, while ensuring the legal structure of intellectual property does not primarily benefit the already developed players, have taken on a variety of names and approaches at the global level. These include the open access movement, the access to knowledge (A2K) groups, the initiative to provide access to medicines, the global Creative Commons model, and the development agenda. Each of these efforts and many more like them are supported by a global network of NGOs and civil society actors, the less developed countries, and activists in the global north that understand the need for less restrictive IP laws.

Those seeking a more flexible global IP structure are without a substantive voice and of course embrace their own set of contradictions. Advocates for a more flexible IP system have created global networks to build a narrative resistance to IP maximalism and the power of their message far exceeds their numbers, in part because their position is far more closely aligned with how most people share to begin with. There are small civil society groups, often with only a few staff, and some of the poorest countries in the world advocating for enhanced sharing against some of the most powerful lobbies and nation-states. However, many poor countries may have policy makers and public officials who, having received training as elites, then advocate for an IP system that fits with the interests of far more powerful nations.

Agencies such as the Knowledge Ecology International (KEI), the Electronic Frontier Foundation (EFF), Public Knowledge, The South Centre and the Third World Network (TNW) provide a combination of political and scholarly advocacy for a more balanced sense of intellectual property enforcement that they argue will lead to a better distribution of wealth for those living in the global south. While advocates for a more limited scope of copyright protection are often called copyright minimalists, this term does not fit their position in part because virtually all advocates deemed 'minimalists' do not reject the concept of intellectual property in its entirety, but rather seek to reduce the terms and scope of ownership and improve the possibilities of the public domain. In other words, while some may advocate for the elimination of all copyright law (Smiers and Van Schijndel, 2008), the vast majority embrace the underlying system of intellectual property but feel it has been skewed too far in favour of industry interests.

Outside the domains of capitalist efforts to own and control the distribution of commercial goods, there is a global flow of innovation, information and creativity that offers a fundamentally different view of the world. In the university system, global research cooperatives in science and technology continue to exist where a balance between secrecy and competition keeps innovation moving forward. The Creative Commons (CC) and Free and Open Source Software (FOSS) efforts have created a global space within which the circulation of ideas can move forward free and unhindered by property barriers, or with less restrictive property barriers than those established under global IP laws. Communications technologies work despite, not because of, IP and the foundation of much of what we understand as the Internet is based upon open source software.

The networks of sharing and the digital citizens it has produced are indicative of a generationally different approach to knowledge production and sharing. When your peer group can be in a gaming environment with global reach, a university setting with international nodes, or a global business, it is technology and not the state that best facilitates the possibility of global exchange. While the reality may not yet live up to the promise, digital generations encounter the world and culture much more differently than past generations. The demand is for instantaneous access to all entertainment regardless of geography, as well as an ability to share it freely with others. It is almost taken for granted that knowledge will be instantly accessible and easily acquired, indicating the future demise or radical alteration of the system of university education. The ongoing and significant digital divide notwithstanding, citizens understand content sharing and user generated content as essential to future progress and innovation. To the extent that copyright gets in the way, there is no use for it. Those taking the minimalist approach are situated in all countries across the globe, putting the vast majority of the world's population in direct opposition with their governments and those that own the intellectual property. MacKenzie Wark conceptualized this as Marx 2.0 (Wark, 2004).

The emergence of the Pirate Party is yet another indication of how different the understanding of content acquisition is for the digital generation. Perhaps more accurately, the digital era has provided a new method to break through the property boundaries established by industry owners of content. Prior efforts to halt copying could be directed at concentrated players – those who produced mass quantities of CDs, knock-off luxury goods, movies, and the like. They remained a central locus of illegal production. The devolution of piracy due to the digital age means that the law must now criminalize everyone if it intends to halt the 'theft'. The future implications of 3-D printers only exacerbate the transformations underway.

Furthermore, as is also prevalent in the IP literature, the boundaries between inspiration and originality versus appropriation and adaptation are at best blurry. While the legal effort is to expand protection to reduce the availability of knock-off products, an effort that is built on clear property boundaries around the intangible, from a more critical perspective, the knock-off, highlights the importance of 'sharing' for future innovation (Raustiala and Sprigman, 2012).

A different example has to do with the global nature of file-sharing that has become the standard method for sharing music and entertainment products in the information age. Piracy as understood by the content industries is a global problem, but it is a problem created by sufficient wealth to be digitally connected – it is a problem of relative affluence. Countries without Internet connections, computers, or even cell phones, remain disconnected even from pirated digital goods. Thus, when states advocate for stronger IP laws to protect the property claimed by the content industries, they act against their own populations who are devising new ways of sharing content and the evolving digital cultures created by the Internet. In other words, they are defending the old against the new. These new tensions and lines of struggle only become visible when one uses a global instead of an international lens to understand the world of intellectual property.

CONCLUSION

Globalization as a field is both critical and reflective, with tendrils moving into different disciplinary avenues. To think within a global frame is to think about issues not just in relation to the state, but to move beyond the nation-state to understand the interconnectedness of the world. While a traditional international view would perhaps understand the only relevant actors to be states engaged in negotiations through member-based international organizations like the UN, in reality the global architecture of IP includes many other dimensions. It includes nations, UN agencies, the World Trade Organization (WTO), civil society actors, NGOs and political activists. While some may disagree with labelling the intellectual positions of those active in fields related to intellectual property as embracing a maximalist or a minimalist trajectory, these categories are useful when providing a description of the political debates over the scope, duration and content of IP regulation. The debate over intellectual property can be characterized through efforts to pull protection towards longer terms, broader protection and more consequences for violations, or towards a more limited scope, shorter periods, or against further criminalization. One should not take these terms as oppositional binaries but instead as trajectories along a continuum of approaches to IP. Furthermore, these trajectories do not map easily along the traditional lines of analysis – north versus south, communism versus capitalism, etc.

Intellectual property has always had global implications. These global trajectories will continue to structure IP debates well into the future. As we move further into the digital future and away from the analogue past, our lived experiences become more implicated in global flows of commercial goods and cultural products. It is important that the shape of intellectual property laws to come adequately reflect the cultural needs and desires of the world's people instead of the short-term interests of an industrial past.

REFERENCES

Adelman M.J., et al. (2010) *Global Issues in Patent Law*, 1st edn. St. Paul: West.

Anon (1993) Convention on biological diversity. Available at: http://www.cbd.int/convention/text/ (accessed 14 January 2014).

Asia Indigenous Peoples Pact (2012) IPs to withdraw from active participation in World Intellectual Property Organization (WIPO) Inter Governmental Committee. Available at: www.aippnet.org/index.php/daily-sharing/724-ipss-decide-to-withdraw-from-active-participation-in-world-intellectual-property-organization-wipo-inter-governmental-committee (accessed 20 June 2014).

Aufderheide P. and Jaszi P. (2011) *Reclaiming Fair Use*. Chicago: University of Chicago Press.

Barlow J.P. (1992) The economy of ideas: Selling wine without bottles on the global net. *IP on the Global Net*. Available at: https://homes.eff.org/~barlow/EconomyOfIdeas.html (accessed 20 June 2014).

Benkler Y. (2006) *The Wealth of Networks: How Social Production Transforms Markets and Freedom*. New Haven: Yale University Press.

Bird R. (2008) *The Global Challenge of Intellectual Property Rights*. Cheltenham, UK and Northampton, MA, USA: Edward Elgar.

Boateng B. (2011) *The Copyright Thing Doesn't Work Here: Adinkra and Kente Cloth and Intellectual Property in Ghana*. Minneapolis: University of Minnesota Press.

Bradley T. (2012) MegaUpload takedown proves SOPA and PIPA are unnecessary. *PC World Business Center*.

Available at: http://www.pcworld.com/article/248469/megaupload_takedown_proves_sopa_pipa_are_unnecessary.html (accessed 21 May 2012).
Constine J. (2012) SOPA protests sway Congress: 31 opponents yesterday 122 now. *TechCrunch*. Available at: http://techcrunch.com/2012/01/19/sopa-opponents-supporters/ (accessed 22 January 2012).
Coombe R.J. (1998) *The Cultural Life of Intellectual Properties: Authorship, Appropriation and the Law*. Durham: Duke University Press.
Cowen T. (2002) *Creative Destruction*. Princeton: Princeton University Press.
da Cunha M.C. (2009) *'Culture' and Culture: Traditional Knowledge and Intellectual Rights*. Chicago: Prickly Paradigm Press.
De Beer J. (2009) *Implementing the World Intellectual Property Organization's Development Agenda*. Waterloo: Wilfrid Laurier University Press.
Drahos P. (2003) *Information Feudalism: Who Owns the Knowledge Economy?* New York: New Press.
El-Said M. (2005) The road from TRIPS-minus, to TRIPS, to TRIPS-plus. *The Journal of World Intellectual Property* 8(1): 53–65.
Erlingsson G.Ó. and Persson M. (2011) The Swedish Pirate Party and the 2009 European Parliament election: Protest or issue voting? *Politics* 31(3): 121–8.
Ernesto (2012a) MegaUpload shut down by the Feds, founder arrested. *TorrentFreak*. Available at: http://torrentfreak.com/megaupload-shut-down-120119/ (accessed 3 March 2012).
Ernesto (2012b) Pirate Bay moves to the cloud, becomes raid-proof. *TorrentFreak*. Available at: http://torrentfreak.com/pirate-bay-moves-to-the-cloud-becomes-raid-proof-121017/ (accessed 7 December 2012).
Gabbatt A. (2012) Richard O'Dwyer's two-year extradition ordeal ends in New York. *The Guardian*. Available at: http://www.theguardian.com/uk/2012/dec/06/richard-o-dwyer-avoids-us-extradition (accessed 18 May 2013).
Gallagher S. (2012) Kim Dotcom's Megabox: Music service or malware? *Ars Technica*. Available at: http://arstechnica.com/business/2012/09/kim-dotcoms-megabox-music-service-or-malware/ (accessed 7 December 2012).
Gervais D. (2003) *The TRIPS Agreement: Drafting History and Analysis*, 2nd edn. London: Sweet and Maxwell.
Gervais D. (2007) *Intellectual Property, Trade and Development: Strategies to Optimize Economic Development in a TRIPS-plus Era*. Oxford and New York: Oxford University Press.
Guarini D. (2013) Kim Dotcom's Mega Cloud sharing service attracts massive traffic, privacy concerns. *Huffington Post*. Available at: http://www.huffingtonpost.com/2013/01/23/kim-dotcom-mega_n_2533751.html (accessed 18 May 2013).
Halbert D. (1999) Intellectual Property in the Information Age: The Politics of Expanding Ownership Rights. Westport: Quorum.
Halbert D. (2005) *Resisting Intellectual Property*. London and New York: Routledge.
Halbert D. (2007) The World Intellectual Property Organization: Past, present and future. *Journal of the Copyright Society of the U.S.A* 54(2): 253–84.
Halbert D. (2008) Mass culture and the culture of the masses: A manifesto for user-generated rights. *Vanderbilt Journal of Entertainment and Technology Law* 11(4): 921–61.
Hamelink C.J. (2004) Intellectual property rights. In: Thomas P. and Zaharom N. (eds) *Who Owns the Media? Global Trends and Local Resistances*. London, New York and Penang: Zed Books, pp. 43–50.
Haupt A. (2008) *Stealing Empire: P2P, Intellectual Property and Hip-Hop Subversion*. Cape Town: Human Sciences Research Council.
Helprin M. (2007) A great idea lives forever. Shouldn't its copyright? *The New York Times*. Available at: http://www.nytimes.com/2007/05/20/opinion/20helprin.html?_r=2&adxnnl=1&pagewanted=2&adxnnlx=1299481200-JSugZnsfzvMzJ4wppST/RA& (accessed 7 March 2011).
Helprin M. (2010) *Digital Barbarism: A Writer's Manifesto*. New York: Harper Paperbacks.
Kato M.T. (2007) *From Kung Fu to Hip Hop: Globalization, Revolution, and Popular Culture*. New York: SUNY Press.
Keating J. (2008) Pirate politics. *Foreign Policy* 164: 104.
Klein N. (2009) *No Logo*, 10th anniversary edn. New York: Picador.
Knake R.K. (2010) *Internet Governance in an Age of Cyber Insecurity*. New York: Council on Foreign Relations.
Latif A.A. (2011) Change and continuity in the international intellectual property system: A turbulent decade in perspective. *The WIPO Journal* 3(1): 36–55.
Lessig L. (2004) *Free Culture: How Big Media Uses Technology and the Law to Lock Down Culture and Control Creativity*. New York: Penguin.
Löhr I. (2011) Intellectual property rights between nationalization and globalization. In: Löhr I. and Siegrist H. (eds) *Intellectual Property Rights and Globalization*. Leipzig: Leipziger Universitätsverlag, pp. 27–45.
May C. (2007) *The World Intellectual Property Organization Resurgence and the Development Agenda*. London and New York: Routledge.
May C. and Sell S.K. (2006) *Intellectual Property Rights: A Critical History*. Boulder: Lynne Rienner Publishers.

Meldrum A. (2006) How much did Picasso's paintings borrow from African art? *The Guardian*. Available at: http://www.theguardian.com/artanddesign/2006/mar/15/art (accessed 2 June 2010).

Netanel N. (2009) *The Development Agenda: Global Intellectual Property and Developing Countries*. Oxford and New York: Oxford University Press.

Oxfam G.B. (2002) *Global Intellectual Property Rights: Knowledge, Access and Development*. Houndsmills: Palgrave/Oxfam.

Raustiala K. and Sprigman C. (2012) *The Knockoff Economy: How Imitation Spurs Innovation*. Oxford: Oxford University Press.

Rossi F. (2006) Free trade agreements and TRIPS-plus measures. *International Journal of Intellectual Property Management* 1(1): 150–72.

Ryan M.P. (1998) *Knowledge Diplomacy: Global Competition and the Politics of Intellectual Property*. Washington, DC: Brookings Institution Press.

Satran J. (2012) Richard O'Dwyer memo leaked to TorrentFreak reveals MPAA's insecurity in piracy fight. *Huffington Post*. Available at: http://www.huffington-post.com/2012/08/08/richard-odwyer-memo-torrent-freak-mpaa_n_1757472.html (accessed 12 November 2012).

Sell S.K. (2003) Private Power, Public Law: The Globalization of Intellectual Property Rights. Cambridge: Cambridge University Press.

Sell S.K. (2011) Everything old is new again: The development agenda then and now. *The WIPO Journal* 3(1): 17–23.

Sengupta S. (2012) US pursues Richard O'Dwyer as intermediary in online piracy. *The New York Times*. Available at: http://www.nytimes.com/2012/07/13/technology/us-pursues-richard-odwyer-as-intermediary-in-online-piracy.html (accessed 12 November 2012).

Smiers J. and Van Schijndel M. (2008) *Imagine – No Copyright*. Barcelona: Gedisa.

Smith L.T. (1999) *Decolonizing Methodologies: Research and Indigenous Peoples*. London: Zed Books.

Steger M.B. (2010) *Globalization*. New York: Sterling Publishing Company, Inc.

Sunder M. (2012) *From Goods to a Good Life: Intellectual Property and Global Justice*. New Haven: Yale University Press.

United Nations (2013) The Universal Declaration of Human Rights. Available at: http://www.un.org/en/documents/udhr/ (accessed 14 January 2014).

United Nations Educational, Scientific and Cultural Organization (UNESCO) (2014) Universal Copyright Convention. *UNESCO: Creativity*. Available at: http://www.unesco.org/new/en/culture/themes/creativity/creative-industries/copyright/universal-copyright-convention/ (accessed 14 January 2014).

United Nations Permanent Forum on Indigenous Issues (2013) *Declaration on the Rights of Indigenous Peoples*. Department of Economic and Social Affairs. Available at: http://undesadspd.org/IndigenousPeoples/DeclarationontheRightsofIndigenousPeoples.aspx (accessed 20 June 2014).

Wark M. (2004) *A Hacker Manifesto*. Cambridge: Harvard University Press.

Winseck D. (2011) NZ feels the throttling effects of new maximalist copyright laws. *The Globe and Mail*. Available at: http://www.theglobeandmail.com/technology/digital-culture/nz-feels-the-throttling-effects-of-new-maximalist-copyright-laws/article4183070/ (accessed 20 November 2012).

World Intellectual Property Organization (2014a) *WIPO-Administered Treaties*. Available at: http://www.wipo.int/treaties/en/ShowResults.jsp?treaty_id=15 (accessed 14 January 2014).

World Intellectual Property Organization (2014b) *Treaties and Contracting Parties: General Information*. Available at: http://www.wipo.int/treaties/en/general/ (accessed14 January 2014).

Yu P.K. (2004) *Currents and Crosscurrents in the International Intellectual Property Regime*. East Lansing: Michigan State University College of Law.

Yu P.K. (2011) ACTA and its complex politics. *The WIPO Journal* 3(1): 1–16.

Zittrain J. (2009) *The Future of the Internet – and How to Stop It*. New Haven: Yale University Press.

PART II

IP and Development

Matthew David and Debora Halbert

The possibility of future economic, social and political development has long been an important factor governing why many in the global south joined international unions, organizations, and the like. With the establishment of the Group of 77 during the first United Nation's Conference on Trade and Development (UNCTAD) in the 1960s, developing countries sought to provide a counter-balance to the power the developed world brought to international negotiations by organizing collectively on issues of trade and development (www.g77.org/doc/). Given the fact that each sovereign nation, despite disparities in wealth and development, has an equal vote to those of the dominant Western powers, it became clear after the decolonizing efforts of the 1960s and 70s that the interests of the global south could be given attention through such global fora.

Broadly speaking, the ambitious United Nations Development Programme (UNDP) global narrative of poverty reduction, universal access to education, enhanced health care, environmental sustainability, and reduction in HIV/AIDS exists because developing countries were able to assert their agenda-making capacity (www.un.org/millenniumgoals/). Issues of economic development similarly frame intellectual property. The World Intellectual Property Organization (WIPO) recently underwent the introduction and implementation of the development agenda, where its state members in association with interested NGOs pushed WIPO to better demonstrate that its actions support the development goals of the United Nations. In part because of the role developing countries can play, organizations such as WIPO remain a more favourable policy space for bargaining than the 'country club' models of multilateral negotiations that frame the post-WTO/TRIPs world (see Gervais and also Yu below).

The much newer World Trade Organization (WTO) has also used economic development and access to trade as a hook to draw developing countries to the table. Perhaps the most significant IP-related change that has affected development in the last 50 years has been the creation of the Trade-Related Aspects of Intellectual Property Agreement (TRIPS). TRIPS is referenced throughout the handbook in part because of its role in intellectual property development, especially for the global south, has been instrumental in framing the legal landscape of intellectual property law today. TRIPS and its impact on development is worthy of focused attention as one of the important and foundational debates within intellectual property scholarship.

The chapters in this Part provide a nuanced and complex assessment of TRIPS as it relates to development. This section begins with the insightful piece by Daniel Gervais. Gervais draws upon the literature that has emerged since the passage of TRIPS to comment on the impact it has had for economic development in the global south. TRIPS development, he argues, has entered its third phase which requires a far more sophisticated critique of the instrument as countries recognize the strengths and weaknesses inherent in the document. However, while (rightfully) critical of TRIPS, Gervais also highlights its redeeming features.

Many have questioned why developing countries signed TRIPS given that it did not appear to be in their best interest. Bargaining power, Gervais argues, is an important answer to this question. Developing countries saw TRIPS and its multilateral dimensions as offering an important setting for future negotiation that could be collective and transparent. Such power was not likely to be found in the bilateral options pushed by the United States. Furthermore, developing countries have long been interested in any method to enhance foreign direct investment and technology transfer. TRIPS, it would seem, might facilitate such practices.

While there may have been reasons to sign TRIPS, Gervais describes some of the problems for development caused by TRIPS. First, while a one-size-fits all patent regime is well suited for the pharmaceutical industry, it does not serve other industries as successfully. In fact, a uniform patent system as required by TRIPS may harm innovation and development in some areas more than help them. Second, while copyright holds more promise for the cultural creation of the global south, the over expansion of copyright needs to be better balanced with protecting the rights of local authors and creators. NGO critics tend to focus on the overexpansion of copyright, especially for digital products, but this broad stroke ignores local collecting societies and governmental efforts to protect local talent, an issue taken up by Perullo and Eisenberg in their chapter on music and copyright in Tanzania and Kenya.

Peter Yu structures his account of change in international intellectual property agreements around three 'sets of recurring developments': firstly, the establishment of a multilateral development agenda in the formation of IP policy; secondly, the shift from multilateral to non-multilateral methods of 'norm-setting' in international IP regulation; and thirdly, the revival of multilateral forms in recent years. Yu concludes by suggesting this pendulum between multilateral and non-multilateral forms of policymaking needs to be fully recognized, as it is misleading only to study short-term trends in one direction or another. What may seem the tide of history at any one moment may well be just a wave about to break and then to recede.

The process of decolonization in the years after the Second World War saw many new states emerge. These new members of what was itself a relatively new United Nations were torn between acceptance of the international treaties created by their former colonial powers (such as the Berne and Paris treaties as relating to IP), to create new arrangements of their own, or to seek reform of existing arrangements. It was in this context that the 'United International Bureaux for the

Protection of Intellectual Property' (BIRPI), the organization founded by IP holders in 1893 to manage the Paris and Berne Treaties on industrial and creative IPRs, transformed itself into the World Intellectual Property Organization (WIPO) in 1967. This new body was no longer simply managed for IP holders by its Swiss administrators. WIPO sought to become a specialized agency of the United Nations (something formally achieved in 1975), and so (it claimed) become a facilitator of UN development goals by means of the promotion of IP. WIPO now has 186 member states. By signing up to the UNs development mandates, WIPO was successful in recruiting and retaining countries that were, and often remain, critical of the role IP plays in maintaining unequal terms of trade between developed and developing countries. Plotting this history, Yu shows how a development agenda has been a recurrent, though fluctuating, force in the shaping of IP policy within one of the most powerful multilateral norm-setting agencies in global IP policy formation. He also sets out the curious history by which WIPO has negotiated its relationship with other such bodies, in particular the more recent World Trade Organization and its founding treaty, the Trade-Related Agreement on Intellectual Property Rights (TRIPS).

In part because of the success of developing countries in pressing for a 'development agenda' within multilateral fora such as WIPO, developed economies (particularly the United States) have more recently sought to bypass the need to 'agree' to multilateral deals by negotiating bilateral and regional free-trade and IP protecting treaties with less powerful actors. This shift to non-multilateralism has produced agreements that enforce developed countries' demands for maximum IP protection, and to diminish even those arrangements that have been negotiated multilaterally that offer limits to IP protection in the interest of promoting economic growth and well-being in less developed countries. Yu documents this return to what he and others call a 'country club' model of deal making.

However, Yu notes that today there is a curious mix of both strands of policymaking in the field of IP, something that can be read as a return to new forms of multilateralism. In particular he notes the recent WIPO-organized Beijing and Marrakesh Treaties on Audiovisual Performances and for Blind readers, respectively, and the potentially – as currently stalled – significant WTO multilateral treaty on generic pharmaceuticals. In conclusion, Yu cautions against assuming that any current direction of travel will last, as fluctuation seems to be the only constant. The balance of economic and political power between developed and developing countries in shaping such developments is also something that should not be assumed will always stay the same.

Many scholars locate their domestic commentary on IP within the larger international sphere established by TRIPS. Important for many are the ways TRIPS has framed development debates on the ground. One such effort is the chapter by Millaleo and Cadenas who discuss TRIPS as it has framed development in Chile. Chile is what Millaleo and Cadenas call a functionally differentiated society where the disparity between the rich and poor is an underlying factor in development discourses. One way in which this functional differentiation manifests itself is through the existence of highly developed policy regimes, such as Chile's intellectual property laws, within a country suffering from on-going and drastic inequality.

Like many post-colonial countries, Chile inherited its original IP laws from Spain and the authors take us through the evolution of IP in Chile. It was TRIPS, however, that posed the most significant change to Chilean IP, in part because signing the TRIPS agreement committed Chile to broadening and strengthening IP rights not under the terms needed for future Chilean development, but under the terms required by an international free trade agreement. Millaleo and Cadenas describe the changes in domestic law made necessary by TRIPS as well as the TRIPS-plus legislation Chile signed with the United States.

This TRIPS-plus agreement further strengthened IP rights in Chile. Chile's reasons for signing these agreements emanate from their interest in accessing American markets, facilitating technology transfer, and enhancing foreign direct investment (Millaleo and Cadenas). While Millaleo and Cadenas comment that Chile did not have the appropriate technological knowledge to fully understand the implications of the deal, they bargained with the intent of enhancing domestic economic development. Despite bargaining for better trade in the context of IP, Millaleo and Cadenas report that to date the benefits of TRIPs and TRIPs-plus treaties have not been realized and conflicts over IP remain visible. However, what Millaleo and Cadenas emphasize is that despite, Chile's seeming sophistication in terms of IP development and negotiations at an international and bilateral level, one must take into consideration the vast inequality in Chile and how the domestic social and economic situation demands a different approach to IP than that advocated by international actors and their elite local supporters. Chile's position in IP negotiations better reflects globalized power in the world, and not Chile as a nation-state actor speaking for its entire population within international fora.

Alex Perullo and Andrew Eisenberg's chapter provides a post-TRIPS analysis of copyright implementation by focusing on the implications of TRIPS for musical copyright in Kenya and Tanzania. Perullo and Eisenberg note that while some domestic interests wanted to see intellectual property laws updated, the primary push for increased IP protection came from the fact that as members of the WTO with an interest in future trading opportunities, countries in Africa needed to be part of the TRIPS agreement as well. Focusing on musical works in their chapter, Perullo and Eisenberg argue that the variable success in the implementation of IP laws as a result of TRIPS in East African countries has more to do with their underlying political, economic and social structures. By using Kenya and Tanzania as case studies and basing their research on interviews with key stakeholders, Perullo and Eisenberg follow two divergent paths towards musical copyright protection to highlight the important fact that local conditions must be taken into consideration when applying international laws, a theme echoed by the other chapters in this section and throughout the handbook.

As Gervais pointed out, developing countries signed TRIPS because membership was seen to provide negotiating advantages and potential trade opportunities. Entrance into the WTO for Tanzania meant, according to Perullo and Eisenberg, that they would become a potential trading partner with other WTO members. From the beginning, however, the implementation of TRIPS in Tanzania faced problems in part because it relied upon foreign experts who conducted meetings primarily in English telling the Tanzanian government how to proceed. Such a gap between understanding (rarely was Swahili used to communicate in these meetings) meant that Tanzanians were frustrated by the implementation process and interest in it diminished as a result.

As a socialist-leaning country, Tanzania followed a different path of IP development in part because it started from a different understanding of property itself. Perhaps more important from the perspective of adequate IP development, was the fact that it cost more to pursue a copyright claim in court than a musician would win, thus undermining the law and its application for all but the wealthy few. Other problems abounded: a corrupt legal structure made the courts a less viable option for any litigation and claims that the domestic collecting societies misused funds undermined trust in the system. As a result, in Tanzania, even with copyright reform after TRIPS, artists were left with little protection and must continue to fend for themselves. However, with lower levels of violence in Tanzania relative to Kenya, Tanzanian musicians enjoy a more vibrant and lucrative live performance economy, even whilst they make less from copyright earnings.

Prior to signing TRIPS, Kenya already had a globally linked music industry and thus signed TRIPS in part to extend better copyright protection to local music and musicians. While Kenya was concerned about musical piracy when it passed its revised copyright laws, there is yet to be any evidence that piracy has diminished as a result of the new laws. However, the new copyright act has changed the domestic collecting societies. The success of Kenya's implementation of TRIPS-led copyright reform is attributed to the internationally educated technocrats that head the collecting societies and understand copyright law in its larger European and American contexts. That Kenya had already been part of the larger international music scene prior to the introduction of new copyright laws and was able, through copyright leaders, to create a sense of copyright consciousness amongst artists and performers, differentiates it from Tanzania that has been mired in problems generated in part from the relation citizens have to the former socialist state. Perullo and Eisenberg conclude that in neither country has the implementation of musical copyright been without problems and that it is the local landscape that makes all the difference in how TRIPS will be adapted and utilized on the ground.

TRIPS has been controversial since its inception, in part because of concerns about its implementation in the global south. There are reasons to remain concerned about the one-size-fits-all international instrument that establishes a specific approach to intellectual property globally. As these chapters suggest, TRIPS may have motivated countries to change their intellectual property laws, and many may have done so because it suited certain domestic interests. However, after several decades of TRIPS-related work, including TRIPS-plus bilateral treaties, larger issues of technology transfer, foreign direct investment, and enhanced R&D remain variable across the globe. These chapters cannot offer a conclusive answer to the issue of development, but they do suggest that further country-by-country analysis of the TRIPS legacy is warranted. Countries may have signed on for a variety of reasons, but the enhanced intellectual property protections that are now in place around the world have yet to mark any pronounced changes in economic development.

5

TRIPS and Development

Daniel Gervais

INTRODUCTION

This chapter examines available data and analyses concerning the impact of the Agreement on Trade-Related Aspects of Intellectual Property Rights (TRIPS) on development. A liminary question that seems inescapable is the definition of 'development' in this context. A full answer would go well beyond the scope of the chapter, but it is worth pointing out that economic indicators do not tell the whole story. One could, for example, embrace the broader approach advocated *inter alia* by Amartya Sen:

> It is simply not adequate to take as our basic objective just the maximization of income or wealth, which is, as Aristotle noted, 'merely useful and for the sake of something else.' For the same reason, economic growth cannot sensibly be treated as an end in itself. Development has to be more concerned with enhancing the lives we lead and the freedoms we enjoy. (Sen, 1999: 14)

This combination of human *and* economic development has in recent years been translated into a series of objectives amenable in part at least to the kind of metrics that evidence-based policy-making might call for, including the United Nations' Human Development Index.[1] Viewed positively, development may be defined, in the words of Professor Okediji, as 'a pseudonym for a complex network of benefits associated with economic growth and human social capital' (Okediji, 2009: 140). Viewed negatively – that is, in terms of factors that encumber development – one could mention income inequality, discrimination, crime, education and a host of other factors.[2]

Tying such broader objectives to intellectual property policy is complex, and determining with precision whether those objectives are achieved (or indeed achievable) remains hard. That said, the main point made here is simple: measuring merely a country's aggregate economic output such as its Gross Domestic Product (GDP) as it may be affected by varying degrees of intellectual property protection does not tell the whole development story. It does, however, tell *a* story, and one worth looking into.

The pivot around which this chapter revolves is, as the title indicates, the Agreement on Trade-Related Aspects of Intellectual Property Rights, better known as TRIPS. TRIPS is Annex 1C of the Agreement Establishing the World Trade Organization (WTO) signed at Marrakech on 15 April 1994 and which entered into force on 1 January of the following year. Developing countries accepted the TRIPS agreement for a variety of reasons, ranging from ignorance to coercion to hard bargaining. These explanations have little to do with proper developmental objectives and strategies. This means that, for several developing countries, TRIPS was accepted not because it would spur development of local innovation but for other reasons. For many of them, a bargaining narrative provides a better explanation: TRIPS was mostly seen as a defense against the use of unilateral trade sanctions imposed bilaterally (by the United States in particular). Those sanctions were used to convince countries better to protect intellectual property rights belonging to multinational companies headquartered in the US and other 'Western' nations. Indeed, before TRIPS the United States used its Trade Act (known as 'special 301') more frequently to threaten or apply trade sanctions against other nations that, in the judgment of the United States Trade Representative (USTR), did not adequately protect US-owned intellectual property rights (Drahos, 2002: 14). The TRIPS agreement multi-lateralized the imposition of such trade sanctions and made the process more fair and transparent in two ways. First, the norms with which each WTO member must comply are contained in the text of TRIPS. Second, sanctions must be pre-authorized by the WTO before they can be imposed. The imposition of trade-based sanctions follows the preparation by a panel of experts of a publicly available report on a dispute and, possibly, also by the WTO Appellate Body. The entire process is governed by the Dispute-Settlement Understanding adopted when the WTO was established in January 1995.[3]

This bargaining-based explanation of TRIPS adds a key dimension to the analysis. The Uruguay Round, a multilateral trade negotiation which started in 1986 at Punta del Este and ended at Marrakech in 1994 with the signing of the WTO Agreement, demonstrated that intellectual property rules and their enforcement could be 'traded' for reductions of tariffs or increases in import quotas on textiles, tropical fruit or other mostly low-tech goods. In other words, intellectual property can be negotiated and traded against anything else with dollars as a common denominator. There is no need to show linkages such as high informational or ideational content. If further evidence for this was required, WTO disputes have since linked intellectual property to both bananas and gambling, to take just two examples.[4]

TRIPS crystallized the highest level of intellectual property rights acceptable to the demanders as of December 1990. That is the year when a text close to the final one signed in Marrakech in 1994 was presented to the negotiators (Gervais, 2012b: 15–29). For proponents of developmental theories based on historical accounts of how developed countries got to where they are economically, namely by copying others first before adopting high intellectual property standards, this was not good news (Gibbons, 2011: 935–937). Indeed, the potential negative impact of TRIPS on development was recognized early after the entry into force of the agreement (Abbott, 1996). Yet, TRIPS was not the first time that developing countries suggested a developmental focus for international IP discussions. A 1979 document prepared for a possible revision of the Paris Convention for the Protection of Industrial Property mentioned specifically the two following objectives:

- To give full recognition to the needs for economic and social development; and
- To facilitate the development of technology by developing countries and to improve the conditions for the transfer of technology.[5]

The etiology of the development of the innovative potential of developing countries is often anchored in transfers of know-how and technology from more industrialized nations to developing ones. While this may not take account of all the dimensions of indigenous innovations (Gervais 2012c), it leads to the conclusion that conditions for such transfers should be established. There is a related perception that technology transfers are more likely to happen if technologies are actually used by and not just sold to people in the developing world, that is, not imported as finished products. This is also not new, having spurred decades of discussions and debate on Article 5A of the Paris Convention and its limits on forfeiture of patents and compulsory licenses for failure to 'work' an invention (Roffe and Vea, 2009). One can see similar arguments in the discussions concerning Foreign Direct Investment (FDI) and the hope that technology-focused FDI will do more for development than 'mere' trade.

The narrative according to which TRIPS (that is, the introduction of higher levels of intellectual property protection and enforcement in developing countries) would spur innovation-based industrial development has been called into question especially when applied to least-developed countries (LDCs). As a result, the WTO has suspended most TRIPS obligations for LDCs until at least 2021.[6] In the following pages, I will thus attempt to assess the impact of TRIPS on developing countries other than LDCs. In doing so, I begin by drawing important distinctions first among the types of countries concerned, then among various industries.

DISTINCTIONS AMONG DEVELOPING COUNTRIES

Developing countries (other than LDCs) are obviously not all identical, far from it. Yet the TRIPS agreement essentially treats them all on the same footing: All developing countries other than LDCs had until January 1, 2000 to implement TRIPS – with up to five more years to apply full patent protection to pharmaceutical products for those, like India, that did not provide such protection. This seems to ignore variables that directly affect how different developing countries were affected by TRIPS.

Developing countries can be grouped in various ways for purposes of this type of analysis. In a recent article (Gervais, 2013), I have suggested that – again leaving aside LDCs for now – one could, in aggregate, distinguish developing countries where innovation benefits outweighed additional rent extraction made possible by TRIPS and those countries where additional rent extraction made possible by TRIPS outweighed innovation benefits. This 'net outcomes' approach led me and others to conclude that, if TRIPS is seen as a given, countries should move from the second to the first group by improving innovation outcomes but also adopting remedial actions (using the so-called TRIPS 'flexibilities') to reduce costs imposed by higher intellectual property protection (Petherbridge, 2001; Straus, 2012: 677–678).

Using a host of factors including domestic market size, diversification and purchasing power (and resulting 'market power'), a similar approach but one more squarely focused on pharmaceuticals was suggested by Benoliel and Salama (2010). They separated developing countries into three groups according to their bargaining power: low, medium and high. The last two categories are reserved for newly industrialized countries (2010: 310). Paradoxically, they suggest that less or non-innovative countries have more bargaining power. This stronger position comes 'because of their ability to issue compulsory licenses' (2010: 312). As we will see below, it seems that this observation is largely correct. By contrast, a stronger pharmaceutical innovation sector in certain countries 'restricts the ability of their governments to issue compulsory licenses that would make drugs more affordable' (2010: 311). Applying these criteria, Benoliel and Salama consider China and India as medium-bargaining power countries, while Brazil, South Africa and Thailand have high bargaining power.

While this chapter is not specifically focused on pharmaceuticals, the notion that domestic market size matters seems intuitively correct. A country that can sell to its own nationals does not depend on favorable international trade rules to the same degree, at least to launch successful new products or services (Acemoglu &

Linn, 2004: 1050). David Lilienthal made the point in the 1950s that a major advantage of the United States in the world economy was the size of its market (1953).

Domestic markets are only part of the equation of course. As the European Union and the US continue to open their borders to more products from developing countries in trade talks, access to those markets becomes a prize coveted by innovators elsewhere. Sudip Chaudhuri noted, for example, that for many Indian and other non-US pharmaceutical companies, access to the US market and its (comparatively) very high drug prices was in many cases more important to generate R&D than access to their local market (2009: 288). This, in turn, suggests that the additional rents that Western drug companies may collect post-TRIPS in developing countries (where prices are typically lower due to economic conditions, price controls, compulsory licensing or a combination of such factors) do not add much to their R&D budgets, while access to the US and EU markets boost their competitors'. This matters because there is market share to be seized by new players. The 'largest pharmaceuticals company reportedly controls a market share lower than 10 percent of the world market. In the United States, the market share of the top five and top ten firms are, respectively, less than 36 and around 60 percent' (Laforgia et al., 2009: 295).

This R&D 'displacement effect' (Gervais 2009a) is compounded by ever increasing intellectual property protection in richer markets. Here again, the 'West' may be giving developing countries' companies the edge. Beyond a certain optimal point, patent protection decreases innovation (Cadot and Lippman, 1995; Gallini,1992; Laforgia et al., 2009: 301). A similar study on patent length seemed to mesh with those results (Horowitz and Lai, 1996). The etiology of sub-optimality of IP protection beyond certain limits or levels is multifactorial, but one could mention the uncertainties (and related negative impact on investment) of an overly generous doctrine of equivalents in patent law, for example, and the inability to produce 'me too' drugs without a serious risk of infringement accompanied by very high exposure to treble, other statutory and/or punitive damages. By the same token, studies have confirmed what seems intuitively correct, namely that in countries without the necessary technology-absorptive capacity, increasing patent protection on pharmaceuticals produces little if any innovation outcomes (Laforgia et al., 2009; Lall, 2003).

In trying to find ways to identify and measure distinctions among developing countries, Chen and Puttitanun's empirical analyses show that, in countries with GDP per capita exceeding $1,260, a growing reliance on stronger IPR regimes is perceptible (Chen & Puttitanun, 2005: 483–489). My sense is that a host of other correlations could be found, such as educational level, corruption indices, etc. Another promising set of factors and taxonomy was proposed by Professor Llew Gibbons (2011: 932–933). He grouped developing countries according to three stages of development:

Stage one (which may be seen as including LDCs):

- Foreign direct investment rare and usually limited to specialized sectors – often relating to the exploitation of natural resources or developing franchise service industries like a major international brand bottling company;
- Unskilled, cheap labor;
- Foreign businesses create the necessary infrastructure and invest in human capital;
- Developing countries ideally are investing in the training of skilled workers and junior managers. Successfully developing a skilled workforce is a prerequisite to entering stage two.

Stage two:

- Economy now able to absorb technology, to imitate technology at some level, and to contribute minor improvements;
- Well-educated workforce adapted to absorbing new technology and incorporating it into the domestic economy;
- Domestic research efforts primarily facilitative or associated with technology transfer. Focus shifts gradually to efforts on more innovative projects.

Stage three:

- Newly industrialized country producing its own intellectual property;
- Nations very selective as to which intellectual property rights they zealously protect and which rights they encourage (mis)appropriation of.

This progression from imitation to absorption to innovation roughly tracks the innovation theorists' view of innovation following a path from imitation to adaptation to true global innovation (Gervais, 2013: 161–162). 'Stage 2' countries likely overlap the group identified previously, namely countries where innovation outcomes do not (yet) outweigh the additional rent extraction made possible by the implementation of TRIPS-compatible norms. As countries build innovation-focused industries, they typically develop, as Professor Gibbons rightly notes, more sophisticated and nuanced views of their intellectual property policies. I had arrived at a similar conclusion (Gervais, 2005). Simply put, they play the IP game better.

Industry players understand that the race to get as many patents as possible does not necessarily mean more innovation. Reliance on secrecy and lead-time often trumps patents (Cohen et al., 2003: 130–147). Hence, while two Chinese companies, ZTE Corporation and Huawei Technologies, had the first and third highest number of international (PCT)[7] patent applications in 2011, China is not necessarily the 'most innovative country' in the world (Yu, 2013: 80). This poses a related question, namely whether China, and possibly other BRICS countries, are a model or rather an exception. In the latter case, most non-BRICS countries would have little interest in high levels of intellectual property protection, because they would be unlikely to benefit in the short or medium term, and would have to accept higher costs due to higher rent extraction. There is no unanimous answer here. The various groupings of countries all point towards a path of progression, however. Along that path, which the evolution of IP rules in developed countries would seem to confirm, countries gradually make more and better use of IP rights (Maskus, 2009: 169; Ragavan, 2012: 12–29).

There is also a widely held view that many developing countries possess negligible technological capacity, so that the points of departure for the progression vary enormously. The timing of the introduction of higher levels of IP matters correlatively. A number of developing countries 'have no meaningful prospects of attracting domestic innovations' (Cheng, 2012: 4).

Benoliel and Salama mention only a handful of countries (BRICS +). Indeed, they opine that 'China and India are effectively the only developing countries that, aside from being scientifically proficient, are also able to produce technology-based products in patent-sensitive industries in large scale' (2010: 288–289). Cheng suggests along similar lines that China 'due to the size of its economy and its unique economic circumstances, should be treated as sui generis, and analyzed separately from the remaining developing countries' (2012: 9).

There are valid arguments for treating large emerging economies, such as some of the BRICS countries, as a special case, and perhaps China as special even among that group. In 2005, while developing countries accounted for only 23% of worldwide research and development, this figure dropped to 14.8% if China was excluded (Cheng, 2012: 9). As possible additional support for this claim, analyses in other developing countries provide mixed results. In Jordan, for example, the government has tried to develop a pharmaceutical industry. It has 'linked its development goals and reform agenda inexorably to the new global economic order, which on the trade side is represented by embracing globalization and open borders; … patent protection periods, copyright protection scopes, trademark registration and categorization mechanisms, to name a few, were globally harmonized' (Nesheiwat, 2010: 365). Yet the policy experiment has yet to bear convincing fruit. As an observer noted after a detailed empirical analysis:

> Absent a national intellectual property strategy that is integrated into developmental goals to optimize knowledge in intellectual property-sensitive goods and services, Jordan and other developing countries stand to continue to pour resources into an area that, for them, is not strongly correlated with economic growth. (Nesheiwat, 2010: 393–394)

The brief discussion in the previous pages shows that differences among countries and their level of human and economic development matter. The next section considers other differences, namely those in the nature of the industries that each country has and can develop.

DISTINCTIONS AMONG INDUSTRIES

In the same way that it put every developing country in a more or less equal position, TRIPS also put all industries on the same footing. And in the same way that this does not map well over distinctions that can be observed among developing countries, treating all industries as equally sensitive to intellectual property protection is simply incorrect. This has a number of unintended consequences.

It has been said that pharmaceutical companies have 'hijacked patent policy both in the United States and globally' (Cheng, 2012: 32). This is not surprising – that industry has been described as an 'archetypical patent-sensitive industry' (Benoliel and Salama, 2010: 267). It is understandable, therefore, that it would push in whichever way it can to get high patent protection in as many markets as possible. However, the costs and restrictions imposed by the 'one-size-fits all' approach of TRIPS means that high patent protection levels – ostensibly adopted for the benefit of commercial pharmaceutical research – will be imposed on all other industries that rely on patents (Carroll, 2009). As Professors Reichman and Lange noted:

> A chronic problem for policymakers even in the most developed countries is that the one-size-fits-all paradigms that underlie classical intellectual property law have proved especially inadequate to deal with the needs of innovators and borrowers in an information age. This problem is compounded many times over in the developing countries, where different players at different stages of development demand different and contradictory approaches to intellectual property rights in their respective fields of interest. (1998: 50)

Then the pharmaceutical industry must deal with complexities of its own. In the wake of the HIV/AIDS crisis, a system was developed under the auspices of the WTO to allow WTO members to issue compulsory licenses to manufacture and export drugs to LDCs who are unable to manufacture complex pharmaceutical molecules. Under the previous legal regime, compulsory licenses predominantly for export purposes were not allowed. The system, put in place in 2003, is not restricted to any specific diseases and essentially works by allowing the issuance of compulsory licenses for export, which are otherwise restricted by TRIPS (Gervais, 2012b: 475–504). Known as the 'paragraph 6 system' (named after the paragraph of the 2001 Doha Declaration on the TRIPS agreement and public health), it has been made effective by a WTO Decision and an amendment to TRIPS, namely article 31*bis*.[8]

As noted above, Benoliel and Salama argue that countries without a domestic pharmaceutical innovation-focused industry may have more bargaining power because they can issue compulsory licenses for domestic use as well without risking retaliation by multinational pharmaceutical companies in the form of withdrawal of R&D dollars, as happened to India after it rejected a patent for a Bayer cancer drug (Halajian, 2013: 1212–1216). Yet this focus on immediate and highly significant short-term public health concerns may mask a risk that incentives to develop new drugs for diseases that affect economically less developed nations will not work (Benoliel & Salama, 2010: 352–353).

The point is not restricted to pharmaceuticals: 'lower levels of protection in a country coincide with poor investment in industries that rely on intellectual property to encourage innovation' (Petherbridge, 2001: 1042). Which industries are those exactly? Beyond pharmaceuticals, it seems that, as far as patents are concerned, this would include at least chemicals and many types of laboratory instruments (Gervais, 2005: 523; Maskus, 2000: 2232). Others suggest other precise industrial fields. Cheng, for example, mentions organic chemicals, plastic chemicals and steel mill products (Cheng, 2012: 35). This classification goes back in part to Mansfield's studies of the field, in which he found that while 90% of pharmaceutical innovations were dependent on patent protection, only about 20% of chemical, electronics and machinery innovations were patent-dependent (Cheng, 2012: 33; Mansfield, 1986; Mansfield et al., 1981). According to Mansfield, patents basically increase the cost of imitation in forcing competitors to invent around, which may itself generate cumulative innovation. The range of increases tended to be from a low near 5% in some electronics-based industries to 40% or more in pharmaceuticals (Mansfield et al., 1981: 913).

Beyond that relatively short list of industries generally considered to be patent-sensitive, major controversies concerning the role and impact of patents on innovation quickly emerge. Do computer software and online commerce benefit more from patents than the aggregate cost of obtaining, enforcing and defending against patent infringement claims, especially those owned by non-practicing entities? This question is front and center in a number of both developed and developing countries (Shrestha, 2010). Proposals to make appropriate differences have been made in the United States: if the legislator is unwilling to separate industries by applying different standards, perhaps courts can (Burk and Lemley, 2010). In a developing country, implementing a *single patent policy for all industries* – as is on the surface required by TRIPS – may thus be sub-optimal. Hence, while TRIPS applies uniform patentability criteria, which a country can define (within reason) to meet its own needs (Petherbridge, 2001), the question whether it makes sense to treat all industries the same should be on any comprehensive innovation agenda. As with trade policy generally, a form of 'discrimination' based on the nature of the industry concerned would be justified if one could develop a proper metric to measure whether and how innovation outcomes are achieved. It would still have to be defensible within a contextual interpretation of TRIPS obligations (Frankel & Gervais, 2013). An inventory of state practice would likely show that courts and in some cases laws themselves treat different industries differently in various contexts (compulsory licensing in patent and copyright; patentable subject matter, etc.).[9]

THE THREE PHASES OF TRIPS

In previously published scholarship, I described the three phases of TRIPS (Gervais, 2009b, 2013). After a first phase which was essentially a 'mad dash' to implement TRIPS quickly – often using model laws prepared by intergovernmental organizations such as WIPO – the HIV/AIDS crisis led to a major backlash and started the second phase. This led to calls to 'resist' TRIPS and aim for a minimalist implementation of its obligational content. The assumptions underlying these first two phases – which I termed addition and subtraction to emphasize the contrast – were radically different, and both were at least incomplete and probably incorrect as well.

During the first (addition) phase, the assumption was that adding relatively high levels of intellectual property protection would produce good outcomes in developing countries (again, I am leaving out LDCs in this analysis). It would also spur economic growth through enhanced trade and FDI. A few years ago, I surveyed the available literature to determine whether there was a basis for the link between FDI and intellectual property (Gervais, 2005). Others have done so more recently (Halydier, 2012). One conclusion one can draw is that TRIPS put the policy cart before the analytical horse. As Professor Maskus observed: 'When the Uruguay

Round negotiations began in 1986, the subject of intellectual property rights (IPRs) was completely unfamiliar to international trade economists' (Maskus, 2000: 2219). Post-TRIPS data suggest a link but also a variegated picture where IP protection is a factor, but only one of many, and one the importance of which varies tremendously. For example, in large markets like China and India, foreign investors might want in, in spite of the presence of perceived failures in IP protection. Indeed, the data shows that it is the 'foreign firms' *perception* of the strength of an IPR regime, rather than the actual strength of the regime within particular industries, that is responsible for determining the level of FDI' (Halydier, 2012: 99). If this is true then it would suggest that countries should 'promote' their IP regimes and pay attention to third party assessments of such regimes.

Edwin Mansfield published a study already mentioned above (1994) which was interpreted as proving that 'if developing countries raise their level of intellectual property protection (especially patents), they will attract foreign investment and technology transfer' (Heald, 2003: 309). Professor Heald suggested that the emphasis on statutory IP rights misread Mansfield's main conclusions, which tended to support the view that the level of enforcement of *trade secrecy* and *contract law* were more important in making foreign direct investment decisions (2003: 316–317). Heald concluded as follows: 'Instead of blindly relying on Mansfield's research, a more rational strategy for developing countries would take into account the costs and benefits of protection in the context of their unique economic situation' (2003: 317).

While recent studies tend to support the view that the perception of stronger intellectual property in LDCs and developing countries may increase the volume of FDI (Qian, 2009: 205), Chen and Puttitanun also mention 'other variables including differences in size, age, political situation, economic freedom, natural resource allocation, technological absorptive capability, WTO accession, and level of development of LDC and developing countries, as well as small sample sizes, poor data collection, and regional instability' (Halydier, 2012: n. 64). Maskus, Fink and Primo Braga's work points in a similar direction (Maskus, 2004: 138–152; Primo Braga and Fink, 1996: 444–454). Maskus also notes that the 'multinational enterprises are more likely to transfer proprietary information to local affiliates or partners that are themselves engaged in adaptive R&D, suggesting that policies to encourage domestic innovation are complementary to inducing inward technology flows' (Maskus, 2009: 171). He then observes that 'elasticity of FDI with respect to patent seems to rise with the abundance of local human capital' (p. 171). This would explain why countries with very low absorptive capacity (such as many LDCs) do not show measurable gains when introducing higher levels of intellectual property rules without a series of accompanying and parallel measures on several different fronts. To that extent, the pro-addition narratives were woefully incomplete. Simply put, standard or mechanical TRIPS implementation with a view to avoiding WTO disputes was and is unlikely to produce net developmental benefits.

Countries implementing TRIPS should thus focus instead on a broad innovation strategy and sets of policies to successfully develop their innovation potential, without having any positives in that area clearly outweighed by the higher costs imposed by a foreign right holder's right to collect additional intellectual property rents. It forms part of what I call the third phase of TRIPS, the calibration process. Dealing with IP rules and their enforcement without dealing with absorptive capacity (including human development and education) and entrepreneurship is unlikely to yield net positives in terms of domestic innovation (Li, 2009). In other words, policy makers are dealing with a complex set of equations with multiple, interpolated considerations and variables (Gervais, 2007). The word used *inter alia* by Michael Birnhack to describe the challenge and 'the meeting of the global and the local', is the 'glocal' (Birnhack, 2009: 397).

China has demonstrated its understanding of this need to be comprehensive in its approach to catch up and perhaps overtake the 'West'. It developed a national intellectual property strategy (Straus, 2012: 667). This includes a strong focus on human capital (Qian 2009: 205). There is, however, a debate as to whether the effort to push domestic industries to develop patent portfolios while slowly accepting the need to enforce rights belonging to foreign rights holders was deliberate or simply the result of a difficult transition (compare Berkow, 2011 and Yu, 2013: 97–199).

The second phase ('subtraction') of TRIPS was incomplete in focusing solely on the need to reduce intellectual property protection. While this was understandable to deal with the major public health challenges facing LDCs unable to pay for necessary medicines, it led to the formation of an anti-intellectual property coalition that sees little good in any form of intellectual property protection. An obvious problem with lowering protection across the board is that some industries are especially sensitive to certain intellectual property protection and will simply not invest in that appropriate intellectual property (and proper enforcement).

This calls for alternative strategies and incentives, from awards and prizes to public funding of research. There are necessarily trade-offs in substituting public funding for private incentives (Carroll, 2009: 1378–1379). Clearly, however, just lowering IP levels is not a strategy. To quote Professor Maskus, 'governments should not view IPR flexibilities as a substitute for sound development policy' (2009: 172). Doing so (especially absent an overall strategy which might secure certain forms of 'compensation' for the removal or weakening of certain IP incentives) is likely to have negative impacts on FDI and local entrepreneurship. Limits on intellectual property rights should be imposed carefully and probably with appropriate distinctions between types of issues and industries. Not all intellectual property rights are the same, nor do all industries respond in the same way to changes in IP protection.

In the field of copyright, it takes relatively little to generate growth in software and book publishing and even in music, where digital sales are picking up and allowing individually-published songwriters and self-promoting artists to support a living outside of major 'record deals'. While it is important to bear in mind that many industries depend on proper limits to copyright, there is an effort in academic and certain NGO circles to jettison copyright for all online content. I find this troubling when the push includes an effort to destroy author collectives trying to support professionals in this area, as the following passage indicates: 'The entities that have the clearest interest in promoting the copyright dogma are collecting societies, who can bring the anti-competitive and the opportunistic motivations to perfection' (Katz, 2012: 1340). Fortunately, a number of developing countries, from Namibia to Nepal, have realized the need to support a fledgling professional 'creative class' and to build and supervise well-managed, transparent author collectives to represent them vis-à-vis major users.[10] The involvement of local composers, songwriters and artists in the governance of such collectives is key in ensuring that collectives attain and maintain effectual levels of (a) the credibility vis-à-vis users needed to get them to license their use of protected content; and (b) the transparency vis-à-vis users and right holders needed for licensing and to have support from all stakeholders. Transparency and credibility will also be required when attempting to negotiate agreements with 'sister' organizations in other territories.

Arguing that all online content should be free or that individual authors are better off negotiating on their own with the likes of Apple, Google or major broadcasters tends not to make all the necessary distinctions among types of copyright content. Conflating all types of copyright material as mere 'content' is rhetorically useful to diminish its value – and the rights attached to it. It is also short-sighted, however. The normative case that, for example, scientific articles based on publicly-funded research should be widely available, and especially so in developing countries, is easily convincing. Is it really the same to argue that the latest song or novel should be freely available to all without payment of any kind because it is online?[11] Policy decisions based on this type of distinction should emphasize both open access to scientific publication and proper mechanisms (a) to facilitate monetization of digital content and (b) to enforce copyright in cases of commercial-scale infringements. As developing countries think about copyright policy as possibly forming part of their developmental strategy, two important changes can be expected in the relevant industries. First, as the vast majority of Hollywood's revenue now comes from overseas markets, it is easy to foresee a future where most movies will be produced outside the United States. India already produces more films than Hollywood and many countries, including Nigeria, are increasing their production. There is fluidity in the market share(s) available for countries that play that game better. This will imply *appropriate* copyright protection. Second, while copyright is necessary for certain industries to prosper, it should be protected appropriately not excessively. This leads in turn to several important policy prescriptions that developing countries can consider.

Copyright needs fundamental rethinking in the digital age. This presents various opportunities for developing countries. Many industries flourish because there are appropriate limits on copyright protection such as fair use that allow them to use, make available and modify existing content in appropriate cases without authorization (Rogers & Szamosszegi, 2011). This does not mean that 'it should all be free', but rather that a proper combination of licensing and exceptions can make the system work best. Professional authors whose works are valued should have a way of getting paid.

If there is a silver lining to the systematic destruction of author collectives in the West, it is that it may create an advantage for authors elsewhere. It also means that distribution systems allowing users to do what they want and like to do with digital content are likely to be more successful in the marketplace. This should allow software start-ups in many countries to win a share in the global intermediation game. What matters online is not scarcity or control of every copy, as many rights-holder-driven business models still try to enforce. It is axiomatic that online business models based on the use of copyright content work best not when enforcing scarcity but rather when connecting content with as many users who value it as possible (Gervais & Hyndman, 2011: 70). Local knowledge in each country and localized social networking could help launch this type of intermediation in several countries. There is a window of opportunity here in patent law as well. While the United States and other Western powers are stuck due to heavy lobbying constraints in the way that they can improve their current intellectual property framework, developing countries can do better and grow certain industries faster. The negative role that patents may play (in aggregate) in software and online business are increasingly well documented. Problems arise because multiple patents – sometimes hundreds – can apply to a single application (e.g. for e-commerce); because patent laws do not typically require full disclosure of the code that is – indirectly at least – protected by the patent; and finally because the term is seen by many as too long for this type of technology because, at the expiry of the patent (20 years after filing), the protected software will probably be obsolete and unlikely, therefore, to lead to follow-on or incremental innovation (Bessen & Meurer, 2009). This suggests a highly cautious approach, which can be implemented by applying proper patentability standards.

PROMOTING STRATEGIC SPILLOVERS

While there is a debate about the optimal scope of intellectual property rights, it seems fair to posit that optimality in that context will depend on a number of factors, the importance of each will depend on the country and industry concerned. Hence, while TRIPS contains uniform norms, it should be implemented taking account of the specific circumstances of each country and region.

In the wake of Nobel Laureate Robert Solow's famous essay (1956), '[t]here has been a general consensus among economists that research and development is a major source of economic growth. ... [M]ost studies show a high correlation between R&D expenditures and productivity growth after accounting for investment in ordinary capital' (Cheng, 2012: 12). As Cheng explains rather convincingly, however, the results of Solow's model have not been borne out empirically. In fact, other economists, including Paul Romer, proposed different endogenous growth models for long-term growth (1990).

This becomes critical in suggesting ways to understand and promote innovation as part of developmental polices because those endogenous growth models identify *R&D spillovers* as a central factor. Such spillovers 'eliminate the problem of diminishing returns to the aggregate knowledge of an economy, which was a main culprit for declining growth in Solow's model' (Cheng, 2012: 13). Put differently, 'what one firm learns from another firm's innovation will improve the productivity of the first firm's R&D' (Helpman, 2004: 34), which suggests considerable yet possibly counter-intuitive positive externalities. Other research in the late 1980s in Canada, Japan and the United States had already identified the existence of R&D spillovers (Bernstein, 1989; Goto & Suzuki, 1989; Jaffe, 1986). In Japan, where patent protection is often described as relatively weak compared to a number of other developed countries, Baumol observed significant spillover effects and abundant innovation (2002: 42).

Developing countries can and should *adopt strategies to maximize spillovers*, including by allowing entrepreneurs to consult patent applications and even attend top trade shows (Levin et al., 1987). If an increase in intellectual property protection leads to more innovation, there should be more spillover effects and, consequently, more imitation. This may sound somewhat counter intuitive (more IP leading to more imitation) but available data do bear this out (Lai, 1998: 135). Studies also suggest something that may be more in keeping with intuitive insights, namely that not all FDI is the same, and that spillovers will happen more frequently and be more beneficial when they are technology related and include a significant technology transfer component. Ideally, developing countries should incentivize the inclusion of R&D elements in appropriate FDI transactions, which could benefit both the investor and the recipient country (Ling, 2011).The suggestion is not to restrict trade by imposing strict FDI rules; it is the opposite, accompanied by positive incentives (Mammone et al., 2012: 116).

There are four main methods to encourage transfer of technological knowledge: licensed technology transfer; unauthorized imitation ('piracy'); patent disclosure; and reverse engineering (Cheng, 2012: 48). All except the second one are legal. The first method, which includes FDI transactions that contain technology transfers, is voluntary; the other three are not, though arguably patent disclosure is consented to when one applies for a patent, because publication of the application after 18 months is part of the patent bargain. Developing countries can help develop patent information systems, informing their local entrepreneurs of published patent applications or at least making it easier for them to find them. They can provide information on and ensure that their laws permit reverse engineering, as do laws in Europe and the United States for example (Evans, 2013; Samuelson & Scotchmer, 2002).

Outsourcing of manufacturing, which typically involves one or more licensing transactions, may weaken the ability of multinational companies to prevent technology from being appropriated, transformed and exploited in recipient countries – or indeed their willingness to do so if those countries prove to be innovative, lower-cost environments. Outsourcing requires the transfer of knowledge, and not all knowledge can or should be protected by intellectual property rights (Sherwood, 2002).

Developing countries wishing to nurture strategic spillover effects may use *antitrust/competition laws* to limit the negative welfare impacts of higher intellectual property protection. In areas in which they are trying to encourage FDI, however, rules that restrict licensing practices (I do not mean to imply abusive practices such as those listed in article 40 of TRIPS) may discourage outsourcing and reduce technology transfers. Cheng goes a step further, arguing that 'the ability to circumvent antitrust restrictions can be said to be an internalization advantage that steers the multinational firm to keep production in-house' (2012: 49–50). Like many other aspects of innovation policy, it is a balancing act. A possible approach would be to use the laws of more industrialized countries as a model and then ensure proper administrative application through training and judicial review.

A related area in which intellectual property may be excessive is access to *essential technologies* writ large (Brown, 2012). I would not limit the definition of essential technologies to patents included in standards, though this is a key point (Mueller, 2002; Zhang, 2011). In this context, one could extend the notion of essentiality using a human rights lens to building blocks of free expression, for example (Brown, 2012: 73–75). It also informed the adoption of TRIPS art. 31bis, where medicines were deemed 'essential' to deal with major public health crises.

Compulsory licensing more generally is subject to two similar caveats. First, any know-how that would be transferred with a voluntary licensing agreement would not be a typical compulsory licensing scenario. There are cases of course where there is very little if any relevant additional know-how not disclosed or otherwise 'enabled' by the patent subject to the compulsory license. Second, as argued by Benoliel and Salama (2010), a firm subjected to a compulsory license may withdraw, delay or cancel other investments in the country. These are factors to bear in mind before issuing a compulsory license. Their relative weight in the decision will vary enormously in each case. Then there is dissemination of information generated by the intellectual property system itself, including patent applications. As Michael Ryan noted: 'Developing countries intent upon closing knowledge gaps and reducing information problems will do so with the help [of] intellectual property institutions – trademark to facilitate consumer knowledge, patent to facilitate technology transfer, copyright to facilitate literary, artistic, and informational expression' (Ryan, 2002: 303).

A more positive and fairly powerful way to develop spillovers is to foster the establishment of *clusters*. Available data and studies suggest that clusters involving *private capital, higher education resources relevant to the area, and government support* (in various forms from subsidies to tax incentives) are a successful form of industrial policy (Gervais, 2009c). They can be used by domestic companies of course, but can also be used to attract FDI with an R&D component by branches of multinational corporations increasingly interested in having a broader geographical R&D footprint. In an age where capital and innovation are mobile, clusters can serve to attract the best minds in both research and business. Often, however, this will also require infrastructural investments by governments (roads and transportation; stable electrical supply; access to the Internet, etc.).

Clusters need to be able to share information. In fact, I would go a step further. Information-sharing, through both formal and informal processes, should be part of the 'culture' of such clusters. Governmental support to make research available, whether using structures such as Creative Commons or otherwise, should be encouraged. In some cases, commercial publishing entities might also see an interest in participating in the formation and development of clusters.

THE ROLE OF WIPO

The World Intellectual Property Organization (WIPO) has been retooling to face the demands of the developing world. It adopted a Development Agenda which is meant to infuse all of its activities with a normative direction pointing towards measurable developmental objectives (Deere, 2009). This 'entails a significant reform of WIPO' (Musungu, 2009: 75). The Organization seems to have responded, noting for example that:

> IP for Development is an emphatic articulation of the notion that IP is not an end in itself but rather is a tool that could power countries' growth and development. WIPO, as the lead United Nations agency mandated to promote the protection of intellectual property through cooperation among states and in collaboration with other international organizations, is committed to ensuring that all countries are able to benefit from the use of IP for economic, social and cultural development.[12]

Even with a retooled WIPO, however, the multilateral future looks bleak for the predictable future. Partly because they were unhappy with WIPO's reshaped mandate, a number of rights holder groups have pushed national and regional governments to implement an agenda seeking to increase rights and enforcement outside of WIPO's aegis. Efforts such as the Anti-Counterfeiting Trade Agreement (ACTA), and the more recent and more positively named Trans-Pacific Partnership (TPP) and Transatlantic Trade and Investment Partnership (TTIP) are examples of this. ACTA was the first international, non-multilateral IP negotiation to be based not on geography but on like-mindedness. I started describing it as the 'country club' model in 2010, an expression I used to contrast this approach with the multilateral one (Gervais, 2012a). TPP and TTIP are broader negotiations including intellectual property. Their broad nature will allow for bargains to be struck across sectors (farm subsidies for longer effective patent terms, etc.). There is an obvious risk of overreach (Frankel, 2011). Those negotiations are not necessarily informed by the latest evidence on the optimal scope of protection. In addition, the secrecy involving the negotiation process is an obstacle for those who would want to inject such evidence into the policy discussions.

There are reasons to remain hopeful, however. First, secrecy is not a fatal obstacle. As with ACTA, leaks will inevitably happen, and democratic institutions, including the European Parliament, should continue to try to obtain information on the process. While I understand the reasons for the secrecy, I continue to believe that in the end it produces more harm than good (Gervais, 2012a). A much better approach is to have a public process – with some side meetings where necessary. Second, to the ideology of 'more is always better', one should not respond with the ideology of 'less is always better'. It is too easy to disprove what are at bottom just ideological claims. A better approach is to debate the desired outcome publicly using available evidence and analyses.

In the end, those regional and country club agreements will not contain identical rules, which will leave us with a patchwork of rules. This is already true in some important respects – even at the multilateral level.[13] This will increase international business costs, because companies will have to comply and live with different rules in different countries and their enshrinement in major trade agreements will decrease flexibilities going forward. On the positive side, however, it will also provide more empirical evidence to determine which policies are working best to promote innovation-based economic development. Variations among countries and regions will provide raw data and it will be up to scholars to parse causation.

CONCLUSION

As policy makers navigate deeper in the calibration waters of phase III of TRIPS, they must avoid the shoals of excessive intellectual property, from patent trolls to patents preventing access to essential medicines to copyright and trademark excesses preventing free expression and other fair uses. To this end, recommendations to maximize the use of TRIPS flexibilities, lessons learned during the second ('subtraction') phase of TRIPS will be helpful. To the Scylla of excessive intellectual property, one must not run to the Charybdis of insufficient intellectual property, however. Excessive exceptions or recourse to compulsory licensing or antitrust restrictions are likely to discourage certain forms of FDI and may thus retard economic development. The focus should be on FDI transactions that include knowledge transfer and ideally a significant R&D component. The lessons of phase I ('addition') of TRIPS, informed by more recent data and analyses, should remain anchored in a strategic policy agenda. TRIPS implementation, even under TRIPS Plus pressures, should remain alert to this type of evidence. This includes the key role of spillover effects in generating both cumulative and breakthrough ('pioneer') innovation.

A country with a large domestic market may have an easier time launching its own innovation-based enterprises, and be less dependent on favorable international trade rules. Countries with a larger population are also more likely to be more diversified. Yet, to translate innovation into commercial ventures requires a host of factors that small countries can also provide. Indeed, sometimes it may be easier for them. Education, infrastructure, legal reforms and the formation of industry-specific clusters should be front and center.

There is little doubt that the overarching objective of policy makers should be *endogenous growth* of their innovation potential within a balanced IP regime, that is, with an emphasis on innovation where there is a reasonable likelihood of success in the country concerned. Smaller countries may have fewer options to diversify. The policy framework should allow entrepreneurship to flourish, which may in turn require a hands-on approach in strategic areas where venture capital and various (e.g. legal) resources may be hard to find locally. Among those, one should not underestimate the role that the extremely limited availability of venture/risk capital in many developing countries plays in retarding innovation-based entrepreneurship and development.[14]

NOTES

1 See http://hdr.undp.org/en/media/HDR_2013_EN_TechNotes.pdf.
2 Blending the attainment of the positive objective with ways to mitigate the negative impacts that introducing higher levels of protection of intellectual property may have, Professor Chon has suggested an approach based on 'substantive equality' in this context (Chon, 2007).
3 See World Trade Organization, *Understanding on Rules and Procedures Governing the Settlement of Disputes*, available at: http://www.wto.org/english/docs_e/legal_e/ursum_e.htm#Understanding
4 See European Communities – Regime for the Importation, Sale and Distribution of Bananas. Recourse to Arbitration by the European Communities Under Article 22.6 of the DSU. Decision by the Arbitrators, WTO document WT/DS27/ARB/ECU, 24 March 2000; and United States – Measures Affecting the Cross-Border Supply of Gambling and Betting Services. Recourse to Arbitration by the United States under Article 22.6 of the DSU. Decision by the Arbitrator. WTO document WT/DS285/ARB, 21 December 2007.
5 Diplomatic Conference on the Revision of the Paris Convention, Geneva, February 4 to March 4, 1980, Basic Proposals, WIPO document PR/DC/3 of 25 June 1979.
6 See Council for Trade-Related Aspects of Intellectual Property Rights. *Extension of the Transition Period under Article 66.1 for Least Developed Country Members*. Decision of the Council for TRIPS of 11 June 2013, WTO document IP/C/64.
7 The 1970 Patent Cooperation Treaty (PCT) makes it easier to apply for a patent in some or all of the 148 countries party to it (as of July 2013).
8 See World Trade Organization, TRIPS and Public Health: Dedicated Webpage for Notifications, http://www.wto.org/english/tratop_e/trips_e/public_health_e.htm
9 In copyright, it is common to treat different categories of works differently. TRIPS does not contain an obligation like art. 27.1, which obligates WTO Members to make patents 'available for

any inventions, whether products or processes, in all fields of technology'. An example of differential treatment would be s. 3(d) of the Indian Patents (Amendment) Act, 2005 (Act No. 15 of 2005), ostensibly designed to tackle certain forms of ever-greening in the pharmaceutical context.

10 A partial inventory of collective management systems can be found in Gervais (2010).

11 I do not wish to bring into the discussion the specialized formats such as Braille copies made available to people with print disabilities. My long-standing support for the recently concluded *Marrakesh Treaty to Facilitate Access to Published Works for Persons who are Blind, Visually Impaired, or otherwise Print Disabled* is part of the public record. Cf. 'Comment submitted by Professor Daniel Gervais to the United States Copyright Office', http://www.copyright.gov/docs/sccr/comments/2009/comments-2/daniel-gervais-vanderbilt-university-law-school.pdf. Conflating this and broad access to commercial works for free strikes me as unfair at best.

12 WIPO, 'Intellectual Property for Development', http://www.wipo.int/cooperation/en/

13 Consider e.g. art. 11 of the *Marrakesh Treaty to Facilitate Access to Published Works for Persons who are Blind, Visually Impaired, or otherwise Print Disabled*, which recognizes four different versions of the 'three-step test'. The text of the treaty is available at http://www.wipo.int/meetings/en/doc_details.jsp?doc_id=241683

14 Marco della Cava, 'A Not-so-crazy Goal to Find, Nurture Talent', *USA Today*, 16 July 2013, at 4B. Interview with Linda Rottenberg, CEO of Endeavor Global, a company that has funded over 500 young companies around the world. She is quoted as saying: 'I think the next Steve Jobs or Oprah could come from emerging markets'. The juxtaposition of a tech entrepreneur and a media personality in her quote is also interesting.

REFERENCES

Abbott, Frederick M. (1996) 'The WTO TRIPS Agreement and Global Economic Development', *Chicago-Kent Law Review*, 72: 385–405.

Acemoglu, Daron & Linn, Joshua (2004) 'Market Size and Innovation: Theory and Evidence from the Pharmaceutical Industry', *Quarterly Journal of Economics*, 119(3): 1049–1090.

Baumol, William J. (2002) *The Free Market Innovation Machine: Analyzing the Growth Miracle of Capitalism*. Princeton: Princeton University Press.

Benoliel, Daniel & Salama, Bruno (2010) 'Towards an Intellectual Property Bargaining Theory: The Post-WTO Era', *University of Pennsylvania Journal of International Law*, 32: 265–368.

Berkow, Jameson (2011) 'Patent Dragon Awakes', *Financial Post* 7 November, http://business.financialpost.com/2011/11/07/patent-dragon-awakes/?__lsa=097c-fdfa (quoting Ikechi Mgbeoji, Associate Professor, Osgoode Hall Law School, York University, Toronto).

Bernstein, Jeffrey (1989) 'The Structure of Canadian Inter-industry R&D Spillovers, and the Rates of Return to R&D', *The Journal of Industrial Economics*, 37(3): 315–328.

Bessen, James & Meurer, Michael J. (2009) *Patent Failure: How Judges, Bureaucrats, and Lawyers Put Innovators at Risk*. Princeton: Princeton University Press.

Birnhack, Michael D. (2009) 'Trading Copyright: Global Pressure on Local Culture', in N. Netanel (ed.), *The Development Agenda: Global Intellectual Property and Developing Countries*. Oxford: Oxford University Press. pp. 363–399.

Brown, Abbe L. (2012) *Intellectual Property, Human Rights and Competition*. Cheltenham: Edward Elgar.

Burk, Dan L. & Lemley, Mark A. (2010) 'The Patent Crisis and How The Courts Can Solve It', *Syracuse Science & Technology Law Reporter*, 23: 1–22.

Cadot, Olivier & Lippman, Steven A. (1995) 'Barriers to Imitation and the Incentive to Innovate', 95/23/EPS, http://ssrn.com/abstract=7187.

Carroll, Michael W. (2009) 'One Size Does Not Fit All: A Framework for Tailoring Intellectual Property Rights', *Ohio State Law Journal*, 70: 1361–1434.

Chaudhuri, Sudip (2009) 'Is Product Patent Protection Necessary to Spur Innovation in Developing Countries? R&D by Indian Pharmaceutical Companies After TRIPS', in N. Netanel (ed.), *The Development Agenda: Global Intellectual Property and Developing Countries*. Oxford: Oxford University Press. pp. 265–292.

Chen, Yongmin & Puttitanun, Thitima (2005) 'Intellectual Property Rights and Innovation in Developing Countries', *Journal of Development Economics*, 78: 474–493.

Cheng, Thomas K. (2012) 'A Developmental Approach to the Patent-Antitrust Interface', *Northwestern Journal of International Law and Business*, 33: 1–79.

Chon, Margaret (2007) 'Substantive Equality in International Intellectual Property Norm Setting and Interpretation', in D. Gervais (ed.), *Intellectual Property, Trade and Development*. Oxford: Oxford University Press. pp. 475–526.

Cohen, Wesley et al. (2003) 'R&D Information Flows and Patenting in Japan and the United States', in Ove Granstrand (ed.), *Economics, Law and Intellectual Property*. New York: Springer. pp. 130–147.

Deere, Carolyn (2009) 'The Politics of Intellectual Property Reform in Developing Countries: The Relevance of the World Intellectual Property Organization', in Neil Weinstock Netanel (ed.), *The Development Agenda: Global Intellectual Property and Developing Countries*. Oxford: Oxford University Press. pp. 111–133.

Drahos, Peter (2002) Developing Countries and International Intellectual Property Standard-Setting (www.bit.ly/13OVlWX).

Evans, Tonya M. (2013) 'Reverse Engineering IP', *Marquette Intellectual Property Law Review*, 2013: 61–101.

Frankel, Susy R. (2011) 'Intellectual Property in New Zealand and the TPPA', in Jane Kelsey (ed.), *No Ordinary Deal – Unmasking the Trans-Pacific Partnership Free Trade Agreement*. Wellington: Bridget Williams Books (http://ssrn.com/abstract=1653591).

Frankel, Susy R. & Gervais, Daniel (2013) 'Plain Packaging and the Interpretation of the TRIPS Agreement', *Vanderbilt Journal of Transnational Law*, 46: 1149 (http://ssrn.com/abstract=2234580).

Gallini, Nancy T. (1992), 'Patent Policy and Costly Imitation', *Rand Journal of Economics*, 23(1): 52–63.

Gervais, Daniel (2005), 'Intellectual Property, Trade and Development: The State of Play', *Fordham Law Review*, 74: 505–535 (http://ssrn.com/abstract=870065).

Gervais, Daniel (2007) 'A TRIPS Implementation Toolbox', in D. Gervais (ed.), *Intellectual Property, Trade and Development*. Oxford: Oxford University Press. pp. 527–545.

Gervais, Daniel (2009a) 'Policy Calibration and Innovation Displacement', in Chantal Thomas & Joel P. Trachtman (eds), *Developing Countries in the WTO Legal System*. Oxford: Oxford University Press. pp. 363–394.

Gervais, Daniel (2009b) 'TRIPS 3.0: Policy Calibration and Innovation Displacement', in Neil W. Netanel (ed.), *The Development Agenda: Global Intellectual Property and Developing Countries*. Oxford: Oxford University Press. pp. 51–75.

Gervais, Daniel (2009c) 'Of Clusters and Assumptions: Innovation as Part of a Full TRIPS Implementation', *Fordham Law Review*, 77(5): 2353–2377, http://ssrn.com/abstract=1408128.

Gervais, Daniel (2012a) 'Country Clubs, Empiricism, Blogs and Innovation: The Future of International Intellectual Property Norm-Making in the Wake of ACTA', in Mira Burri and Thomas Cottier (eds), *Trade Governance in the Digital Age*. Cambridge: Cambridge University Press. pp. 323–343.

Gervais, Daniel (2012b) *The TRIPS Agreement: Drafting History and Analysis*, 4th edn. London: Sweet & Maxwell.

Gervais, Daniel (2012c) 'Traditional Innovation and the Ongoing Debate on the Protection of Geographical Indications', in Peter Drahos & Susy Frankel (eds), *Intellectual Property and Indigenous Innovation*. Canberra: Australia National University Press (www.bit.ly/1bOuQ4E).

Gervais, Daniel (2013) 'TRIPS and Innovation: How Recent Developments Might Inform Canada's Foreign Technology Policy', *Canadian Intellectual Property Review*, 29(1): 141–162.

Gervais, Daniel & Hyndman, Dan (2011) 'Cloud Control: Copyright, Global Memes and Privacy', *Journal of Telecommunications & High Technology Law*, 10: 53–92.

Gibbons, Llewellyn Joseph (2011) 'Do As I Say (Not As I Did): Putative Intellectual Property Lessons for Emerging Economies from the Not So Long Past of the Developed Nations', *SMU Law Review*, 64: 923–973.

Goto, Akira & Suzuki, Kazuyuki (1989) 'R&D Capital, Rate of Return on R&D Investment and Spillover of R&D in Japanese Manufacturing Industries', *Review of Economics and Statistics*, 71(4): 555–564.

Halajian, Dina (2013) 'Inadequacy of TRIPS & the Compulsory License: Why Broad Compulsory Licensing is not a Viable Solution to the Access to Medicine Problem', *Brooklyn Journal of International Law*, 38: 1191–1230.

Halydier, Garrett (2012) 'A Hybrid Legal and Economic Development Model That Balances Intellectual Property Protection and Economic Growth: A Case Study of India, Brazil, Indonesia, and Vietnam', *Asian-Pacific Law and Policy Journal*, 14: 86–151.

Heald, Paul (2003) 'Misreading a Canonical Work: An Analysis of Mansfield's 1994 Study', *Journal of Intellectual Property Law*, 10(2): 309–318.

Helpman, Elhanan (2004), *The Mystery of Economic Growth*. Cambridge, MA: Belknap Press.

Horowitz, Andrew W. & Lai, Edwin L.-C. (1996) 'Patent Length and the Rate of Innovation', *International Economic Review*, 37: 785–801.

Jaffe, Adam B. (1986) 'Technological Opportunity and Spillovers of R&D: Evidence from Firms' Patents,

Profits, and Market Value', *American Economic Review*, 76(5): 984–1001.

Katz, Ariel (2012) 'The Orphans, the Market, and the Copyright Dogma: A Modest Solution for a Grand Problem', *Berkeley Technology Law Journal*, 27: 1285–1346.

Khan, B. Zorina (2002) 'Intellectual Property and Economic Development: Lessons from American and European History, Commission on Intellectual Property Rights', Study Paper 1a (http://www.iprcommission.org/papers/pdfs/study_papers/sp1a_khan_study.pdf)

Laforgia, Francesco, Montobbio, Fabio & Orsenigo, Luigo (2009) 'IPRs and Technological Development in Pharmaceuticals: Who Is Patenting What in Brazil after TRIPS', in N. Netanel (ed.), *The Development Agenda: Global Intellectual Property and Developing Countries*. Oxford: Oxford University Press. pp. 293–319.

Lai, Edwin L.-C. (1998) 'International Intellectual Property Rights Protection and the Rate of Product Innovation', *Journal of Development Economics*, 55(1): 133–153.

Lall, Sanjaya (2003) 'Indicators of Relative Importance of IPRs in Developing Countries', UNCTAD-ICTSD Project on IPRs and Sustainable Development (www.bit.ly/15GHTAb).

Levin, Richard C., Klevorick, Alvin K., Nelson, Richard R. & Winter, Sidney G. (1987) 'Appropriating the Returns from Industrial Research and Development', *Brookings Papers on Economic Activity* (www.jstor.org/stable/2534454).

Li, Lihong (2009) 'Lessons from China's Experience with the TRIPs Agreement', in J. De Beer (ed.), *Implementing the World Intellectual Property Organization's Development Agenda*. Waterloo: Wilfrid Laurier University Press. pp 118–130.

Lilienthal, David (1953) *Big Business: A New Era*. New York: Harper & Row.

Ling, Nan Sze (2011) 'Thailand's Ineffectual Intellectual Property Regime: A Trial and Error Approach to Encouraging Foreign Direct Investment Technology Spillover', *New York International Law Review*, 24: 99–167.

Mammone, Richard et al. (2012), 'Can Developed Nations Make a Fortune by Licensing New Technologies to the World's Poor?', *les Nouvelles*, 47: 115–120.

Mansfield, Edwin (1986) 'Patents and Innovation: An Empirical Study', *Management Science*, 32(2): 173–181.

Mansfield, Edwin (1994) 'Intellectual Property Protection, Foreign Direct Investment, and Technology Transfer', Int'l Fin. Corp. Discussion Paper No. 19.

Mansfield, Edwin, Schwartz, Mark & Wagner, Samuel (1981) 'Imitation Costs and Patents: An Empirical Study', *The Economic Journal*, 91: 907–918.

Maskus, Keith E. (2000) 'Lessons from Studying the International Economics of Intellectual Property Rights', *Vanderbilt Law Review*, 53: 2219–2239.

Maskus, Keith E. (2004) 'The Role of Intellectual Property Rights in Encouraging Foreign Direct Investment and Technology Transfer', *Duke Journal of Comparative & International Law*, 9: 109–161.

Maskus, Keith E. (2009) 'The WIPO Development Agenda: A Cautionary Note', in N. Netanel (ed.), *The Development Agenda: Global Intellectual Property and Developing Countries*. Oxford: Oxford University Press. pp. 163–174.

Mueller, Janice M. (2002) 'Patent Misuse through the Capture of Industry Standards', *Berkeley Technology Law Journal*, 17: 623–684.

Musungu, Sisule F. (2009) 'The Role of WIPO's Leadership in the Implementation of WIPO's Development Agenda', in J. De Beer (ed.), *Implementing the World Intellectual Property Organization's Development Agenda*. Waterloo: Wilfrid Laurier University Press. pp. 70–78.

Nesheiwat, Ferris K (2010) 'The Adoption of Intellectual Property Standards Beyond TRIPS – Is it a Misguided Legal and Economic Obsession by Developing Countries?', *Loyola of Los Angeles Int'l & Comparative Law Review*, 32: 361–394.

Okediji, Ruth L. (2009) 'History Lessons for the WIPO Development Agenda', in N. Netanel (ed.), *Intellectual Property and Developing Countries*. Oxford: Oxford University Press. pp. 137–162.

Parello, Carmelo Pierpaolo (2008) 'A North-South Model of Intellectual Property Rights Protection and Skill Accumulation', *Journal of Development Economics*, 85(1–2): 253–281.

Petherbridge, Lee (2001) 'Intelligent TRIPS Implementation: A Strategy for Countries on the Cusp of Development', *University of Pennsylvania Journal of International Economic Law*, 22: 1029–1066.

Primo Braga, Carlos A. & Fink, Carsten (1996) 'The Economic Justification for the Grant of Intellectual Property Rights: Patterns of Convergence and Conflict', *Chicago-Kent Law Review*, 72: 439–461.

Qian, Yi 'Are National Patent Laws the Blossoming Rains? Evidence from Domestic Innovation, Technology Transfers, and International Trade Post Patent Implementations in the Period 1978–2002', *The Development Agenda: Global Intellectual Property and Developing Countries*, edited by NW Netanel Oxford University Press, 2009.

Ragavan, Srividhya (2012) *Patent and Trade Disparities in Developing Countries*. Oxford: Oxford University Press.

Reichman, Jerome H. & Lange, David (1998) 'Bargaining Around the TRIPS Agreement: The Case for Ongoing

Public-Private Initiatives to Facilitate Worldwide Intellectual Property Transactions', *Duke Journal of Int'l & Comp. Law*, 9: 11–68.

Roffe, Pedro and Vea, Gina (2009), 'The WIPO Development Agenda in Historical and Political Context', in N. Netanel (ed.), *The Development Agenda: Global Intellectual Property and Developing Countries.* Oxford: Oxford University Press. pp. 79–110.

Rogers, Thomas and Szamosszegi, Andrew (2011) 'Fair Use on the U.S. Economy', Computer & Communications Industry Association (http://www.ccianet.org/wp-content/uploads/library/FairUseStudy-Sep12.pdf).

Romer, Paul (1990) 'Endogenous Technological Change', *Journal of Political Economy*, 98: S71–S102.

Ryan, Michael P (2002) 'Knowledge-Economy Elites, the International Law of Intellectual Property and Trade, and Economic Development', *Cardozo Journal of International & Comparative Law*, 10: 271–303.

Samuelson, Pamela & Scotchmer, Suzanne (2002) 'The Law and Economics of Reverse Engineering', *Yale Law Journal*, 111: 1575–1663.

Sangsuvan, Kitsuron (2013) 'Separation of Powers in Intellectual Property Rights: Balancing Global Intellectual Property Rights or Monopoly Power in the Twenty-First Century by Competition Law', *New York International Law Review*, 26: 1–52.

Sen, Amartya (1999) *Development as Freedom.* Oxford: Oxford University Press.

Sherwood, Robert M. (2002) 'Some Things Cannot Be Legislated', *Cardozo Journal of International & Comparative Law*, 10: 37–46.

Shrestha, Sannu K. (2010) 'Trolls or Market-Makers? An Empirical Analysis of Nonpracticing Entities', *Columbia Law Review*, 110: 114–160.

Solow, Robert M. (1956) 'A Contribution to the Theory of Economic Growth', *Quarterly Journal of Economics*, 70(1): 65–94.

Straus, Joseph (2012) 'A Marriage of Convenience: World Economy and Intellectual Property From 1990 to 2012', *AIPLA Quarterly Journal*, 40: 633–680.

Yu, Peter K. (2013) 'Five Oft-Repeated Questions about China's Recent Rise as a Patent Power', *Cardozo Law Review De Novo*, 78–114.

Zhang, Dong (2011) 'Observations from a TRIPS Perspective: Do We Need a Traditional Medicine Exemption for Patent Standards?', *Oregon Review of International Law*, 13: 305–315.

6

Déjà Vu in the International Intellectual Property Regime

Peter K. Yu

INTRODUCTION

In the international intellectual property regime, norm-setting activities take place in cycles. In October 2007, the World Intellectual Property Organization (WIPO) adopted the Development Agenda and its 45 recommendations for action. Based on these recommendations, WIPO introduced a wide variety of pro-development initiatives, ranging from technical assistance and capacity building to norm setting and public policy, and from technology transfer to assessment, evaluation and impact studies. Although considerable scepticism existed when the Development Agenda was proposed in October 2004, the Agenda has now earned the widespread support of the international community.

Notwithstanding this ground-breaking development, developed countries and their like-minded trading partners have continued their aggressive push for the establishment of bilateral, plurilateral and regional trade, investment and intellectual property agreements. Only two weeks after the adoption of the WIPO Development Agenda, these countries formally launched the negotiations on the highly controversial Anti-Counterfeiting Trade Agreement (ACTA). A few years later, they also initiated the negotiations on the equally problematic Trans-Pacific Partnership (TPP). Commenting on ACTA, WIPO Director General Francis Gurry lamented how developed countries and their like-minded negotiating partners had 'tak[en] matters into their own hands to seek solutions outside of the multilateral system to the detriment of inclusiveness of the present system' (Saez, 2010).

Interestingly, just as this handbook went into production, WIPO seemed to have charted a new course by establishing two substantive international intellectual property treaties. On 26 June 2012, close to 50 WIPO members signed the Beijing Treaty on Audiovisual Performances (Beijing Treaty), which offers protection to audiovisual performers under the existing international copyright system. A little more than a year later, WIPO adopted the Marrakesh Treaty to Facilitate Access to Published Works for Persons Who Are Blind, Visually Impaired, or Otherwise Print Disabled (Marrakesh Treaty). Upon ratification, this landmark agreement will provide easy or ready access to copyrighted publications to hundreds of millions of individuals with print disabilities.

Although WIPO already administers two dozen international agreements, the completion of these two new treaties is still quite an achievement. Since the adoption of the WIPO Copyright Treaty and the WIPO Performances and Phonograms Treaty in December 1996, no new substantive international intellectual property agreement has been established at this forum. Moreover, the two recent treaties were negotiated in a highly challenging environment, amid the rapid proliferation of non-multilateral agreements. It is therefore no surprise that Director General Gurry described the Marrakesh Treaty as not only 'a victory for the blind, visually impaired and print disabled, but also for the multilateral system' (World Intellectual Property Organization, 2013).

When these three sets of events and developments are juxtaposed against each other, one cannot help but wonder what the future will hold for the international intellectual property regime. Does the rejuvenation of WIPO norm-setting activities suggest the impending end of a much-feared 'non-multilateral era' (Yu, 2011a: 9–12)? Do the recent norm-setting activities reinforce the Development Agenda painstakingly created by developing countries? Or do these activities indicate just the growing complexity of the international intellectual property regime, within which both multilateralism and non-multilateralism proceed at the same time?

Indeed, if multilateral and non-multilateral developments in this regime are proceeding at the same time – or perhaps even at the same pace – how will they impact the WIPO Development Agenda? Will they further complicate the pro-development efforts at not only WIPO, but also the World Trade Organization (WTO) and other fora governing public health, human rights, biological diversity, food and agriculture, and information and communications (Yu, 2009: 522–40)? Or will these developments merely repeat the experience concerning the ill-fated Development Agenda that developing countries advanced in the 1960s and 1970s (Halbert, 2007; Menescal, 2005: 762–79; Yu, 2009: 468–511)? In short, when describing the recent intellectual property norm-setting developments, would it be appropriate for us to use the quote often attributed to Baseball Hall of Famer Yogi Berra, 'It is like déjà vu all over again!'?[1]

Instead of providing direct answers to each of these questions, this chapter puts the recent multilateral and non-multilateral intellectual property developments in their proper historical contexts. Specifically, the chapter examines three sets of recurring developments: (1) the establishment of development agendas; (2) the negotiation of non-multilateral agreements; and (3) the rejuvenation of multilateral norm-setting activities. From these developments, this chapter draws a simple but valuable historical lesson: international intellectual property developments are influenced by the repeated swings of an invisible pendulum. As this pendulum swings back and forth, history will repeat itself, causing us to feel like it is déjà vu all over again. This chapter concludes by suggesting that this simple lesson provides three key insights into the current and future development of the international intellectual property regime.

THE ESTABLISHMENT OF DEVELOPMENT AGENDAS

In October 2004, Argentina and Brazil introduced a path-breaking proposal to establish a Development Agenda within WIPO. Supported by the Group of Friends of Development,[2] this proposal called upon the WIPO General Assembly to 'take immediate action in providing for the incorporation of a "Development Agenda" in the Organization's work program' (World Intellectual Property Organization, 2004). The proposal sought to reduce and eventually eliminate the historical 'bias against latecomers to the intellectual property policy field – developing countries' (Musungu, 2005: 4). It also aimed to place 'WIPO in a better position to contribute towards tackling the key challenges of the

21st century and thereby the achievement of the [Millennium Development Goals]' (Musungu, 2005: 4).

After three years of deliberation within a provisional committee and multiple intersessional intergovernmental meetings, the WIPO General Assembly finally adopted the Development Agenda in October 2007. This Agenda includes 45 recommendations grouped around six thematic clusters: (1) technical assistance and capacity building; (2) norm-setting, flexibilities, public policy and public domain; (3) technology transfer, information and communication technologies and access to knowledge; (4) assessment, evaluation and impact studies; (5) institutional matters including mandate and governance; and (6) other issues.

Crudely classified, the Agenda's recommendations cover reforms in two different directions. The first set of reforms concerns the need to reform WIPO and enhance its development dimension. These reforms are particularly important in view of WIPO's 'heavy reliance on filing fees from the Patent Cooperation Treaty, the narrow definition of its mandate, and the development of training programs that serve this narrow mandate' (Yu, 2007: 871). The second set of reforms focuses on the need to recalibrate the balance in the international intellectual property system. These reforms 'question whether economic development and wealth creation are the sole metrics for measuring development ... [They therefore] put an end to WIPO's monolithic "IP as power tool of development" approach' (Netanel, 2009: 14).

To be certain, the establishment of the WIPO Development Agenda reflected a growing momentum developing countries had not experienced in decades – since perhaps the establishment of the New International Economic Order in the mid-1970s.[3] The developments also provided a rare opportunity for WIPO members to recalibrate the balance in the international intellectual property system. Nevertheless, these developments are far from unprecedented.

In the 1960s and 1970s, developing countries had already pushed for a similar Development Agenda (Yu, 2009: 468–511). At that time, the decolonization movement had led many colonies and dependent territories to declare independence. These newly independent countries were eager to exercise their newfound independence and sovereignty by affirming international obligations into which their former colonial masters had entered on their behalf (Abi-Saab, 1962: 103). They also harboured a serious concern that the extant obligations were too burdensome, especially in light of their limited economic development and technological backwardness (Johnson, 1970: 93; Ricketson and Ginsburg, 2005: 881–2; Yu, 2009: 472–4).

Consider, for example, the Berne Convention for the Protection of Literary and Artistic Works (Berne Convention), the predominant international copyright treaty. A major decision for these newly independent countries at that time was to determine whether they should continue as Convention members in their own right or whether they should withdraw from the Convention. While India, Pakistan, the Philippines and many former French and Belgian African colonies elected to remain bound, Indonesia withdrew (Ricketson and Ginsburg, 2005: 885).

To entice newly independent states to stay in or join the international intellectual property family, members of the Berne Convention and the Paris Convention for the Protection of Industrial Property (Paris Convention) pushed for reforms within the international intellectual property regime. In the Intellectual Property Conference of Stockholm (Stockholm Conference) in 1967, members of WIPO's predecessor, the United International Bureau for the Protection of Intellectual Property (BIRPI),[4] adopted the Protocol Regarding Developing Countries (Stockholm Protocol) to the Berne Convention. This protocol, if entered into effect, would allow developing countries to make reservations to the Berne Convention in the areas of copyright duration and of reproduction, translation and broadcasting licences (Okediji, 2005: 157; Schrader, 1970). Even though this protocol remained unratified, due in large part to the strong opposition from developed countries and their publishing industries (Ricketson and Ginsburg, 2005: 899; Yu, 2009: 477–8), it paved the way for the development of the now optional Berne appendix. Since its adoption in July 1971, this appendix has been incorporated by reference into the Agreement on Trade-Related Aspects of Intellectual Property Rights (TRIPS Agreement) and the WIPO Copyright Treaty.

Apart from making adjustments to the international copyright system, the Stockholm Conference also sought 'to effectuate the structural and administrative reform of the Paris and Berne Unions as well as of the then existing five special agreements under the Paris Union' (Bogsch, 1992: 24). By revamping the BIRPI's structure, this conference helped prepare the organization's transformation into a specialized agency of the United Nations (UN). Formally established in 1970, WIPO replaced BIRPI, an organization formed as a result of the 1893 merger of the two secretariats that administered the Paris and Berne Conventions (Bogsch, 1992: 21–2). That merger 'mov[ed] control of the organization from the Swiss, who had been exclusively responsible for funding BIRPI, to a more formal governing body that included a structure where delegates from member countries would meet regularly' (Halbert, 2007: 258–9).

The idea of forming an international intellectual property organization dates back to the 1962 meeting of the Permanent Bureaux of the Paris and Berne Unions (May, 2007: 23). The reasons were two-fold. First, as Stephen Ladas (1975: 92) explained, the proposal to establish such an organization:

> was advocated as intended to head off any attempt by outsiders, such as the United Nations Economic and Social Council or the United Nations Conference on Trade and Development [UNCTAD], to deal with the subject of intellectual property and eventually to form a Specialized Agency of the United Nations in this field.

Second, such a change would 'transform [BIRPI] from a developed country club into an organisation with a multilateral character that could attract developing countries including the newly independent ones' (Musungu and Dutfield, 2003: 4). The formation of WIPO therefore would have the same effect as the Stockholm Protocol: by accommodating the needs of developing countries, it would widen the base of both the Paris and Berne Unions (Anderfelt, 1971: 260; Ryan, 1998: 126). At the time of writing this chapter, WIPO has 187 member states.

Although WIPO did not become a UN specialized agency immediately following the Stockholm Conference, 'the draft of the WIPO Convention and the drafts for the revision of the then existing seven treaties, presented by BIRPI to the Stockholm Conference, were proposed with [that] objective in mind' (Bogsch, 1992: 26). In December 1974, WIPO finally became a UN specialized agency. As Árpád Bogsch (1992: 28), the former WIPO Director General, recounted in a booklet commemorating the organization's 25th anniversary, the UN status brought to WIPO three apparent benefits:

> (i) the fact that dealing with intellectual property was the prerogative and the task of WIPO would receive worldwide recognition, (ii) WIPO would have more or less the same members as the United Nations, and in particular, many developing countries would join WIPO (only very few of them belonged to BIRPI), (iii) the governments of Member States would be liberated from having to deal with the fixing of salaries, other working conditions and pensions of the staff, since salaries and pensions would automatically follow the so-called 'common system' of the United Nations and its specialized agencies.

In short, the UN status 'would enable the internal administration of the organization to benefit from the economies of scale available inside the [United Nations]' (May, 2007: 24).

In the years following WIPO's entry into the UN system, developing countries continued to push for reform within the international patent system. Most notable were the demands for the revision of the Paris Convention in the late 1970s and early 1980s (Yu, 2009: 505–11), such as those concerning the local working requirement, remedies to the abuse of intellectual property rights, and the relationship between compulsory licences and the forfeiture or revocation of patents (Roffe and Vea, 2009: 101). These demands eventually led to the notorious stalemate between developed and developing countries over the Nairobi text of the Paris Convention, which precipitated the developed countries' push for new international intellectual property norm-setting activities outside WIPO (Sell, 1998: 123–30; Yu, 2004: 357–8). The Uruguay Round of Multilateral Trade Negotiations (Uruguay Round) was launched in Punta del Este, Uruguay in 1986. The protection and enforcement of intellectual property rights was discussed among 13 other trade or trade-related topics. The Uruguay Round negotiations eventually led to the creation of the WTO and its TRIPS Agreement.

Outside WIPO, developing countries also actively pushed for the establishment of the International Code of Conduct on the Transfer of Technology under the auspices of UNCTAD (Blakeney, 1989: 131–61; Patel et al., 2001; Yu, 2009: 497–505). The development of this Code came at a time when developing countries gained unprecedented momentum in their negotiations with developed countries following the oil crisis and OPEC's success in the early 1970s (Sell, 1998: 79). '[D]rafted on the assumption that transfer of technology to developing countries is desirable and that the transfer process will increase the prosperity of developing countries', the Code sought 'to eliminate those clauses in transfer of technology contracts which are harmful to the economic development of developing countries' as well as other restrictive foreign investment practices (Zuijdwijk, 1978: 563–4).

Although the negotiation of this Code of Conduct was eventually forestalled by the debt crises in Latin America in the late 1980s (Sell, 1998: 105; Thomas, 1999: 2108), along with the US Reagan Administration's radical change of its approach towards competition law and policy (Sell, 1998: 97–8), some of the original provisions in the draft Code did find their way into the TRIPS Agreement. As Abdulqawi Yusuf (2008: 10 fn 18) recounted, some of the provisions in the 'B' text advanced by developing countries during the TRIPS negotiations 'were either directly based on or inspired by those of the [draft Code]. Those provisions are now enshrined in Articles 7, 8, 31(k) and 40 of the TRIPS Agreement, among others' (Yu, 2009: 503–4).

In sum, the WIPO Development Agenda, while path-breaking and important, has its ill-fated predecessor in the Old Development Agenda. It also has parallels at the WTO – through the Doha Development Round of Trade Negotiations (Doha Round) – and in other international fora governing public health, human rights, biological diversity, food and agriculture, and information and communications. If the present Development Agenda is to be successful, it needs to avoid the myriad problems confronting the Old Development Agenda as well as the ill-advised tactics deployed by developing countries (Yu, 2009: 543–4). The WIPO Development Agenda can also benefit from greater collaboration with other development agendas. In view of the rapid expansion and greater complexity of the international intellectual property regime, the impact of an agenda focusing on WIPO activities alone is unlikely to be sufficient.

THE NEGOTIATION OF NON-MULTILATERAL AGREEMENTS

Since the early 2000s, the European Union and the United States have actively established bilateral, plurilateral and regional trade agreements – Free Trade Agreements (FTAs) and economic partnership agreements for the European Union and FTAs for the United States. Consider the United States, for example. This country has used these non-multilateral agreements widely to transplant US laws onto the soil of its less powerful trading partners. As the US Trade Act of 2002 explicitly stated:

> The principal negotiating objectives of the United States regarding trade-related intellectual property are … to further promote adequate and effective protection of intellectual property rights, including through … ensuring that the provisions of any multilateral or bilateral trade agreement governing intellectual property rights that is entered into by the United States reflect a standard of protection similar to that found in United States law …

From the standpoint of the United States' trading partners, however, the transplant of US intellectual property laws has been rather controversial and at times unpopular. Because these laws often provide protections in excess of the levels required by the TRIPS Agreement, and to some extent also the WIPO-administered intellectual property treaties (such as the WIPO Internet Treaties), the intellectual property provisions in US FTAs threaten to ignore the trading partners' local needs, national interests, technological capabilities, institutional capacities and public health conditions.

To illustrate the high TRIPS-plus standards found in US FTAs, consider the Australia–United States Free Trade Agreement, one of the earlier US FTAs. Adopted on 18 May 2004, this bilateral agreement includes in Chapter 17 distinct provisions on copyrights, trademarks, patents and other forms of intellectual property rights. For instance, these agreements require the contracting parties to ratify or accede to the WIPO Copyright Treaty, the WIPO Performances and Phonograms Treaty, the Patent Cooperation Treaty, the Protocol Relating to the Madrid Agreement Concerning the International Registration of Marks and the 1991 Act of the International Union for the Protection of New Varieties of Plants (UPOV), among others. They also require the parties to extend the term of copyright protection beyond the international minimum standard and to provide detailed intellectual property enforcement provisions. Article 17.4.7(a) specifically requires each party to 'provide for criminal procedures and penalties to be applied where any person is found to have engaged wilfully and for the purposes of commercial advantage or financial gain in any of the above activities'. Finally, the Agreement threatens the success and vitality of Australia's Pharmaceutical Benefits Scheme (Ho, 2011: 246–7). Article 17.9.4, in particular, bans the parallel importation of cheap generic drugs.

Although non-multilateral trade agreements are generally initiated by developed countries such as the United States or members of the European Union, large middle-income countries, such as China and India, have also been quite active in pushing for the negotiation of these agreements (Wang, 2010). Beginning in the mid-2000s, China negotiated bilateral agreements with Chile, Pakistan, New Zealand, Singapore, Peru, Costa Rica, Iceland and Switzerland (Gao, 2008; Lanteigne, 2010; Wang, 2010; Yu, 2011b). With the 10 members of the Association of Southeast Asian Nations (ASEAN),[5] China also established a set of regional agreements culminating in the formation of the ASEAN–China Free Trade Area (Wang, 2009; Yu, 2011b: 1007–9).

While these bilateral and regional agreements are quite important from the trade perspective, they do not include many intellectual property provisions. Nor do they introduce new protection and enforcement standards. The only exception is China's FTA with Switzerland, a country heavily involved in the ACTA negotiations. Even though this recently established agreement includes more detailed intellectual property provisions, most of them correspond to the protection levels already required by the TRIPS Agreement. Thus, from the standpoint of international intellectual property norm-setting, agreements negotiated by China and other middle-income countries do not have as significant an impact as those negotiated by the European Union or the United States.

Although countries were already busy negotiating bilateral and regional trade agreements, the United States and the European Union upped the ante by introducing a new form of norm-setting activity. Based on what other commentators and I have described as the 'country club' approach to international norm-setting (Gervais, 2012; Yu, 2014), these countries teamed up with like-minded countries in both the developed and developing worlds to increase obligations concerning the protection and enforcement of intellectual property rights.

A leading example is ACTA, which was negotiated by Australia, Canada, the European Union, Japan, Morocco, Mexico, New Zealand, Singapore, South Korea, Switzerland and the United States. Aiming to set a new and higher benchmark for international intellectual property enforcement, this highly controversial plurilateral agreement was finally adopted on 15 April 2011, after three years and 11 rounds of formal negotiations. Out of the 11 negotiating parties, all but Switzerland and five members of the European Union (Cyprus, Estonia, Germany, the Netherlands and Slovakia) have since signed the Agreement. Because Article 40.1 states that ACTA will not enter into force until six parties have deposited their instruments of ratification, it remains unclear if and when this Agreement will enter into force. Thus far, Japan is the only country to have ratified ACTA.

Another good example is the TPP, an equally controversial agreement that is still under negotiation at the time of this writing. The TPP began as a quadrilateral agreement known as the Trans-Pacific Strategic Economic Partnership Agreement, or more commonly as the 'P4' or 'Pacific 4'. As Meredith Lewis (2009: 403–4) recounted:

> [The negotiations were initially] launched by Chile, New Zealand and Singapore at the APEC leaders' summit in 2002. These original negotiations contemplated an agreement amongst the three participating countries, to be known as the Pacific Three Closer Economic Partnership ... However, Brunei attended a number of rounds as an observer, and ultimately joined the Agreement as a 'founding member'. The Agreement was signed by New Zealand, Chile and Singapore on July 18, 2005 and by Brunei on August 2, 2005, following the conclusion of negotiations in June 2005.

In March 2010, shortly before the eighth round of the ACTA negotiations in Wellington, New Zealand, negotiations began among Australia, Peru, Vietnam, the United States and the existing TPP members for an expanded agreement. Since then, Malaysia, Mexico, Canada and Japan have joined the negotiations.

The TPP is anticipated to include an intellectual property chapter, similar to those intellectual property chapters found in existing US FTAs. As the Office of the US Trade Representative (2011) stated in its update on the TPP negotiations in November 2011:

> TPP countries have agreed to reinforce and develop existing [TRIPS] rights and obligations to ensure an effective and balanced approach to intellectual property rights among the TPP countries. Proposals are under discussion on many forms of intellectual property, including trademarks, geographical indications, copyright and related rights, patents, trade secrets, data required for the approval of certain regulated products, as well as intellectual property enforcement and genetic resources and traditional knowledge. TPP countries have agreed to reflect in the text a shared commitment to the Doha Declaration on TRIPS and Public Health.

As of this writing, the draft text of the TPP intellectual property chapter has yet to be disclosed except through WikiLeaks (Love, 2013).

While the TPP Agreement is to be more inclusive from the standpoint of developing countries, and is likely to include more provisions that could benefit these countries, it could also be quite dangerous from the standpoint of protecting due process, free speech and other civil liberties. Such danger is especially apparent considering the United States' dominance in the intellectual property field and its substantial political and economic leverage over its negotiating partners. For example, the United States could demand greater concessions in the intellectual property area in exchange for concessions in other trade or trade-related areas – such as dairy concessions to New Zealand and textile concessions to Vietnam and Malaysia (Elms, 2013: 386–9).

As if these plurilateral negotiations were not complicated enough, the United States has recently begun negotiating the Transatlantic Trade and Investment Partnership (TTIP) Agreement with the European Union. Similar to the TPP and other bilateral and regional trade agreements, this new agreement is likely to include provisions concerning the protection and enforcement of intellectual property rights. Indeed, it will be no surprise if these provisions raise the standards even higher than those found in ACTA or the TPP. Although the latter agreements have struck some compromises to address the needs and interests of the developing country negotiating parties, an agreement involving the world's two largest and most developed trading powers is unlikely to require similar compromises.

Interestingly and importantly, the European Union and the United States are not the only major trading powers exploring the use of plurilateral agreements, or this new 'country club' approach. Just as the United States was pushing hard on ACTA, the TPP and the TTIP, China and its Asian neighbours began exploring the development of a new trade-based framework known as the Regional Comprehensive Economic Partnership (RCEP). Building on past trade and non-trade discussions under the framework of ASEAN Plus Six (Australia, China, India, Japan, New Zealand and South Korea), this partnership will cover not only the two most economically powerful BRICS countries (China and India), but also two major Asian economies (Japan and South Korea) as well as seven of the TPP negotiating parties (Australia, Brunei Darussalam, Japan, Malaysia, New Zealand, Singapore and Vietnam).

Taken together, ACTA, the TPP, the TTIP and the RCEP have ushered in a new non-multilateral era. Because such an era could greatly undermine the present and future development of the multilateral intellectual property regime, one could suggest that this era will create an unprecedented danger. Nevertheless, bilateral and regional agreements are not new. There were strong historical precedents concerning the use of these agreements before their final consolidation into a multilateral arrangement. As Bryan Mercurio (2007: 217) reminded us:

> By the mid-1800s ... trading nations had created a complex web of agreements in which [most-favoured-nation treatment and national treatment] applied bilaterally. When the 'spaghetti bowl' agreements became unmanageable, practitioners and government[s] realized the rights needed to be formally adopted in an international framework. Such efforts built upon the bilateralism by filling gaps and providing coherence to [intellectual property rights]. This process culminated in the Paris Convention ... and the Berne Convention.[6]

Indeed, before these two cornerstone conventions were established, European countries already began negotiating bilateral treaties to protect the interests of their authors and inventors on foreign soils. Consider, for example, the reciprocity-based protection authors obtained abroad in the 19th century. After the legislature of the Germanic Confederation failed to enact a federal copyright law, Prussia entered into 32 bilateral copyright agreements with other German States from 1827 to 1829 (Ladas, 1938: 44; Ricketson, 1986: 14–15). In 1840, Austria and Sardinia became the first autonomous states to enter into a bilateral copyright agreement (Ladas, 1938: 44). Predominant powers like France and Great Britain followed shortly after (Ladas, 1938: 44–5, 49; Yu, 2003: 346). As Sam Ricketson (1986: 15) recounted:

> By 1886 [the year when the Berne Convention was established], there was an intricate network of bilateral copyright conventions in force between the majority of European states, as well as with several Latin American countries. Of these, France was party to the most agreements (13), followed closely by Belgium (9), Italy and Spain (8 each), the United Kingdom (5) and Germany (5).

While bilateralism was the preferred approach to manage state-to-state intellectual property relationships before the adoption of the Paris and Berne Conventions, it has remained a key strategy used by the US government to promote trade relationships with other countries. In an article examining the development of bilateral trade and investment agreements established by the United States since the turn of the millennium, Ruth Okediji traced the recent bilateral agreements back to those bilateral agreements the country had signed since its founding period. As she explained:

> The so-called new bilateralism is actually more consistent with historical uses of the foreign relations/treaty power of the United States, as well as the general framework of international law, in its dealings with developing countries since the independence era. Consequently, it is probably the TRIPS Agreement that is the aberration in international intellectual property law, and not the recent spates of bilateral and regional agreements. (Okediji, 2004: 130)

Based on Professor Okediji's insightful observation, the TRIPS Agreement should therefore not be considered as the endpoint in the international intellectual property regime (Deere, 2009: 304; Sell, 2003: 121; Yu, 2011c: 523). Nor will the establishment of such plurilateral agreements as ACTA, the TPP, the TTIP or the RCEP be drastic deviations from the traditional path of regime development. Instead, all of these agreements merely reflect the ups and downs of such development.

Given the similarities between the 'new' bilateralisms, plurilateralisms and regionalisms we have today and the 'old' bilateralisms and regionalisms in both Europe and the United States, it is not too far-fetched to suggest that the developments in the international intellectual property regime tend to swing back and forth between non-multilateralism and multilateralism. Notwithstanding this useful observation, it remains unclear whether these developments swing back and forth at the same pace or whether the swings come with pauses and accelerations. As I surmised in an earlier article:

> [I]f ACTA represents the future of international norm-setting, non-multilateralism will not be the passing phase many policymakers and commentators expect – a short, inevitable transitional period before the development of a new multilateral arrangement, such as TRIPS II. Instead, the world will likely go through a long period of non-multilateralism, thereby generating interesting political dynamics that commentators have not yet studied in depth. (Yu, 2011a: 10)

Put differently, what will happen if we are stuck in a long era of non-multilateralism in the near future? That question cannot be answered in greater depth unless we know more about the complex causes behind the old bilateral and regional efforts that eventually consolidated into multilateralism. A deeper understanding and appreciation of past efforts will therefore enable us to better anticipate the future development of the international intellectual property regime.

THE REJUVENATION OF MULTILATERAL NORM-SETTING ACTIVITIES

As noted at the beginning, WIPO adopted the Beijing and Marrakesh Treaties in June 2012 and June 2013, respectively. Although WIPO has not had much success in adopting new substantive international intellectual property agreements since the mid-1990s, it managed to adopt two new substantive treaties in only a little more than a year. In view of these developments, one naturally would ask whether the recent rejuvenation of multilateral norm-setting activities at WIPO indicates a return to multilateralism on the part of both developed and developing countries. Such a return would bode well for not only WIPO, but also the WTO and other international intergovernmental organizations.

For more than a decade now, WTO members have been negotiating in the Doha Round. While this round features important developments in the intellectual property field, including the adoption of the Declaration on the TRIPS Agreement and Public Health and the protocol to amend the TRIPS Agreement by adding Article 31*bis*, the round itself has not been very successful (Abbott, 2005; Abbott and Reichman, 2007; Yu, 2007). Despite four deadline extensions, the amendment, which would allow countries with insufficient or no manufacturing capacity to import generic versions of patented pharmaceuticals, has still not been ratified by more than two-thirds of the WTO membership.

Thus, if developed and large developing countries have indeed chosen to return their focus to multilateral norm-setting, it is logical to look for some major breakthroughs in the negotiations. One potentially qualifying development is the recent adoption of the Bali Package in the Ninth WTO Ministerial Conference in Indonesia, which included the completion of the negotiations on the new Agreement on Trade Facilitation. These negotiations date back to as early as the First WTO Ministerial Conference in Singapore in December 1996.

Although the developments in the Bali Ministerial were quite promising, it is too early to tell whether countries have now re-embraced multilateralism as a primary means to set international intellectual property norms. The rapid developments on the bilateral and plurilateral fronts, including the negotiation of ACTA, the TPP, the TTIP, and the RCEP, seem to suggest that the international intellectual property regime has become much more complex today than in the past. While the recent developments strongly indicate that countries have not abandoned the multilateral norm-setting process, the ongoing developments seem to suggest that multilateralism and non-multilateralism will continue at the same time – and perhaps even at the same pace.

To properly analyse the recent intellectual property developments, it is important to remember that WIPO has always been successful in rejuvenating itself when threatened with marginalization in the international community. A case in point is its success in shaping the development of the international copyright system. When newly independent countries emerged from Africa, Asia and South America in the 1950s and 1960s, they were actively deciding whether they should join the Berne Convention, accede to the Universal Copyright Convention (UCC) or establish their own separate union (Ringer, 1968: 1075).

Developed under the auspices of the United Nations Educational, Scientific and Cultural Organization (UNESCO), the UCC was attractive because it provided an alternative forum for those countries that 'wished to obtain protection for their works abroad but felt unable or unwilling to accord to foreign works the high level of protection required by the Berne Convention' (Ricketson and Ginsburg, 2005: 886). Under the UCC, member states were allowed to grant compulsory licenses for translation purposes and to retain formalities in their copyright systems. The UCC also counted the United States among its members. That country did not join the Berne Union until 1989.

As Barbara Ringer (1968: 1066), the former US Register of Copyrights, recalled, '[t]here was obviously a fear that … Berne would become a moribund old gentlemen's club'. This fear was justified. By the time the Stockholm Conference was held in 1967, the UCC already attracted 26 developing country members, with its total membership lagging behind the Berne Convention by only two (Ricketson and Ginsburg, 2005: 886). While 'the former French African colonies and some of the former British Asian Dominions had preferred Berne … the UCC had attracted the Central and South American countries and a number of former British dependent territories' (Ricketson and Ginsburg, 2005: 886).

Nevertheless, BIRPI, and later WIPO, was able to make itself relevant to these newly independent countries and their neighbours in the developing world. In addition to becoming a UN specialized agency and making adjustments to the international copyright system through the introduction of the Stockholm Protocol (and later the Berne appendix), WIPO collaborated with UNESCO to develop the Tunis Model Law on Copyright for Developing Countries. Devoting a special section to works of national folklore, this model law paved the way for future negotiations on the protection of folklore, or what is now termed 'traditional cultural expressions'. WIPO also 'agree[d] to be listed as co-author on the 1974 UNCTAD report *The Role of the*

Patent System in the Transfer of Technology to Developing Countries, despite the report's thrust being widely divergent from the WIPO's position on the role of patents in technological transfer' (May, 2007: 24).

Fast forward 22 years to the time when WIPO was once again confronted with a major dilemma about its relevance shortly after the adoption of the Marrakesh Agreement Establishing the World Trade Organization in April 1994. Included in this foundational instrument was an annex known as the TRIPS Agreement. Entered into force on 1 January 1995, this agreement not only incorporates the Paris and Berne Conventions, but has also added new norms concerning the protection and enforcement of intellectual property rights. While the provisions on trade secrets and undisclosed information have not appeared in any multilateral intellectual property agreement before (Watal, 2001: 4), the 21 provisions in Part III of the TRIPS Agreement provided for the first time comprehensive intellectual property enforcement norms in a multilateral agreement.

Shortly after intellectual property negotiations moved from WIPO to the WTO, commentators began wondering whether such a 'forum shift' would upset the existing arrangement. As Keith Maskus (2009: 164) colourfully noted, 'WIPO has been hit by a train since TRIPS was concluded'. Nevertheless, WIPO was again able to protect itself from becoming marginalized. To begin with, WIPO made strategic decisions to retain an active role in the new TRIPS-based framework (Musungu and Dutfield, 2003: 11). For example, it was heavily involved in the WTO negotiation process and has since remained an important part of the WTO regime. As Laurence Helfer (2004: 24–5) rightly noted, 'TRIPS itself implicitly acknowledges the continuing importance of WIPO as a forum for negotiating treaties, particularly those embodying "higher levels of protection of intellectual property rights"'. Article 68 of the TRIPS Agreement expressly states that the Council for Trade-Related Aspects of Intellectual Property Rights 'may consult with and seek information from any source it deems appropriate' in carrying out its functions and 'shall seek to establish, within one year of its first meeting, appropriate arrangements for cooperation with [WIPO] bodies'. The consultation required by this provision eventually led to the Agreement Between the World Intellectual Property Organization and the World Trade Organization, which called for cooperation between the WTO and WIPO in the notification of, provision of access to, and translation of national legislation; the communication of national emblems and transmittal of objections pursuant to Article 6*ter* of the Paris Convention; and legal-technical assistance and technical cooperation.

In addition, WIPO was quick to take on leadership in both traditional and new intellectual property matters, including the development of the WIPO Internet Domain Name Process, soft law recommendations on the protection of well-known and Internet-based marks,[7] the WIPO Worldwide Academy and the WIPO Arbitration and Mediation Centre. In September 2000, WIPO established the Intergovernmental Committee on Intellectual Property and Genetic Resources, Traditional Knowledge and Folklore (IGC), which aims to provide 'a forum for international policy debate and development of legal mechanisms and practical tools' (World Intellectual Property Organization, n.d.). Although discussions in the IGC have yet to result in the establishment of new multilateral instruments, the ongoing discussions have undeniably enabled WIPO to draw on its technical expertise and institutional competence to shape a set of issues that are highly important to the developing world. Most recently, the IGC made plans to submit the draft texts of three separate instruments—on genetic resources, traditional knowledge and traditional cultural expressions—for consideration by the WIPO General Assembly (Saez, 2014).

In sum, when WIPO fears that norm-setting activities outside its forum – whether at the multilateral or non-multilateral level – would marginalize the organization, it has always managed to reassert itself. Whether it was in the late 1960s, the early 1970s or the mid-1990s, WIPO has successfully re-injected itself into the forefront of the international intellectual property debate. As Christopher May (2007: 66) observed, since the creation of the TRIPS Agreement, WIPO seems to have undertaken 'a sustained campaign ... to return the organization to the center of global intellectual property policy making'. Likewise, Graeme Dinwoodie (2002: 1005) wrote:

> [T]he sudden emergence of the WTO as part of the international intellectual property lawmaking process seemed to energize WIPO, resulting in the conclusion of several new treaties in copyright, patent and trademark law, as well as the reorganization ... designed to make WIPO fit for the twenty-first century.

Today, international intellectual property norm-setting is still conducted in a largely bimodal regime, with roles divided between WIPO and the WTO and with occasional but growing influences from other related international regimes. Viewed in the light of WIPO's past successes in reinventing itself, the Beijing and Marrakesh Treaties may not necessarily reflect countries' eagerness to return to multilateral norm-setting activities. Instead, it may just be a reminder of WIPO's strong ability to persevere in a rapidly changing international norm-setting environment.

A SIMPLE BUT VALUABLE HISTORICAL LESSON

Based on the three sets of recurring developments discussed in this chapter, one could draw a simple but valuable historical lesson informing both the ongoing and future debates about international norm-setting: international intellectual property developments are influenced by the repeated swings of an invisible pendulum.[8] As I noted in an earlier article, there are both currents and crosscurrents in the international intellectual property regime: 'While the currents of multilateralism push for uniformity and increased harmonization, the crosscurrents of resistance ... protect national autonomy and international diversity' (Yu, 2004: 328).

The idea of having recurrence and repetition in history is nothing new. This idea can be traced back several millennia to ancient history and philosophy. For instance, the *Book of Changes*, an ancient book of divination and Chinese wisdom that dates back to at least the Warring States period (475–221 BC), provided some of the most profound lessons on the inevitability of change and 'how to live one's life in a changing and confusing world' (Balkin, 2002: 3). As Jack Balkin (2002: 197) succinctly observed:

> 'The basic lesson of the *Book of Changes* is that everything changes. Good times turn to bad, and bad times eventually improve. Even during the most peaceful and prosperous conditions, difficulties, decay, and evil are merely held in check and are never completely eliminated'.

Although lessons about change have been around for as long as recorded history, the lesson concerning our proverbial pendulum still provides three key insights into the current and future development of the international intellectual property regime. The first insight concerns the caution needed to identify *new* developments. To be certain, new and transformative developments exist in the international intellectual property regime. Examples immediately coming to mind are the marriage of intellectual property with trade through the TRIPS Agreement and the emergence of non-state interactions brought about by the Internet and new communications technologies (Yu, 2004: 400–6). Nevertheless, many of the existing developments are not entirely new, and they can hardly be described as 'paradigm shifts' within the international intellectual property regime.

Indeed, apart from the three sets of recurring developments examined in this chapter, one could find strong historical parallels between the ACTA negotiations and the push for an anti-counterfeiting code towards the end of the Tokyo Round of Multilateral Trade Negotiations (Yu, 2011c: 513), between the 'common heritage of humankind' concept advanced in the late 1960s and today's free software, open source, free culture and access to knowledge movements (Yu, 2009: 541–2), and between the early transplants of intellectual property laws during the colonial era and the much more recent transplants through the TRIPS Agreement and TRIPS-plus trade, investment and intellectual property agreements (Okediji, 2003: 325–34; Yu, 2006: 373–5).

In his latest book, *Piracy*, Adrian Johns (2009: 498) even recounted the repeated and 'profound shift[s] in the relation between creativity and commerce'. As he warned us about the potential transformation brought about by the Internet and new communications technologies:

> Such turning points have happened before – about once every century, in fact, since the end of the Middle Ages. The last major one occurred at the height of the industrial age, and catalyzed the invention of intellectual property. Before that, another took place in the Enlightenment, when it led to the emergence of the first modern copyright system and the first modern patents regime. And before that, there was the creation of piracy in the 1660s–1680s. By extrapolation, we are already overdue to experience another revolution of the same magnitude. If it does happen in the near future, it may well bring down the curtain on what will then, in retrospect, come to be seen as a coherent epoch of about 150 years: the era of intellectual property. (Johns, 2009: 508)

Whether the Internet and new communications technologies will spell the end of 'the era of intellectual property' or precipitate transformative change in the international intellectual property regime remains to be seen.

The second insight concerns the need to understand intellectual property reform as part of an iterative process, as opposed to a one-off battle between the major players in the international intellectual property regime. What comes as a victory in an early reform battle could easily be eclipsed by losses in later battles. Thus, whether reforms will succeed will ultimately depend on whether the relevant constituencies could sustainably mobilize to protect their gains while challenging the undesirable status quo (Sell, 2004: 319–21; Yu, 2011c: 523). As Susan Sell (2004: 321) reminded us: 'Each new round of contestation and settlement [in the evolution of intellectual property policy] produces new winners and losers. History has shown that depending on how well mobilized and badly threatened the losers are, they can rise up to challenge the settlement'.

Going hand in hand with this key insight are two important but seemingly paradoxical messages. The encouraging message is that countries and their supporters should not be too frustrated even if the international intellectual property regime is not developing in their preferred directions. No matter how unfavourable their current positions are, desirable outcomes will never be out of reach. If these countries and their supporters continue to mobilize, they will eventually achieve greater success down the road. The key to success is not whether the early battles have been won, but whether they can continue to fight strategically towards greater, and at times incremental, gains.

As encouraging as this message is, there is, unfortunately, a discouraging corollary message: no matter how much effort countries and their supporters put in, they should not be complacent over the gains they obtained in reform battles. After all, initial victories do not guarantee future success. In a world where reforms take place in an iterative process, countries and their supporters will need to continue to engage opponents strategically to protect gains and advance positions. After all, few, if any, of their victories will be decisive in the long run.

The final insight concerns the immense benefits historical perspectives provide to enriching our study of the current and future development of the international intellectual property regime. For example, an in-depth study of the failure of the Old Development Agenda could guide us to make the adjustments needed to ensure the success of the New Development Agenda. Similarly, because a considerable volume of bilateral and regional norm-setting activities has already taken place in the past, studying why some of these activities have led to consolidation while others have not could be quite beneficial. A further exploration of the historical roles played by international intergovernmental and nongovernmental organizations could also be highly instructive.

Close to a century ago, US Supreme Court Justice Oliver Wendell Holmes declared, 'a page of history is worth a volume of logic' (*New York Trust Co v Eisner* (1921) 256 US 345, 349). History, however, does not end on a single page. It comes back to haunt us in hundreds of volumes. More importantly for our purposes, history loves to repeat itself. It is not 'just one fucking thing after another', as playwright Alan Bennett (2004: 85) memorably put it in *The History Boys*. Instead, it has a penchant for reinforcing the logic to which Justice Holmes alluded. In the timeless words of George Santayana (1932: 232), 'Those who cannot remember the past are condemned to repeat it'.

CONCLUSION

This chapter draws on three sets of recurring developments to illustrate how the repeated swings of an invisible pendulum have influenced both multilateral and non-multilateral international intellectual property developments. Although we will never be able to see this pendulum in action, or pinpoint its exact movement, history has shown that the pendulum will continue to swing back and forth, making international intellectual property developments intriguing. Thus, the more we study and appreciate the recurrence of these developments, the more deeply we will understand the international intellectual property regime, and the less surprised and disconcerted we will be, even if we feel like it is déjà vu all over again.

ACKNOWLEDGEMENTS

This chapter draws on research from the author's earlier articles in the *Drake Law Review Discourse*, the *Loyola of Los Angeles Law Review*, the *Ohio Northern University Law Review* and *The WIPO Journal*. The author is grateful to Timothy Alberts for excellent research and editorial assistance.

NOTES

1 The 'déjà vu' theme has also been explored in a prior work of one of the editors of this handbook (Halbert, 2007: 271).
2 The Group included Argentina, Bolivia, Brazil, Cuba, the Dominican Republic, Ecuador, Egypt, Iran, Kenya, Peru, Sierra Leone, South Africa, Tanzania and Venezuela.
3 The New International Economic Order sought to bring about fundamental changes in the international economic system by redistributing power, wealth and resources from the developed North to the less developed South. According to Antony Anghie (2005: 313), this Order 'constituted the most important international law initiative taken by the developing world in attempting to remedy colonial inequities'.
4 BIRPI stands for 'Bureaux Internationaux Réunis pour la Protection de la Propriété Intellectuelle' in French.
5 The 10 ASEAN members are Brunei Darussalam, Cambodia, Indonesia, Laos, Malaysia, Myanmar, the Philippines, Singapore, Thailand and Vietnam.
6 Jagdish Bhagwati (1995: 2–3) coined the term 'spaghetti bowl', which refers to 'a mish-mash of overlapping, supporting, and possibly conflicting, obligations' (Lester and Mercurio, 2009: 2).
7 These recommendations include the Joint Recommendation Concerning Provisions on the Protection of Well-Known Marks (1999) and the Joint Recommendation Concerning Provisions on the Protection of Marks, and Other Industrial Property Rights in Signs, on the Internet (2001).
8 The pendulum metaphor has also been used by other commentators (e.g. Okediji, 2004).

REFERENCES

Abbott, Frederick M. (2005) 'The WTO medicines decision: World pharmaceutical trade and the protection of public health', *American Journal of International Law*, 99(2): 317–58.

Abbott, Frederick M. and Reichman, Jerome H. (2007) 'The Doha Round's public health legacy: Strategies for the production and diffusion of patented medicines under the amended TRIPS provisions', *Journal of International Economic Law*, 10(4): 921–87.

Abi-Saab, Georges M. (1962) 'The newly independent states and the rules of international law', *Howard Law Journal*, 8(2): 95–121.

Anderfelt, Ulf (1971) *International Patent-Legislation and Developing Countries*. The Hague: Martinus Nijhoff.

Anghie, Antony (2005) *Imperialism, Sovereignty and the Making of International Law*. Cambridge: Cambridge University Press.

Balkin, Jack M. (2002) *The Laws of Change: I Ching and the Philosophy of Life*. New York: Schocken Books.

Bennett, Alan (2004) *The History Boys*. New York: Faber and Faber.

Bhagwati, Jagdish (1995) 'U.S. trade policy: The infatuation with free trade areas', in Jagdish Bhagwati and Anne O. Krueger, *The Dangerous Drift to Preferential Trade Agreements*. Washington, DC: AEI Press, pp. 1–18.

Blakeney, Michael (1989) *Legal Aspects of the Transfer of Technology to Developing Countries*. Oxford: ESC Publishing.

Bogsch, Árpád (1992) *Brief History of the First 25 Years of the World Intellectual Property Organization*. Geneva: World Intellectual Property Organization.

Deere, Carolyn (2009) *The Implementation Game: The TRIPS Agreement and the Global Politics of Intellectual Property Reform in Developing Countries*. Oxford: Oxford University Press.

Dinwoodie, Graeme B. (2002) 'The architecture of the international intellectual property system', *Chicago-Kent Law Review*, 77(3): 993–1014.

Elms, Deborah Kay (2013) 'The Trans-Pacific Partnership trade negotiations: Some outstanding issues for the final stretch', *Asian Journal of the WTO and International Health Law and Policy*, 8(2): 379–99.

Gao, Henry (2008) 'The RTA strategy of China: A critical visit', in Ross Buckley, Vai Io Lo and Laurence Boulle (eds), *Challenges to Multilateral Trade: The Impact of Bilateral, Preferential and Regional Agreements*. Alphen aan den Rijn: Kluwer Law International, pp. 53–64.

Gervais, Daniel (2012) 'Country clubs, empiricism, blogs and innovation: The future of international intellectual property norm making in the wake of ACTA', in Mira Burri and Thomas Cottier (eds), *Trade Governance in the Digital Age*. Cambridge: Cambridge University Press, pp. 323–43.

Halbert, Debora J. (2007) 'The World Intellectual Property Organization: Past, present and future', *Journal of the Copyright Society of the U.S.A.*, 54(2–3): 253–84.

Helfer, Laurence R. (2004) 'Regime shifting: The TRIPS Agreement and new dynamics of international intellectual property lawmaking', *Yale Journal of International Law*, 29(1): 1–83.

Ho, Cynthia M. (2011) *Access to Medicine in the Global Economy: International Agreements on Patents and Related Rights*. Oxford: Oxford University Press.

Johns, Adrian (2009) *Piracy: The Intellectual Property Wars from Gutenberg to Gates*. Chicago: University of Chicago Press.

Johnson, Charles F. (1970) 'The origins of the Stockholm Protocol', *Bulletin of the Copyright Society of the U.S.A.*, 18(2): 91–181.

Ladas, Stephen P. (1938) *The International Protection of Literary and Artistic Property*. New York: Macmillan.

Ladas, Stephen P. (1975) *Patents, Trademarks, and Related Rights: National and International Protection*. Cambridge, MA: Harvard University Press.

Lanteigne, Marc (2010) 'Northern exposure: Cross-regionalism and the China-Iceland preferential trade negotiations', *China Quarterly*, 202: 362–80.

Lester, Simon and Mercurio, Bryan (2009) 'Introduction', in Simon Lester and Bryan Mercurio (eds), *Bilateral and Regional Trade Agreements: Case Studies*. Cambridge: Cambridge University Press, pp. 1–5.

Lewis, Meredith Kolsky (2009) 'Expanding the P-4 Trade Agreement into a broader Trans-Pacific Partnership: Implications, risks and opportunities', *Asian Journal of the WTO and International Health Law and Policy*, 4(2): 401–22.

Love, James (2013) 'KEI analysis of Wikileaks leak of TPP IPR text, from August 30, 2013'. Available at: http://www.keionline.org/node/1825

Maskus, Keith E. (2009) 'The WIPO Development Agenda: A cautionary note', in Neil Weinstock Netanel (ed.), *The Development Agenda: Global Intellectual Property and Developing Countries*. Oxford: Oxford University Press, pp. 163–74.

May, Christopher (2007) *The World Intellectual Property Organization: Resurgence and the Development Agenda*. London: Routledge.

Menescal, Andréa Koury (2005) 'Changing WIPO's ways? The 2004 Development Agenda in historical perspective', *Journal of World Intellectual Property*, 8(6): 761–96.

Mercurio, Bryan (2007) 'TRIPS-plus provisions in FTAs: Recent trends', in Lorand Bartels and Federico Ortino (eds), *Regional Trade Agreements and the WTO Legal System*. Oxford: Oxford University Press, pp. 215–37.

Musungu, Sisule F. (2005) *Rethinking Innovation, Development and Intellectual Property in the UN: WIPO and Beyond*. Geneva: Quaker United Nations Office.

Musungu, Sisule F. and Dutfield, Graham (2003) *Multilateral Agreements and a TRIPS-plus World: The World Intellectual Property Organisation (WIPO)*. Geneva: Quaker United Nations Office.

Netanel, Neil Weinstock (2009) 'Introduction: The WIPO Development Agenda and its development policy context', in Neil Weinstock Netanel (ed.), *The Development Agenda: Global Intellectual Property and Developing Countries*. Oxford: Oxford University Press, pp. 1–29.

Office of the US Trade Representative (2011) 'Outlines of the Trans-Pacific Partnership Agreement'. Available at: http://www.ustr.gov/about-us/press-office/fact-sheets/2011/november/outlines-trans-pacific-partnership-agreement

Okediji, Ruth L. (2003) 'The international relations of intellectual property: Narratives of developing country participation in the global intellectual property system', *Singapore Journal of International and Comparative Law*, 7(2): 315–85.

Okediji, Ruth L. (2004) 'Back to bilateralism? Pendulum swings in international intellectual property protection', *University of Ottawa Law and Technology Journal*, 1(1–2): 125–47.

Okediji, Ruth L. (2005) 'Sustainable access to copyrighted digital information works in developing countries', in Keith E. Maskus and Jerome H. Reichman (eds), *International Public Goods and Transfer of Technology under a Globalized Intellectual Property Regime*. Cambridge: Cambridge University Press, pp. 142–87.

Patel, Surendra J., Roffe, Pedro and Yusuf, Abdulqawi (eds) (2001) *International Technology Transfer: The Origins and Aftermath of the United Nations Negotiations on a Draft Code of Conduct*. The Hague: Kluwer Law International.

Ricketson, Sam (1986) 'The birth of the Berne Union', *Columbia-VLA Journal of Law & Arts*, 11(1): 9–32.

Ricketson, Sam and Ginsburg, Jane C. (2005) *International Copyright and Neighbouring Rights: The Berne Convention and Beyond*, 2nd edn. Oxford: Oxford University Press.

Ringer, Barbara A. (1968) 'The role of the United States in international copyright – past, present, and future', *Georgetown Law Journal*, 56(6): 1050–79.

Roffe, Pedro and Vea, Gina (2009) 'The WIPO Development Agenda in an historical and political context', in Neil Weinstock Netanel (ed.), *The Development Agenda: Global Intellectual Property and Developing Countries*. Oxford: Oxford University Press, pp. 79–109.

Ryan, Michael P. (1998) *Knowledge Diplomacy: Global Competition and the Politics of Intellectual Property*. Washington, DC: Brookings Institution Press.

Saez, Catherine (2010) 'ACTA a sign of weakness in multilateral system, WIPO head says', *Intellectual Property Watch*, 30 June 2010. Available at: http://www.ip-watch.org/2010/06/30/acta-a-sign-of-weakness-in-multilateral-system-wipo-head-says/

Saez, Catherine (2014) 'Protection of folklore joins TK, GR on way to WIPO General Assembly', *Intellectual Property Watch*, 7 April 2014. Available at: http://www.ip-watch.org/2014/04/07/protection-of-folklore-joins-tk-gr-on-way-to-wipo-general-assembly/

Santayana, George (1932) *The Life of Reason: Or the Phases of Human Progress*. New York: C. Scribner's Sons.

Schrader, Dorothy M. (1970) 'Analysis of the Protocol Regarding Developing Countries', *Bulletin of the Copyright Society of the U.S.A.*, 17(3): 160–233.

Sell, Susan K. (1998) *Power and Ideas: North-South Politics of Intellectual Property and Antitrust*. Albany: State University of New York Press.

Sell, Susan K. (2003) *Private Power, Public Law: The Globalization of Intellectual Property Rights*. Cambridge: Cambridge University Press.

Sell, Susan (2004) 'Intellectual property and public policy in historical perspective: Contestation and settlement', *Loyola of Los Angeles Law Review*, 38(1): 267–321.

Thomas, Chantal (1999) 'Transfer of technology in the contemporary international order', *Fordham International Law Journal*, 22(5): 2096–111.

Wang, Jiangyu (2009) 'Association of Southeast Asian Nations–China Free Trade Agreement', in Simon Lester and Bryan Mercurio (eds), *Bilateral and Regional Trade Agreements: Case Studies*. Cambridge: Cambridge University Press, pp. 192–225.

Wang, Jiangyu (2010) 'The role of China and India in Asian regionalism', in Muthucumaraswamy Sornarajah and Wang Jiangyu (eds), *China, India and the International Economic Order*. Cambridge: Cambridge University Press, pp. 333–86.

Watal, Jayashree (2001) *Intellectual Property Rights in the WTO and Developing Countries*. The Hague: Kluwer Law International.

World Intellectual Property Organization (2004) Proposal by Argentina and Brazil for the Establishment of a Development Agenda for WIPO. WO/GA/31/11.

World Intellectual Property Organization (2013) 'Historic treaty adopted, boosts access to books for visually impaired persons worldwide'. Available at: http://www.wipo.int/pressroom/en/articles/2013/article_0017.html

World Intellectual Property Organization (n.d.) *WIPO Handbook on Industrial Property Information and Documentation*. Available at: http://www.wipo.int/standards/en/part_02.html

Yu, Peter K. (2003) 'The copyright divide', *Cardozo Law Review*, 25(1): 331–445.

Yu, Peter K. (2004) 'Currents and crosscurrents in the international intellectual property regime', *Loyola of Los Angeles Law Review*, 38(1): 323–443.

Yu, Peter K. (2006) 'TRIPS and its discontents', *Marquette Intellectual Property Law Review*, 10(2): 369–410.

Yu, Peter K. (2007) 'The international enclosure movement', *Indiana Law Journal*, 82(4): 827–907.

Yu, Peter K. (2009) 'A tale of two Development Agendas', *Ohio Northern University Law Review*, 35(2): 465–573.

Yu, Peter K. (2011a) 'ACTA and its complex politics', *WIPO Journal*, 3(1): 1–16.

Yu, Peter K. (2011b) 'Sinic trade agreements', *U.C. Davis Law Review*, 44(3): 953–1028.

Yu, Peter K. (2011c) 'TRIPS and its Achilles' heel', *Journal of Intellectual Property Law*, 18(2): 479–531.

Yu, Peter K. (2014) 'The ACTA/TPP country clubs', in Dana Beldiman (ed.), *Access to Information and Knowledge: 21st Century Challenges in Intellectual Property and Knowledge Governance*. Cheltenham: Edward Elgar Publishing, pp. 258–83.

Yusuf, Abdulqawi A. (2008) 'TRIPS: Background, principles and general provisions', in Carlos M. Correa and Abdulqawi A. Yusuf (eds), *Intellectual Property and International Trade: The TRIPS Agreement*, 2nd edn. Alphen aan den Rijn: Kluwer Law International, pp. 3–21.

Zuijdwijk, Ton J.M. (1978) 'The UNCTAD Code of Conduct on the Transfer of Technology', *McGill Law Journal*, 24(4): 562–87.

7

Intellectual Property in Chile: Problems and Conflicts in a Developing Society

Salvador Millaleo and Hugo Cadenas

INTRODUCTION

We live in a society mediated by technology. Technology allows us to participate in various social processes and our world becomes reduced when we have no access to its benefits. For this reason, voices calling for greater inclusion in the technological means possessed within current society are felt with increasing force. A new inequality has arisen, one that differentiates between those who have access to technological resources and those without access. The problem is not only the materiality of the technology, but the way in which technology allows us access to society. Those without access are excluded from participating in countless social situations that may affect them directly.

Along with concern about inclusion in an interconnected world, problems associated with intellectual property (IP) appear with new energy. The emphasis on new technological means not only broadens the horizons of knowledge, but also produces challenges to the fundamentals that governed IP rights for the past two centuries. In this new technologically mediated world, a set of IP-related phenomena appear that do not seem to obey any single principle and whose complexity makes it hard to cover all their breadth in a single chapter.

Conflicts between the use of new information technology and the law of IP are especially acute in regions of the world faced with disparate development within their social structures. In these cases, the interaction between IP and technologies of information have primarily been assessed using a normative scheme that makes an argument for either the obedience to or deviation from the norms that support IP rights. From this perspective, only the oscillation between normative compliance or noncompliance and its consequences are understood as relevant. Nevertheless, this vision ignores not only regional specificities of this compliance/noncompliance, but also leaves open the question of the social construction of this normative scheme to begin with.

In this paper we analyze the issue of IP rights in Chile and a set of conflicts that are associated with them. We argue that Chile is a dramatic case of institutional evolution coupled with social changes of global scope, along with a substratum of deep social inequality. This social and political position has consequences for IP rights in Chile, the nature of which we analyze in this chapter. To present our problem we have divided this text into four sections. In the first section we analyze the structural situation of Chilean society from a socio-systemic perspective. This analysis will serve as a context for the ensuing reflections. In the second section we describe the evolution of IP rights in Chile, from its beginnings up to its current situation. Based on a scheme proposed previously, in the third section we will address the situation of IP rights in Chile in the international context. In this analysis we will focus on four conflicts inherent to this period, namely: the case of access to medicines; the formation of sharing cultures; digital inclusion and exclusion; and the issue of digital piracy. Finally in the fourth section we present the conclusions of our analysis.

MODERNITY AND INEQUALITY IN CHILE: THE CONTEXT OF A DEBATE

To understand the socio-structural situation of Chile a preliminary theoretical explanation is necessary. Chilean society is described as a 'functional[ly] differentiated society' in several different scholarly socio-systemic diagnoses (cf. Cousiño & Valenzuela 2012; Robles 2005; Rodríguez 2007). The concept of 'functional differentiation' comes from the theorizations of the renowned German sociologist Niklas Luhmann (1997), whose influence on Latin American sociology is newly being recognized. The basis of the diagnoses of Chile is the modernization process that occurred in the 20th century.

The concept of 'functional differentiation' was first formulated by Talcott Parsons (1961). According to him, what characterizes modern society is the differentiation of four types of action that form 'systems' – namely, an economic system, a political system, a system of social integration (composed of law, family and other institutions) and a cultural system – in order to maintain a stable social order through the performing of imperative social functions.

The biggest critique of Parsons' theory lay in a lack of evidence to support the claim that his scheme of four systems represented all possible social systems. Parsons was deeply influenced by sociological organicism and by the first currents of open systems theories (Von Bertalanffy 1950). Every social system should fulfill functions to help maintain a stable structure and to propitiate changes that should be at all times consistent with the above mentioned functions. This earned Parsons his well-known reputation as a conservative and many of his ideas were abandoned by later sociologists.

Although the sociological mainstream renounced the Parsonian theoretical project, there were at least two continuations of his work which led his ideas to positions very different from those of their origin. One of them was the theoretical-critical proposal of Jürgen Habermas (1973, 1982, 1994), who used Parsons' ideas to sustain not only a critical position against capitalist society, but also to recapture the ancient question – possible to trace at least from Durkheim – of social integration. Habermas proposed understanding the schema of Parsons as two opposite constructs: economy and politics as self-regulating autonomous action systems and the system of integration and the cultural system as institutions of a different order. These two social realms were called 'system' and 'lifeworld'. The key to achieving social integration, Habermas points out, lies in submitting these self-regulating systems to the rationality of discourse by means of the law as the main tool.

The other variant, less optimistic and much more radical than the last, is that developed for more than 30 years by Niklas Luhmann. Functional differentiation for Luhmann (1997) corresponds to the form of differentiation that can be found in modern society. Unlike Parsons, for Luhmann there is no theoretical or empirical basis to give priority to the maintenance of social order over social change and it is also not possible to reduce the social complexity of modern society to only four systems. In his view, society is a system of communication that possesses its own dynamic. Only communication resulting from current and potential interaction between individuals is social.

In this context, what characterizes modern society is the differentiation of social communication around functions performed by systems. Examples of this differentiation are the existence of a political system concerning the problem of collectively binding decisions (Luhmann 2002), an economic system around the problem of scarcity (Luhmann 1988) or a legal system regarding normative expectations (Luhmann 1995a). Nevertheless, unlike Parsons' scheme, modern society for Luhmann is characterized by the differentiation of additional functional systems, such as art (Luhmann 1995b), science (1992) and education (Luhmann and Schorr 2000). According to Luhmann, there is no theoretical or practical reason to abandon research on the differentiation of other functional systems.

For Luhmann functional differentiation is the result of social evolution, this form of differentiation was preceded by stratification as an organizing principle of society. Functionally differentiated society, unlike stratified society, implies equality of access to all subsystems, since it puts no barriers of strata or origin for participation in the communication. However, a complete or successful participation in such systems is not ensured. For the use of money or financial transactions, for example, certain origins or strata are not required, since all persons can use money if they want to, nevertheless not everyone obtains the same benefits from economic activity and not everyone can get enough money. In a functionally differentiated law, all have rights as individuals, but not everyone can exercise them in the same way.

One of the greatest features of functional differentiation, in this sense, is the universalistic production of services without reference to strata or origin of the persons. Such functional systems cannot be understood as a regional or geographical phenomenon, but as part of the differentiation of a world society. Science, for example, produces the legitimacy of its researches beyond regional boundaries, and the monetary economy trespasses all political or juridical borders. The world society we experience is a product of functional differentiation.

Of course, this globalization/mundialization of functional differentiation does not preclude the fact that differences and transformations occur in local areas. Functional differentiation is a principle of differentiation that overlaps with the previous ones but it does not replace them. But as soon as functional differentiation emerges, social inequalities based on origin or strata lose their legitimacy. In a stratified society the main problem was the justification of equality (e.g. why must patricians be equal to plebeians before the law?), while in a functional differentiated society it is inequality that is, by default, questionable. Nevertheless, functional differentiation does not suppress all inequalities, even whilst they can be exacerbated in some cases. The regional implications of this process are extremely interesting in the Chilean case.

The path towards functional differentiation has been identified by several researchers in Chile. It has been stressed, for example, that since the 1990s an increasing differentiation of the political and of the economic system can be appreciated (Cousiño & Valenzuela 2012). In other cases it has been noted how throughout the 20th century Chilean law has suffered a process – sometimes interrupted – toward its own functional differentiation (Mascareño 2004). Other diagnoses relative to the same process of functional differentiation have put their emphasis upon the consequences for the individuals and the construction of their identities (Robles 2005), or in the ways in which this process is based on relationships of trust or confidence (Rodríguez 2007). In sum, Chilean society would be increasingly pervaded by a process of functional differentiation in various fields of social life. This functional differentiation, however, has had limited resonances in various cases and inequality and social exclusions are problems embedded in this process.

Chilean society can be described as a functionally differentiated modern society with a significant component of inequality (Cadenas 2012). We emphasize this dual condition, since it allows us to understand how it has been possible for Chile to achieve this insertion into the social dynamics of the world society, in spite of maintaining structural conditions of inequality. Chilean society is characterized by a dual socio-structural differentiation. On the one hand, Chile has an increasing tendency to differentiation of functional systems in various aspects of social life, along with, on the other hand, a persistent situation of inequality.

This perspective allows us to observe in a better way the contradictions of a country with highly developed institutions, especially in the case of IP rights, but with a high rate of deviation from its norms. Nevertheless, we will not follow the way suggested by the international institutions that perform measurements on this issue and make recommendations for public policy. For them, the main problem is a lack of control and regulation, and more rigorous investigation of these crimes, as well as stronger penal punishments, is the key to correct this situation. These recommendations, while very plausible, and though they may in some cases achieve the desired effects, do not allow us to understand the socio-structural situation which serves as background to the situation of Chile.

The main factor that encourages and amplifies inequality in Chile is the high level of social exclusion of a significant sector of the population. Just in general terms, international evaluations emphasize that Chile currently suffers a situation of deep inequality and of concentration of wealth in the hands of a small number of persons (OECD 2012). This situation of manifest inequality is replicated in the educational system (Muñoz 2011), in urban distribution (Sabatini et al. 2001), in the health and care systems (Arteaga et al. 2002), in the negative discrimination toward native ethnic groups (Merino et al. 2008), in the situation of the elderly (Thumala et al. 2010), in gender inequalities (PNUD 2010) and in many other social fields. This situation of inequality and exclusion has important consequences for access to the digital world and for IP issues.

EVOLUTION OF IP LAWS IN CHILE

The legal tradition of Chilean IP receives its major influence from Spanish law. Having been part of the Spanish colonies in America, Chile developed its institutional framework from the hand of the colonizers' law. In the first decades of the 19th century Chile became independent of Spain after a long war and began to form its first legal institutions. Although there was a political and economic rupture with the colonizers, in terms of legal traditions, the Chilean legal system inherited much of its organization and jurisprudence from Spain. The Spanish tradition of copyright protection, for its part, was largely influenced by the French Revolutionary Laws of 1793 (Sánchez 2002). The French laws established the author as an independent producer of their own original work and also indicated the rights of their heirs.

The evolution of Chilean IP rights can be defined in two phases. First, there was a phase of internal legal development, which characterized the formation of the Chilean State during the 19th and mid-20th centuries, and second, there has been a phase of opening and adjusting to international law, which began in the 1970s and was consolidated in the 21st century.

Chilean IP protection appears in the beginnings of its republican life. The first law on this matter appears in the constitution of 1833, which explicitly states these rights in its Article 152. A year later (1834) the so-called 'Law of Literary and Artistic Property', which established not only the author's IP rights but also the rights of their heirs, came into force. As noted by Ossa (2008), in the Americas only the United States had older legislation (the Federal Copyright Act of

1790), since Colombia had enacted its IP law only two months before Chile.

The Chilean law of 1834 was recognized in the Civil Code of 1855 issued by the renowned jurist Andrés Bello – who in turn was inspired by the French Enlightenment spirit of his time – and established in its Article 584 the need to elaborate special laws for this type of property. In spite of recognizing the importance of this issue, it was not until 1925 that a new special law was enacted, namely the Decree Law Nº 345, a few months before the promulgation of a new Constitution.

In contrast to the Law of 1834, the Decree Law of 1925 specified in great detail the penal consequences that arise from violation of IP laws and indicated a much wider catalog of protected works, including not only artistic and literary works but also scientific production. This law also extended the term of copyright for the heirs, from five years expandable to ten years – stipulated in 1834 – to 20 years. All these changes were reflected in the Constitution of 1925. The Decreed Law N° 345 of 1925 suffered no substantive changes until 1950, when it underwent one modification relative to the extension of copyright for the heirs, from 20 years to 50 years after the author's death.

During this first period of legal development, a relative stability in matters of IP laws can be observed and only important constitutional transformations seem to produce significant transformations. There is no revolutionary change between the law of 1834 (inspired in the constitution of 1833) and that of 1925, but rather specifications and extensions of rights and their validity. The amendment of 1950 can also be understood as a balanced legal change and not as a deep transformation.

In 1970 there begins a different period relative to the laws of IP. From 1833 until 1950, Chilean legal development relative to IP was marked by changes on policies and internal law; namely, IP was contemplated within the catalog of rights specially defined and protected by the Civil Code and sanctioned by the State. In 1970 a period of adjustments of Chilean legislation in accordance with international law begins.

In 1970 Chile ratified the *Berne Convention for the Protection of Literary and Artistic Works*. This agreement dates from the late 19th century and has been constantly revised. By signing this Convention, Chile was bound to protect the copyright not only of Chilean citizens or foreigners domiciled in Chile, but of the citizens of all signatory countries and to eliminate formalities for the exercise of this right. Due to this agreement, a profound change to the law of 1925 was necessary.

On October 2, 1970, the Law Nº 17.336 on IP was promulgated, which was not intended to change the law of 1925 but to abolish it completely (including the amendment decree of 1950). The commitments of the Berne Convention are evident in its second article, which explicitly states that the IP rights protected by this law not only involve Chilean or foreign authors domiciled in Chile, but all the foreigners protected by international conventions ratified by Chile.

The 1970 law is the basis of the current Chilean juridical arrangements on IP and has been amended seven times,[1] the last of which occurred in 2010. The Chilean constitution promulgated in 1980 recognizes IP rights in its Article 19 (Numeral 25), adding to the artistic and scientific IP rights the concept of Industrial Patent Property. This last change is one of the elements that characterizes this second period of openness to international law.

In addition to the Law of 1970 and its modifications, especially since the return of democracy to the country in 1990 after 17 years of dictatorship, there has been an increase in legislation regarding industrial and commercial activity. Chile has developed an economic growth model based on openness to foreign trade, by means of trade liberalization treaties and the removal of tax barriers. Within this framework, since the 1990s multilateral and bilateral international agreements that incorporate the issue of IP protection have proliferated.[2]

The current institutional framework on the protection of IP in Chile consists of several agencies, including the Ministry of Education, which is responsible for the registration of copyrights, the Ministry of Agriculture, which is in charge of rights of vegetable varieties, agrochemicals and some denominations of origin for agricultural products, and the Ministry of Health which has responsibility for IP in pharmaceutical products. Due to this openness to international law, the role of the Ministry of Foreign Affairs becomes increasingly important in international negotiations and their implementation. Regarding industrial property, the National Institute of Industrial Property is the institution in charge (INAPI-WIPO 2013).

CHILE IN THE GLOBAL EXPANSION OF IP: CONFLICTS AND CONTROVERSIES

The greatest transformations made to Chilean legislation on the issue of IP have been the signing and ratification of *The Agreement on Trade Related Aspects of IP Rights* (TRIPS agreement), the free trade agreement signed between Chile and the US, and the enactment of a set of legal implementation rules – Laws 19.912, 19.914, 19.928, 19.996, 20.160, 20.243, 20.435 and 20.569. This set of normative regulations has had a profound impact on the national Chilean legal system. It is the consequence of a stable international economic relations strategy that has been followed by Chile since the return to democracy. It has involved the inclusion of Chile in world regulation regimes as a binding requirement for different governments. This extends the strategy initiated by the Pinochet regime (Giacaman & Faundez 2003: 7). Therefore, there is an elite consensus in Chile about the assumption of the legal duties of the global IP regime.

By signing these agreements, Chile has been incorporated clearly in the broadening and strengthening process of IP rights (Drahos & Mayne 2002; Matthews 2002; Roffe & Santa Cruz 2006).

The TRIPS agreement was signed by Chile at the Marrakesh Conference, within the framework that created the World Trade Organization, and was immediately ratified in May 1995. This multilateral treaty introduces minimum standards of protection in each of the IP rights categories. Before the TRIPS agreement, the international IP system allowed each country to calibrate their legal regimes to their own national interests. This system allowed countries to differentiate treatment among the industrial sectors and exclude certain subject matter from patent protection (Roffe & Santa Cruz 2006). The main objectives of TRIPS are to reduce distortions in international trade, promote effective and adequate protection of IP rights, and ensure that measures and procedures to enforce IP rights do not themselves become barriers to trade. TRIPS included for the first time ever in an international agreement a systematic set of minimum standards regarding the enforcement of IP rights. These standards mean that it was not enough to recognize a certain minimum level of protection in each country, but countries need to adopt measures to ensure that those rights are effectively applied and protected (Roffe & Santa Cruz 2006).

Under TRIPS, Chile had to adapt its domestic legislation by 1 January 2000. However, despite the early ratification, regulatory effects in the country have been delayed, because the legislative process of implementation started quite late (Schmitz 2010). This delay has two explanations, namely, coordination difficulties over the new obligations taken by Chile under the free trade agreements, and then caution by political elites regarding possible economic impacts of such obligations in the context of the aftermath of the Asian economic crisis in the late 1990s.

The implementation of TRIPS meant the adoption of the following legal regulations:

- Ratification of the WIPO 1996 Treaties: Copyright Treaty and Performances and Phonograms Treaty, in April 2001;
- Law 19.912, which adapts Law 17.336 to TRIPS, November 2003;
- Law 19.996, which adapts Law 19.039 to TRIPS, March 2005;

- Law 20.243, which establishes rules and moral rights for performers of artistic performances fixed in audiovisual format, February 2008.

Particularly Law 19.912 increased protection of copyright in the substantive dimension as in the enforcement if IP. Software protection was formulated more precisely, and protection for databases was added, as well as protection of pictures and textile models; the rights to distribution, reproduction and public communication were secured; border measures and the 'Three Steps Rule' for copyright exceptions and limitations were introduced.[3]

Law 19.996, meanwhile, implemented an increase in the protection of industrial property rights in all dimensions: it allowed the patenting of micro-organisms and microbiological processes, ensured trade secrets and data exclusivity protection in pharmaceutical patents applications; it also widened and strengthened trademark protection and increased the term of patent protection, from 15 to 20 years. It also strengthened enforcement standards through criminal procedures and civil actions for damages, including precautionary measures, it established the possibility of compulsory licenses for patents on the grounds of health, national security, emergency, or in case of anti-competitive practices.

An additional step toward the incorporation of Chile within the global IP legal order has been the Free Trade Agreement (FTA) between Chile and the USA. This FTA was signed on June 6, 2003, and entered into force in both countries on January 1, 2004. This treaty has an extensive chapter on IP rights, which includes issues such as the protection of trademarks, geographical indications, Internet domain names, protection of encrypted satellite signals, copyright, neighboring rights, patents and undisclosed information protection, and enforcement of the agreements rules.

The FTA rules impose TRIPS-plus obligations, i.e. provisions strengthening the protection of IP rights in relation to the TRIPS minimum standards, through various means. These means include increasing protection standards (e.g. duration of protection) or rights available to holders or applicants; reducing the available options for a country's sovereign decision on how to implement a particular TRIPS obligation; or regulating bilaterally matters which previously were regulated multilaterally, affecting both administrative procedures and the criteria that should guide the decisions of national authorities (Escobar 2010).

The interests and information asymmetries were among the main features of the FTA Chile–USA negotiating process, i.e. the divergence of expectations about the outcomes of the negotiating process, and the manifest imbalance of the knowledge basis between the parties for the negotiations. First, Chile sought to consolidate, diversify and increase access to US markets, and to encourage the arrival of foreign direct investment, in return for which the country accepted a drastic strengthening of IP rights, while the USA sought in any case the adaptation of Chilean internal rules to US IP standards (Díaz 2006: 23). Second, the Chilean government did not have adequate technical capacity in IP issues when undergoing the negotiation over the FTA, facing a large knowledge gap about the importance of IP rules for access to science and technology and its impact on development (Díaz 2006: 30).

The implementation of the FTA demanded a reform of Law 17.336 by Law 19.914, in November 2003. This law implies the protection of neighboring rights for performers, phonogram producers and broadcasting organizations, as well as the term extension of copyright protection from 50 to 70 years after the death of the author. Law 17.336 was again amended by Law 20,435 in May 2010, which incorporated a broad reform, establishing a list of exceptions and limitations to copyright, including a restricted fair use, and a system for the limitation of Internet intermediaries' liability for copyright infringements committed by users of their networks, that establishes safe harbors through a special judicial schema of 'notice and take-down'. Moreover, the adaptation of internal rules also demanded the amendment of Law 20.160 by Law 19.039 in 2007, which had as a main effect the granting of an additional period of patent protection for unreasonable delays in the application process.

Unlike what happened with TRIPS, the long delay in the FTA implementation could be explained by the rise of a visible opposition from some social movements against such trade agreements. This opposition highlighted the possible social consequences of the FTA, especially for access to medicines and for prosecution of Internet users who are downloading and sharing copyrighted contents (Alianza por un Comercio Justo y Responsable 2004). In addition to the packed legislative agenda described above, which has produced a large set of adaptation rules with fairly complex regulatory structures in IP issues, there has also been a growing body of disputes over the value of exclusive property rights and protection forms for economic development and access to science, culture and technology in Chile.

The US Government has played a fundamental role in disputes by asserting pressure through the use of the powers of the United States Trade Representative (USTR). The USTR evaluates compliance with the rules of IP for all US trading partners. They use the 'Special Report 301', in which the USTR may recommend trade sanctions, by placing countries on a 'priority watch list', or give warnings to countries that are not accomplishing their commitments in the area of IP, by placing them on a 'watch list'. The USTR makes its decisions based on the information reported by associations of American companies. The USTR has used this mechanism several times against Chile to produce legislative changes to strengthen IP rights.

Regarding produced discursive disputes about compliance with regulatory standards on IP in Chile, we highlight two problematic points.

Access to Medicines

Chile clearly recognized patents on medicines from the enactment of Law 19.039 in 1991, while those drugs whose patents have expired can be traded – usually at lower prices – as generic drugs. This differentiation has given rise to two major sectors within the pharmaceutical industry operating in Chile, i.e., the international laboratory industry, specializing in patented drugs, and the national laboratories industry, specializing in generic drugs.

International laboratories operating in Chile grouped in the Chamber of the Pharmaceutical Industry (CIF) are subsidiaries of large multinational pharmaceutical companies, which are part of the associations that report to the USTR on the damage they claim to suffer from drug piracy, which consists of patented drugs sold without permission and payment of royalties. According to the CIF, national laboratories – grouped in ASILFA and Recalcine – infringe their IP rights, insofar as they sell patented drugs as generic drugs. To guard against this form of piracy, the US Government imposed within the FTA with Chile the obligation to establish a linkage between the patent office and drug health registry – which is part of the Public Health Institute – to prevent drug registrations that are patented by other companies.

The linkage system[4] was introduced into US legislation with the enactment of the Drug Price Competition and Patent Term Restoration Act of 1984 – also called the Hatch-Waxman Act. As a consequence, under American law, new drug applications must include patent information and the FDA considers the existence of valid patents as part of the approval process, so the marketing approval will not be granted to a generic drug until the patent has expired or is found to be invalid. The linkage reduces unnecessary patent infringement litigation by the assessment of whether their drug product is subject to a valid patent; and by acting as a safeguard for patent rights by preventing potential pharma patent violations.

National laboratory associations have organized significant resistance to the implementation of linkage between the two groups. They hold an alternative legal interpretation for the FTA rules, in the sense that the absence of linkage in Chile could be justified because the linkage rule applies when there is a marketing authorization, which does not exist in Chile. There is only an authorization to review the capacity and health properties of drugs for public health purposes (Cárdenas 2011). Thus, the linkage rule is inapplicable in the case of Chile. This interpretation has been supported by the Chilean government, meaning that Chile has not changed its legislation on this subject to date, despite pressures from the US Government. This also explains the delay in the enactment of adapting legal rules for the FTA. On the other hand, the CIF indicates that this interpretation is a legal trick not to comply with the FTA and protect the piracy of patented drugs (Egaña 2010). The CIF position is supported by the US Government.

The rivalry between the two sectors of the pharmaceutical industry has led to a powerful legal conflict between domestic and foreign laboratories in the Chilean courts. Foreign laboratories have accused national laboratories of piracy.[5] Foreign laboratories have in return been accused of using IP monopolies to attack free competition.[6] The US Government has used the inclusion of Chile on the 'watch list' of Special Report 301 and has threatened to apply unilateral trade sanctions to pressure Chile into modifying existing legislation and adapting it to the US interpretation of FTA rules. In parallel, many social movements have been emerging to protect consumer rights and to protest against the high price of patented medicines in Chile. Activists fear that a measure such as linkage would have the effect of increasing the price of medicines still further (Latin American and Caribbean-Global Alliance for Access to Medicines 2013). This fear has already resulted in various protest events in recent years (Salud, un Derecho 2012).

Restrictions to Internet-sharing Cultures

A second source of conflict has been the area that is called by the content and computer industries Internet piracy, i.e. downloading software, applications and cultural content (music, pictures, movies and books) through the World Wide Web. These downloads are made through p2p platforms, direct download and sharing communities, blog posts or websites. In this aspect, the computing and content industries have sought, as in other countries, to move the effort of fighting piracy from judicial reaction to a preventive level, by imposing upon Internet intermediaries, i.e. Internet service providers, obligations in order to block or take down content that is considered an IP violation.

Copyright collecting societies, like the Chilean copyright society (SCD), as well as computer and content companies, like the Association of Science and Technology Companies (ACTI) and the Association of Phonographic Producers of Chile (IFPI), pursue the aim of forcing the Internet intermediaries to collaborate with copyright holders to get quick answers to alleged online infractions.

One of the main FTA objectives was to encourage the cooperation of Internet service providers in copyright protection, through deterrence of actions that would be harmful to IP holders, such as the unauthorized storage and transmission of copyrighted material. By establishing a system of 'notice and takedown', Internet intermediaries' liability can be prevented if these intermediaries block or remove the allegedly infringing material as soon as they receive the information of the infringement, at the same time notifying the content provider of this measure (Jaramillo 2008: 26).

This has motivated much social criticism concerning IP, and different groups and social movements have attempted to influence parliamentary discussions around the adapting of legal rules to the FTA that could affect downloads and file-sharing. Consumer organizations and Internet users associations sought support for access rights to culture and knowledge, rights to privacy and freedom of expression, promoting the consecration of a list of exceptions and limitations to

IP, including the incorporation of fair use and avoiding installation of a 'notice and takedown' system that would fall entirely into private hands (Negron et al. 2010: 8).

Around the parliamentary debate that would lead to the enactment of Law 20.435 in 2010, a long and intense public debate was generated concerning the limits and purposes of IP rights. The end result was a compromise in which supporters of IP sought to minimize the limitations and exceptions to IP, allowing the establishment of a very restricted fair use clause in the law (which only protects eventual and fragmentary use) and failing to allow private copies of copyrighted material. On the other hand, critics of IP rights avoided establishing a safe harbor system to limit the Internet intermediaries' liability similar to the 'notice and takedown' system of the Digital Millennium Copyright Act of the USA, but also managed to include the requirement of a compulsory court decision to authorize the takedown or blocking of any online content.

Because of the degree of influence on public opinion that such critical voices managed to acquire in these discussions, they have generated a favorable climate sufficient to promote the adoption of Law 20.453 in 2010. This is the first ever law of Net Neutrality in the world. This law prohibits Internet Service Providers from enacting any blocking, restriction or hindrance of any data, applications and Internet services for the users on arbitrary discriminatory grounds (Vargas 2013). Law 20.435 and Law 20.453 have in common the recognition of Internet users' rights, ensuring them through the generation of new balances with normative structures that Chile has taken to protect both IP rights and human rights.

In recent years, discussions concerning the relationship between IP and digital cultures have grown around issues that the 2010 reform left pending, as in the case for the regulation of Technical Protection Measures or DRM.[7] Moreover, the US Government continues to press the government of Chile to adopt a notice and takedown system closer to those adopted by the DMCA.

Another controversial issue is the Chilean government's involvement in the negotiation round of the Trans-Pacific Partnership Agreement (TPP), which aims to strengthen IP rights again, and which is being resisted in Latin America by an international coalition of social movements, including activists and organizations from Chile (Busaniche 2011; Public Citizen 2012). Concerning the agreement – still in negotiation – of TPP, a series of initiatives is about to form in Chilean civil society, with the help of international NGOs, that will develop multiple efforts concerning information about and opposition to the TPP.

Due to a series of objections to the negotiated chapter on intellectual property, which is to be found in the draft TPP agreement, several campaigns and protests against it have taken place. An international front of organizations from Chile, Mexico and Peru has been formed – http://tppabierto.net/ – in which international NGOs such as Article 19 and Consumers International also participate.

In July 2013, LAC-Global Alliance for the Access to Medicines, which unites other conglomerates of national (NGO Políticas Farmacéuticas) and foreign NGOs, made a statement that flatly rejects the TPP, because of a lack of transparency in negotiations, probable regulation of TPM and surveillance duties for Internet intermediaries, as well as the threat to access to medicines for the population, particularly due to linkage, data exclusivity protection, extension of patentability scope and term for pharmaceutical patents as compensation for delays in admission (Latin American and Caribbean-Global Alliance 2013).

On August 13, 2013, the Chilean Senate accepted an agreement (Document Nr 647/SEN/13) which, as a consequence of the doubts and criticism voiced by several NGOs, asks the President of the Republic to open up a public debate about the technical, political, convenience and true consequences that TPP could have for Chile.

At the case law level, we would highlight the case of *Cuevana Chile* in 2012, in which the Chilean site administrator of a TV series download platform *Cuevana* – whose website was associated with the Argentine site *Cuevana* – was criminally prosecuted for infringement against copyright in the terms of Law 20.435, due to the links that this website enabled users to find for downloading copyrighted materials, although the links were provided by other actors. In the end, the case concluded without a conviction, but with a reparation agreement, forcing the *Cuevana* manager to teach in poor schools about the meaning of IP.[8]

Digital Inclusion and Exclusion

An additional problem that stems from IP policies in Chile is one that affects the inclusion and exclusion of people in digital communication networks. Digital inclusion can be defined as 'the set of efforts being made to increase the opportunities of integration of persons to social processes that are generated as a result of the relationship with the new technologies' (Raad 2006: 43). Digital inclusion refers to the way in which persons are able to use information technologies and, in this way, to take part in the wide communication network on a global scale that is contemporary society. In short, digital inclusion is a part of processes that support inclusion in functional systems, since they allow a major participation in their communications.

The case of Internet penetration in Chile is very enlightening. Estimates suggest that the number of Chilean households with Internet access has steadily grown and currently is near 60% (SUBTEL 2013). Nevertheless, if households are separated by income quintile, levels of access diverge greatly. In households in the poorest quintile only 10.2% have Internet access. In the second lowest quintile access is 12.2%, and in the third quintile it is 25.5% (SUBTEL-UAH 2009). Internet access is deeply affected by income inequalities, which leads to situations of social exclusion.

Overall, digital inclusion policies developed in Chile have addressed this issue primarily as the result of the relationship between the prices of access to computers and the Internet and personal income. The main Chilean digital inclusion policies in this area have been the subsidy and promotion of access demand (Agostini & Willington 2010).

The design of promotional policies have aimed generally at increasing penetration rates and broadband Internet access, neglecting deeper dimensions regarding access to information and its use and ownership by citizens. Only policies that have as their object an increase in the supply of e-government digital services have been concerned about the social value of the information content offered as one of the critical factors of digital inclusion. Another problem has been the relative homogeneity of the digital inclusion policies implemented, ignoring the special characteristics of different excluded groups of citizens for which public policies are supposed to be designed (Agostini & Willington 2012).

These determinants can explain the characteristics of the long-term direction that digital inclusion policies in Chile have taken. In general these access policies, and functional training for this purpose, are designed to extend the coverage of Internet use (Cabrera 2006). In this sense, we have tried to produce essentially universal access policies. Such universal access policies have traditionally been founded upon two pillars: the initiatives of educational digital inclusion and functional inclusion policies. Educational digital inclusion policies include digital capabilities as part of study plans and proportionate connectivity to the schools; meanwhile functional inclusion policies consist mostly in connectivity possibilities and very little IT training programs for the users. The first emerged from the infrastructure of school education in the country, while functional inclusion policies have emerged from the economic development (Economy Sector) or technological (Telecommunications Sector or State Modernization Programs) agencies, with the public or small businesses and individuals. Initiatives designed to meet the needs of women, youth and other disadvantaged social groups have not been paralleled by digital inclusion policies in Chile.

The most common instruments of inclusion policies have been the expansion of connectivity infrastructure, fiber optic and broadband, demand subsidies, access to computers at subsidized prices, the installation of public access centers (telecentres) and capability training, especially at school level.

Piracy Rates and their Criticism

Although Chile has an institutional framework very similar to developed countries in matters of protection of IP (OECD 2011), the country has a reputation for high rates of copyright infringement, also known as piracy. According to the latest estimates by the Business Software Alliance, 61% of all software in use in Chile was pirated (BSA 2012), which although it has gradually diminished since 2008, is still a very high figure. For the International IP Alliance in turn, more than 50% of the trade in movies and music on optical discs in Chile is carried out by illegal means and 90% of the whole consumption of music in the country comes from Internet piracy (IIPA 2013).

All the above mentioned percentages correspond to indirect estimates based on economic balances and other economic data; nevertheless, in Chile there is no systematic research on the consumption of pirated products, as is the case, for example, in Mexico (ACC-USCC 2008). The Mexican experience shows that the most frequently purchased pirated products are of digital character, especially music CDs and DVD movies. Whilst we cannot corroborate this trend in Chile, some studies have shown a similar situation regarding the consumption of pirated music products in Chile (cf. García et al. 2007).

This situation leads to the phenomenon of deregulated inclusion. On the one hand, the economic inclusion of those who profit by means of copying and trading pirated software and movies, and, on the other hand, what we might call, 'inclusion in the role of the public'. It is possible to be included in functional systems in two ways: in the 'role of performance' [*Leistungsrolle*] or in the 'role of the public' (Stichweh 2009), i.e. as someone who produces an artistic work or as someone who appreciates it, as a sportsman or as a spectator of a sports event, etc. The difference indicates the way in which one person is included in the communication of a functional system and the internal asymmetry in the possible positions in such systems. Unlike other types of IP crimes that are made for the purpose of 'performance', such as the copying of products with industrial ends or artistic plagiarism, the consumption of pirated music and movies produces an effect of inclusion as 'public'. The final consumer of a pirated copy of an artistic work achieves his inclusion inside the public of the art system and thus participates in the communications of this system.

On this problem Chile presents a special situation. On the one hand Chile is a modern institutional order that largely parallels the developed countries (it must be noted that Chile was the first South American country to be part of the OECD) and, on the other hand, IP infringements in Chile, according to the above cited studies of the BSA and IIPA, present an image of a country with very low institutional development. The main structural support of such illegal inclusion is the structure of inequality and exclusion that prevails in Chile. These two elements, a functionally differentiated society, together with inequality and exclusion, offer a favorable structural condition for this type of unregulated inclusion.

Due to IP infringements, Chile appears on the 'Priority Watch List' of countries issued by the government of the United States of America (USTR 2012). The reasons attributed to the persistence of this phenomenon are the lack of control by the government and weaknesses in the prosecution of these crimes by Chile. Nevertheless, it should be stressed that there is no consensus on the validity and accuracy of international statistics on IPO infringement, largely because the economic damage estimates are inaccurately calculated and produced by stakeholders of the industry (GAO 2010).

In Chile, as at the international level and in other countries, piracy figures from IIPA and USTR studies have been criticized. Therefore, it was stated that the claims of these studies are rather data contaminated by conflicts of interest, produced by the same industry representatives that claim to be damaged by these practices (Viollier 2013). According to the NGO *Derechos Digitales*, in particular the figures of unauthorized use of software, as a component of global piracy, related to the *Global Software Piracy Study* conducted by the Business Software Alliance (BSA), 'suffers from multiple defects, which disallowed [it] as a reliable and objective measurement of the rate of unlicensed software use and the monetary amount of losses that this activity causes to the industrial sector' (Viollier 2013: 14). This conclusion was based on the methodological shortcomings of the calculation of the figures, as well as the basis for calculating the study, which used a residual negative system, assuming that everything that cannot be estimated as legitimate software is automatically pirated. Additionally, the methodology unjustifiably assumes an inelastic software demand, calculating industry losses mechanically, and arbitrarily excludes certain unpaid types of web services. According to these critics, all these problems 'converge artificially to increase both the rate and the amount of losses that unauthorized copies of software would cause the industry' (Viollier 2013: 15). These criticisms can be applied to a greater or lesser extent to the calculation of the other components of the USTR data on global piracy, as in the case of infringements of patents on medicines, or the losses of the film and music industry.

These criticisms lead us to note that in Chile, there are appearing increasingly adversarial positions on the semantics of global IP through social movements, especially those that are aimed at the realization of human rights in the digital environment. The construction of the infringement of IP rights as an illegal activity, comparable to other undisputed illegal offenses, by the use of the metaphorical concept of piracy, is a historical and discursive construction (Johns 2010) which is being criticized by the human rights and *copyleft* global movements. Around the world, the opposition to IP (Halbert 2005) has been expanding in connection with the discussion on informational common goods, access rights to health, knowledge and culture, and the protection of traditional knowledge.

In this view, underlying the phenomena known as piracy is the installation of a harmonized world system of IP rights, that would impose common structures on all countries and sectors of world society, and whose technological, economic and social inclusion conditions require differentiated legal regimes (Yu 2003: 135).

Critical positions related to IP rights are being introduced in Chile through free software communities (Hardings & Fuentes 2003) and the social movement for Free Culture, Open Access and Creative Commons (Cerda & Ruiz 2010). For these critical approaches, the epidemics of piracy ought to be seen as a social construction. That is, a product of shifting legal regimes, lobbying activities, rhetorical maneuvers, criminal justice agendas, and interested or partial processes of statistical inference (Yar 2005). As social semantics, the piracy concept reflects the vested interests of companies and groups, urging the strengthening of IP rights through severe legal measures, as well as the delegitimation of sharing practices and free access to knowledge, which don't use exclusive rights (Darch 2011; Mirghani 2011).

Therefore, the area of IP is becoming a conflicting social system, in which the semantics or discursive constructions of involved function systems, namely economics, law, politics, science are connected by symbolic disputes and meaning breaks through flexible and dynamic social forms, such as social movements and the debate arenas in the public sphere, rather than by stable and defined structures (Stäheli 2000: 218ff.). IP offers breaches and uncertainty points, which can't be reduced by legal decisions but accrue to the extent that they occur in both legislative and judicial decisions. These uncertainties are resolved either through a scheme of opposition or from local resistance against global processes, because they involve disputes that are produced and released by processes that, although they are antagonistic – the globalization of IP rights and the globalization of protest against it – share their global nature and reach. The consequences are increasing conflicts over the meaning and value of IP, and these conflicts are part of the ambivalence and indeterminacy of the forms of social differentiation and organization, forms which are more complex than those that were common in Chile during the last century.

CONCLUSIONS

We have analyzed the situation of IP rights in Chile. We indicated that the situation in Chile can be better understood if its socio-structural characteristics are observed. In this context, we characterized Chilean society as a functionally differentiated society with a situation of persistent inequality in various spheres of social life (education, income, health, etc.). Following this premise, we placed our analysis of IP rights within an evolutionary perspective, in which we identified two stages (hierarchical and functionally differentiated societies), the latter being the most relevant to our analysis. In this context we analyzed conflicts emerging in IP rights in Chile. Our reflections on these conflicts can be summarized as follows.

- Inside the international context of IP protection, Chile's current situation deserves special attention due to its structural characteristics. It is clear that in the case of access to medicines, in a society with such high levels of inequality, especially in health, international IP standards must be adapted to this problem. Otherwise, the restrictions imposed on the country in this matter may lead to a worsening of the situation of internal inequality.
- The formation of sharing cultures and digital inclusion strategies in Chile constitutes a means of access for a large number of persons to the knowledge of the digital world. In this context, the negative evaluation that Chile received for this type of practice does not take into consideration the control elements that have already been established in Chilean legislation and the positive effects of this practice to combat the worrying inequality of the country.
- It is necessary to be especially careful when certain judgments on IP violations in Chile are supported by international organization's reports, since several studies suggest that these indicators do not possess sufficient methodological rigor and are affected by a lack of transparency with regard to the interests represented by these organizations. Thus, more rigorous, systematic and independent research becomes necessary.

Our reflections aim to observe IP rights in Chile within a context of wider social changes. The socio-structural situation in Chile can be easily extrapolated to other countries that have experienced uneven processes of modernization and in an accelerated way. Related to this, Chile does not constitute an exception but rather a clear example of this type of socio-structural arrangement. We have tried to establish in our work not only the situation of IP rights in Chile but also the socio-structural aspects that serve as a context to this condition. We noted that Chile presents a situation that combines a high differentiation with an acute social inequality. In other words Chile has high institutional development along with high transversal social exclusion levels. This provides insights into IP tensions generated between the national juridical order and the international, as in the case of the resistances of social movements to the protection of certain drug patents, or against the restrictions on Internet file-sharing. In all these conflicts the dual situation of Chilean society is manifested; namely, one part of the society is directly included in world legal systems demanding higher standards on IP rights protection whilst another part of the society does not have sufficient means to be formally included in such dynamics. Both phenomena cannot be totally justified or demonized. The protection of IP rights is, undoubtedly, a fundamental matter and their violation constitutes a crime recognized worldwide. Nevertheless, requests for social inclusion by means of IP rights that take into account local and social conditions, as well as gradual implementation measurements, should be considered legitimate.

In this context, it is very possible that international agreements which Chile is negotiating on IP will lose their effectiveness and have rather negative effects if the conditions that the country faces at present are not taken into consideration. Without a direct and critical recognition of its own reality by governmental institutions in Chile, the extension of IP may lead to an 'amplification effect' upon the current situation of inequality, with negative effects for the inclusion of large sections of the population.

Chile has been characterized in the last 25 years as adopting global IP standards and accommodating US IP rules. There has emerged an important set of rules that has transformed the intellectual property regime in this country. In this, Chile differs from other countries in Latin America that have sought alternatives and rejected major commitments with the US, such as Brazil and Argentina, who have avoided the FTA and encouraged greater flexibility around intellectual property rules in relation to issues such as public health and national development.

Chilean governments, although they have supported initiatives such as the Development Agenda in WIPO, have not challenged the global agenda of strengthening intellectual property rights.

However, in the practical implementation of the commitments made, and the rules adopted, Chile experiences very similar problems to those of other countries in the region. Access to new technologies, and capabilities for their use, are limited by unequal social opportunities. Social exclusion fragments the public into those who feel incorporated into technological modernity and those who feel excluded, putting intellectual property in an important place in political discussions and social conflicts over the spread of knowledge and technology in Chilean society.

NOTES

1 We refer to the following modifications: Law 18.443 of 1985, Law 18.957 of 1990, Law 19.166 of 1992, Law 19.912 of 2003, Law 19.914 of 2003, Law 19.928 of 2004 and Law 20.435 of 2010. We will return to these reforms later.

2 For a summary of these agreements, see the website of the World Intellectual Property Organization (WIPO): http://www.wipo.int/wipolex/en/profile.jsp?code=CL (retrieved online, October 20, 2013).

3 Established originally in the Berne Convention for the Protection of Literary and Artistic Works of 1967, the rule states: 'Members shall confine limitations and exceptions to exclusive rights to certain special cases which do not conflict with a normal exploitation of the work and do not unreasonably prejudice the legitimate interests of the rightsholders'.

4 The linkage system links patent rights with the marketing approval process, mostly before the health authority. The linkage system for pharmaceutical patents aims to prevent sanitary registrations before the health authority for pharmaceutical products that are covered with a valid patent from being granted. The linkage system requires that patents protecting an innovative pharmaceutical are listed with an official open registry. Generics manufacturers must provide notice to the patent holder of an application of a new generic drug, thereby allowing the patent holder the opportunity to seek enforcement of its patent rights. The health authority refrains from approving the generics drug for a period of time to allow for resolution of any patent dispute (Bouchard et al. 2011). Generic marketing approval is so 'linked' to the expiration of the pharma patent.

5 *Case Laboratorios Recalcine SA v Pfizer Chile SA in Santiago Chile*, March 26, 2003. Retrieved online, October 25, 2013: www.gala-marketlaw.com/membersonly/pdfs/Amsterdam2003.pdf

6 *Case Tecnofarma v Sanofi Aventis*, Free Competition Court, Decision No. 52, of May 2, 2007.

7 Digital Rights Management (DRM) or Technical Protection Measures (TPM) are defined as the set of technological measures by which copyright holders prevent the unauthorized use of

protected digital content by limiting technically the access to and use of digital contents. These restrictions on uses such as downloading, printing, saving and emailing content are encoded directly in the products or the hardware needed to use them and are therefore in immediate effect (Rump 2003).

8 http://noticias.terra.cl/tecnologia/internet/abogados-especialistas-analizan-el-caso-cuevana,e869649ac9f9b310VgnCLD200000bbcceb0aRCRD.html (retrieved online, October 25, 2013).

REFERENCES

ACC-USCC (2008) *Segunda encuesta de hábitos de consumo de productos piratas y falsificados en México*. México D.F.: American Chamber México & U.S. Chamber of Commerce.

Agostini, C. & Willington, M. (2010) Radiografía de la Brecha Digital en Chile: 'Se Justifica la Intervención del Estado'. *Estudios Públicos*, 119, 5–32.

Agostini, C. & Willington, M. (2012) Acceso y Uso de Internet en Chile: evolución y factores determinantes. *Persona y Sociedad*, XXVI(1), 11–42.

Alianza por un Comercio Justo y Responsable (2004) *TLC Chile-Estados Unidos: Un modelo para armar*. Retrieved online, October 25, 2013: http://www.alainet.org/active/6428

Arteaga, O., Thollaug, S, Nogueira, A, C. & Darras, C. (2002) Información para la equidad en salud en Chile. *Revista Panamericana de Salud Pública*, 11(5–6), 374–385.

Bouchard, R. et al. (2011) Structure-function analysis of global pharmaceutical linkage regulations. *Minnesota Journal of Law, Science & Technology*, 12(2), 391–457.

BSA (2012) *Shadow Market 2011: BSA Global Software Piracy Study. Ninth Edition, May 2012*. Washington, DC: Business Software Alliance.

Busaniche, B. (2011) *Propiedad intelectual, acceso a medicamentos y Derechos Humanos. Las amenazas que supone el TPP para la salud pública en Chile*. Buenos Aires: Heinrich Böll Stiftung & Fundación Vía Libre.

Cabrera, V. (2006) Democratización de la información en Chile. El lugar de la apropiación social de las TIC en la agenda digital 2004–2006. *Comunicación y Medios*, 17. Retrieved online, October 30, 2013: http://www.comunicacionymedios.uchile.cl/index.php/RCM/article/viewArticle/11505/11863

Cadenas, H. (2012) La desigualdad de la sociedad. Diferenciación y desigualdad en la sociedad moderna. *Persona y Sociedad*, 26(2), 51–77.

Cárdenas, J. (2011) El uso de la información no divulgada y el linkage en el TLC con EE.UU.: 'A qué realmente se obligó el Estado de Chile y cómo ha cumplido'. *Revista de Derecho Económico Internacional*, 1(2), 4–24.

Cerda, A. & Ruiz, C. (2010) *Internet, Copyright y Derecho: Opiniones Contingentes*. Santiago: Derechos Digitales.

Cousiño, C. & Valenzuela, E. (2012) *Politización y monetarización en América Latina*. Santiago de Chile: IES.

Darch, C. (2011) Ideology, illusion and the global copyright regime. In: Richard A. Danner & Jules Winterton (eds) *The IALL International Handbook of Information Management*. Farnham: Ashgate.

Díaz, A. (2006) *TLC y Propiedad Intelectual: Desafíos de Política Pública*. LC/BRS/R.163. Brasilia: CEPAL.

Drahos, P. (2002) Negotiating intellectual property rights: Between coercion and dialogue. In: Peter Drahos & Ruth Mayne (eds) *Global Intellectual Property Rights: Knowledge, Access and Development*. New York: Palgrave-Oxfam.

Drahos, P. & Mayne, R. (eds) (2002) *Global Intellectual Property Rights: Knowledge, Access and Development*. New York: Palgrave-Oxfam.

Egaña, J. (2010) El Linkage y el Tratado de Libre Comercio con los Estados Unidos. In: *La Propiedad Intelectual en Chile y el Tratado de Libre Comercio con los EE.UU*, edited by AmCham, Series of Technical Studies, AmCham Chile, Documento No. 2. Santiago de Chile: AmCham Chile.

Escobar, B. (2010) *Implementación de obligaciones sobre propiedad intelectual de los tratados de libre comercio con EEUU. Experiencia de Chile*. Santiago: CEPAL-GTZ.

GAO (2010) *Intellectual Property: Observations on Efforts to Quantify the Economic Effects of Counterfeit and Pirated Goods*. Washington, DC: United States Government Accountability Office (GAO).

García, F., Jeldres, A. & Mardones, M. (2007) *Conducta del consumidor y Piratería en la Industria Musical*. Seminario de Título Ingeniería Comercial, Mención Administración. Universidad de Chile. Profesor Guía: Enrique Manzur M. PhD.

Giacaman, V. & Faundez, R. (2003) *Participación Ciudadana en Política Exterior: Un análisis de la participación en foros internacionales*. Santiago: Corporación Participa.

Habermas, J. (1973) *Legitimationsprobleme im Spätkapitalismus*. Frankfurt a.M.: Suhrkamp.

Habermas, J. (1982) *Theorie des kommunikativen Handelns. Band II. Zur Kritik der funktionalistischen Vernunft*. Frankfurt a.M.: Suhrkamp.

Habermas, J. (1994) *Faktizität und Geltung. Beiträge zur Diskurstheorie des Rechts und des demokratischen Rechtsstaats.* Frankfurt a.M.: Suhrkamp.

Halbert, Debora (2005) *Resisting Intellectual Property.* London & New York: Routledge.

Hardings, J. & Fuentes, A. (2003) Desafíos legales en torno a software libre y formatos digitales. Retrieved online, October 25, 2013: http://www.hardings.cl/publications/hardings2003encuentroLinux.pdf

IIPA (2013) *Chile. International Intellectual Property Alliance (IIPA) 2013. Special 301 Report on Copyright Protection and Enforcement.* Washington, DC: International Intellectual Property Alliance.

INAPI-WIPO (2013) *The Use of Intellectual Property in Chile.* Santiago de Chile.

Jaramillo, P. (2008) Acceso a la Cultura y regulación de Derecho de Autor. Desde la perspectiva de los acuerdos comerciales suscritos por Chile. In: Alberto Cerda (ed.) *Acceso a la Cultura y Derechos de Autor. Excepciones y Limitaciones al Derecho de Autor.* Santiago: Derechos Digitales-Ford Foundation.

Johns, A. (2010) *Piracy: The Intellectual Property Wars from Gutemberg to Gates.* Chicago & London: The University of Chicago Press.

Latin American and Caribbean-Global Alliance for Access to Medicines (2013) *Impacto del aumento de las medidas de propiedad intelectual en Colombia, Perú y Chile.* Lima: Ifarma, Latin American and Caribbean-Global Alliance for Access to Medicines & Fundación Misión Salud.

Luhmann, N. (1988) *Die Wirtschaft der Gesellschaft.* Frankfurt a.M.: Suhrkamp.

Luhmann, N. (1992) *Die Wissenschaft der Gesellschaft.* Frankfurt a.M.: Suhrkamp.

Luhmann, N. (1995a) *Das Recht der Gesellschaft.* Frankfurt a.M.: Suhrkamp.

Luhmann, N. (1995b) *Die Kunst der Gesellschaft.* Frankfurt a.M.: Suhrkamp.

Luhmann, N. (1997) *Die Gesellschaft der Gesellschaft.* Frankfurt a.M.: Suhrkamp.

Luhmann, N. (2002) *Die Politik der Gesellschaft.* Frankfurt a.M.: Suhrkamp.

Luhmann, N. & Schorr, K.E. (2000) *Problems of Reflection in the System of Education.* Münster & New York: Waxmann Verlag.

Mascareño, A. (2004) Sociología del derecho (chileno y latinoamericano) *Persona y Sociedad,* 18(2), 63–94.

Matthews, D. (2002) *Globalising Intellectual Property Rights: The TRIPs Agreement.* London & New York: Routledge.

Merino, M.E., Quilaqueo, D. & Saiz, J.L. (2008) Una tipología del discurso de discriminación percibida en mapuches de Chile. *Revista Signos,* 41(67), 279–297.

Mirghani, S. (2011) The war on piracy: Analyzing the discursive battles of corporate and government-sponsored anti-piracy media campaigns. *Critical Studies in Media Communication,* 28(2), 113–134.

Muñoz, V. (2011) *El derecho a la educación: una mirada comparativa: Argentina, Uruguay, Chile y Finlandia.* Santiago de Chile: Orealc/Unesco.

Negron, B., Brodsky, R., Farías, E. & Brodsky, J. (2010) *Propiedad Intelectual y Derecho de Autor.* Santiago: Unión Nacional de Artistas.

OECD (2011) *Enhancing Market Openness, Intellectual Property Rights, and Compliance through Regulatory Reform in Chile.* Washington DC: OECD.

OECD (2012) *OECD Economic Surveys: Chile 2012.* Washington DC: OECD.

Ossa, C. (2008) Apuntes generales sobre derechos de autor y derechos conexos. Manuscrito, Santiago de Chile.

Parsons, T. (1961) An outline on the social system. In: T. Parsons, E. Shils, K.D. Naegele & J.R. Pitts (eds) *Theories of Society,* Vol. 1 (pp. 30–79) Glencoe, IL: The Free Press.

PNUD (2010) *Desarrollo humano en Chile. Género: los desafíos de la igualdad.* Santiago de Chile: PNUD.

Public Citizen (2012) Briefing memo: Chile and the Trans-Pacific Partnership Agreement – Access to Medicines Risks & Continued Bullying from USTR. Retrieved online, August 28, 2013: http://www.citizen.org/documents/Chile-and-the-Trans-Pacific-Partnership-Agreement.pdf

Raad, A.M. (2006) Exclusión digital: Nuevas caras de viejos malestares. *Revista Mad,* 14, 40–46.

Robles, F. (2005) Contramodernidad y desigualdad social: Individualización e individuación, inclusión/exclusión y construcción de identidad. La necesidad de una sociología de la exclusión. *Revista Mad,* 12, 27–58.

Rodríguez, D. (2007) Communication, Confidence and Trust: Functional Differentiation in Chile. *Soziale Systeme,* 13(1+2), 209–220.

Roffe, P. & Santa Cruz, M. (2006) *Intellectual Property Rights in Free Trade Agreements Entered into by Latin American Countries with Developed Countries.* Santiago: CEPAL.

Rump, N. (2003) Definition, aspects, and overview. In: Eberhard Becker et al. (eds) *Digital Rights Management, Technological, Economic, Legal and Political Aspects.* Berlin: Springer.

Sabatini, F., Cáceres, G. & Cerda, J. (2001) Segregación residencial en las principales ciudades chilenas: Tendencias de las tres últimas décadas y posibles cursos de acción. *Revista Eure,* 27(82), 21–42.

Salud, un Derecho (2012) *Manifiesto.* Retrieved online, August 25, 2013: http://www.saludunderecho.cl/el-movimiento/manifiesto/

Sánchez, R. (2002) La propiedad intelectual en la España contemporánea 1847–1936. *Hispania: Revista española de historia*, 62(212), 993–1020.

Schmitz, C. (2010) *El Acuerdo sobre los Aspectos de los Derechos de Propiedad Intelectual relacionados con el Comercio, Diez Años de Vigencia en Chile.* Santiago: ACHIPI.

Stäheli, U. (2000) *Sinnzusammenbrüche. Eine dekonstruktive Lektüre von Niklas Luhmanns Systemtheorie.* Weilerswist: Velbrück Wissenschaft.

Stichweh, R. (2009) Leitgesichtspunkte einer Soziologie der Inklusion und Exklusion. In: R. Stichweh & P. Windolf (eds) *Inklusion und Exklusion: Analysen zur Sozialstruktur und sozialen Ungleichheit* (pp. 29–42) Wiesbaden: VS Verlag für Sozialwissenschaften.

SUBTEL (2013) *Informe sectorial: Telecomunicaciones en Chile. Cifras a Diciembre 2012.* Santiago de Chile: Subsecretaría de Telecomunicaciones de Chile.

SUBTEL-UAH (2009) *Encuesta sobre acceso, uso y usuarios de Internet banda ancha en Chile.* Santiago de Chile: Subsecretaría de Telecomunicaciones de Chile, Universidad Alberto Hurtado.

Thumala, D., Arnold, M. & Urquiza, A. (2010) Opiniones, expectativas y evaluaciones sobre diferentes modalidades de inclusión/exclusión social de los adultos mayores en Chile. *Argos*, 27(53), 91–122.

USTR (2012) *2012 Special 301 Report.* Washington, DC: Office of the United States Trade Representative.

Vargas, P. (2013) Monitoring Social Networks in the First Nation-State that Achieved a Network Neutrality Law, a Case-Study in Chile. Proceedings of the 7th ACORN-REDECOM Conference, Mexico D. F. (Mexico), May 17–18.

Viollier, P. (2013) *Análisis Crítico de Los Mecanismos para la Medición de Piratería de Software, el caso particular del 'Global Software Piracy Study'.* Santiago: ONG Derechos Digitales.

Von Bertalanffy, L. (1950) An outline of General System Theory. *The British Journal for the Philosophy of Science*, 1(2), 134–165.

Yar, M. (2005) The global 'epidemic' of movie 'piracy': Crime-wave or social construction? *Media Culture & Society*, 27(5), 677–696.

Yu, P. (2003) Four common misconceptions about copyright piracy. *Loyola L.A. International & Comparative Law Review*, 126(1), 127–150.

8

Musical Property Rights Regimes in Tanzania and Kenya after TRIPS

Alex Perullo and Andrew J. Eisenberg

INTRODUCTION

During the late 1990s and into the 2000s, over 30 African countries updated their intellectual property rights laws. The push to update these laws, many of which had been in place since the colonial era, came from several interests. Local artists, record companies and musicians' organizations in Kenya, Uganda and Tanzania, for instance, brought concerns about the outdated laws in their countries to government officials and ministers of trade. Through marches, protests, negotiations and court cases, these stakeholders encouraged the government to establish new legislation to better protect original compositions. In Uganda, local artists lobbied the Ministry of Justice and the Office of Constitutional Affairs, beginning in 1988 (Jjuuko 2002). In Kenya, artists established organizations and lobbied for better enforcement. In response, several elected officials in East Africa stated that they understood the cultural significance of the arts but were reluctant to acknowledge the economic potential of local music and, therefore, the need to update laws to protect the rights of artists.[1]

The prevailing push to update copyright legislation in African countries came from the Trade Related Aspects of Intellectual Property Rights (TRIPS Agreement). TRIPS is a World Trade Organization (WTO) agreement that requires any member country to update laws pertaining to patents, trademark and copyright. On January 1, 1995, many countries, including Kenya, Uganda and Tanzania, became members of the WTO, which meant that they officially had to update their intellectual property rights (IPR) legislation by a given deadline. Each East African country needed to comply with TRIPS by either 2005 (for developing countries, such as Kenya) or 2021 (for less developed countries, such as Tanzania and Uganda).[2] In order to address the significantly outdated laws, however, each country passed new legislation well before their deadlines. In terms of copyright law, Tanzania updated their laws in 1999, followed by Kenya in 2001, and Uganda in 2006. Each of these countries also became members of the African Regional Intellectual Property Organization (ARIPO), which requires countries to harmonize their laws with other member countries, and the East African Community (EAC), which aims to promote national and regional protection of IPR.

Despite the passage of relatively uniform copyright legislation throughout East Africa and the formation of regional organizations meant to further standardize these laws, the protection of musical works in East African creative industries has varied significantly within and between each country. While enforcement remains weak throughout East Africa, each country has also taken a different path in the implementation of copyright policies meant to support musical property rights. These different trajectories can be explained, in large part, by the particular political, social and economic paths taken by East African countries toward the neoliberal present. In broad terms, Kenya is often referred to as a commercial center for East Africa with a stronger formal economy, international trade networks, and historic support for the commercialization of music. Kenya, however, has also suffered from high levels of crime, political violence, and despotic leadership, which have collectively hampered the development of a live music scene. Tanzania, in contrast, has been politically stable since independence though cracks in its peaceful image have emerged more recently. More practically, Tanzania supports a large live music scene in part due to the relative safety of its cities and towns, but has never been considered as commercially vibrant as its northern neighbor despite the prominence of Tanzania's music economy during the 2000s.

The particularities of each country's political, social and economic environments shape the daily routines of music in these countries and impact the legal landscapes of musical rights. Each country approaches legal matters from the perspective best suited to the interests of the nation and individuals who work with the laws and music. This can range from the strength of collective management organizations meant to collect royalties on behalf of rights holders to the willingness of local media outlets to pay for the right to play music on their stations. Understanding these differences illustrates the ways that similar legal frameworks can take on new meanings within local contexts. Rather than consider normative properties of intellectual property rights, we argue that it is important to recognize the contexts of law, as well as contestations over who has the power and authority to construct its meaning (Benda-Beckmann et al. 2009: 3). An examination of different trajectories in Tanzania and Kenya can thereby move away from univocal interpretations of law and, instead, recognize the potentially divergent outcomes of similar legal frameworks.

In order to understand the different trajectories of copyright law in East Africa, the next two sections explore political, social and economic circumstances of post-TRIPS reforms on musical property rights regimes in Tanzania and Kenya. We describe the ways in which these different trajectories are animated by historical differences between the two countries with respect to: (1) language and educational policy; (2) the culture of bureaucracy; (3) the organization of musical unions and collective management organizations; and (4) state orientations toward music as national culture. A significant argument is that efforts to harmonize copyright legislation through TRIPS, as well as various regional organizations, has not been strong enough to counter local interests in and conceptions of rights, property and music. Instead, the specific environments that absorb these laws reinterpret their meaning based on the specific lived experiences of those who can exert the most control over them. Without comprehending these differences, attempts to standardize intellectual property rights policy in the region may remain unpredictable and often unsuccessful.

COPYRIGHT LAW AND MUSIC IN TANZANIA

On April 13, 1999, the Copyright and Neighboring Rights Bill was introduced to the Tanzanian Parliament. On the following day, members of parliament debated the law's merits and disadvantages. The Minister of Industry and Commerce, Iddi Simba, started the discussion: 'The law that existed before was blind and left an opening for composers and artists of these works to fail to receive payment from their work, which, from time to time, benefited businessmen in and outside this country' (United Republic of Tanzania 1999: 18).[3] In his speech, Simba went on to explain the importance of protecting the rights of composers and creators. He made it clear that passing a comprehensive and up-to-date Copyright Act would benefit the country's entrance into international trade agreements, namely TRIPS, which would thereby allow Tanzania to continue to be recognized as a trading partner with other members of the WTO. Without passing up-to-date legislation, Tanzania could find itself facing trade sanctions.

The bill quickly passed through Parliament and on June 4, President Mkapa signed the 1999 Copyright and Neighboring Rights Act into law. But, the passing of the law was far easier than what lay ahead. There were numerous conceptions of ownership in Tanzania and little consensus among anyone, including members of parliament and legal scholars, as to the best means of enforcing the Act. Very few lawyers and judges had knowledge of or training in copyright law. Customs officials were unsure of their role in hindering the importation of pirated goods. Even musicians, who were the ones who had potentially the most to gain from the introduction of the law, were unable to agree on the best way to move forward. While it took over a decade to push a copyright bill through Parliament, it appeared far more daunting by the early 2000s to actually administer and enforce the parameters of the Act.

The difficulty in implementing and enforcing the Copyright Act came from a number of sources. Perhaps one of the more obvious problems was that the law was initially only discussed, debated and printed in English. Most Tanzanians rely on Swahili in daily life, including in primary and secondary education, the informal economy and in the home. Most television and radio stations throughout the country use Swahili, though there are a number of significant exceptions. English, on the other hand, tends to be favored by the more elite members of society, including those working in commercial businesses, institutions of higher education and various branches of government. For the law to be effective, particularly in protecting rights holders, it would need to be explained and explored in Swahili.

Over the next decade, many more meetings, organized by international and local organizations, continued to present the importance of intellectual property rights. Those held by international organizations tended to be conducted in English, though translators were present at a few. At these meetings, the task of explaining and debating the implementation, enforcement and effectiveness of copyright law frequently came from non-Tanzanians, such as lawyers, staff of international copyright organizations, or copyright administrators from neighboring countries. While well versed in copyright law, these individuals were far less knowledgeable about issues related to Tanzanian music and business. They also needed to rely on English to discuss copyright matters, which meant that they would alienate many in the audience.

At one conference organized in April 2001 by the United States Embassy, titled 'Understanding and Enforcing Copyright in Tanzania', artists, lawyers, judges, police officers, custom officials, and others heard talks about the meaning of copyright law, its enforcement in East Africa, and particular policies that impacted each of the groups of people attending. Conducted mostly in English, in part because the main speakers came from outside of Tanzania, the long speeches on legal issues frustrated an audience wanting to hear about the basics of the law. During the question session, many people stood up, concerned and angered, asking about the meaning and potential future benefits of the law. All of the questions came in Swahili, and it was clear that few had understood the content of the entire day-long session.

Even when these meetings were well-organized and planned, with specialized workshops on issues that could significantly impact local practices, participants frequently grew frustrated at the use of English and the challenging content of the meetings that often assumed basic knowledge of intellectual property rights. Whereas there was widespread interest in these meetings in the early 2000s, far fewer artists attended later in the decade due to frustration in comprehending the content of the sessions.

Those meetings presented by local organizations in Swahili also tended to be unproductive since the individuals who were given the task of lecturing about IPR in Swahili were often not experts in the field. Organized by state institutions, including the National Arts Council (BASATA), the Business Registration and Licensing Agency (BRELA), and the Copyright Society of Tanzania (COSOTA), as well as independent musicians' organizations, such as the Tanzanian Music Dance Association (CHAMUDATA), meeting organizers often had difficulty finding people knowledgeable about both copyright policies and the local music economy. A few key people, such as Ruyembe Mulimba, who started the organization Rulu Arts Promoters, and John Kitime, a musician and copyright activist, became prominent figures in the local music scene due to their ability to understand the complexities of copyright law and the music business, which they could then communicate in Swahili. Kitime, who is now a board member of BASATA and the chairman of the Tanzanian Musicians Network, was vocal in both lobbying for legislative changes and educating musicians on ways to protect their works. Despite the effort of these individuals, however, there remained a gulf between various stakeholders. Those who had better familiarity with English could read the law, search online for discussions about copyright law, and even contact international rights organizations with questions. Those less familiar with English had to rely on the few organizations, individuals and publications that could provide them with a basic understanding of the law.

The reliance on Swahili, which was historically an effort by the Tanzanian government to unite local populations and promote local traditions, also had broader impacts that indirectly related to people's comprehension of IPR. The lack of fluency in English prevented many citizens from continuing their education overseas or working with individuals from other parts of the world. In the fall semester of 2011, for instance, there were 3,898 new Kenyan students enrolled in American universities, whereas there were only 950 new Tanzanian students (Mugwe 2013, see also Ishengoma 2008: 433). The inability to attain overseas training has meant that there are fewer formalized academic or business relationships between Tanzania and other parts of the world. While language is not the only reason for the paucity of these relationships and partnerships – Kenyans' greater financial wealth and stronger ties to Europe also play a significant role – Tanzania's particular approach to and use of language has prevented stronger knowledge of foreign policies, laws and economic practices among ordinary citizens.

One group that spoke English fluently in Tanzania and used their knowledge of English to better understand copyright law was Asian traders. Asians is a term used in East Africa to refer to people of South Asian descent, most of whom trace their roots in the region to the influx of Indian traders and indentured laborers in the nineteenth century (Mangat 1969). During the 1930s, members of this community became instrumental in the distribution and sale of records imported from either overseas or South Africa. By the 1980s, some Asian traders also expanded their businesses to include the unlicensed sale of both local and foreign cassettes. These traders became so dominant that they managed to saturate markets controlling many music economies in eastern and southern Africa. Their dominance in the 1990s was so significant that copyright officials in other countries, such as Malawi, Uganda and Kenya, commented that their musicians often lost money on the sale of their music to Tanzanian traders only a few days after an album was released in their country.

Part of the success of these traders came from the extensive networks that had been historically established in the region. Asian businessmen often had family or trade networks that stretched from North America and Europe to various parts of East Africa, which allowed them to gain access to the latest music both internationally and locally. They could then duplicate and circulate a wide variety of music throughout the region. Outside of major cities, such as Dar es Salaam and Nairobi, few people were familiar with copyright law, which allowed the traders to continue with their business unimpeded even after the Copyright Act became law. These businesses became so effective that new albums could arrive in Tanzania from another country on the day they were released and be duplicated and redistributed within two days. These unlicensed copies also looked identical to the original cassette tapes or compact discs.

Knowledge of English among Asian traders proved to be an effective tool for keeping track of copyright law and its enforcement. Several of these traders attended copyright sessions, served on boards or committees that aimed to enforce copyright law, and took part in WIPO workshops in East Africa. Their fluency of English gave them a distinct advantage over many other people who attended these meetings, including musicians, artists and other businessmen working in the formal economy. The traders could easily follow the law's development, present their perspective on the best way to enforce the law, and keep up with the latest approaches to preventing the piracy of music. This astute business practice became an advantage as the traders could simultaneously keep track of advances in the law and find alternative methods for promoting their products, whether legally or illegally.

Though many Tanzanian artists and members of foreign music industries label these traders as 'pirates', it is important to realize that they operated in the equally 'informal' (i.e. unregulated) economies that dominated Tanzania during the 1980s and 1990s. Their role in creating vast distribution networks helped to establish a vibrant music economy in the country. Certainly, previous generations of Asian traders benefitted from colonial rule, under which they often became important in local markets. In Kariakoo, for instance, a district of Dar es Salaam currently known as Tanzania's music distribution center, Indian traders controlled 396 of the 420 trading sites as early as 1927 (Brennan 2012: 38). After independence, however, this population was heavily maligned, opportunities to promote their companies were refused, and many had their businesses nationalized. Their political vulnerability meant that they used their extensive regional and international trade networks as a means to fortify their economic positions. By the late 1990s, after socialism ended, these networks ultimately gave the traders an advantage, which some used to promote the commercialization of local music through circulating recordings throughout the region. This would eventually provide opportunities to grow a viable local music market and, through the influence and perseverance of local musicians, encourage the distribution of legitimate albums (Perullo 2011).

Aside from tribulations posed by the use of language and the informal economy, another difficulty in enforcing the 1999 Copyright Act came from the historical relations of ownership and property in Tanzania. Tanzania gained independence from British colonial rule in 1961 and, under the leadership of President Julius Nyerere, the country moved toward establishing unified national policies. Drawing on a combination of neo-traditional ideologies and pan-African notions of community and development, Nyerere promoted racial and ethnic unification with a single-party government that represented the entire population. He emphasized policies that unified over 200 ethnic groups into a population committed to promoting a coherent nationalist vision. And, as already noted, the government promoted a single language, Swahili, in all trade, government activities, education, and even in art (music, theater, literature) to further these efforts. As the Tanzanian writer Godfrey Mwakikagile states, Nyerere was, 'the most successful African leader to unite different tribes and races to achieve national unity. No other African country is as united as Tanzania, in spite of the large number of tribes and racial minorities we have in the country, one of the largest in Africa' (Mwakikagile 2007: 628).

By the late 1960s, the country had moved toward socialist policies, particularly in promoting notions of self-reliance, single-party government and community-based living. Most industries in the country were nationalized, and ownership of land, property and businesses went to the government. Any private entities that remained either struggled to remain solvent or had to work through government agencies to import goods or trade locally. The combination of socialist policies and nationalist efforts encouraged individuals to conceptualize property as either controlled by the state for the betterment of the people or as a national entity. Even today, the concept of private ownership in property, such as land, does not exist. Individuals and/or groups can only have the right to occupy or lease land for a particular duration of time (Sheuya 2010: 3). This notion of temporarily owning physical land in many ways relates to the view that many Tanzanians have toward music, particularly traditional music: it is shared and used, but not owned by individuals.

The development of law in the 1970s and 1980s took on many socialist ideologies and practices. In an article in the journal *Change*, C.K. Mtaki, a lecturer in law at the University of Dar es Salaam, discusses the transition that Tanzania's legal system underwent to accommodate the socialist political system. He writes, 'To give effect to the new [socialist] policies, a well calculated intervention in the legal system ... was made, specifically to inject in some new "socialist tailored legislation" that would cater for an economy dominated by state enterprises' (Mtaki 1996: 4). The movement toward a socialist legal system made individual ownership a contradiction of social practice. In terms of intellectual property rights, most individuals had no legal basis to complain about trademark, patent or copyright infringement, since the government owned, directly or indirectly, most of the works being produced. Even music, typically recorded at state-run studios, became the property of the government. Musicians had no legal basis on which to claim ownership of these works. One of the only options available to musicians to claim rights in compositions was to record their music outside the country, particularly in Kenya.

When the 1999 Copyright Act became law, many musicians understood that they now had rights in their lyrics, music and recordings. They could protect their compositions and attain royalties from the use of their songs on the radio (publishing rights remain elusive in Tanzania). However, many questions persisted. If songs are composed collectively in a group who owns the rights to the music? If a song uses a traditional rhythm, do you have to add the traditional ethnic group as a composer? And, how do you perform songs from the socialist past, which remain popular, if they are potentially owned by the government? These questions were not easily answered. Local organizations, such as COSOTA, BRELA, BASATA and CHAMUDATA, competed with each other to answer these questions for musicians. This meant that the leadership of these organizations often did not agree on the best approaches to handle copyright matters such as hindering piracy, paying royalties, establishing a coherent understanding of authorship, and registering artists' original works. Without an institution that could convincingly resolve these issues, an ad-hoc, informal system emerged within the local music economy to establish rights. Different factions emerged around these organizations, each of which promoted unique ideas for determining rights, ownership and royalties in music. The lack of consensus among all stakeholders ultimately meant that there were divergent efforts to establish rights, ownership and royalties within the local music economy.

While the music community had conflicting views on the enforcement and protection of musicians' rights, many individuals not directly associated with the music economy argued that songs remained a social entity that could not be owned. Many of those who worked in law enforcement, for instance, did not see a reason for confiscating pirated goods. In the early 2000s, customs officials rarely stopped the movement of pirated cassettes because it did not appear illegal. Many members of the public were also unsympathetic with musicians' or artists' claims to royalties. This meant that, many times, artists were criticized for trying to enforce their rights. For instance, in discussions of copyright law with many non-musicians, a consistent argument emerged that there were far more important issues to fight over in Tanzania, including healthcare, poverty, unemployment and education. Copyright, from this vantage point, was a luxury. Even lawyers interviewed as part of this research argued that copyright law in the arts community was less important since there was so little value in litigating a copyright case in court. Legal fees would be more than the amount that could be made from winning a copyright case.

The general malaise among lawyers toward musicians' rights has led to a dearth of legal cases concerning authors' rights. The only cases that have made it before judges are indictments against traders who sell unlicensed sound recordings. These cases are usually filed by the government-run Copyright Society of Tanzania (COSOTA). Even these cases, however, encounter many difficulties. Legal documents are lost or misfiled once they are submitted to the court, while lawyers, adept at foot dragging, stall in bringing cases to court. David Louis Finnegan notes that lawyers in Tanzania often hamper the rule of law through bribing judges, court clerks and other court employees in an attempt to 'obtain either speedier disposition of client matters or beneficial delays' (2008: 103). There are court verdicts (almost comical for their inversion of statutes) in which judges dismiss cases of piracy claiming that the music distributor is simply operating a business and that the plaintiff, whether a musician or legal music distributor, is infringing on the rights of a legitimate and valued local business. Some of these dismissals may be due to a lack of knowledge about the law, but many people argue that some form of corruption is involved. In a 2012 Afrobarometer survey of 2,400 people in Tanzania, the vast majority of respondents only trusted the courts somewhat (42%) or just a little (20%) while some citizens (6.8%) stated that they did not trust the courts at all. The combined lack of trust and regular reports of bribery often equates to a lack of interest in using the local courts for copyright matters.

Despite the very significant obstacles to trying copyright cases, between 2001 and 2012 COSOTA brought lawsuits against several music distributors and had their inventory of unlicensed cassettes confiscated and destroyed. A small portion of these distributors were also asked to pay fines. These efforts put pressure on illegal music distributors to alter their strategies for selling cassettes. Many distributors avoided selling any pirated materials in Dar es Salaam, where the vast majority of artists and lawyers reside, but continued to move materials throughout eastern and southern Africa. Others found ways to transform their illegal operations into successful legitimate businesses. By 2010, the physical piracy of music cassettes had ceased to be a problem, however, as the massive growth in digital piracy replaced analog piracy in many parts of the country. While analog piracy was starting to be dealt with in some ways, digital piracy has thus far proved to be a far more omnipotent challenge for those interested in protecting the intellectual property of local and foreign musicians.

Given all of the issues discussed thus far, including the dominant use of English in copyright matters, socialist notions of ownership, and corruption in the country's legal system, the most significant factor in limiting the success of copyright matters in Tanzania may be the state-controlled Collective Management Organization (CMO). Most countries have organizations set-up to protect the rights of copyright holders. There are unions aimed at educating musicians about their rights and collective management organizations established to collect royalties on behalf of rights holders. While Tanzania has had many of these organizations in the past, only one currently has the authority to enforce, protect, register and collect royalties for all Tanzanian artists: the state-run organization, COSOTA.

Many issues arise from having a state-run organization collect royalties on behalf of artists. First, given that many CMOs work to push new amendments, policies and legislation through government, the lack of separation between the state and the CMO in Tanzania can make it difficult to encourage legislation that is in the best interest of rights holders. Second, many artists, particularly in Tanzania, do not believe that government staff are knowledgeable enough in copyright matters to effectively enforce their concerns. And, third, musicians do not trust the government to handle royalties. In two separate surveys conducted in Tanzania by Perullo in 2007/2009, and 2012/2013, most respondents believe that the government misuses funds collected through taxes, foreign aid or the collective management of music. As in other areas of East Africa, corruption is a common part of people's daily lives. Even if high levels of corruption were just a matter of public perception, many rights holders lack confidence in the government to handle funds collected for them. This means that there are regular and frequent complaints about COSOTA's ability to handle the role that they have been assigned by the state.

Despite these issues with a state-run CMO, COSOTA continues to collect royalties on behalf of artists. In the 2012/2013 fiscal year, COSOTA claimed to have collected Tsh98.8 million (US$62,000) in royalties. COSOTA collects public performance royalties from bars, restaurants, clubs, buses, radio stations, hotels and other establishments that play recorded or live music. The organization also reported that they distributed Tsh88 million to rights holders. In surveys conducted in Dar es Salaam by Perullo in 2012/2013 with 250 Tanzanian musicians, who represent the primary members of COSOTA, 16 individuals stated that they received royalty cheques from COSOTA. Four stated that they received royalties on one occasion from between Tsh30,000 ($18) to Tsh90,000 ($55), and seven stated that they received payments between Tsh50,000 ($31) and TSh300,000 ($124) on two or three occasions (four did not write the amounts that they received). Other musicians stated that they did not join COSOTA as they did not want to pay the annual fees (Tsh10,000 for an individual and Tsh50,000 for a band). The majority of the survey respondents, however, stated that they had never received any royalties from the organization. This latter group included well-established older musicians and younger artists who have had a number of popular songs on the radio over the past few years.

Almost since its inception, artists have complained about the lack of transparency at COSOTA and the potential misuse of funds. After years of criticism, in late October 2013, the Ministry of Information, Youth, Culture and Sports promised a gathering of copyright stakeholders that they would receive their royalties. The Deputy Permanent Secretary of the Ministry, Elisante Ole Gabriel, explained that he was not pleased to see musicians unable to attain the full rights of their labor. Gabriel argued that the lack of protection for artists' rights means that Tanzania falls behind the standard of living of other countries (Mani 2013).[4] After the meeting, rumors in Dar es Salaam were that a foreign government threatened to remove financial aid to Tanzania if the Tanzanian government did not address and more stringently enforce intellectual property rights. The rumor was used as justification for the government's renewed interest in intellectual property rights. Whether valid or not, the rumor was seen as encouraging evidence to many musicians who believed that the government, including COSOTA, was at fault for the ineffectiveness of copyright in Tanzania and that only foreign pressure could strengthen local enforcement.

In response to the confusion over copyright law locally and bureaucratic ineffectiveness nationally, a stronger message now appears to be coming from local leaders and private entities, such as BASATA and the Tanzania Musicians Network, arguing that musicians need to become more self-reliant. Self-reliance, a notion derived from Tanzania's socialist past, promotes the concept that individuals need to take responsibility for the outcomes of their lives. Julius Nyerere famously stated that a self-reliant individual is someone who is willing to help and cooperate with others, but, 'who does not depend on anyone else for his food, clothing, or shelter' (1971: 151). Implied in this statement are the values of hard work, both for the individual and the nation, intelligence and cooperation. By the 1980s, when there was a scarcity of resources in the country, self-reliance took on slightly new meaning that included doing anything to survive (Perullo 2011: 7–12). This included hard work but also developing strategies to make a living with scant resources and limited government support.

In relation to copyright law, the notion of self-reliance means finding ways to exert pressure on those with power in the local music economy to better support local artists and their music. In many meetings, conferences, workshops, and other sessions, artists are told that they need to take action, become familiar with copyright law on their own or through attending meetings, and implement changes in the ways that they do business on a day-to-day basis. This do-it-yourself approach, common in many areas of Tanzania's neoliberal economy, promotes the notion that the individual is responsible for altering his or her circumstances. While many artists still argue that some larger government – whether Tanzania's or a Western state – needs to help local artists, many recognize the long history of failed promises that comes from weak and ineffective laws and regulations in Tanzania. To make a living, these local artists are continuing to rely on their own initiatives and strategies in order to find effective means to benefit from the Copyright Act.

COPYRIGHT LAW AND MUSIC IN KENYA

Kenya's Attorney General Amos Wako brought new copyright and related rights legislation to the Kenyan Parliament in 1999. The decision to move forward six years in advance of the TRIPS deadline was evidently prompted by the glaring deficiencies of the existing IPR enforcement and administrative framework (Ouma 2004: 3), the growing anti-piracy campaign among Kenyan musicians (namely, the Kenya Music Anti-Piracy Association, set up by veteran musician Joseph Kamaru), and the threat of embargos by US entertainment and software companies if the government did not take steps to stem unlicensed distribution (Ondengo 2000). Wako drafted and redrafted the Kenya Copyright Bill between 1999 and 2001 in consultation with WIPO. The Bill ultimately passed in November 2001. It was signed into law a month later, and came into force in February 2003. The vote in Parliament was unanimous, though a couple of MPs who rose in support of the Bill nevertheless voiced skepticism about the benefits of a globalized copyright regime for Kenya, noting that 'people who infringe on copyright in Kenya are … members of the informal sector [and] there are many [Kenyans] who depend on that kind of livelihood' (Republic of Kenya 2001a, statement of Ochilo Ayacko).

As in the Tanzanian case, the discourse around Kenya's millennial copyright legislation emphasized the idea that music artists comprise a class of citizens that need and deserve to be protected. In comments thanking the MPs for passing the Copyright Bill, Attorney General Wako noted that one of Kenya's most famous musicians, Daudi Kabaka, had recently passed away without leaving enough money behind to pay for his own funeral. 'Had this Bill been there in time', he declared, '[Kabaka] would not have died a pauper' (Republic of Kenya, 2001b). Unlike in the Tanzanian case, however, Kenya saw few didactic speeches on the basics of intellectual property law. There was no need, as copyright issues had already been aired within the Kenyan National Assembly multiple times over four decades. Like Tanzania, Kenya first passed copyright legislation a few years after Independence (The Copyright Act, Chapter 130 of the Laws of Kenya, 1966), using the UK Copyright Act of 1911 as a template. But the Kenyan law was amended five times – in 1975, 1982, 1989, 1995 and 2000 – before being superseded in 2001.[5] This greater attention to matters of copyright may be attributed to the historical presence of globally interconnected print publishing and music recording industries in the capital Nairobi.

Kenya's music recording industry has a history that stretches back to the post-World-War-II era, with the establishment of East Africa's first independent record company, East African Sound Studios Ltd, in Nairobi (Harrev 1989). By the 1960s, Nairobi had become a regional hub for commercial popular music production, attracting talented musicians from neighboring countries. By the late 1970s, it boasted a slew of serviceable recording studios (plus a world-class facility owned by CBS), a record pressing plant owned by Polygram, and a collection of multinational record companies. Polygram began operating in Kenya during the early 1970s, after it absorbed two other multinationals with Kenyan operations: Phonogram (Phillips) and Polydor. EMI and CBS both set up subsidiaries in Nairobi in the 1970s, seeking to profit off of an expanding East African market. Both companies partnered with local entrepreneurs. In EMI's case, it turned out to be a disastrous strategy. The company was swindled out of GB£100,000 (Wallis and Malm 1984: 93). But CBS did well for a while, thanks it seems to greater access to local knowledge: 'Peter Bond, who had previously worked for Polygram for thirteen years, was given overall responsibility for CBS African operations. Bond certainly knew Africa well, having done spells in Kenya, Zaire and Nigeria – he is Kenyan by birth and has the added advantage of speaking Swahili' (Wallis and Malm 1984: 94).

In the wake of the passage of the Copyright Bill, Energy Minister Raila Odinga, who would later become one of Kenya's most significant political figures, declared, 'The enactment of this Bill has now put piracy on notice' (Republic of Kenya 2001b). In the past, Kenyan MPs had been focused on the exploitation of musicians at the hands of greedy producers, typically using the figure of 'the *Muhindi*,' the Asian, as a stand-in for carpetbagger capitalist. Take, for example, the comments of Parliamentarian Zephaniah Mogunde Anyieni in 1965:

> There are people here … [who] can play really good music. But the man who takes the copyright is the Asian[;] and it will be found that such people who are the Africans, though they have the talent they are still very, very poor people, and the man who makes the money is the Muhindi. This copyright should not be given to the Muhindi[;] it should be given to the African. (Republic of Kenya 1965)

Stereotypes of the Asian in East Africa as a foreign exploiter have been part of the discourses of nation building in Kenya since independence (see Furedi 1974: 358). As Asians were active in music production and distribution in Kenya (in Nairobi as well as Mombasa and Kisumu) until the 1970s, it was natural for Kenyan politicians to read the struggles of Kenyan musicians as an extension of the problem of Asian 'exploitation' of Kenya's authentic 'African' citizenry.

The emphasis on 'piracy' in the parliamentary debates surrounding Kenya's millennial copyright legislation reveals the pressures from within and outside the country that were driving the legislation process. It also speaks to the common understanding in the country of the damage that unlicensed music distribution has wrought. Nairobi's thriving recording industry had nearly collapsed by 1990. All the multinationals had left, studios were no longer being built or upgraded, and Polygram's record pressing plant was being put in mothballs. This turn of events is generally attributed to the introduction of the audiocassette, which enabled large-scale phonogram piracy and informal sharing ('cassetting') while '[flooding] the market with cheap copies of Western, soul, disco, rock and reggae records' (Graham 1989, 2; cf. Nyairo 2004, 11–13; Wallis and Malm 1984, 6–7). In truth, economic and political factors had already taken a heavy toll on the industry prior to the cassette revolution. Economic decline in the 1980s left Kenyan music consumers unable to pay for luxuries like records and record players (Stapleton and May 1987: 272). At the same time, opportunities for creating music for export diminished due to certain 'institutional changes brought about by [governmental] policies intended to lead to economic development' (Blewett and Farley 1998: 247). These included 'import, visa, and foreign exchange restrictions [which] severely reduced the flows of peoples, ideas, musics, and technologies from the rest of the African popular music world' (Blewett and Farley 1998: 247); and the Kenyan government's Africanization policy during the 1970s, which saw a transfer in the ownership of River Road-based music production and distribution companies to Kikuyu entrepreneurs who lacked the 'contacts, trading history, [and] reputation mechanisms' of their 'Asian predecessors'' (1998: 242). But 'piracy' has always received more attention from the Kenyan media and music industry stakeholders than any other factor negatively impacting local music production and distribution.

It is unclear what effect Kenya's 2001 Copyright Act has had, or will have, on unlicensed music distribution in Kenya. Enforcement activities have certainly intensified in recent years, with high-profile raids and seizures regularly being carried out (and publicized) by a new government body established by the Act, the Kenya Copyright Board (KECOBO), and the Anti-Counterfeit Agency (established by the 2008 Anti-Counterfeit Act). But there is as yet no evidence that the level of 'music piracy' in Kenya, routinely estimated at over 90% of all recorded music sold in the country (e.g. Iseme et al. 2009: 7; KECOBO 2011: 3), is diminishing. Foreign business coalitions attribute the persistence of piracy in Kenya to deficiencies in Kenya's Copyright Act, which they argue depress both 'the levels of fines levied on offenders, and the number of prosecutions' (BASCAP 2013: 17; IIPA 2003). KECOBO, meanwhile, argues that it is due to a lack of knowledge of copyright among law enforcement officers and rights holders, unwillingness among rights holders to follow through on copyright enforcement, and 'the challenge of technology-based piracy represented by downloads, MP3/4, flash disks and other versatile storage media' (KECOBO 2011: 6). Less discussed by these groups, for reasons one can easily intuit, are the obstacles to adequate enforcement posed by 'the pervasiveness of corruption in Kenya' (BASCAP 2013: 12). Kenyan musicians are vocal about this issue, however. Rapper and entrepreneur Nonini (Hubert Nakitare), for example, has been quoted as saying, 'those who pirate our music use their deep pockets to shield themselves from being held to account for their illegal activities' (Ramah 2012).

Where Kenya's Copyright Act has had an undeniable and significant impact on the local music economy is in the administration of musical property rights. In addition to meeting Kenya's obligations vis-à-vis TRIPS and the WIPO Internet Treaties, the Act overhauls the regulation of collective management activities in the country by granting KECOBO the mandate of registering and overseeing CMOs. Setting up and staffing KECOBO was far from a smooth process. But once the body was up and running in 2006, it had an immediate impact on musical property rights administration in Kenya. Under the leadership of Marisella Ouma, a Kenyan lawyer with a doctorate from Queen Mary, University of London, KECOBO fostered a speedy expansion of the institutional network for the administration of musical royalties. Only one music CMO, the Music Copyright Society of Kenya (MCSK), existed as a functioning entity when the 2001 Act was passed. Ouma saw to it that two more were added to collect on behalf of 'neighboring' rights holders (phonogram producers and performers). The Kenya Association of Music

Producers (KAMP) was initially founded by a group of producers in 2003. Ouma walked the Association's leadership through all the necessary steps to become registered as a CMO under the Copyright Act, which they did in 2008. She then worked with some KAMP members and pop singer and human right lawyer Angela Ndambuki to establish the Performers Rights Society of Kenya (PRiSK), which was registered in 2009.[6]

MCSK was also transformed by the implementation of the 2001 Copyright Act. A group of Kenyan musical luminaries with international experience established the Society in 1983. It was the height of the multinational labels' influence in Nairobi, and a number of Kenyan music-industry cooperatives and organizations were emerging to represent the interests of various constituencies (Malm and Wallis 1992: 86). The idea behind the founding of MCSK was to wrest control of public performance royalty collection in Kenya away from the Performer's Rights Society of London. Operating without any official authority or capacity for enforcement, MCSK established a reputation for corruption and general dysfunction. By the time the 2001 Copyright Bill was signed into law, it was undergoing a major restructuring, prompted by an incident in which some members briefly took control of MCSK offices to force the ousting of General Manager Jennifer Shamalla. The advent of the Copyright Act and KECOBO did much to shape this reform process. Aware that the Society would have to be vetted by KECOBO in order to continue operating after 2007, MCSK's Board of Directors brought in Maurice Okoth, a man with experience in both law and administration, as Chief Executive Officer in 2005. With training from WIPO, and financial and logistical support from the International Confederation of Societies of Authors and Composers (CISAC), Okoth succeeded in getting MCSK registered with KECOBO within a couple of years of his appointment.[7]

MCSK grew exponentially, both in terms of membership and income, after becoming a duly registered CMO. Once the Society was operating as a registered CMO, Okoth sought to boost membership, with a view toward forging reciprocal relationships with international royalty collection societies beyond PRSK. He managed to engineer an astounding nearly ten-fold increase in membership, from around 600 to over 5,000, between 2005 and 2011, largely by offering an immediate public performance royalty payout to each new member. (The strategy was controversial, as it brought in fraudulent members who were not actual composers but simply relatives or friends of composers.) At the same time, with the law behind it, the Society moved aggressively to enforce compliance among music users. It became notorious for employing police and private security to carry out checks, levy fines, and even seize property (such as computers from cyber cafés and radios from public service vehicles) from noncompliant users. It also took advantage of opportunities that arose with Kenya's ICT revolution. With the rise of Internet distribution and various forms of music m-commerce (including ringtone and ring-back tone sales and subscriptions), MCSK took on the task of mechanical licensing for digital platforms, adding a mechanical rights rider to the membership agreement (Eisenberg 2012). More recently, it has taken advantage of software provided by WIPO and the entrance of digital media monitoring firms into Kenya to bring radio broadcasters into full compliance while also instituting 'scientific distribution' for its members. The advent of digital media monitoring for collecting and distributing public performance royalties brought an end to the days when even MCSK's most prominent members would receive paltry sums, or nothing at all, from the Society (see Wanyama 2007: 38–39). MCSK is keen to advertise this fact, in light of the lack of trust that has built up between MSCK leadership and its members over the years. Large payouts, such as the nearly $5,000 given out to veteran hotel pop band Safari Sounds in April 2012, are touted in press releases, media interviews and MCSK's annual award 'gala' (Muchangi 2012).

As part of their strategies for increasing collection revenue, all three of Kenya's music CMOs have worked to shape local understandings of how music may be 'owned' and 'used'. MCSK has been most effective in this regard, simply by virtue of its growth. Fraudulent or not, the thousands of new MCSK members began to ask questions about royalty collection, sparking discussion and debate within the music industry and public culture at large (John Katana recorded interview with A. Eisenberg, 1 August, 2012). The result has been an increased copyright consciousness, which is highly evident at annual and occasional industry events. Meanwhile, through lobbying and 'sensitization' activities, KAMP and PRiSK have been working to instantiate a conception of the musical 'rights holder' within Kenya's laws and music industry, so that it is not only copyright holders but also phonogram producers and performers who profit from the sale or use of recorded music. With respect to legal doctrine, they have been successful: a 2012 amendment to the Copyright Act grants producers and performers the right of equitable remuneration through a registered CMO. But transforming understandings of musical property rights among music makers and users in Kenya has so far proven more difficult.

The successes of Kenya's music CMOs to date may be attributed to capable and committed technocrats like Marisella Ouma, Maurice Okoth, and the two women at the helms of the neighboring rights CMOs at the time of writing (June Gachui and Angela Ndambuki, both singers and lawyers with graduate training in intellectual property law), who are all products of Nairobi's Anglophone middle class. Also important have been other music industry stakeholders who were introduced to Euro-American corporate music culture by the multinationals in Nairobi during the 1980s – individuals like John Katana, who has long been active in MCSK and is now a member of KECOBO. While some Tanzanians also engaged with Euro-American corporate music culture – Orchestra Talaka with Remmy Ongala, for instance, 'signed a [generous] contract with Polygram Records Limited in 1982 that allowed the group to maintain the copyright in all their musical works and earn royalties from each of their recordings' (Perullo 2011: 290) – it was Kenyans who had the opportunity to propagate it. The case of John Katana's band 'Them Mushrooms' is illustrative. Signed to Polygram and then CBS Records during the 1980s, they built their own recording studio in 1987 and started up a label shortly thereafter, forming it as 'a fully-fledged record company' in the mold of Polygram and CBS (recorded interview with A. Eisenberg, 1 August, 2012).

Where Kenya's music CMOs have failed so far is in the realm of cooperation. KAMP and PRiSK have worked in partnership since PRiSK's founding. Their ties with MCSK have been fractious, however. The three societies managed to agree in principle on a basic royalty split of 50% (MCSK)/25%/25%. But beyond that, they have not had much success in working together. The situation was exacerbated when KECOBO temporarily deregistered MCSK in 2011 based on an audit that suggested it was spending too much on administrative overhead. Since that incident, MCSK's leadership have been reluctant to incur administrative costs by collecting on behalf of the younger, smaller CMOs (Maurice Okoth, recorded interview with A. Eisenberg, 20 March, 2012). Without an agreement between the three CMOs, the organizations are necessarily less effective at collecting royalties, and sensitizing and lobbying for increased copyright protections.

CONCLUSION

Despite the similarity of their millennial copyright legislation, the distinct political-economic histories of Kenya and Tanzania have fostered divergent trajectories of musical property rights reform over the past decade. In Kenya, the partial formalization and internationalization of the music economy during the 1970s and 1980s established business practices modeled on those of the music recording industries in Europe and the United States. Such practices have always competed with other, less 'Western' ways of doing business. Nevertheless, at the turn of the millennium, Kenya's music economy still comprehended certain 'immutable mobiles' (Latour 1986) from the Global North – formal contracts, royalty payments, and collective management – that stood ready to combine with and reinforce globally 'harmonized' intellectual property law. Additionally, some lawyers in the country had familiarity with or studied intellectual property law. This meant that after the introduction of the 2001 Copyright Act a small but significant population of legal professionals were willing and able to participate in various ways in the difficult process of implementation. Some of these individuals have worked with a missionary zeal grounded in the belief that intellectual property law holds the promise of creating a more just society. Lawyer, former KECOBO intern and prominent blogger Victor Nzomo, for example, developed a passion for copyright law after seeing his mother's academic career negatively impacted by what he saw as intellectual theft (recorded interview with A. Eisenberg, 3 August, 2012).[8] Coupled with the partial formalization and internationalization of the music economy, the presence of professionals with experience and interest in intellectual property law led to a situation in Kenya whereby a set of individuals and institutions, including a trio of music CMOs, emerged as agents of legal, juridical and epistemic change, potentially instantiating functioning, Western-style musical property rights regime in the country (though such a state of affairs is still a long way off).

Meanwhile, Tanzania relied on a combination of state policies and informal practices in the implementation of copyright law. Even after the official end of socialism in the early 1990s, the government attempted to control all issues related to the commercialization of the arts. All bands and artists needed to register with the state-run National Arts Council (BASATA) and all copyright policies were handled by COSOTA. This state-centered control of the arts often became a nuisance for artists who typically found ways to circumvent any government policies that they believed stood in their way of earning a living. Through evading state control, in the early 2000s, the music economy grew at a rate faster than almost any other African country (WIPO 2012). This meant that artists relied on the informal economy to dictate the creation of contracts, authors' rights in music, and the payment of fees related to using other artists' songs. As a result, the standardization of copyright law within the country did not take place given the poor relationship between artists and the state, the lack of legislation aimed at addressing copyright issues, the absence of broader education about copyright law in the country, and the patchy payment of royalties.

It is important to note that the copyright situation is not necessarily enforced or administrated better in one country over another. The hundreds of formal interviews and informal discussions with Kenyan and Tanzanian musicians and music producers carried out by the authors of this chapter reveal that neither country has a musical property rights administration that works to the satisfaction of the citizens whose livelihoods it is meant to protect and creativity it is meant to support. There is substantial corruption in the legal systems of both countries; high rates of digital piracy are present all over eastern Africa; and rights holders continue to struggle to receive royalty payments (though MCSK's increased payouts represent a hopeful improvement in Kenya). Government agencies in both Kenya and Tanzania, particularly those in charge of IPR-related issues, also focus more on patents and technology, particularly biotechnology and pharmaceuticals, since these are seen as both greater concerns for the region and more financially lucrative.[9] This emphasis on patents over copyright has meant less government investment in improving the administration and enforcement of copyright law.

Nonetheless, through detailing the different trajectories of copyright law in Kenya and Tanzania, this article emphasizes the country-specific approaches taken to similar legislation. In discussing human rights in Argentina, Karen Ann Faulk describes the 'vernacularization of human rights discourses' where people and groups imbue international human rights with local meanings (2013: 5). A similar process is at play in East African countries where local histories, ideologies and uses of music shape the meaning of rights, music and ownership. This, in turn, impacts the outcome of copyright law in each country. While these countries also greatly influence each other – a topic not discussed in this article – the linguistic, cultural, economic and political differences between them create divergent approaches to rights. Being able to interpret these differences provides a means to comprehend the dynamic and shifting outcomes of law in African contexts.

ACKNOWLEDGEMENTS

Andrew Eisenberg's contribution to this chapter draws from data collected under the auspices of the European Research Council-funded 'Music Digitization, Mediation' project led by Georgina Born at Oxford University. He gratefully acknowledges the generous ERC funding and essential input from Georgina Born. Both Alex Perullo and Andy Eisenberg would like to thank the Tanzanian and Kenyan musical and legal professionals who freely shared their knowledge and views for this article.

NOTES

1 Before copyright laws were passed in East Africa, Alex Perullo conducted informal interviews there with elected officials from Malawi, Tanzania and Uganda about copyright law and artists' rights. While often sympathetic and supportive of artists' concerns, most believed that the other forms of intellectual property, such as patents and trademarks, were more important for the vitality of the local economy. In later interviews, this relation to the economic viability of the arts shifted in part due to the significant expansion of the music business in East Africa (Perullo 2011).

2 Originally set for 2006, extended to 2013 and then extended again to 2021, the most recent extension on the deadline for least developed countries was made on June 11, 2013 by the World Trade Organization as a means to give these countries more time to protect intellectual property rights.

3 British colonial authorities established the first copyright law in Tanzania on August 1, 1924. The law was an extension of the United Kingdom (Imperial) Copyright Act, 1911, which was enacted in most of Britain's colonies. After gaining independence from the British in 1961, the Tanzanian government created a new copyright law to better protect its interests. President Julius Nyerere officially passed the law, Copyright Act No. 61, in December 1966. The law made provisions for the copyright of literary, musical and artistic works, cinematographic films, sound recordings and broadcasts.

4 The one-day event was called the 'Stakeholders Dialogue Meeting', and took place at the Nyumbani Lounge in Dar es Salaam.

5 For an overview, see Sihanya (2010).

6 PRiSK was abbreviated to PRSK until June 2012, when they voluntarily changed their abbreviation to avoid conflict with the Public Relations Society of Kenya.

7 On an official visit to Nairobi in 2007, officials from CISAC made a 'lobbying visit to the Kenya Copyright Board Chairman and CEO, and the Ministry of Culture to discuss the obtaining of a license to operate as a collection society by MCSK' (CISAC 2007: 20).

8 Nzomo's blog, IPKenya (http://ipkenya.wordpress.com/), is the most prominent blog on IP issues in Kenya. KECOBO and Kenyan CMOs often share and comment on IPKenya posts on social media sites.

9 Kenya's KECOBO, of course, focuses exclusively on copyright matters. But it is situated within the Attorney General's office, which, in the view of a leading Kenyan IP scholar, has not given it the resources it requires (Sihanya 2005, 2010: 17). KECOBO also spends a great deal of time dealing with the matter of software piracy, most recently through an initiative with Microsoft (CIO East Africa 2013). In Tanzania, COSOTA also focuses on copyright matters but has faced numerous setbacks including a lack of funding from the state and a constantly shifting leadership (these details come from interviews with COSOTA staff and other agencies in Tanzania). Meanwhile, patents and biotechnology tend to be an important financial and administrative focus of the government.

The Tanzanian president, Jakaya Kikwete, is said to be an 'enthusiastic supporter' of biotechnology, and there is reported to be constant pressure from 'US driven biotech industry' in many parts of Africa (Visram 2013).

REFERENCES

Afrobarometer. (2012) *Tanzania Round 5 Data (2012)*. Retrieved from http://www.afrobarometer.org.

BASCAP (with the Kenya Anti-Counterfeit Agency). (2013) 'Promoting and Protecting Intellectual Property in Kenya'. International Chamber of Commerce, http://www.iccwbo.org/Advocacy-Codes-and-Rules/BASCAP/BASCAP-Gateways/Country-Gateways/Kenya/Kenya-Reports_-findings-and-documents/

Benda-Beckmann, Franz von, Keebet von Benda-Beckmann, and Anne M. O. Griffiths. (2009) 'Introduction: The Power of Law'. In *The Power of Law in a Transnational World: Anthropological Enquiries*, edited by Franz von Benda-Beckmann, Keebet von Benda-Beckmann, and Anne M. O. Griffiths. New York: Berghahn Books.

Blewett, Robert A. and Michael Farley. (1998) 'Institutional Constraints on Entrepreneurship in Kenya's Popular Music Industry'. In *African Entrepreneurship: Theory and Reality*, edited by Anita Spring and Barbara E. McDade. Gainesville: University Press of Florida.

Brennan, James R. (2012) *Taifa: Making Nation and Race in Urban Tanzania*. Athens: Ohio University Press.

CIO East Africa. (2013). 'Microsoft Partners with Kecobo to Fight Piracy in the Country'. CIO East Africa, November 28, http://www.cio.co.ke/news/main-stories/microsoft-partners-with-kecobo-to-fight-piracy-in-the-country (accessed on December 14, 2013).

CISAC (International Confederation of Societies of Authors and Composers). (2007) *Annual Report 2007*. http://cisac.org/CisacPortal/documentLink.do?sw=on&lang=en&id=13434 (accessed on July 22, 2013).

Eisenberg, Andrew J. (2012) 'M-Commerce and the (Re)Making of the Music Industry in Kenya: Preliminary Notes and Findings'. Paper read at Association for Social Anthropology, at New Delhi.

Faulk, Karen Ann. (2013) *In the Wake of Neoliberalism: Citizenship and Human Rights in Argentina*. Stanford: Stanford University Press.

Finnegan, David Louis. (2008) 'Law and Private Sector Development in Tanzania'. PhD dissertation, University of Michigan.

Furedi, Frank. (1974) 'The Development of Anti-Asian Opinion Among Africans in Nakuru District, Kenya'. *African Affairs* 73: 347–58.

Graham, Ronnie. (1989) *Stern's Guide to Contemporary African Music*. London: Pluto Press.

Harrev, Flemming. (1989) 'Jambo Records and the Promotion of Popular Music in East Africa: The Story of Otto Larsen and East African Records Ltd. 1952–1963'. *Bayreuth African Studies Series 9: Perspectives on African Music* 103–37.

IIPA (International Intellectual Property Alliance). (2003) Special 301 Report: Kenya. www.Iipa.Com/Rbc/2003/2003spec301kenya.pdf.

Iseme, Kamau & Maema, and Mohammed Muigai. (2009) 'Formulation of an EAC Policy on Anti-Counterfeiting, Anti-Piracy and Other Intellectual Property Rights Violations: Final Progress Report Country Specific Findings'. East African Community.

Ishengoma, Johnson M. (2008) 'Tanzania'. In *Higher Education in Africa: the International Dimension*, edited by Damtew Teferra and Jane Knight. Massachusetts, USA: Center for International Higher Education, Lynch School of Education, Boston College, 421–463.

Jjuuko, E.C. (2002) '$250,000 at Stake over Copyright Law'. *Uganda Confidential* 476(January 18–24): 5.

KECOBO (Kenya Copyright Board). (2011). 'The Scourge of Piracy: A Menace to Investors'. *Copyright News* 3 (July–September): 3–7.

Kongolo, Tshimanga. (1999) 'Does the Congo's Copyright and Neighboring Rights Law Conflict with the TRIPS Agreement?' *The Journal of World Intellectual Property* 2(2): 311–327.

Latour, Bruno. (1986) 'Visualization and Cognition'. *Knowledge and Society* 6: 1–40.

Malm, Krister and Roger Wallis. (1992) *Media Policy and Music Activity*. New York: Routledge.

Mangat, Jagjit Singh. (1969) *A History of the Asians in East Africa, c.1886 to 1945*. Oxford: Oxford University Press.

Mani, Imani. (2013) 'Ministry Vow to Help Musicians Get Royalties'. *Daily News*, 2 November.

Mtaki, C.K. (1996) 'The Legal System in Tanzania and the Quest for Rule of Law in a Free Market Economy'. *Change* 4(1–3): 4–12.

Muchangi, John. (2012) 'All Matters Music, Royalties and Copyright'. *The Star*, April 30, www.the-star.co.ke/news/article-20451/all-matters-music-royalties-and-copyright (accessed on November 8, 2012).

Mugwe, David. (2013) 'Fresh Enrolments from EA in American Varsities Drop as Kenya's Numbers Decline'. *The East African*, November 13. Available at: http://www.theeastafrican.co.ke/ (accessed on November 20, 2013).

Mwakikagile, Godfrey (2007) *Nyerere and Africa, End of an Era*. Pretoria, South Africa: New Africa Press.

Nyairo, Joyce. (2004) 'Reading the Referents': (Inter) Textuality in Contemporary Kenyan Popular Music'. PhD dissertation, University of Witwatersrand, Johannesburg.

Nyerere, Julius. (1971) *Ujamaa: Essays on Socialism*. New York: Oxford University Press.

Ondego, Ogova. (2000) 'Time is Running Out for Kenya's Piracy Industry'. *Daily Nation*, April 10, http://allafrica.com/stories/200004100075.html (accessed on November 27, 2013).

Ouma, Marisella. (2004) 'The Copyright Act 2001: A New Era for Copyright Protection in Kenya'. *e-Copyright Bulletin*, July–September.

Perullo, Alex. (2011) *Live from Dar es Salaam: Popular Music and Tanzania's Music Economy*. Bloomington: Indiana University Press.

Ramah, Rajab. (2012) Kenyan Musicians Embrace Technology to Combat Piracy. *Sabahi*, December 14, http://sabahionline.com/en_GB/articles/hoa/articles/features/2012/12/14/feature-02 (accessed on June 19, 2014).

Republic of Kenya. (1965) Parliamentary Debates. National Assembly, 7 December, http://books.google.co.ke/books?id=QeXv3w87y4wC

Republic of Kenya. (2001a) Parliamentary Debates. National Assembly, 20 November, http://books.google.co.ke/books?id=QeXv3w87y4wC

Republic of Kenya. (2001b) Parliamentary Debates. National Assembly, 11 December, http://books.google.co.ke/books?id=QeXv3w87y4wC

Sheuya, Shaaban. (2010) *Informal Settlements and Finance in Dar es Salaam, Tanzania*. Nairobi, Kenya: UN Human Settlements Program (UN-HABITAT).

Sihanya, Ben. (2005) 'Copyright Law, Teaching and Research in Kenya'. *East African Law Journal* 2: 28–63.

Sihanya, Ben. (2010) Copyright Law in Kenya. *IIC-International Review of Intellectual Property and Competition Law*, 41(8): 926–947.

Stapleton, Chris and Chris May. (1987) *African All Stars: The Pop Music of a Continent*. London: Quartet Books.

United Republic of Tanzania. (1999) Parliamentary Debates, April 14.

Visram, Nizar. (2013) 'Tanzania Told to Sever Link with Monsanto'. *Pambazuka News*, June 27.

Wallis, Roger and Krister Malm. (1984) *Big Sounds From Small Peoples: The Music Industry in Small Countries*. New York: Pendragon Press.

Wanyama, Mellitus Nyongesa. (2007) 'Policy and Implementation: A Case of Music Copyright Laws in Kenya'. *Muziki* 4(1): 27–41.

World Intellectual Property Organizatio (WIPO). (2012) *The Economic Contribution of Copyright-Based Industries in Tanzania*. Geneva, Switzerland.

PART III

Branding the World

Matthew David and Debora Halbert

While copyright and patent issues tend to draw the bulk of attention in the literature on intellectual property, trademarks, geographical indications, and other forms of collective rights management are also relevant to a broad understanding of intellectual property law. Trademarks, as Margaret Chon's chapter highlights, have moved well beyond the basic description of a product and are now designed to create identity and even citizenship with specific brands. Chris Rojek's chapter looks at this brand identity from the side of the counterfeit and attempts to delve into why the counterfeit remains popular even when its origins are known to be inauthentic. In both cases, it becomes clear that trademark law must be understood within a far more complex world of human emotion, consumer desires and capitalist markets than today's interpretations allow. While trademark law itself protects a particular mark from the likelihood of confusion in order to ensure brand authenticity, and in some cases safety, the culture of commodities found in modern capitalism means that brands themselves are a commodity to be purchased. The first two chapters in this section deal with the issue of trademarks and branding in this way.

Margaret Chon signals the importance of the trademark as a collective identifier. In other words, while a company might produce a specific mark, it is only in the interaction with consumers and the global market for the good that a brand identity is created and meaning is developed for the mark. Thus, the semiotic interpretation of a mark is substantially different from its descriptive existence. To discuss the complexity of trademarks as meaning makers, Chon develops and uses the concept of 'brand citizenship' and emphasizes the political significance of this concept.

Chon argues that we must go beyond a limited legal analysis of the brand to understand the global flow of culture and meaning making. In doing so, she provides a lens through which to view the globalization of intellectual property articulated by Halbert in the first section. These brand loyalties and citizenships transcend the more limited analysis of nation-state centered international relations. Instead they mark the global flow of contemporary capitalism. Thus, brand citizenship as a concept can better help us understand the symbolic uses of a mark in the global world.

Chon's analysis is important from a development perspective. She is clear that the focus on branding needs to be contextualized within the political economy of production and labour that remains exploitative of people and the environment. What is often forgotten is that under the popular brand lies a global network of exploited garment workers and destructive environmental practices. The recent news regarding deaths in garment factories in Bangladesh has momentarily made these issues visible, yet nothing substantive has been done.

In other words, brand citizenship and meaning making via consumer culture render invisible the costs of production and create what Chon calls an 'ethical distance' between the consumer and the way in which the products they consume were produced. One of the important contributions Chon's chapter makes is her effort to insert ethical thinking into the process of branding and trademarks. The brand, especially as an identifier of a kind of global citizenship, needs to be understood within these larger projects of meaning making. The labour and environmental practices of companies from fashion to big pharma need to be inserted into the discourses of brand citizenship, an alignment with a product that is intentionally cultivated.

Taking up the other side of the branding world, Chris Rojek's chapter looks at counterfeiting in the context of trademarks and branding. Counterfeit goods are those sold under the label of a company, but are not authorized by the company that owns the trademark to the goods. In other words, counterfeit goods are of concern to trademark holders because their existence can undermine trust in a brand if a consumer believes that they have purchased a legitimate product instead of an imitation. Counterfeit goods also challenge notions of authenticity and the value that a brand seeks to create in its product lines.

According to Rojek, trade in counterfeit goods remains significant at the global level and is often linked to organized crime, in part because the penalties for moving counterfeit goods is significantly less than those associated with other illegal goods (like drugs). Rojek's chapter maps counterfeiting as a global enterprise, with markets for counterfeit goods encompassing the entire globe. The ongoing popularity of counterfeit products is one of the underlying motivations for the highly controversial Anti-Counterfeiting Trade Agreement (ACTA). Rojek notes that the fluidity of global counterfeit markets makes them difficult to halt.

The issue is not as clear cut as one might initially think. While Rojek situates counterfeiting within the world of organized crime and as an attempt to confuse or mislead consumers into buying fake products, it turns out that many people willingly and knowingly purchase the counterfeit instead of the original. Rojek seeks to puzzle through why consumers would knowingly purchase counterfeit goods, given the assumptions about the importance of the brand in preserving authenticity. Of course, part of that answer is that there are different types of counterfeiting that must be delineated. Those purchasing a knock-off handbag where there is little consumer threat may simply be looking for a cheaper product, whereas those who unknowingly purchase counterfeit pharmaceuticals must be understood in an entirely different category of consumption. Distinguishing between the types of counterfeiting that occurs can help with the analysis of how one might craft adequate policy to protect consumers against possible threats emerging from some of these illicit markets.

In his analysis of counterfeits, Rojek argues that ultimately the flow of counterfeit goods is simply capitalism through a different lens, one reason why it is so difficult to halt and manage. It is a sort of counterfeit capitalism which runs in parallel to what the law has defined as 'legitimate' markets. Ultimately, Rojek highlights the complexity of the concept of an authentic product, the challenges of understanding commodities as authentic or as having meaning, and suggests that there is more work to be done if we are to understand the ongoing popularity of counterfeit products within global consumption chains. These are indeed worthy topics to consider.

Issues of authenticity, legitimacy and efforts to develop methods of economic preservation for indigenous communities are at the heart of the two-chapter contribution of Coombe, Ives and Huizenga. Building upon their analysis of the role of geographical indications in the global south, Coombe, Ives and Huizenga offer two case studies suggesting that there is a need to critically reflect upon the application of the concept of geographical indications to indigenous communities, despite the fact they are often touted as provided much needed protection and economic development.

Coombe, Ives and Huizenga provide a rich analysis of the concept of the geographical indication as one that creates important economic opportunities for some developing regions while undermining possible sustainable development in others. As with any space where the 'colonization of the life-world' is undertaken, to use a Habermasian term, there are consequences and trade-offs to narrating a way of life as important for a profit-making enterprise. As what had been a non-commodified space becomes commodified, it will generate a different set of winners and losers than existed before.

Geographical indications are one of the newest forms of intellectual property, emerging on the scene in the post-TRIPS world. The field of study is still emerging in terms of how the law is framed in each country. Coombe, Ives and Huizenga provide an excellent overview of the current status and legal complexities of geographical indications and the variety of permutations that are developing as this method of protection becomes popularized. In part, the policy space is complex because GIs are somewhere between a private property regime and 'locally bound public goods' (p. 211).

Coombe, Ives and Huizenga go beyond the description of the status of GIs to think more critically about what they call the 'social imaginary' of GI protection. What emerges in their analysis is the repeated development of a GI as a specific region that can then be narrated as a singular culture with one language and with a defined territory. In other words, the development of an economic system of geographical indications (GIs) is interconnected with the story that people in that region can and will tell about themselves. In this way, GIs tend to reproduce claims of authenticity and 'primordialism' that go unanalysed. Thus, GIs tend to socially construct the cultures they claim to emerge from.

As such, the social construction of a geographical region to sell a specific product might culminate in new permutations of inequality in some areas. However, there is an argument, the authors claim, for its progressive applicability to indigenous cultures and territories. In their two chapters in this section, Coombe, Ives and Huizenga develop an analysis of the costs and benefits of geographic indicators within the Latin American and South African contexts. It must be recognized in both cases, that despite the promise of better economic development, such a priority can also have 'exclusionary and destructive consequences' (p. 217). From mescal to potatoes to Rooibos tea, locally produced items are now wrapped into narratives of geographical and cultural specificity that may ultimately subordinate the historical producers of these products. The first chapter by Coombe, Ives and Huizenga speaks more generally about GIs in the context of South

American development. The second chapter takes up in more detail the case study of the implementation of GIs in South Africa around the issue of Rooibos tea.

Rooibos is a tea that has entered global markets as having a possible health benefit for those who drink it. The geographical origins of the rooibos plant offer a culturally diverse and historically complex example of how a geographical indication for a commercial product comes into contact with a local population and already existing system of production. As the tea has become more globally popular, interest in protecting its trademarks or localized identity has grown. Furthermore, the popularity of the tea has had not altogether positive consequences for the smaller farmers and local residents who have historically produced the product. These issues have been further complicated by issues of land tenure and racialized identity politics.

The focus on Rooibos helps highlight the ways in which the state can and should use the concept of a geographical indication to help establish a framework of social justice for indigenous people within its jurisdiction. South Africa can and should address issues of exploitation, historical discrimination and the need for a redistribution of land in the context of the 'imagined community' of indigenous Rooibos producers. Unless it does, the outcome may be that already entrenched systems of power remain unexamined and unchanged. For Coombe, Ives and Huizenga, GIs may serve as an opportunity for economic development within a context of improved conditions for indigenous peoples, but it should not be assumed that GIs will have this effect.

As should be clear, this section remarks upon a wide variety of property regimes that expand well beyond a traditional focus on copyright and patent law. While seeds also benefit from possible patent coverage, expanding property rights over agricultural products required new ways of understanding intellectual property. Thus, plant variety protection is what is called a sui generis form of intellectual property protection.

Chidi Oguamanam's chapter focuses on farmers' rights as they have evolved within the context of the global effort to assert ownership and control over seeds and thus food itself. His chapter builds upon the global analysis of intellectual property and development articulated in the previous section by looking at the often serious consequences of expanding intellectual property regimes for traditional farmers throughout the global south. Oguamanam provides a detailed history of agricultural production and the transition from small seed businesses to the contemporary corporate agro-business model that has radically changed the tradition of farmers saving, sharing and reusing seeds.

Farmers have become a problem for the seed industry much like music fans have become the enemy of the recording industry, where practices of sharing interfere with efforts to monopolize the economic rewards of the growing corporate agri-business/biotechnology sector. Furthermore, the assertion of intellectual property rights over seeds follows a similar trajectory regarding issues of social justice, labour exploitation, and a wilful ignorance of the contributions of all actors to the system as discussed by Chon in the first chapter of this section.

Oguamanam takes us through the complex international negotiations across multiple United Nations agencies that expanded plant breeders' protection and solidified their rights under the concept of intellectual property. In response to the protection afforded plant breeders, the language of farmer's rights emerged as a form of resistance. Articulating farmer's rights, often in the context of preservation of biological diversity and traditional knowledge, and in opposition to biopiracy, is an effort to insert the interests of farmers, especially those in the global south, back into international negotiations over agricultural products and their development. Defending the interests of farmers from the encroachment of corporate agricultural business interests is a matter of social justice as well as food security. Protecting farmer's rights is an important effort to halt or better balance the ongoing expansion of intellectual property. However, as Oguamanam notes, farmers' rights are not intellectual property rights, but an attempt to articulate an alternative to the growing use of intellectual property. The language of farmers' rights is now part of the international dialogue, but as yet does not hold the same level of power as that of plant breeders.

While the chapters in this section reflect on a variety of types of intellectual property, provide examples from a variety of regions around the world, and reflect upon a diverse set of issues, they share a common theme – a need to broaden the conversation over intellectual property from simply an assertion of private ownership. There are many rights that need to be set against the right to ownership, and even the notion of ownership of property itself is filled with tensions and interpretations that need to be voiced rather than spoken over. The balance between human rights, common heritage, collective rights and private rights over intellectual property must be brought to the forefront of development and IPR agendas.

9

Slow Logo: Brand Citizenship in Global Value Networks

Margaret Chon

INTRODUCTION: LOOKING GOOD

A brand-conscious rather than the typical brand-blind approach to trademarks ('marks') may identify significant gaps in trademark doctrine and theory as it is currently understood. And foregrounding citizenship around a brand can emphasize the importance of belonging to an accountable community, albeit one that may depend upon a fluid, pluralistic and open-ended construction of the value of marks and, importantly, their associated brands. As Seidman (2007: 18) notes:

> citizenship is a protean concept allowing local actors to articulate a wide variety of claims shaped to fit local circumstances. Despite that variation, it is important to recognize that for most of the past two centuries, labor rights have been central to citizenship narratives everywhere.

Presented here, therefore, is the case for a more relevant account of the role of marks in creating discursive and hence economic value: *brand citizenship*.

This proposed approach would acknowledge that the value of a mark is created by everyone and everything exchanging information around its qualities – as signaled in its most reductive form by the legal definition of a mark as a 'sign, or any combination of signs, capable of distinguishing the goods or services of one undertaking from those of other undertakings' (Agreement on Trade-Related Aspects of Intellectual Property Rights (TRIPS Agreement) Article 15(1) 1994). This global exchange of meaning involves not just consumers and firms but also intermediaries and producers as well as others creating meaning around that mark within a media-saturated context (Desai, 2012a, 2012b). In addition, as I have argued elsewhere:

> The current meaning-making environment for [marks] is highly dynamic. It involves overt interplay among the usual suspects: courts, agencies such as the US Patent and Trademark Office (USPTO), competitors in the realms of products and standards, and mark holders and consumers. But, the discourse also expands beyond this predictable epistemic community to include multiple other stakeholders: [standard-setting organizations such as the International Social Environmental Accreditation and Labelling (ISEAL) Alliance]; third-party certifiers (which may or may not be the same as the mark holders); other actors in the value chain; competing standard-setting bodies and their constituents, such as industry associations, consumer organizations, other NGOs, and other intergovernmental agencies; as well as other government agencies. (Chon, 2009: 2329–3)

Thus, brands can be defined for these purposes as the entire dynamic penumbra of functions, symbolic representations and values associated with the marketing of a specific mark, including its cultural, political and social substrates and impacts (Lury, 2004: 15; Arvidsson, 2006: 7–8).

The creation of economic markets through marketing with marks is as old as the existence of marks themselves (Von Staden, 2012; Bently, 2014). Yet the mechanics of marketing and markets are often well beneath the radar of typical current accounts of trademark law, with some limited exceptions (Litman, 1999; Lemley and McKenna, 2010; Desai, 2012a, 2012b). The concept of brand citizenship thus also partly addresses these curious and artificial disjunctures. By emphasizing the political significance of the brand – a presence that exceeds the formal legal boundaries of a mark – as well as its plasticity within the economic and social dynamics of marketing and markets, it has the potential to reveal new, previously invisible or suppressed forms of information exchange. The argument presented here in favor of recognizing brand citizenship builds upon the insights by Ritzer and Jurgenson (2010) that markets have adapted to the pervasiveness of media and that marketing has reinvented itself in this age of what this chapter terms informational or cognitive capitalism. It is critical to extrapolate from these important points to the related insights of new governance (Sabel and Zeitlin, 2008), which includes governance by information.

One premise of this chapter is that a brand usually drives and shapes much of the economic environment that legal scholars tend to see solely through the prism of marks. While not claiming that a brand ought to be exalted to the status of legal personhood (Desai 2013), or even a legally recognized category, the acknowledgement of brand citizenship urged in this chapter may create room for more profound forms of discursive and social relationships among consumers, firms and producers of goods and services marked and re-marked, as these (and they) circulate across territories and exceed the capacities of any one state to regulate for the global public good (Coombe and Stoller, 1994). For example, in 2001, two *Guardian* journalists followed a pair of jeans sold in the UK in its travels around the world. They documented a

> global journey of 40,000 miles by land and sea, starting from the fibre grown in Benin in West Africa to the manufacturing in Tunisia ... The jeans label could have said 'Made in Tunisia, Italy, Germany, France, Northern Ireland, Pakistan, Turkey, Japan, Korea, Namibia, Benin, Australia and Hungary' as all these countries were involved in some way. (Black, 2011: 72–3)

Situating the various informational exchanges associated with marks within territorially cross-cutting global regulatory frameworks, many scholars observe that certification, labeling and marks – along with contract and tort law – are central tools in governance of what are commonly referred to as global supply chains and what will be referred to throughout this chapter instead as *value networks*. The term *value* denotes both economic and non-economic value relevant to marks and brands; in addition to direct monetization, it includes key informational attention that builds brand awareness and recognition within a market (Swann, 2006: 943). The term *network* is intended to underscore a non-linear and domain-specific quality of multiple relationships among relevant market actors (Kaiser, 2006: 139). The term network also corresponds with the network governance based theory underlying certification systems.

For example, actors in a value network focused on the provision of wine may be organized differently in relation to each other than actors in a network focused on the provision of sustainably harvested wood or apparel (Cafaggi, 2010: 26; Blair et al., 2008; Meidinger, 2006; Segerlund, 2010; Büthe and Mattli, 2011; Dimitropoulos, 2011). This is because the industry structures differ, but also because the process of creating brand meaning may differ. And as Cafaggi (2010: 26) notes with regards to the relevant legal framework:

> Not only do consumers have low level[s] of participation in contractual design and standard-setting

within the food supply chain approach, but they also have very weak enforceability powers before courts. The accountability of these regimes is mainly based on the enforcement strengths of NGOs and, to a limited extent, competitors. The strengths and capacities of NGOs may vary across industries and countries.

In the wine industry, for example, brands overlap with other systems that regulate meaning such as geographical indications and cultural and religious proscriptions, as well as (of greatest relevance to this analysis) other regulatory regimes involving sustainability criteria such as fair wages, environmental health and workplace safety.

An emergent literature of inter-firm governance as well as intra-firm governance has linked contract-based oversight to global value networks (Strauss, 2012; Verbruggen and Schmidt, 2012). This genus of private regulation involves trust or at least mostly co-operative behavior between and among firms across spans of time and space, often crossing territories that define national trademark laws (Caldwell and Clapham, 2003). The centrality of maintaining consistent symbolic quality of a mark is linked to its integrity across a global value network – as the goods with which it is associated originate with producers in the network, make their way through the various intermediaries and finally are purchased by the consumer at the other end of an often long series of transactions. Yet, while purporting to represent or guarantee some characteristic, quality or value, no reliable or convincing account exists in current trademark law and theory of how the various facets of a mark's symbolic quality is enforced across far-flung actors throughout these global networks. Again, brand citizenship may operate as a useful heuristic in this regard. In these networked relationships, allegiance, loyalty and trust are key components for value creation (Powell, 1996: 51; Caldwell and Clapham, 2003: 63). The concept of citizenship triggers inquiry about whether and how these components can be mapped onto soft regulatory tools such as exit, voice and loyalty (Hirschmann, 1970; McDuffie and Helfer, 2005), or over-arching governance principles such as accountability, representativeness and transparency (Chon, 2009). Employing the vocabulary of citizenship invites politically meaningful participation in a community, albeit one dominated by an ethos of market-based consumption.

This chapter makes the case for a theoretical departure from existing approaches to trademark law. It first develops the proffered conceptual frameworks in more detail, and then connects informational capitalism to new governance through the heuristic of brand citizenship. Through these suggested analytical lenses, it then examines 'Big Fashion', which like its counterparts 'Big Pharma' or 'Big Tobacco' has become a highly concentrated industry focused almost solely on maximizing shareholder profit without regard to consumer, environmental or labor impact (Siegle, 2011). In this domain, for example, 40 million workers world-wide support the production of apparel, but they are often located thousands of miles from trademark owners and consumers, and their collective contribution to brand value is hidden and devalued (Siegle, 2011: 40). The chapter concludes with some tentative thoughts on the significance of brand citizenship in increasingly globalized markets where downward pressure on prices translates into greater global public 'bads', often imposed upon the most vulnerable. For consumers to 'look good' in both its aesthetic and ethical senses, brand citizenship demands attention to the ethical distance existing between these consumers and other stakeholders in the process of value creation of marks and their associated brands.

FROM SIGNALING FUNCTION TO BRAND CITIZENSHIP

A search cost rationale of marks dominates the current theoretical approaches to trademark scholarship (Landes and Posner, 1987: 265; Dogan and Lemley, 2004: 778). Sometimes also referred to as trademark's signaling function, this posits that marks serve primarily to decrease consumers' search costs by providing them with a shorthand reference or symbol upon which they rely repeatedly. The roles of stakeholders other than consumers and owners of trademark rights are minimized not only in these accounts but also in critiques of them. This section gives a brief overview of the present theoretical frames and identifies some knowledge gaps.

The Troubles with Trust in Trademark

Legal scholars have expanded upon the various assumptions underlying search cost theory. One view extends this theory, for example, to the special case of merchandising (Calboli, 2011), an increasingly widespread marketing practice that arguably leads to consumer confusion. Others have broadened the unilateral focus on the search cost rationale, while still focusing on the consumer as the key relevant stakeholder (Desai, 2012a). For example, Ariel Katz (2010: 1563) has disaggregated the reference function of marks into two major components

> that are related yet distinct: they reduce search costs by condensing complex meanings into concise and unequivocal terms, and they allow buyers to trust and rely upon the signals conveyed by sellers as guarantees for quality, thus helping to prevent the lemonization of markets for goods with experience and credence attributes. Let us call the first function the *linguistic function* of trademarks and the second the *trust function* of trademarks.[1]

This observation exposes an implicit and rather enormous assumption underlying the quality assurance function of trademark law as a species of consumer protection law. That is, trademark law assumes that consumers must be able to trust that the mark represents what the trademark holder tells the consumer it represents. Famously, this representation is supposed to signal source of manufacture and its associated qualities (e.g., the moderately sugary taste associated with Coke as distinguished from the sweeter taste of its main US competitor Pepsi so that consumers can choose between these two products) (Lemley and McKenna, 2012: 2109–11). Trademark law to date centers around disruptions in signaling that occur when false or confusingly similar signals are attached to similar products or services.

This signaling function cannot predict what happens, however, when the qualities of the good to which the trademark is attached are not readily apparent to the consumer (credence attributes). As Katz (2010: 1561) notes:

> Although economists use the terms search, experience, and credence goods, it is more correct to refer to attributes, as most goods or services may have different attributes that correspond to this classification. For example, the fact that a can of tuna looks like a can of tuna is a search attribute. The fact that the content tastes like tuna is an experience attribute. Whether the content is indeed tuna and not a good imitation, or whether it is safe for consumption, are credence attributes. Additional credence attributes may include whether the product contains genetically modified organisms, whether it was derived from organic farming, the age and working conditions of the work force, the environmental impact of the production process, compliance with animal welfare standards, nutritional properties, the geographical origin of the product, etc. – all of which may be important to some consumers.

For example, where a mark may state or suggest that the product is produced without child labor, the consumer has no way of checking on whether this is in fact true and must simply trust the mark and its associated labels. These opaque characteristics are often highly dependent for their accuracy upon intermediaries such as third parties in the value network such as certification bodies. While trust is a highly indeterminate concept (Deutsch, 1958: 265), in this trademark context it surely relates to the degree of alignment of the mark's qualities with consumer expectation of these qualities.[2] In the certification of credence attributes, such as organic cotton or organic avocadoes, trust also extends critically to upstream contractual guarantees between firms of quality assurance (Bachmann, 2006; Cafaggi, 2010).[3]

In this light, the sole doctrinal test for trademark infringement – likelihood of consumer confusion[4] – is woefully inadequate to the task of policing breaches of trust in instances of non-search attributes of marks (Chon, 2009). The core of an infringement action under both UK and US law is preventing passing off by a competitor of related goods with a confusingly similar mark. But if the purpose of marks is not just their signaling function, but increasingly to prevent the corrosive undermining of the mark's so-called trust function, then this doctrinal test falls far short. It is virtually impossible under current doctrine to get at the breach of trust that may occur if the representation of the credence attributes is false (Chon, 2009).

From Producers to Prosumers: The Co-creation of Goodwill

In addition to the protection of consumers from deception or passing off through its signaling function, the other oft-cited principle of trademark law is the protection of corporate goodwill associated with the mark. Goodwill is thought to accumulate through the repeated efforts of the mark owner to frame and consolidate the meaning of the mark's signaling function (McKenna, 2007). Yet a brief examination of this alternate prong exposes further conundrums associated with current prevailing doctrines and theories. One of the issues with this principle is its reliance on a dichotomy between trademark owners and consumers. Along with brand owners, however, consumers are producing enormous value for brands; they can be as involved in the production of meaning, attention and concomitant value as marketing departments.

The growing literature on the construction of brand meaning shows that the goodwill represented by a mark is not produced solely through a firm that technically owns the trademark rights. On the contrary, Arvidsson (2006: 13–14) argues incisively that:

> brands become valuable through their ability to manage and program human communication and appropriate the ethical surplus – the common – that it produces as a source of value. This valuable common is in turn produced by people who employ the generally available … media culture as a resource to enhance the productive potential of their communicative interaction.

Analogous claims about the increasing ubiquity of 'prosumption'[5] and (in the copyright context) 'user-generated content' (Lee, 2008: 1460; Gervais, 2009: 846–50; Hetcher, 2009: 1874–80) suggest that the global circulation of representations and symbols by and for consumers effaces formerly rigidly policed boundaries between producers and consumers of intellectual property-protected content. These pervasive social practices all but destroy the untenable assumptions that trademark value is all about protecting a signal tightly controlled by a corporate owner or content creator and unilaterally delivered to consumers (Gangjee, 2013). As with the trust function associated with credence attributes, these practices of creating goodwill are largely ignored in current legal scholarship. A focus on brands rather than marks makes this widely acknowledged value creation by consumers more explicit.

Poignantly and prominently absent from the discourse surrounding value creation of brands within global value networks is analysis of the value-enhancing activities of the classic producers of goods and services, such as the garment worker, the cotton picker or the coffee grower. For example, in his otherwise cogent analysis of the informational capitalism associated with branding, Arvidsson (2006: 89–90) simply observes, using Nike as an example, that 'material production is outsourced and beyond the formal control of the company' while he observes elsewhere that:

> Brand value is built through the appropriation of solidarity and affect generated in a plurality of different circumstances: in the Nikestore, on the sponsored inner-city basketball court, on the Nike

> goddess website for women, through the surveillance of teenage tastes and, not least by the construction of the company itself as an ambience of identification that permits employees to produce themselves as appropriate Nike people.

Work on the branding of indigenous knowledge (Frankel, 2012) or other forms of culturally-sourced knowledge – what Coombe and Aylwin (2011) have dubbed MICOs (marks indicating conditions of origin) – highlights the key roles of producers of these kinds of intellectual property. The growing literature on so-called sustainable goods such as fair trade also explores the work of the producers. These often include critiques of certification, which are often imposed without input from producers or which assign costs to the producers (Jaffee, 2007; Duguid, 2013). Outside of these bracketed areas, however, the work of articulating brand value created by producers is largely not discussed within intellectual property but rather assigned to labor sociologists (Miller and Williams, 2009), trade analysts (Saxena and Salze-Lozac'h, 2010), consumer activists (Nader, 2004: 196) and/or journalists documenting often deplorable working conditions (Greenhouse and Clifford, 2013). In the apparel industry, moreover, a number of other stakeholders including designers, weavers, dyers, buyers, and others are involved in the complex process of sourcing a garment. A theory of brand citizenship may help to account for the informational value contributed by many stakeholders other than consumers and owners, but the focus here is on the big three: consumers, owners and producers.

Network Dyads of Brand Citizenship within Informational Capitalism

In short, the value of brands (that is, the attention they receive in economic, political and social realms) is co-created by various stakeholders as they exchange meanings with each other. Brands are a type of social performance by consumers to other consumers (C2C). This type of informational exchange is especially true with respect to status goods such as genuine designer clothing (Veblen, 1899; Beebe, 2010; Zimmerman, 2012), but also occurs pervasively with less well known or famous marks (Arvidsson, 2006; Heymann, 2009). Brands exhibit key information from firms to other firms (B2B), for example, to signal information for market-differentiating purposes (Mundlak and Rosen-Zvi, 2011). It goes without saying that brands are performed aggressively by firms to the consumers (B2C) who purchase goods that are marked (Brown, 1948; Lury, 2004). And consumers' expression of feelings, motivations and a set of emotional responses towards a business (C2B) through parody or other means is well documented (Adbusters, n.d.; Klein, 1999). The social knowledge created by consumer practices such as 'playing, worshipping, wining and dining or just looking – that used to be considered part of the wasteful realm of consumption' (Arvidsson, 2006: 6) are viewed as a source of value in its own rights within the frame of cognitive capitalism.

A more precise correspondence of trademark doctrine and theory to evolving social practices would account for these and other informational exchanges. For example, it would also provide space for more meaningful exchange from producers to firms (P2B) – one not confined solely to the logic and metrics of labor law. And it might open the possibility of direct exchange between producers and other stakeholders within a global value network. The art collective known as Superflex has, for example, literally performed (as a type of art) creative, discursive and material collaboration between Brazilian producers of a drink and Danish consumers of the same product (Superflex, 2003, 2014).[6] While perhaps idiosyncratic, Superflex arguably heralds and models the urgent need for a less distanced information flow between consumers and producers (C2P and P2C) than currently exists through certification and labeling regimes.

Brands generate myriad social and environmental consequences in addition to the sales of goods and services. While private regulatory systems hold potential for ameliorating these externalities, they depend unduly on trust mechanisms that are thin (Gargiulo and Ertug, 2006: 165). They also maintain and enforce remoteness between key stakeholders (such as consumer and producers) through their insistence on reliance on voluntary codes of conduct while simultaneously communicating these regulatory norms solely through price and wage mechanisms (Seidman, 2007: 113; Ha-Brookshire and Norum, 2011). This inherent paradox also compartmentalizes away any value (besides in the classic Marxist sense of appropriated surplus value) contributed by producer and renders invisible the value that other stakeholders add to the mark or brand. Brand citizenship tentatively suggests new and creative pathways to participate and claim value-generating activities towards the brand. At the very least, a focus on brands rather than marks per se more accurately depicts the entire governance field in which trademark law operates to ensure consistent and recognizable quality, which is its supposed raison d'être.

BRAND CITIZENSHIP IN THE NEGATIVE SPACE OF IP

The apparel industry (also referred to as fashion or the fashion industry) provides fertile ground for the investigation of brand citizenship. Some have focused on fashion's role in promoting status distinctions (Beebe, 2010) despite the mandate of IP in the US Constitution 'to promote Progress'. Others have focused on fashion's democratizing potential through the provision of lower cost status items, whether genuine or not (Sun, 2012; Zimmerman, 2012). Characterized as a form of semiotic disobedience (Katyal, 2006), forms of free expression around fashion and other IP-protected goods are well-recognized and documented (Dreyfuss, 1990; Coombe, 1991; Ramsey, 2010). Recently, fashion has been recruited to the so-called 'negative space of IP' (Raustiala and Sprigman, 2006: 1687), where the source of competitive advantage derives from copying rather than copyright (Raustiala and Sprigman, 2012).[7] Beyond this initial observation, however, the global industrial sector of apparel design, production, sourcing and distribution bears further scrutiny through brand citizenship, if only because trademark and trade dress laws are the principle regulatory mechanism in the area of design (including fashion) in jurisdictions such as the US (Scafidi, 2006: 115).

Looking Good

In both the ethical and aesthetic senses, human desires to look good exemplify many of the broader issues around information exchange creating value. Fashion is a site for myriad public conversations (C2C, B2C, etc.), possibly around the images of a fashion item and the creation of a consumer 'common' (Arvidsson, 2006: 19–23) or around the aesthetic practices of fashion.[8] As Schor (2005: 446) states:

> What we wear is important to the way we experience our sexuality. Our age. Our ethnicity. It allows us to show respect for others (by dressing specially for a social occasion) or to signal community (through shared garments or styles). Finally, clothing can be part of the aesthetic of everyday life. There is genuine pleasure to be gained from a well-made, well-fitting garment. Or from a piece of clothing that embodies beautiful design, craftspersonship, or artistry. Throughout history, human beings have exercised their creativity through clothing, footwear, and accessories.
>
> In sum, dressing and adorning are a vital part of the human experience. That is why any attempt to put them into a minimalist, utilitarian box will fail. Clothes embody far more than our physical bodies; they are also a measure of our basic values and culture.

From an ethical angle, a distinguishing feature of the fashion sector is its direct intersection with fair labor issues. Persistent out-sourcing of manufacture and consequent lack of direct accountability over producer conditions sharpens many of the challenges associated with global governance in this domain. Unlike the positive valorization associated with distributed and decentralized digital networks to date (Barron, this volume), the decentralized producers of democratizing fashion often are associated with the most recognizably oppressive labor conditions (Traub-Werner, n.d.). Their activities are informalized, according to Fiona Wilson (1991: 191), that is they

> inhabit a social world where [they] sell their labour power but where enterprises are often officially illegal due to non-compliance with labour and tax legislation ... Typically, the labour of women, children and ethnic 'minorities' (in a social sense but not necessarily numerical sense) has been seen as 'outside' the realm of organized labour, and therefore the work they do has been seen as falling 'outside' the orbit of 'formal' industry where labour legislation is considered rightly applicable.

In utter contrast to the glamorous images associated with high-end celebrity consumers and designers who tout fashion brands through red carpet appearances, the factories that are supplying much of the goods in this sector continue to evoke references to the Triangle Waist Company shirtwaist factory fire in New York City resulting in the deaths of mostly young immigrant women (Dickson et al., 2009: 11–13). This tragedy brought into existence the National Consumers League and eventually catalyzed labor regulation at the national level in the US (Dickens, 1842, 1850: 66–70; Dickson et al., 2009: 97–107). For today's US consumers who avail themselves of the myth that 'made in the USA' means sweatshop-free, however, the reality is that poor labor conditions abound in export processing zones and special territorial carve-outs (Dickson et al., 2009: 12–13),[9] not to mention hidden enclaves within the territorial US (Su, 1998). The situation is repeated throughout the developing world.

In addition to the negative externalities in the labor sector, fashion has enormous negative environmental impact. This includes disproportionate use of pesticides, hazards from chemical dying, over-herding or poor treatment of animals, deforestation, over-use of energy in washing and aftercare (which constitutes the lion's share of the energy life cycle), as well as the exponential rise of clothing disposed in landfills (Schor, 2005: 443; Orzada and Moore, 2006: 299–313). The market in second-hand clothing donated by consumers in industrialized countries has also negatively impacted textile markets in developing countries (Dickson et al., 2009: 249–81; Black, 2011: 193–4).

These various concerns have resulted in what is sometimes denoted as the sustainable fashion movement (Cline, 2012: 190). One could call it slow fashion, in contradistinction to so-called fast fashion that dominates apparel consumption today. Fast fashion is inexpensive and designed to be obsolete in a short period of time, an example of 'induced obsolescence' (Raustiala and Sprigman, 2012: 1718–28). It is allegedly democratizing through its accessibility to all income levels, so that high and low as well as fast and slow fashion can be hacked, mashed and remixed. Michelle Obama's fondness for J. Crew and Catherine, the Duchess of Cambridge's occasional forays into Topshop illustrate that even the most privileged can bargain-shop with the rest of us. Biannual product cycles are non-existent in apparel companies such as Zara – its clothes are produced in small batches and are intended to be replaced by buyers as soon as the latest trend appears (Siegle, 2011: 20–5).

Sustainable fashion, by contrast, strives to reduce environmental impact and promote fair labor practices, combining social with economic development. It is associated loosely with socially responsible trade and its brands have grown in impact and attention. Indeed slow fashion has progressed rapidly to the point that distinctions can be made among various sub-sectors such as community and fair trade; ecological and slow design; recycle, reuse and redesign; and other sectors (Brown, 2010).

Apparel and the Limits of New Governance

Apparel is a critical industry for the study of the emergence of new institutional forms of governance because the certification systems in this area appear to be among

> the first programs that have attempted to address the operation of entire industries, rather than building niche markets for products made through uncommon practices, as has been the strategy in organics and Fair Trade products. In this sense … labor standards certification programs are attempting to be more 'regulatory' than some other labeling efforts, *although they clearly mix regulatory strategies with marketing ones*. They are therefore highly relevant for building theories of private regulation and industry governance. (Bartley, 2003: 438, emphasis added)

Responding to the twin pressures of social movements and global trade, brand citizenship – particularly as linked to the trust function of trademarks – is potentially a key frame for this new governance. In short, brands are much more vulnerable to consumer and other social movements when they are well known and where producer conditions are revealed to outsiders. The anti-sweatshop movement targeting Nike in the 1990s is one prominent example of this dynamic.[10] As a result of this public scrutiny, Nike has oddly become one of the industry leaders in social reporting and systems – although given the overall low standards existing with respect to auditing trails and systems, this pinnacle achievement may not be a sign of great progress. As observed astutely:

> Big Fashion will always be fighting against itself: it is predicated on a business model that is too vast and too sprawling for the exercise of proper control. So even while a brand is receiving compliments from the industry on its CSR reporting, that same brand could end up in the newspapers, or at the heart of a sweated labour scandal, in flagrant violation of its own codes of conduct. (Siegle, 2011: 249)

Current public policies addressing the apparel industry's labor practices are arguably forged in the failure of multilateral or intergovernmental solutions to problems posed by transnational markets in goods such as fashion (Bartley, 2003: 454). 'Two types of factors led to the initial emergence of private certification: (1) social movement campaigns targeting companies and (2) a neoliberal institutional context' (Bartley, 2003: 433). The alternative trade approach conveniently relies on certification and labeling by private NGOs or public-private partnerships. These private bodies can perform these tasks in lieu of certain regulatory functions that might be viewed as non-tariff barriers to trade if performed by public agencies under the multilateral framework of the World Trade Organization (Bartley, 2003: 451). And so-called alternative trade is often conflated with effective oversight of the sustainability dimensions of trade, such as labor and environment. Yet many have noted the lack of effective enforcement.

This relates to the larger, important point that even proponents of private governance acknowledge: efforts such as codes of conduct cannot wholly replace functioning public law frameworks (Sabel and Zeitlin, 2008). Public law institutions, including multilateral and other trade regimes, must identify where private frameworks operate optimally and where they fail. Trade pressures in the wake of the recent spate of building fires and collapses has forced at least one government to enact labor legislation to appease the brand owners and consumers in the EU and US (Greenhouse, 2013).[11] The plan

> [u]rges Bangladesh to impose stiffer penalties, including taking away export licenses, on garment factories that violate labor, fire or building safety standards. In addition, the [Obama] administration recommended that Bangladesh create a public database of all garment factories for reporting labor, fire and building inspections, including information on violations found, penalties assessed and violations corrected, with the names of the lead inspectors. (Greenhouse, 2013)

Additionally, any long-term success of privatized regulatory approaches is highly dependent upon collaboration between major brands to higher collective standards, as well as recognition of collective labor practices, combined with greater control by brand owners of their so-called supply chains (Miller and Williams, 2009). None of these conditions for success is likely to emerge quickly or without much public pressure. For example, in the recent debate after the largest apparel industry accident in history, a building collapse in Bangladesh that killed over 1,000 garment workers, most of the big US brands did not join the initial plan implemented by the major European brands (Alderman, 2013). Ultimately, the US manufacturers collaborated on an alternative agreement committing them to far less potential legal liability (Berfield, 2013; Greenhouse and Clifford, 2013).

These and other recent high profile tragedies have made clear that the apparel industry is still not fully internalizing the costs of safety and welfare of workers or the impact on the environment (Anderson, 2013). Global decentralization of so-called cut-make-and-trim or CMT factories has resulted in widespread loss of direct oversight and control by major brands over the way apparel is sourced and produced (Siegle, 2011: 48, quoting Doug Miller). At the same time, the rapid product cycle associated with fashion (particularly fast fashion, often marketed to young demographic groups, at the other extreme end from couture, which was and still is produced in ateliers at great expense by skilled workers) depends heavily upon largely unregulated manufacturing sites.

Among chroniclers of Big Fashion, there is outright skepticism that certification to private standards, the use of audit trails by brand owners or even greater numbers of state inspectors are capable of regulating against poor working conditions, substandard wages or child labor (Siegle, 2011: 75–80). For instance, a US-based non-profit organization, Social Accountability International (SAI), certifies factories to compliance with its private standard, known as SA8000 (Dickson et al., 2009: 230–2). The SA8000 standard 'stipulates that workers be paid enough to meet the basic needs of works and their families, or a living wage' (Dickson et al., 2009: 230–2).[12] However, compliance with this standard does not necessarily guarantee worker safety. As Rainier Braun (2011: 340–41) notes:

> SA8000 certification provides a multistakeholder seal of approval for decent working conditions at a specific farm or factory. In order to obtain certification, individual companies invite third-party auditors to inspect their facilities. SAI trains these auditors to carry out inspections while [Social Accountability Accreditation Services] supervises the auditing companies. SAI does not itself certify facilities ... Certification with SA8000 is a supply-chain management tool, intended to (a) reduce reputational risk for transnational corporations that might be adversely affected by stories about abusive working conditions, and (b) stabilize the supply-chain itself by improving efficiency and reliability. Certification does not lead to the social labelling of products for consumers, as in the case of fair-trade initiatives, and the effects of certification on product marketing are debated.

One of the factories that caught on fire in Pakistan recently, causing the deaths of over 250 garment workers, was allegedly certified to meet this standard.[13] As another observer describes SAI:

> The not-for-profit, industry-controlled auditors ... first emerged in 1996 and 1997 when two associations emerged. The first association was developed by the Apparel Industry Partnership which established the Fair Labour Association and the second association was the Council on Economic Priorities Accreditation Agency, which subsequently changed its name to Social Accountability International. These industry-controlled certification associations were established directly in response to the lack of accountability and appearance of validity of the existing auditing procedures. (Harpur, 2010–11: 57)

The continuing deficit in regulatory effectiveness and oversight, whether US-based or elsewhere, arises also from private regulatory capture combined with the overall lack of trained auditors and certifiers, as well as insufficient incentives and numbers for those who are trained to be rigorously evaluative (Braun 2011; Harpur, 2010–11). Under an increasingly accelerated fast fashion cycle, the apparel industry employs buyers who are under extreme pressure to make deadlines and cut costs, and therefore turn a blind eye to any sustainability issues (Dickson et al., 2009: 296; Siegle, 2011: 80–6). And the consistent failure of industry oversight is due as well in no small part to the reluctance of major brand owners to work collaboratively toward a common industry-wide regulatory standard, to extend financial support to factory owners to upgrade facilities and/or to support national regulation with regard to collective bargaining and other workers' rights (Greenhouse, 2013).

At the same time, consumers are remote in every sense of the word from these practices. Ironically, however, most scholars focus on consumer-based social movements as a key policy lever to change this dynamic. They posit that NGOs and other civil society organizations are a potentially effective counterweight to the decisions of brand owners in their race to the bottom. Before this counterbalancing policy shift can occur within the framework of information capitalism, however, certain informational 'market failures' need to be addressed and remedied.

Brand Citizenship, Information Capitalism and Alternative Trade

Brand owners harness and ultimately appropriate the work of consumers and producers (as well as others) in creating value in brands. Brands are an intensely personal form of identity construction for consumers (Roberts, 2003: 160), and this is reflected in current orthodox marketing strategies and theories. Social media marketing via brands represents an innovative and highly successful adaptation of capitalism to information-driven markets, moving away from a one-way broadcast model toward what could be described as a controlled chaos (Arvidsson, 2006: 16). Brand owners rely overtly on unremunerated labor in the form of consumers embedded within multiple social matrices and dense information networks.

However, the efforts of the heroic consumer enshrined in either narratives of new governance or prosumption inevitably overshadow the work of other key stakeholders in the creation of brand value. Garment workers often do not recognize either the mark or the brand for which they are producing fashion, yet in the words of one of these workers, 'I have lots of feelings about where I work. … Lots of bad feelings, really. I feel like we suffer a lot, particularly if we can't meet the targets we are set' (Arvidsson, 2006: 45). The critical question under the paradigm of brand citizenship is then how to bring these voices into the value networks for meaningful information exchange about the brand, possibly moving the brand into a more sustainable direction. Can encouraging greater information exchange between and among participants function as a type of soft regulatory power – a type of governance by information within informational capitalism – in order to align needed reforms with negative labor or environmental impact?

A Consumer Ethics and Politics of Brand Citizenship

From a consumer perspective, applying socially responsible trade criteria to Big Fashion results in suggestions for reform that include 'exit' from the system: either breaking the addiction to fast fashion (which can be analogized to fast food addiction), buying higher quality clothing (including handcrafted or even artisanal clothing – obviously more within the reach of some than others) or turning to recycled or up-cycled fashion rather than buying new products. These proposals do not intersect with brand citizenship so much as signal a type of boycott from the overall vehicle of branding altogether, to avoid being complicit with the so-called Walmartization of retail.

By contrast, stakeholders who would rather not abandon Big Fashion want to exercise a type of agency or 'voice' with respect to credence attributes. In these cases, brand citizenship may point to avenues ensuring greater informational exchange among stakeholders. These consumer stakeholders yearn to be able to rely on transparency of information so as to make better choices (suggestions include to 'buy like a utility', 'buy the story' or 'buy right') (Siegle, 2011: 279, 286, 288) in the face of incomplete, opaque and outright fraudulent certification and labeling regarding conditions of manufacturing source.

Consumer and other social movement boycotts (in the manner of the Nike-based imbroglio) can be a symbolic stick by threatening brand loyalty through its up-ending of brand trust:

> An interesting sort of politics of legitimacy and information ensues, along with pressures for institutions that can generate credibility and impersonal trust. This dynamic is especially likely to take hold when companies have invested in creating brand images that are cognitively and emotionally significant in the minds of consumers and investors – and thus worth defending in the media and public arena. As social movements increasingly target companies – rather than or in addition to governments – and brands become sites of cultural and political struggle, it may add a new layer to the politics of regulation in the twenty-first century. (Siegle, 2011: 358)[14]

Over-relying on the stick of 'exit' from the brand may be ineffective and have unintended consequences, however. As one labor sociologist notes (Seidman, 2007: 7):

> [c]onsumer pressure has been most successful when it is mobilized through institutions, not by appeals to individual consumers making decisions in supermarket aisles. Rather than relying on individual consumers to make ethical choices, campaigns that have forced corporations to accede to independent monitoring have invariably worked through more organized consumer pressure – through church groups, universities, and major stockholders.

However, these efforts often result in reducing the producer to victim status, and can result in the opposite of what is intended by causing firms to feign compliance (Seidman, 2007: 32–3).[15] Seidman proposes expanding institutional spaces for the direct empowerment of producers (Seidman, 2007).

Slow Logo: Putting the People and Planet into Profit

In the apparel industry and elsewhere, observers across the spectrum realize that the current system of audit trails and reliable certification is inadequate and inefficient. Opinions vary on whether these private forms of regulation can be made more effective (Harpur, 2010–11).[16] In response to a question about the need for urgent reform, one fair trade manufacturer (Minney, 2011: 172) observed:

> Transparency and traceability urgently need to be improved within the fashion industry to help prevent child labour and sweatshops. [We are] working on an exciting project for the EU Geo Fair Trade project which will increase transparency throughout the supply chain. Ultimately, the consumers will be able to scan a barcode into their phone and see our entire production process, from the community-owed plantation on the coast of Ecuador where our straw grows, through to the women's weaving association in the highland region.[17]

And 'by opening channels of communication within functional areas of the business, such as design and product development, sourcing, and logistics', producers can approach embedded institutional customs with new perspectives from their ground-level experiences and knowhow (Dickson et al., 2009: 310). A small but growing segment of Big Fashion reformers have made attempts to increase labeling information to trace production all the way through the value network, and to communicate these provenance characteristics of the brand to their markets.[18] This includes alternative brands, but also internal advocates within Big Fashion who are attempting to hold the brands accountable to the rhetoric of the triple bottom line (people, planet and profits) popularized in corporate social responsibility literature (Minney, 2011: 158, interview with Claire Hamer, who uses the term 'intrapreneur').

The greater capacity of brands and marks to convey these forms of traceability, transparency and tacit knowledge is largely aspirational, but nonetheless well within reach with the assistance of available technologies such as Quick Response ('QR') codes, smart phones and online industry-wide databases with more detailed information around brands. Information made available by brand owners around these characteristics is currently subsumed within marketing claims not subject to accountability or transparency. Yet emerging practices in response to the excesses of Big Fashion suggest possible models for brand citizenship that facilitate the emergence of robust information exchange around brand characteristics that emphasize and evaluate credence qualities.

CONCLUSION

The ruins of conventional trademark doctrine and theory are largely undiscerned, although evidence abounds about the crumbling, if not of trademark law's empire, then at least of many of its foundational assumptions. Examined here is one particular aspect of this claim: the practices of those who participate in informational exchanges to create the meaning of marks (that is to say, all of us who participate in market-based interchanges).

Global consumers are increasingly activist, playful, skeptical and sophisticated regarding marks' linguistic functions, but arguably we are rather more feckless and uninformed about the credence and other trust-based representations of a brand-owner with respect to unseen qualities of a mark.

In the current brand-driven universe, the ethical distance from producers to other stakeholders remains immense (Siegle, 2011: 59). It is fair to say that most prevailing accounts of informational capitalism and new governance add to the almost unilateral focus on consumer agency and consumer efforts in creating or critiquing value through speech. This singular focus concomitantly disregards most other stakeholders who are nevertheless materially if not discursively present. This informational market failure on a grand scale has been tolerated, and even driven by consumer confusion quite different from the passing-off privileged by trademark law. Nevertheless, by operating through collective signifying networks, brand citizenship may hold out a partial solution to the proliferation of credence attributes, the increasing reliance on private governance mechanisms as well as the interdependent yet still too distantly connected interests of producers and consumers within value networks. Thus, slow logo signifies the reintroduction of the

> social – frequently understood as value, meaning or culture – into what are seen as restricted accounts of the rationality of the agents of the economy ... in ways which introduce qualitative intensivity into the extensive but limited rationality of a conventional market economy of price. (Lury, 2004: 6)

The marketing of marks through markets is a key site for future inquiry and action, and brand citizenship through value networks may expand our understanding of brands as a medium for expressing certain qualities into the quantities demanded by markets.

ACKNOWLEDGEMENTS

Versions of this work were presented at the Brand New World symposium at UC Davis Law School, the IP in the Snow meeting, the International Intellectual Property Roundtable at University of San Diego Law School and the Sage Handbook Symposium at Durham University. Special thanks are due to the various organizers (especially Professors Mario Biagioli, Irene Calboli, Anupam Chander, Matthew David, Scott David, Deven Desai, H. Tomás Gómez-Arostegui, Debora Halbert, David Hall, Lydia Loren, Lisa Ramsey, Zahr Said and Madhavi Sunder), and to the other participants of these events who provided helpful advice, encouragement and feedback. Thanks also to Professor Charlotte Garden for her comments about *Nike v Kasky*, to research librarian Kerry Fitz-Gerald; and to Jenny Ling, Seattle University School of Law class of December 2012; David Savage, class of 2013; and Elizabeth Whitney, class of 2015, for their outstanding research support.

NOTES

1 Katz (2010: 1563) also notes, 'I choose the term "linguistic function" to highlight the point that trademarks' capacity to denote complex meanings is similar to the capacity of any word, term or name to denote complex meanings and to highlight the point that trademarks, once used in association with products, enter our communicative vocabulary. I choose the term "trust function" to highlight trademarks' capacity to denote unobservable experience and credence attributes, thus allowing consumers to trust specific sellers or products. The latter depends on the former: being able to trust that the seller provides or the product has the desired but unobservable attributes, the consumer must be able to reliably distinguish between different sellers or products'.

2 Deutsch (1958: 266) notes: 'An individual may be said to have trust in the occurrence of an event if he expects its occurrence and his expectation leads to behavior which he perceives to have greater negative motivational consequences if the expectation is not confirmed than positive motivational consequences if it is confirmed'.

3 Cafaggi (2010): 'Contractual networks directed at information transmission should govern the different sources of safety hazards: some dependent on fraudulent and negligent conduct and some arising out of risks unknown at the time of product safety design … An important yet often neglected role in these networks is played by the certifiers. These are generally third parties paid by suppliers but chosen by retailers, which certify compliance. Given their strategic monitoring function, they ideally should be part of the information network to constitute an additional and more effective source for consumer information'.

4 In the United States, this likelihood of consumer confusion standard is a doctrine based on sections 32(1)(a) and 43(a)(1)(A) of the Lanham Act, which both turn on the use of a mark that is 'likely to cause confusion'. US lawyers often refer to the multi-factor analysis associated with the judicial application of this legal standard as the 'Polaroid Test' after the leading case in this area. See *Polaroid Corp. v Polarad Elecs. Corp.*, 287 F.2d 492, 495 (2d Cir. 1961), *cert. denied*, 369 U.S. 820 (1961). In the United Kingdom, the consumer confusion doctrine is found in section 5(2) of the UK Trade Marks Act of 1994 ('Relative Grounds for Refusal of Registration'), and section 10(2) ('Infringement of Registered Trademark'), as well as under section 56(2) ('Protection of Well-known Trade Marks: Article 6*bis*'). See also Cornish, Llewelyn and Aplin (2010).

5 Ritzer and Jurgenson (2010) define prosumption as: 'Prosumption involves both production and consumption rather than focusing on either one (production) or the other (consumption)'.

6 The concept behind Guaraná Power is described further at: http://sts.ucdavis.edu/csis-sts-special-event-superflex-at-mondavi

7 One could question whether fast fashion with its ever-shortening product cycles is truly about product innovation or whether it is about marketing 'innovation' and expansion through copying combined with unsustainable price competition.

8 See, for example, http://www.luckymag.com/blogs/luckyrightnow/2012/08/Kate-Middletons-Closing-Ceremony-Outfit-Shop-Her-Outfit#/slide=1 (collating low cost versions of Kate Middleton's Olympic outfit).

9 Saipan was described by one lawyer as 'America's worst sweatshop', where more than 50,000 Asians have been recruited with promises of good wages to make clothing tagged 'Made in the USA'. '[These conditions] have persisted for the past decade in the 13-mile-long tropical isle in the Central Pacific … and "make medieval conditions look good", according to [one observer.] The factories stamp their clothing with "Made in the USA" and are able to sidestep duties, tariffs and quotas imposed on imported clothing'; see also Brooklyn Without Limits, available at: http://www.imdb.com/title/tt1635819/ (*30 Rock* episode) (thanks to both Charlotte Garden and Madhavi Sunder for pointing this out). (See Dickson et al., 2009: 12–13).

10 *Nike, Inc. v Kasky*, 539 U.S. 654, 655–8 (2003).

11 Stephen Greenhouse (2013) (outlining plan that 'urges Bangladesh to impose stiffer penalties, including taking away export licenses, on garment factories that violate labor, fire or building safety standards. In addition, the [Obama] administration recommended that

Bangladesh create a public database of all garment factories for reporting labor, fire and building inspections, including information on violations found, penalties assessed and violations corrected, with the names of the lead inspectors').

12 Dickson et al. (2009: 230–2) (explaining that the SA8000 standard 'stipulates that workers be paid enough to meet the basic needs of works and their families, or a living wage'); Paul Harpur (2010–11) ('The Fair Labour Association and SA8000 are both schemes which posit standards and certify third party certification bodies to actually perform the audits. The Fair Labour Association and Social Accountability International do not actually perform audits themselves. The SA8000 scheme, for example, contains extremely detailed standards on labor conditions including safety protection and guards, OSH training, hygiene and other OSH factors. Factories are audited by qualified certification bodies. Auditing firms become certified under SA8000 by applying to Social Accountability Accreditation Services for accreditation. Social Accountability Accreditation Services assesses the expertise of the auditing firm through an impartial assessment procedure, and periodically reviews the accuracy of the certification body's auditing by performing their own audits. This means that a certification body which performs confounded audits may have their certification revoked.')

13 'Despite survivors' accounts of locked emergency exits and barred windows that prevented workers from leaping to safety, the Bhailas' lawyer says their SA8000 certificate, issued under the auspices of Social Accountability International, a respected nonprofit organization based in New York, proves they were running a model ...' This was a state-of-the-art factory that met international standards', said the lawyer, Amer Raza Naqvi. 'The SA8000 is accepted all over the world. They have very strict rules before issuing any certificate' (Walsh and Greenhouse, 2013).

14 Brands convey, among other qualities:

Attributes – e.g. quality, prestige or value for-money.

Benefits – e.g. this expensive product will make me admired.

Values – e.g. this producer always aims for high performance, or cares about the environment.

Culture – the company culture is one that cares for its staff, or is very efficient.

Personality – e.g. this is a cheerful or active type product.

User – e.g. this product identifies me as someone who is involved in the club scene ... (Siegle, 2011: 358).

15 'Most transnational activists recognize the pitfalls inherent in stressing victimization over voice and the danger that global codes will reinterpret local priorities, yet as trade unionists in each of these cases insist, even well-intentioned transnational networks find it difficult simultaneously to respond to local workers' concerns and to mobilize the kind of global support that will get the attention of global brands' (Seidman, 2007: 134–5).

16 'Factories which have SA8000 accreditation are published online, which enables corporations which are concerned with ethical trading to easily identify factories which are accredited as respecting human rights. Social Accountability International is developing the Business Development Database of SA8000-compliant factories. This database will provide details of the certified factories' capacity, current production runs, nature of work, costs and geographic location. This will substantially increase the ability of purchasers to identify SA8000-compliant factories' (Harpur, 2010–11).

17 See also Dickson et al. (2009: 314–15), suggesting the development of industry-wide reporting mechanisms that present accurate evaluative information about practices of brand owners, as well as other measures.

18 The brand Patagonia is often cited as an early innovator in this regard. Its current website has a suppliers' map. See http://www.patagonia.com/us/footprint

REFERENCES

Adbusters (n.d.) https://www.adbusters.org/

Agreement on Trade-Related Aspects of Intellectual Property Rights (TRIPS Agreement) Article 15 (1994).

Alderman, Liz (2013) H&M Led Labor Breakthrough by European Retailers, *New York Times* (May 20).

Anderson, M.T. (2013) Bangladesh's Are Only the Latest in Textile Factory Disasters, *New York Times* (April 30).

Arvidsson, Adam (2006) *Brands: Meaning and Value in Media Culture*. London and New York: Routledge

Bachmann, Reinhard (2006) Trust and/or Power: Towards a Sociological Theory of Organizational Relationships, in Reinhard Bachmann and Akbar Zaheer, (eds) *Handbook of Trust Research*. Cheltenham: Edward Elgar, p. 393.

Barron, Ann (2014) Intellectual Property and the 'Open' (Information Society) in *The Sage Handbook of Intellectual Property*. London: Sage Publications.

Bartley, Tim (2003) Certifying Forests and Factories: States, Social Movements, and the Rise of Private Regulation in the Apparel and Forest Products Fields, *Politics & Society* 31: 433.

Beebe, Barton (2010) Intellectual Property Law and the Sumptuary Code, 123 *Harv. L. Rev.* 809.

Bently, Lionel (2014) The First Trademark Case at Common Law? *The Story of Singleton v. Bolton* (1783), 47 UC Davis L. Rev. 969.

Berfield, Susan (2013) Bangladesh Safety Accord Is Too Binding for American Retailers, *Business Week* (May 15). Available at: http://www.businessweek.com/articles/2013-05-15/bangladesh-safety-accord-is-too-binding-for-american-retailers

Black, Sandy (2011) *Eco-Chic: The Fashion Paradox*. London: Black Dog Publishing.

Blair, Margaret M., Cynthia A. Williams, and Li-Wen Lin (2008) The Role of Standardization, Certification and Assurance Systems, 4 *Comp. Res. L. & Pol. Econ.* 1.

Braun, Rainier (2011) Social Accountability International, in Thomas Hale and David Held (eds) *The Handbook of Transnational Governance: Institutions and Innovations*. Cambridge: Polity Press.

Brown Jr., Ralph S. (1948) Advertising and the Public Interest: Legal Protection of Trade Symbols, 57 *Yale L. J.* 1165.

Brown, Sass (2010) *EcoFashion*. London: Laurence King Publishing.

Büthe, Tim and Walter Mattli (2011) *The New Global Rulers, The Privatization of Regulation in the World Economy*. Princeton and Oxford: Princeton University Press.

Cafaggi, Fabrizio (2010) Private Regulation, Supply Chain and Contractual Networks: The Case of Food Safety, European University Institute, EUI Working Paper RSCAS 2010/10.

Calboli, Irene (2011) The Case for a Limited Protection of Trademark Merchandising, 2011 *U. Ill. L. Rev.* 865.

Caldwell, Cam and Stephen E. Clapham (2003) Organizational Trustworthiness: An International Perspective, *Journal of Business Ethics*, 47(4), Business Ethics in Transitional Economies: Special Issue from the International Conference (November).

Chon, Margaret (2009) Marks of Rectitude, 77 *Fordham L. Rev.* 2311.

Cline, Elizabeth L. (2012) *Overdressed: The Shockingly High Cost of Cheap Fashion*. New York: Portfolio/Penguin.

Coombe, Rosemary J. (1991) Objects of Property and Subjects of Politics: Intellectual Property Law and Democratic Dialogue, 69 *Tex. L. Rev.* 1853.

Coombe, Rosemary and Nicole Aylwin (2011) Bordering Diversity and Desire: Using Intellectual Property to Mark Place-Based Products, 43 *Environment and Planning* 2027.

Coombe, Rosemary and Paul Stoller (1994) X Marks the Spot: The Ambiguities of African Trading in the Commerce of the Black Public Sphere, 7 *Public Culture: Society for Transnational Studies* 249–74.

Cornish, William, David Llewelyn and Tanya Aplin (2010) *Intellectual Property: Patents, Copyrights, Trademarks and Allied Rights*, 7th edn. London: Sweet & Maxwell.

Desai, Deven R. (2012a) From Trademarks to Brands, 64 *Fla. L. Rev.* 981.

Desai, Deven R. (2012b) Response: An Information Approach to Trademarks, 100 *Georgetown L. J.* 2119.

Desai, Deven R. (2013) Speech, Citizenry, and the Market: A Corporate Public Figure Doctrine, 98 *Minn. L. Rev.* 455.

Deutsch, Morton (1958) Trust and Suspicion, *The Journal of Conflict Resolution*, 2(4) (Dec).

Dickens, Charles (1842, 1850) American Notes for General Circulation. Available at: http://www2.hn.psu.edu/faculty/jmanis/dickens/AmericanNotes6x9.pdf (Jim Manis ed., Electronic Classics Series Publication 2013).

Dickson, Marsha, Suzanne Loker, and Molly Eckman (eds) (2009) *Social Responsibility in the Global Apparel Industry*. New York: Fairchild.

Dimitropoulos, Georgios (2011) Private Implementation of Global and EU Administrative Law: The Case of Certification in the Climate Change Regime: Relationships, Issues and Comparison, in Edoardo Chiti and Bernardo Giorgio Mattarella (eds) *Global Administrative Law and EU Administrative Law*. Berlin and Heidelberg: Springer. pp. 383.

Dogan, Stacey L. and Mark A. Lemley (2004) Trademarks and Consumer Search Costs on the Internet, 41 *Hous. L. Rev.* 777.

Dreyfuss, Rochelle Cooper (1990) Expressive Genericity: Trademarks as Language in the Pepsi Generation, 65 *Notre Dame L. Rev.* 397.

Duguid, Paul (2013) California Marketing and Collective Amnesia, 47 *UC Davis L. Rev.* 581.

Frankel, Susy (2012) Branding Indigenous Peoples' Traditional Knowledge, in Andrew T. Kenyon, Megan Richardson and Wee Loon Ng- Loy (eds) *The Law of Reputation and Brands in the Asia Pacific*. Cambridge: Cambridge University Press.

Gangjee, Dev S. (2013) Property in Brands: The Commodification of Conversation in H. Howe and J. Griffiths (eds) *Property Concepts in Intellectual Property Law.* Cambridge: Cambridge University Press.

Gargiulo, Martin and Gokhan Ertug (2006) The Dark Side of Trust, in Reinhard Bachmann and Akbar Zaheer (eds) *Handbook of Trust Research.* Cheltenham: Edward Elgar, p. 165.

Gervais, Daniel (2009) The Tangled Web of UGC: Making Copyright Sense of User-Generated Content, 11 *Vand. J. Ent. & Tech. L.* 841.

Greenhouse, Steven (2013) U.S., Urging Worker Safety, Outlines Steps for Bangladesh to Regain its Trade Privileges, *New York Times* (July 19).

Greenhouse, Steven and Stephanie Clifford (2013) U.S. Retailers Offer Plan for Safety at Factories, *New York Times* (July 10).

Ha-Brookshire, Jung E. and Pamela S. Norum (2011) Willingness to Pay for Socially Responsible Products: Case of Cotton Apparel, *Journal of Consumer Marketing,* 28(5), 344–353.

Harpur, Paul (2010–11) New Governance and the Role of Public and Private Monitoring of Labor Conditions: Sweatshops and China Social Compliance for Textile and Apparel Industry/CS900T, 38 *Rut. L. Rec.* 1.

Hetcher, Steven A. (2009) Using Social Norms to Regulate Fan Fiction and Remix Culture, 157 *U. Pa. L. Rev.* 1869.

Heymann, Laura A. (2009) The Public's Domain: A First Amendment Theory of the Consumer, 43 *Ga. L. Rev.* 651.

Hirschmann, A.O. (1970) *Exit, Voice and Loyalty.* Boston: Harvard University Press.

Jaffee, Daniel (2007) *Brewing Justice: Fair Trade Coffee, Sustainability and Survival.* Berkeley and Los Angeles: University of California Press. pp.226–228.

Kaiser, Susan (2006) Mixing Metaphors in the Fiber, Textile, and Apparel Complex: Moving Toward a More Sustainable Fashion, in Janet Hethorn and Connie Ulasewicz (eds) *Sustainable Fashion: Why Now?* p. 139. New York: Fairchild Books.

Katyal, Sonia K. (2006) Semiotic Disobedience, 84 *Wash. U. L. Rev.* 489.

Katz, Ariel (2010) Beyond Search Costs: The Linguistic and Trust Functions of Trademarks, *Brigham Young Univ. L. Rev.* 1555.

Klein, Naomi (1999) *No Logo: Taking Aim at the Brand Bullies.* New York: Macmillan.

Landes, William M. and Richard A. Posner (1987) Trademark Law: An Economic Perspective, 30 *J. L. & Econ.* 265.

Lanham Act, 15 U.S.C. §§ 1051 et seq. (1946), as amended.

Lee, Edward (2008) Warming Up to User-Generated Content, *U. Ill. L. Rev.* 1459.

Lemley, Mark A. and Mark P. McKenna (2010) Owning Mark(et)s, 109 *Mich. L. Rev.* 137.

Lemley, Mark A. and Mark P. McKenna (2012) Is Pepsi Really a Substitute for Coke? Market Definition in Antitrust and IP, 100 *Geo. L.J.* 2055.

Litman, Jessica (1999) *Breakfast with Batman: The Public Interest in the Advertising Age,* 108 *Yale L.J.* 1717.

Lury, Celia (2004) *Brands: The Logos of the Global Economy.* Abingdon and New York: Routledge.

McDuffie, John Paul and Susan Helfer (2005) Collaboration in Supply Chains: With and Without Trust, in Charles Heckscher and Paul S. Adler (eds) *The Firm as a Collaborative Community: The Reconstruction of Trust in the Knowledge Economy.* New York: Oxford University Press.

McKenna, Mark P. (2007) The Normative Foundations of Trademark Law, 82 *Notre Dame L. Rev.* 1839.

Meidinger, Errol (2006) Multi Interest Self Governance through Global Product Certification Programs. Available at: http://papers.ssrn.com/sol3/papers.cfm?abstract_id=917956.

Miller, Doug and Peter Williams (2009) What Price a Living Wage? Implementation Issues in the Quest for Decent Wages in the Global Apparel Sector, 9(1) *Global Social Policy* 99–125.

Minney, Safia (2011) *Naked Fashion: The New Sustainable Fashion Revolution.* Oxford: The New Internationalist Publications Ltd.

Mundlak, Guy and Issi Rosen-Zvi (2011) Signaling Virtue? A Comparison of Corporate Codes in the Fields of Labor and Environment, 12 (July) *Theoretical Inquiries in Law* 603.

Nader, Ralph (2004) Legislating Corporate Ethics, 30 *J. Legis.* 193.

Nike, Inc. v Kasky, 539 U.S. 654 (2003).

Orzada Belinda and Mary Ann Moore (2006) Environmental Impact of Textile Production, in Janet Hethorn and Connie Ulasewicz (eds) *Sustainable Fashion: Why Now?.* New York: Fairchild Books. p. 139.

Patagonia Footprint Chronicles (n.d.) Available at: http://www.patagonia.com/us/footprint

Polaroid Corp. v Polarad Elecs. Corp., 287 F.2d 492, 495 (2d Cir. 1961), *cert. denied,* 369 U.S. 820 (1961).

Powell, Walter W. (1996) Trust-Based Forms of Governance, in *Trust in Organizations: Frontiers of Theory and Research,* in Roderick M. Kramer and Om R. Tyler (eds). California and London: SAGE Publications.

Ramsey, Lisa P. (2010) Free Speech and the International Obligation to Protect Trademarks, 35 *Yale J. Int'l L.* 405.

Raustiala, Kal and Christopher Sprigman (2006) The Piracy Paradox: Innovation and Intellectual Property in Fashion Design, 92 *Va. L. Rev.* 1687.

Raustiala, Kal & Christopher Sprigman (2012) *The Knockoff Economy: How Imitation Sparks Innovation.* New York: Oxford University Press.

Ritzer, George and Nathan Jurgenson (2010) Production, Consumption, Prosumption: The Nature of Capitalism in the Age of the Digital 'Prosumer', 10(1) *Journal of Consumer Culture* 13.

Roberts, Sarah (2003) Supply Chain Specific? Understanding the Patchy Success of Ethical Sourcing Initiatives, 44 *Journal of Business Ethics* 159.

Sabel, Charles F. and Jonathan Zeitlin (2008) Learning from Difference: The New Architecture of Experimentalist Governance in the EU, 14 (May) *European Law Journal* 271, 289.

Saxena, Sanchita Banerjee and Véronique Salze-Lozac'h (2010) Competitiveness in the Garment and Textiles Industry: Creating a Supportive Environment – A Case Study of Bangladesh, The Asian Foundation (July).

Scafidi, Susan (2006) Intellectual Property and Fashion Design, in Peter K. Yu (ed.) *Intellectual Property and Information Wealth*, p. 115. Santa Barbara, CA: Praeger.

Schor, Juliet (2005) Cleaning the Closet: Toward a New Fashion Ethic, in Leslie King and Deborah McCarthy (eds) *Environmental Sociology: From Analysis to Action*, p. 439. Oxford: Rowman & Littlefield.

Segerlund, Lisbeth (2010) *Making Corporate Social Responsibility a Global Concern: Norm Construction in a Globalizing World.* Surrey: Ashgate.

Seidman, Gay W. (2007) *Beyond the Boycott: Labor Rights, Human Rights, and Transnational Activism.* New York: Russell Sage Foundation.

Siegle, Lucy (2011) *To Die For: Is Fashion Wearing Out the World?* London: Fourth Estate.

Strauss, Peter L. (2012) Private Standards Organizations and Public Law, 22 *Wm. & Mary Bill Rts. J.* 497.

Su, Julie A. (1998) Making the Invisible Visible: The Garment Industry's Dirty Laundry, 1 (Spring) *J. Gender Race & Just.* 405.

Sun, Haochen (2012) Can Louis Vuitton Dance with Hiphone? Rethinking the Idea of Social Justice in Intellectual Property Law, 15 *U. Penn. J. L. & Soc. Change* 387. Available at: http://papers.ssrn.com/sol3/papers.cfm?abstract_id=2055136

Superflex, Guaraná Power (2003). Available at: http://www.superflex.net/tools/guarana_power

Superflex (2014) Keynote Speech: If Value, Then Copy, 47 *UC Davis L. Rev.* 735. Available at: http://lawreview.law.ucdavis.edu/issues/47/3/Symposium/47-3_Superflex.pdf

Swann, Jerre B. (2006) An Interdisciplinary Approach to Brand Strength, 96 *Trademark Rep.* 943.

Traub-Werner, Marion (n.d.) Women in Slavery: Nike's Sweatshops. Available at: http://www.feministezine.com/feminist/modern/Women-in-Slavery-Sweatshops.html

UK Trade Marks Act of 1994.

Veblen, Thorstein (1899) *The Theory of the Leisure Class.* Available at: http://www.gutenberg.org/

Verbruggen Paul and Rebecca Schmidt (2012) The Role of Certification in the Enforcement of Transnational Private Regulation. Available at: http://papers.ssrn.com/sol3/papers.cfm?abstract_id=2255918

Von Staden, Heinrich (2012) Medicinal 'Brands' in Ancient Greece and Rome: Authentication, Falsification, 'Ownership' and the Trade in 'Luxury Goods' (unpublished address at the UC Davis Law Review Symposium: Brand New World (Oct. 5).

Walsh, Declan and Steven Greenhouse (2013) Certified Safe, a Factory in Karachi Still Quickly Burned, *New York Times* (December 7).

Wilson, Fiona (1991) *Sweaters: Gender, Class and Workshop-based Industry in Mexico.* Hampshire: Palgrave MacMillan.

Zimmerman, Diane Leenheer (2012) *Upstairs/Downstairs, Fashionwise: A View of Design Protection from Lower Down the Food Chain.* NYU School of Law, Public Law Research Paper No. 12–48. Available at SSRN: http://ssrn.com/abstract=2147948

10

Counterfeit Commerce: The Illegal Accumulation and Distribution of Intellectual Property

Chris Rojek

INTRODUCTION

Provocatively perhaps, the exchange of counterfeit Intellectual property can be defined as a parade of illegal multiples masquerading as originals. Assuming the expectation of negligible risk for the individual, the attraction of consuming an illegal multiple is obvious. Exclusion from ownership on the grounds of privilege or finance is erased. Leaving aside the question of copyright/trademark infringement for the moment, it would be unwise to deny the connection between reproduction and social inclusion. Reproduction widens access and widening access is a venerated principle in democratic systems (Runciman 2013). Expanding access goes some way towards explaining the conflicted reaction that is often expressed in relation to the question of reproduction. In lectures when I ask students if they feel guilty about illegal downloading, the common response is no. Two reasons are generally given. Firstly, illegal downloading is regarded as maximizing the functionality of the net and digital receiving devices. Secondly, rights holders are dismissed as profiteering and thus are defined as fair game. A third, more sociological reason not often given in class behind the correlation of illegal downloading with low guilt is that it is a victimless crime. The copyright, trademark or patent holder is either invisible or takes the form of a brand or trademark, i.e. an abstract entity.

Counterfeit commerce is different from illegal downloading. It is a form of IP infringement that neutralizes the legal support behind copyright and patent. However, as with illegal downloading, research regularly cites disapproval of alleged legal profiteering and a lack of disapproval for 'victimless' crime as factors influencing the propensity to consume. Additionally, with counterfeits separate issues of authenticity and social distinction in possessing imitation goods are raised. There is a tension in consumer reactions between breaking the law and warrantable crime. Not all types of counterfeit consumption are held to be warrantable.

If my students are generally relaxed about their own participation in illegal downloading, they are indignant about credit card cloning and all forms of identity theft. It is not just a matter of being a victim, there is something disturbing about being deprived of your sense of individuality and uniqueness. The confusion and jousting over identity, priority and privilege that accompany something as basic as biological twinship has been a recurring theme in the sociology of the family and Western literature (Schwartz 1996). The *doppelganger* at the heart of Edgar Allen Poe's story *William Wilson* (1839) continues to unnerve readers. Can an imitation of yourself assume a form that colonizes and dissolves your sense of singularity? If so, what does it say about the matter of being in the world? To propose that identity is socially constructed is one thing, but it is altogether a more troubling matter to propose that personal identity is neither safe nor secure. Poe wrote long before the modern concept of identity theft became common currency.[1] But William Wilson's dilemma is that his individuality has been stolen by someone else. Set against the duplication of credit cards, birth certificates, passports and bio-metric data, Wilson's problem might be called primitive identity theft. It is rendered all the more unsettling because Poe successfully plays with the reader's uncertainty about whether Wilson's dilemma is real or all in the mind of a disturbed man.

In his pioneering essay on mechanical reproduction, Walter Benjamin (2002) extends the issue of ontological insecurity to apply to culture in its entirety. Benjamin, drawing on the thought of Ludwig Klages, contends that the aura that renders works of art unique is lost when art becomes an object of mass production (Eiland and Jennings 2014). Cultural integrity presupposes a relationship of trust between a people and an authentic, original object that operates as a collective representation. In Durkheim's (1917) classic study of tribal society the sacred object was often a feature of nature, such as a rock, a mountain or a river that afforded tribal people with a sense of collective embodiment. More commonly, in contemporary society the original object has cultural provenance. What would American culture be without the Declaration of Independence, or British culture be without the works of Shakespeare? Benjamin's point is not that the copy *per se* corrodes cultural integrity. Rather, it is that the exact reproduction threatens cultural integrity by undermining the relationship of trust that centres upon the authentic object. But this raises the separate question of whether the distinction between an authentic object and a fake is always discernible.

The infringement of copyright/trademark often involves blatant changes in the use of materials, design and brand logo which permit consumers to be reflexively aware that they are buying a fake good. This does not always carry over to the trade in patent infringing goods, i.e. the unauthorized reproduction of patented inventions that have functionality such as drugs, or auto and airplane spare parts. This chapter is focused on counterfeit products – those that to some extent seek to pass for originals, even if the extent of such attempts are not always very great. As such, the focus will be on branded luxury goods more than copyrighted music; and on counterfeit drugs and spare parts that do seek to pass for originals, rather than on patent-infringing 'generic' drugs, which, whilst suspending patent do so openly and which are legally regulated in states that allow them (such as Brazil and India).

AUTHENTICITY, TRUST AND COUNTERFEIT

As the distinguished anthropologist Edward Bruner (1994: 408) remarks, attributions of authenticity, trust and counterfeit are social processes. They always entail interpretation regarding the meaning of the transaction. It will repay us to go a little further into Bruner's discussion. To cite interpretation as central in the matters of authenticity, trust and counterfeit raises dual collateral considerations that are pivotal: namely, who is attributing authenticity and to what uses will attribution be put? We may introduce the term 'authentic reproduction' to capture the nature of a relationship of trust with objects in consumer culture. As soon as we take this step, it is necessary to enter the caveat that authentic reproduction is not a uniform social category. Bruner (1994: 399–401) develops this line of thought by asking the question of what 'authentic reproduction' means. He distinguishes three meanings to the term:

1 A duplicate that conveys *aura*, i.e. even though the object is acknowledged to be a fake, it is still identified as being the closest technical match to the original.
2 A duplicate that conveys *verisimilitude*, i.e. a reproduction that is not presented, and therefore, not accepted as an exact copy. Nonetheless, it is socially authenticated as possessing the 'air' or 'flavour' of the original.
3 A duplicate which is *certified* or 'duly authorized' as 'legally valid'. For example, a corporation may contract to license duplication rights to a sub-contractor while retaining original copyright.

Bruner (1994: 400) goes on to submit that the third meaning is of most interest to anthropologists, for it merges the subject of authenticity with the logically separate question of who has the power to *authorize* authenticity (or counterfeit). In regular exchange, authorization turns upon copyright, trademark and patent. By definition, this does not obtain in counterfeit exchange relations. Counterfeit commerce involves the production, exchange and consumption of illegally duplicated objects.[2] Regulatory guarantees are absent. In ordinary exchange this absence constitutes a disincentive to consume. In counterfeit commerce there is elasticity about the disincentive. If consumers identify the point of exchange and object of consumption as, respectively, irregular and fake, this carries the incentive of prohibiting financial transaction. Yet it is in the nature of counterfeit transactions for irregular exchange and fake objects to increase the propensity for consumers to consume. Deprived or, at any rate, hindered by reason of price, from access to transaction with the object under the protection of copyright, trademark or patent, the copy is welcomed as an affordable substitute. There may also be a sense of getting your own back on corporate super-powers who are deplored for over-pricing or rationing production to manipulate the laws of supply and demand. Needless to say, the same elasticity does not necessarily apply to patent infringement. Where a functional good may conceivably imperil well-being or be a risk to life the incentive to proceed on the basis of good faith in the authenticity of the commodity, rather than knowingly buying a cheap imitation, is higher.

In order to appreciate the cultural significance of buying goods with high (but 'faked') symbolic value, what needs to be taken from Bruner's discussion is the question of authorization. That is, it takes for granted that consumers are actively involved, not only in utility decisions relating to value for money and social positioning, but in moral calculations about the legality and justice of consumption. By extension, it holds that the range of knowledge marshalled by consumers extends much further than the marketplace to encompass topics of class, gender and status positioning, as well as the question of the legitimacy of orthodox market relations.

Here Bruner meets Bourdieu (1984). The influential work of the latter on *distinction* is relevant in shedding light on an additional motivational factor in counterfeit exchange.

Prima facie, the consumer of counterfeit copyright/trademarked goods is the epitome of the reflexive consumer. Undoubtedly, there is a strong tradition in cultural criminology that says as much (Ferrell and Saunders 1995; Presdee 2000; Hayward 2004). Here counterfeit commerce is equated not only with reflexivity, but carries the accent of resistance. Questions of verisimilitude and authenticity are secondary to certification. The question of certification is pursued as a matter of (resistant/oppositional) cultural distinction. That is, the exchange and consumption of the counterfeit articulates judgements about the price inflation of luxury products and the unacceptable face of corporate power. The consumer of counterfeits is magically transformed into an urban bandit who plays the corporations at their own game. In this respect it is interesting to note the high importance of the brand or trademark in the exchange relationship. The consumption of goods that do not possess authenticity or verisimilitude in design or finish possesses attraction because the brandmark or trademark represents access to a luxury sign system. The status that follows this may simply reflect the capacity to possess the brand or trademark. Conversely, following cultural criminology, there may be grounds for reading it as a form of consumer banditry which puts ironical distance between the corporation (with its over-priced, remote products) and the savvy consumer. At all events, counterfeit commerce constitutes a form of intellectual property theft that has direct bearing on everyday life. In all large towns and cities it is possible to find illegal copies of luxury goods and patented commodities at knock-down prices.

WHAT IS COUNTERFEIT COMMERCE?

Counterfeit goods refer to products that illegally duplicate a brand and exchange them at a lower price at point of sale. This entails miscellaneous offences against the law. At the crux of the matter is that the counterfeit trade violates registered trademarks and also infringes any copyrights or patents that have been associated with the brand. It therefore threatens the livelihoods of trademark, copyright and patent holders and those employed by them. There are serious consequences to public finance, since counterfeit commerce is unregistered and therefore makes no contribution to the Exchequer.

Further, counterfeit production, exchange and consumption do not entail compliance with independent regulatory bodies. Therefore, defective copies in, for example, the transport and pharmaceuticals trades may increase risk, ill health and morbidity among consumers.[3]

Thus, the price advantage gained in buying luxury counterfeit products in markets or at shopping kiosks, connects directly to a range of public costs. These stretch from the burden on the public purse arising through uncollected taxes to the loss of profits and jobs in the legitimate economy. In the case of counterfeit patented goods all the above risks apply and in addition avoidable illnesses and deaths may be added.

The formal definition, set down in the Agreement on Trade-Related Aspects of Intellectual Property Rights (TRIPS) is as follows:

> 'Counterfeit trademark goods' shall mean any goods, including packaging, bearing, without authorization, a trademark that is identical to that trademark validly registered in respect of such goods that cannot be distinguished in its essential aspects from such a trademark, which thereby infringes the rights of the owner of the trademark in question under the law of the country of importation. (World Trade Organization 1994)

The trade is estimated to account for approximately 5–7% of global commerce, i.e. $600 billion (Kim and Karpia 2010: 79; Staake et al. 2012; Lee and Workman 2011: 289). Wiedmann et al. (2012) put this as a gross under-estimate. They submit that the trade accounts for 10% of all global consumer transactions. In other words, one in ten of all transactions is illegal (although not necessarily recognized as such).

Whatever the true figure, there is little doubt that counterfeit consumption is a significant part of the global economy and rapidly multiplying in scale. Norum and Cuno (2011: 27) calculate that over the last 20 years the trade has expanded 10,000 times. This is the result of a mixture of factors, namely more efficient supply chains, better design values, deregulation of border controls, the spread of access to copyright design data through hacking, direct/low-risk Internet sales provision, various new forms of intellectual property theft and escalating consumer demand.

The most common duplicated goods worldwide are clothing, shoes, watches, cosmetics, leather goods, pharmaceuticals and jewellery (Lee and Workman 2011). The problem is long standing. A multi-million dollar hidden economy, devoted to the production of fake goods, with international supply points and trade routes and with organized criminal involvement, is well established and thriving. This reflects untapped demand for scarce goods which can be manipulated by price advantage. Not surprisingly, the demand for luxury or remote goods increases when supply expands. The trade is also bolstered by the international nature of supply and exchange chains and the difficulties in effectively policing them.

Rutter and Bryce (2008: 1158) submit that the purchase and consumption of counterfeit goods is a *routine* component of everyday life. It extends over all ages, ethnicities and is gender neutral. In emphasizing the *ordinary* quality of exchange, Rutter and Bryce (2008) problematize the common-sense twinning of counterfeit consumption with crime. I will elaborate upon this point later. Before doing so we need to go into a little more detail about the organization of the trade.

Counterfeit commerce consists of two elements: production and distribution. Significantly, marketing input, which is a key component of the regular copyright goods business, is mostly absent. There is good reason for this. The purpose of marketing is to publicize commodities. Understandably, counterfeiters are wary of doing this because it runs the risk of attracting the unwelcome interest of the authorities to intervene through policing and legal action. Conversely, counterfeiters are encouraged by low penalty laws against the production and distribution of fake goods that obtain in many countries (especially where the counterfeit trade makes a significant contribution to the aggregate level of demand). This means that counterfeiting carries much smaller risks of detection and punishment than comparable, traditional types of crime (Wall and Large 2010: 1097).

Sourcing is concentrated among manufacturers in Far East Asia, principally China, South Korea and Taiwan and West Africa (Ritson 2007). The post-Soviet bloc economies also contribute significantly to the trade. For example, industry reports on one of the most common types of counterfeiting, namely the production of cigarettes, indicate that 65% of counterfeits are produced in China and 20% in Russia. Chow's (2003) research into the counterfeit trade in China unearths deep links with organized crime and the collusion of local populations through protectionism and clientelism. Following an escalation in enforcement effects against illicit recreational drugs such as cocaine and heroin, there is evidence that organized crime syndicates such as the Russian mafia, Mexican drug gangs, Chinese Triads and Colombian drug cartels have switched resources to counterfeit pharmaceuticals (Mackey and Liang 2011).

Factories are run on a 'just in time' principle so that counterfeiters can adapt swiftly to changes in markings, packaging and concomitant design features (McEwen and Straus 2009: 253). Counterfeit goods are transported to affluent metropolitan centres in the West through clandestine trade routes or online auction sites. At every level, the production, carriage and sale of goods are illegal. Producers copy luxury designs illegally, employ workers to produce facsimiles illegally, and shield their activities from the eyes of the authorities. Local distributors stock the products in camouflaged warehouses and supply consumers via underground pathways and bulk cargo trade routes that carry legitimate container material.

With the rise and expansion of the digital economy, the Internet is becoming fundamental to the global expansion of the trade. It is estimated that 'cybersquatting' (using a domain name that capitalizes on an established brand) accounts for 1.7 million websites (Wotherspoon and Cheng 2009: 32). Of course cybersquatting is not confined to the sale of counterfeit goods. Nevertheless, it is a rapidly growing supply route for them.

The spread of the digital economy encourages the growth of counterfeiting. It is a direct form of sale as retailers drive the business straight to consumer digital devices. In addition, for the most part, auction websites, such as eBay, are self-policed and hence attractive to counterfeit commerce. To be sure, eBay has been fined for omitting to efficiently counteract counterfeit trading (Treadwell 2012: 188). However, it has not eliminated the practice. Servers can change identities rapidly and frequently. This makes it difficult for the authorities to pinpoint digital supply chains and finance flows.

Similarly, enforcement measures fall foul of global supply chains that are governed by disjointed jurisdiction. In other words, some nations are more flexible in the provision and enforcement of laws against counterfeiting than others. If producers encounter high barriers in one country, they simply switch operations to regions where anti-counterfeiting provisions are less challenging. In recent years, anti-counterfeiting legislation has intensified. In the USA, the Counterfeit Drug Prevention Act (CDPA) 2007 and the Intellectual Property Enhanced Criminal Enforcement Act (IPECEA) 2007 provide for harsher sentencing for trafficking in counterfeit goods and knowingly supplying counterfeit goods to 'at-risk' groups. In addition, the IPECEA criminalizes the intent to commit copyright infringement and has assigned $12 million to create a special operations unit within the Federal Bureau of Investigation (FBI) to coordinate the investigation of intellectual property crime.

International statecraft has also stepped up anti-counterfeiting provisions. In 2007, the US Trade Representative, Susan Schwab, announced that the USA had started talks with key trading partners to implement the Anti-Counterfeiting Trade Agreement (ACTA). This seeks to strengthen information sharing between law enforcement agencies; increase criminal and civil enforcement of intellectual property rights violations; upgrade border controls; and reform the international law regarding the enforcement of intellectual property rights (Sommers and Kilaru 2008). At the state level, authorities in host countries where supply is concentrated have taken steps to counteract the trade in an effort to enhance international standing. Russia and East Africa have also intensified enforcement against copyright violations (Von Braun and Munyi 2010; Charlton 2012).

However, the opposition to counterfeiting has not been all plain sailing. The European Parliament refused to ratify ACTA in 2012 on the grounds that the proposed legislation threatens individual liberties by infringing personal privacy.[4] As of June 2012, the USA, Australia, Canada and Japan are among countries that have signed ACTA, but neglected to ratify its provisions in national policing. The difficulties illustrate the problems confronting anti-counterfeiting law enforcers who struggle to combat crime, but face resistance from civil liberties groups who maintain that blanket legislation impedes individual rights to duplicate and exchange for private use.

As I have already noted, it is widely agreed that obstacles to policing are formidable. Given the international organization and scale of the trade, Hobbs (1998: 419) suggests that the concept of 'network' is of service in understanding this aspect of counterfeit commerce. Organized crime works through local underworld production points but interconnects with global supply chains. The thrust for illegal profiteering that produces counterfeiters in the first place, reproduces itself in the next place and is supplied by global sourcing and constitutes a global demand. The articulation of the network is influenced by multiple factors. Among the most commonly cited are: demographic distribution; familial structures; ethnic distribution and cohesion; commercial practice; trading patterns and national policing (Hobbs 1998). The coherence of organized criminal networks depends upon perpetual fluidity between the local and the global. Hence, tackling counterfeit commerce requires multi-level, international coordination between police, customs and national regulators of commerce. This level of coordination has proved to be elusive. Periodically, high profile interventions are implemented. For example, in 2010 the Internet-based operation *Pangea III*, involving 45 countries, cracked down on the counterfeit drug trade. An illicit drug cache valued at US$2.6 billion was recovered, 290 illegal websites were closed down and 76 people were arrested (Siva 2010: 1725). But when compared with the extent of the trade and the illegal income streams generated, this is the tip of the iceberg. Most national police resources are insufficient to provide effective multilateral investigation. The majority of police resources are organized to address national concerns. The vested interests behind the counterfeit trade are international, covert and highly mobile. This complicates the tasks of police monitoring, interception and arraignment.

Although counterfeit exchange is a fixture of most high street and shopping mall areas, the retailing arrangements for counterfeit goods are categorically separate from their lawful counterparts. Counterfeit luxury goods typically duplicate the design of high price brands. However, they are not typically sold in department stores, specialist high street retailers or legitimate Internet chains. On the contrary, the commerce is spatially segregated from regular urban vendors and authorised Internet suppliers. Street vendors, off-mall kiosks and markets are the most common point of exchange sites. This sense of outlaw consumption may contribute to the attraction of the trade for some consumers. Certainly, exchange points are a million miles away from regular retail settings dealing in bona fide goods. Typically, sellers employ minimal display, carry limited inventories and are not attired in a recognizable retail uniform. Sales occur in a flexible, informal atmosphere. The problem of illegality is smoothed over by spurning the consumer for looking at a gift horse in the mouth. Haggling and other forms of price bargaining are often permitted. Doubtless, the generally relaxed, flexible nature of exchange is a factor in softening ethical barriers among consumers to engage in counterfeit commerce. In addition, consumers know as well as suppliers that counterfeit transactions carry low risk. While anti-counterfeiting police units exist, and raids on supply chains and retailers periodically occur, their importance is chiefly symbolic. This suggests a wide measure of public acceptance of counterfeit commerce. To be sure, the majority of consumers do not associate the trade with abnormal behaviour. On the contrary, it is widely practised as an orthodox component of consumer culture, albeit totally illegal (Rutter and Bryce 2008; Chaudry and Stumpf 2011).

Turning to the counterfeit trade in patented goods, visibility is much less practised compared with the trade in fake branded/copyright goods. The use of sweeteners and other forms of bribery to encourage purchase and bulk orders is endemic. The purchase of pharmaceuticals and vehicular spare parts involves corporate purchasing chains rather than conventional retail outlets. The compartmentalized purchasing chain is theoretically protected by independent agencies of regulation. However, these agencies are no more invulnerable to illegal incentives than corporate purchasers. Additionally, the margins involved in the legitimate patent trade mean that counterfeiters have a motivation to make fake goods as perfect as the real thing. A significant proportion of trade in counterfeit pharmaceuticals and vehicular spare parts is likely to consist of goods that are purchased and used in good faith as patented items, at least by end-users.

THE MORAL LABYRINTH OF THE TRADE

Prima facie, this is an odd state of affairs. The counterfeit trade supports a global society of producers, retailers and consumers bound together by nothing less than transparent intellectual property infringement (or IP theft). While it is universally acknowledged that the trade involves copyright and patent infringement, in general the police apply a fairly soft policing policy. Doubtless, this reflects the grey status of counterfeit consumption in consumer culture. To some extent, counterfeiters of copyright goods who supply intellectual property (sound recordings, film, books) through the Internet are simply realizing the potential contained in modern technologies of reproduction to increase access to commodities of various sorts.[5]

Although the complete hoodwinking of consumers is not unknown (and is likely to be widespread in counterfeit patented transactions), in most cases of copyright/trademark infringement, there is little doubt that consumers can distinguish between legitimate brands and counterfeits (Vitell, 2003; King and Dennis 2006). That is, consumers in this area of counterfeit trade are mostly reflexive. They knowingly buy goods that violate trademark. The trade is, in fact, organized around a curious moral double standard. While those who engage in counterfeit commerce do not generally believe that they are committing a crime, they simultaneously believe that the sellers of these goods ought to be punished (Norum and Cuno 2011). Crime is imputed to the producer and distributor, while consumers regard themselves neutrally, as merely gaining an opportunist advantage in a luxury goods market that is widely seen as rigged in favour of high income consumers who have the means to accumulate legitimate brands. In short, the counterfeit trade is permeated with profound moral ambivalence. This is compounded by the divided nature of the 'victim' in counterfeit exchange. Research consistently finds that consumers are less willing to engage in counterfeit commerce when the victim is seen as an individual, as opposed to an abstract institution (corporation or state department) or society.

The situation is very different with goods covered by patent, i.e. functional goods such as medicines, auto/airplane spare parts. Although there is very little sociological research into fake reproductions of patent protected inventions, it is probable that the reflexive element in exchange is nominal. Consumers believe that they are purchasing the real thing, albeit often at a competitive price. This brings me to the question of the relationship between reflexive consumption and the perception of victim status. As Wall and Large (2010: 1095) observe, victims in the counterfeit trade fall into three groups, as follows.

At-risk Consumers

At-risk consumers are those who may be exposed to health and safety hazards through the consumption of fake reproductions of patented goods. The counterfeit drug trade carries significant risks of increasing morbidity and mortality. It results in spurious reporting of resistance and toxicity and a crisis in confidence in official healthcare systems. These risks are concentrated in the lowest income quartile of Western society and in the developing world (Newton et al. 2006: 602). Aldhous (2005) reports that research by the Cambodian Ministry of Health examined 230 samples of 24 pharmaceuticals bought in the Cambodian market in 2000, including antibiotics and painkillers. They discovered that 3.5% of them consisted of less than 60% of the labelled quantity of active ingredient.

When the survey was repeated in 2003, 11% of samples fell into this category. Suspicion of the involvement of organized crime in the problem was aroused when researchers found that there was no official record of five of the companies whose products were on sale in the Cambodian market. In such cases the end-user cannot be assumed to be making an informed choice. They are either misinformed, unable to freely choose full priced patented products, or both.

Copyright/Patent Owners

The financial loss to copyright/patent owners is impossible to calculate accurately. However, if the counterfeit trade really does account for 10% of global commerce, revenue loss to aggregated businesses is at least one tenth of potential turnover. Given that counterfeit goods are priced significantly below the market rate, this figure is almost certainly a massive underestimate. The counterfeit trade, then, directly affects the profitability and growth prospects of legitimate business. Needless to say, some sectors are affected more than others. The International Trademark Association estimated that losses to the apparel and footwear industry in 1995 were probably in excess of 20% of sales (ITA 1998: 2). Additionally, in Europe it is estimated that approximately EU7581 million is lost across Europe through counterfeiting in the clothing and footwear industry. The profit drain to European companies in the perfumes and cosmetics sector is put at EU555 million; EU627 million in the toys and sports articles sector; and EU292 million in the pharmaceuticals sector (Blakeney 2009: 7). Counterfeiting is especially prevalent in the spare parts sector of the transport industry, with obvious implications for public well-being. In the USA the Federal Trade Commission (FTC) estimates that counterfeiting deprives the US auto parts industry of $3 billion annually and $12 billion globally (Mele 2004: 16). The US Federal Aviation Administration (FAA) submit that 2%, or 520,000 of the 26 million airline parts installed each year are fakes (Wotherspoon and Cheng 2009: 32).

Above and beyond the question of revenue loss, legitimate business faces a variety of other challenges with counterfeit trade. Counterfeits may damage the brand and thus, diminish goodwill. The trade can increase the risk of being exposed to liability claims that arise from a flood of substandard products on the market carrying the brand name (Wilke and Zaichkowsky 1999; Staake et al. 2012). Moreover, in the long run, counterfeiting may act as a deterrent to the research and development dynamism of legitimate business. For what is the point of investing in R&D if the fruits of this process are hijacked and duplicated by criminals?

General Public

Losses to the public take two main forms. Firstly, since counterfeit goods are exempt from fiscal responsibility, significant tax revenue is lost to the Treasury. It has been estimated that in the UK counterfeiting leads to a loss of £143 million per year in GNP and a £77 million increase per year in Government borrowing (Blakeney 2009: 7). In the sourcing countries, undeclared production and false reporting compounds public revenue loss. Hence, funds that could be used for various types of social investment for the benefit of the public are never generated.

Secondly, several commentators argue that the revenue streams associated with the counterfeit trade are used to finance organized crime and terrorism (Vagg and Harris 1998). Saviano's (2011: 39) study of illegal cartel crime in Italy referred to the production of 'true fakes' in the tailoring industry where dressmakers supply the same dresses for the Mafia using the same design and materials as the 'originals'.[6] The clandestine nature of the financial supply routes generated by the trade make it difficult to accurately compute the scale of these exchanges. Logic dictates that the interlinked profit potential is considerable, thus, making it a reasonable assumption that size of exchange is appreciable.

The moral ambiguities of engaging in counterfeit exchange of copyright/trademark commodities in markets where regular exchange is differentiated by steep hierarchical divisions need hardly be stressed. Where the victim category is cast in abstraction, producers and traders readily psychologically exonerate their criminal acts as exempt from causing real harm. At the same time, beating a rigged system is generally seen as acceptable behaviour even if it involves the transparent violation of IP. The same does not apply to patent infringement. Nearly everyone would see the production of fake pharmaceuticals and aero/auto spare parts as morally objectionable. Yet it is probable that a significant proportion of this trade is made without detection. The counterfeit may only be exposed when illness and death occur and investigators launch enquiries into the causes.

Whilst it may be morally objectionable, the capacity of authorities to end the trade is limited, not because of any 'cultural' acceptance by the public, but rather because it is so profitable and hard to track. Turning the whole issue on its head, one might venture that the legitimated structural inequality of organized capitalism naturally creates counterfeit commerce. The scoundrel in the trade is widely identified as the producer of the counterfeit since they deliberately violate IP. This is reflected in the concentration of police resources and law enforcement in the infringement of IP and supply chains of illegally produced goods. Yet viewed against the yawning price differentials justified and reproduced by regular capitalism, the consumer of reduced priced goods quite rationally takes advantage of opportunities for consumption that the conventional system of consumption rations or debars. This is reinforced by levels of policing and legal action against consumers of counterfeit commodities which are widely perceived as mostly relaxed and low key.

CONSUMER MOTIVATION ISSUES

The question of consumer motivation is fundamental and, on the whole, seriously under-researched. Among the most commonly cited motivations for engaging in counterfeit consumption of copyright/branded goods are, price advantage, one-upmanship, the search for hedonism in engaging in 'risky' transgressive commerce and getting one over on a rigged system (Bloch et al. 1993; Chaudry and Stumpf 2011). The orthodox view of exchange relations in democratic consumer culture is that they are founded upon trust (Jacoby and Chestnut 1978; Rust and Oliver 1994; Alhabeeb 2007). Trust resides in the copyright, trademark or patent of the product and the legality of the exchange relationship. Important residual factors in building trust are packaging and the spatial setting of exchange. Increasingly, Internet purchases are made through 'recognized' servers if they are to be valued as 'legitimate'. The absence of trust generally renders exchange relations forfeit. Counterfeit commerce in copyright/branded goods overturns orthodoxy, even as counterfeit commerce in patent infringing goods conforms to it. Counterfeit symbolic goods (copyright/branded items as distinct from patented goods) are widely, indeed, in most cases, *automatically,* appreciated by consumers as fakes, but consumers buy them anyway. This inevitably poses the question of the character of authenticity in exchange relationships based in such counterfeit products. *What* exactly, is being exchanged?

To answer this question fully requires an engagement with the tradition of cultural criminology. I will turn to this presently. Before coming to this point it is important to take one step back and consider the structural components of consumer exchange which pertain to the question of authenticity. For, basic to the position of cultural criminology is the hypothesis that the legitimacy of authentic consumption in conventional exchange relations under capitalism is at issue. Here we must first return briefly to Edward Bruner (1994). As we have already observed, he remarks (1994: 408) that consumption is a *social* process that involves twin collateral, considerations: namely, who is attributing authenticity, and to what uses will attribution be put? To repeat, for Bruner (1994: 339–401), there are three meanings of authentic reproduction in counterfeit commerce. In the first place, a counterfeit carries the quality of 'authentic' reproduction if it is automatically identified as being the closest technical match to the original. This inverts Walter Benjamin's (2002) thesis that automation decreases the aura of an original object by replacing it with an exact duplicate. What Bruner (1994) is saying, is that some reproductions are so precise that they 'stand in' precisely for objects protected by copyright. Moreover, they are authenticated as such by spectators and consumers. *Contra* Benjamin (2002), it does not follow that the aura of the original object is attenuated. Assuming they can tell the difference, people still value an original *Rolex* more than a precise fake. This level of authenticity is paralleled in the valuation of counterfeit patented goods as well.

A second meaning of authenticity pertains to the *verisimilitude* of the reproduced object. The fake is neither produced nor consumed as an exact copy. Nonetheless, it is socially authenticated as possessing the 'air' or 'flavour' of the original. A fake *Gucci* bag may not be an exact reproduction of the original; nevertheless, the approximate design values and, perhaps above all, the label, communicates the patina of the original. The patina is enough to transmit status. Thus, Bruner moves the question of authenticity more securely from judgements about the technical precision of the reproduced object onto the question of the social process of counterfeit exchange. In the case of counterfeit patented goods the cachet of knowingly buying a fake that is 'almost the equivalent' of the original has a negligible cultural premium, even if cheapness may be at an economic premium for the consumer unable to afford the patented original. It is in the nature of this type of exchange for the fake to be designed, produced and packaged as 'the real thing'. The purchase of cut-price patent infringing 'generic' medicine may be forced by poverty or decided simply by economic calculation. Counterfeit packaging of such an infringing product may deceive the customer into paying more. It does not facilitate reflexive 'cache' or playful resistance.

The third meaning of authenticity in counterfeit commerce is mostly situated at the level of the social process of exchange. When a reproduced object carries neither precision nor an air of verisimilitude, it may be enough for mere representation in the exchange relationship to be certified as socially valid. Hence, in counterfeit copyright transactions, a fake *Omega* may not be a precise copy, nor may it even be an approximation that conveys the 'air' or 'flavour' of the object protected by copyright; however, because it is *authorized* by the counterfeiter as the reproduced object it still carries *cachet*. Of course, the *cachet* in question is not the same as that which derives from the exact reproduction or verisimilitude. It may be conveyed by nothing more than a label or brand. The social value of certification does not reside in the quality of the counterfeit, but in the quality of the social relationships that radiate from exchange. In other words, a sector of counterfeit commerce involves the production and consumption of items which carry *ironic* import. By wearing an obviously fake *Omega*, consumers expose the inflated values of the trade in luxury watches and, perhaps, comment upon more fundamental social divisions in the hierarchy of power and wealth. In doing so they are sometimes theorized as alluding to the 'crass commercialism' that propels the general luxury goods trade (Naylor 2011). Symbolically, they beat the system by exposing its inherent vanity and profiteering tendencies. At point of sale, the attribution of certification does not, of course, involve copyright, trademark or patent holders. It is a matter of a social process of judgement among the excluded, marginalized or, in some other way, *estranged* elements that reside within orthodox consumer culture. Among these strata, at the three levels of meaning specified by Bruner (1994), the authentic reproduction carries the aura of cultural kudos.

By definition, counterfeit commodities are fakes. However, their cultural value cannot be assumed to be primarily a matter of verisimilitude or price advantage. More interesting ways of reading the consumption of counterfeit goods place significance on matters of informal *cultural certification* in relation to hierarchies of power and chains of consumption in relation to which consumers of reduced means are rationed or debarred. Counterfeit commerce certainly breaks the law. The consumer of counterfeit symbolic goods is as much 'in the know' about their violation of corporate intellectual property rights by their gaining access to luxury goods at a cheap point of exchange as is the regular corporate manufacturer of luxury goods 'in the know' about violating workers' human rights when situating their production in low labour cost economies in the developing world. When viewed from this perspective, counterfeit commerce is not a break with orthodox capitalism or a challenge to its fundamental features. More appropriately, it is the logical extension of capitalist 'hyper consumerism' (Hayward 2004: 86).

EXPLAINING CONSUMER MOTIVATIONS: CULTURAL CRIMINOLOGY AND ITS DILEMMAS

What does it mean to propose that counterfeit commerce is the extension of capitalist 'hyper consumerism'? To begin with an obvious observation: at the levels of culture and space, counterfeit commerce is not an episodic feature of social ordering. It is routine and embedded. It is part of the normalization of illegal conduct. Other examples of normalization include the recreational use of illegal drugs, hacking and the illegal downloading of intellectual property (Parker et al. 2002; David 2010). Cultural criminology has sought to provide various explanations of normalization (Ferrell and Saunders 1995; Ferrell et al. 2008). While counterfeit commerce has not figured significantly in this academic field, the analysis of normalization and hyper consumerism may be readily adapted to shed light on the phenomenon.

According to this tradition, the consumption of counterfeit symbolic goods is a strategic response to the general cultural struggle of acceptance and recognition in the context of class divided property relations (Presdee 2000; Hayward 2004). Pivotal to this line of thought is the proposition that emotional, expressive qualities of counterfeit symbolic consumption are inextricably linked to questions of surplus and scarcity in political economy. Seizing symbols of luxury, status and power is analysed as a social reaction to inequality and marginalization. Axiomatically, the counterfeit trade thrives in the context of organized, historically rooted, structural inequality. Counterfeit symbolic consumption is analysed as an illegal practice that arises from the social exclusion of agents from luxury acquisition and associated power hierarchies (by reason of status and property qualifications). Upon this basis, the argument moves on to see reflexive consumption of such counterfeit products as directly or tacitly striking a blow against the system (Hall et al. 2008: 58; Moxon 2011).

Cultural criminology therefore equates consumer motivation with *both* challenging and reproducing the values of capital by dint of engaging voluntarily and reflexively in illegal activity (Ferrell et al. 2004). The consumption of counterfeit commodities is explained either as first, an act of resistance against capitalist power (embodied in copyright and patent law) (Young 1999; Presdee 2000); or it is presented as the inevitable mutation of 'hyper consumerism', i.e. a form of subjective desire that privileges the drive to consume above respect for contract (Hayward 2004: 86; Moxon 2011).

What brings both accounts into contact is the equation of counterfeit consumption with edgy, undisciplined, reflexive consumption. Counterfeit symbolic consumption is a reflexive act of non-conformity linked to expressions of identity. The act provides consumers locked in the ranks of the marginalized and excluded with the temporary experience of control and fighting back in the teeth of a system that emiserates them (Winlow 2001; Hall et al. 2008; Hobbs 2013). By implication, consumers who refrain from engaging in counterfeit consumption are implicitly italicized as passive. By confining themselves to the track of orthodox consumption they reinforce the unequal property relations upon which the system is founded.

But this attempt to break with 'bloodless' criminology and 'mainstream' analysis of consumer culture brings with it problems of its own. Mostly these have to do with the extreme cultural relativism of the approach. It is one thing to cast counterfeit commerce as 'hyper consumerism'. However, it is hardly acceptable to read the effects of consumption as merely, or primarily, 'ironic' and 'resistant'. I have already mentioned Wall and Large's (2010) argument that counterfeit commerce erodes the sale of luxury goods (which contributes to unemployment) and, because it is unregulated, especially in the case of the trade in fake patent goods, may put consumers at risk. Over and above the valid points raised by Wall and Large (2010), is the question of the threat to ontological security in the consumption process by flaunting copyright and patent. If everyone is actually or potentially on the fiddle, consumer rights of fair trade are hardly worth a candle. Without the concept of fair trade, based in responsible and accountable exchange relations, consumption descends into a Hobbesian war of all against all. Given that most goods are not 'fair trade' it might be cynically suggested that the Hobbesian state is precisely what does exist in the global marketplace, but this ignores what regulation (regarding labelling, health and safety, as well as wages) does exist, which counterfeiting acts to undermine at every level. Whilst legitimate production and exchange is far from perfect, it is extremely generous to describe counterfeit consumption as possessing edge or reflexivity simply by evading its limits (Ferrell and Saunders 1995; Presdee 2000; Ferrell et al. 2008). For whatever price advantage or status differentiation that accrues it cannot disguise the fact that the practice is thoroughly parasitic. To expand, suppliers of counterfeit (copyright and patent) goods do not really break with the established business practices of legal providers. Rather, they continue them by other (criminal) means. In particular, they follow the doctrine of buying resources in the cheapest market to sell in the most lucrative for the purpose of profiteering. Just as imitation is the sincerest form of flattery, illegal duplication seeks to gain a slice of the pie of profits by copying the enterprise of the rights holder.

Turning to the level of demand, reflexive consumption of symbolic goods seeks to acquire *cachet* via the illegal possession of desired goods. In doing so it produces leakage in the revenue of rights holders, but ultimately it reinforces the existing power hierarchy. The status of luxury brands is not diminished; it is not even dented by the counterfeit trade. Counterfeit commerce does not produce an *alternative* to the balance of surplus and scarcity in consumer relations. Luxury goods under copyright or trademark are still, on financial grounds, out of reach of the majority of consumers. Nor does the trade challenge the stigma of scarcity or the glamour of surplus. Only at the margins is the ironic consumption of counterfeit symbolic goods privileged over the certified value of commodities inscribed legally by copyright.

By flagrantly flouting legal regulations you might think that counterfeit commerce renders morality forfeit. Nothing could be further from the truth. Producers and consumers behold counterfeit status as serving no moral impediment to exchange. However, most studies show that agents on both sides completely acknowledge the illegality of the exchange relationship. A different kind of consumer judgement about morality and authenticity appears to operate here. In all known types of consumer culture the nexus of transaction (at the point of exchange) involves positional judgements about the status premium of consumption and interpretive analysis about the authenticity of the object of consumption. In other words, irrespective of social context, moral questions about the propriety of consumption are inherent in the exchange process. Most pointedly, they relate to the character of the exchange agents and the setting of exchange. Judgements of morality are certainly affected by property qualifications. However, they cannot be permitted to be viewed as *nullified* by propertyless status. Several consequences for understanding the counterfeit trade follow from these considerations.

In the first place, it is inadequate to read questions of authenticity and trust strictly, or even primarily, in terms of contractual relations. All things being equal, consumers (and producers) will elect to acquire price advantage at the nexus of exchange where the risks of detection and harm to victims are gauged to be negligible. However, it is unsatisfactory to presume that moral questions can be erased by presenting acts of consumption as parts of narrative traditions or subcultures of resistance or hyper-consumerism. For the business of gaining advantage over the declared interests of another agent (registered by copyright and patent law) by knowingly appropriating the design or brand of their commodity, always raises issues concerning the moral responsibility of the act. Not everyone in the propertyless category of wage labour, or the category of the propertied, engages in counterfeit consumption. Similarly, corporate purchasers or regulatory agents who knowingly participate in exchange relations involving fake patent goods are likely to be in the minority. The issue of moral economies and their relation to *habitus* is fundamental. Nor does it follow that the conformist effect of *habitus* is necessarily subordinate to market contingency. While the question of structural inequality is indeed integral to conduct (whether it be law-abiding or criminal) it does not eliminate considering the moral dimension at the nexus of exchange. A middle route between structure and moral choice is desirable.

CONCLUSION

The extent and vitality of the counterfeit trade throws the question of the moral ambivalence of consumer (and producer) practice under capitalism into sharp relief. The evidence demonstrates that consumers and producers are ready to infringe IP and ignore the law by consuming fake goods, providing (a) the risk of detection is low and (b) the reproduced commodity carries the insignia of 'authenticity'. In the tradition of cultural criminology, questions of the functionality, durability and general craftsmanship of the counterfeit symbolic commodity are secondary to consumer meanings of status distinctions. That is, consumers of counterfeit goods communicate an ethic of reflexive copyright consumption that tacitly rejects the over-pricing of luxury branded goods. To some extent producers and (to a lesser extent) knowing consumers of patent infringing functional products (such as purchasers of clearly labelled, yet IP infringing, generic medicines, as opposed to misleadingly packaged counterfeits, also work from the conviction that prices in the legal trade are inflated. However, it would be unwise to push this argument too far.

Critics of the counterfeit trade have a point that the practice breaks the law at every juncture – production, distribution, retailing and consumption. Nonetheless, the trade is not so much a counter-force to legitimate capitalism as a continuation of the same logic of branding and status adoption, by other (criminal) means. Counterfeit consumption should be read as a contribution to criminal innovation and adaptation. This is, of course, consistent with a position made many times since the Chicago School in the 1920s (Hobbs 1993, 2013; Winlow 2001; Hall and Winlow 2007). In particular it highlights the ordinary nature of some forms of 'criminal' behaviour by relating them squarely to the logic of organized inequality that is the foundation of the mature market form. Hence, the consumption of counterfeit symbolic commodities is interpreted as motivated by the desire to make do, and get by, in a commercial context in which access to luxury goods is restricted by property qualifications. Here irony is not necessarily at the crux of consumer motivation. Rather, the pressing logic of capitalism is to find and take opportunities for undercutting the legitimate market and fiddling. As such, it is safe to predict that counterfeit commerce will continue to expand, especially as the digital economy affords new, low risk means of distribution and the direct duplication of intellectual property.

From the standpoint of the producers and vendors of counterfeit goods, effective global policing of counterfeit networks incurs costs that Treasuries will not bear. Faced with a soft deterrent, counterfeiters know that they are located in a low risk economy of illegal trade and unregistered profiteering. As for consumers (and illegal producers), because they are located in structural inequalities based around lines of class, race, gender and status, the incentive to beat the system is unlikely to contract. Getting duplicate goods at a realistic price in a market skewed in favour of organized scarcity and price inflation will always be attractive. Needless to say, where collusion with illicit practice is established as an ordinary or at least – at the level of everyday interaction – *unexceptional* feature of social interaction, the scope for the authorities to act to eradicate the practice is constrained.

This raises separate questions concerning the moral rhetoric of legitimate consumption and the layered, provisional nature of trust in the retail market. It should be noted that cultural relativism is not an adequate way of dealing with the topic of morality. The nexus of exchange raises independent moral considerations which have to be presented as universal if the Hobbesian war of all against all is to be avoided.

The exploration of these questions is a task for a separate study. Perhaps enough has been said here to remind us of the wisdom of Karl Marx's words in the chapter on 'Commodities' in the first volume of *Capital*: 'A commodity appears, at first sight, a very trivial thing, and easily understood. Its analysis shows that it is, in reality, a very queer thing, abounding in metaphysical subtleties and theological niceties' (Marx 1954: 76). It could not have been put better. Yet, as a closing thought, mention of Marx raises an urgent question that has not been asked pointedly enough in the literature on counterfeit commerce. Why is the faith in possessing fakes stronger than a determination to revise the balance between surplus and scarcity in consumer relations? For it is this balance that is the main influence governing the propensity to consume the authentic reproduction. Goods with only symbolic exchange value, rather than any substantial (functional) use value, are deemed 'fair game', yet the desire for such empty commodities is not diminished by such a moral representation of their emptiness. As such, the symbolic counterfeiter's critique of commodity culture, and their 'defence' that they are really only 'stealing' 'nothing' (empty signifiers), remains hollow as long as it perpetuates a parasitical copying of, and desire for, such supposed illusions; whilst failing to engage in, or enable, the production of anything either new or useful.

Anti-consumerist movements like *Black Bloc* and *Occupy* seek to challenge this state of affairs with contrasting degrees of success. *Occupy* certainly made the distinction between the '1 per cent and the 99 per cent' part of the popular vernacular. Consumers were called upon to be reflexive and grasp the manipulation involved in the unequal property and exchange relations of capitalism. Yet despite the optimistic claims of some social commentators, to date, the effect of *Occupy*, seems to be in line with other *temporary* historical protests against power and authority, such as the Paris Commune (1870) and the student uprising (1968) (Castells 2012; Gitlin 2012). When one considers these events it is not so much the dislocation of the set of consumer relations that finally comes to the fore, as the capacity of the system to adapt and eventually find new ways of prospering. To be sure, the burden of this chapter is that the proper way to read counterfeit commerce is as an integral (illegal) component of the legitimated system of production, exchange and consumption, founded upon organized inequality, rather than a genuine alternative.

NOTES

1 Poe's story first appeared in 1839.
2 Needless to say, it is no part of my argument that the capitalist procurement of resources and the lowest cost of point of sale are always licit. Central to the notion of capitalist accumulation is the principle that illegal procurement, via violence and extortion is a layer of conven-

tional capitalist ordering, e.g. in relation to core capitalist economies seizing assets from the periphery.

3 One interesting aspect here that deserves much further investigation is the extent of counterfeit testing and data supply by legitimate brand providers. Healy (2012) argues that major drug companies have a long history of counterfeiting scientific tests in order to expand hugely the market for their products. Healey (2012) recounts how an anti-depressant drug Paxil claiming 'remarkable efficacy and safety in the treatment of adolescent depression' was in reality known to be associated with a threefold increased risk of suicide compared with those on a comparable anti-depressant or on a placebo.

4 Analytically, the point to hold on to is that there are strong continuities between orthodox capitalist production and consumption and the counterfeit trade. Not to be aware of them, risks exaggerating the moral rectitude of branding practices in legitimate corporations and concentrating rule breaking and illegality among illegal counterfeit networks.

5 They are often located in side streets, kiosks or open air markets adjacent to legitimate retail centres. In some places in the developing world there are reports that the practice of over-the-counter selling of counterfeits on request is endemic.

6 Thanks to the eagle eye of my friend, Steve Matthewman in the Department of Sociology, Auckland University, for bringing this reference to my attention.

REFERENCES

Aldhous, P. (2005) 'Counterfeit pharmaceuticals: Murder by medicine', *Nature*, 434: 132–6.

Alhabeeb, M. (2007) 'On trust and product loyalty', *International Journal of Consumer Studies*, 31(6): 609–12.

Baack, B. (2001) 'Forging a nation state', *The Economic History Review*, 54(4): 639–54.

Beckett, A. and Nayak, A. (2008) 'The reflexive consumer', *Marketing Theory*, 8(3): 299–317.

Benjamin, W. (2002) 'The work of art in the age of its technological reproducibility', in Benjamin, W., *Selected Writings, Volume 3: 1935–38*. Cambridge, MA: Harvard University Press, pp. 101–33.

Blakeney, M. (2009) 'International proposals for the criminal enforcement of intellectual property rights', Queen Mary School of Law Legal Studies Research Paper No. 29/2009: www.ssrn.com/abstract=1476964

Bloch, P., Bush R. and Campbell, L. (1993) 'Consumer accomplices in product counterfeiting: a demand side investigation', *The Journal of Consumer Marketing*, 10(4): 27–37.

Bourdieu, P. (1984) *Distinction*. London: Routledge.

Bruner, E. (1994) 'Abraham Lincoln as authentic reproduction', *American Anthropologist*, 92(2): 397–412.

Castells, M. (2012) *Networks of Outrage and Hope*. Cambridge: Polity.

Charlton, J. (2012) 'IFLA raises concerns about ACTA', *Information Today*, 29(6): 14–15.

Chaudry, P. and Stumpf, S. (2011) 'Consumer complicity with counterfeit products', *The Journal of Consumer Marketing*, 28(2): 139–51.

Chow, D.K. (2003) 'Organized crime, locals protectionism, and the trade in counterfeit goods in China', *China Economic Review*, 14(4): 473–84.

Credit Management (1999) 'Warning on Triad counterfeiters', April: 10–12.

David, M. (2010) *Peer To Peer and the Music Industry*. London: Sage.

Durkheim, E. (1917) 'The Elementary Forms of Religious Life', New York: Free Press.

Eiland, H. and Jennings, M. (2014) *Walter Benjamin: A Critical Life*. Cambridge, MA: Harvard University Press.

Ferrell, J. (1999) 'Cultural Criminology', *Annual Review of Sociology*, 25: 395–418.

Ferrell, J. and Saunders, C. (eds) (1995) *Cultural Criminology*. Boston: Northeastern Press.

Ferrell, J., Hayward, K., Morrison, W. and Presdee, M. (eds) (2004) *Unleashing Cultural Criminology*. London: Glasshouse Press.

Ferrell, J., Hayward, K., and Young, J. (2008) *Cultural Criminology: An Invitation*. London: Sage.

Gitlin, T. (2012) *Occupy Nation*. New York: IT Books.

Hall, S. and Winlow, S. (2007) 'Cultural criminology and primitive accumulation', *Crime, Media, Culture*, 3(1): 82–90.

Hall, S., Winlow, S. and Ancrum, C. (2008) *Criminal Identities and Consumer Culture*. Cullompton: Willan.

Hayward, K. (2004) *City Limits: Crime, Consumer Culture and the Urban Experience*. London: Glass House Press.

Healy, D. (2012) *Pharmageddon*. Berkeley: University of California Press.

Hobbs, D. (1993) *Doing the Business*. Oxford: Clarendon Press.

Hobbs, D. (1998) 'Going down the glocal: the local context of organized crime', *The Howard Journal*, 37(4): 407–22.

Hobbs, D. (2013) *Lush Life*. Oxford: Oxford University Press.

International Trademark Association (ITA) (1998) The economic impact of trademark counterfeiting and infringement, International Trademark Association, http://inta.org/downloads/tap_economicimpact1998.pdf

Jacoby, I. and Chestnut, R. (1978) *Brand Loyalty: Measurement and Management*. New York: Wiley.

Kim, H. and Karpia, E. (2010) 'Consumer Attitudes Toward Fashion Counterfeits', *Clothing and Textiles Journal*, 28(2): 79–94.

King, T. and Dennis, C. (2006) 'Unethical consumers', *Qualitative Market Research*, 9(3): 282–96.

Lee, S-H and Workman, J. (2011) 'Attitudes Toward Counterfeit Purchase and Ethical Beliefs Among Korean and American University Students', *Family and Consumer Sciences research Journal*, 39(3): 289–305.

Luca, C., Kemp, S. and Mackenzie, A. (2009) 'Consumer decisions in the black market for stolen or counterfeit goods', *Journal of Economic Psychology*, 30(2): 162–71.

Mackey, T.K. and Liang, B.A. (2011) 'The global counterfeit drug trade: patient safety and public health risks', *Journal of Pharmaceutical Sciences*, 100(11): 4571–9.

Marx, K. (1954) 'Capital', Volume 1, London: Lawrence & Wishart.

McEwen, A. and Straus, L. (2009) 'Counterfeit tobacco in London', *Trends in Organized Crime*, 12: 251–9.

Mele, J. (2004) 'Counterfeit parts: buyers beware', *Fleet Owner*, 99(3): 16–20.

Moxon, D. (2011) 'Consumer culture and the 2011 "riots"', *Sociological Research Online*, 16(4): 19.

Naylor, R.T. (2011) *Crass Struggle*. Montreal: McGill Queen's University Press.

Newton, P.N. et al. (2006) 'Counterfeit anti-infective drugs', *The Lancet Infectious Diseases*, 6(9): 602–13.

Norum, P.S. and Cuno, A. (2011) 'Analysis of the demand for counterfeit goods', *Journal of Fashion Marketing and Management*, 15(1): 27–40.

Parker, H., Williams, L. and Aldridge, J. (2002) 'The normalization of "sensible" drug use', *Sociology*, 36(4): 941–64.

Perry Hobson, J. and Ko, M. (1995) 'Counterfeit credit cards: how to protect hotel guests', *Cornell Hotel and Administration Quarterly*, 36: 48–53.

Poe, E.A. (2004) 'Collected Tales and Poems', London: Wordsworth.

Presdee, M. (2000) *Cultural Criminology and the Carnival of Crime*. London: Routledge.

Ritson, M. (2007) 'Fakes Can Genuinely Aid Luxury Lines', *Marketing*, July 25, 21–21.

Robertson, F. (2005) 'The aesthetics of authenticity', *Technology and Culture*, 46(1): 31–50.

Runciman, D. (2013) *The Confidence Trap*. Princeton: Princeton University Press.

Rust, R. and Oliver, R. (eds) (1994) *Service Quality*. Thousand Oaks, CA: Sage.

Rutter, J. and Bryce, J. (2008) 'The consumption of counterfeit goods: "Here be pirates?"', *Sociology*, 42(6): 1146–64.

Saviano, R. (2011) *Gomorrah: Italy's Other Mafia*. London: Pan.

Schwartz, H. (1996) *The Culture of the Copy*. New York: Zone Books.

Siva, N. (2010) 'Tackling the booming trade in counterfeit drugs', *The Lancet*, 376(9754): 1725–6.

Smart, B. (2010) *Consumer Society*. London: Sage.

Sombart, W. (1967) *Luxury and Capitalism*. Ann Arbor: Michigan University Press.

Sommers, M. and Kilaru, N. (2008) 'Counterfeit corner', *IP Litigator*, 14(1): 41–2.

Staake, T., Thiesse, F. and Fleisch, E. (2012) 'Business strategies in the counterfeit market', *Journal of Business Research*, 65(5): 658–65.

Treadwell, J. (2012) 'From the car boot to booting up? eBay, online counterfeit crime and the transformation of the criminal market place', *Criminology and Criminal Justice*, 12(2): 175–91.

Ungoed-Thomas, J. (2005) 'Designer fakes "are funding Al-Qaeda"', *Sunday Times*, 20 March.

Vagg, J. and Harris, J. (1998) 'Bad goods: product counterfeiting and enforcement strategies', in Gill, M. (ed.) *Crime At Work: Vol 2, Increasing the Risk for Offenders*. Leicester: Perpetuity Press.

Veblen, T. (1899) *The Theory of the Leisure Class*. London: Allen & Unwin.

Vitell, S.J. (2003) 'Consumer ethics research', *Journal of Business Ethics*, 43: 33–47.

Von Braun, J. and Munyi, P. (2010) 'New enforcement mechanism challenge the legality of generics in the name of public-health: the emergence of anti-counterfeiting legislation in East Africa', *African Journal of International and Comparative Law*, 18(2): 238–53.

Wall, D. (2007) *Cybercrime*. Cambridge: Polity.

Wall, D. and Large, J. (2010) 'Jailhouse frocks: locating the public interest in policing counterfeit luxury fashion goods', *British Journal of Criminology*, 50(6): 1094–16.

Wiedmann, K.P. Hennigs, N. and Klarmann, P (2012) 'Luxury consumption in the trade-off between genuine and counterfeit goods', *Journal of Brand Management*, 19: 544–566.

Wilke, R,. and Zaichowsky, J. (1999) 'Brand imitation and its effects on innovation, competition, and brand equity', *Business Horizons*, 42(6): 9–18.

Winlow, S. (2001) *Badfellas*. London: Berg.

World Trade Organization (1994) Trade-Related Aspects of Intellectual Property Rights. Annex 1C of the 'Marrakesh Agreement Establishing the World Trade Organization', Marrakesh, Morocco.

Wotherspoon, D. and Cheng, M. (2009) 'Web of deceit', *Risk Management*, 56(8): 32–6.

Young, J. (1999) *The Exclusive Society*. London: Sage.

Young, J. (2007) *The Vertigo of Late Modernity*. London: Sage.

11

Geographical Indications: The Promise, Perils and Politics of Protecting Place-Based Products

Rosemary J. Coombe, Sarah Ives and Daniel Huizenga

INTRODUCTION

Geographical indications (GIs) are increasingly promoted as a means to protect the livelihoods of rural farmers and serve local and indigenous development needs. States, international institutions, NGOs and development agencies advocate the use of GI protections to promote a form of development that will ensure community security and environmental sustainability while safeguarding intangible cultural heritage. We situate the development of GIs historically and explore the political and economic conditions in which a renewed interest in the use of GIs for rural development and indigenous community aspirations has recently emerged. GIs are promoted through use of a rhetoric that represents a holistic 'community' having a singular tradition, deriving from a singular culture, rooted in a singular place, with its own naturally distinctive ecosystem which it stewards as resources for the future. We call this the 'social imaginary' of GI protections and caution against its literalization. While GIs may serve such laudable objectives, positive social outcomes are not guaranteed, nor are benefits from their use necessarily distributed equally. Historically, they have figured in a politics of privileging elites, reifying cultural traditions and legitimating particular power relations. Focusing on numerous examples, we explore the promise and the perils of using GIs to achieve development objectives and urge consideration of a wider range of social objectives when designing the means of their implementation. Let us start with a simple example:

> The Karoo region presents images of wholesomeness, windmills, sheep farms, endless vistas, hospitality and wholesome food … The region is famous for its sheep meat with its distinct taste and texture. Karoo sheep meat's distinctive character is derived from grazing on indigenous Karoo veldt vegetation. The name 'Karoo' has been abused and misappropriated by many businesses not based in the Karoo. The economic benefits have been taken from the people of the Karoo. Now for the first time a certification mark will guarantee that you are buying true Karoo meat. (Karoo Meat of Origin, 2012–2013)

This is the text that opens the homepage of the Certified Karoo Meat of Origin website written by a Foundation which acts as the 'custodian of the intellectual property rights that vest in the name "Karoo"'. Established in 2009, the Foundation aims to 'trace, record, preserve and commemorate the rich heritage which evolved in the Karoo region', while promoting its economic development by investing in the reputational assets of this arid and economically marginal area of South Africa. To this end, the Foundation has developed a certification scheme in which all those who produce or trade in 'authentic' Karoo sheep meat can use the new mark. Proponents of the mark extoll a regional culture based upon the tranquility and honesty of the Karoo way of life, such that the 'Karoo concept' has become synonymous with quality, tradition and wholesomeness (Kirsten 2006). The Foundation declares that the initiative will create new opportunities for local people to take a more active interest in their natural and cultural heritage, as well as spur development initiatives sensitive to ecological concerns on behalf of 'the beneficiary community in the Karoo'. This example condenses many emergent hopes and expectations for the benefits to be derived from the use of a particular kind of intellectual property known as a geographical indication (GI).

We begin by explaining what a geographical indication is, by situating the term historically and explaining the way it differs in important ways from other forms of intellectual property (IP). We then discuss the political and economic conditions under which GIs have attracted new interest from a diverse group of international actors. We suggest that a certain 'social imaginary' (Castoriadis 1987, 1997; Gaonkar 2002; Maza 2003; Taylor 2004; Touraine 1981; Wagner 2012; Zavela 1992) of a harmonious community with a naturalized relationship to a territory and its resources is fostered by the use of GIs. Those who are encouraged to develop GIs come to understand this as a strategy of legitimation, both for claiming economic revenues and for asserting cultural identity. These rhetorical forms are neither true, nor necessarily false, we suggest, but the deployment of such strategies may bring benefits in some regions while undermining sustainable development objectives in others. We show how such marketing strategies may have unintended social consequences and could give rise to unexpected social disputes, as well as contests over the proper scale for marking the provenance of goods described in cultural terms. While holding social appeal for framing development aspirations in some regions, this social imaginary obscures important social complexities in contexts where tradition and indigeneity are contested terms through which different social groups attempt to maintain or to assert gains in status, income and opportunity, as the following chapter, focused on South African rooibos, will attest.

THE MANY MEANINGS OF GEOGRAPHICAL INDICATIONS

Few forms of intellectual property (IP) are as confusing as geographical indications (GIs). Partly this is because as a form of legal protection, GIs are so recent; only with the passage of the Trade-Related Aspects of Intellectual Property Agreement (TRIPS Agreement) in 1994 did they become known as a distinctive category of intellectual property. Multiple jurisdictions with different legal traditions use a variety of discrete legal vehicles, including indications of source, appellations of origin, denominations of origin and collective trademarks and certification marks, which we will refer to collectively as marks indicating conditions of origin (MICOs). MICOs continue to be the preferred legal means of protecting names and symbols that mark a specific good as having a quality, reputation or characteristic that is attributable to its geographical origin.

The TRIPS Agreement definition adds that the reputation or characteristic be 'essentially' attributable to geographic origin. While this qualification has no clear meaning in the Agreement, the language is significant in that it signals a demand for clear evidence of an *essentialized* natural or cultural linkage between a product and its place of origin.

In some common law jurisdictions, a MICO may be recognized even when it is not registered if it has come to serve as an indication of source for consumers. Although lack of registration makes it more difficult to prevent others from utilizing a mark, because it requires that evidence of use and reputation be established in a court of law, it also eases costs of entry into markets for producers and collective associations seeking to establish a reputation for an indication prior to incurring the costs of registration. Unfortunately, marks do need to be registered in their country of origin to receive international protection under the TRIPS Agreement (Article 24.9), making this less expensive and informal option suboptimal for countries in the Global South.

Having a recognized GI enables the holder of the protection (who may be a certifying authority) to prevent the use of the same mark by others outside of the protected area and by those within it that do not follow the prescribed conditions for producing the goods that bear it. This does not prohibit producers from using the same techniques to make the product as long as they do not use the protected name to market it. It simply sets standards for producers within a geographical region who want to identify their products using the GI. Producers within territories covered by a GI cannot move their production outside of that region and retain the name protected by a GI, as a private owner or a corporation might do with a trademark (Barham 2003: 129). Although over 110 countries have specific GI laws in place, only 22 countries outside of the EU have established public registers (Giovannucci et al., 2009: 39–41) which allow holders of GIs to alert foreign competitors that a mark is already protected. In most countries, expensive litigation or administrative proceedings are necessary to prevent the use of a GI-protected mark in commerce. The broad international obligations set by the TRIPS Agreement do not require that countries commit any particular resources to enforcement. Given the lack of common international commercial law, marks need to be applied for in all relevant countries. Not surprisingly, many countries in the Global South would prefer to see a common international registration system established for all GI-protected goods, not just wines and spirits, which are currently given higher protection.

Clearly a large, diverse and unwieldy group of legal protections already come under the umbrella term 'GI'. Nonetheless, to make the field more confusing, many countries that did not historically protect such indications have used the TRIPS term 'geographical indication' as a generic name for the new forms of protection they have legislatively created to comply with their new international trade obligations. This is particularly true of countries in the Global South, which have only recently developed such protections. However, because the TRIPS Agreement does not specify what form such protection should take, and only requires that unspecified 'basic provisions' be put into place for protection (Article 22.1), countries may call their protections 'GIs', but actually employ governance frameworks historically used for denominations of origin or for collective trademarks. Alternatively, they may combine elements from different legal forms of protection and add new ones (Giovannucci et al. 2009: xiii). For example, many countries that have introduced GIs in the past two decades have established them as forms of state property, when historically they would have been held by producer associations, certifying bodies and collectives that maintained quality controls and were better able to respond to local exigencies. Thus, few generalizations about the promise or performance of GIs as a global category seem warranted without further examination of the actual regulations governing their use and the nature of the quality controls put into place in particular cases.

In the European Union (EU) even further distinctions are made between forms of GI protection, particularly with respect to wines and foodstuffs. For example, a Protected Denomination of Origin (PDO) is the name of a place or region that is used to designate an agricultural product or foodstuff that is both produced and processed within that geographical area; the quality and characteristics of the produce must be due exclusively or essentially to the geographic environment, which has both natural and social dimensions. Parmigiano Reggiano is a well-known example. A Protected Geographical Indication (PGO), on the other hand, is understood to be more flexible: so long as the product exhibits some characteristics attributable to the area, traditional knowledge or local know-how is unnecessary. Darjeeling tea has this status.

The European approach to these issues is considered culturally distinctive and is actively opposed by many other industrialized states. Nonetheless, the European approach is likely to become more widespread for several reasons. The EU sees GI extension as compensation for the reduction of agricultural subsidies entailed by global trade liberalization. In its negotiation of Economic Partnership Agreements with southern countries the EU has pressured states to adopt GIs for local goods in exchange for protecting those established in Europe (Bramley and Biénabe 2013b: 5). European development and environmental NGOs and other transnationally active organizations with funding from European state donors are also promoting the use and development of GIs for a variety of local goods. European approaches to rural development in the agricultural regions of Southern Europe, which depend upon local social economies of collective territorial intellectual property that cultivate and market the culture of the producing territory (Ray 2002) are held out as development models for countries in the Global South (Tregear et al. 2007; Vandecandelaere et al. 2009; Van de Kop et al. 2006).

Even the concept of terroir, long associated with venerable European wines, the most prestigious products of French viniculture, and the oldest appellations of origin, is arguably viable for goods as diverse as Vermont maple syrup (Trubek 2008), Fenland celery from Cambridgeshire, Kalahari melon seed oil, and the microbial qualities of raw milk cheeses (Paxson 2008). One comprehensive overview of the field of GIs defines terroir as:

> (1) a delimited geographic space, (2) where a human community, (3) has constructed over the course of history a collective intellectual or tacit production know-how, (4) based on a system of interactions between a physical and biological milieu, and a set of human factors, (5) in which the socio-technical trajectories put into play, (6) reveal an originality, (7) confer a typicality, (8) and can engender a reputation, (9) for a product that originates in that terroir. (Giovannuci et al. 2009: xv)

The existence of terroir is not necessary for GI protection. However, when the concept is described so broadly, the opportunities that protections for terroir-based goods might hold for producers of goods in the Global South becomes evident. Such a definition is wide enough, for example, to encompass craft traditions in which naturally derived materials such as grass, wood and clay are regularly used in conventional ways, providing that they have some reputation as distinctive.

RATIONALES FOR AND INTERESTS IN EXTENDING GI PROTECTIONS

Many states and international institutions see GIs as providing prospects for new forms of rural development, community autonomy, preservation of cultural traditions, and even conservation of biological diversity when the production of goods encourages the stewardship rather than the depletion of the natural resources from which they are made (Cullet 2005). GIs may enable the sustainable use of genetic resources and aid local conservation efforts (Larson 2007, 2010). Increasingly, the conservation of biological diversity and the safeguarding of cultural diversity are added to developmental objectives in proposals to extend GI protection to new regions and peoples (Wong and Dutfield 2011). Such protections are often idealized as offering the potential to maintain local conditions of production, reward traditional knowledge, and in some formulations even protect cultural practices despite the obvious social transformations they put into play (Broude 2005).

Amongst IP protections, MICOs are unique in creating new forms of inalienable goods rather than alienable commodities. To the extent that many of the legal vehicles employed to protect place-based goods are open to the use of all those who fulfill the underlying conditions, MICOs act more like locally bounded public goods than private properties (Calboli 2006). For example, European PDOs and PGIs are available for the use of all producers within the designated area who adhere to the code of required production practices and who are considered to benefit from the area's reputation (Marty 1997). According to academic commentators, GIs may thus be especially apt for protecting goods produced through collective cultural traditions of knowledge (Bentley and Sherman 2009: 976; Gervais 2009; Sanders 2010; Sherman and Wiseman 2006: 259; Sunder, 2006, 2007).

We have already emphasized that both global and regional trade agreements have put increasing pressure on states to strategically consider these new forms of protection. The geopolitics of trade ensure that developing countries are often forced to compete in the global market without the protection and agricultural subsidies provided in developed countries which, even when reduced in the name of trade liberalization, are still sizeable. Developing countries may also see GIs as one of the few TRIPS-protected IP rights that provide them with some competitive advantage, especially under an agreement that promised them *enhanced access* to markets (Agdomar 2008). GIs 'present long term benefits as they create value, enhance the marketability of goods and give an edge to developing countries to promote exports and rural development, thus generating sustainability and inter-generational equity' (Zografos 2008: 103).

Indeed, the vast increase in the number of states legislatively creating these forms of protection suggests a widespread belief that MICOs have potential value (Bramley and Biénabe 2013a). Nonetheless, far more countries have internationally lobbied for enhanced protections and passed legislation than have registered products at home or abroad, suggesting that the work of implementing regimes of GI governance and marketing protected goods has been far more expensive and complex than anticipated (Das 2009; Hughes 2009; Musungu 2008). For a GI to be effective, strong organizational and institutional structures and well-financed market partners committed to long-term promotion and commercialization are needed to maintain, market and monitor it (Giovannucci et al. 2009: xviii–xix). Moreover, the organization of supply chains, establishment and enforcement of product specifications and development of marketing plans are all daunting and expensive requirements that may be necessary to make GIs successful even in purely economic terms (Rangnekar 2009).

If MICOs are theoretically available to protect an increasing range of goods, they are also attracting the hopes and desires of a greater range of actors because they appear able to meet a number of international policy objectives. The increasing attention to the idea of culture in development theory and practice is another factor that encourages international bodies and civil society organizations to put emphasis on GIs. Coombe has written at length about the growing importance of culture in institutions for sustainable development and the emphasis on both development and tradition by the World Intellectual Property Organization (WIPO), including efforts to devise new forms of protection for traditional cultural expressions (Ahmed et al. 2007; Coombe 2005, 2009). Similarly, the valorization of intangible cultural heritage under global cultural policy instruments has focused attention on viable vehicles for maintaining, protecting and projecting localized cultural properties while rejecting forms of commodification more likely to disrupt social reproduction than to safeguard local forms of meaningful practice (Coombe and Turcotte 2012). MICOs are of interest to cultural heritage practitioners because they have a history of being used to protect collectively held 'traditional cultural expressions' (Aylwin and Coombe 2014: 110–111).

To the extent that NGOs are tasked with furthering projects that carry out objectives under major international policy instruments and human rights norms, they too seek to ascertain whether GIs are appropriate for an ideal of sustainable development in the Global South, that includes the preservation of biological and cultural diversity (e.g., Bramley and Kirsten 2007; Escudero 2001; Gopalakrishnan et al. 2007; Rangnekar 2010; Singhal 2008; Van de Kop et al. 2006). Increasingly, scientists, state research centers and development institutions explore the intersections between regional soil conditions, environmental factors and plant qualities to provide empirical evidence that a product's qualities are attributable to geographic factors and publish their findings in academic journals (Hawkins et al. 2011; Oberthür et al. 2011; Waarts and Kuit 2011).

The fact that MICOs may be collectively managed makes them attractive to development practitioners and NGOs hoping to prevent new forms of inequality and to encourage greater social cohesion by providing new measures of community control over economic activities that tie rural areas into larger markets. Proponents suggest that 'the introduction of GIs can help forge collective rights that are indivisible from locality' (Aylwin and Coombe 2014: 111). Advocates of GIs assume that farmers, large-scale growers and distributors, small-scale producers and residents all share similar interests in developing a region's reputation through the marking of distinctive goods.

> For producers, GIs convey unique characteristics that allow them to distinguish their products and break out of the commodity trap of numerous similar and undifferentiated products trading primarily on price. GIs may also provide a measure of protection for the intellectual or cultural property of a particular group or place and, as such, can contribute to a unique and not easily assailable form of competitive advantage. (Giovannucci et al. 2009: 8)

For rural economies, GIs appear to provide the lynchpin of 'a physical and conceptual structure for affirming and valuing the unique socio-cultural and agro-ecological characteristics of a particular place' (Giovannucci et al. 2009: 8). The reputational effects to which they contribute may influence other products in the region, foster tourism and contribute to regional branding (as anyone who has travelled in rural Italy can certainly attest).

Moreover, a growing number of international legal instruments create state obligations to protect traditional knowledge and indigenous heritage (Coombe 2008). The recognition and acknowledgement of traditional or indigenous knowledge under global biodiversity regimes, and the neoliberal commitment to using market-based vehicles of compensation for benefit-sharing, has motivated a great deal of research and policy that points to GIs. The interests of the UN Permanent Forum on Indigenous Issues in achieving 'development with culture and identity' while protecting 'biocultural heritage' resources and 'biocultural territories' (Wong and Dutfield 2011: xxxvi) has also focused attention on GIs. For indigenous rights advocates, GIs have

> features that respond to the needs of indigenous and local communities and farmers ... [they] are based on collective traditions and a collective decision-making process; reward traditions while allowing for continued evolution; emphasize the relationship between human efforts, culture, land, resources; and environment; and are not freely transferable from one owner to another. (Addor and Grazioli 2002: 865)

This is largely due to their collective ownership:

> One advantage of GIs in this context is that they are a common property instrument. Whereas commercial trademarks are usually owned by individual economic agents who therefore have a monopoly on their use, GIs are instruments that can be used by all genuine economic agents in a specific geographical area, who respect the terms of reference guaranteeing conformity with tradition – not a frozen set of practices but practices judged, after collective deliberation, to be consistent with tradition, i.e. that are genuinely a part of a living culture. (Ilbert and Petit 2009: 504)

The purported confluence of state and indigenous interests make GIs attractive to those concerned with state obligations to protect community heritage, knowledge and expressions. Again and again we see representations and assumptions of a singular tradition, deriving from a singular culture, rooted in a singular place, with its own naturally distinctive ecosystem which a 'community', holistically imagined, stewards as resources for the future. We call this the 'social imaginary' of GI protection.

THE SOCIAL IMAGINARY OF GI PROTECTION

> 'Social imaginaries' are ways of understanding the social that become social entities themselves, mediating collective life ... They are first-person subjectivities that build upon implicit understandings that underlie and make possible common practices. They are embedded in the habitus of a population or are carried in modes of address, stories, symbols, and the like. They are imaginary in a double sense: they exist by virtue of representation or implicit understandings, even when they acquire immense institutional force; and they are the means by which individuals understand their identities and their place in the world. (Gaonkar 2002: 4)

The assertion of naturalized synergies between the qualities of a territory, the characteristics of its goods, the traditions of its people, and the importance of these to their cultural identity has become orthodox for those extolling the virtues of introducing GIs and has often become established in the areas from which the goods they mark originate. The use of GIs tends to imbue products with distinct attributes that unproblematically reflect both a local biodiversity and a local cultural distinction which are presumed to be isomorphic with a 'community'. Thus, a stable, unified and harmonious 'place' is ideally imagined, represented and, ultimately perhaps, even experienced.

The rhetoric used often borrows the tropes of authenticity and primordialism characteristic of discourses of cultural heritage. This is not surprising given the intensity of European involvement in United Nations Educational, Scientific and Cultural Organization (UNESCO) heritage activities, which similarly focus upon the marketing of local cultural distinctions. Let us take a European example to illustrate this phenomenon. Matera, a town of 60,000 people in Southern Italy, is known for its stratified system of formerly inhabited limestone caves which was inscribed as a World Heritage site in 1993. Local crafts such as clay whistles, kitchenware and figurines not only provide tourist revenue, but are also reproduced as signs and symbols iconic of the town and emblematic of its heritage (Bortolotto 2010). In 2003 the Chamber of Commerce launched a publicity campaign for the promotion and appreciation of the DOC (Controlled Denomination of Origin) to further promote the 'culture of typical products underlying their geographical, social and productive roots' through a collective mark for Matera artistic craftsmanship to be used by artisans for the purposes of safeguarding traditional cultural heritage:

> On this point the discourse of the promoters of the label is clear: in the products of the label 'are narrated the events of a region, its territory, its customs, and its people' and the skills of the artisans are considered tools that keep alive a tradition which is assumed to be inherent with a territory. Guaranteed by the collective mark, the authenticity of these goods is produced by the results of the spatial component (geographic origin) and the temporal component (historic depth of the techniques of production). Rooted in the historical-geographic unity which founds the idea of 'territory', authenticity is the product of the crossover point between the natural dimension

> (in relation to the provenance of the primary materials) and the cultural dimension (continuation of know-how and skills) ... This example demonstrates how local heritage stakeholders mobilise and exhibit numerous kinds of evidence in order to prove their conformity with tradition and the embeddedness of the local culture. In so doing they guarantee their authenticity and uniqueness. (Bortolotto 2010: 110)

A form of legal protection that promises new economic benefits and invites communities to trade upon essentialized qualities is sure to find such qualities, or at least to find agents willing and able to project, elicit or inculcate them. Such exercises of social agency are inevitable in the context of enabling legal and political forces at state, regional and international political levels. GIs are being cultivated to promote products, processes and methods 'traditional' to places, and 'traditions' are being cultivated to support these marketing vehicles. Elsewhere, Coombe and Aylwin (2011) have argued that MICOs reify, objectify and socially construct cultural differences, rather than merely reflect a world of traditions that organically pre-exist them. Moreover, the spatialized natural/cultural differentiations which GIs symbolically mark in commerce have social, political and economic consequences, while constituting borders of community and identity (Coombe and Aylwin 2011: 2029).

Anthropologist Paola Filippucci (2004) suggests that the making and marketing of traditional products is the dominant means by which the borders of meaningful cultural difference are marked in modern France. Cheese is understood to be the classic *produit du terroir*, typical of a place and embodying a combination of natural sources and human skills that link people and their habitat. Residents deem such products as exemplary of cultural heritage, representing the enduring presence of a collectivity that displays its identity. Areas that 'do not even have a cheese' appear to lack patrimony (Filippucci 2004: 72). They are unable to demonstrate the essentialized qualities of tradition and authenticity that mark them as having a cultural identity that is legible to the state. Indeed, those who promote the establishment of cultural economies for rural development often advocate the creation of inventories of cultural districts identified by ascertaining goods produced from local cultural traditions (Rojal 2005).

The social imaginary projected by MICO advocates seems to presume a unified community which will receive uniform benefits from it use, a scenario which may have little empirical basis and serves as an aspiration only if GI institutions are shaped with sensitivity to local social relations. Studies of appellations in Europe, for example, suggest that the producers with the most secure marketing networks tend to acquire the lion's share of the added value they yield (Rangnekar 2004). Small producers struggle to build supply chains; without public investments it is virtually impossible to prevent powerful private actors from monopolizing the opportunities that GIs afford. Those most familiar with the use of these legal vehicles in Europe caution against their general promotion and urge careful consideration of their governance when assessing their capacities to serve as engines of equitable rural development (Barham 2003). Even in France, it appears that the oldest appellations of origin were developed to protect aristocratic traditions and continue to reflect class-based privilege (Moran 1993, 1999). Gade's (2004) empirical study of the management of the appellation for cassis in Southern France, for instance, shows how an ever-smaller syndicate of producers came to dictate the conditions of its use in their own favor, limiting the number of eligible producers, preventing tenants who actually grew the grapes from receiving any benefits from its use, and deploying it so as to prohibit the creation of cooperatives that would benefit smaller producers, while entrenching poor working conditions for agricultural workers. The historical use of the GI exacerbates rather than mitigates local inequalities while reducing both biological and cultural diversity, and fails to meet criteria for participatory, democratic governance; for this reason, Aylwin and

Coombe (2014) make the case that new institutions for GI governance should be guided by principles of rights-based development.

Organized indigenous peoples in many areas of the world, however, have developed a concept of territory to describe historical attachments to specific ancestral lands and established forms of governance to further their collective interests in continuing to manage these areas in accordance with culturally distinctive principles of environmental stewardship. For these groups, the social imaginary of GIs may be less pernicious. This is not to argue that indigenous communities are essentially more harmonious. However, where those recognized as indigenous peoples have a political history of managing resources collectively and justifying those practices of resource management in accordance with norms drawn from human rights, environmentalist and sustainable development discourses, as they do in many parts of Latin America (Coombe 2011a, 2011b), GIs may be attractive. This is precisely because indigenous collectivities have made political gains in self-governance using arguments about the cultural significance of their territories in constituting them as a people with specific responsibilities to manage environmental goods in accordance with principles of customary law. They are thus well poised to effectively use this rhetoric, taking advantage of the economic and political opportunities that GI protections afford. To the extent that indigenous collective rights have been forged in a human rights context, many indigenous peoples have a long history of forging rights-based collective institutions based upon participatory principles that avoid entrenching or producing new inequalities.

Some environmental advocates argue that collective trademarks, one variety of GI, are particularly apt for indigenous communities who seek to protect their traditional knowledge, preserve biological diversity and assert indigenous rights. For example, Graham Dutfield (2011), who acknowledges that IP generally does not easily accommodate the collective interests of groups and communities, nonetheless expresses optimism about the prospects for associations of territorially based small producers to use such marks to assert group rights in goods derived from biocultural heritage (2011: 5). Biocultural heritage is a term developed by indigenous peoples and defined by the Convention on Biological Diversity Secretariat as:

> The knowledge, innovations, and practices of indigenous and local communities which are often collectively held and inextricably linked to traditional resources and lands and waters traditionally occupied and used by indigenous and local communities; including the diversity of genes, varieties, species and ecosystems; cultural and spiritual values; and customary laws shaped within the socio-ecological contexts of communities. (CBD Secretariat 2007: 11)

Goods derived from biocultural heritage may include traditional crops and products made from them, foods and beverages, medicines and handicrafts.

THE LIMITS OF THE GEOGRAPHICAL INDICATION'S IMAGINED COMMUNITY

The potential promise that GIs hold for rural sustainable development should not be overestimated. Although there are many community-based enterprises built upon marketing local products that celebrate the distinctiveness of their origins, the most successful of these have involved supports at many scales, including assistance in the constitution of cooperatives, the building of transnational partnerships with CSOs for the creation of marketing strategies, and the facilitation of communications between communities and national institutions. Moreover, states which have recently introduced GIs may play a particularly dominant role in dictating the terms of their use in national jurisdictions, which may not always correspond to community needs or aspirations. Communities have often found it difficult to control the social, ecological and cultural consequences of producing 'traditional' goods for modern mass markets. Two examples from Peru are illustrative.

Anthropologist Anita Chan shows that the Peruvian government has encouraged the use of denominations of origin for the marketing of traditional ceramics. With respect to ceramics marked as 'Chulucanas', she argues, the government has done so while promoting economies of scale and forms of industrialized manufacture that have seriously damaged the social relations of production which historically sustained egalitarian communities of producers, and while driving down prices and increasing competitive relations of mistrust and alienation (Chan 2008, 2014). In the Northern Andes, on the other hand, soft cheeses from the Department of Cajamarca were targeted for development as 'typical products: they are simple, attached to a territory, and the quality of the *mantecosa* is closely linked to the local soils and climate which determine the richness of the pastures and thus the quality of the milk' (Boucher and Gerz 2006: 43). Relying upon traditional knowledge and serving as a symbol of local identity, *mantecosa* is the work of many small farmers in a poor rural area which was seen as likely to benefit from its marketing as a typical product. Efforts to better market the cheese and to promote synergies between cheese, other regional foodstuffs and the development of landscape amenities with the potential to develop regional tourism were promoted through the collective mark 'Poronguito', recognized in 2000. Nonetheless, the work of collective organization has required extensive efforts by NGOs to facilitate dialogue between producers of *quesillo* (the curd used to make the cheese, which is generally provided by poor livestock producers in mountainous regions), small-scale cheese producers, speciality shops and national marketing institutions. In short, brokers were needed to ensure that small cheese makers had their interests respected in this process. Despite these considerable efforts, 'further work must be done to promote a greater sharing of benefits with small producers of *quesillo* (who are often women, often isolated, often exploited by middlemen, and physically and culturally distant from the end-product) as well as to reduce elite family-control of direct marketing to consumers' (Aylwin and Coombe 2014: 115). In both of these Peruvian instances, moreover, infrastructural support is necessary to enforce protection for marks indicating conditions of origin and to prevent their infringement in wider markets.

Such projects of facilitating 'development with identity' (Rhoades 2006) or investing in 'cultural economy' (Ray 2002) have attracted international NGO, indigenous rights, and environmentalist attention and are spreading across Latin America. For example, a 2011 study supported by the Ford Foundation identified multiple poor areas in which 'investment in the valorization of cultural identity can be an effective strategy for sustainable development that includes said territories', citing 'emerging demand for products and services that carry cultural identity associated with rural areas' as a rationale for 'the development of innovations in policies, public investments, and services, and the strengthening of actors, institutions and networks' to generate opportunities for the poor and marginalized (RIMISP 2011: 9).

> In Latin American countries cultural heritage is often associated with very poor and disadvantaged segments of the rural population, including women, indigenous peoples, people of African descent and rural dwellers. Valuation, then, is linked to public recognition of their knowledge and skills, contributing to a rise in self-esteem and sense of citizenship. It has also been observed that governance based on community/collectivity is key as important social capital distinctive of many Latin American countries. Therefore, the rural territorial development with cultural identity processes should include these different dimensions in addition to the economic one. Behind the identity products and services are the real actors and makers of them: people in flesh and blood, communities and their own strategies. To think only of new offerings for new markets leading to higher revenues and consequently, greater well-being, is a simplistic equation … it tends to stifle

> their prospects for a less mercantilist, more comprehensive, and more just and inclusive development. (Ranaboldo 2009: 7, acronyms omitted)

The authors of this report, sponsored by the Latin American Centre for Rural Development (which itself is variously funded by the International Development Research Centre (Canada), the Interchurch Organization for Development Cooperation (Netherlands), the International Fund for Agricultural Development, the Ford Foundation (USA) and New Zealand's Aid Program, indicate that throughout Latin America 'there has been an emergence of actors and networks dedicated to exploring development strategies based on the valuation of cultural assets in rural areas', with women and young people playing prominent roles in these initiatives, and municipal governments increasingly mobilizing to protect cultural heritage assets (Ranaboldo 2009: 8). Although GIs (usually protected denominations of origin) are identified as useful vehicles for this purpose, national and regional laws are described as 'still unfocused, poorly articulated, and little known and used' and in danger of becoming simply marketing instruments, most suitable for powerful business sectors (Ranaboldo 2009: 9).

It is widely acknowledged that Latin American countries face considerable challenges in creating models of culturally based development that do not focus primarily on wealth but also on sustainability and the protection of biodiversity. Efforts, however, are well underway to build and extend models of biocultural diversity territories for 'sustainable inclusive development' (Biocultural Diversity 2013), including capacity-building exercises, diploma programs, coalition-building tools, and the sharing of knowledge management strategies. Not surprisingly, EU partnerships and European models feature prominently in these multi-sectoral, transnational endeavors (e.g., Slow Food Latin America is now a trademark). The recent emphasis upon sustainability and inclusiveness indicates that regional development institutions have absorbed at least some of the lessons that have been drawn from the use of GIs for rural development over the last decade. In particular it has become clear that unless small producers and community actors and institutions themselves are involved in the design of such marketing strategies, the benefits from it are likely to be limited. Current research indicates that MICO programs captured by private interests for primarily economic purposes may destroy the natural and cultural assets upon which the GI is premised (Giovannucci et al. 2009: 118).

GI strategies driven primarily by states in the name of the public interest may also have exclusionary and destructive consequences. One example is a Mexican public–private initiative that aimed to diversify regional varieties of liquor beyond tequila (Mexico's most famous GI, derived from the blue agave) by protecting more varieties of mezcal using new denominations of origin (Coombe and Aylwin 2009). The process was dominated by government and industry elites. It relied upon the introduction of highly industrialized standards and volumes of production which marginalized smaller producers and undermined the characteristics of mezcal's traditional manufacture (Giovannucci et al. 2009: 2, 101). Although agaves and mezcals are endemic to Mexico, the unique aspects of these alcoholic beverages were also derived from culturally diverse processing methods:

> Most of the best quality mezcal is still small-scale artisanal production from rustic installations in remote, poor communities and does not go beyond regional markets. Even though vertically integrated industrial mezcal enterprises are beginning to sprout in different parts of the country, following the tequila model, bottling and commercialization are still generally carried out by small to medium intermediaries who buy up and blend the local productions from the scattered distilleries of small producers. For many poor peasant families of the dry tropics agave and mezcal represent a very important, even if meager, source of income. Because mezcal complements their subsistence economy, mezcaleros are among the few members of the poor and extremely-poor communities who

> do not need to migrate in order to maintain their families. (Giovannucci et al. 2009: 184)

If the denomination of origin publicized and made mezcal more popular amongst consumers, it was also a state property, use of which was restricted to producers, distillers and bottlers who were registered and monitored by a system controlled by a limited numbers of government-approved certifiers. The use of the term was restricted to a particular region, defined by political rather than geographical or cultural borders, excluded many traditional regions and created purely industrial opportunities for people with no tradition of cultivation. Many distinctive mezcals failed to meet the defined product criteria, which were based upon the chemical properties of tequila, not those of mezcal. Diversity in crops, farming methods and in products has been thereby reduced.

The socioeconomic consequences of protecting mezcal have been similarly disappointing. In the traditional cultivation area of Oaxaca, production and commercialization is concentrated in fewer industrial hands, and small agave producers are being pushed out and into migration (Angeles 2007). The federal funds available for developing the maguey-mezcal supply chain are quickly taken by better organized groups and entrepreneurs, often newcomers to the industry. The benefits appear to have been concentrated among large 'commercial interests and bottling enterprises that sometimes buy mezcal cheaply from the smaller producers that are unable to certify themselves and reap the profits … [the former may] establish their own industrial stills and thereby push the original small producers out of business' (Giovannucci et al. 2009: 189). State structures are, in theory, controlled by the public for the public, but, echoing the earlier case of tequila (Bowen and Valenzuela 2006), social conflicts ensued because the Mexican state did not introduce adequate provisions for the participation of smaller producers or traditional farmers or reduce the obstacles they face. With respect to the tequila GI, the entire system became economically and ecologically unsustainable, undermining the sociocultural characteristics of the region which was the cradle of the industry (Bowen and Valenzuela 2006). The future for mezcaleros appears similarly gloomy.

It is evident that many recent GI initiatives are state-driven projects that may have little to do with local communities or their social values and norms. Indeed, in many parts of the world, the issue of whose cultural goods should be protected as whose intellectual property, and thus who should own or control any marks indicating conditions of origin, is becoming a politics of contested scales. For example, Lorraine Aragon and James Leach (2008) showed how the Indonesian government unproblematically used an imagined community of homogenous local cultural groups holding expressive goods such as arts and crafts traditions as collective cultural possessions to declare such goods *national* patrimony. In other words, communities were imagined along the lines of Western corporations who acted as agents for the state. Not only was this a misrepresentation of how local peoples traditionally held rights in cultural goods, it fundamentally undermined local systems of creativity based upon customary trust and reciprocal obligations.

Although the ethnographic work done by Aragon and Leach focused primarily upon the emergence of protections for traditional cultural expressions (the concern of the Ford Foundation mission that funded their research), the implications for development of GI protections are clear. If local norms and practices of transmitting expressive knowledge and practices are ignored in state recognition of 'tradition', it seems highly unlikely that the GIs anticipated under Indonesian law for use on traditional handicrafts from particular areas (Mawardi 2009: 7) will provide participatory rights for communities that respect local social relationships, needs or aspirations. If such handicrafts are deemed to be based on cultural patrimony already considered *national* cultural heritage, these marks are even less likely to provide local community benefits. Indeed, the very use of the term 'traditional' rather than 'indigenous', Aragon (2012: 411) suggests, is designed to foreclose community claims to rights and resources.

It would be a mistake to see forms of development based upon cultural identity as restricted to indigenous peoples, or to understand those territories likely to benefit from cultural economy strategies as more likely to be indigenous. In Latin America, for example, mestizo, maroon, ethnic settler and diasporic communities have also shown capacities to capitalize upon 'cultural distinctions' to foster development (Ranaboldo 2009: 8). Nonetheless, to the extent that indigenous peoples have internationally recognized rights to heritage resources (Coombe, 2008), they are more likely to resist their cultural resources being appropriated by the states in which they are resident, and more likely to receive external support for the exercise of their rights to autonomy in this regard. Indigenous communities in countries where states maintain extensive powers over the use of GIs have sometimes turned to collective marks, which can be held by a community, used and developed informally, without recourse to national registration processes, to develop reputations over longer periods of time, and in distinctive channels of trade.

Collective marks may be used to mark goods made from biocultural heritage resources, pursuant to their own norms or customary laws, and/or in furtherance of non-market values (Coombe 2013). Alejandro Argumedo (2013), a Quechua activist, international indigenous advocate, and founder of the Potato Park in Peru dedicated to the conservation of sustainable use of potato genetic resources using Quchua traditional knowledge under indigenous governance, considers collective marks good vehicles for rural community development, particularly when GIs are held by the state in which they are resident. He argues that marks which can be collectively owned and managed in accordance with community self-determined rules that correspond with customary law principles offer the promise of real economic and political benefits to indigenous communities (Argumedo 2013). Nonetheless, reliance upon a trademark system to enforce rights against infringements of such marks is inefficient, expensive and time-consuming compared to a GI system structured to protect producer interests (oriGIn 2011). Thus, Argumedo believes that regulation of collective marks could be better designed to serve the needs of indigenous peoples, and suggests a new regime of 'biocultural heritage indications' to 'open up the current intellectual property rights system to millions of poor rural communities' (2013: 5).

CONCLUSION

The globalization of IP rights and the spread of IP protections to new parts of the world have engendered hope that GIs will serve processes of sustainable, inclusive development and bring new opportunities and benefits to indigenous peoples and rural communities, particularly in the Global South. We have considered the forces which have coalesced to make GIs appear especially attractive to a wide range of social actors and canvassed research that explores their promise and their perils as vehicles for development with identity, maintaining biocultural heritage, and facilitating the incorporation of traditional knowledge and practice into modern markets. We have argued that the 'social imaginary' of GIs, which supports naturalized synergies between the qualities of a territory, the characteristics of its goods, the traditions of its people, and their cultural identity, may express the experience and enhance the economic sustainability of some peoples in some places, but (as we will further suggest in the next chapter) may socially entrench fundamental inequalities in others. Ultimately, GIs are regimes of governance that need carefully designed institutions to fulfill an optimal range of social and economic objectives.

REFERENCES

Addor, F. and Grazioli, A. (2002) 'Geographical Indications Beyond Wines and Spirits', *The Journal of World Intellectual Property*, 5(6): 865–897.

Agdomar, M. (2008) 'Removing the Greek from Feta and Adding Korbel to Champagne: The Paradox of Geographical Indications in International Law', *Fordham Intellectual Property, Media and Entertainment Law Journal*, 18(2): 541–608.

Ahmed, M., Coombe, R.J. and Schnoor, S. (2007) 'Bearing Cultural Distinction: Informational Capitalism and New Expectations for Intellectual Property', *University of California-Davis Law Review*, 40(3): 891–917.

Angeles, C.G. (2007) 'La conformación de las regiones-mezcalerasen Oaxaca', Memoria del Foro del Tequila y otros Mezcales. Gea, Conabio, Ammchi, Sanzekan, UNORCA, El Poder del Consumidor.

Aragon, L.V. (2012) 'The Problems of Owning Culture: Global Intellectual Property Law and "Traditional" Community Arts in Indonesia', *Asian Ethnicity*, 13(4): 399–417.

Aragon, L.V. and Leach, J. (2008) 'Arts and Owners: Intellectual Property Law and the Politics of Scale in Indonesian Arts', *American Ethnologist*, 35(4): 607–631.

Argumedo, A. (2013) *Collective Trademarks and Biocultural Heritage: Towards New Indications of Distinction for Indigenous Peoples in the Potato Park of Peru*. London: International Institute for Environment and Development.

Aylwin, N. and Coombe, R.J. (2014) 'Marks Indicating Conditions of Production in Rights-based Sustainable Development', in P. Zumbansen and R. Buchanan (eds) *Law in Transition: Human Rights, Development, and Transitional Justice*. Oxford: Hart Publishing. pp. 97–118.

Barham, E. (2003) 'Translating Terroir: The Global Challenge of French AOC Labelling', *Journal of Rural Studies*, 19(1): 127–138.

Bentley, L. and Sherman, B. (2009) *Intellectual Property Law*, 2nd edn. Oxford: Oxford University Press.

Biocultural Diversity and Territories Platform for Sustainable Inclusive Development (2013) (http://www.bioculturaldiversityandterritory.org/)

Bortolotto, C. (2010) 'Globalizing Intangible Cultural Heritage? Between International Arenas and Local Appropriations', in S. Labadi and C. Long (eds) *Heritage and Globalization*. London and New York: Routledge. pp. 97–114.

Boucher, F. and Gerz, A. (2006) 'Mantecoso Cheese in Peru: Organizing to Conquer the National Market', in P. van de Kop, D. Sautier and A. Gerz (eds), *Origin-Based Products: Lessons for Pro-Poor Market Development*, Bulletins of the Royal Tropical Institute, 372. Amsterdam: KIT. pp. 41–51 (http://www.mamud.com/Docs/originbasedproducts_full.pdf).

Bowen, S. and Valenzuela, A. (2006) 'Denominations of Origin and Socioeconomic and Ecological Sustainability: The Case of Tequila', Local Agro-Food Network's Third International Conference 'Food and Territories' ALTER, Baeza: Spain. (http://syal.agropolis.fr/ALTER06/pdf/actes/c40.pdf)

Bramley, C. and Biénabe, E. (2012) 'Developments and Considerations around Geographical Indications in the Developing World', *Queen Mary Journal of Intellectual Property*, 2(1): 14–37.

Bramley, C. and Biénabe, E. (2013a) 'Guidelines for Selecting Successful GI Products', in C. Bramley, E. Biénabe and J. Kirsten (eds) *Developing Geographical Indications in the South*. Dordrecht: Springer Netherlands. pp. 123–136.

Bramley, C. and Biénabe, E. (2013b) 'Why the Need to Consider GIs in the South?', in C. Bramley, E. Biénabe and J. Kirsten (eds) *Developing Geographical Indications in the South*. Dordrecht: Springer Netherlands. pp. 1–14.

Bramley, C. and Kirsten, J.F. (2007) 'Exploring the Economic Rationale for Protecting Geographical Indicators in Agriculture', *Agrikon*, 46(1): 69–93.

Broude, T. (2005) 'Taking "Trade and Culture" Seriously: Geographical Indications and Cultural Protection in WTO LAW', *University of Pennsylvania Journal of International Economic Law*, 26(4): 623–652.

Calboli, I. (2006) 'Expanding the Protection of Geographical Indications of Origin Under TRIPS: Old Debate or New Opportunity?', *Marquette Intellectual Property Law Review*, 10: 181–203.

Castoriadis, C. (1987) *The Imaginary Institution of Society*. Cambridge, MA: MIT Press.

Castoriadis, C. (1997) *World in Fragments: Writings on Politics, Society, Psychoanalysis, and the Imagination*. Palo Alto: Stanford University Press.

CBD Secretariat (2007) Elements for the Development of Sui Generis Systems for Protection of Traditional Knowledge. UNEP/CBD/WG8J/4/7. Convention on Biological Diversity Secretariat. (http://www.cbd.int/doc/meetings/tk/wg8j-05/information/wg8j-05-inf-16-en.doc).

Chan, A. (2008) 'The Fortune of Networks: Neoliberal Seductions, Enterprising Artisans, and the Optimizing of Native Culture in Peru'. Paper presented at the American Anthropological Association Annual

Conference, San Francisco CA, 21 November. [On file with authors.]

Chan, A. (2014) *The Promiscuity of Networks: Digital Universalism and Local Farmers in Information-Age Peru.* Cambridge, MA: MIT Press.

Coombe, R.J. (2005) 'Legal Claims to Culture in and Against the Market', *Law, Culture and Humanities,* 1(1): 32–55.

Coombe, R.J. (2008) 'First Nations' Intangible Cultural Heritage Concerns: Prospects for the Protection of Traditional Knowledge and Traditional Cultural Expressions in International Law', in C. Bell and R. Patterson (eds) *First Nations' Intangible Cultural Heritage and Law, Volume Two: Reconciliation and Reform.* University of British Columbia Press: Vancouver. pp. 313–363.

Coombe, R.J. (2009) 'The Expanding Purview of Cultural Properties and their Politics', *Annual Review of Law and Social Sciences,* 5: 493–512.

Coombe R.J. (2011a) 'Possessing Culture: Political Economies of Community Subjects and their Properties', in M. Busse and V. Strang (eds) *Ownership and Appropriation.* Oxford: Berg Publishers. pp. 105–127.

Coombe, R.J. (2011b) 'Cultural Agencies: The "Construction" of Community Subjects and their Traditions', in M. Biagioli, P. Jaszi, and M. Woodmansee (eds) *The Making and Unmaking of Intellectual Property Law.* Chicago: University of Chicago Press. pp. 79–98.

Coombe, R.J. (2013) 'Marks Indicating Indigenous Values of Production: Marketing Decommodified Socialities'. Presentation at the *Cultural Commodification, Indigenous Peoples & Self-Determination* Symposium, University of British Columbia, 2 May. [On file with authors.]

Coombe, R.J. and Aylwin, N. (2009) 'Branding Traditional Places and their Products: Prospects for Geographical Indications and their Limits', DFG-Forschergruppe Cultural Property Colloquium Series, Institute for European Ethnology, Georg-August-Universitat Gottingen, 17 June. [On file with authors.]

Coombe, R.J. and Aylwin, N. (2011) 'Bordering Diversity and Desire: Using Intellectual Property to Mark Place-based Products', *Environment and Planning A,* 43(9): 2027–2042.

Coombe, R.J. and Turcotte, J. (2012) 'Indigenous Cultural Heritage in Development and Trade: Perspectives from the Dynamics of Cultural Heritage Law and Policy', in C.B. Graber, K. Kuprecht and J.C. Lai (eds) *International Trade in Indigenous Cultural Heritage: Legal and Policy Issues.* Cheltenham: Edward Elgar. pp. 272–305.

Cullet, P. (2005) *Intellectual Property Protection and Sustainable Development.* New Delhi: LexisNexis Butterworths.

Das, K. (2009) 'Socioeconomic Implications of Protecting Geographical Indications in India', Centre for WTO Studies. (http://papers.ssrn.com/sol3/papers.cfm?abstract_id=1587352)

Dutfield, G. (2011) *Intellectual Property Tools for Products Based on Biocultural Heritage: A Legal Review of Geographical Indications, Trademarks and Protection from Unfair Competition.* London: International Institute for Environment and Development.

Escudero, S. (2001) 'International Protection of Geographical Indications and Developing Countries', TRADE WP 10, South Centre, Geneva. (http://southcentre.int/publications/workingpapers/wp10.pdf)

Filippucci, P. (2004) 'A French Place without a Cheese: Problems with Heritage and Identity in Northeastern France', *Focaal-European Journal of Anthropology,* 44(1): 72–86.

Gade, D. (2004) 'Tradition, Territory, and Terroir in French Viniculture: Cassis, France, and Appellation Contrôlée', *Annals of the Association of American Geographers,* 94(4): 848–867.

Gaonkar, D. (2002) 'Toward New Imaginaries: An Introduction', *Public Culture,* 14(1): 1–19.

Gervais, D.J. (2009) 'Traditional Knowledge: Are We Closer to the Answers? The Potential Role of Geographical Indications', *ILSA Journal of International and Comparative Law,* 15(2): 551–567.

Giovannucci, D., et al. (2009) *Guide to Geographical Indications: Linking Products and Their Origins.* Geneva: International Trade Centre.

Gopalakrishnan, N.S., Nair, P.S. and Babu, A.K. (2007) *Exploring the Relationship between GIs and TK: An Analysis of the Legal Tools for the Protection of GIs in Asia.* ICTSD Programme on Intellectual Property Rights and Sustainable Development, International Centre for Trade and Sustainable Development, Geneva, Switzerland.

Hawkins H., Malagas, R. and Bienabe, E. (2011) 'Ecotypes of Wild Rooibos (*Aspalathus linearis* (Burm. F) Dahlg., Fabaceae) are Ecologically Distinct', *South African Journal of Botany,* 77(2): 360–370.

Hughes, J. (2009) 'Coffee and Chocolate: Can We Help Developing Country Farmers through Geographical Indications?', *Report Prepared for the International Intellectual Property Institute, Washington, DC* (http://www.iipi.org/wp-content/uploads/2010/09/Coffee-and-Chocolate-J.-Hughes.pdf).

Ilbert, H. and Petit, M. (2009) 'Are Geographical Indications a Valid Property Right? Global Trends and Challenges', *Development Policy Review,* 27(5): 503–528.

Karoo Meat of Origin (2012–2013) The Official Karoo Development Foundation (http://www.karoomeatoforigin.com/).

Kirsten, J. (2006) 'South Africa: For the Good Name of Karoo Lamb', *Business Day*, 24 April (http://allafrica.com/stories/200604240884.html).

Larson, J. (2007) 'Relevance of Geographical Indications and Designations of Origin for the Sustainable Use of Genetic Resources', *Global Facilitation Unit for Underutilized Species*. Rome (http://www.cropsforthefuture.org/wp-content/uploads/2012/01/Relevance-of-geographical-indications-and-designations-of-origin-for-the-sustainable-use-of-genetic-resources.pdf).

Larson, J. (2010) Geographical Indications, in-situ Conservation and Traditional Knowledge. ICTSD Policy Brief number 3, November 3 (http://www.ictsd.org/themes/environment/research/geographical-indications-in-situ-conservation-and-traditional-knowledge).

Marty, F. (1997) 'Which Are the Ways of Innovation in PDO and PGI Products?', in F. Arfini and C. Mora (eds) *Typical and Traditional Products: Rural Effect and Agro-industrial Problems, 52nd European Association of Agricultural Economics Seminar Proceedings*. Parma, Italy, 19–21 June, pp. 41–58 (http://www.origin-food.org/pdf/eaae97/02_marty.pdf).

Mawardi, S. (2009) *Advantages, Constraints and Key Success Factors in Establishing Origin- and Tradition-Linked Quality Signs: The Case of Kintamani Bali Arabica Coffee Geographical Indication, Indonesia*. Food and Agriculture Organization (http://www.fao.org/fileadmin/templates/olq/documents/documents/Kintamani.pdf).

Maza, S. (2003) *The Myth of the French Bourgeoisie: An Essay on the Social Imaginary 1750–1850*. Cambridge: Harvard University Press.

Moran, W. (1993) 'Rural Space as Intellectual Property', *Political Geography*, 12(3): 263–277.

Moran, W. (1999) 'The Wine Appellation as Territory in France and California', *Annuls of the Association of American Geographers*, 83(4): 694–717.

Musungu, S.F. (2008) 'The Protection of Geographical Indications and the Doha Round: Strategic and Policy Considerations for Africa', *QUNO IP Issue Paper* 8 (http://www.quno.org/resource/2008/12/protection-geographical-indications-and-doha-round-strategic-and-policy).

Oberthür, T. et al. (2011) 'Regional Relationships between Inherent Coffee Quality and Growing Environment for Denomination of Origin Labels in Nariño and Cauca, Colombia', *Food Policy*, 36(6): 783–794.

oriGIn (2011) *Geographical Indications as IPRs: A Word from NGOs*. WIPO-INDECOPI Symposium on Geographical Indications, Lima, Peru, 22–24 June (http://www.wipo.int/edocs/mdocs/geoind/en/wipo_geo_lim_11/wipo_geo_lim_11_26.pdf).

Paxson, H. (2008) 'Post-Pasteurian' Cultures: The Microbiopolitics of Raw-Milk Cheese in the United States, *Cultural Anthropology*, 23(1): 15–47.

Ranaboldo, C. (2009) 'Introduction: Explorations of a Latin American Perspective', in C. Ranaboldo and A. Schejtman (eds) *The Value of Cultural Heritage, Latin American Rural Areas, Experiences and Projections*. Lima and Santiago: IEP and RIMISP. pp. 1–13 (http://www.rimisp.org/wp-content/files_mf/1367855623ValueCulturalHeritagecompleto1.pdf).

Rangnekar, D. (2004) 'Demanding Stronger Protection for Geographical Indications: The Relationship between Local Knowledge, Information and Reputation', Discussion Papers 11. Maastrisht: United Nations University, Institute for New Technologies.

Rangnekar, D. (2009) 'Indications of Geographical Origin in Asia: Legal and Policy Issues to Resolve', in R. Melendez-Ortiz and P. Roffe (eds) *Intellectual Property and Sustainable Development*. Cheltenham: Edward Elgar. pp. 273–303.

Rangnekar, D. (2010) 'No "Lemons" No More: A Sketch on the "Economics" of Geographical Indications', in C. Correa (ed.) *Research Handbook on the Protection of Intellectual Property under WTO Rules*. London: Verso Books. pp. 515–539.

Ray, C. (2002) 'A Mode of Production for Fragile Rural Economies: The Territorial Accumulation of Forms of Capital', *Journal of Rural Studies*, 18(3): 225–231.

Rhoades, R.E. (ed.) (2006) *Development with Identity: Community, Culture, and Sustainability in the Andes*. Wallingford: CABI.

RIMISP (Centro Latinoamericano para el Desarrollo Rural) (2011) *Valuing Our Bio-Cultural Riches: Rural Territorial Development with Cultural Identity*. Narrative Report, 2005–2011. Trans: Peter Kozak.Santiago, Jaurez, and Quito (http://www.bioculturaldiversityandterritory.org/documenti/119_300000176_informe_dtr_ic_ingles.pdf)

Rojal, F. (2005) 'Cultural Districts and the Role of Intellectual Property (Distinctive Signs)', Dipartimento di Economia, International Centre for Research on the Economics of Culture, Institutions, and Creativity, Working Paper No. 02/2005, Università di Torino (http://www.eblacenter.unito.it/WP/2005/2_WP_Ebla.pdf; accessed 22 November 2013).

Sanders, A.K. (2010) 'Incentives for and Protection of Cultural Expression: Art, Trade and Geographical

Indications', *The Journal of World Intellectual Property*, 13(2): 81–93.

Sherman, B. and Wiseman, L. (2006) 'Towards an Indigenous Public Domain?', in L.M.C.R. Guibault and P. Heugenholtz (eds), *The Future of the Public Domain*. Netherlands: Kluwer Law International. pp. 259–278.

Singhal, S. (2008) 'Geographical Indications and Traditional Knowledge', *Journal of Intellectual Property Law and Practice*, 3(11): 732–738.

Sunder, M. (2006) IP3, *Stanford Law Review*, 59(2): 257–332.

Sunder, M. (2007) 'The Invention of Traditional Knowledge', *Law and Contemporary Problems*, 70(1): 97–124.

Taylor, C. (2004) *Modern Social Imaginaries*. Durham: Duke University Press.

Touraine, A. (1981) *The Voice and the Eye: An Analysis of Social Movements*. Cambridge: Cambridge University Press.

Tregear, A., et al. (2007) 'Regional Foods and Rural Development: The Role of Product Qualification', *Journal of Rural Studies*, 23(1): 12–22.

Trubek, A.B. (2008) *The Taste of Place: A Cultural Journey into Terroir*. Berkeley: University of California Press.

Vandecandelaere, E., Arfini, F., Belletti, G. and Marescotti, A. (2009) *Linking People, Places and Products: A Guide for Promoting Quality Linked to Geographical Origin and Sustainable Geographical Indications*. Rome, Viale Terme Caracalla 00155, FAO/SINER-GI, Italy (http://www.fao.org/docrep/013/i1760e/i1760e00.pdf).

Van de Kop, P. Sautier, D. and Gerz, A. (eds) (2006) *Origin-Based Products: Lessons for Pro-Poor Market Development*, Bulletins of the Royal Tropical Institute, KIT Publishers, Amsterdam, 372 (http://www.search4dev.nl/search?identifier=281684;docsPerPage=1).

Waarts, Y. and Kuit, M. (2011) *Intensification and Sustainability in South African Rooibos: Exploring the Conditions for Market-led Sustainable Development in a Biodiversity Hotspot*. LEI, Wageningenur (http://www.sarooibos.co.za/library/cat_view/43-right-rooibos-documents).

Wagner, J. (2012) Water and the Commons Imaginary, *Current Anthropology*, 53(5): 617–641.

Wong, T. and Dutfield, G. (eds) (2011) *Intellectual Property and Human Development: Current Trends and Future Scenarios*. New York: Cambridge University Press.

Zavela, I. (1992) *Colonialism and Culture: Hispanic Modernisms and the Social Imaginary*. Bloomington: Indiana University Press.

Zografos, D. (2008) 'Geographical Indicators and Socio-Economic Development', *4th European Intellectual Property Institutes Network Conference*, Zurich, April 2008 (http://papers.ssrn.com/sol3/papers.cfm?abstract_id=1628534).

Zografos, D. (2010) *Intellectual Property and Traditional Cultural Expressions*. Cheltenham: Edward Elgar Publishing.

12

The Social Imaginary of Geographical Indicators in Contested Environments: Politicized Heritage and the Racialized Landscapes of South African Rooibos Tea

Rosemary J. Coombe, Sarah Ives and Daniel Huizenga

INTRODUCTION

Consumed in more than 30 countries worldwide for its sweet aroma and celebrated medicinal qualities, rooibos tea is still cultivated primarily in the region where it also grows wild: the fynbos biome of southwestern South Africa. The South African Rooibos Council (SARC), a non-profit organization established in its current form in 2005 to promote industry interests, seeks to acquire a geographical indication (GI) for rooibos to protect the term as one that refers uniquely and exclusively to tea cultivated in its traditional region of growth. In this chapter, we will explore the historical, political and ecological context in which rooibos figures as a topical case study of the potential promise and perils of GIs that we introduced in our previous chapter. Multiple stakeholders have strong cultural attachments to rooibos. Historically the subject of trademark battles involving foreigners perceived as usurping a term that should be used exclusively by South Africans, the tea is produced and harvested in an environment characterized by histories of racialized dispossession under apartheid rule, ongoing contestations over land, and shifting identity politics. We suggest that the 'social imaginary' that characterizes many arguments in favor of GIs may obscure the complex historical relationships between the rooibos plant, those who control the lands on which it is grown, those who harvest it, the traditional knowledge of its cultivation and the ecology in which it grows. GI governance regimes should ideally take into account and attempt to ameliorate relations of inequality in the rooibos industry.

Rooibos tea is known around the world for its sweet aroma and medicinal qualities. Celebrated by marketers and scientists for its anti-oxidants and ability to combat stress, sleeplessness and a multitude of other ailments, rooibos is exported to more than 30 countries (South African Rooibos Council, 2014). However, few consumers know that the tea derives from a plant that is cultivated in only one area of the world: the unique fynbos biome of South Africa's Northern and Western Capes. While farmers and many marketers emphasize rooibos's ecological indigeneity, multiple stakeholders also have strong cultural attachments to the plant. Various social groups in the region with distinctive interests describe the tea as central to their cultural heritage. At the same time, rooibos is claimed as a form of national patrimony. Historically the subject of trademark battles involving foreigners perceived as usurping a term that should be used exclusively by South Africans, the tea is produced and harvested in an environment characterized by histories of racialized dispossession under apartheid rule, ongoing contestations over land, and shifting identity politics. Notwithstanding these contestations, the SARC, a non-profit organization established in its current form in 2005 to promote industry interests, has been working to acquire a GI for rooibos to protect the term as one that refers uniquely and exclusively to tea cultivated in its traditional region of growth.

We will explore the historical, political and ecological context in which rooibos figures as a topical case study of the potential promise and perils of GIs that we introduced in our previous chapter. There, we argued that the dominant rhetoric promoting the use of GIs has the tendency to project a particular 'social imaginary' that represents communities holistically, possessing singular traditions and rooted in a particular place characterized by a naturally bounded and distinctive ecosystem. In this chapter, we suggest that although this 'social imaginary' may easily characterize the socionatural contexts of some place-based goods, in the South African context its use may avert political attention from the historical relationship between the rooibos plant, those who control the lands on which it is grown, those who harvest it, the traditional knowledge of its cultivation, and the ecology in which it grows.

Rooibos producers across the socioeconomic and racial spectrum of the region are largely supportive of efforts to retain the *geographical* specificity of the tea known as rooibos and products derived from it. Nonetheless, we will show how the contested ecological, demographic and economic terrain of rooibos complicates any figuration of an undifferentiated 'community' with a naturalized relationship to an indigenous plant. Specifically, we contend that if the prospective GI does not develop institutional forms of governance that take into account the social, economic and political contexts of the tea's cultivation, it has the potential to further entrench existing power relations by conferring benefits primarily upon white farm owners who already control the land and means of production.

ECOLOGICAL, DEMOGRAPHIC AND ECONOMIC TERRAIN

The acquisition of a GI for rooibos tea in South Africa illustrates the complexity of the political, economic, social and environmental factors that may need to be taken into account to evaluate how a GI strategy might impact rural livelihoods and the distribution of industry benefits across an economically and racially diverse socioeconomic terrain. Rooibos tea is a globalized commodity that has become culturally as well as economically significant to South Africa. It is certified as 'Proudly South African', under a decade-long marketing and nation-building campaign, and the tea is known across the South African diaspora as a healthy national product. It is also an icon through which local residents negotiate and claim their belonging in the post-apartheid nation. It is asserted that rooibos, protected by a GI, is 'poised to bring about change that will positively benefit a people, a legal system, and a nation' (WIPO, 2013).

Rooibos grows in a territory that is, nonetheless, unique in South Africa. The demographics of the rooibos-growing region are dramatically different from the rest of the country. It is classified as 80% colored,[1] 15% white, 5% black and less than 1% Asian. The national population is classified as 79% black, 9% colored, 9% white and 2.5% Asian (South African Government, 2011). Ives (2014b: 18) describes this particular racial makeup as characterizing the ways in which both white and colored residents understand the distinctiveness of the rooibos-growing region in which they live; they see themselves as occupying a unique 'haven' from the dominant demographics and racial politics of the country as a whole because of the small number of black South Africans in the area.

Rooibos tea derives from a plant endemic to the Western and Northern Cape Provinces of the country and geographically limited to a particular biome, the fynbos, to which it owes its unique color, flavor, nutrient concentration and its reputed health properties as a rich source of anti-oxidants (Pretorius et al., 2011). The biome comprises just 71,337 km^2 of the extreme southwestern and southern parts of South Africa (Oettle, 2012), which experiences long, hot, dry and windy summers and short, wet winters (Ives, 2014a; Pooley, 2012). Although most accounts acknowledge that wild rooibos had been consumed for centuries, its cultivation for commercial use is generally traced to the turn of the last century after an immigrant trader purchased wild plants from both colored and white farmers. Today, the tea has an established reputation in domestic and international markets. Agricultural economists have argued for almost a decade that rooibos is a product typical of a particular region of South Africa and its geography, thus providing a clear case for GI protection to enhance the area's rural development. For example, Bramley and Kirsten contended that rooibos was ideally suited to be an origin labelled product because the link between the good and its territory was due simultaneously to ecological characteristics, local production practices and local culture, thus ideally engaging both natural and human resources in 'a collective process involving all local actors, thereby activating all the components of the rural economy' (2007: 84). An orthodox case for GI protection is expressed on the World Intellectual Property Organization (WIPO) website:

> Entities such as Rooibos Limited and the South African Rooibos Council are championing the proposed GI for a number of reasons. First, it protects the name from usurpation while allowing all those involved in the rooibos industry in the region – from farmers to exporters – to use it without fear of litigation in foreign markets. Second, a GI comes with specific guidelines for how a product should be produced, and this will ensure that all rooibos is of the same high quality. Third, it adds value for the producers, and a GI would put more power in the hands of the producers and farmers. Fourth, because the GI links an area to a product, it would be a powerful marketing tool for the region, and could be used to promote other activities such as tourism. Fifth, rooibos is produced in a fragile ecosystem, and a GI will help protect the unique biodiversity of the region. Lastly, a GI will ensure that rooibos tea blends are in fact genuine and not diluted, by requiring the product to contain at least 80% rooibos in order for it be labeled as an official rooibos product. (WIPO, 2013)

Although there have been conversations and plans expressed about protecting rooibos as a Mark Indicating Condition of Origins (MICO) for many years, industry efforts accelerated after a French company applied for a trademark on the term in 2012. In July 2013 the Companies and Intellectual Property Commission (CIPC) published a notice for public comment in the Government Gazette to indicate that the South African Rooibos Council (SARC) had applied for protection for the words 'rooibos', 'Red Bush', 'Rooibostee', 'Rooibos Tea', 'Rooitee' and 'Rooibosch' under the Merchandise Marks Act (Act 17 of 1941). Those who would be allowed to use the words include members of the SARC or other parties in the designated region in accordance with the 'Rule of the Use of Rooibos', which dictates that: 'The name ROOIBOS can only be used to refer to the dry product, infusion or extract that is 100% pure Rooibos – derived from Aspalathus linearis and that has been cultivated or wild-harvested in the geographic area as described in this application' (Government Gazette, 2013a). Protecting the mark locally is a necessary preliminary step toward achieving international recognition for it as a GI, particularly in regards to EU registration. International protection is important because over 60% of the annual crop of 12,000 tons of the tea is exported to more than 30 countries around the world (Réviron and Benni, 2012: 317). Large-scale farming is the dominant mode of production, producing 98% of the crop on farms ranging from 1,500ha to 2,000ha (Réviron and Benni, 2012: 320). Today, all farmers turn over their tea to one of eight processors, but Rooibos Limited (a private company which 'inherited' the public apartheid-era Tea Control Board's assets) is the dominant processor, taking a full 70% of all rooibos processed (Troskie and Biénabe, 2013: 100).

Small-scale farmers, many of whom are members of co-operatives that cultivate rooibos for the fairtrade and organic market, produce only 2% of total output (on farms of 0.2ha to 18ha; Réviron and Benni, 2012: 320). For example, small-scale rooibos farmers in the remote, arid, Suid Bokkeveld region of the Northern Cape Province established the Heiveld Co-operative (the Heiveld) in 2001. The goal of the Heiveld, which today has more than 50 members, was initially to provide more economically sustainable livelihoods for small-scale, historically marginalized, largely colored farmers, and to facilitate recognition of the contribution of their traditional knowledge in a rooibos processing and training organization. The Heiveld has received support from local NGOs (the Environmental Monitoring Group and INDIGO Development and Change) and university researchers who have secured research and development grants. Arable land in the region is limited, families are spread out, and collective organization proved challenging before the Co-operative helped residents to participate more directly in the processing and marketing of their tea, instead of relying on larger, predominately white-owned, companies. Today, the Heiveld provides rooibos tea for global fairtrade and organic markets.

Members of the Heiveld developed expertise with geographic information systems (GIS) in order to provide spatial information about production areas to organic certifying agencies (which has also provided them with better knowledge with which to attempt to assert rights to land in the area). Through their work as a co-operative, area residents have become more aware of themselves as a community, investing in local governance, social projects, education, and local packaging of their goods. If fairtrade and organic certification initially enabled these farmers to more than double their profits, both farmers and their NGO supporters worry that fairtrade definitions that allow white commercial farm owners to gain certifications could affect the long-term economic sustainability of such co-operatives:

> Whereas the consumer image of fairtrade tends to be of cooperatively minded smallholders, in South Africa, fairtrade producers mainly consist of White commercial farm owners who wish to support their Black and Coloured workers. An EMG respondent claims that 'small farmers are the least politically empowered within the fairtrade system' and notes that standards are developed in Bonn where smallholders have little voice. EMG likewise notes the difficulty facing producer networks … as they strive to meet increasingly complex standards and certifications that reflect deeply embedded structural inequalities. (Keahey, 2013: 177)

Ironically, the general misrepresentation of rooibos as fairtrade *tea* had negative consequences for small-scale farmers. Had it been classified as an herb (which it more closely resembles) under fairtrade categories, it would have remained a product restricted to smallholders; once it was designated a tea, hired-labor on rooibos farms was permitted. Thus, large commercial farmers facing less challenging conditions for cultivation were able to move into fairtrade channels, lowering prices and capturing the US market (Keahey, 2013: 178). Indeed, in response to these lower prices, many small-scale farmers have emphasized traditional methods of harvesting wild rooibos in the hopes that another niche market can be developed.

The Wupperthal Association has a longer history, originating in NGO, church and European community development efforts in the late 1990s amongst an isolated association of local families, historically described as 'Khoikhoi' in a mission station community founded in the early 19th century (Spath, 2013). Today this area in the Cederberg mountains centers around the Moravian church, and the church owns nearly all of the land in the region, only 7% of which is suitable for farming, of which 4% is used for rooibos (Erasmus, 2013). Most farmers lease their lands from the church, and many can access their rooibos plots only by walking as far as 8km a day. The Association entered fairtrade markets in 1998, and acquired FLO certification as the Wupperthal Cooperative in 2005 (Raynolds and Ngcwangu, 2009). Working with Heiveld, they launched a tea packaging company, Fairpackers, in 2006, in collaboration with an established fairtrade certified rooibos packaging firm. Fairpackers employed ten people, largely women from producer communities, and built a factory to develop flavored blends and package shelf-ready tea to meet varied buyer specifications. It exported the tea to nine countries (Raynolds and Ngcwangu, 2009: 78). The Cooperative loosely connected 'multiple communities separated into distant outstations accessible only by formidable dirt roads' (Keahey, 2013: 181) and faced transportation and communications challenges. Meeting fairtrade and organic standards was difficult, membership quickly outgrew the Cooperative's capacity to provide training, and it lost both organic and fairtrade certification in 2009 (Keahey, 2013: 182). During that time, tea prices also fell in part due to competition from large-scale white commercial farms in the fairtrade sector. With mounting tensions in the community, the rooibos farmers divided into several different farming co-operatives, including the Wupperthal Original Rooibos Cooperative (Keahey, 2013: 183).

The Wupperthal Original Rooibos Cooperative (Wupperthal) has formed a fairtrade organization with a smaller membership base of 93 members (as of July 2013), 39 of whom are female (Erasmus, 2013). Women are represented in management and board positions and the group has developed operations with assistance from the Moravian Church – which provided building access – and preliminary industry support via a processing firm. Members took advantage of their own labor to establish a new tea court, reinvesting its first round of fairtrade 'social premium' funds to complete co-operative infrastructure (Keahey, 2013: 187–188). The premium also enabled the community to provide more teachers in the local school and send more children to a regional high school, with a few receiving university bursaries (Erasmus, 2013). Wupperthal hopes to start using premiums to develop tourism infrastructure and create additional permanent jobs in the region. In recent years, another co-operative, the Driefontein Small Farmers' Cooperative, involving 36 families, has started growing fairtrade and organic rooibos, further south in Redelinghuys. The Driefontein Small Farmers' Cooperative sent the first farmer's child to university less than three years after its 2010 founding (Driefontein, 2013).

Although the formation of co-operatives may enhance peoples' sense of community, the precariousness of colored peoples' livelihoods is nonetheless profound. Rooibos farm workers are concerned about the security of their tenure and recognition of their belonging in the region due to the legacies of colonial violence, apartheid laws and economic inequality. Facing the continual threat of displacement, the colored community appeared trapped in a placeless, liminal state: not white enough under apartheid and not black enough in the post-apartheid nation (Adhikari, 2005). Efforts to secure ownership of lands their families have cultivated for decades have often been unsuccessful and anxiety producing. In the Heiveld area, for example, several families have struggled for years to secure legal title to the rooibos land they farm. This is land on which they have lived continuously for over 70 years and to which they are understood to have customary rights. These families are, however, quite unusual amongst colored peoples for having maintained the capacity to farm their ancestral lands during the apartheid era; most others have been displaced (Legal Resources Centre, 2007). Some farmers claim that the land that co-op farmers hold is insufficient to support their families (Majavu, 2010); legal efforts are underway to obtain restitution of lands in the unusual instances where descendants of ancestral landholders can show historical evidence of dispossession (Majavu, 2013).

In the Wupperthal area, the Rhenish Missionary Society acquired considerable lands, often from local peoples, between 1832 and 1855. Some of these were nominally paid for, but others were 'gifted' to the Society from colonial authorities who did not regard the area's indigenous peoples, denigrated as 'half-castes' or 'bastards' during this era, as having any legal rights to the lands they worked. Many descendants of those whose holdings were subject to transfer continued to regard these transactions as illegitimate well into the 20th century, prompting ongoing legal research into contractual conditions (Strassberger, 1969, cited in Surplus People Project, 2000: 25). Claims to restitution are still outstanding. Driefontein farmers hope that fairtrade premiums on rooibos will eventually allow them to purchase their own lands (Driefontein, 2013).

Reform of South Africa's land tenure security system is perpetually in the offing. In the meantime, colored farm workers face the continual threat of eviction, which, from the perspective of workers is often exercised capriciously, particularly when a worker is about to reach the age when he might be entitled to a pension (Ives, n.d.: 12). White commercial farmers have turned increasingly towards seasonal employment, creating further displacement for colored farm workers. Many of the colored poor now find themselves 'unable to find steady work on farms, obtain urban jobs, *or* make a living as smallholders. The precariousness of livelihoods and the dependencies on white farmers, combined with coloured residents' uncertain claims to belonging, formed a particular kind of dehumanizing structural violence' (Ives, n.d.: 11).

SOCIAL AND CULTURAL TERRAIN

Despite contestations over land, most farmers – colored and white alike – celebrate rooibos and its unique relationship to the local ecosystem. Most rooibos tea is sold in bulk, a matter that almost all those who grow and harvest it consider unfortunate because they feel that a 'Proudly South African' product is not being marketed as such in the wider world, and that little 'value' is being added or returned to the country. The desire to engage in more local marketing of the tea is widespread, but, as we shall demonstrate, the means to communicate the way that it is indigenous to South Africa are not necessarily reflective of local social and ecological circumstances. At least one company has adopted the term 'Khoisan' to market rooibos, despite its being the name of a people and a marker of their heritage, which in most jurisdictions would not be a permissible trademark. The fact that the name was considered public domain may indicate that both industry and consumers consider the Khoisan an 'extinct' people. Marketing images that convey an indigenous lifestyle are also conveyed by words like *Intaba*, from the Xhosa language to denote a general idea of a black African heritage unconnected to the area's local farmers, farm workers, or other residents (Ives, 2014b: 72). Despite a manifest lack of social harmony in the region, the imagined community of a rooibos GI is experienced, evoked and expressed in many ways. As Ives recalls, '… people and plants in the farming region come together in an imagined geographically rooted world. "Rooibos is the fabric of [our] society," one resident said, and indeed, the sights, sounds, and tastes of rooibos were everywhere' (2014a: 311). In many parts of the region, rooibos dominates economic, social, cultural and even family life.

Informants said that rooibos had developed its valuable properties in its 'proper' environment and through its cultivation by its 'proper' stewards, the families in the region who had lived there for generations. Many white Afrikaans farmers claimed a cultural connection to the ecosystem and a personal attachment to rooibos farming so strong that they felt their blood was mingled with the soil; 'People are born rooibos farmers', Henk, an Afrikaans farmer explained. 'It is who they are' (Ives, 2014b: 49).

> Many farmers spoke of 'standing by their land' even in times of drought or low rooibos prices. 'Why protect that land?' I asked Jonas, an Afrikaans farmer. He replied firmly, 'it's our heritage, no more, no less … the specialness of the town is ruined by newcomers.' His language seamlessly moved between natural and cultural preservation. (Ives, n.d.: 32)

An historical survey of the region, its inhabitants, and the racial economy of rooibos production suggests that the issue of rooibos as local heritage is one that evokes pride, passion and considerable pain. As Ives (2014a) delineates it, the rooibos-growing area starts about 200 kilometers north of Cape Town and extends just across the border into the Northern Cape, with most lands lying within the Cederberg municipality. For millennia the area was inhabited by San hunter-gatherers (Adhikari, 2010) with herders, sometimes called Khoi, introducing pastoralism in the first millennium AD (Penn, 2006). These two groups are often referred to by contemporary residents in the rooibos-growing region by the merged name, Khoisan (both the names of these original groups and whether they should be considered distinct peoples is a matter of continuing academic controversy (Wilmsen, 1989)). The mobile Khoisan left thousands of rock paintings, many still visible on rocks in protected areas, on rooibos farms, and on popular walking trails, a matter that may eventually have legal significance for recognition of indigenous territorial claims.

Europeans arrived in the area in the mid-17th century (Mitchell, 2008; Penn, 2006), at first as pastoralists, who, like the Khoi, made claims not to land but to the waterholes that sustained them and their herds. Often protecting these resources at gunpoint, early white colonists have long been seen as setting the Khoisan 'genocide' in motion, killing men and capturing women and children as slave labor for their farms (Adhikari, 2010; Penn, 2006). Private land tenure became codified in the early 19th century, a process characterized by the introduction of surveying, mapping and fencing, all of which served to redefine the landscape and structurally inscribe Khoisan dispossession. As settler colonists built and settled on farms throughout the region they began to demand more labor, which was amassed in the form of chattel slaves (people of African and Asian origins who were often brought from Cape Town) and Khoisan who had been forced into indentured slavery (Penn, 2006). Through this violent history, many of the Khoisan adopted the Afrikaans language and lost both their access to land and their economic autonomy.

COLORED/WHITE FARMING RELATIONS IN ROOIBOS COUNTRY

Land ownership in the rooibos growing region was highly divided by race by the mid-20th century, with nearly all commercial farming taking place on white-owned lands that were worked by colored labor. Although colored farmers grew the tea on the meager holdings they could access, by the time an apartheid-era marketing board was formed to facilitate processing and distribution of the tea (the Rooibos Tea Control Board), the industry was nearly entirely controlled by white land owners. Today, the region's colored residents are the largely landless descendants of the exploited class – a mixture of imported slaves and indentured servants – that served the white agricultural community's need for captive labor. In South Africa the term 'colored' refers to people who are descendants of the Khoisan indigenous peoples, black people who assimilated into the Cape Colonial society, children of marriages between members of these groups and people brought to South Africa as slaves or laborers from other African or Asian countries (Adhikari, 2005: 2). In the rooibos region their linkage to both Khoisan and white histories influences colored people's ideas of foreignness and belonging. 'In this context, white and coloured residents often invoked a distinct *ecological and demographic exceptionalism* in which they saw themselves as part of a specific ecosystem in which other South African people and plants were considered alien' (Ives, 2013: 2).

The rooibos industry was built upon the undercompensated labor of dispossessed colored peoples. Recent years, however, have seen a marked increase in black migrant workers from other parts of South Africa and from neighboring countries. Both colored and Afrikaans farmers refer to rooibos as 'indigenous' to the region and black South Africans and immigrants from other Southern African countries as alien to it (Ives, 2014b: 15). Rooibos and the unique fynbos ecosystem in which it grows provides the basis of a perceived ecological exceptionalism while the region's demographics serves to distinguish the populace 'from what one farmer described as the "black hordes" in the rest of the country' (Ives, 2014a: 317). Some colored and white residents have even considered separatist options for the province (Western, 2001).

In her fieldwork, Ives found that colored and Afrikaans residents alike identified themselves as belonging to the soil and to a natural landscape with resources they regarded as their heritage (Ives, 2014a). Many Afrikaans farmers felt that they were God's chosen people for this land to which they considered themselves 'indigenous', their 'bodies becoming indigenized through exertion in the rooibos soil' (Ives, 2014a: 317). The few colored farmers who did hold land described it as the source of their freedom from employment by whites. They also considered rooibos cultivation to be an expression of the dignity of working with their own heritage and the mark of their authentic belonging in the nation through their connection to the native fynbos landscape. Rooibos farmers regard the plant's cultivation as protecting a natural native landscape against the invasion of new crops that would change the soil composition of one of the last 'properly South African' ecologies (Ives, 2014a: 11).

In other parts of South Africa, many people categorized as colored under apartheid have begun claiming and celebrating their historical relationship to the Khoisan. While these claims have yet to gain many adherents in rooibos country, they are already influencing the ways in which local farmers and farm workers are being identified in the press and by the international certifying bodies with whom they interact, which could have a potential impact on how the equities of a GI dominated by white-owned farms and processing plants are understood. It is important, however, to understand the many differences amongst colored peoples, their representation and their historical experiences. Colored people were codified as a separate 'race' under apartheid laws, occupying an intermediate status between the white minority population and the African majority. They were viewed as descendants of 'extinct' bushmen and products of violent miscegenation, the implication being that colored people were 'deficient in positive qualities associated with racial purity and handicapped by negative ones derived from racial mixture' (Adhikari, 2005: 14). Nonetheless, a vast diversity exists among the colored population. As much as 40% of the population lives in the Cape Town area (Adhikari, 2005), and this urban population has been the focus of most scholarship and activism around the subject of colored identity (Ross, 2010; Salo, 2003). Experiences of colonialism, relationships to land, and contemporary understandings of colored identity are different in the rooibos-growing region than in Cape Town – a place where the majority of colored farmworkers and farmers have never been (Ives, n.d.: 11).

To complicate matters, it is becoming more widely acknowledged that many peoples deemed colored in South Africa have historical relationships with the Khoisan. Despite the apartheid-era myth that San peoples had been exterminated and the Khoi were extinct, historical research shows many colored people to be direct descendants of those formerly known as bushmen (Lee, 2003: 81). Indeed, in many other parts of South Africa, the colored community has undergone a recent ethnographic self-fashioning as Khoisan (Ruiters, 2006), a means, many academics argue, for colored people to understand their heritage in a fashion that better connects them to the land (Lee, 2003; Western, 2001). In rooibos country, however, many colored residents felt that expressing an historical relationship with bushmen might relegate them to a state of primitivism, extinction, or less than fully human status (Ives, n.d.: 4).

In the broader South African context, however, Khoisan identity has enjoyed a resurgence and reinvigoration through the proliferation of Khoisan art and the organization of conferences and scholarly projects in Khoisan studies (Comaroff and Comaroff, 2009; Lee, 2003). Some Khoisan leaders have refused to be part of the Congress of Traditional Leaders, for example, on the basis of their indigenous rather than tribal identity. Proposed changes to the national law contained in a Bill tabled in September 2013, suggest that 'Khoi-San' will now be recognized as having their own communities, leaders and other authorities without reference to them as 'traditional' groups (Government Gazette, 2013b). A variety of NGOs have supported Khoisan political movements, particularly those of the Khomani San in the Northern Cape Province, and intellectual property struggles around traditional knowledge and genetic resources such as the hoodia plant (see Darch, this volume) have brought further attention to what are now widely understood to be indigenous claims (Vermeylen, 2007; Wynberg and Chennells, 2009). A National Khoisan Consultative Conference formed in 2001 represents over 20 communities and acts as an umbrella body for Khoisan peoples across South Africa. In most of South Africa, then, the Khoisan people are no longer regarded as extinct. 'Khoi-San communities, leaders and councils' were described in the press as indigenous peoples when statutory provisions were drafted for their recognition by the Department of Cooperative Governance and Traditional Affairs in 2011, but they are not constitutionally recognized as such (Le Fleur and Jansen, 2013).

The United Nations has long recognized Khoisan indigeneity. Forced dispossession from their lands was acknowledged by the Special Rapporteur on Indigenous Peoples, Rudolfo Stavenhagen as the primary basis for their poverty and an obstacle to intergenerational cultural survival; he suggested that their apartheid-era nomination as 'colored' might consign them to perpetual victimization in the post-apartheid South African occupational structure (Stavenhagen, 2005, cited in Le Fleur and Jansen, 2013: 4). Under international pressure, President Zuma acknowledged in 2013 that Khoisan peoples dispossessed of lands prior to the 1913 Native Land Act would have their land claims considered, and the government implicitly acknowledged their status as indigenous peoples by agreeing that they 'have a right to self-determination', while insisting that they must exercise it 'with the assistance/guidance from the Government' (Majavu, 2013). Nonetheless, some organized Khoisan reject the land claims process as insulting to them as an indigenous nation with whom a treaty would be more appropriate (Majavu, 2013). Some activists argue that in the northernmost rooibos-growing areas, farmers who trace their lineage to the Khoisan have knowledge transmitted through families and are able to point to landmarks which delineate the boundaries of their ancestral lands (Majavu, 2010, 2013).

Embracing a Khoisan identity does not, so far, appear to be widely favored by most colored residents in the rooibos-growing areas, but to the extent that this area is clearly marked by the traditional cultural expressions of Khoisan peoples (rock art to which cultural property claims are now made), there are reasons that it might be considered indigenous ancestral territory. Many researchers see the colored rooibos farmers and workers as descendants of the Khoisan 'First People' whose traditional knowledge of rooibos cultivation has sustained them under conditions of extreme domination and exploitation (Koelle and Oettle, 2010). Indeed, indigenous rooibos is sometimes imagined as a commodity through which the supposedly fraught identity of colored people could be provided with the cultural markers they are seen as lacking, and a more indigenous place-based heritage encouraged through affirmation of their ancestors' cultivation of the tea; as one community worker said, 'The impulse of our project is to restore and bring back heritage to the community, to reinstate lost heritage, give people more a sense of who they are' (Ives, n.d.: 22).

Historical apartheid designations of ethnic homelands and bantustans, however, may make an indigenous territorial strategy less attractive in this region, especially to colored peoples who were historically assigned no such lands. Many white farmers discount or deny the Khoisan origins of commercial rooibos cultivation, and instead celebrate white farmers as the pioneers of the rooibos industry. Indeed, Ives suggests that for colored peoples in the rooibos area, claiming a Khoisan cultural identity to assert a place-based heritage could pose a particular trap, because many white land owners believe that bushmen culture was essentially nomadic, or even less-than-human (Ives, n.d.: 14). Under the pre-apartheid Union of South Africa, they were considered desert animals, allowed to stay in parks as part of the landscape, and, as recently as 1941, classified as part of the country's fauna, destined to disappear (Meskell, 2012). In this context, many residents of the rooibos-growing region were hesitant to celebrate an explicitly Khoisan heritage, Ives (n.d.) found. Although a few of her informants spoke about a Khoisan cultural heritage which included traditional knowledge of rooibos cultivation that had been stolen by industrial interests, most preferred to express indigeneity in aspirations based on an authentic historical relation of belonging with the region's ecosystem (Ives, n.d.). In short, in rooibos-growing territory 'a highly racialized landscape informed people's understandings of their own essentialized – and embodied – belonging in place' (Ives, n.d.: 22).

CONCLUSION: A ROOIBOS GI FOR SOUTH AFRICAN SOCIAL JUSTICE?

Although efforts to obtain a GI are clearly industry-driven, it has broad support in the rooibos-growing region, in the country generally, from the South African government and in international intellectual property policy circles. Authorship of the scholarly literature on the rooibos GI initiative, however, tends to be dominated by those agricultural economists who have championed it in South Africa (Bramley, Kirsten, Troskie) and Europe (Biénabe), as well as by members of the SARC itself. SARC is represented as a collective organization (Bramley and Biénabe, 2013: 132), and while SARC purports to represent smallholders and wild harvesters, few doubt that the governance of the GI will rest with large industry interests (dominated by white South Africans). Internationally, rooibos is represented as a South African product and protection for the name as an assertion of *national* intellectual property. As we have seen, however, the proper holders of goods that are linked to peoples' identities are often disputed; in this instance, rooibos appears to be understood as essential to the emplaced identities of different social groups with diverse, distinctive and sometimes conflicting interests. Moreover, identities are shifting as peoples reinterpret their history and positioning in the still emerging post-apartheid nation.

SARC will determine the conditions under which the rooibos GI may be used, but Keahey (2013) argues that their processes are far from participatory. The vast majority of colored farm workers do not hold lands, and few have the means to become farmers in their own right or to market their crops or goods. Most lack 'confidence, as well as the business, language, and literacy skills required to effectively navigate the commodity network' (Keahey, 2013: 157). In order to better integrate the various constituencies with interests in rooibos, SARC has promoted the Right Rooibos initiative which propounds an integrated management system that captures key protocols in regards to labor, employment and environmental stewardship (Pretorius et al., 2011). This campaign is designed to 'ultimately realize a stringent industry-wide mark that would enable actors to capture multiple standards and certifications in a single auditing stream' (Keahey, 2013: 166). Socially progressive activists have appealed for greater 'emerging farmer' representation so that colored farmers would have a forum to express their collective interests; many would argue that the Right Rooibos initiative while complying with South Africa's laws on employment equity, does not go far enough. In the farming region Right Rooibos is appreciated more for synthesizing the multiple regulatory demands that cultivators face in order to fulfill various global sustainability criteria than as a guide to ethical conduct or social responsibilities.

In the post-apartheid context, is it unreasonable to suggest that the establishment of a rooibos GI might serve South African aspirations to redress economic injustice and achieve greater social equity? The creation and recognition of the rooibos GI is an important *state* activity and its use and governance could be structured as a public institution. The South African Constitution and Bill of Rights is recognized around the world as embracing the fullest range of human rights. For the rooibos GI to be constitutional, the conditions for its use should be based on democratic values, social justice and fundamental human rights, including those of equality and participatory governance. The South African government has constitutionally mandated obligations to provide equality of access to lands, water, food security and employment as well as environmental protections (Forbath et al., 2011). Thus, a rooibos GI could and arguably should be designed to fulfill a wider social mandate. Social rights in South Africa have been developed to address poverty and to remedy the economic injustices of the past (Christiansen, 2008). Conditions in the rooibos industry cry out for the development of rights-based criteria for the use of a rooibos GI that would squarely address long histories of exploitation, dispossession and disenfranchisement, including some form of redistribution of lands to non-white residents to enable them to maximize the livelihood security that rooibos could provide. Moreover, serious consideration needs to be given to the rights of black migrants from other parts of the country to participate in this industry.

Considerations of social justice in the governance of the GI seem especially necessary because the imagined community constituted by a heritage of rooibos cultivation now faces some of its gravest challenges. Despite the emotional attachment that so many people in the rooibos region have to the plant and their desire to limit its cultivation to a particular region designated by the proposed GI, rooibos is unlikely to stay in its proper place. If the imagined community of GI protections promotes and perpetuates essentialized historical relationships between people, place and products, plants have their own needs. However socially dominant residents' ideas about rooibos's ecological and cultural rootedness may be, many scientists now speculate that climate change will shift rooibos's unique ecosystem – its soil, rain and insects – southward, further down the Cape. Droughts and erratic rainfall over the last ten years have negatively affected cultivation (Palitza, 2011), and the insects the plant relies upon for pollination are declining in the region. Just as new opportunities for exports of rooibos are opening up for colored farmers, demand for the tea is expanding and activists seeking restitution for lands taken from them, the *terroir* to which the peoples of this region have such a passionate attachment might literally be moving beneath their feet (Ives, 2014a: 319). It is imperative that the GI be structured so as to provide livelihood security and economic opportunities to a greater number of South Africans, rather than privileging particular people, who hold particular lands at a particular point in time.

Certainly a rooibos GI has the potential to protect a regional industry from having a distinctive crop marketed as a placeless commodity in an increasingly globalized system of production and exchange. By marking the relationship of rooibos to an indigenous South African ecosystem, a GI could provide the product and the people involved with its cultivation some relief from the pressures of industrial agribusiness and its tendencies to globalized monocropping, while maintaining the unique health benefits that rooibos grown in this region offers consumers around the world. However, this South African example also shows how deeply enmeshed place-based goods may be in local relations of power and that identifications with culture and territory may be highly racialized. The promise of GIs may quickly dissolve and their perils be realized if we don't consider how the social imaginary of the GI elides social, political and economic inequities within the territories and communities of producers of GI-certified goods and respect rights-based development principles (Aylwin and Coombe, 2014) in developing their institutions of governance.

NOTE

1 The term colored has a unique meaning in South Africa which we describe in detail later in this chapter.

REFERENCES

Adhikari, M. (2005) Not White Enough, Not Black Enough: Racial Identity in the South African Coloured Community. Athens: Ohio University Press.

Adhikari, M. (2010) A Total Extinction Confidently Hoped for: The Destruction of Cape San Society Under Dutch Colonial Rule, 1700–1795. *Journal of Genocide Research*, 12(1–2): 19–44.

Aylwin, N. and Coombe, R.J. (2014) 'Marks Indicating Conditions of Production in Rights-based Sustainable Development', *University of California Davis Law Review*, 47(3): 753–786.

Bramley, C. and Biénabe, E. (2013) 'Guidelines for Selecting Successful GI Products', in C. Bramley, E. Bienabe, and J. Kirsten (eds), *Developing Geographical Indications in the South*. Dordrecht: Springer Netherlands. pp. 123–136.

Bramley, C. and Kirsten, J.F. (2007) 'Exploring the Economic Rationale for Protecting Geographical Indicators in Agriculture', *Agrikon*, 46(1): 69–93.

Christiansen, E.C. (2008) 'Using Constitutional Adjudication to Remedy Socio-Economic Injustice: Comparative Lesson from South Africa', *UCLA Journal of International Law and Foreign Affairs*, 13(2): 369–405.

Comaroff, J. and Comaroff, J. (2009) *Ethnicity, Inc.* Chicago: University of Chicago Press.

Driefontein, Small Farmers Co-op. (2013) 'Welcome to our World' (http://www.driefonteinrooibos.co.za/index.php).

Erasmus, D. (2013) 'Wupperthal Rooibos Framers Co-operate for a Better Future', *Farmer's Weekly*, Johannesburg, 21 June (http://www.farmersweekly.co.za/article.aspx?id=41908&h=Wupperthal-rooibos-farmers-co-operate-for-a-better-future).

Forbath, W. et al. (2011) 'Cultural Transformation, Deep Institutional Reform, and ESR Practice', in L.E. White and J. Perelman (eds), *Stones of Hope: How African Activists Reclaim Human Rights to Challenge Global Poverty*. Stanford: Stanford University Press. pp. 51–90.

Government Gazette (2013a) Department of Trade and Industry Merchandise Marks Act, 1941 (ACT 17 of 1941) Proposed Prohibition on the Use of Certain Words, Notice 722 of 2013, 12 July (http://www.greengazette.co.za/notices/merchandise-marks-act-17-1941-proposed-prohibition-on-the-use-of-certain-words_20130712-GGN-36637-00722).

Government Gazette (2013b) 'Invitation to Comment on the Traditional Affairs Bill, 2013', *Department of Traditional Affairs*, Notice 947 of 2013, September

20 (www.gov.za/documents/download.php?f=199232).
Ives, S. (2013) 'Uprooting Autochthony in South Africa: Climate Change and Rooibos Tea's Southward Creep'. Presented at the Association of American Geographers Annual Meeting, Los Angeles. [On file with authors.]
Ives, S. (2014a) 'Uprooting "Indigeneity" in South Africa's Western Cape: The Plant that Moves', *American Anthropologist*, 116(2): 310–323.
Ives, S. (2014b) 'Tea Stories: Cultivating Indigeneity in South Africa's Western Cape'. A Dissertation submitted to Stanford University. [On file with authors.]
Ives, S. (n.d.) 'Farming the South African "Bush": Ecologies of Belonging and Exclusion in Rooibos Tea', *American Ethnologist*. [Forthcoming, on file with authors.]
Keahey, J.A. (2013) 'Emerging Markets, Sustainable Methods: Political Economy Empowerment in South Africa's Rooibos Tea Sector'. Unpublished Dissertation, University of Colorado (http://digitool.library.colostate.edu///exlibris/dtl/d3_1/apache_media/L2V4bGlicmlzL2R0bC9kM18xL2FwYWNoZV9tZWRpYS8yMDc1NDI=.pdf).
Koelle, B. and Oettle, N.M. (2010) 'Adapting with Enthusiasm: Climate Change Adaptation in the Context of Participatory Action Research' (http://www.indigo-dc.org/documents/Koelle%20Oettle%20Adapting%20with%20enthusiasm.pdf).
Lee, R.B. (2003) 'Indigenous Rights and the Politics of Identity in Post-Apartheid South Africa', in B. Dean and J. M. Levi (eds), *At the Risk of Being Heard: Identity, Indigenous Rights, and Postcolonial States*. Ann Arbor: University of Michigan Press. pp. 80–111.
Le Fleur, A. and L. Jansen (2013) *The Khoisan in Contemporary South Africa*. Johannesburg: Konrad-Adenauer-Stiftung e.V. (http://www.kas.de/wf/doc/kas_35255-1522-2-30.pdf?130828123620).
Legal Resources Centre (2007) *Annual Report 2006/2007*. Johannesburg: Legal Resource Centre. (http://www.lrc.org.za/publications/annual-reports).
Majavu, A. (2010) 'South Africa's Rooibos Farmers Go Wild to Take On Commercial Growers: Smaller Fair-trade Tea Co-operatives in the Western Cape Choose Wild Rooibos to Beat Climate Change and Large-scale Growers', *Guardian Weekly*, 20 July (http://www.theguardian.com/world/2010/jul/20/south-africa-farming-tea-climate).
Majavu, A. (2013) 'South Africa's First Nations Give Land Claims' Consultation Thumbs Down', The South African Civil Society Information Service, 10 February (http://www.sacsis.org.za/site/article/1585).
Meskell, L. (2012) *The Nature of Heritage: The New South Africa*. New York: Wiley Books.
Mitchell, L. (2008) *Belongings: Property, Family, and Identity in Colonial South Africa (an Exploration of Frontiers, 1725–1830)*. New York: Columbia University Press.
Oettle, N. (2012) *Adaptation with a Human Face*. Suid Bokkveld, South Africa: Environmental Monitoring Group (http://www.emg.org.za/news/99-adaptation-with-a-human-face).
Palitza, K. (2011) 'Making a Hot Cup of Rooibos Tea Unaffordable', *Climate and Development Knowledge Network*, Inter Press Services (http://www.ipsnews.net/news/regional-categories/africa/).
Penn, N. (2006) *The Forgotten Frontier: Colonist and Khoisan on the Cape's Northern Frontier in the 18th Century*. Cape Town: Double Storey Books.
Pooley, S. (2012) 'Recovering the Lost History of Fire in South Africa's Fynbos', *Environmental History*, 17(1): 55–83.
Pretorius, G. Harley, V. and Ryser, L. (2011) *Right Rooibos Handbook*. South African Rooibos Council.
Raynolds, L.T. and Ngcwangu, S.U. (2009) 'Fair Trade Rooibos Tea: Connecting South African Producers and American Consumer Markets', *Geoforum*, 41(1): 74–83.
Réviron, S. and Benni, N.E.I. (2012) 'South Africa: Rooibos Tea', in M. Blakeney, et. al. (eds), *Extending the Protection of Geographical Indications: Case Studies of Agricultural Products in Africa*. New York: Routledge. pp. 314–329.
Ross, F. (2010) *Raw Life, New Hope: Decency, Housing and Everyday Life in a Post-Apartheid Community*. Cape Town: UCT Press.
Ruiters, M. (2006) 'Collaboration, Assimilation and Contestation: Emerging Constructions of Coloured Identity in Post-Apartheid South Africa', in M. Adhikari (ed.), *Burdened by Race: Coloured Identities in Southern Africa*. CapeTown: UCT Press. pp. 104–133.
Salo, E. (2003) 'Negotiating Gender and Personhood in the New South Africa: Adolescent Women and Gangsters in Manenberg Township on the Cape Flats', *European Journal of Cultural Studies*, 6(3): 345–365.
South African Government (2011) Statistics South Africa (http://beta2.statssa.gov.za/).
South African Rooibos Council (2014) The Official Site of South African Rooibos (http://www.sarooibos.co.za/home-mainmenu-1).
Spath, Andreas (2013) 'Without Fair Trade There Was No Future For Us', FairTrade Label South Africa, January (http://www.fairtradelabel.org.za/Pagesetter/viewpub/tid/5/pid/21).
Surplus People Project and the Legal Resources Centre (2000) *An Inventory and Description of the Historical Acquisition of Moravian Church Land: A Report*

Compiled for the Moravian Church of South Africa. Cape Town: Surplus People Project and the Legal Resources Centre (http://www.spp.org.za/reports/moravian.pdf).

Troskie, D. and Biénabe, E. (2013) 'Institution Building and Local Industry Dynamics: Lessons from the Rooibos GI Initiative', in C. Bramley, E. Bienabe and J. Kirsten (eds), *Developing Geographical Indications in the South.* Dordrecht: Springer Netherlands. pp. 95–121.

Vermeylen, S. (2007) 'Contextualizing "Fair" and "Equitable": The San's Reflections on the Hoodia Benefit-Sharing Agreement', *Local Environment,* 12(4): 423–436.

Waarts, Y. and Kuit, M. (2011) 'Intensification and Sustainability in South African Rooibos: Exploring the Conditions for Market-Led Sustainable Development in a Biodiversity Hotspot', LEI, Wageningenur (http://edepot.wur.nl/15298).

Western, J. (2001) 'Africa Is Coming to the Cape', *Geographical Review,* 91(4): 617–640.

Wilmsen, E. (1989) *Land Filled with Flies: A Political Economy of the Kalahari.* Chicago: University of Chicago Press.

WIPO (2013) 'Disputing a Name, Developing a Geographical Indication' (http://www.wipo.int/ipad-vantage/en/details.jsp?id=2691).

Wong, T. and Dutfield, G. (eds) (2011) *Intellectual Property and Human Development: Current Trends and Future Scenarios.* New York: Cambridge University Press.

Wynberg, R. and Chennells, R. (2009) 'Green Diamonds of the South: An Overview of the San-*Hoodia* Case', in R. Wyberg, D. Schroeder and R. Chennells (eds), *Indigenous Peoples, Consent and Benefit Sharing: Lessons from the San-Hoodia Case.* Dordrecht: Springer. pp. 89–124.

13

Farmers' Rights and the Intellectual Property Dynamic in Agriculture

Chidi Oguamanam

INTRODUCTION

The growth and tightening of intellectual property (IP) protection in the last quarter of the twentieth-century century is often analyzed as a combination of private rights expansion and a marginalization of the public interest in global knowledge capital (Maskus and Reichman, 2005). Beyond marginalization of the public sphere, IP overreach implements a neoliberal agenda that evaluates innovation through the prisms of capitalist interests and formal scientific rules. That approach alienates and, often, excludes alternative knowledge production efforts, which reflect fairness and openness in the production and distribution of knowledge. IP overreach accounts for the backlash that has since characterized international IP law and policy making since the Agreement on Trade-Related Aspects of Intellectual Property Rights (TRIPS) came into effect in 1995 (Reichman, 2009; Oguamanam, 2012).

Commentators have analyzed the tension between over protection and moderation in global IP from a variety of perspectives. Global IP debates are often framed using theories of regime complexity, regime shifting, regime tension, regime fatigue, or various forms of counter regime discourses (Oguamanam, 2006a, 2007; Yu, 2007; Helfer, 2009). These analytical frameworks help to map the assertion and reclamation of discursive spaces in which to explore IP issues. They also (re)frame and center the interests of peoples who are marginalized by strong IP protection. In addition, they clarify a number of IP-related issue areas, including public health and access to medicines, access to educational materials, human rights, traditional knowledge, biodiversity conservation, agriculture and food security, etc. (Ho, 2007; Takenaka, 2008; Tansey and Rajotte, 2008; Wong and Dutfield, 2011). These issues have become the rallying sites for re-engaging, scrutinizing and challenging the dominant IP jurisprudence, resulting in calls for a recalibration of IP (Gervais, 2009) to make it responsive to considerations of equity, for example, as evinced in the access and benefit sharing (ABS) movements over genetic resources (Oberthür and Rosendal, 2013). More recently, IP is increasingly confronted with alternative models for protection and promotion of knowledge and innovation through access to knowledge movements, open innovation models, etc. The latter derive impetus largely from the open software movement (Smith et al., 2011; Smith and Reilly, 2013).

This chapter focuses on the evolution of IP in the agriculture sector as part of IP-related issue linkage. It examines the tensions arising from the use of IP to advance a private and formal scientific approach to agricultural innovation, in contrast to using alternative frameworks of agricultural innovation. Such frameworks, which tend to be more open and communal, are usually associated with the practices of farmers in indigenous and local communities (ILCs) across the globe. The chapter surveys the historical context of farmers' rights and their raison d'être, as well as the skepticism that has trailed the concept in the discussion of IP in agriculture. By exploring the ongoing implementation of the 2001 International Treaty on Plant Genetic Resources for Food and Agriculture (the Treaty)[1] and recent developments in related regimes, the chapter argues that even though these initiatives are still at a nascent stage, they represent a mood change, as manifested in the emergence of a concept of 'farmers' rights'. The Treaty and cognate regimes, especially the Consultative Group on International Agricultural Research Consortium (CGIAR Consortium)[2] are important new sites for future negotiations of the IP and farmers' rights interface in agriculture. The feasibility or futility of farmer-centered agriculture in the twenty-first century and the role of IP in that regard is of interest to this chapter.

FARMERS' RIGHTS: HISTORICAL SKETCH AND DRIVING FORCES

> For virtually the entire history of agricultural production, up until the twentieth century, seed collection and distribution resided in the hands of farmers. Farmers collected seeds from their fields after harvest and then used them for the next crop, for feed, for exchange, and for the breeding of new varieties of crops. During the past century, however, these farmer-centered practices became highly controversial, and in many cases came to be regarded as criminal acts of piracy. (Borowaik, 2004: 513)

The pathway through which farmers transitioned from being the bedrock of sustainable agriculture to being perceived as obstacles to agricultural innovation is a complex one. Historically, that transition was championed by commercial seed breeders whose entry into agricultural production resulted in a seismic shift in the balance of interests in agriculture. In the second half of the nineteenth-century in the US and Europe, experimental breeding and the consequent introduction of new seed varieties was essentially undertaken by wealthy land owners and, subsequently, by small family seed firms. The latter were 'descendants' of farmers 'that made it their main business to provide seeds for other farmers who then started breeding programmes to meet the requirement of their customers' (Dutfield, 2008: 31). From this modest origin, the culture of seed breeding became institutionalized through corporate commercial interests and public/private R&D in seeds, or more broadly, plant genetic resources (PGRs). Advancements in science and technological innovations in life forms in general have since resulted in the convergence of agro-allied pharmaceutical, chemical and biotechnology industries, and multi-national agro-business concerns.

In order to consolidate their interests, corporate agro-business stakeholders had to problematize two perceived major obstacles, namely the open, natural biological process of self-propagation of genetic resources, and the customary practices of seed exchange among farmers. Seed exchange is at the core of the ILC farmer-centered approach to agriculture. A multi-pronged solution to these problems was seen to lie in recourse to a technological model of agriculture and co-optation of IP law to further industrial hegemony in agricultural innovation (Oguamanam, 2005). In the techno-scientific realm, the struggle for the control of seeds is evident in many contexts. Breeding scientists were early appropriators of Mendelian genetics in crop improvement, which enabled trait selection and manipulation, with significant influence over yield outcome. In addition, the use of genetics, genomics and various other forms of reproductive science and technology has ensured the development of seeds compatible with ecological and market needs and with various external inputs supplied by agrochemical and allied concerns (Dutfield, 2008: 28). From crossing and selecting across plural parent lines, breeders demonstrated skill in unlocking the potential of self-fertilizing crops. In regard to cross-pollinating crops, notably maize, a breakthrough by George Shull resulted in the adaptation of Mendelian genetics to crossbreed in-bred lines and, thus, opened the world to the wonders of hybridization (Dutfield, 2008: 29).

Hybridization is a symbolic science and technology. It reflects both the power and the limits of technology in the control of seeds. In addition, hybridization provides a means to control the perceived threat that smallholder farmers posed to the profitability of large-scale corporate-driven commercial agriculture through the farmer practice of seed sharing. Hybridization results in high yielding harvests of offspring that have little or no further regeneration or replanting value. Significantly higher yields resulting from hybridization convinced farmers not only of the practical superiority of breeders' innovations but also to concede the futility or non-viability of seed sharing practices. The value of farm-saved seeds was, therefore, radically eroded. Hybridization legitimatized the separation of seed breeders from farmers. That separation is of a prime interest to stakeholders in global transnational corporate agro-business (Borowiak, 2004: 516). The reason is that hybrids created a viable and stable seed market (Dutfield, 2008: 29) while reining in smallholder traditional farmers.

Despite the success of hybrid corn, other biological barriers still constituted a nightmare to the seed industry. According to Borowiak, 'other major crops such as soybeans, wheat, cotton, barley, oats, rice, [and] peanuts proved more difficult and commercially acceptable hybrids were not as forthcoming' (Borowiak, 2004: 517). As such, in addition to hybridization, historically, scientists continued to develop other breeding techniques such as tissue and cell culture used to control plant genetic resources. Through molecular biology and biotechnology in general, scientists continue to improve the efficiency and outcome of conventional and unconventional breeding by way of marker-assisted selections, gene splicing and diverse forms of genetic manipulation even across taxonomic boundaries (genetic engineering). The highpoint of recent technology control measures for plant genetic resources are the controversial 'genetic use restriction technologies', more commonly called terminator technologies (Srinivisan and Thirtle, 2002; Oguamanam, 2005; Kariyawasam, 2009).

Aside from technology, IP law is the second strategy for whittling away at the perceived obstacles posed by farmers to technological innovation in agriculture. On a global scale, before the emergence of plant breeding as a separate preoccupation from farming, agriculture was a farmer-centered endeavor serviced, for the most part, by free exchange of seeds. Prevailing IP protection at both domestic and global levels did not extend to genetic resources or life forms in general. However, plants and animals were indubitably objects of property. But the property rights did not extend to the knowledge or processes associated with the cultivation, composition or manipulation of the genetic characteristics of these life forms (Borowiak, 2004: 514). Plant genetic resources are naturally self-reproducing entities and are perceived to be outside the realm of human creation, invention, manufacture and production – terms often associated with technological innovations that constituted the fulcrum of IP protection, especially through the patent system.

Seed breeding was an entry point for technological intervention in agriculture. That intervention changed the prevailing perception of the nature of agricultural innovation and production. Promoters of transnational corporate agro-business are champions of that change. Largely technology-driven, global corporate agro-business operates within a neoliberal market economic framework, under which the market is regarded as the panacea for socio-economic problems. Not surprisingly, seed breeders had a sense of outrage over the status quo in IP, which neither recognized nor rewarded their contributions (Borowiak, 2004: 520). They were able to frame their activities as falling outside 'natural processes'. Since the latter were excluded from conventional IP protection, breeders 'wanted in' on IP protection. Take hybridization, for example, it is a complex scientific process that does not happen in the context of open pollination, which is a natural occurrence. In hybridization, seeds are *made* in the semblance of production or manufacture as opposed to reproduction (Borowiak, 2004: 515). Furthermore, other complex techno-scientific strategies for agricultural innovation highlighted above are dedicated attempts to 'create' customized genetic materials, through direct or not-so-direct selection of trait preferences and other complex manipulations, not easily evident or possible via non-intrusive natural reproductive options. Indeed, breeders believed that they were in the business of creating, manufacturing, producing and inventing new and improved plant varieties and therefore entitled to IP protection.

In making the case for IP protection in agriculture, scientists, large-scale commercial seed breeders, and other champions constructed a discriminatory and exclusionary understanding of agricultural values and a skewed account of agency in agricultural conservation and innovation. In that perspective, breeders were originators of 'new', 'improved' and 'modern' varieties, while farmers were associated with traditional landraces, which have a close affinity with their wild relatives. Farmers were solely agents for seed exchange, whose activities undermined those of 'real innovators', hence 'rather than being subjects of agricultural innovation farmers are made into discursive and regulatory objects' (Borowiak, 2004: 520). From the late nineteenth century European and American breeders' lobbies laid the ground-work and secured the sympathy of IP policy makers for the full introduction of IP into the agricultural arena via the idea of plant breeders' rights or plant variety protection.

Plant variety protection is a sui generis IP right that accommodates the fluid and dynamic nature of the science and technology of plant breeding. While the details of specific national legislation varied in countries actively involved in plant breeding, such as Germany, the US, the Netherlands, Sweden, etc. (Dutfield, 2008: 31), there was a common focus on curtailing farmers' ability to access or use farm-saved seeds. Plant breeders also made a dedicated attempt to subject farmers' traditional agricultural practices to the seed breeding industry, as evident in the charter of the International Union for the Protection of New Varieties of Plants (UPOV).

With the adoption of the UPOV in 1961,[3] the trend in making farmers discursive objects of regulatory containment through IP was transformed into a global norm. UPOV is 'an international regime designed specifically to protect plant varieties whose seeds could otherwise be easily saved, replanted and sold' (Dutfield, 2008: 31) in the normal course of traditional farming endeavor, especially among ILCs. The UPOV was in essence the law's solution to the inherent limits of hybridization, especially in regard to the failure of the hybridization technique on some important crops mentioned above. Since its introduction, the UPOV has undergone three revisions (1972, 1978 and 1991). Each revision further reduced farmers' *privilege* to use farm-saved seeds and increased breeders' rights, including rights of breeders (as opposed to farmers) to share seeds amongst themselves. Also, the UPOV revisions reflected continuing scientific advances in plant breeding that reinforced the separation of breeders from farmers. Lastly, a notable feature of UPOV through its revisions is its opposition to any form of commercial profit by smallholder farmers and a preference to limit the ability of those categories of farmers to share seeds for subsistence purposes.

Despite the success of the UPOV, sponsors of transnational corporate agro-business, including agro-allied, chemical and pharmaceutical industrial lobbies did not rest. Taking the opportunity of the post-Cold War neoliberal economic awakening and commercial globalization, they were instrumental in the transformation of the global IP system into an instrument of free trade via the World Trade Organization (WTO)'s TRIPS[4] Agreement (Sell, 2003). Specifically, in regard to agriculture, 23 years after the UPOV, TRIPS extended IP protection to micro-organisms, essentially biological processes for the production of plants and animals, as well as to plant varieties (TRIPS, 1994: Article 27(3)(b)). TRIPS provides for the protection of plant varieties 'either by patents or by an effective sui generis system or by a combination thereof'. Significantly, TRIPS' provisions extend the full force of IP to modern biotechnology in general and agricultural biotechnology in particular. The provisions also effect a universalization of plant breeders' rights (PBRs) or plant varieties' protection with all members of the WTO of which TRIPS is a component. The TRIPS framework contrasts to the essentially voluntary and constricted membership of the UPOV.[5] Perhaps more instructively, TRIPS patent provisions and its concurrent endorsement of a sui generis PBRs option help to further boost interest in the UPOV as a preferred 'effective sui generis system'. In essence, TRIPS marks a resounding universalization and consolidation of IP in agriculture and a global 'IPRs regime that is heavily weighed against farmers' (Borowaik, 2004).

The extension of IP in agriculture has not been without friction and resistance from indigenous and local farming constituencies across the world and their sympathizers. Because species' intensity or richness increases from the equatorial poles, disproportionate amounts of global genetic resources are located in tropical and subtropical regions of the world, which largely correspond to the ancestral homelands of most of the world's indigenous and local communities (Oguamanam, 2006b: 50). The correspondence of biological diversity with genetic, cultural and linguistic diversity accounts in part for the status of ILCs, especially those of the tropical and subtropical regions of the global south as centers of origin and genetic diversity. Because of this geo-ecological asymmetry, shared access to global genetic resources and their conservation has been historically justified on the premise of common heritage and common concern of mankind. The common heritage premise provided the justification for the establishment in the second half of the twentieth century of global *ex situ* seed banks of the world's prime genetic resources sourced from centers of global diversity (Kloppenburg, 2004; Mgbeoji, 2006; Aoki and Luvia, 2007). The understanding was that these genetic resources would be freely available for agricultural R&D with the benefits arising therefrom equally accessible to all. However, despite obtaining free access to these genetic resources, pursuant to common heritage, proponents of global corporate agro-business continued to press for a closed and exclusionary regime of IP, as evident in the above analysis.

All the above developments in the IP arena occurred at a time of heightened global environmental consciousness that focused on the depletion of the world's biodiversity (Gillespie, 2011). Part of an emerging strategic response to the global biodiversity crisis is the recognition and promotion of the role of indigenous knowledge in biodiversity conservation and environmental management. Indigenous conservation ethics, often reflected in traditional farming practices (such as multiple cropping, crop rotation, shifting cultivation, use of organic fertilizers, etc.) have since constituted an integral aspect of international environmental law (Oguamanam, 2013). A glaring gap in the emerging debates over biodiversity conservation and the value of local knowledge led developing countries, civil society groups and their allies, in the words of Borowiak (2004: 523) 'to question the asymmetries of a proprietary system that gives free access to farmers' germplasm in the developing world while allowing scientific breeders who develop new varieties out of that germplasm to collect royalties through IPR legislation'.

Debates over biodiversity conservation and environmental sustainability at various United Nations fora, notably the Food and Agricultural Organization, the United Nations Environmental Programme, and United Nations Development Programme, dating back to the 1970s, laid bare the conflict between the common heritage principle as a platform for unrestricted access to genetic resources in centers of origin/diversity and pressure for private rights over innovation in plant genetic resources. For instance, the first instrument to articulate farmers' rights as a counterforce to the pervasive use of IP in agriculture, the FAO 1983 International Undertaking on Plant Genetic Resources for Food and Agriculture (the Undertaking),[6] was premised on unrestricted availability of germplasm as a common heritage. But industrialized countries and other stakeholders in the pharmaceutical and agro-allied industries withheld support for the Undertaking. These stakeholders placed reservations on the implementation of the Undertaking, a development that resulted in temporary suspension of the Undertaking until developed countries were able to extract an interpretive resolution (4/89)[7] to the effect that their commitments to plant breeders' rights pursuant to the UPOV were recognized as not in conflict with the Undertaking's endorsement of plant genetic resources as a common heritage.[8] Consequently, under the interpretative resolution 4/89, states are at liberty to put tolls on access to *improved* germplasm in accordance with their national laws and international obligations, notably the UPOV. The consequence is that despite free access to germplasm pursuant to the common heritage logic, beneficiaries or recipients of plant genetic resources under the common heritage logic reserved rights to levy tolls as a reward for their scientific 'improvements' of freely sourced genetic resources.

In addition to resolution 4/89, the 1989 FAO conference adopted another important Resolution (5/89) on farmers' rights. Resolution 5/89 was a strategy by developing countries to counterbalance the consolidation of plant breeders' rights initiated by their industrialized counterparts in resolution 4/89. The text of resolution 5/89 on farmers' rights notes the historical role of mainly developing country farmers in improving and disseminating the world's plant genetic resources – most of which originate from those countries. It also recognizes that farmers' contributions have 'not been sufficiently recognized or rewarded' (FAO Res 5/89, para. 108).[9] The resolution then *endorses* farmers' rights as:

> arising from the past, present and future contributions of farmers in conserving, improving, and making available plant genetic resources, particularly those in the International Community, as *trustee for present and future generations* of farmers, for the purpose of ensuring full benefits to farmers, and supporting the continuation of their contributions, as well as the attainment of the overall purposes of the International Undertaking.[10]

Resolutions 4/89, 5/89 and another, namely 3/91, were annexed to the Undertaking as its constitutive part. Resolution 3/91 is significant in two respects. Firstly, it clarifies that the common heritage principle in the Undertaking is subject to recognition of the sovereign right of states over genetic resources within their national jurisdictions.[11] This empowers state centers of origin/diversity of plant genetic resources to negotiate from a position of strength in relation to hi-tech users of germplasm and practitioners of industrial agriculture, especially over the preservation of ILCs' interests, notably, in farmer-centered agriculture. Secondly, resolution 3/91 reflects the agreed upon implementation mechanism for farmers' rights. It establishes a proposed international fund on plant genetic resources to support plant genetic resources conservation and utilization endeavors mainly in developing countries. The Undertaking also provides the basis for evaluating the relationship between stakeholders' respective appeals to IP and the emergent concept of farmers' rights, and the justifications of the two approaches on the principles of fairness, equity and justice.

The impetus for advancement of equity in the context of dealing with genetic resources is also associated with biodiversity conservation, especially through the activities of the 1992 United Nations Convention on Biological Diversity (CBD),[12] whose negotiation history predates but largely overlapped with the making of the TRIPS agreement.[13] Although not a treaty on agriculture, the Convention builds on relevant initiatives in the UN system supportive of farmers' rights (Zerbe, 2007: 103). Farmers' rights represent an attempt to reposition farmers as stakeholders in agricultural production. It is a counterpoise to global corporate agro-business's approach to agriculture in which smallholder indigenous and local community farmers were framed not only as obstacles to agricultural innovation but also as discursive targets for regulatory containment. Consistent with resolution 3/91, the CBD recognizes the prin ciple of sovereign rights of states over genetic resources (Article 3, 15) and endorses the link between conservation of global biodiversity and indigenous environmental ethics, as reflected in aspects of traditional farming practices. At its heart, the Convention requires state parties to

> respect, preserve and maintain knowledge, innovations and practices of indigenous and local communities embodying traditional lifestyles relevant for the conservation and sustainable use of biological diversity and promote their wider application with the approval and involvement of the holders of such knowledge, innovations and practices and encourage the equitable sharing of the benefits arising from the utilization of such knowledge, innovations and practices. (Article 8(j))

The Convention has since become pivotal to the desire of ILCs, including constituent traditional farming communities, to seek equity and justice regarding their contributions to biodiversity conservation and various other forms of traditional innovation over genetic resources. It is hardly surprising that nearly two decades after the Undertaking pioneered the articulation of farmers' rights, the latest iteration of the concept in the 2001 FAO Treaty took its inspiration from the CBD and the latter's accomplishments in regard to equitable access and benefit sharing over genetic resources. Article 1 of the Treaty provides that '[t]he objectives of this Treaty are the conservation and sustainable use of plant genetic resources for food and agriculture and the fair and equitable sharing of benefits arising out of their use, in harmony with the Convention on Biological Diversity, for sustainable agriculture and food security'. The Treaty (further discussed below) is the most authoritative instrument on farmers' rights. Aside from its binding status, in contrast to the exhortatory tenor of the Undertaking, the Treaty has moved farmers' rights in the direction of operationalization. It articulates farmers' rights, in Article 9.1 as a subject matter for *recognition*, in almost identical words to those of the Undertaking:

> Contracting parties recognize the enormous contribution that the *local and indigenous communities and farmers of all regions of the world, particularly in the centres of origin and crop diversity*, have made and will continue to make for the conservation and development of *plant genetic resources which constitute the basis of food and agricultural production throughout the world.*[14]

Unlike the Undertaking, the Treaty vests responsibility for realization of farmers' rights on national governments, not the international community. It provides that such responsibilities are to be discharged subject to national needs and priorities of states and to their national laws[15] (Article 9.2).

Between the 1980s and early 2000s when the push for farmer-centered agriculture via the farmers' rights movement was intensified by developing countries and their NGO sympathizers (Zerbe, 2007), the practical effect of a global IP order heavily weighted against farmers was already being felt globally. ILCs' knowledge of genetic resources relevant to food, agriculture, medicine, conservation, environmental management, etc. became targets of appropriation by hi-tech life science industries, provoking a counter narrative of *biopiracy* – a reference to inequitable appropriation of genetic resources in the centers of diversity/origin and associated traditional bio-cultural knowledge without recognition and compensation to the custodians of that knowledge (Arewa, 2006; Mgbeoji, 2006).

Biopiracy is part of the outcome of an IP system that subjects farmers and other practitioners of traditional knowledge to a dominant arrangement that privileges science, technology, commerce and proprietary control over alternative informal frameworks of innovation in genetic resources. Traditional and smallholder farmers have remained primary custodians of genetic diversity over the millennia. They have been able to sustain genetic diversity through diversity in the crops they grow. In addition, through careful observations of randomly occurring mutations in nature, farmers make targeted selections of genetic materials in accordance with ecological and other dynamics in furtherance of sustainability objectives. In agriculture, the dominant techno-scientific and proprietary system devalues such farmers' practices, despite the fact that traditional farmers were engaged in breeding plants and improving the global stock of genetic resources long before seed and contemporary hi-tech agricultural industries existed (Borowiak, 2004: 518). The commercial interests of organized multi-national stakeholders in agriculture, pharmaceutical, chemical and allied life sciences industries were in sync with those of their governments (Sell, 2003). This confluence of interests coordinated actions to transform the depiction of IP from a historically excusable barrier to trade to a trade-facilitating incentive.[16] It was also vital in erroneously portraying industrial laboratories as the main locus of agricultural innovation without regard to the traditional farmers' fields. The symbolic ramification of this state of affairs is the entrenchment of a production as opposed to a re-production and cultural narrative of agriculture. These transformations reconstructed agriculture from a cultural process into essentially a production process in which commercial profitability is the key determinant of value.

Rewarding farmers' historical and future contribution to the conservation and improvement of plant genetic resources, 'which constitute the basis for plant production [including agricultural R&D] throughout the world'[17] is the kernel of farmers' rights. Today, industrialized countries control an estimated 90% of *commercial* seed in an annual global seed market worth over $30 billion (Borowiak, 2004: 524). But it is inconceivable that the lucrative global seed market could have been possible, not to mention sustainable, without the historical and contemporary role of farmers through their perpetual experimentations, improvements and overall stewardship of diverse landraces. Thus, farmers' rights are an attempt to recognize farmers as genuine producers of agricultural value and as foundational actors in the advancement of hi-tech agriculture – facts that commercial seed breeders and proponents of 'scientific' agriculture have consistently downplayed. But the question remains, which we broach in the rest of the chapter, whether farmers' rights can be a counterpoint or a viable substitute to the IP system – a system that has effectively secured for industrialized countries a lopsided control of seed at the expense of farmers and all other informal actors at the centers of plant genetic origin/diversity. We reflect on why or whether farmers' rights have the potential to restore farmer-centered agriculture. We begin by focusing on the content and framework for farmers' rights and examine their amorphous relationship with IP.

FARMERS' RIGHTS: A CONTENT AND CONTEXT ANALYSIS

Both the quest for IPRs in agriculture and farmers' rights are propelled by a sense of justice, fairness and equity. However, breeders and farmers have a different understanding or vision of what constitutes value and how it arises in agriculture. For breeders, agricultural value lies in the commercial profitability of seeds, which is largely a factor of their bred characteristics or properties; however, for farmers, agricultural value arises in the context of the diversity of agro-genetic resources and the socio-cultural processes associated with their relationship with land and agriculture. Similarly, breeders and smallholder ILC farmers also have a different understanding of the appropriate measure of values, between emphasis on commercial profitability on the one hand, and agro-ecological diversity and sustainability on the other. This dichotomy is a key to understanding and mapping the context and the relationship between IP in agriculture and farmers' rights.

IPRs are a state-protected monopoly over knowledge (Drahos, n.d.). Historically, they started as a privilege but have now crystallized as part of conventional rights jurisprudence. IPRs are a closed and exclusionary regime of rights in relation to non-rights holders. Holders of IPRs owe and are owed corresponding duties in their relationship with non-rights holders. These duties may include the responsibility to fulfill statutory obligations or protocols incidental to, or prescribed for the rights holder. Other duties comprise positive and negative forms of obligation on non-rights holders, which enable rights holders to enjoy their rights. For example, patents create an exclusive monopoly for the patentee to exploit their invention for a fixed statutory period, while it strictly forbids everyone else from any conduct that may compromise the exclusive right of the patentee. Similarly, plant breeders' or plant variety rights forbid farmers or third parties from freely accessing or sharing seeds that are subject to protection save under some conditions acceptable to the right holders. Such conditions are spelt out in the applicable statutes, treaties or contractual instruments (such as licensing agreements). Full analysis of the jurisprudence of rights in relation to IP in agriculture (Helfer, 2002; Borowiak, 2004; Oguamanam, 2006c) is outside the scope of this chapter.

The nature of IP in patents and plant breeders' rights is designed to capture and account for 'innovation' arising from the scientific and technological models of R&D practiced within the industrial forms of agriculture (De Schutter, 2011), which comprise plant breeding and related applications of life sciences. For example, patents and plant breeders' rights provide a narrow legal and scientific framework that articulates a number of criteria, including novelty/originality, usefulness, non-obviousness, uniformity, stability, etc. as the basis for determining the legibility of protectable 'innovation'. This framework is not designed to account for informal, collective, cultural, trans-generational and incremental processes through which farmers and ILCs add value and sustain their millennial stewardship of the global plant genetic resources, which are critical for biodiversity conservation (Farley Haight, 1997; Mgbeoji; 2001; Borowiak, 2004: 513–514; Oguamanam; 2004). Through various intervention measures, such as strategic seed selections in response to carefully observed ecological vagaries, farmers' agricultural innovations are incremental. As a result of traditional patterns of seed exchange and the essentially communal orientation of agricultural production, it is not easy to determine at what point a genetic innovation occurs, let alone who is better positioned to take the credit for such innovation to the exclusion of others, as required under conventional IP.

IP operates in sync with formal scientific agriculture in furtherance of a market economic approach for allotting and measuring the value of agricultural innovation. IP recognizes an innovation system that takes credit for originating, creating, manufacturing, engineering or designing new plant varieties, or adding new traits to existing ones. In plant breeding and agricultural genomics such novel qualities include trait selection (even trait suppression) and breeding techniques that result in a wide range of functional possibilities. Traits include high-yields; insect, drought and weed-resistance; ecological adaptation and mitigation; use restriction; agrochemical input compatibility; aesthetics (get-up, look and feel); and brand enhancements. The importance of these and several other techno-scientific augmentations of plant genetic resources covered by IP lie in their economic market value. The latter is the key driver of historic pressure for the displacement of farmers by commercial seed breeders and their modern-day successors. As far as these purveyors of industrial agriculture are concerned, only such qualities with direct economic or commercial benefits are worthy of recognition and protection.

Analysts agree over the ambiguous and indeterminate nature and content of farmers' rights (Helfer, 2002; Borowiak, 2004: 529; Oguamanam, 2006c; Zerbe, 2007; De Schutter, 2011: 341). Few dispute that the Undertaking and the Treaty's articulation of farmers' rights cast the concept outside the framework of IP. First, in accordance with the textual provisions of the two instruments, farmers' rights assume the trans-generational continuum of innovation and knowledge production and not a Eureka 'breakthrough' in the nature of a frontier invention. Second, farmers' rights are directed at an open, collective and communal (as opposed to individual) culture of knowledge production. The concept recognizes that farmers are in the business of conserving, improving, developing and making available/disseminating plant genetic resources and associated local knowledge. Third, farmers' rights are premised on the understanding that this open and shared approach to knowledge is foundational to sustainable global food and agricultural production. An open approach facilitates the exchange of information necessary for unfettered advancement of R&D development in agriculture. In essence, farmers' rights under the key instruments encapsulate a different vision for promoting innovation for sustainable development than the closed and exclusionary model epitomized by IP.

Farmers' rights advocates do not discount claims to economic incentivization for farmers' invaluable innovation over plant genetic resources and conservation (Borowiak, 2004: 528). But the economic dimension of farmers' rights is only an aspect of broader socio-economic and cultural justice implicated in farmers' rights. These include various cultural aspects of traditional farming practices such as seed exchange and the freedom to grow culturally appropriate foods. In addition, socio-economic and cultural aspects of farmers' rights involve farmers' unfettered ability to improve upon crop genetic diversity; their ability to participate in decision making in matters that affect them; and to be entitled to adequate reward for their contributions, for example, through access and benefit sharing schemes. As such, farmers' rights are not a 'me-too' kind of alternative to IP. Yet it is tempting to conflate, if not totally ignore, the nuanced difference between IP and farmers' rights. However, such a conflation risks interpreting farmers' rights as direct or wholesale endorsement of IPRs in agriculture, and thus mistakenly thinking that farmers and all proponents of farmers' rights share a reductionist vision that measures the value of agricultural innovation exclusively in terms of technological efficiency and economic profitability.

Craig Borowiak (2004: 532) expresses apprehension over the conflation of farmers' rights with IP noting that '[g]iven that *farmers' rights campaigns* tend to actually concede recognition of breeders' rights [or IP in general], there seems to be a particular danger that an impracticable [or weak] farmers' rights regime would help [i.e. provide justification for] the very practicable and inequitable IPRs regime …'.[18] The danger of such an outcome is that instead of representing an alternative vision of agricultural innovation and knowledge production, farmers' rights then become an extension of IPRs and part of a monolithic ideology of agriculture embedded in the industrial and market economic forms, which operates at cross-purposes with farmer-centered agriculture. Arguing for the distinguishing of farmers' rights from IP, Noah Zerbe notes that unlike IPRs, farmers' rights do not 'monopolize for commercial purposes what belongs to the communities through privatization … [and] must not be viewed as a form or subset of intellectual property or plant breeders' rights'. He contends that farmers' rights are inherently community-oriented and that linking or equating them with IP amounts to conflation of two distinctly separate concepts (Zerbe, 2007: 111;[19] cited in De Schutter, 2011: 342). Notwithstanding the inchoate nature of famers' rights within conventional rights jurisprudence, the rhetoric of socio-economic, justice and equity campaigns (to which Borowiak alluded) do not necessarily translate into legal texts. In reality, despite the weaknesses in the text(s) of farmers' rights in the two instruments, they do not amount to unsuspecting endorsement of IP, as segments of farmers' rights campaigners are inclined to insinuate.

Farmers' rights reflect a novel type of rights regime constituted referentially or as a counterpoise to IP. The nature of that reference is not an open or uncritical endorsement of IPRs; neither is it a direct rejection of IPRs. At the minimum, farmers' rights reflect farmers' broad-based response to their subjection into discursive objects of regulatory and technological containment by proponents of industrial and corporate-commercial agriculture. Farmers and proponents of farmers' rights do not seek to adopt the same problem (i.e. an IP-centered economic model) as a solution merely by renaming it farmers' rights. Given the history and complex contextual dynamic in the evolution of farmers' rights, the latter symbolize a vision of farmer-centered agriculture. The essence of that vision is that it accounts for salient contributions of farmers to agricultural production, the complex socio-cultural contexts in which farmers operate, and the *positive externalities* of farmer-centered agriculture (as explored below) – all of which are hardly recognized by the IP-focused corporate model of agriculture.

Efforts to justify farmers' rights are often conflated with measures designed to protect them. This conflation provides a confusing or unclear picture of the content of farmers' rights. For example, from the text of the Treaty, traditional knowledge relevant to Plant Genetic Resources for Food and Agriculture (PGRFA) is an integral aspect of farmers' rights,[20] which in turn makes farmers' rights a component of the international indigenous rights movement and emergent jurisprudence. Traditional knowledge relevant to PGRFA is an open-ended concept that captures the variegated traditional farming practices of ILCs, the most central of which is the exchange of farm-saved seeds, directly guaranteed under Article 9.3 of the Treaty. Another broad category of farmers' rights under the Treaty text echoed above is farmers' active and equitable participation in benefit sharing arising from the utilization (by various R&D applications and resulting derivatives) of PGRFA as well as farmers' active involvement in decision-making processes relevant to sustainable use of PGRFA (De Schutter, 2011: 340).

The justifications given for securing these farmers' rights include, but are not limited to, the historic role of farmers in the development, conservation and dissemination of global crop genetic diversity, which constitutes the basis for R&D rclating to new commercial varieties. Farmers' contributions to the development and conservation of plant genetic resources involve a holistic string of value externalities that do not resonate with proponents of IPRs. The open-ended elements of farmers' rights and the plural justifications, therefore, require that measures for their operationalization be equally open-ended and creative so as to meet all the expectations associated with farmers' rights. Without being exhaustive, we sketch some of these unique but highly interrelated farmers' value-addeds (*positive externalities*) in agricultural innovation, not captured by the corporate-centered agricultural model.

First, there is the biodiversity conservation imperative. The role of ILC farmers in biodiversity conservation is a factor of the global ecological disequilibrium in which over 80% of the world's biological resources and, consequently, biological diversity are endemic in centers of origin/diversity, which is home to most of the world's ILCs. The correlation between biological diversity and cultural and ethnic diversity (Borowiak, 2004: 524;

Oguamanam, 2006b: 50) accounts for the complex conservation practices of various practitioners and custodians of traditional knowledge, including farmers. In regard to agriculture, traditional ILC farmers' *in situ* stewardship of a vast portfolio of plant genetic varieties and traditional landraces for food and agriculture constitute the foundation of agro-biodiversity (De Schutter, 2011: 313). Without robust diversity in plant varieties and genetic compositions sustained through farmers' millennial interventions, seed breeding and agricultural biotechnology could not be viable ventures. Indigenous and local community farmers' interests in specific plant varieties are not fundamentally determined by their commercial and economic value. Rather, such interests derive from diverse cultural considerations, food preferences, and endemic ecological and various other endowments that reflect an inclusive and holistic agro-ecological worldview. In sum, the role of farmers as vital agents of conservation and custodians of agro-biodiversity is not one that can be measured on an economic or commercial scale of value alone.

Second, as integral aspects of traditional knowledge, traditional farming practices represent an alternative epistemological approach to agriculture in contrast to technological orientation of transnational corporate agriculture. Farmers' rights aim at the preservation of traditional farming practices. Safeguarding of variegated forms of traditional agricultural practices that are suited to the diverse genetic compositions of complex traditional landraces is the best way to ensure and sustain agro-epistemic pluralism. Scientific intervention has a tendency to add evident commercial value to PGRs such as we have discussed regarding hybridization and various forms of genetic modification. But scientific or industrial agriculture tends to concentrate on a few monocultures because of their commercial advantages (Shiva, 1993, 2000; De Schutter, 2011). Corporate and industrial agriculture's approach to agriculture relies on a single epistemic model, typified by formal science, while traditional agricultural practices' affinity with traditional knowledge offers both diversity and pluralism in agricultural knowledge.

Experience shows that bred or genetically modified products are susceptible to diseases and crop failures. In addition, they tend to depend more on external agro-inputs (which may be unaffordable by smallholder ILC farmers) for their success and sustainability. Moreover, science and technology's approach to shifting ecological dynamics, such as climate change, represent a single epistemic response (De Schutter, 2011). Despite its acknowledged shortcomings,[21] traditional agricultural practices represent desirable epistemic alterity and sources of insights that could complement or serve as a doomsday back-up for the incontrovertible historic uncertainties of industrial agriculture. The multi-dimensional importance of traditional agricultural practices (e.g. in regard to sustainability and global food security) is, however, hardly ascribed any economic value in short-term market calculation.

Third, traditional farming practices, especially seed sharing and exchange represent a site for the legitimacy of an open as opposed to a closed innovation model in agriculture. Seed exchange is a vehicle through which communities exercise control over their food. It is fundamental to food security and food sovereignty, concepts that call attention to the imperative for the majority of the world's most vulnerable people to resist dependence on seed monopolists and proponents of IP in agriculture (GRAIN, 2012: 14). The link between seed sharing, food security and food sovereignty of ILC farmers in the context of threats thereto constituted by IPRs locates farmers' rights within an economic, social and cultural framework of human rights, specifically the right to adequate food (Chapman, 2009; De Schutter, 2011; Oguamanam, 2014).

Statistics indicate that farmer seed exchange is the source of over 80% of traditional agricultural crops cultivated in developed countries (Borowiak, 2004: 525; De Schutter, 2011: 339; GRAIN, 2012). As a consequence, the use of IP to criminalize seed exchange by farmers is a direct threat to the food security of the poor and vulnerable members of the world's population who depend on traditional and subsistence farming for their food. Seed exchange underscores the trans-generational character of traditional farming as a communal and collective as opposed to an individual or corporate endeavor. Perhaps more importantly, like the concept of agro-epistemic pluralism, farmer seed exchange represents an open-model alternative for knowledge protection and promotion in contrast to the exclusive and closed model represented by IP. Without free access to or exchange of seeds, the ability of ILC farmers to experiment and generate new knowledge over genetic resources and to breed new plant varieties is constrained.

IP's potential to stifle R&D in agriculture and the life sciences is a threat to innovation. This weakness in IP warrants the attractiveness of open innovation models (McManis and Seo, 2009; Smith et al., 2011; Smith and Reilly, 2013). Despite the dominance of the IP model, the extent to which it advances innovation in contrast to open models of knowledge governance remains inconclusive or at best debatable (Jaffe Lerner, 2004; and Pugatch, 2004). There is hardly any attempt to understand how the culture of free exchange of farm-saved seeds contributes to agricultural development and the empowerment of vulnerable small-scale ILC famers and other categories of stakeholders in agriculture. Rather, as observed above, seed breeders and their modern incarnations in industrial agriculture have ensured that farmers' culture of seed exchange is stymied in most cases as criminal acts of piracy.

FARMERS' RIGHTS: FROM SKEPTICISM TO HOPE

The previous section underscores the imperative for farmer-centered agriculture. A farmer-centered agriculture includes unaccounted for, but important externalities necessary for sustainable conservation of plant genetic resources for food and agriculture through indigenous and local farming communities and their alternative epistemic orientation. As a concept, farmers' rights speak to the potential of farmer-centered agriculture, which is deliberately ignored within the mainstream farming model based on science, technology, corporate-commercial agriculture and IP. While IPRs have facilitated a successful shifting of agriculture from a farmer-centered endeavor to an industrial and technological model, we now reflect on whether farmers' rights have the potential to restore farmer-centered agriculture or at best bring some balance or parity in the competition over rights in agricultural innovation between stakeholders in global agro-business and ILC traditional farmers.

The weaknesses of farmers' rights are multifaceted (De Schutter, 2011: 341). The textual outline of farmers' rights in both the Undertaking and the Treaty explored above lacks the clarity necessary to identify their concrete meaning or content within the conventional analysis of rights jurisprudence. Second, farmers' rights are cast in terms of 'recognition', an expression lacking legal precision or boundaries in several respects, including the nature or content of the recognition, who is required to provide the recognition, as well as to whom the recognition accrues.

Three subjects of recognition are associated with farmers' rights under the Treaty text: 'local and indigenous communities' and 'farmers' of all regions of the world. None of these terms is easily amenable to legal certainty or precision and they pose an interpretative and legal nightmare (Oguamanam, 2006c). The use of the phrase, 'indigenous and local communities' or 'local and indigenous communities' in international legal instruments, notably the CBD, sidesteps the often troublesome debate on the concept of indigenous people (Farley Haight, 1997). Yet the term local has no settled meaning in law. Similarly, who qualifies as a 'farmer' in the context of farmers' rights is an open question. The particulars for recognition are the historical, future and trans-generational contributions of farmers. As a form of traditional knowledge the different farming practices of ILCs may overlap while sustaining complexly entrenched differences in knowledge systems or approaches to conservation. In such situations, the communal orientation of knowledge generation and knowledge exchange amongst farmers, the incremental process of innovation, and the artificial nature of ILC boundaries collectively render problematic any attempt to identify what contributions qualify for farmers' rights and the appropriate beneficiaries or claimants.

Although the concept of farmers' rights evolved in the context of their role in the conservation of plant genetic resources for food and agriculture, it is hard to discriminate in regard to different categories of farmers. Given the ecological holism imperative for biodiversity conservation, farmers' rights are not the exclusive preserve of crop farmers, but can logically extend to all other categories of farmers (Borowiak, 2004: 530; De Schutter, 2011: 343). The wording of farmers' rights in the Treaty reflects a remarkable shift from the Undertaking by making reference to *farmers of all regions of the world*. In a way, this is a recognition that even though the primary focus of farmers' rights is on farmers operating in the centers of origin/diversity in ILCs, farmers outside those centers can be beneficiaries of farmers' rights in so far as they contribute to the conservation and development of plant genetic resources for food and agriculture and other objectives of both the Undertaking and the Treaty. Technically, conventional and industrial agriculturalists are not excluded from farmers' rights but they have to fulfil expectations in regard to conservation and have to prove that they are 'farmers', a term that is not defined in relevant legal texts. The Treaty's text on farmers' rights also refers to the contribution of *local and indigenous communities* as distinct from the contributions of farmers or such contributions incidental to farming *stricu sensu* toward the conservation and development of *plant genetic resources*. Even though the contributions of local and indigenous communities may overlap with contributions incidental to farming practices, there is recognition of other practices of local communities, which may include cultural and lifestyle proclivities that are conservation-friendly while contributing toward the development of plant genetic resources.[22]

The last point highlights another weakness of farmers' rights, namely their overly wide ambit as open-ended socio-economic rights as evident in the references to the undefined, and indeterminate 'enormous contribution that local and indigenous communities and farmers ... have made and will continue to make ...'.[23] Farmers' rights are associated with the conservation of biodiversity, traditional knowledge, access and benefit sharing, broader considerations of justice, and equity. They are also bound up with ideological struggles around epistemic pluralism, sustainable development in agriculture and in the underexplored issue of the measure of value in agricultural innovation; not to mention the discourse of closed and open approaches to the promotion of innovation in agriculture. Farmers' rights are inevitably and circumstantially over-extended in nature. Consequently, they risk meaning everything and, therefore, nothing in terms of realizable legal rights.

Another aspect of the weakness of farmers' rights is evident from both the text of the Undertaking and the Treaty. The Undertaking vests the responsibility for the realization of farmers' rights on the *international community as trustees and on future generations of farmers*.[24] Under the Treaty, the realization of farmers' rights is the responsibility of national governments, subject to their national and international obligations. The international community and future generation of farmers represent an indeterminate category. The failure of the Undertaking to establish a benefit-sharing fund pursuant to resolution 3/91 demonstrates the weakness of its framework for the realization of farmers' rights. In regard to the Treaty, it is clear that a farmers' rights orientation toward informal and open approaches to knowledge dissemination in agricultural innovation is antithetical to the obligations of many developed countries to an IP-driven closed model of knowledge governance in agriculture, especially under the UPOV and the TRIPS Agreement. Finally, there is a structural weakness evident in embedding farmers' rights within international development and socio-economic frameworks, namely those on biodiversity, indigenous knowledge, access and benefit sharing, etc. Placing farmers' rights within the purview of the international development regime is in contrast to more consequential transformations of IP in plant genetic resources for food and agriculture (through plant variety protection, patents, etc.) in the TRIPS Agreement as part of international trade law with elaborate enforcement powers. Farmers' rights are, for most apparent and practical purposes, on a very low jurisprudential pedestal in relation to IPRs.

An aggregation of the multifaceted weaknesses of farmers' rights accounts for a broadly shared skepticism amongst analysts over the practical impact of farmers' rights beyond denoting a psychological boost of sorts for farmers and farmers' rights proponents. Save for encouraging signals from CBD's access and benefit-sharing-inspired national and regional law-making initiatives, operationalization of farmers' rights at a global level has remained limited. Similarly, the prospect of farmers' rights to restore farmer-centered agriculture is the subject of sustained cynicism (Borowiak, 2004; Oguamanam, 2006c).

Despite the jurisprudential fogginess around farmers' rights, there is ongoing progress toward their operationalization through the Treaty framework and indirectly through recent experimental initiatives at the Consultative Group on International Agriculture Research (CGIAR) Consortium mentioned earlier. It is recognized, however, that the open-ended nature of farmers' rights and their association with socio-economic rights means their operationalization should not be a task limited to a handful of regimes. But here we focus on the Treaty and the CGIAR Consortium for two reasons. First, they are preliminary sites for developments that bear a close resemblance to the operationalization of farmers' rights. Second, the Treaty and the CGIAR Consortium respectively designate a jurisdictional focus on farmers' rights *strictu sensu* and a complementary mandate for the promotion of a public goods approach to agricultural innovation (De Schutter, 2011). The Treaty's operational details have been discussed elsewhere (Marden and Godfrey, 2014), hence the ramifications of the Treaty's implementation for farmers' rights will now suffice.

The Treaty governing body has so far taken control over the governance of global plant genetic resources for food and agriculture. It accomplished this through a number of steps, including (a) the 2006 agreement with 11 International Agricultural Research Centres[25] (who are part of the CGIAR Consortium) possessing in-trust plant germplasm listed in Annex 1 of the Treaty; (b) approval of a harmonized Standard Material Transfer Agreement for dealing in both annexed and non-annexed PGRFA,[26] (c) the setting up of a benefit sharing fund – all of which culminate in (d) the operationalizing of a multilateral system (MLS) of access to and benefit sharing from plant genetic resources for food and agriculture (articles 10–13, 18). The MLS is a co-operative regime through which all stakeholders are encouraged to bring the global stock of genetic resources into a common pool in order to guarantee equitable access and sharing of benefits deriving from their utilization. Thus, the Treaty is the first ever global operational access and benefit sharing regime.

The Treaty commitment to the realization or operationalization of farmers' rights is largely indirect but logically inferred from the overarching framework of its objectives. Farmers' rights language is rooted mainly in scattered references to the transfer of conservation-sensitive and PGRFA-relevant technologies for the benefit of farmers in developing and least developed countries as well as countries with economies in transition, even if those technologies are IP-protected (articles 9–13). There is a presumption that ILC farmers are the mainstay of agricultural production in those regions. At the core of the Treaty's attempt to positively impact farmers is the Benefit Sharing Fund (BSF) – a trust account supported by compulsory and voluntary contributions from users of genetic resources obtained from the multilateral system of access to genetic resources. The BSF is designed to support the implementation of the Treaty objectives. The precursor of the BSF is Resolution 3/91, which was annexed to the Undertaking. That pioneer initiative did not gain the support of industrialized countries (Aoki and Luvai, 2007). So far, while it may be too early to appraise, there has yet to be strong enthusiasm by developed countries over the new BSF system either.

However, unlike the Undertaking's experience, the BSF has actually taken off with modest contributions from a few countries. It is projected that by 2014, the BSF could net about $116 million (Bhatti, 2009). So far, the governing body of the treaty has established an elaborate institutional framework not only for setting agricultural R&D development priorities relevant to farmers in developing countries, but has also funded such R&D initiatives under two funding cycles. The first and second project portfolios involved 11 and 19 pilot projects respectively. [27]

A maiden report by the Secretariat of the Treaty commissioned by the governing body on the benefits sharing fund project highlights the global challenges which the projects were designed to address: safeguarding of biodiversity, strengthening of food security and climate change adaptation. Funding priorities focus on high-impact projects that support farmers in developing countries, especially regarding the promotion of information exchange, technology transfer, on-farm management and sustainable use of crop diversity. The report notes that 'Farmers were directly involved at many stages of project implementation, including in the collection of local crops and the documentation of related traditional practices, seed multiplication and distribution, and a range of awareness raising and training activities'.[28] Farmer participation in R&D and policy sites on PGRFA is part of farmers' rights.

In addition to farmer capacity building, the report emphasized how the first project portfolio and indeed the benefit sharing fund system is boosting the accession of traditional varieties and wild crop relatives to the multilateral system, including the detailing of important new traits for on-farm varieties and those held in gene banks. Given the role of the benefit-sharing-fund-sponsored project portfolio in increasing the multilateral system's global gene pool, the project has potential to support the sustainability of the fund.[29] This income could then further support future positive and strategic farmer-led developments. The benefit sharing fund projects are delivered through formal institutional executing entities and partnership organizations, including universities, specialist research organizations and NGOs. As presently designed, such entities and organizations must be those approved by the contracting party that would host the research project.[30] Even though there are cases of direct involvement of farmers and communities, one of the challenges is to ensure that the interaction between indigenous and local farming communities and these institutional entities yield farmer-centered knowledge translation capable of supporting sustainable traditional agricultural practices as opposed to top-down superimposition of different agricultural knowledge models. The extent to which the Treaty implementation strategies, especially through the benefit sharing fund, promote farmers' rights will depend largely on their ability to make farmers participatory partners in research processes that strengthen multifaceted aspects of traditional farmer-centered approaches to agriculture. The right strategies must aim at putting reform and innovation at the service of farmers from a bottom-up as opposed to a top-down approach.

The CGIAR is a crucial site of complementary initiatives, at least, indirectly focused on the operationalization of farmers' rights. In addition to ceding the control of Annex 1 in-trust plant genetic resources for food and agriculture held by the Consortium's international agricultural research centers through the 2006 agreement with the FAO (on behalf of the Treaty governing body), the CGIAR has been supportive of all the elements of the multilateral system's global gene pool. These include the use of a harmonized special material transfer agreement for ensuring an equitable access and benefit sharing regime in regard to annexed and non-annexed germpalsm under the Treaty framework. Perhaps of more relevance to the operationalization of farmers' rights is the willingness of CGAIR to extend its open access and public good orientation to the sharing of results of R&D in agriculture through its 2012 pilot initiative, the CGIAR Principles on the Management of Intellectual Assets.[31] Constituted by 12 key principles, the document commits all the various funding agencies and partners of the CGIAR and its affiliated research centers to pragmatically mediated use of intellectual assets and IP with a view to enhancing access to the benefits of innovation in PGRFA. The principal objectives of this approach to intellectual asset management are to ensure that intellectual assets, including IP, do not undermine the mission of the CGIAR. Rather, through the intellectual assets management initiative, CGIAR seeks flexible application or redirection of intellectual assets toward the reduction of hunger and rural poverty and for strengthening food security. Central to this strategy is the optimization of knowledge transfer and knowledge translation for widespread diffusion through empowerment of ILC farmers under a public goods framework. The approach is in sync with the overreaching essence of farmers' rights.

Principle 3 specifically addresses farmers' rights to the effect that:

> The CGIAR recognizes the indispensable role of farmers, indigenous communities, agricultural professionals and scientists in conserving and improving genetic resources. The CGIAR seeks to be respectful of national and international efforts to protect and promote farmers' rights as envisaged by the Treaty and support the development of appropriate policies and procedures for their recognition and promotion.

In addition to the above specific provision on farmers' rights, the entire CGIAR initiative on intellectual assets is a significant step toward the realization of farmers' rights. It builds upon previous and ongoing initiatives to break down institutional barriers and legal bottlenecks to the dissemination of knowledge over dealings in plant genetic resources. Perhaps more importantly, the CGIAR principles on the management of intellectual assets offer flexible and creative ways to constrain and to adapt IP to advance the public goods ideology of open dissemination and access as opposed to a closed framework of knowledge governance in plant genetic resources for food and agriculture. The open framework is a sharp counterpoise to the traditional emphasis on strong, closed and exclusionary intellectual or proprietary control of innovation in agriculture. The CGIAR principles do not problematize farmers as targets of regulatory containment, nor do they sanction farmers' practice of seed exchange as a criminal act of piracy. Rather, through its elaboration of the principles of partnership[32] in the sound management of intellectual assets and IP,[33] it seeks operational melding of industrial agricultural stakeholders and 'others' toward widespread diffusion of knowledge for optimal impact, especially on ILC farmers in developing countries. Its major challenge is how to ensure that the intervention does not replicate the discredited top-down model of engagement that undermines farmer-centered approaches to agriculture.

CONCLUSION

We have moved beyond skepticism over the operationalization of farmers' rights. But the stage of operationalization is still in its infancy. However, given the widespread domains of the farmers' rights movement as part of the broader socio-economic, equity, and justice movement, the two sites of its operationalization explored in this chapter are hardly sufficient. However, they are symbolic for a couple of reasons. First, they reflect a transition or mood change from perceiving farmers as objects of regulatory containment and control through technological and IP interventions to targets of empowerment. Second, they also reflect a positive, even if faintly evolving shift from a hard-edged closed approach to IP and intellectual assets in plant genetic resources to a more collaborative and open framework, one that is conducive to addressing the social justice gaps highlighted in the farmers' rights movement. Despite the inching of farmers' rights toward some form of operationalizing, it is illusory to believe that these initiatives are capable, in the present and near future, of resulting in the re-direction of global agricultural evolution toward farmer-centered agriculture. Nonetheless, in the next couple of decades, entrenching the CGIAR principles (which is an experimental initiative) and the Consortium's collaboration with the Treaty's governing body in the progressive implementation of the Treaty will perhaps be the pivotal sites for securing further advancement of farmers' rights in the context of a more progressive intersection with IPRs.

NOTES

1 Available at http://www.planttreaty.org/content/texts-treaty-official-versions
2 Available at http://www.cgiar.org/who-we-are/
3 Adopted in Paris in 1961 and came into force in 1968; Texts of the Acts of the Convention, available at http://www.upov.int/upovlex/en/acts.html
4 1869 UNTS 299; 33 ILM 1197 (1994); available at http://www.wto.org/english/docs_e/legal_e/27-trips_01_e.htm
5 Since the implementation of the TRIPS Agreement, state membership of the UPOV has continued to grow across geopolitical and economic divide. Through bilateral free trade agreements, industrialized countries demand of their developing country partners' compliance with the UPOV standard, as part of a trend in the TRIPS-plus standard.
6 Available at http://www.fao.org/Ag/cgrfa/iu.htm.
7 Agreed Interpretation of the International Undertaking.
8 Farmers' Rights, Conference Resolution on FR, available at http://www.farmersrights.org/about/fr_history_part4.html
9 FAO Resolution 5/89 (1989), available at http://www.fao.org/docrep/x5588E/x5588e06.htm
10 Ibid., emphasis added.
11 The subjecting of the common heritage principle to sovereign rights of states over genetic resources was endorsed by the commission on genetic resources at its inaugural meeting in 1985. See para. 9 Report of the First Session of the Commission on Plant Genetic Resources, 11–15 March, 1985, available at ftp://ftp.fao.org/docrep/fao/meeting/015/aj367e.pdf
12 1760 UNTS 79; 31 ILM 818 (1992), available at http://www.cbd.int/convention/
13 Although the CBD was signed in 1992 and came into effect in 1993, its evolution predated the TRIPS agreement (which was signed in 1994 and came into effect in 1995). Essentially, the two treaties overlap in terms of their implementation from the early to mid 1990s.
14 International Treaty, note 1 (emphasis added).
15 And relevant international obligations such as the UPOV and TRIPS.
16 As a guarantor of monopoly, IP is fundamentally a barrier to free trade. But it is an excusable barriers justified on the need to provide temporary reward to those who expend energy, resources and talent to bring a new product to the market.
17 Resolution 4/89 para 108(3); see note 7, above.
18 Emphasis added.
19 Zerbe's observation was made in the context of the African Model law, which, among other things, is an African regional template for adoption of farmers' rights across national jurisdictions.
20 Article 9.
21 Notably, skepticism over the ability of traditional farming practices to feed a rapidly growing global population, the suboptimal use of agricultural land under the traditional agricultural model, etc.
22 There is yet a distinction regarding farmers or ILCs dealing in annexed genetic resources and those dealing in non-annexed genetic resources. While the former readily engage farmers' rights under the Treaty, the latter fall within the CBD framework.
23 See note 14.
24 See note 10.

25 ftp://ftp.fao.org/docrep/fao/meeting/014/j7496e.pdf
26 This is a reference to those PGRFA not listed in Annex 1, but which were collected and held by the IARCs before the treaty entered into operation. Those were hitherto under the term of the 1994 agreement with the FAO.
27 See Report on the First Round of the Project Cycle of the Benefit-Sharing Fund, available at http://www.planttreaty.org/sites/default/files/Report_BSF.pdf.
28 Ibid. P. 1 (Executive Summary).
29 Third parties who use genetic resource under accession to the MLS for commercial purposes are required to make mandatory contribution to the BSF at 0.5% of sales over the first ten years of their exploitation of the crop.
30 Projects are awarded to country parties as beneficiaries and not the executing institutions.
31 Available at http://www.cgiarfund.org/sites/cgiarfund.org/files/Documents/PDF/cgiar_principles_management_intellectual_assets_7march_2012.pdf
32 Principle 2.
33 Principle 5.

REFERENCES

Aoki, Keith and Luvai, Kennedy (2007) 'Reclaiming Common Heritage Treatment in the International Plant Genetic Resources Regime Complex', *Michigan State Law Review*, 35: 35–70.

Arewa, Oluwafunmilayo, B. (2006) 'Piracy, Biopiracy and Borrowing: Culture, Cultural Heritage and Globalization of Intellectual Property', *Case Legal Studies Research Paper* No. 04–19.

Bhatti, Shakeel (2009) 'Technology Transfer Aspects of the Multilateral System of the ITPGRFA', paper presented at FAO International Technical Conference on Agricultural Biotechnologies in Developing Countries, Guadalajara, Mexico, March 3. Available at: http://www.fao.org/fileadmin/templates/abdc/documents/itpgrfa.pdf

Borowiak, Craig (2004) 'Farmers' Rights: Intellectual Property Regimes and the Struggle over Seeds', *Politics and Society*, 32(4): 511–543.

Chapman, Audrey R. (2009) 'Toward an Understanding of the Right to Enjoy the Benefits of Scientific Progress and its Application', *Journal of Human Rights*, 8: 1–36.

De Schutter, Olivier (2011) 'The Right of Everyone to Enjoy the Benefits of Scientific Progress and the Right to Food: From Conflict to Complementarity', *Human Rights Quarterly*, 33(2): 304–350.

Drahos, Peter (n.d.) 'The Universalization of Intellectual Property: Origins and Development', available at http://www.wipo.int/edocs/mdocs/tk/en/wipo_unhchr_ip_pnl_98/wipo_unhchr_ip_pnl_98_1.pdf

Dutfield, Graham (2008) 'Turning Plant Varieties into Intellectual Property: The UPOV Convention', in Geoff Tansey and Tasmin Rajotte (eds), *The Future Control of Food: A Guide to International Negotiations and Rules on Intellectual Property, Biodiversity and Food Security*. London: Earthscan. pp. 27–47.

Farley Haight, Christine (1997) 'Protecting Indigenous Knowledge: Is Intellectual Property the Answer?', *Connecticut Law Review*, 30(1): 1–57.

Gervais, Daniel (2009) 'Of Clusters and Assumptions: Innovation as Part of a Full TRIPS Implementation', *Fordham Law Review*, 77(5): 2353–2377.

Gillespie, Alexander (2011) *Conservation, Biodiversity and International Law*. Cheltenham: Edward Elgar.

GRAIN (2012) *The Great Food Robbery: How Corporations, Control Food, Grab Land and Destroy the Climate*. Barcelona: Pambazuka Press.

Helfer, Laurence R. (2002) 'Intellectual Property Rights in Plant Varieties: An Overview with Options for National Governments', *FAO Legal Paper Online* #31, available at: http://www.fao.org/fileadmin/user_upload/legal/docs/lpo31-2.pdf

Helfer, Laurence R. (2009) 'Regime Shifting in the International Intellectual Property System', *Perspectives on Politics*, 7(1): 39–44.

Ho, Cynthia M. (2007) 'Agricultural Biotechnology under TRIPS and Beyond: Addressing Social Policies in Pro-Patent Environment', in Jay Kesan (ed.), *Agricultural Biotechnology and Intellectual Property: Seeds of Change*. New York: CABI. pp. 304–319.

Jaffe, Adam, B. and Lerner, Josh (2004) *Innovation and Its Discontent: How our Broken Patent System is Endangering Innovation and Progress and What to Do About It*. Princeton: Princeton University Press.

Kariyawasam, Kanchana (2009) 'Terminator Technology as a Technological Means of Forcing Intellectual Property Rights in Plant Germplasm: Its Implications for World Agriculture', *European Intellectual Property Review*, 31(1): 37–44.

Kloppenburg Jr., Jack R. (2004) *First the Seed: The Political Economy of Plant Biotechnology 1492–2000*, 2nd edn. Madison: University of Wisconsin Press (1st edn 1988).

Marden, Emily and Godfrey, Nelson (eds)(forthcoming 2014) *Innovation in Agricultural Genomics; Overcoming Complexities in Intellectual Property-Regulatory Complex*. Vancouver, Canada: UBC Press.

Maskus, Keith H. and Reichman, Jerome H. (eds) (2005) *International Public Good and Transfer of Technology:*

Under a Globalized Intellectual Property Regime. Cambridge, UK: Cambridge University Press.

McManis, Charles R. and Seo, Eul S. (2009) 'The Interface of Open Source and Proprietary Agricultural Innovation: Facilitated Access and Benefit-Sharing Under the New FAO Treaty', *Washington University Journal of Law and Policy*, 30: 405–464.

Mgbeoji, Ikechi (2001) 'Patents and Traditional Knowledge of Uses of Plants: Is a Communal Patent Regime Part of the Solution to the Scourge of Bio Piracy', *Indiana Journal of Global Legal Studies*, 9(1): 163–186.

Mgbeoji, Ikechi (2006) *Global Biopiracy: Patents, Plants and Indigenous Knowledge*. Vancouver: UBC Press.

Oberthür, Sabestian and Rosendal, G. Kristin (eds) (2013) *Global Governance of Genetic Resources: Access and Benefit Sharing after the Nagoya Protocol*. London: Routledge.

Oguamanam, Chidi (2004) 'Localizing Intellectual Property in the Globalization Epoch: The Integration of Indigenous Knowledge', *Indiana Journal of Global Legal Studies*, 11(2): 135–169.

Oguamanam, Chidi (2005) 'Genetic Use Restriction (or Terminator) Technologies (Gurts) in Agricultural Biotechnology: The Limits of Technological Alternatives to Intellectual Property', *Canadian Journal of Law and Technology*, 4(1): 59–72.

Oguamanam, Chidi (2006a) 'Regime Tension in Intellectual Property Arena: Farmers' Rights and Post-TRIPS Counter Regime Trends', *Dalhousie Law Journal*, 29(1): 413–453.

Oguamanam, Chidi (2006b) *International Law and Indigenous Knowledge: Intellectual Property, Plant Biodiversity and Traditional Medicine*. Toronto: University of Toronto Press.

Oguamanam, Chidi (2006c) 'Intellectual Property in Plant Genetic Resources: Farmers' Rights and Food Security in Indigenous and Local Communities', *Drake Journal of Agricultural Law*, 11: 273–305.

Oguamanam, Chidi (2007) 'Agro-Biodiversity and Food Security:Biotechnology and Traditional Agricultural Practices at the Periphery of International Intellectual Property Regime Complex', *Michigan State Law Review*, 215–255.

Oguamanam, Chidi (2008) 'Local Knowledge as Trapped Knowledge: Intellectual Property, Culture, Power and Politics', *Journal of World Intellectual Property*, 11(1): 29–57.

Oguamanam, Chidi (2012) *Intellectual Property in Global Governance: A Development Question*. New York: Routledge.

Oguamanam, Chidi (2013) 'Rio+20: Indigenous Knowledge and Intellectual Property in Coastal and Ocean Law', *Ocean Year Book*, 27: 121–146.

Oguamanam, Chidi (2014) 'Intellectual Property, Agricultural Biotechnology and the Right to Adequate Food: A Critical African, Perspective', *African Journal of International and Comparative Law* (forthcoming).

Pugatch, Perez, M. (2004) *The International Political Economy of Intellectual Property Rights*. Cheltenham: Edward Elgar.

Reichman, Jerome R. (2009) 'Intellectual Property in the Twenty-First Century: Will Developing Countries Lead or Follow', *Houston Law Review*, 46(4): 1115–1185.

Sell, Susan K. (2003) *Private Power, Public Law: The Globalization of Intellectual Property Rights*. Cambridge: Cambridge University Press.

Shiva, Vandana (1993) *Monocultures of the Mind: Perspectives on Biodiversity and Biotechnology*. London: Zed Books.

Shiva, Vandana (2000) *Stolen Harvest: The Hijacking of Global Food Supply*. Cambridge, MA: Southend Press.

Smith, Matthew, Laurent, Elder and Heloise, Emdon (eds) (2011) 'Open Development: A New Theory of for ICT4D', *Information Technologies and International Development*, 7(1) (Special Issue: Open Development), available at http://www.itidjournal.org/itid/article/view/692/290

Smith Matthew, L. and Reilly, Katherine, M.A. (2013) (eds) Open Development: Networked Innovations in International Development. Cambridge, MA: MIT Press.

Srinivasan, C.S. and Thirtle, Colin (2002) 'Impact of Terminator Technologies in Developing Countries', in T. Swanson (ed.) *Biotechnology Agriculture and the Developing World*. London: Edward Elgar. pp. 150–176.

Takenaka, Toshiko (ed.) (2008) *Patent Law and Theory: A Handbook of Contemporary Research*. Cheltenham: Edward Elgar.

Tansey, Geoff and Rajotte, Tasmin (2008) (eds) *The Future Control of Food: A Guide to International Negotiations and Rules on Intellectual Property, Biodiversity and Food Security*. London: Earthscan.

TRIPS (1994) Available at http://www.wto.org/english/docs_e/legal_e/27-trips_01_e.htm.

Wong, Tzen and Dutfield, Graham (eds) (2011) *Intellectual Property and Human Development: Current Trends and Future Scenarios*. New York: Cambridge University Press.

Yu, Peter K. (2007) 'International Enclosure, the Regime Complex and Intellectual Property Schizophrenia', *Indiana Law Journal*, 82: 827–907.

Zerbe, Noah (2007) 'Contesting Privatization: NGOs and Farmers' Rights in the African Model', *Global Environmental Politics*, 7(1): 97–119.

PART IV

Between Economy and Culture

Matthew David and Debora Halbert

Contemporary intellectual property law is designed, its advocates claim, to support innovation and the creation of knowledge-based products. These laws have been largely drafted by the most powerful states and driven by the most powerful interests in those states; but are said to be best applied everywhere and to benefit everyone. Copyright specifically, but intellectual property generally has been reshaped over the last few decades to assert ownership over digital products and rethink creative work as an engine for contemporary economic growth in what is now globally understood to be the information age. The traditional narrative of intellectual property describes the important benefits of these legal regimes for the emerging digital economy and claims that far reaching protection is essential for further progress to be achieved. Without these incentives, the traditional story suggests, innovation and creativity will halt. This narrative is asserted by governments and already established industries seeking to cement their economic future in an otherwise volatile flow of ideas and innovations.

This section brings together four different approaches to the intersection of intellectual property, economic motivations, and how one might strike the balance between too much and too little protection. Drawing on themes that have emerged in the previous sections about political economy, economic incentives, development and the role of intellectual property, the chapters in this section further explore the relationship between economic incentive and cultural progress. The chapters here suggest that economic development in the sphere of culture may not be as contingent upon strong intellectual property rights as those in industry might have one believe. Rather, there are a wide variety of viewpoints on the role of copyright as the basis of economic development that can be explored. First, Colin Darch in the first of two chapters for the Handbook provides a critical overview of the ways in which intellectual property influences development and culture in South Africa. By providing a comprehensive view of the way the global framework of IP has changed conditions on the ground in South Africa, Darch positions the myriad issues of traditional knowledge, trademark protection and copyright within a critique of their potential to help support further economic development in the country. While other authors commenting on issues in Africa (see Perullo and Eisenberg, this volume) provide some insight into possible benefits of copyright law, especially for musicians, Darch makes visible the way intellectual property primarily enhances the ability of transnational corporations to further control economic development on the continent.

Much as Coombe, Ives and Huizenga warn of the problems and complexities of using geographical indications to protect traditional knowledge, Darch warns that efforts to place traditional knowledge within a framework of IP more generally may not lead to the types of benefits touted by IP advocates. He also seeks to put efforts to use geographical indicators and trademarks to protect traditional knowledge and smaller farming operations within the wider economic context of larger firms who tend to benefit from these laws. His chapter provides a multitude of important examples of the intersection between state action to promote intellectual property policy, often done in order to meet the government obligations under TRIPS, and efforts by local creators and others to find a way to make a living. As with many contributors to this volume, Darch suggests we must think carefully about who benefits and who loses with the balance of power struck by contemporary intellectual property law.

Lillian Álvarez provides an essential perspective on copyright that proposes a different balance between copyright protection and the public welfare. Viewing intellectual property from a Cuban perspective gives us a rare insight into the alternatives that can and do exist to those that dominate the debate over copyright in countries driven by capitalist economies. In this way, Cuba can stand as a case study of a country that has sought to balance economic rights and creativity differently than most other countries in the world.

Cuba is one of the few places from which we can get a socialist perspective on intellectual property. Álvarez situates Cuba's laws within the larger international framework which, from a Cuban perspective, can be seen to enhance the power of multinational corporations at the expense of local creators. While Cuba had intellectual property laws long before the TRIPS agreement, its socialist approach has meant that a different balance was struck between users and owners of copyrighted materials. Cuba has been especially vigilant in assuring access to knowledge by providing Cuban students with free access to textbooks and expanding the concept of fair use far beyond that seen in capitalist countries like the United States.

From a Cuban perspective, the spread of knowledge is an important public asset, and as long as there is no profit from the copied materials, their use and value as part of public culture outweigh the individual rights of the original author. Striking the balance between profit maximalization and public use differently in Cuba has meant that the country has been able to continue to develop its science, engineering and medical fields despite the persistent US blockade and the ensuing lack of access to crucial educational materials. Cuba, according to Álvarez, is able to provide a balance that is fundamental to a people-centred economic development. Thus, for Cuba, the users of what we call intellectual property are also an important factor in the debate.

Edwards, Klein, Lee, Moss and Philip are also concerned with how users of copyrighted materials are framed in contemporary copyright debates. Users are often vilified as pirates and it is clear that there is a chasm between the types of uses made of copyrighted works by users and the efforts to expand ownership in the digital age supported by copyright owners. Because most countries have not affixed the balance of rights to favour the public as Cuba has, it means that rights in most of the world are skewed towards copyright owners. Edwards et al. argue that the voice of the user is not taken seriously enough in copyright discussions and thus intellectual property policy does not reflect the reality of use. In part, it might be argued from the perspective of Cuba, that the problems Edwards et al. have highlighted are the logical extension of the capitalist perspective on intellectual property. Edwards et al. make clear that the public has not been considered in the changes in copyright law developed to protect digital culture emerging from the UK and elsewhere. Instead, the public is categorized as pirates and every effort is made to restrict their uses of copyrighted materials.

While copyright dependent industries have gone through a variety of overarching narratives to justify expanded copyright laws, Edwards et al. point out that these narratives continue to place industry itself as a copyright owner central to future innovation and economic development. In doing so, alternative perspectives are marginalized. Edwards et al. are interested in the voices of users and have utilized focus groups to better understand their perspectives on the issue of digital copyright. Users, it turns out, value sharing, they value the ease of copying things, and while willing to pay for downloads, they do so within an ethical political economy that does not reflect the expectations of the music industry. However, there is an ethics to file-sharing that informs consumer choices. For example, if a user cannot access material legally and at a price they feel is fair most see no problem with finding that material through other channels. To use the language of the economist – they are simply filling a market failure where industry has left a gap.

Cuba has not gone to war on users as the UK and other countries have done. In part, they have recognized the legitimacy of private sharing as important for cultural and economic development and the public good. These notions of private sharing were developed by Phythian-Adams in her chapter on the economics of copyright. Edwards et al. begin from the level of stories told by users and conclude that sharing culture is an important part of user behaviour. To that end, in a cultural environment that is designed for profit-making, one must determine a way to modify the extremes of profit maximalization's logic. By focusing on users, Edwards et al. seek to contribute another voice to the larger copyright discourse and understand how economics and culture interact from the perspective of the consumer.

O'Brien is also critical of the expansiveness of copyright in the context of the so-called cultural/creative industries. He argues that despite their advocacy for strong intellectual property rights, the creative industries themselves have a much more complex relationship to these rights. Thus, to the degree that culture produces a new type of economy, intellectual property may not be as important as one is led to believe. Much like Edwards et al., O'Brien focuses on the UK (and to a lesser extent the US) experience. Despite this focus, the concept of an information economy he develops transcends the UK and also frames debates in the EU and beyond. In an information-based economy, even knowledge itself becomes a commodity. As pointed out by those critical of the political economy of information, O'Brien notes that the creative labourers in the new information economy rarely own their creative work, but rather work for the corporate structures that control copyrighted knowledge and creativity. Policies aimed at protecting IP are presented as ones that protect all those working in the 'cultural' sector. However, in reality, giving more control to copyright, patent and brand holders has gone hand in hand with reducing the security of employment and reward for the vast majority who work in this so-called 'creative' sector.

These chapters as a whole provide different starting points for understanding the economy of culture but all offer substantive critique of the claims that copyright is essential for future economic and cultural development. For Cuba, culture, education, the arts and music form a foundation upon which economic progress and development can be laid. To that end, the country has chosen to strike a different balance between producers and users of copyrighted materials while developing alternative means to ensure authors and artists are paid for their work. From the US/UK perspective, however, the 'creative' user is almost always seen as a pirate and the 'culture' industries themselves commodify culture as a product to be bought and sold. O'Brien's critique of copyright would have us divide culture from industry and more clearly define what we mean when we seek to protect information and creativity via copyright and trademark. Rather than simply accepting that protection for informational 'capital' is synonymous with the greater good and protection of all (artists, employees, audiences and consumers), we should, as Edwards et al. suggest, integrate all users into the debate and as Álvarez notes, make central the value and defence of the public good.

14

The Political Economy of Traditional Knowledge, Trademarks and Copyright in South Africa

Colin Darch

INTRODUCTION

This chapter, together with my 'Politics, Law and Discourse: Patents and Innovation in Post-Apartheid South Africa', also published in this Handbook, was written to constitute a general overview of the contested terrain of South African intellectual property (IP) policy and law since the fall of apartheid in 1994 and the end of the country's international isolation. Nevertheless, it can also be read alone as a discussion of the dominant and competing narratives around the political and judicial aspects of trademarks, copyright and the protection of traditional knowledge, using exemplary cases from contemporary South African jurisprudence. Like its companion text, it links current South African policy and law to developments in the international IP and trade environment. For an analysis of the broader South African legal and economic context, and a description of the current development of government policy towards IP at the macro level, readers are referred to 'Politics, Law and Discourse' (Chapter 33, in this volume). This field of policy is one in which change occurs in unpredictable ways, and for up-to-date information, readers are advised to consult, *inter alia*, the blogs cited at the end of this chapter.

PROTECTING TRADITIONAL KNOWLEDGE

The protection of 'traditional knowledge' (hereafter TK) through IP mechanisms is a 'real but amorphous problem' (Hughes, 2012: 1224), and one that is acute in the South Africa context. The Cape 'floral kingdom' is the smallest of the six scientifically recognized botanical kingdoms, and is particularly diverse in terms of indigenous species. The rest of the country is also especially rich in different kinds of plants, many of which have been and continue to be used by local communities for a wide range of medicinal, nutritional and other uses. This means that the country is especially vulnerable to 'bio-prospecting' and the related practice of 'bio-piracy', in which products are developed and marketed from plant or other natural resources with little or no recognition of prior knowledge within local communities, without permission and often without compensation. The twin risks are first that knowledge is appropriated and privatized, and second that the physical resource itself may be harvested to the point of near extinction. Both practices frequently involve the registration of patents, and therefore become an issue of IP rights (IPRs). South Africa has added to this problem, if not to its solution, both an iconic piece of jurisprudence and a legislative proposal that has been severely criticized for its general approach. These are respectively the San-Hoodia case – probably the best known but certainly not the only South African case fought out in public and judicial arenas – and the much derided IP Laws Amendment Bill.

The *amorphousness* of the concept of traditional or indigenous knowledge is evidenced by what Hughes has called the 'definitional instabilities' of the field (2012: 1216). It is difficult to delineate exactly what TK is and what it is not, as well as how it relates to core IP concepts. Although the idea of TK can be traced back to the 1960s, the defining moments in the development of the now global drive towards IP protection for TK were the Convention on Biological Diversity of 1992, which included provisions in article 8 (j) for the regulation of TK; TRIPS, which *excluded* certain materials from patenting in its article 27.3 (b); and the Doha Declaration of 2001. Even the terminology is contested: 'local knowledge', 'indigenous knowledge', and 'traditional knowledge' are all used, as are 'traditional environmental knowledge' and 'traditional cultural expression' (previously called folklore). The phrase 'traditional knowledge' is preferred here as being broader than 'indigenous knowledge' and indeed encompassing it (Mugabe, 1999). TK is an aspirationally nomothetic concept: a broad definition would include techniques and theories, often preserved orally, of botany, agriculture, the environment, astronomy and other subsistence-and-survival fields of knowledge within a community.

The problem arises at the interface between globally dominant 'Western' values and subaltern systems of knowing, and is fundamentally political in nature. IP and TK are – and by and large remain – quite simply 'worlds apart' (Patel, 1996: 318). Nineteenth- and twentieth-century imperialism and colonialism helped to produce a structural, persistent and global asymmetry of information and knowledge, in which what is 'known' in industrialized countries is contrasted with what is merely 'believed' in the global south. At the same time, selected TK was and continues to be appropriated and absorbed into the knowledge systems of the (former) colonizing powers: 'indigenous cultural knowledge has always been an open treasure box for the unfettered appropriation of items of value to Western civilization' (Greaves, 1996: 25). The contradiction, which has been frequently pointed out, lies in the literal acceptance of the 'property' metaphor into TK discourse by indigenous peoples, and the idea that Western IP is an appropriate instrument to control access to non-Western forms of knowledge that are not fixed in form, not used for trading, nor necessarily innovative:

> intellectual property has a unique European derivation and this informs its modes of classification, identification and operation. Intellectual property law promotes particular cultural interpretations of knowledge, ownership, authorship and property. These do not necessarily correspond to or complement indigenous peoples' understandings about the role and function of knowledge and knowledge practices. (Anderson, 2010: 1)

The issue of the uncompensated appropriation of TK arose famously in South Africa when the Council for Scientific and Industrial Research (CSIR), having identified the active appetite-suppressing agent in the *hoodia* cactus, applied for local and international patents without taking into account the interests of the impoverished San people, who had used the plant in this way for centuries (Wynberg et al., 2009: 3).

Of course, bio-piracy is probably as old as empire, but it has always required enabling technologies to truly flourish. As soon as the invention of the Wardian case in the nineteenth century enabled plants to survive long sea journeys, imperial powers began their systematic plundering of the botanical riches of the global south, culminating in the 'greatest theft of protected trade secrets that the world has ever known' (Rose, 2010: 245), i.e. Robert Fortune's clandestine removal of tea plants from China in 1848–1849. It is evident that this tradition continues to the present day: the CSIR needed 'high-field nuclear magnetic resonance spectography' before it was finally able to identify the relevant molecules in the *hoodia* (Wynberg and Chennells, 2009: 95).

The San-Hoodia case attracted intense media attention and has been the subject of journal articles, dissertations and film documentaries in recent years (Wynberg and Chennells, 2009: 90). The appetite-suppressant qualities of the *hoodia*, known to indigenous people for centuries, were first documented in the scientific literature in the 1930s. After years of research, the CSIR identified and patented the active agents in the *hoodia* plant in the mid-1990s, but made no contact with the San. A natural appetite suppressant attracted the interest of pharmaceutical companies marketing dietary remedies to the overweight, and over the next few years license and royalty agreements were duly concluded between the CSIR and various partners: Phytofarm, Pfizer, Unilever and, in the final stages, Phytofarm again.

In mid-2001, alerted by Rachel Wynberg and others at Biowatch South Africa, the British Sunday newspaper *The Observer* broke the story about the appropriation, with the objective of 'making us thin', of what it termed the 'secret' of *hoodia* (Wynberg and Chennells, 2009: 101). The issue became an international scandal, in which 'big pharma' was seen ripping off the impoverished and marginalized San. The negative publicity effectively forced the CSIR to begin negotiations with a cross-national representation of San people from Botswana and Namibia as well as South Africa. It soon became clear that the situation was complex. Not only the San, but interrelated indigenous groups such as the Nama and the Damara shared knowledge of the *hoodia*'s medicinal properties (Wynberg and Chennells, 2009: 104–106).

In 2003, an agreement was reached in terms of which the San would get six per cent of royalties received by the CSIR from Phytofarm (Wynberg and Chennells, 2009: 107). This would increase to eight per cent when certain milestones were reached, and the revenue would be held by a trust whose objective was to 'to raise the standard of living and well-being of San peoples of southern Africa' (Wynberg, 2010: 23). There were some obvious problems: the agreement was between the San and the CSIR, not the companies, so the revenue was a percentage of a percentage. In addition, the patent rights were traded around: Pfizer lost interest in 2003 and left the rights with Phytofarm, who then reached agreement with Unilever (Wynberg, 2010: 22–23). Last, the original assumption that *hoodia* would be marketed as a drug turned out to be false; by 2007 it was to be commercialized as a food supplement (Vermeylen, 2007: 430). It is clear that expectations had risen to unrealistic levels. Such high hopes were inevitably dashed: the San apparently believed 'that they [were] sitting on a potential goldmine and that they [would] become multi-millionaires overnight' (Vermeylen, 2007: 432). Even the modest amounts that have in fact been received bring new problems: by 2010 'only US$100,000 [had] been received by the San Hoodia Trust, but already the challenges of distributing this money [were] immense, and [diverted] energy away from other needs' (Wynberg, 2010: 24).

One of the problems in negotiations between commercial companies and local 'communities' is the lack of definition of what the membership of the community consists of, and who is authorized to speak on its behalf. In Bushbuckridge in Mpumalanga province a solution to this problem was found through a participatory and facilitated process to develop a 'biocultural community protocol' (BCP) for local traditional healers, who had little experience of working together. The area is poor, with high levels of unemployment; in addition 'commercial-level harvesting of medicinal plants for use in South Africa's cities threatens many [local] plant species' (Sibuye et al., 2012: 103). The process of facilitating a BCP led to an agreed text that defines the 'community with shared values' and which 'clearly sets out their combined views on conservation and the sustainable use of medicinal plants, including the use of their traditional knowledge' (Sibuye et al., 2012: 107). The healers established the Kukula Traditional Health Practitioners Association, which now has around 300 members, is legally registered as a non-profit, and has negotiated agreements with a local cosmetics company about potential uses of local TK (Sibuye et al., 2012: 101, 106).

Another recent case that attracted some media attention involved the exploitation by a German company, Schwabe Pharmaceuticals, of the medicinal properties of the two very similar plant species *Pelargonium sidoides* and *Pelargonium reniforme*. The pelargonium is used as an ornamental plant in Europe, but has been used in southern Africa to produce a traditional herbal remedy, *umcka-loabo*, used to treat symptoms of the common cold such as coughs, as well as diarrhoea and chest pain (European Medicines Agency, 2011: 3). Schwabe had patented extracts from the plant, but in 2010 the patents were challenged before the European Patent Office's Opposition Division by the African Centre for Biosafety (ACB) and a Swiss NGO, representing Eastern Cape communities, and the patents were revoked (McKune, 2010: 4). This was the first successful challenge to a patent by an African organization, but Schwabe announced their intention to appeal the judgement (Parkes, 2010: 5).

The desire to provide IP protection for TK is rooted in an expansionist and maximalist paradigm; similarly, the concept of bio-piracy is located in a discourse of communitarian and nationalist identity politics in which the 'accidents' of birth, geography and local environment are seen to determine rights of 'ownership'. Ironically, 'un-owned' communal knowledge ends up being appropriated, in the name of community, into a Western system that turns it into private property, as the only way of protecting it from complete alienation. Dutfield has pointed to an analogy between the physical displacement of indigenous peoples by colonialism and the appropriation and privatization of their knowledge:

> open access is the rule for … traditional knowledge and resources, whereas enclosure is the rule as soon as these are proved to have economic value … one type of IPR system is being universalized and prioritized to the exclusion of all others, which causes the most legitimate disquiet among those peoples and communities that are least able to benefit from what, to them, is an imposed system. (2004: 59)

Can the global IP system be retro-fitted to the needs of TK? Patel posed this blunt question in 1996, and concluded that there was 'no possibility of modifying the IPR system in the foreseeable future in any way or manner in order to promote the rights of indigenous people … the door is simply not open' (Patel, 1996: 319). The South African government (or at least the Department of Trade and Industry, the DTI; the Department of Science and Technology, the DST, appears to have its own views) disagrees, and at the time of writing is in the process of pushing legislation through parliament to protect TK. The IP Laws Amendment Bill is the legislative expression of a maximalist position that believes the prevention of bio-piracy to be an urgent matter: as Minister Rob Davies remarked in parliament when introducing the Bill in October 2011: 'failure to act will … encourage further unabated exploitation of communities' heritages by unscrupulous private interests'. The Minister also referred to on-going but unidentified 'rampant exploitation of IK through the IP system' (Davies, 2011).

The Bill rejects the *sui generis* approach, and instead amends existing legislation – the Performers' Protection Act of 1967, the Copyright Act of 1978, the Trade Marks Act of 1993 and the Designs Act of 1993 – setting up a National Council, a National Database and a trust fund. It also establishes an Alternative Dispute Resolutions (ADR) system. This overall approach attracted strong – perhaps intemperate – criticism from the highly-respected Professor Owen

Dean, probably South Africa's best-known IP attorney in recent decades, and presently holder of the chair in IP law at Stellenbosch University. He described the legislation variously as 'an exercise in futility', 'an outright slap-stick farce' and 'a proverbial white elephant' (Dean, 2011). By mid-2012 he had drafted an alternative statute, which was tabled in the legislature in 2013 by the opposition Democratic Alliance (Jooste, 2013).

The DST had earlier taken a different line, publishing a policy document on TK systems in which the emphasis was on defensive measures to protect knowledge from appropriation. This document cautiously identified the establishment of a database of TK as an efficient method of anchoring TK in the public domain, with *sui generis* legislation – to be administered by the DTI – required as well (DST, 2005: 21, 29). The multi-pronged strategy recommended in the DST document involved four steps: the recording of IK by IK holders; minimum standards for benefit sharing; an agreement on public domain declarations of knowledge; and an agreement on the certification of IK holders and their IK rights (DST, 2005: 29).

TRADEMARK AND GI DISPUTES IN SOUTH AFRICA

The Trademarks Act (no. 194 of 1993), together with case law, governs this area of IP in South Africa. Protection is extended to registered trademarks under the act, and to some extent even to unregistered trademarks under common law. Importantly, trademark use is also governed by other legislation, such as the Counterfeit Goods Act (no. 37 of 1997), the Consumer Protection Act (no. 68 of 2008), and the Companies Act (no. 71 of 2008) (Wimpey, 2012: 255–256). The Trademarks Act came into force in May 1995, introducing 'two new forms of trademark infringement, namely: protection of well-known trademarks … and the anti-dilution provisions' (Webster, 2005). The two most important trademark cases since the end of apartheid have hinged on the clarification of these principles, but have not resulted in an entirely coherent jurisprudence, as lower courts have not necessarily followed the principles established by the Constitutional Court in the second case discussed here. Indeed, the contradictory trends discernible in the recent jurisprudence have been described by one specialist as constituting 'a fundamental collision of values' within the judiciary (Wheeldon, 2007: 253).

South Africa is a member of the Paris Convention for the Protection of Industrial Property (1883), administered by WIPO, but has not acceded to the Madrid Agreement Concerning the International Registration of Marks (1891). The national register of trademarks is maintained by the CIPC. Applications to register trademarks are examined and registration may be renewed every ten years upon payment of a fee, a process that may be repeated indefinitely. South African trademark law includes non-use provisions, which provide for the de-registration of a trademark if it was not registered in good faith (i.e. with an intention to use it), if it has not been used for a period of five years, or if the owner has died or gone out of business. The particular issue of the lapsing and removal of marks, and whether or not international brands were 'well-known' locally, was the basis for the first major trademark dispute of the post-apartheid era, a group of closely-interrelated cases of which the best-known is *McDonalds Corporation v. Joburgers Drive-Inn Restaurant*.

The movement to enforce sanctions on South Africa was an important weapon in the struggle against apartheid, especially in the 1980s. The objective was to isolate the country by enforcing economic, academic, cultural and sporting boycotts, including pressure on international brands to disinvest. In the United States, the Sullivan Principles played an important role, requiring US companies to ensure non-discrimination in their South African operations. These struggles, especially the disinvestment campaign, succeeded in triggering capital flight from the country and played an important part in the eventual collapse of apartheid.

After the advent of non-racial democracy with the 1994 elections, several large companies that had disinvested decided either to return to South Africa or to begin trading. In the latter group was the hamburger franchise McDonalds, which had registered a range of trademarks in South Africa in 1968, and had renewed them at regular intervals, although up to 1993 it had never actually used any of them. The company claimed that it believed in respecting sanctions against apartheid and had been awaiting an appropriate political moment to enter the market (Dean, 1996b: 409).

The South African fast food market in the 1990s was dominated by 'several strong home-grown brands, specifically catering to South African tastes' and was to prove a harder nut to crack than the company had anticipated (*The Economist,* 1997). Indeed, the battles over trademark registration were only one aspect of a difficult journey to local acceptance by a corporation that at least initially failed to take into account the specific character of the new market that it was entering. Aspects of this specificity included black consumers' overwhelming preference for chicken over beef products. South Africans in general found McDonalds' burgers overpriced and under-sized (*The Economist,* 1997: 80). The path to success – in the marketplace as well as in the IP arena – was neither simple nor straightforward.

In this context, a South African company, Joburgers Drive-Inn Restaurant, applied in 1993 to have McDonalds' trademarks deregistered and re-registered in its own name in order to use them in South Africa. Joburgers was the franchiser of a successful local fast food chain, Chicken Licken. McDonalds immediately and successfully sued Joburgers for infringement, and obtained an interdict against their future use of any of the disputed marks (Dean, 1996b: 409). There is, incidentally, no tradition of arbitration of IP disputes in the South African system; in essence, everything is litigated (Alberts and Brand, 2008). Joburgers subsequently acquired Asian Dawn Investments, which owned an existing restaurant in Durban called MacDonalds, with the minor spelling variation. The US corporation quickly applied to prevent Joburgers from continuing to trade under that name as well; in response, Joburgers sold the company on to a third party, Dax, which operated other Chicken Licken franchises, and which in due course applied to register McDonalds' trademarks in its own name (Dean, 1996b: 410).

In May 1995, while these matters dragged on, the new Trademarks Act came into force, including the provision allowing the owner of a 'well-known' foreign trademark to sue for infringements. McDonalds instituted proceedings against both Joburgers and Dax on the grounds that its trademarks were indeed well-known – the idea that they might not be was considered 'preposterous' (*The Economist,* 1997: 79). When the case was heard in the Transvaal Provincial Division in 1996, McDonalds produced a couple of market surveys, conducted in the white suburbs of Johannesburg and Durban, as evidence in support of the claim that their marks were well-known (Dean, 1996a: 102). Brand recognition was around 80 per cent. However, the judge was unconvinced, and ruled that McDonalds had failed to show that the marks were well-known to all groups at all levels of society, across the whole country, or that its use 'by other parties would be likely to cause deception or confusion' (Dean, 1996b: 414). The judgment in effect said that McDonalds was not a well-known brand in South Africa, and that the trademarks must be cancelled.

Opinion was sharply divided on this decision, especially its impact on foreign attitudes towards South Africa. Visser, for example, regarded McDonalds' failure to demonstrate serious intention to use the mark in South Africa itself or through licensees as 'fatal' (1996: 16). Both Visser and Job noted that failure was also the result of the weakness of the survey evidence that McDonalds presented in court (Visser, 1996: 16; Job 1996b: 317). Indeed, Job lamented the fact that media coverage of the case had created the *false* impression that 'South African law and its courts pay scant regard to the protection of foreign trade marks and foreign investors are now left to the mercy of unscrupulous local entrepreneurs' (1996b: 317). Dean, on the other hand, made no bones about his disapproval of the lower court judgment and endorsed the subsequent reversal on appeal, referring in articles published at the time to 'trademark hijackers', and 'rustlers' (1996a, 1996b). He reported that the lower court ruling was

> greeted with incredulity in trademark legal and business circles around the world, particularly in the United States of America. It had far-reaching and significant legal, political, and commercial implications, and gave rise to the contention that South African trade-mark law does not comply with international standards for protecting foreign trademarks. (Dean, 1996b: 408)

The judgment was soon reversed in the Supreme Court of Appeal, which decided that it had been proved that the trademarks were 'well-known', since a sector of the population was aware of them, and dismissed the application to have the trademarks removed from the register (Job, 1996a: 677). This outcome was described as 'rather unexpected', and the appeal court's reasoning left some issues unresolved. For example, did a failure to trade in South Africa because of sanctions in fact constitute 'exceptional circumstances'; and did McDonalds' renewals of their unused trademarks amount to 'abuse' of the system? (Job, 1996a: 680).

Contemporary newspaper reports allege that these decisions had an impact on investor confidence, although the evidence remains largely anecdotal. What is clear is that there was widespread concern among IP professionals about national reputation (something that can still be detected in the discourse even today). For example, the president of the South African Institute of Intellectual Property Law (SAIIPL) commented in September 1996 that the appeal judgment would help to dispel the perception that South Africans were 'trademark bandits' and would encourage foreign companies to go to court to protect their IPRs (Russell, 1996: 11). Similarly, the City of Cape Town was then preparing an eventually unsuccessful bid to host the 2004 Olympic Games, and it was widely believed that the International Olympic Committee took local IP enforcement standards into consideration in making its decisions (Zaina, 1996: 9). The subsequent ruthless exploitation by FIFA of its trademarks, even before the World Cup in 2010, with over 500 registered or applied for, would tend to support this view (Kelbrick, 2008: 328).

The second major piece of trademark jurisprudence to emerge from South African courts is the Laugh It Off case, which was finally decided on appeal in a Constitutional Court judgment in May 2005. This case (2006 (1) SA 144 (CC)) raised the issue of IP law versus constitutionally-guaranteed freedom of expression, in the broader context of the practice of 'culture-jamming', a term coined in the mid-1980s to describe the process of hacking into corporate communications (such as trademarks) to offer a counter-message (Haupt, 2008: 127–128). In this particular case, a small South African company, Laugh It Off Promotions, had produced a t-shirt which parodied the trademark of Carling Black Label beer, produced in South Africa by South African Breweries (SAB). The shirt took the original trademark and re-worked it; thus the phrase 'Carling Black Label Beer' became 'Black Labour, White Guilt', and the subordinate text was changed to read 'Africa's lusty, lively exploitation since 1652. No regard given worldwide'. The success of such a subversion of the original message, as Haupt points out, depends on public familiarity with the brand and its marketing methods (2008: 129). Laugh It Off had also produced shirts parodying such brands as Standard Bank, Diesel and Lego, but the reaction from these companies was mixed: First National Bank reportedly bought the shirts and gave them to its employees (Haupt, 2008: 129).

SAB were much less accommodating however, and sought a remedy for dilution of its trademark through the courts. Both the High Court of South Africa and the Supreme Court of Appeal found in favour of SAB, commenting that the race-related content bordered on hate speech. The case was finally appealed to the Constitutional Court. Although section 34(1)(c) of the Trademarks Act (no. 194 of 1993) protects trademarks from 'detrimental' use, the Court decided that the section had to be interpreted in conjunction with the constitutional guarantee of freedom of expression. SAB had failed to produce any evidence that harm to its brand would result from the sale of the shirt, merely arguing that the harm was self-evident since the shirt associated the brand with racism. The 'discomfort of a trademark proprietor with criticism' was insufficient (Rens, 2005: 21).

This innovative Constitutional Court judgment was not generally well received by specialist IP lawyers in South Africa. A representative of one of the country's leading firms described it as 'a serious setback for any trade mark proprietor wishing to enforce rights in its well-known trade marks' (Webster, 2005). Another practitioner of IP law argued that the impact of the Constitutional Court decision was effectively to create a new avenue for appeal in trademark matters, beyond the Supreme Court of Appeal (Dean, 2005: 11). Indeed, Dean suggested that the effect of the judgment was to 'shake the foundations of trade mark law as known and practiced in the past' (2005: 11). Commentators later expressed doubt over whether IPR cases were constitutional issues at all, describing the Constitutional Court as 'ill-suited' for IP cases, given the inadequate 'IPR expertise and … commercial litigation skills' of the justices (Harms and Dean, 2012: 105).

Historically, geographical indications (GIs) are the oldest form of trademark, a rough and ready guarantee of quality based on public knowledge of regional reputation. Examples of this were oranges from Seville or wine from Burgundy (Blakeney, 2006: 295–296). GIs are included in the TRIPS regime, but there is little international agreement about this form of protection, especially between the US and the EU, but also between industrialized and developing countries:

> many problems about the legal treatment and level of protection of GIs continue to be debated … This has been a long-term source of international controversy … it may be true that GIs are similar to trademarks in that they function as source indicators, [but] these two different types of intellectual property rights are governed by very divergent systems of laws and bodies of beliefs … [some] countries disregard the validity of such protection because such names do not deserve protection under trademark law and many product names are considered to be generic terms. (Cortès Martín, 2004: 287–288)

The absence of clear international agreements on GI standards has exposed South African producers to risk on at least two occasions. Rooibos [*Afrikaans*: 'red bush'] tea is a popular caffeine-free herbal beverage that South Africa exports to the EU and the US. It is grown only in the Cederberg region of the Western Cape, mainly by small-scale black and coloured farmers, and about half the annual production of around 12,000 tons is exported. It is also used in some cosmetic products. In the 1990s, a US company, Burke International, registered 'rooibos' as a trademark, at a time when the tea was virtually unknown in the North American market. Subsequently the company began to demand royalties from tea importers, and in 2004 the matter went to court. Burke agreed to limit its control to cosmetics (Gardiner, 2004: 1), but this was refused. In January 2005 a US court ruled the trademark invalid, and it was voluntarily surrendered six months later (AHPA, 2005)

In 2010 the NGO Natural Justice launched a campaign to draw attention to five patent applications lodged in 2009 by Nestlé related to the use of rooibos and honeybush plants in cosmetics applications. The patents conflicted with the requirements of South African and international legislation, and after negative media coverage the company dropped the applications (Natural Justice, 2011).

In March 2013 the issue arose yet again, this time in France, where Compagnie de Trucy applied to register both 'rooibos' and 'South African rooibos' as trademarks (Marais, 2013b: 9). The move attracted wide press coverage in South Africa. The French position, in summary, was that in the absence of protection in South Africa itself, such protection could not reasonably be claimed in other countries. At the time of writing, the DTI had intervened, requesting the EU to grant protection not only for rooibos, but also for honeybush tea and Karoo lamb (Marais, 2013a: 1). In an analysis of the question, including the fact that it has now surfaced for the second time, Dean suggested a solution under the Merchandise Marks Act of 1941, which allows for the prohibition of the use of a particular word in any trademark, and would amount to local protection. Dean also criticized the government for what he called its failure to take any 'concrete or effective steps to protect and control the use of this term in South Africa or elsewhere' (Dean, 2013b: 6); another report in a popular magazine referred to the government as 'weak' on the issue (McGarrity, 2013: 20).

However, in this case as in others, there are moralizing narratives at work, with casts of characters assigned their roles as heroes or villains. The dominant rhetorical representation has rapacious foreign companies (whether French or American) appropriating GIs to the disadvantage of poor black and coloured farmers without agency, and incompetent government bureaucrats fumbling for a solution. This is not to say that the narrative is a misrepresentation, merely that the relationship of rooibos producers and exporters to their IPRs is more complex than such oversimplification allows. There are poor black and coloured farmers, certainly, but the rooibos export market is dominated by three local firms (including a cosmetics company) as well as several smaller ones (Biénabe et al., 2009: 65). These smaller players have also been very active in claiming IPRs. In fact, three years ago there were 13 rooibos-related trademarks either registered or applied for in the United Kingdom; 16 in the United States; five in Australia; five in Germany; and nine in South Africa itself (Biénabe et al., 2009: 78–82).

COMPETING NARRATIVES IN SOUTH AFRICAN COPYRIGHT

South African copyright law is comprehensively covered in Dean's authoritative *Handbook of South African Copyright Law*, a loose-leaf publication that is regularly updated; the most recent revision was issued in April 2012. The *Handbook* includes a synopsis of the law of copyright, a digest of authorities, a compendium of legislation and a section on precedents (Dean, 2012). Given the current availability of Dean's book, therefore, this section will focus on aspects of the political economy and discourse of copyright. Competing narratives have emerged around the most famous of all South African copyright disputes, the Solomon Linda case; copyright protection is contested terrain in education, and government policy in this area, as in others, remains seriously underdeveloped.

The current South African legislation, the Copyright Act no. 98 of 1978, is outdated. It has been amended eight times, most recently by the Copyright Amendment Act no. 38 of 1997, which incorporated TRIPS-related alterations to the law. Currently, the legislation lists nine categories of work eligible for protection, including computer programs. South Africa has not submitted to pressure to harmonize with US practice, and the copyright term remains at the author's lifetime plus 50 years. Government publications are also protected for 50 years, except for 'official texts of a legislative, administrative or legal nature' (section 12(8)(a) of the Act). There is no presumption of copyright in South African law. The South African publishing industry is highly developed, with a strong emphasis on the English language and to some extent the Afrikaans markets, but with little activity in widely-spoken African languages such as isiZulu or seSotho other than in the school textbook market. Annual turnover for the industry in 2011 was calculated at R3.6 billion (US$498 million) (PASA, 2011: 210).

The best-known South African copyright case is the lawsuit brought against the Disney Corporation in 2004 by the daughters of

Solomon Linda, a black South African musician who in 1938 had written and recorded a song, *Mbube*. This later became the basis for a series of hits by US musicians, none of whom credited Linda or paid any royalties to him or his descendants. The song was also used in the Disney animated film *The Lion King*. In 2000 the story was broken in a *Rolling Stone* article by Rian Malan, who estimated that *Mbube* earned about US$15 million just in the film version. In the ensuing court case, with backing from the South African government, Owen Dean, then still practicing rather than teaching law, relied on a little-noticed quirk of the Copyright Act of 1916, which incorporated the Imperial Copyright Act of 1911, and under which Linda's daughters had re-acquired rights to their father's song. An out-of-court settlement was reached in early 2006, for an undisclosed amount and the right to future royalties (Dean, 2006: 10).

This narrative has been told many times and is regarded as a triumph by most commentators. Essentially, the moral of the tale is that the IP system may be abused sometimes, but it can also deliver just outcomes. The *New York Times*, for example, headlined a story about the settlement, published on 22 March 2006, 'In the jungle, the unjust jungle, a small victory'. Dean himself wrote that 'from a South African perspective the saga has a happy ending and there is some pride in having successfully championed the cause of the small creator among entertainment industry giants' (2006: 10). In a recent assessment, he added that this was 'a rags-to-riches fairy tale … in true fairy tale fashion, the victors ought to live happily ever after' (Dean, 2013a). 'Ought to', perhaps: but there is some evidence that even at the most mundane level things did not work out so well. Some years later, a press report suggested that the Linda family was seriously dissatisfied and relations between them and Dean had soured (Oliphant, 2009c: 6).

There are other possible readings of the story, which do not necessarily serve to legitimize the IP status quo. As Ovesen and Haupt point out, the de-racialized rhetorical structure of the Linda case fits the 'grand narrative' of post-apartheid South Africa in which justice is eventually done, however belatedly and at whatever cost. The problem is that the property relations and the structures of power

> that enable the continuation of huge socio-economic disparities are still in place … key problems … persist in dominant assumptions about intellectual property, the ill-treatment of countless other black musicians during apartheid, as well as racialised class inequalities that persist nearly two decades after apartheid. (Ovesen and Haupt, 2011: 74)

Erlmann argues that the settlement had an impact on 'African cultural industries', not as a correction of injustice, but as the perpetuation of 'power imbalances in post-apartheid South Africa … both in terms of judicial practice and, more especially, in light of the persistence of race in public discourse pertaining to the appropriation of the country's cultural heritage' (Erlmann, forthcoming). The Linda case provides ideological support for the perpetuation of existing power and property relations. Both the government and the private sector want South Africa to become a 'player' in global IP industries, an effort that

> involves and, at the same time, legitimizes the massive expansion of proprietary rights to cultural practices and artifacts … Increasingly this IP expansionism is supplemented by the thinly veiled claim that the individual rewards to be reaped from a new spirit of musical entrepreneurship by far outweigh the broader social goods realized in communal, 'traditional' forms of cultural practice as a source of innovation and economic growth. (Erlmann, forthcoming)

The misleadingly titled Copyright Review Commission (CRC) chaired by Judge Ian G. Farlam was set up by the DTI in November 2010 to investigate music royalties, and submitted its report in 2011. When it was established, 'nine years after the enactment of needle-time legislation in 2002, *not a cent had been paid in royalties to musicians and record companies*' (CRC, 2011: 3, emphasis added) and the CRC's primary task was to find out why. The amounts involved totalled 'millions of rand' (CRC, 2011: 3). The report concluded that the problem lay in legislation that failed to protect rights-holders sufficiently, but evidence in court cases has pointed to less comforting explanations. The Southern African Music Rights Organization (SAMRO) was sued in early 2009 over royalties allegedly owed to the deceased South African singing star Brenda Fassie. Despite a string of hits, Fassie had received only a few cents in royalties from SAMRO between 1989 and 2003 (Oliphant, 2009a: 3); a former SAMRO CEO commented drily that the record business was 'a mafia industry' (Oliphant, 2009b: 3).

The recording industry is not the only arena of struggle over copyright. Students at South African universities and colleges, like their counterparts elsewhere, need but often cannot gain access to affordable learning materials, such as textbooks and course readers (collections of photocopied articles, chapters and excerpts put together by the lecturers themselves). Over the past decade or so, another South African collecting society, the Dramatic, Artistic and Literary Rights Organization (DALRO), has persuaded many universities either to adopt transactional processing of permissions or, more efficiently, to sign blanket licences for the production of course packs, which has 'progressively ... brought [the problem] under control' (PICC, 2004: 14), although sometimes at the cost of giving up fair dealing rights. But the market for complete photocopied textbooks continues to thrive, since the

> prevailing form of infringement [is] the unlawful copying by students of whole books as a substitute for buying them. Most piracy takes place off campus, in copy shops usually strategically situated near the gates of the university or technikon ... Publishers are aware of schools in which entire textbooks are being copied and sold by teachers and cases taken up by publishers have revealed wholesale production of pirated, photocopied textbooks being supplied to state schools. (PICC, 2004: 14)

The cost of the original textbooks is a major factor favouring the production of these infringing photocopies (Luthuli, 2012: 7). In recent years SAFACT has largely taken over from DALRO in running raids and sting operations against the copy shops. This may be an indication either of DALRO's limited capacity and general unwillingness to engage in litigation, or of its new orientation as a 'copyright asset management' organization rather than a mere collecting society (Kennedy, 2012: 7).

There has been no landmark Kinko-type case in South Africa to determine the limits of fair dealing (see *Basic Books v Kinko's* (758 F. Supp. 1522)), and collecting societies and universities alike tend to avoid litigation. This is not to say that prosecutions never happen; in 1996, in a high-profile action, DALRO went after Prontaprint, a copy shop chain that was offering students pre-bound photocopies of standard textbooks (*Mail and Guardian,* 1996: 10).

With the growth of the loosely-structured global 'Access to Knowledge' or A2K movement, however, perspectives have begun to shift. A2K takes as axiomatic the idea that access to knowledge is fundamental to social and economic development and to the exercise of other rights. Hence, it has itself the character of a fundamental human right (Armstrong et al., 2010: 1, 128, 205). The role of the copyright system in limiting rather than facilitating access, especially in poor countries, has been the subject of research by such groups as the heterogeneous Copy South research network, which included South African participants (Story et al., 2006). Similarly, the South African Open Copyright Review was carried out in 2008, and showed that it is almost impossible for a South African citizen to live a copyright-compliant life (Rens et al., 2008: 4–5). The Review argued that permitting parallel imports of non-medical products would have a major impact in facilitating access to learning materials (Rens et al., 2008: 73).

The African Copyright and Access to Knowledge (ACA2K) research network investigated access to learning materials in eight African countries – Egypt, Ghana,

Kenya, Morocco, Mozambique, Senegal, South Africa and Uganda – and found that existing fair use and fair dealing exemptions are inadequate in meeting the needs of learners (Armstrong et al., 2010). The project found that legislation in six of the eight countries studied included provisions forbidding the 'circumvention' of technological protection measures (TPMs). These laws made it illegal for users to perform, in the digital environment, actions that would otherwise be entirely permissible (Schönwetter and Ncube, 2011: 65). Indeed, in the case of South Africa, the Electronic Communications and Transactions Act (no. 25 of 2002) has established standards of such rigidity that they are considered stronger than those in force in the US:

> It is incomprehensible that South Africa, a developing country, should opt for a system of protecting TPMs that is far more destructive of research and education than the systems adopted in the United States and Europe. Were the United States to conclude a free trade agreement with the Southern African Customs Union (SACU), and were such agreement to mandate the adoption of protection of TPMs along American lines, researchers and educators in South Africa would be better off than they are now. It is a supreme irony that the South African negotiators have been resisting the inclusion of such protection in an FTA, probably because the left hand (one government department) does not know what the right hand (another government department) has done. (Visser, 2006: 62)

It is probably too early to comment on the impact of the 'Marrakesh Treaty to Facilitate Access to Published Works by Visually Impaired Persons and Persons with Print Disabilities' that was signed in June 2013 by 51 countries. The treaty, which has been widely welcomed, formalizes the reproduction of copyright-protected materials without the permission of the rights-holder for the use of the visually-impaired, and makes it legal to transport such copies from jurisdiction to jurisdiction. It is worth noting that South Africa was not one of the 51 signatories; the South African delegation to the conference that agreed to the document was headed only by a deputy minister (who was not from the DTI); and last, the treaty is not mentioned at all in the government's draft IP policy published in September 2013 (DTI, 2013). This last omission was criticized by at least one commentator (Low, 2013).

CONCEPTUALIZING IP ANEW: THE SOUTH AFRICAN ROLE

An analysis of the different sectors of South African IP shows various narratives at work, each one largely self-contained and failing to intersect with the others. There is a dominant 'industry discourse', driven by the interests of multi-national entertainment corporations, relying on questionable data on piracy levels and pushing for strict enforcement practices and the criminalization of infringement. The general public is bombarded with propaganda equating infringement with theft; 'newspaper readers and TV audiences ... are exposed to a flood of industry-generated stories about the negative effects of piracy' (Primo and Lloyd, 2011: 120). Unsurprisingly, however, there is evidence of

> a significant disconnect between the media narrative and actual consumer attitudes, which show much greater diversity and widespread tolerance of piracy ... pirate practices [are] completely normalized and integrated into daily life. (Primo and Lloyd, 2011: 120–121)

There is also resistance to the enforcement agenda for IP infringements from the massively over-stretched judicial system, which generally imposes lenient sentences and fines rather than the more stringent penalties demanded by industry rhetoric.

The discourse of the community of IP practitioners reveals anxiety about South Africa's global status and a commitment to upholding the letter of the law, but little interest in interrogating basic assumptions about IP. There is academic analysis from a legal-realist perspective, concerned to discover what the impact of the IP system is on society at large. Finally, there are civil society organizations impatient with the failure of IP to take into account the urgent health and other needs of the desperately poor, or to respect fundamental human rights when profits are at stake.

This has as much to do with the globalization of IP as a regime as it does with specifically South African conditions. The doctrine of national treatment, established in the Berne Convention in 1886, has a long history; both domestic and foreign copyrighted works are equally protected in a given jurisdiction by that jurisdiction's rules. Holders of patents, by contrast, have no easy way of enforcing their rights across national borders (Trimble, 2012: 81–125). What both systems share, however, is the idea that national jurisdictions should establish what is protected, and the question, to what extent? In reality, this is no longer entirely the case. Despite formal recognition of 'national treatment' by TRIPS and the WTO, 'harmonization' is now a much more important concept, meaning the adoption of US standards for copyright terms, anti-circumvention and enforcement measures. IP law is fast becoming a nomothetic, one-size-fits all, global system:

> States around the globe are converging upon the same set of intellectual property standards in areas of law such as copyright, patents, trademarks and industrial designs, as well as upon the remedies available for the enforcement of these rights. Moreover, in many cases states are shifting to higher standards than previously prevailed in their domestic law – longer terms of protection, fewer exceptions to the scope of rights and sometimes new rights ... the case for the globalisation of intellectual property rights is anything but persuasive ... [and] intellectual property rules may well be an obstacle to development. (Drahos, 2002: 1)

The WIPO Development Agenda represents a push-back from the countries of the global south in the opposite direction. The history of the development agenda has been told before (e.g. May, 2007a, 2007b), and is dealt with in detail elsewhere in this volume; disappointingly, South Africa has not played a leading role. WIPO's job, as a specialized UN agency, has always been to *promote* IP on the assumption that strong IP supports development. The Development Agenda, by contrast, is based on the idea that, as an agency of the United Nations, WIPO can and should only be promoting IP *to the extent that it supports the developmental objectives of the UN as a whole* (May, 2007b: 76). Nevertheless, the Agenda is a cautious rather than radical programme; it seeks

> neither to generally reduce the protection for IPRs, nor to suggest that intellectual property [is] the only problem. Rather the Development Agenda seeks a re-orientation of the WIPO towards a more developmental set of concerns, and sets out the argument that the protection and enforcement of IPRs cannot be seen as an end in itself. (May, 2007b: 78)

In this context, is there a shift within South Africa towards a more nuanced understanding and application of IP, an IP that in whatever way supports economic development? Some of the South African jurisprudence seems to indicate that this may be the case; but government policy remains confused and confusing, and is seen by many as uncritically maximalist. The government's position remains that the construction of an appropriately developmental national IP system is best achieved in the context of South Africa's BRICS membership, and using the opportunities of the WIPO Development Agenda (Davies interview, 2013).

There are indications of government support for a new continent-wide IP organization, the Pan-African IP Organization (PAIPO), supported by the African Union (Daniels, 2013). It is possible that South Africa, which does not belong to either of the two existing African IP bodies (Anglophone ARIPO and Francophone OAPI), will lead the new organization. The draft statute of PAIPO – 'drafted by true believers of IP-maximalist ideology' (Baker, 2012) – has been sharply criticized for its failure to take account of any of 'the challenges facing Africa with respect to access to medicines and learning materials' (Ncube and Lailtaika, 2013: 116).

The South African IP landscape is not a well-cultivated garden in which order reigns; to mix metaphors, it is instead a cacophonous environment in which different voices strive to be heard above the others, and in which agreement about the social, economic and legal function of the elements of IP is rarely found. It is, above all, a fiercely contested terrain, and it is clear that popular awareness of its importance – first of all in public health and then in education – is rapidly growing. It is unlikely that IP will ever again be seen, in South Africa at least, as a boring technical subject best left to the specialists.

ACKNOWLEDGEMENTS

I gratefully acknowledge the assistance of Dilshaad Bray, Gino Cocchiaro, Matthew David, Adam Haupt, Judith Head, Caroline Ncube and Tobias Schönwetter in the preparation of this chapter. An earlier version was presented at the 'Sage Handbook of Intellectual Property' Symposium, University of Durham, 29–30 June 2013, and in the seminar series of the IP Unit, Faculty of Law, University of Cape Town, 11 November 2013, and I am grateful to participants in those meetings for their supportive criticism and feedback. Full responsibility for any errors of fact or interpretation is mine alone.

REFERENCES

Blogs About South African IP

Afro-IP – www.afro-ip.blogspot.com/

Owen Dean – http://blogs.sun.ac.za/iplaw/news-3/from-ipstell/

Caroline Ncube – www.carolinebncube.wordpress.com/

Denise Nicolson – www.africanlii.org/blogs/denise/

Interviews

Rob Davies (Minister of Trade and Industry), Cape Town, 25 April 2013.

Moosa Ebrahim (Chief of Staff, Ministry; DTI), Cape Town, 25 April 2013.

Published Sources

AHPA (2005) 'Rooibos trademark abandoned', American Herbal Products Association, 27 June, (http://newhope360.com/supply-news-amp-analysis/rooibos-trademark-abandoned).

Alberts, Wim and Jonathan Brand (2008) 'Arbitration and mediation in trade-mark disputes: a survey of the field', *Juta's Business Law* 16(1): 5–8.

Anderson, Jane (2010) *Indigenous/Traditional Knowledge and Intellectual Property.* Durham NC: Center for the Study of the Public Domain, Duke University School of Law.

Armstrong, C. et al. (eds) (2010) *Access to Knowledge in Africa: the Role of Copyright.* Cape Town: UCT Press.

Baker, Brook (2012) 'Intellectual property policy incoherence at the African Union threatens access to medicines: proposed Pan-African IP organization a terrible idea', 26 October (www.lists.keionline.org/pipermail/ip-health_lists.keionline.org/2012-September/002463.html).

Biénabe, Estelle et al. (2009) 'An economic analysis of the evolution in intellectual property strategies in the South African agricultural sector: the rooibos industry', in: David Kaplan et al. (eds) *The Economics of Intellectual Property in South Africa.* Geneva: WIPO, pp.56–83.

Blakeney, Michael (2006) 'Geographical indications and TRIPS', in: Michael Pugatch (ed.) *The Intellectual Property Debate: Perspectives from Law, Economics and Political Economy.* Cheltenham: Edward Elgar, pp.293–304.

Cortès Martin, José Manuel (2004) 'The WTO TRIPS agreement: the battle between the Old and the New World over the protection of geographical indications', *Journal of World Intellectual Property* 7(3): 287–326.

CRC (2011) *Copyright Review Commission Report.* Pretoria: Department of Trade and Industry.

Daniels, Linda (2013) 'South Africa leaning toward support of Pan-African IP office, minister says', *Intellectual Property Watch*, 28 February (www.ip-watch.org/2013/02/28/south-africa-leaning-toward-support-of-pan-african-ip-office-minister-says/).

Davies, Rob (2011) Speech delivered by the Minister of Trade and Industry, Dr Rob Davies, MP, in the National Assembly on the Intellectual Property Laws Amendment Bill. 27 October (http://www.dti.gov.za/delegationspeechdetail.jsp?id=2288).

Dean, Owen (1996a) 'Just desserts for rustlers', *Financial Mail* 20 September: 102.

Dean, Owen (1996b) 'McDonalds turns the tables on trademark hijackers', *South African Mercantile Law Journal* 8: 408–423.

Dean, Owen (2005) 'Trade mark misuse is a laughing matter', *The Marques Newsletter* 84: 10–11.

Dean, Owen (2006) 'The return of the lion', *WIPO Magazine* April: 8–10.

Dean, Owen (2011) 'The Mad Hatter in Wonderland', *Anton Mostert Chair of Intellectual Property Blog* 1 November (http://blogs.sun.ac.za/iplaw/2011/11/01/the-mad-hatter-in-wonderland/).

Dean, Owen (2012) *Handbook of South African Copyright Law* [Service 14]. Cape Town: Juta.

Dean, Owen (2013a) *Awakening the Lion: The Case of the Lion Sleeps Tonight*. Cape Town: Tafelberg. [Unpaginated e-book.]

Dean, Owen (2013b) 'Beating about the rooibos', *Without Prejudice* 13(3): 6–7.

Drahos, Peter (2002) 'Introduction,' in: Peter Drahos and Ruth Mayne (eds) *Global Intellectual Property Rights: Knowledge, Access and Development*. London: Palgrave Macmillan, pp.1–9.

DST (2005) *Indigenous Knowledge Systems*. Pretoria, Department of Science and Technology.

DTI (2013) 'Draft national policy on intellectual property (IP) of South Africa: a policy framework', Government Gazette 36816, 4 September: 3–43.

Dutfield, Graham (2004) *Intellectual Property, Biogenetic Resources and Traditional Knowledge*. London: Earthscan.

The Economist (1997) 'Johannesburgers and fries', *The Economist* 27 September: 79–80.

Erlmann, Veit (forthcoming) 'Lion's share: intellectual property rights and the South African music industry', in: Mamadou Diawara and Ute Röschenthaler (eds) *Copyright Africa: How Intellectual Property, Media and Markets Transform Immaterial Cultural Goods*. Canon Pyon, Herefordshire: Sean Kingston Publishing.

European Medicines Agency (2011) *Assessment Report on Pelargonium Sidoides DC and/or Pelargonium Reniforme Curt., radix*. London: EMA, Committee on Herbal Medicinal Products 31 March (EMA/HMPC/560962/2010).

Gardiner, Bryan (2004) 'New US deal on rooibos an insult to South Africa', *Cape Argus* 27 May: 1.

Greaves, Thomas (1996) 'Tribal rights', in: Stephen B. Brush and Doreen Stabinsky (eds) *Valuing Local Knowledge: Indigenous People and Intellectual Property Rights*. Washington DC: Island Press, pp.25–40.

Harms, Louis and Owen Dean (2012) 'South Africa's specialized Intellectual Property Courts regime', in: *Study on Specialized Intellectual Property Courts*. Washington DC: International Intellectual Property Institute; US Patent and Trademark Office.

Haupt, Adam (2008) *Stealing Empire: P2P, Intellectual Property and Hip-Hop Subversion*. Cape Town: HSRC Press.

Hughes, Justin (2012) 'Traditional knowledge, cultural expression, and the siren's call of property', *San Diego Law Review* 49: 1215–1266.

Job, Chris (1996a) 'The McDonalds appeal decisions', *De Rebus* October: 677–680.

Job, Chris (1996b) 'The McDonalds decisions', *De Rebus* May: 317–322.

Jooste, Cobus (2013) 'Sui Generis TK Bill Published in the Gazette', *Anton Mostert Chair of Intellectual Property Blog* 9 April (http://blogs.sun.ac.za/iplaw/2013/04/09/hot-off-the-presses-sui-generis-tk-bill-published-in-the-gazette/).

Kelbrick, Roshana (2008) 'The W**d C*p of 2*1*: FIFA's intellectual property rights in South Africa', *Journal of Intellectual Property Law and Practice* 3(5): 327–333.

Kennedy, Christina (2012) 'When it is easy, all have the right to copy', *Business Day* [Johannesburg] 19 July: 7.

Low, Marcus (2013) 'Blind sidelined by Department of Trade and Industry', *GroundUp* 2 October (www.groundup.org.za/content/blind-sidelined-department-trade-and-industry).

Luthuli, Nosipho (2012) 'Shops warned on copying books', *Daily News* [Durban] 1 February: 7.

McGarrity, Emma (2013) 'Small farmers in a stir as government remains weak on tea trademark', *The Big Issue* 17(208) April–May: 20–23.

McKune, Craig (2010) 'Ground-breaking victory for community against drug giant', *Cape Times* 28 January: 4.

Mail and Guardian (1996) 'Publishers crack down on illegal copying', *Mail and Guardian* 22–28 March: 10.

Marais, Jana (2013a) 'Davies goes to war over rooibos trademark', *Sunday Times* [Johannesburg] 24 March: 1.

Marais, Jana (2013b) 'Rooibos fights to protect its name', *Sunday Times* [Johannesburg] 3 February: 9.

May, Christopher (2007a) 'The World Intellectual Property Organization and the Development Agenda', *Global Governance* 13(2): 161–170.

May, Christopher (2007b) *The World Intellectual Property Organization: Resurgence and the Development Agenda*. London: Routledge.

Mugabe, John (1999) 'Intellectual property protection and traditional knowledge', in: *Intellectual Property and Human Rights*. Geneva: World Intellectual Property Organization, pp.97–125.

Natural Justice (2011) *Biopiracy/Nestle-Rooibos Case* (www.naturaljustice.org/our-work/campaigns).

Ncube, Caroline and Eliamani Laltaika (2013) 'A new intellectual property organization for Africa?', *Journal of Intellectual Property Law and Practice* 8(2): 114–117.

Oliphant, Lumka (2009a) 'Brenda got five cents in 14 years', *City Press* 22 February: 3.

Oliphant, Lumka (2009b) 'Fassie funds queries open up hornet's nest', *City Press* 15 February: 3.

Oliphant, Lumka (2009c) 'Lion King's heirs in painful fight', *City Press* 21 June: 6.

Ovesen, Håvard and Adam Haupt (2011) 'Vindicating capital: heroes and villains in *A Lion's Trail*', *Ilha do Desterro* 61 (July–December): 73–107.

Parkes, Kathryn (2010) 'Germans to fight E[astern] C[ape] town over ban on cough mixture patent', *Daily Dispatch* 3 February: 5.

PASA (2011) *Annual Book Industry Survey 2011*. Pretoria: Publishers Association of South Africa.

Patel, Surendra J. (1996) 'Can the intellectual property rights system serve the interests of indigenous knowledge?', in: Stephen B. Brush and Doreen Stabinsky (eds) *Valuing Local Knowledge: Indigenous People and Intellectual Property Rights*. Washington DC: Island Press, pp.305–322.

PICC (2004) *PICC Report on Intellectual Property Rights in the Print Industries Sector*. Cape Town: Print Industries Cluster Council.

Primo, Natasha and Libby Lloyd (2011) 'South Africa', in: Joe Karaganis (ed.) *Media Piracy in Developing Economies*. New York: Social Science Research Council, pp.99–147.

Rens, Andrew (2005) 'A powerful, symbolic victory', *Rhodes Journalism Review* 25: 21.

Rens, Andrew et al. (2008). *Report on the South African Open Copyright Review*. Durbanville: Shuttleworth Foundation.

Rose, Sarah (2010) *For All the Tea in China: How England stole the World's Favourite Drink and Changed History*. New York: Penguin.

Russell, Susan (1996) 'Intellectual property law up to scratch', *Business Day* 18 September: 11.

Schönwetter, Tobias and Caroline Ncube (2011) 'New hope for Africa? Copyright and access to knowledge in the digital age', *Info* 13(3): 64–74.

Sibuye, Rodney, et al. (2012) 'The Bushbuckridge BCP: traditional health practitioners organize for ABS in South Africa', *Participatory Learning and Action* 65: 101–108.

Story, Alan et al. (2006) *The Copy/South Dossier: Issues in the Economics, Politics and Ideology of Copyright in the Global South*. Canterbury: Copy/South Research Group.

Trimble, Marketa (2012) *Global Patents: Limits of Transnational Enforcement*. New York: Oxford University Press.

Vermeylen, Saskia (2007) 'Contextualizing fair and equitable: the San's reflections on the Hoodia benefit-sharing agreement', *Local Environment* 12(4): 423–436.

Visser, Coenraad (1996) 'McDonalds fried: foreign trademarks in South Africa', *Juta's Business Law* 4(1): 15–18.

Visser, Coenraad (2006) 'Technological protection measures: South Africa goes overboard. Overbroad', *Southern African Journal of Information and Communication* 7: 54–63.

Webster, Charles (2005) 'The laughing is over: setback for trade mark dilution', *Spoor and Fisher* 1 June (www.spoor.com/home/index.php?ipk ArticleID=150).

Wheeldon, Ron (2007) 'South Africa, trade mark law: where is it heading?', in *Building and Enforcing Intellectual Property Value*. London: IP Media Group, pp.253–255.

Wimpey, Brian (2012) 'South Africa', in: *World Trademark Review Yearbook 2012/2013*. London: IP Media Group, pp.255–262.

Wynberg, Rachel (2010) 'Hot air over hoodia', *Seedling* October: 22–24.

Wynberg, Rachel and Roger Chennells (2009) 'Green diamonds of the south: an overview of the San-Hoodia case', in Rachel Wynberg et al. (eds) *Indigenous Peoples, Consent and Benefit Sharing: Lessons from the San-Hoodia Case*. Dordrecht: Springer, pp.89–124.

Wynberg, Rachel et al. (2009) 'Introduction,' in Rachel Wynberg et al. (eds.) *Indigenous Peoples, Consent and Benefit Sharing: Lessons from the San-Hoodia Case*. Dordrecht: Springer, pp.3–10.

Zaina, Jacqueline (1996) 'Olympic hope boosted by cabinet agreement', *Business Day* 3 September: 9.

15

Author and Cultural Rights: The Cuban Case

Lillian Álvarez

INTRODUCTION

The opportunity for all to gain access to the results of a creation is a supposition of creation itself. Above all, the citizen must have the possibility of gaining access to knowledge and interacting with existing cultural wealth. Prior protection of a creation has the implicit recognition of precedence and offers the possibility of effectively exercising other basic human rights that the vast majority of people lack today. Universal access to education, the opportunity for people to increase their capacity for art appreciation, the opportunity to express themselves, the opportunity to access specialized teaching and other cultural options that allow for the enrichment of their spirituality and would help develop their talent, constitute a series of values that transcend the acquisition of profit for authors as the basis of creation. In Cuba, the execution of a defined cultural policy where the principle of author's rights is subordinated to the broader interests of social necessity has made possible a widespread diffusion of science, technology, education and culture. This policy has been fundamental to Cuba's educational and cultural achievements.

This chapter begins with several stories that have not seen widespread distribution, but help reveal some of the abuses and absurd situations provoked by the laws protecting author's rights. These stories also help highlight the contradictions that can be generated by the contemporary application of copyright regulations.

The first example concerns the publication of an art history book in Canada. In 2012, the publication of *Global Vision and Culture Information: Prehistory to 1800* by a Canadian university press made the news because the textbook included no pictures. The book was published for a course on the history of art without images because no agreement could be reached regarding the rights to the pictures. However, despite the lack of images, students were required to purchase the book for $180 dollars.[1]

The second example deals with a 2012 report regarding the author's rights collection society in Belgium, SABAM. SABAM notified public libraries that they would have to pay for the right to read aloud to children in the library. The library programs, designed to promote reading, required communication in a raised voice that, although done by volunteers, was directed to groups of ten or more small children and was thus considered a public performance. According to calculations made by a representative of the Dilbeek library, reading aloud to children would require a payment of 250 euros a year.[2]

The third case refers to the work *White Dove* by Picasso. Many people have taken up this image as a symbol of peace, but copyright law prohibited its free use until 2013. One group caught by copyright law was the University of Malaga. The University of Malaga's heraldic shield 'has a white dove, a reproduction that appears in the lithography of the Malaga citizen Pablo Ruiz Picasso', according to its statutes in 2004. Despite Picasso's well-known anti-fascist and pacifist affiliations, his heirs sued the University over the use of the symbol. A long negotiation was necessary and the University ultimately decided to change the image to a different dove painted by the author himself to avoid payment of a reclaimed economic remuneration, although it must still pay for the merchandizing of products that carry the new logo of the University (Bravo, 2005).

The fourth case comes from Spanish jurist, David Bravo, who in his essay 'Copy this Book' tells the story of a New Jersey restaurant owner who tried to register the name 'World Trade Center' at 14: 40 on September 11 2001 so that he would become the 'owner' of the name and according to his own declaration, participate in the monetary benefits (Bravo, 2005).

Also little known is the case of the Argentine Horacio Potel, philosophy professor at the University of Buenos Aires who published on his website, and free of charge, the Spanish translations of the works of Nietzsche, Heidegger and Derrida. The professor was sued by the Argentine Chamber of Books in 2009 for infringing the copyright owners' rights. After a strong international campaign, the prosecution withdrew the charge since it had no effective proof of any damage caused by Potel's actions.

More dramatic was the case of 26-year old Aaron Swartz, programmer, writer and Internet activist, who was accused of downloading 4.8 million documents to allegedly share them on the net. The young co-author of the RSS 1.0 specifications, and collaborator on the Creative Commons license and the Open Library system was found hanged in his apartment. At the time of his death, Swartz was under federal indictment on 13 different counts for the downloads and if found guilty could have been fined up to 4 million dollars and could have served 50 years in prison.[3]

These are just a few examples that demonstrate the absurdities of copyright laws that increasingly promote the appropriation and mercantilist exploitation of the results of human ingenuity. In contrast to these introductory stories, in this chapter I deal with the Cuban case and seek to explain the principles that govern contemporary Cuban law, which prioritizes educational and cultural policies.

AUTHOR'S RIGHTS

There are two predominant legal systems in the world today. First, the Anglo-Saxon system of author's rights: copyright. Second, the continental system embodied by France, which is much closer to protecting personal rights. In both cases, the influence of corporate interests is so strong that international, regional and bilateral agreements, as well as national laws, have been invaded by the more utilitarian principles of copyright and differences between the two legal systems of rights have faded. In this manner, the original objectives of protecting *author's* rights have slowly disappeared in favor of protecting the economic interest of *owner's* rights.

In the context of author's rights, international agreements recognize two objectives: protection of the creator of a specific international work and protection of all human beings as receptors, or 'consumers', who must be guaranteed access to creative results. This double protection is defined in the Universal Declaration of Human Rights. Article 27 sets down, first, that:

> (1) All persons have the rights to freely take part in the cultural life of the community, to enjoy arts

> and participate in scientific progress and its benefits. (UN, 1948)

And secondly:

> (2) All persons have the right to the protection of moral and material interest that correspond to him/her regarding scientific, literary or artistic productions of which he or she are the authors. (UN, 1948)

'Persons' in their condition as 'authors' are not favored in the interpretation of how these rights are exercised. Instead, corporate interests have dramatically infringed upon the right to 'freely take part in the cultural life of society'. For this reason, the classification of author's rights as a human right (a claim supported by artists) is now questioned. However, legitimizing intellectual property in the hands of companies and corporations is not a human right but an effort to monopolize the circulation of works and is opposed in essence to the concept of cultural rights.

EVOLUTION OF CULTURAL RIGHTS

The first legal regulations of culture emanate from French rights that regulated legal storage in the 19th and 20th centuries (Prieto de Pedro, 2002). There were three areas of fundamental rights defined in the law: cultural heritage and centers of cultural storage (museums, archives and libraries); cultural industries (press and print regulations); and author's rights. No constitutional text explicitly mentions cultural rights until the 1917 constitution born of the Mexican Revolution, a document that used the concept of culture for the first time in the context of cultural rights.[4] The 1917 constitution signified a qualitative jump in the recognition of cultural rights that had been treated, until that point, in a dispersed manner. The new constitution demonstrated the interest of the state in protecting cultural rights. It is now the case that many constitutions established the obligation of public power to promote and spread national culture, and constitutions now include articles referring to the protection of cultural and linguistic heritage in defense of traditional knowledge and the rights of minorities, articles protecting the freedom of creation, and articles focused on the role of libraries and other institutions.

The important step of revolutionary Mexico during the early part of the 20th century paved the way for such cultural rights – as part of law – to achieve a general social balance among the different actors involved in cultural processes. However, far from embarking on a coherent and balanced effort to protect and safeguard these cultural rights, we have instead witnessed, on a worldwide level, an unbalanced development openly privileging economic interests. Today this is characterized by a hypertrophy of protection for some individuals and economic relations while at the same time it has led to an abandonment of the regulation and practical implementation of protection for other more necessary rights.

In the UN, for example, more than 60 years since the approval of the Universal Declaration of Human Rights and more than 40 years after the ratification of the International Pact of Economic, Social and Cultural Rights, there are still explanatory processes going on regarding the content, reach and effective implementation of cultural rights. No goal has yet been achieved in the international community to place economic, social and cultural rights on an equal standing and give them the same weight as civil and political rights. The so-called 'progressiveness' has not favored the full realization of the rights acknowledged in these international instruments but, on the contrary, the last 60 years has seen a retreat in the commitment of states to achieve these goals. It has also meant that for the majority of human beings from the underdeveloped world and for millions of persons in the developed world there has been a clear retreat in the enjoyment of these rights.[5]

Within the UNESCO framework, such significant instruments as the Convention for the Protection of Cultural Goods in the case of an Armed Conflict (protocols of 1954 and 1999); the Convention for the Safeguarding of Immaterial Cultural Heritage (2003); and the Convention for the Protection and Promotion of Cultural Expression (2005) are just three examples of efforts to protect culture that have been adopted. These conventions establish agreements that should be complied with by the signatory states and are of great importance for subsequent work. The execution of these protocols demonstrate, after all, that if there is no coherent political will regarding these commitments, their adoption is dead letter. And this is, unfortunately, what happens all too often. It is clear that the UNESCO Convention for Protection and Promotion of the Diversity of Cultural Expressions, for example, could be in conflict with the norms of the World Trade Organization. How this tension will be resolved is still to be determined, and there is no evidence of an open debate on the subject.[6]

While Conventions adopted by the community of nations within the framework of the United Nations Organization involve multiple clarifications and implementation issues to be put into practice, the fabric around the Berne Convention for the Protection of Literary and Artistic Works is a mesh of regulations set to become the most extended agreement on author's rights and it includes 164 countries.

The rights of intellectual property are today regulated by administrative treaties, primarily overseen by WIPO. This organization has worked diligently in favor of regulating each new use, including each new form of reproduction or public communication of a work in an effort to give rights owners real possibilities of guaranteeing their incomes. For example, between the inception of the World Wide Web in 1991 and regulations promoted by WIPO in the Treaty of Author's Rights[7] and other related rights[8] for the digital sphere, only five years passed. It is significant that WIPO achieved a normative instrument in such a short time for a subject that was so new and complex. On the other hand, the World Organization of the Blind called on WIPO, UNESCO and representative organizations of rights owners to collaborate on the evaluation of a detailed national and international legal rights protocol that would permit the blind and poor of vision to have full and equal access to all materials protected by author's rights without posing a threat to the legitimate interests of the authors and editors.[9] Thirteen years had to pass before a treaty in 2013 on this subject was made.[10]

The majority of author's rights laws currently in force in the countries of the South are laws very similar to the legal regulations of their old metropolises. These laws of eurocentrist[11] tone were transported to the old colonies without any change and served as a perfect basis for the subsequent adoption of the Berne Convention of 1886. The neocolonial homogenization forged through the Berne Convention made possible the TRIPS agreement, one of the basic agreements of the WTO.[12] The United States and industrialized nations have applied pressure on countries of the South to carry out the homogenization of national legislation required by TRIPS. They have even demanded the adoption of stricter regulations through international, multilateral and bilateral trade agreements (initiatives known as TRIPS Plus).[13]

The alleged protection that comes from Berne, which was ratified by the TRIPS agreements and extends to the treaties of free trade, clearly benefits authors and grants them authority to defend their privileges without taking into account rights of access. TRIPS includes enforcement mechanisms demanded by the WTO in the form of economic sanctions – a provision that is not at the disposition of any country through UNESCO conventions or available to defend cultural rights. Additionally, it should be pointed out that historically economic sanctions within the WTO framework have been a tool for legal action between developed nations or to impose sanctions upon underdeveloped nations.[14] From this framework of coercion a system is born that is a universal straitjacket and undoubtedly presents an analogy in the four continents. No international effort, not in the framework of the United Nations nor outside of it, has achieved a higher force against that system.

Using the deceit of liberalizing trade benefits, the large and small promoters of these concepts force the underdeveloped nations (in exchange for an alleged access to the most powerful markets) to invest resources in defense of business rights. States that are losing the languages and cultural practices of their original inhabitants find themselves committed to setting aside scarce resources to persecute those who copy products of large corporations, at the risk of economic sanctions. The debts owed to the developed nations rapidly become larger and important. It can be assured that the international regulatory instruments and the majority of national legislations on intellectual property have no bearing on the needs of the creators or the requirements of access by the citizens.

AUTHOR'S RIGHTS AND CREATION

The theoretical basis of author's rights begins with the recognition of originality as the prerequisite for protection of the work. The author (in its non-Anglo Saxon definition) has the exclusive right over the unique work that he/she has created. This idea corresponds to the so-called 'myth of genius' typical of Romanticism. According to Adolfo Colombres (2004), romanticism inverts the concept of originality as an anchor to an origin to convert it into an innovation that breaks or intends to break with the origin, with tradition. The 'I' becomes the object of the work itself. The concept of genius is linked to the cult of personality by taking the artist as the center of the world, around which turns, or should turn, the large majority of people, converted into passive receptors of their works, without any creativity at all. According to this theory, the individual is the genius that creates culture and not the whole of society, in its constant symbolic interaction (Colombres, 2004: 243).

At the end of the 1960s Roland Barthes (2013) broke with this idea and made a radical critique of the author as an institution. He stripped away the character of the author as the only one able to manipulate matter that no one else could mold. Literary work became something born from the writing of the author but that was significantly altered through time where, from an active position, the reader was a protagonist. In that manner Barthes returns written literature to the collective character of oral literature.

It can never be known who writes, whether the author or others that somehow force him, the individual or his personal experience, the psychology of the time or, in reality, the writing itself, for the simple reason that writing is renouncing individuality and becoming collective. From the moment we take up the pen, write as we have been taught, with a determined rhetoric, with a syntax, a grammar and some figure of speech set since antiquity, with a language that surrounds us and wraps us in an incessant murmur, a great store of references and signs of very diverse centers of culture operate as inter texts (Pérez Parejo, 2013).

Throughout history we have received a notable number of artistic and literary works in which we do not know the author. In reality, the author is a modern personage and has been assimilated according to the concept of each period: medieval anonymity, the individualism of the romantic genius, and the exaltation of the superstar author with commercial success. But this personage, as well as the forms of narrating, of making music, of making art in general and of reaching its fruits, is historically and socially conditioned and changing. And this is a more than sufficient reason to produce a change in the legal framework that regulates these processes.

We are in truth confronting a new epoch (Silva and Browne, 2006: 137–147). The aesthetic frontiers dissolve and technique acquires a radical 'status' as validity. Technology, therefore, is no longer a vehicle of transmission but a means as part of the media that opens up a breach or crossroads for the widespread symbolic universe of literature. It is no longer possible to refer to the media but to the inter media of images, sounds and texts and even biological experiences that are bonded to the technique. The authors who express themselves through new technologies do not find room in archaic laws that presuppose a finished piece, an extreme originality that ignores the aesthetics of a remix and ignores the constant inter-textual game of contemporary art, to mention just some examples.

At the same time the new technologies have caused changes that affect or modify the exercise of hereditary rights such as the right of reproduction, to the revolutionary speed and quality of the copies, and some works are lost in the limit of difference between the original and its duplicates. Speed has multiplied the degree of public communication of intangible copies, the facility to modify works, etc. But the owners of the rights (editorial companies, producers and software companies) have reacted by turning the screw once more regarding legislation with an increasing and more prohibitive tendency. If originally referring to artistic and literary works, today the author's rights extend to computer programs, databases, photographs and casual videos and much more. The times of protection have extended to an evident economic purpose, but such laws that benefit the monopolies guaranteeing a false scarcity are confronted by the infinite potential for reproduction at minimum costs.

In a world saturated by information and cultural 'content', what is disputed every minute is the eye or ear of the human 'consumer'. It becomes increasingly difficult to prevent copying or make it more difficult. The essential logic of new media's mechanisms for the 'all rights reserved' system is suicidal self-destruction.

At the same time texts transformed oral culture and the press revolutionized the means of the diffusion of knowledge, with the same force. This burst the audiovisual, hyper-text and hyper-media appearing with incalculable possibility for the public to navigate on their own within the work and construct their own actions in the diversity of spaces, times and points of view with images, sound and other scenarios and effects.

Concurring at the same time as authorships of very different origins and different degrees of participation a conflict is produced with current norms that demand identification of the author of a 'finished work'. These regulations do not respond to the broad spectrum of creative interactivity presented by new artistic expressions.

We are attending the announced death of the author. There is no doubt that there is a lack of authority present in this ancient personage. New relations have appeared in which rights cannot be left unscathed. Pseudonyms, 'collective names' and nameless pages constructed between authors and readers are an example of the rupture of the limits between 'emitters' or 'producers' of a text that modify the linear process of communication.

In an era of post-production, of genesis and collective re-appropriation through the Web, art can no longer continue to be seen as a series of finished works, in isolation, for its receptors to venerate or attempt to surpass; but as an immense bazaar in which the necessary elements are collected to recombine and re-create them. In spite of this, regulations included in international treaties continue to demand an author and a finished work, restricting its use and stubbornly and obsessively attempting to collect payment.

But it is necessary to make a basic distinction: although voices and images reach a larger media resonance, the creators are not only the few well paid stars, publicized, under contract and represented by multinationals – 'famous' objects to be admired or imitated but as unreal as the careers they sell. The majority of creators cannot even live by their artistic incomes. In the campaigns of the media, those who defend an alternative to rights of access are an irresponsible mass of usurpers who, armed with their computers, want to strip the creators of what is theirs, rob them and make them live in destitution. This is accompanied by the 'victimization' of the industry confronted by the problem called 'piracy', with figures that demonstrate the profits not collected or investments lost.

When a record by an author is sold he earns only seven or eight percent (and the interpreter a similar figure), and the rest is distributed between companies, editorials and societies of management; then we have to redefine the concepts of usurpers and usurped. When contracts with an infinite number of pages allegedly for the artists' benefit leaves little room for the right to take a photograph without the permission of their producer nor even to know exactly, as authors of literature may know, how many books were sold, then we have to clarify 'author's' rights. We are in the presence of a recognized inequality in the relation between large rights holding companies and the negotiating power of the artists and real creators. Again new obstacles, montages, mirages of rights emerge calling themselves 'author's rights'.

AUTHOR'S RIGHTS AND CULTURAL DIVERSITY

The UNESCO report on our creative diversity states that:

> In truth the majority of the [world's] cultural traditions have a less important role in the individual expression of the creative process [than] in the West.
>
> Very large art works continue to be collective creations such as the gothic cathedrals of Europe several centuries ago. In these contexts, the artist or craftsman, man or woman, are certainly one person but not necessarily a 'personality'. This contrasts also with the emphasis of the world mass culture of the 'stars' of the day, film celebrities or sports champions who are idolized out of proportion in relation to their creative contribution. Active participation of persons in the forms of cultural expression continues to be scorned. Frequently forgotten is that creation is a social force, whether by an amateur artist or the efforts of a community. (UNESCO, 1996)

International treaties and conventions referring to author's rights have universalized a system of protection (in truth of appropriation) in the 'Western' style, inadequate for many cultures, especially those of native peoples in which, for centuries, creation has been and is, in essence, collective. This system assumes colonial concepts of the theory of art that excludes manifestations of many peoples and has forced and imposed forms of appropriation that distorts and dulls them.

For certain historical reasons, modern Western art requires conditions of individual geniality, renovating rupture and uniqueness of the work for its products. These conditions, spurred by the strange logic of colonialism and regulatory demands, have been improperly applied to all forms of art. But native art – such as the *campesino*, like all forms of art that is not modern – does not abide by these conditions: it is neither the fruit of an absolute individual creation (although each artist reinterprets in his own way the collective deeply rooted codes), nor is it produced through transgressing innovations (in spite of the development that supposes a constant mobilization of the social imaginary), nor is it manifest in unrepeatable works (even when each specific form had to conquer the individual expressive and aesthetic talent) (Escobar, 2012: 29–30).

Well known is the process of extermination by the colonialist, in addition to the exploitation of natural resources. The devastation of the environment is the loss of human lives and has implied a cultural clash that laid waste to a large portion of the cultural and religious lives of the peoples conquered when the culture of the invader was imposed. As a continuation of this process, the neo-colonial period persists in the logic of assimilation according to European canons that assume as valid the concept of art-merchandise. This system requires the renunciation of traditional clothing, tattoos, body paint and all the other forms of inherited artistic expression that are not saleable – or they become catalogued as non-art.

The cultural and intellectual heritage of indigenous peoples includes much more than finished works shown or commercialized. This cultural and intellectual heritage is formed by the practices, knowledge and ways of life that characterize it. Also, individual creativity – many times relegated and deformed in function for its saleable quality – which is born from cultural heritage, persists and is enriched as heritage is modified to answer new and circumstantial moments. Culture cannot be conceived as static and dissociated from the real life of the peoples, designed only to acquire a space in the market, not in conquered lands or even in Europe.

Processes of creation, nourished from its many sources, pass through the sieve of time and experiment with decantation and natural assimilation. Not everything creative is able to transcend and be significant. These processes require adequate, flexible norms that protect and promote creative works as natural processes that are alive and that can confront the threat of being displaced because they are incapable of guaranteeing a profit. The most diverse cultures are moving toward extinction because there has been a loss of proper routes for their preservation and enrichment.

Despite numerous theoretical discussions and some small achievements in the definition of terms employed for international instruments linked to cultural rights, there has been no substantive advance in the protection of cultural rights worldwide. Take for example the 2005 UNESCO Convention on the Protection and Promotion of the Diversity of Cultural Expression. To date little can be demonstrated to show that there has been an efficient and significant move toward compliance with the objectives outlined in the 2005 convention.

AUTHOR'S RIGHTS AND RIGHT OF ACCESS

The possibility that everyone has access to the results of creation is a presumption of creation itself. Above all, the citizen must have a space for interaction with the entire cultural wealth created by society. They should have the opportunity of gaining access to and interacting with the wealth of existing knowledge formed by previous generations. Individual creation is not born in a vacuum. Although personal talent implants a particular seal on cultural expression, from our location in a language to the basic texts of our disciplinary knowledge, creativity is the result of what we inherit and have on loan from others. Thus, access to these sources, traditions and bodies of knowledge is an essential condition for the creation of new works. To gain access to the legacy of knowledge accumulated throughout history is a necessary condition for the recognition and effective exercise of basic human rights that is denied to many today.

Some time ago the Brazilian theologian Frei Betto (2003) said: 'To speak of human rights in Latin America is a luxury because we are still fighting for the rights of animals since eating, protective clothing, educating the young are animal necessities'. That is why referring to the cultural rights of the global South first implies analyzing not only the legal formulas adopted but the conditions of existence under which many live. A viable conversation about cultural rights must begin with the exercise of such basic rights as the rights to life, to food, to health, to work, to education, to an attended childhood, among others.

Soon after the adoption of the Universal Declaration of Human Rights, the deep-rooted ideological divisions in the world during the 1950s led to these rights being categorized. Unfortunately, these ideological divisions informed the later elaboration of human rights in ensuing treaties during the early 1960s and have left their mark on the present. For this reason, the First World Conference on Human Rights (Teheran, 1968), firmly established the interdependence and indivisibility of all human rights, an approach to human rights that was ratified in subsequent resolutions of the General Assembly of the United Nations. Of utmost importance is the recognition of the universality, the indivisibility and the interdependence of all human rights. What meaning can the right to freedom of expression have, for example, without the right to education? Or how can any right be enjoyed without the right of health or life? Cuba defends this integrationist viewpoint.

To understand cultural rights we must begin with such an integrationist view of human rights. The individual must have free and universal access to education, to the possibility of developing his capacity of appreciating the arts, to opportunities to access specialized training and to other cultural options that can lead to the enrichment of his spirituality and development of his talent. The exercise of these rights effectively constitutes the basis for the promotion of the protection of creation and its authors. For the full exercise of cultural rights, it is also necessary to count on a minimum of infrastructure available equally to all and a responsible cultural policy in tune with the obligation of the state to its population.

Today, enormous sums are paid to a few famous authors and artists that have created commercially accepted works. However, the majority of citizens lack support to even develop their creative potential. Legislation to protect authors' rights tends to benefit those that charge for the puerile use of works of the intellect and that pursue and viciously condemn any copy or participation in the exchange of works. The monopoly of the cultural industry destroys the diffusion of works and genres that have no commercial acceptance; it also destroys the possibility of promoting creation at a social level and dangerously acts against cultural diversity. Confronted by an absence of an inclusive cultural policy, the market becomes the supreme judge and it establishes hierarchies and decides what to spread and consume based upon those who can pay the high prices for cultural goods and services.

Cultural rights today should protect the creator and society from interests that mutilate and weaken the spiritual potential of the human being. Access to works cannot depend on the ability to pay by the citizens – today very limited in these times of crisis – nor can protection be based only on the capacity to generate profits. Payment for many kinds of uses and persecution of the offender has not produced results for the betterment of conditions of the large majority of creators, nor more spiritual wealth, nor more tolerance, nor has a dialogue between the cultures been promoted. Quite the contrary, the large spaces of promotion and distribution have become more exclusive and selective and have favored their monopolization

The effective exercise of the rights of access of the citizens to culture and knowledge mentioned in article 27 of the Declaration of Human Rights has suffered a clear and evident impairment through laws allegedly 'for the author'. This system has meant that libraries are besieged by the lack of funds to pay for subscriptions, editorial houses try to impose payments for loans to the library and they prohibit photocopies of books used in universities; furthermore, management societies hound citizens that use musical scores. A world ever more connected technologically becomes increasingly more prohibitive, and what technology could allow is closed with padlocks on intellectual property.

Undoubtedly, filmmakers are the largest consumers of films, musicians accumulate larger and better collections of music, writers are the most voracious readers, whether books are bought, exchanged, given as gifts or loaned. What person who considers themselves a creator has not copied the work of another author that cannot be found in the market for their enjoyment? The creator is the first and most avid 'user' of culture. Creators and users are not two distinctive parts with different interests.

> Most creators would not be what they are today if what has been called piracy did not exist ... The principal instruction of many musicians comes to us precisely because they jumped the barrier built by the market and accessed a culture to which they were denied. It would be good sincerely to survey and know how many authors who now shout against piracy were not nourished by it. (Bravo, 2005)

But the most outstanding tendencies in the evolution of author's rights in the last two decades seem to bet on the opposite:

1. **Increase in the duration of protection of the rights**

   The first law of author's rights established a limit of 14 years and could be extended for an additional 14, counted from the publication date of the work. Currently laws, such as those being proposed by the European Community, will last for 70 years after the death of the author. Others extend 100 years for corporate bodies from the publication date. The constant prolongation of these periods unfairly precludes the users from the information, lengthens the time until creative and intellectual sources reach the public domain and distorts the balance that should exist between rights of the author and society.

2. **Intent to reduce exceptions to author's rights (even those for educational purposes, training of professionals, library use and others) and the ever more restrictive interpretation of the 'fair use of copyright'**

   Decree 2001/29 of the European Parliament, for example, included several exceptions to author's rights but left it to the will of national governments to include them or not in their domestic legislation and establish, or not, its free use. Among these was the private use of copies by cultural or educational institutions, illustrations for teaching or scientific research, as well as exceptions for the benefit of disabled persons, etc. Regarding 'fair use' in the United States, legislation sets unclear limits to the law and extraordinary legal penalties if these limits are crossed and thus creates a state of fear in the use of works under these exceptions.

3. **Strengthening of protection of owner's rights for works that are not their own**

   The ownership of author's rights only coincides initially with the real authors (original authors). Those owners of the rights, mostly businesspersons, editors or other agents – companies that have made great economic power monopolies– who through fierce contracts obtain the rights from authors or their heirs, pay incredibly low sums and assume a minimum of risks. But their rights tend to be lumped together as author's rights and connected with the rights of the original authors together as 'rights of intellectual property', equaling the treatment of subjects that are different.

4. **Elimination of the free loan in libraries**

   The loss of a free loan system contravenes the very purpose of the public library and its purpose as a social and educational institution, so important for readers.[15] Directive 92/100/CEE of 1992 of the European Union regulated 'public lending rights' consisting of a rule of payment of compensation to the authors and editors for the public loan to libraries. Although this Directive admits several national regulations, it recognizes that a public loan causes 'economic damage' instead of understanding it as one of the limits of author's rights in favor of the right of access of the citizen. This norm and later legal regulations of the member countries of the European Union raised protests by librarians, professors and writers in Italy, Spain and Portugal.

5. **Broadening of the sphere of protection of author's rights to totally uncontrolled protection of investments**

   Protection of computer programs as established by the TRIPS agreement and national laws have no precedent even when a license is obtained to legitimately exploit the 'work'; its code is not revealed, limiting the use of the program to those who obtain the license. This kind of regulation protects the investment of the owner of the license more than the creation itself by forming a technological dependence that should not be confused with authorship laws. In some countries the law has been too all encompassing and includes photographs or casual videos with no artistic intention. This is the situation established by Spain's intellectual property law. Not only does the law protect what we know as snapshots without any artistic intention, but it includes heredity rights of reproduction, distribution and public communication, albeit for only 25 years. These photographs also retain no moral rights (article 128).

6. **Use of online license contracts**

   Online licenses prevent negotiation and exclude the possibility of exercising exceptions. For example, to download software online, it does not matter if the use qualifies as a fair use, but instead the download is only allowed if the proposed contractual conditions are accepted.

7. **Implementation of technological measures of security**

   Technological security measures are another method used to evade the enjoyment of the limitations and exceptions to author's rights that national legislations and international treaties grant. If an archive is technologically protected, it's not worth anything for the user, nor is the user's intention considered, because the technological measure is self-exclusive.

8. **Private appropriation of the contents of the public domain**
   Appropriation of information and research that belong to the public domain or that has been financed by public funds (for example research done in public universities) is a common practice by knowledge companies. Databases are common in the provision of public information but once the database is the property of a company, access to the information is privatized.
9. **Use of different forms of pressure by developed national governments and powerful corporate lobbies to universalize a restrictive concept of author's rights and persecute alleged offenders**
   There are several ways the pursuit of a more restrictive concept of author's rights can be seen. First, the inclusion of the protection of author's rights into trade treaties is an expansion of the concept. Second, it can be seen in the support provided for underdeveloped countries to implant allegedly 'efficient' intellectual property regimes that ignore the real priorities of the global South, but instead require the rapid implementation of IP regulations that favor the owner of those rights. The WIPO has been criticized for this tendency.[16] Third, the expansion of rights is part of the demand to mobilize efforts and resources to fight piracy and the demand that the damages to private companies be taken into account as if it were a damage to society. Fourth, the constant monitoring by the United States of the protection of intellectual property throughout the world through the Special 301 report that berates other governments regarding the state of their legislation and observance is an indication of this expansive concept. Finally, the continued effort of powerful groups in the US to intensify action against copyright offenders, including those outside its borders, of which most notorious are the efforts favoring the Sinde Law in Spain and the Hadopi Law in France, among others.[17]
10. **Indiscriminate practice of 'legal' piracy by transnational companies to appropriate and protect, in their favor, cultural expressions or traditional knowledge that belongs to native communities or nations of poor resources**
   Traditional expressions of the underdeveloped nations suffer plundering and systematic appropriations. Very noteworthy is the 'ethnic' motif seen on European and US fashion catwalks under labels that have nothing to do with their origins. Another common practice is the action of companies which appropriate and illegally exploit songs, legends and traditional stories that solely belong to communities without any legal protection. This is done usually by falsifying the contents and modifying them according to market interests.[18]
11. **Proposal of new international agreements that strengthen the observance of intellectual property in both the physical and digital spheres**
   The Anti-Counterfeiting Trade Agreement (ACTA) that was initially presented as a broad treaty against the falsification of brands and physical goods was secretly negotiated[19] and had the purpose of creating a new standard of application of intellectual property that went beyond existing label patterns of the WTO, criminalizing and restricting the free circulation of information on the Internet. Also, the Trans-Pacific Partnership (TPP) included US proposals that would make more rigid the obligation of its members regarding author's rights.[20]
   It should not be forgotten that there have appeared in the US situations where large companies such as Google, Amazon, Facebook and eBay have joined together to lobby against restrictions on the Internet. The interest of these companies is to achieve unlimited traffic, a goal that bonds them with citizens, although they are defending their corporate interests.

This moment we find ourselves in is characterized by an unprecedented strengthening of the laws of intellectual property and, paradoxically, by a widespread and immense exchange of knowledge and information, as well as the multiplication of centers of resistance that defend the rights of the citizens to intervene creatively in cultural processes. A free culture, as an alternative, proposes a system of production, consumption and diffusion based on cultural expressions that are an inalienable right of humanity. This proposal implies the liberation of creative forces and their diffusion, and the guarantee of broad social participation. It is based on the promotion of a social economy of culture, assuming it as a right of self-management and new sustainable models (such as crowd-funding and other forms of social financing). It recognizes cultural processes associated with new technologies and searches for collaboration between creators, intermediaries and consumers. It promotes the public domain and open licensing and sees the Internet as a social space and not as a channel of commercial distribution depending on old models of business.

These principles are also valid for the generation of, and access to, scientific and technical knowledge, a sphere that develops initiatives based on its character of a social good. Open Access is an initiative that allows free access to digital resources derived from scientific or academic production without economic barriers or restrictions derived from the rights of copyright on them.[21]

AUTHOR'S RIGHTS AND CULTURAL RIGHTS: THE CASE OF CUBA

It is useful to analyze the case of Cuba, albeit briefly, since it is a small underdeveloped nation subjected to special harassment – specifically, an economic and financial blockade of more than 50 years. There is much disinformation about Cuba and thus some facts are necessary:

- Cuba complies with the Objectives of Development of the Millennium proposed for 2015 by the UN (UNDP, 2010).
- Cuba has a high index of human development and occupies 59th place in the world, according to the 2013 report on the subject (UN, 2013).
- Cuba has a high educational level and is 14th in the world according to the Index of Development of Education for All (Cubaminrex, 2012).
- Cuba has two thousand scientists and researchers for every million inhabitants, in a population of 11 million (Cubadebate, 2011).
- Cuba had a university enrolment for the 2011–2012 school term of approximately 500,000 students.

Cuba has a system of professional artistic teaching that is totally free, from the most elemental level to the university level. Despite serious resource limitations, it has maintained a network of cultural institutions in the communities, notably the culture centers, the public libraries and museums. More than 20,000 art instructors teach in the schools and hold workshops on creation and art appreciation (Cubadebate, 2013). Also, Cuba has an education system that covers more than 99 percent of children and adolescents and an institutional system of culture that reaches all corners of the country and constitutes an appropriate basis for the exercise of cultural rights.

During the first half of the 20th century, Cuba was a real laboratory of cultural absorption. Invaded by Hollywood films and US lonely hearts magazines, the island did not identify with the Latin American condition and much less with the Caribbean. It had generalized a racist view of its African extraction. Valuable intellectual and artistic efforts were isolated by governmental indifference. From 1959, steps were taken to 'decolonize' culture. This occurs in what is known as 'high culture', as in popular traditional culture with a new public (audience and participant) of Cuban and universal culture of all varieties.

The first objective at that time was important: the population had to be made literate. More than 700,000 Cubans learned to read and write through a campaign that placed illiteracy at 3.9 percent for the entire population. Goals were designed for the population to first achieve a sixth grade reading level and then later ninth and twelfth grade reading levels. The point was to count on a more prepared citizenry to appreciate literature and art and to express itself in these fields. Furthermore, culture received an important boost from within, from creation itself. During the 1960s, basic transformations also occurred and an institutional structure to support culture began to be created.

The group of Cuban laws regarding cultural rights demonstrates acceptable progress, although some features are not yet in correspondence with the level of creativity achieved on the island. A well-oriented policy has led to increasing actors and cultural spaces that, today, support the capacities and possibilities of the institutions.

The Cuban constitution recognizes the right to free education at all levels, including free educational material given to each child and young person regardless of the economic situation of the family, as well as the opportunity to promote study in accordance with students' aptitudes. The State encourages and promotes constitutional rights to education, to culture and science in all their manifestations as well as art education, a vocation for cultivating art and literature and the ability to appreciate them.

It is proper to point out that as long ago as April 29, 1967 in anticipation of current debates, the former Prime Minister Fidel Castro asked hundreds of students:

> How is it possible to intend to deny ... to billions of human beings who now live in poverty, in underdevelopment, how to prevent them to gain access to the technology that ...they need so much such as feeding themselves, something so necessary that is living? ... We believe that all technological knowledge is a heritage that is a right for all humanity and this is a special right of the peoples that have been most exploited ... Usually technical books are produced in developed nations ... then the poor countries, the countries most exploited for centuries do not have the right to access these techniques when from their bones were stripped – for centuries – of many of the resources taken from those countries, armed with modern technology? (Castro, 1967: 3)

Thus, for more than four decades Cuba denounced as unfair the system of monopolizing knowledge.

Then, to confront the challenges of under development the island was forced to make a risky decision. In the face of the tragic situation of not having the technical books needed to educate university youths to confront the development needs of the country, Cuba decided to publish these texts and explain to the authors the reasons behind this desperate decision. In this manner, publications called 'Ediciones R' (Ediciones Revolucionarias) began. These texts by foreign authors, mostly from the US were of utmost importance for the technical formation in such important fields as medicine and engineering because the highly qualified workforce had emigrated.[22] The 'Ediciones R' books could only be used inside the country and were given to the students free of charge. But this declaration and corresponding decision did not imply the abolishment of intellectual property. In 1977 the National Assembly of Popular Power enacted Law 14 of 1977, the 'Law of Author's Rights'.

To find earlier versions of the Cuban author's rights law, we would have to go back to 1879 when Cuba was regulated – as was the practice in the colonies – through the Spanish Law of Intellectual Property and its Regulations, based in the continental system.[23] In the neo-colonial period of the Republic (1902–1958), there is no indication that there was any intention to adapt Spanish laws to national necessities. The majority of regulations of this period referred to rules for the registration of newspapers and magazines, formal requirements in the press and other bureaucratic controls.

In June of 1946, during the Inter American Conference of Experts for the Protection of Author's Rights held in the Pan-American Union (today the Organization of American States [OAS]) in Washington, the Cuban government subscribed to the Inter American Convention on Rights of Authors of Literary, Scientific and Artistic Works. This unbelievable step should be understood as a result of the call by the US government that attempted to achieve, with its influence, an extension of the system of protection of author's rights according to its regulations against others, in the face of European systems that were already advancing in some Latin American countries. These regulations were in force in Cuba until their repeal by the current Law 14.

In 1960 an institution was created with its own attributions as a management institution[24] and later the Office of Music and Intellectual Property Rights. In 1987 the Ministry of Culture founded the National Center of Author's Rights (CENDA).[25]

Law 14 of December 28 1977 recognized the right of authors to ownership and to the integrity of their work, to defend against deformation, mutilation or modification, anonymous, pseudonym rights, to make or authorize translation, adaptation, rearrangement or any other transformation of their work and the right to receive payment for the intellectual work done when the work is used by other natural or corporate bodies. But although recognition of these author's rights was important, much more so was the introduction of a principle very advanced for its time and stipulated in Article 3:

> Protection of author's rights established in this Law is subordinated to the higher interest imposed by social necessity of a broader diffusion of science, technology, education and culture in general. The exercise of these rights recognized in the Law cannot affect social and cultural interests. (*Gaceta Oficial Ordinaria* [official gazette], 30 December 1977: 1)

This principle has been indispensable to the results in terms of educational and cultural development that Cuba has demonstrated to the present. The policy formulated and applied for scientific publications and for education is intended to promote free access as a means of converting science to a common good and promote its advance. Textbooks for education are published under licenses granted by CENDA in the case that a right cause authorization from the authors has not been obtained.

Law 14 stipulates in its Article 37 that for reasons of social interest, the competent authority can grant a license for the use of the work without requiring authorization or payment specified in the Law. For this requirement the work must be necessary for the development of science, technology, education or professional improvement; its distribution or diffusion should be free of charge or with no intent of profit; and its distribution or diffusion should be done exclusively within the territory of the Cuban State. Specific works of libraries, centers of documentation, scientific institutions and institutions of education are also protected by this law which grants the right to reproduce works if there is no profit motive and use is limited to the needs of its activity.

In education centers in Cuba, the reproduction of texts to support teaching is done through mechanical or digital means and is a common practice – assumed as a right – by professors and students alike and, luckily, large corporations have no real influence. There is no awareness within society that these acts are not legal, since the concept of solidarity and free exchange is deemed most important.

An important experience of democratization of knowledge in view of the possibilities that the new technologies offered by the Net can bring, is *Infomed*, from the Ministry of Public Health of Cuba. This is dedicated to scientific information in the field of medicine and allows Cuban health professionals constant and updated information on subjects of vital importance, to and from very remote locations.

Cuban publishing houses of scientific and educational material, although they do not count on laws that promote the different kinds of free licenses, have taken up these principles as a policy and, protected by law, have been granted the right for necessary uses. For example, *Acimed*, the publishing house for medical sciences established, since its inception, that: 'allowed is the total or partial reproduction of works published always if the source is cited', which made it in fact a journal of open access. Now it is under the Creative Commons License 'non-commercial – and equally shared 2.0'.

The law also allows for the representing or execution of works, without authorization or payment to the authors in all cases that do not seek a profit. This article is important since it allows the diffusion of culture through the movement of amateur artists, culture centers, with important repercussions for the artistic formation and capacity of the appreciation of the arts.

The duration of author's rights in Cuba is 50 years after the death of the author according to what is established in Decree Law No. 156.

Regarding software, the blockade imposed by the United States against the island has, by denying the possibility of user licenses, led to an extended use of non-authorized copies of proprietary software. This does not increase the costs of information, but it does not solve the problem of technological dependence, rather it worsens it. There is a strategy designed by the government for the use and learning of free software as well as for the migration of all sectors of the public administration of the country regarding these types of programs. However, this has moved slowly. The Cuban government is emphasizing the development of a Cuban software industry that has invested in important human and material resources. There are more than 400 Young Computer Clubs with localities in all municipalities of the country in which young people learn about and exercise, free of charge, the new technologies.

To solve litigation that could arise for non-compliance or violation of the author regulations, interested parties are directed to the National Center of Author's Rights. Still open, however, is the possibility of going to the competent civilian courts. For conduct that infringes author's rights, each state establishes sentences that go from the exclusively financial to prison terms. But the current Penal Code in Cuba (Law No. 62, modified by Law No. 87 of 1999) only applies prison sentences or fines in cases where the perpetrator, to the detriment of the creator or cultural heritage, falsifies a work of art or traffics in them. Nonetheless, this classification is included in the article 'TITLE VI: Crimes against Cultural Heritage' and can only be applied to fine arts, excluding recognition by the law of author's rights as a legal good that deserves criminal guardianship (imprisonment). In its modification, Law 87 decriminalized plagiarism. The absence of penal sanctions associated with the protection of author's rights has been criticized by authors' defenders. In this sense, the Cuban state considered the criteria of social danger that should guide all penal regulations.

Cuba today is part of the Berne Convention and as a condition of its membership of the World Trade Organization, the TRIPS Agreement is also applicable. Law 14 has had a few modifications, although these do not depart from its basic principles. Their formulations do not answer current requirements of the development of technologies and the manner of contemporary creation. However, Cuban legislation has been positive in setting aside an avalanche of modifications that many Latin American countries made during the 1990s that have favored the appropriation of new creative results, recognized the length of time of protection or heightened criminal punishment for re-appropriation, the remix or so-called unauthorized copy. Nevertheless it is time to begin searching for legal solutions to adapt the law to cultural practice. New methods of licensing in the style of Creative Commons and copyleft should appear without setting aside all regulative structures of the 20th century. The regulations should refer to reality and in Cuba there is an advanced culture that coexists with the conditions of an underdeveloped nation and a model of economic renovation.

Law 14 was an example of clarity from those in charge of writing and passing it, professionals who knew how to interpret the needs of a different society and that, required different formulations. The ethical and legal principle that guided this law is, at present, the great absence in the legislation of the 'more developed' Europe and the rest of the American continent; that is a principle of balance, of protection against the all exclusive monopolies, for the interests of society.

The state today complies with the payment to authors for the use of their works, be they national or foreign, although economically they can be insufficient as compared to other countries. It is part of the Cuban cultural policy that a creation is not only protected but that other means of protection are also used. These means can include measures of safeguard and promotion of popular traditional culture, protection and conservation of heritage, a boost of creation through events and festivals, the subsidy of publications, musical products and audiovisuals and genres and significant artistic collectives with little or no possibility of surviving in the market, and other programs of impact in the development of talent and diffusion of their results.

Thanks to the practice of a humanist cultural policy that places the needs of the citizens above economic factors, contradictions caused by rigid author laws seen in the rest of the world are not felt in Cuba. Co-existing in the island are forms of distribution and cultural consumption that take part in the market and a widespread cultural life remote from the harmful effects of these which is accessible to all.

Teaching in this field of rights, however, has left behind the demands of a cultural practice and many factors that are encumbered by eurocentrist concepts in the history of art and author's rights. Still pending in our universities is a critical approach to the discipline and systematization on a theoretical plane of the contributions made by Cuba in the socialization of knowledge and culture without neglecting individual creators.[26]

The academic sphere has suffered at times from an excessive attitude towards foreign author laws and the doctrine of neo-liberal author's rights that extended throughout the continent under the umbrella of the WIPO/OMPI, the WTO and the TRIPS agreements during the 1990s. These organizations went on the offensive in the training of professionals; courses and congresses flourished in the continent that taught all the actors implicated (authors, artists in general, promoters, intermediaries, officials and even cultural officials, judges and prosecutors) the doctrines and necessary legal changes to adapt to the 'international system of author's rights', convinced that they were the only possible canons. This offensive has borne fruit in Latin America but in Cuba, although somewhat influenced, it has not caused substantial changes in the legislation nor did it modify the cultural policy.

Referring to legal regimes in other spheres of culture, there is a certain development in areas of heritage (Law No. 1 'Law of Protection of Cultural Heritage' and Law No. 2, aimed at the protection of national and local monuments and complemented later with more precise specifications) and in strengthening and promoting creativity (decrees that regulate the working condition of the artist and the regimes of social security). There are also regulations, not sufficiently systematized nor at the height of vitality of these activities, referring to the functioning of library systems, the work of compiling national references, to archives and museums (Law No. 23 of the Municipal Museums) and for the creation and functioning of the culture houses system.

Cuba lacks a harmonious legislative development that integrates regulations of a different dispersed character and a hierarchy that regulates the functioning of institutions, the relations with creators and participation of the actors that are not state directed but that intervene in the cultural processes, such as associations and foundations.

But, in this case, a weak legislative development does not mean cultural impoverishment. Equally it cannot be said that an extensive legislative development is a synonym for a vigorous cultural life. Legislation, technically impeccable, does not guarantee a massive participation in culture and the rights granted without any condition to exercise them. The market acts like a force that censures and excludes crudeness and in the world inequality in economic power can override the effectiveness of better regulation. That is, the economic differences may impede the exercise of rights duly recognized.

National and foreign producers and editors flock to Cuba. The existence of these national and foreign influences allows artists and creators to relate to individuals of different societies (mercantile societies – in many cases dependent on transnational companies) as well as interacting with independent labels and state institutions. In the case of state institutions, income from intermediaries is redistributed at a social level, meaning such income reverts to the promotion of artistic teaching, social security, and the subsidy of non-commercialization projects that protect cultural heritage, etc. In contrast, incomes obtained from transnational companies or independent labels only enrich its own patrimony.

Confronted by the disparity between these systems of protection, national legislation must exist to protect creators and citizens while guaranteeing a space for participation for both Cuban state institutions and foreign companies, while avoiding the disfigurement of Cuban cultural policy. Balancing these concerns while dealing with the exceptional circumstances found in Cuba is a significant challenge. Specifically, the problem of the economic and financial blockade imposed against Cuba by the US for more than 50 years, and condemned 21 times in the General Assembly of the United Nations, creates significant problems.[27]

This blockade prevents commercial cultural activities[28] and, consequently, these types of activities cannot be used to generate income for the country. The blockade not only prevents Cuba from developing relationships with US companies but, due to the extraterritorial nature of the blockage, it also affects all countries with US capital, even when US capital is based in a third party country. The majority of the large companies involved in entertainment and software are either from the US or have some type of US support. When looking at the rights of music authors, for example, it has been impossible to sign contracts of reciprocal representation between Cuba and the US with societies of collective management for the exploitation of musical repertoires in both territories and obtaining the corresponding benefits. Furthermore, the US editorial market is closed to Cuban authors living on the island. Cuba is also prevented from engaging in any monetary transactions using the US dollar and US banks or their foreign branches.

Restrictions regarding the possibilities of access to US technology are manifest in the impossibility of purchasing equipment directly from America. Cuba is prohibited from signing software licenses that guarantee information securities, such as those attached to anti-virus software and that directly relate to Web development or that provide efficient tools for Internet management. Additionally, permission to work on computer information platforms for our placement in the Internet, as well as for help with statistical evaluation of websites associated to searches is prevented.[29] In view of this analysis, the particularities of the Cuban case can be understood in the solutions applied to its reality.

CONCLUSIONS

There is much to be done in the sphere of protection of cultural rights in the world. Existing regulatory instruments established by current international organizations are merely well intentioned declarations when they lack the force found in other international agreements. As a result of the force exerted by companies that own rights, there has been an imbalance in legislation and its application. Author's rights have become an instrument in the hands of large corporations to establish monopolies over knowledge and other cultural content to guarantee their optimal commercial exploitation to the detriment of further creative efforts. Such monopolies affect the exercise of cultural rights by all citizens.

The new forms of creating and consuming culture that have emerged, as well as the collective creation found in many native cultures, just to mention two examples, have no place within the archaic laws that presuppose a finished piece, based upon a strong originality and a lineal discourse. One effective protection of creation implies dealing with the issue integrally with all factors that act upon it: technologies, culture, society, economics and law. The basis for the promotion of creation in Cuba includes access to all pre-existing creations and the possibility for participating in cultural life as routes to guaranteeing the proper place in society for creative work instead of premising its protection on just the economic remuneration for the sale of the work. But this condition is also implied, as precedence, in the recognition and possibility of the effective exercise of other essential human rights of which many individuals are deprived, considering the principles of the indivisibility, universality and interdependence of these rights.

Cuba is an underdeveloped country with its own particularities. It has an educational and cultural policy defined to integrally protect creation and the principle of author's rights while at the same time embracing the social interests of the people to access science, technology, education and culture. The balance between these rights acknowledged by Cuban law has been key to the educational and cultural achievements of Cuba today.

NOTES

1 For more information see: 'Students required to purchase the art book for 180 dólares without images due to copyright problems', Alt1040, consulted July 29, 2013 at: www.alt1040.com/2012/09/alumnos-libro-arte-sin-imagenes-copyright
2 For more information see Robin Wauters, 'Belgian rights holders group wants to charge libraries for reading books to kids', consulted October 22, 2013 at: www.thenextweb.com/media/2012/03/13/belgian-rightsholders-group-wants-to-charge-libraries-for-reading-books-to-kids/
3 A few days after the death of Swartz, a contributive initiative was unleashed on Twitter urging researchers and professors around the world to make their articles freely available on the Web.
4 References are to culture as an object of rights and fundamental rights of culture and legal guarantees.
5 MINREX (Ministry of Foreign Affairs of Cuba), 'Position of Cuba regarding the Project of the Optional Protocol of the Pact of Economic, Social and Cultural Rights', consulted June 19, 2014 at: http://anterior.cubaminrex.cu/Multilaterales/Articulos/Archivo/NotasVerbales/2002/11.html
6 It would be worthwhile to remember the obstacles that the international community had to overcome in 2005 for the adoption of the Convention on Protection and Promotions of Diversity of Cultural Expression including the blatant blackmail by the US delegation of Ministers present in the plenary session. The then Secretary of State of the United States, Condoleeza Rice, in a letter dated October 5 to the Ministers of Foreign Affairs of the UNESCO member nations expressed that: 'The adoption of this convention could cool negotiations in the WTO. For this reason it can become a tool for abuse by enemies of democracy and free trade ... The United States is preparing an explicative declaration that would conserve the text of the treaty explaining that it cannot be correctly interpreted in the sense that authorizes dictators to prohibit the flow of information or industries to impose protectionist measures to justify protecting culture' (Rice, 2006).
7 World Intellectual Property Organization: 'WIPO Copyright Treaty', consulted July 20, 2013 at: www.wipo.int/treaties/en/ip/wct/
8 World Intellectual Property Organization: 'WIPO Performances and Phonograms Treaty', consulted July 2013 at: www.wipo.int/treaties/en/ip/wppt/trtdocs_wo034.html
9 'Function of exceptions to author's rights in the promotion of equal access to information and full social integration of the blind and poor of sight in society', Initial Memory of the World Union of the Blind, UNESCO, Bulletin of author's rights, consulted June 19 2014 at: http://portal.unesco.org/culture/es/files/9754/10669225361WBU_S.pdf/WBU%2BS.pdf
10 OMPI, 'Marrakesh Treaty to Facilitate Access to Published Works for Persons Who are Blind, Visually Impaired or Otherwise Print Disabled' adopted by the Diplomatic Conference in June of 2013. Consulted October 22, 2013 at: www.wipo.int/edocs/mdocs/diplconf/es/vip_dc/vip_dc_8.docx
11 Laws are qualified as eurocentrist because they are based on artistic and legal concepts from Europe. The culture of the majority of peoples and native communities in colonized countries do not take into account their works or expressions as a product of individual genius and they should not be appropriated by an individual. Also the concept of originality is not recognized. For more information consult 'The Copy/South Dossier Issues in the economics, politics, and ideology of copyright in the global South', consulted June 20, 2014 at: http://eprints.rclis.org/7563/1/CSdossier.pdf
12 Homogenization of legislation is considered a neo-colonial issue because to be able to participate in world trade through the WTO, countries of the underdeveloped South had to accept the ADPIC without reservation and with this a new form of domination by the North. This agreement establishes a series of basic principles on intellectual rights and forces national legislation in member countries to guarantee the conditions for the defense of owner's rights in the developed world with an adverse effect on such matters as education, health, technology transfer, etc. for less developed nations. The Treaty on Aspects of Rights of Intellectual Property related to commerce (TRIPS Agreement), is Annex 1C of

the Convention created by the WTO and signed in 1994. It came into effect on January 1, 1995.

13 ADPIC Plus are dispositions in issues of intellectual property included in other commercial agreements (outside of the OMPI sphere) that limit the possibility of using flexibilities of the ADPIC including, for example, more restrictive interpretations, enlarging duration periods of the rights, and expansion of materials subject to protection, etc. Examples of the agreements are clauses considered in ADPIC Plus: the failed Free Trade Area for the Americas (FTAA), and bilateral treaties of free trade such as the Chile-US, Euro-Korea or the ACTA.

14 In general few developing countries make use of these sanctions to demand trade rights since the cost of these sanctions, in the case of poor countries, can be larger for those who impose than those who receive them. They also run a high risk of being inefficient.

15 For more information see Platform Against Payment for Libraries: www.noalprestamodepago.org/adhesiones/

16 'Proposal to establish an OMPI Program for development, detailed analysis of the issues set down in the WO-6A-31-11', Document IMM/1/4/, consulted June 20, 2014 at: http://www.wipo.int/edocs/mdocs/mdocs/es/iim_1/iim_1_4.doc

17 Lillian Álvarez, 'Inside Views: The Contributions of Julian Assange to the Debate on Intellectual Property', consulted July 29, 2013 at: www.ip-watch.org/2012/09/08/the-contributions-of-julian-assange-to-the-debate-on-intellectual-property/

18 See section 3 of 'The Copy/South Dossier Issues in the economics, politics, and ideology of copyright in the global South', consulted June 20, 2014 at: http://eprints.rclis.org/7563/1/CSdossier.pdf

19 ACTA (Trade Agreement Against Falsification). This agreement was made by a group of officials (initially from the US and Japan). It would be negotiated in a first phase between similar countries but their main objective was to impose it, like the ADPIC Plus on developed countries. For the US it is important that the reach of ACTA be as broad as possible. However, the secret nature of the negotiations undermined the legitimacy of the entire process and led to problems in many countries, including the European Union that rejected ACTA in December of 2012. For more information see: http://www.laquadrature.net/en/ACTA, consulted June 20, 2014.

20 For more information see: www.tppabierto.net/nosotros

21 For more information see the Budapest Declaration (2002), the Bethesda Declaration on Publication of Open Access (2003) and the Declaration of Berlin (2003).

22 Note one significant figure: of the more than 6,000 doctors the country had, 3,000 emigrated. Today Cuba has more than 70,000 doctors as a solution to the previous loss of medical expertise.

23 Royal Order of January 14 1879.

24 Law No. 860 created the Cuban Institute of Music Rights (ICDM) on August 8, 1960.

25 Decree 20 of February 21, 1978 created the National Center of Author's Rights (CENDA).

26 Identification continues in many cases regarding the term 'protection' for the creator with payment for commercial exploitation of their works even when a large part of the process of creation and diffusion passes outside the market and when there is a system of social security for the artists.

27 More information on the blockade can be found here: http://www.cubavsbloqueo.cu/en, consulted June 20, 2014.

28 See 'Impact of the Economic, Financial and Trade Blockade of the U.S. Against Cuba in the Sphere of Culture'. Period: March 2011 to March 2012. Consulted June 20, 2014 at http://www.min.cult.cu/estadisticas/informe-del-bloqueo-2012.pdf

29 Ibid.

REFERENCES

Alt1040, 'Exigen a los alumnos un libro de arte de 180 dólares sin imágenes por problema de copyright', consulted July 29, 2013 at: www.alt1040.com/2012/09/alumnos-libro-arte-sin-imagenes-copyright

Álvarez, Lillian, 'Inside Views: The Contributions of Julian Assange to the Debate on Intellectual Property', consulted July 29, 2013 at: www.ip-watch.org/2012/09/08/the-contributions-of-julian-assange-to-the-debate-on-intellectual-property/

Álvarez, Lillian, Derecho de autor. El debate de hoy, Editorial Ciencias Sociales, la Habana (2006), consulted July 29, 2013 at: www.especieenpeligro.org/index.php/privatizacion-de-la-vida/1471-derecho-de-autor-el-debate-de-hoy

Argentine and Brazilian Proposal to establish an OMPI program for development discussed in the thirty first session of the General Assembly of that organization in Geneva from September 27 to October 5, 2004, consulted June 20, 2014 at http://www.wipo.int/edocs/mdocs/mdocs/es/iim_1/iim_1_4.doc

Barthes, Roland, La muerte del autor, consulted October 22, 2013 at: www.teorialiteraria2009.files.wordpress.com/2009/06/barthes-la-muerte-del-autor.pdf

Betto, Frei, 'Derechos humanos o derechos animales?', ADITAL, (2003) consulted October 22, 2013 at: www.adital.com.br/site/noticia2.asp?lang=ES&cod=9856

Bravo, David, Copia este libro, Editorial Dmem S.L., España, (2005) consulted October 22, 2013 at: www.copiaestelibro.bandaancha.st/

Budapest Open Access Initiative (BOAI), (2002) consulted October 22, 2013 at: www.madrimasd.org/informacionidi/e-ciencia/documentos/docs/BOAI.pdf

Castro Ruz, Fidel, Speech delivered by Fidel Castro in Guane. Pinar del Río, on April 27, 1967, and in Granma, April 30, 1967, p. 3.

Colombres, Adolfo, Teoría transcultural del arte. Hacia un pensamiento visual independiente, Ediciones del Sol, Buenos Aires, 2004, p. 243.

Copy/South Research Group, 'The Copy/South Dossier Issues on the economics, politics, and ideology of copyright in the global South', consulted June 20, 2014, at: http://eprints.rclis.org/7563/1/CSdossier.pdf

Cuba vs Blockade, 'Cuba is More than a Blockade', consulted June 20, 2014 at: http://www.cubavsbloqueo.cu/en

Cubadebate, 'Cuba posee dos mil científicos e investigadores por millón de habitantes', 7 August 2011, consulted July 29, 2013 at: www.cubadebate.cu/noticias/2011/08/07/cuba-posee-dos-mil-cientificos-e-investigadores-por-millon-de-habitantes-afirma-experto/

Cubadebate, 'Informe de Cuba al Examen Periódico Universal (EPU) del Consejo de Derechos Humanos', 30 April 2013, consulted July 29, 2013 at: www.cubadebate.cu/noticias/2013/04/30/234231-2/

Cubaminrex, 'Cuba ostenta el lugar 16 en el Índice de Desarrollo de la Educación para Todos presentado por la UNESCO', 2012, consulted October 22, 2013 at: www.unesco.org/new/es/education/themes/leading-the-international-agenda/efareport/reports/

Cuban Ministry of Culture, Impact of the Economic, Financial and Trade Blockade of the U.S. against Cuba in the Sphere of Culture. Period: March 2011 to March 2012., consulted July 29, 2013 at: http://www.min.cult.cu/estadisticas/informe-del-bloqueo-2012.pdf

Declaration of Berlin, (2003) consulted October 22, 2013 at: www.geotropico.org/1_2_Documentos_Berlin.html

Declaration of Bethesda on the Publication of Open Access. Published June 20, 2003, consulted October 22, 2013 at: www.ictlogy.net/articles/bethesda_es.html

Escobar, Ticio, La belleza de los otros, Editorial Casa de las Américas, La Habana, 2012, pp. 29–30.

La Quadrature du net, 'Wikileaks Cables Shine Light on ACTA History', consulted June 20, 2014, at: http://www.laquadrature.net/en/ACTA

MINREX (Cuban Ministry of Foreign Affairs), 'Posición de Cuba en relación con el Proyecto de Protocolo facultativo al Pacto de Derechos Económicos, Sociales y Culturales', consulted June 20, 2014, at: http://www.cubaminrex.cu/Multilaterales/sociohumanitarios/Notas%20verbales%202002/sociohumanitarios_nota%20verbal_posicion%20de%20cuba%20en%20relacion%20con%20el%20proyecto%20de%20protocolo_tc.htm

Official Ordinary Gazette of the Republic of Cuba, December 30, 1977, 'Law No. 14, Law of Author's Rights, December 28, 1977'.

OMPI, 'Marrakesh Treaty to Facilitate Access to Published Works for Persons Who are Blind, Visually Impaired or Otherwise Print Disabled', adopted by the Diplomatic Conference in June of 2013, consulted October 22, 2013, at: www.wipo.int/edocs/mdocs/diplconf/es/vip_dc/vip_dc_8.docx

OMPI, 'OMPI Treaty on Author's Rights', 1996, consulted July 29, 2013, at: www.wipo.int/treaties/en/ip/wct/

OMPI, 'OMPI Treaty on Interpretation or Execution and OMPI Treaty on Interpretation or Execution, and Phonogram Execution', 1996, consulted July 29, 2013 at: www.wipo.int/treaties/en/ip/wppt/trtdocs_wo034.html

OMPI, 'Proposal for establishment of an OMPI Program for the development, detailed analysis of issues that appear in the document WO-6A-31-11', document IMM/1/4/, consulted October 22, 2013 at: www.wipo.int/edocs/mdocs/mdocs/es/iim_1/iim_1_4.doc

Pérez Parejo, Ramón, 'La crisis de la autoría: desde la muerte del autor de Barthes al renacimiento de anonimia en Internet', consulted October 22, 2013 at: www.ucm.es/info/especulo/numero26/crisisau.html

Prieto de Pedro, Jesús (2002) 'Cultura, economía y derecho, tres conceptos implicados', consulted June 19, 2014 at: http://www.laciudadhumanizada.es/wp-content/uploads/2010/09/Cultura-econom-y….pdf

Rice, Condoleeza, 'Letter to the Ministers of Foreign Affairs to UNESCO Member Nations', consulted June 19, 2014 at: http://firgoa.usc.es/drupal/files/da.pdf

Silva Echeto, Víctor; Browne Sartori, Rodrigo, Literatura y ciberespacio: 'creación' de simulacros y simulacros de 'creación', Revista Chilena de Literatura 69 (2006): 137–147, consulted October 22, 2013 at: www.scielo.cl/scielo.php?pid=S0718-22952006000200009&script=sci_arttext

Story, Alan, 'An Alternative Primer on National and International Copyright Law in the Global South:

Eighteen Questions and Answers', consulted June 20, 2014 at: http://www.manzanamecanica.org/files/manual-alanstory-espanol-con-portada.pdf

Tppabierto, consulted October 22, 2013, at: www.tppabierto.net/nosotros

UN, United Nations System in Cuba 'Cuba in the Report on Human Development 2013', consulted October 22, 2013 at: www.onu.org.cu/news/e8a887868cd111e-2b6a23860774f33e8/press-release-2013-hdr-cuba/

UN, Universal Declaration of Human Rights proclaimed by the General Assembly of the United Nations (Paris, December 10, 1948), consulted October 22, 2013, at: www.un.org/en/documents/udhr/

UNDP, 'National Reports on Compliance of the ODM', Cuba: Third National Report on Compliance of the Millennium Objectives of Development, 2010, consulted July 29, 2013 at: www.cu.undp.org/content/dam/cuba/docs/Informe%20ODM%20espanol%20cuba%202010.pdf

UNESCO, 'Our Creative Diversity', Report of the World Commission of Culture and Development, summarized version, Paris, September, 1996, consulted June 19, 2014 at: http://unesdoc.unesco.org/images/0010/001055/105586sb.pdf

UNESCO, Bulletin of Author's Rights, 'The function of exceptions to author's rights and promotion of equal access to information and full social integration of the blind and visual handicapped in society', Initial Memory of the World Union of the Blind, June 2003, consulted June 20, 2014 at: http://portal.unesco.org/culture/es/files/9754/10669225361WBU_S.pdf/WBU%2BS.pdf

WTO 'Agreement on Issues of Intellectual Property related to Trade, 1995', consulted October 22, 2013 at: www.wto.org/spanish/docs_s/legal_s/27-trips.pdf

16

Communicating Copyright: Discourse and Disagreement in the Digital Age

Lee Edwards, Bethany Klein, David Lee, Giles Moss and Fiona Philip

INTRODUCTION

Digitization of media has brought longstanding tensions about the purpose and scope of copyright law to the fore, not only for those with a financial stake in copyrighted materials, but for ordinary users as well. This chapter considers modern copyright debates as involving a range of implicit and explicit justifications communicated by government, industry, artists and users. While certain discourses are prioritized and naturalized, often others (and particularly those of users) are given little serious attention, thus constraining discussions about and innovation in intellectual property policy. Drawing on an analysis of various sources of communication about copyright – from government-commissioned reviews and industry campaigns, to public relations materials and the voices of users themselves – this chapter locates the issues underpinning the disagreement between involved groups. While changing industry communication has re-positioned users as partners, and not simply pirates, the division between the beliefs of users and the norms expressed in copyright regulation persists. The act of communicating copyright has often been a one-way street with powerful corporations and policy-makers attempting to persuade ordinary media users to modify their attitudes and behaviour. By opening space for a lane in the other direction, users may be rightly recognized as sources of legitimate justifications that could feed into copyright policy and regulation.

As a result of the changes and challenges presented by the digitization of media, copyright has emerged as a central element of contemporary debates about a range of issues related to the creative industries, creative labour and media consumption. Current events and news stories have brought the content of usually obscured media policy and law to the attention of ordinary media users. Proponents of a more transparent and democratic media regulation environment could view the public spotlight on copyright as cause for celebration. However, with users largely implicated as current or potential infringers of the law, an open discussion of copyright remains a hope rather than a reality.

In the absence of alternatives, the justifications that are most frequently expressed through communication to the public and communication about public behaviour begin to form a taken-for-granted common sense about the purpose and logic of copyright: intellectual property is equivalent to physical property; infringing copyright is tantamount to theft; and the success of the creative industries is reliant on copyright. Yet changing relationships between producers and consumers, the continuing presence of conservative limitations to copyright exceptions, and the disconnect between everyday behaviour and what is allowed, have together encouraged a debate over the foundations and details of copyright law. In the most recent UK government-commissioned review of copyright, Hargreaves writes, 'The copyright regime cannot be considered fit for the digital age when millions of citizens are in daily breach of copyright, simply for shifting a piece of music or video from one device to another' (2011: 5). The failure of the UK government to act quickly and decisively in response to recent reviews speaks to the power of the lobbying industries, but also ensures the conversation about the suitability of copyright in the digital age continues (a conversation that might not take place if quick fixes were applied).

We characterize these modern copyright debates as involving a range of implicit and explicit justifications communicated by government, industry, artists and users. Rather than a struggle to encourage or force users to abide by the law, the copyright crisis is viewed as a disagreement structured by the justifications of invested actors, including ordinary users. We draw on Boltanski and Thévenot's (2006) theoretical understanding of justification as a fundamental societal process enacted by different groups in society as they try to legitimize their practices. Justifications are structured in the context of internally coherent 'cités', or justificatory regimes, each governed by a particular perception of the 'common good' that defines the relative value of different groups. For example, in a market-oriented cité, groups and practices that help markets function effectively (such as CEOs, technology companies, or individual consumption) are valued more highly than those who do not contribute to markets in the same way (such as file-sharers or illegal downloaders). A range of justificatory regimes co-exist at any one time, and each may be criticized on the basis of either the *definition* of the common good that governs it, or the evidence supplied for claims that a particular act, individual or group actually *contributes to* the common good. In the face of critique, new processes of justification arise and it is this dialectical process, according to Boltanski and Thévenot (2006), that can eventually lead to social stability. However, the process of critique must be taken seriously if the dialectic is to be fulfilled and stability achieved.

Boltanski and Thévenot's work helps us shift the focus from an examination of the mechanisms used to enforce copyright towards an analysis of the justificatory discourses that constitute the foundation on which copyright legislation and enforcement are built. We argue that certain discourses are too often taken-for-granted by policymakers, while discourses (particularly those of users) that critique normative justifications are not taken seriously enough: as a result, discussions about and innovation in intellectual property policy are limited, and it is unlikely that a stable outcome will be achieved under such conditions. Through analysis of government-commissioned reviews and reports, websites and campaigns, public relations materials, and focus groups with users, we identify key issues behind the disagreement between involved groups. Industries are changing how they address media users, yet there remains a division between the beliefs of users and the norms expressed in copyright regulation. While the goal of communicating copyright to media users has been to persuade them to change their attitudes and behaviour, users could instead be treated as sources of legitimate justifications that may inform copyright policy and regulation.

THE WAR ON PIRACY (AND THE PUBLIC)

Current issues and debates around copyright, from balancing author rights with the public interest and determining the appropriate length of a copyright term to attempts to tackle copyright infringement, continue to be rooted in specific historical events, frames and decisions. The Statute of Anne – enacted in 1710 and widely considered to be the first copyright law – embedded two key copyright concepts: firstly, it moved rights from printers to authors, entrenching ideas about ownership and reward of creative works. Secondly, it incorporated an understanding of the relationship of copyright to the public interest in two respects: as encouraging the availability and accessibility of creative works to the public through exceptions and limited terms, and as driving creativity, which ensures that a wealth of creative works circulate in society.

The author's role and right with respect to the 'property' (drawing on Locke) of creative work was revisited in numerous cases in the decades that followed: 'the representation of the author as creator who is entitled to profit from his intellectual labor came into being through a blending of literary and legal discourses in the context of the contest over perpetual copyright' (Rose, 1993: 6). The ultimate rejection of a perpetual copyright in the *Donaldson v Beckett* case (1774) again considered the benefit to the public in the decision-making process. As Deazley explains:

> Copyright, in eighteenth century Britain, was never simply concerned with the bookseller or the author. What emerges from a close study of the movement of the law during this period is that copyright, with both the passing of the Statute of Anne and the factual decision of *Donaldson*, was primarily defined and justified in the interests of society and not the individual. (2004: 226)

Davies notes a shift resulting from the emergence of digital technology, where

> the public interest has been invoked, not in favour of strengthening the protection afforded to authors and other right owners to protect them against piracy in cyberspace, but in favour of free and unfettered access by the public to copyright works combined with the means of copying them for personal use. (2002: 7)

Yet, if the public interest has been invoked in debate, the shift has not resulted in changes to policy in favour of the public, despite recommendations in government-commissioned reviews to, for example, allow for more private copying exceptions. Instead, recent changes to copyright law (e.g. the 2011 European Union directive extending the copyright term for sound recordings from 50 to 70 years) have fortified copyright protection, and reinforced an understanding of copyright as primarily rewarding and protecting creative work, ignoring persuasive arguments that question the reality of such claims. As Vaidhyanathan puts it, 'Powerful interests have argued for stronger restrictions that intimidate artists, musicians, and computer hobbyists into respecting "property rights" at the expense of creativity' (2001: 4). Furthermore, through their forays into illegal downloading and distribution of media, ordinary media users have inherited the historical characterization of infringers as pirates, suggesting that there are good guys (authors/owners) and bad guys (pirates) and naturalizing claims that copyright must be protected and infringement punished (Edwards et al., 2013a).

The recent public debate about copyright has focused overwhelmingly on how copyright holders can protect their intellectual property and tackle online copyright infringement, continuing to emphasize the piracy frame while neglecting the aspect of the public interest argument that favours more open access. Corporate rights holders have waged war on 'piracy' in various ways, not just through legal actions but also through marketing and educational campaigns and the promotion of legal and more controllable forms of digital distribution (Edwards et al., 2013b;

Murray, 2010). They have lobbied governments forcefully for new legislation designed to tackle online copyright infringement, such as the HADOPI law (*Haute Autorité pour la diffusion des œuvres et la protection des droits sur internet*, or 'law promoting the distribution and protection of creative works on the Internet') in France (2009) and the Digital Economy Act in the UK (2010). Meanwhile, efforts to regulate digital copyright have been resisted by an intransigent public, who continue to break copyright law in significant numbers, and from vocal campaign and user groups, who argue that overly strict copyright regulation is contrary to the public interest.

Rights holders initially turned to the law to tackle piracy. In a well-known early case, the Recording Industry Association of America (RIAA) took legal action against the file-sharing site *Napster*, resulting in its closure in 2001, and there have been numerous subsequent cases since then, such as the high-profile case against *The Pirate Bay* in Sweden (for an overview of key cases, see Murray, 2010: 234–254). More controversially, rights holders have also targeted individual file-sharers. In 2003, the RIAA initiated hundreds of lawsuits against members of the public in the United States (Yu, 2005). Meanwhile, in 2007, it was reported that law firms in the UK were practising 'volume litigation', where suspected infringers were sent letters *en masse* and given the choice of either settling out of court for a fee of approximately £600 or facing legal proceedings (Murray, 2010: 258–259). The aim of such legal actions is not simply to sanction individual infringers and to recoup money for the industry, it is also to send out a message to others. As the RIAA President Cary Sherman (cited in Yu, 2005: 658) explains, 'lawsuits are a very potent form of education'. In practice, however, the use of what have been viewed as 'strong-arm tactics' has generated negative publicity and threatened to anger and further disaffect the public (Yu, 2005: 655).

As well as using the law, rights holders have sought to address piracy through technology. In his well-known account of Internet regulation, Lessig (2006) underscores the importance of 'code' (which he defines broadly as technical instructions embedded in software and hardware) as a form of regulation. Code can be easily programmed and reprogrammed to achieve different regulatory goals and, unlike the law, it regulates behaviour automatically, without the need to take legal action (McIntyre and Scott, 2008). Digital rights management (DRM), for example, controls the ways in which users can use and access digital files by putting in place limits on the copying of files and other restrictions. While the early use of DRM for music files proved unpopular and was opposed by users (as a result, Apple decided to remove its FairPlay DRM restrictions for music files on iTunes in 2009 (Murray, 2010: 69–70)), DRM protection is still widely employed by rights holders to protect their intellectual property and is used by more recent music services such as Spotify. Furthermore, the move away from the PC towards cloud computing (where files are stored centrally rather than on people's own computers) and what Zittrain (2009a) calls 'tethered devices' (which can be controlled centrally by companies) offers greater regulatory control. In 2009, to take a notorious example, Amazon remotely removed the novel *1984* by George Orwell from the Kindle e-readers of those who had purchased a copy since the company did not own the rights to the book (Zittrain, 2009b: para. 4).

In recent years, rights holders have sought to enlist the help of Internet service providers (ISPs) in policing copyright infringers. They have lobbied governments for new so-called 'three-strikes' or 'graduated-response' legislation, where ISPs are required to impose 'technical measures' on users who disregard initial warnings about copyright infringement. In the UK, for example, the Digital Economy Act 2010 includes provisions for ISPs to limit and suspend the Internet accounts of recidivist copyright infringers (Digital Economy Act 2010, section 10). Although laws establishing systems of graduated response have been passed in other countries (e.g.

the French HADOPI law mentioned above), such legislation has proven contentious. In the United States, the Stop Online Piracy (SOPA) and Protect Intellectual Property (PIPA) Acts were opposed by user groups as well as by large Internet and technology corporations such as Google and Facebook. However, while the legislation was eventually abandoned, rights holders have been able to negotiate and implement a private system of graduated response (the 'Copyright Alert System') through voluntary arrangements with ISPs (Electronic Frontier Foundation (EFF), 2013); the fairness and effectiveness of this new system remains unsettled. Meanwhile, in the UK, courts have required that ISPs apply filters in order to block access to sites involved in copyright infringement such as *The Pirate Bay*.

At the same time as seeking to combat infringers directly by using the law and technical measures, rights holders have also had success in promoting legal forms of digital distribution through set-top boxes, video and radio streaming services such as YouTube and Spotify, and digital platforms for purchasing music and films like iTunes. Revenues are increasing from digital services as a result, be it through online subscriptions, advertising, or per-copy payments. In the case of the music industry, for example, the International Federation of the Phonographic Industry (IFPI) reported that digital revenues were up by 9 per cent in 2012 and that recorded music revenues rose by 0.3 per cent overall (including digital revenue streams). The IFPI (2013: para. 4) confidently concludes that 'the global recorded music industry is on a path to recovery, fuelled by licensed digital music services and rapid expansion into new markets internationally'.

Given growth in digital revenues, rights holders may, it seems, be winning the war on 'piracy'. Zittrain (2012: para. 1) has concluded that, while there is still 'plenty of fighting' over piracy, 'the lines for détente on straight-out copying are drawn: there's been uptake of all-you-can-eat subscriptions through services such as Spotify or Netflix, and pay-per-item stores such as the iTunes store'. However, even if Zittrain's (2012) forecast is correct, the emerging settlement around digital copyright is not necessarily the most legitimate one. As already noted – and as implied by the continuing efforts of industry and government bodies to limit and penalize illegal access to and distribution of copyrighted material – copyright infringement persists among large sections of the public, something which can be read not simply as a case of people seeking 'something for nothing', but also as an implicit rejection of industry claims that current copyright regulation is fair, balanced and in the public interest (Edwards et al., 2013b). Rejection of current copyright policy is explicit in public campaigns against new legislation, as was the case with SOPA/PIPA in the United States, and in the voices of oppositional groups, from digital rights organizations to creative workers themselves, who challenge the claims of corporate rights holders about the public benefits that follow from current copyright policy.

The assumption behind the industry war on piracy has tended to be that users are self-interested utility maximizers who commit piracy simply because it is easy and they can get away with it. In this view, copyright infringement is best tackled by imposing ever stronger sanctions on infringers and by the development of technologies and the imposition of technical measures that limit and control access to and uses of copyrighted material. This regulatory approach towards infringement offers little to no appreciation of the complexity of user practices around copyrighted material or any sense that the direction of copyright policy could itself be open to question. The possibility that users might have more reasoned and ethical justifications for their practices around copyrighted material, let alone that they might be sources of legitimate perspectives that could contribute meaningfully to debates about media policy and regulation, is overlooked from the start (Boltanski, 2011; Boltanski and Thévenot, 2006).

Consideration of the attempts by industry to regulate copyright and the public resistance that has ensued begins to point to the competing perspectives that characterize the copyright debate. However, to gain a clearer sense of the way in which the public and the public interest are positioned and addressed requires a closer examination of the different justificatory discourses employed in the current copyright debate. How do rights holders explain and justify the current copyright system? Does the public understand these justifications and find them credible and convincing? Rather than approach the copyright crisis as simply a struggle to force delinquent users to acknowledge and abide by the law, we can approach copyright – drawing on Boltanski and Thévenot's (2006) sociology of justification – as a site of disagreement which is structured by the competing justifications of invested actors, including ordinary users. Drawing on an analysis of industry communication and discussions among media users, in the following sections we identify and examine the justifications employed by industry and users in order to better understand the apparent gulf between those seeking more effective regulation and the seeming refusal of others to be regulated.

THE CREATIVE INDUSTRIES AND JUSTIFICATORY DISCOURSES

Since the turn of the 21st century, industry discourses that represent or communicate copyright to users have tended to fall into three main areas: those that seek to criminalize the user-as-infringer; those that seek to shame users into adopting legal behaviour; and those that attempt to educate supposedly naive and ill-informed users. More recently, there has been a shift to representing the (paying) user as a crucial cog in the audio/visual industries, and thus responsibilizing them as partners of industry. Before unpacking these more recent shifts in industry discourse, we contextualize them in relation to earlier dominant depictions of infringing media users.

With the spread of domestic copying technologies in the 1980s, the media user, rather than just the commercial infringer of copyright, came under the scrutiny of the creative industries. Despite clear differences between everyday users of media and the pirates demonized in historical iterations of debates about copyright infringement, the pirate label was applied and users were consequently viewed as a substantial threat to the creative industries. Perhaps the most famous – and extreme – instance of the discourse of criminalization and threat was the Motion Picture Association of America (MPAA) president Jack Valenti's statement that 'the VCR is to the American film producer and the American public as the Boston strangler is to the woman home alone' (US House of Representatives, 1983). In the UK the connection between crime and illicit domestic copying was taken up by the British Recorded Music Industry (BPI) in its 'Home-taping is Killing Music' campaign: adapting the Jolly Roger flag to include a cassette above the cross-bones, the campaign rendered the fan practices of taping the top 40 from the radio and producing mixed tapes as piratical and as foreshadowing the collapse of the British recorded music industry.

The dominant discourse of criminalization persisted into the 2000s, with the MPAA's prominent 'Piracy: It's a Crime' campaign (MPAA, 2004) pairing illegal downloading of media with the theft of physical objects, like handbags, cars and DVDs (see also Rutter, 2010). As with the BPI's earlier campaign – whose Jolly Roger insignia was re-configured by *The Pirate Bay*, and whose central claim was parodied in TalkTalk's anti-Digital Economy Act campaign (Bull and TalkTalk, 2010) – the MPAA's campaign became the butt of user and televisual lambastings (e.g. the 2007 'Moss and the German' episode of *The IT Crowd*). Such parodies may arguably have discouraged the BPI from launching a similar, modern campaign, yet it continued to contribute to the discourse of criminalization more generally through its enforcement and lobbying activities. While the discourse of criminalization persists in select industry material, such as that produced by trade organizations like the Alliance Against IP Theft (AAIPT, which has since tellingly re-branded as the Alliance for Intellectual Property) and the Federation Against Copyright Theft (FACT), a different tack was developed towards the end of the 2000s, as the British film and TV industry sought to shame its viewers into lawful behaviour. For instance, in 2007 the Industry Trust released the 'Knock-off Nigel' campaign (Industry Trust, 2007), which depicted media users who download illegitimate copies of films as cheap and grubby.

Despite industry claims to the contrary (see Parkes, 2013), the failure of anti-piracy campaigns like 'Knock-off Nigel' to make a dent in illegal downloading figures has led the creative industries in the UK to change gear in their communications to and about users. For example, subsequent campaigns by the Industry Trust – 2010's 'You Make the Movies' (Industry Trust, 2010) and the ongoing 'Moments Worth Paying for' (2014) campaign – adopt a much gentler approach to users. The theme of partnership replaces that of criminality: the campaigns thank consumers for supporting the British film and TV industry and highlight the enjoyment that users derive from audio-visual products as a rationale for legal consumption. Similarly, the ongoing BPI-sponsored campaign 'Music Matters' (BPI, 2014) stresses the role of artists in the production of the music 'that you love', thus seeking to responsibilize users into 'good' or 'ethical' consumption habits.[1]

The shift in emphasis from criminalization to partnership observed in the UK makes sense in the context of ongoing user rejection of criminalization (exemplified by continued high levels of illegal downloading) and the evolution of sharing as a normative practice in the digital communications environment; the discourse had to change because the audience was itself evolving in the context of an information-rich, empowering digital environment. However, central to both the criminalization and partnership discourses is a conception of the creative industries as an important locus of economic growth, a sector that must be protected in order to sustain the UK's international competitiveness in the now global cultural industries, and to protect jobs and creativity domestically. Legal consumption is framed as a way of ensuring that industry workers receive a return for their effort and, implicitly, that existing industry structures – which facilitate this return – remain intact. Alternative models of achieving a fair return for creative work are thus deemed unnecessary and excluded.

As well as appealing to users, industry bodies engage with policy-makers about copyright through government consultations, offering another source through which industry discourse can be located and examined. Submissions to consultations are framed by the calls for evidence to which they are responding. They present industry knowledge as a form of expertise, and the notion of 'evidence' leads to an academic, scientific style of writing, with plentiful use of statistics and categorical language – the latter often masking opinion-based statements as fact. This contrasts with the marketing campaigns outlined above, where communication is a pedagogical exercise enacted through advertising, movie trailers and websites, with language that is emotional rather than scientific, appealing to users' feelings and identities rather than to their rationality.

And yet despite differences in delivery, industry discourses directed towards users and those directed towards policy-makers share a common justification in the argument that creative industries are a major source of economic growth and consumer satisfaction. Many policy submissions use statistics to back up the argument that the creative industries sector is a valuable contributor to GDP, citing numerous statistics as evidence. For example, the BPI's submission to the Gowers Review (BPI, 2006) includes figures for the trade surplus generated by the sector, the diverse repertoires it offers, per capita consumption and export growth, while Warner Brothers describes IP protection as 'the cornerstone to facilitating, creating, distributing, and monetizing creative works' (Warner Bros., 2006: 2). Correspondingly, any action that might open up markets or loosen the protection that copyright affords equates to the potential destruction of markets for creative work. Exceptions to copyright law, such as fair dealing or limited terms for copyright, are dismissed as strategies that will introduce risk rather than security, reducing creativity rather than enhancing it. For example, in relation to the advent of many older works falling into the public domain, the BPI paints a dismal picture:

> Far from this auguring in a golden age in which thousands of obscure recordings are suddenly rescued from the vaults and made available to a grateful public, the likelihood is that this will result mainly in a slew of poorly packaged 'hits' collections of variable quality, with none of the proceeds finding their way back to the original creators and investors. They will occupy already restricted shelf space in retail outlets and paradoxically REDUCE the availability of rare works to the consumer. (BPI, 2006: 26–27, emphasis in original)

Industry justifications of copyright are presented differently to different audiences, based on the genre (Fairclough, 2001, 2003) that will be most effective for those audiences: marketing and pedagogy for direct communication to users; scientific and industry expertise for policy-makers. The different genres are crucial to the effectiveness of the justifications and hardly conflict despite their very different persuasive rationales, not least because these audiences rarely share the same discursive space. Nonetheless, while the strategies may differ the conclusions are the same: the market is the most effective way of ensuring creativity circulates and generates economic and creative benefits for society. Copyright protects artists and industry workers because it ensures creativity is rewarded. Users' only legitimate role is as legal (i.e. paying) consumers of creative work, and providing users with opportunities to access creative work in other ways (described as piracy, theft or illegal downloading) is constructed as the potential source of industry collapse rather than an indication of the failures of a pre-digital model of intellectual property regulation.

However, copyright's effectiveness depends upon users adopting the role of paying customer that the market prescribes for them, a logic which forms a 'regime of truth' (Foucault, 1980: 131) where there is little space for alternative perspectives about users, their roles, and the validity of industry structures or of copyright. As a result, a gap is revealed between industry discourses and those that are promoted by groups that represent broader public interests. Moreover, the latter are relatively few in number: users themselves are barely visible in policy-making processes, while groups that seek radical changes to existing copyright laws, such as the Open Rights Group and the Electronic Frontier Foundation (EFF), are scarce compared to their corporate counterparts.

The marginalization of alternative perspectives is exacerbated by the fact that the principles on which the arguments of such groups are based reverse the industry story. Creativity is enhanced, rather than endangered, through an open, flexible information and communications environment. Open Rights Group (2013), for example, argues that the digital environment is not a source of risk, but a route to different types of freedom: democracy, information, creativity and connection. Greater access to creative work is a 'public right' that ensures future creativity: file-sharing may be understood as the manifest desire for greater access rather than a pathological behaviour. With users as likely to innovate as the 'creatives' formally recognized in industry structures (for example, artists, writers or composers), wide circulation of work (not stronger protection of work) becomes essential to creativity.

As the following Creative Commons excerpt explains, the constantly changing creative environment is full of potential, but pre-digital copyright systems promoted by industry prevent potential from being 'leveraged'. By implication, social benefits can only be delivered through more flexible copyright regulation that accommodates both private and public interests:

> [T]he status quo 'all rights reserved' copyright protection increasingly serves as the standard business model for most copyright-based industries to date, whether it be publishing, music or education. The restrictive nature of maximized copyright protection is thrown into stark relief by the potential for access, use and reuse of content made possible by digital technologies. Digital technologies enable the storage, availability, dissemination and, perhaps most importantly, repurposing of content greater than was possible in the analogue world. However, this potential cannot be leveraged in an 'all rights reserved' world. (Creative Commons, 2006: 2)

Users are positioned by Creative Commons discourse as both creators and consumers, and are trusted to enact both roles responsibly through their re-use of content, innovation and experimentation, emphasizing the public benefit that a limited copyright regime should deliver.

In summary, the construction of notions of piracy and the public in early debates about copyright have led to entrenched principles about what constitutes good or bad use, even as contemporary accounts and characterizations of users have shifted. While space for alternative characterizations of users has been opened, the foundation of good versus bad behaviour is perpetuated: industry implicates users as either law-abiding or criminal, ethical or unethical, good or bad fans. Furthermore, the goal remains the same: to stop copyright infringement. Emergent discourses linked to copyright have created space in which to imagine alternative models of creative production and distribution (Lessig, 2004), but struggle to be heard in a world where industry voices are so dominant. Both industry and advocacy groups advance their agendas in part by communicating to and about users, but if we are to understand how users make sense of the discourses communicated to and about them, and how they view and justify their attitudes and behaviour, they must be given their own platform from which to speak.

USER PERSPECTIVES ON COPYRIGHT

The growth of media sharing and copying that has resulted from digitization has put the behaviour and attitudes of everyday users under the spotlight of policy, industry and academic researchers. In the UK, interest in the everyday activities of ordinary users can be seen in policy research funded through the Intellectual Property Office (IPO) (BOP Consulting, 2010; Hunt et al., 2009); in Ofcom's recent consumer survey into online copyright infringement and 'wider digital attitudes and behaviours' (Ofcom, 2012); in recently published industry research into business models for copyright infringing sites, which amongst other things considers the 'users' journey to each site' (PRS for Music and Google, 2012); and in the establishment of a national research centre for copyright and new business models at the University of Glasgow (CREATe, 2013). There is no doubt that understanding users is high on the agenda for several parties. However, while users are framed and positioned through various inquiries and communication and while alternative voices can be viewed as speaking for ordinary users, the voices of users themselves are generally absent from the debate and from the policy-making process.

The importance of user voices is clear. From the perspective of industry and policy-makers, effective regulation relies on getting users on side and, as we have demonstrated, strategies that have relied on particular assumptions about or characterizations of users have not been successful. From our perspective, the copyright crisis must be approached not as a struggle to encourage users to abide by the law but as a disagreement structured by the justifications of all involved actors (Boltanski and Thévenot, 2006), including ordinary users. Drawing on an analysis of focus group discussions, we seek to elevate the attitudes of users to the status of legitimate justifications, which a deliberative and democratic policy-making process will allow into the arena to sit beside and interact with the justifications communicated by industry.

We carried out 12 focus groups of participants based in Yorkshire, England. The groups included between three and ten participants, ranging in age from 16 to 84, and involved discussions about copyright, the creative industries, digital media, downloading and piracy which lasted between 1¼ and 1¾ hours. The reliance on pre-existing groups was intended to produce conversations that resemble the conversations about copyright that may take place naturally between friends and acquaintances. Anonymized transcripts were analysed inductively using an interpretive approach through a combination of manual and computer-assisted techniques.

The emergence of user voices, in this case through focus group discussions, unsettles the dominant and simplistic categorizations of users by industry and policy, by showing the complexity of media use and the variegated, yet well-informed ways in which media users engage with the issue of copyright in the digital age. Recurrent themes point to ways forward in terms of how policy-makers and industry might begin to re-conceptualize users and re-imagine the form and purpose of 'data' related to user behaviour and attitudes in order to develop a more holistic and sustainable approach to copyright protection. Media users challenged justifications that form the basis of industry discourse to policy-makers and the public, putting forward their own complex, rational and cynical perspectives on copyright, the creative industries and appropriate media use.

As the focus groups demonstrated, ordinary media users spill over the bounded categories frequently deployed in industry and government research and communications material: confused versus educated consumer; intentional versus accidental criminal; good versus bad fan; legal versus illegal downloader; producer versus consumer. Instead, users displayed a range of views and an array of practices in relation to their consumption of copyrighted media.

Focus group participants described accessing media in various ways and via multiple platforms: users of illegal downloading or file-sharing platforms also rely upon a variety of legal platforms, from set-top boxes to video and radio streaming services, from online stores to subscription services. Many purchased CDs and DVDs, and used freeware or open source software. Consumption of a single film was charted from its release at the cinema to its availability as a reduced-price DVD:

> a film comes out in the movies. And if it looks really good, I'll go watch it. And then, I dunno, a couple of weeks go by, and you can get a relatively good quality [copy] online and download it illegally. And, I'll do that so I can watch it at home. And then another few months go by and I can buy the DVD for a quid.

As Ofcom's recent survey (2012) noted, users who access media both illegally and legally claim to spend more on legal content than those who only consume media legally. The value of such consumers to the creative industries underlines the importance of understanding the varied methods of access users may pursue.

The division between producer and user was also challenged in focus group discussions. While industry communications frequently address consumers as distinct from producers, many media users engage in non-professional creative activities that mean that they consider copyright from multiple perspectives, reflecting the emergence of web 2.0 interactive technologies which encourage user participation and cultural collaboration. Focus group participants confirmed such behaviour, focusing on the legitimacy of sharing copyrighted material, viewing the circulation of their own creative products as encouraging interest and engagement, and expressing a Creative Commons attitude even in the absence of the phrase.

The observations of participants and descriptions of their own actions also challenged the depiction of copyright infringers as thoughtless and unethical consumers of creative work. Although illegal downloading can be dismissed as a simple lack of consumer responsibility, their comments suggest that the choice to illegally download may in fact be the result of a balancing act of various ethical decisions: 'You know, you are so into other things and you just cannot think about every single thing you're doing in life. Like is this movie alright? Is this music alright now? Are these socks I'm buying alright and organic and Fairtrade?' The recognition that users consume digital media both legally and illegally, and consume goods more generally both ethically and less ethically, challenges the more simplistic positioning of illegal downloaders as representing a certain type of (bad) consumer. In contrast, the use of illegal platforms is accompanied by ethically-informed justifications, highlighting another significant characteristic of media users: media users are rational.

Given the opportunity to share their views, focus group participants justified their media choices with reasoned explanations. While perspectives on copyright (generally supportive of its basic tenets) and creative labour (understood as deserving reward) may often be inconsistent with everyday behaviour, the explanations of behaviour we heard in the focus groups were grounded in logic and displayed internal consistency. Counter to characterizations of media users as knowing criminals, specific circumstances were viewed as legitimizing technically illegal access to digital media. For example, participants defended file-sharing as a sensible solution in cases where legitimate copies of media products were not available to them. Out-of-print material was fair game, as were products without simultaneous (or reasonably fast) global release. Thus, using P2P or streaming sites to watch 'good American shows' was justified by UK-based viewers who knew 'it was going to be like a year until it came out'.

Copyright infringing access was also justified by users as a transitory phase. Younger users understood file-sharing as a practice that was temporary, a life stage that they anticipated moving on from once they became independent earners. Likewise, not being able to afford media was seen by some users as a legitimate justification for sharing, highlighting the perception of media as a public good. Their arguments suggest that media users project mitigating circumstances on to instances of illegal media use and cast copyright as potentially limiting availability for some users: 'Maybe that guy's not got any money and his friend's given him a DVD or whatever and he's got one week of, you know, watching something nice for once. You know, like, should he be a criminal for that?' In this way, users voiced the aspect of the public interest relevant to copyright exceptions rather than the aspect of the public interest that justifies copyright protection as driving creativity, and that dominates industry campaigns intended to appeal to users as partners.

A rational framework for decision-making was likewise displayed by the tendency of focus group participants to combine legal and illegal access, and to report sampling practices ('We tend to download a film we want to see … and then if we really like it we'll buy it on Blu-Ray'). Use of P2P sites was justified through their value as both a promotional tool and a successful means of wider distribution: 'it gets their music out to me and then I will buy it afterwards'. Hybrid practices (of consuming the same product both illegally and then legally) are not the thoughtless acts of rampant criminals, but a considered response to the free market by media users adapting to neoliberal discourses of consumer-citizenship (Marquand, 2004), a reaction to its central notion of choice and the call to be a discerning consumer, especially in economically-straitened times.

The sharing of both digital and hard copies with friends and family was another technically illegal activity justified by the participants as situated within a broader promotional and distribution system, and not connected to the criminal activities used as metaphors in industry campaigns (e.g. theft and piracy). Rational defences of behaviour highlighted parallels between online and offline norms, particularly in terms of social activities: sharing between friends and family was understood by focus group participants as legitimate and normal, and sharing legally purchased material was considered a fair consumer right and akin to inviting a friend round to watch a television programme together or lending a book or CD to a peer. The lack of a private copying exception in current UK copyright law was viewed as making a 'normal person a criminal' and restrictions around sharing were viewed as out of alignment with shared norms around media consumption: 'It's become so commonplace I don't even feel guilty about downloading'. Despite offering support for casual sharing, users drew a line at profiting from sharing media or sharing media online with a wider, unknown audience. However, widespread use of illegal file-sharing platforms suggests that the line is blurred when users are on the receiving end of sharing or when an online forum is considered a community or fan group. Such activities may be classified by the creative industries as 'bad fan' behaviour in financial terms, but can also be understood as actions arising from 'good fan' tendencies to share with like-minded individuals, illustrating the competing moral frameworks activated by users and the creative industries.

Disagreement between user perspectives and the evidence provided by public campaigns for the benefits of copyright can be a source of tension. Far from being convinced by campaigns, media users often respond cynically to industry claims: the pervasiveness of campaign parodies (David, 2013) is one demonstration of user perspectives. Rather than finding anti-piracy campaigns persuasive, focus group participants were able to highlight holes in the claims and rationales communicated, and underline the limitations of applying the framework of piracy to ordinary user behaviour. While more sympathetic to the artists' perspective than general industry pleas, they were nonetheless suspicious of artists' pleas for fans to abide by copyright law. Focus group participants were critical of the nature of the commercial music industry and questioned the legitimacy of anti-piracy claims. For example, some highlighted the discrepancy between commercially successful artists, whose wealth contradicts industry claims that it is ailing, and less successful artists, whose situation can be seen as resulting from exploitative record labels rather than disloyal fans. Participants expressed the view that creative industries remain financially successful in the face of illegal downloading, were aware of alternative revenue streams available to artists and industry, and identified mixed messages coming from different actors in the music industry, with some bands and artists actively encouraging fans to share their music.

Although industry and government communication has frequently suggested that greater education would decrease copyright infringement, users are more cynical when they have a stronger grasp of the detail of copyright law and creative industry processes. More detailed knowledge allowed focus group participants to engage directly with current UK copyright law and regulation, particularly in terms of the length of copyright and fair dealing exceptions. For example, awareness of the recent EU ratification of an extension of music copyright from 50 to 70 years opened the door to critique:

> I think it's fair to protect the income stream of the property owner to a point. I mean, there comes a point where you might even say, do you know what, I think the world has paid you amply for your intellectual property, and you should now say, thank you very much, world, and hand it over.

When focus group participants discussed the current laws around private copying, they were flummoxed by the misalignment of the law with their everyday, ordinary activities. Hargreaves describes a private copying exception as long overdue and necessary to address 'a growing mismatch between what is allowed under copyright exceptions, and the reasonable expectations and behaviour of most people' (2011: 43). Yet, as the user attitudes and behaviour detailed above suggest, private copying is but one area of copyright law into which user responses and perspectives might contribute to change.

Challenging existing industry and policy norms and characterizations, real media users evade easy categorization. Corporate and government approaches to copyright, which tend to focus narrowly on capital accumulation and the free market development of the creative industries, for the most part fail to recognize or respond to media user perspectives on issues relevant to copyright and their own activities. While industry communication takes the foundation of copyright (and attendant notions of piracy) for granted, users can complicate such discourses, particularly when 'educated' with the details of copyright law. The role of the public in the copyright debate is confused by competing senses of the public interest activated through discourse: industry tends to push one aspect of public interest (driving the creative economy) while the public highlights another (access and availability). Evidence of the real, rich voices of users demands that industry and policy-makers communicate with (and *listen* to) media users as complex, rational and cynical citizens, rather than as errant consumers or willing criminals. The disjuncture between industry and user perspectives can only be healed if the creative industries acknowledge the media users on whose patronage they rely as sources of legitimate justifications and valuable contributions to the policy-making process.

CONCLUSION

This chapter has outlined and analysed some of the competing discourses driving the copyright debate, from powerful and pervasive industry perspectives to the challenges of advocacy groups, to the opinions of media users themselves. We have suggested that the battle over copyright suffers under the weight of historical baggage: the piracy frame continues to activate the 'driving creativity' public interest argument while obscuring the 'open access' public interest argument. By challenging the dominant industry perspective, this analysis hints at the possibility that 'pirates' are not simply damaging the creative economy but are pointing towards different and more flexible models.

The last decade has produced half a dozen government-commissioned reviews related to intellectual property in the UK, with an uneven relationship between recommendations and policy change. Policy reviews tend to echo the justifications of well-resourced players over others and, as a result, recommendations have not been especially surprising or progressive. At the same time, even the least controversial recommendations are subject to lengthy implementation processes and can be viewed as minor fixes that might be less likely to raise user eyebrows but that do not address some of the fundamental objections to copyright terms or the social acceptance of certain (still illegal) forms of sharing. Thus, despite the government's support of the recommendations from the most recent review (IPO, 2011), planned changes can be understood as just the start of a bridge, with a wide gulf remaining.

The question remains as to how the gulf can be effectively bridged. From the perspective of Boltanski and Thévenot's justificatory discourses, the analysis shows that disagreement in the current crisis operates on different levels. First, the different parties to the debate disagree about the 'common good', or the meaning and role of the public interest that can be realized through copyright regulation. Second, there is disagreement about the route to realizing the public interest, both in terms of the type of model which forms the foundation of a successful creative economy and the appropriate response to infringement. Finding a resolution to the crisis requires policy-makers to acknowledge all positions in the debate, including that of users, as important, thus offering a more balanced approach than one which favours the input from large, resource-rich rights holders. Such a balanced approach would require a significant change to the policy-making process to accommodate greater public engagement and more deliberative consultation. The copyright crisis will not be resolved through tougher regulation, greater education or appeals from the most powerful to the least powerful: resolution must begin through the establishment of a shared sense of the 'common good' and an openness, from all parties involved, to various models and the routes through which they might be achieved.

ACKNOWLEDGEMENT

This work was supported by the Economic and Social Research Council [grant number RES-062-23-3027].

NOTE

1 While the responsibilization approach towards users has increased with recent campaigns positioning users as partners in the creative economy, there are earlier precedents, such as the Software Publishers Association (SPA) campaign 'Don't Copy that Floppy' (SPA, 1992).

REFERENCES

Boltanski L (2011) *On Critique: A Sociology of Emancipation*. Cambridge: Polity.

Boltanski L and Thévenot L (2006) *On Justification: Economies of Worth*. Trans. C Porter. Woodstock and Princeton: Princeton University Press.

BOP Consulting (2010) Changing attitudes and behaviour in the 'non-internet' digital world and their implications for intellectual property. Available at: www.ipo.gov.uk/ipresearch-attitudes-201001.pdf

BPI (2006) The Gowers review of intellectual property: A response from the British Phonographic Industry. Available at: http://webarchive.nationalarchives.gov.uk/+/ and http://www.hm-treasury.gov.uk/d/british_phonographic_industry_306_160kb.pdf

BPI (2014) Music matters. Available at: http://www.bpi.co.uk/music-matters.aspx

Bull D and TalkTalk (2010) Home-taping is killing music. Available at: www.youtube.com/watch?v=R3jkUhG68wY

CREATe (2013) Theme 6: User creation, user behaviour and community norms. Available at: www.create.ac.uk/research-programme/theme-6/

Creative Commons (2006) Submission to the Gowers review of intellectual property. Available at: webarchive.nationalarchives.gov.uk/+/http://www.hm-treasury.gov.uk/d/creative_commons_418_p1_936kb.pdf

David M (2013) File-sharing and beyond: Cultural, legal, technical and economic perspectives on the future of copyright online. In: Dutton W (ed) *The Oxford Handbook of Internet Studies*. Oxford: Oxford University Press, 464–485.

Davies G (2002) *Copyright and the Public Interest*. 2nd Edition. London: Sweet & Maxwell.

Deazley R (2004) *On the Origin of the Right to Copy: Charting the Movement of Copyright Law in Eighteenth Century Britain (1695–1775)*. Oxford: Hart Publishing.

Digital Economy Act 2010 (2010) London: The Stationery Office. Available at: www.legislation.gov.uk/ukpga/2010/24/contents

Edwards L, Klein B, Lee D, Moss G and Philip F (2013a) 'Isn't it just a way to protect Walt Disney's rights?': Media user perspectives on copyright. *New Media & Society*[onlinefirst].doi:10.1177/1461444813511402

Edwards L, Klein B, Lee D, Moss G and Philip F (2013b) Framing the consumer: Copyright regulation and the public. *Convergence: The International Journal of Research into New Media Technologies* 19(1): 9–24.

Electronic Frontier Foundation (EFF) (2013) The copyright alert system FAQ. Available at: www.eff.org/deeplinks/2013/02/six-strikes-copyright-alert-system-faq

Fairclough N (2001) Critical discourse analysis as a method in social scientific research. In: Wodak R and Meyer M (eds) *Methods of Critical Discourse Analysis*. London: Sage, 121–138.

Fairclough N (2003) *Analysing Discourse: Textual Analysis for Social Research*. London: Routledge.

Foucault M (1980) *Power/Knowledge*. Brighton: Harvester.

Hargreaves I (2011) *Digital Opportunity: A Review of Intellectual Property and Growth*. London: HM Treasury.

Hunt R, Williams P, Rowlands I and Nicholas D (2009) Copycats? Digital consumers in the online age. Available at: www.ipo.gov.uk/ipresearch-copycats-200905.pdf

IFPI (2013) IFPI publishes Digital Music Report 2013. Available at: www.ifpi.org/content/section_resources/dmr2013.html

Industry Trust (2007) Knock-off Nigel: downloading. Available at: www.youtube.com/watch?v=GlhdK5Yl8u0

Industry Trust (2010) You Make the Movies. Available at: www.industrytrust.co.uk/campaigns/you-make-the-movies

Industry Trust (2014) Moments Worth Paying For. Available at: www.industrytrust.co.uk/campaigns/moments

Intellectual Property Office (IPO) (2011) Modernising copyright: A modern, robust and flexible framework. Available at: www.ipo.gov.uk/response-2011-copyright-final.pdf

Lessig L (2004) *Free Culture*. New York: The Penguin Press.

Lessig L (2006) *Code 2.0*. New York: Basic Books.

McIntyre TJ and Scott S (2008) Internet filtering: Rhetoric, legitimacy, accountability and responsibility. In: Brownsword R and Yeung K (eds) *Regulating Technologies*. Oxford: Hart, 109–125.

Marquand D (2004) *Decline of the Public: The Hollowing-Out of Citizenship*. Cambridge: Polity.

MPAA (2004) Piracy. It's a crime. Available at: www.youtube.com/watch?v=HmZm8vNHBSU

Murray A (2010) *Information Technology Law: The Law and Society*. Oxford: Oxford University Press.

Ofcom (2012) *OCI Tracker Benchmark Study Q3 2012: Introduction and Key Findings*. London: Ofcom.

Open Rights Group (2013) Our work. Available at: www.openrightsgroup.org/ourwork/

Parkes N (2013) Making plans for Nigel: The Industry Trust and film piracy management in the United Kingdom. *Convergence* 19(1): 25–43.

PRS for Music and Google (2012) The six business models of copyright infringement. Available at: www.prsformusic.com/aboutus/policyandresearch/researchandeconomics/Documents/TheSixBusinessModelsofCopyrightInfringement.pdf

Rose M (1993) *Authors and Owners: The Invention of Copyright*. Cambridge, MA: Harvard University Press.

Rutter J (2010) Consumers, crime and the downloading of music. *Prometheus* 28(4): 411–418.

SPA (1992) Don't copy that floppy campaign. Available at: www.youtube.com/watch?v=up863eQKGUI

US House of Representatives. Subcomittee on Courts, Civil Liberties and the Administration of Justice (1983) *Home Recording of Copyrighted Works, Part 1*. April–September 1982. Available at: www.cryptome.org/hrcw-hear.htm

Vaidhyanathan S (2001) *Copyrights and Copywrongs: The Rise of Intellectual Property and How It Threatens Creativity*. New York: NYU Press.

Warner Bros. Entertainment UK (2006) Submission to the Gowers review of UK IP laws. Available at: webarchive.nationalarchives.gov.uk/+/http://www.hm-treasury.gov.uk/d/warner_brothers_entertainment_uk_097_35kb.pdf

Yu PK (2005) P2P and the future of private copying. *University of Colorado Law Review* 76. Available at SSRN: www.ssrn.com/abstract=578568

Zittrain J (2009a) *The Future of the Internet: And How to Stop It*. New edn. London: Penguin.

Zittrain J (2009b) Lost in the cloud. *The New York Times*, 19 July. Available at: www.nytimes.com/2009/07/20/opinion/20zittrain.html

Zittrain J (2012) Don't let software patents stop us standing on the shoulders of giants. *The Guardian*, 18 April. Available at: www.guardian.co.uk/commentisfree/2012/apr/18/software-patents-shoulders-of-giants

17

Creativity and Copyright: The International Career of a New Economy

Dave O'Brien

This chapter argues that the idea of intellectual property at the centre of the creative industries is a construction that has little to do with the reality of work in these sectors of the economy. The focus is on three areas: (1) the rise of creative industries discourse; (2) the creation and effects of the British model of creative industries; and (3) creative work and labour. The bulk of the discussion is around the 'career' of creative industries discourse as it intertwines itself with intellectual property. The chapter shows how creative industries held out the promise of a new form of economic activity to replace the supposedly declining heavy industries of the West. In fact creative industries have, so far, offered forms of labour and visions of culture that are deeply problematic. The chapter concludes by assessing the usefulness of a model of the economy based on a version of intellectual property that is set against the reality of work in the creative industries.

INTRODUCTION

> We will soon begin to see the 'creative industry' phenomenon as something specifically linked with the Blair and post-Blair years, starting 1997 and in effect lasting for just more than a decade. (McRobbie 2010: 32)

The chapter explores the rise of the creative industries and their relationship to intellectual property. The main argument in the chapter is that although intellectual property, in the UK model, seems to be inextricably linked with creative industries and the creative economy, in fact it has a complex and often peripheral role in the practices of those industries and that economy. This is because the term 'intellectual property' was used in a specific way as part of the development of the concept of creative industries. Rather than referring to the legal regime surrounding the protection and exploitation of property rights, intellectual property in the UK's version of creative industries became a catch-all term for an economic and an arts policy. The chapter will demonstrate how this version of intellectual property is deeply problematic, particularly as its usage elides several different ideas.

The chapter begins by outlining the various iterations of the creative industries, from the cultural industries of the 1980s to the digital economy described by recent European Union (EU) policy documentation. Following this overview the chapter uses existing research to consider the extent to which the initially central place given to a problematic idea of intellectual property in the UK's highly influential definition of creative industries is a reality. In fact, for many in the creative economy, their labour is not primarily concerned with intellectual property, and the exploitation of the intellectual property they produce provides an uncertain basis for their lives. The chapter concludes by surveying the most recent debates defining creative industries. It questions the sustainability of economic activity that is defined by the Department for Culture, Media and Sport (DCMS) version of intellectual property. The DCMS conception of intellectual property is, as this chapter indicates, both at odds with British and international legal frameworks of intellectual property, such as copyright, and at odds with the working lives of those within the creative industries.

MAKING MONEY FROM IDEAS: THE CREATIVE INDUSTRIES

The idea of the creative industries became well known because of work in the UK. In 1998 the UK's ministry of culture, the Department for Culture, Media and Sport (DCMS) produced a definition of cultural and business activities that were seen to be part of a new form of economic activity (DCMS 1998). DCMS began by using 13 sectors of economic activity as the basis for the creative industries: advertising, architecture, arts and antiques markets, crafts, design, designer fashion, film and video, interactive leisure software, music, performing arts, publishing, software and computer services, and television and radio. The 13 sectors were controversial as the definition included such things as database design and computer games that, on the surface, seemed only tenuously linked to cultural activities (Campbell 2013). Indeed academic discussions over what was and what was not a creative industry provoked a rich and intensive debate (e.g. see Flew (2012) for a summary).

Debates over the definition of creative industries focused on the question of what, exactly, brought these 13 sectors together. In the DCMS work on defining the creative industries, the common link and theme between the disparate sectors was the idea of intellectual property. This idea was focused on the economic importance of the 13 cultural and business sectors, as their economic similarities were seen to be that they derived revenues from their use of intellectual property:

> those industries which have their origin in individual creativity, skill and talent which have a potential for job and wealth creation through the generation and exploitation of intellectual property. (DCMS 2001: 5)

The DCMS thus placed intellectual property at the root of the creative industries in terms of its importance. However, this definition of intellectual property is highly problematic. This is because, in the initial development of creative industries and the mapping of what was and what was not a creative industry, the understanding of intellectual property was not at all clearly defined. Two examples, from a series of critiques of the DCMS 13 by various authors and organizations (Hesmondhalgh 2012; NESTA 2013; Work Foundation 2007), illustrate the problem with the use of the term intellectual property in this context.

In the first instance there is an issue of how the markets for the goods and services captured by the 13 sectors functions. Recent debates (NESTA 2013) have shown that particular sectors of the 13 tended to have little or nothing to do with intellectual property in the sense of the exploitation of ownership and control over property rights, such as copyrights or patents. The market for art and antiques, for example, has elements of economic value that are the direct result of the ownership of the intellectual property that subsists in a painting or sculpture. However, much of the economic value in this sector is generated by the physical property, suggesting the market is more akin to the buying and selling of land. In particular it is the sale and resale of the physical property, the painting or sculpture, and the associated processing, auction and brokerage fees (Velthuis 2007) that are the drivers of economic value.

Sectors such as publishing have a closer relationship to the intellectual property protection regime associated with copyright, although 30 years ago this would have been more linked with the activity of selling the physical object. Film and computer games represent the opposite end of the scale, whereby an important (but not the only) source of economic value comes from the control and exploitation of the copyrights over creative and cultural content, although this has begun to change when confronted with the challenge of new technology for content dissemination and delivery (David 2010).

The second example is to do with the activities and working lives of those labouring with the 13 sectors. This is a point that the chapter will explore in much more detail in later sections. Before turning to issues of work and labour, it is worth considering other debates over creative industries that can help to clarify why the idea was so seductive to policy makers and how this seductive aspect has ensured the global dissemination of an, at best, very specific understanding of intellectual property.

The DCMS definition of the creative industries, with its focus on intellectual property, generated extensive criticism and debate. In the first instance, the 13 sectors chosen as the relevant creative industries seemed to rely heavily on the sectors that were more closely associated with technical expertise, such as database design, rather than those sectors most usually associated with the arts, such as performing or visual arts. Peter Campbell (2013) has shown how, when faced with the exclusion of software-related activity that was not computer game creation, the claims as to the strong, or above average, contributions to British GDP and employment were hard to sustain. Part of the attractiveness of the creative industries, as subsequent sections will show, was their capacity to generate economic impact that would be above and beyond other areas of economic activity. If the less artistic sectors were the drivers for this growth, what would that mean for the claims for a new economy based on DCMS's definition of intellectual property?

This first point bleeds into a second question, which concerns the use of intellectual property by DCMS as a basis for defining the creative industries. The use of intellectual property, in the DCMS's understanding, meant that the boundaries around what was, and was not, considered creative industries were unclear. For example, activities that are grouped together as the Galleries, Libraries, Archives and Museums (GLAM) sector, which are all crucial drivers of tourism revenue and have a clear relationship and dependence on the DCMS's 13 sectors, were excluded from the DCMS's original map of creative industries. If the boundaries between particular forms of cultural activity, such as those of the GLAM sector, and creative industries seemed arbitrary (Hesmondhalgh 2012) then the boundaries between the rest of the economy, almost all parts of which have (as subsequent sections of this chapter will describe) a relationship with the DCMS version of intellectual property, were equally problematic. Why the creative industries comprised specific parts of the economy and why they merited the special and particular attention of policy makers was, therefore, difficult to discern, beyond the DCMS policy's faith in its version of intellectual property. Indeed, as Bilton and Leary (2002: 50) assert: 'it is difficult to think of a product which does not exploit some intellectual component in the form of patents, design elements or other intangible, symbolic properties that make that product unique'.

DCMS's 13 sectors reflected several longer-term trends surrounding discussions about culture and the economy, summarized by Garnham's (2005) paper exploring the shift from the term cultural industries to the use of the concept of creative industries within policy discourses. The term cultural industries was most famously associated with the work of the Frankfurt School, who saw the production of cultural artefacts as closely related to the need to create order and submission within the power structures of monopoly capitalism (Adorno and Horkheimer 1997). Creative industries, grounded in the work of

DCMS and its version of intellectual property was the policy application of a longer-term emergence of cultural industries as a viable part of economic life.

Garnham argues the roots of the creative industries in the UK can be found in the strategies for funding the arts during the 1980s, whereby arts organizations made the case for the economic impact that they could have, if given sufficient funds by the state. By the 1990s the cultural aspect of the arts' claims to industrial status had been superseded by the rhetoric associated with a transformation within capitalism to an economy based on information and knowledge. This transformation is discussed in more detail later in this chapter, but at this juncture its importance stands as part of the explanation for the term 'creative' in creative industries and the focus on intellectual property as the key driver for the role of creative industries in the economy.

The development of an information economy was crucial to European Union attempts to remain competitive in a globalized economic order. The broad definition of creative industries used by the DCMS, with an important role for software production and advertising (Garnham 2005: 26), would not exist without the background of the information society and the EU's insistence on the need to employ knowledge as a central aspect of economic production. The employment of knowledge as a central aspect of economic production, although not spelt out in detail in EU documentation (Garnham 2005), has a similar status to intellectual property in DCMS's creative industries, as a seemingly established and coherent term, but one which bears little relation to the legal regimes surrounding knowledge or the realities of work and labour in this economy.

A range of British policy documents and ministerial speeches and statements show how the creative industries are currently understood in the UK. The most recent of those followed the change of government in 2010. By 2012 David Cameron (Cabinet Office 2012), who had said comparatively little on the specifics of art and cultural policy, framed comments on film policy through the lens of that sector's economic contribution:

> Our role, and that of the BFI, should be to support the sector in becoming even more dynamic and entrepreneurial, helping UK producers to make commercially successful pictures that rival the quality and impact of the best international productions … Just as the British Film Commission has played a crucial role in attracting the biggest and best international studios to produce their films here, so we must incentivise UK producers to chase new markets both here and overseas.

Cultural activity offered the chance to create an export industry that could contribute to British growth and competitiveness, staffed by entrepreneurial workers. Its primary product would be the intellectual property associated with the film industry and it seemed to be an area in which the British could not only compete with international rivals, but could also be seen to be excelling. This is, of course, in contrast to the narratives associated with labour intensive manufacturing and other forms of heavy industry that had seen a decline, for a variety of reasons, in the UK since the 1960s. Film, as an example of one of the creative industries, offered a chance to replace these jobs with a new type of work. This conception of creative industries would prove to be seductive beyond the UK, when framed within the DCMS definition of the 13 sectors of the economy that were creating intellectual property, as DCMS saw it, capable of being exploited.

GETTING CREATIVE WITH THE CREATIVE INDUSTRIES: THE UK AND USA

The previous section suggested that creative industries had been founded on a hopeful, but unclear, conception of intellectual property. The potential offered by this British understanding of creative industries and their role in the economy proved massively influential across the globe, even in contexts where the term itself was rejected. Ross's

(2007) narrative of the differing understandings of creative industries, in connection to the dissemination of the British model, is an important way of beginning to illustrate the distinction between the DCMS definition and the reality of creative practices. He identifies DCMS's creative industries model as itself a commodity to be exported, drawing interest from a range of nations seeking to develop a new form of economy, whether as a substitute for supposedly declining industrial activities, or as a means of short circuiting the prescriptions of developmental programmes.

The success of the British model of creative industries parallels similar successes in the cultural sector – an innovative repackaging of existing material that is clear or catchy enough to transcend linguistic or cultural barriers. The DCMS 13 created an economic sector, in the first instance, then coupled this sector to a narrative explicitly suggesting that this sector was growing at a much faster rate than the rest of the economy in the UK (Campbell 2013). The union of cultural activity, such as the traditionally publicly funded arts, with software and database design constructed a concept that appealed to aspects of individuals' identity, the need for economic growth and a difficult to refute appeal to the idea that work would no longer be the back-breaking labour of the factory, but would be some combination of individual artistic endeavour within a technologically advanced digitally literate society.

Ross (2007: 20) succinctly captures the objections to this model of the creative industries, which cuts across a range of policy and academic disciplinary areas:

> It will not generate jobs; it is a recipe for magnifying patterns of class polarisation; its function as a cover for the corporate intellectual property (IP) grab will become all too apparent; its urban development focus will price out the very creatives on whose labour it depends; its reliance on self-promoting rhetoric runs far in advance of its proven impact; its cookie-cutter approach to economic development does violence to regional specificity; its adoption of an instrumental value of creativity will cheapen the true worth of artistic creation. Still others are inclined simply to see the new policy rubric as 'old wine in new bottles' – a glib production of spin-happy New Labourites, hot for naked marketization but mindful of the need for socially acceptable dress. For those who take a longer, more orthodox Marxist view, the turn toward creative industries is surely a further symptom of an accumulation regime at the end of its effective rule, spent as a productive force, awash in financial speculation, and obsessed with imagery, rhetoric and display.

But the issue most pertinent to this discussion that Ross's work identifies is the status of intellectual property within the DCMS definition. This is especially clear when the rather glib reference to intellectual property in the DCMS version of creative industries is compared internationally. In the USA, the concept of creative industries has gained little traction, within a national setting that has placed intellectual property at the centre of its conception of the economic role of culture has shown how commercial cultural activity in the USA, in this instance film production, is tied up with complicated forms of state subsidy, benevolent tax regimes and the politics of US foreign policy, both in the Cold War era and after.

State support for this cultural industry is bound up with an insistence, internationally, by the US that overseas markets must open their boarders to US cultural exports, that nation states must be prevented from offering other forms of support, for example the French cultural exception, and that intellectual property rights must be afforded the strongest forms of protection. This situation has underpinned the point Ross makes, that in the USA the creative industries do not exist, rather they are known only as the copyright industries, reflecting the acknowledgement of the basis for their revenue and business models.

CREATIVITY GOES GLOBAL

Although the previous section introduced a range of challenges to the DCMS version of creative industries, this model has generated much interest and a variety of policy engagements across the world. Interest is partially a result of what Peck (2005: 751) neatly identifies as the ephemeral character of the creative industries, in the sense that the 'creativity' which is supposedly at their root is like apple pie and motherhood – hard to be against, yet ultimately a concept that is hard to coherently define.

The nebulousness of creativity was useful when it brought together software and the arts in the DCMS definition. Not only would creative industries offer the vision of a new economy, alongside an economic role for artistic practices, they would be open to anyone and everyone. After all, we are all creative, in our own way.

Arts organizations, start-up businesses, consultants and government bureaucracies all embraced the idea that the economy would now follow a blueprint driven by artistic and cultural production. Whilst the terms for this new economic system vary, being known as the knowledge economy (Foray and Lundvall 1996), as post-industrial (Bell 1974), as financialized capitalism (Engelen et al. 2011), as neo-liberal (Harvey 2007), as the network society (Castells 2000), as digital capitalism (Betancourt 2010) and as post-Fordism (Amin 1994), all of the various labels sought to focus on how the era of large-scale factory production of standardized goods via the physical labour of the worker was being overtaken by another economic system.

The new economy, detailed by Garnham (2005), would be characterized by industrial activity that had high fixed costs of production, for example newspapers or films, but almost no costs of reproduction and distribution, as digital technology made marginal costs of new products close to zero. Other writers have drawn attention to the wider aspects of the new economy that build on this business model, with terms such as 'cognitive capitalism' (Moulier Boutang 2011). Moulier Boutang's description ascribes a range of characteristics to cognitive capitalism (15 in total), with immaterial labour as perhaps the most important. This is the labour of thinking, of interacting with people, the labour that was traditionally contrasted with the manual work of the factory or the docks. Immaterial labour is now crucial to the economy, even in sectors that are still concerned with the production of material goods. Moulier Boutang gives the example of how even farming depends on mechanization, ICT and digitized forms of information.

In the information-based version of the economy, knowledge becomes the centre of economic life. Privileging knowledge creates a new division of labour, celebrating those able to exploit their cognitive endeavours, for example through possession and acquisition of intellectual property rights, whilst excluding those unable to adapt to the new paradigm, which shifts work away from physical labour and the factory. For Moulier Boutang (2011) firms adopt individualized and flexible forms of production, that even when producing material goods are more dependent on large-scale information about the potential consumer, client or customer than earlier industrial models. Eventually the division between producer and consumer itself is blurred, as the production of economic value is led by the consumer. The blurring of producer and consumer can easily be seen in the business model of the poster child company of the new economy, Facebook. For Facebook, the user is the product itself and the company derives revenue from users' activity and engagement.

In the cognitive age:

> the object of accumulation consists mainly of knowledge, which becomes the basic source of value ... issues such as property rights, positioning in networks, alliances and project management become major institutional and organisational factors. Their role is crucial. The strategies of this capitalism are determined by the quest for a spatial, institutional and organisational positioning likely to increase its capacity for engaging in creative processes and for capturing their benefits. (Moulier Boutang 2011: 57)

The means of capturing the benefits of knowledge, and exploiting those benefits, are not confined to intellectual property. Networks, as described in the work of sociologist Manuel Castells (2000), become the organizational form and the set of practices for the cognitive age, mirroring the practices and organizations of the cultural sector from which, in the DCMS narrative, it draws much of its inspiration (Garnham 2005).

PRODUCING CREATIVE INDUSTRY POLICY

> [I]t would be difficult to identify a non-creative industry or activity. (Pratt 2005: 33)

The crossover between cultural practices and the new economy finds its most obvious expression in theories of convergence culture, theories that have been important to the way creative industries policy is currently understood.

Cognitive capitalism (as one of the many related terms to describe the new economy) is marked by forms of what Henry Jenkins calls convergence culture (Jenkins 2006). In cognitive capitalism, the economic and the cultural become closely intertwined (DuGay and Pryke 2002). It would be easy to say such intermingling had always been the case; however, as Lash and Lury (2007) summarise, it is not that economic practices depend on cultural norms, but rather that forms of culture are now commodified and thus their interchangeability underpins the economy:

> when, for example, movies become computer games; when brands become brand environments, talking over airport terminal space and restructuring department stores, road billboards and city centres; when cartoon characters become collectables and costumes; when music is played in lifts, part of a mobile soundscape. (Lash and Lury, 2007: 8)

The overlap and convergence between cultural forms, media and spaces reflects the crossover between culture and economy. In the initial critical theoretical discussions of *cultural* industries (Adorno and Horkheimer 1997) there was a lament about the enveloping of culture by the economy. Under convergence culture this is celebrated, as cultural artefacts and practices can be the source of considerable value for national economies and can provide forms of work that are 'cognitive' and dependent on individuals' creativity.

The celebration of the convergence between economy and culture is vitally important to the DCMS understanding of creative industries, with its related vision of intellectual property. In the UK, creative industries are now placed within this broader economic narrative that links culture with many forms of economic activity that would not usually be seen as part of the arts, such as manufacturing. The Work Foundation (2007) and most recently the National Endowment for Science Technology and the Arts (NESTA) (2013) have both attempted to chart the relationship between state subsidized forms of cultural and artistic practice and market orientated commercial cultural forms, including design, advertising, film and music, alongside manufacturing and services. This reflects precisely the arguments of Moulier Boutang (2011), whereby cognitive activity is narrated as central to even the most mundane parts of the industrial or manufacturing economy. Indeed for NESTA (2013) the centrality of cultural and creative activity to the rest of the economy is an important justification for state funding and intervention in favour of cultural and artistic organizations.

Policy research argues that cultural practice is embedded in the wider economy, influencing innovation in a range of sectors in a diffused way (Work Foundation 2007). The policy research literature also argues that the metaphor of ecosystems (Leicester and Sharpe 2010) is the appropriate way of understanding the relationship between artistic practice and more traditional economic spheres (Bakhshi et al. 2008). In both the UK (Vaizey 2011) and the USA (NEA 2012) not only are the art schools, subsidized galleries, higher education institutions, advertising firms, film makers and designers seen as part of a cultural ecosystem, but this ecosystem is seen as relating directly to organizations such as the manufacturers of domestic appliances, computers and aircraft. The ecology is, to return to the DCMS definition of creative industries, one that has intellectual property at its very centre, because the sources of innovation, the avant-garde arts, and the commercial forms of cultural production depend on 'the generation and exploitation of intellectual property' (DCMS 2001: 15)

THE CREATIVE CLASS: INTELLECTUAL PROPERTY'S IDEAL TYPE?

The previous section described how policy research following the initial DCMS definition of creative industries developed into a much wider vision of how economy and society should be organized. This work extended the DCMS definition from an ill-defined idea about intellectual property to a blueprint for policy questions that went beyond just creative industries. However, in this extended version of creative industries, the idea of intellectual property moved further away from the specific aspects of copyright or patents that make up the legal regime protecting and exploiting intellectual property. Rather the eventual meaning of intellectual property in the DCMS definition of creative industries elided the fixed forms of intellectual property in records or paintings with the creative practices and activities that make up most forms of work and labour in the arts. This elision justified the expansion of the enforcement of intellectual property rights for those in control of them, via legislation such as the Digital Economy Act 2010, using the story of promoting and developing the individuals and practices that are supposed to be the source of the value generated by intellectual property.

However, as the remainder of this chapter will show, the DCMS understanding of intellectual property, which elides artistic and cultural practice with the ownership and control of property rights in fixed creative expressions, is far from the reality of those who work in the sectors of the economy defined as creative industries.

In the DCMS definition of creative industries, intellectual property comes from the 'individual creativity, skill and talent' of the creative worker. Centring creative work as essential for the economy seems like a seductive strategy to a range of political positions. On the political left it offers a non-exploitative vision of work that escapes the manual labour associated with the nineteenth and twentieth centuries. For the political right, it is associated with a form of entrepreneurialism that will do away with the need for state intervention and will give rise to, in essence, a nation of creative shopkeepers, selling their individual intellectual property.

However the reality is very different. Oakley (2009) argues that cultural work is filled with similar pains and pleasures that workers were supposed to escape as they became creative labourers. There remains a great deal of exploitation in this work. The creation of the DCMS version of intellectual property is often irrelevant to the working lives of creative labourers, whereby they are using their creativity, skill or talent, but derive little revenue and often do not control the copyrights or patents that they produce (Gill and Pratt (2008), Hesmondhalgh (2012), Oakley (2009) and Schlesinger and Waelde (2012) all give introductions to these issues). This raises questions as to the capacity for creative industries to genuinely transform economy and society.

The creative worker became prominent during the late 1990s, based on a range of discussions, but figuring most obviously in the ideas of Richard Florida (2002) in the United States. Florida's work offered similar narratives to those displayed in previous sections, whereby creative individuals could transform local and city economies as they represented new forms of labour to replace declining manufacturing and industrial activity. This version of creative individuals was important in British government policy and rhetoric, across a range of areas, including urban, cultural and education policies (Evans and Shaw 2004; Jowell 2004). Creativity, therefore, has an apple pie banality, identified by Peck (2005), that has allowed it to march beyond just economic policies, into social and health policies (Galloway 2008;

Garnham 2005). The fundamental lack of definition has also allowed the concept of creativity to be applied to the entire population, making it a personal quality that everybody possesses. As a result, individual creativity can be the basis for an untapped form of capital, akin to a coal seam or a diamond mine that the British economy can use to return to global pre-eminence.

Although creativity is something that the entire population is said to possess, it is also a quality that is associated with specific occupations. For DCMS it was those occupations in the creative industries. For other writers, such as the consultant Richard Florida (2002), it was a whole section of society that he called the 'creative class'. The creative class has three traits. First, they are highly individualistic, seeing themselves as having moved beyond the discussions of social structures of class, gender, ethnicity and other aspects that characterized debates over the workforce in the twentieth century. Second, as part of their individualism they have an open and tolerant attitude to diversity. Finally they are highly meritocratic. Everyone is creative, so it is by virtue of hard work and having good ideas that the creative class have managed to get where they are (Banks 2009).

WHAT DOES THE CREATIVE CLASS DO WHEN IT CREATES?

The traits of the creative class play out in a highly uneven economy, which has only a limited and contradictory relationship to the idea of intellectual property that DCMS thought was important to the 13 sectors that make up the creative industries. DCMS's act of constructing the creative industries, by defining them in terms of exploitation of intellectual property based on individual creativity that only then has the potential for job and wealth creation, missed much of the reality of how both the supposed creative class and the creative economy functions. For example, the two mapping documents, of 1998 and 2001, have little detailed engagement with the core protection regime of 'creative' intellectual property – copyright – but are rather concerned with identifying and measuring contributions to economic activity Gross Value Added (GVA), employment and prospects for growth in the 13 sectors.

David (2010) and Schlesinger and Waelde (2012) have explored how intellectual property is most commonly exploited. It is rare for individuals to control their intellectual property in a form that can be used for substantial 'wealth creation'. For example to exploit copyright requires the ability to regulate reproductions of work, the right to copy. It is far more common that larger corporate structures control (legally and economically) such copyrights, even whilst intellectual property ownership remains nominally in the 'artist's' legal possession. The music industry is the paradigmatic example. Schlesinger and Waelde's work is especially important here, as is the cross-industry study conducted by Searle (2011). These authors suggest that creative work is not an individual process. In the case of the avant-garde musicians and dance professionals, researched by Schlesinger and Waelde, there is a sense of community and communality that is part of the creation of artistic artefacts. This larger community makes it difficult to attribute particular intellectual property rights to individual creative acts. In Searle's work, most notably in her discussion of computer games, there is a lack of clarity over ownership within the crowd-sourced nature of modern computer games. Most creative work is collective and non-proprietorial. Much that is created is not owned, nor claimed, by its creators. Much that is owned is claimed by actors who cannot be said to have been its sole creators. This raises questions as to the potentially exploitative structure of computer game generation. Likewise for the owners of indie record labels, the broader community of which they are part is crucial to their economic models. Intellectual property exploitation is, however, the core practice of the major labels.

The communality of creative work casts doubt on the role of the individual at the heart of the British model of creative industries. Intellectual property is not the source of revenue that allows these workers to live. Rather it is often given away free as a method of making a living in other ways. Avant-garde musicians and dancers, for example, are often occupied by work in state-funded institutions, most notably university music and dance departments, which serve as their main source of income (Schlesinger and Waelde 2012).This practice is mirrored in other parts of this economy. A range of work across creative industries, whether new media (Gill 2010), television (Hesmondhalgh and Baker 2011) or music (David 2010) shows how the majority of fiction writers, journalists, musicians, actors, dancers and visual artists make either none or very little of their earnings from intellectual property rights (royalties from reproductions of their works), but rather make their livings predominantly from the sale of original works, live performances and work for hire; and/or related employment, such as teaching, tutoring, talks, mentoring, training, or working at and managing events/venues, etc. These positions are a useful illustration of the problems of the DCMS approach to intellectual property and creative industries. These individuals are creative workers, but their relationship to forms of intellectual property such as copyright is in most cases peripheral compared to the importance of their status as performers. Moreover it is their cultural value or worth as producers and performers that secures them jobs and incomes, rather than reproduction revenue from copyright. In the DCMS version of creative industries intellectual property is the source of value. In reality the fixed forms of property, such as copyright, are only tenuously related to job and wealth creation for most creative individuals. The value of their work results from its reputation amongst critics and peers, rather than its commodity value as a product to be exploited. In Searle's work, these debates between the cultural and economic (or copyright) values of a given piece of work illustrate how non-economic forms of value that come from culture as an expression of identity or as a contribution to a canon or field outweigh the DCMS vision of an ill-defined intellectual property system that is supposed to motivate, protect and reward the participants in the creative economy.

THE EFFECTS OF CREATIVITY

If research has suggested that intellectual property protection is at times peripheral to creative workers, then what is the reality of the creative economy and the role of intellectual property in this new economy? The rest of this chapter turns to a series of key issues within the creative economy, focusing on the effects of maintaining the idea that the new economy will be premised upon strong intellectual property rights. As examples from the disciplines of economic geography, the sociology of work and critical political economy will show, the effects of the myths underpinning policy surrounding creative industries are at best unevenly distributed rewards and at worst perniciously exploitative.

In the UK, home of the British model of creative industries, there is a major split between the dominant position of London, with knock-on effects into the south east of England, and the rest of the UK. London is a global and globalized city, with a range of creative industries that are both globally connected and interrelated across industrial sectors. Outside of London the story is different, with a much more local creative economy served by localized creative industries (Chapain and Comunian 2010).

The uneven geography of the creative industries produces an uneven distribution of work and rewards in this sector. The lack of clarity over the boundaries of what actually constitutes a creative industry, especially given the unclear relationship between work, reward, motivation and intellectual property for those labouring in the sector, impacts upon the day-to-day realities of work as well (McRobbie 2010). Individuals, communities and societies have differing views of what constitutes good and bad work in these sectors. These views of what is good work and what is bad work are divided around two specific forms of labour. The first is associated with positive forms of self-expression and creativity, thus requiring sacrifice in the form of long hours, low pay and precariousness, whilst other forms of work are maligned because of the supposed lack of creativity associated with them.

McRobbie's work places this division within a longer historical trend, whereby the cultural practices of emerging entrepreneurs of the 1980s UK gave way to much more exploitative labour structures as creative industries became codified and taken up by policy makers. During the 1980s in the UK, the fashion industry micro-businesses associated with subcultural scenes and the related informal and alternative publishing and media channels were a response to deindustrialization, reflecting the rise of identity politics and the birth of a specifically cultural form of entrepreneur. By the late 1990s and into the 2000s, these subcultural entrepreneurs gave way to a night-time economy driven model of cultural work (Chatterton and Hollands 2001) that spilled over into more traditional service and leisure sector businesses, of bars and clubs (Thornton 1995). Very often the specific service sector jobs associated with subcultural scenes had very little to do with intellectual property, at the very same point when the British government was drawing on their symbols and signs of success, in the form of such hideous tropes as 'Cool Britannia' (Oakley 2004), to underpin the DCMS model of creative industries. Rather, this work reflected the aestheticization of services and leisure as culture and economy became increasingly intertwined. This aestheticization is part of the broader trend towards cognitive capitalism outlined earlier in the chapter, but is also part of the increasing importance given to the labour of consumers in producing the culture that owners of intellectual property seek to control and exploit.

The rise of creative jobs that are not about the production of intellectual property, but rather reflect the aestheticization of the service sector, for example event managers, is influential in carrying over the negative working conditions experienced within the night time economy, into other parts of the creative industries. These include insecurity, poor working conditions, long hours and a lack of professional status. The convergence culture discussed by Lash and Lury (2007) manifests itself in work, whereby jobs become hybrid forms of work and multiple forms of employment are necessary to make a living. For some this can be both empowering and rewarding. For example, the workers in Schlesinger and Waelde's (2012) research into avant-garde musicians and dancers were not making money from copyright exploitation but often held stable and relatively high status positions within higher education institutions. However, for others the results are far less benign.

As with the rest of the cognitive capitalist economy, much work is low paid, with the resulting poor standards of living. Whilst this is true for those working as cleaners, care workers or in other supposedly low skilled, but often highly affective, areas of the economy, it is particularly important in the creative industries. This is because the narrative of poor pay and poor conditions is linked to the narrative that creative industries offer good work, or at least work that is better than both the factory and the low-skilled sector. For writers such as McRobbie the consequences are that 'the creative sector finds itself full of young people who are burnt out, exhausted, unable to consider having children and often self-exploiting on the basis of the "pleasure in work" factor' (McRobbie 2010: 2).

WORK, THE SELF AND THE MARGINALIZATION OF INTELLECTUAL PROPERTY

Recent research into work in the creative industries (Gill 2010; Hesmondhalgh and Baker 2011) points very straightforwardly to the idea that a major part of what is produced in this sector of the economy is not the version of intellectual property that the British model sees at the heart of creative industries, but rather is selves and individuals. Economic value depends on the cultivation and maintenance of an individual identity that can be used to generate revenues. Gill (2010) summarizes this trend neatly in the idea drawn from one of her research participants, that 'life's a pitch'.

Fundamentally the idea of constantly pitching oneself for various types of work within the creative industries is deeply ambivalent. On the one hand this form of labour is empowering, offering autonomy and the chance to express oneself in exchange for very flexible employment patterns. On the other hand the promise of self-expression and self-realisation can equate to long hours, low pay and a range of damaging effects that locate themselves in the individual psychology of the creative worker. Hesmondhalgh (2012: 243) summarizes this ambivalence:

> The cultural industries might not provide good, meaningful work as reliably as many policy makers claim. But such work is available there and it remains plausible to suggest that it might be more available in making television programmes, music and magazine journalism than in other industries.

The self-realization and self-expression of what allegedly comes from work based on culture and creativity can be framed within a larger narrative of ambivalence, whereby the pleasures and pains of creative work can be seen as a highly privileged position when compared to other forms of work. The creative industries offer what Hesmondhalgh and Baker call a 'very complicated version of freedom' (2011: 13).

This complicated version of freedom is bound up with the aesthetic positions that are related to DCMS's intellectual property based vision of the creative industries. Within this reading artistic and individual genius is protected by intellectual property rights, but in fact this idea of individual genius is highly problematic (David 2010) and has pernicious effects on the reality of work in the creative industries. Whilst it is large corporate bodies that tend to own and control property rights in culture, the narrative of individual genius leads creative production to be is seen to be unlike other forms of work. Rather workers are seen as being 'paid for their hobby', rather than working at all (Gill 2010).

The idea of being paid for one's hobby and that one's work should rise above both the market and its monetary concerns creates a demand for constant self-discipline in the face of a need to reject claims for high pay, decent conditions and professional status. Work, as one's hobby, with the worker's self as a commodity, in association with the creative ethos discussed earlier in this chapter leaves little room for the individual to consider structural questions of class, gender or ethnicity.

Gill and Pratt (2008) describe how the creative industries are mainly populated by young, able-bodied, well-educated and socially networked people. The sector's composition by this section of society goes hand in hand with high levels of gender inequality and specific forms of exclusion. Ball et al.'s (2010) study of recent graduates in the creative industries illustrates this point:

> 42% of [survey] respondents had undertaken unpaid or voluntary work or work experience since graduating. Those most likely to have done so were: women, older graduates, graduates with disabilities and those from fine art courses. Findings showed that those from more advantaged backgrounds had more chance of gaining relevant work experience (by working unpaid or undertaking internships, before or after graduation) because their parents could support them. (Ball et al. 2010: 12)

The practical reality of exclusions based on class or gender, with an associated meritocratic assumption to justify these exclusions is the key point in McRobbie's (2010) critique of the promise of the new economy and the role of creative industries. The idea of working at one's hobby, expressing one's self and one's identity creates a stark division between success and failure. Failure is not just the failure to get work or to have a sustainable career. Failure is in fact a failure of the self, that one's own identity is somehow unworthy of work in this new economy. Moreover, taking work in the institutions associated with normal or regular work (McRobbie gives the examples of teaching and social work) means one has failed to be a creative worker. Thus, the individual's identity and the categories of work that are not seen as creative are all lessened and undermined, despite their obvious social and economic importance. To get a non-creative job is to admit defeat in the struggle associated with the life of the artist, a myth that is important for the DCMS version of the creative industries:

> this would in many ways mark a moment of personal failure to live up to the dream of a talent led economy, where the myth of personal creativity is so dominant and everything else is second or third best. (McRobbie 2010: 2)

And, as Ross (2008: 34) comments, the legacy of the artistic myth continues to drive the naive hopes of a policy that has really not understood the real meaning of work in the industries that policy thinks is grounded on the exploitation of a rather incoherent idea of intellectual property:

> No doubt it is ritually assumed that creative jobs, by their nature, are not deficient in gratification. If anything, their packaging of mental challenges and sensuous self-immersion is perceived to deliver a surplus of pleasure and satisfaction. Proponents of this line of thinking may well concede that the life of creatives, in the past, has also been associated with misery, frustration and deprivation, but the given wisdom is that those pitfalls were primarily the result of economic inattention and social marginalization. In a milieu where creativity is celebrated on all sides, such drawbacks will surely dissolve.

The various strands of research described in this section of the chapter all suggest that what drives creative industries' success is not DCMS's idea of intellectual property, nor are the 13 creative industries sectors primarily staffed by people exploiting the intellectual property they create. This is because there is a range of employment types in these sectors and even where there are workers who derive revenues directly from intellectual property, most often as copyright, those revenues are too small for almost all of those that do to make a living from them (Schlesinger and Waelde 2012). Rather, what is created and exploited is the self, with creative industries based on an army of low-paid, insecure, artistic and service-based labour searching for the 'one big hit' of intellectual property that will allow them to enjoy the promise offered by the DCMS definition of creative industries. Intellectual property may, therefore, be seen more as an act of seduction to potential creative workers, as opposed to both the protection and the form of economic value that policy has been keen to assert.

CONCLUDING THOUGHTS: CAVEATS TO THE CREATIVE INDUSTRIES

Writing in 2013 it seems as if, McRobbie's caution notwithstanding, the creative industries are now firmly embedded within the policy discourses of both government and academia. The term survived academic dissent to give rise to a range of books (e.g. Flew 2012, 2013), journals, courses and academic institutions, as well as surviving a change of government in the UK. If creative industries have embedded themselves within UK policy discourses, irrespective of whichever party is in power, it is unlikely that the global promulgation of this configuration will cease. However, there are challenges to these conceptions of the creative industries, with intellectual property at the heart of the government's definition. These challenges cast doubt on the prospects of the term and the continued insistence on defining the sector based on a form of property exploitation that does not create much, or possibly any, benefit for the types of individuals who are seen to be its standard bearers. Indeed, one may question the extent to which policy has ever understood the challenges identified by this chapter. Indeed, in the UK, the home of the British model of creative industries:

> public policy has concerned itself with skills and training issues, and asserted the importance of entrepreneurship and business skills within the arts education tradition, but beyond that it has paid little attention to the issues of cultural work. (Oakley 2009: 59)

If the promise of creative industries, founded on intellectual property has been unfulfilled, what is the future in this area? Fundamentally, the idea of creative industries will need to be re-founded, with a basis that moves away from the DCMS's version of intellectual property. This is because, as Towse's discussion of intellectual property and the creative industries identifies, the narrative of creativity, the apple pie, has too closely conflated intellectual property's legal protection and the economic benefits a creative or cognitive economy is supposed to bring to workers labouring in such sectors:

> it is very easy to slip between the use of copyright as a way of defining the creative industries and the idea that their contribution to the economy is caused by the presence of copyright. (Towse 2010: 382)

As this chapter has indicated, the creative industries were meant to solve the problem of the supposed transformation of Western economies from manufacturing of tangible goods, based on the institution of the factory, to the creation of a service-led economy with a radically different type of labour. This vision has, of course, been subject to the sorts of debates outlined by this chapter. However, the cultural activities that became problematically conflated with the production and exploitation of a specific version of intellectual property in the creative industries might still have potential as an alternative form of creative work.

The first way to study this is by raising the question of how creative industries are defined. The definitional question concerning creative industries is still on-going, in terms of settling what is or is not a creative industry. For example, DCMS removed certain forms of software design from the DCMS 13 in 2011, and the specific methods by which to measure creative industries' activity have witnessed the production of an on-going series of papers, most recently by the UK's National Endowment for Science Technology and the Arts (NESTA 2013). Following both of these developments, DCMS has subsequently issued a consultation on how best to define the creative industries. But the question of definition that the British government is currently grappling with is secondary to a proper analysis and discussion of the role and function of culture and its relationship to the economy. The lack of this discussion has allowed DCMS to elide the reality of cultural work with corporate dominated forms of making money from intellectual property rights such as copyright.

Culture, stripped of its context and meaning and repackaged as creativity, runs the risk of merely replicating the dominant and longstanding economic structures it might appear to be rebelling against. Indeed, as Ross (2009) points out, creativity is now the 'new oil' for the new economy. The connection between economy and culture, in the face of the potential misuse of culture to support continuing economic inequality, means there is a need to understand the interdependence between culture and economy.

There are also interdependences within cultural production itself. In the models of creative industries (Leicester and Sharp 2010) that sought to move away from the individualist production of intellectual property assumed by DCMS's definition, there is interdependence between large organizations, smaller organizations, firms, entrepreneurs and state funded arts institutions, as well as government. This interdependence is part of the way the utopianism associated with figures such as the artist can thus diffuse across the rest of the economy. If cultural labour is somehow emancipatory, as seen in the understanding of both Richard Florida (2002) in the United States and in left-wing discourses in the United Kingdom, then this aestheticized new economy forces us to ask what this cultural labour is and what its 'emancipatory' relationship to the economic world actually is. Freedom is a potentially double-edged sword. Thus, the critical role of culture investigated by the Frankfurt School's original use of the term 'cultural industries', which saw the revolutionary potential of forms of culture that were not mass produced to transform the monopoly capitalist settlement, can be remade. Whilst, as Lash and Lury (2007) show, the division between culture and economy has become even further blurred since the era of the Frankfurt school, in the discussions in this chapter creative industries activity has raised critical questions for the rest of the economy and society surrounding payment, ownership and the ability of individuals to have fulfilling and rewarding work in the age of an aesthetic, cognitive capitalism.

Without this critical interrogation the assumption that creative industries are fundamentally based upon individual creativity protected by intellectual property rights will continue to function as a rhetorical mask for what are, at best, deeply problematic changes within the contemporary economy. Within this economic settlement it seems as if the responsibility for one's labour, indeed as Gill (2010) indicates, for one's self, is no longer a social matter, and it has been left to the individual to produce the intangible goods that will sustain them, based on our own sense of creativity. The risks posed by this settlement have been made clear by the discussion in this chapter and they are risks that have been, to a lesser or greater extent, compounded by the policy decisions associated with the definition of the creative industries as intellectual property based sectors of the economy. The question such policy documents leave us with is whether we really are, indeed, all creative? If we are not then the consequences seem to be punishment, rather than the sorts of protections supposedly associated with intellectual property, in exchange for the admission of a failure to be a member of a fantasy vision of a creative class.

REFERENCES

Adorno, T. and Horkheimer, M. (1997) *Dialectic of Enlightenment.* London: Verso.

Amin, A. (1994) *Post-Fordism: A Reader.* Oxford: Blackwell.

Bakhshi, H., McVittie, E. and Simmie, J. (2008) *Creating Innovation.* London: NESTA.

Ball, L., Pollard, E. and Stanley, N. (2010) 'Creative graduates creative futures', available from www.employment-studies.co.uk/pubs/report.php?id=471 (accessed 18 May 2013).

Banks, M. (2009) 'Fit and working again? The instrumental leisure of the "creative class"', *Environment and Planning A* 41(3): 668–81.

Bell, D. (1974) *The Coming of the Post-Industrial Society.* London: Heinemann.

Betancourt, M. (2010) 'Immaterial value and scarcity in digital capitalism', available from www.ctheory.net/articles.aspx?id=652 (accessed 10 March 2013).

Bilton, C., and Leary, R. (2002) 'What can managers do for creativity? Brokering creativity in the creative industries', *International Journal of Cultural Policy* 8(1): 49–64.

Boltanski, L. and Chiapello, E. (2007) *The New Spirit of Capitalism.* London: Verso.

Cabinet Office (2012) 'PM backs "dynamic and entrepreneurial" film industry', available from www.gov.uk/government/news/pm-backs-dynamic-and-entrepreneurial-uk-film-industry (accessed 5 November 2013).

Campbell, P. (2013) 'Imaginary success? The contentious ascendance of creativity', *European Planning Studies* DOI:10.1080/09654313.2012.753993.

Castells, M. (2000) 'Materials for an exploratory theory of the network society', *British Journal of Sociology* 51(1) 5–24.

Chapain, C. and Comunian, R. (2010) 'Enabling or inhibiting the creative economy: the role of the local and regional dimension in England', *Regional Studies* 44(6): 717–34.

Chatterton, P. and Hollands, R. (2001) *Changing our 'Toon': Youth, Nightlife and Urban Change in Newcastle.* Newcastle-upon-Tyne: University of Newcastle Press.

David, M. (2010) *Peer to Peer and the Music Industry.* London: Sage.

DCMS (1998) *Annual Report.* London: DCMS.

DCMS (2001) *Creative Industries Mapping Document.* London: DCMS.

DuGay, P. and Pryke, M. (eds) (2002) *Cultural Economy.* London: Sage.

Engelen, E., Erturk, I., Froud, J., Johal, S., Leaver, A., Moran, M., Nilsson, A. and WIlliams, K. (2011) *After the Great Complacence: Financial Crisis and the Politics of Reform.* Oxford: Oxford University Press.

Evans, G. and Shaw, P. (2004) *The Contribution of Culture to Regeneration in the UK.* London: London Met.

Flew, T. (2012) *The Creative Industries.* London: Sage.

Flew, T. (2013) *Global Creative Industries*. London: Sage.

Florida, R. (2002) *The Rise of the Creative Class*. New York: Basic Books.

Foray, D. and Lundvall, B. (1996) *Employment and Growth in a Knowledge-Based Economy*. Paris: OECD.

Galloway, S. (2008) *The Evidence Base for Arts and Culture Policy*. Edinburgh: Scottish Arts Council.

Garnham, N. (2005) 'From cultural to creative industries', *International Journal of Cultural Policy* 11(1): 15–29.

Gill, R. (2010) '"Life is a pitch": managing the self in new media work', in Deuze M. (ed.) *Managing Media Work*. London: Sage.

Gill, R. and Pratt, A. (2008) 'In the social factory? Immaterial labour, precariousness and cultural work', *Theory, Culture & Society* 25(7–8): 1–30.

Harvey, D. (2007) *A Brief History of Neo-Liberalism*. Oxford: Oxford University Press.

Hesmondhalgh, D. (2012) *The Cultural Industries*. London: Sage.

Hesmondhalgh, D. and Baker, S. (2011) *Creative Labour*. New York: Routledge.

Jenkins, H. (2006) *Convergence Culture*. New York: New York University Press.

Jowell, T. (2004) *Government and the Value of Culture*. London: HMSO.

Lash, S. and Lury, C. (2007) *Global Culture Industry*. Cambridge: Polity.

Lash, S. and Urry, J. (1994) *Economies of Signs and Space*. London: Sage.

Leicester, G. and Sharpe, B. (2010) *Producing the Future: Understanding Watershed's Role in Ecosystems of Cultural Innovation*. Bristol: Watershed.

Luxford, J. (2010) 'Art for art's sake – was it ever thus? A historical perspective', in Beech, N. and Townley, B. (eds) *Managing Creativity: Exploring the Paradox*. Cambridge: Cambridge University Press.

McRobbie, A. (2002) 'Clubs to companies', *Cultural Studies* 16(4): 516–31.

McRobbie, A. (2010) 'Rethinking creative economy as radical social enterprise', paper presented at 'Art and Labour' conference, Glasgow, November.

Miller, T., Govil, N., Mcmurria, J., Maxwell, R. and Wang, T. (2011) *Global Hollywood*. Berkeley: University of California Press.

Moulier Boutang, Y. (2011) *Cognitive Capitalism*. Cambridge: Polity.

NEA (2012) *How Art Works*. Washington DC: NEA.

NESTA (2013) *A Dynamic Mapping of the Creative Industries*, available from http://nesta.org.uk/areas_of_work/creative_economy/assets/features/a_dynamic_mapping_of_the_uks_creative_industries (accessed 29 May 2013).

Oakley, K. (2004) 'Not so cool Britannia', *International Journal of Cultural Studies* 7(1): 67–77.

Oakley K. (2009) *Art Works*. London: CCE.

Peck, J. (2005) 'Struggling with the creative class', *International Journal of Urban and Rural Research* 29(4): 740–70.

Pratt, A. (2005) 'Cultural industries and public policy', *International Journal of Cultural Policy*, 11 (1): 31–44.

Ross, A. (2007) 'Nice work if you can get it', in Lovink, G. and Rossiter, N. (eds) *My Creativity Reader*, available from www.networkcultures.org/_uploads/32.pdf (accessed 18 May 2013), pp. 17–41.

Ross, A. (2008) 'The new geography of work', *Theory, Culture & Society* 25(7-8): 31–49.

Ross, A. (2009) *Nice Work If You Can Get It: Life and Labor in Precarious Times*. New York: New York University Press.

Schlesinger, P. and Waelde, C. (2012) 'Copyright and cultural work: an exploration', *Innovation: The European Journal of Social Science Research* 25(1): 11–28.

Searle, N. (2011) *Changing Business Models in the Creative Industries: The Cases of Television, Computer Games and Music*, available from http://ipo.gov.uk/ipresearch-creativeind-full-201110.pdf (accessed 10 March 2013).

Thornton, S. (1995) *Club Cultures*. Cambridge: Polity.

Towse, R. (2010) *A Textbook of Cultural Economics*. Cambridge: Cambridge University Press.

Vaizey, E. (2011) '"The creative ecology": speech at state of the arts', available from www.gov.uk/government/speeches/the-creative-ecology-speech-at-state-of-the-arts (accessed 10 March 2013).

Velthuis, O. (2007) *Talking Prices*. Princeton: Princeton University Press.

Work Foundation (2007) 'Staying ahead', available from www.theworkfoundation.com/assets/docs/publications/176_stayingahead.pdf (accessed 18 March 2013).

PART V

Commons

Matthew David and Debora Halbert

An integral part of debates over intellectual property concerns the creation and defence of spaces that contain and maintain the absence of intellectual property rights. When terminated either at the end of the length of IP protection or because they were not protected in the first place, much that is of value is in the public domain, and those spaces considered the public domain have helped ignite a vigorous debate over the relevance and value of an intellectual commons. The public domain as a concept, offers conceptual challenges since its existence is predicated upon commercial copyright and patent regimes that at some point terminate to allow for free public use. However, those parts of culture that were never protected under such regimes, or have long fallen out of protection, also pose challenges given that they problematize ownership and blur the lines between what can be protected and what might be in the public domain.

Traditional knowledge (see Oguamanam, Dutfield, Darch, Coombe et al. and others in this Handbook) can also pose problems for the concept of the public domain, as knowledge that was never commercialized under legal regimes of copyright or patent law is deemed free to be taken and used, and this has led to the accusation of 'biopiracy' (framed as a form of 'stealing' from the commons). As a result, there are numerous dimensions of the concept of the commons that must be investigated. The chapters in this section take up different ways of viewing the value and necessity of a vibrant intellectual commons and the political struggles that have emerged over the contested space of knowledge exchange.

Jyh-An Lee's chapter on the role of nonprofits in the production of the commons offers a new and insightful contribution to our understanding of the commons and how it might be protected. Lee observes the creation and evolution of non-profits that have an interest in creating, preserving and protecting the commons. Utilizing Boyle's analysis of the environmental movement, Lee maps the growing importance of these non-profit organizations to an intellectual commons-based movement. Lee situates his chapter within the organizational context of non-profits and demonstrates that the non-profits that have taken up the cause of an intellectual commons provide a crucial infrastructure for the commons environment. These organizations also play a critical role in political advocacy and in efforts to mitigate the harms of expanding intellectual property laws. While often located in the United States, the non-profit organizations dealing with issues of intellectual property look globally at the harms of expansive intellectual property laws and their scope is far reaching. Creative Commons, the GNU licensing, and others demonstrate the global scope of these efforts. In the long run, a critical role these non-profits can play in the intellectual policy space is through policy experimentation and implementation.

Pradip Thomas's chapter takes up the tension in India between copyright advocacy and the opportunity to see a broader and more vibrant public domain. As with other country-specific chapters in this volume, Thomas locates the problems of copyright in India within the global context of TRIPS and the resulting responsibilities of India to formulate its domestic IP laws in conjunction with international mandates. His underlying critique of the neo-liberal economic order helps frame some of the difficulties faced by India in balancing economic development with strong intellectual property enforcement. What is powerful about Thomas's analysis here is that he shows how India remains an 'ambivalent' state when it comes to strong copyright protection and has instead embarked upon a policy effort to expand access to knowledge in the context of its copyright laws rather than reduce access. Thomas focuses specifically upon India's efforts, much maligned by the powerful content lobbies from the United States, to protect and expand access to knowledge. Three such efforts include: first, the Indian inclusion of protections for those with visual impairment into their copyright laws; second, the creation of the traditional knowledge digital project which makes an effort to preserve and protect traditional knowledge from exploitation and biopiracy along with providing Indians access to their cultural heritage; and third, the creation of a public sector software project premised upon the Free and Open Source Software (FOSS) movement. FOSS, one of the non-profits discussed by Lee, has played an inspirational role in software innovation around the world. India has opted to work towards a FOSS inspired public software system instead of relying upon proprietary software for its public institutions.

Thomas's view from India, where the state is pulled in opposing directions – firstly to work both to improve its domestic economy within the rules established by the primary international organizations and, secondly, by other efforts to further develop and provide access to knowledge that better reflects traditions of sharing and cultural exchange – exemplifies the tensions remarked upon by numerous authors throughout this volume in developing and developed countries across Africa, North and South America, Europe, Asia and Australasia. In each case, the existence of a commons outside intellectual property protection and the ability to draw from this commons has remained a critical part of the debate as well as a critical resource for development.

Lee positions the non-profit organizations that have emerged to protect the commons within the larger social movement of intellectual property critique. Lisa Dobbin and Martin Zeilinger make an intervention into similar territory by discussing one of the more recent additions to the intellectual property movement – the Pirate Parties. The Swedish Pirate Party emerged in the aftermath of the efforts to sink Sweden's popular file-sharing site, The Pirate Bay. Other national Pirate Parties have emerged across Europe, and beyond, since then. The emergence of digital file-sharing has been one of the most significant challenges to the old order of copyright law to emerge. While many call file-sharing piracy, as others in this volume have noted, different norms of sharing and use of cultural products within digital culture have surfaced amongst user groups than those the content industries would most like to see embraced.

The Pirate Party, still nascent in terms of its political development, marks the visible and vocal political advocacy of a different copyright balance and, more broadly, for a different and more transparent method of governance from the local to the global. As Dobbin and Zeilinger note, while piracy may not be the most suitable international platform, the existence and success of Pirate Parties to date does indicate that copyright reform is of interest to many. As they argue, Pirate Parties 'functions as an international arena of experimental (often playful or mocking) dissent' (p. 371).

Pirate Parties, Dobbin and Zeilinger point out, are difficult to position on the traditional left/right political spectrum. Some call them leftist, some libertarian, and some right-wing. Indeed, according to interviews completed by the authors, members and organizers of different Pirate Parties do not espouse a singular traditional political ideology but attempt to move beyond these categories towards something bound by 'humanism and civil liberties' (p. 374). Part of the Pirate Party goal is to determine new and information age relevant boundaries between information ownership and information sharing. To that end, they take up the concept of the commons as central to an understanding of how the law must be balanced. In the US this means adopting the concept of fair use in a broader digital framework that might allow for file-sharing. As with other advocates of intellectual property reform, the goal of the Pirate Party is not to reject in its entirety the concept of copyright but to better reflect the balance between contemporary social norms of file-sharing and ownership of creative content.

What is central about the political call of the Pirate Party is that it mirrors the international academic and legal community's efforts to protect and enhance the public domain. As others in this volume have noted, orphan works that are not officially in the public domain and have gone out of print or out of publication, but whose legal ownership is unknown, leading to an inability to secure permissions to reproduce, detract from our ability to fully engage in our cultural heritage. The Pirate Party understands these dilemmas and thus calls for a much shorter copyright term than the current lengths.

This section provides important insight into intellectual property's other side – the public domain. The need to create appropriate policy to protect and enhance the intellectual commons threads throughout this volume and helps highlight one of the central debates between intellectual property's critics and those who advocate for the maintenance of the status quo.

18

Non-Profits in the Commons Economy

Jyh-An Lee

INTRODUCTION

Protecting what has come to be known as the intellectual commons has been one of the most important goals underlying recent innovation and information policies. Awareness of the importance of preserving the intellectual commons has increased dramatically because of expanding intellectual property (IP) laws and the digital technologies that control the flow of information. Over the past 20 years, the creation of institutions and organizations, such as Creative Commons (CC), Electronic Frontier Foundation (EFF), Free Software Foundation (FSF) and Public Knowledge (PK), have created a social movement that has laid the essential building blocks for the development of the intellectual commons. Significantly, these entities are primarily non-profit organizations (NPOs). This chapter focuses on the NPOs that have come to occupy an increasingly critical and visible position in the intellectual-commons environment in recent years. It highlights the importance of the non-profit sector in the digitally networked environment, a topic that has been neglected by mainstream IP and Internet law scholarship. By illustrating the role of NPOs in shaping the commons environment, this study provides a new lens through which we can better understand the intellectual-commons environment.

Intellectual resources that anyone can use with or without permission granted beforehand are what constitute the intellectual-commons. Since access to intellectual resources is crucially important to creativity, innovation and human development, the shrinkage of the intellectual-commons environment is a profound loss for cultural freedom. Therefore, although some would argue that expanding IP protection fosters more innovation, in recent years, protecting what has come to be known as the intellectual-commons has been one of the most important goals of recent innovation and information policies.

One way societies deal with various problems is by constructing institutions; therefore, it is important to understand the effectiveness of different institutions, such as the government, for-profit businesses and NPOs. By the same token, in any discussion of preserving and strengthening the intellectual-commons environment, it is crucial for researchers to understand how different institutions affect this environment. Boyle (2003) argues that a number of intellectual-commons focused organizations, such as CC, EF, and PK, parallel the functions of environmental groups like Greenpeace, the Environmental Defense Fund, and Environmentally Concerned Scientists. Significantly, these organizations are primarily NPOs.

This chapter focuses on the NPOs that have come to occupy an increasingly critical and visible position in the commons economy in recent years. These organizations have been involved in current IP reform via litigation, political advocacy, public interest grant-making, as well as various private ordering activities, such as producing free licensing schemes and repositories of commons resources. The unique features of these NPOs enable them to serve important social aims that neither the proprietary sector nor the government may fulfil very well.

Through a detailed description of these NPOs, I argue that such organizations have provided the social structures that are necessary to support what can be understood as following Boyle's typology as cultural environmentalism. Moreover, this chapter tests the robustness of two dominant NPO theories – *contract failure theory* and *government and market failure theory* – in the commons movement context. By applying these theories in a new territory, this study not only broadens the scope of NPO scholarship but also provides a new lens to understand the commons economy and cultural environmentalism.

Although NPOs have a unique value for the cultural commons, I do not suggest that they can or will completely supplant the government and for-profits in the commons environment. Neither do I suggest that NPOs are adversaries to the market and the state. In fact, these three sectors share many characteristics and perform complementary tasks. Their complementary co-existence and relative salience as organizational forms for various social activities determine the allocation of resources in our society.

INTELLECTUAL COMMONS

To many legal scholars who study intellectual property (IP) and information technology (IT), a commons is a shared resource that is not under private control and that anyone can use without permission (Benkler, 2003, 2006; Lessig, 2002, 2006b). Expressed differently, the essential nature of a commons is the opposite of the essential nature of property in terms of exclusiveness. IP scholarship indicates that the commons is not subject to exclusive private control, whereas exclusivity is one of the most important characteristics of property (Benkler, 2006). The commons, in contrast to the proprietary aspect of IP, refers to intellectual resources, including culture, knowledge and information, which are openly accessible and not under private control. By contrast, one can prevent the transformation of one's intellectual resource into a commons by keeping it secret or by exercising IP rights over it.

Free and Open Source Software (FOSS) is a typical example of a commons described in this chapter. FOSS is software whose source and object code are distributed and made available to the public, a step that allows for use and modification by anyone. FOSS is distributed under a licence that requires source code authors, distributors and users to comply with certain conditions. Similarly, the content of Wikipedia is a commons because it is licensed under the Creative Commons Licence, which allows various uses by any user.

NPOS, INSTITUTIONAL FORMS AND INTELLECTUAL RESOURCES

This section will introduce the concept of the NPO and the roles of different institutional forms in the proprietary and commons environments. By providing an overview of three primary institutional forms in two intellectual arenas, this section situates the study within current scholarship. Thereafter, this section will focus on NPOs' legal and social functions in the commons communities.

What is an NPO?

Non-profit organizations (NPOs), sometimes collectively referred to as 'the voluntary sector' (Frumkin, 2002: 16; DiMaggio & Anheier, 1990), are private organizations that are restricted from distributing any profit to anyone associated with the organizations. Scholars have regarded such a *non-distribution constraint* as NPOs' most important institutional characteristic and developed NPO theories based on that characteristic (Hansmann, 1980; Weisbrod, 1988). As a result, NPOs do not seek to maximize financial profit for distribution. Nonetheless, an NPO can earn surpluses and use them for its own purposes or for other charitable purposes. United States law promotes NPOs by exempting them from certain taxes and by subsidizing them on the basis of the belief that NPOs provide outputs that are not obtainable from proprietary firms. In countries, such as Italy (Defourny & Nyssens, 2010), Sweden (Evers & Laville, 2004), the United Kingdom (Kerlin, 2006), and Taiwan, the *non-distributive constraint* is an important element in non-profit regulations. Some other European countries' laws similarly place limits on the distribution of nonprofits' profits (Evers & Laville, 2004).

Institutional Forms and Intellectual Resources

There are three major types of formal organizations in every society: proprietary, public and voluntary. Each type has its own strengths and weaknesses in meeting various societal demands. Proprietary firms are usually more flexible and efficient in meeting consumer demands because these firms have to maximize the profit they distribute to owners and managers. If they fail to satisfy consumer demands efficiently, they would not survive in a competitive market. However, as IP is designed to offer monopolies that suspend aspects of the competitive market, IP may insulate private firms from such an orientation to their customers' preferences (at least temporarily – such as in the case of the recorded music industry prior to file-sharing). Proprietary firms, however, are unlikely to respond to public-interest issues, such as pollution control and safety protection, as actively and efficiently as the other sectors because profit-motivated firms usually consider only activities that affect their revenues and not their externalized costs.

Governments, in contrast, have the potential to correct market failure because of their sovereign control typically granted by citizens to allocate resources within specific territorial boundaries. With the power to tax, governments can encourage public goods provision through subsidies or can discourage unwanted private activities through tax levies. Governments can also use coercive power to overcome the free-rider problem (Douglas, 1987). Nevertheless, government decisions are frequently influenced by industries and pressure groups. Contrariwise, the policy-making process usually more easily ignores the interests of weakly organized groups (Weisbrod, 1988).

NPOs, as the third sector in society, mirror the organizational advantages and disadvantages of the proprietary firms and the government. NPOs are usually much more responsive than proprietary firms to public-interest issues. Moreover, in contrast to the government, they are less subject to transaction costs stemming from the political process. NPOs, however, have their own limits. They cannot levy taxes, and they are much more restricted than proprietary firms in the types of activities they pursue. Charges against NPOs also include the notion that without an effective incentive mechanism, NPO managers are usually less efficient than those in proprietary firms in terms of organization operation and meeting customers' demands (Weisbrod, 1988). In other words, when efficiency cannot be financially rewarded in legal ways, NPOs themselves are more likely to be less efficient than proprietary firms. Nonetheless, this deficiency may be overcome if NPO managers obtain personal fulfilment from their work.

Accordingly, as Table 18.1 reveals, different institutional forms exist in both proprietary and commons production systems. In the proprietary system, the government plays a critical role in designing IP laws as well as

Table 18.1 Examples of institutional forms in the proprietary and the commons environments

		Degree of Exclusiveness	
		High	*Low*
		Proprietary Environment	*Commons Environment*
Institutional forms	Government	Provide IP laws and enforcement as incentives	Subsidies for Open Source Software
	Proprietary firms	Disney, Microsoft	IBM, Red Hat
	NPOs	ASCAP, BMI, MPAA	ASF, FSF, Wikimedia

maintaining public IP administration through agencies. The government's monopoly over coercive power also supports the IP system through the public enforcement of law. Arguably, an IP system provides incentives to proprietary firms to create and to innovate, and proprietary firms appropriate IP rights to gain business advantages. Some NPOs also are critically important in the commercial IP system. For example, the American Society of Composers, Authors, and Publishers (ASCAP) and Broadcast Music, Inc. (BMI) are NPOs that assist their members in collecting royalties from licensees. Likewise, the Motion Picture Association of America (MPAA) is a trade association of movie studios advocating strong copyright protection.

These three primary sectors play specific roles in the commons environment as well. For example, governments may subsidize basic research and the development of FOSS. An increasing number of for-profit firms, such as Dell, Google, Hewlett-Packard, Hitachi, IBM, Intel, Motorola, Nokia, Oracle, Philips and Sony have also begun to invest in the production of the intellectual commons in computer code. Although these firms cannot directly appropriate the value of such commons, they either donate code to the FOSS communities or encourage their employees to actively participate in FOSS development (Lerner & Tirole, 2002; Mann, 2006; Merges, 2004). Other commercial FOSS companies, such as Red Hat and SourceForge, make their money by selling updates, support and services to companies that use FOSS, rather than from the upfront licence fees that traditional software companies charge.

Among these three sectors, the NPO sector is probably the most active in the commons environment. A number of NPOs, including ASF, CC, EFF, the Mozilla Foundation and the Wikimedia Foundation, have played important roles in cultivating the commons environment. The roles of these organizations are the focus of this article.

NPOS IN THE COMMONS ENVIRONMENT

Most current NPO theories treat the nonprofit sector as a response to gaps in the supply of public goods (Frumkin, 2002; Hansmann, 1981). In this section, I attempt to identify the primary public goods produced by these NPOs. By categorizing these public goods, a general picture of how various NPOs operate in the commons ecology will emerge. It should be noted that many of the public goods introduced in the following pages provide crucial infrastructure resources for the commons environment.

Social Norms and Licensing Terms

There are two important premises underlying the commons movement: the reinforcement of sharing norms, and the licensing terms that enforce such norms. Interestingly, NPOs have played a crucial role in both reinforcing the norms of sharing and producing the licensing terms. Many community norms now enforced by FOSS licences existed before any specialized NPOs were formed and before FOSS licenses were introduced. In the 1960s and 1970s, code sharing between programmers in commercial and academic institutions was quite common (Lerner & Tirole, 2002). According to Richard Stallman, when he worked at the Massachusetts Institute of Technology (MIT) Artificial Intelligence Lab in the 1970s, the community recognized software-sharing customs and members could ask to see a source code, and could make changes or modifications to the code (Stallman, 2002). Stallman embraced this sharing culture and its openness. Nevertheless, such norms were quickly eroded by increasing proprietary control over software.

In the early 1980s, the informal norm of sharing basic operating code was threatened when AT&T decided to enforce its IP rights over the Unix System. This decision illustrated that norms may easily weaken without a formal support structure (Weber, 2004). As a result, Stallman institutionalized the norms of free code distribution and modification by establishing the FSF in 1985. This was the first NPO to support the idea of protecting a software commons from enclosure and privatization.

One of the most important innovations of the FSF is its formal licensing procedure. The licensing process has been recognized as a key factor in the success of FOSS because it facilitates the enforcement of FOSS community norms and clarifies the distinctions between FOSS and proprietary software. By defining ownership functionally, FOSS movement leaders have designed many of the FOSS licences to protect the norms of sharing and related freedoms (Lessig, 2004). Professor Steven Weber (2004) even regards the licences as constituting the social structure in the FOSS world. Although many other NPOs have designed other FOSS licences for their own projects, the GNU Public License (GPL), developed by the FSF and adopted by the GNU/Linux operating system, is the most famous and dominant licensing mechanism among all the FOSS licence models (Benkler, 2006; Deek & McHugh, 2008).

The Open Source Initiative (OSI) is another NPO that constitutes a mechanism for enforcement of certain industry norms. The OSI was established because many software developers felt that the FSF free software movement had a tarnished reputation in the business world due to the more radical ideas associated with free software. In contrast to the FSF's 'ethical position focused on the freedoms associated with software', the OSI takes a 'pragmatic position' regarding the market merits of the FOSS (Feller & Fitzgerald, 2002: 41–44). The OSI has published its Open Source Definition (OSD), which enumerates several criteria for an open source licence, and the OSI analyses licences' consistency with the OSI definition of 'open source'. License approval from the OSI has become a precondition for any software to be regarded as open source. In this sense, the OSI plays the role of 'a standard builder', 'a watchdog' and 'a trusted standards body' for the FOSS community (Feller & Fitzgerald, 2002).

Similarly, licensing plays a decisive role in facilitating commons production other than FOSS. Creative Commons (CC) is an NPO that has worked to adapt the FOSS movement model to other forms of creative works. Through a wide range of licensing terms, CC offers a web application that enables users to donate their works to the public domain, or to freely license their works for certain uses and to simultaneously retain copyright. Scholars have recognized that CC has initiated a global social movement, advocating for the norms of information sharing and reusing (Elkin-Koren, 2005).

Through the production and promotion of licences, the FSF, the OSI and CC are enabling creativity to spread more easily and promoting the philosophy underlying the commons movement. They use private ordering to build a commons environment and introduce an innovative way of exercising legal rights to bring about social change.

Organizational Support for Peer-production Projects

Some commentators have the impression that commons communities are primarily informal. Indeed, over 100,000 FOSS projects do not constitute legal entities, such as formal corporations or foundations. They instead use the free project hosting service provided by SourceForge, which provides free coordination mechanisms, such as a Concurrent Versions System (CVS) repository, mailing lists, message forums, bugging tracking tools, and others. The majority of the prominent FOSS projects, however, have their own hosting NPOs. For example, the Free Software Foundation (FSF) is the institutional host for the GNU project. The Apache Software Foundation has been successfully supporting Apache-server software development and other FOSS. The Mozilla Foundation exists to support and provide leadership to Mozilla projects, which are derived from the Netscape browser software. Table 18.2 provides a list of NPOs that support certain FOSS projects.

Although these NPOs similarly serve as institutional umbrellas for FOSS projects, they can have different origins and different development models. Some NPOs, such as the Apache Software Foundation, originated from grassroots communities of user developers (Lerner & Tirole, 2002). More recently, however, a second model has emerged, in which for-profit organizations spin out internally developed code and incorporate NPOs to attract and build FOSS communities. Examples of this model are the Eclipse Foundation, spun-off from IBM, and the Mozilla Foundation, formed by AOL (Deek & McHugh, 2008). Businesses making such spin-off decisions may have numerous strategic reasons for doing so. Some businesses view the spin-off as a more active investment in FOSS projects, whereas others may use the spin-off strategy to withdraw from a specific type of technological development. Outside the FOSS world, there are other NPOs hosting platforms that facilitate online collaborative creation of the commons. For example, the Wikimedia Foundation supports the Wikipedia project, an extensive online encyclopaedia written and amended by any user who wants to participate. Although volunteers are involved in much of the administrative work, the Wikimedia Foundation still needs to administer Web pages and to resolve conflicts in the community (Tapscott & Williams, 2006). Furthermore, the Project Gutenberg Literary Archive Foundation (Project Gutenberg Foundation) provides individuals with a platform on which volunteers can collaboratively scan and proofread public domain books. The Internet Archive, also an NPO, provides the public with a depository of and free access to text, audio, images, software and archived Web pages.

The institutional support provided by these NPOs may vary according to the nature and history of the underlying commons projects.

Table 18.2 FOSS foundations

NPO	*I.R.C. Category*	*Main F/OSS Project Hosted*
Apache Software Foundation	501(c)(3)	Apache Projects
Eclipse Foundation	501(c)(6)	Eclipse Platform
FreeBSD Foundation	501(c)(3)	Free BSD Projects
Free Software Foundation	501(c)(3)	GNU Project
GNOME Foundation	501(c)(3)	GNU Network Object Model Environment Project
Mozilla Foundation	501(c)(3)	Mozilla Projects, including Firefox Web browser and Thunderbird e-mail software
Open Source Application Foundation	501(c)(3)	'Chandler,' a desktop PIM application, and 'Cosmo,' a server system
Linux Foundation	510(c)(6)	Linux system
Perl Foundation	501(c)(3)	Perl programming language
Python Software Foundation	501(c)(3)	Python programming language
XMPP Standards Foundation	501(c)(6)	Extensible Messaging and Presence Protocol (XMPP) messaging software

Nonetheless, many of these organizations function similarly for their communities. They act on behalf of communities to manage property rights, to transact or communicate with other entities, to provide collective decision-making mechanisms, and to protect individual contributors from potential liability.

Legal Support

Proprietary firms have tended to threaten customers and contributors by asserting that FOSS products involve high potential for patent infringement. Therefore, individuals and organizations participating in commons production, distribution or consumption face a number of legal uncertainties, which may ultimately hinder distributed creative activities. As a result, some NPOs have devised mechanisms to provide legal support to reduce the legal risks facing participants in the commons settings. Such support is most common in the FOSS world in the aftermath of a series of suits brought by the SCO Group. For example, OSDL, one of the predecessors of the Linux Foundation, sponsored the Linux Legal Defence Fund to defray the legal expenses of Linux users and some key developers in legal suits brought by the SCO Group.

The Software Freedom Law Center (SFLC) is probably the most representative NPO that provides legal support for FOSS development. The SFLC was founded in 2005 to supply pro-bono legal services to protect and advance FOSS development. The organization provides legal representation for both individuals and other NPOs that participate in FOSS development. The SFLC assists the represented parties in enforcing copyrights in both the United States and other jurisdictions. Moreover, it also offers licensing assistance and NPO formation for FOSS communities. The public goods provided by the SFLC include not only legal support, but also, and more importantly, assists in providing legal certainty among FOSS developers.

Beyond the FOSS world, several NPOs have endeavoured to protect the commons through litigation. The Electronic Frontier Foundation (EFF) is dedicated to fighting for individual freedoms in the digital economy. In the context of copyright, the EFF has been involved in milestone lawsuits such as *Metro-Goldwyn-Mayer Studios Inc. v. Grokster, Ltd. (MGM v. Grokster)*, *Online Policy Group v. Diebold, Inc.*, *Kelly v. Arriba Soft Corp.* and *Lenz v. Universal Music Corp*. The result of this series of litigations is certainly a public good for consumers of intellectual commons. If, through litigation, NPOs successfully sustain the freedom to consume commons, all consumers will benefit from the results without fear of infringing.

Political Advocacy

NPOs have played an active role in the policy-making process in many areas of the United States. They educate the public and policy-makers in a broad range of issues and their policy implications. As many public-interest advocates worry that the expanding IP laws may damage the existing commons environment, some of these advocates have formed NPOs in order to influence legislation through lobbying activities.

For example, Public Knowledge (PK) is an NPO that aims to protect the intellectual commons by 'monitor[ing] Congress, US Agencies, State Legislatures and International Bodies for any proposed legislation or policy that relates to intellectual property or technology policy'. It participates actively 'in the debate about proposed legislation and discusses its position with key policymakers, the press … [and] industry'. PK has primarily focused on opposing 'policies that would slow technology, impede innovation, shrink the public domain, or limit fair use' (Public Knowledge, 2013). Other NPOs involved in international IP legislation include EFF, Knowledge Ecology International (KEI), and the Open Society Institute.

Although lobbies may sometimes produce a *public bad* for society (Sandler, 1992), the potential benefits that result from lobbying can also constitute a public good that every individual in the society may automatically enjoy. It depends on whether the result of lobbying increases social welfare. In this sense, by promoting good IP laws or stopping bad IP laws, it is possible that PK and the EFF engage in lobbying activities whose public goods spill over into the entire society. However, the well-established copyright industry has also been intensely involved in the copyright lobby, which aims to further strengthen current copyright protection. Since such lobbying has been supported by a well-organized and financially resourceful proprietary industry, it is not easy for NPOs, such as PK and the EFF, to fully achieve their goal through similar lobbying activities.

Information Access and Repositories

One may not have access to a commons due to physical constraints. It is estimated that only a small portion of public domain materials are digitalized for public access (Lasica, 2005). In order to allow more people to benefit from the commons, some NPOs have provided access to and repositories of these resources. For example, the Public Library of Science (PLoS) is an NPO dedicated to 'making the world's scientific and medical literature a freely available resource' (PLoS, 2013). It publishes both online and physical academic journals, and the articles all appear under a CC licence that allows unrestricted reproduction, distribution and modification in any medium, provided that the original work is properly cited. In 2003, the PLoS launched a series of open access journals beginning with PLoS Biology. All of the articles published in the PLoS journals are immediately available online without charge.

The PLoS is certainly not the only NPO involved in open access academic publishing. Universities, a unique type of NPO, have historically been viewed as important social institutions that produce and disseminate knowledge. They have also begun to provide access to their researchers' publications. For instance, the University of California has plans to initiate an open access academic journal. Moreover, many other reputable universities have adopted DSpace, a repository software platform, to provide free access to their faculties' publications. Another interesting example of the access to knowledge provided by universities is MIT's OpenCourseWare (OCW). In September 2003, MIT launched its OCW initiative, which made the content of its course materials freely available online. All of the OCW materials are licensed under CC Attribution-Noncommercial-Share Alike 3.0 licences. Through OCW, MIT has published almost all its course materials since 2007. After MIT initiated the OCW project, Rice University, the University of Notre Dame, Yale University and the University of California, Berkeley also decided to make their educational materials freely available online.

Other universities have also begun to provide access to information digitally, which was not available before the Internet era. For example, the University of Michigan has built the Internet Public Library (IPL), which provides 20,000 books in full-text, a collection of links categorized by various topics, and a reference service at no charge. The IPL enables users to freely reproduce its pages and resources in print sources for non-commercial use, provided that the users comply with specific conditions, such as citing appropriately and informing the IPL. Tufts University is running the Perseus Digital Library project that collects texts and images pertaining to the Archaic and Classical Greek world, late Republican and early Imperial Rome, the English Renaissance and nineteenth-century London. The Perseus Digital Library allows online users to freely search for and read information about specific people, places and dates in its digital collections.

Several NPOs treat information as a public good by making it available to the public. For instance, the online library Internet Archive provides the public with open and free access to text, audio, images, software and archived web pages in its collections. It operates Web crawlers – programs that index information stored on the Internet – and offers the Wayback Machine, which allows Internet users to find previous versions of Websites. Similarly, Project Gutenberg, hosted by the Project Gutenberg Literary Archive Foundation, has provided the public with free online access to a large number of public domain books. It is worthwhile to note that by archiving a variety of digital information, these organizations have preserved important social memory.

Public-interest Grant-making

Grant-making foundations are legally distinct from other NPOs in the sense that the latter have to spend '85 percent of [their] income on the active conduct of [their] charitable program' (Simon et al., 2006: 269). In contrast, grant-making foundations usually endeavour to improve social, economic or political life through funding for other intermediary organizations (Hall, 2006). In other words, grant-making foundations do not provide public goods directly to society. These grants can often be more than just cash transfers: they often affirm beliefs that accomplish public purposes while providing grant-makers with the satisfaction of seeing their values put into action.

A number of grant-making foundations have also provided indispensable funding for NPOs to help support the creation of an intellectual commons. For example, the Open Educational Resources (OER) programme of the William and Flora Hewlett Foundation invested $68 million from 2002 to 2006 to stimulate the OER movement, which included $43 million for the 'creation and dissemination of open content', and $25 million for 'reducing barriers, understanding, and/or stimulating use' (Atkins et al., 2007: 7). The Hewlett Foundation's grantees have included CC, Internet Archive, MIT OCW, and other academic institutions opening up their educational resources online. Further, the Hewlett Foundation requires that all products from its grants be licensed under a CC licence. Other grant-making NPOs in the commons environment include the Center for the Public Domain, the John D. and Catherine T. MacArthur Foundation, the Rockefeller Foundation, the Open Society Institute, affiliated with the Open Society Foundation, and the Andrew W. Mellon Foundation.

NPO THEORIES AND THEIR APPLICATIONS

The heterogeneous nature of the non-profit sector has greatly complicated the work of theorists who seek to model the origins and the behaviour of NPOs. In this section, I introduce two principal NPO theories – the contract failure theory, and the government and market failure theory – both of which suggest that NPOs are a private response to certain failures in society. These theories highlight NPOs' social value, and suggest that their value rests on their particular failure-correcting devices.

By applying both theories to the commons context, I will test the strengths and weaknesses of these theories. Although I seek to expose some gaps in both theories, I do not reject their central insights, which are necessary tools to understanding NPOs' role in cultural environmentalism.

Contract Failure Theory

Theory

The 'contract failure theory' was first proposed by Professor Henry Hansmann (1980). The central concept behind contract failure theory lies in the idea that the monitoring mechanism that occurs naturally in a normal market, in which buyers pay when the suppliers perform acceptably, cannot discipline the supplier of certain goods or services. As a result, when consumers are under-informed, in relation to the suppliers, the proprietary sector tends to perform badly because consumers pay too much for goods and services. In other words, the basic hypothesis of contract failure theory is that poorly informed consumers are unlikely to discover proprietary firms supplying higher quality when low quality items can be sold at the same price. Thus, contract failure, which leads to inefficient services provided by proprietary firms, is a particular type of market failure and occurs in venues in which services are difficult to evaluate (Hansmann, 1980).

Hansmann uses charity as an example to articulate the essence of contract failure theory. He believes that NPOs function as a trusted channel when donors of specific services or goods and the corresponding recipients have no connections with each other. The non-distribution constraint of NPOs can assure donors that their contribution, in fact, meets the costs of the organizations' production. Conversely, a for-profit firm has both the opportunity and the incentive to exploit the customer in such a circumstance (Hansmann, 1980).

NPOs seem necessary when there is this kind of contract failure – where the donor cannot directly contact the intended beneficiary of the donation or gift. In circumstances where contributors know the quality of the tendered service, contract failures still occur when contributors have little assurance about whether their payment will be appropriately used on the service they receive. An NPO form may, therefore, inspire greater trust (Hansmann, 1980).

In sum, according to contract failure theory, 'contract failure is the essential factor in the role of nonprofit enterprise' (Hansmann, 1980: 845). NPOs' non-distribution constraint solves the problem of market failure that stems from the information asymmetry between the parties involved in the transaction. Therefore, NPOs offer the purchaser a degree of assurance that the goods or services being purchased meet adequate standards of quality and quantity.

Applications

It may be the case that contract failure theory satisfactorily explains public-interest grant-making NPOs. Donors trust that NPOs, as opposed to for-profit firms, will make use of the donors' monetary donations according to the organizations' mission statements. Therefore, some philanthropists use the NPO as a tool to fulfil their charitable projects.

In the commons economy, there are also several grant-making foundations, such as the aforementioned Hewlett Foundation, the MacArthur Foundation, and the Open Society Institute. These foundations fulfil their public-interest function by channelling financial resources to other NPOs and entities in the commons environment. Such public-interest grant-making activities exemplify how, by connecting the donors with the recipient NPOs, grant-making NPOs can alleviate contract failure.

Nonetheless, an important distinction between the traditional contract failure scenario and the contract failure that occurs in commons peer production comes in the form of the types of donation people make. In traditional contract failure theory, the type of donation, including money, food and other supplies, consists of private goods, typically characterized by rivalry and exclusiveness. Although typical private goods can be delivered and consumed physically, the delivery and the consumption of intellectual resources unfolds differently and in a unique way. Consequently, in the commons economy, new types of contract failure may occur as depicted in the following two scenarios. The first scenario deals with two cases resulting from a contract failure related to physical obstacles existing between information donors and information recipients. The second scenario results from existing legal constraints leading to the market failure. By successfully correcting these failures in both scenarios, a number of NPOs have created indispensable social value for our cultural environment.

Scenario One: Case One – Access Failure

Access to information has always been an important policy consideration in contemporary copyright law. The purpose of the IP system has been to balance private incentives to engage in creative activity with the social benefits that arise from broad access to creative works. The trade-off between 'access' and 'incentives' has been an important decision for IP policy-makers. Nonetheless, with for-profit entities' increasing control over information, the policy goal of public access to information has been difficult to achieve.

When individual creators fail to provide ready access for consumers, access failure – a new type of contract failure – occurs in the market for information access. Access failure was first perceived in the market for academic journals. In recent years, although digital technologies have substantially decreased the cost of disseminating journal articles, the average cost of a journal subscription has increased significantly (Litman, 2006; Tapscott & Williams, 2006). The prices that users pay to access scholarly journal articles have drastically increased due to publishers' adoption of digital technologies that restrict access to academic works. Publishers typically charge by the number of users or by the number of articles downloaded (Armbruster, 2008; Litman, 2006).

With strong copyright and market control, commercial publishers usually bundle journals in a licence package. As a result, small libraries, institutions in developing countries, independent scholars, and the general public cannot afford the tremendous cost of these bundles. This problem has existed for at least 15 years (David, 1996), but has become more serious in recent years. This cost prohibition is most problematic in scientific and medical research because journal subscriptions in such fields are usually very expensive, yet access to the published articles is critically important for the advancement of research in progress. What is worse about the digitalization of journal articles is that the entities with centralized control may have the power to remove them completely from circulation (Hess & Ostrom, 2003). Once the subscription period ends, subscribers will have nothing left in their libraries or databases. This feature of digital journal subscription illustrates another serious access failure in the digitally networked environment.

The access failure stemming from increasing journal subscription fees may be detrimental to the advancement of human knowledge because the knowledge contained in a proprietary journal may not be open enough to rigorous criticism. From their perspective as authors, scholars usually place much more importance on professional recognition than on pecuniary profit. Therefore, rather than choosing to earn substantial profits from copyright, most scholars prefer to have their works disseminated and cited as widely as possible. Furthermore, from their perspective as readers of academic articles, it is critically important for scholars to have access to others' work because scholarly discussion is a continuous process based on previous research. A reader of an academic article is very possibly an author of another article. Accordingly, in academia, authors' willingness to disseminate their works is usually consistent with the public's interest in free access to information. Such consistency indicates that the academic journal market does not need copyright as an incentive for intellectual creation.

Nonetheless, in *American Geophysical Union v. Texaco*, 802 F. Supp. 1 (S.D.N.Y. 1992), the court stated that copyright still plays an important role in the dissemination of scholarly research. The court argued that in the academic journal market, copyright's primary role was not to protect authors' scholarly works, but rather to induce the professional publication, reproduction and distribution of these works. Some scholars also argue that because authors generally do not seek to profit directly from their published work, they would rather relinquish the underlying copyright to commercial publishers in exchange for publication and distribution of their works (Litman, 2006).

However, behind this type of exchange lies a potential conflict that arises between the interests of authors and the interests of publishers, which leads to access failure in the academic journal market. As noted previously, authors wish to distribute their works as widely as possible, whereas for-profit publishers are not incentivized to make journal articles widely and cheaply available. These publishers, instead, prefer to strengthen and extend the copyright protection of information in order to maximize their profits. As a result, copyright has become a tool with which commercial publishers extract all potential commercial value from works of authorship.

In the midst of this mismatch between the interests of scholars and the interests of commercial publishers, the PLoS has adopted a new approach to the academic journal publishing market. The PLoS provides scientists with an opportunity to take charge of their own IP and to bypass the market control of commercial publishers. Because the Internet has significantly decreased the costs of disseminating academic journals, the copyright system is not the only mechanism that can be relied upon to publish and distribute academic journals. In other words, with the Internet's capacity to transmit information efficiently, it becomes problematic to justify commercial publishers' control over the copyright of published papers.

In the interests of publishing quality academic journals, a formal organizational structure is desirable to cover various transaction costs required by a professional publication. Such costs include, for example, the costs of running the server, and administering peer review, editing, layout, typesetting processes and publication itself. Therefore, in order to simultaneously eliminate access failure and internalize transaction costs that stem from journal publication, the NPO emerges as an ideal organizational form for the PLoS. Through the Internet connection, the PLoS has successfully corrected the contract failure that has long existed between academic writers and academic readers. In recent years, PLOS journals have successfully increased their impact factors in a number of scientific fields (Davis, 2013). This accomplishment has revealed the fact that PLoS's non-profit open access model and its publication quality have been preliminarily recognized by the academia.

Scenario One: Case Two – Collaborative Failure

Commons production requires successful collective action either among individuals or among organizations. The organizational structure of NPOs has become an effective tool to enable such collective action. In fact, the relationship between collective action and NPOs is not new to academia. Nobel laureate Kenneth Arrow has long pointed out the collective action problems for organizations besides the government and for-profit firms (Arrow, 1974). In the commons realm, NPOs also facilitate collaboration among individuals. Therefore, this chapter argues that NPOs are capable of correcting *collaborative failure*, which is a mutation of the original contract failure scenario.

As peer production has become the central means for commons production, collaboration has been one of the key features of the commons. Commons-based peer production projects range from Wikipedia to large FOSS tasks, such as Apache and Linux. Although peer production itself can address certain market failures and generate production activities whose costs are relatively low, it may fail owing to disincentive problems or to collective action problems arising from coordination among participants, property rights management, resources provision and potential liabilities. Such failure constitutes the collaborative failure among dispersed participants in the commons-production system. By internalizing or reducing the costs of distributed participants' collective action in the peer-production process, many NPOs play an important role in rectifying the collaborative failure by managing property rights, providing resources, dealing with other entities, protecting individuals from liability, and formalizing the decision-making process.

A casual observation of the NPOs' presence in the commons environment suggests that these organizations exist only around large-scale projects. There are at least two possible explanations for the relationship between NPO incorporation and the size of these commons projects. The first explanation is that only when a peer-production project achieves a critical mass of volunteers will the project have enough resources to form an NPO. According to the second explanation, a formal organization is needed only when the underlying peer-production project's complexity and scale increase substantially. Moreover, the nature of the NPO is especially suitable for large-scale, peer-production projects because the NPO is less likely than a for-profit organization to impair the diverse motivations of distributed contributors. To harmonize these diverse interests and motivations, NPOs' structures provide organizational arrangements for various stakeholders in large commons communities.

Scenario Two: Licensing Failure

As copyright law protects creators by default when copyrightable materials are first created, it is necessary for users to secure permission for each use of every copyrighted resource. In addition, because US copyright law does not require any formalities, such as copyright notice and registration, it is difficult to ascertain whether a work falls under copyright protection or has shifted into the public domain. As a result, users may hesitate to consume such resources due to fear of infringement. Even if the potential users decide to get a licence from copyright holders, it may be extremely expensive to identify, locate and negotiate with the right holders (Boyle, 2008; Lessig, 2004).

Because of the default rule in copyright law, creators must take affirmative action if they want to opt out of the full copyright protection. Although some of the creators may initially be willing to allow a particular use of their work, they are ultimately likely to conclude that granting permission is unwise because of the high costs of legal fees for the licensing process (Elkin-Koren, 2005). As a result, this first type of licensing failure typically occurs between individual creators and users of intellectual resources, and can be attributed to prohibitively high information and transaction costs.

In this type of contract failure scenario, the most desirable free licensing arrangement is one that facilitates the free distribution of copyright protected works. Such licences can allow creators to release and distribute their works for public use under certain conditions. Among all these licences, the CC licences are most flexible for reflecting creators' preference regarding reuse of the creators' works. Legal devices like the CC Attribution License allow the creators to waive some of their copyrights and to simultaneously retain other copyrights, such as the right to prevent dissemination of altered or commercialized copies. Such free licenses not only enable creators to exercise their rights flexibly and economically, but also facilitate users' efforts to identify creative works that are readily available for reuse without bargaining. Therefore, by producing and freely distributing the licences, CC, the FSF, and other NPOs provide the public with greater access to copyrighted materials than the default legal rules would otherwise allow.

Theoretical Implications

Hansmann's contract failure theory is sometimes referred to as *trust theory* because one of the theory's most important propositions is that donors must voluntarily entrust and contribute their resources to the NPOs (Dollery & Wallis, 2003). Contract failure theory focuses on circumstances in which customers are more likely to trust NPOs than their for-profit counterparts because the former are not motivated by profit, and, thus, may be less likely to act opportunistically towards consumers. Trust functions as both the catalyst for the formation of the NPO and as the key ingredient for its survival.

Hansmann (1980) argues that donors usually aim to donate their resources to a specific group of recipients. In the case of commons production, however, there are usually no specific recipients. Because all of the resources are donated as commons, the intended beneficiary of the donations is actually the whole society or community. Nonetheless, the two types of donors, donors in Hansmann's theory and donors in the commons scenario, are concerned about whether or not their donations will eventually fall into the hands of the intended beneficiaries. In the commons arenas, stealing a commons and converting it into proprietary information is a serious infraction of accepted norms (Feller & Fitzgerald, 2002). Consequently, NPOs supporting peer-production projects may serve as trusted intermediaries that will not privatize intellectual resources donated by volunteers.

It is not surprising that for-profit companies can rarely play the role of trustworthy institutions. These companies may not be able to credibly internalize the philanthropic objectives of commons communities (Lerner & Tirole, 2002). Moreover, they may adjust or withdraw their commitment to commons communities because of their profit-making concerns. By contrast, NPOs' non-distribution constraint constitutes an assurance that voluntary contributions from the communities will reach the intended recipients. Therefore, NPOs' non-distribution constraint provides a certain degree of trust that enables stakeholders in the commons environment to act collectively in their mutual interests. NPOs' neutrality can also help to convince commons contributors that their contribution will not be managed for the interest of a specific proprietary business (Lee, 2010).

In commons operating beyond the FOSS world, NPOs similarly provide trust, which is indispensable for the sustainability of communities. As an NPO, the Wikimedia Foundation has decided not to run the Wikipedia project using revenue from commercial advertisements because its founder, Jimmy Wales, believes that commercial ads may be harmful to the project's credibility and community trust (Lessig, 2008). In summary, by enabling trust that is difficult for for-profit enterprises to gain, NPOs provide a proper organizational incentive structure for commons production.

Many commons communities operate according to principles that differ greatly from the principles driving proprietary firms. Conventional wisdom attributes the success of FOSS and other peer-production projects to the Internet and characterizes the Internet as the most important medium connecting contributors and users to one another (Benkler, 2002; Feller & Fitzgerald, 2002). Many commentators similarly suggest that the Internet is a perfect medium for eliminating the middleman and transaction costs stemming from organizational structure (Shirky, 2008; Weber, 2004).

Indeed, by removing the temporal and geographical obstacles of interpersonal communication, the Internet gives individuals the ability to distribute their contributions quickly and broadly, and to collaborate with other participants all over the world. Nonetheless, although the Internet has radically transformed the boundaries of traditional organizations, the Internet-based arguments overlook the fact that new forms of organizational structures have arisen to reconfigure information production processes. The analysis of contract failure in the commons discourse demonstrates how humans come together, create communities and organizations, and make decisions and rules to sustain a common resource or to achieve a desired outcome. This analysis suggests that in addition to the Internet, many NPOs help to connect people to each other and pool resources in the digital world.

Market and Government Failure Theory

Theory

Another important theory, proposed by Professor Burton A. Weisbrod (1977), traces the existence of NPOs back to both 'market failure' and 'government failure', where obstacles limit both the private market's and the government's ability to provide public goods. Providing public goods purely through the market will, in effect, ensure that they will be under-supplied because few consumers will volunteer to pay for products that they could enjoy at no expense. Consequently, the producer will produce less of a public good than the public really needs. In traditional economic theory, this 'free-rider' problem is the major rationale for the government because a government can overcome market failure by taxing people to produce public goods.

Nevertheless, the government also encounters certain restraints as a public goods producer. In a democratic society, the government will provide the public with only a limited range and quantity of public goods to obtain majority support (Weisbrod, 1977). With limited resources, the government can only respond to 'majoritarian interests'. The limitation of the public goods means that some unsatisfied demand will persist. Certainly, some dissatisfied customers will purchase substitute, but not necessarily the same, commodities in a private market. However, when the substitute goods offered by the market do not fully meet the unsatisfied demand for collective goods, consumers can resort to NPOs (Weisbrod, 1988). According to Weisbrod (1988: 59–60, emphasis original),

> '[A] class of voluntary organizations will come into existence as *extragovernmental providers of collective-consumption goods*. These organizations will "supplement" the *public* provision (which can be zero) and provide an alternative to the *private*-sector provision of the private-good substitutes for collective goods.'

Application

NPOs in the commons environment produce various public goods which are provided neither by the government nor by the market. Therefore, Weisbrod's theory may explain why many of these NPOs exist at all.

According to Weisbrod's theory, to satisfy diverse societal demands, NPOs have emerged as a private response, not only to market failures, but also to government failures. In this sense, Weisbrod's theory can explain some of the circumstances associated with government activities that are not mentioned in the contract failure theory. Weisbrod's insight into government failure is especially useful in analysing NPOs in the commons environment, many of which were established as responses to government copyright laws. As Hunter (2005) indicates, a number of public-interest groups, including the CC, the Center for the Public Domain, and the Open Knowledge Network, emerged in the aftermath of the Digital Millennium Copyright Act (DMCA) and the Sonny Bono Copyright Term Extension Act (CTEA). Other commentators also indicate that DMCA and CTEA engendered the free culture movement (Lasica, 2005).

The most common government failure associated with copyright laws is that the legislative process was captured by powerful copyright industries (Bohannan, 2006). Litman (2001) vividly describes how, in the past century, the legislative process has evolved into an industry-negotiated and industry-drafted process. The industry-drafted copyright legislation tends to tilt copyright law in the direction of increasingly stronger protection. Litman (2001) suggests that the resulting copyright legislation is due to the industry's generous campaign contributions and the government's intrinsic incompetence. Examples given by Litman (2001) include the DMCA legislative process, where established players such as the sound recording and movie industries exercised their considerable influence.

Similarly, the CTEA reflects Disney's intense lobbying for an extension of copyrights that would protect Disney's copyright on Mickey Mouse. Although CTEA was challenged in the US Supreme Court in the *Eldred v. Ashcroft* case, the court ruled that it was Congress's decision to make. The consequence of this decision is to foster further collective action in cultural environmentalism (Kapczynski, 2008).

Market failure in the commons discourse has been the focus of many NPOs. According to Weisbrod's theory, for-profits fail to provide certain public goods due to the free-rider problem (Weisbrod, 1977). Since for-profits have difficulties in profiting from producing these public goods, they will have no incentive to provide them in the marketplace. Because these public goods are crucial to certain creative activities, market failure occurs as a result of for-profits' incapability of supplying these goods. This hypothesis resonates with the commons scenario in which NPOs play an increasingly important role in producing public goods.

Because contract failure is a type of market failure, the above-mentioned *contract failures* pertaining to commons can also exemplify market failures when we apply Weisbrod's theory to the NPOs studied here. In addition to contract failure, Richard Steinberg (2006) identifies two types of market failures that NPOs aim to correct: under-provision and over-exclusion. Under-provision means that the intellectual resources are not sufficiently supplied to meet societal needs, while over-exclusion refers to when IP has prevented the ideal number of citizens from accessing the underlying intellectual resources. In fact, sometimes contract failure may take place in the form of under-provision or over-exclusion. For example, *access failure*, which is a new type of contract failure identified in this chapter, occurs as a result of proprietary publishers' or other enterprises' over-exclusion of information. *Collaborative failure* takes place when the market fails to provide sufficient resources for large-scale peer-production and other collective activities. *Licensing failure*, resulting from the significant transaction costs imposed by the default rules in copyright law, leads to the under-provision of intellectual resources for building culture upon the past. Moreover, the NPOs studied in this chapter produce certain public goods that both the government and the market have failed to provide in the first place. Society's extensive consumption of these public goods thereafter indicates that an under-provision problem existed prior to the NPOs' efforts, regardless of whether the function of these goods is to cure contract failure or the over-exclusion problem.

Since copyright law and its captured legislative process are the primary causes for government and market failure in the information society, it is no surprise that some NPOs exist to influence copyright legislation. For example, PK was established as a response to copyright lobbying activities. This organization seeks to preserve the intellectual commons and expose related market failures by documenting which segments of the general public are trying to influence specific legislation. Since the government is not always perfectly informed regarding its policy-making, it may fail due to the significant information costs in the decision-making process. PK may correct such failure, to some extent, by providing important information to the government regarding certain legislation, which would otherwise be unavailable. To this end, PK also collaborates with other NPOs, such as the EFF. As PK's President Sohn explained in an interview with the author: 'What we try to do is ... to work with those organizations like the EFF ... and move on. They have grassroots. So we provide the content and they'll provide the network. We'll seek out organizations that have grassroots presence and we'll activate them.'

To this end, several NPOs function as common platforms for collaborations between different groups. For instance, PK, KEI and the Open Society Institute, have invested significant resources in coalition building to integrate voices from individuals, business and other NPOs that share similar ideas of an ideal copyright system. Nonetheless, the impact of NPOs' advocacy efforts is often difficult to evaluate.

Given the obvious difficulty of convincing Congress to pass ideal legislation, litigation has emerged as an alternative to prevent the overexpansion of IP rights. Therefore, NPOs, such as the EFF and the SFLC, have sought remedies for the public in court. Other NPOs, such as the FSF and CC, are involved in enacting *private law*. By providing creators with non-exclusive licences, these organizations are building a broader scope of commons for creative activities. The FSF-designed GPL has acquired a reputation as a contractual mechanism 'cutting back' the scope of background IP rights (Radin & Wagner, 1998). Similarly, CC, established in the aftermath of *Eldred v. Ashcroft*, is a more obvious example of a private response to the imperfect copyright system. CC deems current copyright law to be a major obstacle to creative activities and seeks to change the default rule that it created (Lessig, 2008).

Numerous other NPOs have built architecture to preserve the commons environment. For example, the PLoS, MIT, and other academic institutions have provided access to valuable scholarly information. Internet Archive and similar organizations have created digital artefacts that preclude cultural memory from fading. Moreover, through the production of licences and architecture, NPOs have reshaped the market for online information. In the past, the use of information was constrained by considerable legal costs and uncertainties. In summary, these NPOs help to correct under-provision and over-exclusion failures through 'a model of property based more on *amplification* than scarcity' (Harold, 2007: 149).

Theoretical Implications

Based on NPOs' responses to government and market failures, it is apparent that some NPOs provide resources for social experimentation. Since governments are discouraged from using taxpayer money to make new policies on the basis of trial and error, NPOs can help fill the role of experimenters for future policy-making. More often than not, governments then implement new policies that imitate successful NPO programmes (Frumkin, 2002).

Historically, it is not uncommon for NPOs to financially support such social experimentation. For example, the Rockefeller Foundation sponsored remedial social and economic sciences in England during the interwar years, because it believed that the levels of poverty and unemployment were misinterpreted (Douglas, 1987). Likewise, the NPOs that use their funds to stimulate commons development recognize that there is something fundamentally wrong or insufficient with government policy concerning creative activities. For example, the Open Society Institute has aimed to influence policy by the funding of a series of experiments. The PLoS has successfully influenced the funding policy of National Institutes of Health (NIH) through its experiment on open access publishing. Starting in 2005, the NIH, the largest funder of science research in the US federal government, began requiring every scientist who receives an NIH research grant, and who publishes the result in a peer-review journal, to deposit a digital copy of the article in PubMed Central (PMC). PMC then provides free online access to its copy sometime after the article is published in a journal.

Many other NPOs also aim to influence government policy through their social experimentation. For example, after their own experience with a digital archive, the Internet Archive began assisting governments in preserving digital culture. In order to avoid the threat to the collaborative process that produces the FOSS, the FSF has advocated a top-down legal change regarding software patents. Through the anti-software patent campaign, the FSF aims to demonstrate to policy-makers the potential innovation opportunities arising in the absence of software patents via its free software experiment.

The Hewlett Foundation has invested substantially in open textbooks for K-12 students and other OER projects. By making OER grants, the Foundation is attempting to force the government to recognize OER's value from a policy perspective. Therefore, the way that the Hewlett Foundation responds to government failure is to prove OER's value through a set of social experiments. The organization believes that the result of these experiments will provide policy-makers with essential information that is unavailable through the traditional and formal policy-making process.

The most ambitious NPO project in the commons environment with the goal of changing the law through social experimentation is probably Creative Commons (CC), which aims to help IP policy-makers understand authors' desire to control their creative works as well as the importance of the public domain to various types of creative genres (Lessig, 2004). As CC's founder, Lawrence Lessig (2006a: 199) states: '[the] lesson [from CC] may help policy makers recraft copyright law in the future'. Through the private reform initiated by CC, Lessig (2006b: 74) desires to 'awake recognition of the need for [public] reform'. He envisioned that, only when the free culture movement promoted by CC has gained significant public support will

Congress be more likely to engage in copyright legislative reform to protect the freedom of the general public.

The NPOs studied in this chapter have formed an unprecedented ecosystem that makes various commons-related activities possible. Without NPOs, the commons environment might be much less vigorous than it now is. Currently prevailing NPO theories aid our understanding of NPOs' role and behaviour in the commons environment. Nevertheless, neither contract failure theory nor government and market failure theory provides a complete picture of NPOs' role in the commons realm. Given the diversity of various NPOs, a theory about one type of NPO does not translate easily to other types. Therefore, these theories may be regarded, to a large extent, as complementary rather than mutually exclusive efforts to understand a heterogeneous sector operating in diverse economies.

CONCLUSION

This chapter has identified access failure, collaborative failure and licensing failure as the three major types of contract failure in the commons economy. NPOs have played a critical role in various commons activities. Some of these problems may be ameliorated significantly by good governance structures. By clarifying the role of NPOs in correcting contract failures in the digitally-networked world, this chapter illustrated how trust provided by NPOs is indispensable for commons governance. Diverging from the conventional wisdom associated with the Internet's disintermediation effect, this chapter uses NPOs in the commons arena to argue that formal organizations are still necessary for decentralized production activities in cyberspace. The organizational and governance form of NPOs is appropriate to coordinate contributions and mediate between the interests of participants and sponsors.

Moreover, NPOs are a private response to various market and government failures. These failures include the captured copyright legislation, the copyright law itself, contract failure, and the under-provision and over-exclusion of intellectual resources. Through the lens of market and government failure theory, we can understand the role of NPOs in conducting social experimentation and empowering individuals in our intellectual ecology. Moreover, NPOs occasionally act as independent innovators that harness individual values and that direct them toward significant collective ends. NPOs can, therefore, be analysed as an organizational form able to correct various failures in our society.

REFERENCES

Armbruster, Chris (2008) 'Cyberscience and the Knowledge-Based Economy, Open Access and Trade Publishing: From Contradiction to Compatibility with Nonexclusive Copyright Licensing', *International Journal of Communications Law and Policy,* 12(Winter): 20–41.

Arrow, Kenneth J. (1974) *The Limits of Organization.* New York: Norton.

Atkins, Daniel E. (2007) *A Review of the Open Educational Resources (OER) Movement.* Palo Alto: The William and Flora Hewlett Foundation, at http://www.hewlett.org/uploads/files/ReviewoftheOERMovement.pdf

Benkler, Yochai (2002) 'Coase's Penguin, or, Linux and the Nature of the Firm', *Yale Law Journal,* 112(3): 369–446.

Benkler, Yochai (2003) 'Freedom in the Commons: Towards a Political Economy of Information', *Duke Law Journal,* 52(6): 1245–76.

Benkler, Yochai (2006) *The Wealth of Networks: How Social Production Transforms Markets and Freedom.* New Haven: Yale University Press.

Bohannan, Christina (2006) 'Reclaiming Copyright', *Cardozo Arts & Entertainment Law Journal,* 23(3): 567–634.

Boyle, James (2003) 'The Second Enclosure Movement and the Construction of the Public Domain', *Law and Contemporary Problems,* 66(1): 33–74.

Boyle, James (2008) *The Public Domain: Enclosing the Commons of the Mind.* New Haven: Yale University Press.

David, Matthew (1996) 'Information: Culture or Capital', *Radical Philosophy,* 79: 56.

Davis, Phil (2013) 'The Rise and Fall of the PLoS ONE's Impact Factor', *The Scholarly Kitchen*, at http://scholarlykitchen.sspnet.org/2013/06/20/the-rise-and-fall-of-plos-ones-impact-factor-2012-3-730/

Deek, Fadi P. and McHugh, James A.M. (2008) *Open Source: Technology and Policy*. Cambridge: Cambridge University Press.

Defourny, Jacques and Nyssens, Marthe (2010) 'Conceptions of Social Enterprise and Social Entrepreneurship in Europe and the United States: Convergences and Divergences', *Journal of Social Entrepreneurship*, 1(1): 32–53.

DiMaggio, Paul J. and Anheier, Helmut K. (1990) 'The Sociology of Nonprofit Organizations and Sectors', *Annual Review of Sociology*, 16(1): 137–59.

Dollery, Brian E. and Wallis, Joe L. (2003) *The Political Economy of the Voluntary Sector: A Reappraisal of the Comparative Institutional Advantage of Voluntary Organizations*. Cheltenham: Edward Elgar Publishing.

Douglas, James (1987) 'Political Theories of Nonprofit Organization', in Powell, Walter W. (ed.), *The Nonprofit Sector: A Research Handbook*. New Haven: Yale University Press. pp. 43–54.

Elkin-Koren, Niva (2005) 'What Contracts Cannot Do: The Limits of Private Ordering in Facilitating a Creative Commons', *Fordham Law Review*, 74(2): 375–422.

Evers, Adalbert and Laville, Jean-Louis (2004) 'Defining The Third Sector in Europe', in Evers, Adalbert and Laville, Jean-Louis (eds), *The Third Sector in Europe*. Cheltenham: Edward Elgar. pp. 1–42.

Feller, Joseph and Fitzgerald, Brian (2002) *Understanding Open Source Software Development*. Boston: Addison-Wesley/Pearson Education.

Frumkin, Peter (2002) *On Being Nonprofit: A Conceptual and Policy Primer*. Cambridge: Harvard University Press.

Hall, Peter Dobkin (2006) 'A Historical Overview of Philanthropy, Voluntary Associations, and Nonprofit Organizations in the United States, 1600–2000', in Powell, Walter W. and Steinberg, Richard (eds), *The Nonprofit Sector: A Research Handbook*. New Haven: Yale University Press. pp. 32–58.

Hansmann, Henry B. (1980) 'The Role of Nonprofit Enterprise', *Yale Law Journal*, 89(5): 835–901.

Hansmann, Henry B. (1981) 'Reforming Nonprofit Corporation Law', *University of Pennsylvania Law Review*, 129(3): 497–623.

Harold, Christine (2007) *OurSpace: Resisting the Corporate Control of Culture*. Minneapolis: University of Minnesota Press.

Hess, Charlotte and Ostrom, Elinor (2003) 'Ideas, Artifacts, and Facilities: Information as a Common-Pool Resource', *Law and Contemporary Problems*, 66(1–2): 111–45.

Hunter, Dan (2005) 'Culture War', *Texas Law Review*, 83(4): 1105–36.

Kapczynski, Amy (2008) 'The Access to Knowledge Mobilization and the New Politics of Intellectual Property', *Yale Law Journal*, 117(5): 804–85.

Kerlin, Janelle A. (2006) 'Social Enterprise in the United States and Europe: Understanding and Learning from the Difference', *Voluntas: International Journal of Voluntary and Nonprofit Organizations*, 17(3): 247–63.

Lasica, J.D. (2005) *Darknet: Hollywood's War Against the Digital Generation*. New Jersey: Wiley & Sons.

Lee, Jyh-An (2010) 'Organizing the Unorganized: The Role of Nonprofit. Organizations in the Commons Communities', *Jurimetrics: The Journal of Law, Science, and Technology*, 50(3): 275–327.

Lerner, Josh and Tirole, Jean (2002) 'Some Simple Economics of Open Source', *Journal of Industrial Economics*, 50(2): 197–234.

Lessig, Lawrence (2002) 'The Architecture of Innovation', *Duke Law Journal*, 51(6): 1783–801.

Lessig, Lawrence (2004) *Free Culture: How Big Media Uses Technology and the Law to Lock Down Culture and Control Creativity*. New York: Penguin Press.

Lessig, Lawrence (2006a) *Code Version 2.0*. New York: Basic Books.

Lessig, Lawrence (2006b) 'Re-Crafting a Public Domain', *Yale Journal of Law & the Humanities*, 18(3): 56–83.

Lessig, Lawrence (2008) *Remix: Making Art and Commerce Thrive in the Hybrid Economy*. New York: Penguin Press.

Litman, Jessica (2001) *Digital Copyright*. New York: Prometheus Books.

Litman, Jessica (2006) 'The Economics of Open Access Law Publishing', *Lewis & Clark Law Review*, 10(4): 779–96.

Mann, Ronald J. (2006) 'Commercializing Open Source Software: Do Property Rights Still Matter?', *Harvard Journal of Law & Technology*, 20(1): 1–47.

Merges, Robert P. (2004) 'A New Dynamism in the Public Domain', *University of Chicago Law Review*, 71(1): 183–203.

PLoS (2013) Public Library of Science (www.plos.org/).

Public Knowledge (2013) *About Public Knowledge: Our Work*, (at https://www.publicknowledge.org/about-us/).

Radin, Margaret Jane and Wagner, R. Polk (1998) 'The Myth of Private Ordering: Rediscovering Legal Realism in Cyberspace', *The Chicago-Kent Law Review*, 73(4): 1295–317.

Sandler, Todd (1992) *Collective Action: Theory and Applications*. Ann Arbor: University of Michigan Press.

Shirky, Clay (2008) *Here Comes Everybody: The Power of Organizing Without Organizations*. New York: Penguin Press.

Simon, John et al. (2006) 'The Federal Tax Treatment of Charitable Organizations', in Powell, Walter W. and Steinberg, Richard (eds), *The Nonprofit Sector: A Research Handbook*. New Haven: Yale University Press. pp. 267–99.

Stallman, Richard (2002) 'The GNU Project', in Gay, Joshua (ed.), *Free Software, Free Society*. Boston: GNU Press. pp. 17–32.

Steinberg, Richard (2006) 'Economic Theories of Nonprofit Organizations', in Powell, Walter W. (ed.), *The Nonprofit Sector: A Research Handbook*. New Haven: Yale University Press. pp. 117–39.

Tapscott, Don and Williams, Anthony D. (2006) *Wikinomics: How Mass Collaboration Changes Everything*. New York: Portfolio.

Weber, Steven (2004) *The Success of Open Source*. Cambridge: Harvard University Press.

Weisbrod, Burton A. (1977) *The Voluntary Nonprofit Sector: An Economic Analysis*. Lexington: Lexington Books.

Weisbrod, Burton A. (1988) *The Nonprofit Economy*. Cambridge: Harvard University Press.

19

Copyright and Copyleft in India: Between Global Agendas and Local Interests

Pradip Ninan Thomas

INTRODUCTION

The Indian government's position on intellectual property and in particular copyright has been shaped by the compulsions of geopolitics and international trade, the interests of domestic and global copyright industries and by differing understandings of the overall goals and objectives of digital policy in India. The government's position is further shaped by the tension between those who are supportive of the increased privatization of these industries on the one hand and those who are supportive of the country's sovereignty and independence on matters related to hardware and software on the other. To some extent, its position is also influenced by civil society lobbies and NGOs. Given the multiple interests involved, it is hardly surprising that Indian policy related to copyright is fluid, open, and in process. This changing, and what might seem to be inconsistent, approach to copyright is often critiqued by the global copyright industries that are keen that India draft copyright laws that are in tune with global legislation. One can argue, however, that the approach taken by the Indian government is not only consistent but reflects policy that is attuned to the evolving nature of digital information ecosystems and the national interest in information as a resource, service and product that has increasingly begun to contribute towards its GDP. I have characterized India as an ambivalent state torn between its commitments to economic globalization and growth on the one hand and its commitment to its citizens on the other. This ambivalence is clearly expressed in its policies related to intellectual property, including copyright.

While copyright law in India has been governed by the Copyright Act (1957) that has been amended on a number of occasions, most recently in 2012, the issue of copyright became a political and economic issue in the context of India's involvement in the Trade Related Intellectual Property Rights (TRIPS) agreement that was negotiated at the end of the Uruguay Round of GATT talks. TRIPS led to intellectual property rights (IPR) becoming the cornerstone of multi-lateral trade under the World Trade Organization (WTO). The progressive liberalization of all trade in goods and services, a requirement for accession to the WTO, rather inevitably led to pressure on India to tighten its IP legislation across the board, create new legislation for emerging industries, particularly those connected to the hardware and software of the digital economy, and harmonize domestic with international IP legislation. Why copyright only became an issue in the 1990s, when India already had for decades a strong and vibrant tradition of cinema (Bollywood), publishing and music is an interesting question. To a large extent the accentuation of pressure to harmonize India's copyright laws with global laws corresponds with economic liberalization and the entry of foreign capital into India's cultural industries. Chowdhury (2008: 109) proffers the following explanation:

> Unlike Hollywood, the studio system, barring a few prominent production houses, has been almost non-existent in Bollywood since post-1950s. This explains the absence of any Hollywood-style oligopolistic corporation with vertical integration of production-distribution-exhibition in the Indian motion picture business. This aspect of Bollywood also explains the lack of initiative for lobbying for copyright reforms in India by the members of this unintegrated sector, although piracy remains a serious problem.

The reason for the Motion Picture Association of America's involvement in copyright protection of local film products becomes clearer when seen against the investments made by one of its members, Sony Entertainment TV, that was launched in October 1995 in the Indian subcontinent and has bought rights to 300 Hindi films, and secured exclusive rights for cultural and sporting events in India. Sony also hosts the top-rated show *Aahat*, currently has access to and owns 1500 hours of exclusive programming, has invested millions of dollars in dubbing Hollywood films into Hindi and in the making of local feature films, and is also involved in making profits from its Sony music label. Similarly, another member of the Motion Picture Association of America (MPAA), Fox Star Studios, part of News Corporation, has invested in film production both in Bollywood and the South Indian film industry. Its co-production *My Name is Khan* grossed US $23 million in India. In 2010, Disney entered the market with its animated Hindi movie *Roadside Rome* (Thomas, 2010). With such investments at stake, India can look forward to the active involvement of the MPAA in the matter of copyright enforcement.

The Indian government's stance related to copyright has not been predictable and it is this unpredictability, best illustrated by its refusal to follow the international script to the letter, that makes it an interesting case study. Stronger copyright enforcement in line with its advocates at the Business Software Alliance and the MPAA has been accompanied by the Traditional Knowledge Digital Library and among the most progressive laws in favour of access to information for the visually impaired. This chapter will begin with a brief introduction to the contemporary terrain of copyright in India, followed by a section on the Indian state and global copyright pressures, and then go on provide examples of three proactive copyright policies enacted by the state in India, namely the Traditional Knowledge Digital Library (TKDL), the Copyright Act (2012) amendment on the rights of the visually impaired to accessible resources, and public sector software in Kerala. The final section provides a reflection on the future of copyright in the context of an 'ambivalent' state.

THE CONTEMPORARY TERRAIN OF COPYRIGHT IN INDIA

The amendment of the Indian Copyright Act (2012), the sixth since its enactment in 1957, is especially significant for its provisions related to Digital Rights Management (DRM) thus bringing the Indian act in line with WIPO's Copyright (WCT) and Performances and Phonograms (WPPT) treaties. Other amendments include provisions on the rights of artists, disability provisions, compulsory licensing, strengthening enforcement and the reform of the Copyright Board (Thomas, 2013). Interestingly enough, India is not a signatory to either of these WIPO treaties, despite pressure from the WIPO to sign them. The refusal to sign the treaties suggests that the Indian government is confident enough to amend its copyright laws only when such amendments will be in line with national development objectives. The government has held its ground despite multiple pressures from both global and local copyright industries to expand the law, with the key goal being the curbing of piracy. Furthermore, amendments such as that of the DRM, are by no means exact replicas of the WIPO treaties or the US Digital Millennium Copyright Act (DMCA). While the circumvention of DRM can invite fines and jail sentences, there are exceptions and these technologies can be circumvented in specific circumstances such as in the interest of national security.

A recent (2010) case in point is the government's conflict with the Canadian company Research in Motion (RIM), makers of the mobile phone Blackberry. Blackberry communications are difficult to decrypt and the Indian government has been keen to monitor information flows and access the formats it uses for communication. Heightened speculation related to terrorist outfits and their potential use of Blackberry as a preferred tool for communication has led the government to place extraordinary pressure on Blackberry. In 2012, the company handed over encryption keys to the government of India after it 'recently demonstrated a solution developed by a firm called Verint that can intercept messages and emails exchanged between Blackberry handsets, and make these encrypted communications available in a readable format to Indian security agencies, according to an exchange of communications between the Canadian company and the Indian government' (Philip, 2012). The DRM amendment does not criminalize the actual facilitation of circumvention or the tools used for this purpose – thus ensuring space and opportunities for technological innovation (see Krishnakumar and Saha, 2013). This stands in marked contrast to clauses in the DMCA that criminalize all attempts to circumvent DMAs.

Without a doubt, the extraordinary growth that the knowledge industry and the entertainment sector have witnessed in India over the last two decades has played a major role in efforts to strengthen the copyright regime. The 2012 FICCI-KPMG Indian Media and Entertainment Industry Report, entitled *Digital Dawn: The Metamorphosis Begins* (*Digital Dawn*, 2012: 4) presents a picture of a dynamic industry that seems to have weathered the economic slow-down that has otherwise affected the growth rate in India, projected to be in the range of 5.4 per cent for 2013, down from the steady 9–10 per cent experienced in earlier years. This report estimates a 12 per cent increase in growth in the entertainment industry in 2012 to reach INR823 billion (US$15.3 billion) from its base of INR728 billion (US$13.6 billion) in 2011. The key areas for growth are in TV, print, film, radio, music, outdoor advertising, animating and VFX, gaming and digital advertising.

While exact calculations are difficult to come by, and the projected buoyancy in these markets may be based on optimism rather than reality, there has been enormous growth in media environments over the last few decades. Such growth is best illustrated by the fact that in 1991 there were five TV channels while today there are around 800. The Indian print market tells a similar story and is second only to Japan in terms of circulation. There are ten newspapers that command a daily readership of between 6 and 17 million, with the Hindi-based *Dainik Jagran* leading at 16.4 million. The only English newspaper in this group is the *Times of India* that commands a circulation of 7.4 million.

There are a couple of observations that need to be made. Firstly, the growth that is occurring is predominantly in the vernacular language markets that cater to audiences in Tier 1 and increasingly Tiers 2 and 3 cities (this ranking system corresponds with population size). Secondly, and in the absence of strong regulatory reform, particularly cross-media ownership regulations, there has been an increase in the already dominant media houses diversifying into other media and non-media areas, established conglomerates investing in media and established political families controlling the media and in particular news channels. The 300 or more news channels in existence certainly do not all make profits – and it is clear that they are subsidized. For example, the Sun media network in the South Indian state Tamilnadu is run by members of a dominant political family. The decidedly populist politics in this state led to the government giving away free television sets to the poor, with the result that it has the largest TV viewing audiences in India and the largest TV-based advertising revenues. The Sun network has major interests in cable and satellite TV, FM radio, print, cable distribution, and film production (Thomas, 2010).

Thirdly, there have been both vertical and horizontal integrations in the media environment. As Thakurta (2012) notes:

> what is perhaps more significant in the current context are new forms of 'diagonal' mergers or 'lateral' expansion that are now taking place – almost as an extension or evolution of horizontal and vertical mergers – where there is a strategic association between a telecommunications company and a media company to use common infrastructure. Two recent examples are: (a) the strategic association of Reliance Industries Limited (RIL), India's largest corporate entity in the private sector, with the Network 18 and the Eenadu groups and (b) the Aditya Birla group acquiring a substantial holding in the Living Media group.

Increased copyright controls need to be seen in the light of the growth of this sector, the thriving software business, as well as the increased availability of content over a variety of digital platforms including mobile phones – that has also experienced massive growth over the last decade.

During the last two decades, the government of India has invested in strengthening the institutions, procedures and enforcement of copyright. These attempts at harmonizing domestic IP legislation with international TRIPS, WIPO and other related legislations have been complemented with major investments in strengthening and modernizing the infrastructure of IP and institutional mechanisms to aid coordination, monitoring, training, sensitization and enforcement. These include the establishment of the Copyright Enforcement Advisory Council (CEAC) under the Ministry of Human Resource Development and the setting up of special copyright enforcement cells:

> in 23 States and Union Territories, i.e. Andhra Pradesh, Assam, Andaman & Nicobar Islands, Chandigarh, Dadra & Nagar Haveli, Daman & Diu, Delhi, Goa, Gujarat, Haryana, Himachal Pradesh, Jammu & Kashmir, Karnataka, Kerala, Madhya Pradesh, Meghalaya, Orissa, Pondicherry, Punjab, Sikkim, Tamil Nadu, Tripura and West Bengal. States have also been advised to designate a nodal officer for copyright enforcement to facilitate easy interaction by copyright industry organizations and copyright owners. (Zinnov LLC, n.d.: 4)

The Copyright Enforcement Advisory Council under the Copyright Office is constituted of senior director generals of the police along with representatives from the key societies linked to the copyright industries in India such as the national Association of Software Service Companies, the Film Federation of India, along with others. India's efforts and increasing IP protection also includes joint enforcement activities between international trade bodies such as the Business Software Alliance and the Motion Pictures Association, bodies that represent in the main US-based organizations such as Microsoft and Disney, and local trade bodies such as the Society for Copyright Regulations of Indian Producers of Films and Television (SCRIPT), the Indian Performing Rights Society Limited (IPRS) and the Phonographic Performance Limited (PPL) (Thomas, 2010).

BOLLYWOOD, HOLLYWOOD, PIRACY AND THE IIPA

India's negotiations at the Uruguay Round of GATT had included a commitment to the progressive liberalization of trade in the audio-visual sector. Hollywood had lobbied hard to reverse the 20-year-old quota policy that restricted the annual import and distribution of Hollywood productions in India to 100 films. It had urged the US government to enforce Section 301-based trade sanctions against India for content piracy. The US-based International Intellectual Property Alliance (IIPA) had, in 1995, estimated trade losses to the US service industry as a result of piracy in India alone to be in the region of US$119 million, out of which $58 million was incurred in film, $10 million in recorded music, $26 million in entertainment software and $26 million in the book trade (quoted in Mansell and Wehn, 1998: 212).

The issue of piracy was turned into the means by which the MPAA, representing the seven major film and television producers in the US (i.e. Walt Disney Company, Sony Pictures Entertainment, Metro-Goldwyn-Mayer, Paramount Pictures Corporation, Twentieth Century Fox Film Corporation, Universal Studios and Warner Bros), made a determined effort to enter the Indian market. With a potential audience of 200 million, including cable and satellite television viewers, the Indian film market was perceived as a potential source of revenues for Hollywood. Box office returns of US$6 million for the Hindi version of *Jurassic Park*, US$12.5 million for *Titanic* and a similar amount for local blockbusters such as the Hindi-language *Dil To Pagal Hai* supported the notion that the Indian market was worth investing in. In fact, as Sidhva (1996: vi) has noted, Hollywood planned to carve out 10 per cent of the Indian film market by 2000, through the consolidation of a production, distribution and exhibition strategy, the latter aided by the establishment of multiplexes in Mumbai.

By 2011, the presence of Hollywood had become stronger with their growing investment in regional cinema markets in India, joint productions and dubbing of films in regional languages, resulting in returns from the top ten box office hits of around INR260 crores (US$55 million). Major companies such as Sony, Fox Star, Viacom 19 and Disney have invested in the Indian film market. Their ability to raise capital and invest in marketing has been a critical advantage to their success. While Bollywood continues to command the majority of audiences, advertising tie-ups are steadily moving towards Hollywood films. As Subramaniam (2012) has observed:

> in the last couple of years, Hollywood movies have also found steady appeal amongst brands which seek co-branding in association with films leading up to their release. Brands like Reebok, Seven Seas Codliver Oil, Kelloggs, Horlicks and MAAC among others, have put their money on big ticket Hollywood films. Another factor aiding their popularity is wider distribution than before. If a Hindi film saw a release with 400 prints, Hollywood films earlier would see around 50 prints. This has changed today. For instance, *The Amazing Spider-man* was released with 1236 prints in four languages – English, Hindi, Tamil and Telugu and in 3D, 2D and IMAX formats. *The Dark Knight Rises* released with 650 prints and 800 shows across the country.

The US government, through the United States Trade Representative (USTR) and Section 301 reports, and lobbying groups such as the IIPA, MPAA and the BSA continues to exert pressure on India. Recent Wikileaks reports confirm the close relationship between the US state department, the private sector and lobbying carried out by the US Embassy in Delhi, including talks with Mr N.N. Prasad, Joint Secretary with the Ministry of Commerce and Industry, regarding frustration with progress related to IP protection (www.cablegatesearch.net/cable.php?id=08NEWDELHI1683&q=special-301). The *2012 Special 301 Report on Copyright Protection and Enforcement* (IIPA, 2012) cites music industry source estimates of losses of around US$430 million in 2011 to piracy, representing 95 per cent of all downloads of music (in other words only 5 per cent of online music downloads are legal). The report also highlights losses worth US$1.4 billion incurred as a result of a 64 per cent rate of software piracy. In other words only 36 per cent of software in circulation in the Indian market is considered legal and therefore legitimate (IIPA, 2012).

This report recommends that India remain on the Priority Watch List in 2012 given that:

> Physical, online, and mobile piracy (through both mobile uploading/downloading, as well as mobile applications being used to infringe), circumvention of technological protection measures (TPMs), e.g., through the use of mod chips and game copiers, illegal camcording of movies from cinema screens, print and photocopy piracy, pay TV theft, and unlicensed use of business software, stifle the market and keep India's creative industries from reaching their potential. (IIPA, 2012: 63)

The methods used to calculate media piracy estimates remains contested. Appendix B. in the 2013 IIPA *Special 301 Report on Copyright Protection and Enforcement* (IIPA, 2013) details the methodology used to calculate estimates of piracy. Data on legal software is calculated on the basis of market data of legal software sales in 80 countries, and 20 countries on a custom basis. However, the quantity of unlicensed software is calculated on the basis of the BSA Global Software Piracy Study, for which data has not been included.

However, the Social Science Research Council (SSRC) Report on Media Piracy in Emerging Economies (Karaganis, 2011: 9) highlights issues with the measurement of piracy.

> Despite the tone of certainty that accompanies industry press releases about piracy, most of the industry researchers we spoke with showed considerable circumspection about their ability to accurately measure either rates or losses. Increasingly, industry researchers and representatives talk in more general terms about the magnitude of piracy, rather than about precise numbers. The USTR, for its part, appears to share this reticence and no longer includes top-line estimates for rates or losses in its Special 301 reports.

The report recommends a national anti-piracy task force, judicial reform, the reinvigoration of IP cells within state police units, a national database to track copyright criminals, increased raids, software audits of companies, along with other measures to combat piracy.

Joint Bollywood–Hollywood enforcements have grown and there is evidence that courts have begun to take violations seriously. Rhys Blakely reports in *The Australian* (2009: 12) on the US$200,000 out of court settlement by the Indian film company BR Films to Twentieth Century Fox for the film *Banda Yeh Bindaas Hai* (*This Guy is Fearless*), an illegal remake of the Oscar winning *My Cousin Vinny*, as the very first payment of its kind for the copying of a Hollywood film. The settlement suggests that Bollywood will find it harder to tread the copy route in the future. This is a turnaround from what used to be the norm even as late as 2003, when the romance novelist Barbara Taylor Bradford lost her bid to take the Indian company Sahara TV to court for basing their 260-part television series *Karishma – Miracles of Destiny* on her novel *A Woman of Substance.*

However, this enforcement approach to copyright is arguably out of sync with the reality of digital piracy, the complex nature of informal pirate networks in India and differing attitudes to piracy exhibited by the courts, and between the central government and the various state governments in India. To the dominant, mainly US-based cultural industries, cultural piracy is a relatively straightforward matter of unscrupulous foreigners ripping off creators of culture. Piracy is seen in terms of black and white, good versus bad, the legal versus the illegal and right versus wrong. This attitude is best exemplified in the US government's annual global survey of media piracy through the office of the US Trade Representative. The inability to grasp the reality of alternative circulations of culture, or to understand the multiple reasons for the growth of cultural piracy, or to implement alternative approaches to dealing with IP infringement are major blind spots for the dominant copyright industries. An adherence to restrictive copyright standards is a global reality for cities located in the developed as well as in the developing world. Ravi Sundaram's (2009: 338) description of the nature of contemporary piracy is the stuff of nightmares for both governments and their cultural industries.

> Postcolonial piracy is typically a post-liberal (if not a post-Marxist) cultural effect. Piracy destabilizes contemporary media property and, working through world markets and local bazaars, both disrupts and enables creativity, and evades issues of the classic commons while simultaneously radicalising access to subaltern groups in the Third World. Post-colonial piracy works more through dense local networks of exchange and face-to-face contact, rather than individual online downloads ... Piracy ... occupies a field the edges of which move all the time, margin to centre, international to local.

The complex nature of media markets in India and the ambivalent response of the state to piracy are reflected in its investments and interest in strengthening the basis for local innovation rather than the enforcement agenda. In practice, piracy is dealt with on an ad hoc basis (Liang and Sundaram, 2009). I have argued that we simply have to deal with piracy in India in the context of poverty, access to knowledge, the diffusion of personal devices such as mobile phones and the fact that the digital remains a contested entity, a site for claims and counter-claims in a revolution that is still unravelling and remains 'unfinished business' (Thomas, 2012).

ACCESS TO KNOWLEDGE AS A PUBLIC GOOD

The following three sections describe India's stance on copyright and people with disabilities, traditional knowledge, and its commitment to public sector software based on free and open source software (FOSS) principles. These sections highlight the Indian government's attempt to devise IPR policies that are consonant with its national interests. I am not, by highlighting these examples, arguing that the Indian government has established a wholly independent position on IPR. That is by no means the case, given continuing wrangles over patenting software and the alarming capitulation to global patent interests in areas such as agriculture. Rather, these examples reveal the government's commitment to balancing national and global interests, private and public interests, as well as seeking to maintain the relative autonomy of states such as Kerala to pursue software agendas that can be deemed Copyleft. US-based copyright industries understand the complexity of centre-state relationships and actively lobby at the state levels as well, especially in the states that have major knowledge and cultural industries, including Maharashtra (Bollywood), Tamilnadu (Kollywood), Karnataka (software) and Andhra Pradesh (software).

Arguably, India's strategic interests, during the last two decades have become more aligned with the interests of the USA. The US government is grooming India to be a countervailing force to China in the region. A good example of US influence is the shift in the government of Tamilnadu's initial decision to include open source platforms based on Linux in all laptops in its free laptop scheme, to proprietorial software (Windows Starter Edition) following a visit from Hilary Clinton in July 2011 and senior Microsoft representatives (Manish, 2011) This change needs to be viewed in the context of the state being a major beneficiary of US investments in manufacturing. US manufacturing companies in Tamilnadu include Ford, John Deere and Caterpillar, and the state is also the location for major service industries including healthcare, software, Business Process Outsourcing (BPOs), cinema and animation. However, and in spite of such correspondences, the Indian government has recognized the need for IP legislation that is supportive of domestic interests. The following three examples illustrate initiatives that are in the interest of the Indian 'public'.

WIPO Treaty for Visually Impaired Persons/Persons with Print Disabilities and Indian Copyright Law

India is home to 40 per cent of the world's visually impaired people. Traditionally, people with disabilities in India have been among the most culturally and socially marginalized people in the country. Despite constitutional guarantees and special legislation, such as the Persons with Disabilities (Equal Opportunities, Protection and Full Participation) Act, 1996, including Sections 27 and 28 that require the government to both design and invest in research in assistive devices and make accessible resources in relevant formats, there has been a disconnect between policy and practice. However, and over the preceding decade, State–NGO collaborations related to disability access have led to significant progress in national commitments to people with disabilities. Key NGOs include the Bengaluru-based Centre for Internet and Society (CIS), the Daisy Forum of India and the work carried out by the Kerala-based NGO Inclusive Planet. Special mention needs to be made of the efforts by the lawyer activist Rahul Cherian, whose untimely passing in February 2013 has been a loss to both international and national advocacy related to rights for people with disabilities. This section follows the lobbying work carried out by Rahul Cherian, especially in connection with the WIPO Treaty for the Visually Impaired. A number of documents related to his efforts at WIPO are available on the CIS website.

As a result of lobbying by disability activists and NGOs in India, the Copyright Amendment Bill, 2012, promises access commitments for the visually impaired that are amongst the most progressive in the world today. Previously, any conversion of cultural resources into special formats required the prior permission of the copyright holder and conversions were restricted to 'special formats'. The process of clearing permission was often an onerous one made difficult by the lack of interest shown by copyright holders. 'Special formats' automatically marginalized those who were not versed in the Braille language. The amendments made to the 2012 Bill have turned access for the visually impaired into a national right.

As Prakash (2012) has commented:

> Section 52(1)(zb) allows any person to facilitate access by persons with disabilities to copyrighted works without any payment of compensation to the copyright holder, and any organization working for the benefit of persons with disabilities to do so as long as it is done on a non-profit basis and with reasonable steps being taken to prevent entry of reproductions of the copyrighted work into the mainstream.

Clause 52(1)(zb) allows for fair use including the adaptation, reproduction and production of material for personal educational use and the sharing of such material among people with disabilities. This can be carried out by any organization involved either primarily or secondarily in disability rights. This clause nullifies the previous requirement that any organization applying for a compulsory licence to reproduce material for the disabled had to be registered, work solely in this area and be recognized by the government.

Furthermore, people with disabilities could not, by themselves apply for such licences (Saikia, 2010: 8). Section 31(B) allows any person working in the area of disability to apply for a compulsory licence to publish any copyrighted work for the benefit of the disabled. Furthermore, there is now a correspondence between the amended copyright act and domestic disability legislation such as the Draft Rights of People with Disabilities Bill, 2012, that is yet to become law.

Progress on the domestic IP front has been in marked contrast to the negotiations at WIPO. WIPO Negotiations on the Treaty for the Visually Impaired have been fraught and have pitched the developing world, in particular the contingent from Africa and India, against the USA and EU countries. Since the beginning of negotiations in 2008, the EU and the USA have lobbied for a soft, non-binding instrument that limited 'authorized entities' who were licensed to convert material to accessible formats to only recognized players, thus ignoring the rights of the vast majority of disability organizations to undertake such conversions. Moreover, the rules and procedures related to licensing were made intentionally complex.

As McClanahan (2012) writing in the *Guardian* has observed,

> A binding agreement would mean people in the global south could get immediate access to books that have already been translated into accessible formats in other countries. A treaty would also lead to enormous cost savings, as expensive translation has to be replicated in every country that wants to produce an accessible form of a given book.

Visually impaired people face a book famine in which close to 95 per cent of all books published are not accessible in friendly formats. Rahul Cherian (2012a), who had been involved in the negotiations in Geneva on behalf of the World Blind Union, wrote a very forthright piece on the negotiations in Geneva, the lack of transparency, the marginalization of accredited organizations such as the World Blind Union and closed door discussions to which only representatives of nation states were invited. This marginalization of 'civil society', the term used to describe one of the stakeholders at these negotiations consisting of an aggregation of NGOs, independent academics and practitioners, is by no means unusual given the experience of such actors at the first iteration of the World Summit on the Information Society held in Geneva in 2003. Cherian (2012b) has attempted to demystify the 'legal' language – as for example the phrase 'commercial availability' and its links to exceptions that would make any practical and effective solutions related to access impossible. The copyright industries in the USA in particular, and in this case, the Association of American Publishers, played a key role in limiting meaningful progress in the negotiations. At the 25th Standing Committee on Copyright and Related Rights (SCCR/25) at WIPO, held in November 2012, and in line with the European Parliament, the EU agreed to a treaty for the blind, leaving the USA as the only country against the road map towards the Diplomatic Conference in 2013 and eventually to a fully-fledged, binding treaty.

The Traditional Knowledge Digital Project (TKDL) Project

The eight-year TKDL project is the result of a collaboration between the Council of Scientific and Industrial Research (CSIR), the National Institute of Science Communication and Information Resources (NISCAIR), the Ministry of Science and Technology, the Department of Ayurveda, Yoga, Unani, Siddha and Homeopathy (AYUSH) and the Ministry of Health and Family Welfare. It contains 54 textbooks on ayurvedic medicine, nearly 150,000 entries based on ayurvedic, unani and siddha medicine and over 1,500 postures in yoga that have evolved over many millennia, including the Yoga Sutras of Patanjali that are over 2,000 years old, among other content. Protecting India's traditional knowledge from cultural and bio-prospectors intent on patenting and copyrighting India's many and diverse traditions – from yoga to traditional medicine – was the primary motive behind the compilation of this database. Jishnu (2012), writing in the Indian environmental magazine *Down to Earth*, has observed that:

> This treasure trove of knowledge is being plundered by a range of enterprises, from multinationals such as Nestle, Procter & Gamble, Johnson & Johnson, L'Oreal and Avon to domestic companies such as Avesthagen and Lupin and first-time entrepreneurs, for commercial profit by filing wrongful patents on known formulations.

During the ensuing decade, the Indian government was involved in expensive litigation in US courts over patents given to traditional medicinal and food plants from India – turmeric (Udgaonkar, 2002), neem, basmati rice (the Agricultural and Processed Food Products Export Development Authority, for example, took seven years and 7.62 crores (US$1.5 million) to fight the battle related to basmati rice), and yoga positions, the last popularized by the California-based yoga guru Bikram Choudhary. Choudhary claimed copyright over a yoga routine consisting of 26 asanas that is completed in 90 minutes in an environment with a temperature of up to 46 degrees centigrade and sent notices to yoga studios that infringed his copyright (see Srivastava, 2007).

In fact in 2007 alone, 130 patents and 1,000 trademarks were given to yoga postures and products in the USA (Hodge, 2009). Yoga is a multi-million dollar business. The TKDL, available in English, German, Japanese, Spanish and French will provide examiners evidence of 'prior art' when confronted with patent applications related to TK.

It would seem that India has now begun to benefit from this database. A report in the *Economic Times* (2012) points out that 1,000 cases of bio-piracy have been identified and 105 claims withdrawn as a result of the TKDL. Plans are also afoot to create a South Asian Association for Regional Cooperation (SAARC)-wide database of traditional knowledge modelled on the TKDL (Padma, 2005). The TKDL has become a model to be emulated and a number of countries around the world have begun exploring setting up similar databases.

The TKDL presents us with an opportunity to question larger issues related to nomenclature. For example, is the multi-accentuality of the term 'traditional knowledge' problematic, and an obstacle to understanding and clarifying the worth of traditions in a context in which 'big traditions' are given precedence over 'little traditions'? In India, traditional knowledge (TK) is the preferred term that is used to cover all traditions – from that of the big traditions associated with ayurveda and yoga to the little traditions of indigenous groups such as the Irulas and Kurumbas, among literally hundreds of other groups throughout India. Would it make sense to disinter the notion of the traditional and reintegrate it into categories that reflect contemporary traditions in India – dominant traditions, small and large 'living' traditions, traditions on the edge, reinvented traditions? And would such a categorization enable a clearer understanding of advocacy and commitment to TK? While from a personal point of view, my sympathies lie with traditions on the edge, I do sympathize with, and recognize the efforts made by the government and organizations in India to protect TK, including that allied to the dominant traditions, from commercial interests outside of the country.

At the same time, it is equally important that one acknowledges that there are equally rapacious exploiters of dominant traditions within the country who probably have a lot to gain from protecting its IP (see Thomas (2010) for a more detailed discussion of TKDL). Additionally, what becomes of traditional knowledge when the state makes a claim to it? Reddy (2006: 175) recalls some of the critiques of the TKDL:

> within Ayurvedic practitioner circles, the technocratic, top-down nature of the electronic database has not escaped criticism. In the first instance, Indian library and technology experts suggest that digital media technologies are far more fragile, prone to degradation, and obsolescence than earlier thought; now they wonder if TKDL funds might have been better focused on the preservation or conservation of the texts themselves. A more important and far-reaching set of critiques comes from the critical development literature, which argues that this headlong rush toward digitizing knowledge transforms the very nature of medical heritage: specimens are turned into derivatives and practical knowledge is decontextualized, raising serious questions about the commensurability of indigenous knowledge with Western science.

The politics of TK includes fraught issues related to inclusion and exclusion. In the context of culturally diverse India, the issue of what traditional knowledge merits protection and preservation remains contested. And, as it is clear from this section, the digitization of TK based on an abstraction of practices from its context, does have its own shortcomings.

Public Sector Software (PSS)

The final example of proactive state support for copyleft is that of the Kerala government's IT@Schools project. The government of Kerala explicitly made the decision to use FOSS rather than proprietorial software platforms in its public education projects. Kerala is the best known of a number of state governments currently exploring the use of non-proprietorial software including Karnataka and Assam.

Public Sector Software refers to software designed on principles drawn from FOSS and whose unique qualities derive from the fact that software is a public good.

The move to explore the possibilities for public sector software in India was precipitated by several factors:

1. the realization by the government of the breadth and depth of public sector investments in the digital revolution inclusive of the informationalization of services and infrastructure developments;
2. the recognition of the critical roles played by information and knowledge in society and the economy;
3. the evidence of vendor lock-in, particularly the overwhelming presence of Microsoft as the single, dominant software player in the public sector, and the financial costs associated with licensing along with the political economy of intellectual property (IP);
4. a recognition of the benefits, particularly access to software code, interoperability, and the lowering of costs associated with free and open source software (FOSS).
5. the billions of dollars' worth of investments in e-governance and issues related to software deployment and access to information;
6. broader public domain issues articulated by champions of open access, both within and outside of the public sector in different parts of the world.

PSS's objectives are explicitly linked to the goals of furthering universal access, participation and affordable software for the majority of people in India. Notwithstanding issues related to increased possibilities for the state to extend its surveillance capacities via e-governance, the positive freedoms associated with PSS should not be discounted; namely, the potential to unleash creativity and innovation through collaborative learning, applications and co-creation. In the context of the right to information, PSS can also be leveraged by ordinary people to reform governance and make the public sector accountable to its publics.

The space and opportunities for public sector software are best illustrated by current investments in e-governance, such as the US$4.46 billion investment by the Government of India in the National e-Governance Plan (Kanungo, 2010), pre-existing research and development initiatives related to FOSS, and policy initiatives like the Ministry of Information and Communication Technology's draft policy on Open Standards for e-Governance (2009). To some extent, PSS as an aspect of the new approach to public management in India is an outcome of internal reform as well as external pressure – such as public sector adoption of the right to information and adoption of 'transparency' as a key principle of governance. This new approach is based on increased efficiency, decentralization, increased accountability, improved resource management and marketization (Heeks, 1998).

While PSS shares a number of characteristics with FOSS, including the freedom to modify and share software:

> Public software is all software that is essential for participating in the digital society and thus needs to be provided to everyone as an [sic] universal right and entitlement … Public software needs to be free software, providing the freedom to use, study, modify and share, to ensure universal access as well as participation in its creation and modification … Software developed for public service has a unique context and objectives deriving from those of public service; with its imperative of providing public goods and ensuring equity and social justice … public software is also a public good. While Free Software requires the freedoms of the individual user to use, study, share and modify the source code, in addition to this, public software emphasises its 'public good' nature and vests on government the responsibility of ensuring that basic software required for negotiating the digital world is freely available to all. (Public Software Centre, n.d.)

The partnership between the state and civil society is best illustrated by the relationship between the government of Kerala's IT@School project and the NGO the Society for Promotion of Alternative Computing and Employment (SPACE). To a large extent, the commitment to public sector software in Kerala is the consequence of bi-partisan support from both the major political parties, the Congress and Communist Party of India

(Marxist). Kerala is home to a number of committed civil servants and civil society activists who are passionate about the need for free and open source software solutions in public arenas. The relationship between the Government of Kerala and SPACE has been especially significant. Since 2005, SPACE has been involved in supporting extensive, free software-based government projects in the areas of education, local language computing, e-governance, micro-enterprise and in the social sector, inclusive of e-training and support for people with disabilities, hospitals and community libraries. The objectives of SPACE are to:

- Promote the use of FOSS in the public, private, and governmental sectors as well as for personal/home use
- Develop a model for FOSS-based employment generation that is appropriate to Kerala's context, by identifying appropriate business opportunities and providing support services including training and micro-business incubation
- Carry out research and development activities for the development of essential prototypes that bridge existing gaps in software, so as to enable widespread use of FOSS
- Ensure that Kerala is able to develop sufficient numbers of high-quality human resources in the FOSS domain. (SPACE, n.d.)

The FOSS-based IT@School project in Kerala has led to ICT-enabled education in 8,000 schools in the state and the training of 200 master trainers and 5,600 IT coordinators (selected from teaching staff). The publically owned software has been bundled into a single CD for a one-point installation – which would not have been achievable in the context of the use of proprietary software (Thomas, 2011).

Using the GNOME Desktop, Ubuntu operating system and the assistive technology and screen-reader software ORCA (created by Sun Microsystems), SPACE has pioneered the combinations of speech synthesis technology, Braille and magnification to create a powerful aural tool for the visually impaired (via a program called Insight) that is complemented with an audio magazine, *Swaram*. An important aspect of ORCA is that it is free software. Its proprietary counterpart costs about US$1,300. SPACE works collaboratively with state actors such as the National Informatics Centre and the Centre for the Development of Advanced Computing (C-DAC), quasi-governmental bodies, NGOs and civil society.

What is perhaps the most significant aspect of this project is that there has been a massive investment in teachers and students as co-learners and foot soldiers of FOSS in Kerala. From the very beginning there was a strong commitment to teachers and students taking responsibility for the development of FOSS. This was an important innovation given that the norm regarding IT in education projects is for outside consultants and/or vendor employees to fix bugs and malfunctioning hardware and software. Such dependence can be costly both in terms of time and expenditure, and accentuating 'disintermediation' is one of the most important characteristics of this project. Mobile hardware clinic teams regularly visit schools. As Kasinathan (2009: 2) has highlighted in a Policy Brief:

> The program has created 'mobile hardware clinic' teams, which regularly visit schools for inspection, checking hardware and doing most of the required maintenance and repair work. A policy of cannibalising computers that cannot be repaired has two benefits; it substantially lowers costs of maintenance while ensuring higher uptime. Teachers are trained to install software and to also do routine software upgrades. The program disproves a commonly held belief that school teachers in India's public education system are not capable of, and/or are unlikely to be interested in, engaging with ICTs beyond being simple users.

I would argue that this approach is in the Freirean tradition, of demystifying technology-assisted learning, strengthening critical consciousness, enabling users to understand how it works and getting people to use software for their own ends (Freire, 1982). Furthermore, the story of FOSS in Kerala is that of people realizing that software is a tool that can and should be adapted to local ends and that knowledge making is a process involving teachers, students and technology. Hardware clinics and content development classes are frequently held and the school wikis help in the creation of collaborative content. Not only has FOSS been customized to teachers' needs, it is available in Malayalam, the local language, and all material is owned by the public and is shareable.

CONCLUSION

This brief overview of copyright and copyleft in India has attempted to highlight and engage with numerous contestations over access to knowledge. Copyleft, by its very nature, is a fluid project that embraces a great variety of attempts to gain affordable access to information, entertainment and knowledge. Given the existence of deep economic, social and cultural divides in India and uneven development, copyleft is bound to remain a key means by which a level playing field is established. India's efforts to globalize its economy have led to numerous attempts to harmonize domestic IP laws with their global equivalents. In the light of the country's intent to become a global entertainment and knowledge hub, it has attempted to modernize its IP framework and in particular, has invested in efforts to criminalize copyright violators, create awareness of copyright, and enforce the law. It has, in other words, responded to pressure from the global copyright industries and governments such as the USA that have linked better IP protection to preferential trade agreements.

Adherence to international standards, however, is just one side of the equation. India, as an ambivalent state, has also responded to the need to expand spaces for local innovation and creativity, increase opportunities for employing FOSS-based solutions in its public sector efforts at education, enacted progressive 'access' related policies for the visually impaired and created databases supportive of traditional knowledge. It is this ambivalence, expressed in and through a multi-faceted response that makes the study of copyright in India an abidingly intriguing prospect.

REFERENCES

Blakely, R. (2009) 'Bollywood pays up for plagiarism', *The Australian*, 8 August, p. 12.

Cherian, R. (2012a) Ring-side view: Update on WIPO negotiations on the Treaty for the Visually Impaired, August 13, Centre for Internet and Society. Available at: www.cis-india.org/accessibility/ring-side-view (accessed on February 10, 2013).

Cherian, R. (2012b) Linking commercial availability and exceptions in the Treaty for Visually Impaired/Persons with Disabilities, January 23. The Centre for Internet and Society. Available at: www.cis-india.org/accessibility/blog/linking-commercial-availability-and-exceptions-in-tvi (accessed on February 10, 2013).

Chowdhury, A.R. (2008) The future of copyright in India, *Journal of Intellectual Property Law and Practice*, 3(2): 102–114.

Digital Dawn: The Metamorphosis Begins, FICCI-KPMG Indian Media and Entertainment Industry Report, 2012. Available at: www.kpmg.de/docs/FICCI-KPMG_Report_2012.pdf (accessed on August 28, 2013).

Draft National Policy on Open Standards for e-Governance (2009). Available at: www.fosscomm.in/OpenStandards?action=AttachFile&do=get&target=Policy_On_Open_Standards_V2.pdf (accessed on September 28, 2010).

Freire, P. (1982) *Pedagogy of the Oppressed*. Harmondsworth: Penguin Books.

Heeks, R. (1998) Information Age reform of the public sector: The potential and problems of IT for India (1–21), Information Systems for Public Sector Management, Working Paper Series No. 6. October, Institute for Development Policy and Management, University of Manchester. Available at: http://unpan1.un.org/intradoc/groups/public/documents/NISPAcee/UNPAN015479.pdf (accessed on June 19, 2014).

Hodge, A. (2009) India acts to keep tradition safe for all. *The Australian*, 24 February. Available at: http://www.theaustralian.com.au/archive/news/india-acts-to-keep-tradition-safe-for-all/story-e6frg6t6-1111118941896 (accessed on June 19, 2014)

IIPA (2012) *India: International Intellectual Property Alliance (IIPA): 2012 Special 301 Report on Copyright Protection and Enforcement*. pp. 63–78. Available at: www.iipa.com/rbc/2012/2012SPEC301INDIA.PDF (accessed on February 9, 2013).

IIPA (2013) *International Intellectual Property Alliance 2013 Special 301 Report*, Table of Contents, Appendix B – Methodology used to calculate value of unlicensed software, other estimated piracy losses, piracy levels. International Intellectual Property Alliance. Available at: www.iipa.com/2013_SPEC301_TOC.htm (accessed on September 14, 2013).

Jishnu, L. (2012) Safeguarding ancient wisdom, *Down to Earth*, October 15. Available at: www.downtoearth.org.in/content/safeguarding-ancient-wisdom (accessed on February 10, 2013).

Kanungo, V. (2010) Government of India to invest in Rs. 20,000 crores on e-Governance by 2014, e-GovWorld 2010, July 19. Available at: http://67.223.235.55:8081/eGovWorld/newsupdate/opportunities-for-indian-it-companies-to-beat-global-demand-in-it-services-as-government-of-india-decides-to-invest-rs-20-000-crore-on-e-governance-projects-1 (accessed on June 19, 2014).

Karaganis, J. (ed.) (2011) *Media Piracies in Emerging Economies*. New York: Social Science Research Council.

Kasinathan, G. (2009) IT for change, policy brief: ICTs in school education – outsourced versus integrated approach. Available at: www.itforchange.net/sites/default/files/ITfC/Policy_Brief_on_ICTs_in_School_Education_from_IT_for_Change_August_2009.pdf (accessed on June 17, 2012).

Krishnakumar, T. and Saha, K. (2013) India's new copyright law: The good, the bad and the DRM, *Journal of Intellectual Law and Practice*, 8(1): 15–17.

Liang, L. & Sundaram, R. (2009), Chapter 8: India (339-397), in Karaganis, T. (Ed.) Media Piracy in Emerging Economies, Social Science Research Council, NY.

Manish, S. (2011) The deadly Microsoft embrace, *Tehelka Online*, October 10. Available at: http://archive.tehelka.com/story_main50.asp?filename=Ws101011MICROSOFT.asp (accessed on September 10, 2013).

Mansell, R. and Wehn, U. (1998) Institutional innovations or the governance of information services: Enforcing intellectual property rights and protecting security and privacy, in Mansell, R. & Wehn, U (eds.), *Knowledge Societies: Information Technology for Sustainable Development*, Oxford University Press. Oxford. pp. 203–224.

McClanahan, P. (2012) US and EU blocking treaty to give blind people access to books, *The Guardian*, 30 July. Available at: www.guardian.co.uk/global-development/2012/jul/30/us-eu-blocking-treaty-blind-books (accessed on February 10, 2013).

Padma, T.V. (2005) 'Digital library to protect indigenous knowledge', *Science and Development Network News*, January 10.

Philip, J.T. (2012) Blackberry maker Research in Motion agrees to hand over its encryption keys to India, *The Economic Times*, 2 August. Available at: http://articles.economictimes.indiatimes.com/2012-08-02/news/33001399_1_blackberry-enterprise-encryption-keys-corporate-emails (accessed on February 9, 2013).

Post recommends modified IPR strategy for India (2008) New Delhi, Unclassified. Available at: www.cablegatesearch.net/cable.php?id=08NEWDELHI1683&q=special-301 (accessed on February 9, 2013). See also www.keionline.org/node/1245 for Wikileaks cables related to Section 301 (Countries G to Y).

Prakash, P. (2012) Analysis of the Copyright (Amendment) Bill, 2012, Centre for Internet and Society, May 23. Available at: www.cis-india.org/a2k/blog/analysis-copyright-amendment-bill-2012/ (accessed on February 10, 2013).

Public Software Centre (n.d.) What is public software. Available at: www.public-software.in/Public-software (accessed on September 18, 2013).

Reddy, S. (2006) Making heritage legible: Who owns traditional medical knowledge, *International Journal of Cultural Property*, 13: 161–188.

Saikia, N. (2010) Disability and the Indian Copyright (Amendment) Act, 2010, Social Science Research Network. Available at: http://papers.ssrn.com/sol3/papers.cfm?abstract_id=1600621 (accessed on February 10, 2013).

Sidhva, S. (1996) *A Target for Hollywood, Financial Times*, July 11, p.vi.

Society for Promotion of Alternative Computing. (SPACE) (n.d.) About Space. Available at: www.space-kerala.org/node/10 (accessed on August 27, 2013).

Srivastava, S. (2007) Lotus in the muck, *Outlook India.com*, 25 June. Available at: www.outlookindia.com/article.aspx?234960 (accessed on November 3, 3010).

Subramaniam, A. (2012) Hollywood on an aggressive mode to market their films in India, bets big on brand tie-ups, *Business Today*, 25 July. Available at: www.businesstoday.intoday.in/story/hollywood-market-their-films-in-india-aggressively/1/186594.html (accessed on February 9, 2013).

Sundaram, R. (2009) Revisiting the Pirate Kingdom, *Third Text*, 23(3): 335–345.

Thakurta, P.G. (2012), Good for Business, Bad for Freedom, in The Hoot. Available at: http://thehoot.org/web/home/story.php?storyid=6169&mod=1&pg=1&sectionId=&valid=true (accessed on June 20, 2014)

The Draft Rights of People with Disabilities Bill, 2012. GOI, Ministry of Social Justice and Empowerment,

Department of Disability Affairs. Available at: www.socialjustice.nic.in/pdf/draftpwd12.pdf (accessed on February 10, 2013).

The Economic Times (2012) India may win patent claims due to Traditional Knowledge Digital Library: Manmohan Singh, *The Economic Times*, October 16. Available at: http://articles.economictimes.indiatimes.com/2012-10-16/news/34498963_1_traditional-knowledge-digital-library-patent-examiners-patent-offices (accessed on February 10, 2013).

Thomas, P.N. (2010) Traditional knowledge and the Traditional Knowledge Digital Library: Digital quandaries and other concerns, *International Communications Gazette*, 72(8): 659–673.

Thomas, P.N. (2011) *Negotiating Communication Rights: Case Studies from India*. New Delhi: Sage.

Thomas, P.N. (2012) *Digital India: Information, Communication and Social Change*. New Delhi: Sage.

Thomas, Z. (2013) Overview of changes to Indian copyright law, *Journal of Intellectual Property Rights*, 17: 324–334.

Udgaonkar, S. (2002) The recording of traditional knowledge: Will it prevent bio-piracy, *Current Science*, 82(4): 413–419.

Zinnov LLC (n.d.) *Intellectual Property Rights Protection in India: An Analysis*. Available at: www.software-ceo.com/downloads/file/sceo/white_papers/IP_Research.pdf (accessed on September 11, 2013).

20

Treasuring IP: Free Culture, Media Piracy and the International Pirate Party Movement

Lisa Dobbin and Martin J. Zeilinger

INTRODUCTION

This chapter concerns the emergence and growing popularity of the international pirate party movement. We survey critical approaches to the phenomenon of piracy, consider the usefulness of this concept in discussions of digital practices commonly labelled 'media piracy', and discuss the role of the pirate parties in opposing conflicts around these practices. Contrasting the international pirate party movement with the historical figure of the maritime pirate, we approach the modern-day pirates through Christopher Kelty's concept of the 'geek', which describes individuals motivated by the desire to preserve their ability to use digital tools for the sharing of information, communication and creative purposes. Our discussion highlights some of the gross imbalances imposed by current copyright laws on digital culture and on the private use of digital technologies, and proposes that the activities of today's so-called pirates can be understood as a critical commentary on the vilification and criminalization to which everyday users of digital technologies are often subjected. In considering how these imbalances are reflected in the rhetoric of the pirate party movement, ultimately we suggest that the movement represents an experimental arena of political dissent and policy reform efforts.

Vitriolic debate over conflicting definitions of 'digital media piracy' and the future of cultural ownership abounds domestically as well as internationally. For many, media piracy is a derogatory term imposed on everyday digital practices that should be protected rather than vilified (e.g. Lessig 2004). For others, the downloading and sharing of digital artifacts amounts to systematic, large-scale theft. Out of this fundamental disagreement, a central question often arises: does our nearly universal ability to copy media content threaten the foundations of property-based economies of free enterprise, or, conversely, are universal ideals of freedom of expression and free access to information threatened by the restrictions which intellectual property (IP) policy places on our dealings with digital culture? An important emerging voice in this debate is that of Pirate Parties International (PPI), a non-governmental organization offering guidance to the growing number of independent 'pirate parties' springing up around the globe. While these loosely affiliated parties have yet to produce a unified political vision, many of them have achieved an impressive amount of visibility and legitimacy in national party systems.

The popularity of the international pirate party movement is fed by everyday users of digital technology as much as by informed anti-IP activists opposing conservative policy reform efforts. Overall, this popular base indicates that a powerful dissonance exists between the practice of everyday digital life and the legal regimes designed to regulate digital commodities. While lobby groups representing corporate IP owners wield a disproportionate amount of power to influence law-makers, progressive legal scholarship frequently sides with the 'pirates'. In this chapter, we document and analyze some of the debates surrounding PPI. In doing so, we position it as a political movement that resists the restrictions imposed by conservative intellectual property policies on the new creative, productive, communicative and educational opportunities that are afforded us by freely accessible, copyable and redistributable digital media technologies. PPI is still far from representing a sustainable policy perspective on the use and regulation of digital media. However, we believe that the loosely connected pirate parties play an important role in delineating the ongoing conflict between IP owners and the large, international communities of users who share copyright protected materials online. And, while we doubt that embracing the concept of 'piracy' is the most productive way to enter into dialogue with political opponents, there can be no doubt that the international success of the various pirate parties is symptomatic of an urgent need for progressive IP policy reform.

By embracing the self-ascribed image of a group of 'media pirates', the pirate party movement subscribes to the idea that peer-to-peer (P2P) users – or, more generally speaking, digital users with the ability to exchange information freely across open networked communication systems – should be able to freely distribute copyright-protected materials online. Unsurprisingly, this is a problematic agenda. Nevertheless, PPI's uncertain status as well as the tensions and conflicts to which its activities give rise provide rich grounds for critical reflection on existing definitions of media piracy, as well as on the place of activism in countering the negative impact of restrictive IP policy on ubiquitous opportunities to copy and share digital artifacts.

Both the history and the current shape of 'piracy' are decidedly international. This fact is reflected in the kind of growth the pirate party movement has enjoyed, as well as in the nature of the digital practices and the technological infrastructures with which the movement is concerned. Therefore, rather than limiting our focus on a specific country, jurisdiction, or national cultural landscape, our aim in this chapter is to engage in a comparative discussion that touches on different national pirate party branches and on policy issues based in different legal systems. We begin this chapter by tracing the emergence of several existing pirate parties, and by suggesting that members and supporters of these groups are generally not media pirates – i.e., professional thieves – in the traditional sense. We interpret the pirates' enthusiastic embrace of this misnomer as a critical comment on the vilification and criminalization to which everyday users of digital technologies are frequently subjected. We then go on to contextualize this overview with a genealogy of the more general concept of piracy, as well as with a comparative discussion of maritime and media piracy. In highlighting some of the imbalances imposed by current copyright laws on digital culture and on the use of digital technologies, and in showing how these imbalances are reflected in the rhetoric of the pirate party movement, ultimately we suggest that the pirate party movement functions as an international arena of experimental dissent. In this arena, shortcomings of current IP policy are exposed and transposed from the virtual margins of user practice to the center stages of national party politics and, thus, back into the realm of policy. In participating in this push, self-proclaimed 'pirates' defend their cultural terrain and shed light on complex legal inadequacies. Ultimately, we conclude that if the diverse pirate parties can be said to have a shared agenda at all, it is that they take the concerns and activities of everyday digital users seriously, not as an area of legally dubious goings-on, but rather as a source of inspiration for much-needed progressive policy reform.

PIRATE PARTY INTERNATIONAL – HISTORY AND VISION

Originally an offshoot of the P2P website *The Pirate Bay* (TPB), which allows users to share links to downloadable media and software content, and the Swedish organization *Piratbyrån* (in English: 'Bureau of Piracy'), Pirate Party International (PPI) has shifted the conflict between digital media 'pirates' and intellectual property holders into the policy sphere. Established in 2003, *Piratbyrån* emerged in opposition to the *Svenska antipiratbyrån* ('Swedish Anti-Piracy Bureau'), a lobby group consisting of media industry stakeholders. While most pirate parties are today locally registered political organizations, *Piratbyrån* (now defunct) understood itself to be a think-tank, and acted as a hub for public discussions about intellectual property law as it relates to digital culture. The first proper pirate party took shape in Sweden in December 2005 by way of an online petition protesting Swedish copyright reform and advocating for the right to creative and expressive freedom online. As support for the petition grew, founder Rick Falkvinge was soon able to officially register the pirates as a political party (Miegel & Olsson 2008: 208). In 2009, the party received a total of 7.13% of Swedish votes in the European Parliament elections, and currently holds two parliamentary seats (www.val.se/val/ep2009/slutresultat/rike/index.html).

Since 2006, pirate parties have spread all over the world as part of a larger body of cultural and political movements protesting restrictive IP laws. Today, these parties exist from Brazil to the United Kingdom, from Canada to Morocco, from Slovenia to the United States. In mid-2014, the PPI website listed 69 countries in which Pirate Parties have been registered (www.pp-international.net/). The growing number of Pirate Parties demonstrates the vast gap experienced by many digital media users between the everyday practices in which they engage and the parameters of (il)legality imposed on these practices by intellectual property law. In part, this discrepancy is the result of a period in the twentieth century in which many owners of copyright protected content did not take legal action against individuals who created copies for private, non-commercial use. In many national legislations, consumers could make a non-commercial recording for a friend from a compact disc they purchased. In the United States, for example, the *Audio Home Recording Act* specified levies collected from blank media such as compact discs (CDs), and in turn allowed for copies of IP-protected content to be produced on a small scale, for private use. As Jessica Litman points out in *Digital Copyright*, this created a preference among listeners for free use and sharing of music, and also normalized and legitimized this behavior (Litman 2001: 154). Seen in this light, the copying and sharing of digital media content entails 'the same sort of things unlicensed users have always done – making copies for their own personal use, sharing copies with friends, or reverse-engineering the works embodied on the copies to figure out how they work' (Litman 2001: 85).

According to Ipoque's *Internet Study 2008–2009*, P2P 'generates by far the most traffic in all monitored regions – ranging from 43% in Northern Africa to seventy percent in Eastern Europe' (Schulze & Mochalski 2009: 2). Research suggests that the majority of file-sharers do not see their activities as part of a broader, more politicized resistance movement, but rather, in more pragmatic terms, as an affordable and accessible way to access and share information (Andersson 2009: 93). Copyright laws, however, tend to be drafted by stakeholder industries who represent commercial interests, rather than the public, and contain complex exclusions and privileges designed to protect these interests (Litman 2001: 72). Copyright, as a result, is overly complex, counterintuitive, and represents the interests of industry stakeholders who can afford to have their lawyers present at the drafting table. Powerful lobbying groups for the international recording, motion picture and software industries take advantage of this and engage in high-stakes policy reform campaigns to protect their business, rather than to keep copyright law meaningful and relevant in an era in which more users than ever before are equipped to copy, share and reuse intellectual property.

The popularity of P2P technology frequently leads content industry associations like the Recording Industry Association of America (RIAA) to describe online piracy as 'devastating', and to accuse it of the destruction of 'the livelihoods of artists, musicians, songwriters, retailers, and everyone in the music industry' (2003). Such descriptions invoke the myth of the romantic author as a moral justification for copyright law's clearly economic bias. In this discussion, piracy is framed as a practice that fundamentally opposes the idea that creators should be rewarded for their labor. If creators are not financially rewarded for their contribution to society, so the story goes, they will have no incentive for further creative activities. In this scenario, and without protection through intellectual property laws, cultural progress would cease entirely. William Patry calls this particular rationalization of copyright law 'the myth of natural rights and geniuses', and argues that it produces an idea of authors as unique individuals whose creations came to them in a vacuum (2009: 65). The narrative of the romantic author is often used in enforcement efforts surrounding media piracy, which are designed to persuade the public of pirates' lack of moral responsibility.

Copyright law is meant to grant a limited monopoly right to reproduce, distribute, make derivatives, perform and display a work (Hettinger 1989: 34). In its beginnings in the eighteenth-century British legal system, copyright law was intended to enact a 'wise utilitarian bargain' (Vaidhyanathan 2001: 9), taking the interests of a text's creator, publisher/distributer, and the public, equally into account. In this bargain, the public was seen to need access to copyrighted texts in order to benefit from the ideas contained within them; simultaneously, the author of that text, and the industry that financed its production, must also have an incentive to create it in the first place. Vitally, copyright was meant to place a limit on the amount of time an author or publisher could hold a monopoly over a certain work before it fell into the public domain. However, the length of copyright terms has, virtually everywhere, been extended from its original, reasonably short duration (Great Britain's 1710 *Statute of Anne*, commonly considered to be the first copyright statute, initially outlined a duration of 14 years with the possibility of one 14-year renewal). Today, copyrights tend to outlast an author's life by many decades, with the result that fewer and fewer works fall into the public domain within a reasonable timeframe. As Lawrence Lessig argued in *Eldred v. Ashcroft* (2003), a landmark case in which the constitutionality of the United States' *Sonny Bono Copyright Extension Act* was challenged before the US Supreme Court, the increasing length of time during which copyrighted texts are protected contradicts the very purpose of the legal mechanism. Today, as Lessig and many other legal scholars have observed, copyright protects the monopoly, rather than the social bargain, which prioritized the public domain alongside the right of the author to benefit from his or her work.

PIRATE PARTY POLITICS

Like those involved in the creation and maintenance of TPB, the pirate parties and their supporters often articulate the belief that copyright law should accommodate file sharing, again often relying on the rhetorics of 'media piracy'. For instance, in 2011 the United States Pirate Party published *No Safe Harbor: Essays About Pirate Politics*, a freely downloadable essay collection that represents an effective public relations campaign, featuring contributions from vocal free culture proponents including Cory Doctorow, Travis McCrea, danah boyd and Kembrew McLeod, among others. Lawrence Lessig's contribution reflects on the well-documented fact that before using someone else's creative intellectual property became an act of 'piracy', it had in fact been integral to the establishment of the mass media industry, and was therefore normalized and legitimized: 'The history of the content industry,' Lessig concludes, is itself 'a history of piracy' (Lessig 2011: 81, 84). A different campaign strategy utilized by PPI members is to reveal 'scandal' in their opponents' camps. The Canadian Pirate Party for instance, recently announced that using Internet protocol-scraping tools similar to those 'used by the RIAA and MPAA [Motion Picture Association of America] to assemble computer addresses for class action copyright lawsuits', they had discovered a number of IP addresses, registered to the Canadian House of Commons, which had been used by staff to pirate films, music and software (Pirate Party of Canada 2012). This political tactic works to expose hypocrisy on the part of those who publicly denounce digital media piracy but privately participate in it.

Despite such tactics, to many it remains unclear where on the political spectrum the various pirate parties are actually located. A recent controversy, wherein a Berlin Member of Parliament claimed that the German Pirate Party was rising as fast as the Nazis did, has led some to question whether the party panders to far-right extremists (*Spiegel Online International* 2012). However, only three days later, the same publication described the party as 'a new left-wing force'. Many observers have also claimed that the pirate party movement champions libertarian values. The French newspaper *Le Monde*, for instance, has called pirate party politicians 'the spiritual heirs of the libertarian hackers from the late 20th century, who dreamed of a free circulation of culture and knowledge on the Internet' (Eudes 2012). An article in the UK's *The Guardian* similarly claims that, 'in their mistrust of the state and calls for transparency, [pirate party politicians] are reminiscent of libertarian movements of Anglo-Saxon origin, be they Ayn Rand fanatics or anarchically-minded socialists' (Zeh 2012). But giving the libertarian title to the movement is hardly helpful; while the term does literally mean 'of or about freedom', 'people have very different ideas of what situation embodies the opposite of authoritarianism' (Widerquist 2004: 1). In the United States, for example, libertarians have become associated with free-market capitalists, while in many other parts of the world libertarian ideology is still associated with anarchist socialism and anti-authoritarianism (Widerquist 2004).

The pirate movement's lack of political coherence, however, is neither an oversight nor a campaign strategy. The Pirate Party UK's (PPUK) *Manifesto 2010* states that theirs is 'a new type of political party … A party that is not left wing or right wing' (Pirate Party UK 2010: 2). Similarly, Canadian Pirate Party member Travis McCrea, a parliamentary candidate in central Vancouver, asserts that his party does not 'fall on the political spectrum, that's what makes our movement so unique. We are libertarians and socialists, liberals and conservatives. We are all here because we believe in humanism and civil liberties' (2012: email correspondence). Patrick Fitzgerald, another Canadian Pirate Party member, concurs: 'I do not believe that the Pirate Party falls into the traditional political spectrum … I have always liked to say that if the Pirate Party has a direction we are moving forward' (2012: email correspondence).

How might this uncertainty impact the pirate parties' potential to retain enough momentum to hold parliamentary representation and achieve policy reform? Some research indicates that most voters rely on relatively fixed, pre-existing norms regarding what it means to be politically 'left' or 'right' throughout their lifetimes, with little consideration for exceptional events such as recessions or wars (Green et al. 2002: 2). This suggests that the lack of a clear political program could turn out to be a poor long-term campaign strategy for the pirate parties. Then again, the recent successes of the German Pirate Party challenge this argument. In the May 2012 regional elections, the party took 8% of the vote in Germany's biggest state, Schleswig-Holstein (RT.com 2012). As of June 1, 2013, the party holds 45 seats in the German parliament, having won between 7% and 9% of the vote in four regional elections since fall 2011 (Eudes 2012). In May 2012, *The Guardian* cited a new poll that put the party at 11% of the German national vote (Zeh 2012). Impressively, some have estimated that 25% of the German Pirate Party's total base of support comes from previous non-voters (RT.com 2012). According to *Time World*, the pirate win in the German state of North Rhine-Westphalia (in May 2012) attracted 30,000 first-time voters and 70,000 previous 'non-voters' (Adams 2012). In addition, the party attracted 60,000 votes from Angela Merkel's Christian Democratic Union (CDU), 80,000 votes from the Green Party, and 90,000 from the Social Democrats (Adams 2012).

This massive switching of established alliances suggests that Manfred Guellner, head of Germany's Forsa Institute for Social Research and Statistical Analysis, may have been right in stating that 'whoever votes for the pirates, is unhappy with the established parties' (Scheven 2012). Instead of moving 'forward', to use Pirate Party member Patrick Fitzgerald's phrase, the group may be more aptly described as situated in the here-and-now: as a protest movement that does not articulate a particularly holistic vision for the future. In 'A Party is Not a Movement and Vice Versa', Joachim Hirsch (1998) paints a strikingly familiar picture when he describes the German Green Party's emergence amid the global economic crisis of the 1970s. This era seemed to reveal the limit of capital accumulation, and with it came rising unemployment and a continuation of the late 60s' unprecedented protest movements. When the German political apparatus could not address the concerns of these movements, it began to approach them through a strategy of 'political marginalization and criminalization' (1998: 181–182). In turn, the German Green Party self-identified as the extended, parliamentary, arm of the marginalized protest groups.

Though the broader pirate party movement has not yet officially recognized such a role for itself, the Pirate Parties International website does provide links to the US-based Electronic Frontier Foundation (EFF) and the UK's Open Rights Group, both of which advocate for digital freedom and openness. Moreover, party members and individual candidates tend to emphasize the pirate party system's ideological links to social movements advocating for open culture, as well as to groups known for producing harsh critiques of repressive corporate and governmental structures of knowledge exchange and information sharing. Travis McCrea, for example, states that 'You can't really mention the Pirate Party without mentioning Anonymous and you can't really mention the Arab Spring without mentioning the Pirate Party' (2012: email correspondence). In an interview with *Framablog*, French Pirate Party candidate Pierre Mounier, in a similar vein, stated his belief that the Pirate Party is an ally of Occupy, Anonymous, Wikileaks, as well as 'le phénomène des casseroles à Montréal', the Montréal student protests (2012), and proposed that the Pirate Party should officially represent these movements at the political level (*Framablog* 2012).

In a 1998 essay on the German Green Party, Claus Offe argued that the German Greens had to 'switch from a style of politics that is naïvely and expressively obsessed with the immediate solutions of problems to a more complex style of politics that at least methodologically does not shy away from also considering the problems of solutions' (Offe 1998: 174). By this Offe meant that protests should be accompanied by designs for reform, which, in turn, must demonstrate insight into the potential problems arising from their implementation (Offe 1998: 175,

176). To extend this argument to the pirate party movement, it follows that it, too, must work to create a more nuanced and specific political program to succeed as a cluster of related, proper political parties. Some observers believe that the pirate parties have yet to do so because they have not approached the issues at hand with an adequate combination of analytical rigor and political expertise (see Becker et al. 2012). One can indeed imagine the waning of the pirate party movement once a few of its ideas have been adopted by law-makers and mainstream political parties, and once its protests become less unique. But at least until then, the pirate parties are in a unique position to pursue what political theorist Hannah Arendt called 'politics as action' – the freedom to pursue something completely new, rather than relying on pre-existing trajectories.

PIRATE POLICY REFORM

Many of the 'pirates' discussed in this chapter have outlined their agenda in party programs; a comparative approach that draws on cultural scholarship can yield a nuanced understanding of the movement and its possible benefits to the global landscape of digital culture. A 2005 essay by Christopher Kelty provides a useful conceptual framework for this purpose: it describes groups of like-minded individuals who have no formal affiliation beyond their shared interest in digital technology as collectives of 'geeks'. Geeks, in Kelty's sense, are primarily interested in preserving and improving their ability to use digital tools for communication, the sharing of information, dissent and creative purposes. The Internet and other networked communication systems are the subject of their discussions as well as their primary medium of interaction. In this sense, collectives of geeks are 'constituted by a shared, profound concern for the technical and legal conditions of possibility for their own association' (2005: 185). In many ways, this definition also aptly describes the pirate party movement. For example, Christian Engström, Member of European Parliament for the Swedish Pirate Party, and Rick Falkvinge, founder of the first pirate party, are both not only politicians and activists, but, like many other pirate party members, they are also trained programmers and software developers.

Integrating these different backgrounds and interests, Engström and Falkvinge believe that 'writing software and configuring networks are as essential to freedom and public participation as speaking to a public about such activities. The right to create software is seen in a similar light as the right to state an opinion' (Kelty 2005: 187). Seen through the lens of Kelty's concept of the geek, the pirate parties thus emerge as defenders of an important socio-cultural terrain, rather than as the enemies of cultural producers that they are made out to be by culture industry lobbyists. Here, it also becomes clear that the policy debates in which the pirate parties are involved are not only about copyright, but, more broadly, about the technologies and communication systems through which copyrighted works are being copied and distributed. In a freely distributed book on copyright reform, Engström and Falkvinge thus write that 'free operating systems and communications software are at the heart of all our future freedom of speech, as well as the freedom of speech for regime topplers today. The software that is being built by these hero activists is a guarantee for our civil liberties' (Engström & Falkvinge, 2012: 13).

It may seem surprising that the authors build their arguments on the admission that all uses of a copyrighted work should be protected in commercial scenarios (Engström & Falkvinge, 2012: 3). They thus do not fundamentally oppose the view that intellectual property rights can be attached to cultural works. Building on this admission, however, their schema immediately posits that non-commercial copying and distribution of protected texts should never be perceived to infringe on the rights of their owners. In this, Engström and Falkvinge approximate the US concept of 'fair use' and its common law equivalent, 'fair dealing', both of which outline permissible, non-infringing uses of copyrighted materials for which no permission needs to be sought by the user. Jessica Litman has advocated for similar steps toward relinquishing the monopoly right of the owner to make copies of a work in favor of the more limited and specific right to exploit that work commercially (2001: 182). For Litman, establishing the necessary balance between authors and users in copyright law starts with defining the 'compensable units' protected in the work (2001: 175). Historically, it made sense to define the copy as the compensable unit of a text: copies were produced and controlled by industry professionals, and, as material artifacts, were easily trackable. Today, argues Litman, this is no longer the case (2001: 177). Copyright owners can now benefit from a host of other rights, including the right to perform, display, adapt and translate a work. It is thus unrealistic and impractical to approximate financial losses suffered through copyright infringement (i.e., 'media piracy') by simply counting illegal copies of a work. In many cases, users may never have purchased a legitimate copy of a pirated text; in other cases, as Matthew David has pointed out, whilst an illegitimate copy may raise the commercial value of the copied original by making it more widely known and prompting further sales, what is certainly a fact is that the free circulation of recorded music has increased the price and volume of live-music ticket sales (2010).

Engström and Falkvinge continue their call for copyright reform with a demand for what they call 'quotation rights' for audio-visual material, which they see as an extension of existing conventions regarding the permissible quotation of properly cited text passages (2012: 6). This mirrors Litman's concern that the abolishment of non-commercial protection could harm the integrity of an original work (if, for instance, it is altered by a user). As a remedy, Litman suggests that in the digital age, adaptations (both commercial and non-commercial) can easily 'be accompanied by a truthful disclaimer and a citation (or hypertext link) to an unaltered and readily accessible copy of the original' (2001: 185). We find a similar approach spelled out in several widely used Creative Commons licenses, which explicitly allow users to produce non-commercial copies of originals as long as proper attribution is attached (www.creativecommons.org/). Both legal theory and existing alternative IP practice is thus in agreement with Engström and Falkvinge's emphasis on the importance of avoiding wide-scale vilification of all copying practices, and distinguishing between commercial and non-commercial copying, as well as copying for educational or creative purposes. Tied to this is a further request levied by Engström and Falkvinge, namely that digital rights management (DRM) locks should be abolished alongside the sole right of the owner to make copies. While Litman does not go quite so far, she does state that circumvention of DRM should be allowed if someone is using a part of a text that is within the public domain (Litman 2001: 184). The existence of DRM locks can also create problematic contradictory situations (such as in the 2012 *Canadian Copyright Modernization Act*), in which the law permits users to create copies for backup and personal use, but disallows the circumvention of digital locks.

Overall, Engström and Falkvinge's proposal for copyright reform resembles similar calls from international communities of legal scholars in that it reflects a concern for creating a more robust public domain. To strengthen and fortify the public domain, Engström and Falkvinge would like to see copyrights restricted to a 20-year maximum duration, with an additional requirement to register a copyrighted work five years after it is published (2012: 5). Such a rule could ensure that works remain protected only if the rights owners deem this to be worth the effort; the overwhelming majority of protected cultural works, which cease to produce significant revenue after a few years, could thus enter into the public domain sooner, and be available to inspire further uses and creations. This measure would have the added benefit of reducing the number of orphan works which currently remain protected by copyright even though they are unclaimed by their owner, and which therefore remain unavailable to many users.

The official copyright reform platforms of other pirate parties are remarkably similar to the one outlined in Engström and Falkvinge's *The Case for Copyright Reform.* Canada's Pirate Party, for example, campaigns for the legalization of sharing for personal use, and a five-year copyright term, with a possible renewal of five more years. The PPUK offers a slightly more in-depth plan for reform. It, too, seeks the legalization of non-commercial sharing, but also calls for the inclusion of mandatory warning labels with DRM-protected items, which would alert users to 'the potential defects' built into these uncopyable artifacts (PPUK 2011). As an ideal duration for copyright protection, the PPUK suggests ten years, with the possibility of a five-year renewal. As an interesting addition, the PPUK also demands that the British Broadcasting Corporation (BBC), whose programming is funded by the public, should be prohibited from using DRM technology, and that its programming should furthermore be protected under Creative Commons licenses, which would make content more easily available to a public that, it is argued, has already paid for it. In this approach, members of the public are essentially seen as co-producers of BBC content, who should share in the user rights of the protected works, at the very least for unrestricted uses for critique, teaching and the creation of derivative texts. As the platform rightly argues, securing this kind of access was copyright law's intention in the first place.

The PPUK also advocates for strengthening the penalties for frivolous copyright infringement allegations. Presently, copyright owners are able to send a high volume of infringement warnings to users, effectively without having to fear repercussions. Such warnings tend to have a powerful intimidating effect for those unfamiliar with copyright law. Recipients of such warnings require education regarding their rights (such as outlined in fair use and fair dealing provisions), rather than reminders of the ownership rights allegedly infringed, composed in language that can be impossible to understand for laypeople. The negative impact of such frivolous 'warning' practices on learning and research, creativity, productivity and innovation has already been highlighted by a range of legal scholars (e.g. Jaszi and Aufderheide 2004). Like the PPUK, legal scholars Eduardo Penalver and Sonia Katyal identify the establishment of legal guidelines to diminish copyright misuse as a potential tool for the restoration of the owner/user balance in copyright law. Alongside increased penalties for copyright owners who overstate their intellectual property entitlements, the defendant would be allowed to use the copyright owner's property without consent and would be eligible for compensatory damages (Penalver & Katyal 2010: 220).

We suggest that the overlap between some of the ideas put forward by the pirate party movement and legal scholarship is symptomatic of a widespread concern with bolstering digital user rights. User rights, in legal scholarship, offset the monopoly granted to the copyright owner of a cultural property. They represent the public's interest and emphasize the important creative and educational possibilities lying dormant in every cultural expression, as long as it remains widely accessible for further uses. As the Canadian law professor Abraham Drassinower argues in 'Taking User Rights Seriously', these rights are encompassed, most importantly, in fair use and fair dealing provisions. In the Canadian context, states Drassinower, 'fair dealing is a user right rather than a mere exception because it arises from and affirms the very same principle that gives rise to the plaintiff's entitlement' (2005: 471). In other words, defending a particular use as 'fair dealing' often entails the argument that the work in question has undergone sufficient transformation to establish the user as an author in their own right. In this sense, fair dealing emerges as a fundamentally important user right that enables users to become authors themselves. Legal scholar Carys Craig develops a similar argument in 'Locking Out Lawful Users: Fair Dealing and Anti-circumvention in Bill C-32' (2010), with a focus on the ways in which digital locks infringe on Canadian users' fair dealing rights. Like Drassinower, Craig argues that fair dealing should not be conceptualized as an exemption to the rights of an owner, but rather as a user's positive claim that copyright owners have a duty to respect. As Craig notes, '[w]here fair dealing is recognized as a "user right," it can be argued that copyright owners have a correlative obligation to permit users' fair dealings with their works' (2010: 181).

Members and supporters of pirate parties would surely agree with Craig when she writes that users who cannot access a 'locked' digital work are inhibited from dealing fairly with it (2010: 193). In a piece called 'The Pirate Party is More Libertarian than the Libertarian Party', Phil Hunt, the PPUK foreign policy spokesperson, emphasizes this fact, and argues that users should not only have the right to format-shift, but also the right to tinker with a legitimately acquired copy of a text once it has been digitized: 'if I have a hard disk, it's my property and I can arrange the patterns of magnetic alignment on it in any way I choose; and if I cannot, because copyright law forbids me, my property right in the hard disk has been reduced' (Hunt 2010).

The calls by various national pirate party platforms for copyright reform reflect their desire to continue discussion and development of their means of association, communication and creative expression. To wit, Hunt writes:

> When you use a computer or other digital electronics, who do you think should control what you can do? (A) yourself, (B) big government, (C) big business. If you answered A, the Pirate Party agrees with you, and we exist to protect your rights from governments and corporations that would usurp them. (Hunt 2010)

Approached via Kelty's concept of geek culture, the pirate parties' initial involvement in the 'copyright wars' can be seen as incidental; their intent is to continue to share, create and communicate via Internet technology, not to inflict harm on others via intellectual property infringement. Accordingly, the pirate party movement's proposals for copyright reform indicate an awareness that 'the need for self-expression must always be weighed against the legitimate claims of hard-working creators and balance what is desired with the basic needs of others' (Penalver and Katyal 2010: 223).

The fact that so many people unwittingly break copyright laws on a daily basis, without any intention to engage in illegal activities, indicates that the law is obscure and incomprehensible:

> It is unrealistic to imagine that we could make members of the public conduct their daily affairs under rules thought up by and for major players in copyright-affected industries simply by announcing they must. If the public is to play by copyright rules, then those rules must be designed with the public's interests in mind. (Litman 2001: 72)

Work by other legal scholars echoes the same sentiment (see e.g. Lessig 2004; McLeod 2010). As this research shows, the rules governing intellectual property in the digital sphere have yet to establish a suitable balance between authors/creators/owners, on the one hand, and the public of users, on the other.

Rather than adopting a radical approach that delegitimizes intellectual property rules altogether, and therefore the incentive for the production of creative new works that benefit the public, the pirate party movement has put forward suggestions that are animated by the positive notion of an empowered user, and by an understanding of the moral and social implications of cultural ownership that goes beyond copyright law's current economic bias. Rather than promoting 'piracy' in the conventional sense of the term, their copyright reform efforts should be seen as an attempt to enable what Coombe, Wershler and Zeilinger call 'dynamic fair dealing', namely 'emergent approaches to the creation, circulation and management of digital cultural objects that challenge traditional paradigms of intellectual property or pose alternatives to them' (Coombe et al. 2014: 5).

PIRACY AND 'MEDIA PIRACY'

Having surveyed some of the characteristics and merits of the Pirate Party movement, we now turn to a more theoretical discussion of piracy, and consider how PPI challenges contemporary understandings of the term. In the context of immaterial goods, Lawrence Lessig, best known as the initiator of the Creative Commons licensing system, defines media piracy as the use of another person's creative property without their permission (2011: 81). A 2011 report funded by the American Social Science Research Council (SSRC), entitled *Media Piracy in Emerging Economies*, defines the term piracy as 'the ubiquitous, increasingly digital practices of copying that fall outside the boundaries of copyright law' (Karaganis 2011: 2). In an earlier formulation, media scholar Siva Vaidhyanathan writes, similarly, that the pirating of intellectual property 'is an offense created by the notion of copyright', but adds an important qualification, namely that media piracy 'could not exist as a concept without the granted monopoly of copyright that it violates' (2001: 67). While these authors refer specifically to digital media piracy, their perspective retains a tenuous conceptual link to maritime piracy, which has, likewise, been theorized in terms of its relationship to property law.

In a recent history of piracy written from a philosophical perspective, the sea pirate's relation to the law is reminiscent of Vaidhyanathan's description of media piracy: 'The classical pirate is a creature of legal authority: more precisely, he is its own presupposition, that against which the civil order must variously strive, and in whose absence it would not be itself' (Heller-Roazen 2009: 38). All these theoretical articulations, then, portray piracy and the law as co-constitutive: piracy importantly derives its meaning as a cultural practice from the legal institutions that frame it; the law, in turn, legitimizes itself in opposition to the perceived transgressions of the pirate.

In this perspective, piracy, as the 'definitive transgression of the information age' (Johns 2010: 6), cannot be said to have straightforward, *a priori* characteristics. As Gary Hall clarifies in the introduction to a journal issue devoted to pirate philosophy, we must describe all types of piracy in terms of 'the decisions that are made in relation to it, the specific tactics and strategies that are adopted, and the particular conjunction of time, situation and context in which such actions and activities take place' (Hall 2009: 2). Piracy thus emerges as a contingent concept devoid of inherent, independent qualities. This perspective can be usefully applied both to sea piracy and in media piracy contexts. Discussing the re-emergence of maritime piracy in Somali coastal waters, for example, Shannon Dawdy develops a similar approach and proposes that Somali piracy has flourished not in a vacuum, but in response to officials' inability to protect coastal areas from overfishing and illegal dumping by foreigners (Dawdy 2011: 365). Somalia's pirates thus self-identify not as violators, but rather as unappointed protectors of their country's sovereignty: 'We consider sea bandits those who illegally fish in our seas and dump waste in our seas and carry weapons in our seas. We are simply patrolling our seas. Think of us like a coast guard' (Dawdy 2011: 368).

This hybridization of seemingly contradictory roles – law-enforcing and law-breaking – significantly complicates questions regarding the ethics of 'pirate activities'. Could it indeed be in the international legal system's best interest to have Somali pirates patrol their own coasts, at least until the civil war has ended and the self-appointed 'coast guards' can return to their previous occupations as fishermen and farmers? While Somali pirates play a constructive (though not legitimate) role as 'coast guards', they also perform criminal acts. Transposed to different contexts, this double role can serve to expose the ambivalent role of law in validating or discouraging contentious activities depending on who carries them out and why. In the present case, depending on one's perspective, both the Somali pirate activities and the over-fishing and waste-dumping which they prevent can be described as illegal. It is important to note, then, that piracy here functions as a way of exposing weaknesses within the political-economic framework in which it takes place.

The Somali pirates' interpretation and justification of their activities is reminiscent of the historical phenomenon of privateering, which occurred until the late nineteenth century. Historically, pirates were defined as the 'enemy of humankind' (*hostis humani generis*), since they did not fall under the jurisdiction of any one nation-state; privateers, in turn, were legally sanctioned by individual states to raid the ships of enemy states. Governments would present these men with so-called letters of marque, a license that entitled them to attack and pillage shipping or navy vessels from other nations. Privateers owned their own ships and arms, and could keep whatever bounty they accrued, while the state gained additional combative power without spending public funds. Undoubtedly, the line between piracy and privateering was blurry and mutable. In times of conflict, seamen of the former designation would be solicited by the state to act on its behalf, thus becoming privateers by contract. The very same type of activity, undertaken by the same individuals, could thus be seen as illegitimate (i.e., as piracy) at one time, and as legitimate (i.e., as privateering) at another.

This conceptual interplay between pirate and privateer has an important analogy that reaches through the cultural and legal history of intellectual property into the present. As many legal scholars have pointed out, after Great Britain's history of copyright legislation began with the *Statute of Anne* in 1709, it took the United States until 1891 to begin acknowledging international copyright law for printed works (Vaidhyanathan 2001: 62). American printers produced cheap pirate copies of British classics, which was justified as a necessary boost for the emerging American publishing industry. This practice was also justified as promoting literacy and learning, by giving the American public access to printed matter at a fraction of the cost charged by the foreign publishers (Vaidhyanathan 2001: 51). Again, 'piracy' can be interpreted both as harmful and as beneficial. Indeed, from a certain perspective it could be argued that the American business of copying continental books for its domestic market was 'An Act for the Encouragement of Learning', which happens to be the subtitle of the very statute violated by the early American print-based pirating.

It did not take long, however, before prominent American authors such as Mark Twain recognized that American writers were losing income from the lack of international copyright protection (Vaidhyanathan 2001: 61). In other words: American piracy of foreign works was perceived as legitimate, while the international piracy of American works was condemned. After persistent international lobbying efforts, the US Congress eventually passed an international copyright bill in 1886, ending a period of nearly 200 years during which the US publishing industry illegitimately copied British literature. However, the USA did not sign the Berne Convention until 1988, and up to that point did not fully recognize copyright in foreign authors' works unless they were published in the US itself. During that time, many British and American authors alike may have conceptualized the US book industry's piracy as theft; the industry itself, however, had been able to convince law-makers of the social benefits arising from its production of cheap English literature, and thus of the legitimacy of its activities. As Heller-Roazen puts it:

> To the question of the point at which illegitimate plundering at sea could be told apart from legitimate depredation – that of 'the line,' in other words, 'where wrong became right' – these various authorities furnished one answer: 'it is not the

act that renders itself legitimate, nor the actor, but the authorization'. (2009: 81)

The examples of contemporary Somali pirates and early American piracy of British print works can be extended into the present day of contested digital media practices. In the contexts of maritime as well as media piracy, the pirate and the privateer have never held stable, discrete roles. They represent, rather, a set of practices that take on fluid meanings and (il)legitimacy only in context.

As indicated in these examples, the law plays a role of great importance in defining acts of piracy, and thus pirates. But since the concept of piracy is imbued with multiple and often contradictory meanings that shift based on time, context and perspective, a definition of piracy based purely on the law is inadequate. We argue that one function of 'media piracy' is indeed often to highlight the law's shortcomings by means of provocation and transgression. In this sense, copying activities that the proponents of strict IP regulation condemn as piracy often have an activist dimension, and should not be said simply to constitute the theft of intellectual property. Indeed, alleged 'media piracy' of the kind that the international pirate parties condone takes place almost exclusively in the arena of social and cultural practiccs, rather in that of commercially motivated, unfair violations of property rights.

CONCLUSION

Through its various political platforms, the international pirate party movement seeks to highlight the need to contextualize 'media piracy' practices as well as the authorized practices with which they correlate both socially and culturally. This is well articulated in a set of guiding principles published by Pirate Parties International in 2011. These principles describe 'media pirates' as activists who defend strong ideals of freedom of expression and access to information. In line with our discussion above, they suggest that a working definition of piracy cannot be based solely on a legal approach, and that creative and socially productive dimensions of the practices in question must also be taken into consideration. Thus, according to the PPI document, pirates:

- Defend the freedoms of expression, communication, education; respect the privacy of citizens and civil rights in general.
- Defend the free flow of ideas, knowledge and culture.
- Support politically the reform of copyrights and patents laws.
- Have a commitment to work collaboratively, and participate with maximum transparency.
- Do not accept or espouse discrimination of race, origin, beliefs and gender.
- Do not support actions that involve violence.
- Use free software and open protocols whenever possible.
- Politically defend an open, participative and collaborative construction of any public policy.
- Promote solidarity with other pirates.
- Share whenever possible. (Pirate Parties International 2011)

These principles, intended as guidance to the international platforms, clarify the pirate party movements' political vision as one that integrates democratic idealism and cultural inclusivity with the right to freely share information. This multivalence of piracy is reflected in Salvatore Poier's historical survey of the concept, which argues that pirate practices should be seen as experimental forms of social organization (2009). Sea pirates have surely committed violent and illegal acts, but, as indicated in historical accounts as well as the example of present-day Somali, pirates also developed democratic systems of governance (both aboard their ships and through their actions) amongst men who had little or no opportunity for self-governance or self-determination in the larger society. For many, piracy thus offered realistic access to social and economic upward mobility and, as Poier suggests, the opportunity to participate in the creation of a locally contained, fair and quasi-democratic social order.

Without glorifying piracy as an 'outside' to power, Poier writes that in the maritime context, 'piracy represented for many of the poor the opportunity to get out of an unavoidable life of deprivation and misery' (2009). Read against the PPI principles cited above, it becomes clear that media pirates and sea pirates, despite certain undeniable failings, may share important values and ideals. Like sea pirates during the golden age of maritime piracy, media pirates, through their legally dubious activities, seize the opportunity to experiment with the construction of radically new moral economies of social, cultural and economic exchanges that oppose the shortcomings of existing rules and regulations.

Today, copyright laws created for traditional, pre-digital media are experienced by many as inadequate for the fair regulation of cultural and economic activities in the digital era. The mass infringements occurring day by day on P2P networks and other file-sharing platforms around the globe are, we argue, indicative not only of legal transgressions, but also of the inability of the law to meaningfully and fairly accommodate the everyday lives of digital subjects. Issues surrounding digital media piracy do indeed have precedents in pre-digital arenas of trade and cultural exchange; but what is often overlooked in both contexts is that considering the economic implications of the infringement of property rights is not enough. In the digital context, the international pirate party movement argues, the implications of many infringing copying activities that the law perceives as transgressions are, in fact, qualitatively different from simple acts of intellectual property theft. It is argued, in other words, that the social and cultural benefits produced by modern-day 'pirates' in their capacity as 'geeks' can be fundamentally positive even when they involve IP law violations.

The ability to explore and develop these benefits depends on the continued openness of the Internet as well as open access to immaterial cultural works, a conviction that forms a central pillar of most pirate party platforms. To ensure that this openness can be retained or even expanded, they advocate for copyright reforms that will allow for non-commercial copying of IP-protected content. If the public is expected to comply with copyright law, this law must be brought back in step with the needs and desires of digital communities, as well as with the opportunities that digital technologies afford them. Until copyright laws are reformed to reflect the evidently widespread belief that writing code and collaboratively creating digital networks are socially and culturally productive activities benefitting the public at large, the international pirate party movement can be expected to gain momentum and grow both regionally and internationally.

REFERENCES

Adams, W.L. (2012) 'More Trouble for Merkel as Pirate Party Raids Its Fourth State Parliament'. *Time World, Global Spin Blog*. Located at: www.globalspin.blogs.time.com/2012/05/14/more-trouble-for-merkel-as-pirate-party-raids-its-fourth-state-parliament/

Andersson, J. (2009) 'For the Good of the Net: The Pirate Bay as strategic sovereign'. *Culture Machine* 10: 64–108.

Arendt, H. (2005) *The Promise of Politics*. New York: Random House.

Becker, S., Fleischhauer, J. & Pfister, R. (2012) 'Artists Turn Against Pirate Party'. *Spiegel Online International*. Located at: www.spiegel.de/international/germany/authors-and-musicians-rebel-against-pirate-party-policies-in-germany-a-827877.html

Bergh, A. (2011) 'The Rise, Fall and Revival of the Swedish Welfare State: What are the Policy Lessons from Sweden?' IFN Working Paper No. 873. Available at SSRN: http://papers.ssrn.com/sol3/papers.cfm?abstract_id=1884528 or www.dx.doi.org/10.2139/ssrn.1884528

Bergh, A. & Erlingsson, G.O. (2009) 'Liberalization without Retrenchment: Understanding the Consensus on Swedish Welfare State Reforms'. *Scandinavian Political Studies* 32(1): 71–93.

Bhabha, H. (1987) 'Of Mimicry and Man: The Ambivalence of Colonial Discourse'. In *October: The First Decade, 1976–1986*. A. Michelson, R. Krauss, D. Crimp and J. Copjec (eds). Cambridge: MIT Press.

Coombe, R. (1998) *The Cultural Life of Intellectual Properties: Authorship, Appropriation, and the Law*. Durham: Duke University Press.

Coombe, R. (2001) 'Is there a Cultural Studies of Law?' In *A Companion to Cultural Studies*. Toby Miller (ed.). Hoboken: Blackwell Publishing.

Coombe, R., Wersher, D. & Zeilinger, M. (Eds.) (2014) *Dynamic Fair Dealing: Creating Canadian Culture Online*. Toronto: University of Toronto Press.

Craig, C. (2010) 'Locking Out Lawful Users: Fair Dealing and Anti-circumvention in Bill C-32'. In *From Radical Extremism to Balanced Copyright: Canadian Copyright and the Digital Agenda*. M. Geist (ed.). Toronto: Irwin Law (177–203).

David, M. (2010) *Peer to Peer and the Music Industry: The Criminalization of Sharing*. London: Sage Publications.

Dawdy, S. (2011) 'Why Pirates Are Back'. *Annual Review of Law and Social Science* 7: 361–385.

Drassinower, A. (2005) 'Taking User Rights Seriously'. In *The Public Interest: The Future of Canadian Copyright Law*. M. Geist (ed.). Toronto: Irwin Law.

Druckman, J.N. (2001) 'The Implications of Framing Effects for Citizen Competence'. *Political Behavior* 23(3): 225–256.

Engström, C. and Falkvinge, R. (2012) *The Case for Copyright Reform*. Located at: http://www.copyright-reform.eu/sites/copyrightreform.eu/files/The_Case_for_Copyright_Reform.pdf

Ernesto (2008) 'The Pirate Bay Tops 20 Million Peers'. *TorrentFreak*. Located at: www.torrentfreak.com/the-pirate-bay-tops-20-million-peers-081101/

Eudes, Y. (2012) 'The Pirate Party's Next Target: The French Parliament'. *Le Monde/Worldcrunch*. Located at: www.worldcrunch.com/pirates-about-embark-french-parliament/5488

Fitzgerald, P. (2012) 'Re: Copyright and Pirate Party Issues'. 10 Jan. 2012. Email.

Framablog (2012) 'Entretien avec trois candidats du Parti Pirate aux legislatives 2012.' Located at http://www.framablog.org/index.php/post/2012/06/04/parti-pirate-legislatives-2012

Geist, M. (2012a) 'Beyond Users' Rights: Supreme Court Entrenches Technological Neutrality as a New Copyright Principle'. *Michael Geist Blog*. Located at: www.michaelgeist.ca/content/view/6592/125/

Geist, M. (2012b) 'Canadian Music Industry Lobby: Put SOPA Into C-11 Or Stand With Illegal Sites'. *Michael Geist Blog*. Located at: www.michaelgeist.ca/content/blogsection/0/125/10/10/

Geist, M. (2012c) 'Ten Key Questions and Answers about Bill C-11, SOPA, ACTA, and the TPP.' *Michael Geist Blog*. Located at: www.michaelgeist.ca/content/view/6275/125/

Geist, M. (2012d) 'The Battle over C-11 Concludes: How Thousands of Canadians Changed The Copyright Debate'. *Michael Geist Blog*. Located at: www.michaelgeist.ca/content/view/6544/125/

Goodman, D. (2012) 'In Sweden, Twitter Is Democratic, and File Sharing Is a Religion'. *The New York Times*. Located at: http://thelede.blogs.nytimes.com/2012/01/18/in-sweden-twitter-is-democratic-and-file-sharing-is-a-religion/

Green, D., Palmquist, B. & Schickler, E. (2002) *Partisan Hearts and Minds: Political Parties and the Social Identity of Voters*. New Haven: Yale University Press.

Halbert, D. (2005) *Resisting Intellectual Property*. London: Routledge.

Hall, G. (2009) 'Introduction: Pirate Philosophy'. *Culture Machine* 10: 1–5.

Heller-Roazen, D. (2009) *Enemy of All: Piracy and the Law of Nations*. Cambridge: Massachusetts Institute of Technology.

Hesmondhalgh, D. (2010) 'Music, Digitalization, and Copyright'. In *Digital Dynamics: Engagements and Disconnections*. G. P. e. New Jersey: Hampton Press.

Hettinger, E. (1989) 'Justifying Intellectual Property Law'. *Philosophy and Public Affairs* 18(1): 31–52.

Hirsch, J. (1998) 'A Party is Not a Movement and Vice Versa'. In *The German Greens: Paradox Between Movement and Party*. M. (eds). Philadelphia: Temple University Press.

Hunt, P. (2010) 'The Pirate Party is more Libertarian than the Libertarian Party'. *Amused Cynicism* Wordpress Blog. Located at: www.cabalamat.wordpress.com/2010/02/16/the-pirate-party-is-more-libertarian-than-the-libertarian-party/

Jaszi, P. and Aufderheide, P. (2004) *Untold Stories: Creative Consequences of the Rights Clearance Culture for Documentary Filmmakers*. Washington, DC: Center for Social Media. Located at: http://www.cmsimpact.org/sites/default/files/UNTOLDSTORIES_Report.pdf

Johns, A. (2010) *Piracy: The Intellectual Property Wars from Gutenberg to Gates*. Chicago: University Of Chicago Press.

Judas (2004) 'RE: Electronic Notice of Infringement – the piratebay.org'. *Legal Threats*. Located at: http://thepiratebay.se/static/adv_response.txt

Karaganis, J. (2011) 'Chapter 1: Rethinking Piracy'. In *Media Piracy in Emerging Economies*, The Social Science Research Council.

Kelty, C. (2005) 'Geeks, Social Imaginaries, and Recursive Publics'. *Cultural Anthropology* 20(2): 185–214.

Krebs, R.R. & Jackson, P.T. (2007) 'Twisting Tongues and Twisting Arms: The Power of Political Rhetoric'. *European Journal of International Relations* 13(1): 35–66.

Lessig, L. (2004) *Free Culture*. New York: Penguin Press.

Lessig, L. (2011) 'Pirates'. In *No Safe Harbor: Essays About Pirate Politics*. United States Pirate Party (81–84). Located at: http://pp-international.net/no_safe_harbor/No%20Safe%20Harbor%20-%20United%20States%20Pirate%20Party.pdf

Li, M. (2009) 'The Pirate Party and the Pirate Bay: How the Pirate Bay Influences Sweden and International Copyright Relations'. *Pace International Law Review* 21(1): 281–307.

Litman, J. (2001) *Digital Copyright*. New York: Prometheus Books.

Logie, J. (2006) Peers, Pirates, and Persuasion: Rhetoric in the Peer-to-Peer Debates. West Lafayette: Parlor Press.

McCrea, T. (2012) 'Re: Pirate Party'. 19 Jan. 2012. Email.

McLeod, K. (2001) *Owning Culture: Authorship, Ownership and Intellectual Property Law*. New York: Peter Lang.

McLeod, K. (co-producer) (2010) *Copyright Criminals*. Film.

Miegel, F. & Olsson, T. (2008) 'From Pirates to Politicians: The Story of the Swedish File Sharers Who Became a Political Party'. In *Democracy, Journalism and Technology: New Developments in an Enlarged Europe*. N. Carpentier, P. Pruulmann-Vengerfeldt, K. Nordenstreng, M. Hartmann, P. Vihalemm, B. Cammaerts, H. Nieminen & T. Olsson (eds.). Tartu: Tartu University Press (203–215).

Minow, M. (1996) 'Stories in Law'. In *Law's Stories: Narrative and Rhetoric in the Law*. P. P. e. New Haven: Yale University Press (24–36).

Offe, C. (1998) 'From Youth to Maturity: The Challenge of Party Politics' in *The German Greens: Paradox Between Movement and Party*. M. (eds) Philadelphia: Temple University Press.

Patry, W. (2009) *Moral Panics and the Copyright Wars*. Oxford: Oxford University Press.

Payne, R.A. (2001) 'Persuasion, Frames and Norm Construction'. *European Journal of International Relations* 7(1): 37–61.

Penalver, E. and Katyal, S. (2010) *Property Outlaws: How Squatters, Pirates and Protestors Improve the Law of Ownership*. New Haven: Yale University Press.

Pirate Parties International Wiki (2011) 'Building the Principles of PPI'. Located at: https://int.piratenpartei.de/Building_the_principles_of_PPI

Pirate Parties International Wiki (2012) 'Members of the PPI'. Located at: http://wiki.pp-international.net/Members_of_the_PPI

Pirate Party of Canada (2012) 'Press Release: Copyright Infringement in Canadian House of Parliament'. Located at: https://www.facebook.com/piratepartyca/posts/10150557194856438

Pirate Party UK (PPUK) (2010) *Manifesto*. Located at: www.pirateparty.org.uk

Pirate Party UK (PPUK) (2011) *Manifesto*. Located at: www.pirateparty.org.uk/policies/

Poier, S. (2009) 'Hostis Humani Generis: History of a Multi-Faceted Word'. *Dark Matter: In the Ruins of Imperial Culture*. Located at: www.darkmatter101.org/site/2009/12/20/hostis-humani-generis-history-of-a-multi-faceted-word/

Pontusson, J. (2011) 'Once Again a Model: Nordic Social Democracy in a Globalized World'. In *What's Left of the Left? Democrats and Social Democrats in Challenging Times*. J. (eds). Durham: Duke University Press.

Recording Industry Association of America (RIAA) (2003) 'Recording Industry Begins Suing P2P File Sharers Who Illegally Offer Copyrighted Music Online'. *Gold and Platinum News*. Located at: www.riaa.org/newsitem.php?id=85183A9C-28F4-19CE-BDE6-F48E206CE8A1

RT.com (2012) 'German Pirate Party to Rock Merkel's Boat?' Located at: www.rt.com/news/pirate-party-support-merkel-186/

Sample, I. (2012) 'Free Access to British Scientific Research Within Two Years'. *The Guardian*. Located at: www.guardian.co.uk/science/2012/jul/15/free-access-british-scientific-research?newsfeed=true

Scheven, N. (2012) 'Support for German Chancellor Merkel's Party Falls'. *Nasdaq*. Located at: www.nasdaq.com/article/support-for-german-chancellor-merkels-party-falls-20120613-00162

Schmidtt, C. (1937) 'The Concept of Piracy'. *Humanity* Spring 2011: 27–29.

Schulze, H. & Mochalski, K. (2009) *Ipoque Internet Study 2008–2009*. Located at: http://www.ipoque.com/sites/default/files/mediafiles/documents/internet-study-2008-2009.pdf

Spiegel Online International (2012) 'Pirate Politician Says Party "Rising as Fast as Nazis"'. Located at: www.spiegel.de/international/germany/outrage-after-pirate-party-member-says-party-growing-as-fast-as-nazis-did-a-829166.html

Stallman, R. (2005) 'Biopiracy or Bioprivateering?' *Information Ethics: Privacy, Property, and Power*. A. Moore (ed.). Seattle: University of Washington Press.

Supiot, A. (2010) 'A Legal Perspective on the Economic Crisis of 2008'. *International Labour Review* 149(2): 151–162.

The Pirate Bay (n.d.) 'About'. Located at: www.thepiratebay.se/about

The Pirate Bay (2001) 'POwr, Broccoli, and Kopimi'. Located at: http://torrentfreak.com/pirate-bay-manifesto-powr-broccoli-and-kopimi-090225/

The Pirate Bay, 'Legal Threats'. Located at: www.thepiratebay.se/legal

United States Pirate Party (2011) *No Safe Harbor: Essays About Pirate Politics.* United States Pirate Party. Located at: http://pp-international.net/no_safe_harbor/No%20Safe%20Harbor%20-%20United%20States%20Pirate%20Party.pdf

Vaidhyanathan, S. (2001) *Copyrights and Copywrongs: The Rise of Intellectual Property and How It Threatens Creativity.* New York: New York University Press.

Weisberg, R. (1996) 'Proclaiming Trials as Narratives: Premises and Pretenses'. In *Law's Stories: Narrative and Rhetoric in the Law.* P. Brooks & P. Gerwitz (eds.). New Haven: Yale University Press.

Widerquist, K. (2004) 'Libertarianism'. Located at: http://www.widerquist.com/karl/Articles–scholarly/Libertarianism.doc

Yar, M. (2008) 'Rhetorics and Myths of Anti-Piracy Campaigns'. *New Media and Society* 10: 605–623.

Young-Bruel, E. (2006) *Why Arendt Matters.* New Haven: Yale University Press.

Zeh, J. (2012) 'The Pirate Party Fits the Political Gap'. *The Guardian.* Located at: www.guardian.co.uk/commentisfree/2012/may/18/germany-pirate-party-political-gap

PART VI
Creative Copying

Matthew David and Debora Halbert

To 'steal' a great line, when it comes to producing original work, we all stand on the shoulders of giants! Whether it be in the sciences, arts or more directly commercial fields of practice, progress always involves the use of past works in the creation of anything new. The question of when such 'use' becomes 'infringement', and when it should/is regarded as itself an original piece of work, is the subject of this section, though it is of course a thread that runs throughout the handbook. Raizel Liebler, Claudy Op den Kamp, and John Tehranian approach the tension between originality and infringement directly in this section, if from a number of different angles. Whilst Tehranian and Liebler combine legal and literary scholarship in their approaches to the question of creative copying, Op den Kamp approaches the question of past works in relation to future uses from the perspective of an archivist and historian of film. Respectively they explore the concepts of 'fanfiction', 'orphan works' and, 'aesthetic neutrality' as prisms through which to explore how law and society shape the boundary between permitted and prohibited, rewarded and punished, forms of creative appropriation.

Raizel Liebler draws parallels across fictional genres (from science fiction films, comics, novels, music and cult television series), historical periods, and national legal and cultural traditions, to explore the relationship between popular forms of copyright protected fiction and the diverse forms of fanfiction that develop in relation to such works. Fanfiction is one form of what is often called user-generated content, but not the only type of user-generated content (see Lastowka in this collection). Whilst fans of various fictional works revere the authors whose works they like, this reverence often takes the form of a kind of 'guardianship' or 'stewardship' that does not directly conform with authorial/corporate conceptions of copyright control. Fans are not passive recipients of content (see Whiteman, this collection), but active in their engagement with it. Often this involves creative copies, extensions and revisions.

Whilst parody is protected as 'fair use' in US law, much fanfiction, precisely in so far as it reveres the original, cannot be so regarded and thus can be seen as a copyright infringement under the law. However, to the extent that fanfiction is rarely produced or circulated for commercial gain, its existence has often been regarded as harmless to copyright holders. Liebler notes fanfiction is also, for the most part, highly beneficial to rights holders in holding and extending interest in their creative work (whether that be *Star Trek*, *Firefly* or *Harry Potter*). Nonetheless, disputes have arisen when it is suggested that fanfiction is either commercially oriented or might harm legitimate sales or the reputation of the original works. Non-commerciality is itself disputed, as this raises the question of whether fans are themselves being exploited in the work they do in promoting and adding to commercial works. Look up 'Jayne Hats' online to see how Fox recently issued a 'cease and desist' order against a fan who created *Firefly* bobble hats despite long since cancelling the (now) cult series.

Whilst Sir Arthur Conan Doyle was 'forced' to bring back Sherlock Holmes ten years after 'killing him off' in *The Final Problem* in 1893, it is unlikely that fanfiction – that repeatedly revived and revised the great detective – was responsible for Doyle's decision to do so too. Rather, it was Holmes's other 'fans' (those that did not revive their hero) that were most insistent that Doyle did so. Nonetheless, authors may feel compelled to respond to the way fans take their characters over. The question of whether authors truly own, or should own, the characters they create is a fascinating one. Overly litigious controls may kill off fan support, whilst giving free reign may mean authors lose control entirely. When fans set up Twitter feeds and Facebook accounts; and assume the identities of characters from their favourite fictional books, films and programmes – what then? Disputes over JD California's 'take' on *Catcher in the Rye* (the prohibited *60 Years Later*) and various law suits involving 'takes' on the Harry Potter franchise, are amongst a range of illustrations drawn upon to highlight tensions between creativity and copying, help and harm. In her chapter, Liebler then goes on to look at Japanese comic book fanfiction (*doujinshi*), a form that has achieved relatively high status in Japan and which may offer an example of a more harmonious way of dealing with author/fan relations than simply asserting the exclusivity of copyrights. Whether Don Quixote (and his creator Miguel de Cervantes) could have better revenged himself (themselves(?)) on those that parodied him if he had used the legal framework of 'moral rights' rather than those of Anglo-Saxon 'copyright' is then debated, as are the IP implications of making a music video in which your fans sing along with you.

The 1962 film *De overval* (*The Silent Raid*) tells of events in occupied Holland in 1944. Whilst the film is only 50 years old, its copyright holders cannot be identified as the original production company no longer exists and, unlike in a novel for example, a film has a string of potential copyright holders. This example begins Claudy Op den Kamp's account of the 'orphan works problem', the difficulty of identifying ownership in vast numbers of creative works. The problem of orphan works applies to a range of different creative fields, but film helps illustrate the wider problem well. Extension of copyright terms to 70 years after the death of the author is triply problematic when it comes to knowing whether a work has fallen out of protection. With no singular owner, it is not clear when the clock starts, and with such a long duration the likelihood increases that owners, and their beneficiaries, will become lost. Added to this is the absence of any requirement to register copyright in the first place.

It is not just that many works have no identified copyright holders. It is the case that the current absence of an identified owner is not enough to protect a user of such work against any subsequent claim made by someone who then comes forward with a valid claim to be that (until then 'orphaned') work's copyright holder.

Some work exists in the public domain because its copyright has expired. However, as three-quarters of all silent film content has long since ceased to exist, the volume of work securely in the public domain is modest. Of what films remains most of it is from dates that could realistically leave them within copyright, yet the British Library estimate that 40% of its film archive is 'orphaned'; and Cornell University's film archive estimates 58%. By different methods of calculation various continental European estimates vary from between 5% and 21%. These figures say as much about inconsistent measurement as they do about the reality of what is being measured. It is simply the case that vast swathes of our common heritage are beyond the scope of 'safe' use, by historians, documentary makers and other film makers, because it is impossible to calculate the cost of using that material in the event of a copyright holder coming forward. Public archives with limited budgets are not able to release such material, nor even warrant the cost of digitizing material that they cannot then make available. Private film archives (such as those of film studios themselves) tend to re-release only what they can be sure they own the rights to themselves. The problem of orphan works then gives us a very different angle on the question of creative re-use, or the danger of chronically inhibiting it. Op den Kamp suggests the need for, and the possibility of, a number of solutions, from collective licensing schemes, contractual liability limits and statutory exemptions for certain kinds of use. Various national schemes of this kind have been proposed and developed, but international agreement remains elusive.

On questions of aesthetic value, the judiciary are not supposed to take a view, at least not in terms that would sway their judgement regarding whether or not a work should be granted copyright. Originality is supposed to be the criteria, not whether that originality is more or less aesthetically pleasing or superior (however that might be defined). John Tehranian, however, documents how this supposed 'aesthetic neutrality' is only ever a convenient fiction behind which lie judgements about what should and should not be defended as 'worthy' or 'sacred' texts. Tehranian explores three cases in depth. The first concerns Alice Randall's *The Wind Done Gone*, a 'take' on Margaret Mitchell's *Gone with the Wind*. The second is the case brought by JD Salinger (author of *Catcher in the Rye*) against JD California's *60 Years Later*. Third is the case of the appropriation artist Richard Prince's use of original works by the photographer Patrick Cariou in the construction of 30 works of his own.

In each case the 'fair use' principle was invoked as grounds by which one author/artist might legitimately draw upon and use the characters/narrative/content of another without infringing their copyright. What Tehranian is able to do in juxtaposing these three cases is to highlight how in each case differences in interpretation allow the copyright of the 'original' author/artist to be either upheld or suspended depending upon whether or not the 'original' artist/author retains or has lost their 'sacred' status as 'creative genius' relative to their challenger. For many decades the estate of Margaret Mitchell had successfully defended her/their exclusive right to control the use of any story, character and relationship between characters 'taken' from *Gone with the Wind*. In 2001, however, Mitchell's estate lost its attempt to prevent the publication of Alice Randall's *The Wind Done Gone*, a 'take' on Mitchell's work that radically revised the racial and sexual politics of the original. In refusing to enjoin the publication of Randall's work, the US courts determined that the book was a parody, and hence entitled to fair use protection. Counterwise, in the case of JD California's 'take' on JD Salinger's *Catcher in the Rye*, the courts found California's work to be a 'sequel', rather than a 'parody' and hence not entitled to First Amendment (fair use) protection. Tehranian outlines the arbitrary nature of this distinction, and its application, and hence the need to explain such decisions in terms of other criteria, in particular the extent to which each original work was (or in the case of *Gone with the Wind* was no longer) deemed canonical. That Richard Prince could use a series of photographs by Patrick Cariou in the composition of his work was (finally) deemed not to be copyright infringement on the grounds that Cariou's prior sales were so diminutive relative to Prince's multi-million dollar order book. Unable to directly cite aesthetic criteria to determine Prince a 'real' artist, relative to Cariou, the court rather canonized 'real' art with reference to prevailing valuations in cash terms.

21

Copyright and Ownership of Fan Created Works: Fanfiction and Beyond

Raizel Liebler

INTRODUCTION

What do one of the first novels ever published, the second most popular book series of all time, and a music video for a modern Korean pop star have in common? They are influenced by the communities of fandom that both consume and produce additional stories and media related to their interests. The use of existing stories, creative works and ideas as the basis of new works is a centuries-old practice employed by writers, storytellers and others. Within the law, this practice has ranged in acceptance – with original authors and copyright owners sometimes encouraging and sometimes suing creators of fanworks.

Fanworks are works of creativity that build upon the works of others, usually within the context of a larger fan community. As exemplified by Japanese fan-made comics (called *doujinshi*), one definition of whether a work may be categorized as fan-based is if it is '(1) undertaken as a complement to, rather than in competition with, the underlying work, and (2) enhances, in aggregate, the author's economic and creative interests' (Noda 2010: 139). The creation of these fanworks is usually done as an expression of belongingness, as part of a larger fan community, regardless of whether they have been granted permission to use the original work. The majority of legal scholarship on fanworks have focused on fanfiction, starting with Rebecca Tushnet's pioneering article where fanfiction (also called fanfic) was described as 'any kind of written creativity that is based on an identifiable segment of popular culture, such as a television show, and is not produced as "professional" writing' (Tushnet 1997: 655). Another term used to refer to these works is user-generated content. However, user-generated content can also include works whose creation is prompted by the copyright owner (such as in a contest. Because this chapter focuses on works based on being part of a larger fan community, the term 'fanworks' will be used throughout this chapter.

This chapter will discuss issues of how fanworks may be simultaneously original and imitative, engage in sharing as well as control, and of course raise intellectual property concerns, such as possible copyright infringement. Overall, in the United States, fanfiction and fanwork creators have more legal leeway and flexibility than in other countries. However, Japan's flexibility for fanworks outside of the legal system provides for a very loose and permissive environment for transformative works, even for fanworks that earn money for their creators. Generally, countries that have 'moral rights' protecting the rights of authors without accompanying 'fair use' or 'fair dealing' provisions put the creation of fanworks at greatest risk.

THE TENSION BETWEEN FANS, AUTHORS AND OWNERS

There is a natural tension between fans, the authors of creative works, and the media owners/copyright holders. This tension is based on the differing sets of perceived value placed on said creative work by the stakeholders in question. Fans often value a work based on intangible motivations: a sense of community through fandom, a personal connection to the story, a creative or emotional outlet through the work itself. Rebecca Tushnet says fans view themselves as 'guardians of the texts they love, purer than the owners in some ways because they seek no profit. They believe that their emotional and financial investment in the characters gives them moral rights to create with these characters' (Tushnet 1997: 657). Jenkins, Ford and Green (2013: 294) state how important it is to not see audiences as passive, but instead 'they transform the material through active production processes or through their own critiques and commentary, so that it better serves their own social and expressive needs'. What this means is that content 'does not remain in fixed borders but rather circulates in unpredicted and often unpredictable directions, not the product of top-down design but rather the result of a multitude of local decisions made by autonomous agents negotiating their way through diverse cultural spaces' (2013: 294).

Most fanwork creation, and specifically fanfiction writing, rather than being considered the work of individual writers attempting to assume authorship of another author's original text, or to claim a piece of someone else's intellectual property, is more accurately described as a collective, a creative community in which the original source medium exists as shared, communal property, which is modified and distributed not for profit, but for enjoyment. The non-commercial use of this property is the standard practice, and writers do not claim to own particular characters or ideas exclusively, nor do they claim to have created the source medium themselves. The longer the time that the creative community is allowed to grow, the larger this collective becomes, and the possible interpretations and revisions of this communal property are more varied.

Creating fanworks provides a legitimate creative outlet for novice and professional writers and other types of creators to experiment with the craft. There are a number of reasons why fans and writers engage in the creation of fanworks and these reasons vary based on the motivation of the audience. Some fanworks are created as a commentary on, parody of, or response to an original author's work, at other times it is as an extension of the original work of the media creator. Traditionally, fans see their role as the stewards of a media text, and they create fanworks in an attempt to maintain fidelity to a story that may be unduly influenced by commercial considerations (Lichtenberg 2013: 94–95).

Fans often view their re-workings as part of an overall cultural experience, meaning that once a mainstream work is released to the public, it is too late for the author or owner to hold it back from use by others. As Jane Gaines in *Contested Culture: The Image, the Voice, and the Law* points out, 'The owners of popular forms, which constitute our most widely shared culture … are in the contradictory position of encouraging the widespread uses of Batman, Superman, and Snow White. But when those forms are used spontaneously … the owners want to take them back' (Gaines 1991: 228).

Media owners predictably, and many would say rightfully, base a creative work's value on its commercial viability. Fox cultivated a popular online fandom from 2003 through 2006 for the TV show *Firefly* and follow-up movie *Serenity* and encouraged the creation of fanworks, not out of an altruistic desire to spread the word about Joss Whedon's characters and fictional universe but to market their product in order to create a hit. When *Firefly* was cancelled and the marketing campaign for the movie ended, these fanworks lost value for the media owner (Fox) but increased in value for the fans, as they were now the only outlet to keep Whedon's universe and characters alive, and they formed a platform for fans to connect around the text.

As Jenkins, Ford and Green (2013) note in one specific example involving fan created *Mad Men* Twitter feeds, owners/authors frequently want to limit fanworks whether or not the fans are specifically monetizing their work. In this example, fans created Twitter accounts from the perspective of their favorite characters, 'speaking' in their voices. For a time, these fan created accounts were shut down, due to the efforts of the owners of *Mad Men*. This conflict exemplifies two different narratives for interaction with copyright works by fans. The traditional interaction model is one where 'fan-created material off official *Man Men* channels is in competition with the show, and any traffic those outlets receive dilutes the reach of the show's official response. This approach assigns no value to how fan-created-and-circulated content might drive awareness and engagement … because it cannot be easily quantified' (Jenkins et al. 2013: 34) On the other hand, a more permissive model also exists that shows that 'content often gains traction when people are given the latitude to use "official" media texts to communicate something about themselves' (2013: 34). In this model, owners giving up exclusive control benefit more in the long-term because they create strong fan ties to their work that help spread the work widely.

At the same time, mainstream authors and media creators often exist in the grey area between the oft-conflicting motivating factors of commerce and creativity. Authors create an original work with the hope of finding an appreciative audience and earning an income from said work. They may personally encourage fan interaction with their work, while at the same time keeping a close eye on their own legal representation and economic benefit as the primary creator of that work.

Acknowledging the symbiotic relationship between media creators and fan communities, and between fanworks and copyrighted properties, can allow for greater acceptance of fanworks, based on an acknowledgement that fanworks would not exist but for the original work. As a result, generally, distribution for free is acceptable, but payment requires the permission of both fanfic and original writers.

While fanworks are generally viewed as non-commercial within the communities that create them, the lines between commercial and not are becoming increasingly blurred. Rebecca Tushnet states that:

> commercial and noncommercial spaces interpenetrate, and cannot readily be disentangled. Fans generally don't make money from fandom; particularly in female-dominated media fandoms, there is a strong norm against anything that smacks of commercialization. This is thought to be both legally and ethically protective: fans argue that they are good consumers and that their fandom encourages them to buy more of the official product. This position, however, entails that other people and entities – professionals, convention organizers, Google – regularly do make money from fans. (Tushnet 2010: 3–4)

Therefore, because fans are focused on the object of their fandom, offering up their fan activities, such as creating fanworks, their creative activities generally are considered to be part of a gift economy, rather than an economic economy. Considering that one of the major justifications for copyright protection is that creativity will be diminished without a system built around compensation, the creators of fanworks belie that argument.

As stewards of texts, fans see their interests as sometimes superseding the interests of authors and owners to keep works alive. Authors and owners do decide to permanently or temporarily end works, usually for reasons of commercial viability; fanworks help to keep interest going for official releases that often have pauses – either temporary or permanent. At least as far back as the 'death' of Sherlock Holmes in 'The Final Problem' in 1893, fans have written fanfiction to keep characters 'alive' (Doyle, 1894). While Holmes returned from the dead ten years later in 1903, the tradition of writing additional stories moving forward continued (Doyle, 1905). More recently, fan communities have kept subcultural interest in *Star Trek*, *Doctor Who* and other properties alive long enough for their owners to return to making money on years of official mainstream releases, often through the creation of fanworks.

Despite fanworks being in existence for quite some time, the present platforms help to throw into sharp relief the differential between those who create content and those who are able to benefit monetarily from it. The conflict between fans and owners is inherent in many of the platforms fans use to create and share their fanworks. As Jenkins, Ford and Green demonstrate throughout their book *Spreadable Media*, too much control can lead to fans disconnecting from the original work due to the unstable relationship between the parties, where only owners have the right to pull the plug. They state (2013: 83):

> Web 2.0 discourse assumes that fan participation is highly generative – yielding new insights, creating new value, reaching new audiences – but the business model often isolates the resulting texts from the social contexts within which they were produced and circulated, thus devaluing notions of reciprocity. Many Web 2.0 companies have sought to assert total ownership over content generation by the fans, even after having sought to strengthen participants' sense of personal interests in order to placate the contested assertion of intellectual property claims posed by other commercial interests.

WHO GETS PAID? FANDOM AS FREE LABOR

One of the most important elements regarding fanworks is the continued principle that fans are not to be paid for their efforts. Abigail De Kosnik (2013) has therefore asked whether fan culture's insistence on non-commerciality is lining the pockets of everyone but fans. Tushnet states that 'fans are only noncommercial in a particular sense, and that sense is that if there is any money on the table, it certainly won't be flowing towards the fans' (Tushnet 2010: 4). As De Kosnik puts it (2013: 105):

> because fans generally conceive of their activities as 'resistive' to consumerism, they refuse to consider that their works might constitute either promotional materials or ancillary products that increase the value of the objects of fandom and therefore might be deserving of compensation, either from official producers or from other consumers.

Fanworks do have value – but determining the impact of each individual work is nigh on impossible:

> Fan-made videos, websites, commentary, posters and other artworks, stories, songs, and reviews merge with the stream of official advertising and promotion that surrounds any given product – fan labor can ramp up the buzz and reputation of the product, and it can reinforce the pull or allure that the product exerts on would-be consumers, but it would be impossible to tell what percentage of sales of the product had resulted from fans' efforts versus those of the paid corporate marketers. (De Kosnik 2013: 109)

Adjusting the present formula where authors and owners hold the legal right to attempt to shut down fanworks without much legal pushback from fans, will take changes from all sides. It would take 'both fans and corporations acknowledging that fandom is a form of labor that adds value to mass-produced commodities and is worthy of compensation' (De Kosnik 2013: 110).

There have been attempts to pay fans in small ways. In 2013, Amazon launched Kindle Worlds, a platform for fanfiction writers to publish and make money from their works, mostly through royalty payments for copies sold to other fans. Many fandom communities had a skeptical approach, partially because there are a limited selection of titles and fandoms, and there are content limitations on the works authorized through this platform. Another concern was the loss of control fanwork creators would face when signing away their rights in order to use this platform. The only real advantage most fans saw to the Amazon effort was the ability to create in a sandbox where they would not be sued for creating fanworks, due to the fanfiction.

THE STATE OF THE LAW IN THE UNITED STATES

Is the main question regarding the status of fanworks one of law or of practice? Some legal experts view it as primarily an issue of the interpretation of copyright, while others have a more interdisciplinary view: an issue of balancing the law with a widespread cultural practice that is only now being brought to the forefront by the Internet. More traditional legal experts tend to view fanfiction as a copyright concern: 'It is still an open question whether much fanfiction is an infringement of the derivative work right under copyright law or rather may be excused as a fair use' (Lipton 2011: 579). Media studies experts view the concern with fanworks as an issue now bubbling to the surface, even though many of the qualities in the creation of fanworks have existed for quite some time. With increased access online, these works become more visible, placing previously hidden and private activities in the public eye. Within the United States:

> some people describe these shifts as a crisis in copyright and others a crisis in fair use. Fans defend perceived rights and practices that have been taken for granted for many years. ... Corporations, on the other hand, want to constrain behaviors they see as damaging and having a much larger impact in the digital era. Both sides accuse the other of exploiting the instability created by shifts in technology and media infrastructure. (Jenkins et al. 2013: 54)

United States copyright law allows for copyright owners to control the creation of derivative works. However, additionally within United States law, the use of the works of others is acceptable within specific limits. The fair use doctrine, a flexible four-factor test, allows non-licensed use of copyrighted materials, to avoid 'stifl[ing] the very creativity which that law is designed to foster' (*Campbell v. Acuff-Rose Music*, 1994: 577). The factors must be used together in each individual case and no one factor can make the determination, codified in the Copyright Act of 1976:

> (1) the purpose and character of the use, including whether such use is of a commercial nature or is for nonprofit educational purposes;
> (2) the nature of the copyrighted work;
> (3) the amount and substantiality of the portion used in relation to the copyrighted work as a whole; and
> (4) the effect of the use upon the potential market for or value of the copyrighted work.

As the Supreme Court in *Campbell v. Acuff-Rose Music* (1994: 577) has warned, '[t]he task is not to be simplified with bright-line rules', and courts must always keep in mind 'the purposes of copyright'.

Fanworks are an example of secondary creativity. Generally used within the context of the 'fair use' copyright doctrine, the concept of secondary creativity is a useful way to distinguish between an original work – primary creativity – and secondary creativity, which allows creators to build on the prior creativity of others. Some examples of secondary creativity include timeless ones such as folk tales and folk songs. There are also more recent types of fan creation such as musical 'mash-ups' (when the vocals or instrumentals of two or more original songs are combined into a new song). As the Supreme Court stated in *Campbell*, the important question when dealing with the value of secondary creativity is 'whether the new work merely 'supersede[s] the objects of the original creation ... or instead adds something new, with a further purpose or different character, altering the first with new expression, meaning, or message; it asks, in other words, whether and to what extent the new work is "transformative"' (*Campbell v. Acuff-Rose Music* 1994: 578).

Generally, the idea of thinking about and speculating on what could happen to characters is still within the realm of rights copyright owners possess for in-copyright works. In its discussion of JD California's *60 Years Later*, an unauthorized sequel to JD Salinger's *The Catcher in the Rye* (Salinger, 1951), for example, the District Court acknowledged the importance of audience speculation, 'what ifs' about characters' potential futures, but left the control for anything beyond a discussion between fans in the hands of the copyright owner. The court found that fair use should not protect the ability to publish unauthorized sequels:

> [B]ecause some artists may be further incentivized to create original works due to the availability of the right not to produce any sequels. This might be the case if, for instance, an author's artistic vision includes leaving certain portions or aspects of his character's story to the varied imaginations of his readers, or if he hopes that his readers will engage in discussion and speculation as to what happened subsequently. (*Salinger v. Colting* 2009: 268)

Depending on one's viewpoint, this can mean that fanworks are protected by fair use if they are transformative enough – or if they do not affect the marketplace. But because each fanwork requires an individualized determination through the fair use factors, uncertainty persists. And especially now, whether a work is parody (versus satire) or of high quality matters more than ever before.

WHY SATIRE, PARODY, AND QUALITY MATTER, YET ACCEPTANCE BY THE COPYRIGHT OWNER USUALLY DOESN'T

Within the context of United States copyright law, the distinction between satire and parody causes differences in how fanworks are treated. Parody copies from the object it mocks, while satire uses recognizable elements from the original work to mock something else or society in general. Parody is 'fair use' and thus protected, it is much more difficult to prove that satire is fair use.

This definition seems very straightforward, but real world examples show how difficult it is to work within the distinction between parody and satire. For example, with many mash-up videos created by fans, there can be two or more fandoms and original works at issue. What happens to the analysis when a fanwork is a parody of one work, a satire of two more, using elements from a couple more, and uses the music from yet another? For example, *Yu-gi-oh: The Abridged Series* overdubs episodes of the Japanese children's card game show *Yu-gi-oh* with multiple elements, leading to a series that is a pastiche of many different copyrighted works. All episodes include elements that are a parody of the original show (such as making fun of the concept of a children's card game being the focus of the lives of the characters, with incongruities added into the English original dub, and developing the rich inner lives of the characters) and satirize other parts of popular culture, such as memes and gaming culture, while at the same time generally using elements of popular culture in ways that are outside of both satire and parody. The show also serves as a meta-commentary about itself – the fair use issues the show has faced through its use of clips, sounds and more during the now over six years of this show's running. Without the satirical elements, the show would not be as interesting to those that watch it. Only by combining these varied elements can this web series retain its humor (Little Kuriboh 2006–2014). By using multiple properties, the fan creator is more and more likely to have at least one of the copyright owners object, but the multitude of different influences is more likely to make the work transformative and less likely to serve as a market substitution for any of the starting works.

The importance of whether a work is satire in determining whether fair use exists was the focus of *Salinger v. Colting* (2009, 2010), a case about the novel *60 Years Later: Coming Through the Rye*. The protagonist in *60 Years Later*, Mr C, is an aged Holden Caulfield, the main character in JD Salinger's acclaimed novel *The Catcher in the Rye*. While *60 Years Later* follows many of the elements of a fanwork, such as using a recognizable character and taking them in a different direction from the original, the court determined that the work was not a permissible fair use and enjoined its publication. The court concluded that *60 Years Later* was not a parody because it 'contain[ed] no reasonably discernible rejoinder or specific criticism of any character or theme of Catcher' (*Salinger v. Colting* 2009: 258). Rather than commenting on Holden Caulfield as a character, the purpose of *60 Years Later* was to 'satisfy Holden's fans' passion' (*Salinger v. Colting* 2009: 260). While reviewing the District Court's order, the Second Circuit agreed 'the defendant and his work lack a transformative purpose' (*Salinger v. Colting* 2010: 83).

Another complicating factor is the quality of fanworks. Copyright owners would not be likely to want fanworks to be as good as the original, and thus serve as a replacement work, but they would also not prefer for them to be poor quality either, causing potential fans or purchasers to avoid the original work. While some fanfiction writers do succeed in creating interpretations of existing fictional works that may rival these works in quality, there is no shortage of fan-writing of dubious quality. However, 'even poorly written fanworks are representative of the fan's own desires and/or viewpoint. … In fact, one of the positives of fanfiction is that unsophisticated voices still get to have a say' (Montano 2013: 704). In either case the actions taken by the authors of original works to protect what they see as the artistic integrity of their original creation is understandable. From the perspective of content owners, a fanwork of too high quality could serve as a replacement for the original; thereby they may prefer low quality fanworks. However, authors of the original work may not want their work to be 'disparaged' by low quality work either. While a high-quality fanwork may take away some of their market, if it is in the 'right voice' it at least does not insult the overall 'feel' of the original.

One of the important lessons from the Harry Potter Lexicon case is that walking the line between high and low quality is an important one for creators of fanworks to make – at least within the context of fair use determinations in the United States. (*Warner Bros.* 2008). Overall, the decision in favor of the copyright owner gives a distinct impression that if one is to base a work on that of another, it should be of high quality – and that means not too much direct copying:

> The Lexicon's verbatim copying of such highly aesthetic expression raises a significant question as to whether it was reasonably necessary for the purpose of creating a useful and complete reference guide. … Verbatim copying of this nature demonstrates Vander Ark's lack of restraint due to an enthusiastic admiration of Rowling's artistic expression, or perhaps haste and laziness as Rowling suggested … in composing the Lexicon entries. (*Warner Bros.* 2008: 547–548)

Regardless of the quality, however, the copyright owner/author always has the ability to attempt to shut down the use of their owned property at any moment, even if direct acceptance have occurred. Acceptance by the original author doesn't prevent lawsuits by the copyright owner, frequently leaving fans in a precarious position. Also, authors or copyright owners can pull their tacit or stated acceptance of fanworks at any time, meaning that any fanwork could lead to litigation even if originally created within a different, and more accepting context.

As stated by Ann Bartow, *Twilight* series author Stephenie Meyer generally allows for fanworks, however:

> Meyer can make content-based decisions about which actionable, unauthorized uses she will tolerate and which she will smite … Perhaps Meyer simply ignores the reader-driven choices her characters make that she would never permit them. But, she could attempt to control Bella's fan-based sexuality selectively based on her own moral, social, or political views. The statutory bulwark that could constrain this – facilitating freer expression

> by her fans, critics, or emulators and less control by Meyer – is fair use. (Bartow 2010: 78–79)

However, courts could potentially rule in favor of either Meyer or the fans. Furthermore, except in rare instances, the fans have fewer means to fight for their fair use rights than authors or owners have in attempting to minimize such use. The issue of having to walk the line of acceptance by the work's owner is part of what has led to most fan communities remaining subcultural in most countries. However, Japan has a unique model for fanworks that benefits all – fans, original creators and copyright owners.

INTERNATIONAL INFLUENCES: DOUJINSHI

Japan's fan culture is different from other countries in its acceptance of fanworks. At the same time, these works are technically illegal. *Doujinshi* (sometimes written as *dōjinshi* or *dojinshi*) are fan-made comics, 'written by authors using the well-known characters of another, more famous, author' commonly deriving elements from *manga* (comics), *anime* (animation) or video game sources (Mehra 2002: 156). *Doujinshi* creators create and distribute their works under two very different conditions than most creators of fanworks – first, many create with the purpose of making money, and second, their work tends to be supported by the copyright owners. Japanese copyright law (*chosakuken*) has not been changed to allow for these *doujinshi* markets – these creations still technically infringe Japanese copyright law. These works are frequently called parody, but such a description minimizes the breadth of possibilities contained in the new works.

As described by Lawrence Lessig in *Free Culture*, *doujinshi* require an important creative difference from the original to be accepted:

> It is not doujinshi if it is *just* a copy; the artist must make a contribution to the art he copies, by transforming it either subtly or significantly. … There is no formula for what makes the doujinshi sufficiently 'different.' But they must be different if they are to be considered true doujinshi. (2004: 25–27)

While the default is to allow *doujinshi* to flourish without interference from the copyright owner, there have been at least two well-publicized incidents of copyright owners challenging *doujinshi* – both where the specific *doujinshi* had the potential to impact the market. An 'adult' version of Pokémon and an imagined 'final' episode of Doraémon with the artistic quality to compete with the original were both challenged as copyright violations (Ingulsrud and Allen 2009: 49). These cases were settled out of court, and the creator of the Doraémon 'ending' issued a public apology and shared profits with the copyright owners. However, generally, large mainstream media owners participate and support many of the *doujinshi* markets, like Comiket, the world's largest *doujinshi* fair, held twice a year, with attendance figures of around half a million people. The reasons for the acceptance of these unauthorized works are quite complex. Generally, it is seen as *anmoku no ryokai*, meaning an unspoken, implicit agreement, because 'the dojinshi are creating a market base, and that market base is naturally drawn to the original work' (Pink 2007).

One notable aspect of this acceptance of fanworks in Japan is how the line between what is an official author or creation and what is an unofficial work is drawn. *Doujinshi* can cover anything that is not released by the official publisher, officially. In addition to being created by fans, amateurs and others, *doujinshi* is frequently used as the same way 'spec scripts' are used in the entertainment industry – allowing aspiring official *manga* creators to show their talents to potential employers and to also allow official *manga* artists to release manga outside of official publishing channels, due to publishing regulations or schedules. Additionally, as seen within Western fan creator communities, *doujinshi* can help keep interest alive in completed or slumbering properties – and help to keep up fan interest in active media properties.

Generally, the creation of these fanworks is seen as highly positive, with most academics viewing these markets as parallel to, or supportive of, rather than competing with, the official copyright market. As Foster emphasizes:

> of particular note, doujinshi do not necessarily steal profits from the original, but enhance the market for the original by causing customers and fans that enjoy the parodies to seek out the original. It is perhaps for this reason that copyright holders and the authors of the original works have generally let doujinshi authors continue with their art. (Foster 2013: 315–316)

Others view the acceptance of *doujinshi* as a result of its being of direct benefit to the mainstream industry, through increasing loyalty in a way that supports the most intense fans, and creating market data that cannot be duplicated at any cost by highlighting which properties create the most popular, long tail or upswell in *doujinshi* (Pink 2007).

As Pink (2007) states, balancing the interests of owners and fans is extralegal:

> instead of rewriting a national statute or hashing out separate individual contracts or crafting special licenses, it leaves everything unsaid ... It takes the situation out of the realm of law... It places the established publishers and the dojinshi creators in something resembling the prisoners' dilemma: If they cooperate – that is, if they honor the terms of *anmoku no ryokai* – they both gain. But if one overreaches – if publishers crack down aggressively or if dojinshi creators go too far – they both suffer.

Either everyone wins or everyone loses.

INTERNATIONAL INFLUENCES: MORAL RIGHTS

Moral rights are additional rights that creators receive for investing themselves in authorial and artistic expressions. They attach to copyrighted works separate from the copyright in the work itself. These rights are generally recognized in civil law jurisdictions, having originated in France and Germany. Generally, these rights are considered to be so important in European civil law jurisdictions that they cannot be assigned, meaning that even if the author of a work sells the copyright to another, the author still has moral rights in the work. There are some limited moral rights in common law jurisdictions, including in the United Kingdom, Canada and other jurisdictions formerly under the British crown. In the United States, moral rights are smaller than in other common law jurisdictions, restricted only to a very limited set of visual art.

There are two moral rights that are the most popular. The right of attribution (*droit à la paternité*) is the author's right to be recognized as the author of the work and the right of integrity (*droit au respect de l'oeuvre*) is the author's power to prevent any tampering with the work as a whole. Moral rights are different than the rights given under traditional copyright law because they focus on a continued connection between the creator and the work – rather than economic incentives. The right of attribution and integrity are contained in Article 6bis(1) of the Berne Convention, obligating signatory countries to protect an author's rights of attribution and rights of integrity:

> Independently of the author's economic rights, and even after the transfer of the said rights, the author shall have the right to claim authorship of the work and to object to any distortion, mutilation or other modification of, or other derogatory action in relation to, the said work, which would be prejudicial to his honor or reputation. (Berne Convention 1979: Article 6bis(1))

It is possible that the creation of fanworks is pre-emptively forbidden within a strict moral rights system, considering that fanworks do not keep the original work as a whole. Instead, fanworks purposely reinterpret and change the work's meaning, giving it greater cultural resonance as it departs from the integrity of the original. How would a fanwork creator in a jurisdiction with strong moral rights protection ensure that they do not possibly create 'a false impression about the [original] author's intended meaning or message' so as to protect themselves from the possibility of litigation (Lipton 2011: 578–579)? While copyright has a theoretical endpoint of approximately the life of the author plus some number of years, moral rights – or at least raising them, does not seem to have an ending. After all, despite the fact that the copyright term had long since expired worldwide, the descendants of Victor Hugo attempted to protect his reputation from unauthorized works such as sequels to *Les Misérables* using a moral rights framework. These attempts failed overall, because the right of adaptation did not survive the copyright term (*Les Misérables* 2007).

DON QUIXOTE, HARRY POTTER AND G-DRAGON

To illustrate the complications inherent in works created as fanworks, this section will focus on a few examples that blur the lines of ownership and creativity. Starting in 1615 and moving to the present, these examples span three different cultures – Spain in the 1600s, the worldwide reinterpretation of the British Harry Potter book series over the past decade, and a South Korean official music video with footage by fans.

Don Quixote, written by Miguel de Cervantes Saavedra in 1605 and 1615 is viewed as the first modern novel and deals with the issue of unauthorized sequels within the text of the novel itself. The second half of the book, written ten years after the first half, specifically responds to the unauthorized, not parody, sequel written by the pseudonymous author, Alonso Fernández de Avellaneda. The characters are 'aware' of the first authorized book – and how wrong the unauthorized sequel gets their characters.

While there was no copyright lawsuit, considering that *Don Quixote* predates the first copyright law, the Statute of Anne, enacted in Great Britain, by a hundred years, there is a legal-ish solution built into the novel. Don Quixote 'meets' one of the unauthorized characters Don Alvaro Tarfe, and convinces Tarfe to swear an affidavit, confirmed with a notary that he has never previously encountered the real Don Quixote or Sancho Pancha. (Cervantes 1615: Chapter 72). Therefore, Cervantes has managed to co-opt a character from another's unwanted sequel into his own work. In a moral rights regime, both the unauthorized sequel and Cervantes' response would not be allowed. Because the fake sequel's author also has moral rights regarding his storytelling elements, Cervantes would be unable to turn his moment of humiliation – having his characters 'stolen' by another – into an opportunity to turn the critique back on itself.

The next two examples of fanworks are from within a time when copyright not only exists, but where copyright protection is strong. Since the publication of the Harry Potter books and the release of the licensed movies, several fan communities have built up around the 'Potterverse'. These communities include those who write fanfiction, those who play a non-magical version of Quiddich (the sport created by Rowling), those who write and perform songs (generally called wizard rock) related to the 'Potterverse', as well as many other fan-related activities. Generally, J.K. Rowling is accepting of those who write fanworks, but there are exceptions. Fanworks that are 'adult' in nature or compete with actual or potential authorized works are deemed highly problematic. An additional wrinkle is that the trademarks in Harry Potter are not owned by J.K. Rowling, but by Warner Brothers.

The line between acceptable and non-acceptable fanworks has led to several lawsuits. For example, a Harry Potter reference book, created as an online encyclopedia with a large number of fans helping to make the entries accurate, was enjoined from publication. In *Warner Bros. Entertainment, Inc. and J. K. Rowling v. RDR Books*, the court stated:

> In striking the balance between the property rights of original authors and the freedom of expression of secondary authors, reference guides to works of literature should generally be encouraged by copyright law as they provide a benefit [for] readers and students; but ... they should not be permitted

> to 'plunder' the works of original authors ... 'without paying the customary price' ... lest original authors lose incentive to create new works that will also benefit the public interest. (*Warner Bros.* 2008: 551)

When Vander Ark, the author of the Lexicon, signed his book deal there was no consideration of any compensation to the countless fans that contributed and made the website a success. So the lawsuit was a fight between the author and the compiler/host of a fan-created work. But the fans that have contributed to the Lexicon got neither money nor recognition for their contributions.

The Lexicon case was mostly conceived as a struggle between the competing interests of an author trying to protect her copyrighted work (the derivative works right) and the interests of a sole author creating a new work (fair use). During the Lexicon trial, the larger fan community and their input adding to the Lexicon or their interest generally in making fanworks was not directly considered because fans were not party to the case. The exclusion of any mention of fan labor and fan contributions is unfortunate. However, there are helpful nuggets for those who are engaged in fanworks in the District Court's ruling finding for Warner Brothers and Rowling.

The key to the determination that the Lexicon was not protected by fair use was that the Lexicon copied too much of the original text – and did a poor job in creating a reference work. Somewhat snarkily, the court held that:

> Perhaps because Vander Ark is such a Harry Potter enthusiast, the Lexicon often lacks restraint in using Rowling's original expression for its inherent entertainment and aesthetic value. ... Although the Lexicon is generally useful, it cannot claim consistency in serving its purpose of pointing readers to information in the Harry Potter works. Some of the longest entries contain few or no citations to the Harry Potter works from which the material is taken. (*Warner Bros.* 2008: 544)

The poor quality of the Lexicon continues to be an issue in the court's analysis, leading to the conclusion that 'the Lexicon disturbs the balance' between using copyrighted material of others and imparting useful information, by using too much the original Harry Potter books, through verbatim copying (*Warner Bros.* 2008: 548). Fanworks rarely copy verbatim as the Lexicon did, focusing instead on characters, settings and plots, so by stepping further away from the original, most fanworks are sufficiently transformative.

The final example uses the work of multiple fans to help build a music video. What happens when the copyright owner directs the fans to generate content for him? While not a fanwork in a more traditional sense, this last example investigates what happens when the work of multiple fans is then used in a way that only supports the economic interests of the copyright owner/author. What becomes clear is that for many fans, the loss of 'ownership' in their work is less important than being included within the larger fan culture and sometimes being acknowledged by the object of their fandom.

In 2013, a major K-pop (a South Korean popular music genre) star, G-Dragon relied on his fans to provide footage for his music video, 니가 뭔데 (WHO YOU?). This is not an original idea for musical acts with intense fandoms – both Metallica and the Beastie Boys released long-form concert videos taken from fan-recorded videos. However, what makes this music video unique is twofold – the acknowledgement of fan contributions is the first text that appears on the screen in both Korean and English – 'This video was made by G-Dragon and the personal recordings of 1,000 of [his] fans'. Additionally, the fans are actively included within the video as fans – they are participants in the process, appearing in the snippets recorded by other fans. The end of the video includes the names of all of the fans that contributed. Thinking about the fan recording in a solely copyright context (assuming that their entrance to the recording studio allowed each fan recording), each fan has a copyright in the portion of the video in which they appear, but the sound recording is still copyrighted by whomever owns that copyright. However, what these fans are looking for more than copyright in their own recordings is the ability to participate in fan culture, which they are able to do here, and specifically to have their contribution acknowledged. This example is one that works for both the original artists and the fans – they share in the credit, though not the money.

CONCLUSION

Thinking about fanworks solely as the production of individual fans or even as the cultural production of fan communities is too limiting to the contributions of fans; yet fans are not on one side with authors and owners on the other. However, at present, the contributions of fans in making the intellectual property of others valuable is not fully understood or appreciated by copyright owners. Our present legal regimes honor the sanctity of original works, their owners and creators, without appreciating the impact fans have in making those properties valuable. The ability of fans and fanfiction to keep the works of others alive should not be minimized, especially considering the long tail of copyright and of works that are no longer being 'exploited'. Fans also allow for multiple streams of interest for works in the public domain. There are separate fandoms for all of the recent Sherlock Holmes properties, for example – including the American and UK television shows, the Hollywood movies, as well as more niche programs based on Sherlock Holmes. Jenkins, Ford, and Green (2013: 297) state that:

> fans 'act as "multipliers" who attach new meaning to existing properties, as "appraisers" who evaluate the worth of different bids on our attention, as "lead users" who anticipate new markets for newly released content, as "retro curators" who discover forgotten content which may still hold cultural and economic value, as "pop cosmopolitans" who seek cultural difference and help to educate others about content they've discovered from other parts of the world'.

There are plenty of opportunities to balance the needs of fans with those who currently have more control. In writing about the Kindle Worlds platform for 'authorized' fanworks, Chaney (2013) suggests a potential market that could benefit a number of parties:

> I recently had a thought about where there might be a happy medium between profit motive and fan inspiration, in a way that is (less) exploitative for fans and perhaps beneficial for all: copyright holders, production companies and fan creators alike. What if Kindle Worlds (or a similar licensed fanworks publisher) specialized exclusively in fanworks for dormant or dead fandoms? Cancelled shows, older films, etc. Working with the license holder for said show and coming up with a partnership to create 'semi-canonical' fanworks for sale. It keeps interest in a fandom alive for fans but also keeps interest in a media franchise alive for media owners. It would be America's equivalent to Japan's (mostly) live-and-let-live approach to *dōjinshi*.

Everyone has something to gain – and alternatively to lose – in our present legal regime, assuming the proper balance is struck around creative works. To make the system of sharing creative works not grind to a halt, all parties need to make it work because:

> 'any party can block or slow the spread of texts: if creators [or content owners] construct legal or technical blocks, if third-party platform owners choose to restrict the ways in which material can circulate, or if audiences refuse to circulate content which fails to serve their own interests' (Jenkins et al. 2013: 294)

The creation of fanworks is only one part of the creative system, but it is an essential one, as another example of the continued diffusion of culture.

REFERENCES

Bartow, Ann (2010) 'Bloodsucking Copyrights', *Maryland Law Review*, 70(1): 62–86.

Berne Convention for the Protection of Literary and Artistic Works (1928, 1979, as amended).

Campbell v. Acuff-Rose Music, (1994) 510 U.S. 569 (United States Supreme Court)

Cervantes Saavedra, Miguel de (1605, 1615) *Don Quixote [El ingenioso hidalgo don Quijote de la Mancha].*

Chaney, Keidra (2013) 'Fanfiction For Sale: Could Kindle Worlds Keep Dormant Fandoms Alive?', *The Learned Fangirl*, 11 August 2013. www.thelearnedfangirl.com/2013/08/11/fanfiction-for-sale-could-kindle-worlds-keep-dormant-fandoms-alive/

De Kosnik, Abigail (2013) 'Fandom as Free Labor', in Trevor Scholz (ed.), *Digital Labor: The Internet as Playground and Factory*. New York: Routledge. pp. 98–111.

Doyle, Arthur Conan (1894) 'The Final Problem', in *The Memoirs of Sherlock Holmes*. London: George Newnes.

Doyle, Arthur Conan (1905) 'The Adventure of the Empty House', in *The Return of Sherlock Holmes*, New York: McClure, Phillips & Co.

Foster, Mariko (2013) 'Parody's Precarious Place: The Need to Legally Recognize Parody As Japan's Cultural Property', *Seton Hall Journal of Sports & Entertainment Law*, 23(2): 313–344.

Gaines, Jane (1991) *Contested Culture: The Image, the Voice, and the Law*. Chapel Hill: University of North Carolina Press.

G-Dragon. (2013) 니 가 뭔데 (WHO YOU?).

Ingulsrud, John and Allen, Kate (2009) *Reading Japan Cool: Patterns of Manga Literacy and Discourse*. Lanham: Lexington Books.

Japanese Copyright Act [Chosakuken] (2013) http://www.cric.or.jp/english/clj/cl2.html

Jenkins, Henry, Ford, Sam and Green, Joshua (2013) *Spreadable Media: Creating Value and Meaning in a Networked Culture*. New York: New York University Press.

Les Misérables (2007) No. 04-14.543 (Cour de cassation [French Supreme Court]).

Lessig, Laurence (2004) *Free Culture: How Big Media Uses Technology and the Law to Lock Down Culture and Control Creativity*. New York: Penguin.

Lichtenberg, Jacqueline (2013) 'Recollections of a Collating Party', in Anne Jamison (ed.), *Fic: Why Fanfiction is Taking Over the World*. Dallas, Texas: BenBella Books, pp. 91–99.

Lipton, Jacqueline (2011) 'Moral Rights and Supernatural Fiction: Authorial Dignity and the New Moral Rights Agendas', *Fordham Intellectual Property, Media & Entertainment Law Journal*, 21(3): 537–580.

Little Kuriboh (2006–2014) *Yu-gi-oh: The Abridged Series* www.yugiohabridged.com/?p=about

Mehra, Salil (2002) 'Copyright and Comics in Japan: Does Law Explain Why All the Cartoons My Kid Watches Are Japanese Imports?', *Rutgers Law Review*, 55(1): 155–204.

Montano, Natalie (2013) 'Hero with a Thousand Copyright Violations: Modern Myth and an Argument for Universally Transformative Fan Fiction', *Northwestern Journal of Technology & Intellectual Property*, 11(7): 689–705.

Noda, Nathaniel (2010) 'Copyrights Retold: How Interpretive Rights Foster Creativity and Justify Fan-Based Activities', *Seton Hall Journal of Sports & Entertainment Law*, 20(1): 131–164.

Pink, Daniel (2007) 'Japan, Ink: Inside the Manga Industrial Complex', *Wired*, 15(11): 216–223, available at http://archive.wired.com/techbiz/media/magazine/15-11/ff_manga?currentPage=all

Rowling, J.K. (1997) *Harry Potter and the Philosopher's Stone*. London: Bloomsbury.

Salinger, J.D. (1951) *The Catcher in the Rye*. Boston: Little, Brown.

Salinger v. Colting, (2009) 641 F. Supp. 2d 250 (Southern District of New York).

Salinger v. Colting, (2010) 607 F.3d 68 (Second Circuit Court of Appeals).

Tushnet, Rebecca (1997) 'Legal Fictions: Copyright, Fan Fiction, and A New Common Law', *Loyola Los Angeles Entertainment Law Journal*, 17(3): 651–686.

Tushnet, Rebecca. (2010) 'Hybrid Vigor: Mashups, Cyborgs, and Other Necessary Monsters', *I/S: A Journal of Law and Policy for the Information Society*, 6(1): 1–12.

United States Copyright Act of 1976, (2006) 17 United States Code §§ 101–22.

Warner Bros. Entertainment, Inc. and J. K. Rowling v. RDR Books, (2008) 575 F.Supp.2d 513 (Southern District of New York).

22

Copyright and Film Historiography: The Case of the Orphan Film

Claudy Op den Kamp

INTRODUCTION

The 1962 Dutch feature film *De overval* (*The Silent Raid*, dir. Paul Rotha, Sapphire Film Productions NV, NL, 1962) tells the story of a silent raid on the House of Detention in the city of Leeuwarden in the north of the Netherlands in December 1944. In this raid, a small group of men forced their way into the penitentiary and liberated 51 members of the resistance movement. The film holds a special place in Dutch history and film history since it was the first feature film that dealt with the Second World War resistance movement.

In 2003, the Nederlands Filmmuseum and the Frisian Resistance Museum made an attempt to publish *De overval* on DVD. The project had been placed on hold several times before. What had stalled the project before was the failure to answer the question of who owned the copyright of the film as it was not obvious. Publishing the film on DVD entailed both reproducing the work and communicating the work to the public, both copyright restricted activities, and so permission needed to be obtained from the rights owner. The Frisian Resistance Museum had a large constituency of interested consumers with an appetite for the film, but held no original film elements. The Filmmuseum held the original film material, but not the copyright.

The first step in determining the film's current copyright owner was to establish whether the film was still in copyright at all. Article 40 of the Dutch *Auteurswet* states that the:

> copyright in a cinematographic work shall expire 70 years after 1 January of the year following the year of death of the last of the following persons to survive: the principal director, the author of the screenplay, the author of the dialogue and the composer of the music created for use in the work.

The author of the screenplay, Dr Loe de Jong was still alive in 2003 (he died in 2005) so the term of protection was indeed still active.

The next step in establishing who owned the copyright was trying to uncover who owned it first. Although the contracts that would prove ownership were missing, it was assumed that the film was made in the course of employment and that therefore Sapphire Film Productions as the employer was the first copyright owner of the film. To track the production company's history, trade papers were researched at the Chamber of Commerce in Amsterdam. In 1973, Sapphire Film Productions went bankrupt and was purchased by Tuschinski Film Distribution BV. Information in the trade papers, such as names of former owners as well as bankruptcy curators were thought to be instrumental in helping to determine what happened to Sapphire's assets after its purchase. However, none of the contact information was up-to-date. Less official leads were also investigated and contact was established with numerous individuals connected to the film or its production company: former owners of Tuschinski, the company that bought Sapphire upon their bankruptcy and their children (as possible heirs); the archivist at Pathé, the company who now owns the Tuschinski archive; directors of the other films produced by Sapphire and their children, as the copyright situation of their films might help elucidate what happened to *De overval*; film distribution companies that distributed the film and audio-visual archives that had film prints and donation files as information in those records and a possible financial trail might help clear up the copyright situation. After several months of research the turning points in Sapphire's company history remained obscure and there was no conclusive answer to the copyright ownership question.

Despite the lack of an identified copyright owner, the Filmmuseum decided to pursue the DVD production of the film. A different archive might, of course, have taken a different decision. The particular risk was taken based on the assumption that the record of the attempts that were undertaken to trace the possible owner could possibly be used as a future indemnification.

In 2003, *De overval* was one example of a problematic title in one specific archive, and in 2013, ten years after the initial research took place, the copyright situation has not been resolved and the film's ownership has not been claimed.[1] *De overval* is a so-called *orphan work*, a work without an identified or located copyright owner, and is part of a larger *orphan works problem*. The film is an illustrative case study to show how untraceable copyright owners, and the consequent inability to clear the rights in such a work, can halt or significantly delay the distribution of archival film. Strictly legally speaking, if the permission for re-use cannot be obtained, the re-use should be withheld, and potentially beneficial uses are hindered.

It may be clear that having to trace a copyright owner is a time-consuming process and not possible at this level for every title, and that the relation between the steps that have to be taken in order to trace someone and the actual benefit of that process, making the material available so it can 'reach its potential for film history making' (Jones, 2012: 119), is unbalanced. In as much as the availability of materials to view shapes our understanding of cinema's past, and arguably our sense of history in a wider context, the chapter argues that a resituating of the debate is needed and highlights how the orphan works problem in the context of an audio-visual archive is not to be understood as the effect of a specific legal discourse but as part of a more complex issue – the relation between the audio-visual archive and the dynamics of film history – in which film history is co-constructed by the institutions that control the evidentiary products.

THE AUDIO-VISUAL ARCHIVE, COPYRIGHT OWNERSHIP AND THE HISTORICAL NARRATIVE

In UNESCO's *A Philosophy of Audiovisual Archiving*, Ray Edmondson (1998) quotes a definition[2] of an audio-visual archive as 'an organization or department of an organization which is focused on collecting, managing, preserving and providing access to a collection of audiovisual media and the audiovisual heritage' (1998: 7). The image of a professional and well-run institution with certain protocols and collection policies in place is often a realistic one. It is, however, worth zooming in on the material reality of an archive, as the provenance of the material will highlight why some of the legal metadata is incomplete with lacunal access as a consequence.

In his 1983 book *Les Cinémathèques*, Raymond Borde indicates 'collective destructions' (1983: 18), such as the replacement of silent film by sound film in the 1930s and the abandonment of the inflammable nitrate film stock in favour of the acetate one in the 1950s, as some of the major motivations for the emergence of film archives. Historically, but also nowadays, large parts of archival holdings start as 'stuff' arriving at the archive's back door. Distributors deposit multiple copies of feature films in the film archive after their theatrical run is over. Also, individuals, such as filmmakers and collectors, donate or deposit their private holdings with an archive. It might even happen that a collection of materials is donated anonymously.

An archive's intentional selection, acquisition and exchange choices will further shape the haphazard nature of the archive's collection. An archive is not a collection of exclusively complete titles; it houses a heterogeneous collection of, amongst others, multiple versions of the same title, out-takes, unedited camera negatives, incomplete films, unidentified films and fragments. There might also be projectors, posters, film stills, filmmakers' paper archives or even film props. These holdings comprise innumerable types of different formats, only some of which have become worldwide standards while some others will be no longer playable.

Film archives around the world are different in their origins, sizes, organizational structures and funding; they can be funded publicly, privately or in some other way that is a combination of the two. Some of these organizational structures might have consequences for the composition of their respective collections, as the holdings of most public archives seem to be characterized by a national or regional focus, whereas the holdings of most privately held archives seem to be characterized by copyright ownership (Fossati, 2009). Public sector institutions usually own the copyright to only a small portion of their collections; the majority of the holdings will be owned by an outside party. Material that no one owns (public domain material) or of which it is unknown who owns it (orphan works) make up the other parts. Donations or deposits to these archives can be large parties and often there is not enough manpower to immediately identify and catalogue the material correctly. This backlog means that the origins of notably older parts of collections will not always be clear, which has immediate implications for locating copyright holders at a later stage.

A 're-categorization' of archival holdings according to their legal status, as outlined in the next two parts of the chapter, will unravel some of the contemporary economic factors at work in archival access. The re-categorization will further be used to show that in the context of an audio-visual archive the orphan works problem, which initially can be seen as an exclusively legal problem, masks a much larger problem; the problem of history. The archive as an institution is itself an artefact of a historical narrative, while at the same time it is an instrument for the formation of such a narrative. Audio-visual archives can be seen as a sort of 'grab bag' of history; there are many stories to be told and through their preservation strategies, for instance, archives help shape the particular narrative that is told. The re-evaluation of colour in early cinema by means of new restoration techniques can be seen as a classic example (Meyer, 2011). Based on the same material, an alternative story can be told, just by sieving the material differently.

Moving image archives, housing a remnant of historical filmic evidence, and the availability of that material influence the way in which film history is understood; film historians describe and analyse film history based on the films that film museums have collected, restored and provided access to over the course of the years (Lameris, 2007). Film professor and founder of the Orphan Film Symposium, Dan Streible, emphasizes that the visible part of the archive is only a partial picture, as for various (political, economic, curatorial, etc.) reasons 'historians are not seeing most of the films that exist to be studied' (2009: ix). By scrutinizing where the specific intersection of copyright and the audio-visual archive meets with the outside world – in providing access to archival film – it becomes clear that the visibility of important works of film that are arguably crucial to our understanding of the past are not only shaped by the rather arbitrary filter of copyright, but, as keeper of the material evidence, the archive has the power to shape all the narratives that can be found there and therefore co-constructs the way film history is understood.

RE-CATEGORIZATION I: THE ORPHAN FILM

A re-categorization of audio-visual archival holdings according to legal status exposes orphan works as those that raise the most particular problems in the archival access debate. When a work is still assumed to be under copyright and the copyright owner of a work cannot be identified or located (so that permission for duplication and dissemination can be obtained), the work is said to be an orphan work. Orphan works – like all works – cannot be used without this permission and collections often remain dormant. In the realm of audio-visual archives, the works most at risk are documentaries, commercials, newsreels and educational films, particularly those from before the Second World War, as well as commercially produced films by production companies which have subsequently gone out of business or have transferred their rights to another entity (NFPF, 2004; HLG, 2008).

Particular obstacles to successfully identifying and locating the copyright owner have been identified by the United States Copyright Office (USCO) in their large-scale orphan works study *Report on Orphan Works* (2006) as including:

> (1) inadequate identifying information on a copy of the work itself; (2) inadequate information about copyright ownership because of a change of ownership or a change in the circumstances of the owner; (3) limitations of existing copyright ownership information sources; and (4) difficulties researching copyright information. (USCO, 2006: 2)

The report concluded that the 'orphan works problem is real' while at the same time 'elusive to quantify and describe comprehensively' (USCO, 2006: 7). A follow-up publication in 2012, on orphan works and mass digitization particularly, added that the problem of orphan works 'affects a broad cross-section of stakeholders including members of the general public, archives, publishers and filmmakers' (Pallante, 2012b: 64555).

Differences in the interpretation of what constitutes an orphan work (and for instance the concept of 'untraceability') and estimations of the dimension of the orphan works problem (including those beyond the specific constraints of the audio-visual archive) have ranged from '40% of all holdings' at the British Library to 58% at Cornell University library (Elferink and Ringnalda, 2008: 25). Recent estimates by several European audio-visual archives range from 5% to 21% of all holdings.[3] Not being able to gauge the problem precisely has direct consequences for the daily archival practice: in terms of access to the work, potential creative and productive use of the work will be delayed and possibly halted as long as the legal status of the work is unclear. On a larger scale, access to orphan works seems to call attention to the tense relationship between the audio-visual archive and the dynamics of film history. It has been estimated that no more than 25% of the entire silent film production survives in archives today (Hediger, 2005), and that amount of material forms the basis of our entire understanding of that period of film history. In a time in which 'ubiquitous access' seems to be the norm, the estimates by audio-visual archives of how many film works are currently 'dormant' because of copyright restrictions could in the worst case correspond to roughly the same amount, and the consequences for film historiography seem self-evident.

The orphan works problem is not new. There have been copyright owners that were untraceable or impossible to contact much further back in time than the recent study of the phenomenon suggests. However, in the light of burgeoning digitization discussions, aggregated initiatives that promote access to cultural heritage, and public archives whose funding applications often stress the necessity for (online) dissemination, the problem has come to the fore rather quickly in the last decade.

Scope, Content and Causes

Before turning to some of the underlying causes of the orphan works problem, it is important to briefly look at the scope and content of the material under scrutiny. The large majority of films that are considered to be orphan will be found in public archives. Films housed by commercial archives, such as studio archives, will most likely have clear legal ownership, and such collections will therefore include few or no 'true' orphan works. However, some of the rights to the underlying works of film, such as a play or a novel, might belong to an external party and the costs for renewal of those underlying rights can be prohibitive to the extent that the work, although physically available, might be considered to be legally 'lost' *within* the archive (Allen, 2010).

The legal and administrative causes that underlie the orphan works problem forge a larger network of factors, none of which individually can be seen as the sole reason for the challenges faced by archivists but taken as a whole create an untenable situation. Arguably, the most important legal causes of orphan works are threefold: (1) the term of copyright lasts a long time, which does not only mean it will take a long time before a work will enter the public domain but also that the longer the term, the greater the chance that a copyright holder will go missing; (2) there is no complete record of whose is what, partially due to a lack of copyright registration formalities (when there once were such registration formalities the record was not necessarily complete or correct either; however, there seemed to be a clearer place to start); and (3) for a film there are many possible copyright owners, differing from country to country, making a search more complicated. These specifically legal causes are supplemented by a set of more administrative causes, such as unclear archival origins of (parts of) an archive's collection; lack of identifying information on the works themselves; and a lack of manpower and financial infrastructure to do the necessary research on a title-by-title basis. As argued by van Gompel and Hugenholtz (2010), the orphan works problem can be seen as an information problem; the problem need not exist and when it does, it need not progress as long as there is enough manpower and financial infrastructure available to do the necessary research. In general, however, it seems that works with 'copyright issues' have a tendency to sink to the bottom of the list of works to be preserved, especially if there is a (funding) obligation to make the work (digitally) available.

Existing and Proposed Solutions

Legal research and the resulting literature suggests that a 'legal solution is required' (Elferink and Ringnalda, 2008: 6). This would take such forms as collective licensing schemes, contractual agreements or statutory exemptions, as administrative solutions alone cannot legitimize the re-use of a work. The legal solutions would have to be focused on bringing rights holders and (good faith) users together so that a transaction, most often in relation to a dormant collection, could take place. Several legal amendments are in the process of being implemented, but there is as yet no 'ready-made' solution to the orphan works problem. The administrative solutions seem to be mainly directed at keeping collections workable and manageable on a daily basis, so solutions include such measures as risk assessments. Again, legal and administrative measures go hand in hand, and are collectively part of a more complex network of factors.

The context in which orphan works literature emerged has changed considerably in the decade or so since the topic first came to significance in archival access debates. The focus shifted away from licensing uses of individual orphan works to issues of mass digitization. Not only has the context in which the literature emerged changed. The content of the studies has also changed. Over the course of the last decade the focus of the literature on orphan works has shifted from international and comparative survey/overview works that identified and tried to map the problem, including underlying causes to the problem and the realization that a diligent search was necessary to reduce the number of orphan works, to studies that lay out the particular necessities of possible solutions to the orphan works problem, partially reformulated in the light of mass digitization efforts (Duke Center for the Study of the Public Domain, 2005; IViR, 2006; USCO, 2006; Elferink and Ringnalda, 2008; Vetulani, 2008; Pallante, 2012a). There has also been a shift in authors, as representatives from the archival practice (heritage institutions and libraries, but also collective rights agencies, etc.) have become involved in thinking about shaping some of the legal initiatives, such as establishing due diligence guidelines or databases of legal metadata on the basis of a voluntary registration scheme (HLG, 2008; EFG, 2009; JISC, 2009).

Legislative Measures

A legal solution to regulate the use of orphan works is not simple as it has to address a range of issues at stake: a comprehensive orphan works definition; the development of adequate due diligence guidelines (as well as the establishment of a regulating body); the kind of permitted uses (educational, commercial, etc.), which ideally should apply to all uses and all users, in accordance with previous directives and international conventions, all in an international framework with different legal traditions;[4] and remuneration schemes with precisely defined moments of payment, be it at the time of actual re-use of the material or at the time of the rights owner's potential claim. In what follows, a brief overview will be given of existing and proposed legislation at the time of this writing.[5]

In a notice of inquiry of late 2012, in which the US Copyright Office seeks comments regarding the current state of play for orphan works, Maria Pallante, Register of Copyrights and Director of the US Copyright Office, addresses the present state of orphan works legislation in that country. There is an ongoing focus on orphan works in the US (not least because of the Google Book Search Litigation) and '[b]oth the 109th and the 110th Congresses considered the orphan works problem. … Congress came very close to adopting a consensus bill shortly before the presidential election in 2008, but did not enact orphan works legislation before adjourning' (2012b: 64556).

Pallante continues to address recent and proposed legislation elsewhere as follows: 'The European Council formally approved the proposed orphan works directive ("Directive") in October 2012, for which Member States have two years to implement the Directive in national legislation' (2012b: 64559). Several countries, such as Canada, France, Hungary, Denmark and Finland, have already adopted forms of orphan works solutions in national law. The Canadian Copyright Act, for instance:

> permits users to file applications with the Copyright Board of Canada for the use of certain types of orphan works on a case-by-case basis. If an applicant demonstrates that it has made a reasonable effort to locate the rights holder and the rights holder cannot be located, the Board will approve the request and issue a conditional non-exclusive license. (2012b: 64560)[6]

The UK has seen two large national copyright reviews, both of which included some focus on orphan works. The first was the *Gowers Review of Intellectual Property* in 2006, but it wasn't until *The Hargreaves Review of Intellectual Property and Growth* in 2011 that a recommendation on orphan works was given. In the previously mentioned notice, Pallante summarizes:

> the United Kingdom issued proposed legislation in 2012 that would amend the Copyright, Designs and Patents Act of 1988 to permit the commercial and non-commercial use of orphan works under a licensing scheme that would include both individual licensing of orphan works as well as a form of voluntary extended collective licensing. The scheme

> would require a diligent search, the results of which would be verified by 'an independent authorising body.' The proposal would also establish an orphan works registry and, if the name of the rights holder is unknown (and therefore cannot be credited), any licensed use of the work would have to include a notice that refers back to the registry. (Pallante, 2012b: 64559)

Various kinds of copyright registries, based on voluntary registration, feature in both legislative and administrative measures. In practice, a great quantity of legal metadata is missing and the orphan works problem can therefore be seen as an information problem. Partially, this is due to the lack of copyright registration formalities (van Gompel and Hugenholtz, 2010), so one of the most obvious solutions would be to reinstate copyright registration formalities. However:

> Except for purely national situations, it is prohibited under the Berne Convention to establish mandatory registration systems or to mandate a copyright notice, including information on the identity and whereabouts of a copyright owner and the date of copyright, on each copy of the work. On the other hand, it is not prohibited to establish measures that stimulate rights owners to voluntarily provide information concerning copyright ownership and licensing conditions. (van Gompel and Hugenholtz, 2010: 4)

The obvious drawback of a database with voluntary registration for the orphan works problem – a so-called *opt-in* scenario – is that rights holders who sign up to these databases will most likely be aware of their property.[7] An obvious part of the orphan works problem is that some of the rights holders might be missing or ignorant of their rights.

Administrative Measures

One of the most practical solutions to deal with the orphan works problem is to put a large legal staff in place who research the historic and current legal status of the archival holdings including up-to-date contact information on the current rights owners so that a transaction can take place between a good faith user and the rights owner. In principle, the problem need not exist, but obviously, clearance of rights, in particular in large collections, may not always be possible at the level of each unique item.

Due Diligence Guidelines

In practice, trying to identify and locate a copyright owner can be a time-consuming process. In the framework of the European Digital Libraries Initiative, which aims to 'provide a common multi-lingual access point to Europe's cultural heritage', a work-group at the EU-level compiled of representatives of right holders and cultural institutions, such as ACE (Association des Cinémathèques Européennes), FIAPF (Fédération Internationale des Associations de Producteurs Films), FERA (Federation of European Film Directors) as well as the British Library, the British Screen Advisory Council, and many others, have come up with a *Memorandum of Understanding on Diligent Search Guidelines for Orphan Works*. Due diligence guidelines include such factors as who must participate in the search process; the nature and extent of the search required and the types of resources, tools, registries or other information-sharing mechanisms required or allowed in completing a search (Hansen et al., 2013). In 2012, the European Parliament passed a directive on certain permitted uses of orphan works which recognizes the diligent search (as 'complementary to its legislative proposal') as outlined in the above-mentioned Memorandum.

Risk Assessment

Long-term solutions to the orphan works problem are being sought in regulating it legally. However, it is difficult to implement the various solutions in an official, and more importantly, an international context, as digital access, and more specifically online distribution, of a work is by definition international. As mentioned before, some of the obvious solutions would not comply with international agreements; while 'it does not further the objectives of the copyright system to deny use of the work, sometimes for decades. … it is not good policy to protect a copyright when there is no evidence of a copyright owner' (Pallante, 2012a: 1). In the archival practice, putting a research team at work is a time-consuming and costly process and will not always be a successful strategy, as seen in the example of *De overval*. When the permission needed for duplication and dissemination cannot be obtained the archive will have to determine what risks are involved in making the work public anyway. In order to unravel some of the contemporary economics of archival access, the next section will focus on those works which should be free from legal restrictions.

RE-CATEGORIZATION II: THE PUBLIC DOMAIN FILM

A re-categorization of audio-visual archival holdings according to legal status distinguishes the public domain works as works that should be free from rights restrictions and can be used 'without the need for permission for use from the copyright owner' (Deazley, 2006: 107). New artistic works are mostly built on older, extant works, and a large public domain, in which works are freely available, is generally accepted as a stimulant for further creativity. However, these works are, paradoxically, not necessarily publicly available: the works are often deposited behind archival institutional layers and archives do not necessarily have the possibility of releasing the work. What access to orphan and to public domain films shows is that film history is co-constructed by the institutions that control them; access is not only controlled by those who own the rights, but also by those who own the physical assets, with far-reaching consequences for the visibility of the films.

Exclusive Ownership

After works have fallen into the public domain and are no longer owned intellectually, what is left in the archives is the material property.[8] There seem to be great differences in the ways in which different kinds of archives provide access to their public domain materials; commercial archives will often own the copyright to most of their holdings and will therefore frequently exploit those materials in favour of their public domain holdings, as will be illustrated here by a studio archive example. Non-profit archives, on the other hand, own mostly material property and seldom the rights to the films they safeguard (Thompson, 2007), so for distribution purposes, they benefit from the rights to their works having expired. Whether they are commercial or non-commercial in nature, all audio-visual archives have become involved in what Law Professor Ronan Deazley in *Rethinking Copyright* characterizes as the 'interplay between the ownership of the physical object … and the ability to control the subsequent use and dissemination' (2006: 124).

Aside from the different philosophical shapes the public domain apparently can take based on what one believes is in or out of the public domain, there is also a distinction between what could be considered a 'practical' versus a 'theoretical' public domain. A theoretical public domain comprises works that are in the public domain in theory, but as Samuelson demonstrates, in practice do not really 'reside there':

> A painting from the mid-nineteenth century that remains in a private collection or was destroyed in a fire is, in theory, in the public domain as a matter of copyright law, but its non-public nature or its destruction mean that it may, in fact, be there only in theory (2003: 149, n. 12).

Public domain works are subject to appropriation by anyone, as they can be used without the need for permission from a copyright holder, but exclusive ownership of the physical materials and a resultant control of the works' dissemination seem to adversely influence this situation as they can make the works less accessible. This chapter argues that, just like a mid-nineteenth-century painting that remains in a private collection, some of the public domain works held by audio-visual archives also reside only in a theoretical public domain. They do not reside in a practical public domain, because of their non-public nature combined with the archive's exclusive ownership of the physical materials.

For-Profit Initiatives

The following two case studies show that when it comes to digital distribution in the for-profit environment, fewer public domain titles seem to be being made available. As will be illustrated, in the case of an on-demand initiative of a studio archive, public domain titles are fading from public view, and in the case of a specific high-end DVD label, the works will not even be acquired for possible distribution.

Warner Brothers Collection Online

The holdings of a studio seem to fall into clearly distinguishable legal categories: they are either in copyright or they are not. In cases where they are, the studio will probably own the copyright to most of the works and therefore an upfront investment in the preservation and subsequent dissemination of the work can be made relatively easily. In cases where the works are not under copyright anymore, the materials are said to be in the public domain, because the rights have expired, for instance, or because the rights have been forfeited because of legal technicalities.[9] For the studio, it will almost always be easier to recoup some of the preservation and access costs when a work is in copyright, so when it comes to providing digital access to the works online, commercial actors are most likely to invest time and money in such clearly copyrighted works, rather than in those works from which a commercial return is less easily secured. Not being able to control the potential infringement of a distributed public domain title seems to lessen the attraction of pursuing the digital or online dissemination of such a title.

In the case of online access to public domain works, it seems that the studio chooses to reduce their availability, as was illustrated by George Feltenstein[10] during his presentation at the 'Reimagining the Archive' conference at UCLA in November 2010. While presenting Warner Brothers' new DVD-on-demand website,[11] he outlined that of the circa 7,800 Warner feature films,[12] some 4,100 were distributed on VHS and in 2009, 1,700 features had come out on DVD. The DVD-on-demand website was launched in March 2009, and what started with 150 digitized titles, had grown two years later to approximately 1,000 titles, including '10% of the library that likely would not have made it to DVD before' (Feltenstein, 2010). An apparently new niche for archival material had been tapped into; the 1,000 titles were not exclusively theatrical feature films that were released before; they also included 'short subject collections' previously not distributed. At the same time, however, while the ultimate goal is to 'make the whole Warner library available to everyone with the best possible quality' (Feltenstein, 2010), the site features hardly any public domain titles. The lack is most visible in the absence of films with a theatrical release date of before 1923,[13] the cut-off date in the US before which all creative works are deemed public domain automatically. In the case of Warner Bros., this chapter suggests that in the shift from analogue to digital distribution, fewer public domain titles are being made available and are fading from public view.

Criterion Collection

Another example in which titles that are still under ownership appear to be favoured over public domain titles is in the DVD distribution of the Criterion Collection. An immediate and important distinction with the previous example of Warner Bros. is that the Criterion Collection does not own a film collection as such, but is in the business of issuing DVDs of films ('filmschool in a box'; Parker and Parker, 2011), the licensing rights to which they have to acquire from an external party. In his role as advisor and consulting producer for Criterion, Robert Fischer affirmed in his presentation during the 2010 Gorizia International Film Studies Spring

School that the label would never distribute public domain titles: of the various selection criteria, a 'secure rights situation' is the very first, only then followed by whether the particular title fits within the rest of the collection.[14] This is not to say that Criterion does not encounter other rights problems: over the years it has become increasingly hard to obtain licensing rights to produce DVDs from popular studio films. 'One unfortunate result of this situation is that many of the excellent supplements [that were] available on the company's laserdiscs languish without an outlet' (Parker and Parker, 2011: 184, n. 72).

Although Warner Bros. currently seems to be making their material available in an interesting 'hybrid' situation between a push ('making available') and a pull ('on-demand access') model (Fossati and Verhoeff, 2007: 331), these are but two examples of large-scale digitization efforts in which little or no attention seems to be given to public domain titles. Selling attractive products for which some of the re-mastering and restoration costs can be recouped requires a clear copyright ownership or clear licensing agreements. An arguably more important result of a clear copyright ownership is the potential protection against possible infringement, so an upfront investment in said preservation costs can be made at all. There is, however, a big difference between the business model of a studio and the mandate to making works available of, for instance, a national audio-visual archive.

Initiatives by Non-Profits

The same possibilities concerning the legal status of the holdings apply to a non-profit archive: the material is either in copyright or it is not. If the material is in copyright, it is possible that the archive itself is the owner of the films' rights. This will most probably, however, only apply to a relatively small proportion of the materials. As mentioned before, non-profit archives seldom own the rights to the material film holdings they own, so the bulk of the holdings of these kinds of archives will consist of material to which the owner is an external party. If the material is in the public domain, archives benefit from the rights to their works having expired, especially for distribution purposes. However, as in a for-profit environment, selections will have to be made as to what material will be made available. High costs are involved in the restoration, the digitization and the continued preservation of film material, so even if a non-profit archive operates under a mandate which requires that material must be made available, it will not blindly provide online access to all the holdings that they either own themselves or that are in the public domain. Not only the commercial archives, but also the public ones appear to be involved in the 'interplay between the ownership of the physical object ... and the ability to control the subsequent use and dissemination' (Deazley, 2006: 124).

Internet Archive

Most of the online access provided by public archives appears to emphasize public domain works in favour of the more 'difficult' copyrighted works, and some online initiatives seem to be made up in large part or even exclusively by public domain material. One example is the Internet Archive, a non-profit initiative established in the mid-1990s in San Francisco, which aside from open access to public domain books also provides online access to historical audio-visual collections, through collaboration with external partners, such as the Library of Congress. The site contains 'only public-domain items, including the ever-popular *Duck and Cover*, allowing [the archive] ... to avoid the problem of copyright' (Thompson, 2007).

Images for the Future Projects

Other examples of initiatives by non-profits include projects made possible by the Dutch national digitization project 'Images for the Future',[15] such as video-on-demand platform *Ximon* and online remix contest

Celluloid Remix. One of the ideas behind the video-on-demand portal *Ximon* was to avoid a situation where the legal status of the material would dominate the character of the portal. However, the most important factor that determined what was presented online first was 'what was available and what was clearable' and therefore the platform initially included a large proportion of public domain works (Rechsteiner, 2010). In order to determine what was available, various other factors, such as the physical condition of the material or how much restoration a film would need, were also taken into consideration. *Celluloid Remix*, an online remix contest with early Dutch films, which took place in 2009 (for the first time), was made up exclusively of public domain material.

The consequences for film historiography seem clear in the case of the accessibility of public domain works. In a commercial context, the public domain status of the films in combination with the exclusive ownership of the source materials leads to an invisibility of the materials. In a non-profit context, that same combination seems to facilitate an 'easier' online distribution and can even lead to what curator of the Danish Film Institute Thomas Christensen labelled a 'freak show':[16] a unilateral representation of audio-visual public domain materials on various online platforms, or a *hyper-visibility* of certain titles.

CONCLUSION

In the last decade, legal literature has come to define orphan works as a consequence of a particular legal discourse but it has become clear that a reframing of the debate is needed. Just as with some of the public domain films, some of the orphan works have also to be seen as pertaining to a theoretical as opposed to a practical domain; for in practice they do not really 'reside there'. And therefore, the orphan works problem is not to be understood as a purely legal issue, but as a more complex one in which the archive itself plays a fundamental and shaping role.

Aside from the principal objectives of acquisition and preservation, the remit of an audio-visual archive is to provide access to their holdings and in doing so to engage with the dynamics of history. If an audio-visual archive cannot or will not provide access to their holdings, it cannot and does not engage with the dynamics of history, in the sense that there is an inhibited visibility of important works of film that are arguably crucial to our understanding of the past. What the focus on the particular case study of orphan works in this chapter has made visible is that a deeper understanding of what access to orphan works means in a historiographical context becomes essential. For the archive, as keepers of the evidentiary products of film history, legitimization of the orphan works problem might not be the entire issue, as one neglected, orphaned, area will only expose another.

For a more inclusive way of looking at orphan works, we might need to revisit one description from 1992 in which 'the "orphans" of film' were defined as 'the bread-and-butter features which enjoyed a screen life and then faded from view, but which have an honourable place in the still-primeval history of the twentieth century's unique art form, the motion picture' (Jeavons in Eyles and Meeker, 1992: 9), or embrace the definition put forward by Dan Streible, as including 'the curatorial and intellectual energy associated with the phenomenon':

> Orphan films can be conceived as all types of neglected cinema. While a film might not be literally abandoned by its owner, if it is unseen or not part of the universe of knowledge about moving images, it is essentially orphaned. Its orphan-ness might be material, conceptual, or both. Physical deterioration obviously puts films at risk. In this sense, more moving image works are orphaned – or headed to the orphanage – than not. But even a preserved and well-stored film is orphan-like if its existence is unknown outside of the archive. (2009: x)

Indifference of the film industry to the survival of its past product, neglect, loss, decay or willful destruction and other political, economic and curatorial issues are amongst the factors that have helped shape the particular partial picture of the available film history to be studied. Copyright might be added to the line of historic and contemporary factors that influence what material is available and consequently how we understand film history. These factors are all particular 'sieves' through which the numerous narratives that can be found in an archive can be filtered. In that sense, copyright in the context of an audiovisual archive can be seen as a smokescreen for the problem of history, the telling of which is necessarily a partial and provisional story, told from the present.

NOTES

1 The Nederlands Filmmuseum (now EYE Film Institute Netherlands) has never had any cases in which untraceable copyright owners have come forward after a film has been made public. Email from Ronny Temme (Sales, Eye Film Institute Netherlands) to author, 10 May 2010.

2 The definition originates from SEAPAVAA's constitution. The South East Asia-Pacific Audiovisual Archive Association was founded two years prior to the publication of the UNESCO report.

3 Numbers expressed by representatives of the EYE Film Institute and the Danish Film Institute at the 'Taking Care of Orphan Works' conference in May 2011 in Amsterdam.

4 In the EU, it is a prerequisite that all member states have solutions which are interoperable and that they agree to mutually recognize any mechanism that fulfils the generally accepted core principles. Mutual recognition is important with a view to the cross-border nature of the use (HLG, 2008: 5).

5 For an extensive discussion of possible solutions to the orphan works problem as well as the advantages and disadvantages of each, leading up to the current state, please refer to van Gompel and Hugenholtz (2010).

6 For a fuller discussion of the already adopted forms of orphan works solutions in several national laws, please refer to Pallante, M. (2012b).

7 Although both primarily geared towards the literary world, some examples of databases based on voluntary registration are ARROW and WATCH. ARROW, the acronym for Accessible Registries of Rights Information and Orphan Works towards Europeana, was a project of a consortium of European national libraries, publishers and collective management organizations, also representing writers – working through their main European associations and a number of national organisations – which was launched in November 2008 and lasted for 30 months (www.arrow-net.eu/faq/what-arrow.html [last accessed: 11 May 2013]). WATCH is a database of copyright contacts for writers, artists and prominent people in other creative fields. It is a joint project of the Harry Ransom Center (The University of Texas at Austin) and the University of Reading Library in the UK. Founded in 1994 as a resource principally for copyright questions about literary manuscripts held in the US and the UK, it has now grown into one of the largest databases of copyright holders in the world (http://norman.hrc.utexas.edu/watch/about.cfm [last accessed: 11 May 2013]).

8 There are several ways in which works can become public domain. 'Copyright in any given work we know comes into existence from the point of creation' (Deazley, 2006: 102) and one of the most straightforward ways in which a work is said to enter the public domain, is when that copyright expires. Alternatively, the copyright in a work might have been forfeited because of a failure to comply with the technical formalities of copyright in effect at the time or the works might be non-copyrightable at all because they are categorically excluded from copyright protection, such as some governmental works (Samuels, 1993).

9 For numerous classic studio film examples, see Pierce (2007).

10 Senior Vice President, Theatrical Catalogue Marketing, Warner Archive Collection Online

11 What started as www.warnerarchive.com now redirects to www.wbshop.com, where other WB products are sold, such as clothing and toys. 'The DVDs are created on demand, professionally authored, and ship within two or three days' (currently to the US only) (Feltenstein, 2010). [Site last accessed on 9 October 2012.]

12 These titles are not exclusively Warner produced feature films: several mergers and take-overs have led to what is currently a quite eclectic film collection, including several other film libraries, such as the pre-1986 MGM one.

13 More research would be needed not only to establish whether any of the later titles featured on the site are in the public domain (there are several ways in which a film can become public domain) but also to establish more precisely how

many titles currently owned by WB were released pre-1923 and still survive. As Warner Brothers was officially incorporated in 1923, pre-1923 films would include such titles as those produced by First National Films, which later merged with WB (Finler, 2003). Additionally, titles that can be purchased on the same website from both the MGM Limited Editions and Sony Pictures Choice Collection do also not include any pre-1930s titles.

14 Obvious exception to this policy seems to be *Nanook of the North* (US, 1922, dir. Robert Flaherty), which was released on DVD by Criterion in 1999 (as #33). The title is a US film with a release date before 1923, the defining reason that makes the film a public domain title.

15 Participating partners included film, television and audio archives. www.imagesforthefuture.org

16 In his presentation at the 'Archiving the Future' conference in York, UK, February 2010.

REFERENCES

Allen, B. (2010) Interviewed by Claudy Op den Kamp. Philadelphia, 4 November.

Auteurswet (Copyright Act 1912) Unofficial translation [Online]. Available at: www.ivir.nl/legislation/nl/copyrightact.html

Borde, R. (1983) *Les Cinémathèques.* Lausanne: Éditions L'Âge d'Homme.

Deazley, R. (2006) *Rethinking Copyright: History, Theory, Language.* Cheltenham: Edward Elgar Publishing.

Duke Center for the Study of the Public Domain (2005) *Access to Orphan Works.* [Online] Available at: http://web.law.duke.edu/cspd/pdf/cspdorphanfilm.pdf (last accessed: 23 June 2013).

Edmondson, R. (1998) *A Philosophy of Audiovisual Archiving.* Paris: UNESCO.

Elferink, M. and Ringnalda, A. (2008) *Digitale Ontsluiting van Historische Archieven en Verweesde Werken. Een Inventarisatie.* Utrecht: CIER.

European Film Gateway (EFG) (2009) *D5.1 Report on Legal Frameworks in European Film Gateway (EFG) Consortium Member States* [Online]. Available at: www.efgproject.eu/downloads/D.5.1_legal_frameworks_in_EFG_consortium_a.pdf (last accessed: 3 June 2013).

Eyles, A. and Meeker, D. (eds) (1992) *Missing Believed Lost: The Great British Film Search.* London: BFI Publishing.

Feltenstein, G. (2010) 'New Platforms', *Re-imagining the Archive. Remapping and Remixing Traditional Models in the Digital Era*, UCLA, 10–12 November.

Finler, J. (2003) *The Hollywood Story.* London and New York: Wallflower Press.

Fossati, G. (2009) *From Grain to Pixel: The Archival Life of Film in Transition.* Amsterdam: Amsterdam University Press.

Fossati, G. and Verhoeff, N. (2007) 'Beyond Distribution: Some Thoughts on the Future of Archival Films', in Kessler, F. and Verhoeff, N. (eds) *Networks of Entertainment: Early Film Distribution 1895–1915.* Eastleigh: John Libbey Publishing, pp. 331–339.

Gowers, A. (2006) *Gowers Review of Intellectual Property.* London: HM Treasury.

Hansen, D., Hinze, G. and Urban, J. (2013) 'What Constitutes a Diligent Search Under Present and Proposed Orphan Work Regimes?' *Berkeley Digital Library Copyright Project White Paper #5* [Online]. Available at: www.copyright.gov/orphan/comments/noi_11302012/Berkeley-Digital-Library-Copyright-Project.pdf (last accessed: 15 October 2013).

Hargreaves, I. (2011) *The Hargreaves Review of Intellectual Property and Growth.* Independent report [Online]. Available at: www.ipo.gov.uk/ipreview-finalreport.pdf (last accessed: 23 June 2013).

Hediger, V. (2005) 'The Original is Always Lost: Film History, Copyright Industries and the Problem of Reconstruction', in de Valck, M. and Hagener, M. (eds) *Cinephilia: Movies, Love and Memory.* Amsterdam: Amsterdam University Press.

High Level Expert Group (HLG; i2010: Digital Libraries) (2008) *Report on Digital Preservation, Orphan Works, and Out-of-Print Works* [Online]. Available at: http://ec.europa.eu/archives/information_society/avpolicy/docs/library/studies/heritage/final_report_en.pdf (last accessed: 23 June 2013).

IViR (2006) *The Recasting of Copyright & Related Rights for the Knowledge Economy* [Online]. Available at: http://ec.europa.eu/internal_market/copyright/docs/studies/etd2005imd195recast_report_2006.pdf (last accessed: 23 June 2013).

JISC (2009) *In From the Cold.* Cambridge: Collections Trust.

Jones, J. (2012) *The Past is a Moving Picture: Preserving the Twentieth Century on Film.* Gainesville: University Press of Florida.

Lameris, B. (2007) 'Opnieuw Belicht: De Pas de Deux Tussen de Filmmuseale Praktijk en Filmhistorische Debatten'. PhD Dissertation, Universiteit Utrecht.

Memorandum of Understanding on Diligent Search Guidelines for Orphan Works. [Online]. Available at: http://www.ifap.ru/ofdocs/rest/rest0001.pdf (last accessed 19 August 2014).

Meyer, M.P. (2011) 'Authenticiteit en fotografische materialiteit', in de Jong, A. (ed.) *Zorgen voor Onzichtbare*

Assets: Over het Behoud van Digitale AV- Collecties. Hilversum: Nederlands Instituut voor Beeld en Geluid.

National Film Preservation Foundation (NFPF) (2004) *The Film Preservation Guide*. San Francisco: NFPF.

National Recording Preservation Board (NRPB) (2010) *The State of Recorded Sound Preservation in the United States: A National Legacy at Risk in the Digital Age.* Washington, DC: The Library of Congress [Online]. Available at: www.clir.org/pubs/reports/pub148/pub148.pdf (last accessed: 8 September 2013).

Pallante, M. (2012a) 'Orphan Works & Mass Digitization: Obstacles & Opportunities' [Keynote Address]. *Berkeley Digital Copyright Project*, Berkeley Center for Law and Technology, 12 April.

Pallante, M. (2012b) 'Orphan Works and Mass Digitization', *Federal Register*, 77(204), Washington, DC: Library of Congress, Copyright Office, pp. 64555–64561.

Parker, M. and Parker, D. (2011) *The DVD and the Study of Film: The Attainable Text.* New York: Palgrave Macmillan.

Pierce, D. (2007) 'Forgotten Faces: Why Some of Our Cinema Heritage is Part of the Public Domain', *Film History*, 19(2), pp. 125–143.

Rechsteiner, E. (2010) Interviewed by Claudy Op den Kamp, Philadelphia, 5/6 November.

Samuels, E. (1993) 'The Public Domain in Copyright Law', *Journal of the Copyright Society*, 41, pp. 137–182.

Samuelson, P. (2003) 'Mapping the Digital Public Domain: Threats and Opportunities', *Law and Contemporary Problems*, 66, pp. 147–171.

Streible, D. (2009) 'The State of the Orphan Films, Editor's Introduction', *The Moving Image*, 9(1), pp. vi–xix.

Thompson, K. (2007) 'The Celestial Multiplex', *Observations on Film Art*, 27 March. Available at: www.davidbordwell.net/blog (last accessed: 11 February 2012).

United States Copyright Office (USCO) (2006) *Report on Orphan Works.* Washington, DC: Library of Congress.

van Gompel, S. and Hugenholtz, B. (2010) 'The Orphan Works Problem: The Copyright Conundrum of Digitizing Large-Scale Audiovisual Archives, and How to Solve It', *Popular Communication, The International Journal of Media and Culture* [preprint], pp. 1–11.

Vetulani, A. (2008) *The Problem of Orphan Works in the EU.* Brussels: European Commission.

23

Dangerous Undertakings: Sacred Texts and Copyright's Myth of Aesthetic Neutrality

John Tehranian

INTRODUCTION

At a rhetorical level, courts have maintained a steadfast commitment to aesthetic neutrality in their copyright jurisprudence. Consider Justice Oliver Wendell Holmes's enduring admonition from over a century ago. Writing for the majority in *Bleistein* v. *Donaldson Lithographing Co.* (*Bleistein* 1903), Holmes famously rejected claims by both the lower courts and defendants that the plaintiff's works in an infringement case did not qualify for copyright protection. Cautioning judges to expurgate aesthetic judgments from the courtroom, Holmes found no basis to deny the benefits of copyright to an advertisement featuring renderings of circus performers, despite its prosaic commerciality (*Bleistein* 1903: 251). Holmes held that the perceived aesthetic value of a work could not and should not determine its copyrightability (1903: 252–53).[1] In theory, therefore, commercial copy should receive the same protection as high art. As Holmes famously reasoned: '[i]t would be a dangerous undertaking for persons trained only to the law to constitute themselves final judges of the worth of pictorial illustrations, outside of the narrowest and most obvious limits' (1903: 251).

For more than a century, judges have ostensibly heeded Holmes's charge, and the rhetoric of aesthetic neutrality has become a dominant trope in modern copyright jurisprudence. Robert Gorman notes, 'It is indeed the rare judge who purports to assess, in explicit terms, whether the art, literature or music before it is good or bad' (Gorman 2001: 2). One need look no further than the emphatic language of the Seventh Circuit: 'judges can make fools of themselves pronouncing on aesthetic matters' (*Gracen* 1983: 304).

Yet for all this rhetorical solicitude against the 'dangerous undertaking', courts inevitably make aesthetic judgments when approaching copyright cases. In his ground-breaking work on the subject, Alfred Yen (1998: 266–97) argues that the palaver of aesthetic neutrality has belied the common judicial practice of assessing aesthetics factors in deciding fundamental issues of copyright law. To illustrate this point, Yen examines jurisprudence on the issue of originality, the useful arts doctrine, and substantial similarity. At a certain level, copyright hermeneutics necessarily implicate aesthetic considerations. For example, the Constitution's Copyright Clause – which appears to limit copyright protection to the extent that it promotes 'the Progress of Science and useful Arts'[2] – virtually demands such 'aesthetic determinations' (Gorman 2001: 2). In addition, judges have introduced aesthetic considerations into the copyright calculus in a variety of ways through doctrines having their origins in the common law (Liu 2003: 415–20). For example, in assessing productive or transformative uses under the first factor of the fair use defense, courts have often elevated certain types of work (e.g., parody) over other types of work (e.g., satire) (Madison 2004: 1559).[3] Construing conceptual severability for the purposes of distinguishing between works of applied art (which receive copyright protection) and works of industrial design (which do not) inevitably involves aesthetic judgments about what constitutes art and what defines the proper relationship between form and function as needed to secure legal protection.

Aesthetic judgments appear in many forms. In the narrowest sense, they reflect a judge's feelings about a work's beauty, as embodied in its inherent elements – color, tonality, shape, melody, rhythm and composition, for example. But, aesthetic judgments also come in other guises, including judicial determinations motivated by or based on a work's worth or social value. Indeed, as we shall see, courts will often draw on a work or artist's commercial success as a proxy to determine the work's legal worth and, subsequently, the level of protection it deserves. As Robert Gorman notes, 'it is not at all rare to find courts addressing the question, "what is art?" And it is quite common to find copyright courts assessing – sometimes covertly, sometimes openly – whether a work has merit, worth or social value' (Gorman 2001: 2). The normative dangers of these undertakings may be the subject of reasonable debate. After all, we may or may not want courts to deny copyright protection to certain types of work that are without 'worth' – whether that means works lacking sufficient creativity so as to constitute a true product of authorship or works whose social impact is much more harmful than good. That debate is the subject of a different conversation. Rather, we focus here on the indisputably far-reaching positive, rather than normative, consequences of such aesthetic adjudications. As Yen (1998: 248–49) argues, the influence of such aesthetic judgments in our copyright jurisprudence inextricably affects the type of works we, as a society, receive from our artists. Economically motivated artists might 'prefer creating works that meet the aesthetic preference of judges because other works would either not get the benefits of copyright protection or wind up being suppressed' (Yen 1998: 248–49). Even more fundamentally, however, aesthetic judgments can serve to both maintain and preserve existing power structures. After all, aesthetic judgments are imbued with cultural norms. The seemingly neutral laws of copyright, therefore, have the potential to create a hierarchy of culture that can preserve entrenched interests or solidify particular (often elite) narratives.

Consider the way in which application of the fair use doctrine, in combination with other copyright principles, has violated ostensible norms of aesthetic neutrality in deciding which works will remain consecrated and hallowed and which works will not. Fair use, of course, serves as an affirmative defense to claims of infringement and, where successfully raised, excuses all liability.[4] Codified in Section 107 of the United States Copyright Act and equitable in nature, the fair-use defense weighs at least four factors – namely, the purpose and character of the use; the nature of the copyrighted work; the amount and substantiality of the portion used in relation to the copyrighted work as a whole; and the impact of the use on the market for and value of the copyrighted work – to determine whether a particular unauthorized and uncompensated use of a copyrighted work will be immunized from infringement liability.[5] With a narrow reading of fair use, a court can protect a work from remix, reinterpretation, and unauthorized mutilation. In short, it can preserve a work's aura, inviolability, and canonic status and promote its economic value to its rights holder. With a broader reading of fair use, a court can open the floodgates for the work's use and abuse. Indeed, if the time has come for a work to be metaphorically rejected from the modern canon, there is perhaps no more defining moment than when that work loses its strong copyright protection in court. A careful exegesis of copyright jurisprudence reveals that aesthetic decisions, driven by implicit cultural considerations, can dramatically affect the fair use calculus. In the process, fair-use determinations can readily become inquisitions as to which cultural works are – to quote a celebrated parable about the seductive sway of aesthetics – the 'fairest of them all'.

To explore this point, this essay conducts a close reading of the decisions in two high-profile copyright infringement suits targeting unlicensed derivatives of canonical literary works. The first suit, *Suntrust v. Houghton Mifflin* (*Suntrust* 2001b), concerned infringement claims against Alice Randall's *The Wind Done Gone*, an unsanctioned recasting of Margaret Mitchell's *Gone with the Wind*. The second suit, *Salinger v. Colting* (*Salinger* 2010), dealt with infringement claims against John David California's *60 Years Later*, an unauthorized postmodern riff on J.D. Salinger's *Catcher in the Rye*. The results of the two cases differed. In the former, an injunction against publication of the unauthorized work was lifted, and in the latter, the injunction ultimately stood. However, in both cases, aesthetic considerations – namely juridical conceptions of history, hierarchy and value pertaining to the underlying works and their allegedly infringing alter egos – dominated the fair-use analysis and ultimately enabled the law's selective consecration of cultural meaning, its development of epistemological narratives and its beatification of sacred texts. And such an approach to infringement questions does not appear isolated to suits involving the most iconic of works. As the recent *Cariou v. Prince* suit (*Cariou* 2013) over the unauthorized use of a series of Rastafarian photographs in the works of appropriation artist Richard Prince demonstrates, the types of aesthetic judgments animating both *Suntrust* and *Salinger* can all too easily permeate copyright jurisprudence. In the end, therefore, to better understand the adjudication of copyright questions, we must not only recognize the elusive nature of aesthetic neutrality, we must also appreciate the power of embedded cultural norms and assumptions in driving copyright law's development.

THE CONSECRATION DONE GONE: THE DE-CANONIZATION OF *GONE WITH THE WIND* AND THE BATTLE TO DEPICT THE ANTEBELLUM SOUTH.

In *Suntrust v. Houghton Mifflin* (*Suntrust* 2001a), the estate of Margaret Mitchell sued to enjoin publication of Alice Randall's *The Wind Done Gone* on the grounds that it constituted an unauthorized derivative work based on *Gone with the Wind*. The main conceit of Randall's novel was its recasting of the *Gone with the Wind* story and world from the point of view of the African-American slaves and mulattos rather than the white aristocrats. In Randall's work (*Suntrust* 2001b: 1270–71), Ashley Wilkes is gay, interracial sexual relationships are discussed, and the travails of daily life for the victims of the South's rigid and racist social hierarchy are vividly depicted.

A district court initially enjoined publication of *The Wind Done Gone*, accepting the Mitchell estate's contention that it constituted an infringing work and rejecting Randall's fair use defense (*Suntrust* 2001a: 1386). Specifically, the trial judge found that *The Wind Done Gone* was a sequel and not a parody, and therefore not the type of transformative use granted fair-use protection (*Suntrust* 2001a: 1378). The tenor of the judge's opinion is particularly revealing. It begins by immediately emphasizing *Gone with the Wind*'s place in the cultural canon and its commercial significance –noting both its 'widespread acclaim' and its impressive sales in the 'tens of millions' (*Suntrust* 2001a: 1363). These facts are, of course, largely irrelevant to any aesthetically neutral analysis of infringement and fair use. But, they set the tone for the court's opinion, which reflects a strong deference to the work's favored aesthetic status – its presumed import and cultural and economic value.[6]

The existing body of fair use precedent all but mandates that parodic works enjoy exemption from infringement liability. The key portion of the trial court's decision therefore comes when it characterizes *The Wind Done Gone* as not primarily a parody but, rather, a sequel or some other form of unauthorized derivative work.[7] While acknowledging that the book has numerous parodic elements, the court somehow divines that 'the book's overall purpose is to create a sequel to the older work and provide Ms. Randall's social commentary on the antebellum South' (*Suntrust* 2001a: 1378). The court's attempt to segregate the parodic elements of the work from the sequel-like elements is difficult to understand when the two concepts are not at all mutually exclusive and, quite often, intertwined. For example, Mel Brooks's classic *Spaceballs* is, in some senses, both an unauthorized sequel to and parody of *Star Wars*. Indeed, the dialectic that casts parody in opposition to sequel is, at its core, an aesthetic judgment. As a parody, the work is presumed to be transformative and, consequently, entitled to fair use protection for its contribution to progress in the arts.[8] As a sequel, the work is seen as nothing more than an effort to free ride off of the copyrighted work of another. In this sense, the *Suntrust* court ends up conflating its analysis of commercialism with its analysis of transformative use, later concluding that: 'the purpose of putting the key characters of *Gone with the Wind* in new settings is to entertain and sell books to an active and ready-made market for the next *Gone with the Wind* sequel' (*Suntrust* 2001a: 1379).[9] To the court, Randall is nothing more than a leech sucking economic value away from Mitchell's genius. But, at some level, all parodies can be portrayed as such. After all, they all rely upon the original and its status as a recognized work to reach a certain audience. Moreover, we are avowedly fine with such unauthorized recastings once a work has fallen out of copyright. To take one example, consider *Wicked*, the Tony-award-winning musical based on the *The Wonderful Wizard of Oz*. Because the underlying source material (L. Frank Baum's novel) resides in the public domain, the creators of *Wicked* could freely retell the story of Oz from the point of view of the witches without getting permission from Baum's estate. Choices about what constitutes fair use determine which parts of our cultural output remain sacred and which do not.

As it turns out, a careful parsing of the court's decision reveals that its conclusion stems from aesthetic judgments about the inviolability of *Gone with the Wind*. As the court tautologically posits, 'If the defendant is permitted to publish *The Wind Done Gone*, an unauthorized derivative work, then anyone could tell the love story of *Gone with the Wind* from another point of view and/or create sequels or prequels populated by Ms. Mitchell's copyrighted characters without compensation to the Mitchell Trusts' (*Suntrust* 2001a: 1382). With these words, the court presupposes that the latter result simply cannot occur (despite the existence of the fair use doctrine that plainly creates no such hard-and-fast rule). Put another way, the court assumes, and thereby ensures, that the work must remain inviolate. As a sacred text, *Gone with the Wind* should be protected from unauthorized individuals telling the story from a different point of view.

Consecration is at the heart of the court's concern because a world where the sacred text has been defiled is unimaginable: '[B]y killing two core characters from *Gone with the Wind* and marrying off another, *The Wind Done Gone* has the immediate effect of damaging or even precluding the Mitchell Trusts' ability to continue to tell the love story of Scarlett and Rhett' (*Suntrust* 2001a: 1382). Read literally, the court's admonition fails to distinguish between real life – where an individual's death typically precludes the possibility of resurrection – and fiction – where no such limitations exist. The statement not only reflects a startling failure of imagination by the court – doubtlessly provoked by the inability to envision the bastardization of the consecrated work – but also does not hold weight empirically. For example, the *Star Trek* franchise has continued to thrive in telling the stories of Captain Kirk, Mr. Spock, and the U.S.S. Enterprise, despite the fact that both Kirk[10] and Spock[11] were killed at various points during the *authorized* movies. Moreover, audiences can readily discern between authorized and unauthorized sequels of a franchise, and, if they cannot, that is something that the federal Lanham Act could help police through its prohibition of unfair competition and false advertising. Indeed, the universe of fan fiction – which typically appeals to the most fervent connoisseurs of a franchise – is often occupied with works featuring storylines and character developments that are often inconsistent with one other. Despite these apparent contradictions with the authorized canon (and even with other fanfiction), these derivatives are no less enjoyable to their readers.

Of course, the Scarlett and Rhett characters do not die just because Randall says they do. But, what the court really fears is that *The Wind Done Gone* will sound not the literal death knell for the characters, but for *Gone with the Wind*'s untouchability. Stripped of unadulterated idealization, the work and its characters can no longer survive in the exact form they once possessed. Thus, it is not whether the work is parody or sequel that truly appears to drive the court's decision; it is destruction of the work's romanticism – a romanticism that is grounded in a distinctly whitewashed vision of the antebellum South that painfully ignores the harsh realities of life for that society's underclass. Thus, the court's reading of copyright law, driven by aesthetic judgments, has an impact on the discourse about what is perhaps the most famous and popular vision of Southern life during the years of slavery. With the District Court's opinion, copyright law is used to preserve a hegemonic vision of the South that has historically prevailed in the American consciousness.

By sharp contrast, the Eleventh Circuit (*Suntrust* 2001b) found *The Wind Done Gone* protected by the fair use doctrine and the First Amendment and reversed the District Court's injunction.[12] Despite its differing logic, however, the Eleventh Circuit's opinion was similarly influenced by aesthetic judgments.[13] To the Eleventh Circuit, criticism, ridicule, and even scorn for a work, serves as a social good that trumps any harm it may do to a copyright holder's economic rights.[14] Citing the Ninth Circuit's *Fisher* case that immunized *When Sonny Sniffs Glue* from liability as a parody of *When Sunny Gets Blue*, the court's concurring opinion by Judge Marcus asserts that '[d]estructive parodies play an important role in social and literary criticism and thus merit protection even though they may discourage or discredit an original author' (*Suntrust* 2001b: 1283).[15] Works are not to be treated as sacred cows and the preservation of immutability does not serve public interests. 'Because the social good is served by increasing the supply of criticism – and thus, potentially, of truth' posits the court, 'creators of original works cannot be given the power to block the dissemination of critical derivative works' (Suntrust 2001b: 1983).[16]

In particular, the Eleventh Circuit found *Gone with the Wind* especially ripe for deconstruction (*Suntrust* 2001b: 1275). And this becomes a critical point when considering identity interests and how the copyright holders may draw on intellectual property rights as a means to preserve and maintain existing power structures, visions of inclusion and exclusion, and critical historical narratives. The Eleventh Circuit specifically singles out the Mitchell estate's control of prior authorized derivative works and its desire to limit certain themes as a basis *for*, rather than *against*, its ruling (*Suntrust* 2001b: 1274–75). By sharp contrast to the District Court, which sought to retain the aesthetic integrity of Mitchell's saccharine depiction of Dixie and protect it from unwanted mutilation,[17] the appeals court viewed Mitchell's work as one ripe for, if not in need of outright, deconstruction.[18] As the court takes pains to point out, the Mitchell estate was particularly horrified at the idea that the *Gone with the Wind* milieu might be adulterated with depictions of interracial relationships or homosexuality.[19] Indeed, the court quotes the Mitchell estate as having told a potential writer of the authorized sequel for *Gone with the Wind*, 'You're not going to like this, but the estate will require you to sign a pledge that says you will under no circumstances write anything about miscegenation or homosexuality' (*Suntrust* 2001b: 1282). Ultimately, therefore, the court's decision sought to vindicate Randall's right to transform 'Ashley Wilkes into a homosexual' and to depict 'interracial sex, and … multiple mulatto characters' (*Suntrust* 2001b: 1282).

All told, the struggle over the scope of the *Gone with the Wind* copyright becomes a struggle over the right to present an alternate vision of Old Dixie, using the familiar terrain of the romanticized antebellum South to bring long-suppressed issues of race, class, and even sexual orientation to the forefront of the story. In the end, the Eleventh Circuit found that the preliminary injunction enjoining publication of *The Wind Done Gone* constituted 'an unconstitutional prior restraint' (*Suntrust* 2001b: 1259) – not just of free speech broadly speaking, but of the right to challenge the idealized notions of the Old South that have historically resided in the national subconscious precisely because of such works as *Gone with the Wind*.[20] To the Eleventh Circuit, the time had come to de-canonize *Gone with the Wind* and end its inviolability.[21] And the decision to do so stemmed from aesthetic judgments supporting the subversive power of Randall's broadside in novel form.[22] Painfully out of sync with more modern views, *Gone with the Wind* had to face the fact that the time to lose its consecrated status had come.

60 YEARS LATER J.D. SALINGER AND THE PRESERVATION OF THE CANON

Indeed, a revealing contrast emerges when one considers the ultimate outcome of *The Wind Done Gone* suit – which effectively excommunicated *Gone with the Wind* from the realm of sacred texts – in comparison to the more recent controversy involving an unauthorized send-up of *The Catcher in the Rye*. Entitled *60 Years Later: Coming Through the Rye* and purportedly authored by one John David (J.D.) California,[23] the fanciful reverse postmodern bildungsroman features Holden Caulfield, now a 76-year-old on the run from a nursing home, confronting his creator, J.D. Salinger himself.[24] In 2009, J.D. Salinger came out of hiding, at least legally speaking, to seek an injunction restraining publication of *60 Years Later* on the grounds that it constituted a blatant infringement of his copyright.[25] The defendant objected, claiming fair use and First Amendment protection.[26]

The District Court issued an injunction to enjoin the publication and distribution of *60 Years Later* after finding Salinger was likely to prevail on the merits of the case.[27] On appeal, the Second Circuit affirmed that part of the holding.[28] A central part of the decision came when the court distinguished the case from the suit involving *The Wind Done Gone*.[29] Specifically, the court opined that *The Wind Done Gone* was clearly a parody – thereby entitling it to a fair use defense – while *60 Years Later* was a sequel (Salinger 2009: 258–60). But, as discussed earlier, *The Wind Done Gone*'s purported status as a parody, sequel or both is wrought with complexity. And, at a minimum, it was a close call – with the United States District Court for the Northern District of Georgia ruling one way and the Eleventh Circuit ruling the other.[30]

Moreover, there were several key facts that actually should have given *60 Years Later* a *better* fair use defense than *The Wind Done Gone*. First, with respect to market harm – the fourth (and most important, according to some courts)[31] fair use factor – *The Wind Done Gone* was certainly more damaging to the Mitchell estate's *economic* interests than *60 Years Later* was to Salinger's. Specifically, the Mitchell estate had demonstrated a concrete and manifest interest in entering the market to create derivative works based on *Gone with the Wind*.[32] In 1991, they authorized publication of a sequel entitled *Scarlett*.[33] And, at the time of the *Suntrust* case, they had sold the rights to an authorized sequel.[34] Indeed, St Martin's Press had paid dearly for the privilege of publishing the latter – to the tune of seven figures (Reardon 2001). By sharp contrast, whatever the moral offense to Salinger, the publication of *60 Years Later* did not raise the same specter of economic harm as did the publication of *The Wind Done Gone*.[35] After all, Salinger was a notorious recluse who had categorically refused to publish anything for the last half century of his life (Alexander 2000: 26). He never betrayed any interest in publishing a sequel to *Catcher in the Rye*. The work, *60 Years Later*, is therefore highly unlikely to dilute a derivative market, as this was a market in which Salinger had no desire whatsoever to participate. Admittedly, the jurisprudence applying the market harm test has suggested that harm to potential markets is enough for a plaintiff to prevail on this element of the fair use test.[36] The *Salinger* court noted as much:

> [A]lthough Salinger has not demonstrated any interest in publishing a sequel or other derivative work of *Catcher*, the Second Circuit has previously emphasized that it is the 'potential market' for the copyrighted work and its derivatives that must be examined, even if the 'author has disavowed any intention to publish them during his lifetime,' given that an author 'has the right to change his mind' and is 'entitled to protect his *opportunity* to sell his [derivative works]'. (*Salinger* 2009: 268)[37]

But, potential must at least be plausible and, at the end of the day, it is utterly disingenuous to read Salinger's suit as an attempt to preserve his right to change his mind should he decide to enter the market for derivative works.[38]

Secondly, large parts of *The Wind Done Gone* actually retold the story from *Gone with the Wind* (Schur 2003: 6), thereby engaging in more actual borrowing, both literal and structural, than *60 Years Later* did from the *Catcher in the Rye*. *The Wind Done Gone* even appropriated entire sentence structures from the original work. As an example, the first page of *The Wind Done Gone* states, 'She was not beautiful, but men seldom recognized this, caught up in the cloud of commotion and scent in which she moved' (Randall 2001: 1), while *Gone with the Wind* begins, 'Scarlett O'Hara was not beautiful, but men seldom realized it when caught by her charm …' (Mitchell 1936: 1). In *60 Years Later* the author certainly used the Holden Caulfield of *Catcher in the Rye*, but this borrowing was largely limited to the use of certain (common and non-protectable) catchphrases or idioms related to the Caulfield character.[39] In fact, the *Salinger* ruling was notable as it represented the first time that a court in the Second Circuit had found that copyright protection extended to a single character who had appeared in a single novel.[40]

Nevertheless, while *The Wind Done Gone* ultimately received fair use protection, *60 Years Later* was enjoined from publication.[41] And aesthetic judgments on the relative value of unauthorized derivative works appear to have made a key difference in the court's decision to issue the injunction. Consider the only mention that the *Salinger* court makes of the overarching goals of the copyright system.[42] Seeking to reconcile its ruling with copyright's role in promoting progress in the arts, the *Salinger* court reasoned that 'some artists may be further incentivized to create original works due to the availability of the right *not* to produce any sequels' (*Salinger* 2010: 268, emphasis in original). As a first matter, the court's speculation on this point strains all credulity. But regardless of how one feels about the bizarre conjecture that the right not to produce sequels can incentivize creation, it is clear that the court's statement rests on a tacit aesthetic judgment: that it is better to preserve (ex post) the incentive to create *The Catcher in the Rye* than it is to stimulate the creation of unauthorized sequels. The calculus here is fairly remarkable: the court chooses to enjoin *definitely* the publication of unauthorized derivatives – works that could contribute to progress in the arts – on the *chance*, based on idle speculation, that some artists may create more because they can rest secure in the knowledge that no one can create sequels of their works. The hierarchy at play is simple: the original work implicitly trumps the sequel(s) and/or derivatives, especially those of the unauthorized variety. Certainly, for every *Godfather II* and *Return of the Jedi*, there are dozens of *Blues Brothers 2000*'s. But in deciding the fate of *The Wind Done Gone*, the Eleventh Circuit certainly did not seem bothered by this possibility, as it adopted a radically different aesthetic judgment of the unauthorized derivative. At a more subconscious level and in the context of our times, it perhaps feels less wrong to allow someone to skewer the dated artistic vision of Margaret Mitchell than to permit the adulteration of J.D. Salinger's beloved Holden Caulfield.

PRINCE, PRIVILEGE AND CULTURAL HIERARCHY

The seepage of aesthetic judgments into copyright infringement analysis occurs with regularity. And, it is not a phenomenon limited to cases featuring such iconic works as *Gone with the Wind* or *Catcher in the Rye*. The Second Circuit's recent decision in the widely watched *Cariou v. Prince*[43] case illustrates both of these trends. In its opinion (*Cariou* 2013: 712), the appellate court reversed a judgment finding that 30 works by appropriationist artist Richard Prince infringed the Rastafarian photographs of Patrick Cariou. Prince had taken numerous parts of Cariou's photographs, altered them in various ways (including by painting 'lozenges' over the faces of the subjects) and combined them with other appropriated art to form pastiche compositions.[44] The Second Circuit ruled that at least 25 of Prince's 30 allegedly infringing works were transformative as a matter of law and, therefore, immunized from liability under the fair use doctrine (*Cariou* 2013: 712).[45] Though the Second Circuit putatively framed its analysis around the application of the four fair use factors enumerated in Section 107 of the Copyright Act, extraneous aesthetic considerations permeated the court's reasoning.[46] In the end, therefore, the resulting opinion appeared dominated more by obeisance to cultural hierarchy (as reified by elite sensibilities) than by fealty to precedent.[47]

The central narrative undergirding the court's decision is its oppositional casting of Prince as the rightfully celebrated high artist of the cognoscenti and Cariou as a merely slavish and obscure chronicler of the Rastafarians. The court begins by detailing Prince's success along two axes – economic and cultural.[48] His works, we are told, sell for millions of dollars.[49] Meanwhile, he has exhibited at the world's most prestigious museums and in such internationally renowned galleries as the Gagosian.[50] These references are not merely sundry facts peppering the opinion, a fact made plain by the court's bizarre effort to regale the reader with a lengthy list of representatives from the celebrity and art worlds who attended the opening of Prince's exhibit: '… musicians Jay-Z and Beyoncé Knowles, artists Damien Hirst and Jeff Koons [to whom the Second Circuit had recently granted a high-profile fairuse victory],[51] professional football player Tom Brady, model Gisele Bundchen, *Vanity Fair* editor Graydon Carter, *Vogue* editor Anna Wintour, authors Jonathan Franzen and Candace Bushnell, and actors Robert DeNiro, Angelina Jolie, and Brad Pitt' (*Cariou* 2013: 709).[52] Repeatedly, the court fetishizes Prince's size – that of his pocketbook, of his cultural capital and even of his literal works (by, among other things, continually emphasizing the enormity of Prince's compositions) (Sarmiento 2013).[53] As Sergio Muñoz Sarmiento (2013) has noted, the court's fascination 'would have one think we were reading a narration of what transpires in a boy's high-school gym'. With this selective introduction, the court implicitly legitimizes the critical accolades and monetary rewards Prince has enjoyed. The court then explicitly heralds Prince's work with effervescent language to highlight the magnitude of his apparently unique artistic vision.[54] We are told that, by employing 'new aesthetics with creative and communicative results' (*Cariou* 2013: 708), Prince has created works that are 'jarring', 'provocative' and 'expressive' (*Cariou* 2013: 706).

Meanwhile, the decision takes pains to convey Cariou's inferior status in the cultural landscape by denigrating the creative worth of his vision and his success (or lack thereof). This binary casting – with Prince as transformative visionary and Cariou as pedestrian tradesman – ultimately drives the Second Circuit's decision to reverse the lower court's judgment of infringement. Specifically, the majority opinion presents Cariou as merely a competent photographer who happens to 'depict the natural beauty of Rastafarians and their surrounding environs' – language that paints the plaintiff as more of a factual observer than inspired *auteur*. Throughout the opinion, the court highlights just how little the plaintiff has achieved in the marketplace. Thus, the court informs us that Cariou's book, which featured the allegedly infringed Rastafarian photographs, 'is currently out of print' and that Cariou only earned $8000 in royalties from the work as 60% of the sales of the book 'sold below the suggested retail price' (*Cariou* 2013: 699). Such details are largely irrelevant to the question facing the court; after all, the Second Circuit has only the issue of liability, and not damages, before it. Indeed, the monies earned by Cariou for his photographs have no real bearing on the fair use analysis. However, they implicitly undercut any notion that Cariou's works should enjoy the inviolability assured to works at the apex of copyright's protection regime.

Meanwhile, to the extent that Cariou's commercial interests could conceivably come into play in the fourth fair-use factor – the harm to the potential market for the value of Cariou's work – the analysis follows a fundamentally different logic than that embraced in the *Salinger* case only a few years earlier.[55] Specifically, in *Salinger*, the court had protected the plaintiff's right to market potential sequels to or derivatives of his work even though J.D. Salinger was a notorious recluse who had not published any work in half a century and had vehemently disavowed any interest in doing so.[56] An author, according to the *Salinger* court, has the full right to decide when, how and even if he or she might enter the licensing market.[57] By contrast, in *Prince*, the court gives little weight to such interests for Cariou. Instead, the majority opinion emphasizes Cariou's meager success and notes that '[e]xcept for a handful of private sales to personal acquaintances, he has never sold or licensed the individual photographs' (*Cariou* 2013: 699). Further, in a sharp departure from the reasoning of *Salinger*, the court asserts that '[t]here is nothing in the record to suggest that Cariou would ever develop or license secondary uses of his work in the vein of Prince's artworks. Nor does anything in the record suggest that Prince's artworks had any impact on the marketing of the photographs' (*Cariou* 2013: 709). Both statements, however, were equally true of J.D. Salinger in his dispute with John David California; yet these facts gave the court no pause in issuing an injunction against the publication of *60 Years After*.

In the end, it appears that the Second Circuit cannot deem Prince's artistic efforts actionable because it is unfathomable that such celebrated works could be infringing. To wit, the court deigns Prince's works 'transformative' as a matter of law, thereby lending judicial confirmation to what high society has already declared to be true.[58] Meanwhile, the Second Circuit has no problem denying Cariou the sacralization that courts have offered to the works of J.D. Salinger (and so many others) over the years, largely as a consequence of its relative aesthetic judgments about the litigant's art. As the court euphemistically concludes, 'Prince's work appeals to an *entirely different sort* of collector than Cariou's' (*Cariou* 2013: 709, emphasis added).

As the *Suntrust*, *Salinger* and *Prince* cases illustrate, competing notions of inviolability, artistic merit and cultural hierarchy can suffuse the federal courts' treatment of infringement claims. And the use of these aesthetic considerations has significant social and political consequences. The decision to open up *Gone with the Wind* to *The Wind Done Gone* effectively freed the literary property – and, more generally, the popular interpretation of a critical era in our nation's history – to different narratives and perspectives. By sharp contrast, the injunction against the publication of *60 Years Later* effectively consecrated and deemed inviolable J.D. Salinger's Holden Caulfield and his particular vision of innocence, adolescence and adulthood. Meanwhile, although many observers quickly heralded the *Prince* decision as a victory for the expressive freedom of artists to build on the works of others, that right was grounded in particular notions of cultural hierarchy, elite acceptance and commercial success. Indeed, as this exegesis of the *Suntrust*, *Salinger* and *Prince* cases suggests, the battle over copyright protection can often become a clash between the hegemonic power of cultural reproduction and subversive effects of semiotic disobedience. Through the subtle use of aesthetic judgments – both conscious and subconscious – our intellectual property laws can achieve something much broader than merely 'progress of the arts'. Instead, by consecrating meaning and value, patrolling cultural hierarchy, and regulating the semiotic signposts of our society, intellectual property transcends its small corner of the legal universe and plays a fundamental role in shaping social structures and regulating individual behavior as part of a broader cultural project.

NOTES

1 As Holmes argued, 'That these pictures had their worth and their success is sufficiently shown by the desire to reproduce them without regard to the plaintiffs' rights', at 252.
2 U.S. Constitution, art. I, § 8, cl. 8.
3 Michael J. Madison: 'Whether "productive" or "transformative" use guides the first fair use factor, either inquiry threatens to trap courts and litigants into making the kinds of aesthetic judgments that the copyright system expressly disclaims' (2004: 1559, n. 137). See also *Hanley v. DeVore*, (2010: 1156–57) (holding that politicians' unauthorized use of musical compositions during campaigns constituted 'satire' rather than 'parody' and, therefore, did not qualify for a fair use defense as it did not adequately comment upon or criticize the direct content of songs).
4 17 U.S.C. § 107.
5 Ibid.
6 *Suntrust Bank v. Houghton Mifflin Co.*, 136 F.Supp.2d 1357, 1363 (N.D. Ga. 2001), *vacated*, 252 F.3d 1165 (11th Cir. 2001) and *rev'd*, 268 F.3d 1257 (11th Cir. 2001).
7 Ibid. at 1378.
8 See *Campbell v. Acuff-Rose Music, Inc.*, 510 U.S. 569, 575 (1994) (stating that '[f]rom the infancy of copyright protection, some opportunity for fair use of copyrighted material has been thought necessary to fulfill copyright's very purpose, "To promote the Progress of Science and Useful Arts"').
9 'The court finds that *The Wind Done Gone* is unquestionably a fictional work that has an overarching economic purpose. … [T]he commercial purpose of *The Wind Done Gone* weighs strongly in favor of the plaintiff on the first factor' (*Suntrust*, 136 F. Supp. 2d at 1379).
10 'Well. Kirk may have been dead in the movies, but there was no reason he had to be dead in the publishing industry. I sold my treatment to Simon & Schuster and *Star Trek: The Return* became a best-selling novel' (Shatner & Fisher 2008: 287).
11 Kraemer et al. (2003: 161).
12 *Suntrust Bank v. Houghton Mifflin Co.*, 268 F.3d 1257 (11th Cir. 2001).
13 Ibid. at 1271.
14 Ibid. at 1276–77.
15 Marcus, J., concurring (citing *Fisher v. Dees*, 794 F.2d 432, 438 (9th Cir. 1986)).
16 Quoting *Leibovitz v. Paramount Pictures Corp.*, 137 F.3d 109, 115 n.3 (2d Cir. 1998).
17 *Suntrust*, 136 F. Supp. 2d at 1386.
18 *Suntrust*, 268 F.3d at 1276–77.
19 *Suntrust*, 136 F. Supp. 2d at 1364.
20 Ibid. at 1270.
21 Ibid. at 1283 (Marcus, J., concurring) ('The law grants copyright holders a powerful monopoly in their expressive works. It should not also afford them windfall damages for the publication of the sorts of works that they themselves would never publish, or worse, grant them a power of indirect censorship').
22 The Eleventh Circuit's decision is also significant in another light. What the district court saw as

property – an interest in the preservation and consecration of something over which the Mitchell Trusts was said to possess dominion – the appeal court saw as speech. This is arguably an aesthetic judgment as to the nature of a copyrighted work – whether it is simply a piece of private property, outside of the scope of the First Amendment, or whether it constitutes a form of speech, subject to First Amendment protection.

23 John David California is the pseudonym of author Fredrik Colting (*Salinger v. Colting*, 641 F.Supp. 2d 250, 253 (S.D.N.Y. 2009)).

24 See *Salinger v. Colting* (*Salinger I*), 641 F. Supp. 2d 250 (S.D.N.Y. 2009) (granting injunction enjoining the sale of *60 Years After* as an unauthorized derivative work based on *Catcher in the Rye*, regardless of the originality of contributions by the author of *60 Years After*).

25 Ibid.

26 Ibid. at 258.

27 Ibid. at 254.

28 *Salinger v. Colting*, 607 F.3d 68 (2d. Cir. 2010) (affirming the district court's finding that Salinger was likely to prevail on the merits of the case but remanding the case for full consideration of the factors from *eBay, Inc. v. MercExchange*, L.L.C., 547 U.S. 388 (2006) before the injunction issues).

29 *Salinger*, 641 F.Supp.2d at 257–58.

30 *Suntrust Bank v. Houghton Mufflin, Co.*, 136 F.Supp.2d 1357, 1363 (N.D. Ga. 2001) *vacated*, 252 F.3d 1165 (11th Cir. 2001) and *rev'd*, 268 F.3d 1257 (11th Cir. 2001).

31 See, e.g., *Harper & Row, Publishers, Inc. v. Nation Enters.*, 471 U.S. 539, 566 (1985) (noting that market harm 'is undoubtedly the single most important element of fair use').

32 Ibid. at 1363.

33 Ibid.

34 Ibid.

35 *Salinger*, 641 F. Supp. 2d at 268 (noting that Salinger has not demonstrated any interest in publishing a sequel or other derivative of *Catcher in the Rye*).

36 See *Castle Rock Entm't, Inc. v. Carol Pub. Group, Inc.*, 150 F.3d 132, 145–46 (2d Cir. 1998) (finding that the fourth factor of fair use favors the plaintiff even where it has 'evidenced little if any interest in exploiting this market for derivative works'); *J.D. Salinger v. Random House, Inc.*, 811 F.2d 90, 99 (2d Cir. 1987).

37 Quoting *J.D. Salinger v. Random House, Inc.*, 811 F.2d 90, 99 (2d Cir. 1987) (emphasis added).

38 *Salinger*, 641 F. Supp. 2d. at 267–68.

39 *Salinger*, 641 F. Supp. 2d at 264 (noting *60 Years Later's* use of such Caulfield catchphrases as 'phony', 'crumby', 'lousy', 'hell' and 'bastard').

40 Of course, while Holden Caulfield appeared in only one book, his character did appear in two published short stories, see Salinger (1945, 1946), and his family appeared in at least one other, see Salinger (1944).

41 *Salinger*, 641 F. Supp. 2d at 254.

42 Ibid. at 268.

43 *Cariou v. Prince*, 714 F.3d 694 (2d Cir. 2013).

44 Ibid. at 699–703.

45 The court remanded the analysis over the remaining five works to the District Court. Ibid.

46 Ibid. at 705–11.

47 Ibid.

48 Ibid. 699–704.

49 Ibid. at 709.

50 Ibid. at 609–704.

51 See *Blanch v. Koons*, 467 F.3d 244 (2d Cir. 2006).

52 *Cariou*, 714 F.3d at 709.

53 Sergio Muñoz Sarmiento (2013) (noting that the court's opinion is littered with the following size-conscious phrases: 'measuring approximately', 'several times that size', 'ten times as large', and 'Prince's collages ... measure between ten and nearly a hundred times the size of the photographs'). Among other things, the court gives a series of precise measurements for Prince's works and mentions that the 'smallest of the Prince artworks measures 40' x 30', or approximately ten times as large as each page of *Yes Rasta* [which contained *Cariou's* photographs]'. *Cariou*, 714 F.3d at 700.

54 *Cariou*, 714 F.3d at 707–08.

55 Cf. ibid. at 708–09, with *Salinger v. Colting*, 641 F. Supp. 2d 250, 267–68 (S.D.N.Y. 2009).

56 *Salinger*, 641 F. Supp. 2d 250, 268 (quoting *J.D. Salinger v. Random House, Inc.*, 811 F.2d 90, 99 (2d Cir. 1987)).

57 Ibid.

58 Ibid. at 708 (explaining that despite the fact that Prince's artworks are commercial, 'we do not place much significance on that fact due to the transformative nature of the work').

REFERENCES

Alexander, P. (2000) *Salinger: A Biography*. New York: Renaissance Books.

Blanch v. Koons, 467 F.3d 244 (2d Cir. 2006).

Bleistein v. Donaldson Lithographing Company, 188 U.S. 239 (1903).

Campbell v. Acuff-Rose Music, Inc., 510 U.S. 569 (1994).

Cariou v. Prince, 714 F.3d 694 (2d Cir. 2013).

Castle Rock Entertainment, Inc. v. Carol Publishing Group, Inc., 150 F.3d 132 (2d Cir. 1998).

Gorman, R.A. (2001) 'Copyright courts and aesthetic judgments: Abuse or necessity?', *Columbia Journal of Law & the Arts* 25: 1–19.

Gracen v. Bradford Exch., 698 F.2d 300 (7th Cir. 1983).

Hanley v. DeVore, 733 F.Supp.2d 1144 (C.D. Cal. 2010).

Harper & Row, Publishers, Inc. v. Nation Enterprises, 471 U.S. 539 (1985).

J.D. Salinger v. Random House, Inc., 811 F.2d 90 (2d Cir. 1987).

Liu, J.P. (2003) 'Copyright law's theory of the consumer', *Boston College Law Review*, 44: 397–431.

Kraemer, R.S. Cassidy W. & Schwartz (2003) *Religions of Star Trek*. Boulder, CO: Westview Press.

Madison, M.J. (2004) 'A pattern-oriented approach to fair use', *William and Mary Law Review*, 45: 1525–690.

Mitchell, M. (1936) *Gone with the Wind*. New York: Macmillan.

Randall, A. (2001) *The Wind Done Gone*. New York: Houghton Mifflin.

Reardon, P.T. (2001) 'Frankly, my dear, the literati give a damn', *Los Angeles Times*, 24 April, available at: http://articles.latimes.com/2001/apr/24/news/cl-54756

Salinger, J.D. (1944) 'Last day of the last furlough', *Saturday Evening Post*, 15 July.

Salinger, J.D. (1945) 'I'm crazy', *Colliers Magazine*, 22 December.

Salinger, J.D. (1946) 'Slight rebellion off Madison', *The New Yorker*, 21 December.

Salinger v. Colting, 641 F. Supp. 2d 250 (S.D.N.Y. 2009).

Salinger v. Colting, 607 F.3d 68 (2d. Cir. 2010).

Sarmiento, S.M. (2013) 'Judicial activism and the return of modernism in the Cariou v. Prince Decision', *Hyperallergic*, 29 April, available at: http://hyperallergic.com/69939/judicial-activism-and-the-return-of-modernism-in-the-cariou-v-prince-decision/

Schur, R. (2003) 'The Wind Done Gone controversy: American studies, copyright law, and the imaginary domain', *American Studies*, 44(1–2): 5–33.

Shatner, W. & Fisher, D. (2008) *Up Till Now*. New York: St Martin's Press.

Suntrust Bank v. Houghton Mifflin Co., 136 F.Supp.2d 1357 (N.D. Ga. 2001a).

Suntrust Bank v. Houghton Mifflin Co., 268 F.3d 1257 (11th Cir. 2001b).

Yen, A.C. (1998) 'Copyright opinions and aesthetic theory', *Southern California Law Review*, 71: 247–302.

United States Constitution (1788).

PART VII

Audiences and Sharing

Matthew David and Debora Halbert

Intellectual property is a non-rivalrous good. By this, it is meant that whilst two people cannot use a hammer at the same time, two (or any number of) people can use the idea of using a hammer. Even sharing a hammer would potentially wear it out, whereas sharing the idea of using a hammer has no detrimental effect upon the idea itself. By extension, informational goods can be shared without reducing the utility of the informational content. What is lost in such sharing is the scope to sell such information to each successive/simultaneous user. It is precisely the fact that intrinsic scarcity is not a characteristic of informational goods that requires the legal imposition of restrictions on sharing if some level of scarcity is to be created such that these goods will retain a price value to their owners. The 'problem' (from the point of view of those wishing to sell information-rich goods) of having to fabricate scarcity by legal means where such goods lack physical or 'natural' scarcity gets a whole lot worse in the kind of information-rich society and economy that Manuel Castells refers to as 'the network society', a globalized system of distributed networks designed to enable information to circulate freely across national and institutional/regulative boundaries, and where any blockage to such circulation is regarded as a form of 'damage' to be navigated around.

The network society, and in particular the rise of the Internet, arose hand in hand with the development of new digital media corporations able to sell copyrighted content to ever wider global markets in the post-Cold-War era of worldwide de-regulation, deterritorialization and neo-liberalism. Castells calls this an era of 'capitalist perestroika'. However, since the end of the last millennium, the Internet has allowed audiences to share copyrighted content in forms of de-regulated, deterritorialized digital networking that challenge the capacity of corporate IPRs holders to control (in fact) what they continue to claim rights over (in law).

The chapters in this section of the collection address the capacity of audiences to suspend IPRs, their willingness to pay where sharing has become an option, and to explore how far law can contain such practices. The relationships between technology, law and culture are also examined. Where technology affords the by-passing of IPRs, and where attempts to lock down content with digital rights management have all failed, can cultural campaigns to persuade audiences not to share fill the gap? The work of David, Kirton, Millward and Whiteman (variously combined) rather suggests it cannot.

Matthew David, Andrew Kirton and Peter Millward address the rapid rise in the value of sports broadcasting rights in the age of global digital media, with a particular focus upon the rights arrangements for English Premier League (EPL) football. Other leagues and other sports are also addressed to show how the EPL really is a paradigmatic case. The EPL was launched in 1992 alongside Sky Sport's digital subscription television service. As a result, top flight English football (for the most part) ceased to be free to view via terrestrial national television channels; something replicated in popular sports the world over. The value of EPL broadcasting rights packages rose from tens of millions, to hundreds of millions, to billions of pounds. Domestic rights auctions were complemented by exponential growth in the sale of overseas rights, with rights now sold to more countries than are even recognized by the United Nations. Across the world, rights to other leagues and sports were increasingly bought up by global broadcasters able to maximize the value of such rights by a combination of legal monopoly, distributional closure (a control over the digital delivery channels – whether these were cable or satellite), and (curious as it may seem) digital openness (the ability to go global in whom they could reach and sell access to).

This 'first' revolution in digital sports media was not, however, the end of the story. Whilst a decade later than in music and then in film, broadband Internet and radically improved compression technology eventually meant that live sport could be streamed over the Internet to domestic users via their computers at a level of image quality comparable to what commercial broadcasters were able to offer using dedicated channels. This 'second' digital revolution is more fully 'networked' than its commercial rival. Once technical affordances enabled live sports streaming over the Internet, sports' broadcast rights holders started to express concern. Whilst the challenge is real, and is documented in the chapter, it is worth noting that, unlike in the recorded music industry, live sports broadcasting has not seen a sales crash, and rights values continue to rise. However, as the chapter shows, the situation is more complex than might first appear. In part, free streaming has actually consolidated the position of dominant commercial players, as new entrants to the commercial broadcast market have not been able to build a market share capable of generating revenues sufficient to out-bid established players for new rounds of rights. The double digital revolution has created something of a curious stand-off.

For a time it appeared that sports fans were simply less willing to break the law (at least when it came to infringing copyright) than were music fans. This was in part because live sport required more bandwidth and compression than was, until recently, available to most domestic Internet users. Reasonable image quality for live visual content was beyond the capacity of the Internet (at least to almost all domestic users) until very recently indeed, and to view such content in a domestic setting required dedicated cable or satellite services. The Internet revolutionized access to music at the end of the 1990s. Film could be downloaded slowly and watched at leisure, but live-sport 'was' different. However, this is increasingly not a sufficient explanation.

Super-fast broadband means live sport can be streamed at high quality over the Internet, just as music, film and television can. David and Whiteman explore the history of music-sharing. The language of 'theft', 'piracy' and 'stealing' is something questioned in their chapter. The attempt, by rights holder lobbies to use the term 'piracy' as a negative label against file-sharers has rather backfired. It is generally taken as a positive accolade – even if it is not a very accurate term for non-commercial sharers. Attempts to prevent music sharing by legal means has systematically failed because each time a legal target is identified within the architecture of Internet sharing, that 'bottle-neck' within the sharing software is removed. This has led to ever more fully distributed forms of sharing, from central server models, to peer to peer systems, to peers to peer (torrents) and, now, to streaming services. Technical locks have also all been broken. This has led content industry lobbies to focus upon 'cultural' strategies – seeking to create a 'moral panic' about file-sharing, seeking to associate online sharing with terrorism, people trafficking, child-exploitation, plagiarism and more.

David and Whiteman explore whether such cultural strategies have 'worked'. In so doing they address the question of whether the very notion of 'moral panic', a term created in an age where far fewer media channels, and greater editorial control, meant 'moral entrepreneurs' had more scope (if successful) to control the news agenda. If the Internet suspends the 'editorial nexus' characteristic of traditional print and broadcast media, is it still possible for 'moral entrepreneurs' to create 'moral panics' in an age of new media? It is certainly true that no panic is evident amongst the general public over 'Internet piracy', but even the classic 'moral panic' theories did not assume that media coverage would induce actual public hysteria. Rather, the creation of media outrage was seen as part of 'moral entrepreneurs'' attempts to lobby for tougher forms of regulation on whatever it was they were agitating about. This chapter certainly highlights the success of IPRs lobbyists, in using media coverage of their claims, to press pliant legislators for tougher laws and punishments. However, given that such laws have then been themselves bypassed by newer technical affordances, such formal success has not translated into any substantive prohibition in practice. That file-sharers can parody and invert the messages put out by IPRs lobbyists, and that these messages can be disseminated as widely as those they seek to challenge, also means that 'panic' messages online tend to cancel one another out.

Natasha Whiteman develops the analysis of audience empowerment in an age of new media through further exploration of how Internet file-sharers construct their own practices in ethical terms. She rejects models of ethical action that seek to measure audience behaviour against a legal yardstick, measuring them in terms of their 'competence', by which is meant compliance with rights holders' control. Rather, Whiteman is interested in examining ethical performances, the accounts given by file-sharers of their actions and their attempts to show how their behaviour is or is not 'ethical' in their view. In this sense, the 'good' audience is not simply one that does what it is told, and demonstrates the ability to do so even when it is not being told (in other words when people have internalized 'the correct' way to act). Rather, how audiences construct and orient themselves towards notions of property, authorship, ownership, reciprocity and fair use become significant.

Interestingly, 'the audience' has always been a source of anxiety, whether this be in relation to public executions, religious congregations, early urban theatre audiences, and film; or more recent anxieties about the private viewer of television, computer games and the Internet. Audiences are supposed to take an interest, to be aroused by what is put before them; but such emotional responses are always, equally, a source of disquiet. Audiences – so pleased – may seek to take matters into their own hands. Fear that audiences are passive dupes is set against a counter fear that they may well, rather, become active performers in their own right. Rendering audiences passive was itself an active part of the 'civilizing process'. Audiences were not supposed to seek possession of performances, to themselves become actors in events. Yet, in the case of popular music in particular, the audience continued to play its role in creating the event (something also true in sport – see David, Kirton and Millward in this Part of the handbook).

Music fans don't accept that the music simply does not belong to them. Audience involvement makes 'live' music 'alive'. Singing along at a concert, or with the radio is part of taking possession and being possessed by the music. Sharing music with friends and fellow fans is also a part of the normative practice of being part of the audience, of being part of the music. Attempts to prohibit such practices, in the case of litigation against file-sharing, sees record company conceptions of music as private property running up against alternative notions of public participation and possession. In distinguishing dominant narratives around conformity through ethical competence, and counter narratives that locate ethics within alternative modes of performance; Whiteman shows that the huge array of literature concerning audiences and file-sharing from around the world can be made sense of. It is not contradictory to say you would download music but would not steal a car. That IPRs lobbyists equate a car with IP is one way of constructing reality. It is not reality, and it is certainly not the construction of reality most music fans hold.

24

Sports Television Broadcasting and the Challenge of Live-streaming

Matthew David, Andrew Kirton and Peter Millward

INTRODUCTION

As the affordances of developing technologies are appropriated and realized we often see how emergent practices challenge, disrupt and even outmode established social, economic, political and cultural arrangements. Such disruption has been particularly well illustrated since the mid-1990s, when emergent practices of free online content reproduction and circulation presented some significant challenges to established arrangements for the commercial production and circulation of various kinds of 'content'. The challenge of free online content reproduction and circulation is now being experienced in a range of industries, including those broadcasting industries with which sport became irrevocably bound up over the course of the 20th century. Chief among those industries is the television broadcast industry, which, since the mid-20th century has been the dominant medium for the circulation of sports content and has concomitantly experienced burgeoning audiences and revenues during this period. Such content continues to be in high demand, with sports fans paying substantial amounts of money to access content either via subscriptions or one-off payments to broadcasting companies. The economic value of the exclusive rights to broadcast sporting events have in turn been escalating at a dramatic rate, providing lucrative returns to those sporting leagues that own them.

Whilst the development of global digital broadcasting led to a period of rapid growth in sports television broadcasting rights revenues, developments in networked distribution and digital compression have more recently become associated with a significant challenge to sports television broadcasting arrangements. Just as digital communications and networking technologies have been widely appropriated for the purposes of free music, film and other content circulation, these technologies are increasingly being used to reproduce and circulate television broadcasts via the Internet. Rights holders broadcast live sport with a view to selling access. 'Live-streaming' represents an infringement of rights holders' control over distribution when such live events are re-routed via streaming channels over the Internet, and hence made freely available to anyone in the world who can access the web. The unauthorized 'live-streaming' of legitimate broadcasts threatens to significantly disrupt the economic arrangements that accumulated and solidified over the course of the late 20th century and into the 21st century.

In this chapter, while other cases will be examined, we focus our analysis on the broadcasting arrangements surrounding English Premier League (hereafter EPL) football as a paradigmatic case in order to illustrate the challenges that 'live-streaming' presents to the established sports television broadcasting economy. We consider the broadcasting industry's responses to live-streaming and the potential outcomes of this struggle for control over content circulation in the digital network age. The EPL is a paradigmatic case of those 'hyper-commoditized' (Giulianotti 2002; Walsh and Giulianotti, 2007) sporting leagues that have developed as part of today's global sports-media complex, which is itself a characteristic of the network society. Yet this complex relies upon hierarchical (legal, technical and corporate) structures of regulation that a fully networked mode of distribution brings into question. The study of the challenges that live-streaming presents to the EPL is therefore of a broader relevance. The birth and rise of the EPL was based upon the greater rights revenues that could be generated through subscription-based digital satellite broadcasting models, relative to former broadcast arrangements in which national (terrestrial) channels bought rights and broadcast for free to domestic audiences (funded either by licence fees or advertising). This primary digital revolution is challenged by new forms of free digital network distribution, but this challenge has, so far at least, only proved limited. The challenge of network distribution and the limits of such a challenge both lie in the fact that IPR-dependent content industries like sports broadcasting are far less networked than theorists of the 'network society' (such as Manuel Castells) have suggested.

CASTELLS' NETWORK SOCIETY AND GLOBAL INTELLECTUAL PROPERTY RIGHTS

Information and communication technologies (ICT) have been amongst the defining technological transformations of late 20th century and 21st century society. The Internet became widely available to the public in the 1990s – and has proved central to this (Castells 2000b [1996]; 2001; Dyson 1997). 'New' media technologies – such as personal computers, MP3 players, smart phones and other digital communications/storage devices – proliferated as a result of the Internet, and have afforded the Internet itself further capabilities (Gane and Beer 2008). The Internet and new networked media devices hold a reciprocal relationship in the way both have been and are being used. How these new media developments have and are impacting upon sports broadcasting, and fan practices is what will be examined in the following pages.

The 'network society' developed as a global restructuring of human interaction since the 1980s and has been based upon a distributed system of digitally interconnected nodal points (Castells 2000b [1996]). The network society is one built upon the possibilities of global digital connections and the temporal/spatial compressions these networks afford. These connections and compressions intensified in the 1990s with a rapid acceleration of Internet adoption by citizens, particularly in the most affluent societies, but elsewhere as well. However, the transformation of action and affordances was not only at the level of end-users/consumers. The capitalist 'mode of production' underwent fundamental changes as well. Capitalism's 'mode of development' altered from one based upon the primacy of industrial innovation (energy supply and physical force/manipulation), to the primacy (in production and distribution) of information storage, manipulation and global circulation. Such informational flexibility, coordination and dissemination allowed immaterial capital to flow globally. Not only this, but the coordination of the physical production of goods could be similarly (though to a lesser extent) achieved across diverse sites within a global system of interchangeable manufacture.

The emerging society is one of networks of geographical spaces, people and objects; discrete points are connected by networks of digital links. For Castells at least, capital and ideas can now flow between such nodes, spread across multiple and distant spaces, in what he refers to as 'a space of flows'. The speed with which such action takes place leads to what he has called a form of 'timeless time' (Castells 2000a). Castells (2000b [1996]) suggests networks are the primary form of social organization across the globe today. He gives emphasis to the transnational socio-cultural and economic significance of such connections. This made previously established and unquestioned national boundaries – and state regulations – increasingly porous or 'lighter' in both perception and practice.

The rise of the network society coincided, and was bound up with the final stages of the Cold War, the collapse of the Soviet Union, and the rise of a neo-liberal global economy in the 1990s. Castells saw (2000b [1996]: 99) the birth of the World Trade Organization as central to the rise of market interpenetration between increasingly open nation-states, a trade infrastructure programme that paralleled the rise of the digital architecture of the network society.

> The 1996 US telecommunications Act, the founding of the World Trade Organization in 1995 [the treaty signed in 1994 created both the WTO and TRIPS], and support for media privatization from the International Monetary Fund (IMF) and other international institutions helped to denationalize the processes of media production and distribution. (Castells 2009: 86)

Just as the 1886 Berne Convention for the Protection of Literary and Artistic Works reflected the desire to regulate copyright in an age of increasing international trade in creative works, so WTO and TRIPS represent regulative responses to the rise of the network society.

On the one hand Castells (2000b [1996]) argued that the main reason this change occurred was because new networked actors were more effective in taking up globally dispersed and digitally mobilized affordances. On the other hand, such de-territorialization was also premised on new forms of legal and political regulations in the form of IP-related treaties. In his analysis during the 1990s, the key actors were primarily seen as firms and other 'corporate' funded actors; in concert with states and transnational state agencies. What Castells (2009: 63–71) calls 'mass self-communication' – the rise of individual citizen 'broadcasters' networked to each other across the world, premised upon new media connections – became a focus only in later work.

The network society witnesses the rise of the 'network enterprise'. In a 'network society' action bounded by national customs and state laws is out-paced and out-manoeuvred by action able to exploit advantages, and evade inhibitions – wherever these might be encountered. This change leads to what Castells (2000b [1996]) refers to as 'capitalist perestroika'. The efficiency of network organizations depends upon their ability to integrate useful nodes into their 'space of flows' and to bypass any 'places' that obstruct transnational organizational goals. The most dynamic form of capital in a network society is mobile and informational. However, such fluid capital also drives transformations in material capital configurations, as well as altering 'traditional' symbolic forms of status and distinction. As this chapter will suggest, one version of the network enterprise has been the new global media corporation, able to exploit global distribution channels to sell exclusive access to copyright protected digital content, in particular sports content. However, a very different network enterprise is the live-streaming channel provider that today enables viewers to access the same content without the permission of its monopoly rights holder.

The above tension between different forms of network enterprise gives a specific importance to Castells' (2000b [1996]) suggestion that new technologies empowering the space of flows in the network society have generated 'timeless time', or the globally simultaneous 'now'. The particular significance of the simultaneous 'now' for the emergence of global networked sports media is that what makes such content sell is that it is 'live', and that today even 'live' content can be copied and re-distributed 'now'. Hutchins and Rowe (2012, 2013) identify the 'digital revolution' in sports media with the rise of Internet and mobile technologies in the mid-2000s. This combination challenged (in both legal and copyright infringing forms) existing broadcast television based models of sport mediation. However, we note that what had become the mainstream business model in sports broadcasting by the mid-2000s, when Internet and mobile technologies started to challenge it, was already the result of an earlier digital revolution. Where the first digital revolution afforded the rise of a new global and hyper-commercial sports media industry, able to use global digital distribution to maximize the value of broadcasting rights, the second created the possibility of global free-sharing of mediated sports coverage. The digital, in allowing global distribution, actually increased the market for sporting events and so increased the value of its IPRs, but this was only as long as such distribution could be controlled. Fully networked digital distribution disrupts the very flow of copyright income global digital distribution initially promoted.

Nonetheless, Hutchins and Rowe (2012) are correct to point out that new commercial applications of Internet and mobile media have not replaced television as the dominant medium for the circulation of sports content. The modification of digital affordances to support free circulation challenges commercial expectations currently governing pay-per-view and subscription digital television worldwide, but large numbers continue to watch sport on television screens. What is not certain is whether this audience will all continue to spend money to do so or at least spend as much as broadcasters anticipated sports content would make them spend (see Giullianotti and Robertson 2009 below). How elite and globalized sports leagues such as the EPL might be positioned in a 'networked' new 'new'-media-supported transnational society needs ongoing scrutiny. Here we now detail the two digital revolutions: firstly, the digital revolution that afforded the rise of a global hyper-commercial digitally mediated set of sports leagues (see Millward 2011); and secondly, global sport in the age of a networked revolution that affords global sharing of digital products (see David 2010). The EPL is taken as the key illustration in each case. However, it is also interesting to show how other leagues and other broadcasters have acted to highlight both parallels and some differences.

THE GLOBAL EXPLOITATION OF DIGITAL INTELLECTUAL PROPERTY IN SPORT

Intellectual property rights, particularly copyright, underpins the economic relationship between sports organizations and media corporations. Television broadcasting corporations in particular invest huge sums of money in securing the exclusive right to broadcast sporting events, especially those considered to be of global interest and significance. For example, The BBC is believed to have paid about £60m for the right to broadcast four Olympic Games starting with the 2012 Olympic Games in London (Gibson, 2012). The sale of other such rights generates huge sums of money for sporting organizations. The sale of rights to broadcast the 2010 FIFA World Cup in South Africa is believed to have generated US$2.4bn for the organization (WIPO, 2013). When national broadcaster rights payments (such as those above) are compared to the sums paid for rights by global media organizations who aim to sell access to billions rather than to millions of domestic viewers (see below), the significance of global digital networks becomes all the more obvious (cf. Castells 2000b [1996]).

The most successful and powerful agents in the global network media world will occupy the most lucrative space, which in the contemporary network society is increasingly global. The EPL has become global in not just the players on the pitch but with respect to the geographical make up of fans across the world and the involvement of overseas' investors (Millward 2011). Interest in access to broadcast EPL games is high across the whole planet. The number of countries in which it is possible to subscribe to authorized digital broadcasts of EPL games has now grown to 211 (which is in fact more 'countries' than are officially recognized by the United Nations). With this level of demand, the total financial value of the EPL's overseas broadcasting rights have witnessed a dizzying rise over the last two decades. Broadcasting companies have proven willing to pay increasingly large amounts of money for the exclusive right (within limited and specific territories) to broadcast matches overseas. For instance, the three-year overseas broadcast rights deals that were signed in 2001 were worth £178m in total to the EPL. Those relating to 2004 were valued at £325m and 2007's were valued at £625m (Wilson 2007), whilst 2010's deal hit an estimated £1.437bn (Harris 2013). As such, the total value of such rights roughly doubled with each renewal in the years from 2001 and 2010. The most recent set of such contracts – for the 2013/14 to 2015/16 period – did not grow at quite the same rate but showed a 55% increase to be cumulatively worth £2.23bn to the EPL, of which £941m comes from Asian broadcasters (Harris 2013).

Domestically, this revolution in digital broadcasting changed the landscape for elite English clubs too. For instance, in 1988 *the British Satellite Broadcasting company (BSB)* challenged the then analogue broadcasters *BBC* and *ITV*'s rights to screen games, and although they did not succeed in securing matches, the fee rose from £3.1m to £11m per season, of which 75% was retained by clubs in the top division. With English football's restructuring into the FA Premiership, later rebranded to the FA Premier League, in 1992, the first five-year broadcast contract was won by *BSkyB* (a merger of *Sky TV* and *BSB)* for a reported £304m, rising to £670m for the three years from 1997, whilst 2009's three-year domestic broadcast renewal was worth £1.782bn. The most recent deal, from 2013/14 to 2015/16, was worth a total of £3.018bn (*The Guardian* 2012). National rights remain greater in total than do overseas rights, but a global network enterprise (such as *BSkyB*) is not limited and will work across all possible markets.

BSkyB has been more than the principal broadcaster of EPL games; rather it can be understood as its 'marketing partner'. Broadcasting contracts have encouraged football fans to take up subscription offers (Boyle and Haynes 2004), but, in return, *BSkyB*'s advertising of the EPL has opened up new markets for the league to attract new supporters that did not previously follow football (King 2002 [1998]). Within two decades of the rise of the EPL, elite English football shifted from a state of 'recession' (Taylor 1984) to a 'global football league' (Millward 2011). In the process top flight English football had moved from being mainly watched through match attendance to being predominantly watched via digital television subscription (Buraimo 2008).

The EPL is an important case because it illustrates a wider pattern. Hutchins and Rowe (2012: 13 and 177) document how far rising sports media finance, itself driven up by the global digital revolutions in cable, satellite and now Internet/mobile rights revenues, has intensified commercialization in the Olympics as well as all varieties of football (Association, i.e. international, American, Australian and Rugby). With respect to the National Football League (NFL in American football), *Sports Illustrated* (2012) suggested that the competition generates over $4bn (USD) each year from its global digital broadcasting rights sales, with the Super Bowl XLVI (2012) drawing in a global television audience of 166.8 million people through *NBC*'s coverage of the game (Florio 2012). Meanwhile, the Indian Premier League (IPL in cricket), a tournament that is still in its infancy, broadcast to audiences of 145 million in its home country (see Haigh 2010 and Majumdar 2011 – cited in Hutchins and Rowe 2012: 23), but drew in viewers from across the world – specifically in Europe, Australia, North America and the Middle East – which were facilitated through new media advances (*Sport On The Box* 2012).

Just as terrestrial broadcasters could not compete with Sky in terms of rights bids, so other national football league coverage has been 'de-territorialized'. Evens and Lefever (2013) examine the digitally afforded revolution in football coverage in Belgium. As in England, what occurred was a migration away from free terrestrial broadcasting to pay-per-view/subscription-based digital coverage. On the one hand, there is now more 'choice' in terms of channels and events being broadcast. On the other hand, for those that cannot afford to pay, there is less choice. Whilst prices vary, one common fact around the world has been that when sports rights migrate from free to air terrestrial providers to globally distributed digital providers the audience is required to pay more.

Just as in the UK, Belgian state regulators have sought to defend some events as free to view, regarding them as both a citizens' right and also part of the nation/community-building process. Nonetheless, over time, the number of events that remain free to view has declined. Other interesting parallels and divergences with the EPL can be seen in other top flight association football leagues in relation to digital television rights revenues. A number of the highest performing Spanish clubs have brokered independent digital rights deals to maximize revenues relative to rivals in their top national league. This has resulted in Barcelona and Madrid each earning around €140 million from television revenues per season.

In the same period of time the next-highest earner, Atletico Madrid, makes around one third of this value at €47 million. Smaller clubs receive just a fraction, with Rayo Vallecano's share of broadcasting money being worth €14 million in the 2013/14 season (*ESPN* 2013). The way in which Spain's elite division, La Liga, sells its broadcasting rights could, however, change in the future to something more akin to the collective sale agreement that exists in the EPL. Prior to the 2010/11 season, television broadcast rights were individually sold by Serie A clubs – Italy's premier football division – but since then they have switched to a collective sale agreement (not unlike in the EPL) in an attempt to ensure a competitive league (Evens and Lefever 2013; Hutchins and Rowe 2012). Whilst there are differences in how digital rights revenues have been distributed, the common characteristic of the first digital revolution in sports media coverage (that of global digital commercialization) is that more fans pay and each of these fans pays more.

Just as there is tension over how revenues are distributed amongst sporting actors (sports, leagues, clubs, players, etc.), so there is now competition emerging between new media platforms, something that in a sense parallels the earlier challenge posed by the first wave of digital media players to terrestrial broadcasting. The Internet has been seen as a commercial challenger to digital (satellite or cable) television. However, Goldsmith (2013) points out that whilst Internet rights to distribute Australian Football League coverage raised AU$153m for the 2012–16 period, the television rights were sold for over AU$1bn, a ratio of over six to one. He notes that this is not dissimilar to the situation in other sports and countries. Goldsmith observes that in these contexts, television remains the dominant medium, but that it is evolving within an increasingly integrated digital environment. New new media/the Internet is not replacing digital television (the older form of new media as it were); rather it offers to reinvent the relationship between fans and television viewing. Thus, as television migrates to an almost exclusively digital format, so its distinctiveness from other digital media may decline. This could mean that television becomes the digital hub around which other digital media circulate – computers, tablets, games consoles and even mobile telephones connecting with, and displaying images on, a television screen.

This confluence of hardware, the integration of multiple screens with one another (linking television, tablet and smart phone, etc.), and the integration of computing functions within devices (the fusion of telephone, email, web, apps services, music, film, camera, banking services, word processing, GPS and banking to name but a few options), is key to the logic of the network society, what Castells (2000b [1996]: 62) calls the fifth and most powerful dimension of the informational mode of development: 'the growing convergence of specific technologies into a highly integrated system'. Such devices can – under normal circumstances – receive new media images, such as broadcasts of images and/or sounds.

Digital broadcasters have responded to this 'new new' media by launching Internet platforms, for instance *Sky Go* is a subscription-based online television service offered by *BSkyB* that allows users to watch live and on-demand content on their computer, smart phone and even some computer game consoles through an Internet connection. Similarly, *ESPN* offers a 'goals' app that promises viewers that they need 'never miss a goal, wicket, try, set or knockout again', meaning, not that owners of the technology will physically see the 'goal' being scored, the 'wicket' being taken, the 'try' being scored, the 'set' being won or the 'knockout' taking place, but they can see text reportage of the 'event' on their hardware device. The first digital revolution continues to transform the practice of 'watching' sport (from the stadium, to the television, and now synchronized with screens), but what defines this revolution remains the extent to which the viewer's access remains doubly mediated, both digitally and financially. In Castells (2000b [1996], 2009) the Internet has non-uniform impacts on established practices and so the integration of digital television broadcasting with the Internet may forward or challenge this dynamic of global hyper-commercialization.

THE GLOBAL SHARING OF DIGITAL INTELLECTUAL PROPERTY IN SPORT: THE CHALLENGE OF FREE ONLINE CIRCULATION IN THE FORM OF LIVE-STREAMING

Free sharing 'hit' record companies before it seriously impacted upon visual media, and in particular live visual media. Yet, file-sharing was itself based on technical developments that emerged from research into the more efficient distribution of digital television images. The 1980s saw extensive research carried out by various (academic and commercial) research teams under the umbrella of the Moving Picture Expert Group into methods of compressing visual data so as to be better able to distribute it digitally, by either cable or satellite (Musmann 2006). This research was carried out by commercial companies like Bell Labs and Phillips, who sought to commercialize digital distribution, and by university research teams across the world (David 2010).

The Motion Picture Expert Group created/harmonized various MP (Moving Picture) compression formats, and the move to MP3 was initially part of the first (i.e. commercial) digital revolution in music (see David 2010). The initial drivers for compression were in developing the potential for relatively cheap (and hence profitable) digital television, for which sports broadcasting was the spearhead. Whilst MP1 and 2 coincided with the launch of both Sky Sports and the EPL, it was the MP3 (audio layer III) version of the MPEG compression format that was to revolutionize the distribution of music online. MP3 was first released in 1993 and underwent various revisions up until 1998. Initially, its use was envisaged as something that would render commercial distribution of music files more efficient (digital revolution one – something to follow on from the hugely profitable digital format switch to CDs a decade earlier), but it was in 1999, that Sean Fanning's Napster showed the world the potential of the MP3 format for digital revolution two: free sharing

(David 2010). Highly compressed MP3 music files, held on networked computers, could, once linked to simple search and share software lead to a form of music distribution that would shake mainstream record companies to their foundations.

When Napster's central server was successfully targeted for 'contributory infringement'; new 'peer to peer' software emerged that did not require a central server to facilitate exchanges between peers. When uploaders using such P2P software were targeted for distributing/making available copyright infringing music (and film) files, torrent based 'peers to peer' (Ps2P) software emerged that allowed downloaders to make copies from a torrent of uploads, making it impossible to identify individual liability in providing the material that was copied. Prosecutions of torrent location software providers (such as The Pirate Bay) led to the migration of such servers to distributed jurisdictions and to a balancing of torrent copying and streaming (where the viewer watches but does not actually make a copy of the content being viewed). The movement towards streaming has had monumental consequences for the distribution of television, and in particular live sport. How those consequences will play out in terms of challenging today's dominant media corporations, or in fact strengthening them, remains to be seen, as will be pointed out below.

Music compression (such as in MP3) relies on high levels of 'filling in' by the human brain when listening. For this reason MP3 audio files can undertake a level of data-reduction that makes them sufficiently small to share at speed via domestic computers, even with the kinds of bandwidths most domestic Internet users had at the turn of the millennium. MPEG researchers had spent so much time working on the compression of visual data prior to developing audio formats because the commercial market for digital distribution was in television, and in particular live sport. Live broadcasting of digital content required more than just the ability to download content. It required that such content could be downloaded at the same speed as it was being performed (in other words without the need to 'cache' data until it was ready to view).

Whilst downloaders could wait for a large film file to download before watching it, live sports broadcasters relied upon the faster bandwidth available via satellite and cable television providers to ensure they could offer higher quality live images than could be viewed over the Internet. The claim that 'you cannot see the ball' (something said of the first live television sports broadcasts in the 1930s – Barnett 1990) were true in the early days of live sports Internet streaming. However, this has long since ceased to be true – at least if you look at the best quality streams. Because of this lag in domestic network user capacity the second digital revolution only really took off in sport a decade after it had effected change in relation to recorded audio content.

These technological developments are helping to expose commercial television broadcasters to the same kind of challenges that have been plaguing the music, film, games and software industries since 1999. As with *all* those commercial enterprises whose business models involve providing access to content in return for payment, commercial broadcasters of television rely upon a certain level of 'scarcity' in terms of access. However, in the last 20 years we have moved rapidly from a situation of 'broadcast scarcity' to 'digital plenitude' (Hutchins and Rowe 2009). As we know from the experiences of the music, film, book, games and software industries, digital and networking technologies have been crucial in affording people alternative means of accessing content that would otherwise be restricted, and may have significant consequences for existing economic systems.

Ten years of cat and mouse manoeuvring in court and in software design led music sharers to torrents and streaming. This infrastructure for free sharing that evolved to combat the need for legally targetable 'bottle-necks' (actors within the process of exchange who could easily be identified and prosecuted), combined with ongoing improvements in bandwidth to mean that today's Internet users can stream free live sport broadcasting at a level of quality comparable with the level of service offered by commercial suppliers. Sports leagues and commercial broadcasters now make available, in digital form, live coverage of sporting events that are often not allowed to be broadcast in the event's home territory, to hundreds of other territories. Live broadcasts to foreign audiences is not thought to threaten domestic 'gate' receipts at stadiums, whilst domestic broadcasts are sometimes deferred to avoid this perceived threat. As such, the scope to re-route such content, via live-streaming channels on the Internet, means that streams are not only free, they are actually more likely to be available live in the home territory than are the commercial (and legal) alternatives.

The availability of EPL matches via live-streaming became apparent to the English Premier League in 2009. The EPL's Chief Executive, Richard Scudamore, came to see live-streaming as 'a very real threat' to the commercial attractiveness of the broadcasting rights deals, rights deals that had come to underwrite the EPL, and its member clubs (see David and Millward 2012). Scudamore (2009) famously proclaimed: 'Call it by its name – this is theft'. Whilst 'theft' is not quite the correct way to describe online infringement, the bigger ambiguity, for Scudamore, and all those involved in the sale of live-sports broadcasting rights at least, is different. Unlike primitive (early) downloading services that had infringing content pass through their central servers, streaming channels host transitory content. If the streaming-channel-providing services investigate reports of infringement and take down channels found to be streaming copyright infringing content, the channel itself cannot be held liable for the content its users choose to stream (Birmingham and David 2011).

The speed with which rights holders can scan and contact streaming channel providers has increased. Some streams are now taken down mid-match. However, jurisdictional differences, speed of legal action relative to event duration, and the vast numbers of alternative streams available (usually in proportion to the popularity of the event itself amongst fans) make it impossible to prevent fans from accessing high-quality streams free of charge if they choose to do so. Prosecution of streaming services is not an option (as pointed out above). Taking action against those up-loading content onto channels provided by streaming channel services is highly problematic as such actors may be anywhere in the world. Trying to chase individual viewers is the very worst case scenario as these viewers are not 'downloading', but only viewing streamed content, and so are both hard to find, and are not liable to anything like the kinds of fines that might apply to those found to be distributing content. The minimal deterrent effect of such actions, when set against the reputational harm of prosecuting their own fans makes such a course of action deeply unattractive.

Live streaming does require more bandwidth and greater data-compression than music downloading. However, this has become less technically problematic over time. This has posed problems commercially for those seeking to prevent it. In the very years when file-sharing was rising and sales of recorded music was in sharp decline, the commercial value of digital sports broadcasting was rising by every measure, and in all significant markets (Hutchins and Rowe 2012). Yet, since 2009, the idea has had to be questioned as to whether sports fans will continue to pay for digital access (because loyalty to 'club' might bind them to team, management, league and broadcasters), even whilst music fans increasingly do not (because identification with artists is often in direct opposition to the commercial machinery that surrounds them). At least things are not as clear cut as they once appeared to be. Birmingham and David (2011), David and Millward 2012, and Kirton and David (2013) identify in more detail the rising numbers both of streams and viewers of them.

Castells (2004 [1997]) argues that a form of 'power' in the network society is affective, cognitive, emotional and connected to 'identity'. The ways established broadcasters dissuade viewers from watching live-streams takes two forms – 'bad' quality and/or 'sad' viewers (David and Millward 2012). First, traditional broadcasters have given a platform to EPL executives to frame Internet streaming as 'poor' quality. The Advocate General's 2011 recommendation to the European Court of Justice (ECJ) that parallel imported broadcasts (where a match played in one country has rights sold to broadcast it in multiple countries, and where a viewer in the 'home' country then pays a foreign broadcaster for access) should be allowed within EU/EFTA (in February 2011), illustrates this. EPL chief spokesman Dan Johnson told *BBC News* (2011) viewers that 'what they [the fans] care about is the quality; and they care about the quality of the broadcast so a broadcast you know, where the broadcasters invest very heavily in production – like the *BBC*, like *[B] Sky[B]* – they produce a quality product and people will choose it on that basis'. Whilst some live-streams are low quality relative to televised broadcasts, time and technological advances have caused an exponential improvement. Media consultancy firm *NetResult* concede that there are now 'good quality streams' available (Christopher Stokes, quoted in Smith 2009). The 'bad' quality frame is therefore losing credibility. The second frame, the 'sad' consumer, is affective, emotional and identity-based. For instance, the BBCs 'Internet football piracy' alert (*BBC News,* 2009) framed the typical live-stream viewer as someone alone watching illicitly in a darkened bedroom. For a large number of fans 'going to the match' is the pinnacle of commitment and sociability (Giulianotti 2002; King 1997; Millward 2011). Who would want to be the 'solitary fan', alone and sad – especially when for most non-attending fans the appeal of watching football still lies in its social nature? The sad loner portrayal of live-stream viewers, given by *BBC News*, stands in clear contrast to this positive collective representation.

While many fans watch matches at home, the isolated individual frame stands in stark contrast to the broadcasters' own presentation of television football viewing as a communal activity (whether at home with family/friends or in public places). Watching matches on a relatively small computer screen limits scope for watching with others, and hence the 'sad' frame may hold some continued resonance with audiences. Yet this may be about to change. As digital television and PC/computer convergence mean that the 'private small screen/public big screen' distinction falls away, the 'sad' frame may go the same way as the already outdated 'bad' (quality) frame.

Ironically, the UK's 2010 Digital Economy Act, which did introduce a tougher regime designed to reduce online copyright infringement by requiring Internet service providers (ISPs) to cooperate more with IP rights holders in identifying users who are thought to be infringing, may have the opposite effect. Attempts to compel ISPs to hand over user names to copyright holders just on the basis of 'suspicious' Internet use (patterns of use that suggest illicit content viewing/copying) have stalled in the UK courts. ISPs, if contacted by copyright holders may in fact write to their customer 'warning' them that their Internet use has led them to be identified, and suggesting they modify their usage – which may be read as a need to stop infringing, or to stop using downloading services and switch to less easily identifiable streaming services (David and Millward 2012). Yet, the one thing the Act did push through was a definitive 'cut-off' date for analogue broadcasting. This means that from late 2015 all functioning televisions in the UK will have to be digital. As a result, anything one can now watch on a 'small' computer screen (such as Internet streamed sport) will (using a simple cable) also be watchable on however large a television that person happens to own. The Act in effect abolishes the computer/television distinction and any vestigial security that distinction might have afforded those selling broadcast television as in some ways visually superior, and less socially 'sad', relative to what can be watched via the Internet.

Beyond the confines of English football, Hutchins and Rowe (2012: 17) argue that sports with more limited global geographical appeal (such as Australian Rules football) will generate smaller revenues from globalized commercial digital rights deals. However, such sports will also suffer fewer losses from unauthorized 'piracy'. The converse, they suggest, is that sports and leagues with a global reach in the digital broadcasting age will be those that suffer the greatest loss of paying customers to unlicensed streaming and file-sharing services. The EPL is the most extreme case, but, Hutchins and Rowe argue, this threat also challenges commercial stakeholders invested in other increasingly global sports distribution deals. They list Formula One motor racing, Italian and South American association football, and Indian as well as Australian Cricket.

It is odd then, that the earliest case of legal action against a live-streaming channel was the failed attempt, by the Australian broadcaster *FoxSport*, to pre-emptively bar US 'Channelsurfing.net' from streaming the A-League Australian Football Cup Final in 2007. This was an event *FoxSport* had bought the exclusive rights to broadcast (Hutchins and Rowe 2012: 37). The fixture was very popular in Australia, but had limited outside appeal. The free streaming of the event was advertised five days in advance of the match. Nevertheless, *FoxSport* could not get a 'cease and desist' order enforced on a foreign-based company in that timeframe.

Hutchins and Rowe highlight similar actions for infringement against streaming channels in relation to Ultimate Fighting Championship coverage, the US NFL, NBA and MLB, and the Australian Tennis Association. As was the case for the EPL in its attempts to close down streaming channels, what success there is in closing channels and even blocking channel hosting sites has been circumvented by the time delays involved in issuing, checking and enacting 'cease and desist' orders combined with jurisdictional differences, distributed hosting and the simple diversity of alternative sites in the event of one being closed mid-stream (Birmingham and David 2011; David 2011; David and Millward 2012). The International Olympic Committee claimed a degree of 'success' in identifying (and blocking/closing) over 4,000 unauthorized streaming channels worldwide during the 2008 Beijing Olympiad (Hutchins and Rowe 2012: 38). However, this success cannot easily be calibrated. Any such number needs to be set against the time it took for such channels to be blocked in each case, as well as the number of alternatives that were available at any given time.

By the 2012 London Olympics, LOCOG (the organizing committee) set out elaborate restrictions for both athletes and spectators regarding what they could and could not do with their mobile phones in terms of both filming content and/or blogging commentary (Goggin 2013: 31–2). This was designed to protect the lucrative and highly complex set of digital rights (by format and by geographical area) which had been negotiated and paid for by an array of broadcasters and advertisers. The prohibitions issued were both an indication of the significance of digital rights to the modern Olympics, and evidence of the threat posed by unauthorized digital coverage, or, in Castells' (2009) argument, new networked affordances were challenging the hierarchical structures involved in the 'official' selling of rights. Five days was not enough to enact a cease and desist order in 2007. By 2012 timescales had shrunk radically, with many streaming channel providers reducing the time they take to close down channels found to be streaming copyrighted content to a matter of hours, or, in some cases much less. However, in the 'space of flows' (Castells 2000b [1996]) all blocked nodes are bypassed and in the age of 'timeless time' new streams emerge faster than older ones are closed down. The Internet is built to respond to blockages, which it is designed to treat as damage, by routing around them. Whilst deregulation of global and digital media corporations in the 1990s may have seemed compatible with such a bypassing of specific restrictions upon global distribution, such commercial players are threatened when their desire to retain control over the distribution of copyrighted content is challenged by just such a network form of deregulated global digital distribution.

THE CONTEMPORARY BALANCE OF COMPETING AND REINFORCING PRESSURES

The consumer market release of the compact disc in 1982 led to a golden age in recorded sales, with reformatting and radically reduced costs. However, the golden age came to an abrupt end in 1999, after which recorded music sales started to decline dramatically (Sandall 2007). In step, but ten years behind, 1992 saw the creation of the EPL and its 'marketing relationship' with *BSkyB*'s Sky Sports. This first order digital revolution in sports broadcasting saw a parallel golden age in profitability for both the EPL and *BSkyB*. In a similar fashion, one decade after Napster's wide-scale release in 1999, 2009 saw a 'signal' event in relation to digital sport broadcasting's golden age.

In what may or may not come to be seen as sport's 'Napster Moment', *Setanta UK*, a digital broadcaster of a multitude of elite sports, including the EPL, filed for bankruptcy in June 2009. It had failed to generate the subscription revenues it anticipated and on which it had based its bidding for rights. *Setanta UK*'s failure to generate sufficient subscription revenues flowed from a combination of things. It only secured a limited number of EPL matches in the bundle of rights it had secured. It could not out-bid *BSkyB* for a bigger share. It could not afford to bid anything like as much as its larger rival, and the number of matches it was able to secure rights to show was far less than *BSkyB*. Until 2007 *BSkyB* held a full monopoly of domestic EPL broadcast rights, and had built a large enough subscription base to allow it to bid very high amounts in subsequent rights auctions (see above). With its limited rights secured *Setanta UK* was not able to realize the levels of digital television subscriptions that analysts had been predicting, and which its bid reflected.

Giulianotti and Robertson (2009) report 'expert' analysis that had predicted that 80% of UK households would have taken up a satellite television subscription by the early years of the millennium. However, they note, in reality the figure reached just under half that amount. Whilst digital television subscription rates have risen, such increases have not been as great as had been expected. This left *Setanta UK* unable to pay the EPL for the rights it had bid for. *Setanta UK* was very quickly replaced by the Disney owned and heavily subsidised *ESPN*. However *ESPN* soon found it could not prosper either and withdrew from the next round of EPL rights bidding. *ESPN* was then replaced by *British Telecom* (hereafter *BT*) which, like all other earlier bidders (including *BSkyB* at its inception) sought to run its services as a loss leader in the hope of building a market that would generate profits in the future. It should be noted that whilst *BSkyB* was successful in that early costs did lead to later profits, all subsequent broadcasters have failed in this regard.

Setanta UK's collapse and the subsequent withdrawal of *ESPN* was not a death blow to global digital sports broadcasting in its commercial form. The availability of free alternatives has rather meant that new commercial providers have been unable to gain a sufficient foothold to establish themselves relative to the one dominant and formerly fully monopolistic provider (*BSkyB*). Nonetheless, many, like Richard Scudamore, saw new media free streaming as a direct and significant threat to digital sport's fundamental business model (David 2011; Birmingham and David 2011). This has, to date, not proved to be the case for *BSkyB*, even if it may be said to have formed part of the environment that led *BSkyB*'s competitors to fail. The EPL's £3.018bn domestic rights deal for 2013/14–2015/16 with *BSkyB* and *BT* suggests that even if a second (free) digital revolution is underway, the first (hyper-commercial) digital revolution is not dead. It remains active in its attempt to fend off its newer new media rival.

A court order in July 2013 brought by the EPL required UK ISPs to block access to the popular live-stream site, *FirstRow1.eu*. First Row Sport, which operates from Sweden, was found to systematically encourage copyright infringing live-streaming (Lee 2013). This victory mirrors multiple site blocks and prosecutions of software providers brought by the music industry in its unsuccessful attempt to stamp out music sharing (see David 2010). The blocking of First Row Sport will not result in a reduction of live-streaming as streams still exist on other channels. Unable to block alternatives, legal rights holders are also creating their own alternative channels. *BT*, for example, has created a new digital channel, *BT Sport* to broadcast the matches they have bought the rights to show. *BT* followed up its purchase of EPL rights with those to screen rugby union's Premiership for four seasons from 2013/14, paying £152m (Rees 2012). As the EPL and *BSkyB* had acted as marketing partners in building each other's 'brands' in football over the last 20 years (Millward 2011), so *BT* hope that sport can help to build its market share in the provision of Internet broadband. *BT Sport* is given free to view on televisions and/or computers for customers who subscribe to the parent company's broadband. Those who have paid *BT* for the Internet access that would allow them to live-stream can now legally watch those matches whose broadcast rights are owned by the company.

An irony exists here. *BT* and *Sky* are two of the UKs leading suppliers of broadband Internet, and between them control all domestic broadcast rights for EPL matches. In order to watch all live matches broadcast legally a viewer would have to subscribe to both companies. Just paying one digital broadcaster would leave them either unable to watch all the matches being broadcast, or having to stream those not provided by the broadcaster they were paying for. Subscribing to one broadcaster and broadband Internet supplier would allow legal access to one set of matches and the means of streaming the others. However, once you have decided to stream, then the incentive to still pay for accessing any matches would be diminished.

The double payment situation, created since 2007, in an attempt to break monopoly control over pricing, has created a polarization whereby for those not willing to infringe copyright, prices have increased further, whilst at the same time creating even greater incentives to stream. This makes it hard for *BT* to 'break into' the subscription market. Unless someone is willing to pay for both services, taking up *BT* means giving up *BSkyB*. If a user was willing to drop one for the other because they were willing to stream the matches they were giving up the right to watch legitimately, they might as well stick with *BSkyB* and stream the matches *BT* have rights to show, assuming they have access to the Internet already (something Sky also provides). Neither company can actively point out that their Internet service would allow customers to stream their competitor's 'content'. This would leave them in exactly the position that early file-sharing service providers were in – i.e. being deemed liable for user infringement because they actively and explicitly encouraged it (see David 2010). Nonetheless, unless *BT* really expected large numbers of EPL fans to pay both them and *BSkyB*, they must have known that bundling sports broadcasting into an Internet package would be primarily attractive because it would allow the user to access both sets of matches through one service (even if only one of these sets would have been accessed lawfully).

Whatever their motivations and expectations, *BT*'s strategy (at present) does not, however, seem to be any more successful than either of its predecessors (*Setanta UK* and *ESPN*). A little over two months after *BT Sport* was launched, there were concerns expressed amongst investors that the company had overestimated the size of the market for its sports television channels (Martin 2013). The company's share price fell as a result. Less than 30% of *BT* customers were using the channel and *BT* has – as yet – failed to make serious further gains in the broadband market. *BT* responded by purchasing exclusive rights to UEFA Champions League matches in the UK, for three seasons beginning in 2015/16 and paying £897m. *BT*'s large-scale investment is designed to gain enough content to make their new channels attractive in order to grow their audience share. However, unlike *BSkyB*, which grew its market with a monopoly over both rights and the delivery infrastructure, *BT*, like *Setanta UK* and *ESPN* before it, have to contend with both a dominant existing commercial rival, and an array of free, new media facilitated, alternatives. *BT* is caught between free alternatives that limit its scope to grow the market just on price, and a dominant player able to bid vast amounts based on a subscriber base far larger than that which *BT* has, or which it can expect to gain, given *BT*s inability to outbid *BSkyB* for the most popular EPL content.

CONCLUSIONS

Castells' (2000b [1996]: 18–22) informational 'capitalist perestroika', the transition to networked capitalism, is partial. Commercial success in sports media remains bound to non-networked digital distribution (dedicated cable and satellite) and legal monopolies. The networked 'mode of development' has not been either fully subordinated to the prevailing (capitalist) 'mode of production', nor have new technical affordances 'overthrown' the dominant (non-network based) economic order. Castells' vocabulary, his non-reductive account of the relationship between the mode of technical development and the mode of economic production, is helpful in comprehending new (new) media dynamics. However, his focus upon how far capitalism has reinvented itself in the last few decades (relative to the Soviet Union's failure to adapt to network affordances – Castells 1998: 55–8) underestimates the extent to which capitalism remains dependent upon forms of 'control' that the network mode of development does not protect and may weaken. That copyright reliant content industries such as sports broadcasting still remain profitable (at least some of its dominant players remain so) suggests that hierarchical control (such as is achieved through the maintenance of dedicated satellite and cable delivery) remains significant even whilst fully networked forms of distribution afford alternative possibilities.

REFERENCES

Barnett, S. (1990) *Games and Sets: The Changing Face of Sport on Television*. London: British Film Institute.

BBC News (2009) 'Internet Football Piracy Alert', 6 March http://news.bbc.co.uk/1/hi/uk/7927818.stm [accessed 6/2011]

BBC News (2011) 'Premier League TV football choice "upheld" by EU Advice', 3 February www.bbc.co.uk/news/business-12355022 [accessed 6/2011].

Birmingham, J. and David, M. (2011) 'Live-streaming: will football fans continue to be more law abiding than music fans?', *Sport in Society*, 14(1): 69–81.

Boyle, R. and Haynes, R. (2004) *Football in the New Media Age*. London: Routledge.

Buraimo, B. (2008) 'Stadium attendance and television audience demand in English league football', *Managerial and Decision Economics*, 29(6): 513–23.

Castells, M. (1998) *End of Millennium*. Oxford: Blackwell.

Castells, M. (2000a) 'Materials for an exploratory theory of the network society', *British Journal of Sociology*, 51(1): 5–24.

Castells, M. (2000b [1996]) *The Rise of the Network Society*. Oxford: Blackwell.

Castells, M. (2001) *The Internet Galaxy*. Oxford: Oxford University Press.

Castells, M. (2004 [1997]) *The Power of Identity*. Oxford: Blackwell.

Castells, M. (2009) *Communication Power*. Oxford: Oxford University Press.

David, M. (2010) *Peer to Peer and the Music Industry: The Criminalization of Sharing*. London: Sage.

David, M. (2011) 'Music lessons: football finance and live streaming', *Journal of Policy Research in Tourism, Leisure and Events*, 3(1): 95–8.

David, M. and Kirkhope, J. (2006) 'The impossibility of technical security: intellectual property and the paradox of informational capitalism', in Lacy, M. and Wilkin, P. (eds), *Global Politics in an Information Age*. Manchester: Manchester University Press, pp. 88–95.

David, M. and Millward, P. (2012) 'Football's coming home? Digital reterritorialization, contradictions in the transnational coverage of sport and the sociology of alternative football broadcasts', *British Journal of Sociology*, 63(2): 349–69.

Dyson, E. (1997) *Release 2.0: A Design for Living in the Digital Age*. New York: Broadway Books.

ESPN (2013) 'Spain to sell TV rights', 27 June, www.espnfc.com/news/story/_/id/1486306/spain-sell-collective-tv-rights-liga-clubs?cc=5739 [accessed 11/2013].

Evens, T. and Lefever, K. (2013) 'The struggle for platform leadership in the European sports broadcasting market', in Hutchins, B. and Rowe, D. (eds), *Digital Media Sport: Technology, Power and Culture in the Network Society*. New York: Routledge.

Florio, M. (2012) 'Super Bowl draws record total audience of 166.8 million', *NBC Sports*, 6 February, http://profootballtalk.nbcsports.com/2012/02/06/super-bowl-draws-record-total-audience-of-1668-million/ [accessed 11/2013].

Gane, N. and Beer, D. (2008) *New Media: The Key Concepts*. Oxford: Berg.

Gibson, O. (2012) 'BBC scores rights to broadcast next four Olympic Games', 18 July, www.theguardian.com/media/2012/jul/18/bbc-rights-next-four-olympic-games [accessed 1/2013].

Giulianotti, R. (2002) 'Supporters, followers, fans and flaneurs: A taxonomy of spectator identities in football', *Journal of Sport and Social Issues*, 26(1): 25–46.

Giulianotti, R. and Robertson, R. (2009) *Globalization and Football*. London: Sage.

Goggin, G. (2013) 'Sport and the rise of mobile media', in Hutchins, B. and Rowe, D. (eds), *Digital Media Sport: Technology, Power and Culture in the Network Society*. New York: Routledge.

Goldsmith, B. (2013) '"SporTV": the legacies and power of television', in Hutchins, B. and Rowe, D. (eds), *Digital Media Sport: Technology, Power and Culture in the Network Society*. New York: Routledge.

Greenfield, S. and Osborn, G. (2001) *Regulating Football: Commodification, Consumption and the Law*. London: Pluto Press.

Harris, N. (2013) 'REVEALED: Asia driving boom as Premier League foreign TV cash hits £2.23bn', *Sporting Intelligence*, 9 September, www.sportingintelligence.com/2013/09/16/revealed-asia-driving-boom-as-premier-league-foreign-tv-cash-hits-2-23bn-160901/ [accessed 11/2013].

Hutchins, B. and Rowe, D. (2009) 'From broadcast scarcity to digital plenitude: the changing dynamics of the media sport content economy', *Television & New Media*, 10(4): 354–70.

Hutchins, B. and Rowe, D. (2012) *Sport Beyond Television: The Internet, Digital Media and the Rise of Networked Media Sport*. New York: Routledge.

Hutchins, B. and Rowe, D. (eds) (2013) *Digital Media Sport: Technology, Power and Culture in the Network Society*. New York: Routledge.

King, A. (1997) 'New directors, customers and fans: the transformation of English Football in the 1990s', *Sociology of Sport Journal*, 14(3): 224–40.

King, A. (2002 [1998]) *The End of the Terraces: The Transformation of English Football in the 1990s*. London: Leicester University Press.

Kirton, A. and David, M. (2013) 'The challenge of unauthorised online streaming to the English Premier League and television broadcasters', in Hutchins, B. and Rowe, D. (eds), *Digital Media Sport: Technology, Power and Culture in the Network Society*. New York: Routledge.

Lee, D. (2013) 'Premier League wins piracy block of First Row Sports', *BBC Online* www.bbc.co.uk/news/technology-23342349 [accessed 11/2013].

Malcolm D., Jones, I and Waddington, I. (2000) 'The people's game? Football spectatorship and demographic change', in J. Garland, D. Malcolm and M. Rowe (eds), *The Future of Football: Challenges For The Twenty-First Century*. London: Frank Cass.

Martin, B. (2013) 'BT slips on sports channel worries', *The Telegraph*, 23 October, www.telegraph.co.uk/finance/markets/marketreport/10400527/BT-slips-on-sports-channel-worries.html [accessed 11/2013].

Millward, P. (2011) *The Global Football League*. Basingstoke: Palgrave.

Millward, P. (2013) 'Spatial mobilities, football players and the World Cup: evidence from the English Premier League', *Soccer and Society*, 14(1): 20–34.

Musmann, H.G. (2006) 'Genesis of the MP3 audio coding standard', *Consumer Electronics, IEEE Transactions*, 52(3):1043–9.

Rees, P. (2012) 'BT signs exclusive deal to broadcast Premiership rugby from 2013', *The Guardian*, 12 September, www.theguardian.com/sport/2012/sep/12/premiership-rugby-bt-deal-broadcast [accessed 11/2013].

Rowe, D. (2011) *Global Media Sport: Flows, Forms and Futures*. London: Bloomsbury Press.

Sandall, R. (2007) 'Off the Record', in *Prospect Magazine*, 137 (August), www.prospectmagazine.co.uk/magazine/offtherecord/ [accessed 20/11/2013].

Scudamore, R. (2009) 'Call it by its name – this is theft', *The Guardian*, 23 November, G2: 4.

Smith, P. (2009) 'Interview: NetResult CEO Christopher Stokes on tackling football TV pirates', http://gigaom.com/2009/09/22/419-interview-netresult-ceo-christopher-stokes-on-tackling-football-tv-pira/ [accessed 6/2011].

Sport On The Box (2012) 'CRICKET: ITV secures new four-year IPL deal', 30 March, www.sport-onthebox.com/2011/03/30/itv-secures-new-four-year-ipl-deal/ [accessed 11/2013].

Sports Illustrated (2012) 'Inside NFL's money making machine', http://sportsillustrated.cnn.com/multimedia/

photo_gallery/1103/nfl-inside-money-machine/content.1.html [accessed 11/2013].

Taylor, I. (1984) 'Professional sport and the recession: the case of British soccer', *International Review for the Sociology of Sport*, 19: 7–30.

The Guardian (2012) 'Premier League sells domestic TV rights to Sky and BT for £3.018bn', 13 June, www.theguardian.com/football/2012/jun/13/premier-league-tv-sky-bt [accessed 11/2013].

Walsh, A., and Giulianotti, R. (2007). *Ethics, Money and Sport: This Sporting Mammon*. Routledge: Abingdon.

Wilson, J. (2007) 'Premier League is world's favourite league', *The Telegraph*, 6 November.

WIPO (2013) 'Broadcasting and media rights in sport', http://www.wipo.int/ip-sport/en/broadcasting.html [accessed 1/2014].

25

'Piracy' or Parody: Moral Panic in an Age of New Media

Matthew David and Natasha Whiteman

INTRODUCTION

This chapter addresses attempts to foster a 'moral panic' around file-sharing. The attempt to foster associations between online sharing and various illicit/illegal practices – to demonize sharing in order to reduce its incidence, by persuasion or by warranting prohibitions – has been recurrent (Litman, 2000). Yet efforts to establish such connections have consistently been undermined by consumers' apparent unwillingness to accept, and in some cases willingness to subvert and reject, anti-piracy messages. By placing attention on audience re-workings of anti-piracy messages in productions and descriptions of media use, this chapter explores the contestation of panic messages relating to copyright violation. Not only is the moral character of file-sharing contested, but the very resources deployed in its rhetorical demonization are key to making such challenges; the inversion of the pirate from folk devil to folk hero being only the most manifest example. The chapter then goes on to highlight downloader inversions of dominant moral claims, and concludes with a discussion of the challenges to, but continued value of, the idea of moral panics in the study of intellectual property disputes in the new media and cultural field. Elite policy makers, lobbyists and mainstream media remain a primarily self-referential nexus in the production of moral panic discourses and policy responses to file-sharing. The rise of alternative media channels does little to dilute this. However, the affordances of new media do allow the 'folk devils' scapegoated in such panics, not so much to talk back, but more importantly to talk to each other and most importantly of all – relative to the effectiveness of moral panic discourse to warrant new forms of regulation – to carry on sharing, irrespective of what elites might say and do about it.

The Motion Picture Association of America's most widely circulated, and parodied, anti-piracy trailer contains the following assertions:

YOU WOULDN'T STEAL A CAR
YOU WOULDN'T STEAL A HANDBAG
YOU WOULDN'T STEAL A TELEVISION
YOU WOULDN'T STEAL A MOVIE
DOWNLOADING PIRATED FILMS IS STEALING
STEALING IS AGAINST THE LAW
PIRACY. IT'S A CRIME

This bold and simple string of claims seeks to associate the downloading of films (file-sharing) with physical theft. This trailer can be seen as part of a broader attempt to create a 'moral panic' around file-sharing activity. In this, file-sharing joins a group of issues that have threatened dominant interests and been configured as social problems in the media. To date, however, those who have sought to manufacture panic discourses in the mass media regarding file-sharing have failed to evoke a moral panic within the general public (even as their campaign is received favourably by law makers and control agencies who take such panic discourse as justification for attempts to intensify and extend their existing authority – as has been extensively documented by Patry (2009)). Why is this, and to what extent might the contemporary media landscape enable resistance to the sorts of panic messages that classical moral panic theory documents?

In exploring these questions, this chapter considers the strength of the moral panic concept in an age of new media alternatives. One of the key contributions of moral panic research for the study of intellectual property, we suggest, is the way that it places attention on cultural and technical modes of regulation, rather than simply studying legal changes and disputes in isolation. Traditional moral panic theory assumed the primary significance of the mainstream media–policy maker nexus in defining folk devils and moral panics (Cohen, 2002/1972; Hall et. al, 1978; Young, 1971). Yet the rise of alternative and new media communications can be seen to bring such an assumption into question (McRobbie and Thornton, 1995). There are now more channels through which counter constructions can be distributed and, in this context, mainstream media content may lose much of its supposed significance. From this perspective, the challenge to copyright owners from Internet file-sharing is doubly interesting, as the Internet facilitates both the deviant practices copyright owners wish to prevent, and the distribution of alternative representations of those who copyright defenders would cast as 'folk devils'. However, new media does not automatically undo the mainstream media–policy maker nexus, even if in practice it may limit the efficacy of such a nexus in achieving certain kinds of outcome.

These developments have significant implications for the management/regulation of IP. If technical change deregulates the flow of media representation, how far does this challenge attempt to use cultural forms of regulation (moral panics) to warrant legal forms of regulation? How effective can any legislation be (if enacted) if it lacks both cultural credibility and technical enforceability? The continued utility/redundancy of moral panic theory itself hinges exactly upon this question of whether or not new media plurality abolishes the significance of (and perhaps even the existence of) a mainstream media–policy maker nexus. The results of that debate are therefore useful in laying the ground for a more intelligent analysis of conflicts over file-sharing. In exploring audiences' interpretations and reworkings of 'anti-piracy' and 'anti-anti-piracy' messages, we argue that online sharers subvert the entertainment industry's definition of 'piracy' and that the channels through which such resistant messages travel are also those that limit the capacity of regulative reactions to successfully limit online sharing.

APPROACHING A 'FAILED' PANIC

In a paper on the failure to generate a moral panic around the issue of child pornography on the Internet, Peter Jenkins (2009: 45) notes the significance of both (1) 'the supply of official information and interpretation designed to promote concern' and (2) the audience's demand for the panic for the 'successful' generation of moral panics. In this chapter we examine both 'supply' and 'demand' aspects of the failed panic surrounding file-sharing by looking at three forms of text: anti-piracy campaigns, amateur-created anti-piracy parodies circulated on the Internet, and interviews with media consumers. Whilst our analysis of the first enables a consideration of the way that anti-piracy messages are conveyed, our engagement with the latter two forms of text enable a consideration of the 'complex realm of reception' (McRobbie and Thornton, 1995: 572) in which panic messages are situated. Our consideration of 'demand' aspects of this failed panic within a new media context also enables a consideration of the place of the audience in moral panic theory. The assumption that audience demand is a factor in determining the success of a moral panic was not part of the original theorization of this concept, and, as we will argue, the role of the audience has been somewhat neglected by moral panic researchers ever since. Finally, in moving between these texts, we seek to explore the contemporary landscape, in which values relating to file-sharing are asserted, interpreted and contested, and the role of new media technologies in providing a platform for commenting on, as well as engaging in, file-sharing activity.

A brief account of moral panic theory and attempts to create a moral panic over online music sharing precedes an analysis of the Motion Picture Association of America's (MPAA) 'You wouldn't steal a car ...' campaign, which examines how this campaign attempts to fix file-sharing as a deviant phenomenon. We then examine parodic re-workings of the MPAA campaign which subvert anti-piracy messages and articulate counter-messages regarding the moral status of file-sharing. Finally, we examine the ways that individuals construct alternative positions regarding the ethics and dangers of file-sharing in accounts of media use.

THE IDEA OF MORAL PANICS: ORIGINS

Stan Cohen's (2002/1972) conception of moral panic extends earlier conceptions of deviancy amplification, by making the suggestion that institutional reactions to initial actions themselves turn such actions into higher forms of deviancy. Cohen's account is of the media amplification of fighting between young people at English seaside towns during bank holiday weekends in the mid-1960s. Cohen is primarily concerned with mass media representations, not their causes or their effects upon audiences. He defines a 'moral panic' (2002/1972: 19) in terms of: (1) exaggeration and distortion; (2) prediction; (3) symbolization; and (4) reaction (pp. 59–119). Particular events are blown up and said to be only foretastes of more to come (often acting as self-fulfilling prophecies); these events are represented as indicative of deeper problems, ones that necessitate tough new regulations and actions. The final stage, reaction, involves sensitizing authorities to 'the problem', making it more visible and then using the problem as justification for control extension in terms of diffusion, escalation and innovation. By diffusion Cohen means the involvement of a widening range of agencies across a widening range of locales in regulating the 'problem' as its definition is extended. By escalation Cohen draws attention to what he sees as the intensification of threat claims being made. Finally, by innovation Cohen refers to new forms of regulative techniques that moral panics are used to justify (for a detailed outline see Cohen (2002/1972: 66–68)).

Cohen compared 'moral panic' constructions in the media with public opinion surveys suggesting that the public are far more modest in their reactions to events than the media. Moral panics rarely occur at the level of the general population. Rather, it is those in positions of power who seize upon panic stories as warrants for extensions of their power, which Cohen refers to as 'exploitation culture': the take up and use of moral panic stories and constructions for ideological and/or political purposes. Cohen's initial work does not develop the notion of exploitation culture fully. The practices of the 'exploiting' moral entrepreneurs, those that actively set out to manufacture 'moral panics' rather than just to ride stories already under way, are documented but not theoretically elaborated. Later work (Hall et al., 1978) makes more of such action, but Cohen's theory of moral panics is first and foremost a theory of media content, of panic discourse in the media, and the immediate nexus of media, authorities and politicians in making the news.

THE IDEA OF MORAL PANICS IN AN AGE OF NEW MEDIA PLURALITY

Disputes have marked the 40-year history of moral panic research (for more detail see David et al., 2011). Young (1971) placed greater emphasis upon the amplifying effect of reactions upon the initial actors, the way that the criminalization and demonization of drug users increased their marginalization from mainstream work and society, and thereby intensified both their economic and cultural identification as drug dealers/users. Cohen placed greater emphasis upon documenting the moral entrepreneurs that seek to generate moral panics. Hall et al. (1978) suggested that Cohen's account of ideological reactions was insufficient and sought to integrate moral panic research within a Gramscian version of Marxism. Cohen (2002/1980) conceded that his initial account had given insufficient attention to the cultures of the supposed 'folk devils', even whilst questioning the 'romantic' attributions of authentic cultural resistance that he felt characterized 1970s British cultural studies of sub-cultures.

Much discussion has arisen since the 1970s as to the continued relevance of the concept of moral panics. Those most relevant to current challenges to copyright by Internet file-sharers have hinged around the scope of counter-voices to be heard in new media environments. On this question Angela McRobbie and Sara Thornton's (1995) work is most significant. McRobbie and Thornton acknowledge that Cohen's (2002/1972) focus was on media representations, and that Cohen never suggested that a 'moral panic' required audiences to actually panic. However, McRobbie and Thornton argue that the rapid expansion of electronic and paper-based media outlets/outputs in the 1980s and 1990s radically undermines Cohen's conception of media consensus and audience engagement with media content.

Cohen's work suggested that audiences were passively resistant to 'media panic' discourses. When surveyed as to whether they believed media claims, Cohen (2002/1972: 49) found that audience members displayed higher levels of caution, scepticism and even outright disbelief, than was to be found in media coverage. McRobbie and Thornton argue that subsequent media plurality has given audiences scope to look for alternative representations and that this enables a more active form of resistance than simply remaining sceptical about what is being served up in media coverage. They suggest that previously silenced groups that might, in the past, have been scapegoated, have been given greater voice, whilst an increasingly professionalized array of lobby group spokespersons is now primed to counter panic discourses. McRobbie and Thornton give the example of how the music press and record companies sought to label rave music as transgressive to boost publicity and sales during a panic surrounding the drug ecstasy in the UK in the 1990s. Yet it is important to note that the music industry was not the only voice contributing to the discourse surrounding this event. Although McRobbie and Thornton draw attention to the role of new and alternative media in creating channels for alternative representations and claims, the diversity they describe does not eliminate the significance of a core media–policy maker nexus. For all the alternatives, mainstream media, law enforcement agencies and politicians carried on expanding their 'panic' discourse and their 'war on drugs'. To date, alternative media and changing public beliefs and behaviour regarding drugs appear to have had little inhibiting impact on the criminalization of drugs as the primary state regulative mechanism at least in the UK (Moore and Measham, 2012).

Sean Hier (2002) examined disputes around rave culture and the risks associated with the drug ecstasy in Toronto. Here, both authorities and 'pro-rave' lobbies sought to generate anxieties regarding the legal or illegal conduct of raves, with the pro-rave lobby suggesting that making such events illegal increased risks to participants and hence lead to more deaths and injuries. In the work of Cohen (2002/1972), Young (1971) and Hall et al. (1978), 'mods and rockers', drug-users and young Afro-Caribbean men respectively were demonized in media coverage, and each suggests that the construction of such groups as 'folk devils' (human embodiments of moral depravity and wickedness) was used to justify new forms of legal regulation and tougher punishments. In the case of 1990s Canadian rave parties, new media plurality (including the development of the Internet) gave the 'folk devil' scope to air alternative views to the moral entrepreneurs at City Hall. Hier (2002) does not describe the pro-rave lobby as themselves engaged in a moral panic discourse (in their concern with death and injury), as he locates moral panics within a wider account of ideological regulation, but in many ways his account is of reciprocal constructions of moral panic discourse. To reiterate, McRobbie and Thornton's challenge to the earlier works of Cohen, Young and Hall et al. was to suggest that as a wider range of media outlets appeared, it became more difficult for a dominant editorial line to command attention. This case of rave parties in Toronto therefore supports McRobbie and Thornton's (1995) claim that media diversification limits the scope for a singular editorial line, and hence the ability to present a singular 'panic' discourse as 'the' truth. However, as long as policy makers orient themselves towards mainstream media and vice versa, the significance of these alternatives may be limited. The extent to which such alternatives inhibit policy making based on panic discourses in the mainstream media has to be studied on a case-by-case basis. In the case of drugs and drugs policy there is little evidence that cultural change and media liberalization has impacted upon legislative policy (Moore and Measham, 2012).

With the above example in mind, questions regarding file-sharing and the Internet, and the findings we are going to present, can be better presented, as follows:

1. Have lobbyists sought to create moral panic discourses in mainstream media around the supposed threat of file-sharing? We will demonstrate below that this clearly is the case.
2. Have such panic discourses been used to warrant increased legal regulation? Again, we will argue below that it is the case that lobbyists have succeeded in persuading legislators to enact new laws and toughen existing ones.
3. Has new media plurality allowed counter voices to challenge mainstream representations? This, we will show, is also the case.
4. Does such new media plurality seriously undermine the power of lobbyists in influencing both mainstream media and legislation? To this we will suggest the answer is no.
5. Does such new media plurality seriously undermine the capacity of such mainstream representations and legislative mechanisms to regulate the communicative practices of file-sharers? To this, we suggest the answer is yes.

Whilst points one and two above sit comfortably with traditional moral panic theory, point three appears to confirm Thornton and McRobbie's critique of it. However, as point four seems to confirm the traditional view, and point five its critique, our conclusion must be that neither view is fully correct, and that a more nuanced account of regulation and deregulation in the age of new media is necessary.

THE ABSENT AUDIENCE

Ever since Cohen (2002/1972) noted how the general public did not take up the invitation to panic that was presented to them in media coverage of 'mods and rockers', moral panic researchers have rather ignored the audience. This neglect of the audience parallels the actions of the media and moral entrepreneurs being studied. Cohen (2002/1972: 140) uses Howard Becker's distinction between two kinds of moral entrepreneur; the rule enforcer (mainly state based) and the rule creator (the morally crusading politician, editor, journalist or evangelical campaigner). Moral entrepreneurs are not static 'moralists' as such, but rather agents that seek enterprising new ways of extending their moral authority. To this extent, Cohen argues, rule enforcing and rule creating moral entrepreneurs naturally orient towards one another. The media, lobby groups seeking to create new moral rules, and control agencies keen to further justify and/or extend their scope for action, primarily orient towards each other, even as each evokes (but does not consult) the audience/public as the victim in whose name they claim to speak and act. McRobbie and Thornton (1995) suggest that talk of 'panic' tends to anthropomorphize society into a single personality gripped by some kind of psychological over-reaction. Whilst the use of the term 'panic' has just such connotations in its everyday usage, such audience reaction is rarely found to occur in the accounts of moral panic researchers. Goode and Ben-Yehuda (2009/1994) come closest to mass society, collective behaviour and mass hysteria theories in their construction of moral panics, but even these writers admit that such reaction is rare and unnecessary in defining a moral panic. In almost every case it is rather the mainstream print and broadcast media that are the locus of panic discourse, along with control agencies and lobby groups. This nexus is also the locus of almost all moral panic research.

To the extent that this chapter focuses attention upon audiences, and their active engagement with, as well as their reconstruction and redistribution of, media messages, we certainly accept, to a degree, McRobbie and Thornton's (1995) challenge to traditional moral panic theories. However, just because the 'folk devils' have a greater voice today, attention to mainstream media panic discourse remains important in understanding legislative reactions, even if the distributed nature of new media dilutes the scope for such discourse and legislation to control sharer interactions.

FILE-SHARING: LEGAL/TECHNICAL EVASIONS

To understand the significance of cultural strategies designed to create a moral panic around file-sharing it is necessary to know how unsuccessful other strategies have been in limiting the practice of online sharing. Undertaken in unison; legal, technical and cultural strategies have all been pursued. The legal and technical genealogy of lobby group and legislative/technical actions in relation to file-sharing is a cat and mouse history of move and countermove (David, 2010). Law and technology shape each other's development just as do the legal and technical actions of copyright defenders and those of sharers. Since Napster's closure for contributory infringement in 2001/2, sharers have developed ever more distributed forms of sharing to overcome legal liability, encryption and surveillance. The failure to secure copyright protection by legal or technical means has made the attempt to persuade people to adhere to copyright 'laws' increasingly significant. It is perhaps unsurprising that, in this context, those wishing to protect their copyright interests have focused attention on promoting anti-piracy messages. However, as this chapter shows, audience indifference/rejection means that such messages only 'resonate' with the very policy makers whose legislative tools have so far failed to prevent globally distributed network sharing.

FILE-SHARING: PANIC DISCOURSES AND AUDIENCE INDIFFERENCE

The attempt to create a moral panic around file-sharing has taken many forms and involved the promotion of different rhetorical tropes. This in part reflects the importance placed on such attempts by copyright defenders, but also reflects the limited success of each prior attempt to associate file-sharing with something more widely seen to be 'bad'. Organizations such as the Motion Picture

Association of America (MPAA) and the Recording Industry Association of America (RIAA) in the United States, and the BPI (formally the British Phonographic Industry) and the Federation Against Copyright Theft (FACT) in the UK, alongside innumerable other bodies across the world, have sought to fix the deviant status of copyright violation by fostering associations between file-sharing and just about every kind of negative, amoral and immoral practice imaginable. Sidestepping the complex status of copyright law and contradictory evidence relating to the impact of file-sharing on the media industries, the narratives they have produced have sought to fix the illicit status of file-sharing through favourable simplifications of copyright law and via the association of copyright infringement with an array of other practices that are more generally regarded as unacceptable (Gillespie, 2009/1994; see also Gates, 2006; Halbert, 1997b; Logie, 2006; Yar, 2008 for analyses of anti-piracy campaigns/rhetoric). Repeatedly, attempts to connect file-sharing to other illicit/illegal activities (such as terrorism, human trafficking, commercial piracy, drug dealing, and even student plagiarism) have been undermined by the tenuous fit between file-sharing and the criminal activities cited. These attempts have also been undermined by the ease with which such dubious connections can be challenged in alternative media spaces. This undermining of such associations in alternative media is very much in line with McRobbie and Thornton's (1995) argument that media plurality undoes the mainstream editorial consensus assumed in traditional moral panic theory.

This rolling attempt to condemn by dubious association can be seen in a brief survey of some of the crimes that file-sharing has been linked to in the past. Some of the anti-file-sharing campaigns have been specifically targeted at young consumers. As far back as 1999, FACT and the RIAA sought to equate online sharing of copyrighted material with student plagiarism (Snapper, 1999). As Gillespie suggests, this was strategic 'to the extent that plagiarism arguably carries more ethical valence in the classroom than copyright does' (Gillespie, 2009/1994: 297). Anti-piracy campaigns in US and UK schools have also promoted the idea of file-sharing as theft, equating copyright infringement with stealing material goods, and emphasizing the financial threat that this poses to producers (Gillespie, 2009/1994). In 2008 the UK recording industry began funding a charity called 'Childnet', with the aim of educating children about the dangers of file-sharing, which, it was said, could land them in trouble with the law (BPI, 2008). The RIAA similarly funded 'What's the Diff?', a campaign supposedly to protect children by educating them into 'respecting' intellectual property.

File-sharing has also been linked to more extreme forms of criminality. Ken Fisher (2003, 2005) notes how the MPAA sought to equate the longstanding US 'war on drugs' with its developing war on file-sharing. The conflation of illicit dealing and mixing of drugs and music created an image of innocent 'kids' experimenting with apparently harmless 'recreational' drugs/sharing and then gradually becoming drawn into more dangerous practices and circles of people. After September 11th 2001, the MPAA and FACT sought to link file-sharing and terrorism, by blurring the distinction between 'piracy' (commercial infringement) and free-sharing (Bagchi, 2003; Burkeman, 2004; Patry, 2009). Only three months after the September 11th 2001 attacks in the United States, president of the Motion Picture Association of America Jack Valenti, during testimony at a congressional hearing, sought to suggest that film 'piracy' was a key source of terrorist funding, and that, therefore, in fighting against 'piracy', he claimed of his organization: 'We're fighting our own terrorist war' (cited by Patry, 2009: xxii). 'Online piracy' became a synonym for file-sharing in press releases and statements from that time. In 2003 Jack Valenti, then president of the MPAA, testified before a US Senate Committee that piracy funded terrorism (Bagchi, 2003), citing reports regarding a range of commercially pirated goods vaguely linked with terrorist funding. Reference to

Internet piracy included file-sharing in with this litany of terror. That free online sharing funds nothing as it's free did not deter either Democrat or Republican representatives on the committee from taking Valenti's lead. Speakers from both parties agreed that to 'bust a couple of these college kids …' (Gross, 2003, cited in David 2010: 100) would teach 'them' a lesson. How these 'college kids' were associated with 'terrorists' was not explained. At the same time in the UK, FACT set about equating file-sharing with piracy and then went on to claim, 'Piracy funds terrorism and will destroy our society and your future enjoyment. FACT' (Advertising Standards Authority 2004, cited in David 2010: 101). Such 'textbook' attempts to create moral panics were the most extreme cases in relation to digital copying.

By 2004 Jack Valenti had moved on from trying to equate file-sharing with terrorism to claiming that networks of pirates and people traffickers in Pakistan and Russia were flooding Europe with both illegal immigrants and pirated DVDs. Equating file-sharing with piracy, and piracy with people trafficking allowed Valenti to claim that the struggle against IP violation was equivalent to preventing Western countries from being 'invaded' (2004). Isabella Alexander (2007) equates UK campaigns at this time, which sought to link piracy with illegal immigrants through advertising showing rats pouring out of sewers, with similar campaigns a century earlier against pirated sheet music sellers, when newspapers sought to link the trade with a network of supposedly Jewish organized criminal gangs operating across Europe.

US legislators (both Democrat and Republican) appeared willing to accept the highly questionable claims made to them by the president of the MPAA, as they have been passing increasingly maximalist copyright extension legislation in recent years, on the questionable advice of such bodies as the MPAA and RIAA (Vaidhyanathan, 2003). William Patry (2009: 30–34, 94–96, 136–137 and 139–170) documents a catalogue of erroneous statistics and associations put forward by copyright industry lobbies. He also shows how this fabricated 'evidence' has been repeatedly and uncritically used by legislators in warranting new laws to suit powerful IP lobbies. In similar fashion legislators around the world have tended to be more attuned to the lobby messages of such bodies as the World Intellectual Property Organization (WIPO) in framing domestic legislation than they have to their own domestic civil society campaigners (May, 2007). The recent example in the UK of the 2010 Digital Economy Bill saw heavy industry lobbying pay off when, according to Wilson (2011), a freedom of information request demonstrated that the then Secretary of State, after consultation with media industry executives, gave his approval to the inclusion of tougher regulations against file-sharers in the legislation two months prior to the closure of the public consultation exercise that was supposed to have preceded the drafting of the bill.

Even amidst rapid change, and despite the different forms of deviance that have provided axes around which anti-piracy narratives have been constructed, there remains one consistent theme in the discourse surrounding file-sharing. This is the recurrent use of the term 'piracy' to refer to this activity. Non-commercial file-sharing is a civil offence, that of copyright infringement. It is not 'piracy' if it is not conducted commercially. However, it is interesting to note how the piracy = file-sharing link has been accepted (e.g. 'The Pirate Bay' and 'Pirate Parties') in a way that none of the other associations marked out above appear to have been. For copyright defending lobbyists this is a resounding own goal (self-inflicted defeat) in as far as the pirate label carries more positive than negative connotations in contemporary culture. As noted earlier, when examining how deviance amplification increased the deviance levels of those 'drug-users' so labelled by the state, Jock Young (1971, 2009) subsequently asked how long it would take for a demonized person to become a demon. Here, deviance amplification creates a heroic identity (David et al., 2011; Young, 2011).

These attempts to connect file-sharing with forms of criminality have failed to capture public interest. Yar, for example, links efforts by media industries to promote a 'moral pedagogy about copyright violation' in classrooms to the 'reality of widespread public indifference' (2008: 608), noting how: 'Despite the de facto and ever-tightening legal prohibition of such activities, there is little resonance in public sentiment about either the inviolability of intellectual property rights or the harmfulness of their traduction [transmission]' (2008: 609). Media consumers continue to be nonchalant about engaging in such behaviour and regard file-sharing as less deviant than other forms of profit-based criminality (Bryce and Rutter, 2005; Freestone and Mitchell, 2004; Lysonski and Durvasula, 2008; Yar, 2008). Even the reporting of file-sharing stories in the mainstream media is ambivalent. Whilst UK tabloids have routinely and uncritically replicated the press releases of copyright defending lobby groups, the BBC and broadsheet newspapers have been neutral at best and often directly challenging of the claims made by copyright defenders (David, 2010: 96–115). As such, copyright defending lobbyists have been required to pay to advertise their message, or attach such messages to their products. The most widely circulated of these is discussed below.

YOU WOULDN'T STEAL A CAR

Having given some indication of the range of cultural strategies deployed to defend copyright and demonize file-sharing, this chapter now turns to a more detailed account of the most pervasive and long-lasting example of this strategy in order to highlight how particular anti-piracy campaigns have been inverted and redistributed by means of new media channels. Our starting point is the MPAA's 'You wouldn't steal a car …' campaign, first launched in 2004 as a trailer on DVDs. This trailer has been dubbed, subtitled and re-used by copyright defending bodies across the world and remains in use today, displayed on official DVDs in a form that cannot be fast forwarded past or skipped over. To view this trailer, simply type in 'MPAA' and 'You wouldn't steal a car' to any Internet search engine.

The trailer is 40 seconds long and contains no dialogue. It shows the perpetration of four criminal acts – the thefts of a car, handbag, television and a DVD – by four (male) criminals, and one averted action, the downloading of a film by a girl in her bedroom. This download provides the trailer with a unifying narrative: it is shown starting at the beginning of the ad, continues throughout the trailer (intercut with glimpses of the 'other' crimes), and is halted at the very last moment when the girl cancels the download and leaves her room, picking up her (school?) bag as she exits.

These five events are linked by text; 34 words which appear in jumpy typeset capitals on a black background, building into lines one or two words at a time in seven short bursts that are spliced between the tightly edited visual material that represents the four crimes and the cancelled download:

YOU WOULDN'T STEAL A CAR
YOU WOULDN'T STEAL A HANDBAG
YOU WOULDN'T STEAL A TELEVISION
YOU WOULDN'T STEAL A MOVIE
DOWNLOADING PIRATED FILMS IS STEALING
STEALING IS AGAINST THE LAW
PIRACY. IT'S A CRIME

The commercial uses a slick combination of visual devices to punctuate and reinforce this message. Colour filters give an air of menace and disturbance to the four scenes in which the four acts of stealing referred to in lines one to four of the text are enacted. Jumpy editing, high/low camera angles, and an absence of faces in close up shots of the criminal acts increase the sense of menace and present the perpetuators as anonymous threats. These visual devices contrast with the brighter and more colour-rich scenes in which the girl is shown *almost* downloading a film.

The trailer's musical background – punctuated by the sound of police sirens – also creates a sense of tension, movement and resolution. Flat, repetitive, thumping background music builds tension during the first four scenes and lines (as the download steadily edges towards completion). The music then gives way to a rewinding sound that is matched with a similar visual effect before returning to a build-up of tension during the three more heavily punctuated later lines of text. There is a final musical release as the last line of text hangs on the screen. Always on the lookout for hypocrisy, online commentators have noted that this music bears an uncanny resemblance to the Prodigy track 'No Man's Army' and might itself be a breach of copyright (Nelhans et al., 2013).

Editing, camera angles, scene setting, lighting, sound and textual content therefore combine to create a sense of narrative force. These formal elements convey a central message: that file-sharing is stealing, and hence a crime. The viewer is invited to identify with the girl, who is presented far more sympathetically than the four menacing criminals and, unlike them, is shown to act appropriately in pulling back from the brink of engaging in a 'criminal' act. The 'you' of the audience is presumed not to be like 'them', but instead encouraged to be like her (with the girl's age reflecting, perhaps, the intended audience that is being addressed).

Yet there are contradictions within the narrative's supposedly logical construction. Take the last three lines of text. This makes up something approximating a logical syllogism. The first four lines (You wouldn't steal a car … handbag … television … movie) engage in a form of rhetorical repetition by which a framework of common sense moral prohibition is asserted. The last three lines construct an argument of sorts. If piracy is stealing and stealing is against the law, therefore piracy must also be against the law. The exact wording does not quite make up a formal logical syllogism, such that if A is a case of B and B is a case of C it must be concluded that A is also a case of C. For this to be the case the third line would have to read 'Piracy is against the law'. The wording instead seeks to equate 'against the law' with 'crime'.

This slippage is potentially significant. As we have described, downloading is copyright infringement, but does not constitute piracy. Non-commercial copyright infringement is a civil offence, not a criminal offence. As such, whilst an infringement of the law, non-commercial infringement is not in fact a 'crime'. In contrast, piracy – the act of commercially making and selling copyright infringing goods – *is* a crime, even if this is technically not the same as 'stealing', as insinuated in the four prior examples that seek to establish the 'stealing' frame of reference. The seven lines therefore present rhetorical forms of repetition and apparent logical necessity to construct what appears to be true, but which is precisely only the appearance of truth by means of vague and sometimes simply false premises. The claim being put forward is built upon questionable parallels, questionable assertions of fact, and misleading forms of reasoning. In particular the seemingly logical assertion that if piracy is stealing, and if downloading equals piracy, then downloading must be stealing, has a logical structure, but as piracy is not the same as physical theft, and as file-sharing is not commercially based infringement (piracy), downloading is doubly not 'stealing'.

PARODIES

The MPAA campaign appears highly pervasive, and seems to have high levels of audience recognition. In a survey of 100 university students carried out by David in 2011, for instance, over three-quarters recognized the trailer, with over 60 per cent being able to identify the topic of the trailer (anti-piracy) just from hearing the background music. Yet the argument that the trailer presents has not proved wholly persuasive. Almost all these students, for instance, routinely downloaded music and films irrespective of whether or not they recognized the music or the message in this anti-piracy trailer.

Challenges to the argument that downloading is a serious criminal offence are evident in the many thousands of parodies of this campaign available on the Internet, alongside the original MPAA trailer, on sites like YouTube and elsewhere. These parodies mimic or simply repeat the MPAA trailer's very distinctive formal characteristics and then modify the content in different ways. Some are political whilst others are simply playful. Some seek to discredit the claims of the MPAA campaign by means of alternative and/or absurd parallels and assertions. Others seek to use the same formal structure of the MPAA trailer to make counter-claims about social and political 'crimes' the makers see as more serious than those being asserted by the MPAA. With such a robust set of formal characteristics it is relatively easy to re-insert pretty much any textual content in place of that given by the MPAA, as the following examples suggest:

Example 1

'You wouldn't invade Poland' (can be found at: www.youtube.com/watch?v=wdSFe0UgB3E, but is also widely circulated elsewhere) uses the same music and text format. Here, however, the central text is accompanied by various clips of film footage from the Second World War.

You wouldn't steal a car
You wouldn't remilitarize the Rhineland
You wouldn't invade Poland
You wouldn't commit genocide
Downloading pirated films is genocide
Genocide is against the law
Over the top examples – They're a crime

Example 2

'ABUSE OF POWER' (can be found at many locations including: www.criticalcommons.org/Members/adiab/clips/SF_Anderson_AbuseOfPower.mov/view) uses the same music and type format. Visual images show various US Republican politicians involved in the invasion of Iraq in 2003, corporate executives found guilty of fraud, and lobby group representatives including the former head of the MPAA.

You wouldn't start a war
You wouldn't loot a pension fund
You wouldn't circumvent the constitution
You wouldn't monopolize the media
Who are the real pirates?
Defend your rights
Protect the commons

Example 3

Share – It's Fair (can be found at: www.youtube.com/watch?v=qmXv3naV_IQ and elsewhere) was made by a group of Berlin based sharers. A man runs with a handbag. A hoody wearing woman checks a car door handle. A man puts on gloves and a mask and picks up a television set. In the second half of the feature it transpires that the runner is returning the handbag, the woman is trying to release a dog trapped in the overheated car, whilst the masked man is taking a TV around to friends who are having a 'Darth Vader' costume party.

I wouldn't steal a handbag
I wouldn't steal a car
I wouldn't steal a TV
But I do download films
The entertainment industry lobbies to adapt laws to suit them
They exploit artists and sell propaganda
Share. It's fair

In the face of the MPAA campaign's attempt to discursively fix the meaning of file-sharing as a negative, criminal endeavour, these parodies demonstrate the recruitment of formal elements of the MPAA trailer to both undermine/invert its central message and comment on other issues. As we have noted, whilst some of these videos adhere to the topic and seek to subvert the regulative drive of the campaign, others (such as the 'You wouldn't start a war' video) recruit the formal principles of the trailer to critique other objects/issues. In each case the drive is parodic, involving an imitation that opens critical distance from the original (Hutcheon, 2000). Whilst these examples and most other anti-anti-piracy parodies reject the original text, Hutcheon's claim that the 'ironic inversion' of parody is 'not always at the expense of the parodied text' (2000: 6) is radically borne out by the way that the 'piracy' label has been accepted and recruited as a resource in the construction of communities and identities by some of those most involved in file-sharing activity.

The critical significance of parody has been asserted by scholars in different ways. Whilst Judith Butler's work has emphasized parody's role in de-familiarizing normative assumptions about sex and gender, others have focused on the value of parody in challenging the authority of institutions (Kenny, 2009). These parody videos could be seen to reveal the constructed character of naturalized expectations. Yet the idea that file-sharing is immoral, or equivalent to other forms of stealing or criminal activity, does not appear to hold widespread acceptance. What is being re-worked here is therefore not the taken-for-granted (even if the MPAA are attempting to encourage a sort of standardized belief). What these parody videos achieve, is to textually reject and challenge the institutional position that is being conveyed in the original source material. Excessive exaggerations of acts that 'you' would not engage in serve to ridicule the simultaneously authoritarian and hysterical tone of the original campaign, as well as its assertion that file-sharing is equivalent to other serious criminal acts, and shifts attention onto other, apparently more serious forms of piracy and misdemeanour.

The formal elements of the MPAA campaign are so distinctive and so open that they provide easily convertible resources for the construction of such messages. Almost anything could potentially be targeted through this rhetorical/narrative structure. Yet what makes such parodies interesting is not simply the fact that the MPAA's trailer appears so very open to inversion. In the contemporary context of new media technologies, attempts to foster moral panics about Internet users' own peer-to-peer exchange can be challenged through the very means that are said to be of concern. Such parodies have become widespread by means of the Internet. Alternative constructions such as these parodies can be spread as far and as fast as those of mainstream media actors, in this case the MPAA. In this regard McRobbie and Thornton (1995) are right to suggest that the folk devil can speak out, now as often and as far and as wide as can their demonizers. Selective listening, in particular from policy makers and enforcement agents, however, remains significant, and will be returned to later.

FROM PARODIES TO ACCOUNTS OF INTERNET USE

The anti-piracy parodies described above present an explicit invalidation of the MPAA campaign's perspective on file-sharing and seek to establish positions that stand in opposition to that of the MPAA and its interests. What of the audience that is involved in file-sharing activity but not involved in the production of such texts – the 'everyday' Internet users who may engage in sharing media content online but are not driven to publish their responses to anti-piracy material in this way? As we have suggested, the evidence is that contemporary audiences are unconvinced, or at least unmoved to change their own file-sharing behaviour, by the sort of arguments promoted by the MPAA (Bryce and Rutter, 2005; Freestone and Mitchell, 2004; Lysonski and Durvasula, 2008; Yar 2008). How do downloaders regard the messages circulated by those attempting to promote a 'panic' around file-sharing?

Here we turn our attention to accounts of the use of new technologies to access and exchange media content gathered by Whiteman during a small-scale study of the ethics of contemporary media consumers (2009–2010).[1] Whiteman's study was based on one-to-one qualitative interviews with 15 adult Internet users (7 female, 8 male, aged approximately 20–50 years) – an older demographic than the students and young people who have typically been the focus of file-sharing-related audience research (see Whiteman, also in this volume). The sample included two postgraduate students, with the remaining participants working in different professions, including IT, new media, publishing, law and the media. Each interview moved from an exploration of the participant's patterns of use of the Internet, related new technologies and more general media consumption practices, towards a more detailed exploration of their experiences of, and attitudes towards, file-sharing.

Before looking at two of these accounts in more detail, it is worth outlining some of the broader patterns of engagement and positioning articulated in the interviews. Thirteen of the participants had first-hand experience of streaming/downloading copyrighted media content. The two participants who did not engage in file-sharing activity included an individual who worked in media production and voiced the strongest criticism of media 'piracy' (describing how they would be very upset if they found out that their children were involved in this practice). The other participant described themselves as happy to rely on 'legitimate' sources of media content, such as radio, television, YouTube and iPlayer, rather than rejecting file-sharing on moral grounds.

The majority of participants were therefore involved, to some extent, with file-sharing activity. The interview accounts described varying degrees of involvement in file-sharing activity – from regular, 'everyday' uses of torrent and streaming sites, to the description of more anxious (and sometimes unsuccessful) attempts at obtaining content online. The interviews also established contrasting positions in respect of the acceptability of different behaviours. Streaming content, for instance, was regarded as more 'acceptable' than downloading files by a majority of participants. In a similar way, participants defined digital file-sharing activity as more acceptable than the purchasing of counterfeit products (DVDs, software, etc.), or other forms of commercialized piracy. These distinctions were tied to the articulation of concerns about risk and understandings of the (il)legality of different online activities (such as the idea that streaming might constitute a safer activity in contrast to peer-to-peer file-sharing, or that downloading television programmes might be less risky than downloading films or music). Confusion also emerged in a number of the interviews in respect of the relative legality of other activities (the use of iPlayer without a TV licence, for instance, or the legality of downloading television programmes that have been aired in the US).

Participants framed their downloading activity in relation to media producers and a broader context of regulation and increasing surveillance of online activity. Four of the interviewees described (and justified) their participation in the streaming or downloading of content as explicitly oppositional actions carried out in defiance of the media industry and its workings. These interviewees voiced hostile reactions to the threatening tone of anti-piracy campaigns ('the moment that someone tells you that you're a thief, my reaction is I don't want to help these people any more'), rejecting the authority of regulators and politicians to control their online actions and voicing scepticism regarding the potential for file-sharing activity to be successfully regulated/policed ('everybody's sharing and downloading like crazy so they're welcome to try and do something at home and then there is all of Russia, there is China and there is India and so what if they manage to restrict it here? They can't, you know, these are huge, huge ... all the servers are in China or Russia or Eastern Europe'). Such views were aligned with criticism voiced across the interviews regarding legitimate routes to accessing content (such as the excessive cost of cinema-going and the frustrating nature of television advertising).

The interview accounts also included the reporting of moments in which the growing regulatory regime surrounding file-sharing was described as having impacted upon individuals' online behaviours, or having led them to be more/less concerned about their participation in file-sharing activity. One of the participants in the study described how they had stopped downloading media content after a letter was sent to their employer warning of file-sharing going on within the company. Another described how a friend had been banned from a University network for engaging in file-sharing activity and how this had made them reconsider and amend their online activities (increasingly relying on streaming rather than downloading content).

We now want to look at extracts from two of the interviews where participants discussed the legal and moral status of file-sharing. In exploring the positions these participants construct in these examples, we are interested in signalling the ways that, at an individual level, audience members articulate messages about piracy and its moral status; how the notion of file-sharing as deviant is asserted or denied in these accounts, and how this relates to a construction of themselves as 'ethical'. The participants concerned – whom we are calling 'Tim' and 'Sara' – described different levels of experience of file-sharing activity. Tim was one of the most apparently confident participants in his discussion of file-sharing, with Sara being much more hesitant in relation to this activity. Their accounts also differ in respect of the extent to which each participant articulates a more or less strongly fixed position regarding the acceptability/legality of file-sharing activity.

The first extract is from the interview with Tim, an experienced downloader who relies on the Internet for downloading TV content and does not have a TV licence. At the start of the interview he described his experience of taking part in early file-sharing activity by using telephones to download computer software. Later in the interview he explained his understanding of this activity at that time:

> Did you have a sense of the legality of what you were doing then?
>
> Oh absolutely. I mean at no point, at no point in time was I under any doubt that this was not kosher, or that it was kosher, sorry. I always knew that this, that I could get busted for this and I knew of guys who got busted for running a server like that and then there will be hell to pay. Yes absolutely there's never been a doubt for a second that it's legal. However not, and this is the interesting aspect of it, it's never stealing for the very simple reason that they wouldn't have got a penny out of me anyway. So I might be freeloading but I'm never going to be a customer anyway. So the thing which companies don't seem to get about piracy, at least non-industrial piracy, because the sort of industrialized piracy that you get in China where people actually sell stuff, that's clearly a problem, but when you have a consumer who decides to just watch something for free or download some music track for free, at least in my case I was never a customer in the first place and they didn't lose any business. So I never, I always knew it was illegal. Ethically it's perfectly fine because they're not losing inventory because of what I do, they still have the opportunity to sell it as merch, and in fact if I talk about it to somebody who is actually of slightly different moral persuasion, they may actually go out and buy it because of my recommendation. So if anything they're getting through word of mouth out of it, so yeah.

This extract is underpinned by a basic assumption that downloading is illegal. Tim states that he always knew that downloading software was illegal and that participation involved running the risk of being 'busted'. This status is then extended to the downloading of media content ('music tracks') which is also presented as being illegal. However, the extract also introduces a key distinction between illegal file-sharing and stealing. The former, being 'non-industrial' is presented as being equivalent to 'freeloading'; it does not equate with stealing material goods because the producers didn't lose any 'business' or 'inventory' through his actions. Stealing, in this framework, is presented as taking away a sale from the producers of these goods. It is those out for financial gain, rather than mere consumption – those involved in 'industrialized piracy' ('in China') – that are the 'real problem'. Towards the end of the extract Tim also suggests that his file-sharing activity may actually be advantageous to media producers, as his recommendations may lead to sales through word-of-mouth. A separation is therefore marked out between the status of engaging in illegal file-sharing and being a criminal. The true criminals are not, in this formulation of the ethics of file-sharing, the girl in her bedroom downloading movies.

Tim identifies himself as an 'ethically perfectly fine' 'non-industrial pirate'. He accepts the 'piracy' label, even as he splices it in two.

Tim's account of the moral status of file-sharing can be contrasted with that of the second participant, Sara. Sara was far less experienced in the use of technology to access media content, having only engaged in file-sharing on a couple of occasions and voicing concern about the technological risks of downloading content from the Internet (computer viruses, etc.). When asked during the interview about her opinion of the acceptability of downloading different types of media content (films, television and music) she offered the following response:

> Actually you know having said that films I think is slightly different because I ... yeah, TV I don't have such a strong feeling about and I think it's because of the ... from what I understand and the knowledge I have about TV companies, oh sorry TV stations, broadcasters, they're kind of doing all right. The film industry I think is a little bit, it's hard for people to get funding for films, to get distribution for films and films to make money and I like cinemas and I like films and maybe it's because I see those ads at the cinema saying don't download and don't illegally watch this and I wouldn't want to feel like I'm doing something wrong there but at the same time if there's a film I want to see and I can't get access to it legally and I can watch it, my motivation to watch the film would, I believe, in fact I'm pretty, I'm certain, would overcome any ethical qualms.

Here we find the articulation of an understanding of the (possible) impact of file-sharing on media producers but also differentiation in respect of the type of content that is being downloaded (suggesting that it is more acceptable to download TV than film). The focus on the film 'industry' and the financial challenges that film producers face resonates with more recent MPAA campaigns that have focused on the impact of piracy on those working within the film industry (Gates, 2006) rather than the more negative equating with crime. Sara accepts the MPAA line that file-sharing is illegal. However, she claims, her actions are based on right and wrong, rather than lawful and unlawful ('I wouldn't want to feel like I'm doing something wrong'). Yet at the end of this extract she shifts her position, noting that her desire for content would probably override her concern with doing wrong, or indeed her concern for the interests of the film industry. Being persuaded about the illegality of downloading film content would therefore not prevent her from downloading such content.

What we have in these two extracts are two very different ways of dealing with these issues. Both accept that file-sharing activities are not legal, and both still choose to engage in them. Yet these two individuals construct different stances in respect of this activity. In the first, ideas of 'legality' and 'illegality' are strongly separated from a sense of 'ethical action' and harm. The second extract is not based consistently on this distinction, deploying it at first, but then abandoning 'justification' in favour of self-interest, with the positioning sliding around. The manoeuvring in the second of these extracts can be contrasted with the certainty of Tim's account, but also with the certainty of the MPAA message: 'Piracy: It's a crime'. Yet, like the MPAA rhetoric, the accounts offered by sharers correspond with their practices, not to any logically compelling construction of evidence. Whilst downloading is a civil offence (that of copyright infringement), it is not 'stealing'. As such, the string of claims made by the MPAA in which we are taken from not stealing a car to not downloading films through the implied logical consistency of not stealing, is not a logical set of steps. To this extent, despite the pretence of being a logical sequence, the MPAA's 'logic' is no less inconsistent than is Sara's leap from not wanting to do anything wrong to then setting aside ethical qualms and doing it anyway. Each sequence is logically inconsistent but totally consistent with the interests of the person/organization expressing them.

Tim and Sara's words demonstrate the complex rationalizations and justifications that media consumers construct in their descriptions of their online activities and media use. Such accounts suggest the ways that the sort of messages promoted by the MPAA in their anti-piracy campaign may become accepted and/or understood, whilst not being acted upon. Looking at the accounts in detail enables an interrogation of how individuals negotiate the complex 'moralizing discourses' (Hier, 2008) surrounding file-sharing, and more generally, the way that 'people in their everyday articulations of their moral beliefs and concepts … offer an alternative moral voice to that of institutional morality' (Zigon, 2008: 164).

A FAILED MORAL PANIC – SOMETHING NEW?

There have, of course, been other examples of failed panics. Jenkins (2009) argues that a moral panic around child pornography on the Internet in the United States around the year 2000 did not arise because law enforcement agencies made no effort to publicize the problem. He refers to this as a 'failure to launch' a moral panic (Jenkins, 2009). Whilst many parallels exist between Jenkins' focus and our own – not least in the unregulated, expanding, global and Internet-based sharing of illicit materials – rather than a failure to launch, constructing the 'problem' of piracy displays multiple launches and yet a consistent failure to ignite.

The MPAA campaign is situated within a terrain in which anti-piracy messages are being explicitly undermined in amateur-produced parodies. These parodies are replicated and circulated widely and many are viewed millions of times over. Whilst it cannot be determined whether content 'influences' viewers' attitudes, or simply reflects the preference of the viewer who chooses to watch it, their existence, and their profusion indicates the widespread circulation of the anti-anti-piracy message, and hence the inability of dominant lobby groups to fully control representations of the issue. Infringers are negotiating and rejecting aspects of the messages that are being promoted by the copyright lobbyists. These infringing 'folk devils' make use of the possibilities of new media to work around the restrictions that regulators would seek to impose on media consumers. New media affordances not only allow evasion of restrictions but also allow sharers to share their counter messages, justifications for infringing and their critiques of the status quo. The question that arises in such conditions is whether any attempt to create a moral panic by means of media constructions, as suggested by Cohen in 1972, can succeed today. If new media allows those being labelled in the mainstream media to counter and invert the messages being broadcast about them, to circulate alternative perspectives that challenge attempts to fix moral positions in ways that favour dominant economic interests, is the original theory of moral panics either redundant or, at the very least, rendered insignificant to the extent that mainstream media content loses what force it might once have been assumed to have?

Some parody trailers bemoan the way the original MPAA trailer was placed on legal DVDs and could not be fast forwarded or skipped past, thus inconveniencing the very people who were not watching downloads. Yet this ability to control the viewer's access to content is precisely what the Internet abolishes. Whilst mainstream media channels can be saturated with a particular construction of events, alternative channels exist. The absence of editorial control over the Internet has meant that the very characteristics that are supposed to enable the construction of a moral panic, exaggeration, prediction, symbolization and reaction, can be inverted and played back to global audiences in the form of parodies that use exactly the same rhetorical devices to achieve similar, if inverted, forms of rhetorical effect.

If 'moral panic' language, as depicted by Cohen, is one of excess, fear, conspiracy and exploitative reaction, as the above parodies suggest, the Internet ensures that it is not just elites who can indulge in such discursive creativity. It is not a question of asserting that once audiences believed what they were told but now question mainstream messages. As Cohen observed in 1972, audiences did not simply believe what they read/saw. Whilst the Internet has reduced trust in mainstream media (Poster, 2006), such trust was never strong (Mann, 1971). What is new is how the inversion and rejection of mainstream media messages has become so visibly and globally shared. Parodies on the Internet provide a chorus of alternative interpretations, ones that can be seen to relate to those articulated by individual consumers. To this extent they are not a simple counter-message. They do, however, undermine the rationale for paying particular attention to the content of mainstream media messages as any kind of proxy for audience beliefs, but this was always a mistaken proxy. Does the rise of new media then undermine the value of research on mass media content, something that has been central to Cohen and 40 years of moral panic investigation?

A FAILED MORAL PANIC – WAS IT NOT ALWAYS EVER THUS?

One defence of the study of moral panics in an age of new media counter-messages is that Cohen's original formulation is not focused primarily upon whether audiences are persuaded or have alternative sources of information. Cohen's original account of moral panic is an account of mainstream media representation and its exploitation by policy makers and authorities, not actual panicking behaviour amongst the general public. So it might be suggested that studying attempts to create a moral panic over downloading should focus upon mainstream media representations and the responses of authorities, not the reactions of others.

The earlier example, where US elected representatives responded to claims from then MPAA president Jack Valenti regarding piracy and terrorism with calls for tougher punishments for file-sharers, shows a shared underlying symbolization held by media lobbyists and politicians, irrespective of whether such equations were believed by anyone else. The passing of the UK Digital Economy Act in 2010 can be seen as just such an accord between industry-based copyright lobbies and government (David and Millward 2012). The Act's race through parliament and into law side-lined questions of whether any but the lobbyists and politicians needed to be convinced. Like politicians and industry lobbyists, Tim and Sara articulate rhetorics compatible with their practical interests; though the others don't display Sara's honest inconsistency when articulating moral justification and amoral self-interest, as she says, 'at the same time'. It would appear that corporate lobby groups, politicians and sharers do what suits them best, construct compatible moral frameworks accordingly, and thus insulate themselves from moral constructions founded upon alternative interested practices.

CONCLUSIONS

Surely the idea of moral panic can have no purchase in such a cynical world. But have things radically altered? What has changed is not the absence of audience panics (these always having been rare and incidental). Nor is it the primary orientation of moral entrepreneurs to policy makers rather than to the wider public (this was always true). Rather, it is the visibility of non-compliant and counter messages. The centrality, in sociological accounts such as Cohen's, of mainstream media content to the maintenance of social order, is much diminished, though not abolished; squeezed between active new-media networked 'audiences' and elite oriented lobbyists. Do new voices within an increasingly diverse media landscape impact upon the success or failure of moral panics, as McRobbie, Thornton and Hier suggest? If the measure of success is not public reaction, but rather the reaction of control agencies, then even if alternative voices get coverage, as long as control agencies continue to warrant legislative reactions by reference to lobbyist's claims making, such moral panic discourses can be called 'successful' at this level. Counter-discourses may limit such warrants to react. They may not. We have not sought to suggest here that new media counter-discourses have mobilized a political counterforce to challenge dominant economic lobbyists at the level of policy making (though research on Pirate Parties in this collection does suggest some evidence of this starting to happen). Just as moral entrepreneurs want control agents to 'react', so counter-voices have to connect with actors if they are to enact a counter-force of some kind.

This chapter's examination of file-sharing, constructions of, as well as challenges to, intellectual property rights, and the open ended character of the piracy label suggests that new media give far greater scope for alternative messages to be distributed than would have once existed. Legislators, nonetheless, tend only to listen to the voices they are attuned to hear (see above). Legislative success, getting control agencies to react (the classic measure of the success of a moral panic), may be tempered by the failure of such laws to 'bite', that is, if they cannot be enforced. The inability of anti-piracy moral panic discourses, and legal/policy reactions warranted by such media panic discourses, to stop file-sharing is linked in no small part to new and alternative media communications channels. However, the failure of this mainstream panic discourse in substantively regulating practices has as much to do with what such new media channels enable people to do (the de facto suspension of copyright law) as it has with what such channels enable them to say about themselves in response to the (de jure and in media) labels they are given by elites.

NOTE

1 Whiteman's study was funded by a British Academy Small Research Grant (SG-54626).

REFERENCES

Alexander I (2007) Criminalizing copyright: a story of publishers, pirates and pieces of eight. *Cambridge Law Journal* 66(3): 625–656.

Bagchi J (2003) File-sharing and piracy linked to terrorism? *Commons Law*, posted 31 March online at: www.kuro5hin.org/story/2003/3/14/234939/956 (accessed 6 August 2008).

BPI (formally the British Phonographic Industry) (2008) *More than the Music: The UK Recorded Music Business and Our Society*. London: BPI.

Bryce J and Rutter J (2005) *Consumer Engagement with Counterfeit Goods. Report for the Organised Crime Task Force*, Northern Ireland Office. Executive Summary published as Fake Nation? A Study into an Everyday Crime, Organised Crime Task Force, http://www.allianceagainstiptheft.co.uk/downloads/pdf/Fake-Nation.pdf (accessed October 2007).

Burkeman O (2004) Terrorism actually. *The Guardian*, 4 February. Available at: www.guardian.co.uk/film/2004/feb/04/1 (accessed 14 August 2008).

Cohen S (2002/1972) *Folk Devils and Moral Panics*. London: Routledge.

Cohen S (2002/1980) Symbols of trouble. Introduction to the second edition of *Folk Devils and Moral Panics*. London: Routledge: xlvii–lxxiv.

David M (2010) *Peer to Peer and the Music Industry: The Criminalization of Sharing*. London: Sage.

David M and Millward M (2012) Football's coming home: digital reterritorialization, contradictions in the transnational coverage of sport and the sociology of alternative football broadcasts. *British Journal of Sociology* 63(2): 349–369.

David M, Rohloff A, Petley J and Hughes J (2011) The idea of moral panic – ten dimensions of dispute. *Crime, Media, Culture* 7(3): 215–228.

Fisher K (2003) Is P2P the next 'drug war'? *Arstechnica*, posted 17 July online at: www.arstechnica.com/news.ars/post/20030717-70.html (accessed 1 August 2003).

Fisher K (2005) MPAA equates pirated DVDs to 'drugs on the street'. *Arstechnica*, posted 15 November online at: www.arstechnica.com/news.ars/post/20051115-5580.html (accessed 2 August 2008).

Freestone O and Mitchell VW (2004) Generation Y attitudes towards e-ethics and internet-related misbehaviours. *Journal of Business Ethics* 54: 121–128.

Gates K (2006) Will work for copyrights: the cultural policy of anti-piracy campaigns. *Social Semiotics* 16(1): 57–73.

Gillespie T (2009/1994) Characterizing copyright in the classroom: the cultural work of anti-piracy campaigns. *Communication, Culture & Critique* 2: 274–318.

Goode E and Ben-Yehuda N (1994) *Moral Panics: The Social Construction of Deviance*. Cambridge, MA: Blackwell.

Halbert D (1997a) Discourses of danger and the computer hacker. *The Information Society* 13(4): 361–374.

Halbert D (1997b) Intellectual property piracy: the narrative construction of deviance. *International Journal for the Semiotics of Law* X(28): 55–78.

Hall S, Critcher C, Jefferson T and Clark J (1978) *Policing the Crisis: Mugging, the State and Law and Order.* Basingstoke: Palgrave Macmillan.

Hier S (2002) Raves, risks and the ecstasy panic: a case study in the subversive nature of moral regulation. *Canadian Journal of Sociology/Cahiers canadiens de sociologie* 27(1): 33–57.

Hier S (2008) Thinking beyond moral panic: risk, responsibility, and the politics of moralization. *Theoretical Criminology* 12(2): 173–190.

Hutcheon L (2000) *A Theory of Parody: The Teachings of Twentieth-Century Art Forms.* Urbana and Chicago: University of Illinois Press.

Jenkins P (2009) Failure to launch: why do some social issues fail to detonate moral panics? *British Journal of Sociology* 49(1): 35–47.

Kenny K (2009) 'The performative surprise': parody, documentary and critique. *Culture and Organization* 15(2): 221–235.

Litman J (2000) The demonization of piracy. Paper Presented at CFP2000: Challenging the Assumptions, Tenth Conference on Computers, Freedom and Privacy, Toronto, Canada. Available at: www-personal.umich.edu/~jdlitman/papers/demon.pdf

Logie J (2006) *Peers, Pirates, and Persuasion: Rhetoric in the Peer-to-Peer Debates.* West Lafayette, IN: Parlor Press.

Lysonski S and Durvasula S (2008) Digital piracy of MP3s: consumer and ethical predispositions. *Journal of Consumer Marketing* 24(3): 167–178.

McRobbie A and Thornton SL (1995) Rethinking 'moral panic' for multi-mediated social worlds. *British Journal of Sociology* 46(4): 559–574.

Mann M (1971) *Consciousness and Action Among the Western Working Class.* London: Papermac.

May C (2007) *The World Intellectual Property Organisation: Resurgence and the Development Agenda.* London: Routledge.

Moore K and Measham F (2012) Impermissible pleasures in UK leisure: exploring policy developments in alcohol and illicit drugs. In Jones C, Barclay E and Mawby R (eds) *The Problem of Pleasure: Leisure, Tourism and Crime.* Abingdon, Routledge. pp. 62–76.

Nelhans G, Maurin Söderholm H, Nolin J, Klang M and Lassi M (2013) Spontaneous reactions to an anti-piracy initiative: a Youtube clip micro analysis. *iConference 2013 Proceedings,* 985–989. www.ideals.illinois.edu/bitstream/handle/2142/41278/507.pdf?sequence=4

Patry W (2009) *Moral Panics and the Copyright Wars.* Oxford: Oxford University Press.

Poster M (2006) *Information Please: Culture and Politics in the Age of Digital Machines.* Durham, NC: Duke University Press.

Snapper J (1999) On the web, plagiarism matters more than copyright piracy. *Ethics and Information Technology* 1(2): 127–136.

Vaidhyanathan S (2003) *Copyrights and Copywrongs: The Rise of Intellectual Property and How it Threatens Creativity.* New York: New York University Press.

Valenti J (2004) Testimony of Jack Valenti President and CEO Motion Picture Association of America, before the Committee on Foreign Relations, United States of America, 9 June 2004. Available at: https://archive.org/details/PressReleaseMPAAValentiCallsOnSenateCommitteToRatifyWIPOTreatiesProtectingU.S.IntellectualProperty (accessed 1 August 2008).

Wilson D (2011) Documents show the Digital Economy Act was a done deal all along. *The Inquirer,* 1 August. Available at: www.theinquirer.net/inquirer/news/2098344/documents-digital-economy-act-deal (accessed 29 August 2013).

Yar M (2008) The rhetorics and myths of anti-piracy campaigns: criminalization, moral pedagogy and capitalist property relations in the classroom. *New Media & Society* 10(4): 605–623.

Young J (1971) *The Drugtakers: The Social Meaning of Drug Use.* London: Paladin.

Young J (2009) Moral panic: its origins in resistance, ressentiment and the translation of fantasy into reality. *British Journal of Criminology* 49(1): 4–16.

Young J (2011) Moral panics and the transgressive other. *Crime, Media, Culture* 7(3): 245–258.

Zigon J (2008) *Morality: An Anthropological Perspective.* New York: Berg.

26

Intellectual Property and the Construction of Un/Ethical Audiences

Natasha Whiteman

INTRODUCTION

A 2012 report to the UK Government, 'A Future for British Film' (Film Policy Review Panel), describes the possibilities and challenges of 'a marketplace that is shifting away from physical media' (p. 18). Seductive opportunities for building film audiences are suggested, if only producers can harness the affordances of new media; from the development of a legitimate downloading and streaming market, to possibilities for transmedia storytelling. Yet, the report suggests, these opportunities will only be realized if industry and regulators are able to rein in the illicit practices of film audiences. A number of threats to industry are set out: a collapsing DVD rental/ownership market, 'the fear that new distribution technologies will cannibalise established revenue streams' (p. 19) and – significantly – the need to reduce copyright infringement and theft. As well 'as greater enforcement of IP rights', the report argues, there is a need 'for greater understanding of the motivations for unlawful downloading and an exploration of potential new ways to engage audiences' (p. 23). At the heart of this report is a conceptualization of the audience as a site of potential profit, but also as an increasingly misbehaving, unruly body that needs to be regulated in order to be constrained and successfully exploited.

Yet audiences have long been a 'subject of concern and objects of regulation' (Butsch, 2008: 1), key participants in an ongoing 'struggle over obedience and disobedience' (Kernfeld, 2011: 2) between media producers and those who challenge their interests. The visibility of the sorts of activities suggested in this report – from file-sharing activity to the actions of online communities that engage in the appropriation and creative re-working of commercial media content – has seen scholars focusing renewed attention onto the rights and responsibilities of audiences. Defining 'good' and 'deviant' users has always been an important activity for an industry seeking to protect its intellectual property (Halbert, 1997) and, increasingly, negotiating this distinction has also become a concern for academics. In doing so, audience researchers have contributed to a complex and messy discursive terrain – and are themselves part of wider hegemonic struggles surrounding intellectual property law (Coombe, 1998) – that presents mixed messages about the 'rights' and 'wrongs' of different audience behaviours and uses of media content.

This chapter examines the ways in which the ethics of audiences have been conceptualized in research that takes as its focus the intersection of forms of media entertainment, the activities of 'participatory' audiences (Livingstone, 2013), and intellectual property. This chapter draws attention to a danger evident in this literature: the danger of asserting apparently naturalized ethical values/positions in the presentation of analyses of the ways that audiences themselves negotiate the ethical challenges of the contemporary media environment. As I will describe, the concept of 'audience' has long been the focus of deconstructive efforts that seek to challenge essentialized, apparently 'straightforward' understandings of what the media audience 'is'. The audience's status as obedient/disobedient participant in the media sphere is also historically contingent, with different norms and expectations being asserted at different times. Today, as technologies evolve, and as the activities of audiences continue to press at the interests of corporations, this chapter argues that there is a need to deconstruct conceptualizations of moral value that are attributed to or denied from different audience practices, and consider the ways that assertions of what constitutes 'ethical' conduct can serve to reinforce or deny the interests of audiences, industry and policy makers.

This is important for a number of reasons, not just because there are inherent risks in asserting generalized or universalized ethical positions that fail to consider the context-specificity of research (see Whiteman, 2012), but because debates regarding intellectual property and copyright involve the stating of assertions, rather than the recruitment of natural rights and responsibilities. It is also important because the actions of audiences are the focus of regulatory initiatives, and the basis of these initiatives needs to be interrogated (Silverstone, 2004). In this context – a context in which researchers are increasingly being encouraged to contribute to public debate (even if the nature and quality of this contribution might be questioned (Buckingham, 2013)) – researchers may also be seen to have a responsibility to reflect on the ways that they reinforce or challenge particular understandings of the authority of audiences.

This chapter begins by introducing recent arguments that suggest that the development of new media technologies has led to a significant destabilization of established ethical foundations relating to media use. It then examines the concept of the audience, considering the development and current status of this term, before going on to trace the historical development of normative conceptualizations of 'unruly' audiences. The concept of audience 'sovereignty' is introduced, in order to demonstrate the instability of the rights of audiences and notions of audience 'dis/obedience' over time (Butsch, 2000). I then turn to contemporary forms of audience 'misbehaviour'. I consider the contested rhetoric that surrounds audience practices that appear to present threats to intellectual property holders and the complex ethical terrain this presents to academics as well as audiences. In the final part of the chapter, I explore how media researchers have interrogated the ethics of contemporary audiences and mark out a distinction between *ethical competence* and *ethical performance*. This, I suggest, provides a way of opening up researchers' assessments of the ethics of audiences and the slippages between normative and descriptive formulations in this growing field of literature.

A CRISIS OF NORMATIVITY?

It has been argued that the contemporary media environment is suffering from 'an acute, endemic crisis of normativity' (Duff, 2008: n.p.; see also Edwards et al., 2013; May, 2003) in which established understandings of rights, wrongs and responsibilities developed in a pre-digital era, no longer appear to 'fit'. Sinnreich, Latonero and Gluck (2009), for example, have described how new forms of 'configurable culture' (e.g. remixing, modding and the production of user-generated content) have unsettled foundational dichotomies - such as that between artist and audience, production and consumption - that were established in relation to earlier forms of media distribution. They suggest that this has led to tensions because regulatory responses to these activities have remained problematically rooted in the 'black and white' ethics of earlier periods (2009: 1243).

As technologies have developed, users have played with new possibilities for interaction, publication and exchange, and existing frameworks for thinking about authorship and ownership have become outdated (DeVoss and Porter, 2006), 'social consensus, law provision and subsequent ethical guidelines' have been left 'playing a game of "catch-up"' (Freestone and Mitchell, 2004: 127). In the absence of common ethical frameworks, and with industry, regulators, policy makers and the public struggling to keep up with the provocations of the new, rules of acceptable conduct are being contested and negotiated in online and offline environments (see Whiteman, 2012).

Such developments have particular implications for those concerned with the protection of intellectual property. Here too, discrepancies have been identified between established values and emergent practices. As May describes:

> The social norms that have up until recently supported copyright are now breaking down because technological change is enabling content owners (and others) to violate the previously largely legitimised bargain between private rewards and public goods. (May, 2003: n.p.)

In this way, tensions have been identified between 'our dominant systems of cultural evaluation' and emerging practices (Sinnreich et al., 2009: 1243). For these reasons, audiences engaged in consuming, sharing, making and reworking forms of media entertainment find themselves operating within a highly unstable ethical terrain.

It would be wrong, however, to overstate the uniformity of the normative expectations and systems of cultural evaluation that have been destabilized by recent technological and cultural developments. If we consider how the 'audience' was understood in previous eras, we can see that societal expectations/fears of the audience, and understandings of what obedience to authority (whether that be the authority of producers, regulators or policy makers) might mean, have always been fluid constructs, historically and culturally defined rather than impermeable or essential values/states (Butsch and Livingstone, 2013; also Butsch, 2000, 2008). It is to these audiences that I now turn.

The Concept of the Audience

> [T]he audience as such does not actually exist except as idealization. (Grossberg et al., cited in Bratich, 2005: 243)

The 'audience' is a familiar term with an 'everyday usage' (McQuail, 1997). It is also an intensely unstable signifier with an 'abstract and debatable character' (McQuail, 1997), one that has inspired diverse theoretical and methodological efforts to bring its meaning into being. Early understandings of the category 'audience' drew on a 'common-sense reality' (Bratich, 2005). Apparently unproblematic referents, such as the notion of collectives of 'readers of, viewers of, listeners to one or other media channel or this or that type of content or performance' (McQuail, 1997: 1), for instance, appeared to provide stable points of reference for scholars interested in the effects of the mass media on audiences during the early development of the field of audience research.

As this field of scholarship matured and researchers examined localized contexts of media reception and use, its central concept was destabilized. Audience research became informed by a constructionist/discursive framework, which focused attention on the diverse discourses by which its central category was produced (Alasuutari, 1999; Bratich, 2005) and the vested interests involved in the discursive formation of this category. These included mechanisms of industrial audience measurement (Ang, 1991) which served to commodify and commercially exploit the audience category (McQuail, 1997; Smythe, 1977), popular discourses, and 'the audience's notion of themselves as the "audience"' (Livingstone, 2003). This way of thinking promoted an understanding of the audience as a construct, rather than social phenomenon 'out there' (Alasuutari, 1999: 6). In this way, the straightforward 'audience' was reconfigured by scholars as an 'impossible subject' (Erni, 1989); a 'moving target' (Livingstone, 2003), with a 'fugitive' object (Bratich, 2005), formed of 'shifting constellations' (Grossberg, cited in Alasuutari, 1999: 6). In this formulation, the audience: '… inhabits no real space, only positions within analytic discourses' (Allor, 1988), its only existence being as an 'imaginary entity' (Ang, 1991).

As '20th-century media migrated away from public to private screens, and from shared sitting rooms to solitary bedrooms' (Silverstone, 2004: 442), and new and social media technologies exerted a grip on media subjects' daily lives, the security of the audience concept was further unsettled. Audiences engaged in more diversified, individualized, privatized and convergent practices, and new opportunities for interaction and participation saw audiences reconfigured as 'users' and 'produsers' (see Livingstone, 2003, 2013). The resulting emphasis on audiences' creative and social participatory efforts challenged the audience/producer distinction, in ways that extended beyond earlier notions of the 'active' audience (Livingstone, 2013: 24). It is worth observing that notes of caution have been voiced regarding the generalizability of such claims to transformation, not least because much audience research has focused on Western and industrialized societies (Bird, 2011). As Carpentier et al. (2013) argue, such narratives of technological 'progress' can also be regarded as problematic when they wholeheartedly embrace or reject new developments, or imply a linear development of processes of social change. In the first instance, the problem is that more nuanced analyses of technological 'transformation' may be prevented, and in the second, 'the complexities of these processes, and the many discontinuities that characterise them' (Carpentier et al., 2013: 2) may be seen to be ignored.

The developments in audiencing described above lead to a questioning of the boundaries of audience research, as the audience dispersed across different fields of research. As Bratich describes, today:

> The audience is everywhere being studied, but rarely named as such. Audiences are problematized as mobile, interactive, and highly technologized media subjects in a variety of disciplines and fields, including organizational communication, computer-mediated communication, library studies, telecommunications, information science, social network analysis, distance education, media literacy, and technology studies, to name a few. (2005: 261)

One might ask: if the audience does not exist, and if individuals now engage in such diverse media practices, what is the value of retaining and using this term? It has been suggested that the concept still plays an important unifying role, acting as 'a relational or interactional construct, a shorthand way of focusing on the diverse relationships among people mediated by historically and culturally specific technological forms' (Livingstone, 2003: 25). As I will demonstrate later in the chapter, used in this way – and without essentializing its referential object – the term enables us to draw connections between varied audience practices relating to intellectual property, and to draw together a diverse body of scholarship that has examined the social nature of the contemporary 'copyfight' (Andersson, 2009).

Historical Audiences: Fears, Rights and Disobedience

The language used to bring historical audiences into existence demonstrates that public discourses relating to audiences have always been 'intensely normative' (Butsch and Livingstone, 2013: 3). Yet these norms have shifted, as the hopes and fears that audiences have inspired have changed over time. As Butsch (2000: 2) notes:

> In the nineteenth century the problem lay in the degenerate or unruly people who came to the theatre, and what they might do, once gathered. In the twentieth century, worries focused on the dangers of reception, how media messages might degenerate audiences. In the nineteenth century, critics feared active audiences; in the twentieth, their passivity.

Such fears were not simply assigned to popular entertainment. As Appleby (2006) describes, in the seventeenth century, restoration authorities feared the agency of listeners, linking attendance at sermons to public unrest: 'the authors of the [1661] Act to Preserve the Person and Government of the King sought to place a large part of the blame for the political carnage of the 1640s upon scurrilous and seditious sermons' (p. 12). By the 'moral panics' of the twentieth century – media events that cast a moral gaze on the apparent vulnerabilities and pathologies of audiences – audiences had been 'redefined from active to helpless, dependent, passive, from dangerous to endangered' (Butsch, 2000: 2).

Assessments of audience actions have also demonstrated changing attitudes towards audiences' morals and participatory rights. Butsch's (2000) study of historical American theatre audiences is a valuable source for thinking about the ways that the rights of audiences have been both encouraged and constrained. He explores forms of audience 'sovereignty' from the sixteenth to the mid-nineteenth century; the ways that audiences 'insistently constructed themselves as active' by 'assert[ing] their rights to judge and direct performances' (p. 4). As he describes it, these rights were recognized by theatre owners and authorities:

> They acknowledged audience prerogatives to call for tunes, chastise performers and managers, hiss, shout and throw things at intransigent performers on the stage, even riot to enforce their will. During the colonial period, gentry exercised an aristocratic sovereignty over the nascent theatre. After the Revolution, common folk employed the anti-aristocratic rhetoric of the Revolution to assert their own plebeian sovereignty in the theatre. (Butsch, 2000: 5)

Whilst these prerogatives were respected, audiences also engaged in forms of 'misbehaviour' that were regarded as disrupting; from extreme rowdiness to inattention. What followed was a period in which the (inter) actions of audiences were constrained:

> managers in many theatres (and the courts) began to strip audiences of their 'sovereignty' and to prohibit vocal and rowdy behaviour, to bolt chairs to the floor, and in other ways restrict audiences' actions and movements. The changes culminated in the latter part of the century with darkening the theatre during performances, a 'benefit' of electric lighting. (Butsch, 2000: 15)

These moves served to 'quieten', isolate and privatize audiences (Butsch, 2000). Working-class sovereignty was reconfigured as a form of 'Rowdyism,' with notions of citizenship and obligations to authorities setting out expectations regarding participation in civil(ized) public life. These regulative efforts, along with increasing realism in dramatic forms, served to separate audiences and performances (a distinction that, as Butsch notes, 'is of modern origin' (2000: 8)). In this way, the 'resistant vitality' of early audiences was repressed (Kershaw, 2001). 'Rowdy' elements continued, but were restricted to certain locations and types of entertainment (such as the 'lower class' houses 'where rowdiness was tolerated' (Butsch, 2000: 6)). By the twentieth century, with entertainment now delivered directly into the home, and recorded rather than live forms of entertainment dominant, audiences had been re-configured from unruly participants in media performances to vulnerable receivers of transmitted media messages. Earlier fears regarding the threatening agency of the audience-as-collective were replaced by concerns relating to the vulnerability of isolated individuals in the face of the powerful influence of the mass media (vulnerabilities that appeared to have been dramatically exploited via the use of propaganda during the 1930s, for instance). In this, the focus of concern shifted to the perceived passivity of audiences in the face of the narcotizing effects of the media (see Ruddock (2001) for discussion of these developments).

Alongside changing notions of audience agency and passivity, rowdiness and sovereignty, another important development that helps to situate contemporary debates relating to audiences and IP within a historical context relates to the changing physicality of media forms. The ubiquity of reproductive technologies in the twentieth century (Cummings, 2013) and more recent expansion of media options into digital forms have liberated audiences from the need to purchase physical media products, presenting multiple channels and possibilities for the acquisition, sharing and appropriation/creation of content. The Internet and related digital technologies have supported mass participation in individualized sharing/downloading/publishing activities, activities that have seen the distinction between audiences and producers and between audiences and performances unsettled once again.

This is not to suggest that sharing/reworking of media content hadn't taken place before. Again, there are historical precedents to contemporary activities. Fan communities demonstrated both pre-and-post digital forms of textual circulation, production and exchange, challenging copyright as well as revealing potential sources of the 'unexploited value that remains in the texts after broadcasting' (Nightingale, 2009: 243; see also Jenkins, 1992, 2006). In the context of music and copyright, scholars have documented pre-Internet practices that challenged the intellectual property of producers in different ways; from the consumption of bootlegging recordings, out-takes and live recordings (Marshall, 2005) to forms of disobedient/unauthorized music distribution 'via song sheets, fake books, music photocopying, pirate radio, phonograph radio piracy, tape piracy, album bootlegging, compact-disc piracy' (Kernfeld, 2011: 2). Technological developments have made the creation and distribution of content much easier than in the past. As Kernfeld describes, distribution of music content transitioned from the 'mass production of phonograph records in pressing plants' to a period in which:

> the private manufacture and distribution of tapes and CDs became available to individuals with the introduction of low-end tape duplicators and CD burners. Then later, when songs became digital files, the whole field shifted: point, click, distribute. (Kernfeld, 2011: 14)

These developments have provoked renewed concerns, new regulative efforts to address perceived 'disobedience', and new forms of discursive contestation regarding the legitimacy of audience practices.

CONTEMPORARY AUDIENCES, INTELLECTUAL PROPERTY AND ETHICS

The Internet and new media technologies can perhaps be regarded as offering new opportunities for the exertion of audience sovereignty. As Andersson (2009: 64) suggests, sites like The Pirate Bay 'have begun to appear less as a reactive force (i.e. "breaking the rules") and more as a proactive one ("setting the rules")'. Yet to others, the Internet may be regarded as a site of unacceptable 'rowdiness'. Differences can, of course, be identified between the rowdiness of theatre audiences and contemporary audience practices such as copying. Institutional responses to illicit sharing, for instance, can be seen to take as their focus the protection of economic interests in respect of activities carried out in private domains, rather than concerns relating to civic behaviour in public settings. Yet certain aspects persist. Audiences' actions continue to be cast in moral terms, with authorities attempting to mark certain forms of behaviour as deviant and endeavouring to 'quieten' audience activities in new ways. Ripening disobedience to copyright authority (Lee, 2005) and 'rampant copying' (Spinello, 2005) have provoked sustained responses from those seeking to protect copyright, as an 'increasing discrepancy between the emerging participatory networked culture and the hegemonic copyright and intellectual property regime' (Cammaerts, 20011: 1) has emerged. Copyright breaching activities have been asserted as forms of misbehaviour through technological and legal initiatives, as new technologies demonstrate their capacity to enclose as well as liberate content (Spinello and Tavani, 2004). Yet the effort of regulators to respond to new assertions of audience sovereignty meets resistance. As Green and Jenkins have suggested, the relationship between consumers and producers has increasingly become one of distrust and antagonism, with '[b]oth sides suspect[ing] the other of exploiting the instability created by shifts in the media infrastructure' (Green and Jenkins, 2008: n.p.).

Kernfeld's (2011) distinction between 'equivalent' and 'transformational' uses of songs – a distinction that draws attention to the different ways that media products may be taken up and acted upon by individuals – helps to mark out the varied copyright-challenging activities that contemporary audiences may engage in. By 'equivalence' Kernfeld (2011: 4) refers to the 'venal practice' of illegal for-profit 'pirate' copying of counterfeit reproductions to sell on, with the use of the term 'venal' suggesting the author's own moral position on this activity. He contrasts this with 'transformational' uses, by which he refers to 'functional' transformations, such as making songs available in ways that were not previously possible, rather than modifying the original song content (Kernfeld, 2011: 7). He notes that he is not using the term to suggest more creative transformations (these would be more akin to the notions of 'reconfiguration and creativity' in the practice of fan 'poaching', such as the way that media fans 'borrow, remix and manipulate textual materials as part of their consumption' (McCulloch et al., 2013: 319; see also Jenkins, 1992)). McCulloch et al. (2013) provide an example of what might be thought of as functional transformation: how fan communities may 'collectively source copies of films to rip, then convert these to alternative file types, provide subtitles if necessary, upload them within a closed community and then prefect them in response to community feedback' (p. 322). As Kernfeld describes, such activities meet a need that is not met by those officially distributing the content. He notes that uses can shift from equivalence to transformation and from criminality to disobedience (for example, when an illegally copied version of a CD might be used to create a new compilation of songs, not previously available (2011: 8)). Audiences may move across these different activities, from exact copying and sharing (whether for financial purposes or not), to reworking for circulation in a new form, towards the modding and creative transformation of content. These possibilities demonstrate that just as the audience is not a stable construct, media texts and products are also mutable, with the instability of texts opening up spaces for struggles over ownership between audiences and producers.

The sharing of copyrighted media content is perhaps the most contested activity that audiences engage in, and one that demonstrates the complexity of discourses relating to audiences and intellectual property. Following unsuccessful attempts at generating moral panics around such activity (see David and Whiteman in this volume), a failure to rein in file-sharing activity through educational initiatives (Yar, 2008), and in the face of increasingly decentralized file-sharing activity (Gillespie, 2007), industry bodies have used encryption, alongside law and surveillance, as weapons against copyright theft (2007) (in an attempt to 'bolt' audiences down?). To date, attempts to regulate audiences' practices through heightened enforcement and punitive efforts have had limited success. As Gillespie has argued:

> These control strategies have thus been of limited effectiveness in the face of persistent hackers, the efforts of commercial bootleggers, the powerful appeal of free and accessible entertainment for a generation that has known little else, and the ubiquitous cultures of sharing pervasive to the societies and economies of India, China, and elsewhere. (2007: 7)

Despite attempts to control the actions of media consumers, and the efforts of industry to impose a meta-narrative on this activity, audience 'disobedience' (as perceived by copyright holders) persists.

For industry, the situation is not helped by the fact that public messages relating to the moral status of copyright violation are mixed. Media coverage of file-sharing has increasingly presented this activity as 'unequivocally immoral and illegal', and public discourse has increasingly veered towards 'punitive extremes' (Rodman and Vanderdonckt, 2006). Jack Valenti's efforts as President of the Motion Picture Association of America to demonize audiences as 'file-stealers' who engage in 'assaulting' the industry is a prominent example of efforts to render file-sharing deviant (Yar, 2005). Yet, as in previous struggles over audience sovereignty, alternative positions also exist. Challenges to the evidence regarding the economic impact of file-sharing (particularly the idea that a download equates with a lost sale, (Lessig, 2004; Rodman and Vanderdonckt, 2006)), the public interventions of media artists apparently supporting file-sharing activity, and input of campaigning groups such as the Open Rights Group in the UK (who also challenge the notion that file-sharing causes 'substantial damage to the income of key industries' (ORG, n.d.), undermine attempts to pathologize such activity. In this way, society sends out 'ambivalent signals about downloading pirated material … Even if copying is wrong, it's not seen as a serious offence, but as a minor and victimless crime' (Spinello, 2005: 35). The conflicting discourses, rationalizations and evidence surrounding file-sharing mean that 'what may seem at first a simple injustice perpetuated by an uncaring public against hard-working artists is rich with complexity' (Edwards et al., 2013: 10).

Audiences can therefore be seen to be uncomfortably positioned at the 'intersections of culture, technology, legal settings, and business practices' (Condry, 2004: 345). Of course, it is not just the copying/sharing of content that has been deemed problematic. More creative transformational uses of copyright have also incited the efforts of regulators (as cease and desist letters delivered to fan communities by lawyers working on behalf of media corporations have demonstrated in the past (see Ogbu, 2003)). In each case, the absence of fixed (or persuasive) moral codes and different normative drives sees the legitimacy of audience activities being thrown into question. In this context, copyright defenders' attempts to colonize ethical values and exert a possessive regime by seeking to establish a 'claim to the principles of evaluation' (Chung et al., 2004) of what it means to be an 'ethical' media consumer, come into conflict with audiences' continued presentation of unruly, localized instantiations of ethical manoeuvring. I am now going to turn to the scholarship on contemporary audiences and intellectual property to consider how this manoeuvring takes shape within this field of research.

STUDIES OF AUDIENCES AND INTELLECTUAL PROPERTY

Scholarship exploring relationships between contemporary audiences and intellectual property has settled into different areas of research (in which the audience emerges 'in scattered and masked forms' (Bratich, 2005: 261)). This includes work on consumer ethics and Internet use (Freestone and Mitchell, 2004); studies of intellectual property and fan cultures (Condry, 2010; Denison, 2011; Schwabach, 2011); the ethics of hacking (Taylor, 1999; Thomas, 2005); studies of the ethics of young people (Freestone and Mitchell, 2004; James et al., 2009); and work on intellectual property, 'piracy' and video games (Grimes, 2006; Herman et al., 2006; Humphreys et al., 2005; O'Donnell, 2013; Postigo, 2008; Taylor, 2006).

There is a substantial body of literature surrounding file-sharing: from work on Internet users' attitudes towards file-sharing (Hughes and Lang, 2004); studies of file-sharing cultures (Condry, 2004; Lindgren and Linde, 2012; Sano-Franchini, 2010); work on the sharing of music (Jones and Lenhart, 2010; Lysonski and Durvasula, 2008; Rodman and

Vanderdonkt, 2006) and film (Bounie et al., 2006; Kwok, 2004; Yar, 2005). This work displays particular empirical orientations. Geographically, there has been an emphasis on studies of North American and European audiences, although recent studies have examined characteristics of file-sharing cultures in other national contexts including the Ukraine (Haigh, 2007, 2008, 2009), Australia (Jackson et al., 2005), Singapore (Cenite et al., 2009), Japan (Condry, 2004) South Korea (Lee, 2005) and Hong Kong and China (Kwok, 2004). There has also been a focus on young people, particularly university students who are seen as the core participants in file-sharing activity (see for example, Altschuller and Benbunan-Fich, 2009; Bounie et al., 2006; Chiang and Assane, 2008; Gerlich et al., 2007; Lysonski and Durvasula, 2008; Moore and McMullan, 2004, 2009).

This scholarship has provided certain lay lines for understanding the behaviour of audiences. In relation to file-sharing activity, for instance, the literature has provided different answers to the question that so perplexes industry and scholars of why citizens who would not steal property in the 'real world' think that it is acceptable to download copyrighted media content. Diverse explanations for this discrepancy have been presented in the literature. These include moral ambivalence around the topic, the draw of free content, distinctions between digital and material goods, absence of fear of the law, and a 'disconnect between law and ethics' (Altschuller and Benbunan-Fich, 2009) which suggests that 'what is legal is not always broadly regarded in society as moral and legitimate and what is illegal as immoral and illegitimate' (Pardo, cited in Zigon, 2008: 65). As Edwards et al. have argued 'rational individualistic theories, which assume that individuals just download illegally because it is free, easy, and they can get away with it' (2013: 14), have been particularly influential in explanations of why audiences behave as they do.

While the findings of these studies helps us to understand the behaviour of contemporary audiences, I am interested in how this research articulates notions of what is right and wrong and in doing so positions the audience in relation to industry. In their discussion of the tension between producers and consumers introduced earlier in this chapter, Green and Jenkins (2008) acknowledge that *not all* producers take a straightforwardly antagonistic approach towards the unruly audience. They mark out a distinction between two broad approaches that companies can be seen to position themselves in relation to: a collaborative perspective that embraces and seeks to exploit the vivacity and digital creativity of audiences, and a more prohibitionist posture that attempts to 'tighten control over intellectual property, trying to reign in the disruptive and destabilizing impact of technological and cultural change' (Green and Jenkins, 2008: n.p.)

Like the media producers described by Green and Jenkins, and like the public discourse that surrounds audiences and intellectual property, researchers relate to contemporary audiences in different ways. Some seek to contribute to regulatory efforts to constrain the audience, marking certain activities as forms of misbehaviour and deviance, whilst others are keen to celebrate the audience's vivacity and productivity. As audience resistance 'has cast user attitudes and behaviours as a crucial focus for government and industry research with a view to producing more effective regulation', many researchers have been closely aligned to industry interests in presuming the need to protect copyright (Edwards et al., 2013, 14). Yet others have adopted more critical stances. Critics of the contemporary copyright regime have argued that it downplays 'the public interest element of copyright's history' (Edwards et al., 2013: 10) and may itself be outdated (the idea that UK copyright is 'obviously misaligned with current consumer practice and expectation' (2013: 10)). Others have been more radical in arguing that insurgency is necessary to challenge increasingly globalized copyright 'ideologies', and calling for user resistance and insubordination to copyright (Lee, 2005).

In positioning the audience within contemporary debates regarding media use and intellectual property, researchers can be seen to recruit different values and assumptions regarding the moral landscape in which audiences and producers operate. These values and assumptions are often presented as if they are natural or stable entities, providing a secure ground for the evaluation of audience practices. Yet, just as discursive/constructionist approaches to the audience focused attention on how the category of 'the audience' was discursively brought into existence, and in doing so rejected straightforward notions of this category, it is also worth considering the ways that the ethics of audience have been brought into being in this research.

I am going to mark out two broad approaches to the ethics of audiences in this work which position the audience differently in relation to the values asserted by an increasingly globalized copyright regime. In doing so, I make a distinction between *ethical competence* and *ethical performance*. This conceptual distinction serves to focus attention on the way in which the actions of audiences have been interpreted – both celebrated and denigrated – by academics. My recontextualization of this distinction (which resonates with a number of theoretical antecedents including Saussure's distinction between *langue* and *parole* (1974[1916]) and Noam Chomsky's (1965) distinction between linguistic competence and performance), refers to the degree to which researchers recruit institutionalized norms/ values in their 'reading' of the actions of audiences, or remain at the level of the individual act or utterance (see Dowling, 2005). Here, then, I am concerned with the extent to which an action is assessed in relation to institutionalized ethical expectations about what constitutes acceptable behaviour. If the interpretation of a specific action focuses on the extent to which the action satisfies the expectations of an institutionalized understanding of what is 'right' and 'wrong', the emphasis is on competence. In contrast, if the specificity of the action is examined on its own terms (so to speak), without evaluative recourse to such external framework, the emphasis is on performance.

This analytical distinction provides a way of exploring the tensions that are visible in the literature between the descriptive desire to present an analysis of the values/ethical manoeuvring of different audience members/ formations, and efforts to align with, and assert, different normative principles and standards regarding what constitutes 'good' and 'bad' audiencing. These tensions can be seen in both approaches to the ethics of audiences that I am introducing here. As I will suggest, the distinction between competence and performance does not suggest reified categories that research accounts can easily be fitted into. Tensions reside in those descriptions which appear to privilege either competence or performance.

Ethical Competence

Examples of the first approach to ethics can be found in academic work that assesses the actions of media consumers from the perspective of 'copyright ideologies' that increasingly operate at a 'global level' (Lee, 2005). Such work may seek to understand, but also, and significantly, make a contribution towards reigning in the disruptive actions of audiences. In this way it can be seen to resonate with the 'prohibitionist posture' suggested by Green and Jenkins.

In its approach to the ethics of audiences, this work can be seen to privilege *ethical competence*; competence which involves the 'deployment of a skill, which is to say the realisation of an attributed competence – attributed, that is, in and by the establishing of an emergent regularity of practice' (Dowling, 2005: n.p.). From this perspective, ethical competence is evaluated in relation to institutionalized frameworks of values and criteria, etc., and must be learnt or acquired (it is through the repetition and codification of expectations/admonishments that we learn how to behave, for example). Failure to demonstrate an anticipated competence might then lead to a deficit interpretation of the utterance or action, one that emphasizes failure and attributes ethical 'incompetence' to the action.

A key question in scholarship that emphasizes ethical competence is often 'why' individuals violate the law – an attempt at understanding 'abhorrent consumer behaviour' and 'misdemeanour' (Freestone and Mitchell, 2004). In studies of file-sharing, this activity is equated with piracy, which is configured as a threat. Scholars asserting this position make straightforward reference to 'pirates' (Bounie et al., 2006) and appear to accept the negative narratives perpetuated by industry. For example, Chiou, Huang and Lee (2005: 161) note that: 'Piracy is the greatest threat facing the music industry worldwide today. This study developed and empirically tested a model examining the antecedents of consumer attitude and behavioural intention toward music piracy behaviour'.

Another example of a research account that emphasizes ethical competence is Freestone and Mitchell's (2004) study, which uses questionnaires and ethical scenarios to explore young peoples' attitudes towards 'piracy'. The authors link this activity to other 'misdemeanours' including fraud, 'pornography, cyberstalking, online pharmacies, organ sales and identity theft' (Freestone and Mitchell, 2004: 121). The authors are interested in how young people interpret and relate to different actions, and how they justify their behaviour (the extent to which they are 'permissive of software piracy' (p. 126), for instance), noting how different ethical theories might establish different positions in relation to its rightness/wrongness (p. 122). Whilst this interest in audience justifications suggests a degree of openness to the practice, the activity of file-sharing is presented as a form of abhorrent behaviour. The study's aim is presented as 'to describe the methods by which young consumers seek to *exploit* organisations via the Internet and related technologies, and to assess generation Y consumers' ethical attitudes towards these' (p. 122), and towards the end of the paper the authors suggest the introduction of a hotline for 'reporting unethical activities' (p. 126).

In this way, certain underpinning normative values are asserted, which enable the activities of media consumers to be evaluated in relation to those of market/regulatory forces. Some practices become 'unethical' and a particular distinction between industry and audience is reinforced (restricting the rights of audiences whilst presenting industry as the rightful right-holders). Ethical competence can therefore be seen to be here established in relation to the external hegemonic norms of market and regulatory bodies which mark some practices as disobedient and configure the subject as a good/bad citizen/consumer.

Another example, Lysonski and Durvasula's (2008) report on consumer and ethical 'predispositions' to the sharing of MP3s, demonstrates the way that in positioning the audience as unethical, and emphasizing ethical competence, researchers also position themselves. The study uses a number of instruments (including scenarios and measures of attitudes and beliefs regarding the acceptability of different activities) to gather quantitative data on the 'mindsets of college students regarding illegal downloading' (p. 170). Throughout the paper, the authors identify with institutionalized regulations and concerns of industry, anchoring particularly strongly to the concerns of the Recording Industry Association of America (RIAA). The paper begins with a quote from the RIAA Chairman and CEO that asserts the negative economic and cultural impact of downloading on the industry:

> Even as we continue to transform ourselves and transition to the digital marketplace, the music community is still suffering enormously from the impact of various forms of music theft. ... One of the stories we need to repeatedly tell in the coming months is that illegal downloading and burning continue to compromise the industry's ability to invest in the new bands of tomorrow. (Lysonski and Durvasula, 2008: 167)

As the paper proceeds, the idea that file-sharing is a serious problem/threat is repeatedly reinforced. The narrative of harm to industry is presented and supported via references to a number of industry studies and press reports that provide quantitative data on the prevalence of file-sharing, its impact on industry and the resulting growth of lawsuits (pp. 167–168). Reference to the work of other scholars is used to establish the 'magnitude of the problem'. Citing a study of music downloading on consumer expenditure, for instance, they note that the 'analysis supports the contention that the proliferation of P2P file-sharing networks since 2000 has been responsible for a significant decline in music format sales' (p. 168).

Whilst the authors align themselves with industry interests, they distance themselves from those engaged in file-sharing activity. Young people and particularly students – the focus of the study – are presented as the key problem group, who are disproportionately involved in this activity. Early on, the authors present the study as having been partly motivated by discussion with their students (Lysonski and Durvasula, 2008: 168). They go on to make reference to those 'interested in acquiring "free" copyrighted music by engaging in digital piracy' (p. 167) and their intention to 'examine the mindset of those who are involved in this illegal activity' (p. 168). Value judgements are asserted in relation to this distant other through the rhetorical choices of the authors: see references to 'violators' (p. 168), 'perpetuators' (p. 169), references to audiences' 'lack of scruples' (p. 170), the 'stealing of music' (p. 170), 'offenders' (p.175), and industry attempts to encourage 'more ethical conduct' (p. 170) as well as equating illegal downloading with 'cheating the system' (p. 175). In this way the activity – and its 'perpetrators' – is othered from themselves (p. 168).

Instead, their study addresses the interests of industry ('the paper contributes to inform[ing] industry representatives that appeal[s] to ethics or guilt are not likely to deter illegal downloading measurably' (Lysonski and Durvasula, 2008: 167)). *Deterrance* is the key aim. Understanding this audience is presented as a way to 'assist in developing measures to discourage such piracy' (p. 168). There are therefore two levels of ethics here – one is the level of the values being asserted by the authors, another is their measuring of ethics of the individuals who participate in the study. The moves the authors make privilege subjects within the field of industry rather than the audience – establishing an allegiance to the values and interests of the former and seeking to rein in the latter.

While these examples of scholarship present an interest in the positioning of the audience, this interest is examined in relation to a relatively fixed understanding of the (il)legitimacy of the referential activity, against which the research subjects' positioning (and ethical in/competence) is interpreted/assessed. The use of scenarios of 'unethical' behaviour, categorizes practices in relation to a scale of values that are set from outside of the referential activity. These scenarios can therefore be seen as leading (in framing the scope of ethical positioning in ways that are interpreted as more/less appropriate, rather than being open to the positioning of audiences as legitimately valid in itself). Apparently natural and straightforward values are recruited and promoted in a way that serves to reinforce one understanding of the relationship between, and rights of, media audiences and copyright holders.

Ethical Performance

In contrast to studies that assess the ethical competence of audiences, alternative positions can be identified in scholarship that legitimates the ethical manoeuvring of audiences by examining the localized *performance* of ethics within audience formations. Rather than generalizing to a broader category (against which a specific act/utterance might be evaluated), an emphasis on ethical performance focuses attention onto the specificities of the individual utterance/stance. This can involve the reification of individual/authorial will (Dowling, 2005), and may be linked to the idea of resistance in emphasizing the localized production of actions that may go against institutionalized efforts to encourage certain types of behaviour. This emphasis has been particularly prevalent in qualitative studies of fan, file-sharing and video gaming cultures.

From the perspective of ethical performance, we find a willingness to assert the legitimacy of what might – from a prohibitionist perspective – be regarded as illicit activities. Rather than the evaluation of audiences' ethics in relation to a broader category of normative expectations (such as that imposed by copyright defenders), the primary focus is on the contextual production of ethics. This interest in the localized production of ethics is evident in studies of culturally situated performances of ethical positioning – descriptions of the ways that young people 'repurpose existing cultural criteria in innovative ways' in judgements regarding the ethics of media appropriation (Sinnreich et al., 2009: 1250), and the need to understand audiences as value-producers (Postigo, 2008: 61). It is also evident in Cenite et al.'s assertion that; 'file sharers – so stigmatized for allegedly unethical and illegal activity [may] have their own informal file-sharing ethics, an ethics of the unethical' (2009: 207). Wholesale negative connotations of 'piracy' are rejected, with scholars instead exploring the ways that individuals construct ethical positions and identifications in relation to notions of property, authorship and creativity. Alternative positions to the hegemonic copyright regime are given equal footing. In this way, studies that emphasize ethical performance over ethical competence demonstrate the very different ways that media scholars have established ethical stances in relation to the moral status of audiences.

Work on fansubbing of Japanese anime is an example of this. Fansubbing fan communities are devoted to the translation and subtitling of media products, creating what Denison calls, 'fan texts that are at the liminal edge between fan creativity and piracy' (2011: 450). Such activity breaks copyright but also presents the development of a set of localized working expectations about what is and is not appropriate. Denison identifies splits in this community, arguing that as the activity grows: 'It is heterogeneity of practice, rather than morality, that seems to rest at the heart of discourses around the ethics of fansubbing' (2011: 463). She argues that these communities can 'make some claims to legitimacy ... based on the fact that a significant proportion of the works that anime fans enjoy never make it as far as legitimate distribution beyond the domestic market' (p. 451). In this way, Denison suggests that fansubbing activity represents a form of acceptable functional transformation; what fansubbers do addresses an unmet need, and can therefore be defended (as without the subtitles they create, fans would not be able to fully enjoy these texts).

Condry (2010: 194) similarly emphasizes the 'ferocity of debate' amongst fan communities regarding the sharing of media files, the ways that participants distinguish between the law and ethics and 'principles are developed by a citizenry'. Condry suggests that activities such as fansubbing challenge the neoliberal idea that the market works 'as an appropriate guide – an ethic – for all human action' (Harvey, cited in Condry, 2010: 199). He demonstrates how, within this context, moral distinctions are made by fans between different types of activity – from more ethical (subtitling unlicensed programmes) to less ethical (copying released DVDs) (Condry, 2010: 204). The study demonstrates openness towards the legitimacy of these practices, in the suggestion that 'fans are an integral part of what may be an emerging consensus on the appropriate boundaries of commodification and legitimate sharing' (p. 207). This analysis shifts the focus away from the evaluation of audience practices in relation to deviant notions of sharing, to examine the configuration of ethical actions within a specific audience context. The account also suggests the institutionalization of ethical values at a local level, a point to which I will return shortly in thinking about how the distinction between competence/performance comes undone.

Another work by Condry – an ethnographic examination of file-sharing culture in the US and Japan (2004) – presents an affiliation to the music industry, and a stated interest in encouraging the development of a healthy creative industry, but does so without anchoring itself to the prohibitionist model. Like Lysonski and Durvasula's paper, the article begins with reference to the actions of the RIAA (and its attempts to manage the audience through lawsuits). Rather than accepting the legitimacy of these efforts, however, Condry questions this initiative – stating that he seeks to understand, rather than constrain the culture of file-sharing:

> The RIAA hopes the dragnet, and ensuing publicity, will change the 'culture' of file-sharing online by convincing computer owners that using software to share music files is identical to shoplifting from a neighbourhood store. But what is this *culture* of file-sharing, and what is at stake in trying to change it? (Condy, 2004: 344)

Rather than denigrating the activity, he argues that 'moving forward requires enlisting the enthusiasm of fans' (p. 346). To some extent, the author establishes an identification with other music fans (by including himself in those with an interest in music – making reference to 'Our interest in music') and making reference to the pleasures of sharing music with friends and family in order to challenge the representation of file-sharers as 'selfish, improperly socialized people who simply want to get something – the fruits of someone else's labor – for free' (p. 348). At the end of the article, he contrasts industry attempts to regulate audiences through lawsuits, legislation and educational campaigns, and their 'commitment to "protecting property" as the basis for a healthy business' with his own personal experience of knowing 'many people who have used p2p downloads to develop new love affairs with music' (p. 360).

Condry also attempts to distance himself from value judgement inherent in the terrain ('Please note that I use the terms "file-sharing" and "piracy" interchangeably, not to emphasize their "good" or "bad" sides. Part of my point is that determining whether file-sharing is good or bad depends upon looking at the issue from multiple angles' (2004: 345)). However, he does establish a distinction between commercial and non-commercial piracy, which suggests that the former is, perhaps, 'bad' ('Pirated CDs and DVDs sold on sidewalks around the world are a separate issue' (p. 345)). In sum, the paper is open to, and emphasizes the value of the activity, arguing that piracy is pro-consumption and emphasizing the value of the network (p. 348). Again, we have a distinction between the ethics of the researcher and those being attributed to the audience; however, here it is one that is open to the ethics of file-sharing cultures, rather than rooted in the discourses of industry. Whilst the emphasis of performance appears less evaluative than that which emphasizes competence, different values are therefore evident in the analysis.

Unsettling the Distinction between Ethical Competence and Performance

The two broad perspectives that I have marked out here configure the audience in different ways: firstly – in work that emphasizes ethical competence – as subject to certain generalized, institutionalized values that they either adhere to successfully or are shown to be deviant or lacking in relation to (or need to be carried towards through a process of education); and secondly – in work that emphasises ethical performance – as individuals engaged in the localized construction of values and ethical expectations which may be more or less strongly institutionalized, and more or less explicitly codified within formations of social relationships between audience members, with this institutionalization/codification involving the formation of normative expectations in informal or everyday social contexts. Both position the actions of consumers in relation to a hegemonic copyright regime that is increasingly seeking to colonize ethics. There are, perhaps unsurprisingly, disciplinary and methodological emphases in this work. As Edwards et al. (2013) have suggested, policy and industry research, as well as scholarship within criminology and marketing, etc., have been more closely aligned with the norms of industry. Those taking sociological and anthropological approaches have often appeared more critical of these norms.

There is another distinction that emerges from that between competence and performance, between what might be thought of as descriptive and normative tendencies in the literature. I want to emphasize that these are not clear cut, and do not provide neat containers in which to place specific studies. Work that emphasizes the localized production of ethics within audience cultures appears to be more descriptive in its approach to documenting the ethical values and practices of particular individuals and contexts. It also presents the rejection of normative values set partly by industry and traditional distinctions between producer and consumer. However, we can also recognize the promotion of alternative normative values in this work. Different values are asserted, with creativity, agency and affiliation being presented as alternative goods. Scholars emphasize the affective bonds that hold audience activity together (Herman et al., 2006), and argue that 'value depends on community as much as markets' (Condry, 2010: 193), or that file-sharing involves 'affectively charged social relationships' rather than just the exchange of commodities (Rodman and Vanderdonkt, 2006: 248). There is, then, a different form of normative positioning going on in this work.

At the same time, it is possible for a study to emphasize both competence *and* performance. Studies that emphasize ethical performance may also emphasize ethical competence when the ethics of individuals are considered in relation to the formation of social norms, values and expectations within fan/audience communities. These social contexts present norms and expectations that may compete with those of the hegemonic copyright regime, suggesting alternative institutionalizations of expectations and practices. It is notable, for instance, that work emphasizing performance over competence, also tends to emphasize the collective, rather than individual nature of audiencing – therefore moving away from the narrow focus on the individual within much policy and media research (Edwards et al., 2013). These 'performances' are therefore not isolated, but contextually situated, and can therefore be assessed in relation to the expectations of the collective/community (file-sharing, hacking, fan cultures, etc.).

Denison's account of fansubbing communities, for example, makes reference to the establishing of institutionalized codes of conduct, such as the 'New Ethical Code for Digital Subtitling' of the Anime News Network (Denison, 2011), which strongly recommends that fansubbers should not seek profit or compensation for their work. As Denison notes (and despite the conflict over ethics within the community she describes): 'The guidelines attempt to legitimate the practice of fansubbing, while at the same time creating clearer demarcations between acceptable fan practice and piracy' (2011: 460). This involves an institutionalization of the ethics of fansubbing from which the actions of specific fans can be assessed – an approach which would emphasize ethical competence. Scholarship that recruits the notion of the 'moral economy' in considering convergent media (e.g. Jenkins, 2008) similarly suggests a degree of institutionalization and consensus, but also that moral economies are open to redefinition at a vernacular level.

This focus on the communal, collective value of contemporary audiences may be considered a strength of this work (in moving away from the individualist focus on motivation and attitudes). However, there are also potential problems here. Key concerns include the risk of slipping into the celebration of these audiences, or neglecting audience members who do not participate in the sorts of cultures that these scholars have tended to examine (fan communities, interest groups, etc.). This resonates with Bird's reminder that, in the focus on fannish and creative Web 2.0 practices/formations, audience researchers 'should not lose sight of the more mundane, internalized, even passive articulation with media that characterizes a great deal of media consumption' (Bird, 2011: 504).

There is also the danger of overstating the stability of audiences' affiliations to different sites of media consumption and reception. As audiences move across and between on/offline settings, focusing on specific locations/contexts in considerations of audiences' relations to intellectual property may be limiting. Because many of the studies of file-sharing and fan cultures focus on participants within institutionalized contexts, a key challenge for researchers remains to explore audiences' more casual, spontaneous and/or sporadic participation in copyright breaching activities/intellectual objects. We also need to understand the ethical manoeuvring of individuals who would not self-identify as fans or as downloaders, and are not strongly affiliated to institutionalized positions (see David and Whiteman in this volume).

CONCLUSION

As this chapter has examined, the contemporary media environment is marked by ethical uncertainty and conflict. Exploring what it means to be a 'good' audience member in this context raises important questions about audiences' affective relations to property, notions of authorship/ownership, ideas regarding reciprocity and fair use, and the ways that ethical codes emerge and are institutionalized within different formations of audiences (from online communities to offline relationships and sites of reception).

I have situated contemporary debates relating to audience and IP within the context of historical discourses and expectations regarding the 'audience'. Images of the audience from the sixteenth to the twentieth century 'were always evaluative and normative, and the standard of evaluation was the conscientious, cultivated, and informed citizen' (Butsch, 2008: 2). How different are things today? Irr (2010: 4) suggests that, in the US copyright model, for instance: 'Only those citizen-subjects assumed to possess moral purpose (that is, educators, and clerics) or to refrain from market competition are normally trusted to handle the work freely; others must pay for the privilege'.

Increasingly, however, other citizen-subjects – or in the terms that I have been thinking about them in this chapter, audiences – are appropriating and using content without permission. Contemporary assertions of 'sovereignty' see individuals claiming possession of rights and authority in ways that are different from the actions of earlier audiences, yet also similar in their active assertion of audience prerogatives. At the same time, we seem to be moving away from physical forms of media (back) towards (new digital) experiences. It would therefore be a mistake to reify a relatively modern state of affairs in the discussion of the ways that new technologies have 'transformed' relationships between audiences and producers/media productions. As we have seen, these relationships have always been in flux, and narratives of transformation and progress can be problematic. The contemporary situation can instead be understood as an extension of historical developments by which the 'audience' asserted its rights and became the target of protection, regulation and mobilization (Bratich, 2005: 258) via moral assertions and in the name of market interests.

I have also drawn attention to the discursive construction of audiences and intellectual property. The idea that the audience does not exist is now well established. The idea that the ethics of audiences also do not exist is perhaps more controversial. Both, however, can be regarded as a product of discursive positioning and forms of evaluation and measurement that reflect specific perspectives and interests. Debates relating to intellectual property and copyright have also been understood as constituting an ideological terrain, involving the hegemonic fixing of positions rather than natural rights. Any hegemonic discourse 'selects, limits, and constructs the possibilities of a more expansive field of social practices' (Dyer-Witheford, cited in Bratich, 2005: 245). Against this backdrop, I have argued that attention needs to be placed on who is given and/or denied moral rights in the contemporary media environment and the manner by which this is done. Alongside popular and policy discourses relating to the practices of contemporary audiences, academic scholarship on audiences and intellectual property also constructs and reinforces ways of thinking about the 'sovereignty' and 'unruliness' of audiences, and therefore has a political dimension that demands consideration.

The conceptual distinction that I have introduced between ethical competence and ethical performance (one that, as I have suggested, itself should not be reified) provides a framework for interrogating the way that ethical stances relating to audiences and intellectual property are brought into being in audience research. As I have described, this distinction draws attention to the way that the actions (and, with this, ethics) of audiences are interpreted; the extent to which the actions of audiences are assessed in relation to institutionalized frameworks of values, or considered at the level of the utterance/act. In setting out the distinction between ethical competence and performance, I have not intended to present certain studies or perspectives as 'more' ethical than others. Instead, my intention has been to demonstrate how, in producing such accounts, academics are involved in inscribing themselves into positions in relation to the audience/industry (positions that, as we have seen, may involve the articulation of personal affiliations). Attending to these moves also raises important methodological questions relating to researchers' openness to the audience as 'other' (as well as the distinctions that are made between 'us' and 'them'). In examining the positioning in this literature, this chapter has therefore encouraged a reflection upon not just how researchers conceptualize the audience, but also the value judgements that underpin our work. As Silverstone (2004) argues, 'There is inevitably and necessarily a need for caution in any kind of moral position lest it be seen as, or become, moralistic' (p. 446). This is an important warning for those contributing to the terrain of discourses regarding intellectual property, audiences and the media. The framework presented in this chapter provides one way of approaching these ongoing debates.

ACKNOWLEDGEMENTS

I would like to thank the editors for their comments on this chapter as it developed. I am also very grateful to Helen Wood for reading a previous draft and for her valuable insights and suggestions.

REFERENCES

Alasuutari, P. (1999) 'Introduction: Three Phases of Reception Study', in *Rethinking the Media Audience: The New Agenda*, P. Alasuutari (ed.), London/SAGE, 1–21.

Allor, M. (1988) 'Relocating the Site of the Audience', *Critical Studies in Mass Communication*, 5, 217–233.

Andersson, J. (2009) 'For the Good of the Net: The Pirate Bay as a Strategic Sovereign', *Culture Machine*, 10, 64–108.

Ang, I. (1991) *Desperately Seeking the Audience*, London/Routledge.

Altschuller, S. and R. Benbunan-Fich (2009) 'Is Music Downloading the New Prohibition? What Students Reveal through an Ethical Dilemma', *Ethics Information Technologies*, 11, 49–56.

Appleby, D.J. (2006) 'Issues of Audience and Reception in Restoration Preaching', in *Readers, Audiences and Coteries in Early Modern England*, Geoff Baker and Ann McGruer (eds), Newcastle/Cambridge Scholars Publishing, 10–27.

Bird, S.E. (2011) 'Are We All Produsers Now? Convergence and Media Audience Practices', *Cultural Studies*, 25(4–5), 502–516.

Bounie, D., M. Bourreau and P. Waelbroeck (2006) 'Piracy and the Demand for Films: Analysis of Piracy Behavior in French Universities', *Review of Economic Research on Copyright Issues*, 3(2), 15–27.

Bratich, J.Z. (2005) 'Assessing the Multitude: Revisiting Early Audience Studies', *Communication Theory*, 15(3), 242–265.

Buckingham, D. (2013) 'Representing Audiences: Audience Research, Public Knowledge, and Policy', *The Communication Review*, 16, 51–60.

Butsch, R. (2000) *The Making of American Audiences: From Stage to Television 1970–1990*, Cambridge/Cambridge University Press.

Butsch, R. (2008) *The Citizen Audience: Crowds Publics and Individuals*, London/ Routledge.

Butsch, R. and S. Livingstone (eds) (2013) *Meanings of Audiences: Comparative Discourses*, London/ Routledge.

Cammaerts, B. (2011) 'The Hegemonic Copyright-Regime vs. the Sharing Copyright Users of Music? *Media, Culture & Society*, 33(3), 491–502, http://eprints.lse.ac.uk/32835/

Carey, J.W. (1989) *Communication as Culture: Essays on Media and Society*, Boston/Unwin Hyman.

Carpentier, N., K.C. Schrøder and L. Hallett (2013) 'Audience/Society Transformations', in *Audience Transformations: Shifting Audience Positions in Late Modernity*, N. Carpentier, K. C. Schrøder and L. Hallett (eds), Abingdon and New York/Routledge, 1–12.

Cenite, M., M.W. Wang, C. Peiwan and G.S. Chan (2009) 'More than Just Free Content: Motivations of Peer-to-Peer File Sharers', *Journal of Communication Inquiry*, 33(3), 206–221.

Chiang, E.P. and D. Assane (2008) 'Music Piracy Among Students on the University Campus: Do Males and Females React Differently?', *Journal of Socio-Economics*, 37(4), 1371–1380.

Chiou, J., C. Huang and H. Lee (2005) 'The Antecedents of Music Piracy Attitudes and Intentions', *Journal of Business Ethics*, 57, 161–174.

Chomsky, N. (1965) *Aspects of the Theory of Syntax*. Cambridge, MA: MIT Press.

Chung, S., P. Dowling and N. Whiteman (2004) '(Dis) possessing Literacy and Literature: Gourmandising in Gibsonbarlowville', in *The World Yearbook of Education 2004: Digital Technology, Communities and Education*, Andrew Brown and Niki Davis (eds), London/Routledge.

Condry, I. (2004) 'Cultures of Music Piracy: An Ethnographic Comparison of the US and Japan', *International Journal of Cultural Studies*, 7(3), 343–363.

Condry, I. (2010) 'Dark Energy: What Fansubs Reveal about the Copyright Wars', in *Mechademia, Volume 5: Fanthropologies*, F. Lunning (ed.), Minneapolis/ University of Minnesota Press, 193–208.

Coombe, R.J. (1998) *The Cultural Life of Intellectual Properties: Authorship, Appropriation, and the Law*, Durham and London/Duke University Press.

Cummings, A. (2013) 'Inherent Vice: Bootleg Histories of Videotape and Copyright, by Lucas Hilderbrand', reviewed by Alex S. Cummings, *Visual Resources: An International Journal of Documentation*, 27, 4, 371–375.

Denison, R. (2011) 'Anime Fandom and the Liminal Spaces between Fan Creativity and Piracy', *International Journal of Cultural Studies*, 14(5), 449–466.

DeVoss, D.N. and J.E. Porter (2006) 'Why Napster Matters to Writing: Filesharing as a New Ethic of Digital Delivery', *Computers and Composition*, 23, 178–210.

Dowling, P. (2005) 'A Timely Utterance', invited contribution to the European Systemic Functional Linguistics Conference and Workshop, presented 4 August 2005. Available at: www.pauldowling.me/publications/dowling2005/timely_utterance/index.htm

Duff, A. (2008) 'The Normative Crisis of the Information Society', *Cyberpsychology: Journal of Psychosocial Research on Cyberspace,* 2(1). Available at: www.cyberpsychology.eu/view.php?cisloclanku=2008051201&article=1

Edwards, L., B. Klein, D. Lee, G. Moss and F. Philip (2013) 'Framing the Consumer: Copyright Regulation and the Public', *Convergence: The International Journal of Research into New Media Technologies,* 19(1), 9–24.

Erni, J. (1989) 'Where Is the "Audience?": Discerning the (Impossible) Subject', *Journal of Communication Inquiry*, 13(2), 30–42.

Film Policy Review Panel (2012) 'A Future for British Film: It Begins with the Audience', Report to Government http://culture.gov.uk/images/publications/DCMS-film-policy-review-report-2012.pdf

Freestone, O. and V-W. Mitchell (2004) 'Generation Y Attitudes Towards E-ethics and Internet-related Misbehaviours', *Journal of Business Ethics*, 54, 121–128.

Gerlich, R.N., N. Turner and S. Gopalan (2007) 'Ethics and Music: A Comparison of Students at Predominantly White and Black Colleges and their Attitudes Toward File Sharing', *Academy of Educational Leadership Journal*, 11(2).

Gillespie, T. (2007) *Wired Shut: Copyright and the Shape of Digital Culture*, Cambridge, MA/MIT Press.

Green, J. and H. Jenkins (2008) 'The Moral Economy of the Web'. Available at: www.henryjenkins.org/2008/03/the_moral_economy_of_web_20_pa.html

Grimes, S.M. (2006) 'Online Multiplayer Games: A Virtual Space for Intellectual Property Debates', *New Media & Society*, 8(6), 969–990.

Haigh, M. (2007) 'Downloading Communism: File Sharing as Samizdat in Ukraine', *Libri*, 57, 165–178.

Haigh, M. (2008) 'The "Goodbye Petrovka" Plan: Moral Economy of File Sharing in Post-Soviet Ukraine', *Working Paper Series of the Research Network 1989*. Available at: http://gesis.org/knowledgebase/1989/papers/haigh_wp7.pdf

Haigh, M. (2009) 'Of Ducks and Downloads: The Moral Economy of Intellectual Property in Post-Soviet Society', *Libri*, 59, 248–258.

Halbert, D. (1997) 'Intellectual Property Piracy: The Narrative Construction of Deviance', *International Journal for the Semiotics of Law*, X, 28, 55–78.

Herman, A., R.J. Coombe and L. Kaye (2006) 'Your Second Life? Goodwill and the Performativity of Intellectual Property in Online Digital Gaming', *Cultural Studies*, 20(2–3), 184–210.

Hughes, J. and K.D. Lang (2004) 'Issues in Online Focus Groups: Lessons Learned from an Empirical Study of Peer-to-Peer Filesharing System Users', *Electronic Journal of Business Research Methods*, 2(2). Available at: http://ejbrm.com/vol12/v2-i2/vol2-issue2-art5-hughes.pdf

Humphreys, S., B. Fitzgerald, J. Banks and N. Suzor (2005) 'Fan Based Production for Computer Games: User Led Innovation, the "Drift of Value" and the Negotiation of Intellectual Property Rights', *Media International Australia*, incorporating Media and Culture, 114, 16–29.

Irr, C. (2010) *Pink Pirates: Contemporary American Women Writers and Copyright*, Iowa City/University of Iowa Press.

Jackson, M., S. Singh, J. Waycott and J. Beekhuyzen (2005) 'DRMs, Fair Use and Users' Experience of Sharing Music', *Proceedings of the 5th ACM Workshop on Digital Rights Management*, November 7, Alexandria, Virginia.

James, C., with K. Davis, A. Flores, J.M. Francis, L. Pettingill, M. Rundle and H. Gardner (2009) '*Young People, Ethics, and the New Digital Media: A Synthesis from the Good-Play Project,* John D. and Catherine T. MacArthur Foundation Report on Digital Media and Learning.

Jenkins, H. (1992) *Textual Poachers: Television Fans and Participatory Culture*, New York/Routledge.

Jenkins, H. (2006) 'Quentin Tarantino's Star Wars: Grassroots Creativity Meets the Media Industry', in *Convergence Culture: Where Old and New Media Collide*, New York and London/New York University Press, 135–173.

Jenkins, H. (2008) 'The Moral Economy of Web 2.0: Part One'. Available at: www.henryjenkins.org/2008/03/the_moral_economy_of_web_20_pa.html

Jones, S. and A. Lenhart (2010) 'Music Downloading and Listening: Findings from the Pew Internet and American Life Project', *Popular Music and Society*, 27(2), 185–199.

Kernfeld, B. (2011) *Pop Song Piracy: Disobedient Music Distribution Since 1929*, Chicago/University of Chicago Press.

Kershaw, B. (2001) 'Oh for Unruly Audiences! Or, Patterns of Participation in Twentieth -Century Theatre', *Modern Drama*, 44(2), 133–154.

Kwok, S.H. (2004) 'File-Sharing Activities Over BT Networks: Pirated Movies', *ACM Computers in Entertainment*, 2(2), 11.

Lee, K. (2005) 'The Momentum of Control and Autonomy: A Local Scene of Peer-to-Peer Music-Sharing Technology', *Media, Culture & Society*, 27(5), 799–809.

Lessig, L. (2004) *Free Culture: How Big Media Uses Technology and the Law to Lock Down Culture and Control Creativity*, New York/Penguin Press.

Lindgren, S. and Linde, J. (2012) 'The Subpolitics of Online Piracy: A Swedish Case Study', *Convergence*, 18(2), 143–164.

Livingstone, S. (1998) 'Relationships between Media and Audiences: Prospects for Audience Reception Studies', in *Media, Ritual and Identity: Essays in Honor of Elihu Katz*, T. Liebes and J. Curran (eds), London/Routledge, 237–255.

Livingstone, S. (2003) 'The Changing Nature of Audiences: From the Mass Audience to the Interactive Media User', London: LSE Research Online. Available at: http://eprints.lse.ac.uk/417/

Livingstone, S. (2013) 'The Participation Paradigm in Audience Research', *The Communication Review*, 16, 21–30.

Lysonski, S. and S. Durvasula (2008) 'Digital Piracy of MP3s: Consumer and Ethical Dispositions', *Journal of Consumer Marketing*, 25(3), 167–178.

Marshall, L. (2005) *Bootlegging: Romanticism and Copyright in the Music Industry*, London /SAGE.

May, C. (2003) 'Digital Rights Management and the Breakdown of Social Norms', *First Monday*, 8(11). Available at: www.firstmonday.org/ojs/index.php/fm/article/view/1097

McCulloch, R., V. Crisp, J. Hickman and S. James (2013) 'Of Proprietors and Poachers: Fandom as Negotiated Brand Ownership', *Participations: Journal of Audience & Reception Studies*, 10(1), 319–328.

McQuail, D. (1997) *Audience Analysis*, Thousand Oaks, CA/SAGE Publications.

Moore, R. and E. McMullan (2004) 'Perceptions of Peer-to-Peer File Sharing among University Students', *Journal of Criminal Justice and Popular Culture*, 11(1), 1–19.

Moore, R. and E. McMullan (2009) 'Neutralizations and Rationalizations of Digital Piracy: A Qualitative Analysis of University Students', *International Journal of Cyber Criminology*, 3(1), 441–451.

Nightingale, V. (2009) 'Contemporary Television Audiences: Publics, Markets, Communities and

Fans', in *The SAGE Handbook of Media Studies*, J.D.H. Downing, D. McQuail, P. Schlesinger and E.Wartella (eds), Thousand Oaks, CA/SAGE, 227–249.

O'Donnell, C. (2013) 'Mixed Messages: The Ambiguity of the MOD Chip and Pirate Cultural Production for the Nintendo DS', *New Media & Society*. Published online before print 12 June.

Ogbu, C. (2003) 'I Put Up a Website about my Favorite Show and All I Got Was This Lousy Cease-and-Desist Letter: The Intersection of Fan Sites, Internet Culture, and Copyright Owners', *Southern California Interdisciplinary Law Journal*, 12: 279.

ORG (n.d.) 'Open Rights Group briefing: Illicit P2P file sharing'. Available at: www.openrightsgroup.org/assets/files/pdfs/p2p-briefing-print.pdf

Postigo, H. (2008) 'Video Game Appropriations through Modifications: Attitudes Concerning Intellectual Property Among Modders and Fans', *Convergence: The International Journal of Research into New Media Technologies*, 14(1), 59–74.

Rodman, G.B. and C. Vanderdonckt (2006) 'Music for Nothing Or, I Want my MP3: The Regulation and Circulation of Affect', *Cultural Studies*, 20(2–3), 245–261.

Ruddock, A. (2001) *Understanding Audiences: Theory and Method,* London /SAGE.

Sano-Franchini, J.L. (2010) 'Intellectual Property and the Cultures of BitTorrent Communities', *Computers and Composition*, 27, 202–210.

Saussure, F. (1974[1916]) *Course in General Linguistics*, trans Wade Baskin, London/Fontana Collins.

Schwabach, A. (2011) *Fan Fiction and Copyright: Outsider Works and Intellectual Property Protection*, London/Ashgate.

Silverstone, R. (2004) 'Regulation, Media Literacy and Media Civics', *Media, Culture & Society*, 26(3), 440–449.

Sinnreich, A., M. Latonero and M. Gluck (2009) 'Ethics Reconfigured: How Today's Media Consumers Evaluate the Role of Creative Reappropriation', *Information, Communication & Society,* 12(8), 1242–1260.

Smythe, D.W. (1977) 'Communications: Blindspot of Western Marxism', *Canadian Journal of Political and Social Theory,* 1, 120–127.

Spinello, R. (2005) 'Beyond Copyright: A Moral Investigation of Intellectual Property Protection in Cyberspace', in *The Impact of the Internet on Our Moral Lives*, Robert J. Cavalier (ed.), Albany/State University of New York Press.

Spinello, R. And Tavani, H. (eds) (2004) *Readings in Cyberethics (2nd edition) Sudberry*, MA/Jones and Bartlett Publishers.

Taylor, P.A. (1999) *Hackers*, London/Routledge.

Taylor, T.L. (2006) *Play Between Worlds: Exploring Online Game Culture*, Cambridge, MA/MIT Press.

Thomas, J. (2005) 'The Moral Ambiguity of Social Control in Cyberspace: A Retro-assessment of the 'Golden Age of Hacking', *New Media & Society,* 7(5), 599–624.

Whiteman, N. (2012) *Undoing Ethics: Rethinking Practice in Online Research*, New York/Springer.

Yar, M. (2005) 'The Global "epidemic" of movie "piracy": crime wave or social construction?', *Media, Culture & Society*, 27(5), 677–696.

Yar, M. (2008) 'The rhetorics and myths of anti-piracy campaigns: criminalization, moral pedagogy and capitalist property relations in the classroom', *New Media & Society*, 10(4), 605–623.

Zigon, J. (2008) *Morality: An Anthropological Perspective*, Oxford and New York/Berg.

PART VIII

Creative Origins and Limitations

Matthew David and Debora Halbert

Core to the notion of intellectual property rights is the ability to assign them to a specified holder and for the form of such rights (whether copyright, patent or other) to be clearly specified. A number of difficulties with classification of both creative origin and form are explored in the three chapters of this section. It is a longstanding question as to whether or not computer software should be classified as a patentable invention or copyrightable creation. The consequence of whether something is covered by patent or by copyright has very significant implications for disclosure and for duration of protection. Whether certain types of code are eligible for any kind of protection at all is also significant as it touches on the relationship between language and expression. When might a piece of code simply be said to be a necessary expression for communicating a particular idea/function, and when might it become something that could be said to be a genuinely original piece of work? This is disputed territory. The question of what constitutes progress, and what best fosters the motivation necessary to generate such progressive innovation is again open to dispute. On a parallel theme, should an industrial design be said to be less creative than a non-functional piece of art precisely because its utility means its composition is inevitably tied to necessary characteristics that thereby limit the true originality that might be said to reside in its creator's expression?

Greg Lastowka addresses the question of whether copyright can be applied to computer games, and if so to whom (claims to have created 'original' content arise at various stages)? These may seem rather unusual questions as copyright protection is routinely granted to creative forms such as novels and films, so what makes computer games (potentially at least) different? Lastowka notes a catalogue of good reasons, though each such reason can also put into question the routine assumptions of copyrightability in relation to other creative works. In the mere half-century since the creation of the first computer games (*Tennis for Two* in 1958 and *Spacewar!* in 1961) much has changed. The earliest games were created by academic researchers as a geekish distraction and were circulated freely to the limited audience able to copy and run the relevant code. Only later did arcade games and then home consoles make for a commercial market. Yet these earliest commercial products were graphically very primitive and it was not easy to separate what made a game unique/original when most involved a simple playing out of basic real-world games or generic fantasy scenarios, basic movements within geometric patterns, and/or elementary genres (space/war/crime/sport, etc.). Only when games gained a sufficient level of both sophistication and commerciality did the lawsuits begin. Lastowka documents this even shorter, but highly intriguing, history.

Once games become sufficiently sophisticated to gain copyright protection as being more than just generic structures and scenarios, a number of additional complexities came into play. Courts found it difficult to evaluate patterns of similarity and difference in actual computer coding to identify 'copying' as it was not easy for judges or juries to distinguish necessarily identical from non-essential coding. Only non-essential coding (if repeated) would suggest copying. This meant most attention was paid to similarity and difference in the experience of playing the game itself. However, precisely as games became more sophisticated, so the player's unique choices within the game made it harder to claim that any two plays of one game, let alone any two different games were essentially the same. Whilst games are not narrative films, a desire to establish unique and fixed content has led game producers to insert more and more non-user controlled film-like excerpts between levels of game-play, precisely to have definitive elements of 'authorial' uniqueness. This is, however, contradictory. Using (increasingly graphically sophisticated) film-like segments, as evidence of copyrightability, only draws further attention to its distinctiveness from the user-controlled game-play that may then be said to stand in distinction from creator claims to overall ownership of the game.

Lastowka sets out the distinction between narrative-based accounts of games (which draw parallels between games and narrative forms of fiction) and ludological accounts that explain games as rule-based action created by the player, not the rules' creator. When seeking to determine when, and where, copyright can be applied and when it cannot, US court decisions have swung between these two poles. Narratives and fictional characters can gain copyright protection, but sets of rules and systems cannot. Computer games contain variations of all of these; and, to make things more complex still, as games have moved from single console platforms to Internet-based community environments, earlier questions about player involvement in creating the action have expanded into questions of whether players should be able to hold copyright in their own 'user-generated content'. Court cases over the possibility of claiming copyright at all has now been joined by a set of disputes over whether protectable creativity stops at the point where the game is released or whether it continues in the objects and characters created by users in the course of their play.

Jessica Silbey takes further this question concerning the origins of creativity. She questions the legal and economic assumptions that see creative work as motivated primarily by the aspiration for personal material advantage. Her chapter is based upon five years of qualitative research interviewing patent and copyright holders as well as lawyers and IPRs managers. Silbey is keen to locate contemporary intellectual property debates in a longer historical context, in particular in relation to the United States' Constitutional debates over property and intellectual property. She notes how the founding fathers in the United States deemed the granting of intellectual property protection (time limited monopoly powers) as something to be given as part of a social contract that offered such protection only in return for a contribution to the common good, understood in terms of 'progress' in the practical and creative arts. Progress required both value and significant limits on exclusivity to ensure private protection did not harm the public good. Intellectual property was not to be seen as property like any other, but rather a balance between private and public benefits where the latter in the end should predominate.

Silbey's twenty-first-century interviews with copyright and patent holders unearthed an overwhelming similarity with the public mindedness propounded by the US founding fathers in their deliberations over allocating IPRs. Scientists and creative artists alike tended to see the primary benefit of their IPRs as being in their identification as inventor/author, rather than in the financial returns garnered by exclusive rights. Motives to create were similarly tied to recognition from which careers were made, rather than direct rewards for selling access. IPRs lawyers and managers seemed to have to press their clients to enforce rights, and it was these professional IP workers who tended to be the ones suggesting rights to control use were the appropriate means of benefiting from creative works. If inventors/authors are motivated, and rewarded primarily, by recognition, Silbey suggests current laws are misplaced. Shorter, not longer, IP terms would serve the purpose of recognizing creativity, enabling its reward through various forms of licensed use and speeding up the process by which such innovation circulates within society. That would, Silbey suggests, produce more progress all round.

Uma Suthersanen explores the question of how best to deal with industrial designs; three-dimensional, usually in some sense functional, objects, within the intellectual property rights system. In many jurisdictions three-dimensional objects have been offered less scope for copyright protection than have two-dimensional ones. Objects that may be said to have some kind of utility have been offered even less. Suthersanen gives a number of examples: 'designer' lamps and 'reproduction' furnishings, stormtrooper helmets from the Star Wars film franchise, industrial machines and Frisbees. The rise of industrial manufacture saw a bifurcation of the traditional artisan into the industrial worker and the creative artist. Suthersanen documents how courts and legislatures, in Europe, the United States and elsewhere came to perceive a problem in assigning full copyright to useful, and prospectively mass produced objects; not least because copyright terms in such elementary artefacts of the new industrial consumer age would create far more powerful impacts on the supply and price of 'basic' goods than might be said to flow from copyright control over unique and more specific art works (whether these were books, paintings or pieces of music).

Whilst different legal jurisdictions came to different conclusions as to how to balance the issues at stake in this question, what is highlighted in this chapter is that assignment of protection was not just a question of creativity itself. The suggestion that 'pure art' works are intrinsically 'more creative' than 'applied art' is a convenient fiction if it can be used to warrant a lower level of protection, and if such a lower level of protection is deemed to serve a deeper purpose, that of avoiding long-term monopolies over basic designs that underpin large-scale industrial production. Whilst a painter or a novelist is not hemmed in by the necessity of making her work perform certain essential functions, as might be true of a designer of a kettle, dress, armchair or lamp, such 'artists' do work within parallel domains of (aesthetic) constraint, with certain principles governing their field of practice. As such, their creativity is just as much an exercise in the innovative manipulation of possibilities within specific constraints. As such, Suthersanen rejects the rationale for discrimination against three-dimensional objects and designs, and rather supports recent European Court of Justice moves to overcome it. This is very much in line with public perceptions that today elevate 'designer' goods to the status of high art.

27

Copyright Law and Video Games: A Brief History of an Interactive Medium

Greg Lastowka

INTRODUCTION

Throughout their short history, video games have posed challenges to intellectual property laws. This chapter explores how courts in the United States have struggled to apply the traditional laws of copyright to video games. The primary problem that video games pose to copyright is that they, like all games, are interactive processes. Players of video games both experience the games as creative works and perform those works during the course of their play. From the perspective of copyright law, the interactive nature of video games makes players somewhat like authors and undermines the authorial status of the game creator. A video game creator does not design a single scripted experience, but instead designs an interactive system.

Early case law in the United States has suggested that video game design, to the extent it is not traditionally authorial, is not fully protected by copyright law. Video games receive protection under copyright only to the extent that they resemble non-interactive authorship. Traditional copyright law may therefore be insufficiently protective of game designers as authors.

Additionally, video games today are increasingly social and rich with creative affordances. Those who provide video games as platform technologies often benefit from the creative labor of authorial players. Copyright law may therefore be insufficiently protective of player authorship by channeling the economic benefits of player authorship toward platform owners.

DEFINING VIDEO GAMES

Video games are very popular today, but the serious academic study of video games is a comparatively recent enterprise. This is due, in large part, to the fact that video games were only recently invented. The birthdate of the video game genre is often debated. Some histories point to William Higginbotham's 1958 *Tennis for Two*, created on an early analog computer and oscilloscope at the Brookhaven National Laboratory. Others point to 1961's *Spacewar!*, a game created by graduate students tinkering with very expensive systems at Boston's MIT. Ford (2012) states that in 1972, Atari's *Pong* marked the beginning of the cabinet arcade game industry. Ralph Baer's Magnavox Odyssey console, also released in 1972, marked the origin of household video games. Hobbyist computers, and the early games written for them, first arrived in the 1970s, but became more mainstream with each passing year. Which of these events marked the origin of video games?

As Kent (2001) explains, video game historians acknowledge the uncertainty concerning how 'video games' should be properly defined. If video games consist of any form of electronic and interactive graphical amusement, Higginbotham's *Tennis for Two* or even early electronic amusements like pinball could be the first video games. If video games are defined by computer-based entertainment technologies and legions of fans, then *Spacewar!* would qualify. If they must be consumer commodities involving display screens, Ralph Baer's Magnavox Odyssey system might be the first video game. But however one defines the word 'video game', it must be noted that the term is often used synonymously with 'electronic games', 'digital games', 'computer games', 'entertainment software', and the broader category of 'interactive media'. Literal interpretations of these terms would encompass separate genealogies, such as: hand-held electronic devices, client-server technologies (including early MUDs and new social network games), and other forms of digital art (Kerr, 2006; Kline et al., 2003; Mortensen, 2009). As Kerr (2006) explains, this mélange of terminology creates significant slipperiness in academic discussions of the video game medium.

However they are defined, video games account for a significant segment of today's media landscape. As Kerr (2006) explains, contemporary video games have a significant market penetration in developed countries, ranging from roughly a quarter to over half of the populations identifying as regular players. While video game players do skew toward younger and male audiences, a growing number of games are targeted at older demographics, and woman are actually the dominant consumers in particular market segments (Kerr, 2006). Extrapolating from Kerr (2006), we can estimate that the size of the contemporary global market for video games today is likely upwards of US$40 billion, rivaling the size of the motion picture and music industries (Kerr, 2006; Kline et al., 2003).

This rivalry, however, is often more of a partnership, given that many popular video games today are based on motion pictures and sometimes (less frequently) motion pictures can be based on video games. Even in the early days of video gaming, one of the most popular hobbyist computer games was Mike Mayfield's *Star Trek*, an unlicensed text-based space battle written in BASIC (Kent, 2001). However, not all adaptations have been so successful. It is commonly claimed that the terrible quality of Atari's *E.T. the Extra-Terrestrial* video game played a significant part in the crash of the industry in the early 1980s (Montfort and Bogost, 2009). The destruction and burial of thousands of copies of the game in a New Mexico landfill (Guins, 2009) demonstrates that video games and motion pictures are indeed separate media forms. While a successful book may not lead to a successful movie, both novels and motion pictures have similar narrative structures. It is no trivial task, however, to adapt a successful book or film into a successful video game – the characteristics of interactive electronic media are quite different than the characteristics of traditional media (Bogost, 2007; Ryan, 2001).

Much of the work of game studies scholarship has been focused on understanding how video games are unlike other textual and audiovisual media. Over the past two decades, numerous scholars have drawn out the formal characteristics of games in many papers and monographs (Aarseth, 1997; Bogost, 2006, 2007; Elias et al., 2012; Juul, 2005; Mortensen, 2009; Murray, 1997; Myers, 2003, 2010; Ryan, 2001; Salen and Zimmerman, 2003). However, the first individuals to collaboratively theorize the unique nature of video games were surely video game designers themselves.

Perhaps the most notable early work by a game developer was published in 1984 by Chris Crawford, who wrote a book entitled *The Art of Computer Game Design: Reflections of a Master Game Designer*. Crawford was largely dismissive of the state of the video game art circa 1984, when Taito's *Space Invaders* was still a flagship arcade game. He acknowledged that skeptics might claim 'computer games are too trivial, too frivolous to be called art. They are idle recreation at best' (Crawford, 2011, loc. 24). However, he aspired to put game design on a par with other media and to create an aesthetic theory of video game design.

Crawford explained that the key appeal and aesthetic potential of video games resided in their ability to combine player participation with representational media: 'the highest and most complete form of representation is interactive representation. Games provide this interactive element, and it is a crucial factor in their appeal.' (Crawford, 2011, loc. 214) However, the works that Crawford valorized were not games, i.e. the artistry and authorship of Michelangelo, Beethoven, and Hemmingway.

It may seem curious that Crawford faulted video games for failing to meet the standards of great visual, musical and literary art, given that traditional games are generally not understood as art, but as rule-based leisure activities. A footrace or a game of hopscotch is generally not appreciated by participants or spectators as an artistic work, but as a rule-based activity that motivates and gives meaning to pleasurable physical performances (Huizinga, 1950; Lastowka, 2010; Suits, 2005). Play and games are sometimes associated with creative performances, yet traditional theorists of play and games did not generally equate the design of game rules or game environments with art (Caillois, 1961; Huizinga, 1950; Suits, 2005; Sutton-Smith, 1998).

Video games, however, are unlike traditional games. Game rules are encoded into software constraints. Players use common digital interfaces (keyboards, buttons, joysticks, trackpads) to manipulate and explore symbolic representations that are projected on screens. Unlike sports practices, video game titles are sold as reproduced copies of information that are marketed similarly to books and films (e.g. featured new releases and sequels). Video games are generally developed by commercially-motivated firms and distributed by industry publishers. The consumption of video games is tied to specific technological platforms that are also consumer commodities, such as consoles, computers, or handheld devices (Kline et al., 2003). And certainly the contemporary complexity (and industrial scale) of video game animation, music, and acting can make a modern video game share more in common with a motion picture than with a child's game of noughts and crosses. Given all of this, perhaps Crawford's expectation that computer games would someday possess visual, musical and narrative complexity rivaling traditional media was prescient, given contemporary titles such as *Grand Theft Auto V* and *Journey*. However, despite their increased complexity and artistry, video games remain interactive *games*.

The schism between traditional forms of artistry and the medium of the video game is reflected in the game studies literature as a tension between so-called 'narratological' and 'ludulogical' approaches to game studies. Narratological approaches emphasize the similarities between video games and traditional narratives. Ludological approaches emphasize the similarities between video game play and traditional game play. It should be emphasized that these two categories are not camps within game studies. In fact, no game studies scholar has ever explicitly adopted the cause of narratology and those who claim to be ludologists are often eager to admit that games can have fictive elements and narrative structures (Frasca, 2003). Nonetheless, the narratology/ludology divide helps to describe the variance between traditional textual approaches and rule-based approaches to understanding games (Kerr, 2006; Mortensen, 2009).

The narratological approach to video games derives from the past traditions, methodologies and vocabularies for interpreting literary and audiovisual texts. Alvin Toffler, as early as 1980, claimed that video games were changing the way their players interacted with media:

> [T]hrough such seemingly innocent devices millions of people are learning to play with the television set, to talk back to it, to interact with it. In the process they are changing from passive receivers to message senders as well. (Toffler, 1980: 163)

Early game studies scholars made similar observations. Janet Murray emphasized that game players were granted agency over the unfolding events in a game (Murray, 1997). Espen Aarseth, in *Cybertext* (1997), contrasted the passive consumption of conventional literature with the laborious and multi-directional 'reading' practices of interactive fiction and electronic games. It is common to see claims among those who study games that players actively collaborate with the game's interface to shape the game's narrative (e.g. Gee, 2007; McGonigal, 2011; Papert, 1993; Ryan, 2001). The narratological approach frames reader–text interactivity as a novel development and contrasts video games with past media.

The ludological approach, by comparison, frames video games as a medium related to non-electronic games, such as card games or sports (Costikyan, 2013; Elias et al., 2012; Juul, 2001; Salen and Zimmerman, 2003). Games have always involved purposeful activity constrained by rules, so interactivity, from the ludological standpoint, is a given. At the extreme, ludological approaches downplay or even reject the salience of representation and narrative to game studies, focusing on games as formal systems characterized by, for example, players, objects and rules defining goals and constraints (Juul, 2001).

Perhaps not surprisingly, many of the early ludologists were often video game developers who were interested in games generally and believed that academic commentary on video games should not begin and end with post-structural literary theory. The ludological approach to video game studies is also more congruent with video game development practice. In large-scale game development, the traditional forms of authorship (e.g. fine artwork, music and writing) are certainly present, but are generally created by specialists (e.g. fine artists, musicians and animators). Artwork, music and writing are sometimes referred to as the 'assets' of a game and distinguished thereby from the design of the game.

Debates about the proper formal categorization of video games may seem rather obscure, but the question has also been raised in legal proceedings. While the United States Supreme Court has never considered a case involving copyright law in video games, it has considered the question of whether video games constitute a form of speech protected by the First Amendment.

Put simply, the legal question confronted by the Supreme Court in *Brown v. EMA*, 131 S.Ct. 2729 (2011), was whether video games were fundamentally different than books, films, artwork, and other forms of traditional media. Some early decisions on this issue suggested that video games were so simple and crude that they amounted to trivial electronic amusements devoid of expressive value. More recent decisions, including the lower court decision in *Brown*, had extended First Amendment protections to video games. If video games were protected speech, then California's effort to limit the sale of violent video games to minors would face the strict scrutiny that would attend a similar restriction on the sale of violent books or artwork.

Justice Scalia, writing for the majority, extended full First Amendment protections to video games. In the course of doing so, he downplayed the salience of video game interactivity. He stated that textual interactivity:

> is nothing new: Since at least the publication of The Adventures of You: Sugarcane Island in 1969, young readers of choose-your-own-adventure stories have been able to make decisions that determine the plot by following instructions about which page to turn to ... As for the argument that video games enable participation in the violent action, that seems to us more a matter of degree than of kind. As Judge Posner has observed, all literature is interactive. (p. 2738)

In essence, Justice Scalia played the narratologist, stressing the continuity between past forms of experimental literature and the modern video game. Justice Alito, concurring in the judgment, played the ludologist. He argued that conflating interactive video games with other media was premature and could lead to erroneous decisions. Justice Alito explained that reading the murder scene in Dostoyevsky's *Crime and Punishment* was a far different experience than enacting it:

> When all of the characteristics of video games are taken into account, there is certainly a reasonable basis for thinking that the experience of playing a video game may be quite different from the experience of reading a book, listening to a radio broadcast, or viewing a movie. (p. 2751)

But even though Scalia and Alito disagreed about whether video games were a significantly different medium, both agreed that the efforts of California to regulate the sale of violent video games to minors violated the constitutional protections of the First Amendment. So the Supreme Court's disagreement about interactivity ultimately had no practical import in the *Brown v. EMA* decision.

In the next section, I will describe how similar debates about interactivity appear in copyright law decisions. The presence of video game interactivity has influenced the contours of copyright protection for video games and continues to create difficulties for courts today.

PROTECTING EARLY VIDEO GAMES WITH COPYRIGHT

In this section and the section to follow, the analysis of video games and copyright law will focus on the statutory and case law of the United States. United States copyright law is not radically different from the copyright laws of other countries, but different countries may have slightly different approaches to copyright protection for interactive media. That said, jurisdictional differences may be somewhat less important to this field than they are to other legal domains. This is because today's major video game studios, such as Blizzard/Activision, Rockstar, Ubisoft, Bethesda, and Mojang, generally produce games for an international marketplace (Kerr, 2006; Kline et al., 2003). Historically, given the US origins of the video game industry, the copyright law of the United States has exerted a significant (perhaps overly significant) influence on the practices of the video game industry. Due to the importance of the United States market, game companies will generally attempt to comply with United States copyright law when developing any title that might be marketed in the United States.

However, it is still worth noting that there are sizeable, geographically-limited markets for the production of video games outside the United States. Smaller-scale game production in Europe and some large commercial game companies in Asia may be unaffected by the rules of United States copyright, to the extent that United States law does not track the law of other jurisdictions. Even outside the United States, however, the discussion below should illustrate the general contours of the copyright problems posed by interactive video games.

Some of the most popular early video games, such as *Spacewar!*, were not consumer commodities, but were instead the hobbyist works of computer technicians toying with expensive equipment that they did not own (Kent, 2001). These games were labors of love, not commerce. They were often copied and shared across early digital networks. Their creators had no expectation – or at least no practical hope – of monetary compensation.

This state of affairs changed, gradually, during the 1970s as popular computer software attained commodity status. Arcade games like *Pong* and *Space War* took the early hobbyist games and combined them with quarter-consuming cabinets. Competitors often copied the designs of these simple games with impunity (Ford, 2012). Even though, in theory, copyright law might have been asserted against certain unauthorized imitators during the 1970s, the industry's innovation-oriented and cash-strapped pioneers generally chose to invest in innovation rather than litigation – with a handful of exceptions that led to no significant recorded opinions (Ford, 2012). Additionally, given the novelty of the machines and interfaces and the simplicity of the early representational elements (e.g. a *Pong* paddle), patent law may have seemed more appropriate than copyright. Indeed, it may have been unclear whether copyright law could protect a very simple form of electronic amusement, such as *Pong*.

It took over a decade for courts to address the question of copyright in very simple video games. Years after the game's advent, Atari sought to register a copyright in its *Breakout* game. *Breakout* was essentially a *Pong* variant, originally developed for Atari by both Steve Jobs and Steve Wozniak, the founders of Apple. Instead of playing against an opponent, the player used a paddle to rebound a ball into a wall of bricks, with each collision removing an additional brick from the wall.

By the late 1980s, the original 1976 *Breakout* arcade game had been replaced by a slew of computer and console-based successors. Atari was, no doubt, eager to assert its exclusive rights to the game design and force infringers to obtain licenses for *Breakout* clones. However, the Copyright Office initially rejected Atari's copyright registration for *Breakout*, stating that the game was insufficiently creative to constitute an authorial work.

According to the Register, the *Breakout* game was composed of simple colors, sounds and geometric shapes, and therefore lacked the originality requisite for copyright protection. Atari appealed the Register's decision in *Atari Games v. Oman*, 693 F. Supp. 1204 (D.D.C. 1988), to no avail. Judge Pratt, writing for the Federal District Court, affirmed the Register's decision. Judge Pratt explained that *Breakout* was:

> little more than a stock description of a paddle-and-ball game, inseparable in any principled manner from the idea which it embodies. This is quite distinct from video games which feature expressive and artistically creative renditions of an idea, and which thereby merit copyright protection. (p. 1207)

Appealing Judge Pratt's ruling, however, Atari found a panel of more sympathetic jurists. In *Atari Games v. Oman*, 888 F. 2d 878 (D.C. Cir. 1989), then-Judge (later Justice) Ruth Bader Ginsburg, writing for the Federal Court of Appeals for the District of Columbia Circuit, faulted the Register's analysis for failing to appreciate how *Breakout* consisted not just of simple shapes, but presented a sequential audiovisual combination of simple elements. According to Judge Ginsburg, the whole of *Breakout* was greater than the sum of its parts. Adopting a narratological viewpoint, she stressed that *Breakout* was fundamentally no different than a complex audiovisual work (e.g. a motion picture), and should be analyzed as such.

On remand, the Copyright Office again refused registration, finding that, even considered as a whole, *Breakout* contained no original authorship in either the selection or arrangement of the images or their components. The case worked its way up to Judge Ginsburg again, who, in *Atari Games Corp. v. Oman*, 979 F. 2d 242 (1992), again faulted the Register for failing to appreciate the dynamic and interactive nature of the game. She stated that it was improper for the Register to 'focus on the individual screens, rather than the flow of the game as a whole. The hallmark of a video game is the expression found in the entire effect of the game as it appears and sounds, its sequence of images' (p. 245). Once again, the case was remanded. Atari's *Breakout* registration was finally issued (Boyd, 2006), giving Atari the legal right to pursue those who reproduced the game without permission.

It is possible that the Register's decision on Atari was biased by the Copyright Office's late 1980s vantage point. Even by the early 1980s, the majority of commercially prominent video games were much more complex than *Breakout*. Games like *Pac-Man*, *Defender* and *Donkey Kong* featured crude but effective characters acting in crude but effective stories.

In the 1980s, companies like Atari had transitioned into more traditional corporate practices, were flush with cash, and were ready to litigate against pirates (Lipson and Brain, 2009). When the first wave of video game copyright cases reached the courts in the early 1980s, judges seemed eager to reward the plaintiffs who had designed these new forms of interactive media. Cases in which a defendant had copied a plaintiff's software wholesale were quickly resolved in favor of plaintiffs and against the pirates.

There were, however, some novel questions, especially in cases where a defendant's copying was inexact. Perhaps the primary question concerning courts in the 1980s was the same question concerning game studies scholars in more recent history: as a form of artistic expression, how are video games different than traditional media? This question was prompted by the difficulty of comparing the authorial work in video games with the allegedly infringing work.

Defining the scope of copyright protection is an essential step in any copyright infringement case. The scope of an intellectual property right is analogous to the metes and bounds of a piece of real property. With traditional works, courts and juries generally look at sculptures and two-dimensional artworks side-by-side, noting similarities and differences. According to doctrinal standards, the copying of certain elements in authorial works may be allowed, but even if discrete elements are not subject to protection (e.g. facts in a biography), their creative arrangement by the author (e.g. how the facts are expressed linguistically) is generally still subject to copyright protection.

Courts do make similarity comparisons across media. An author's novel can be compared to an allegedly infringing film adaptation. Courts have also analyzed complex media, for example, dissecting two allegedly similar songs and enlisting the aid of expert musicologists to testify about usual and unusual melodic sequences. The practice of determining substantial similarity, though it has its doctrinal complexities, is certainly more of an art than a science: the fundamental issue is whether the defendant has taken 'too much' or has misappropriated 'the heart' of the authorial work. However, even given the ambiguity inherent in that standard, courts generally feel comfortable that they understand the two works at issue. A song has a beginning and an end. A photograph has four corners.

Video games, by contrast, are inchoate media. They must be played to be experienced, and no two players will play a video game in exactly the same manner. So when comparing two video games, how can a court obtain a firm sense of the copyright-protected work? Contemporary video games like *Skyrim* or *World of Warcraft*, which often feature vast imaginary continents and require hundreds of hours to fully explore, make this even more difficult.

Courts might have analogized video games to scripted plays, which are also inchoate media in a sense. Each actor's performance of any given script does vary. Yet the text of the play's script remains the same. Video games do have a sort of script analogous to the script of a play – their unchanging core is their software code. Jurists concluded that they were obligated by copyright law to protect this software code as a 'literary work', but this did not always make matters simpler. Without expert testimony, most jurists and jurors found the software and its relation to the video game's output incomprehensible (Montfort and Bogost, 2009). It was (and still is) quite difficult for the average legal professional to distinguish between code that is creative and code that is routine and functional. Therefore, in cases where the code was not admittedly copied verbatim, the 'script' of the video game was actually less accessible to the jurist than the game's performance, even though the performance varied according to the player. So, in comparing two works, the court struggled to discern the work of the video game's author from the variable interactions of the player with the video game's interface.

An additional concern was presented by copyright's requirement that protected works be 'fixed' in some tangible medium of expression. Given that video game play requires collaboration between the player's actions and the game's software, it could be argued that no particular video game performance is ever fixed. Each performance of a video game, like each performance of a game, is arguably dependent on the specific actions of particular players. If this were true, copying the mere appearance of a video game without copying the game's underlying code might not be infringing, given that the audiovisual appearance of the game would fall outside the scope of copyright's protection.

Invariably, courts managed to overcome both of these objections. With regard to the latter fixation objection, courts found that because it was uncontested that the game's software code was static and permanently fixed, and that software code was perceived through the game's interface, variances in any individual performance of the game did not undermine the fixed nature of the resulting audiovisual work. (Some have argued against this conclusion, see for example, Burk (2013).)

But even accepting that the audiovisual work of the video game was fixed, this just led to the prior question about the appropriate scope of the protected work: if the work varied with each player, how much of the game was actually protected by copyright and how much was simply attributable to the game's performance by the player? Could the player's contribution be separated from the game? Or, as Yeats once put it, could the dancer be separated from the dance? (Yeats, 1928).

Some litigants essentially dodged the interactivity question by successfully arguing that their 'attract sequences' – the animated sequences that served to entice customers to insert a quarter – were never controlled by players and therefore presented an invariable audiovisual display. Courts accepted these arguments, finding that when defendants had exactly copied attract sequences, they infringed. A similar litigation strategy entailed operating the video game without the interaction of the player. Some courts observed how, when the two compared games were initiated and players did not operate their controls, identical audiovisual sequences would be presented: for example, a player's ship would crash and be destroyed in an identical manner. One might query how often this particular scenario occurred outside of courtrooms, but enacting a counter-factual game play situation allowed courts to avoid the thorny questions of interactivity. It also allowed judges and lawyers to avoid playing video games during judicial proceedings.

Still, many courts accepted that, in their normal course of operation, video games were played, and that, at their core, video games were an interactive medium. In close cases, this recognition led to some curious judicial opinions. These will be discussed in the next section.

THE PROBLEM OF INTERACTIVE COPYRIGHT

For the strategic reasons mentioned above, defendants, not plaintiffs, were more likely to argue that the player, not the game's creator, was the true author of the audiovisual work. This argument did have some initial appeal to some jurists. Indeed, in the *Breakout* case discussed above, the Copyright Office asserted this argument, determining that *Breakout* as played (the audiovisual work) was 'created randomly by the player and not by the author of the video game' (*Atari Games v. Oman*, 888 F. 2d 878, 880).

The Register's arguments did not win the day, however, and Atari prevailed by pointing to discrete elements and sequences that could not be altered. Similar strategies were pursued by other plaintiffs confronting claims of player authorship. For example, in many games, the background playing fields (e.g. mazes and buildings) were fixed. Copying those playing fields as an element of a new game, therefore, could contribute to copyright infringement. The appearance of player avatars (e.g. the 'gobbler' character in *Pac-Man* or the spaceships in *Scramble* or *Asteroids*) was also not subject to player modification. Courts concluded that these fixed components and sequences of video games were, essentially, the protected work, and dismissed the actions of players as choosing and 'reading' the elements. So a player might control how Pac-Man moved through a maze, but the player had no control over Pac-Man's color or shape, the design of the maze, or the animation sequence associated with Pac-Man's death. A defendant making a video game that copied Pac-Man, the maze shape, and the death sequence could therefore infringe on the *Pac-Man* copyright.

The analysis of Chief Judge Cummings, writing for the Seventh Circuit Court of Appeals in *Midway Mfg. v. Artic International*, 704 F. 2d 1009 (1983), is typical of the analytical approach used to defeat a defendant's claim that players engaged in 'authorship'. With regard to the video game *Defender*, he stated:

> The person playing the game can vary the order in which the stored images appear on the screen by moving the machine's control lever. That makes playing a video game a little like arranging words in a dictionary into sentences or paints on a palette into a painting. The question is whether the creative effort in playing a video game is enough like writing or painting to make each performance of a video game the work of the player and not the game's inventor.
>
> We think it is not ...
>
> Playing a video game is more like changing channels on a television than it is like writing a novel or painting a picture. The player of a video game does not have control over the sequence of images that appears on the video game screen. He cannot create any sequence he wants out of the images stored on the game's circuit boards. The most he can do is choose one of the limited number of sequences the game allows him to choose. He is unlike a writer or a painter because the video game in effect writes the sentences and paints the painting for him; he merely chooses one of the sentences stored in its memory, one of the paintings stored in its collection. (pp. 1011–12)

This sort of approach did not resolve all the difficulties of video game infringement, but it did make many cases more straightforward. If player authorship was largely marginal and the invariable component features of video games were dominant, a substantial similarity comparison could proceed largely in the same manner it occurred with respect to traditional authorial media. Infringement could be established without reference to the game's underlying software code or how the games were actually played.

So, for instance, in *Atari v. North American*, 672 F. 2d 607 (1982), involving Atari's claim that the copyright in *Pac-Man* was infringed by a game called *K.C. Munchkin*, the court found infringement, noting a list of close similarities between the original and infringing works:

> North American not only adopted the same basic characters but also portrayed them in a manner which made K.C. Munchkin appear substantially similar to PAC-MAN. The K.C. Munchkin gobbler has several blatantly similar features, including the relative size and shape of the 'body', the V-shaped 'mouth', its distinctive gobbling action (with appropriate sounds), and especially the way in which it disappears upon being captured. An examination of the K.C. Munchkin ghost monsters reveals even more significant visual similarities. In size, shape, and manner of movement, they are virtually identical to their PAC-MAN counterparts. K.C. Munchkin's monsters, for example, exhibit the same peculiar 'eye' and 'leg' movement. Both games, moreover, express the role reversal and 'regeneration' process with such great similarity that an ordinary observer could conclude only that North American copied plaintiffs' PAC-MAN. (p. 618)

Of course, this sort of analysis raised the question of how to understand and map conventional narrative notions like 'stock characters', 'genre', and 'plot' – all of which influenced the substantial similarity test in narrative media – to the context of video games. In a young medium featuring constant innovation and imitation, notions of 'genre' were quite fluid and perhaps were constructed by copyright law as much as copyright law constructed them.

For instance, in *Atari v. Amusement World*, 547 F. Supp. 222 (1981), an early case involving a *Meteors* version of Atari's *Asteroids*, a district court in Maryland determined that the defendant had copied only the concept of the *Asteroids* game, but not the particularized expression. The court explained that any similarities between the two games were dictated by the 'idea' of a video game involving spaceships and free-floating space rocks – essentially transforming *Asteroids* into a genre of video games:

> There are certain forms of expression that one must necessarily use in designing a video game in which a player fights his way through space rocks and enemy spaceships. The player must be able to rotate and move his craft. All the spaceships must be able to fire weapons which can destroy targets. The game must be easy at first and gradually get harder, so that bad players are not frustrated and good ones are challenged. Therefore, the rocks must move faster as the game progresses. In order for the game to look at all realistic, there must be more than one size of rock. Rocks cannot split into very many pieces, or else the screen would quickly become filled with rocks and the player would lose too quickly …
>
> All these requirements of a video game in which the player combats space rocks and spaceships combine to dictate certain forms of expression that must appear in any version of such a game. In fact, these requirements account for most of the similarities between 'Meteors' and 'Asteroids.' Similarities so accounted for do not constitute copyright infringement, because they are part of plaintiff's idea and are not protected by plaintiff's copyright. (p. 229)

The *Meteors* decision was issued when *Star Wars* had re-ignited a popular interest in spaceships and asteroid fields, an interest that was part and parcel of the commercial success of *Asteroids*. However, if the *Meteors* court was right that video games involving spaceships blasting space rocks constituted an unprotectable genre, then could one not also conclude that K.C. Munchkin had simply copied the 'idea' of a maze game where a pie-shaped 'gobbler' vied with four ghost monsters? What made a video game involving 'spaceships and space rocks' an unprotected idea, but a video game involving a pie-shaped gobbler and four ghost monsters a particularized form of expression?

Commentators have long complained about the metaphysical muddiness involved in copyright law's requirement of separating the idea of an artistic work from its particular expression. The doctrine is clearly no better – and perhaps somewhat worse – when applied to the constantly evolving medium of interactive video games.

GAMES AS UNPROTECTABLE SYSTEMS

There is an additional wrinkle in the idea/expression dichotomy that is arguably unique to video games and the copyright law of the United States. The idea/expression dichotomy is set forth in Section 102(b) of the copyright statute. That section specifically bars protection for 'any idea, procedure, process, system, method of operation, concept, principle, or discovery, regardless of the form in which it is described, explained, illustrated, or embodied in such work'. While Section 102(b) expresses the historic prohibition against securing a copyright in an 'idea' (e.g. the genre of asteroid shooting games), it also prohibits copyright protection for any 'system' or 'procedure'. To the extent that games are primarily systems and procedures that guide player behavior (as the ludologists would have it), certain elements of video game design may also be barred copyright protection for that reason.

Professor Bruce Boyden has written extensively about this rationale for denying copyright protection to games, arguing that games, insofar as they consist of systems of rules, properly should not be subject to copyright protection (Boyden, 2011a, 2011b). Boyden's argument draws on various case law as well as the Nimmer copyright treatise, which reaches a similar conclusion. The gist of this argument is not specific to video games, but encompasses all game forms.

Notably, the prohibition has limits. Both the Nimmer treatise and Boyden accept that games may have independently copyrightable components (such as a *Monopoly* game board or a sculpted playing piece) and that these artistic components ('assets' in game development parlance) can and should be subject to copyright protection. So it is not the game elements, but their combination in a game system that the Nimmer treatise and Boyden argue must be excluded from protection. As Boyden himself notes, this rule seems somewhat incongruous: 'Imagine there were a rule that "novels are not copyrightable", but that a novel's plot, characters, setting, dialog, and cover art all were. What would be the point of such a rule?' (Boyden, 2011a, p. 445)

Boyden's answer is that games, as abstract systems (composed of constraining rules, players, motivating goals, etc.) should not be protected, and therefore instances of game play should fall outside the scope of copyright law. Boyden applies this understanding to video games specifically by stating:

> the experience of play is supplied by the players, not the game designer ... Even video games, despite being comprised of software, audiovisual elements, plots, graphics, and characters, nevertheless have an uncopyrightable core: the actual play of the game ... Systems are shells into which users pour meaning. (Boyden, 2011a: 479)

In subsequent work (2011b), Boyden has made additional arguments that the scope of copyright protection for video games cannot include the player's performance of the game. For Boyden, the actual experience of game play is akin to an individual reader's encounter with a book or an individual viewer's perception of a film – it combines the reader's activity with the text. Building on this claim, Boyden states that unauthorized recordings of video game play should provide a compelling case for fair use due to 'the limited nature of copyrightable information captured in a recording and its dissimilarity from the original work, a noninteractive recording as opposed to an interactive game' (Boyden, 2011b: 8). Boyden concedes, however, that his argument is in conflict with at least one opinion, *Red Baron-Franklin Park v. Taito*, 883 F. 2d 275 (1989), a case involving the arcade game *Double Dragon*, where a court found that unauthorized player performances of the game infringed on the performance rights of the game's owners.

In essence, Boyden's 'systems' approach recalls the ludological perspective, identifying video games with rule-based performance rather than traditional narrative. However, not all commentators agree that Boyden's proposed 'systems' exclusion is warranted. Dan Burk, in a recent article (2013), argues that certain forms of art (e.g. ballet performance or haiku) operate under constraints that are similar to the constraints imposed by game rules. Just as a video game player acts creatively within the game space, so a poet composing a Haiku must work within the constraints of that genre. Hence, according to Burk, the historic prohibition against copyright in games as systems is essentially a prohibition against copyright in a genre as an idea. Works constructed within the genre of Westerns, for instance, can be protected by copyright, but the stock elements of that genre (showdowns, bar fights, cowboy hats) fall outside the scope of copyright. Essentially, Burk plays the narratologist to Boyden's ludologist, pointing out the analytic congruence between traditional artistic genres and game performances.

What are the practical consequences of failing to protect video games as systems? Consider two hypothetical games, both based on Atari's *Asteroids*. The first game is *Squid Attack*, which borrows *Asteroid*'s system, but adorns that framework with a different fiction. In *Squid Attack* a submarine shoots torpedoes at waves of oncoming squids and octopi that then break down (*contra* realism) into multiple smaller units of squids and octopi. *Squid Attack* is a ludological copy of *Asteroids*. The optimal play strategy is identical, as is the scoring system.

A second game, *Space Miner* is visually identical to *Asteroids*. It uses vector graphics and displays a triangular spaceship on a black screen amid drifting geometric outlines of asteroids. *Space Miner* embraces the *Asteroids* outer space fiction, but changes the game play. The goal of *Space Miner* is to collide with space rocks, resulting in the same animated explosion of *Asteroids*, but with this graphic scoring points for the player who is deemed to have 'mined' the asteroid. In *Space Miner*, the player has unlimited ships, but limited time.

From the perspective of a game developer, *Squid Attack* is simply *Asteroids* with different art assets, but *Space Miner* is a different game using identical art assets. For players, which game would be understood as the closer copy of *Asteroids*? The answer depends on what makes video games appealing – fiction or rules? However that question is resolved, a court applying the logic of the *Meteors* and *K.C. Munchkin* cases would likely find *Space Miner* a form of copyright infringement, but would find *Squid Attack* to be a non-infringing copy of the unprotected rule system of *Asteroids*.

In reality, there is rarely a game that only copies game rules or game fiction. Indeed, it isn't clear that the line can be clearly drawn. For instance: were the unlimited spaceships in *Space Miner* merely a change in *Asteroid*'s rules (as I suggested) or did *Space Miner* change the *Asteroids* narrative? Two recent cases, both involving fairly simple games designed for mobile devices, show the problems that courts have in separating interactive games into unprotected rules and traditionally protected art and narrative.

In *Spry Fox v. LOLApps*, No. C12–147RAJ (W.D.Wash. 2012), the creators of the puzzle game *Triple Town* sued the makers of *Yeti Town*, alleging infringement of copyright. *Yeti Town* was essentially a clone of *Triple Town*, but, somewhat like *Squid Attack*, it replaced the medieval pastoral setting of *Triple Town*, featuring trees and bears, with an arctic setting, featuring Eskimos and yetis. The court first explained that the ludological structure of *Triple Town* was outside the scope of copyright protection:

> the idea underlying Triple Town is that of a hierarchical matching game, one in which players create objects that are higher in the hierarchy by matching three objects that are lower in the hierarchy. Frustrating the player's efforts are antagonist objects; aiding the player are objects that destroy unwanted or ill-placed objects. Spry Fox's copyright gives it no monopoly over this idea. 6Waves (or anyone else) is free to create a video game based on the same idea

The court continued, however, by stating:

> A video game, much like a screenplay expressed in a film, also has elements of plot, theme, dialogue, mood, setting, pace, and character. Spry Fox took the idea underlying Triple Town and expressed it with its own characters, its own setting, and more. These objective elements of expression are within the scope of Spry Fox's copyright ...
>
> Spry Fox's allegations are more than adequate to illustrate plausibly the objectively similar expression embodied in Yeti Town. The object hierarchy is similar. Progressing from grass to bush to tree to hut is similar to progressing from sapling to tree to tent to cabin. Perhaps more importantly, the object hierarchy coupled with the depiction of the field of play comprise a setting and theme that is similar to Triple Town's. A snowfield is not so different from a meadow, bears and yetis are both wild creatures, and the construction of a 'plain' is not [sic] plausibly similar to the construction of a 'patch', at least as the two games depict those terms.

In a typical copyright substantial similarity analysis, it would be absurd to equate a tent with a tree. Yet the court here engages in what amounts to a very high-level comparison of fictional elements, equating bears and yetis as wild creatures, in order to find infringement. The court seems to be saying that when two game elements are situated in similar locations within a ludological system, lesser similarities between those elements may be sufficient to establish infringement. Allowing *Triple Town*'s ludological structure to influence the infringement analysis affords a weak form of copyright protection to the game's ostensibly unprotected rules.

Another recent case involved a claim by the owners of *Tetris* against a cloned version of that game. In *Tetris Holding v. Xio Interactive*, 863 F. Supp. 2d 394 (2012), Judge Wolfson of the District of New Jersey struggled with 'the unenviable task of dissecting a game's ideas from its expression'. She stated that the idea of *Tetris* consisted of 'the game at an abstract level and the concepts that drive the game'. After explaining the basic rules and concept of *Tetris*, Judge Wolfson concluded that the defendant had infringed by copying not only the idea of *Tetris*, but also its protected expression:

> In addition to the design and movement of the playing pieces as discussed above (including the use of bright colors, the individually delineated squares within the pieces, and the downward, lateral, and rotating movement), I find the following elements are also protected expression and further support a finding of infringement: the dimensions of the playing field, the display of 'garbage' lines, the appearance of 'ghost' or shadow pieces, the display of the next piece to fall, the change in color of the pieces when they lock with the accumulated pieces, and the appearance of squares automatically filling in the game board when the game is over. None of these elements are part of the idea (or the rules or the functionality) of Tetris, but rather are means of expressing those ideas. (p. 32)

What this analysis demonstrates is that separating *Tetris* into ideas and expressions is, as Judge Wolfson indicated, an unenviable task, and one prone to raise difficult questions in the context of interactive games. While the court places the rotational movement of the *Tetris* pieces, the 'ghost pieces', and the display of the upcoming game piece in the realm of protected expression, all are arguably part of the rules of *Tetris*. They all clearly influence optimal play strategy. Judge Wolfson even found that the twenty-by-ten grid of Tetris was included in the game's protected expression, given that the defendant could have just as easily copied the idea of *Tetris* and used a fifteen-by-eight grid. The court rejected the defendant's argument that the size of the *Tetris* grid was part of the game's idea.

The *Triple Town* and *Tetris* cases both suggest that courts either cannot or will not disentangle video game rules from video game fiction. Courts know that copyright law requires them to divorce the abstract ideas in games from their particularized expressions in specific characters, objects and settings. In practice, however, drawing this line invariably involves rendering arbitrary judgments. Even if it could be done successfully, it would still leave the hallmark of video games, the ludological design of interactive systems, with the least amount of copyright protection.

COPYRIGHT AND VIDEO GAMES IN THE 21ST CENTURY

More than 40 years after the first commercial video games were introduced, some aspects of the industry are largely unchanged today. Although there have been many new platforms for video game play, most of the early genres of games (e.g. racing games, sports games, shooting games, and multi-player combat games) are still popular in more detailed modern incarnations. Joysticks, keyboards, and buttons are still the most common tools that players use to interact with represented environments portrayed on flat screens.

Certain aspects of the industry have changed. Myriad new business models have replaced the quarter-guzzling arcade machines of the 1980s, and there is intense competition among large and small (and 'indie') creators making mobile and handheld games, console games, PC games, and social network games. For the most part, video game graphics, audio and animation have grown much more detailed and complex, buoyed by technological advances in data storage, processing, transfer, and image display.

With some notable exceptions, like *Tetris*, very few of today's most popular games are characterized by the geometric simplicity of *Pong* or *Breakout*. While simple games, such as *Triple Town* and *Tetris*, are still popular, many games today have very rich and detailed creative assets and stories, making it that much easier for courts, like the Supreme Court in *Brown*, to narratologically equate video games with motion pictures. As one court stated in 2004, finding that video games had become worthy of free speech protections:

> The early generations of video games may have lacked the requisite expressive element, being little more than electronic board games or computerized races. The games at issue in this litigation, however, frequently involve intricate, if obnoxious, story lines, detailed artwork, original scores, and a complex narrative which evolves as the player makes choices and gains experience. (*Video Software Dealers Association v. Maleng*, 325 F. Supp.2d 1180 (2004))

The elements of player interactivity in most games today are also more complex. Players interact not only with the game during play, but often compete and collaborate with other players in a multitude of game contexts (Banks and Deuze, 2009; Boellstorff, 2008; Grimes and Fields, 2012; Malaby 2009; Nardi, 2010; Taylor 2006, 2012). This is because contemporary video games are increasingly integrated into Internet-based networks. Though online game play dates back to the 1970s, early arcade machines, consoles and PC games were rarely networked with other machines. Today, even when a video game is not directly dependent on a constant link to the Internet, Internet-based resources invariably serve as the central site for player community interactions.

Video game companies are therefore increasingly playing a governance role as they host and supervise interactions within online player communities (Humphreys, 2009). Many popular games are played exclusively online and the current home game consoles (the Xbox One, Wii U, and PlayStation 4) are designed to take advantage of online interactions. When player communities use proprietary technologies to interact with each other via the Internet, this gives rise to new forms of technological and legal control over player behavior (Burk, 2010; Lastowka, 2010).

For instance, game companies can use passwords, encryption, digital rights management, click-through contracts, anti-hacking and computer trespass laws, and other techno-legal means to police player behaviors. Copyright becomes another tool that can be used to govern the interactions of player communities. Some courts have even found, in some cases, that players violating game rules can face liability for violations of copyright law, provided there is a nexus between the unauthorized player activity and the protected work of the game company. Of course, the same holds true today with respect to non-game, Internet-based social websites, such as Facebook or Twitter: where communities interact online, the owners of platforms effectively become the governors of virtual communities (Lastowka, 2010).

From a copyright perspective, the ability of communities of players to interact online within and around video games raises novel issues. As this chapter explained previously, courts deciding earlier video game cases generally concluded that the claimed interactive authorship of players did not withdraw video games from copyright protection. As the court in the *Midway* case stated, a player could only 'choose one of the limited number of sequences the game allows him to choose' (*Midway Mfg. v. Artic International*, 704 F. 2d 1009, 1012 (1983)).

However, game studies scholars have observed the various ways that game players today co-create the experience of game play (Banks and Deuze, 2009; Consalvo, 2007; Postigo, 2007, 2008, 2010; Taylor, 2006; Wirman, 2011). This game studies literature overlaps, to some extent, with the study of various forms of media fandom, such as communities of *Star Trek* or Japanese anime enthusiasts who enjoy sharing fanfiction, homemade character costumes and props, and fan artwork among their community (Jenkins, 2008). It also overlaps with broader claims about the rise of 'user generated content', 'crowdsourcing', 'remix culture', 'peer production', 'Web 2.0', 'prosumption', 'produsage', and other terms describing popular creativity that is shared (primarily) online (e.g. Banks and Dueze, 2009; Baym, 2010; Benkler, 2006; Bruns, 2008; Burri-Nenova, 2010; Coombe, 1998; Jenkins, 2008; Lessig, 2008; Shirky, 2010; Tapscott and Williams, 2010). Within the legal academy, many copyright scholars are similarly attempting to map out the implications of user-generated content for copyright law (e.g. Fiesler, 2008;

Gervais, 2009; Halbert, 2009; Hetcher, 2009; Nichols, 2007).

Game players can certainly be 'fans' in much the same manner that television audiences might be fans of a particular series, such as *Star Trek* or *Buffy the Vampire Slayer*. However, there are many game-specific creative practices, such as sharing play strategies, composing 'walkthroughs' that explain how to win solo games, creating 'skins' and 'cheats' that change the appearance and nature of play, and providing other software modifications that enhance or alter the play experience (Consalvo, 2007). In some video games, players collaborate during game play, assisting each other and forming social groups like 'clans' and 'guilds' (often with elaborate Web-based systems of recruitment, governance, scheduling and resource management) (Taylor, 2006). Finally, in a growing number of games, players use in-game and out-of-game tools to create their own original works (avatars, objects and environments) that they share, by various means, with other players.

For game studies scholars and those who study fan communities, there is a lively debate over whether the labor that fans and players invest in producing new information resources is ultimately exploitative or empowering (Banks and Deuze 2009; Terranova, 2004). Critics of the rise in video game co-creation point to the fact that game companies retain the majority of the economic value produced by free player labor (Kline et al., 2003; Scholz, 2013; Terranova, 2004). A related complaint is that game owners do not sufficiently respect the value contributed to their companies by player communities, refusing to listen to their players and sometimes treating them with contempt (Taylor, 2006).

Those with more optimistic views of co-creativity in video games generally make arguments that are essentially consistent with those made by early proponents of Web 2.0. For instance, they claim that greater player participation in shaping video game culture leads players to feel empowered with respect to media. They claim that active media participation is intrinsically beneficial for players insofar as it teaches new communicative and interpersonal skills. They point out the ways that player co-creation of game content increases the diversity of ethnic and cultural perspectives. They claim that player participation in video games operates in a non-market cultural sphere that is normatively superior to domains of commoditized culture (see e.g., Benkler, 2006; Burri-Nenova, 2010).

Those who defend the importance of video games often make similar claims about the benefits of video games vis-à-vis other more 'passive' media forms. Whatever one's position on the social harms and benefits of co-creative technologies, the practice clearly raises new questions for copyright law. Players who author game modifications, create fan fiction and artwork, or build elaborate avatars, objects and environments are not merely choosing a particular pre-authored sequence already fixed within the video game's code. They are creating works of authorship as part of the process of video game play. Such user-generated game content should lead us to re-examine earlier jurisprudence on copyright in interactive media.

USER-GENERATED CONTENT IN VIDEO GAMES

'User-generated content' has been defined in a number of ways (Burri-Nenova, 2010). An often-cited definition (Gervais, 2009) is from the OECD's 2007 Report entitled 'Participative Web: User-Created Content'. That report, while acknowledging the variable uses of the term, defined 'user-created content' (a synonym of 'user-generated content') as content: (1) made publicly available over the Internet; (2) which reflects a certain amount of creative effort; and which is (3) created outside of professional routines and practices. Clearly, this OECD definition is a broad one – it essentially encompasses all non-commercial Internet-based creative content.

In order for this definition to dovetail neatly with copyright law, it might be helpful to re-define 'a certain amount of creative effort', to denote such creative effort that rises to the level of originality necessary for copyright protection. Under this definition, a mundane tweet might not amount to user-generated content (UGC) (since it would not be protected by copyright), but a series of lengthy tweets might cross the UGC threshold. This definition would make UGC a subset of copyright-protected works generally.

Defined this way, video game UGC is both familiar and novel. It is familiar because there is no requirement that authorial works should be professional in order to be protected by copyright. Under contemporary copyright law, copyright subsists in original works upon their fixation, regardless of their authorship or their authorial motivations. Copyright law, in theory, subsists in the billions of new amateur works created online every day, including amateur stories, photographs, journalism, videos, music and software.

The term 'user-generated' arguably adds nothing new to traditional copyright law, given that, historically, almost all authors (e.g. poets, painters, musicians, sculptors) have 'used' particular technologies as part of their artistic practices. Given the OECD's broad definition, any non-professional author, artist, or musician uploading a text, image, or song to the Internet would be characterized not as an author but as a 'user' – a somewhat strange substitution. Much like 'player' is a term that defines an individual in relation to a game, 'user' is a term that defines an individual in relation to a technology (the Internet) rather than highlighting the individual's role as an author (Lastowka, 2008).

Player-created UGC can be divided into three general categories. First, player UGC might include video game 'fan works' that are not directly incorporated into the video game experiences. Many video game players create stories, artwork, costumes, videos, walkthroughs, fan websites, and other works of authorship that do not directly borrow audiovisual assets from the video game. The copyright implications of these sorts of fan works are largely indistinguishable from the copyright implications of fan works based on other popular media (Wirman, 2009).

A second category of fan works includes traditional works of authorship (e.g. poems, songs, or paintings) that are authored outside the context of the video game and then inserted into game play in some manner (Reuveni, 2007). For instance, a player might compose a poem and then read it to other players within a multi-player game. In such a case, the player would clearly own the copyright to the poem, at least initially. After the player included the poem in the game, ownership and licensing would depend on the game's contract and one's interpretation of applicable copyright doctrines. Most online games that permit players to upload new content generally demand that players license the platform owners to make use of those works. Some even demand an assignment of the uploaded content to the game company.

The third, and most confusing, situation is where players create works of authorship that directly incorporate and depend upon the software of the video game, either with or without permission of the game developer (Scacchi, 2010). This differs from the second situation insofar as the player works are not first created independently of the video game, but are reliant on the video game's software or audiovisual presentation for their creation.

There is a long history of these sorts of creative tools in games. Some video games, past and present, have been designed to allow players to create and save a variety of in-game works: for example, avatars, narratives, in-game objects, new environments and animation sequences. An early example is the 1983 game, *Pinball Construction Set*, authored by Bill Budge, which, as the title suggests, allowed players to build virtual pinball tables with flippers, bumpers, spinners, magnets, lanes, gates, etc. More recent examples include games like *Spore*, *Little Big Planet*, and *Minecraft*, all of which provide players with sophisticated authorship tools.

Even in cases where players are not provided with authorship tools, many players today use third-party software and technologies to copy and reproduce particular elements of video games. This sort of practice can range from the use of simple technologies to capture game performances to more complicated interventions, such as 'modding' games (Postigo, 2007, 2008, 2010; Scacchi, 2010) or using a game's graphic assets to create the combination of video game animation and cinematography known as machinima.

As Tyler Ochoa (2012) has explained, many forms of software are used today as authorial tools. If we put aside the contractual issues surrounding player authorship within the context of video games, there seems to be no reason that players cannot qualify under copyright law as authors when they use robust creative tools provided by video games. Ochoa notes that typical word processing software constrains the creative freedom of the user in some ways. Yet no one would argue that Microsoft owns all creative output from literary works created by authors who use its program. It follows that video game players can author works in video games using tools that are equivalent to paint programs and 3-D modeling software.

Ochoa uses the example of player-created video game avatars, and in particular those created in the multi-player game *City of Heroes*. Given that, by conservative estimates, *City of Heroes* enabled players to create trillions of possible avatars, Ochoa concludes that such avatars should qualify as copyright-protected works of authorship. Ochoa concludes that the existing law with respect to collaborative copyright is not ideal, but argues that the optimal way of understanding avatar copyright is to view player avatars either as joint or independent works (dependent on their qualities and mode of creation) and to view them as contributions to the 'collective work' of the game space.

Similarly, as mentioned previously, Burk (2013) argues that, barring contractual modifications to the *status quo ante*, game play performances might be subject to copyright protection. Burk analogizes sophisticated video game play performance to improvisational music, dance or theater. He explains that both forms of activity are creative and that skilled performances can be constrained by technological limitations and cultural conventions. He concludes, therefore, that athletic performance (including e-sports performance) could qualify as original expression under copyright law. Burk does recognize, however, that this position is in tension with a leading case in point, *National Basketball Association v. Motorola*, 105 F.3d 841 (1997). In that case, Judge Winter, citing the same section of the Nimmer treatise cited by Boyden, explained:

> Sports events are not 'authored' in any common sense of the word ... Unlike movies, plays, television programs, or operas, athletic events are competitive and have no underlying script ... If the inventor of the T-formation in football had been able to copyright it, the sport might have come to an end instead of prospering. Even where athletic preparation most resembles authorship – figure skating, gymnastics, and, some would uncharitably say, professional wrestling – a performer who conceives and executes a particularly graceful and difficult – or, in the case of wrestling, seemingly painful – acrobatic feat cannot copyright it without impairing the underlying competition in the future.

Even if we reject Burk's arguments and agree with Judge Winter (and Nimmer and Boyden) that video game performances should be generally excluded from copyright authorship, Tyler Ochoa's example of player-created avatars and more traditional forms of in-game authorship (e.g. creating in-game artworks, stories, or sculptures) would seem to fall within Judge Winter's conception of the appropriate limits of copyright's scope. Creating an avatar is more like painting a portrait and less like playing basketball, hence it would not seem to be barred by a legal rule excluding game play from authorship.

It is an open question whether most games will feature player authorship tools in the future, but an increasing number of popular games today include some built-in tools for player creativity. Even in cases where such tools are not part of the game, players increasingly use third-party creative technologies to increase their creative control over games.

As Ochoa and Burk both acknowledge, the application of copyright law to player authorship presents difficult questions for copyright. These new questions may take some time to reach courts, if they are litigated at all. As numerous game studies scholars have noted, technological powers and click-through contracts have already proven to be effective mechanisms enabling game companies to monetize various forms of player productivity. Whether copyright law theoretically protects specific forms of player creativity may not be as important as more pragmatic questions about the likely assertion and enforcement of player copyright interests. Even if we conclude that video game players should hold copyright in particular recorded play performances, the majority of recorded performances will be of low value. Only those who seek to monetize expert performances (e.g. e-sports leagues) will have the commercial motivation to enforce their copyrights, provided they have power to do so under contract law. Like the early video game pioneers, these e-sports innovators may lack the funds to pursue expensive litigation in order to enforce uncertain rights.

The vast majority of player authors today are sharing amateur works that lack market value when they are considered individually. Collectively, such works may add significant value to video game cultures and technological platforms, but they are unlikely to form the basis of active markets for copyright claims.

CONCLUSION

Although video games are increasingly part of the 21st-century media landscape, their protection under copyright law still poses complex doctrinal questions. This is despite the fact that their key distinguishing feature – player interactivity – has existed since their earliest inception. Early cases largely discounted the importance of video game interactivity, focusing on the similarities between video games and prior media. The traditional doctrine prohibiting copyright in games bolstered this approach, suggesting to courts that interactive play practices were outside the appropriate scope of copyright. However, in recent years, authorial tools are increasingly embedded into video games, making it clear that video game software can actually give rise to various forms of player authorship. This makes video games a technologically, doctrinally and formally unique realm of interactive media within the domain of copyright law.

In coming years, with the rise of more powerful tools for player authorship, we may see the questions of interactivity once again challenge courts. However, it seems equally possible that players will simply contribute their creative work to game platforms without the expectation of receiving the economic and legal rewards that normally accompany copyright productivity.

REFERENCES

Aarseth, Espen J. (1997) *Cybertext: Perspectives on Ergodic Literature*. Baltimore, MD: Johns Hopkins University Press.

Banks, John A. and Deuze, Mark (2009) 'Co-creative Labour', *International Journal of Cultural Studies* 12: 4194.

Baym, Nancy (2010) 'Embracing the Flow', research memo for the Convergence Culture Consortium.

Benkler, Yochai (2006) *The Wealth of Networks: How Social Production Transforms Markets and Freedom*. New Haven: Yale University Press.

Boellstorff, Tom (2008) *Coming of Age in Second Life: An Anthropologist Explores the Virtually Human*. Princeton: Princeton University Press.

Bogost, Ian (2006) *Unit Operations: An Approach to Videogame Criticism*. Cambridge, MA: MIT Press.

Bogost, Ian (2007) *Persuasive Games: The Expressive Power of Videogames*. Cambridge, MA: MIT Press.

Boyd, Greg (2006) 'Litigations that Changed the Games Industry', *Gamasutra*, available at: www.gamasutra.com/view/feature/1757/litigations_that_changed_the_games_.php

Boyden, Bruce E. (2011a) 'Games and Other Uncopyrightable Systems', *George Mason Law Review* 18: 479.

Boyden, Bruce E. (2011b) 'Copyright's Middle Ground: The Interaction of Players and Video Games', in proceedings of The Game Behind the Video Game: Business, Regulation, and Society in the Gaming

Industry, New Brunswick, New Jersey, April 8–9, 2011.

Bruns, Axel (2008) *Blogs, Wikipedia, Second Life, and Beyond*. New York: Peter Lang Publishing.

Burk, Dan L. (2010) 'Authorization and Governance in Virtual Worlds', First Monday 15(5).

Burk, Dan L. (2013) 'Owning E-Sports: Proprietary Rights in Professional Computer Gaming', *University of Pennsylvania Law Review* 161: 1535.

Burri-Nenova, Mira (2010) 'User Created Content in Virtual Worlds and Cultural Diversity', in C.B. Graber and M. Burri-Nenova (eds), *Governance of Digital Game Environments and Cultural Diversity*. Cheltenham: Edward Elgar, pp. 74–112.

Caillois, Roger (1961) *Man, Play, and Games*. Urbana and Chicago: University of Illinois Press.

Consalvo, Mia (2007) *Cheating: Gaining Advantage in Videogames*. Cambridge, MA: The MIT Press.

Coombe, Rosemary J. (1998) *The Cultural Life of Intellectual Properties: Authorship, Appropriation, and the Law*. Durham: Duke University Press.

Costikyan, Greg (2013) *Uncertainty in Games*. Cambridge, MA: MIT Press.

Crawford, Chris (1984) *The Art of Computer Game Design: Reflections of a Master Game Designer*. Osborne/McGraw-Hill. Revised edition 2011 [Kindle edn].

Elias, George Skaff, Garfield, Richard and Gutschera, K. Robert (2012) *Characteristics of Games*. Cambridge, MA: MIT Press.

Festinger, Jonathan B. (2005) *Video Game Law*. Dayton, Ohio: LexisNexis Butterworths.

Fiesler, Casey (2008) 'Everything I Need To Know I Learned from Fandom: How Existing Social Norms Can Help Shape the Next Generation of User-Generated Content', *Vanderbilt Journal of Entertainment and Technology Law* 10: 729.

Ford, William K. (2012) 'Copy Game for High Score: The First Video Game Lawsuit', *Journal of Intellectual Property Law* 1: 1.

Frasca, Gonzalo (2003) 'Ludologists Love Stories, Too: Notes from a Debate that Never Took Place', in Marinka Copier and Joost Raessens (eds), *Level Up: Digital Games Research Conference Proceedings*. Utrecht: DiGRA and University of Utrecht.

Gee, James Paul (2007) *What Video Games Have to Teach Us About Learning and Literacy*. New York: Palgrave Macmillan.

Gervais, Daniel (2009) 'The Tangled Web of UGC: Making Copyright Sense of User-Generated Content', *Vanderbilt Journal of Entertainment and Technology Law* 11: 841.

Grimes, Sarah M. and Fields, Deborah A. (2012) *Kids Online: A New Research Agenda for Understanding Social Networking Forums*. New York: The Joan Ganz Cooney Center at Sesame Workshop, available at: http://dmlhub.net/sites/default/files/jgcc_kidsonline.pdf

Guins, Raiford (2009) 'Concrete and Clay: The Afterlife and Times of E.T. The Extra-Terrestrial for the Atari VideoComputer System', *Design and Culture* 1: 345.

Halbert, Debora (2009) 'Mass Culture and the Culture of the Masses: A Manifesto for User-Generated Rights', *Vanderbilt Journal of Entertainment and Technology Law* 11: 921.

Hetcher, Steven A. (2009) 'Hume's Penguin, or, Yochai Benkler and the Nature of Peer Production', *Vanderbilt Journal of Entertainment and Technology Law*, 11: 963.

Huizinga, Johan (1950) *Homo Ludens: A Study of the Play Element in Culture*. Boston: The Beacon Press.

Humphreys, Sal (2009) 'Discursive Constructions of MMOGs and Some Implications for Policy and Regulation', *Media International Australia* 130: 53.

Jenkins, Henry (2008) *Convergence Culture: Where Old and New Media Collide*. New York: NYU Press.

Juul, Jesper (2001) 'Games Telling stories? A Brief Note on Games and Narratives', *Game Studies* 1: 1.

Juul, Jesper (2005) *Half-Real: Video Games Between Real Rules and Fictional Worlds*. Cambridge, MA: MIT Press.

Kent, Steven L. (2001) *The Ultimate History of Video Games: From Pong to Pokemon – The Story Behind the Craze That Touched Our Lives and Changed the World*. New York: Three Rivers Press.

Kerr, Aphra (2002) 'Representing Users in the Design of Digital Games', in Computer Games and Digital Cultures Conference Proceedings.

Kerr, Aphra (2006) *The Business and Culture of Digital Games: Gamework and Gameplay*. London: Sage Publications Ltd.

Kline, Stephen, Dyer-Witheford, Nick and DePeuter, Greig (2003) *Digital Play: The Interaction of Technology, Culture, and Marketing*. Montreal: McGill-Queen's University Press.

Lastowka, Greg (2008) 'User-Generated Content & Virtual Worlds', *Vanderbilt Journal of Entertainment and Technology Law* 10: 893.

Lastowka, Greg (2010) *Virtual Justice: The New Laws of Online Worlds*. New Haven, CT: Yale University Press.

Lessig, Lawrence (2008) *Remix: Making Art and Commerce Thrive in the Hybrid Economy*. New York: Penguin Press.

Lipson, Ashley S. and Brain, Robert D. (2009) *Computer and Video Game Law: Cases, Statutes, Forms, Problems & Materials*. Durham, NC: Carolina Academic Press.

Malaby, Thomas (2009) *Making Virtual Worlds: Linden Lab and Second Life*. Ithaca, NY: Cornell University Press.

McGonigal, Jane (2011) *Reality Is Broken: Why Games Make Us Better and How They Can Change the World.* New York: Penguin Press.

Montfort, Nick and Bogost, Ian (2009) *Racing the Beam: The Atari Video Computer System.* Cambridge, MA: The MIT Press.

Mortensen, Torill Elvira (2009) *Perceiving Play: The Art and Study of Computer Games.* New York: Peter Lang.

Murray, Janet (1997) *Hamlet on the Holodeck: The Future of Narrative in Cyberspace.* New York: Free Press.

Myers, David (2003) *The Nature of Computer Games.* New York: Peter Lang Publishing.

Myers, David (2010) *Play Redux: the Form of Computer Games.* Ann Arbor: University of Michigan Press.

Nardi, Bonnie A. (2010) *My Life as a Night Elf Priest: An Anthropological Account of World of Warcraft.* Ann Arbor: University of Michigan Press.

Nichols, W. Joss (2007) 'Painting through Pixels: The Case for a Copyright in Videogame Play', *Columbia Journal of Law and the Arts* 30: 101.

OECD (2007) Participative Web and User-Created Content. Web 2.0, Wikis, and Social Networking. Paris: OECD, available at: http://www.oecd.org/sti/38393115.pdf

Ochoa, Tyler (2012) 'Who Owns an Avatar? Copyright, Creativity, and Virtual Worlds', *Vanderbilt Journal of Entertainment and Technology Law* 14: 959.

Papert, Seymour (1993) *The Children's Machine: Rethinking School in the Age of the Computer.* New York: Basic Books.

Postigo, Hector (2007) 'Of Mods and Modders: Chasing Down the Value of Fan-Based Digital Game Modifications', *Games and Culture* 2: 300.

Postigo, Hector (2008) 'Video Game Appropriation through Modifications', *Convergence: The International Journal of Research into New Media Technologies* 14(1): 59–74.

Postigo, Hector (2010) 'Modding to the big leagues: Exploring the space between modders and the game industry', *First Monday* 15.

Reuveni, Erez (2007) 'Authorship in the Age of the Conducer', *Journal of the Copyright Society of the USA* 54: 285.

Ryan, Marie-Laure (2001) *Narrative as Virtual Reality: Immersion and Interactivity in Literature and Electronic Media.* Baltimore: John Hopkins Press.

Salen, Katie and Zimmerman, Eric (2003) *Rules of Play: Game Design Fundamentals.* Cambridge, MA: MIT Press.

Scacchi, Walt (2010) 'Computer game mods, modders, modding, and the mod scene', *First Monday* 15(5).

Scholz, Trebor (2013) *Digital Labor: The Internet as Playground and Factory.* New York: Routledge.

Shirky, Clay (2010) *Cognitive Surplus: How Technology Makes Consumers into Collaborators.* New York: Penguin.

Suits, Bernard (2005) *The Grasshopper: Games, Life and Utopia.* Toronto: Broadview Press.

Sutton-Smith, Brian (1998) *The Ambiguity of Play.* Cambridge, MA: Harvard University Press.

Tapscott, Don and Williams, Anthony D. (2010) *Wikinomics: How Mass Collaboration Changes Everything.* New York: Portfolio Trade.

Taylor, T.L. (2006) *Play Between Worlds: Exploring Online Game Culture.* Cambridge, MA: MIT Press.

Taylor, T.L. (2012) *Raising the Stakes: E-sports and the Professionalization of Computer Gaming.* Cambridge, MA: MIT Press.

Tehranian, John (2011) *Infringement Nation: Copyright 2.0 and You.* New York: Oxford University Press.

Terranova, Tiziana (2004) *Network Culture: Politics for the Information Age.* Pluto Press.

Toffler, Alvin (1980) The Third Wave. New York: Morrow.

Wirman, Hanna Elina (2009) 'On Productivity and Game Fandom', *Transformative Works and Cultures* 3.

Wirman, Hanna Elina (2011) 'Playing The Sims 2: Constructing and Negotiating Woman Computer Game Player Identities through the Practice of Skinning', PhD dissertation, University of the West of England.

Yeats, W.B. (1928) 'Among School Children,' in *The Tower.* New York: Macmillan.

28

Promoting Progress: A Qualitative Analysis of Creative and Innovative Production

Jessica Silbey

INTRODUCTION

For five years, I have been conducting interviews with artists and scientists in diverse fields, as well as with their lawyers and business partners. My goal in doing so was to learn how intellectual property functions in their professional lives devoted to creative and innovative work. The scholarly literature defending and explaining intellectual property in the United States is largely dominated by a theoretical economic approach to law with its assumptions about human motivation and the benefits and values of creative and innovative work to those making it. In contrast to a law and economics approach to IP's function and optimal form, this qualitative investigation of creators and innovators investigates the roles of intellectual property (and entitlement claiming more generally) from the ground up.

The interview data contain rich accounts and reflections about how and why individuals create and innovate and also about how complex industries devoted to creative and innovative products and services sustain their businesses. Beyond the interest in these details from creative and innovative people and industries, this study has broader implications for intellectual property law reform specifically and our understanding of IP-rich communities generally. Whether readers are lawyers, local or national political leaders or business people, the data from these interviews should shape our conversations about the individual and socio-economic benefits and pleasures that creative and innovative work brings. Historically, many nations (and the United States in particular) protect intellectual property production in order to enhance its output to promote 'progress'. But the content of 'progress' remains ill-defined. This project addresses precisely that question in an effort to learn from those creating or innovating (and those that facilitate creativity and innovation) the nature of the progress for which they aim.[1] One hope for this project, then, is to infuse our discussion of intellectual property with grounded facts about what people really care about when they are engaged in work protectable through intellectual property law so that when we engage in policy reform discussions about intellectual property we might debate the issues with concrete details from those driving the innovation and creativity. In the United States, the Constitutional prerogative 'to promote the progress of science and the useful arts' (U.S.

Const., Art. 1, Sec. 8, Cl. 8.) drives the congressional mandate for intellectual property regulation, but 200 years since our constitutional beginnings, we remain unsure – indeed deeply conflicted – about whether the laws that protect intellectual property work as we hope.[2] This is in part because of our failure to study those who create and innovate and instead to base existing laws on theoretical models of commercial transactions and hypothetical business practices.[3] This study aims to refocus the inquiry on the creators and innovators themselves to learn how and why they work in order to investigate whether or how intellectual property law functions in their professional and innovative activities.

The interviews are semi-structured and open-ended conversations about the interviewees' work: its origins, its personal and organizational contours, challenges, pleasures and desires. I interviewed a wide variety of artists, scientists, engineers, lawyers and business managers. All own or manage intellectual properties. However, in the interviews, I do not ask directly about intellectual property or specifically about progress goals until the end of conversation. But from the detailed accounts and reflections throughout the open-ended conversation, I gleaned specific categories and diverse roles for intellectual property in the development and fulfillment of artistic and scientific work towards the achievement of progress.

In the interviews, progress features centrally despite its elusive nature. Notably, it is not a value-neutral or subjective concept but a tall order and one that interviewees describe as demanding objective evaluation. Progress is explicitly directional and qualitative: it is about novelty and correction vis-à-vis the past, and it is valued for the kinds of things produced and their associated benefits rather than for how much is made or money earned. Everyday work, professional identity and sustainable social welfare are signs of progress for almost all of the people and industry leaders I interviewed. Part II of this chapter will discuss these dimensions in more detail. But it is worth noting now that these standards are much higher than current intellectual property regimes in the United States require.

Instead of conducting and analyzing interviews for a qualitative analysis of creative and innovative work, I could study outcomes and pursue a quantitative study. For example, I could ask instead: Do pharmaceutical companies with more patents make more socially beneficial medicines? Do filmmakers and production companies who exploit the full range of their copyrights remain viable for longer? Measuring outcomes would be easier – there is a tangible dependent variable to count. But such quantifiable outcomes are deeply ambiguous metrics. How do we determine which medicines fulfill the constitutional 'progress' rationale? By how many lives saved? By how much profit generated? And, importantly, how do we know whether intellectual property law that protects the output is the mechanism that is causally responsible for it?

Instead of focusing on outcomes, this qualitative project focuses on processes. It unpacks the assumption and mystery of incentives and the amorphous claims about progress by analyzing the accounts people provide about (1) how and why they do what they do, and (2) how intellectual property law has enabled or constrained their work. Without exception, courts, legislators and lawyers describe the purpose of intellectual property law in the United States as providing the necessary incentive for creativity and innovation, assuming that as long as creative and innovative work gets done, progress will follow under the right circumstances (*Bowman v. Monsanto*, 569 U.S. __ (slip op. 8) (2013); Landes and Posner, 2003: 37–84; Zimmerman, 2011). However, this utilitarian justification speaks of incentive without evidence of connection to lived experience. And it makes no claim to substantively describe what 'progress' might mean except tautologically as the creation of creative and innovative work. Despite a vast theoretical literature on intellectual property, and a growing body of quantitative research on IP law and policy, qualitative research that could document or challenge the function of IP regulation is rare.[4]

Moreover, qualitative research and its attention to language and narrative accounts help us understand things that surveys and other quantitative research cannot. The language people use to describe their lives and work offers access to the cultural milieu of creativity and innovation, including the law that regulates their work and livelihood. Language – words and stories – make sense of the world (Lakoff and Johnson, 1980). Whether called narrative, rhetoric, or interpretation, stories explain or justify the situation in which we find ourselves (Chambers, 1984: 212–213). This includes the legal situation that frames (enables and constrains) creativity and innovation. At the same time, stories are inherently political (White, 1980: 11). They can justify the status quo or affect change.[5] Their repeated use (along with repeated words and phrases) reify or transform categories and expectations, which in turn structure relationships and obligations (including legal ones) in our communities.[6] Studying the stories told and the language used is important for understanding how we live together in organized communities and the rules that govern us.[7]

The 50 transcripts at the foundation of this project tell remarkably consistent stories about what constitutes artistic or scientific progress. Despite diverse industry actors and organizational structures, the nature of 'progress' sought and valued is varied but coherent. Before getting to these common threads in Part II, however, this chapter first discusses the historical and theoretical roots of the United States Constitution's clause in order to later contextualize the grounded research. The second part of the chapter catalogues the variations in the notions of 'progress' as described by the creators and innovators themselves and highlights their common themes as well as some notable distinctions. Despite being a study of United States law and communities, I hope that the implications for this study will speak to an international audience concerned, as most of us are in our digital age, with how to make the most of our increased connectedness by improving lives and achieving individual and communal goals globally. As will become clear, 'progress' is an aspect of both personal and public life, although personal welfare may differ from the public good. As it turns out, connecting the individual with a collective view of progress is a central preoccupation of creators and innovators. Although many struggle to find a role for intellectual property regulation in making that connection, most make the connection in and through their work. Central to this paper's conclusions, therefore, is the sometimes overlapping and frequent misalignment of IP protection with progress-related ambitions.

PROGRESS IN HISTORY AND THEORY

There is relatively little documentary history about the genesis of Article 1, Section 8, Clause 8 of the US Constitution, which grants power to Congress 'to promote the Progress of Science and useful Arts by securing for limited Times to Authors and Inventors the exclusive Right to their respective Writings and Discoveries' (the 'IP Clause') (Oliar, 2006: 1790–1791). Compared to other parts of the Constitution – for example, its tripartite structure, its dual sovereign system and the Civil War Reconstruction Amendments – contemporary debates over the IP clause were neither lengthy nor public. Several scholars have written detailed historical analyses of the genesis of the IP Clause and have come to different conclusions about its meaning. (Bugbee, 1967; Heald and Sherry, 2000; Nachbar, 2004; Oliar, 2006; Walterschied, 1995).

Interestingly enough, the debate over the IP Clause is rarely about the meaning of 'progress' or 'science' (Pollack, 2001; Snow, 2013) the way debates about the Commerce Clause (Art. I, Sec. 8, Cl. 3) are about the meaning of 'commerce'. (Balkin, 2010; Merritt, 1995). Instead, investigations of the IP Clause concern its relation to other enumerated powers of Congress in the Constitution: whether Congress can 'promote progress' through other means, for example by drawing on its Treaty Power or its Tax Power, or whether the IP clause limits other powers of Congress (Fromer, 2012). Most scholarly debates concern the internal limitations of the IP clause: whether Congress may only grant patents and copyrights if by doing so it is 'promot[ing] the progress of Science and useful Arts' (Fromer, 2012: 1336). These are important debates as they focus upon a central issue of United States constitutionalism: the limited authority of the federal government and instances when the exercise of federal power may exceed this. In most of these cases, however, the central question concerns the operative verb 'promote,' and the shape and nature of 'progress' is taken for granted.

The pithy documentary evidence of the genesis of the IP clause shows a coordinated submission during the Constitutional Convention by James Madison (Virginia) and Charles Pinckney (South Carolina) that does not shed much light on the substantive meaning of 'progress'. Interestingly, both Madison and Pinckney made proposals that overlapped in purpose and substance and largely focused on the role of institutions rather than individuals. Madison proposed granting patents and copyrights to inventors and 'literary authors' for limited times, as did Pinckney (although Pinckney proposed the more general 'exclusive rights' instead of Madison's more specific 'copy right').[8] Both men also proposed a form of institutionalized learning of science and the arts. Madison suggested that Congress be empowered to establish a university and Pinckey proposed a seminary. The men also proposed that Congress be empowered in other ways. Madison suggested that Congress 'encourage by proper premiums and provisions, the advancement of useful knowledge and discoveries' (also known as the proposed 'encouragement' power) and Pinckney proposed that Congress 'establish public institutions, rewards and immunities for the promotion of agriculture, commerce, trades and manufactures' (Oliar, 2006: 1789).

These proposals came late to the Constitutional Convention, which began on May 25, 1787. Madison and Pinckney did not offer the above-described submissions until August 18. And on September 5, after less than a week of deliberation behind closed doors, the proposals were shortened, revised and submitted for adoption. The revised recommendation that came from committee was the same IP Clause contained in the ratified US Constitution. There was no recorded debate about the clause and the vote to accept it was unanimous (Farrand, 1991: 505). Apparently Madison and Pinckney tried later to revive only the university power before final ratification of the Constitution, but they were unsuccessful (Farrand, 1991: 616).

Scholars have interpreted the shortening and streamlining of Madison's and Pinckney's proposals to have various implications on the breadth and meaning of the IP Clause. For some, the combination of the progress provision (taken from Madison's proposed encouragement power) with his proposed patent and copyright power *limits* Congress's award of patents and copyrights to only those instances when doing so will 'promote the progress of Science and the useful Arts' (Waltersheid, 2002: 1). For others, the exclusion of universities and prizes from the final version as ratified expressly excludes Congress from establishing a university or issuing prizes under the IP Clause (Oliar, 2006: 1792). Whether and how Congress can otherwise establish a university (which it hasn't) or facilitate the issuing of prizes and grants for research (which it has) is also debated in the literature (Fromer, 2012: 1379–1391).

In contrast to 'progress', the meaning of which is largely assumed without analysis, the IP clause's language of 'science' and the 'useful Arts' is well researched and believed to be understood. 'Science' at the time of the founding meant the systemized study of a branch of learning, as in the 'science of commerce', 'political science', or the 'science of war' (Snow, 2013: 290–291). It did not mean, as it might today, the specific sciences of biology, chemistry, or physics, for example. 'Useful Arts' referred to practical skills, applied sciences and trades, including manufacturing, agricultural trades and civil engineering (Waltersheid, 2003).[9] Whether the fine arts (e.g., poetry, painting, sculpture) was meant to fall within the 'Sciences' remains a subject of on-going inquiry and mystery (Beebe, 2014), although today, to be sure, federal copyright law protects works of fine art. All of this is against the backdrop of enlightenment ideology, a belief system deeply held by the founders and rooted in the power of directive investigation, one goal of which is to break with stagnating tradition and aim for a better future through scientific and literary inquiry.

The addition of 'promote the progress' to 'Science and the useful Arts' does not clarify the scope of the IP Clause. Some scholars insist that 'promote' and 'progress' must have different meanings otherwise Congress would not have included both in relation to 'Science and the useful Arts' (Pollack, 2001: 755–757, 794–795). Most commentators agree that 'promote' means to 'stimulate', 'encourage' or 'induce' and that 'progress' is a substantive noun: a betterment, an advancement or a move in a forward direction (Fromer, 2012: 1373).

In legal scholarship, there is considerable focus on the appropriate levers needed to 'promote … Science and the useful Arts' (Burk and Lemley, 2003). For example, legal scholars and economists routinely ask what precisely (and how much) effectively incentivizes scientists or businesses to invest in researching and developing new medicines (Johnson, 2012; Lemley, 2004; Mann, 2005). Others ask whether moral rights, protected in parts of Europe under copyright law, are necessary to encourage the widespread distribution of certain works of art in the United States (Ginsburg, 2011; Kwall, 2001; Lipton, 2011; Sprigman et al., 2013). The *promotion* language of the IP Clause is central to the literature on intellectual property law. But what about the *progress* language?

Dictionaries now and at the founding define 'progress' as 'advancement' or 'betterment'. But to me, this begs the question. 'Progress' is a subjective label for a movement or trend. What may be an advance in biological science on the one hand may not necessarily be a state of 'betterment' for others. For example, is progress achieved if we know more today about breast cancer than we did ten years ago, but diagnostic tests are widely inaccessible because of costs related to legal barriers, specifically patent law (Chon, 1993)?[10] Or, what may be an advance in music-making technology (the growth of self-recording and self-publication of music on the Internet) may not necessarily be 'better' for musicians and audiences because fewer reliable filters exist for promotion and quality. Moreover, what may be easily understood as a scientific or technological advance in terms of an 'accumulationist' view of progress is not so easily understood for aesthetic works (Beebe, 2014: 28). We may comfortably evaluate the accumulation over time of positive scientific knowledge as it supersedes or refines previous understandings of the natural world. And we may experience the accumulation over time of technological discoveries as more efficient means to accomplish specific ends. As Barton Beebe has written, these forms of progress are 'unidirectional and ratchet-like and may be measured objectively' (Beebe, 2014: 28). But what can we say that an aesthetic work 'does' or that its accumulation supersedes or refines? There may exist a 'weak accumulationist' account of artistic work getting 'better' over time. But since the twentieth century modernist and postmodernist art movements, the 'relative merit [of the artwork] can only be assessed subjectively' (Beebe, 2014: 28).

Given that United States copyright doctrine abjures evaluations of traditional aesthetic judgment, what is aesthetic progress today? To this question, Barton Beebe offers the pragmatists and their theory of aesthetics (Beebe, 2014: 28).[11] This gesture towards the pragmatists intuits a theme in the interview data, but not the only one. As Beebe summarizes, the pragmatists, such as Dewey: (1) emphasize popular aesthetic experiences over 'museum' art; (2) reconceptualize as productive and essential the interdependence between consumer and producer; and (3) value practice (the making) over objects (the made). The interview data *across industries* strongly supports these three values. Although Beebe's exploration focuses only on fine art and aesthetics, the interview data covers scientific and technological work as well. These and other themes alongside the descriptions and analysis of the data itself are highlighted in the next section.

Although US constitutional understanding demands a method of interpretation rooted in history and legal practice, the discussion that follows is not tied to any one modality of constitutional exposition. If I were to consider how a court or a legislature in the US would or should interpret the IP clause today, my guess is that it would track the legal analyses which I have already cited (Fromer, 2012; Pollack, 2001; Snow, 2013).[12] In doing so, the interpretation would begin with an originalist approach but would also rely upon evolving precedent and contemporary socio-historical and economic contexts to render the clause meaningful and consequential today (Balkin, 2009; Strauss, 2010). This is the typical way of proceeding with US constitutional interpretation and application when the language is otherwise opaque.

This project's goal is to infuse into our understanding of the US IP Clause contemporary conceptions and appreciations for what 'progress' might mean to those engaging in science, technology and art. Thus, my contribution is not from legal history or precedent, but from the 'bottom up' (Oliar, 2006: 1837) in a form of 'grounded practice' (Strauss and Corbin, 1997) to advance 'arguments about what "promotes progress" in specific contexts or areas of creativity'(Oliar, 2006: 1837).[13] This chapter's contribution to the US constitutional debate, therefore, relates to the theory of living constitutionalism (Balkin, 2009). It appreciates the ambiguity of the term 'progress' as contained in the US Constitution and develops a contemporary understanding of 'progress' for the clause's application in contemporary society. Doing so hopefully reaches beyond United States policy, however, with implications for a broader debate that focuses on the role of IP regulation and international relations, both for local and national communities with an eye towards global welfare.

PROGRESS ON THE GROUND

Progress is not Value-neutral

For many interviewees across a range of creative and innovative professions, 'progress' has two characteristics. It is explicitly directional: for example, we learn new facts that surpass or refute what we previously knew, or we alter old form and media to produce new works. Progress is also (or uniquely) qualitative: for example, what has been created is better than what came or was before and 'better' is thereafter explained. Notably, progress is rarely measured by an amount of things made or money earned, but instead on the kind of things produced and the kinds of benefits that accrue from them. And these qualities of progress set a higher standard for protected output than current copyright or patent law provide. Thus, strong claims to origination and ownership are less frequent among the interviewees than IP law would otherwise support because the kind of work worthy of exclusive dominion that embodies 'progress' is described as atypical if not also rare.

As an example of both directional and qualitative progress, interviewees describe work that *challenges existing paradigms*, *fills a niche* or *solves an identified problem* as worth doing and sometimes also protecting through legal claims. Typically, scientists, engineers, business agents and lawyers, describe their good work in these ways. But artists in the study do as well. (To be sure, many interviewees don't describe the manner in which they protect their work in IP terms, but many anticipate that the 'law' broadly construed will help them continue their work by protecting their output when necessary.)

Many of the IP lawyers with whom I spoke described their clients' work and business structures in the above progress-based terms. One particular lawyer, who was herself a biologist before becoming an attorney, describes her client's scientific breakthrough as 'a complete sea change' in the science and the subsequent patent process as fairly straightforward. This lawyer is a partner in a law firm that specializes in intellectual property law; and she speaks eloquently, displaying a habit of mind I recognized in many effective attorneys who seek to deeply understand their clients' needs, desires and limitations. She spoke from a conference room in her law firm about her client, a molecular biologist:

> [I]t's not about the money for him: he's interested [in patenting his invention] because it fits into what he does every day, which is his science and his lab, and his recognition at meetings, and now everyone associates his name with this particular thing. I don't think it's about royalties with him. And I think that generally speaking, it isn't with these guys. It's more about being recognized for some type of scientific achievement, and [having] his or her name being associated with that. And generally, that's through publications, not through patent applications. … It's because of the subsequent papers he published in this field. But [the patent is] generating institutional interests … he is out on the circuit more, getting invited [by] … organizations, corporations. You know, people in Europe are now interested in him.
>
> I think for him, that the interesting [thing] for him [about his discovery] is it went contrary to every scientific theory that was out there. … He is very smart, and very friendly; gets along very well with people. And he's very proud of what he's done. It's also helping a population of people for which there has been very little hope for many years, and he is very touched by that. It's a very emotional thing for him. And when he sat there with the [patent] examiners and he talked about, you know, the theories that were out there for this particular condition, and he said to them – he goes, 'Look, I am just a scientist, you know? I go into my lab, and I come up with theories.' And he said, 'This was a complete sea change' – and that was his word: a complete sea change. No one – and no one believed him. And we wrote a patent, and we got him an application, and we got his patents allowed, and he's in Europe, and he's all over – worldwide jurisdiction. And now, people are using, employing this particular method to help a population of people for which there was very little hope, and it's working. And he's just – so he is very touched by that, that he did something that … He looked at the data with one of his students, and he was like, 'You know what? I don't think it's that – I think it's *this*.' And so let's test it.'

Beyond the absence of a pecuniary motive, this passage is notable for its identification of reputation and professional growth as benefits that accrue from good work and sometimes also from IP rights. Admittedly, the scientist about which this lawyer talks is a salaried employee and does not worry about earning a living from patent royalties. Generally, he is not motivated to do the research by the possibility of receiving a patent on his invention. It doesn't 'incent' him as intellectual property law sometimes presumes. But once received, the patent has value as a symbol of the scientist's good work: his recognition for discovering something new, being sufficiently insightful and courageous to pursue a path not previously taken, and doing so in order to solve a problem that will improve the well-being of an underserved population of people worldwide. This scientist considers his work progress for all of these reasons. In other words, patenting his invention does not seem unreasonable or incongruous because he recognizes it as representing a kind of progress. If, however, his high standard was the standard for patentability, there would be significantly fewer patents, to be sure.

Notably, this same lawyer describes most of her scientist and engineer clients as being uninterested in the patent process, rarely discussing their patents and patenting strategies unless doing so achieves their personal and professional goals. She says:

> They're annoyed; you're an annoyance, generally. You take up their time [and] they could be doing other things. They're generally not interested. ... there's an inventor ... that I've dealt with ... he founded a small company. Even when he founded [a] small company, he really didn't want to spend any time talking to me about [patents] – he'll talk about baseball, but he didn't want to talk about his patent applications.

In other words, the patent process is only worth the effort when it facilitates other personal and professional progress as described above. Although the patent itself did not facilitate the invention of which the scientist is so proud, it enabled him to grow his reputation and thereby share his research and his research agenda with a larger audience. And he believes – although whether this is in fact true is a different question – that the patent enables the widespread distribution of the invention to communities in need.

Artists also describe the value of their work as directionally forward-looking or a qualitative improvement beyond what came before or exists currently. I interviewed a wide range of artists, including painters, writers, sculptors, photographers and filmmakers. Most of them spoke, as did the scientists and engineers, about the value of challenging existing paradigms in their work, filling a niche among similar artists, or solving an identified problem. For example, a novelist describes her everyday process of writing this way:

> I'm obviously using my brain, it's *my* brain, but I don't have that much control over it. I can just – I can set the rules for the day, I can set the project for the day, but I can't force myself to come up with stuff. You know, I can say, 'This is the problem that needs to be solved', or, you know, 'I need to get this character from point A to point B ..., but I can't think, 'I am going to work on a really felicitous way of saying this.' You know, it just doesn't ... happen [like that]. I mean, what you really have to do is focus on a slightly larger problem, and then hopefully something felicitous will come as you go.

Problem-solving of a more general nature is at the root of creative expression, she says. And that process generates excellent work. This novelist believes she can distinguish between excellent and mediocre writing. Excellent writing is both timeless and yet also 'timely' in that it is different than writing that has come before and responds to life currently.

> I feel like human nature has been pretty stable for a long time, and we have probably said everything there is to say about it [laughter]. But conditions, the conditions of human nature, of humanity, do change, have changed. You know, we produce new foodstuffs, and we *whatever*, you know? And there are always these specific details that are new. So come up with a new story to tell me about those things.

This is similar to the view of scientific progress as discoveries that stand the test of time and develop existing paradigms of understanding.

I interviewed many sculptors, some whose work is displayed in museums and others whose art is commissioned for public installation. These artists focus routinely as a goal on the marriage of form and function in their sculpture. They also regularly discuss the importance of their audiences and physical contexts in which their work is situated. One such artist, well-established and trained as an architect, describes his goals and philosophies when choosing projects. Although his professional identity as a combined sculptor and architect was unique among the interviewees, his outlook was not. Many artists – writers, painters, photographers, filmmakers – similarly described their interests in making art as focusing on intellectual challenge, uniqueness or novelty (aesthetic and otherwise) and the accomplishment of a particular social or public end. He says:

> I see [public art] as an interesting way to do certain things, which is kind of a hard crossover, towards community-building. [Because] I guess what I tend to do anyway is to try to make things work as well as be art. I'm not content to just sort of be a commentary, which a lot of art is, sort of 'This is a way of creating a metaphor, or commenting on some, like a social, or some issue.' I mean, I was recently involved in designing for a streetcar line, and doing shelters for the thing. And the issue became whether these shelters were too much like architecture, or were they sufficiently art, and I think

> sufficiently art by some of the art people … was considered to be less functional and more whimsical, or something. And you know, I kind of had a problem with that. … 'cause those things turn into one-line jokes, and if they're there for ten years, it gets kind of old, and so I think that there's a place to put things in an urban, or any kind of community environment, that work[s] on both levels. And in fact, that's what I would consider really my goal.

This artist's goal was both particular and broad. Particularly, he sought to design structures that were both functional as shelters and beautiful as enduring art. He didn't prioritize either aspect and, indeed, considered optimal output as melding the two. Broadly, he sought to create works that united and enriched the communities in which they were situated. Like the scientist/inventor who describes the public benefits from a new method of treatment for an orphan disease, this artist conceives of good work as new, filling a need, and establishing or sustaining a community.

Compare a geneticist's critique of patenting medical technology with a filmmaker's description of why she makes films. The geneticist visited my office for an interview and spoke mostly about her eight years in graduate school and more time completing her postdoctoral work and working as an assistant clinical professor in a medical center. She later went to work for a large, publicly-owned pharmaceutical company. She expressed concern for and disaffection with the industry despite the services rendered to patients, particularly because of the perceived conflicts between medical ethics, business needs and patent law:

> I would say clinical utility [is a major problem] … and health care reform will put pressure on this one – is the test a benefit to the patient? Or are you just offering it as a revenue generator?

This geneticist describes directional progress but qualitative progress only vaguely. Compare these concerns with a filmmaker's description of how she got into filmmaking.

> In college, I could take literature classes in Spanish, I could do that, or politics, you know, I could learn about that. But Latino culture, it was nonexistent. … And I knew very well that media was the most powerful thing. So I ended up taking a film and anthropology class … and it became the thing that I thought, 'It's so powerful, it's a way to talk to other people about these cultures that live right here.' So it's a way, in the same way that when radio technology was invented, and suddenly black people's music could enter the home, could enter the living room. … So these stories could enter into your consciousness, into your living room, in an intimate way that you would never experience, and I feel that you know, our divisions in society are about ignorance, basically. So to me that was a powerful medium.

Old stories told in fresh ways could teach something new to the uninitiated as well as foment harmony within a community through shared experiences of culture. Both the geneticist and the filmmaker describe goals of helping people or communities, either through health benefits or political and social cohesion. Both industries (medical technology and film) are IP-rich, claiming dependence on the exclusivity that patents and copyrights provide to generate sustaining revenue. And yet as described by industry actors, the progress they seek to achieve is less related to an IP business strategy that facilitates the return on investments; progress is detached from exclusivity and from the idea of wealth or, simply, 'more'. Instead, the progress they seek aims at the effect the work has on the particular field and relevant population.

Skeptics might say that business managers, CEOs and lawyers are the pertinent actors to focus on for discerning how IP can help achieve certain progress goals of creators and innovators. Artists and scientists may not focus on legal regulation, exclusivity and profit, but their business agents or intermediaries do. The interviews do not support this conclusion. Instead, business people describe ambitions similar to the hands-on creators, albeit sometimes in vaguer terms, both for themselves and on behalf of their clients. They describe the desire to solve problems to grow a business. They describe the pleasure of engaging in an intellectual challenge to discover as-of-yet unexplored processes, services or goods that will address an identified need or generate new joys. And IP doesn't always help achieve these goals. A seasoned IP attorney, working for more than three decades in the profession, explains:

> In the area that IP protects … it hasn't been solved by IP protection. I mean, the theory of intellectual – the underlying theory of the whole thing is if you create property rights in it, you'll create a market; that will create an incentive to make these things, right? And I am saying in this case, you know, we have NDAs, we have provisional patents, we have copyright – we have all sorts of things. It hasn't worked. Many, many inventions don't make it to market that are perfectly good inventions, for a variety of reasons. … the idea that if you create private property ownership of things, magically the market will take care of everything else is a complete fantasy.

For this attorney, making 'good inventions' is the goal (and he later describes 'good' in the way already mentioned, for example, filling a niche, new and imaginative). This kind of work is worthy of recognition and remuneration because it builds affections, efficiencies and adds to the sum total of things people care about. But IP doesn't necessarily help promote these goals. For this lawyer, as with many other interviewees, the misalignment between the progress goals and the IP mechanisms is stark.

I interviewed many business people, ranging from those managing public companies to those working at start-ups. Although not all were as disaffected as the above-quoted lawyer regarding IP's benefits, many disavowed as overstated the ability of IP to achieve their entrepreneurial goals. In the living room of his suburban home, I interviewed an Internet entrepreneur who is the CEO of his second company that specializes in online marketing. He sold his first company for many millions of dollars within ten years of his college graduation. He is a self-described workaholic and has four school-aged children. Below, he responds to my question about his choice to quit his stable and lucrative job as an investment banker soon after college to start his own company with all the risks it entails.

> I've found that I like the challenges around problem-solving. I like growing things. I like finding solutions, and puzzles, and so, one of the things about a business particularly [of] this size is like, there's a lotta challenges. Some of 'em suck. Some of 'em are good. But like if you like problem-solving, and challenges, there's a never-ending supply [of] intellectual challenges. Some of them are human, I don't necessarily love managing human capital, but I've gotten pretty good at it, I think. But you know, what markets should we go at, and why is the pricing not working, and how do we win this customer, and just all kinds of interesting things, so if you like to figure things out, and you like to grow things, it's a good place to be. And I think it's part of the reason why I also like to garden.

The progress this entrepreneur describes effecting through his innovative company (and for which he believes he deserves credit and payment) is about building something 'real', making valuable connections between people and serving various social or economic niches. He seeks challenges and particularly loves seeing them resolved and blossom into solutions that grow his company. His company is rich with intangible assets (software, brands, customer and client databases), but the value of his company he describes in different terms. He says:

> I feel like we have built a real product. Where we provide real value to real companies, who pay real money, right? So it was not like dollar in, dollar out kinda stuff, it's like, hey … these companies are getting value, they're building on our platform, they're using it to grow their own companies, and they're willing to pay for that. It's much more rewarding. I feel like it's building something real.

Rather than just pushing money around (a reference, I believe, to his investment banking days), he perceives in his company something sustaining and self-generating about the services it provides. Progress is not only the scaling up of his company's platform, but the way it is mobilized, sustained and grown through relationships with other companies. For him, building this company's work is a very worthwhile way of spending his time, and, as he says, something for which he is proud to earn a living. But he doesn't claim the need for IP exclusivity to develop his business. Indeed, aside from trademarks, he rejects copyright and patents as retarding agents in his industry.

At the end of the interview, he became wistful, telling me:

> [I]f we can view the notion of creating a company, as actually pushing around electrons and changing energy, then perhaps we never die as entrepreneurs, right, because what we create enriches the lives of others, whether it's people who work for you, or companies, and like so all that gets dispersed, no matter if you succeed or failed, by definition you've influenced the timeline of life.

References to immortality and to a life well lived permeated the interviews of artists and scientists, business folks and lawyers. People describe wanting to contribute to the communities of which they were a part and not just by adding things to it, but by adding things that helped, that brought pleasure, that connected people. One might think these are vague and clichéd personal or professional goals. And perhaps they are, explaining their ubiquity throughout the interviews. *But* they are not the goals we hear with reference to 'progress' and intellectual property in an accumulationist and market-driven framework, which is the dominant framework in the United States. As currently described by US courts, *any* rational basis for promoting more art and science, and not particularly these lofty public-oriented purposes, is good enough to qualify for IP protection.[14] To be sure, standards of patentability and bars for prior art are intended to restrict the issuance of patents (in contrast to the very low standard for copyrights which permits almost anything with a modicum of originality to receive copyright protection). But the debates about patent thickets and a dysfunctional patent system raise the specter of not enough restrictions, insufficiently discerning filters and too many bad patents (Bessen and Meurer, 2008; Jaffe and Lerner, 2004; Lemley et al., 2005: 12–13).

A further dimension of qualitative or directional progress includes a particular focus on novelty. I heard throughout the interviews how newness and uniqueness was a primary basis for ownership claims over creative expression and inventions. As already mentioned and to be discussed more fully below, these claims are not as durable or exclusive as current intellectual property rights. But the basis for a claim, according to the interviewees, is nonetheless its novelty and its origination by the creator or innovator.[15] For example, the above-quoted businessman believes his unique team of employees and his personalized business structure distinguish his company from many others and that distinction drives its growth and profitability. He admits that first mover advantage and his tireless work habits also play a part in his success. But bringing something new to customers is the value he sells.[16] In some form or other, the importance of uniqueness united scientists, engineers, business people and artists in their identification of value in their work. We heard it above when the scientist described his invention as a 'complete sea change' and with the novelist who demands a 'new story'. Confirming this value, a professional photographer in his late fifties who survived his industry's evolution from celluloid to digital, speaks from his studio, where he proudly displays a new, mammoth-sized printer he recently purchased.

> Every time you do something, you establish a series of rules and rule number one is that you cannot do twice the same thing. That forces you to step up the notch a little bit every time you do what you do. Sometimes that comes easy, sometimes it doesn't, but you need to plant the element there.

The interviewees do not eschew the value of borrowing or copying in creative and innovative work. To the contrary, most describe how both are catalysts for learning and inventing. But an elevated standard of novelty and distinctiveness – identified by challenging existing paradigms and addressing a particular need or desire – are features they value above others and is evidence of progress happening and worth protecting. Creative and innovative output with these features will stand the test of time and that, too, is sought after and respected as exemplary of enduring progress which, given limited times, eventually returns to the public domain, a fact interviewees expect, applaud and upon which they appear to rely.

Porous and Contingent Ownership Claims

From the above discussion, one might think that existing patent standards of novelty, non-obviousness and utility already satisfy the progress values described. One might also think that creators and innovators resemble classic utilitarians in thought and process. But the identified standards for 'progress' are higher than those administered by the patent office (and certainly higher than those that determine copyrightability). Also, the interviewees should not be misunderstood as driven by function above process. The interviewees' reasons for and ways of controlling their work and situation expound claims for control that serve ends associated with everyday practice, professional identity and sustainable social welfare. They are functional only insofar as they serve these relational and social goals. And they are often misaligned with or underserved by IP rules in part because these are on-going concerns that resist finite measurement. They are not assets but ambitions. They are described as opportunities and developing capacities with hoped-for positive effects on others. That they are realized or maintained through creative and innovative work (work as *labor* not *output*) undermines a strict utilitarian approach to their achievement. It furthermore discourages as unworkable or undesirable a rule of exclusion defined in traditional property terms.[17] The following describes in more detail these progress goals in terms of claims related to work, identity and welfare.

Everyday Practice

We often hear that patents provide a company with the 'freedom to operate' or 'room to run'. Interviewees confirm this reason for asserting their patents against others. Several lawyers and scientists celebrated a patent's ability to defend and enable a research agenda by preventing others from hijacking or blocking the research.[18] Below, an in-house lawyer at a pharmaceutical company describes persuading otherwise reluctant scientists to participate in the patenting process in order that the scientists' own research may continue:

> I said [to the scientists], 'What I want is something that I can trade … I'm not interested in necessarily asserting these against anybody. I'm looking for something that either (A) gives me a quid to trade with somebody, or (B) we patent it first so that some other company can't patent it and then come to us for $100,000 a year royalty.'

Notice in this quote how the lawyer explicitly defends against the implied accusation that he will assert the patent against anyone for revenue or as an injunction (presumably against other scientific companies). He recognizes his scientific colleagues' perspective that patents may thwart collaboration and scientific development instead of promoting it. And he assures his colleagues that he has noble (read 'progressive' or welfare-enhancing) motives for patenting. The lawyer may in fact be describing forms of cross-licensing (revenue generation) or ways to prevent patent infringement actions against the company (risk management),[19] but the enduring value of the exclusivity in the IP is characterized in broad terms as freedom-enhancing: working and keeping working. He is explicitly not describing how to maximize the financial value of the patented invention and, in the opinion of some, is under-enforcing the patent. Other interviewees describe a similar dynamic and urge compulsory licensing schemes in lieu of exclusive rights to promote on-going work and effort in the field.

Artists (filmmakers, musicians, painters, sculptors, writers) describe picking and choosing when to assert their copyrights. Most avoid claiming infringement when others borrow material and reuse it in a complimentary or minimally transformative way. (Photographers were a notable exception to this rule. Although the photographers I interviewed accepted some forms of copying and fair use, their tolerance seemed lower than other artists.) Indeed, most artists cared more about attribution and misattribution and much less (if at all) about exclusivity in their work. Assertions of exclusivity arose during accounts of situations in which continuity of work was at stake. For example, a music composer and opera director complained about the contours of copyright being too strict and ill-defined so that he is regularly afraid of receiving cease-and-desist letters concerning his new versions of others' older work (some uses which may be protected by fair use and some of which may not be). When he sought his own copyrights, he enforced them only for derogatory uses of his work in hopes of minimizing risk and maintaining stability in his company. Several other musicians describe feeling squeamish about asserting copyright over their songs as forcefully as their publishers might require, especially given that digital distribution of music (illegal or not) foments an appreciative fan-base. But when selling a particular song or performing for a television or radio commercial would generate more royalties than they expected to receive from their entire album over several years, they could be convinced to agree to the copyright license they would not normally agree to in order to support their interest in continuing to write and play music on their own terms.

The interviews illustrate the importance of everyday work with stories about practice, routine and attention to detail. As Alasdair MacIntyre described in his ground-breaking *After Virtue*, the value – indeed the virtue – of practice and routine is that its embodiment as everyday activity binds people within particular communities around shared standards (MacIntyre, 1981). In his influential book, MacIntyre discusses the ethics of practice and everyday work as a defense to the corrosive effects of capitalism and that routine work binds communities around shared values. MacIntyre means 'practice' quite literally, the way musicians practice, atheletes train and artists and scientists study (or anyone else who works repetitively everyday within a community with common goals). In this vein, within the interview data, writers talk about developing the pacing of stories and working on consistency of characters. They talk about the number of pages they write every day and the details of character and plot development as physical milestones. Painters and other visual artists, such as filmmakers and photographers, talk about refining color and lines and losing track of time as they manipulate their equipment. Scientists and engineers talk about how long it took them to become proficient in their field – years of schooling and working alongside mentors in laboratories with equipment and machines – so that they could eventually be on the cutting edge to develop science and technology. Here, a musician contrasts her love of recording music, which is detail-oriented and painstaking, with performing.

> I love performing, but my favorite part is that secret place where you are all alone and you are writing, and ... you are really living in a world as an artist. And I love the recording process. I love just, like, tinkering away in the workshop doing – crafting it, and having that time to, like, polish it and sculpt it, and, like, perfect it in a way.

When asserting intellectual property rights enables everyday practice (with material support, risk management or providing protection from others), creators and innovators embrace and assert the right granted to them, although rarely in its full capacity. Working everyday at their chosen field is a virtue and a good. Doing so is a precursor to, if not an embodiment of, progress and thus one of its critical dimensions. But because intellectual property protections are infrequently the basis of revenue-generating business models for most creative professions (performance and payment for services being much more common), the focus on everyday practice (and thus on service and performance) most often avoids or omits assertions of exclusion by others.

Identity

The interviews contain scores of stories describing charged disputes over proper attribution for work. Individual writers, artists and musicians commonly expressed significant concerns regarding attribution and misattribution – naming or misnaming with reputational effects. This is unsurprising in light of the literature on the importance of attribution in the arts and sciences (Fisk, 2006; Goldman, 2011; Sprigman et al., 2013). For example, an opera composer said that although he is fine with people copying his music and 'reiterpret[ing] a character in a non-offensive way, … to make something which would be offensive and then put my name on it would be a problem'. Likewise, a famous author who sometimes employs a ghostwriter for her sequels and voluminous series explains how she has 'to have very close control over [the book series]. My name is on the books'. A music agent describes an upsetting situation in which one of her client-musician's eponymous albums was placed, without approval, all over a kitschy candle store chain as part of a marketing ploy by a marketing professional. In each of these examples, of which there are many more in the interviews, subjectively misusing a name – which stands for a person and her work – is disturbing. It is almost a form of *name-calling*. Concerns about professional reputation collide with wounded egos and resemble defamation claims rather than copyright, patent or trademark disputes where market harm structures the legal action. More than a physical harm, harm to one's 'good name' is, as Cassio says in Shakespeare's *Othello*, harm to 'the immortal part of myself'.

But US intellectual property law does not facilitate accurate attribution or prevent misattribution in the way that most interviewees seek. Other than fairly thin protection for certain rights of integrity and attribution (so-called 'moral' rights) in the US Copyright Act for particular forms of visual art, the requirement that creative or innovative work be accurately attributed or maintained (and not changed or destroyed) does not exist in US IP law.[20] Before the US Supreme Court decided *Dastar Corp. v. Twentieth Century Fox Film Corp* (539 U.S. 23, 2003), there existed some possibility that trademark and copyright owners might succeed on a claim for misattribution or mutilation of their work via section 43(a) of the Lanham Act that prohibits false designation of origin.[21] But in 2003, the US Supreme Court decision in *Dastar* finally closed the door on the possibility that IP law could require attribution or prevent misattribution in the way authors or artists desire (539 U.S. at 31). And yet the interview data is full of explanations of the importance of attribution and promises of maintaining the work's integrity (as a measure of personal and professional reputation) to facilitate the work's optimal promotion and dissemination whether or not for profit.[22] As the interviewees describe, this is because attribution (or the prevention of misattribution and mutilation) is central to safeguarding and managing one's professional identity and relationships with their audiences, which are primary concerns for those in creative and innovative fields. Interviewees consider it both mysterious and frustrating that IP law does not facilitate accurate attribution. In their mind, it frustrates their professional development and therefore may also stymie their engagement with work. This is antithetical to progress, in their mind.

Concerns over attribution take many forms. Some interviewees describe being very particular – in one interviewee's word 'anal' – about when people are permitted to use their name as a reference and when they themselves will claim a work as 'theirs'. Several academic scientists discussed the importance of inclusive attribution in scientific research (recognizing a group of contributors rather than single authors without accounting for relative size of each individual contribution). But these academic scientists (a biologist and a chemist, both of whom have been engaged later in life in successful entrepreneurial projects) also said that when hiring or evaluating colleagues in their field, it was critical to discern those from among the multiple-authors of works who were the primary and secondary contributors. From this I understood that inclusiveness was helpful for building community and maintaining on-going relations, but when according substantial rewards (a job or a promotion, for example), understanding proper attribution was also important. In both these instances, attribution was about accurately conferring credit so the reputational benefit would accrue to the right person.

The desire to be named – to be called out as special in your profession or at work – was a strategy used by many lawyers who sought cooperation from their clients. An in-house counsel in a high-technology company incentivizes innovative disclosures by appealing to 'bragging rights'. He created a company-wide contest in which every month employees submit as many 'cool ideas' as they discover while working, and at the end of the month, the company votes on the 'coolest idea' (whether it's protectable by intellectual property or not).

> They aren't fully baked enough to consider for IP purposes. ... people basically just get bragging rights. We then rank them, and we announce the winners. We incent people, it's like a $10 gift certificate or something. Anyone who submits a cool idea gets the $10 gift certificate. ... And so [eventually, if we can protect it or commercialize it] that particular piece of IP [is] ... held up as 'This was Sarah's. She was cool idea number one, and here it is.'

The desire to be known as someone who contributes good ideas is strong. This helps develop a reputation as a smart or able person (with the likely benefits of emotional well-being and work advancement). According to the above in-house attorney, being identified as the origin of a 'cool idea' is more effective for building community and workplace effectiveness than if the originator gets to own the idea in the future. According to these interviews, building and nurturing reputation develops feelings of belonging to a certain community (a work community), of a secure affiliation within it, and that the community is better off for it. Although some of the interviews describe negative feelings about the perceived arrogance of those who overstate their contributions and are less worthy of attribution, the motivation behind the attribution claims is both self and other-directed. These examples of attribution claiming – naming and identifying oneself as belonging within a particular professional space and to a particular work outcome – demonstrate the constitutive relationship between identity and work. It further underscores this relationship's driving role in community building and professional settings.

The forceful and emotionally charged nature of these stories about professional identity and reputation may explain the tendency of owners and originators of creative or innovative work to overreach when the nature and quality of their work (or the name attached to it) is disparaged or described inaccurately. Seeking protection through IP or other legal means makes sense in these contexts as a defensive reaction, but IP law's lack of likely redress undermines its relevance to artists and scientists hoping to protect these particular reputational concerns.[23] Given this lack of relevance, it makes sense that the interviews contain many examples of managing or controlling reputation without strong property claims or other legal entitlements. They do so to control their identity in a competitive or crowded field and to selectively build professional relationships to enrich their work. For most, this is a lifelong undertaking that demands regular nourishment and attention, and it is inseparable from the work and communities to which they are devoted. In the end, because of the centrality of reputation to their own commitment to the work and its effects on others they find ways to develop and sustain their professional identities outside the parameters of IP law.

Enhancing Welfare through Access

I already mentioned the interviewees' attention to community benefits and welfare through the work in which they engage. By identifying particular needs, solving problems in their field, or addressing a gap in the market for goods or services they can provide, interviewees describe themselves and their work as contributing to and shaping their communities. Distribution of and access to the work is central to this participation and interviewees describe diverse ways in which to maximize access to their work.

The public function of intellectual property (its reliance on and default to a public domain) depends on dissemination and access. Both scholars and courts have contended that dissemination is the *ultimate* goal of IP law and incentivizing creation the penultimate goal (Goldstein, 2003: 216; *Golan v. Holder*, 132 S. Ct. 873, 888 (2012)). The statutory basis of intellectual property confirms the important role of serving the public through distribution and access. Until 1976, the federal copyright did not attach until the work was *published*, which was interpreted to mean publicly available on a reasonably non-restrictive basis. For patents, exclusive rights are typically considered a quid pro quo for disclosure to the public of the invention by filing invention specifications and written descriptions with the Patent and Trademark Office so others can benefit from and build on these inventions during the patent term and after the patent expires. Courts confirm this understanding of IP, reminding us that 'private motivation must ultimately serve the cause of promoting broad public availability of literature, music, and the other arts' (*Sony Corp v. Universal City Studios, Inc.*, 464 U.S. 417, 431–432 (1984)) and that the 'sole interest of the United States' lies not in authorial or inventor reward but in 'the general benefits derived by the public from the[ir] labor' (*Sony v. Universal*, 464 U.S. at 429).

Evidence from the constitutional founding, what little there is, confirms the importance of dissemination as a basis for both institutional and independent learning and as well as for 'improvements' to commerce, trade, manufacturing, agriculture (Farrand, 1911; Madison, 1788; Hamilton, 1791). Access to new developments in these areas is critical for the constitutional prerogative of the public good to be fulfilled. Exclusive dominion in the form of a durable property right may be one way to encourage broad access; control over the work's reproducibility may encourage dissemination free of fear of those who would otherwise take the work when initially distributed, copy and claim it for themselves, and profit from it by competing with the originator in the market.

Evidence from the interviews does not reflect this fear. Indeed, the diversity of methods interviewees describe (including businesses) to disseminate work in ways that lack substantial control over its subsequent use indicates that strong and broad intellectual property rights are unnecessary for achieving this and other progress goals. Most blatant (or even surreptitious) forms of infringement do not frustrate dissemination or access, although they may reduce revenue or feel like a personal or emotional trespass. To be sure, in some instances widespread unlawful distribution – counterfeits are the most obvious example – can eliminate the shared benefits of fair competition and professional development that is based on expected norms of borrowing and excused copying (downloads or sharing between fans, for example). But these are the rare exceptions in the interviews. Most often, creative and innovative professionals describe the 'progress' that attends to distribution happening without strong IP claims.

Across the interviews, there appear to be five distinct modes of distribution: broad distribution, selective distribution, sharing, gifting and hold-out (no distribution). Interviewees, particularly those in the pharmaceutical, medical device, software and publishing businesses, describe distributing their work as broadly as possible through the manufacture or reproduction of many copies of their work. The goal in this instance is to blanket audiences with more than, or as much as, is achievable. Many of these examples (although not all) are from interviewees concerned that distribution should not occur through unlawful copying, although enforcement is weak and litigation over infringement is avoided at almost all costs. Software companies are an exception. Although they too refrain from assertions of infringement, most do so because they care little about unlawful copying. Indeed, many software engineers and entrepreneurs I interviewed predicated their success on unlawful copying and distribution of programs because doing so built a fruitful consumer base. To be sure, their businesses relied in part on licenses to software, but unlawful copying and distribution also fueled their business because it grew the number of users, who would eventually pay for software and services, and it increased brand recognition.

Interviewees also describe a more selective form of distribution akin to an in-person performance. This kind of distribution benefits from exercising more control over distribution and reception because controlled dissemination tends to enable productive audience feedback that enhances subsequent work. Three industries dominate this distributive category: publishing/writing, music and sculpture. Folks in these fields describe cultivating opportunities to 'perform' their work either through controlled in-person environments or closed-digital environments for three primary purposes: revenue generation, establishing desired relationships with collaborators or customers, and nourishing professional identity and autonomy. However, many other creative and innovative industries, including scientific and manufacturing industries, also describe how a 'managed performance' of the work (sharing certain diagnostic tools under highly controlled circumstances) exercises and challenges their own (and others') competencies, which leads to improved and evolved goods and services.

Many industries, such as text publishing, music, manufacturing, e-commerce and Internet companies engage in diverse distributional forms. The most common form of dissemination across all industries is a widespread distribution that makes available the work at low or no cost for personal or limited professional use ('sharing'). This is a kind of dissemination among people who may be unknown but who are presumed well-intentioned, like a friendly audience. This kind of sharing may generate revenue by the sheer volume of its distribution but it also builds an attentive audience who consumes both for pleasure and to reuse and create. Like the 'managed performance', this kind of 'sharing' expects an engaged audience but it is purposefully less controlled and without immediate or directed feedback. Perceptions of unlawful copying in this category are rarely mentioned given the nature of the distributive impulse and form.

Most industries and individuals describe sharing as a way to ensure their work will penetrate and endure. Here is a musician who describes tolerating the ripping of CDs so that her fans can enjoy her music and other musicians can build on it, especially when purchasing the music is an unlikely option.

> [Ripping CDs] It's just free marketing. I mean, because … the people that actually buy CDs is still there, you know? But I feel like if you're not going to buy it, but you're going to give it to your friend, great. If you're going to give it to five friends, that's fine. Because I'd rather you have it if you're not going to buy it. I mean, I'm not saying I want everyone to do that, obviously, because like I said, I'm still depending on the sales. But I mean, I discover a lot of good stuff by someone just bringing me a CD, you know?

Filmmakers with whom I spoke expressed a similar sentiment in terms of the desire to make 'evergreen' films: films that have staying power, that continue circulating and growing in culture but without having necessarily strong exclusive rights of distribution.[24] In fact, filmmakers appreciate the sharing of their work that occurs beyond their control.

> [W]hen you make broadcast programs … there is a cycle to it. You work so hard and then it airs, and then it's just kind of, like, *done*. And you know, now with the Web and with DVRs and stuff, there is more life to it … You meet history professors [who have unauthorized copies of the film], and they say, 'Oh, I love using your film in my class.' And it makes you feel better. I mean, it makes you feel like, 'OK. Well, then people are still watching it.' You know, it – there is a life after the [televised] program.

This filmmaker tolerates unauthorized uses of her film because she wants it to have a life beyond the singular (or rerun) episode on television or in the theaters. To be sure, she expects to generate renown and revenue from its diffuse distributions, but what she really seeks is the film's reuse, its continued life with others. Another filmmaker echoes this sentiment, saying, 'I love the idea of a … broadcast, which [this film will] have, but to me that's just a blip in the world … I want [it] to enter the schools, and I want it to have an impact on how we learn about [its subject matter]'. These conversations with filmmakers concern relationships with diverse audiences (other filmmakers, teachers, interested viewers) as much as they involve the challenge of producing content that will reach an 'evergreen' status. This filmmaker believes sharing her work enhances its quality, both in its potential to affect people and in its future development.

Scientists and engineers, academics and firm employees, describe their desire to share in comparable terms. They describe sharing in terms of *talking* and as *a conversation*, i.e., the modus operandi of research is to talk about it with others. As one biologist said, 'You think about developing your research program. The thing that's most important to you is being known as a scientist, not as an inventor on a patent application. Because what scientists do is they disclose: they share, they talk'. University technology licensing professionals, corporate counsel and firm executives confirm this yearning and tendency among scientists and engineers to 'share … talk'. Business managers and lawyers describe the sharing and talking by scientists and engineers as sometimes appealing and other times frustrating, because sharing and talking can lead to a loss of exclusivity in intellectual property rights.

A pharmaceutical consultant describes the tensions he faces convincing scientists to refrain from disclosures

> They are researchers. … So they are proud of [the work], and they love to talk about it. So they go to conventions and industry forums and there is – 'I want to present a paper on this.' 'No, you can't. I know you want to. You can't.'

A licensing officer confirms this belief, saying about the scientists and engineers with whom she works that they're 'setting out to do research, which [they're] going to publish and, get … tenure, or get the medal in obscure biology or whatever'. In these instances, the sharing accomplishes at least two goals. It is reputational, cultivating an identity in a community and contributing to self-definition and autonomy within one's field. And it is relational, forming collaborations and acquaintances that advance one's research. Despite frustrating corporate agents and lawyers who work with scientists and engineers, these sharing impulses and desires are strong among the individuals doing the work and are often operationalized within the workplace in order to maximize job satisfaction and performance (Goleman and Gardner, 2008; Pink, 2009: 72–73).

Sharing widely so that others will experience the work is so important to some interviewees that they describe taking costly steps to assure their work is in circulation. One such inventor, a computer scientist who describes his motives for inventing and disseminating in reputational, problem-solving and financial terms, laments how one of his inventions, which was sold to a small company, became entangled in a bankruptcy proceeding. And so he bought his own invention out of bankruptcy in order to put it back into circulation.

> *A:* I made a deal with the guy who had the small company, and the shysters who stole it from him in bankruptcy, to get [the invention] back, if I gave 'em each 25 percent stake.
>
> *Q:* You knew at this time it was valuable. That's why you wanted it back?
>
> *A:* No, I was just really frustrated that the patent was stuck in bankruptcy, and nothing was being done with it. … I just didn't like it being stagnant. You know, and iPhone's coming, and you know, something's gonna happen. … it took about ten years to get the patent. So the original patent issued in '95. The patent was paid for by the small company, and then by 2000 or so they had gone bankrupt, and it was all locked up.

Visibly upset at the 'stagnan[cy]' of his invention and the patent, this individual (who has a well-paying and stable job otherwise) bought back his own patent so that it would be free to be used and licensed in the future. He did so not only in hopes of financially benefiting from the patent, but, as it seemed, primarily to experience the intrinsic pleasure of witnessing the invention's use by a large and appreciative audience.

Two other forms of distribution were present across the interviews. The fourth form looks like outright donative distribution, a form of gifting. Interviewees describe offering their work in various ways with no strings attached (e.g., an outright transfer of the work or copies of the work, abiding (even encouraging) unlawful copies like when musicians post free downloads despite recording label restrictions). In these instances, interviewees describe having no expectations except that the work circulate and be enjoyed. The antithesis of gifting is the fifth form of distribution. It is the non-distribution or 'hold-out' category, which is preferred by some interviewees when the benefit of creating or inventing is entirely internalized and may be squandered by the imagined harm or anxiety of dissemination to the public. Here, there is no public good achieved (and therefore no 'progress') except as an aggregate of self-satisfaction.

Although is it not possible to generalize about the distribution of these categories over a larger population, the existence of the variations within this data and the fact that single industries engage in a variety of distributional mechanisms is evidence of IP's malleability and perhaps also its limited relevance. Moreover, it is notable that within the data, the overwhelmingly common distributional form in which *all* industries engaged was the third: sharing. Listening to professionals describe the benefits of this loose form of distribution convinced me that our IP regimes are too rigid for the accomplishment of their professed goals. To be sure, I am not the first to say this or to document it.[25] But this data is further evidence that exclusive control through IP laws is unnecessary for progress that matters to those who are engaged in creative and innovative work.

Public Comes First

What may be most surprising about the interview data is that personal gain and wealth aggregation are subsidiary interests for most creative and innovative individuals and organizations. The view of 'progress' as contained in the data is not an accumulationist account. There are intrinsic and extrinsic values associated with creative and innovative work separate from the function that money provides. Creating or discovering something truly new and helpful is worthy of protection and dissemination, but the latter (dissemination and access) takes precedence over the former (protection) in nearly all the examples in the interviews.

The characteristics of progress concerning on-going everyday work, protecting and developing one's identity, and sustaining access to promote community welfare are values that undergird a civil society with democratic aspirations. These values articulated throughout the interviews in relation to creative and innovative activities reflect strong interests at the constitutional founding. James Madison famously said that:

> [Man] has an equal property in the free use of his faculties and free choice of the objects on which to employ them. … [It] is not a just government, nor is property secure under it, where arbitrary restrictions, exemptions, and monopolies deny to part of its citizens that free use of their faculties, and free choices of their occupations which … are the means of acquiring property. (Madison, 1906: 102)

Property in this sense concerns fundamental rights of persons, rights without which a person cannot be free. In other words, access to knowledge and the protection of a commons in which exclusivity is an exception and not the expectation appears to be a constitutional default. Such is not the case today. It is easy to forget that the granting of copyright and patents is the exception and not the rule concerning the status of creative expression and novel ideas.

If from the interview data we were to generate a normative account of 'progress' as achieved and sustained through creative and innovative work, we would find a lesser role for the exclusive rights of copyright and patents. We would also find a misalignment between the rights granted under the current IP regimes and the expectations and desires of those creating and innovating. According to the interviewees, not everything that is creative or innovative is or should be owned in the Blackstonian sense of total dominion and control. Themes throughout the interviews make clear that there is too much claiming, too much exclusivity and it hurts the everyday work and the relations (professional or otherwise) they seek to develop. Strong property claims to exclude others' use or exploitation of copyrighted works or patented inventions make sense when the work is truly novel and when unauthorized exploitation jeopardizes on-going work and its further dissemination and use. This happens rarely, as the dominance of the sharing model of distribution shows.

Progress is achieved when work and practice can continue and when its harvest can be enjoyed, used and repurposed within the community. As the founders explained, and later scholars repeated, the value of knowledge 'lies not in its mere possession but in the range of possible uses and users for it' (Fuller, 1991: 109). Although the artists and scientists I interviewed were self-directed and individualistic, the progress they sought had less to do with their own particular circumstances and more to do with public benefits and relations among communities and populations that their work could stimulate. Sometimes these goals required qualified exclusivity to manage the risk of loss that would prevent their future work and injury to their dignity. But much of the time the breadth of exclusivity available to assert was unnecessary or cumbersome. The various dimensions of progress could be achieved without it.

This leaves US intellectual property protection in an awkward place – available but unnecessary, unwieldy and even exasperating for many individuals and industries. If reform were on the horizon, we might do well to heed the accounts in this data and reset the public availability baseline in our statutory regimes for broad access and use. This would comport both with original understanding of the progress clause and contemporary values embodied in creative and innovative communities.

NOTES

1 In other publications, I explore different aspects of the interviews (Silbey, 2011, 2013, 2014).
2 The amount of literature calling into question the necessity or utility of intellectual property law in the United States is too vast to cite here. But as examples see Bessen and Meurer (2008); Boldrin and Levine (2008); Burk and Lemley (2009); and Ku et al. (2009).
3 The literature on law and economics is largely theoretical, based on frictionless transactions and rational-actor models, despite these models' lack of significant correlation to lived experiences. For a seminal article in the area, see Landes and Posner (1989) (see also Arrow, 1962; Kitch, 1977: 265–290). The literature tends to admit this failing (Landes and Posner, 2003) but nonetheless continues to dominate case law, statutory reform and, by consequence, legal advice and counsel.
4 The well-regarded 2008 Berkeley patent survey is a quantitative study of motives and incentives (Graham et al., 2009). Some recent qualitative research on intellectual property from the legal academy includes Schwartz (2012); Gallagher (2012); Silbey (2011, 2013). There has been significant ethnographic research in other fields, including anthropology and sociology, which studies innovative communities, such as computer programmers (Kelty, 2008), musicians (McLeod and DiCola, 2011) and university technology transfer offices (Owen-Smith, 2005). But their focus has not explicitly been on the connection between legal incentives and productivity.
5 For other work on IP and narrative theory, see Jessica Silbey (2008) (describing the origin stories of intellectual property law as justifying certain social hierarchies); and (2010) (describing changing narratives in relation to changing political structures of property entitlements).
6 The isolation and analysis of narrative components of selection, time and relationality coalesce to form a particular moral ordering or authority (White, 1980: 22).

7 For in-depth descriptions of the methodology behind this qualitative project, I direct the reader to Silbey (2011, 2013, 2014).

8 There is some debate over whether Madison proposed a patent power, but that debate is irrelevant to the arguments and analyses I present here (Oliar, 2009).

9 In an unpublished manuscript discussing the problem of 'aesthetic progress' in US copyright law, Barton Beebe (2014) reminds us that the IP clause does not contain the common 'arts and sciences' phrase and instead says 'Science and the useful Arts', suggesting that the latter phrase intentionally omits the fine arts from its ambit.

10 For recent advocacy asking this question, see *Association for Molecular Pathology v. Myriad*, 569 U.S. 12-398 (2013) and Senator Leahy's call for the government to exercise its 'march in' rights under the Bayh-Dole Act to compel access to genetic testing for certain forms of breast cancer. Tony Dutra, 'Leahy Calls for NIH March-In Against Myriad But Some Patents Not Subject to Bayh-Dole', *Bloomberg Law*, July 12, 2013, available at http://www.bna.com/leahy-calls-for-nih-march-in-against-myriad-but-some-patents-not-subject-to-bayh-dole//

11 For other legal scholars writing about the problem of aesthetics and copyright see Yen (2008) and Haight-Farley (2005).

12 For past US Supreme Court cases engaging in such an exercise, see *Eldred v. Ashcroft*, 537 U.S. 186, 211–214 (2003) (deferring to Congress's judgment as rational that longer copyright terms may incentivize the creation of more work) and *Golan v. Holder*, 132 S.Ct. 873, 887–890 (2012) (arguing that preserving work and incentivizing its dissemination is a form of progress).

13 We may anticipate that 'over time, through our system's adversarial and appellate process, we may either have various conceptions of progress in different industries, or may be able to generalize from particular examples to a general concept of progress as a constitutional limitation' (Oliar, 2006: 1837).

14 *Eldred v. Ashcroft*, 537 U.S. 186 (2003) (holding Congress was rational to presume that adding 20 years to copyright terms would promote the creation and dissemination of more original expression); *Golan v. Holder*, 132 S.Ct. 873 (2012) (holding that Congress was rational to presume that restoring copyright to foreign works, even after they have been in the public domain for decades, will incentivize the production and dissemination of original expression).

15 This coincides with the rhetorical justification for intellectual property, which is that it 'originates' with an author or inventor (Silbey, 2008).

16 Several entrepreneurs and business people described the value of their business in these terms.

17 Barton Beebe (2014) makes a similar claim about the pragmatist theory of aesthetics in terms of its priority of *work* not *works*.

18 Jason Schultz and Jennifer Urban wrote an intriguing article about how Open Innovation Communities (OICs) may or should opt back into the patent system for precisely this reason, to defend their on-going research from interference by patentees. They suggest a 'defensive patent license' as a compromise (Schultz and Urban, 2012).

19 Stuart J.H. Graham et al. (2009) report that both cross-licensing and avoiding patent infringement suits are motives for patenting by start-ups.

20 For an overview of moral rights in the US and Europe in the context of film history in the US, see Peter Decherney (2011: 277–280).

21 In the name of reputational injury, early film and television producers and actors wrangled for control over their creative work product to prevent changes, such as colorization, adaptations and sponsored advertising. In doing so, they relied on an amalgam of copyright, trademark, unfair competition and defamation law. But as Peter Decherney describes in his work on copyright and the film industry, court decisions were unpredictable because of warring policies between technological innovation, market growth and author's rights to control their reputation through control of their work (Decherney, 2011: 304–305). Eventually, the majority of court decisions reached a consensus that US IP law protects economic not personal or moral rights.

22 Peter Decherney describes a situation in which in order to protect their work's integrity, Monty Python would rather (and did) upload their content for free in a form they approved, than sell their work and have it be altered without their permission or approval (Decherney, 2011: 316).

23 Copyright law protects the substance of original expression, not attribution or misattribution. And patent law (like copyright law) facilitates the disaggregation of ownership from inventorship (or authorhship) such that inventors may be credited on the patent but may lack control over the uses of the invention. US Patent law requires that accurate inventorship be listed on every patent, but patentees who are employees rarely have any control or ownership over their inventions that would direct or protect the use of their name or the invention.

24 The term 'evergreen' in the film context is not the same as in the patented invention context, where 'evergreening' a patent elongates the life of the patent exclusivity through continuation

filings. Where 'evergreening' in the film context does not presume exclusivity, evergreening in the patent context does. For a discussion of the economic effectiveness of evergreening in patented pharmaceuticals, see Hemphill and Sampat (2012).

25 Notably, Margaret Chon (1993) published a paper that described the potential inconsistency been IP incentives and progress in terms of the flow of information and commerce.

REFERENCES

Arrow K.J. (1962) Economic Welfare and the Allocation of Resources for Invention. In: *The Rate and Direction of Inventive Activity: Economic and Social Factor.* Princeton: Princeton University Press, pp. 609–626.

Association for Molecular Pathology v. Myriad, 569 U.S. 12–398 (2013).

Balkin J.M. (2009) Framework Originalism and the Living Constitution. *Northwestern University Law Review* 103(2): 549–614.

Balkin J.M. (2010) Commerce. *Michigan Law Review* 109(1): 1–51.

Beebe B. (2014) Bleistein; or, Copyright Law and the Problem of Aesthetic Progress. (unpublished manuscript on file with author).

Bessen J. and Meurer M.J. (2008) *Patent Failure: How Judges, Bureaucrats, and Lawyers Put Innovators at Risk.* Princeton: Princeton University Press.

Boldrin M. and Levine D. (2008) *Against Intellectual Monopoly.* New York: Cambridge Press.

Bugbee B.W. (1967) *Genesis of American Patent and Copyright Law.* Washington: Public Affairs Press.

Burk D. and Lemley M. (2003) Policy Levers in Patent Law. *Virginia Law Review* 98(7): 1575–1614.

Burk D. and Lemley M. (2009) *The Patent Crisis and How the Courts Can Solve It.* Chicago: University of Chicago Press.

Chambers R. (1984) *Story and Situation: Narrative Seduction and the Power of Fiction.* Minneapolis: University of Minnesota Press.

Chon M. (1993) Postmodern 'Progress': Reconsidering the Copyright and Patent Power. *DePaul Law Review* 43(Fall): 97–146.

Decherney P. (2011) Auteurism on Trial: Moral Rights and Films on Television. *Wisconsin Law Review* 2: 273–330.

Farrand M. (ed) (1911) *The Records of the Federal Convention of 1787, Volume 2.* New Haven: Yale University Press.

Fisk C. (2006) Credit Where It's Due: The Law and Norms of Attribution. *Georgetown Law Review* 95(1):49–117.

Fromer J. (2012) The Intellectual Property Clause's External Limitations. *Duke Law Journal* 61(7): 1329–1414.

Fuller S. (1991) Studying the Proprietary Grounds of Knowledge. *Journal of Social Behavior and Personality* 6(6): 105–128.

Gallagher W. (2012) Trademark and Copyright Enforcement in the Shadow of IP Law. *Santa Clara Computer & High Technology Law Journal* 28(3): 453–497.

Ginsburg J. (2011) 'European Copyright Code' – Back to First Principles (with Some Additional Detail), *Journal of the Copyright Society of the USA* 58(3): 223–241.

Goldman E. (2011) Regulating Reputation. In: Masum H and Tovey M (eds) *The Reputation Society: How Online Opinions are Reshaping the Offline World.* Cambridge, MA: MIT Press, pp. 51–62.

Goldstein P. (2003) *Copyright's Highway: From Gutenberg to the Celestial Jukebox.* Stanford, CA: Stanford University Press.

Goleman D. and Gardner H. (2008) Good Work: Aligning Skills with Values (Wired to Connect: Dialogues on Social Intelligences, More than Sound Productions, 2008) (Audio Recording).

Graham SJH, et al. (2009) High Technology Entrepreneurs and the Patent System: Results of the 2008 Berkeley Patent Survey. *Berkeley Technology Law Journal* 24(4): 1255–1328.

Haight-Farley C. (2005) Judging Art. *Tulane Law Review* 79(4): 805–858.

Hamilton A. (1791) Report on Manufactures (5 December). In: Kurland P and Lerner R (eds) *The Founders' Constitution.* Indianapolis: Liberty Fund, p. 41.

Heald P. and Sherry S. (2000) Implied Limits on the Legislative Power: The Intellectual Property Clause as an Absolute Constraint on Congress. *University of Illinois Law Review* 4: 1119–1198.

Hemphill C.S. and Sampat B.N. (2012) Evergreening, Patent Challenges, and Effective Market Life in Pharmaceuticals. *Journal of Health Economics* 31(2): 327–339.

Jaffe A.B. and Lerner J. (2004) *Innovation and its Discontents.* Princeton: Princeton University Press.

Johnson E. (2012) Intellectual Property and the Incentive Fallacy. *Florida State University Law Review* 39(3): 623–680.

Kelty C. (2008) *Two Bits: The Cultural Significance of Free Software.* Durham: Duke University Press.

Kitch E.W. (1977) The Nature and Function of the Patent System. *Journal of Law and Economics* 20(2): 265–290.

Ku RSR, Sun J. and Fan Y. (2009) Does Copyright Law Promote Creativity? An Empirical Analysis of Copyright's Bounty. *Vanderbilt Law Review* 62(6): 1669–1748.

Kwall R.R. (2001) Preserving Personality and Reputational Interests of Constructed Personas through Moral Rights: A Blueprint for the Twenty-first Century. *University of Illinois Law Review* 1: 151–172.

Lakoff G. and Johnson M. (1980) *Metaphors We Live By*. Chicago: University of Chicago Press.

Landes W.M. and Posner R.A. (1989) An Economic Analysis of Copyright Law. *The Journal of Legal Studies* 18(2) 325–364.

Landes W.M. and Posner R.A. (2003) *The Economic Structure of Intellectual Property Law*. Cambridge, MA: Harvard University Press.

Lemley M. (2004) Ex Ante Versus Ex Post Justifications for Intellectual Property. *University Chicago Law Review* 71(1): 129–150.

Lemley M., Lichtman D. and Sampat B. (2005) What To Do About Bad Patents? *Regulation* 28(4): 10–13.

Lipton J.D. (2011) Moral Rights and Supernatural Fiction: Authorial Dignity and the New Moral Rights Agendas. *Fordham Intellectual Property, Media & Entertainment Law Journal* 21(3): 537–580.

MacIntyre A. (1981) *After Virtue: A Study in Moral Theory*. London: Gerald Duckworth & Co. Ltd.

McLeod K. and DiCola P. (2011) *Creative License: The Law and Culture of Digital Sampling*. Durham: Duke University Press.

Madison J. (1788) Federalist No. 42, 288 (23 Jan 1788). In: Kelsler et al. (eds) *The Federalist Papers*. New York: Penguin, pp. 232–239.

Madison J. (1906) Property. In: Gallard Hunt (ed), *The Writings of James Madison*, Vol. 6. New York: G.P Putnam's Sons, p. 106.

Mann R.J. (2005) Do Patents Facilitate Financing in the Software Industry? *Texas Law Review* 83(4): 961–1030.

Merritt D.J. (1995) Commerce! *Michigan Law Review* 94(3): 674–751.

Nachbar T.B. (2004) Intellectual Property and Constitutional Norms. *Columbia Law Review* 104(2): 272–362.

Oliar D. (2006) Making Sense of the Intellectual Property Clause: Promotion of Progress as a Limitation on Congress's Intellectual Property Power. *Georgetown Law Journal* 94(6): 1771–1846.

Oliar D. (2009) The (Constitutional) Convention on IP. *UCLA Law Review* 57(2): 421–480.

Owen-Smith J. (2005) Dockets, Deals, and Sagas: Commensuration and the Rationalization of Experience in University Licensing. *Social Studies of Science* 35(1): 69–97.

Pink D.H. (2009) *Drive: The Surprising Truth about What Motivates Us*. New York: Riverhead Books.

Pollack M. (2001) What Is Congress Supposed to Promote? Defining 'Progress' in Article I, Section 8, Clause 8 of the United States Constitution, or Introducing the Progress Clause. *Nebraska Law Review* 80(4) 754–815.

Rumsey J. (1789) Letter from James Rumsey to Thomas Jefferson (June 6, 1789). In: Boyd, JP (ed) *Jefferson Papers* (Volume 15, 1958). Princeton University Press: Princeton, p. 170, 171–72.

Schultz J. and Urban J.M. (2012) Protecting Open Innovation: The Defensive Patent License as a New Approach to Patent Threats, Transaction Costs, and Tactical Disarmament. *Harvard Journal of Law & Technology* 26(1): 1–68.

Schwartz D.L. (2012) The Rise of Contingent Fee Representation in Patent Litigation. *Alabama Law Review* 64(2): 335–388.

Silbey J.M. (2008) The Mythical Beginnings of Intellectual Property. *George Mason Law Review* 15(2): 319–446.

Silbey J.M. (2010) Comparative Tales of Origins and Access: Intellectual Property and the Rhetoric of Social Change. *Case Western Reserve Law Review* 61(1): 195–268.

Silbey J.M. (2011) Harvesting Intellectual Property: Inspired Beginnings and 'Work-Makes-Work', Two Stages in the Creative Processes of Artists and Innovators. *Notre Dame Law Review* 86(5): 2091–2132.

Silbey J.M. (2013) Patent Variation: Discerning Diversity among Patent Functions. *Loyola Law Review* 45: 441–478.

Silbey J.M. (2014) The Eureka Myth: Creators, Innovators and Everyday Intellectual Property. Stanford, CA: Stanford University Press.

Snow N. (2013) The Meaning of Science in the Copyright Clause. *Brigham Young University Law Review* 2: 259–318.

Sprigman C.J., Buccafusco C.J. and Burns Z.C. (2013) What's a Name Worth? Experimental Tests of the Value of Attribution in Intellectual Property. *Boston University Law Review* 93: 1.

Strauss A. and Corbin J.M. (eds) (1997) *Grounded Theory in Practice*. Thousand Oaks, CA: Sage Publications.

Strauss D.A. (2010) *The Living Constitution*. Oxford: Oxford University Press.

Walterscheid E.C. (1995) Inherent or Created Rights: Early Views on the Intellectual Property Clause. *Hamline Law Review* 19(1): 81–106.

Walterscheid E.C. (2002) *The Nature of the Intellectual Property Clause: A Study in Historical Perspective*. Buffalo: William S. Hein & Co.

Walterscheid E.C. (2003) To Promote the Progress of Science and Useful Arts: The Anatomy of a Congressional Power. *IDEA: The Journal of Law and Technology* 43(1): 1–82.

White H. (1980) The Value of Narrativity in the Representation of Reality. In: Mitchell WJT (ed) *On Narrative*. Chicago: Chicago University Press, pp. 1–23.

Whittington K.E. (1999) *Constitutional Interpretation: Textual Meaning, Original Intent, and Judicial Review*. Lawrence, KS: University Press of Kansas.

Yen A.C. (2008) Copyright Opinions and Aesthetic Theory. *Southern California Law Review* 71(2): 247–302.

Zimmerman D.L. (2011) Copyrights as Incentives: Did We Just Imagine That? *Theoretical Inquiries in Law* 12(1): 29–58.

29

Copyright and Industrial Objects: Aesthetic Considerations and Policy Discriminations

Uma Suthersanen

Whatever is beautiful is useful, because beauty gives pleasure and pleasure is a kind of happiness, and happiness is a kind of utility. (*Magic Ruffle Co. v Douglas*, 1863)[1]

The law does not, therefore, judge works: it weighs neither their merit, nor their importance; it protects them all, blindly; short or long, good or bad, useful or dangerous, fruit of genius or of the mind, simple product of labour or patience, every literary or artistic work is admitted and may benefit from the provisions of the law. (Pouillet, 1894: 38)

INTRODUCTION

A vast range of creations of different genres and modes of manufacture are conferred copyright protection without reference to the quality or merit or aesthetics of such creations. Past jurisprudence, in the major European Union (EU) Member States as well as in the United States, shows that copyright law mercilessly equates the creations of Dan Brown, Roy Orbison and Margaret Mitchell[2] with more pedestrian compositions such as fertilizer labels, letter/numeral square grids, consumer guides, and shopping catalogues (see discussion on UK below). Although copyright law does employ certain tools, including the idea–expression dichotomy, and the criterion of originality (in common law countries) or personality (in civil law countries) to distinguish between protectable and non-protectable elements, it eschews discourses on the merit of the creation, except in the case of industrially manufactured objects expressed in three-dimensional forms.

This chapter looks at the legal policies with respect to the copyright protection of such manufactured objects as employed within different jurisdictions. In doing so, one realizes the intense discomfort experienced by judges, jurists and legislators in extending copyright protection to such objects. Indeed, there is a particular difficulty in viewing such objects without indulging in qualitative considerations based on merit, worthiness, functionality and aestheticism. This occurs irrespective of the mode of production, or the nature of the substrate manifesting the form, or the purpose of the creator, or the value, or the final contextual use, of the product. We can begin to understand the discrimination against such objects by employing a comparative law approach, and viewing legal policies and decisions in a historical light within the EU. First, there has been much international and national ambivalence concerning the proper intellectual property regime to house industrial objects. Secondly, this ambivalence has had a domino effect in that different policies have sprouted in the different legal systems as to the proper treatment of manufactured objects within copyright law itself. Thirdly, in order to pigeonhole industrially manufactured objects into one or the other legal system, judges and tribunals have employed artificial legal tests, including obfuscatory interpretations within legally constructed classifications of subject matter, arbitrary criteria of protection, and subjective considerations of aestheticism and functionalism.

What emerges is a landscape of varying legal tools employed by the legislators and courts to drive two overwhelming historical policies. One was that copyright law was the proper legal construct for 'artistic works'. Within this classification, some, but not all, industrial objects could be protected. The second was that the proper vehicle of protection for 'industrial objects' was a separate species of law, which could be industrial copyright, unregistered design law or registered design law.

This chapter questions these policy trends, with emphasis on the exclusionary nature of copyright law. It is not easy to accept the illogical, and often bewildering, interpretations of art and function which are used to classify manufactured objects, in order to implement these policies. The doubt that this is the right path is reinforced by two landmark decisions in 2011 handed down by the Court of Justice of the European Union, and by the UK Supreme Court, in relation to industrially manufactured objects. The Court of Justice questioned this approach in the EU, declaring that all Member States within the EU were compulsorily obliged to protect industrially manufactured objects under copyright law, subject to the object fulfilling the *normal* copyright criteria. The UK Supreme Court, on the other hand, expressly approved the current UK legislative policy in discriminating against 'three-dimensional objects in a graduated way',[3] which is, it admitted, unlike the 'indiscriminate protection of literary copyright'. The chapter concludes that the correct approach is that of the Court of Justice which adopts the traditional French approach of non-discrimination between 'pure art' and 'industrial art'. This approach further coincides with some of the factors taken into account by German courts when traditionally assessing the level of creativity of a work under copyright law, especially the prevailing cultural norms as to how a particular industrial object functions within society. Finally, the non-discriminatory treatment is very much in accordance with current societal perceptions of the role and meaning of an industrial object.

EVOLUTION OF INTERNATIONAL POLICIES

The origins of the dilemma in relation to manufactured objects can be critically viewed through three lines of analysis: the international and national treatment of industrial objects under intellectual property rights; the different approaches adopted nationally in order to implement the non-harmonized policies as to the appropriate mode of protection; and the legal tools employed in order to classify industrially manufactured objects.

Parallel Regimes of Protection

Copyright law is premised on various philosophical, economic, moral and social theories, depending on the provenance of the legal system.[4] Some of these theories are complementary – thus, for instance, the theory that 'copyright is a social good' has a similar resonance to the dictate that 'copyright is necessary to prevent market failure'. Other justifications tend to be contradictory. Arguments based on the author's right to dignity, or on the author's right to benefit from his moral and material interest tend to be focused on the individual,[5] as opposed to those laws based on communitarian and social functions.[6] Most of these theories do converge on one point; namely, certain genres of creations should be excluded *ab initio* from protection. Thus, ideas and principles are not protected under international and national copyright laws; similarly, courts have struggled with the protection of factual or commonplace data. The reasons vary: such creations lack originality or creativity or the author's personality; or copyright protection may impede innovation, or may offer monopolistic positions in the marketplace; or copyright law must not pre-empt the function of other intellectual property rights.

One primary reason why certain types of industrially manufactured objects were historically removed from copyright protection and placed into a separate *sui generis* intellectual property regime was the concern over lengthy monopolies on functional products (Budd, 1978; Drysdale, 1980); whereas a long term of protection for creations categorized as *fine arts* would not affect other artists as the scope of freedom and creativity would remain broad. Indeed, a similar rationale applied to two-dimensional manufactured objects, especially engravings and textile patterns (Suthersanen, 2009: 43–4).[7] This benevolent treatment changed with the Industrial Revolution where manufactured objects were viewed increasingly as utilitarian and functional objects, made by the new mechanical technologies. The artist/craftsman had metamorphosed into a nameless industrial worker making mass-produced objects. The massive organizational changes wrought by the Industrial Revolution, coupled with new manufacturing techniques, with greater production units at lower costs, catered for the growing consumer market. Competitive pressures led to demands for product innovation, notably in the application of some characteristic feature or aspect of skill to distinguish a manufactured product and attract the interest of customers. This additional stage of adding 'art' to the manufactured object gave rise, in turn, to the profession of 'art-workers' who 'translated the ideas of fine artists into mass production' (Sparkes, 1987: 4; also, Forty, 1986: 36; Walker, 1989: 23).[8] Foremost of their tasks was to determine the commercial viability and desirability of consumer products.

While the 'aesthetic effect' of manufactured goods was something to be rewarded and protected, the fact that the effect was tied, in their eyes, to the utility of the product, made legislators' concern shift from the protection of the 'art', to the protection of the 'decorative art' or 'applied art' which had to be balanced against allowing such copying to preserve and promote competition.[9] A parallel regime of intellectual property rights – design law – was adapted by the late 19th century as the legislative solution to accommodate the rights of creators whilst promoting a product competitive market. Design law was considered more suitable for manufactured objects circulating within the general products market for several reasons, including the fact that it had higher thresholds of protection (often novelty), and that it offered a much shorter duration of protection as compared to copyright law. This would have the effect of releasing the industrial object from the grasp of intellectual property law into the public domain (Jehoram, 1992; Kur, 1993). This policy subsequently became one of the cornerstones of judicial decisions in some countries (including the UK and Germany) as to why manufactured objects should be discriminated against under copyright law, namely, to avoid the usurpation of the *sui generis* design regime.

Once design law was viewed as the vehicle of protection for industrially manufactured objects, an inchoate set of international and national policies started to mushroom within international and national copyright laws. In respect of the former, the position is still primarily governed by the 1886 Berne Convention which adopted an expansive definition of protectable subject matter, and is, in turn, supported by the 1883 Paris Convention for the Protection of Industrial Property and the 1994 TRIPS Agreement.

International Legal Landscape

Article 2(1) of Berne Convention for the Protection of Literary and Artistic Works specifies that Union Countries must protect 'literary and artistic works' which are defined as follows:

> (1) The expression 'literary and artistic works' shall include every production in the literary, scientific and artistic domain, whatever may be the mode or form of its expression, such as books, pamphlets and other writings; lectures, addresses, sermons and other works of the same nature; dramatic or dramatico-musical works; choreographic works and entertainments in dumb show; musical compositions with or without words; cinematographic works to which are assimilated works expressed by a process analogous to cinematography; works of drawing, painting, architecture, sculpture, engraving and lithography; photographic works to which are assimilated works expressed by a process analogous to photography; *works of applied art*; illustrations, maps, plans, sketches and three-dimensional works relative to geography, topography, architecture or science. (emphasis added)

However, the non-discriminatory and inclusive definition of literary and artistic works under the Convention must be read together with the provision dealing specifically with industrially manufactured objects. Thus, Article 2(7) of the Convention states that:

> it shall be a matter for legislation in the countries of the Union to determine the extent of the application of their laws to works of applied art and industrial designs and models, as well as the conditions under which such works, designs and models shall be protected.

The issue of whether 'works of art applied to industrial purposes' should be included within the scope of the international copyright law had been a matter of much contention at preceding Berne revision conferences, and was finally adopted in Brussels (1948). It is clear that attempts to bring manufactured objects under the umbrella of full artistic copyright protection under the Berne Convention was not entirely successful. The final position adopted in the Berne Convention was derived from the fact that no compromise policy could be reached given the various approaches to the copyright protection of manufactured object under national laws (discussed below). Subsequent international intellectual property instruments did not clarify matters, with the 1883 Paris Convention (on industrial property) being another contender for industrial objects, under the separate classifications of designs and utility models.[10] However, the mode or criteria of protection, whether by a registered design regime or by copyright, was left entirely to the discretion of Member States.[11] An analogous treatment can also be recognized in the subsequent TRIPS Agreement 1994, which adopts the Berne position while obliging WTO states to give a minimum standard of protection, and suggesting specifically that copyright protection may be the best approach for the protection of textile designs.[12] More noteworthy is that no definitions of 'applied art' or 'industrial design' are offered in any of these instruments.[13]

Why is there such an ambivalent attitude towards this area? Part of the reason is that the policy question as to whether copyright should include or exclude art as applied in the manufacture of objects, which may serve a utilitarian purpose, was not new. Prior to the Berne Convention, various approaches to this question were to be seen at the national level. Some nations had historically accorded limited protection to artistic patterns which were industrially applied to articles, the earliest examples being found both in the UK[14] and France[15] in relation to textiles and other materials. However, a growing hesitation can be seen in protecting manufactured objects. At the doubting end of the spectrum, countries were eager to demarcate between objects created by different modes, and for different purposes. This goes some way to explain, for example, the insistence within the Anglo-American common law countries of categorizing objects as either belonging to the genre of *fine arts*, falling within the purview of copyright law, or as *industrial objects*, to be relegated to industrial property protection, i.e. patent, utility model or design law. Most civil law *droit d'auteur* jurisdictions tried not to fall into the classificatory trap, and instead adopted an inclusive definition of protected subject matter, which was in turn judged on the extent to which the work evinced authorial personality or creativity. Nevertheless, the test of personality or creativity was pressed into service as a means of detaching industrial objects from the potentially wide scope of protectable subject matter. The common policy position was that there could only be, at best, partial cumulative protection of industrial objects under copyright law and the separate design law. Countries such as Italy went further to exclude all objects with fused artistic and utilitarian features.[16]

At the other end of the spectrum, one finds the converse approach adopted in some countries, with France leading this position, that all objects, whether classified as pure art or manufactured industrially, deserved the same treatment under copyright law – called the cumulative protection approach. While this may be thought to be an extreme view in its all-embracing nature, it was thought by French jurists to have the virtue of being logical and avoiding the manifold difficulties that arise when an attempt is made to fix a boundary beyond which works of industrial art will not be protected. We now turn to look at these approaches and policies in France, Germany and the UK, and the manner by which qualitative judgements and subjectivism creep into the evaluation of whether an object qualifies as an artistic work.

NATIONAL LANDSCAPES WITHIN THE EU

France: Non-discrimination and the Unity of Art Doctrine

Article L.111-1 of the French copyright law states:

> The author of a work of the mind shall enjoy in that work, by the mere fact of its creation, an exclusive incorporeal property right which shall be enforceable against all persons.[17]

Further on, Article L112-1 emphasizes:

> The provisions of this Code shall protect the rights of authors in all works of the mind, *whatever their kind, form of expression, merit or purpose.*[18]

The current approach under French copyright law is clearly to embrace a generous cumulative stance whereby copyright law will protect all works, irrespective of its genre, method of production and expression, value or purpose. Under such a philosophy, copyright law has unhesitatingly protected laser light shows,[19] displays of objects in a museum,[20] articles of fashion[21] (as well as fashion shows)[22] as copyright works. The Court of Cassation, France's highest court, has also reminded the legal fraternity that judges should not take into account the artistic value or the aesthetic merit of creations.[23] The sole threshold for works is that they must show the mark or stamp of the author's personality (*l'empreinte de la personnalité d'auteur*),[24] taking into account the degree of freedom the author has to create.[25] Nevertheless, this doctrinal position is the culmination of a century of confusion and debate as to whether qualitative considerations should have a place in copyright jurisprudence, especially in relation to industrially manufactured objects.

Since the inception of the first copyright law in the 18th century,[26] French judges have debated on the status of manufactured objects as creative works of the mind, and as copyright subject matter. It was clear from the prevailing 1793 law that both propositions could be linguistically supported – the Act referred to '*beaux-arts*', as well as to 'any other production of the mind or of genius'.[27] One school of thought was that protection should be limited to higher forms of art, leaving the world of everyday consumer objects to be protected by the then *sui generis* design law.[28] In order to demarcate between the fine arts and the other industrial, manufactured and commercial arts, the courts employed a variety of imaginative tests, some of which recur repeatedly in other jurisdictions, including: the purpose of the work;[29] the character of the mode of production, and whether it was handmade or machine-made;[30] the message conveyed by the object;[31] the creator's intention and his profession;[32] and finally the eventual audience or market of the object, namely whether the object had been commercialized or presented to the public as an artistic work.[33] Inevitably, attempts to separate copyright law from manufactured, industrial objects resulted in different and erratic approaches being advocated, and a series of subjective value and aesthetic judgements ensued (Strowel, 1993: para. 313).

Conversely, the second, and eventually, victorious school of thought was that the law should be extended to all genres and manners of creative works, including fine arts, applied arts and manufactured arts.[34] This was a reflection of what was occurring in practice, where courts eschewed all aesthetic or meritorious considerations to award copyright to advertisements, trade circulars, tables of contents and technical drawings (Laligant, 1991). An early 19th-century Court of Cassation decision on commercial sculptures sets out the non-discrimination principle clearly. Despite the argument made that the 1793 law was silent on sculptures, the Court saw no reason to doubt the intent of legislators

> to protect, against counterfeiting, works of sculpture, which, with as much right as the works of literature, painting, engraving, and music – which are named specifically – ought to figure amongst the productions of the mind and of genius.[35]

Further on, the Court agreed with the counsel's view that there was no need to enquire into the purpose or destination of the work:

> But is it appropriate to distinguish between a sculpture belonging to the *fine arts* proper, and the sculptures which are meant for commerce? This distinction is not acceptable ... All paintings, all drawings, regardless of whether they are good or bad, of whether they are the work of an artist or not, are the exclusive property of their author, on the sole condition that they should have been *created* by the person who claims them as his property. *Production within the domain of the fine arts* (in the law of 19 July 1793) means simply *production analogous* to the arts of painting and drawing, but does not in any way imply a production which, on account of its *merit*, is considered worthy of being classed amongst the objects of art. (Robin v Romagnesi, Cour de Cassation, 1814)

A similar battle was fought in respect of photographs as an object of copyright protection. In an 1862 Court of Cassation decision, the supreme court judges had to grapple with two options: whether photography should be discriminated against due to it being a product manufactured under the aegis of a machine with little authorial input, or whether it should be protected on the basis that the images,

> although obtained by the use of a dark chamber and the influence of light, may indeed, to a certain extent and degree, be the product of the thought, of the mind, of the taste, of the intelligence of the operator ... [and] may give to the photographer's work the mark (*l'empreinte*) of his personality.[36]

What is clear is that the judicial reasoning did eventually culminate in the legal status of manufactured objects within French intellectual property law being *ab initio* protectable, unless authorial personality was absent. The doctrinal and subsequent legislative stance currently is that the French copyright law adopts a non-discriminatory classificatory system, and it does so by employing the doctrine of *l'unité de l'art* (unity of art) as chiefly set out by the French jurist E. Pouillet. The principle advances the view that it is impossible and unjustifiable to distinguish one form of creative effort from another (Duchemin, 1976: 84; Gaubiac, 1982: 42ff.; Lucas and Lucas, 1994: para. 74; Mott, 1964; Pouillet, 1911: 52; Strowel, 1993: para. 311). Just as art can descend to commercial trivia, the opposite also holds true – that industrial works can ascend to great art. Both works of pure and applied art must be treated alike. One commentator explains the doctrine as follows:

> The theory of 'unity of art' has its basis in the refusal to make any distinction between 'pure art' and 'industrial art'. It extends protection insured by the copyright law to all creations of form, even the most modest, those which, on the 'lower' frontier of applied art, depend on what is called 'industrial aesthetics'. It finds its explanation – and, we think,

> its justification – in the idea that an adequate distinction is impossible between 'major art' and 'minor art', all criteria to which one may have recourse to this effect being subject to the accusation of subjectivity or being powerless, in other ways, to solve the borderline cases. (Finniss, 1964: 516)

Applying this thesis, the French conviction is that any attempt to apply a criterion of demarcation between art and industry must entail a value judgement on the part of the courts and its judges, based on a subjective perception of aestheticism. All works must, thus, be protected by copyright (and design) law, irrespective of the merit or purpose of the work, and irrespective of the mode of manufacture of the work or the context or audience for the work.[37]

We return to this notion of cumulative protection as perhaps being the only logical basis upon which copyright law can function in relation to industrial objects when we investigate the EU Court of Justice's position and societal perspectives.

Germany: Discrimination through the Schöpfungshöhe *Doctrine*

Article 1 of the German copyright law states:

> The authors of works in the literary, scientific and artistic domain enjoy protection for their works in accordance with this Act.[38]

In Germany, the *de jure* position has long been that copyright law will not discriminate against all manner of subject matter, as long as the object under consideration passes the singular threshold of creativity as set out in Article 2(2) of the law:

> Only the author's own intellectual creations constitute works within the meaning of this Act.

A related determining factor is the notion of '*Spielraum*', whereby the work is judged by measuring the margin or degree of freedom the author possesses within which to create the work, and whether the author of the work has a wealth of choices available to him.[39] As one commentator stated:

> The presence of individual character in a work presupposes that the work is a result of a creative act within the '*Spielraum*' and that the author's personality has thus been incorporated within the work.[40]

However, the courts have frequently subjected industrially manufactured objects (or as termed under German law 'works of applied art') to a higher degree of creative individuality,[41] authorial freedom and aesthetic considerations. This is to be contrasted to the courts' position vis-à-vis the level of creativity required for 'works of literature, music and the "pure" purpose-free arts'.[42]

It is not the art expert's opinion which is paramount, but

> '... the aesthetic impression that the work communicates according to the assessment of a person sensitive to and, to a certain extent, familiar with art. In the process, account must be taken of the conditions at the time of the creation of the work.[43]

Thus, any accusations of subjective aesthetic observations under German copyright law can be countered by the assertion of the legal doctrine of *Schöpfungshöhe*, whereby courts only evaluate the level of creativity of the object in question rather than the artistic merit of the work. This, in turn, is supported by decisions which list the objective factors to be considered when evaluating the *Schöpfungshöhe* present in an object including, *inter alia*: the environment within which the work circulates (is it primarily a consumer product, or a display in an exhibition or museum?); the categorization of the object as 'art' by the prevailing societal and cultural norms (is it an 'art chair' or a mass-produced one?); and even the status of the creator (is he a designer/artist or an average designer).[44] A product will be protected by copyright if the spectator-society classifies it as such, irrespective of the purpose or destination of the object.[45]

This is decidedly odd. Historically, the German 'high' level of creativity has never been applied with equal vigour to all categories of works and objects. It varies according to the nature of the subject matter under review. Accordingly, the creativity level can be low for literary, musical and fine art works; indeed, copyright protection is often justified under the '*kleine Münze*' ('small coins' or 'small change') doctrine for mundane works such as catalogues and technical documents, with little evidence of high creative input.[46] One rationale for the accepted discrimination against manufactured objects is that creativity tends to be both incremental and cumulative in nature. Thus, protection should be accorded to pedestrian literary and musical works displaying very small changes as compared to pre-existing works. The doctrine cannot extend to manufactured objects, however, since there is an alternative layer of protection available under *sui generis* design law, or even utility model or trademark laws.[47]

This attitude has changed dramatically, however, in light of the EU Court of Justice's decision in *Arco*, discussed below. In November 2013, the German Supreme Court, in a landmark decision concerning children's toys, overturned its own jurisprudence to hold that the level of creativity required for works of applied art will be no higher than that required for works of fine art.[48] This volte-face was primarily due, held the court, to the change in EU design legislation. This is slightly unconvincing as the changes to EU and national laws were implemented in 2001 and 2004 respectively. Instead, it is submitted that the real reason for the change in German jurisprudence, which follows the changes made within UK copyright law in 2013 as well, was the EU's line of reasoning in the *Arco* decision. The full impact of the German Supreme Court's decision has yet to take effect, but it is to be presumed that Germany will reverse its policy of discrimination and adopt the full cumulative protection approach.

UK Law: Classificatory Discrimination

Section 1 of the British copyright law states that copyright subsists in the following 'descriptions of work':

(a) original literary, dramatic, musical or artistic works,
(b) sound recordings, films or broadcasts, and
(c) the typographical arrangement of published editions.[49]

As evident from the above provision, objects must fulfil two hurdles in order to be protected under the law. First, they must fall within the strict, closed classificatory system in relation to subject matter. Secondly, certain types of works, including artistic works, must fulfil the criterion of originality. Originality in the UK has traditionally not required any qualitative considerations of creativity or merit (aesthetic or otherwise). Since the 18th century Chancery Court rulings, the rationale of copyright protection in the UK have been accepted as protecting labour and investment (Birrell, 1899: 170–1; Saunders, 1993: 456). This has led to a very modest threshold of originality, namely 'skill, labour and judgement'.[50] From this, one can easily accept that UK copyright law protects all sorts of things, 'irrespective of the question whether the quality or style is high'.[51]

British legislators and judges have, by and large, accepted that the law must be blind to the aesthetic quality and merit of the subject matter at hand, especially where literary, musical or dramatic works are concerned. And, by and large, it is. It is clear from the statute that quality is not a consideration for most works, as the classificatory system is based on a technical approach, where copyright works are categorized according to the way in which they are made (Booton, 2003: 40–41). Thus, although the classificatory system is exhaustive, it has been applied in a generous and inclusive manner, according to the mode of production. A literary work, for example, is defined as any work that is 'written, spoken or sung', and includes tables, compilations and computer programs.[52] Moreover, the concept of 'writing' includes 'any form of notation or code, whether by hand or otherwise and regardless of the method by which, or medium in or on which, it is recorded'. Thus, newspaper headlines,[53] circuit diagrams,[54] fertilizer labels,[55] legal dictionaries,[56] computer programs and shopping catalogues,[57] have all been accorded copyright protection in the past.

And to a certain extent the courts have also eschewed aesthetic and other qualitative considerations in extending copyright protection to *some* forms of two-dimensional graphic works, including navigational charts,[58] architectural plans,[59] sketches of hairstyles,[60] technical or engineering blueprints,[61] typefaces,[62] dress or knitting patterns,[63] and cartoon characters.[64]

Yet, this munificent spirit is absent when one views the law's relationship to industrially manufactured objects. The difficulty is not the criterion of originality, but rather the fiendishly difficult category of 'artistic work', defined as follows:[65]

(a) a graphic work, photograph, sculpture or collage, irrespective of artistic quality,
(b) a work of architecture being a building or a model for a building, or
(c) a work of artistic craftsmanship.

Most three-dimensional industrial objects would fall under the sub-categories of sculpture or work of artistic craftsmanship. It is clear that the word 'artistic' is not meant to incorporate any criterion of quality or merit, with the exception of works of artistic craftsmanship and works of architecture. The clear implication is that courts must not involve themselves in subjective reasoning, but instead must apply objectivity in determining whether the object in question falls to be treated as an 'artistic work'. This necessitates returning to the technical approach and determining whether the object has been made according to the technique suggested by the sub-categories within the statute. One commentator summarizes the inherent difficulties in applying a technical approach universally to all works, especially in relation to three-dimensional industrial objects:

> notwithstanding the attempts by courts to do so, 'works of artistic craftsmanship' and 'sculpture' cannot be defined technically since neither of these sub-categories is susceptible to an approach to definition based on a consideration of the ways in which they are made. In the case of the former this is because, even if it were possible to specify a range of techniques that fall within the notion of 'craftsmanship', this is not sufficient to define such works since that craftsmanship must be 'artistic'. In the case of the latter, the difficulty is that 'sculpture' may be produced by any number of techniques, none of which are unique to the production of sculpture as that term is ordinarily understood.[66]

Indeed, the illogicality of this demarcation was noted in a parliamentary debate prior to the enactment of the current copyright law:

> [It is] odd that on the matter of artistic craftsmanship a court must look at the question of what is or is not artistic when that is something at which it is forbidden to look in relation to graphic works, photographs and sculpture. Where the distinction is drawn between sculpture and artistic craftsmanship seems to be an area of supreme difficulty.[67]

The Herculean task faced by courts with this distinction is clear from *George Hensher Ltd v Restawile Upholstery (Lancs) Ltd*,[68] where copyright protection was denied to a prototype model of a furniture suite as a 'work of artistic craftsmanship'. Although there was unanimity among the five House of Lords judges that the object did not qualify as one of artistic craftsmanship, none of them was able to agree as to why, nor could they arrive at a universally acceptable definition of this category. Lord Kilbrandon noted wryly that the court had 'rejected, or at least refrained from adopting, nine solutions of the problem'.[69] One solution, which was to find favour again in relation to sculptures in the 2011 *Lucasfilm* decision (discussed below) was to concentrate on the status of the creator and whether the product was the work of an artist craftsman; indeed, all aesthetic considerations, including the artistic merit of the object, were irrelevant.[70] A slightly re-formulated test was put forward by another Law Lord:

> [the] conscious intention of the craftsman will be the primary test of whether his product is artistic or not; the fact that many of us like looking at a piece of honest work, especially in the traditional trades, is not enough to make it a work of art.[71]

It is unsurprising that the *Hensher* decision has effectively closed this sub-category for industrial objects.[72] The judicial discourse in relation to the other relevant sub-category of sculpture – where no aesthetic merit is required – has proven to be equally challenging to comprehend. In *Wham-O Manufacturing Co. v Lincoln Industries Ltd.*[73] the New Zealand Court of Appeal was faced with the task of determining whether wooden moulds used in the industrial production of the plastic flying Frisbee toys could be sculptures. In accepting that such moulds could be sculptures, the court sought refuge in several dictionary definitions, and concluded as follows:

> According to ordinary acceptation a sculpture is the product of the art of forming representations of things or abstract objects in the round or in relief by chiselling stone, carving wood, modelling clay, casting metal, or similar processes.

As one commentator notes, this is an extremely limiting definition that would exclude much of modern sculpture (Booton, 2003: 59–61). The antipathy for allowing copyright protection to extend to industrial objects goes further. Even where an object is classified as an artistic work, the law curtails copyright protection of the object should it be 'applied industrially' to 25 years.[74]

What is perhaps more intriguing is that the courts, in accepting the wooden moulds as sculptures, declined to extend this reasoning to the flying discs themselves, noting that:

> [it] seems to us inappropriate to regard utilitarian objects such as plastic flying discs, manufactured as toys, by an injection moulding process, as items of sculpture for the purposes of the Copyright Act. They lack any expressive form of the creator and any idea which the creator seeks to convey.

The reference to utilitarianism as being in some way explanatory of the concept of sculpture (and other artistic works) has been taken up in subsequent judgements, not only in UK copyright law but in EU design law – which is discussed in the next section.

EU LAW AND CUMULATIVE PROTECTION

In 2011, the Court of Justice of the European Union (CJEU) handed down its *Flos SpA v Semararo*[75] decision. This changed the copyright landscapes of Italy, Germany and the UK – three jurisdictions that have clung to the notion that copyright protection of industrial objects should be curtailed. This decision controversially[76] sought to end the long-running saga within the EU as to whether industrially manufactured objects can be artistic works. To understand its ground-breaking effect and consequences not only on Italian law but also UK and German copyright laws, one has to appreciate the attempt within the EU to harmonize the copyright/design dilemma.

EU Copyright/Design Interface

After years of discussion, the EU legal community finally agreed on a harmonized approach to the protection of designs under a new *sui generis* design law, as set out in the Community Design Regulation (CDR).[77] The law deliberately eschews any qualitative requirement of artistry or aestheticism. In addition to this, the CDR deliberately omits the requirement of 'industrial character' or 'industrial application', and a product can be the result of an industrial process or be the result of craftsmanship. The traditional demarcation between fine art, applied art, decorative art, and industrial product or design was to be discarded where the new design law was concerned.[78] While the CDR set out a unitary design law regime, a harmonizing directive was also issued in order to align national design laws throughout the EU.[79] The thorny question of whether countries could pursue their own diverse approaches to copyright protection of designs (including industrial objects) was ostensibly done away with by the following provision:

> A design protected by a design right registered in or in respect of a Member State in accordance with this Directive shall also be eligible for protection under the law of copyright of that State as from the date on which the design was created or fixed in any form. The extent to which, and the conditions under which, such a protection is conferred, including the level of originality required, shall be determined by each Member State.[80]

This was presumed to require that registered designs be eligible for protection under copyright law, while expressly leaving Member States free to determine:

(i) the conditions under which such designs were protected (this would allow the German higher threshold of creativity for applied art, and the UK to maintain its closed classificatory system in relation to artistic works), and
(ii) the extent of such protection (this would allow countries to tinker with the scope of protection, such as the UK which limited copyright protection of artistic works to 25 years should such art works be industrially produced).

Flos v Semeraro

In this decision, the CJEU was faced with the Italian transitional provisions in relation to copyright protection of industrial objects. The object in question was the famous Arco lamp, designed and created by the Castiglioni brothers.[81] Flos claimed that Semeraro imported from China and marketed in Italy the Fluida lamp design that imitates all the stylistic and aesthetic features of the Arco lamp, in breach of its copyright in that lamp. The defendant, Semeraro, conversely argued that this was legally incorrect.

At the time of the allegedly infringing act, copyright protection of manufactured artistic works was heavily circumscribed by the condition of separability (*scindibilità*), namely industrially manufactured objects were only protected by copyright if their artistic value could be separated from the industrial character of the product with which they were associated. This requirement predictably excluded a large number of objects from copyright protection in Italy, including the Arco lamp. The condition of separability was removed in 2001 and cumulative protection under copyright and design laws was permitted as per the Design Directive. Copyright protection was restricted to post-2001 artistic works having a creative character and an artistic value; pre-2001 works were subjected to various transitional provisions which effectively curtailed any possibility of copyright protection to industrial art objects.[82] Semeraro argued that it was lawfully entitled under the moratorium period to imitate the Arco lamp. Moreover, the Italian Government argued that it had a right to impose such transitional provisions under Article 17 of the Directive which allowed Member States to choose the manner in which copyright protection was applied. The CJEU disagreed, stating that Art. 17 of the Design Directive:

> cannot be interpreted as meaning that Member States have a choice as to whether or not to confer copyright protection for a design protected by a design right registered in or in respect of a Member State if the design meets the conditions under which copyright protection is conferred.[83]

One view of this is that the CJEU in *Flos* was indicating that irrespective of any position under national law, all designs (including industrial objects) were entitled to protection under *EU copyright law*.[84] Support for this interpretation can be found in the passage where the *Flos* court held that although Member States are entitled to determine the extent of copyright protection under Art. 17, this does not allow these countries to tinker with the duration of copyright protection – such as the situation under UK law, which curtails protection to industrially manufactured objects. This is because the term of protection under EU copyright law has been harmonized.[85] Moreover, the court found it inconceivable that Member States could determine conditions of protection, since this position, it assumed, was harmonized under EU law.[86] The assumption, it should be noted, is actually based on the CJEU's own interpretation of the conditions of protection in relation to issues governed by EU law; namely, that copyright will be conferred on any object constituting the 'author's own intellectual creation' – no further criteria being applicable.[87]

The effect, as stated earlier, has been dramatic. In 2013, the German Supreme Court shifted its century-old jurisprudence dramatically to hold that there should no longer be any discrimination against industrial objects under copyright law.[88] Likewise, the UK Government rushed through a legislative amendment of the copyright law to repeal the notorious s.52 provision curtailing copyright protection upon industrial application of an artistic work.[89] It thus seems that theoretically all industrial objects are eligible for copyright protection if they fulfil the criterion of originality – which should be at the same level as applied to other genres of works.

But will this entirely remove the subjective reasoning that any aesthetic-based legal test entails? In the next section we look at how the legal landscape does, and should, look after the CJEU's firm stance on a non-discrimination principle.

Ex post Flos: *Institutional or Purposive Approach?*

The German Supreme Court's new approach is that the *Flos* decision has invalidated its approach of adjusting the test of creativity to suit its national policy of discriminating against industrially manufactured objects. Its new jurisprudential policy is to be non-discriminatory: the level of creativity doctrine which was applied to discriminate between literary and artistic works is to be relinquished in favour of a level playing field for all subject matter. *Ex post* the *Flos* decision, the Italian appellate courts have accepted that copyright protection should be available as a matter of course to industrial objects (especially furniture).[90] Under Italian law, objects that can be regarded as industrial designs must 'possess in themselves creative character and artistic value'.[91] In the *Panton Chair* decision,[92] the Milan Court of Appeal held that the 'artistic value' had to be assessed objectively, and that:

> a particular indicator of the artistic value of a design work is the fact that some cultural institutions have commonly recognized it to emanate from or be the expression of trends and influences of art movements, beyond the intentions and awareness of its author, having regard to both the intrinsic value and the representation and communication ability that a work of art has, and is recognized to have, by a circle of persons not limited to the consumers of that specific product.[93]

This line of analysis was also applied in the *Flos* decision which was remanded back to the Court of Milan. The court, this time round, considered the following factors in order to ascertain the 'artistic value' of the Arco lamp:

(a) whether there was widespread appreciation of the work in the cultural and institutional sector (e.g. critics, cultural institutions, museums, etc.), irrespective of the fact that it is of daily use;
(b) Flos's evidence that a consensus had been reached among cultural and institutional fields on the 'Arco' lamp's ability to represent the trends of post-war Italian industrial design.
(c) the fact that the 'Arco' lamp had been included in the collection of the New York Museum of Arts and Design for over ten years.[94]

This approach to evaluating artistic value, dependent on societal and institutional perceptions, differs markedly from the UK courts' evaluation, as the latter appears to depend largely on notions of utilitarianism and the creator's original artistic intention. The recent 2011 decision in *Lucasfilm Ltd. v Ainsworth*[95] is an example of why this approach may be short-sighted and unreflective of the role the industrial object in question plays in everyday life. One of the primary issues in the case was whether the Imperial Stormtrooper helmet as used in the original Star Wars films could qualify as an artistic work.[96] The two appellate courts concurred with the first instance court as to the approach to be applied: it was important to keep to the normal English usage of the word 'sculpture', though this usage was not necessarily determinative; and no judgment must be made about artistic worth – the task, instead, is to discern artistic purpose or 'the artist's hand' and 'artistic expression'.[97] It is not clear why the courts subsequently veered from concentrating on the technical definition of sculpture, i.e. *how* a sculpture is made, to issues of functionality. Nor is it clear how functionality is tied to the creator's intent. Counsel for the claimants had argued that the issue of functionality could not possibly arise as the articles in question had no functional purpose *in themselves*: the helmets did not exist in order to keep their wearers warm or decent or to protect them from injury in an inter-planetary war – their sole purpose was to make a visual impression on the filmgoer.[98] The first instance judge stated that the primary function of the helmet was utilitarian because:

> While it has an interest as an object, and while it was intended to express an idea, it was not conceived, or created, with the intention that it should do so other than as part of character portrayal in the film. That, in my view, does not give it the necessary quality of artistic creation inherent in the test suggested by Laddie J.

The Court of Appeal also adopted the view that functionality was a deciding factor as to whether copyright should be conferred:

> Although invented, the helmet and armour are still recognisable as such and have a function within the confines of the film as the equipment of the stormtrooper.[99]

Thus, in addition to an evaluation as to the mode of production, the courts have included a further subjective element in that the *intention* of the creator has to be clear from the beginning:

> Put simply, it has, broadly speaking, to be a work at least intended to be a work of art.[100]

One can thus conclude that the UK judiciary deliberately eschewed societal perceptions and usage of the object, and instead opted for the more subjective 'purposive nature of the object' test, whereby one discerns the 'intrinsic quality' of the object with reference to the artist's intention.[101] Here, the judges are saying, is a helmet that is utilitarian because it was intended to be an element in the process of production of the film; *ergo* it has no intrinsic artistic value.[102] In thus concluding, the court did not look at other factors which their brethren courts in the EU have done in recent times. If they had, it would have been clear to them that far from merely functioning as the equipment of soldiers in a film, the Stormtrooper helmet manifests itself in diverse forms in the amorphous world of fashion, symbolism, culture and image identifiers.

For instance, there are countless websites retailing Star Wars paraphernalia and costumes where one can purchase a Stormtrooper helmet to suit every age, taste and budget. The ever-popular infant-sized Stormtrooper costume, with a look-alike helmet, retails at £22, whilst an adult-sized Stormtrooper replica helmet alone can cost approximately £240.[103] These are made from 'unauthentic' moulds (i.e. these will not have been made using the original moulds used to cast the first helmets utilized in the original Star Wars movies). If one wished an 'original' Stormtrooper helmet cast from the 'original Ainsworth' mould, it would cost between £300 and £500 (hence explaining, in part, the consternation and resulting lawsuit from Lucasfilm Inc. in this case). If one accepts that artistic value is something adjudicated not only at a judicial level using the creator's intention as its sole yardstick, but also at an institutional and societal level, it will be of interest to note that an original Ainsworth-made *unfinished* Stormtrooper helmet sold at the Christies auction house in 2002 for £4,465.[104]

Not many art works, including conceptual and performance art, are produced by the artist themselves, but are, instead, the product of a collective. Studio production, apprenticing and outsourcing have long been accepted historically in the art world.[105] Consider Rubens and Damien Hirst. Nevertheless, armed with a historical policy of discrimination, the UK Supreme Court was understandably not about to embark on an analysis of institutional and societal valuations, including the market prices for helmets originating from the original moulds, or the current purposes of the helmets by end-users or modern collectors' tastes.[106] This attitude has come to also signify to the outside world that the UK stands quite alone now within the EU in its reluctance to view iconic furniture or designer goods as protectable copyright works. And this would be the result, irrespective of the societal evaluation. Louis Vuitton handbags, for example, may have been exhibited in the past in the Guggenheim Museum in New York (as 'art'), and in the Victoria and Albert Museum in London (as 'design'). But to the UK Supreme Court, such considerations do not matter (Thompson, 2008: 11). Unfortunately, in this author's view, the approach – the creator's intent – has also found root in the *sui generis* EU design law regime.

Barron (2002: 374) notes, quite correctly, the following in respect of the classificatory nature of British copyright law:

> the *effect* of this taxonomic approach to defining the objects of copyright is certainly discriminatory, simply because the narrowness of the law's classifications causes it to fail to reflect the diversity of contemporary art.

One could press her observation further and argue that in addition to the classificatory system, the approach that artistic works are *only* to be considered via their technical modality and the intent of the creator is incorrect. And perhaps this is the policy rationale behind the CJEU's stance in the *Flos* decision, as well as the French *l'unité de l'art* doctrine, and the current Italian treatment of artistic value – that legislators and judges are ill-positioned to determine how an object actually functions without reference to the final judgment made by institutional and societal actors.

SOCIETAL PERCEPTIONS OF ART AND INDUSTRIAL OBJECTS

Often, objects play various different roles. A pair of spectacles is both a medical appliance and a fashion accessory: they should be hardy and fit for the purpose of corrective vision, but they also modify the appearance and may connote scholarly maturity. Are these inherent qualities of the object? Or are many aspects nowadays accepted as inherent values or qualities of the object acquired over time through constant repetition, familiarity and social conventions? The legal perspective is but one lens through which objects are viewed. The extreme position that we have seen above is that of the UK classificatory system where the 'artistic work' and its subcategories have been defined with respect to the physical media through which the visual elements of the work are displayed; and also upon the technical processes which produce the physical objects, which in turn correspond to the different categories of artistic works. As Barron notes, this categorization is a result of historical lobbying and piecemeal law making, but the resultant classifications of art are no longer relevant (Barron, 2002).

Many of the rationales for not accepting industrial objects as *beaux arts* are no longer convincing in our current society. Some manufactured objects eschew practicality to embrace value and emotion-laden sentiments of beauty, aesthetics and pleasure. Other manufactured objects, albeit destined to be anonymous mass-produced objects, are still passionately created 'by people who spend a lot of time worrying about injection moulding, or about the precise degree of curve needed to blunt the sharp edges of a monitor screen' (Sudjic, 2009: 31). And yet, the only way to judge how the industrial object sits within our culture and lives is to at least attempt to investigate its reflection by reference to creators, audiences and consumers.

Societal Factors: The Audience Matters

An institutional theory of art apparently does not define artworks by their intrinsic properties or by reference to a critic's subjective evaluation, but rather by reference to their recognition as art by the art world.[107] A more market-orientated observation is that 'The easiest definition of contemporary art … is what is sold by major auction houses in contemporary art sales' (Thompson, 2008: 10).

The approach advocated in the above views is that art only becomes 'Art' when the reaction and input of the spectator (or market) has been assimilated into the work. It may look and feel functional and be made without any specific artistic intent, but society may treat it otherwise. Thus, a fashion object may be transformed into a powerful medium of information conveying political and social messages. The Court of The Hague certainly understood this when it allowed the artist Nadia Plesner to incorporate an exact reproduction of a Louis Vuiton Audra handbag in her mural painting entitled *Dafurnica*, inspired by Picasso's *Guernica*. Despite the intellectual property rights subsisting in the design of the bag, the artist's right to freedom of expression allowed her to usurp the original intent of the creators and employ the object as a symbol to contrast poverty and consumptive tastes.[108]

Lord Reid, in the *Hensher* decision discussed above, came the closest to advocating the societal approach to objects:

> I think that by common usage it is proper for a person to say that in his opinion a thing has an artistic character if he gets pleasure or satisfaction or it may be uplift from contemplating it … if unsophisticated people get pleasure from seeing something which they admire I do not see why we must say that it is not artistic because those who profess to be art experts think differently. After all there are great differences of opinion among those who can properly be called experts … If any substantial section of the public genuinely admires and values a thing for its appearance and gets pleasure or satisfaction, whether emotional or intellectual, from looking at it, I would accept that it is artistic although many others may think it meaningless or common or vulgar. ([1976] A.C. 64)

Moreover, to reward a creator for his intent on producing an art object does threaten to be counter-productive to the actual role and purpose of the product at hand. Papanek uses the term 'cancerous growth' to describe the creator who over-emphasizes aestheticism at the expense of the consumer (Papanek, 1984: 40). His particular angst is in relation to chairs, which ironically have been one of the few industrially manufactured objects readily accepted into the pantheon of art works by courts within the EU. Papanek (1984: 41) illustrates his point with his own user experience of the de Stijl chair:

> These square abstractions painted in shrill primaries were almost impossible to sit in; they were extremely uncomfortable. Sharp corners ripped clothing, and the entire zany construction bore no relation to the human body … A whole elitist nostalgia craze has elevated some of the most uncomfortable seating arrangements yet devised by man into trendy and expensive status symbols that lie halfway between refined torture racks and 'art objects'. The chairs are enormously expensive, unspeakably uncomfortable, and the movement affects only small bored cliques in New York, Milan, or Paris.

Of course, it is perverse to construct and then approve a law that seeks to reward such exhibitionist and non-consumer orientated behaviour. But, as the discussion above on traditional German legal theory on this matter indicates, the query is framed thus: is this a 'pure' purpose-free art object? In contrast, perhaps we can turn to the 'artist' Marcel Duchamp who set out, from a legal perspective, a cumulative and societal view of art. According to him, the audience (who can be another creator or a parodist) has a vital role in validating something as an artwork:

> The artist may shout from all the rooftops that he is a genius: he will have to wait for the verdict of the spectator in order that his declarations take a social value and that, finally, posterity includes him in the primers of Artist History. (Duchamp, 1957)

Duchamp's view of the artist is that he is but one consideration when determining whether a work is artistic or not. For him, the artist is merely the medium of the work, without full consciousness of what is being produced. This goes against the grain of heavy reliance on the intention of the designer/artist.

The Duchamp approach would go even further to treat all industrial objects in a similar manner, in which case protection might logically be extended without debate to computer programs, advertising posters, drawings, maps, plans, and even perfumes.[109] It is the view of the spectator/consumer as to whether such works convey valuable, aesthetic, functional or moral value or information. Moreover, courts would need to look not only at the intention of the creator, the process of creation and manufacture, and the initial purpose of the object, but also at the acquired meaning the object gains with time and societal appreciation. What was once utilitarian (e.g. the design of a train engine) can become popular, fashionable and even artistic (e.g. Hogwarts Express). The design of the GWR 4900 Class 5972 Olton Hall locomotive is highly functional, being purpose-built in 1937. Only subsequently did the need arise to make an authentic visual representation of J.K. Rowling's Hogwarts Express in the visionary world of Harry Potter. For *this* film purpose the 1937 locomotive was captured and then admitted into a highly stylistic and lucrative merchandising world.[110] On the other hand, what was once avant-garde 'art' (for example, the Alvar Aalto Armchair) can become a commonplace mass-manufactured piece of anonymous furniture (for example, Ikea's POÄNG chair).

Societal Factors: Functionality and Market Considerations

Of course, part of the problem as to why copyright doctrines have discriminated against industrial objects lies in the need to demarcate between copyright and patent law. In *British Leyland Motor Corporation v Armstrong Patents Co. Ltd.*, a case dealing with the scope of protection of technical drawings depicting an exhaust pipe, the House of Lords' instinctive stance was that it is anomalous for manufacturers of 'purely functional objects' to have a monopoly under copyright law when the object is not patentable or registrable as a design:

> First, copyright protection for functional designs, as extended to articles of functional utility manufactured in accordance with those designs, would certainly seem to be capable of abuse as a means of obtaining many of the advantages conferred by patent monopoly while circumventing the many stringent conditions and safeguards to which patent protection is subject.[111]

This is entirely understandable. The concern as to the anti-competitive effects of copyright protection is that the creativity imbued within a three-dimensional manufactured object is manifested physically. One appreciates then the aversion to protecting patentable inventions under copyright law, and thus bypassing the strict thresholds of protection under patent law (namely novelty and inventive step). The step which is harder to realize is the relevance of functionality and the intention of the creator as being the main determinants of whether copyright law will be extended to an industrial object or not. When one is dealing with everyday objects, the main 'function' may lie in its visual significance and product differentiation. And therein lies the second dilemma when encountering judicial statements on functionality and aestheticism – there is a strong sense that their decision making capacities are strongly swayed by a historical aversion to extend copyright protection of art works to objects created by machinery; there is, on the other hand, no attempt to understand that objects can look, but not be, functional.

An object may look functional but this can be a deliberate deception by the object designers to seduce the user in a crowded field of technology. A consumer is being led to believe that a revised model of a particular product is technically superior to the previous model in the market due to its visual 'functional' appearance. A historical case study on point is the styling policy of General Motors in the mid-twenties and thirties in the United States. A crowded technology motor vehicle market introduced art-designers and stylists into the production equation to give their products the artificial appearance of innovation and progress. Thus, General Motors, in 1923, introduced the Chevrolet Superior which sold extremely well considering, in one expert's opinion, that it 'offered nine-year old technology clothed in a body of the newest style, with a lower roof, higher hood and more rounded lines' (Gartman, 1995: 126).

O'Shaughnessy further highlights the fact that societal perceptions as to which attributes contribute to high performance do not necessarily coincide with reality. Thus, computer firms have, in the past, added weights to their home computer when it was found that lightness suggested poor quality. This, has of course, changed with Jonathan Ive's philosophy of aesthetics (O'Shaughnessy, 1987: 113–14).

Despite Barron's views on the out-of-date structural concepts of the classificatory approach, one finds her nonetheless empathic about the 'no copyright protection to functional items' argument, whilst simultaneously suggesting a preference for the 'materialist' or 'physicalist' approach because it is a way to 'avoid giving judges licence to enforce their own subjective aesthetic preferences in the process of adjudicating in copyright disputes' (Barron, 2002: 396). Yet again, this has the danger of throwing the baby out with the bathwater. We are not advocating that the creator's intention or mode of production be ignored; instead one is asking that a more holistic notion of what constitutes an artwork be taken into account when considering an industrial object.

CONCLUSION

Industrially manufactured objects are devised to satisfy societal needs and conditions. The industrial object lies perilously in the intersections between science, culture and commerce. Most objects live in the nebulous and grey area where multiple definitions of the object and their purpose exist. A society comprising of business entities, creators and consumers understands and navigates this grey area on a daily basis. Business entities understand that the manufactured object has long since ceased to be an object for a specific purpose, acquired only when needed. Instead, objects are shaped to promise and sell a lifestyle. Creators understand that the object must be designed in such a way as to tell a story, using elements of functionalism or symbolism or aestheticism. Consumers understand that objects are investments and that functional objects can be icons.

All these actors also understand that 'art' no longer originates solely from professional painters, sculptors and artists but can arise from a complex relationship between public taste, merchandising, consumption habits, branding, visual appeal, and most importantly, pricing. If successful, the work will be misappropriated, copied, counterfeited and pirated.

The hybrid nature of a product, as an icon, as museum exhibits, as collectors' items, as practical everyday objects, and as industrial functional products, has made legal categorization difficult. The stance of demarcating a manufactured object into the copyright-art hemisphere, on the one hand, and into the industrial property/applied art-function/commerce hemisphere on the other hand, has had a real effect on the commercial market. Thus, unlike Germany and France, the UK has been the base for reproduction furniture – which even the retailers dub 'designer' furniture or goods. On both sides of the Atlantic, 'designer' objects can be sourced for a fraction of the cost of the original as unauthorized reproductions are lawful. Thus, an Eames original would cost approximately £4,200, whereas a reproduction would be £900; an Arne Jacobsen's Egg chair would be around £300, whereas the original would cost approximately £3,996.[112]

As Hillel Schwartz points out, the notion that art loses its authority and aura in an age of industrial reproduction is inaccurate. Instead, he asserts:

> Only in a culture of the copy, do we assign such motive force to the original … the more adept the West has become at the making of copies, the more we have exalted uniqueness. (Schwartz, 1996: 140, 211)

This chapter has investigated these policy trends and analysed how different countries manage to effectively bar the copyright protection of industrial objects. The best approach may be the current French approach, which has been recently adopted by the CJEU: that protection should be accorded without regard to the nature and quality of the work. This approach coincides with the attitudes taken in other EU countries, as well as the institutional approach towards art. Finally, the non-discriminatory treatment is very much in accordance with current societal perceptions of the role and meaning of an industrial object.

NOTES

1 (1863) 2 Fisher's Pat. Cas. 330, Fed. Cas. No. 8,948.
2 See for example, *Baigent and anor v The Random House Group* [2007] EWCA Civ. 247 (CA); *Campbell v Acuff-Rose Music*, 510 U.S. 569 (1994); *Suntrust v Houghton Mifflin Co.*, 252 F. 3d 1165 (11th Cir. 2001).
3 *Lucasfilm Ltd v Ainsworth*, Supreme Court, [2011] UKSC 39, [2011] 6 E.C.D.R. 21.
4 For an account of the various justifications, and writings on them, see Dutfield and Suthersanen (2008: Chapter 3); Hughes (1988); Waldron (1993); Fisher (2001).
5 For example, Article 15 (1)(c), International Covenant on Economic, Social and Cultural Rights 1966.
6 For example, Article 1.8, US Constitution.
7 A clear policy has always been in place in relation to textile patterns and designs; even the current TRIPS Agreement suggests that copyright protection may be the best form of protection for this subject matter. See Art. 25(2), TRIPS Agreement.
8 A related aspect is the initial stirrings of standardization of goods such as the sizing of ready-made clothing, shoes and hats. Thus, component parts of consumer products were manufactured to standard dimensions, especially in relation to certain textiles, where yarn counts and cloth dimensions were standardized by law by the 18th century (Styles, 1994: 527–53).
9 *Gorham Mfg. Co. v White,* 81 U.S. (14 Wall.) 511 (S. Ct., 1872) (the first US Supreme Court decision in design law which stated that the 'acts of Congress which authorize the granting of patents for designs were plainly intended to give encouragement to the decorative arts'); also Ricketson and Suthersanen (2012: Chapter 8).
10 Art. 1(2), Paris Convention. These two categories only entered the Convention under the 1925 Hague Revision Conference.
11 Art. 5 *quinquies*, Paris Convention. See also Bodenhausen (1967: 73–4, 86).
12 Articles 9(1), 25 and 26 of the Agreement on Trade-Related Aspects of Intellectual Property Rights, Including Trade in Counterfeit Goods, Annex 1C of World Trade Organization Agreement (April 15, 1994) (hereinafter, TRIPS Agreement). See also Jehoram (1991). For an international perspective, see Duncan (1993).
13 For a full discussion on the Conventions, see generally, Ricketson and Ginsburg (2005: Chapter 8); Mangué (1990).
14 The Designing and Printing of Linens Act 1787 (27 Geo 3, c 38); the Designing and Printing of Linens Act 1794 (Geo 3, c 23); the Designs Copyright Act 1839 (2 & 3 Vict c 17).
15 The first *sui generis* law to specifically protect industrial art works was in respect of textile designs and patterns – Ordinance of the Consuls of Lyons (1711), approved by the Council of State (1712) and registered in Parliament (1717). This was subsequently followed by the French Law of 1806 (*Bulletin des Lois*, 4th ser, IV, 352, 354). See generally Prager (1944); Miller (1999).
16 For a summary of the position not only in Europe but also in the United States, see Reichman (1983: 1153ff.). For a historical account of design patent protection in the US, see Janis and Du Mont (2013).
17 French Intellectual Property Code, 1992 (as amended). The official French translation of the law is available at: www.legifrance.gouv.fr/content/download/1959/13723/.../Code_35.pdf. In relation to this discussion on French law, newer cases are generally available from www.legalis.net or www.legifrance.gouv.fr. All translations are the author's, unless otherwise indicated.
18 Ibid., emphasis added.
19 *Eiffel Tower*, Cass. civ, I, March 3, 1992, DS 1993, 358.
20 *Association Henri Langlois et autres v Cinémathèque française et autres, CA Paris 2 October 1997*, D.1998, p. 312 note B. Edelman; English translation in (1998) 176 *Revue internationale du Droit d'auteur* (RIDA) 422 (mise en scène of the collection of the Paris Musée du Cinéma was awarded copyright and the heirs of the creator could thus successfully invoke moral rights).
21 For instance, fashion wear was granted protection against Zara, a well-known pan-European high street store – *Vanessa Bruno v. Zara France*, CA Paris, Oct. 17, 2012; *Céline v Zara France*, CA Paris, Feb. 27, 2013.
22 *Roberts A. D. et al. v Chanel et al.*, Cass. Civ. Crim., 5 February 2008, available at www.

legalis.net/?page=jurisprudence-decision&id_article=2185

23 Cass. civ. 1ère, 11 February 1997, Sté Zip Zag, JCP G 1997, II, 22973, note X. Daverat (copyright protection given to a clothing button in the shape of a marine node).

24 Cour de Cass., 29 May 1996; English translation in (1996) 170 RIDA 174. The Court of Cassation has affirmed this position recently in relation to earring designs – Cass.civ 1ère, 10 July 2013, available at www.legifrance.gouv.fr/affichJuriJudi.do?oldAction=rechJuriJudi&idTexte=JURITEXT000027704683&fastReqId=2140450450&fastPos=1

25 *Cts Lemaître v Guerlain*, Paris Court of Appeal, 11 June 1997; English translation in (1997) 174 RIDA 174.

26 French Decree of 19–24 July 1793 on the property rights of authors of writings of all kind, of music composers, of painters and of designers

27 Article 7, of the 1793 Law: 'The heirs of authors of works of literature or of engravings, or of any other production of the mind or of genius (*ou de toutes autres productions de l'esprit ou du génie*) within the domain of the fine arts (*beaux arts*), shall have exclusive property in those works for a period of ten years'. For a transcription of the original text, and translation, see *Primary Sources on Copyright Project (1450–1900)*, http://copy.law.cam.ac.uk/cam/index.php

28 O. Laligant, 'La révolution française et le droit d'auteur ou pérennité de l'objet de la protection', English translation in (1991) 147 RIDA, at 50–53; and Cass. Civ. 2 December, 1814 (doubt as to width of law to include commercial designs, since the Act also explicitly mentioned works of music, works of 'beaux arts' and works of engravers).

29 This test was particularly effective, and led to the following instances where copyright was denied to: works of bronze consisting of elaborately twisted brass coils of shovel and tong, Cass. 8 June 1860, Ann. Prop. Ind. 1860, 94; ceramic table pieces, Cass. 18 August 1868, Ann. Prop. Ind 1869, 191; a poster illustrating the sign '*Les noces de chocolat*', Trib. civ. Seine 20 June 1891, Ann. Prop. Ind. 1894, 51. Cited Greffe and Greffe (1994: para. 5).

30 Decision of Conseil d'État, 30 May 1823, cited in Greffe and Greffe, (1994: para. 5.

31 One commentator set the following test: if the design dispalyed intelligence and sentiment, thus it was an artistic design; however, if the design did not arouse any artistic sentiment, but merely satisfied the whims of fashion, then it was a manufactured design (Greffe and Greffe, 1994, para. 5).

32 This test was offered by a 19th-century jurist, Vaunois. Thus, if the author was a manufacturer, the 1806 law would apply; if the work was that of an artist, the 1793 law would apply (Greffe and Greffe, 1994: para. 5).

33 Cass. Civ. 17 January 1882, DP 1883, 1, page 119, cited in Greffe and Greffe (1994: para. 5).

34 Cass. Civ. 2 August 1854, D.P. 1854, 1, page 395.

35 *Robin v Romagnesi*, Cour de Cassation, 17 November 1814, available in English at *Primary Sources on Copyright (1450–1900)*, http://copy.law.cam.ac.uk/cam/tools/request/showRecord.php?id=record_f_1814; for a subsequent confirmation, see Cass. Civ. 2 August 1854, D.P. 1854, 1, p. 395 cited in Lucas and Lucas (1994: para. 74).

36 *Betbéder and Schwalbé C. Mayer and Pierson*, Court of Cassation. 21 November 1862, available in English at Primary *Sources on Copyright (1450–1900)*, http://copy.law.cam.ac.uk/cam/tools/request/showRecord.php?id=record_f_1862. The debate on photographs was carried on in various other legal fora. The Berne Convention, for instance, was equally ambivalent as to the legal classification of photographs and opted for the same formula as applied to works of applied art in that both these categories of works had a minimum term of protection of 25 years – Art. 7(4), Berne Convention.

37 Article 1 of the 1793 law was subsequently amended in 1902 to codify the case law to include the phrase: '*Le même droit appartiendra aux sculpteurs et dessinateurs d'ornements, quels que soient le mérite et la destination de l'Œuvre*' ('The same right shall belong to sculptors and ornamental designers, whatever the merit and the purpose of the work). The phrase subsequently found its way into the current Act (Greffe and Greffe, 1994: para. 7).

38 Copyright Act of 9 September 1965 (Federal Law Gazette Part I, p. 1273), as amended. The official English translation is available at: www.gesetze-im-internet.de/englisch_urhg/englisch_urhg.html

39 Strowel (1993): paragraph 331 *et seq*.

40 U. Loewenheim, in G. Schricker (ed), *Urheberrecht Kommentar*, §2, page 97, as translated and cited in Strowel (1993): para. 331.

41 *Silberdistel* decision, BGH, June 22, 1995, GRUR 1995, 581; (1997) 28 IIC 140 (mass-produced silver thistle earrings served a utilitarian purpose and were works of applied, rather than pure, art); further confirmation of this principle is also to be found in the following German Supreme Court decisions: BGH, GRUR 1958, 500 (501) *Mecki-Igel* (configuration of a hedgehog granted *droit d'auteur* protection); BGH, GRUR 1959, 289 (290) *Rosenthal-Vase* (an asymmetric vase granted *droit d'auteur* protection); BGH, GRUR 1961, 635 (638) *Stahlrohrstuhl* (tubular steel chair granted

protection); BGH, 10 December.1986 I ZR 15/85, GRUR 1987, 903 *Le Corbusier Möbel*; BGH, 14 April 1988, I ZR 99/86, GRUR 1988, 690 (692) *Kristallfiguren*. For a discussion of these cases, see Henning-Bodewig and H. Ruijsenaars (1992).

42 OLG Hamburg, 3 May 2001, 3 U 130/00, GRUR 2002, 419 (*Move*); English translation at [2003] 34 IIC 461

43 OLG Hamburg, 3 May 2001, 3 U 130/00, GRUR 2002, 419 (*Move*); English translation at [2003] 34 IIC 461, at 462

44 *Freischwinger* BGH, February 17, 1989, 1990 GRUR 356; English translation at [1991] IIC 280.

45 BGH, 10 December 1986, I ZR 15/85, GRUR 1987, 903 *Le Corbusier Möbel*; OLG Hamburg, 3 May 2001, 3 U 130/00, GRUR 2002, 419 (*Move*); English translation at [2003] 34 IIC 461, at 462.

46 For example, *Bedienungsanweisung* (Operating Instructions) decision, BGH, (1992) 23 IIC 846 (where copyright was granted to an operating manual for a technical device which consisted of drawings, photographs and text).

47 *Silberdistel* decision, BGH, June 22, 1995, GRUR 1995, p. 581; (1997) 28 IIC 140.

48 BGH, 24 November 2013, I ZR 143/12 *Birthday Train*; unreported as yet; German Supreme Court press release available at: http://juris.bundesgerichtshof.de/cgi-bin/rechtsprechung/document.py?Gericht=bgh&Art=en&Datum=Aktuell&Sort=12288&nr=65848&linked=pm&Blank

49 Copyright, Designs and Patents Act, c. 48, 1988 (as amended).

50 *Ladbroke (Football) Ltd. v William Hill (Football) Ltd.*, 1 All E.R. 465 (1964, HL). This position is currently in flux as the CJEU has begun, on its own initiative, to harmonize the concept of originality. See *Infopaq International A/S v Danske Dagblades Forening* (C-5/08) [2009] E.C.D.R. 16; *Bezpečnostní softwarová asociace – Svaz softwarové ochrany v Ministerstvo kultury* (C-393/09), *Football Association Premier League Ltd. et al v QC Leisure et al*; *Karen Murphy v Media Protection Services Ltd* (joined cases C-403/08 and C-429/08), [2012] ECDR 8.

51 *University of London Press Ltd v University Tutorial Press Ltd* [1916] 2 Ch. 601 (Chancery Division, 1916), at 608.

52 Article 3, Copyright, Designs and Patents Act, c. 48, 1988.

53 *Newspaper Licensing Agency Ltd v Meltwater Holding BV* [2011] EWCA Civ 890.

54 *Anacon Corporation Ltd v Environmental Research Technology Ltd [1994] F.S.R. 659; Electronic Techniques (Anglia) Limited v Critchley Components Limited* [1997] F.S.R. 401

55 *Elanco Products Ltd. v Mandops (Agrochemical Specialists) Ltd.* [1979] FSR 46 (CA).

56 *Waterlow Directories Ltd. v Reed Information Services Ltd.* [1992] FSR 409 (Ch.D.).

57 *EMAP Business Communications Ltd v Planet Media AB* [2000] E.C.D.R. 93.

58 *Macmillan Publishers Ltd. v Thomas Reed Publications Ltd.* (1993) FSR 455.

59 *Chabot v Davies* (1936) 3 AER 221.

60 *Nicol v Barranger*, MacG. Copyright Cases (1917–1923) 219 (Ch.D).

61 *British Leyland Motor Corp v Armstrong Patents Co.* (1986) RPC 279 CA, HL; *Solar Thomson Engineering Co. Ltd. v Barton* (1977) RPC 537, CA; *LB (Plastics) Ltd. v Swish Products Ltd.* (1979) RPC 551; cf. *Canon Kabushiki Kaisha v Green Cartridge Company (Hong Kong) Limited* (1997) FSR 817.

62 *Stephenson, Blake & Co v Grant, Legros & Co.* (1916) 33 RPC 406.

63 *J. Bernstein Ltd. v Sydney Murray Ltd.* (1981) RPC *303*; *LA Gear Inc v Hi-Tech Sports plc* (1992) FSR 121; *Lerose Ltd. v Harwick Jersey International Ltd* (1974) RPC 42.

64 *King Features Syndicate Inc v O&M Kleemen Ltd.* (1941) AC 417, HL; *Mirage Studios v Counter-Feat Clothing Co. Ltd.* (1991) FSR 145.

65 S.4, Copyright, Designs and Patents Act 1988. Further definitions are given in relation to graphic work, and the term sculpture will include models or casts.

66 Ibid.

67 *Hansard*, House of Lords, vol. 490 col. 849 (30 November 1987).

68 [1976] A.C. 64. For a thorough discussion of this decision, see Booton (1996).

69 [1976] A.C. 64. at p. 99.

70 Ibid at pp. 92, 95–6.

71 Ibid at pp. 97–8.

72 *Merlet v Mothercare* (1986) RPC 115 (prototype of a waterproof raincoat with cape for a baby was not a work of artistic craftsmanship as the purpose of the maker was to protect the child from the harsh Scottish climate, as opposed to creating a work of art); *Komesaroff v Mickle* (1988) RPC 204 (copyright denied to a container with two glass windows for observing the movement of coloured sand and glycerine making 'sand pictures' as no craftsmanship on the part of the creator was involved to produce these sand landscapes).

73 (1985) RPC 127 (New Zealand High Court). Section 2(1)(a), New Zealand Copyright Act 1962 is *in pari materia* with s.4, UK CDPA, in relation to artistic works.

74 S.52, Copyright, Designs, and Patents Act 1988 offers a defence to anyone who copies the work so as to make articles of any description. See also Copyright (Industrial Process and Excluded Articles) (No. 2) Order 1989, S.I. 1989/1070 (explaining that industrial process means where more than 50 articles are made).

75 *Flos SpA v Semeraro Casa e Famiglia SpA*, Case C-168/09, [2011] ECDR 8.

76 For a vehement position on why the CJEU was wrong in *Flos*, see Bently (2012).

77 Council Regulation (EC) No. 6/2002 of 12 December 2001 on Community designs (OJ EC No L 3 of 5 January 2002, p. 1), amended by Council Regulation No 1891/2006 of 18 December 2006, OJ EC No L 386 of 29.12.2006, p. 14.

78 Recital 10, CDR states: 'Technological innovation should not be hampered by granting design protection to features dictated solely by a technical function. It is understood that this does not entail that a design must have an aesthetic quality'.

79 Directive 98/71 of the European Parliament and of the Council of 13 October 1998 on the legal protection of designs [1998] OJ L289/28.

80 Art. 17, Design Directive; a similar provision can be found in Art. 96(2), CDR.

81 www.flos.com

82 Law No 633/1941, Art. 2(1)(iv) (as amended by Law No 95/2001); Article 239, Italian Intellectual Property Code (as amended by Law no. 14/2012).

83 *Flos SpA v Semeraro Casa e Famiglia SpA*, Case C-168/09, [2011] ECDR 8, para. 36; see also *Cassina SpA v Alivar Srl and Galliani Host Arredamenti Srl*, Case C-198/10, 9 September 2011

84 See Advocate General's Opinion in *Criminal Proceedings against Donner*, Case C-5/11, [2012] ECDR 18, para. AG32 (concerning sale of well-known pieces of furniture, which were technically purchased in Italy – where no copyright protection was available for such objects – but conveyed to purchasers in Germany – where copyright protection was available for well-known furniture).

85 Directive 2011/77/EU of the European Parliament and of the Council of 27 September 2011 amending Directive 2006/116/EC on the term of protection of copyright and certain related rights.

86 Directive 2001/29/EC of the European Parliament and of the Council on the harmonization of certain aspects of copyright and related rights in the information.

87 This remains a controversial point, especially in the two common law countries within the EU – UK and Ireland. Three prior directives have stated the definition of originality to be 'the author's own intellectual creation', but only in relation to photographs, computer programs, and databases. The CJEU has extrapolated this position to *all* works in its own jurisprudence, and thereby bases its assumption of an EU harmonized criterion of originality on its own jurisprudence. As Advocate General Jääskinen observed in *Criminal Proceedings against Donner*, Case C-5/11, [2012] ECDR 18, note 14: 'Recent case law of the Court has established that when a copyright issue is governed by EU law, only works that amount to the author's own intellectual creation, and are therefore original in this sense, will be eligible for copyright protection'. For the line of jurisprudence, see *Infopaq International A/S v Danske Dagblades Forening* (C-5/08) [2009] E.C.D.R. 16 at para. 37; and *Painer v Standard Verlags GmbH* (C-145/10) [2012] E.C.D.R. 6 at para. 87.

88 See discussion on Germany in Part 2.2 above.

89 S.74, Enterprise and Regulatory Reform Act 2013 c.24.

90 Barbieri and De Santis (2012).

91 However, it should be noted, that the protection does not cover works that were already in the public domain prior to 2001; hence the *Flos* situation.

92 *Vitra Patente AG v High Tech s.r.l.*, Case No. 1983/2007, Court of Milan, September 13, 2012; a similar decision was reached in respect of the Le Corbusier chair – *Cassina v High Tech S.r.l.*, Court of Milan, July 7, 2011. See Barbieri and De Santis (2012).

93 Author's translation.

94 *Flos/Arco* decision, Court of Milan, September 20, 2012. See Barbieri and De Santis (2012).

95 *Lucasfilm Ltd v Ainsworth*, High Court [2008] EWHC 1878 (Ch), [2008] ECDR 17; Court of Appeal, [2009] EWCA Civ 1328; [2010] E.C.D.R. 6; Supreme Court, [2011] UKSC 39, [2011] 6 E.C.D.R. 21

96 The helmet, it was claimed, constituted a work of artistic craftsmanship and a sculpture; only the latter claim was pursued at the appellate stages.

97 *Per* Mann J, [2008] EWHC 1878 (Ch), [2008] ECDR 17, para. 112; this refers to the oft-cited definition of Laddie J. in *Metix (UK) Ltd v G H Maughan (Plastics) Ltd* [1997] FSR 718, at pp. 721–2.

98 [2011] 6 E.C.D.R. 21, at para. 39.

99 [2011] 6 E.C.D.R. 21, at paras 40–41.

100 *Per* Lord Justice Jacob, [2009] EWCA Civ 1328; [2010] E.C.D.R. 6, at paras 66 and 70.

101 *Per* Lord Justice Jacob, [2009] EWCA Civ 1328; [2010] E.C.D.R. 6, at paras 73–5.

102 *Per* Lords Walker and Collins, [2011] UKSC 39, [2011] 6 E.C.D.R., at para. 44.

103 See, for example, www.funwarehouse.co.uk/ and www.stormtroopershop.com/. A Google search for these item retrieves over 260,000 websites. The original Ainsworth site is available at http://www.originalstormtrooper.com

104 Sale 9538 (Film & Entertainment), December 2002, London, available at www.christies.com/lotfinder/star-wars-1977/4036538/lot/lot_details.aspx?from=searchresults&pos=3&intObjectID=4036538&sid=de84c410-0056-4209-a068-f87e281f5684&page=10

105 Damien Hirst's polka dot murals come to mind; but for a contemporary global studio production instance, note Sam Durant's 'Nine Chairs' which are porcelain chairs where the entire labour is outsourced to Chinese artists. Sam Durant, 'Nine Chairs', www.samdurant.com/porcelain-chairs.

106 The Supreme Court admitted this much when it pointed out that UK Parliamentary policy had been to develop three separate tiers of graduated protection for industrial objects; and that this was to be contrasted to the 'indiscriminate protection of literary copyright'. The Court stated that there were 'good policy reasons for the differences in the periods of protection, and the Court should not, in our view, encourage the boundaries of full copyright protection to creep outwards', at para. 48.

107 For example, see Dickie (1974).

108 *Plesner v Louis Vuitton*, [2011] ECDR 4.

109 *Kecofa BV v Lancome Parfums* [2006] ECDR (26) 363.

110 This steam locomotive is used to haul the 'Hogwarts Express'. One can obtain an exact miniature reproduction made by Hornby, the leading producers of model railways in the UK since 1901 (the 'Harry Potter Hogwarts Express' set) for around £45 from eBay.uk.

111 [1986] UKHL 7 (27 February 1986), available at www.bailii.org/uk/cases/UKHL/1986/7.html

112 See 'Samantha Cameron counts the cost of her repro lamp', *The Guardian*, 3 October 2011, available at www.theguardian.com/artanddesign/2011/oct/03/sam-cam-arco-repro-lamp

REFERENCES

Barbieri, A. and De Santis, F. (2012) 'Copyright protection of design: Approach of Italian courts and Italian law after ECJ's decision in Flos vs Semeraro', available at http://www.portolano.it/wp-content/uploads/2012/10/Copyright-Protection-of-Design-Approach-of-Italian-Courts-and-Italian-Law-after-ECJ%E2%80%99s-Decision-in-Flos-vs-Semeraro-.pdf

Barron, A. (2002) 'Copyright law and the claims of art', *Intellectual Property Quarterly*, 4: 368–401.

Bently, L. (2012) 'The return of industrial copyright?', *European Intellectual Property Review*, 10: 654–672.

Birrell, A. (1899) *Seven Lectures on the Law and History of Copyright in Books*. London, Paris, Melbourne: Cassell and Co.

Bodenhausen, G. (1967) *Guide to the Application of the Paris Convention for the Protection of Industrial Property as revised at Stockholm in 1967*. Geneva: BIRPI.

Booton, D. (1996) 'Legal determinations of artistic merit: Works of artistic craftsmanship under United Kingdom copyright law', *Art, Antiquity and Law*, 1(2): 123–138.

Booton, D. (2003) 'Framing pictures: Defining art in UK copyright law', *Intellectual Property Quarterly*, 1: 38–68.

Budd, B (1978) 'The future of industrial copyright', *European Intellectual Property Review*, 2.

Dickie, G. (1974) *Art and the Aesthetic: An Institutional Analysis*. Ithaca: Cornell University Press.

Drysdale, J. (1980) 'The application of UK copyright law to manufactured articles', *European Intellectual Property Review*, March: 75–78.

Duchamp, M. (1957) 'The creative act', a paper given at the Convention of the American Federation of Arts, Houston, available at www.eunchurn.com/mvio/Duchamp_Creative_Act.pdf

Duchemin, W. (1976) *Protection of the Works of Artist-Craftsmen – a Study for the EC Commission*, SPADEM.

Duncan, L. (1993) 'Improvement of international protection of designs and models', *Australian Intellectual Property Journal*, 32.

Dutfield, G. and U. Suthersanen (2008) *Global Intellectual Property Law*. Cheltenham: Edward Elgar.

Finniss, G. (1964) 'The theory of "unity of art" and the protection of designs and models in French law', *Journal of the Patent Office Society*, 46: 615, 618–619.

Fisher, W. (2001) 'Theories of intellectual property', in *New Essays in the Legal and Political Theory of Property*, S. Munzer (ed.). Cambridge: Cambridge University Press.

Forty, A. (1986) *Objects of Desire – Design and Society Since 1750*. London: Thames and Hudson.

Gartman, D. (1995) 'Harley Earl and the art and colour section: The birth of styling at General Motors', in *Design History: An Anthology*, D.P. Doordan (ed.). Cambridge: MIT Press.

Gaubiac, Y. (1982) 'La théorie de l'unité de l'art', *Revue internationale du Droit d'auteur*, 111: 2.

Greffe, P. and F. Greffe (1994) *Traité des Dessins et Modèles*. Paris: Litec.

Henning-Bodewig, F and Ruijsenaars, H. (1992) 'Alternative protection for product designs – a comparative view of German, Benelux and US law', *International Review of Intellectual Property and Competition Law*, 23: 643–669. .

Hughes, J. (1988) 'The philosophy of intellectual property', *Georgetown Law Journal*, 77: 251–314.

Janis M. and Du Mont J. (2013) 'The Origins of American Design Protection', *Indiana Law Journal*, 88: 837–879.

Jehoram, H.C. (1991) 'Hybrids on the borderline between copyright and industrial property law', *Australian Intellectual Property Journal*, 2: 190.

Jehoram, H.C. (1992) 'The EC Green Paper on the legal protection of industrial design: half way down the right track – a view from the Benelux', *European Intellectual Property Review* 14(3): 75.

Kur, A. (1993) 'The Green Paper's "design approach" – what's wrong with it?', *European Intellectual Property Review* 15(10): 374.

Laligant, O. (1991) 'La révolution française et le droit d'auteur ou pérennité de l'objet de la protection', Revue Internationale du Droit d'Auteur, 147: 32–47.

Lucas, A. and H.J. Lucas (1994) *Traité de la Propriété littéraire et artistique*. Paris: Litec.

Mangué, P. (1990) 'The international protection of industrial designs under the international conventions', *University of Baltimore Law Review*, 19: 393.

Miller, L.E. (1999), 'Innovation and industrial espionage in eighteenth-century France: An investigation of the selling of silks through samples', *Journal of Design History*, 12: 271–92.

Mott, K.M. (1964) 'Analysis of the "unity of art" concept in European legal systems', *Bulletin of the Copyright Society*, 11: 242.

O'Shaughnessy, J. (1987) *Why People Buy*. Oxford: Oxford University Press.

Papanek, V. (1984) *Design for the Real World*. London: Thames & Hudson.

Pouillet, E. (1894) *Traité théorique et pratique de la propriété littéraire et artistique et du droit de représentation*, 2nd edn. Paris: Imprimerie et librairie générale de jurisprudence; translation from Rideau, F. (2008) 'Commentary on the Court of Cassation on compilations (1814)', in *Primary Sources on Copyright (1450–1900)*, eds L. Bently and M. Kretschmer, www.copyrighthistory.org

Pouillet, E. (1911) *Traité théorique et pratique des dessins et modéles*. Paris: Marchal & Godde.

Prager, F. (1944) 'History of intellectual property from 1545 to 1787', *Journal of the Patent Office Society* (November), 26(11): 711–60.

Reichman, J.H. (1983) 'Design protection in domestic and foreign copyright law: From the Berne Revision of 1948 to the Copyright Act of 1976', *Duke Law Journal*, 1143–1264.

Robin v Romagnesi, Cour de Cassation, 17 November 1814, Primary Sources on Copyright (1450–1900), Ibid. Bently, L. and Kretschmer, M. (eds), available at http://www.copyrighthistory.org" www.copyrighthistory.org

Ricketson, S. and J. Ginsburg (2005) *International Copyright and Neighbouring Rights: The Berne Convention and Beyond*, 2nd edn. Oxford: Oxford University Press.

Ricketson, S. and U. Suthersanen (2012) 'The design/copyright overlap: Is there a resolution?', in *Overlapping Intellectual Property Rights*, N. Wilkof and S. Basheer (eds). Oxford: Oxford University Press.

Saunders, D. (1993) 'Early Copyright and the Court of Chancery', *European Intellectual Property Review*, 12: 452–456.

Schwartz, H. (1996) *The Culture of the Copy: Striking Likenesses, Unreasonable Facsimiles*. New York: Zone Books.

Sparkes, P. (1987) *An Introduction to Design and Culture in the Twentieth Century*. London: Allen & Unwin.

Strowel, A. (1993) *Droit d'auteur et copyright – Divergences et convergences – Etude de droit comparé*. Paris: LGDJ.

Styles, J. (1994) 'Manufacturing, consumption and design', in *Consumption and the World of Goods*, J. Porter and R. Porter (eds). London: Routledge.

Sudjic, D. (2009) *The Language of Things*. London: Penguin.

Suthersanen, U. (2009) *Design Law: European Union and United States of America*. London: Sweet & Maxwell.

Thompson, D. (2008) *The $12 Million Stuffed Shark: The Curious Economics of Contemporary Art and Auction Houses*. London: Aurum Press.

Waldron, J. (1993) 'From authors to copiers: Individual rights and social values in intellectual property', *Chicago-Kent Law Review*, 68: 842–887.

Walker, J.A. (1989) *Design History and History of Design*. London: Pluto Press.

PART IX

Regulating Innovative Technology

Matthew David and Debora Halbert

Technological change creates new affordances for action. Some of these possibilities may challenge 'business as usual' when it comes to selling IP-rich commodities, even whilst they may enable new creative ways of doing business and generating new ideas. The three chapters in this section address this tension. Technological 'solutions' to perceived technical 'problems' can themselves become 'problems' for those for whom the initial 'problem' was in fact a 'solution'. Technical cat-and-mouse developments occur when new waves of technique are developed, each designed to overcome the affordances of earlier developments.

Where the law comes to be added into this mix is interesting, as the law is often an afterthought, brought in to 'fix' perceived difficulties introduced or enabled by new technologies. However, the law can itself become a spur to various forms of technical development. Ian Brown's examination of the relationship between intellectual property rights and other rights (such as those over health, privacy, freedom of expression and social inclusion) highlights the conflict, when seeking to uphold 'rights'. To uphold one right by means of legal prohibition on certain technologies, and by upholding the right to use other techniques (of encryption/surveillance), will most often impinge on other rights. Andrew Kirton's account of the history of the music industry highlights that law and technology have always been intimately bounded together in both disrupting and re-stabilizing forms of economic and cultural valuation. Where the Internet enables large-scale content sharing of copyrighted material, it can also enable a tracing of the IP addresses of those doing the sharing. If legal professionals are able to force Internet Service Providers (ISPs) to provide them with the real-world identities of these IP address holders, they can engage in what David Wall calls 'speculative lawyering', a form of legal 'trolling' where tens of thousands of Internet users receive demands for money to avoid court action. Wall highlights the questionable legal standing of this practice, tracks the rise and fall and then geographic migration of this practice, and also notes how such 'extortion', that started around music downloading, has now moved over to pornography, as those accused are far less likely to take their case to court, where such en bloc actions have never actually succeeded.

Ian Brown explores the tension between intellectual property rights and other human rights. To say other immediately raises the question of whether or not intellectual property rights (and property rights in general) should be considered human rights as well (see Darch, this volume). Various national, regional and international conventions have identified IPRs as human rights, but at the same time noted that such rights cannot be considered absolute or irreversible when set against other conflicting human rights. The balance between IPRs and other rights such as health, privacy, social and cultural inclusion, as well as freedom of expression, have been hotly contested, as Brown demonstrates.

It is also the case that one strategy to regulate innovative technology has been to develop various forms of technical prohibitions and intrusions. Another is to legislate to prohibit technologies that bypass such locks or which inhibit such surveillance. Digital rights management systems, whether these be hard DRM, in the form of digital locks, site blocks or user exclusions, or soft DRM, in the form of various kinds of surveillance and data collection, have raised a number of concerns regarding the scope of technical mechanisms to overstep or replace legal decision-making in determining what might be 'fair use', even when it is not in accordance with the wishes of an IP rights holder. While in some countries blocking access to the Internet for someone found to have infringed IP is mooted as a legitimate punishment/deterrent, in others it is considered a fundamental denial of human rights. Some jurisdictions have means by which 'take down' requests can be challenged, and potentially 'put back'; but others do not.

It is, nonetheless, the case that attempts to develop secure forms of encryption by which IPRs could be put under technical lock and key irrespective of any legal demands for 'fair access' have failed, as have attempts to create absolute surveillance. What is viewed in the US and UK as a threat to IPRs has itself been praised (and in part encouraged) by those same states in relation to freedom of expression in countries deemed 'repressive'. The history of attempted technical regulation shows that attempted closure simply creates incentives to create new forms of evasion. Brown nicely illustrates how those countries most active in attempting to block their citizens from accessing The Pirate Bay, are also those countries with the highest use of proxy servers to allow them to get around such blockages. Whilst IPR-holding lobbies are instrumental in driving much of the legal and technical regulation that has been introduced of late, such lobby groups have been less successful in curbing users in claiming and enacting what they (Internet users) think their rights are/or ought to be. Creating rules is not the same as being able to make everyone comply with them.

The history of intellectual property is bound up with changes in technology and the affordances such new artefacts bring to the making and circulating of copies and multiples of original innovations. Andrew Kirton highlights that this tension between the desire to increase access and the desire to maintain an element of scarcity has been central to the history of 'the music industry' long before even audio 'recording', let alone more recent conflicts over the scope of Internet-based digital copying. The history of musical 'reproduction' moves from print, to recording, to digital distribution over centuries, and this history saw much interaction between market, technical and legal actors in the production of particular forms and innovations, which, in turn, but only for a short time, came to stand as 'normal' and 'necessary' modes of valuing music (both culturally and commercially).

In one sense, fatally perhaps, law has always lagged behind technology in this construction of musical consumption, but the power of dominant interests was routinely served in legal reconfigurations that naturalized their position. At various junctures new technologies appeared to threaten the interests of intermediaries relative to performers and audiences; but, as Kirton documents, the history of the music industry is one of recurrent re-assertions of dominance, and this has involved various attempts to integrate new technology within a system that needs to maintain scarcity even whilst attempting to make the most of new opportunities to reduce costs and increase distribution. Kirton shows that copyright law, even as it was formally extended to give IP rights to composers and performers, acted to separate intellectual property itself from the right to commercially control it. This in turn made possible the rise of musical publishing and then recording industries where artists are required to sell their copyrights in exchange for a share of technical and market distribution benefits. As long as record companies maintain monopoly rights over distribution, the share taken by artists can be pressed to a minimum (often nothing at all once costs are 'recouped' from the artists' royalties), even whilst prices to audiences can be kept high.

Yet, music takes us to the heart of the tension between cultural and economic conceptions of owning and belonging, and between private and public. The rise of new digital technologies, not for the first time, highlights these tensions, and can enable us to re-question the relationship between creative artists and performers, commercial actors, and audiences. However, just as has happened during earlier ruptures in the technical, cultural and economic 'status quo', Kirton warns that we cannot, and should not take it for granted that such disruption will automatically bring into being a more equitable system of exchange and reward.

David Wall explores the practice of 'speculative lawyering' in cases where legal professionals take it upon themselves to request large numbers of real-world details from ISPs of Internet Protocol (IP) address holders they claim (evidence being a key question mark in this process) have infringed IPRs holders' 'property'. This usually involves the claim that the Internet Protocol (IP) address holders have downloaded a file containing music belonging to 'their client' (the IPRs holder). For some time courts in the UK, US and elsewhere, and increasingly now in other counties, have been willing to compel ISPs to provide this information. Having obtained names and addresses, lawyers have been writing, en bloc, sometimes sending out 10,000 letters at a time, 'notifying' Internet users that they are accused of infringing copyright and demanding 'pre-court' settlements of up to £500/$1,000 to prevent further action. Such firms have been able to generate large amounts of money by such means, even when only a portion of those written to pay up.

However, the legal status of such actions has been questioned, and Wall documents the rise and fall of such speculative practices in a range of jurisdictions. The practice has led to overstretch in some instances, and these cases have led to judgments that effectively curtail the willingness of most mainstream IPRs holders (such as record companies) to instruct law firms to engage further in such actions. Wall notes that cold feet on the part of mainstream record companies has led to 'entrepreneurial' law firms migrating towards using claims that Internet users have accessed copyright protected pornography as a way of 'extorting' money from those they contact. Claiming that someone has accessed 'illegal pornography' is an even better way of ensuring payment, as those who think they might have viewed 'questionable' content will pay up to avoid the risk of having themselves exposed in court. If innocence is no defence in the eyes of public opinion, regarding such things as the accusation of having viewed child pornography for example, just the accusation may be sufficient threat to make even the entirely guiltless pay to avoid court proceedings, especially when non-attendance may be taken as sufficient grounds for conviction.

Wall notes that law firms who engage in such work, whilst initially paid to represent IPRs-holding companies, then began actions of their own, rather than taking instruction from clients. He also notes that such firms rely on pre-court settlement, and have never successfully prosecuted the individual cases that have come to court as a result of such bulk mail-outs. This brings into question the very legality of such actions. The 'evidence' claimed may be really nothing of the sort. Simply being identified as having visited a website or having clicked on a file with a name indicative copyrighted content does not – on its own – prove infringement. If firms make such content available themselves, to ensure that they know what it is that has been downloaded by the person they then accuse, they may be accused of 'honey pot' entrapment. Whilst overstretch, as well as court and public reaction to it, seems to have limited the spread of such 'trolling' in certain countries and for certain content, the practice has now spread to other jurisdictions and other kinds of content.

30

Copyright Technologies and Clashing Rights

Ian Brown

INTRODUCTION

As the Internet and personal computers have given most consumers in advanced economies the ability to make unlimited numbers of perfect, cost-free, copies of digital works, copyright law has become increasingly difficult to enforce. Billions of songs are shared without authorization every year, over peer-to-peer file-sharing networks, streaming sites and 'file lockers', with unauthorized downloading of music and films being the most common offence committed by 10–25-year-olds in the UK (Wilson et al. 2006). Pirate Parties demanding copyright reform have successfully stood in local and national elections, with Swedish German voters electing Pirate members to the European Parliament and Icelanders sending three Pirate Party members to the world's oldest legislature, the Althing.

Rights holders, claiming 'the answer to the machine is in the machine' (Clark 1996), have persuaded governments around the world to target new copyright regulation at personal computers, media devices and Internet Service Providers. In particular, new legal protection has been given to Technological Protection Measures that restrict access to digital works, while more recently some governments have required ISPs to police the behaviour of their users. The potential sanctions range from warning letters, through restrictions on connection speed, to disconnection.

As well as effectiveness challenges, these measures have also raised difficult questions related to human rights. The Universal Declaration of Human Rights and its implementing international and regional covenants and conventions give authors a right to protection of their 'moral and material interests'. But they also give individuals rights to freedom of expression (International Covenant on Civil and Political Rights § 19), privacy (ICCPR § 17), 'to take part in cultural life' and 'to enjoy the benefits of scientific progress and its applications' (International Covenant on Economic, Social and Cultural Rights § 15). Can automated restrictions on the use made of digital works, and on individuals' access to the Internet, support all of these rights?

This chapter assesses the outcome and broader lessons of these attempts to regulate the technology underlying the control of creative works. It first sets out the public policy objectives of copyright, including the

Anglo-American incentivization of creativity, Continental European protection of authors' rights, and balancing these considerations with the maximization of social welfare and the protection of human rights. The latter includes protection of freedom of expression and privacy, as well as broader economic, social and cultural rights in international law – all of which can be difficult to take into account in technologies that attempt to restrict copying or block access to infringing copies. The chapter then considers the economic impact of new digital playback and copying tools, linked via the global Internet.

Encouraged by rights holders, governments and intergovernmental organizations have attempted to shape the development and use of these digital technologies. This chapter traces the co-evolution of these legal provisions and 'Technical Protection Measures', analysing the institutional political economy that has resulted in poor outcomes that over-privilege the interests of rights holders against those of technology innovators, users and society. It suggests mechanisms for policy makers to take better account of these interests in future, and suggests that technological 'magic bullets' are unlikely to play a significant role in more balanced outcomes.

PUBLIC POLICY OBJECTIVES

Since the 18th century, governments have granted exclusive rights of reproduction to authors in an attempt to incentivize the creation of printed books 'for the Encouragement of Learning' (Statute of Anne 1710) and 'To promote the Progress of Science and useful Arts' (US Constitution 1787). The continental European approach to 'authors' rights' additionally emphasizes the natural right of individuals to control their works (Hugenholtz 2002, 241).

Most governments have now recognized non-economic 'moral' rights, such as the right to be identified as the author of a work, and to object to distortion or mutilation of a work (Berne Convention art. 6bis 1886). Economic and natural rights are both included in article 27 of the Universal Declaration of Human Rights, which declares: 'Everyone has the right to the protection of the moral and material interests resulting from any scientific, literary or artistic production of which he is the author'.

However, there are significant social costs to providing these exclusive rights to authors. Information goods are non-rivalrous in consumption; as Thomas Jefferson wrote in 1813, 'He who receives an idea from me, receives instruction himself without lessening mine; as he who lights his taper at mine, receives light without darkening me' (Jefferson 1854, 180–181). This is one reason why most copyright protection is time-limited – although the copyright term has been greatly extended in most countries, for example in the US from 14 years (renewable once for another 14 years) in the original Copyright Act of 1790, to 70 years after the death of the author in 1998.

Information goods are recognized as essential to democracy, education, research and other public goods. Copyright also has the potential to stifle freedom of expression. Hence, copyright policy must try to balance the rights of authors and their incentives to create against potential social losses resulting from over-protection. In the US this led the courts to develop a 'fair use' doctrine that allows certain uses of copyright works without prior authorization, so long as this does not damage the commercial market for the work. In the EU, an exhaustive list of optional exceptions is included in the 2001 Copyright Directive, including parody, research and news reporting. The 30 Member States of the European Economic Area have implemented different combinations of these exceptions in national law, creating an extremely fragmented 'single market' for copyright works (Hugenholtz 2000). While such an enumeration of exceptions gives greater legal certainty – Lessig has characterized fair use as the right to take expensive, lengthy and uncertain legal actions (2008, 187) – it can significantly constrain innovation in areas unforeseen by legislators (Hugenholtz 2013).

Human Rights

Copyright interacts in several areas with the UN's 'Bill of Rights' developed following the Second World War: the Universal Declaration (UDHR), the International Covenant on Economic, Social and Cultural Rights (ICESCR), and the International Covenant on Civil and Political Rights (ICCPR).

Amplifying article 27 of the UDHR, article 15 of the ICESCR declares three rights: 'to take part in cultural life'; 'to enjoy the benefits of scientific progress and its applications'; and 'to benefit from the protection of the moral and material interests resulting from any scientific, literary or artistic production of which he is the author'. Article 15 emphasizes the social nature of copyright: to protect authors' rights, but also to enable everyone to participate in cultural life and benefit from scientific progress.

The authors of the ICESCR and ICCPR excluded a right of property, although this is included in the regional versions of these treaties. For example, Article 1 of the First Protocol to the European Convention on Human Rights (ECHR) states: 'Every natural or legal person is entitled to the peaceful enjoyment of his possessions. No one shall be deprived of his possessions except in the public interest and subject to the conditions provided for by law and by the general principles of international law'. The European Court of Human Rights has interpreted this to include copyright (Helfer and Austin 2011, 516).

Most recently, the EU's Charter of Fundamental Rights includes a specific article specifying 'Intellectual property shall be protected' (§17(2)). This is most plausibly read as an explicit confirmation that copyright protection is included within the more general right to the protection of property – an important, but qualified right to be balanced against conflicting public interests (Griffiths 2011). As the EU Court of Justice observed in *SABAM v. Netlog* (Case C-360/10): 'The protection of the right to intellectual property is indeed enshrined in Article 17(2) of the Charter … There is, however, nothing whatsoever in the wording of that provision or in the Court's case-law to suggest that that right is inviolable and must for that reason be absolutely protected' (§41). There is greater scope for state interference with the right to property in Article 1 Protocol 1 of the ECHR than other qualified rights (ARTICLE 19 2012, 10).

These property rights sit within the wider human rights framework and must be balanced with others, particularly freedom of expression and privacy. As the England and Wales Court of Appeal has stated:

> copyright is antithetical to freedom of expression. It prevents all, save the owner of the copyright, from expressing information in the form of the literary work protected by the copyright … It is stretching the concept of freedom of expression to postulate that it extends to the freedom to convey ideas and information using the form of words devised by someone else. Nonetheless there are circumstances … where this freedom is important.

The court determined that:

> rare circumstances can arise where the right of freedom of expression will come into conflict with the protection afforded by the Copyright Act … we consider that the court is bound, insofar as it is able, to apply the Act in a manner that accommodates the right of freedom of expression. (*Ashdown v. Telegraph Group plc* [2001] EWCA Civ 1142 §§30–31, §45)

Freedom of expression can be greatly damaged by technologies that prevent lawful uses of copyright works, or the blocking of Internet sites or users alleged to be infringing copyright without a full judicial proceeding (La Rue 2011). The US Digital Millennium Copyright Act (DMCA) encourages websites to immediately take down content when served with notice, but users are rarely in a position to make use of the DMCA's put-back provisions (Lemley 2007). The EU's E-Commerce Directive (2000/31/EC) does not even include put-back provisions.

Demands from rights holders that ISPs disconnect allegedly infringing customers and block access to infringing sites are particularly dangerous for freedom of expression. In a report to the UN Human Rights Council, the UN's Special Rapporteur on Freedom of Expression said he was 'alarmed by proposals to disconnect users from Internet access if they violate intellectual property rights' (La Rue 2011). A report for the Organization for Security and Cooperation in Europe (Akdeniz 2011, 35) stated:

> Since blocking mechanisms are not immune from significant deficiencies, they may result in the blocking of access to legitimate sites and content. Further, blocking is an extreme measure and has a very strong impact on freedom of expression and the free flow of information. Participating States should therefore refrain from using blocking as a permanent solution or as a means of punishment … Blocking of online content can only be justified if in accordance with these standards and done pursuant to court order and where absolutely necessary. Blocking criteria should always be made public and provide for legal redress.

The European Court of Human Rights has determined:

> The right to Internet access is considered to be inherent in the right to access information and communication protected by national Constitutions, and encompasses the right for each individual to participate in the information society and the obligation for States to guarantee access to the Internet for their citizens. It can therefore be inferred from all the general guarantees protecting freedom of expression that a right to unhindered Internet access should also be recognised. (*Yildirim v. Turkey*, no. 3111/10, 2012, § 31)

Copyright laws to some extent 'internalize' a balance with freedom of expression through limits such as: the protection of expression, not ideas; term limits; and exceptions and limitations. This has been the justification for the US Supreme Court's rejection of a significant tension between copyright and the First Amendment (and that both are explicitly specified in the US Constitution as mechanisms to promote free speech). But Pamela Samuelson's comment still rings true: 'all too often in recent years, when courts have perceived a conflict between intellectual property rights and free speech rights, property has trumped speech' (2001, 2028). The First Amendment has a limited impact on private action (although it can be argued copyright enforcement implicates this (Yu 2010, 1398)), but European governments have no such excuse given their ECHR 'positive obligations' to secure their citizens' rights.

In some cases, courts also need to take account of the 'external' conflicts of copyright law with rights to freedom of expression (Birnhack 2003). These external considerations are important in ensuring the interests of users and future authors are taken into consideration alongside those of authors and other rights holders (Helfer and Austin 2011, 509). The right to impart, seek and receive information is a critical underpinning of democracy, and of other civil and political rights (UN Human Rights Committee 2011).

The main tension between privacy and copyright comes with the introduction of enforcement mechanisms that involve covert surveillance, by public or private bodies. Under the ECHR, such measures require a clear justification, and must be proportionate to their goals and include safeguards against abuse. The EU Court of Justice in its *Promusicae* case (C-275/06) acknowledged this 'fair balance.' It has been especially stressed by the European Data Protection Supervisor in his opinion on the Anti-Counterfeiting Trade Agreement (ACTA), which emphasized that some proposed ACTA measures were 'highly invasive', entailling 'generalised monitoring of Internet users' activities' affecting 'millions of law-abiding Internet users, including many children and adolescents' (EDPS 2010, 3).

Intellectual property rights have also become a key part of global discussions on a 'right to development'. Many low-income countries have complained about the high price of software and textbooks resulting from international intellectual property agreements. These types of copyright-protected goods are essential for development in a global knowledge economy. As the Government of Pakistan told the United Nations Commission on Human Rights in 2001:

> [T]he fundamental objectives of these agreements are not being realized. There may perhaps be reasons to believe, at best on theoretical grounds, that in the long term, benefits could accrue in the form of increased investment, innovation and transfer of technology. However, it is painfully evident that in the short and medium term, the costs being borne by the developing countries are higher than the gains, and that the balance between the rights holder (mostly from the developed countries) and the user of intellectual property has shifted dramatically in favour of the former.

The production of copyright policy in private, government-facilitated corporate discussions worked reasonably well pre-Internet, when the main affected parties had at least partial representation. It has become increasingly problematic as sanctions against the unrepresented user have become the main topic of behind-closed-doors discussion. It violates a core democratic right of interested parties to participate, in the words of the United Nations Committee on Economic, Social and Cultural Rights, in 'any significant decision making processes that have an impact on their rights and legitimate interests' (Helfer and Austin 2011, 513). Without care, copyright enforcement measures can also damage individual freedom of expression and privacy, which are core civil and political rights that underpin democracy itself.

THE ECONOMIC IMPACT OF TECHNOLOGY

Technological shifts during the 1980s led to intensive discussion of the 'modernization' of copyright law. The World Intellectual Property Organization (WIPO), the United Nations agency responsible for global copyright treaties such as the Berne Convention, debated model copyright laws during the 1980s to respond to the still-novel personal computer, as well as new audio and video recording equipment. But it was the arrival of the Internet as a mass medium in the mid-1990s, and especially the development of file-sharing software such as Napster, that drove government and industry discussions concerning the impact on copyright law of users' abilities to share copyright works without permission on a grand scale.

Data on levels of such sharing are difficult to gather, and are often modelled using proxies such as levels of peer-to-peer file-sharing traffic on large networks. Cisco Systems estimated such traffic would see a compound annual growth rate of 23% between 2010 and 2015 (2011, 9). Market research companies conduct frequent surveys asking respondents about their downloading behaviour. One of the largest recent surveys, covering 8,000 adults across 13 countries, found that 29% had downloaded music without payment (Synovate 2010).

It is difficult to use such statistics to produce accurate estimates of economic effects, especially on the wider economy. Different types of downloading activity are legal in different jurisdictions. Survey respondents may be afraid to report illegal activity, or exaggerate it. The rate at which consumer access to infringing copyright works reduces expenditure on legitimate works is extremely hard to measure (Hargreaves 2011b, 1–2). Infringement has a complex range of economic impacts, some positive, for different stakeholders, as analysed in Table 30.1 from the US Government Accountability Office (GAO).

The GAO found that even within the US government, three widely used estimates of the costs of infringement (from the Federal Bureau of Investigation, Customs and Border Protection, and the Federal Trade Commission) could not be substantiated (2010, 19). It found that it is 'difficult, if not impossible, to

Table 30.1 Economic impact of copyright infringement

Stakeholder	*Positive effects*	*Negative effects*
Consumers	Perceived benefits from lower prices of pirated goods	
Industry	Increased sales of legitimate goods based on consumer 'sampling' of pirated goods	Lost sales Lost brand value or damage to public image Cost of IP protection Decreased incentive to invest in research and development
Government		Lost tax revenue due to illegal sales of pirated goods Cost of IP enforcement
Economy as a whole		Lower economic growth as a result of reduced incentives to innovate Lost revenue from declining US trade in countries with weak IP rights regimes

Source: GAO (2010, 9–10).

quantify the net effect of counterfeiting and piracy on the economy as a whole' (p. 15).

An independent review for the UK government concluded that 'sales and profitability levels in most creative business sectors appear to be holding up reasonably well … many creative businesses are experiencing turbulence from digital copyright infringement, but … at the level of the whole economy, measurable impacts are not as stark as is sometimes suggested' (Hargreaves 2011a, 6). The review noted that music industry revenues have continued to grow year-on-year, up 5% in 2009 (with rising live performance revenues compensating for a limited stabilization at radically reduced levels of revenues from the sale of recorded music), as did book sales from 2004 to 2009 (p. 74).

As a matter of policy, copyright is a limited monopoly, rather than a market intervention to promote competition. Most information goods also have high fixed costs but low marginal costs of production. It is therefore unsurprising that many industries structured around copyright ownership are highly concentrated. The three major record labels (Sony, Universal Music Group and Warner Music Group) control around three-fifths of the world market. There are only five major US film studios, which control three-quarters of the world market (Patry 2012, 111–112). The limited interventions that have been made by competition regulators have been at the periphery, for example with attempts by the European Commission to increase competition between the national collecting societies that collect royalties for music performances in each Member State.

TYPES OF CODE REGULATION

From its inception, Anglo-American copyright law regulated reproduction of creative works to ensure the remuneration of authors and later songwriters, performers and directors. This was effective because all of these industries required capital-intensive investment in printing presses, radio and television broadcast networks, and vinyl, videocassette and optical disk reproduction equipment, encouraging market concentration and creating significant barriers to entry to those seeking to ignore the law. Expensive reproduction machinery presents an easy seizure target for civil and criminal action against those failing to comply with requirements to gain approval from rights holders for making copies.

A range of new reproduction technologies throughout the 20th century was first seen as a significant challenge to copyright regulation, but then successfully developed into new industries that ultimately benefited rights holders. Player piano rolls, phonograph records, jukeboxes, radio and cable television were all developed in the US with the aid of copyright exemptions and compulsory licences, while the video rental industry depended on the first sale doctrine permitting a wide variety of uses for lawfully owned works (Ginsburg 2001; Lesk 2003; Litman 2001, 106–107).

Home audiotape and video-recording equipment became mass-market items during the final third of the 20th century, for the first time putting cheap high-quality reproduction machinery into consumers' hands. Industry lobbyists complained furiously that 'home taping is killing music' and that 'the VCR is to the American film producer and the American public as the Boston strangler is to the woman home alone' (Anderson 2009). The executive secretary of the American Federation of Television and Radio Artists, Howard Wayne Oliver, told the US Congress that the electronics revolution could 'undermine, cripple, and eventually wash away the very industries on which it feeds and which provide employment for thousands of our citizens' (Litman 2001, 106–107). It was only a close (5–4) decision by the US Supreme Court in the 1984 *Sony v. Universal Studios* case that protected the manufacturers of technologies with 'substantial non-infringing uses' from liability for copyright infringement by users.

Primitive attempts were made to limit the capabilities of these technologies, with restrictions on Amstrad tape-to-tape recorders (*CBS Songs Ltd v. Amstrad Consumer Electronics plc* (1988) 11 IPR 1; *Australian Tape Manufacturers Association Ltd v. Commonwealth of Australia* (1993) 25 IPR 1 at 4). The Cartrivision system prevented consumers from rewinding rented videotapes for viewing a second time, requiring the payment of a fee to a rental store with specialist equipment (Patry 2009, 144).

The first sophisticated attempt to regulate home copying through regulation of home copying technologies came with the introduction of the Digital Audio Tape (DAT) standard. The Recording Industry Association of America opposed the US sale of DAT recorders in the late 1980s, threatening legal action against anyone selling DAT machines (Patry 2009, 95). The recording industry (particularly CBS Records) lobbied Congress for a legal requirement for DAT machines to implement a system called CopyCode, which would prevent the reproduction of pre-recorded music. CBS's opposition weakened when they were bought by DAT manufacturers Sony.

Eventually rights holders settled for a requirement that DAT recorders implement a Serial Copy Management System (SCMS) that prevented the reproduction of first-generation copies. This became part of the US Audio Home Recording Act of 1992, which also levied taxes on recorders and blank media (Ginsburg 2001, 1628). SCMS was also included in the later MiniDisc and Digital Compact Cassette formats. At the same time, the US introduced a ban on the supply of devices that assisted with unauthorized decryption of satellite programmes. This provision was later included in the North American Free Trade Agreement (§1707(a)).

Technological Protection Measures and Rights Management Information

The UK was the first country to introduce a more general legal provision that banned devices designed or adapted to circumvent copy-protection (or even the publication of information intended to enable circumvention). While these provisions did not immediately influence other countries' legal frameworks, they had a strong impact at the World Intellectual Property Organization (WIPO).

The UN agency debated including in their model copyright law provisions a requirement of copy-protection functionality in all devices used to access copyright works. However, because of concerns about the impact on competition and innovation, WIPO developed provisions closer to the new UK law (Ficsor 2002). WIPO's 'Internet treaties' (the Copyright Treaty and Performances and Phonograms Treaty), agreed in 1996, both contain provisions that parties 'shall provide adequate legal protection and effective legal remedies against the circumvention of effective technological measures'. By increasing rights holder control over uses of works, technological protection measures (TPMs) are likely to increase their revenues (Halderman and Felten 2006).

The US used this broader language to ban the circumvention of 'effective access controls', as well as circumvention devices and services. The European Union mirrored this restrictive language in Article 6 of its Copyright Directive (2001/29/EC). However, some Member States that joined the EU in 2004 gave users more flexibility in national laws, allowing them to circumvent access controls in order to make legitimate use of copyright works (Brown 2003; Gasser and Ernst 2006; Kerr 2010).

Because all access to and use of digital works involves temporary reproduction within computing devices and communication networks, copyright has a much greater impact on the use of digital than analogue works. It has moved from regulating duplication to regulating access. This has given rights holders much greater influence over the design of digital media technologies than they ever had over paper mills, radios, televisions or videotape players. It has been backed up by anti-circumvention laws that cover all access to protected works, the seeming consequence of ambiguous language in WIPO's Internet treaties (Cunard et al. 2003).

Also included in these treaties are protections for 'rights management information' that identifies a copyright work, its author, or terms and conditions of use. This information can be used to protect the moral rights of authors, such as attribution. It can also facilitate lower transaction costs in acquiring rights to use specific content. These rights-management provisions have been much less controversial than the equivalent anti-circumvention provisions, mainly because they do not prevent users of such works from exercising their fair use/dealing rights under copyright law.

While WIPO and its members were busy giving legal protection to content-protection mechanisms, TPMs initially received little support from major technology companies and were easily hacked. The mechanisms tested in the 2000 Secure Digital Music Initiative (SDMI) challenge were immediately broken by just one academic research team (Craven et al. 2001). Widely deployed systems, such as the Content Scrambling System used in the DVD video format, were so easily circumvented they became a joke. Many came from small companies with a greater appetite for risk than large rights holders, eager to gain market share (and power) for their platform. This encouraged the deployment of poorly-tested systems that could easily be broken and sometimes threatened the security and privacy of users (Halderman and Felten 2006).

Only later did rights holders get support from the major companies producing computing hardware (e.g. Intel and Apple) and operating system software (Microsoft and Apple). These were the only companies that could introduce even vaguely effective digital 'locks'. But while these technology giants all now include TPMs in their core product lines, market developments – particularly the triumph of the unprotected MP3 music format, driven by ease of use and interoperability – have rendered them irrelevant in the music market. New high-definition restricted video formats such as HD-DVD, designed with much greater care and industry input than earlier TPMs, are still being broken (Waters 2007).

Rights holders with hardware divisions (such as Sony) had a strong incentive to push the use of protected formats best suited to their own players and recorders (Halderman and Felten 2006). But ironically, the market power that Apple gained with the success of the iTunes Music Store allowed the company to demand better access to unprotected content from the major recording labels. Very little music is now sold in TPM-protected formats, although Apple still applies it to TV programmes, films and applications in the iTunes store.

Infrastructure operators

In addition to statutory protection for Technological Protection Measures and Rights Management Information, rights holders have attempted to co-opt the operators of Internet infrastructure into copyright enforcement action. This has included lawsuits against the operators of peer-to-peer systems such as Napster, Grokster, Kazaa and The Pirate Bay; attempts to gain injunctions requiring Internet Service Providers to block access to infringing sites; and legislation to introduce 'notice and takedown' liability safe harbours.

The operators of the first peer-to-peer file-sharing systems were obvious targets of legal action for rights holders. In the first major case, *A&M Records v. Napster* (239 F.3d 1004), the US Court of Appeals for the Ninth Circuit found that Napster was liable for contributory and vicarious copyright infringement. Napster claimed its system was 'capable of substantial non-infringing use', a defence under the 1984 Supreme Court Betamax decision. But the court found that Napster, which indexed the files being shared by its users, could segregate and prevent infringing uses. By not doing so, it was guilty of contributory infringement, since it 'had actual knowledge that specific infringing material is available using its system' (p. 1022).

The trial court ordered Napster to prevent the trading of copyrighted works using its system. The company agreed to pay a $26m settlement to rights holders, and attempted to design a subscription service that would use audio fingerprinting software to block infringement. Because the company could not meet the 'near perfection' standard demanded by the trial judge, it instead shut down the network (Samuelson 2006). In the meantime, a judge blocked the sale of the company to Bertelsmann, which led to its bankruptcy (Evangelista 2002).

Later generations of peer-to-peer systems were designed so that operators could claim to be lacking such actual knowledge of infringement. Grokster, Streamcast and Sharman Networks (running KaZaa systems) and The Pirate Bay (running a search engine and tracker for the BitTorrent system) were still, however, found by courts to be 'inducing' (in the US), 'authorizing' (in Australia) or 'assisting' (in Sweden) infringement.

In the US, the Supreme Court found that 'one who distributes a device with the object of promoting its use to infringe copyright, as shown by clear expression or other affirmative steps taken to foster infringement, is liable for the resulting acts of infringement by third parties'. Grokster distributed an e-newsletter promoting users' ability to access popular copyright music, didn't use filtering tools, and profited from increased advertising revenue as infringement increased. The Court decided that the Betamax defence was not relevant given this active inducement (Ginsburg and Ricketson 2006, 5). Grokster then settled with the plaintiffs, stopping distribution of its software and support for the associated network. It agreed to pay up to $50m in damages, but lacked the resources to meet this promise (Leeds 2005).

The Australian Federal Court reached its decision because it found that Sharman had given ineffective warnings to users about infringement, but taken no technical measures to reduce it. Since Sharman's business model depended on maximizing sharing, it did 'authorize' infringement – an Australian and UK law concept developed to fill gaps in the general principles of joint tortfeasorship and vicarious liability (Ginsburg and Ricketson 2006, 10–11). Sharman Networks ultimately agreed to pay $100m to settle the case and became a legal download service (BBC 2006).

In Sweden, a district court found that Pirate Bay's monitoring of the location of tracker file components and search facility for torrents meant that the site operators were criminally liable for assisting users in making copyright works available (Carrier 2010). On appeal, the four defendants were sentenced to several months each in prison and fines totalling 46 million kronor.

In all of these cases, the on-going relationship between the P2P system operators and users was a key element in a finding of liability. Unlike the sale of tape-to-tape recorders, these organizations' relationships with their users continued post-sale, with upgrades and even help lines as well as the provision of server capabilities. This principle was included in Australia's Copyright (Digital Agenda) Amendment Act 2000, reflecting existing case law, since an ability to prevent infringement and a commercial benefit from an ongoing relationship are both relevant to liability (Ginsburg and Ricketson 2006, 14).

More generally, there was widespread concern as the Internet industry developed in the 1990s that intermediaries such as ISPs could become liable for hosting or carrying infringing material from third parties. Many legal systems include principles such as vicarious and contributory liability (for example, the US) and authorization of distribution (UK and Australia), which could have led to serious damages being awarded by courts (OECD 2011, 10–11). In response, many jurisdictions created 'safe harbours' that protected intermediaries against liability so long as they took specific actions to reduce infringement. These are often known as 'notice and takedown' regimes (created in Title II of the US Digital Millennium Copyright Act and articles 12–15 of the EU's E-Commerce Directive), since they protect service providers from liability until they have 'active knowledge' (usually supplied by notice from a rights holder) of infringing content. At this point providers must expeditiously remove or block access to such content. The DMCA further requires that providers will identify infringing customers in response to a subpoena, and terminate the accounts of repeat infringers. Both regimes specifically protect ISPs that merely transmit or temporarily cache data for their users; the DMCA also explicitly protects 'information location tools' such as directories and search engines.

One question that has remained somewhat open is the extent of these safe harbours, and particularly the scope of 'actual knowledge' of infringement. In reviewing US cases, Ginsburg (2008, 20–21) suggested that some courts had required an 'immense crimson banner' rather than a red flag identifying infringement. In *Perfect 10 v. CC Bill*, the Ninth Circuit found that the use of domain names such as 'illegal.net' and 'stolencelebritypics.com' did not in itself provide knowledge the featured photographs were infringing, since it could simply be an 'attempt to increase their salacious appeal' (488 F.3d 1104, 2007). However, the use of specific movie, TV programme or record titles might raise greater concern, especially if those titles had been repeatedly included in takedown notices or uploaded by a user that had previously posted infringing content.

A further question is how well these regimes will adapt to new Internet technologies and business models, in particular in the US, where the DMCA safe harbour is limited to specific types of intermediaries (Lemley 2007) and courts have so far refused to impose any obligation on intermediaries to use more sophisticated technology that might automatically identify infringing works, such as YouTube's ContentID system. Viacom's attempts to force YouTube to undertake such proactive monitoring have to date been decisively rejected by US courts (*Viacom Int'l Inc. v. YouTube, Inc.*, No 1:07-cv-02103-LLS (S.D.N.Y. Apr. 18, 2013)):

> If, as plaintiffs assert, neither side can determine the presence or absence of specific infringements because of the volume of material, that merely

> demonstrates the wisdom of the legislative requirement that it be the owner of the copyright, or his agent, who identifies the infringement by giving the service provider notice ... The system is entirely workable: in 2007 Viacom itself gave such notice to YouTube of infringements by some 100,000 videos, which were taken down by YouTube by the next business day.

The E-Commerce Directive explicitly prevents a general monitoring requirement being placed on intermediaries, or a requirement to 'seek facts or circumstances indicating illegality'. On this basis, as well as the rights to freedom of expression and privacy in the EU Charter of Fundamental Rights, the EU Court of Justice rejected attempts by a Belgian collecting society to obtain injunctions imposing filtering systems on an ISP (*Scarlet v. SABAM*, Case C-70/10) and a social networking site (*SABAM v. Netlog*, Case C-360/10). Samuelson (2006) suggested that *Grokster* was a Pyrrhic victory for rights holders, since it leaves open the possibility of P2P system operators avoiding liability for 'inducement' by operating the same technology, while avoiding making any statements encouraging its use for infringement.

That said, the DMCA and E-Commerce Directive both allow rights holders to take action for injunctive relief against intermediaries; and this is explicitly required by Article 8 of the Copyright Directive. A recent test case in the UK saw movie studios obtain a High Court order against the country's largest ISP, British Telecom, requiring BT to block customer access to a site, Newzbin2, that allowed users to search for indexes of infringing Usenet files. The judge agreed with the applicants that the order would be justified 'even if it only prevented access to Newzbin2 by a minority of users'. The judgment referred to a number of similar orders granted by courts in Denmark, Belgium, Italy, Sweden and Austria ([2011] EWHC 1981 (Ch) §96).

Injunctions have subsequently been extended to the other largest UK ISPs, and to additional sites such as The Pirate Bay. The latter stated in May 2013 that 8% of its traffic was now coming through proxy services that enable the circumvention of blocks, with one of these services receiving the most visits from countries attempting to block The Pirate Bay (TorrentFreak 2013).

More aggressive enforcement action was taken by New Zealand and US law enforcement agencies against the streaming 'cyberlocker' site Megaupload. The US Department of Justice indicted the operators of Megaupload on the basis that they had committed, conspired to, and aided and abetted infringement, as well as committing racketeering, money laundering and wire fraud (*U.S. v. Dotcom*, No. 1:12CR3, ECF Doc. 34, at 2–3 (E.D. Vir. Feb. 16, 2012)). New Zealand anti-terrorism police arrested the defendants, and they were, at the time of writing, on bail waiting for an extradition hearing. US, New Zealand and Hong Kong authorities also seized associated domain names, computer servers and other electronics, bank accounts and vehicles (Martin and Newhall 2013).

A New Zealand court has since ruled that the warrants used to raid residences were unlawful, and that the FBI acted illegally by cloning seized hard disks and sending them to the US. Remarkably, New Zealand's Prime Minister has declared that he was 'quite shocked' to discover that the Government Communications Security Bureau had illegally wiretapped the defendants; an investigation is underway (Saarinen 2012). Chief Executive Kim Dotcom has meanwhile launched a new encrypted locker service, Mega, which has no ability to monitor the content being shared by its users.

'Three Strikes'

A more recent rights holder strategy has been to lobby for the introduction by ISPs of 'three strikes' or 'graduated response' schemes, either by statute (Taiwan, France, South Korea) or through negotiations following legal action (Ireland) or threats of such (US). Under these schemes, ISPs send warnings to customers alleged by rights holders to have been detected committing copyright infringements. After several such warnings to an individual customer, ISPs take further action such as requiring customers to review an 'educational' website about infringement, reducing bandwidth, imposing download caps, blocking access to specific sites or peer-to-peer protocols, or terminating customer accounts (Yu 2010).

Irish ISP Eircom agreed to introduce such a scheme after legal action by four multinational record companies, who wanted to require Eircom to monitor all subscriber traffic for evidence of infringement. The Irish Data Protection Commissioner investigated this scheme after 300 users claimed they had wrongly been accused of infringement (McIntyre 2011), but took no further action.

The first version of France's so-called HADOPI three strikes law was found to be unconstitutional, because it allowed users to be disconnected by an administrative agency. The revised law, approved by the Constitutional Council, allowed for judicial ordering of disconnection. However, this provision was repealed following political controversy and doubts that the system was cost-effective (*Décret n° 2013-596 du 8 juillet 2013*). The UK's Digital Economy Act 2010 included powers for the government to introduce 'obligations to limit Internet access' and 'injunctions preventing access to locations on the Internet', although for now these are not to be introduced following the High Court's Newzbin2 injunction, which was issued under earlier legislation.

In its first nine months of operation the HADOPI agency received 18 million notifications from rights holders, identified around 900,000 alleged infringers, and sent 470,000 first warnings and 20,000 second warnings (Columbus 2011). As Patry observed of earlier takedown notices in the US, they are sent by outsourced companies 'who rely on automated processes, indirect evidence of infringement, but who have a direct financial incentive to send out as many notices as possible' (2009, 169). HADOPI has been so unpopular that the current French government has threatened to scrap the agency. Its budget has been cut from €11.8m in 2011 to €8.5m in 2013, with a review underway (Farivar 2012).

A recent review suggests that HADOPI has led to iTunes song and album sales increasing in France by 22.5% and 25% relative to a control group, suggesting increased annual revenues of €9.6m (Danaher et al. forthcoming). Interestingly, sales increased before any sanctions were imposed, likely as a consequence of increased public awareness following intense media discussion of the law.

Internet Service Providers were very successful in lobbying for notice and takedown regimes during the late 1990s, protecting them from broader liability for copyright infringement by their users. They have been less successful in resisting 'three strikes' regimes. The industry costs associated with these regimes can be significant. An Industry Canada study showed that sending a single notification of alleged infringement cost large ISPs C$11.73 and small ISPs C$32.73 (2006). The UK government estimated that the three-strikes regime in the Digital Economy Act would cost ISPs £290m–£500m (Department for Business 2009, 13).

This difference in political efficacy may reflect the fact that ISPs have more divided interests with three strikes regimes than over secondary liability protection. Peer-to-peer traffic is often the largest single category of data flowing over ISP networks, which can lead to significant congestion and bandwidth usage charges. Many ISPs are trying to develop businesses as premium content providers, and some are part of larger telecommunications companies that supply cable TV and other paid-for video content. Both of these provide incentives for ISPs to reduce customer copyright infringement, even where they are protected from secondary liability.

INSTITUTIONAL POLITICAL ECONOMY

Copyright policy has traditionally been settled in 'dark, smoky rooms' between major corporate stakeholders, facilitated by government (Litman 2001). This produced reasonably stable outcomes so long as these stakeholders were themselves the major target of regulation. Litman characterized this as a process in which publishers, movie studios, record companies and TV broadcasters 'jointly controlled the playing field', and that it was now 'nearly impossible to wrest that control away' (2009, 313). Upstart market entrants were the main innovators, breaking in using radical new technologies and often initially paying little attention to copyright concerns (Wu 2010).

This pattern has been reproduced in the last two decades. Individual developers and start-ups developed MP3 storage and peer-to-peer distribution systems that became extremely popular but were subject to extremely adverse legal decisions. They gained legitimacy when adopted by companies such as Apple and Spotify that were eventually able to overcome great resistance from the major record labels, revolutionizing the music market. Innovative business models squashed by rights holders during the 2000s, such as My.MP3.com (Ginsburg 2001, 1617), have been resurrected in forms that give less control to rights holders.

This has also been a problem at the international level. After becoming frustrated with the influence of developing countries at WIPO, major rights holders shifted the debate to the GATT trade discussions. Here they successfully pushed the process that led to the Agreement on Trade-Related Aspects of Intellectual Property Rights (TRIPS), created as part of the establishment of the World Trade Organization (Drahos and Braithwaite 2003, 108–147).

TRIPS contains a broad range of provisions concerning copyright term, scope and enforcement. However, it came too early to include anti-circumvention provisions protecting Technological Protection Measures (TPMs). These provisions were taken up enthusiastically in the US during the 1990s. President Clinton's Intellectual Property Working Group proposed a new Copyright Act chapter to ban circumvention devices or services, acknowledging that this 'provision will not eliminate the risk that protection systems will be defeated, but it will reduce it' (Intellectual Property Rights Working Group 1995, 177).

The chair of the working group, Bruce Lehman, was also the US representative to WIPO, and saw this route to get international agreement on these provisions as a way to bypass Congressional objections (Samuelson 1997). At WIPO, the US pushed detailed model provisions on circumvention devices or services. However, in the run-up to the finalization of the Internet treaties, the developing world – led by South Africa and with significant input from civil society groups – resisted this language. As a result, Articles 11 and 18 of the Copyright Treaty and the Performances and Phonographs Treaty, respectively, contain much more generic language (Ficsor 2002).

Further development of protection for TPMs has taken place in bilateral negotiations of Free Trade Agreements (FTAs) with less powerful developing-world nations, and in multilateral groupings of advanced economies. Broad anti-circumvention provisions have subsequently appeared in US Free Trade Agreements with a wide range of countries (Brown 2006) and more recently in EU Free Trade Agreements (such as art. 10.12 of the EU–South Korea FTA agreed in 2010). They are also included in article 27(5) of the Anti-Counterfeiting Trade Agreement (ACTA) agreed in 2010 by the US, EU, Japan, Canada, Australia, Mexico, Morocco, New Zealand, Korea, Singapore and Switzerland – although the European Parliament has since blocked EU implementation of ACTA.

During a decade of discussions at WIPO over a proposed broadcasting treaty, civil society and developing country representatives complained of exclusion from key decision-making processes, a lack of transparency, and even of public-interest briefing papers being thrown into a lavatory rubbish bin (Gross 2007). Most recently, negotiations over ACTA took place in secret for two years between rich-world economies, with negotiating texts circulated by the US government to industry representatives but withheld from civil society groups as 'classified in the interest of national security' (Love 2009).

Even academic copyright experts complain of being ignored. Amsterdam University's Institute for Information Law wrote to the European Commission in 2008, warning that two studies it carried out for the EC had been 'almost entirely ignored' in a way that 'seem[s] to reveal an intention to mislead the Council and the Parliament, as well as the citizens of the European Union' and that 'reinforces the suspicion, already widely held by the public at large, that its policies are less the product of a rational decision-making process than of lobbying by stakeholders' (Hugenholtz 2008, 2). Two independent reviews for the UK government felt the need to emphasize that policy should be based on evidence and not 'lobbynomics' (Gowers 2006; Hargreaves 2011a, 18). As Jessica Litman has written: 'the copyright war has been intensely polarizing. The conflict has been protracted and venomous. The middle ground seems to have disappeared' (2009, 317).

This is not only a theoretical problem. The exclusion of major stakeholders (users and bodies responsible for fundamental rights, and to a lesser extent ISPs and technology companies) from negotiations over Internet-era copyright reform has produced unbalanced and impractical outcomes, at the national and international level. And it has allowed rights holders to block innovative new business models that could have increased revenues for creators while better meeting consumer needs, but perhaps threatened short-term revenues (Patry 2009, 171–199). In some cases, large rights holders have merged with telecommunications providers (such as NBC Universal and Comcast). These conglomerates have the same types of incentives for copyright enforcement as Sony after it purchased Columbia Pictures Entertainment in 1989 (and later Metro-Goldwyn-Mayer).

Civil society groups have campaigned consistently for stronger user protections to be included in new copyright laws, with varying success. The Electronic Frontier Foundation (EFF) led a successful campaign for a DMCA provision that allows the Librarian of Congress to exempt certain classes of works from anti-circumvention provisions, where users are being 'adversely affected … in their ability to make noninfringing uses' (§1201(a)(1)(c)). As eastern European countries implemented EU law while becoming members, members of the European Digital Rights coalition campaigned for them to make maximum use of flexibilities in the Directive to protect user rights, particularly over anti-circumvention rules (Brown 2003). But generally civil society has been kept out of or side-lined in the negotiations leading to copyright law revisions (Litman 2009), and has had to battle for influence in legislatures and courts. At the OECD, the civil society information society advisory council refused to approve Internet policy making principles developed in a multi-stakeholder process, since they included liability for copyright infringement in some circumstances for intermediaries (Civil Society Information Society Advisory Committee 2011).

Governments and rights holders have found it extremely difficult to extend effective copyright regulation from a relatively small number of companies to the billions of individual users of the Internet. A UK government review found that downloading was the most common offence committed by 10–25 year olds, and that 63% of downloaders had full knowledge that it was illegal (Wilson et al. 2006). Courts simply cannot process quickly enough lawsuits against the vast numbers of unauthorized sharers of music, and mistakes and disproportionate punishments seen in such cases have provoked enough negative publicity for the recording industry to cause them to focus on more automated, code-based strategies.

However, these strategies have generally been blunt attempts to bludgeon users of copyright works into compliance, rather than nudge them towards legal use of works. The first has been to file an automated blizzard of lawsuits and takedown notices against individuals, using software to indicate the sharing of copyright works. This software has proven to be 'notoriously inaccurate, leading to lawsuits against people who don't even have computers or who are dead' (Patry 2009, 13) – and even against computer printers. Entirely original videos have been taken down from sites such as YouTube as infringing. It can be expensive and time-consuming for affected individuals to have suits dismissed, or works put back up, especially if a fair use or dealing defence is involved (Patry 2009, 13).

Motion Picture Association of America (MPAA) president Dan Clickman reportedly responded to these problems by stating: 'When you go trawling with a net, you catch a few dolphins' (Doctorow 2007). But such an industrial fishing approach is hardly appropriate where, in 'three-strikes' systems, inaccurate allegations could lead to individuals' disconnection from the Internet and all of the online services they rely on (Yu 2010, 139–167).

While courts have found against the suppliers of software and services enabling large-scale infringement via peer-to-peer file-sharing (most notably in the *Grokster* and *Pirate Bay* cases), this has not been enough to stop individual developers from continuing to supply such software. Indeed, P2P systems have continued to evolve in the face of legal action, removing the central points of failure that enabled Napster to be shut down by the Californian courts.

The legal protection of TPMs has done little to stop the unauthorized access to and sharing of protected works, but has had a negative impact on competition, interoperability, innovation and security research. TPMs can stop the design and production of compatible or interoperable devices that allow access to protected content, while blocking scientific research into the quality of security mechanisms. They stop users from exercising their fair use or dealing rights, since machines are unable to judge the sometimes-subtle factors that courts would assess in allowing these exceptions (Electronic Frontier Foundation 2010) – meaning, for example, that the World Blind Union is still finding that TPMs are preventing the visually impaired from using text-to-speech software to access protected e-books. They even sometimes threaten the safety of users' computers, and the Internet more broadly – to the point where officials from the US Department of Homeland Security warned that 'in the pursuit of protection of intellectual property, it's important not to defeat or undermine the security measures that people need to adopt in these days' (Mulligan and Perznowski 2007, 1771–1174).

Consumer resistance eventually resulted in the abandonment of TPM restrictions on most downloaded music, although these are still a central part of the strategy of the movie industry, where they may better fit consumer desires to rent rather than own films. It is not yet clear whether the greater efforts to provide consumer-friendly, legal services for online movie access will be sufficient to avoid the widespread infringement suffered by recorded music once sufficient bandwidth becomes widely available to consumers.

CONCLUSION

Large rights holders have spent nearly two decades trying to alter the nature of the Internet and the personal computer to fit business models relying on scarcity and the control of copies, with little success. After trying all of the alternatives, they are now finally beginning to work seriously with innovators developing technologies that can remunerate creators without taking control of individuals' PCs or Internet connections.

These alternatives include systems such as YouTube's content ID fingerprinting system, which allows rights holders to choose whether automatically-detected infringing videos should be investigated and taken down, or alternatively to share in the advertising revenues generated by such videos. 'All-you-can-eat' subscription services such as Spotify give paying customers streaming access to very large libraries of licensed musical works, coming close to the 'celestial jukebox' envisaged in the early days of the Internet. Major Chinese search engine Baidu has reached a deal with Universal, Warner and Sony to allow users access to a large catalogue of works on an advertising-supported basis (Xinhua 2011). And a review for the UK government has suggested the development of a 'digital copyright exchange', which would enable the automated trading of licences and reduce the cost of dispute resolution (Hargreaves 2011a, 28–35).

Many of these technologies could have been developed much earlier given cooperation from rights holders. The BBC has complained that it took 'nearly five years' to put together the licences required to launch its iPlayer service. Technology start-ups complain that licensing negotiations can take an inordinate amount of time, have inconsistent results, and sometimes result in threats of legal action (Hargreaves 2011a, 29). The US Register of Copyrights (2007) observed:

> licensors have rarely turned down the opportunity in the digital age to seek royalties, even where the basis for their request is weak at best. Online music companies rightly complain that they need certainty over what rights are implicated and what royalties are payable so that they can operate without fear of being sued for copyright infringement.

An international group of experts convened by the civil society group ARTICLE 19 has developed a set of principles on freedom of expression and copyright, building on international law, which could provide a starting point for a better balancing of these issues. They specifically recommend no user disconnection from Internet access on copyright grounds, strict limits on filtering and blocking, and minimization of intermediary liability, along with a number of other broader principles (ARTICLE 19 2012).

The evolution of digital copyright policy provides an abject lesson in the damage caused to innovation and the public interest of allowing self-interested industry groups to drive policy, excluding other stakeholders, and basing regulatory decisions on 'lobbynomics'. One can only hope that policy makers in future will think more carefully about ways to better incentivize cooperation between *all* stakeholders.

There are no technical options that will magically balance the range of interests implicated by copyright policy. Maximizing social welfare while incentivizing creativity and protecting human rights, all in the face of massive technological change, may not be easy, but there is a growing evidence base on which to base better attempts than we have seen so far.

ACKNOWLEDGEMENT

This chapter is an expanded and updated version of Chapter 4 of *Regulating Code* by Ian Brown and Chris Marsden (MIT Press 2013).

REFERENCES

Akdeniz, Y. (2011) *Freedom of Expression on the Internet: Study of Legal Provisions and Practices Related to Freedom of Expression, the Free Flow of Information and Media Pluralism on the Internet in OSCE Participating States*. Vienna: Office of the Representative on Freedom of the Media, Organization for Security and Co-operation in Europe. Available at www.osce.org/fom/80723

Anderson, N. (2009) '100 years of Big Content fearing technology – in its own words'. *Ars Technica*. Available at www.arstechnica.com/tech-policy/2009/10/100-years-of-big-content-fearing-technologyin-its-own-words/

ARTICLE 19. (2012) *Balancing the Right to Freedom of Expression and Intellectual Property Protection in the Digital Age*. Available at www.article19.org/data/

files/medialibrary/3716/13-04-25-share-BACKGROUND-PAPER.pdf

BBC, (2006) 'Kazaa site becomes legal service', 27 July 2006, at http://news.bbc.co.uk/1/hi/technology/5220406.stm

Birnhack, M. (2003) 'Acknowledging the conflict between copyright law and freedom of expression under the Human Rights Act'. *Entertainment Law Review*: 24.

Brown, I. (ed.) (2003) *Implementing the European Union Copyright Directive*. London: Foundation for Information Policy Research.

Brown, I. (2006) 'The evolution of anti-circumvention law'. *Law, Computers and Technology* 20(3): 239–260.

Carrier, Michael A. (2010) 'The Pirate Bay, Grokster, and Google'. *Journal of Intellectual Property Rights* 15(1): 7–18.

Cisco Systems. (2011) *Visual Networking Index (VNI) Global Mobile Data Traffic Forecast*. Available at www.cisco.com/en/US/solutions/collateral/ns341/ns525/ns537/ns705/ns827/white_paper_c11-520862.html

Civil Society Information Society Advisory Committee. (2011) *CSISAC Statement on OECD Communique on Internet Policy-making Principles*. Available at http://statewatch.org/news/2011/jun/internet-CSISAC-statement.pdf

Clark, C. (1996) 'The answer to the machine is in the machine'. In *The Future of Copyright in a Digital Environment*, ed. P.B. Hugenholtz, 139–148. The Hague: Kluwer Law International.

Columbus, S. (2011) 'France to disconnect first Internet users under three strikes regime'. *OpenNet Initiative blog* at https://www.opennet.net/blog/2011/07/france-disconnect-first-internet-users-under-three-strikes-regime

Craven, S.A., Wu, M., Liu, B., Stubblefield, A., Swartzlander, B., Wallach, D.S., Dean, D. and Felten, E.W. (2001) 'Reading between the lines: Lessons from the SDMI challenge'. *Proceedings of the 10th USENIX Security Symposium*, Washington DC (August).

Cunard, J.P., Hill, K. and Barlas, C. (2003) 'Current developments in the field of digital rights management'. Paper prepared for World Intellectual Property Organization Standing Committee on Copyright and Related Rights, Tenth Session.

Danaher, B, Smith, M.D., Telang, R. and Chen, S. (forthcoming) 'The effect of graduated response anti-piracy laws on music sales: Evidence from a natural experiment in France.' *Journal of Industrial Economics*. Available at http://papers.ssrn.com/sol3/papers.cfm?abstract_id=1989240

Department for Business. (2009) 'Digital Economy Bill impact assessments'. Available at http://webarchive.nationalarchives.gov.uk/+/interactive.bis.gov.uk/digitalbritain/wp-content/uploads/2009/11/DEB-Impact-Assessments.pdf

Doctorow, C. (2007) 'Online censorship hurts us all'. *The Guardian*, 2 October.

Drahos, P. and Braithwaite, J. (2003) *Information Feudalism: Who Owns the Knowledge Economy?* New York:: Free Press.

Electronic Frontier Foundation. (2010) 'Unintended consequences – twelve years under the DMCA'. Available at www.eff.org/wp/unintended-consequences-under-dmca

European Data Protection Supervisor (EDPS). (2010) 'Opinion on the current negotiations by the European Union of an Anti-Counterfeiting Trade Agreement (ACTA)'. O.J. C (147).

Evangelista, B. (2002) 'Napster runs out of lives – judge rules against sale'. *San Francisco Chronicle* (September). Available at www.sfgate.com/cgi-bin/article.cgi?file=/chronicle/archive/2002/09/04/BU138263.DTL

Farivar, C. (2012) 'French anti-P2P agency's funding to fall by 23 percent in 2013', *Ars Technica*, 24 October, at http://arstechnica.com/tech-policy/2012/10/french-anti-p2p-agencys-funding-to-fall-by-23-percent-in-2013/

Ficsor, M. (2002) *The Law of Copyright and the Internet: The 1996 WIPO Treaties, their Interpretation and Implementation*. Oxford: Oxford University Press. pp. 359–373.

Gasser, U. and Ernst, S. (2006) *EUCD Best Practice Guide: Implementing the EU Copyright Directive in the Digital Age*. Berkman Center Research Publication No. 2006–10.

Ginsburg, J.C. (2001) 'Copyright and control over new technologies of dissemination'. *Columbia Law Review* 101(7): 1613–1647.

Ginsburg, Jane C. (2008) 'Separating the Sony sheep from the Grokster goats: Reckoning the future business plans of copyright-dependent technology entrepreneurs'. *Arizona Law Review* 50: 577.

Ginsburg, J.C. and Ricketson, S. (2006) 'Inducers and authorisers: A comparison of the US Supreme Court's Grokster decision and the Australian Federal Court's Kazaa ruling'. *Media & Arts Law Review* 11(1).

Government Accountability Office. (GAO). (2010) *Observations on Efforts to Quantify the Economic*

Effects of Counterfeit and Pirated Goods. GAO-10-423.

Gowers, A. (2006) *Gowers Review of Intellectual Property.* London: The Stationery Office.

Griffiths, J. (2011) 'Criminal liability for intellectual property infringement in Europe – the role of fundamental rights'. In *Criminal Enforcement of Intellectual Property: A Blessing or a Curse,* ed. C. Geiger. Cheltenham: Edward Elgar.

Gross, R. (2007) 'World Intellectual Property Organisation, Global Information Society Watch'. Available at http://giswatch.org/institutional-overview/civil-society-participation/world-intellectualproperty-organisation-wipo

Halderman, J.A. and Felten, E. (2006) 'Lessons from the Sony CD DRM episode'. Proceedings of the USENIX Security Symposium (August).

Hargreaves, I. (2011a) *Digital Opportunity: A Review of Intellectual Property and Growth.* London: UK Intellectual Property Office.

Hargreaves, I. (2011b) *Data on the Prevalence and Impact of Piracy and Counterfeiting.* London: UK Intellectual Property Office.

Helfer, L.R. and Austin, G.W. (2011) *Human Rights and Intellectual Property: Mapping the Global Interface.* Cambridge, UK: Cambridge University Press.

Hugenholtz, P.B. (2000) 'Why the Copyright Directive is unimportant, and possibly invalid'. *European Intellectual Property Review* (11): 499–505.

Hugenholtz, P.B. (2002) 'Copyright and Freedom of Expression'. In *The Commodification of Information,* eds N. Elkin-Koren and N.W. Netanel. Amsterdam: Kluwer International.

Hugenholtz, P.B. (2008) 'Open letter concerning European Commission's "Intellectual Property Package"' (August). Available at www.ivir.nl/news/Open_Letter_EC.pdf

Hugenholtz, P.B. (2013) 'Fair use in Europe'. *Communications of the ACM* 56(5): 26–28.

Industry Canada. (2006) 'Assessing the economic impacts of copyright reform on Internet Service Providers'. Available at www.ic.gc.ca/eic/site/ippd-dppi.nsf/eng/ip01083.html

Intellectual Property Rights Working Group. (1995) *Report on National Information Infrastructure (NII) Task Force on Intellectual Property and the National Information Infrastructure.* September.

Jefferson, T. (1854) *Writings of Thomas Jefferson,* ed. H.A. Washington, Vol. 6. Washington, DC: Taylor and Maury.

Kerr, I. (2010) 'Digital Locks and the Automation of Virtue'. In *From 'Radical Extremism' to 'Balanced Copyright': Canadian Copyright and the Digital Agenda,* ed. Michael Geist. Toronto: Irwin Law.

La Rue, F. (2011) *Report of the Special Rapporteur on the promotion and protection of the right to freedom of opinion and expression,* Human Rights Council, Seventeenth Session Agenda item 3, A/HRC/17/27 of 17 May 2011. Available at www2.ohchr.org/english/bodies/hrcouncil/docs/17session/A.HRC.17.27_en.pdf

Leeds, J. (2005) 'Grokster calls it quits on sharing music files'. *New York Times,* 8 November. Available at www.nytimes.com/2005/11/08/technology/08grokster.html

Lemley, M.A. (2007) 'Rationalizing ISP Safe Harbors'. *Journal of Telecommunications and High Technology Law* 6: 101.

Lesk, M. (2003) 'Chicken Little and the recorded music crisis'. *IEEE Spectrum* 1(5): 73–75.

Lessig, L. (2008) 'Remix: Making Art and Commerce Thrive in the Hybrid Economy'. London: Bloomsbury Academic.

Litman, J. (2001) *Digital Copyright: Protecting Intellectual Property on the Internet.* New York: Prometheus Books.

Litman, J. (2009) 'The politics of intellectual property'. *Cardozo Arts and Entertainment Law Journal* 27: 313–320.

Love, J. (2009) 'Obama administration rules texts of new IPR agreements are state secrets'. *Huffington Post,* March.

Martin, B.C, and Newhall, J.R. (2013) 'Criminal copyright enforcement against filesharing services'. *North Carolina Journal of Law and Technology* 15(1): 101–152.

McIntyre, T.J. (2011) 'Data Protection Commissioner investigating Eircom's "three strikes" system'. Available at www.tjmcintyre.com/2011/06/300-false-accusations-data-protection.html

Mulligan, D. and Perznowski, A. (2007) 'The magnificence of the disaster: Reconstructing the Sony Rootkit Incident'. *Berkeley Technology Law Journal.* 22: 1157.

OECD. (2011) 'Communiqué on principles for Internet policy-making'. OECD High Level Meeting on the Internet Economy (June). Available at www.oecd.org/dataoecd/40/21/48289796.pdf

Patry, W. (2009) *Moral Panics and the Copyright Wars.* New York: Oxford University Press.

Patry, W. (2012) *How to Fix Copyright.* New York: Oxford University Press.

Saarinen, J. (2012) 'New Zealand Intel Agency investigated for unlawful spying on Kim Dotcom'. *Wired Threat Level,* 24 September.

Samuelson, P. (1997) 'The U.S. digital agenda at WIPO'. *Virginia Journal of International Law* 37: 369.

Samuelson, P. (2001) 'Anticircumvention rules: Threat to science'. *Science* 293 (5537): 2028–2031.

Samuelson, P. (2006) 'Three reactions to MGM v. Grokster'. *Michigan Telecommunications Technology Law Review* 13.

Synovate. (2010) 'Summary: Music Matters/Synovate/ MidemNet Global Survey'.

TorrentFreak. (2013) *At Least 8% of All Pirate Bay Traffic Now Provided By Proxy Services.* Available at http://torrentfreak.com/at-least-8-of-all-pirate-bay-traffic-now-provided-by-proxy-services-130505/

UN Human Rights Committee. (2011) *General Comment No. 34*, CCPR/C/GC/34, 12 September 2011. Available at www2.ohchr.org/english/bodies/hrc/docs/gc34.pdf

US Register of Copyrights. (2007) *Statement of Marybeth Peters before the Subcommittee on Courts, the Internet, and Intellectual Property.* Committee of the Judiciary, United States House of Representatives, 110th Congress, 1st Session.

Waters, D. (2007) 'DRM group vows to fight bloggers'. *BBC News* (May). Available at http://news.bbc.co.uk/1/hi/technology/6623331.stm

Wilson, D., Patterson, A., Powell, G. and Hembury, R. (2006) *Fraud and Technology Crimes: Findings from the 2003/04 British Crime Survey, the 2004 Offending, Crime and Justice Survey and Administrative Sources.* Home Office Online Report 09/06.

Wu, T. (2010) *The Master Switch: The Rise and Fall of Digital Empires.* New York: Knopf.

Xinhua. (2011) 'Baidu makes deal with world music giants' (July). Available at http://news.xinhuanet.com/english2010/china/2011-07/19/c_13995900.htm

Yu, P.K. (2010) 'The graduated response'. *Florida Law Review* 62: 1373–1430.

31

Music, Technology and Copyright: The Makings and Shakings of a Global Industry

Andrew Kirton

INTRODUCTION

Nowhere has debate about copyright been so publically animated than it has in relation to music since the end of the twentieth century. The rapid development and adoption of technologies enabling the free sharing of music online sparked a debate that has seen copyright laws, their articulation, and their enforcement in particular, receiving an unprecedented level of attention. In this context, critiques of copyright law and the socio-economic arrangements they support have proliferated. And yet, despite some significant challenges, established legal frameworks and the socio-economic arrangements and activities they support, have shown remarkable resilience. Despite all the initial hype regarding the impending demise of copyright and the emergence of alternative socio-economic arrangements for the production and circulation of music, copyright law remains in rude health. In fact, given recent legislative actions across the globe, we should recognize that copyright has become a more prominent feature of the music industry than ever before. This chapter offers an account of the relationship between the music industry and copyright law that may help us further understand and explain these recent developments.

In accounting for recent developments in copyright law this chapter draws particular attention to the place of technology. One cannot fully understand the relationship between copyright law and music without also understanding the place of technology. On the one hand, the development of the music industry represents the commercial appropriation of developing technical capacities to capture, store, reproduce and circulate music. On the other hand, wider appropriations of those same technical capacities have frequently presented challenges to established commercial interests and practices. In the twenty-first century more than ever, the seemingly paradoxical role of technological development has been clear to see. Established commercial actors have been working hard to exploit the opportunities that new digital and networking technologies have presented in terms of the marketing, promotion, distribution and retail of music online. At the same time these same technologies have afforded practices (namely unauthorized file-sharing) that directly challenge established commercial systems and logics. It is in relation to this particular dynamic that the development of copyright law in relation to music can be fully understood.

The production and circulation of music as an industry is of course heavily dependent upon copyright laws. The legal recognition of music as a form of intellectual property (hereafter IP) enables the effective commoditization and commercial exploitation of music as a commodity. In affording exclusive rights of ownership, copyright laws provide a legitimate means of restricting the practices of others. In this sense, copyright laws provide a means of dealing with the challenge of those technologically afforded practices that threaten existing commercial arrangements. The account developed here will acknowledge that copyright law constantly lags behind technological developments, however, and they have often appeared inadequate in allowing for the restriction of emergent and conflicting/competing appropriations of new technical capacities. In an attempt to establish and maintain preferable (profitable) socio-economic arrangements in the face of changing technological environments, commercial actors have throughout the history of the music industry frequently called upon legislators to extend or enhance the scope of copyright laws and their enforcement. The history of copyright law in this particular context subsequently presents itself as one in which we may observe the gradual extension and expansion of rights in the interests of established commercial actors and economic interests, often at the expense of equally legitimate others.

In brief overview, this chapter ultimately offers a critical account and analysis of the role and place of copyright in relation to music. It highlights the apparent power of commercial and corporate actors in inducing and directing legislative change, and the way in which copyright laws have as a result moved increasingly away from principles of rewarding creators, to protecting established economic interests in the form of corporate investors and exploiters of IP. Modern copyright law underpins a set of socio-economic arrangements that see the creators of musical IP economically exploited in ways that are actually detrimental to the creative production that copyright laws are often said to incentivize. It will be acknowledged in this sense that recent extensions of copyright and its enforcement in particular convey no obvious benefit to the original creators of IP or to society at large in terms of creating any additional wealth, improving access to or circulation of IP, or further incentivizing IP production. In fact, recent legislative actions may be said to have potentially detrimental implications for technological innovation, rival sectors of capital accumulation, principles of privacy, freedom of speech, access to valuable informational goods, and the development of alternative socio-economic arrangements that may better reflect the desires and interests of those beyond a small group of established corporate actors.

The chapter begins by outlining the general role of both technological development and copyright laws in relation to the evolution of the music industry along the lines discussed above. This first part outlines a historical account that illustrates the way in which the development of copyright law has closely followed changes in the technological environment. It focuses on early developments in this context, from developments in printing to the recording of sound. Changes in laws are furthermore shown to be the result of pressure placed on legislators by commercial actors, who in the face of a changing technological environment seek to protect established and preferable (profitable) socio-economic arrangements. The second half of the chapter focuses on events following the 'digitization' and subsequent emergence of music online. These more recent developments suggest the continuation of a well-established trend. The changing technological environment brings both opportunities and difficulties for existing commercial interests and actors. These actors have responded in their usual way, striving to exploit the opportunities presented by technical development via the articulation of exclusive rights afforded by existing copyright laws, and placing pressure on legislators to further enhance the scope of those existing laws and their enforcement in order to restrict what others may do. Legislators' response to this pressure also appears somewhat typical – the legislative environment has been modified in ways that appear to protect the interests of established commercial actors, allowing existing socio-economic arrangements to be maintained at all costs.

UNDERSTANDING THE PLACE OF TECHNOLOGY AND COPYRIGHT IN THE DEVELOPMENT OF THE MUSIC INDUSTRY

'Music is, by its nature, non-material. It can be heard but not held. It lasts only as long as it plays. It is not something that can, in any direct way, be owned' (Frith, 2001: 26). The question of how music became 'commoditized' offers a useful way of introducing and explaining the crucial roles of both technological development and copyright in the development of the modern music industry.

Technological Development and the Music Industry

The development of the modern-day music industry has in a very clear sense been dependent upon the development of what Simon Frith (2001) describes as technological capacities to 'store' and 'retrieve' music. To elaborate on Frith's conceptualization, technical capacities to 'store' music in such a way as to allow its subsequent 'retrieval' have throughout history proven to have a certain commercial potential. As a highly valued cultural 'good' or 'product', people have paid money to access these musical 'stores' and 'retrieve' the music held within them, whether that 'store' be an actual person (e.g. a musician), or some 'functional artefact' (Gendron, 1986) such as a written score, Compact Disc or digital file. As this suggests, people themselves may be thought of as the most fundamental of such musical 'stores' (Frith, 2001). People 'store' music in their memories and bodies, and it is 'retrieved' via physical performance. People were also the first kind of musical store to be commercially exploited of course; 'a musician would retrieve – perform – music in return for payment, whether from secular or religious patrons, from communities or passing individuals (Frith, 2001: 28). The professional musician in this sense has existed for many thousands of years, and the live performance of music remains an extremely important activity in today's broader music industry.[1] Other important aspects of the music industry have been established following the appropriation of other important developments in the technical means to store, distribute and retrieve music, however.

The most important technological developments in this regard have of course been those in printing and sound recording, which in turn gave rise to a print music publishing industry and a recorded music industry (as discussed further below). Today's music industry as a result represents something akin to a 'networked economy' (Leyshon et al., 2005) consisting of a range of (commercial and non-commercial) actors, institutions and operations all connected via the flow of both product and capital. We might distinguish between the live music industry, the music publishing industry, and the recorded music industry today, but each sector is connected, and they perform complementary functions in terms of accumulating capital through the production and circulation of music. The production and circulation of music for the purposes of capital accumulation has been far from unproblematic, however.

Firstly, demand for such products remains largely unpredictable and unstable and the music industry as such represents something of a 'risky business', though certain practices have been developed in order to off-set the high proportion of commercial failures (as discussed further below). A second and much more practical difficulty stems from the fact that the appropriation of new technical capacities has often had unanticipated, unintended and extremely disruptive consequences for established socio-economic arrangements. The development of a recorded music industry in the twentieth century had unintended and unpredicted consequences for other pre-established sectors of the industry including live performers, sheet music publishers and instrument makers, for instance (Martin, 1995). More pertinent of course is the way in which music fans and consumers have often appropriated technologies. In this regard we often see the emergence of practices that fundamentally conflict with, undermine and contradict established socio-economic relations for the production and circulation of music. Most obviously, music fans and consumers have used available technologies to freely reproduce recorded music, a practice evident in the 'home-taping' phenomenon of the 1980s and the on-going 'file-sharing' movement of the twentieth century. In both cases, the free reproduction and circulation of recorded music has been construed by the established recording industry as a major threat to established profit accumulation strategies and activities.

For those who seek to profit from the production and circulation of music as a commodity, the widespread availability of capacities to reproduce and recirculate music presents a major challenge that must be addressed if a viable market is to be maintained. The logic behind these concerns is, of course, that people are less likely to pay to access something they can access freely elsewhere. The empirical reality and validity of such a concern has become the subject of much debate within the discourse surrounding online music file-sharing in particular.[2] This challenge is not a new one, however. Music industry operations have frequently faced this kind of technologically afforded disruption. But, whilst it is true that technological development has often brought disruption to the established socio-economic arrangements of the music industry, it is also true that the music industry has displayed a remarkable resilience in the face of these technologically afforded challenges. This is where an account of the music industry must necessarily turn to the concept of intellectual property and to the place of copyright laws.

Intellectual Property Rights and the Music Industry

The modern music industry is clearly reliant upon copyright laws. Indeed, as Frith and Marshall (2004) encourage us to recognize, the music industry is a rights industry before it is any other kind of industry. Copyright, they assert, 'is the currency in which all sectors of the industry trade' (Frith and Marshall, 2004: 2). Crucially, the legal recognition of music as a form of intellectual property subject to associated rights of ownership is the mechanism through which established socio-economic arrangements for the production and circulation of music can be protected against the technologically afforded challenges outlined above.

'Intellectual property' (IP) may be understood as a general name given to those products of some creative or innovative thought. Understood as a form of property, the products of creative work come to be treated like any other form of private property, in which one would expect to benefit from certain exclusive rights of 'ownership'. Intellectual property *rights* (IPRs) are precisely those rights that one would expect to have over the creations of the mind if they were indeed to be classed as a form of private property. In other words, IPRs conventionally express property ownership's legal benefits. These rights are enshrined in the patent, trademark and copyright laws of many modern states and indeed all those states that wish to participate in international trade must incorporate minimum levels of legal IPRs under the 1994 Trade-Related Aspects of Intellectual Property Rights (TRIPS) agreement and various other international conventions/agreements. The principle piece of legislation enshrining IPRs in the UK, for instance, the jurisdiction from which many of the examples in this chapter are taken, is the Copyright, Designs and Patents Act 1988 (c.48), though this act has been amended and extended a number of times since it came into force in 1989 in order to keep up with international conventions and most often following lobbying pressure from commercial actors both nationally and internationally.

The key function of IP and its establishment in law has in a very clear sense been to allow the products of creative work to be brought into the marketplace as a form of private property (May, 2006). As May and Sell highlight, the legal recognition of IP conventionally affords its producers rights which are best understood as *economic* rights: (1) the right to charge rent for use; (2) the right to receive financial compensation for loss or damage; and (3) the right to demand payment for transfer to another party (2004: 7). In relation to copyright laws specifically, Martin Kretschmer (2000) suggests that *four exclusive* rights are actually afforded: (1) the exclusive right to publish the work; (2) the exclusive right to reproduce and distribute the work; (3) the exclusive right to perform the work in public; and (4) the exclusive right to authorize another party to do these things (adapted from Kretschmer, 2000). The use of the term 'exclusive' is crucial here of course. Under copyright laws no one but the copyright holder has the legal right to do the things outlined by Kretschmer[3] without their permission. Gaining permission of course typically involves financial compensation. The copyright holder may bring legal action against anyone who does the things outlined by Kretschmer without their permission and/or (typically) without paying financial compensation. Kretschmer and Kawohl (2004) suggest that all such property rights can thus be defined negatively as the 'right to exclude'. To use Simon Frith's (1987) terminology, they are the rights to say 'no'. In other words, copyright laws allow copyright holders to say what may and may not be done with their property, even when a *copy* of that property has been legitimately purchased.

Copyright laws afford rights to restrict practice then. The function of these legally endorsed rights to restrict is to manufacture a form of scarcity in goods that are in practice freely reproducible, especially once fixed or stored in some functional artefact (which is precisely the point at which music becomes subject to copyright). In other words, copyright laws, in providing a means for practices of reproduction to be restricted, establish conditions in which a 'pay to access' market for music can be established and exist. The historical development of the music industry clearly illustrates the way in which copyright law, its interpretation and/or enforcement has been continually modified in order to sustain this market in the face of technologically afforded challenges. It is to this history that the account and analysis now turns.

EARLY DEVELOPMENTS IN THE MUSIC INDUSTRY

What follows is an attempt to provide an account of the development of the music industry which further illustrates the inextricably intertwined roles of both technological development and copyright in relation to music. Ultimately, the account highlights that in this particular context copyright laws clearly develop in line with established commercial interests in the production and circulation of music as a commodity. It is suggested that the interests driving the evolution of copyright in relation to music do not necessarily correlate with those of artists whom copyright laws are often said to protect. Nor do they necessarily benefit society at large. Unfortunately, the account offered here must necessarily omit much detail – it does not chart every twist and turn in the development of the music industry, nor does it fully convey the long and complex history of copyright law. These narratives can be found expertly written elsewhere. Rather, the account offered here seeks to develop a narrative that *succinctly* illustrates the way in which copyright law develops in relation to the music industry – as a response to commercial interests in establishing and protecting profit accumulation practices from technologically afforded disruption. It does so by highlighting two significant examples. The first relates to the development and commercial appropriation of technical capacities to print music, and the subsequent application of copyright law to music. The second relates to the development and appropriation of technical capacities to record music, and the subsequent extension of copyright law in relation to the new commercial opportunities and challenges this presented.

Printing Technology and Copyright

Popular music scholar, Reebe Garofalo (1999), quips that when Gutenberg invented the printing press around 1450 he actually laid the foundations for the modern music industry. The basic process of producing and marketing music was established in England by at least the late Middle Ages (Lloyd, 1975). But with the invention of the printing press, mass (re)production of musical scores became possible as a commercial activity. Skilled musicians were still required to retrieve the music stored within the musical score via performance, and thus people would most often need to pay for the services of a musician to access music stored in a printed score. Thus, the invention and subsequent appropriation of the printing press for the commercial production and distribution of sheet music led to a growth in several interrelated markets: (1) that for live performance of the music stored within scores; (2) that for the printed music itself; and (3) that for the instruments which were required in order to retrieve the music stored in print.

Crucially, the growth of an industry based on the mass production of printed music saw an interest in the concept of copyright developing. Basic proto-copyright mechanisms evolved during the fifteenth century. As the reprinting and selling of popular books became commonplace, the granting of crown/sovereign 'privileges' emerged as a means of solving the 'non-scarcity' problem. These privileges granted individual printers and publishers the exclusive rights to print and sell particular books for a limited period of time (Kretschmer and Kawohl, 2004). It is understood that some musical scores were protected via the granting of individual privileges over the course of the sixteenth and seventeenth centuries, but that most composers would have simply handed over manuscripts in return for a small 'one-off' fee from publishers (Deazley, 2008). There was little concern for the rights of the author in this early period, highlighting the notion that those mechanisms out of which copyright laws emerged were themselves developed to protect and incentivise *investors* in IP, not creators themselves. Manuscripts were often sold between publishers without the involvement, consideration, or financial compensating of authors, according to Kretschmer and Kawohl (2004).

The first formal copyright law enacted in Britain, the Statute of Anne 1709, came into force in 1710 for the protection of 'Books and other Writings'. The so-called 'Act of Anne' provided publishers with 'the sole right and liberty of printing' for 14 years upon registration of a manuscript in Stationers' Hall, London (Kretschmer, 2000: 198). Initially music was not thought to be protected under the terms of the 'Act of Anne', and it appears that music publishers did little in the way of joining the rest of the book trade in lobbying for statutory protection. Deazley (2008) suggests that music publishers had felt statutory protection unnecessary or even undesirable in the early eighteenth century. Firstly, most musical works would not remain in demand for more than a few years at most. Secondly, dominance in the market at this time relied not upon copyright but rather upon the quick and cheap reproduction of material originally printed by others. Copyright was not simply irrelevant then, but was perceived to be a potential obstacle in establishing an otherwise financially lucrative business (Deazley, 2008). In 1777, however, J.C. Bach and C.F. Abel famously won a case against a London publisher for the unauthorized publication of a J.S. Bach lesson, thus establishing that printed music was protected under the terms of the 1710 Act. This case reflected what by then had become a growing concern on the part of music publishers to secure the same kinds of protections that the book printing and publishing industry had been enjoying since 1710. In the context of rapidly developing and diffusing printing technology, the economic value of such protection was apparently clear to see. Through this case, music was pushed, for the first time, firmly into the realm of copyright by those seeking to exploit it commercially.

The next significant development came with The Copyright Amendment Act of 1842. Like the preceding 1814 Act it extended the term of copyright further. What was new was that it recognized a performing right in musical compositions for the first time. This would grant the copyright holder the exclusive right to authorize and receive financial compensation for not just the reproduction of a score, but also the public performance of the music stored within. There was no institutional mechanism for monitoring such musical activity at that time, however. For any individual composer or publisher, it was impossible to know when and where a composition to which one exclusively held the copyright was being performed. It was not until the Copyright Act of 1911 and the setting up of the Performing Rights Society (PRS), as a collection body able to monitor usage and recover and distribute performance 'royalties' that performing rights became fully acknowledged in the UK (Kretschmer, 2000). This represented the extensions of rights to cover a wider range of commercial uses of music, effectively allowing their monetization and incorporation as a revenue stream into the emerging 'music industry'.

It was the publisher and not the author who remained the primary beneficiary of the emerging copyright system of course. Individual creators still lacked access to the technical means of reproduction and distribution of their work that might allow them to benefit financially from the products of their creative effort and work. Instead, they could only sell their products to those who did have access to such capacities in return for a fee. In doing so, publishers effectively purchased the rights that were now afforded to authors of work with their purchasing of compositions. Thus, there is little sense of the developing copyright system conveying any notion of incentive or reward for creative effort on the part of the original producers of IP. The emerging framework simply provided investors in IP with a means of benefiting financially from the technical capacities to reproduce musical works stored in scores.

Sound Recording and the Music Industry

The next major development in technical capacities for the storage and retrieval of music was sound recording. Following the invention and development of Thomas Edison's phonograph and Emile Berlinger's Gramophone at the end of the nineteenth century, actual sound could now be stored in functional artefacts for later retrieval or 'playback'. Recorded music was entirely different to sheet music in terms of what it gave people. With records, music could now be 'retrieved' more freely at home, but as a matter of consumption rather than technique, skill or work. This had some interesting cultural implications of course, but crucial for the current discussion, is the notion that with the advent of sound recording and its embodiment in functional artefacts, music itself – actual sound – became even more object-like, a 'thing' that could be individually possessed or owned (Eisenberg, 1988).

The immediate commercial implication of recording technology was the development of an entirely new industry sector – the manufacture and retail of recordings. By 1910 the recording industry had established itself in most countries throughout the world (Martin, 1995). Sales of recorded music accelerated in the years after the First World War, but the 1920s and 1930s brought a decline and then a virtual collapse, mainly due to broader economic conditions. The business did revive, but in a different form, with major recording companies linked to film and radio interests. At the start of the post-war period the basic structure and organization for the modern recording industry was in place (Frith, 1988). Records soon eclipsed sheet music as the dominant medium for storing and disseminating music as a commodity. Record companies thus displaced publishing houses as the dominant institutions of commercial music production (Garofalo, 1999). By the 1960s recorded music sales surpassed the gross revenues of all other forms of entertainment for the first time (Petersen and Berger, 1975). The commercial exploitation of recorded music also challenged the role of live music, with various conflicts of interest emerging around the use of recorded music in live music venues.[4]

Copyright was first applied to sound recordings in the UK under the Copyright Act of 1911. Recording companies apparently agreed at this point, that the purchaser of a gramophone record acquired the right to play that sound recording in public. By the end of the 1920s, however, a drastic decline in record sales was being observed. This decline coincided with a worldwide economic recession but the recording industry pinned the decline in recorded music sales specifically on increased public performance in the form of radio airplay. This led to a major rethink on the part of recording companies (Frith, 1987). In 1934 a court upheld the Gramophone Company's claim that *only* the manufacturer of the record as the copyright holder (not the author of the music embodied in those artefacts, nor the owner of the artefact itself), had the right to play that recording in public (Frith, 1987). In winning this right, the recording industry not only managed to prevent a practice that they saw as economically threatening (the public broadcast of recorded music) but simultaneously establish a new revenue stream – that for the licensing of such public performances of recordings. Phonographic Performance Limited (PPL) was set up to administer these new rights and appropriate the income generated. The newly formed International Federation of the Phonograph Industry (IFPI) began lobbying governments around the world for the amendment of domestic laws along similar lines (McFarlane, 1980). The public performance of recorded music remains restricted under the terms of copyright law today of course, and its broadcast via radio and TV or performance in shops, bars and restaurants, represents a major revenue stream for the recording industry as producers of recorded music (Hull, 2004).

The next major technological challenge to the recording industry's profit accumulation strategies, and around which further debates about copyright ensued, came after a sharp decline in the value of recorded music sales in 1978–1983 (Frith, 1987). Again this period coincided with economic recession, but the recording industry apparently construed the rising sale of blank cassette tapes and portable cassette players as directly responsible for the decline. Cassette technology had been introduced during the 1960s following developments in magnetic recording techniques, and had become the industry's preferred means of product dissemination by the mid-1970s (Garofalo, 1999). But precisely because of the format's superiority in terms of usability it became increasingly popular among consumers for using recorded music in ways unintended by rights holders. The IFPI's response to the apparent threat of this particular technological development was to embark on an international campaign for a levy to be placed on blank tape and/or recording equipment sales on behalf of the recording industry (*The Case for a Home-taping Royalty*, 1984). Though there was scant concrete evidence to support their claims, the IFPI asserted that there was little doubt that 'private copying is seriously affecting the profitability of the phonograph industries' (IFPI; cited by Frith, 1987: 60). The result of this campaign was the Audio Home Recording Act 1992 in the US, which introduced said royalty.

The reaction and response to home-taping illustrates a number of important things. Firstly, it is broadly illustrative of the way in which established commercial actors have responded to the challenges that technological developments often bring. Rather than adapt to the new technological environment in a way that benefits anyone, they tend to respond by lobbying for legislation that they hope will protect established socio-economic relations proven to be inefficient and outmoded by the very fact that they are being challenged by practice. Secondly, the fact that the IFPI were successful in their campaign to induce a legislative response illustrates the apparent power of these interests in directing legislative action. Thirdly, this particular example illustrates the way in which legislative action lags behind technological innovation and practice. By the time the Audio Home Recording Act came into force, technology had already moved on, and people were already using home computers to copy CDs, and of course it wouldn't be long before people were using the Internet to circulate music freely. It is to these more recent developments in the relationship between technological development, the music industry and copyright law that the discussion now turns.

'DIGITIZATION' AND THE RISE OF MUSIC ONLINE

The previous sections illustrated the way in which copyright law has evolved in line with economic interests in the production and circulation of music. In particular, it highlighted the way in which copyright laws have developed in response to the changing technological environment, and the challenges that this often presents to established socio-economic arrangements. The latest of these technological developments is 'digitization'.[5] The term digitization refers to the process of converting information into a digital format; a process whereby information is represented numerically in a series of 1s and 0s, rendering it amenable to processing by computers. The 'digitization' of recorded sound has in the longer term presented the recording industry with a major problem. Profit-making in the recording industry depends largely on the production of artificial scarcity (most crucially via the articulation of intellectual property rights as discussed above). The accuracy and ease with which recordings embodied in digital files can be copied and circulated presents a major threat to such artificial scarcity and its preserving through the enforcement of copyright laws, however.

Digitization has not been 'all bad' for the recording industry. After arriving on the market in 1982, the appropriation of the Compact Disc (CD) format brought about the biggest boom in recorded music sales ever seen by the recording industry. Leyshon et al. (2005) refer to the subsequent 15 or so years of recorded music sales growth (in terms of units shipped, turnover and profit) as a 'golden era' in the history of the recording industry. The introduction of the CD persuaded music consumers to replace their vinyl and cassette collections, and by the mid-1990s the CD had become the predominant format for recorded music and thus the primary source of sales revenue for the recording industry. In 1999 CDs accounted for 2.5 billion or around 66% of the 3.8 billion 'units' shipped by the recording industry, with cassettes accounting for 0.9 billion and LPs 0.02 billion (IFPI, 2001). CDs also enabled recording companies to exploit their own back catalogues via the reissuing of old recordings in the new format. As Robert Sandall (2007a) points out, as a digital format, the CD contained the seeds of its own destruction, however:

> Anybody who owned a CD could indeed use it as record companies had traditionally used master tapes: to clone thousands more, and quickly, using kit available on any high street. And at home, CD burning hardware on computers made it simple to produce copies in seconds. (Sandall, 2007a: 30)

There is a familiar story here of unexpected consequences: the industry's adoption of the digital CD format in the early 1980s, and its successful campaign to persuade consumers to shift from vinyl to CD, can be seen to have lifted the recording industry out of a period of economic decline. But in storing music as bits of information, record companies were also undermining the *material* distinction between production and reproduction on which copyright law rests (Frith and Marshall, 2004: 3). The industry had apparently been warned about the dangers of what amounted to giving away master tapes, but they were too concerned with immediate profits to debate the potential problems of this new technical capacity (Sandall, 2007a).

Using freely available software, digital content could be 'ripped' from CDs and converted into an MP3[6] file for storage on any computer. With the release of CD 'burners' to the public in 1998, people could now transfer MP3 files from their computers onto recordable CDs (CD-Rs), and a black economy in counterfeit CDs soon proliferated. The IFPI claim that the global traffic in pirated disks was worth US$4.5 billion in 2005, with pirate CD sales outnumbering legitimate sales in a total of 30 national markets (IFPI, 2006). The IFPI, funded by the recording industry, pumped vast amounts of money into combatting physical piracy during this period. But rapidly expanding Internet access and developments in digital computing and networking technology were to bring a new challenge. The vast technological assemblage of digital devices and networks that was already taking shape at the end of the 1990s meant that once embodied in a digital file, the recording could be freely reproduced any number of times without loss of quality, and, crucially for the recording industry, without engaging in any associated financial transaction.

By the end of the 1990s, people were uploading large collections of MP3 files to the Internet where anyone with Internet access could in turn make a copy of their own, for free. The proliferation and spread of music online, plus the difficulties in trying to find a particular recording, inspired North American college student, Shawn Fanning, to create the now famous *Napster*, a software application that enabled people to search for and obtain music online by remotely accessing each other's hard drives. Soon after its launch in 1999, millions of *Napster* users were sharing billions of copyrighted sound recordings embodied in digital files over the Internet.[7] The illegal or illicit status of file-sharing today means it is impossible to derive any truly accurate measure of the practice, which probably leads to some gross inaccuracies. In highlighting the difficulties in measuring file-sharing, economist Stan Liebowitz (2006) asserts that while file-sharing is carried out through computers – devices capable of measuring such activities – the desired data has yet to live up to its full promise. The sources currently available give extremely varied accounts of the extent of file-sharing and studies have generally suffered from one or more serious limitations.

Following Bakker, Hesmondhalgh (2009) acknowledges how a number of distinct but interrelated technological developments have been important in the rise and proliferation of online music file-sharing. He summarizes four important developments as follows:

1. The development of the MP3 compression standard which allows digital audio files to be reduced in size making them easier to store and circulate.
2. The spread of high-bandwidth Internet connections.
3. The introduction of multi-media computers with increased storage capacity, soundcards, CD-Roms and speakers.
4. The development of relatively easy to use software that allows users to rip music from CDs and convert them into various digital audio file formats, and software that allows users to search for, locate, download and upload digital audio files via the Internet (Hesmondhalgh, 2009: 59).

Hesmondhalgh (2009) acknowledges that these innovations were primarily driven by the telecommunications and software industries, which in relation to the recording industry he describes as representing rival sectors of economic capital accumulation.

Whilst the recording and other content industries might have liked restrictions to have been placed upon the development of some of these technological capacities, the industries behind those developments were able to resist those measures. What is particularly interesting about recent legislative actions is the way in which the interests of recording companies have been prioritized above the interests of these other sectors of capital, even though they are in fact more valuable in terms of economic activity.

The Nature of File-sharing

A definitive definition of file-sharing is difficult to find. Authors and commentators tend to discuss the phenomenon and associated issues without explicitly or clearly defining the practice or thinking too much about what distinguishes this particular practice from other forms or methods of information sharing (which is what file-sharing is a form of in essence). One of the difficulties associated with defining file-sharing is that, as a technologically mediated and in some cases 'illicit' practice (depending on precisely what is being shared), the technical characteristics of file-sharing are constantly evolving. Definitions of file-sharing are as such in danger of becoming quickly outdated. The Internet was being used to share music files from the mid-1990s via Internet Relay Chat (IRC), email and personal web spaces. What is referred to as 'file-sharing' generally refers to the process of sharing digital files via specifically designed computer programmes or applications. In essence, as Michael Einhorn describes, file-sharing applications 'provide to web users the ability to find and download files from other computer hard drives by typing an appropriate title, word or phrase' (2004: 79). 'Downloading' refers to the act of obtaining such files via file-sharing networks, whereas 'uploading' refers to the act of making these files available for others to download. Though the specific nature and design of file-sharing applications have evolved over time, simply put, file-sharing applications allow anyone with access to the Internet to search for and freely copy recorded music.

In his book, *Peer to Peer and the Music Industry: The Criminalization of Sharing*, Matthew David defines file-sharing as 'the circulation of compressed digital computer files over the Internet using an array of location and exchange software' (2010: 2). This definition remains suitably broad so as to encompass the range of forms that file-sharing has taken to date, whilst also providing a clear indication of what 'file-sharing' actually is. In essence, as David's definition indicates, file-sharing logically refers to the *sharing* of *files*. As David's definition further indicates, however, the term file-sharing is typically used to refer to the sharing of *digital* files *online* specifically. In other words, the term file-sharing is not typically used to refer to the sharing of any other kind of 'file', or the sharing of files – even *digital* files – offline. Individuals may share digital files offline via the circulation of physical artefacts such as CDs, memory sticks and portable hard drives for instance, but this would not normally be referred to as file-sharing, despite the fact that it simply represents a different method of transferring digital content from one device to another.

The term file-sharing is also used to refer to the transfer of files in the absence of an economic transaction. This latter distinction, between transfers that take place as part of an economic transaction and those that do not, draws attention to perhaps the most important characteristics of file-sharing. The term *sharing* is used precisely because the activity to which it refers is said to constitute an act of 'sharing'. Within the networks of sharing that file-sharing applications afford, a kind of 'gift economy' (Leyshon, 2003) is often said to be at work, where reciprocation is understood to be an important aspect of 'appropriate' behaviour.[8] As Hesmondhalgh notes, a certain ethos or ethic is often espoused by users of these networks, which resembles 'a version of freedom located in an anti-commercial anarchism of the "property is theft" variety' (Slater, 2000, cited by Hesmondhalgh, 2009: 60). As Hesmondhalgh asserts though, we must not lose sight of the fact that many of these file-sharing networks operate as commercial enterprises supported by advertising and often backed by venture capital, further illustrating the fact that the conflict surrounding file-sharing is not simply one involving a tension between commercial and anti-commercial interests, but one that also involves tensions between competing sectors of economic capital (Hesmondhalgh, 2009). In fact, it might even be the case that some of these file-sharing operations generate more revenue than traditional recording companies themselves, further adding weight to the argument that existing copyright laws, which allow these sites to be shut down at the request of recoding companies might actually be stifling further economic development.

We must also bear in mind that the sharing of information is something of an anthropological given (music itself is, after all, fundamentally a communicative endeavour and *social* practice). The sharing of information embodied in digital files via electronic networks simply represents a logical continuation and extension of a fundamental human practice in this sense (which is what makes any attempt to restrict it so philosophically troubling for some perhaps). There is a tendency to talk about anything associated with technological development as 'new' – a promotional discourse usually instigated by the developers of those technologies. Quite often however, it's the technological means that's new, and not the practice itself. This is certainly the case with music file-sharing. Whilst the specific technologically mediated forms which the sharing of information takes today are 'new', the fundamental practice of sharing information is not. The notion that file-sharing simply represents the continuation and evolution of such a fundamental social practice and good is perhaps one that makes attempts to curb it in the interests of capital accumulation so abhorrent for some.

The Recording Industry's Response to the Emergence of Online Music File-sharing

Recording companies have been asserting that file-sharing is the primary cause of an economic downturn being experienced since the turn of the century. Leading companies in the sector began posting disastrous results and projections from 2000 onwards. EMI, for example, posted a financial loss £54.4 million in the six months leading up to 2001 (Leyshon et al., 2005). David Sandall (2007a) also highlights how the period since 2000 has seen some drastic cost-cutting exercises among major recording companies including significant culls of staff and artists. The closure of several well-known high street music retailers would appear to be further evidence of the decline in sales of recorded music embodied in physical artefacts since the turn of the century.[9]

In 2006, the UK recording industry trade body, the British Phonograph Industry (BPI), asserted that 'the overwhelming majority of reputable third party research shows that illegal file-sharing has been a key factor in the recording industry's 22% worldwide sales decline between 1999 and 2004' (BPI, 2006: 5). They also provided a substantial list of studies and reports whose conclusions and findings support this claim. The apparent links between the dramatic decline in the value of global music sales and the emergence of file-sharing naturally led to a proliferation in econometric studies attempting to measure and demonstrate the relationship (Liebowitz, 2006). The majority of this evidence seemed to support the conclusion that file-sharing has brought significant economic harm to the recording industry. Liebowitz (2006: 24) declares that, 'the birth of file-sharing and the very large decline in CD sales that immediately followed is a powerful piece of evidence on its own'. The logic behind such a claim is simply that a significant proportion of people have stopped buying music now they can now get it quickly and easily for free via file-sharing networks.

This seems like a logical argument, but there may be other factors at work also, and it is certainly a zero-sum argument.

As Leyshon et al. (2005) acknowledge there is evidence to suggest that the rise of file-sharing cannot be held solely responsible for the depth and severity of the apparent decline in recorded music sales. Both Laing (2004) and Sanghera (2002) suggest entirely alternative explanations for the apparent decline in people's expenditure on recorded music. One argument suggests that competition for consumer spending on entertainment has intensified greatly with the launch of DVDs, new video game systems, and so on. These two authors also argue that the mid-1990s represented the end of the 'CD replacement cycle' that gave rise to a 15-year boom in recorded music sales (Laing, 2004: 89). Laing also highlights the obvious implications of general economic circumstances and points to a global economic stagnation from the turn of the century. He draws on Snell's (2001) conclusion that 'historical trends confirm a strong correlation ... between music sales and consumer confidence' (Snell, 2001, cited by Laing, 2004: 89). The extent of *physical* piracy which has proliferated since the 1990s must also be taken into account when considering the reduction in legitimate music sales since the turn of the century of course.

Despite the value of these alternative explanations for the decline in the value of global music sales, they have paled into insignificance next to the weight of evidence that the music industry has gathered (via commissioned research) to show the direct link between the emergence and proliferation of file-sharing on the one hand and a significant decline in the economic value of global music sales on the other. There have also been moves to forcefully debunk some of the alternative arguments. In his review of these alternate arguments, Stan Liebowitz (2006) systematically dismisses each of them. He asserts in his review that all of the studies of which he is aware, except one, find that file-sharing brings about some significant degree of harm to copyright owners. The recording industry as represented by the IFPI is keenly aware of this supporting evidence, as demonstrated by their regular reference to it in publications and on their website.

Whether file-sharing is directly responsible for the decline in revenues and sales or not, the phenomenon has provoked a severe reaction and response within the global recording industry. This has involved large-scale litigation and public awareness campaigns, and intense lobbying of governments/legislators. The major global recording companies apparently felt so threatened by *Napster* as the first major file-sharing application, that they joined forces to sue it out of service. Found to be falling foul of US copyright law and faced with lawsuits filed on behalf of major recording companies, the original *Napster* was shut down in 2001. Since then, recording companies and their representative organizations have been lobbying hard for the extension and enhancement of copyright laws and enforcement in the context of the new technological environment.

Even before the emergence of *Napster* and the proliferation of other file-sharing systems, content corporations including music corporations were moving to make sure that the Internet could be successfully exploited in commercial terms. As Hesmondhalgh (2009) discusses, the first major response to the rise of the Internet came with the World Intellectual Property Organization's Geneva conference in 1996 where signatories agreed to update their national laws to allow rights holders to extend their rights in relation to the changing technological environment. The result was the Digital Millennium Copyright Act (DMCA) in the USA in 1998, and the EU *Copyright Directive of 2001.* The UK Government implemented this directive via The Copyright and Related Rights Regulations 2003 as a statutory instrument. Crucially, these acts contained clauses which made it illegal to counter the Digital Rights Management (DRM) systems that were being developed and used by content industries to protect their products from unauthorized reproduction. As Hesmondhalgh acknowledges, such an extension of copyright law into the digital terrain was to be expected, and was an early sign that 'the digital environment was being fruitfully presented by copyright industries, such as the recording industry, as a threat, one against which legislation was needed to protect them' (2009: 66).

After successfully seeing the original file-sharing network *Napster* closed down in 2001, the recording industry and their respective trade associations continued to pursue litigation against the developers and providers of file-sharing applications including *Grokster*, *Morpheus*, *OiNK*, and more recently and famously *The Pirate Bay*. These seeming 'successes' on the part of the recording industry can be seen as an indication of the 'continuing legal and regulatory power of the oligopoly of corporations that dominate global music circulation and rights ownership' (Hesmondhalgh, 2009: 61). More controversially, recording companies have also pursued litigation against individual *users* of such file-sharing applications. In the UK context, the BPI began a rolling programme of legal action against individual uploaders in 2004. By May 2005, around 90 cases against individuals had been launched with 60 settlements by July of the same year. By May 2006, more than 100 cases against individuals had been settled without the need for court action, with an average settlement of over £2,000.

Elsewhere, led by the Recording Industry Association of America (RIAA) and backed up by US copyright law including the newly implemented Digital Millennium Copyright Act 1998 (DMCA), record companies in America were most active in this respect, bringing cases against thousands of individuals. The RIAA were the first to announce that individuals would face legal action in 2003. Again, most cases of copyright infringement brought against individuals were settled out of court, one of the most famous such cases being that brought against a 12-year-old girl from New York, which was settled for $2,000. The first case brought against an individual file-sharer to reach trial represented an important 'victory' for music corporations. In 2007 a Native-American woman was found guilty of copyright infringement and ordered to pay $222,000 damages for making 24 songs available for others to download via the *Kazaa* file-sharing application – a cost of $9,250 per song. These various litigation campaigns proved hugely controversial, of course, representing what Hesmondhalgh describes as a 'public relations disaster' for the companies and corporations involved (2009: 61). Recording companies have continued to pursue litigation against individual file-sharers regardless, but much of their collective efforts have been put into securing further enhancements of existing copyright laws and their enforcement.

In the face of the continued proliferation of file-sharing, music corporations have continued to exert pressure on legislators to further enhance the scope and enforcement of existing copyright laws. In the UK the result of this intense lobbying pressure has been the passing of the Digital Economy Act 2010 (DEA), which formally affords recording companies the right to have individuals suspected of sharing their property online temporarily disconnected from the Internet.[10] At the time of writing, the Stop Online Piracy Act (SOPA) and the Protect IP Act (PIPA), which would likewise seek to enhance enforcement of copyright law in the online environment, have recently been making their way through legislative processes in the US (though unsuccessfully to date). Again, the recording industry, this time represented by its US trade body, the RIAA, has been heavily involved in the formulation of measures contained in these acts and in lobbying for approval for these Acts. On an international scale, the EU, US, and many other countries have signed up to the Anti-Counterfeiting Trade Agreement (ACTA), a multinational treaty intended to establish an international framework for the combatting of online copyright infringement, among other things.

International treaties that introduce requirements for minimum levels of protection in all signatory states have a long history of course, from the 1886 Berne Convention for the Protection of Literary and Artistic Works through the World Trade Organization's 1994 treaty on Trade-Related Aspects of Intellectual Property Rights (TRIPS) to the 1996 WIPO Copyright Treaty. As highlighted earlier, this latter international treaty was crucial in efforts to bring all Member States into line on issues of IP protection in the digital environment. Activity at the international level, in terms of the development of unilateral agreements of course reflects the fact that the modern industry is itself global and the corporations that constitute it are multinational in nature. Their markets extend beyond national jurisdictions and thus they have an interest in the legal frameworks that would support their operations around the world. Furthermore of course, file-sharing itself, as a practice, crosses national boarders and boundaries. The enforcement of copyright laws thus requires international cooperation. The enhancement of existing laws and their enforcement that corporations have been lobbying for in the new technological environment are deserving of some further critical attention.

CRITIQUING RECENT DEVELOPMENTS IN COPYRIGHT LAW IN RELATION TO MUSIC

Recent extensions of copyright laws and enhancement of their enforcement, as typified by the UK's Digital Economy Act for instance, are for most critical analysts and observers somewhat problematic – for various reasons. As Frith suggests, to apply copyright law is to ultimately and in principle restrict usage – the copyright owners' basic power is to prevent their work being used in certain ways; 'The history of copyright law is the history of the steady extension of legal clauses on what can't be done' (1987: 71). Kretschmer and Kawohl concur that in the current legal environment, 'access to property becomes conditional on the discretionary decision of the owner. Property entails the right to say no' (2004: 41). As laws which place restrictions on what people may and may not do, and which afford rights to certain groups to have the practices of others restricted, these legislative actions clearly need careful and thorough legitimation. Traditionally, copyright and related laws have often been justified in terms of incentivizing the creators of IP through the creation of a secure legal environment in which economic rewards can be realized. The incentivization of creators is in turn often said to have broader social benefits. As May and Sell discuss, it is often assumed or asserted that:

> Without IPRs there would be little stimulus for innovation. Why would anyone work toward a new invention who would be unable to profit from its social deployment? Therefore, not only does intellectual property reward intellectual effort, it actually stimulates activities that have a social value and most important, it serves to support the social good of progress. Underlying this argument is a clear perception of what drives human endeavour; individual reward. Only by encouraging and rewarding the individual creator or inventor (with property and therefore market related benefits) can any society ensure that it will continue to develop important and socially valuable innovations, which will serve to make society as a whole more efficient. (May and Sell, 2006: 22)

As commercial and corporate actors have continued to call for changes to copyright laws, they have often attempted to justify these calls in the above sense. Frith highlights how in their campaign against home-taping, the IFPI argued its case in both general and particular terms:

> In general, the loss of revenue has implications for future investment, employment, talent development and so on; in particular, people are getting pleasure from music makers who are getting nothing back in return. The whole point of copyright is to ensure that the author of the work, its absolute owner, is duly rewarded for other people's enjoyment of that work – without such rewards there would be no economic incentive to make musical or literary works in the first place ... The question that is evaded by IFPI is the precise relationship between the author's copyright (as creator of the work) and the record company's copyright (as

> owner of the material on which the work is recorded). (Frith, 1987: 61)

The same is true when it comes to recent calls for enhancements to copyright laws, where representatives of the recording and broader music industry have essentially argued that the death of the established recording industry equates to the death of music in society. These claims, whilst perhaps containing some internal logic, lack any real empirical validity whatsoever. As well as the obviously problematic nature of the assumption that individual financial reward is what drives creativity, those creators who would seek financial reward are rarely in a position to do so themselves. Creators invariably need the financial help of others today – namely recording companies. Enlisting the help of recording companies, however, usually means the creator ceding both extensive creative control and the exclusive rights of ownership afforded to them via copyright law. In return for their investment in creative production, recording companies and publishers acquire the rights of ownership over what the creator produces in terms of sound recordings. In the pursuit of profit maximization, recording companies actively seek to minimise returns to creators, in most cases leaving artists in debt to their record labels. Critiques of these economic relations have proliferated since the 1990s – most paint a clear picture of the way in which corporate investors are able to exploit artists via the utilization of a legal framework often said to reward creators.[11]

The dominant copyright paradigm, as it exists today, does not clearly function to the economic benefit of creators, at least not in the case of music production and circulation. It is not clear how enhancing copyright law enforcement to protect a system that endebts more than it pays music creators will further incentivize creativity. As Kretschmer (2000) concludes, the chief beneficiaries of copyright law and its continual enhancement are commercial investors in creators, not creators themselves. Copyright laws are now being extended and their enforcement enhanced without any real consideration of the interests of those for whom copyright laws were supposedly developed to protect. Rather, it seems, these laws are now being rationalized and legitimated in reference to the much broader economic visions and strategies of governments. Thus, as Hesmondhalgh asserts, 'the original stated purpose of copyright, to stimulate creativity within society, is being sidelined in favour of the protection of corporate interests' (2009: 67).

In terms of the supposed public and social benefits of the copyright system, copyright laws and the restrictions they place on what may and may not legally be done with the products of creativity, should in principle balance a public interest in access with the interests of producers in financial reward. As has been asserted above however, the history of copyright law is one of frequent extensions of this right to say 'no' and restrict usage, to the benefit of investors in musical IP rather than the creators. In placing further restrictions on new technologically afforded cultural practices, recent developments in copyright law and its enforcement ultimately represent a continuation of this theme. What's more, these measures create no *additional* wealth for investors in IP – they only seek to function to protect pre-established socio-economic arrangements and activities from technologically afforded disruption, which in the digital network environment of direct marketing look increasingly outmoded. The measures that many recent Acts contain clearly raise concerns about privacy and surveillance of Internet users. The placing of restrictions on what may and may not be done with developing technological capacities may actually hinder innovation and further economic development in terms of the development of alternative socio-economic arrangements for the production and circulation of musical and creative IP more broadly.

Finally, the fact that the unauthorized circulation of IP online continues to proliferate points towards some the practical difficulties that copyright holders will continue to face in terms of materially restricting these practices. As increasing amounts of time and money are spent trying to combat the practice, equal amounts of time, effort and money are being spent on developing new, more efficient, and less easily detected and restricted ways of practising the activity.[12] Copyright laws will continue to lag behind the constantly changing and evolving practices of content sharing in this sense. Sharing technologies necessarily become increasingly efficient and effective, thus increasing their appeal. One might ask in this case, whether the time, effort and resources being spent on finding ways to stop people sharing what, according to copyright laws, does not belong to them, might be better spent looking for and developing alternative legal and economic frameworks which better represent the interests of creators and consumers of IP.

In thinking further about the ways in which these various agreements and acts have been justified and might be explained, we should further point out how they reflect not just the lobbying power of multinational corporations in influencing legislative frameworks, but the power of these interests within a particular economic-ideological context. Recent developments in copyright law and their enforcement clearly relate to the pervasiveness of information society and knowledge based economy (KBE) discourses and thinking. In the UK, for instance, recording companies were clearly able to exploit the (1997–2010) New Labour government's expressed concern to secure the UK's competiveness in the global KBE by securing enhancements to copyright law enforcement measures that would protect those industries whose health was seen as central to that overarching goal. This receptiveness did not dissipate with the 2010 change of government. The question of whether the enhanced enforcement of copyright laws in the online environment was of any consequence to the creators of IP, or society at large, became marginalized as an apparently irrelevant issue in this context.

Even more interesting in this context perhaps, is the privileging of recording companies, as one sector of economic production, over others, particularly Internet Service Providers (ISPs). Many of the recent developments in copyright law (proposed and actual) effectively impose obligations on ISPs which they have understandably been extremely reluctant to accept. As corporations with interests in protecting their customers, ISPs made robust cases against proposed measures to release information on subscribers that could lead to the termination of their accounts. The interests of ISPs were subjugated to those of corporate rights holders. This is surprising given that the telecommunications sector, of which ISPs are a part, is, even more so than the creative industries, an industry that governments construe as being central to securing success in the global information economy. Still, such centrality in innovation and growth may also explain why de jure subjection is being bypassed de facto.

CONCLUDING DISCUSSION

This chapter has offered a critical account of the development of copyright law and its enforcement in relation to music and the music industry. In accounting for the development of copyright laws in this context it has highlighted the intertwined roles of technological development and copyright law. The recorded music industry in particular was one of the first industries to experience the threat of digital technology (Frith and Marshall, 2004) and has been at the forefront of calls and attempts to extend and enhance the scope and enforcement of intellectual property rights in the face of changing technological environments. As Hesmondhalgh (2009) asserts, those seeking to make money from the production and circulation of music have always had to fight to enforce the boundary between what they define as 'legitimate' forms of music consumption – those involving financial compensation, monetary exchange, and flows of income – and those they wish to define as illegitimate – those practices which do not involve financial compensation for reproduction and distribution, such as online music file-sharing. People often wish to appropriate new technical capacities in ways that others would rather they did not, and when it comes to music – a good of immense cultural and social value that plays such a prominent part in people's everyday lives – this tension has been particularly visible. As Simon Frith asserted in relation to the music industry's attempts to restrict people's uses of technology and music in the 1980s, 'they [consumers] own records/radios/cassette players, so why can't they do what they like with them? Copy a record for a friend? Tape the best tracks from a John Peel show?' (1987: 60). At the turn of the century, Théberge suggested that:

> It is important to recognise that what is at stake in the various controversies surrounding the MP3 file format is not simply the issue of copyright *per se*. The case of Napster needs to be understood as a clash between radically different value systems – between a particular notion of what constitutes a legitimate form of social interaction between fans, on the one hand, and the commercial needs of the industry, on the other. (Théberge, 2001: 21)

Whilst it is in the interests of music corporations to appropriate the Internet and other technologies for the purposes of profit accumulation and maximization, music fans and consumers, as well as creators of course, may appropriate these same technical capacities, according to conflicting interests, to share music, thus bypassing what the industry defines as legitimate practices and what statutes define as legal. The established socio-economic arrangements and practices of the music industry have frequently been disrupted in this sense, as discussed throughout this chapter.

Whilst it is true that technological developments have often brought disruption to established music industry arrangements, Garofalo (2001: 94) reminds us that it is also true that the recording industry in particular has 'generally ended up benefiting financially from every technological innovation of the twentieth century'. In this sense, the recording and broader music industry has been well-supported by copyright law-making and enforcement. When it comes to music, as one particular form of IP, one can clearly see how the development of copyright laws and their enforcement prioritize and privilege established interests in producing and circulating music for the purposes of profit accumulation. The enhancement of existing copyright laws and their enforcement in the years since the world wide web emerged represents a continuation of a well-established and long-observed pattern in this sense.

Of particular concern is the way in which the development of copyright laws in this context appears to be systematically moving away from principles of encouraging creativity and innovation, to the principle of protecting established socio-economic arrangements and interests, even when those arrangements can be seen to be problematic and relatively unproductive. Copyright law has, over the last decade increasingly come to be legitimated and rationalized in terms of protecting corporate rights holders from economic harm and as a means of securing national economic performance, rather than in terms of incentivizing individual creative production for the good of society, as was initially intended. What's more of course is that recent developments convey no obvious benefit, economic or otherwise, to the original creators of IP or to society at large. They do not create any additional wealth, improve access to, or circulation of, IP, or further incentivize IP production. In fact, recent legislative actions may be said to have potentially detrimental implications for further technological innovation, rival sectors of capital accumulation, principles of privacy, freedom of speech, access to valuable informational goods and the development of alternative socio-economic and legal arrangements that better reflect the desires and interests of music creators and the public at large.

However, we should finally acknowledge the level of resistance to recent developments in copyright law that have been witnessed. On the one hand, we may point to the fact that despite the continued efforts of the recording industry to restrict practice, file-sharing and variants thereof continue to proliferate, and will by most accounts continue to do so. Despite legal threats and technical locks, people have continued to share what according to existing laws is not theirs to share at all. This has exposed what Frith and Marshall (2004) described as a radical disjuncture between the law and the social practices it supposedly governs. They summarized the situation a decade ago as follows:

> Copyright law has an effect on how we act but it does not determine our actions. When we consider the law (any law), we do not just obediently follow it, but bend it and, significantly, follow the law as we think it should be. If copyright law is counter intuitive, if it contradicts widely held beliefs about the avaricious nature of the recording industry, then it is unlikely to be followed. Many musicians and most music consumers seemingly do not believe in existing copyright laws, and so rights holders are trying to make us believe in them through legal threats and technological locks. The outcome of this struggle cannot be predicted; it depends upon the particular power relations involved. And as Toynbee rightly concludes, wishful thinking apart, to promote copyright change requires us to acknowledge that there are powerful actors out there with vested interests in strengthening the existing regime. (Frith and Marshall, 2004: 213)

The powerful actors to which Frith and Marshall allude are clear to see in the history of copyright law and the music industry. 'Victory' on the part of the established music industry is not a foregone conclusion. 'Victory' for the recording industry would be if people stopped appropriating technologies for the purposes of sharing music and stopped innovating in this regard. File-sharing continues to evolve and proliferate however. Furthermore, alternative socio-economic arrangements, for the production and circulation of music *are* developing.[13] Whether this growing critique and dissent will be effective in forcing governments to reconsider the enhancement of copyright laws in the interests of corporations is unclear. Critical voices *are* being effectively marginalized in legislative processes currently, but the growing mass of people simply ignoring copyright law in this context cannot be simply ignored. If attempts to restrict practice through the enforcement of these laws, continues to be as unsuccessful as it has been, then those laws and their enforcement clearly need to be re-evaluated.

NOTES

1 The live performance of music can actually be said to have become more important as a source of income today than it has been for some time. In the context of the free online circulation recorded music sales, live performance represents a relatively secure product to be exploited economically. Furthermore, live performance may boost sales of merchandise (and potentially recorded music). Furthermore, the wide circulation of recorded music can in turn boost interest in live performance. Of course, those artists signed to recording companies are increasingly expected to sign contracts ('360 degree contracts') that see revenues from these wider activities flowing back to the recording company and not the artist.

2 This is a complex debate. There is a great deal of conflicting argument and evidence. Whilst it is relatively clear that recording industry revenues have been declining since the turn of the century, that this is due *entirely* to file-sharing is not. Furthermore, it may be legitimately argued that the wide and free circulation of recorded music online is actually beneficial to other revenue streams, such as that generated through live performance for instance.

3 What exactly may and may not be done legally, and for what purpose, represents a key point of contention in debates surrounding copyright of course, especially in the context of continually evolving technical capacities to reproduce and share music, as discussed further below.

4 The setting up of the Musicians Union in the UK provides a good example of how the emergence of new music industry sectors following the appropriation of new technical capacities disrupts established socio-economic arrangements on the one hand, and also of the way in which musicians and performers have been pushed into a position where it is necessary to protect their interests from the commercial exploiters of musical IP. See 'The Musicians' Union: A Social History' at www.muhistory.com for a discussion of the history of the MU and Kirton (2010) for an analysis of the role of such organizations in relation to debates about file-sharing in particular.

5 Hesmondhalgh (2009), along with others, uses the term 'digitalization'. I have proposed using the term 'digitization' instead since the term 'digitalization' is used elsewhere to refer to the administration of 'digitalis' for the treatment of certain heart conditions. Confusion is unlikely among readers of this work of course!

6 MP3 is shorthand for Moving Pictures Experts Group (MPEG) 1 Audio Layer 3, an audio compression and encoding format that uses an algorithm to reduce the amount of data required to represent an audio recording digitally by a rate of about 12:1, consequently reducing the size of the original file dramatically (Anestopoulou, 2001: 320).

7 See John Alderman's *Sonic Boom: Napster, P2P and the Future of Music* (2001) for a comprehensive commentary on these early developments in online file-sharing.

8 Economist Stan Liebowitz (2006) argues that the term 'file-sharing' is actually somewhat of a 'misnomer' since participants hardly 'share' music in the true sense of the word. Rather it should be called 'anonymous file copying' since that reflects what actually occurs, he argues.

9 In the UK, recorded music retailer Music Zone went into administration in January 2007. This was followed by the closure of 105 Fopp stores across the UK in June 2007. HMV announced significant profit warnings in 2007. Richard Branson also dumped Virgin Megastores in 2007.

10 See Kirton (2010) for a full analysis of the formulation of the UK Digital Economy Act and its progress through the legislative process.

11 See Alibini's (1993), Love's (2000), or the FMC (2001) critique of recording industry practices in this regard.

12 The development of file-sharing as a technologically mediated practice provides an interesting case study in the way that the criminalization of culturally prevalent activities may not only act to displace those practices spatially but may also act as a catalyst for creativity, adaptation, resourcefulness and ingenuity among those criminalized. Note how as one file-sharing network is shut down users simply shift to another; how the providers of file-sharing services have sought to (re)locate their operations within certain spatio-legal territories; and how the technical characteristics of file-sharing have evolved as methods for identifying and restricting it have developed.

13 We must be cautious about celebrating and/or embracing alternatives too quickly, as some of these alternatives have begun to display equally troubling dimensions as economically oriented arrangements involving inequitable divisions of labour and rewards.

REFERENCES

Albini, S. (1993) 'The Problem with Music' [online]. Available at: http://www.thebaffler.com/past/problem_with_music [last accessed, 1 July 2014].

Alderman, J. (2001) *Sonic Boom: Napster, P2P and the Future of Music*. London: Fourth Estate.

Anestopoulou, M. (2001) 'Challenging Intellectual Property Law in the Internet: An Overview of the Legal Implications of the MP3 Technology'. *Information & Communications Technology Law* 10(3), pp. 319–337.

Bakker, P. (2005) 'File-Sharing – Fight, Ignore or Compete: Paid Download Services vs. P2P-Networks'. *Telematics and Informatics* 22(1–2), pp. 41–55.

BPI. (2006) *Sound Recording Copyright Term: The Benefit to the UK of Extending Term – Five Reasons to Support British Music: One of the UK's Most Valuable Industries*. London: BPI Ltd.

Copyright Designs and Patents Act 1988 (c.48). London: HMSO.

David, M. (2009) *Peer to Peer and the Music Industry: The Criminalization of Sharing*. London: Sage.

Deazley, R. (2008) 'Commentary on Bach v. Longman (1777)', in: Bently, L. and Kretschmer, M. (eds) *Primary Sources on Copyright (1450–1900)* [online]. Available at: http://copy.law.cam.ac.uk/cam/tools/request/showRecord?id=commentary_uk_1777 [last accessed 27 November 2013].

Digital Economy Act 2010 (c.24). London: HMSO.

Ehrlich, D. (1985) *The Music Profession in Britain since the Eighteenth Century*. Oxford: Oxford University Press.

Einhorn, M.A. (2004) *Media, Technology and Copyright*. Cheltenham: Edward Elgar.

Eisenberg, E. (1988) *The Recording Angel: Music, Records and Culture from Aristotle to Zappa*. London: Picador.

FMC. (2001) *Major Label Contract Clause Critique* [online]. Available at: http://futureofmusic.org/article/article/major-label-contract-clause-critique [last accessed, 1 July 2014].

Frith, S. (1987) 'Copyright and the Music Business', *Popular Music* 7(1), pp. 57–75.

Frith, S. (1988) *Facing the Music*. New York: Pantheon.

Frith, S. (2001) 'The Popular Music Industry', in: Frith, S. Straw, W. and Street, J. (eds) *The Cambridge Companion to Pop and Rock*. Cambridge: Cambridge University Press. pp. 26–52.

Frith, S. and Marshall, L. (Eds) (2004) *Music and Copyright* (2nd ed.). Edinburgh: Edinburgh University Press.

Garofalo, R. (1999) 'From Music Publishing to MP3: Music and Industry in the Twentieth Century', *American Music* 17(3), pp. 318–353.

Garofalo, R. (2001) 'A Discussion about Napster', *Journal of Popular Music Studies* 13, pp. 93–102.

Gendron, P. (1986) 'Theodor Adorno Meets the Cadillacs', in: Modleski, T. (ed.) *Studies in Entertainment: Critical Approaches to Mass Culture*. Bloomington IN: Indiana University Press. pp. 272–308.

Harker, D. (1997) 'The Wonderful World of IFPI: Music Industry Rhetoric, the Critics and the Classical Marxist Critique', *Popular Music* 16(1), pp. 45–79.

Hesmondhalgh, D. (2009) 'The Digitalisation of Music', in: Pratt, C. and Jeffcutt, P. (eds) *Creativity, Innovation and the Cultural Economy*. Abingdon, Oxon: Routledge, pp. 57–73.

Hull, G.P. (2004) *The Recording Industry* (2nd Ed.). London: Routledge.

Hunter, D. (1986) 'Music Copyright in Britain'. *Music & Letters* 67, pp. 269–282.

IFPI. (1984) *The Case for a Home Taping Royalty*. London: IFPI.

IFPI. (2001) *The Recording Industry in Numbers*. London: IFPI.

IFPI. (2006) *The Recording Industry Piracy Report 2006* [online]. Available at: www.ifpi.org/content/library/piracy-report2006.pdf [last accessed 20 November 2013].

Kirton, A. (2010) 'Discourse and Power in the Formulation of UK Anti-file-sharing Legislation: The Place of Recording Company and Music Creator Interests'. PhD thesis, University of Liverpool.

Kretschmer, M. (2000) 'Intellectual Property in Music: A Historical Analysis of Rhetoric and Institutional Practices', *Studies in Cultures, Organizations and Societies* 6, pp. 197–223.

Kretschmer, M. and Kawohl, F. (2004) 'The History and Philosophy of Copyright', in: Frith, S. and Marshall, L. (Eds) *Music and Copyright* (2nd ed.). Edinburgh: Edinburgh University Press. pp. 21–53.

Kusek, D. and Leonhard, G. (2005) *The Future of Music: Manifesto for the Digital Music Revolution*. Boston MA: Berklee Press.

Laing, D. (2004) 'World Record Sales 1992–2002', *Popular Music Studies* 23(1), pp. 88–89.

Leyshon, A. (2003) 'Scary Monsters? Software Formats, Peer-to-Peer Networks and the Spectre of the Gift', *Environment and Planning D* 21, pp. 533–558.

Leyshon, A., Webb, P., French, S., Thrift, N. and Crewe, L. (2005) 'On the Reproduction of the Musical Economy after the Internet', *Media Culture & Society* 27(2), pp. 177–209.

Liebowitz, S. (2004) 'Will MP3 Downloads Annihilate the Recording Industry? The Evidence so Far'. *Advances in the Study of Entrepreneurship, Innovation, and Economic Growth,* 15, pp.435–473.

Liebowitz, S. (2006) 'File Sharing: Creative Destruction or Just Plain Destruction'. *Journal of Law and Economics* 6(1), pp. 1–28.

Lloyd, A.L. (1975) *Folk Song in England.* St Albans: Paladin.

Love, C. (2000) 'Courtney Love Does the Math' [online]. Available at: www.salon.com/technology/feature/2000/06/14/love/print.html [last accessed 20 November 2013].

Lukes, S. (2005) *Power: A Radical View* (2nd Ed.). Basingstoke: Palgrave Macmillan.

Marshall, L. (2005) *Bootlegging: Romanticism and Copyright in the Music Industry*. London: Sage.

Martin, P. (1995) *Sounds and Society: Themes in the Sociology of Music*. Manchester: Manchester University Press.

May, C. (2006) 'The Denial of History: Reification, Intellectual Property Rights and the Lessons of the Past', *Capital & Class* 30(1), pp. 33–56.

May, C. and Sell, S. (2006) *Intellectual Property Rights: A Critical History*. London: Lynne Rienner.

McFarlane, G. (1980) Copyright: The Development and Exercise of the Performing Right. Eastbourne: J. Offord.

Peterson, R.A. and Berger, D.G. (1975) 'Cycles in Symbol Production: The Case of Popular Music', *American Sociological Review* 40(2), pp. 158–173.

Sandall, R. (2007a) 'Off the Record', *Prospect,* August 2007.

Sandall, R. (2007b) 'The Day the Music Industry Died', *The Sunday Times,* 7 October.

Sanghera, S. (2002) 'Rock 'n' Roll Suicide', *Financial Times,* 14 November, pp. 19.

Théberge, P. (2001) 'Plugged in': technology and popular music', in: Frith, W., Straw, W. and Street, J. (eds.) *The Cambridge Companion to Pop and Rock*. Cambridge: Cambridge University Press. pp. 3–25.

32

Copyright Trolling and the Policing of Intellectual Property in the Shadow of Law

David S. Wall

INTRODUCTION

If you are a file-sharer of songs, films or books, there is a distinct possibility that you may receive a letter asking for a payment to represent the cost of something you have downloaded. The letter, usually from a lawyer, will accuse you of illegally downloading content and indicate that failure to pay the amount demanded will result in you being taken to court. Most people choose to pay up rather than go to court, especially when it refers to an action that you may have undertaken – but not always! In fact, recipients do not tend to consider their options because the letter comes from a lawyer and looks authoritative. But, they do have options, because such practices are contestable and exploit human vulnerabilities and various loopholes in law in order to encourage them to settle the invoice. These practices are regarded in some quarters simply as 'creative lawyering',[1] but in others as 'copyright trolling'. Regardless of the view held, the practice mocks the creative artefacts that their creators seek to protect and is also indicative of the emerging, adaptive and darker side of the anti-piracy industry (Lobato and Thomas, 2012). Ironically, copyright trolling is a by-product of the same networked technologies that enable file-sharing and which have transformed the business model of the music industry. It exhibits many of the same contradictions and complexities, not least the precarious balance that is required between the 'policing' of intellectual property in order to control access to the intellectual artefact and the simultaneous need to circulate the signs and symbols in order to maintain their value.

This chapter explores the phenomenon of 'copyright trolling',[2] which is the (il)legal practice often referred to as 'speculative invoicing' that sows discord and seeks to either upset or embarrass people so that they will pay for downloaded material (paraphrasing Campbell, 2001). It will look at the policing of digital copyright in the UK, US and Germany by exploring the practice of copyright trolling as well as some recent examples of litigation in those countries. More specifically, it will ask the question to what extent have some intellectual property lawyers been creatively and entrepreneurially seeking to use the threat of court or exposure to embarrass defendants into making payments. It will also ask whether or not this form of litigation has actually had the effect of policing (regulating) copyright under the shadow of law? This chapter will also contribute to the emerging criminological debate over organizational crime by providing an example of how organizational and professional corruption takes place as well as detailing the process of corruption. It illustrates an aspect of the criminalization of civil space by the private sector, in this case the brutal aim is to neutralize opposition and maximize income generation whilst protecting the income stream.

The first part will explore key trends in the changing business model of the music industry and outline the main issues and arguments relating to the debate over sharing music files. The second section outlines the case for file-sharing. The third part looks at who the creative industries are in terms of creative assets and artists and at how networked technologies have changed the power relationships between the two. The fourth part contemplates what is being protected and outlines the case against file-sharing. In so doing, it evaluates what intellectual property rights are and what their purpose is. The fifth section examines the practice of speculative invoicing to 'police' illegal file-sharing. The following part considers how speculative invoicing has turned into copyright trolling by exploring the case study of ACS:Law and also the US copyright trolling experience and seeks to draw some lessons from the UK and US experiences. The final part draws some conclusions.

THE CHANGING BUSINESS MODEL OF THE CREATIVE ARTS AND THE FILE-SHARING DEBATE

At the heart of the file-sharing debate is the fact that Internet and e-commerce-based forms of the distribution of files containing creative works have changed the business model of the creative arts. This is particularly the case with peer-to-peer (p2p) file-sharing networks such as BitTorrent, but previously Napster, Gnutella and later Kazaa[3] (Nguyen, 2006). Peer-to-peer file-sharing networks operate globally by linking users together so that downloads made by one sharer are effectively uploads from another person's file (for the early history of downloading and file-sharing, see Carey and Wall (2001)). Full p2p management systems, in contrast to the earliest sharing software such as Napster, only contain information about who holds particular files in order to link users together, which makes the system more effective and also harder to regulate.

The popularity of p2p is at the heart of the changes in the business model of the creative industry as it shifts the main point of sale from the artefact to the live event. Where musicians used to release records and then tour to promote them, the new business environment of music encourages artists to give their music away free to promote their tour. There is arguably a similar effect with cinema and other creative works. The dominant incomes streams have changed, as have control over them. In the words of David Bowie: 'You'd better be prepared for doing a lot of touring, because that's really the only unique situation that's going to be left. It's terribly exciting. But on the other hand it doesn't matter if you think it's exciting or not; it's what's going to happen' (David Bowie, quoted by Pareles, 2002). A, now classic, example of this shift can be found in the case of 'the artist formerly known as Prince'. In 2007 Prince gave away his album in the *Daily Mirror* to advertise a series of 21 shows at the O_2 Arena in London (BBC, 2010; Bryant, 2010). The shows sold out quickly (The O_2, 2007). There is anecdotal evidence that this business practice is also happening with cinema and other creative arts. Moreover, it will be argued later that this transformation is the result of a broader change in consumer behaviour whereby creative industry products (intellectual property) are creatively consumed (prosumed, see later). In short, consumers now demand what they want to consume and also how they want to consume it, disrupting long-standing power relations between the cultural industries and the public.[4]

The creative industries have long claimed that file-sharers are stealing creative products from them and the artists they represent. One such claim is that file-sharing is causing declining CD music sales and declining revenue streams and removing artists' incentives to produce. Whilst it is not doubted that there has been a continued decline in music sales, whether or not this decline is due to file-sharing is questionable. Firstly, the music CD market (recorded CD sales) declined once buyers had replaced their vinyl collections with CD versions. The CD market also experienced considerable competition from DVD and video game sales. Furthermore, the entry of mass retailers such as Wal-Mart into the music market led to falling prices and the deleting of older titles that sold in smaller quantities. Secondly, in the digital age, the Internet and networked technologies have caused some significant transformations, the main being that networked technologies have helped democratize intellectual property by allowing it to be more freely circulated, especially via peer-to-peer (p2p) file-sharing groups. The traditional (zero-sum) take on this transformation is that it kills important revenue streams. In contrast, the revisionist view is that it arguably increases the cultural value of the property by allowing the further exchange of symbols and signs, and it ultimately increases its financial value by creating new revenue streams. Moreover, this potential for 'people power' or 'people-sourcing' has led to 'prosumption' where consumers of intellectual property relate to it in an individualizing manner, producing or re-authoring it as they consume it (Tapscott and Williams, 2007). Prosumption allows signs and symbols to continue to evolve and keeps them fresh, but causes problems for the 'conventional' business models of intellectual property rights-holders. Rights-holders rely upon exclusive forms of control to exercise their rights, however, control is lost when the artefacts in question are non-physical. This process, or shift, not only challenges the doctrines of intellectual property law, but it also requires IPR owners to restructure business models; which is not an easy thing to do.

CONSTRUCTING THE CASE FOR FILE-SHARING (AGAINST THE TRADITIONAL BUSINESS APPROACH)

Orthodox arguments over intellectual property consumption both overplay control and underplay and undervalue the creative role played by consumers in the life of an artefact. Intellectual property law has the effect of binding a popular sign to a single source of meaning and functions as if it were the only possible source (Gaines, 1992: 236). To protect their intellectual property rights and police 'copyright theft' in their interests, the creative industries have tended to use three tactics, with varying degrees of success.[5]

Firstly, the industries sought to introduce a range of new forms of technological access control; see for example the Sony anti-copying technology which prevented CDs from being copied, but also from being played on certain types of players (Borland, 2001). In practice, the anti-copying technology meant that some Sony CDs became non-interoperable and could not be played on all computers, effectively limiting the freedoms of owners to legitimately copy for their own use and raising important questions about ownership of digital goods. Furthermore, the technological controls did not stop unauthorized copying, because sharers found ways of circumnavigating the control mechanisms. When it was subsequently found that the technology could also be a form of spyware, the outcry and public scorn from consumers led to class actions and its suspension (BBC, 2006).

Secondly, the creative industries tried, with limited success, to criminalize the shared virtual space that uploaders and downloaders use to share copyrighted materials by using criminal narratives. The 'Knock off Nigel', 'You wouldn't' steal a ...' campaigns[6] actively confused *homo economicus* with *homo criminalis* (see later) and sought to send a strong derisive message to downloaders that they were criminals, when in most cases the dispute was the subject of civil law (for a very full explanation of the criminalization of sharing see David (2010), also David and Whiteman in this collection). The early derisive anti-counterfeiting campaign was subsequently replaced by short advertisements thanking consumers for buying CDs, without any mention of piracy (Cellan-Jones, 2009). The anti-piracy advertisements effectively punished the best customers by threatening them through their legitimate purchases about the consequences of copying – one of which was allegedly helping to fund organised crime.[7]

Thirdly, the creative industries and their representative organizations in many Western countries have sought to use legal process by pushing hard for stronger laws to protect their interests. They have also pursued means of recovery that rely upon cease and desist orders (US and Canada) (Enigmax, 2010; Espiner, 2010), letters before action and speculative invoicing (UK) and *Abmahnungen* (Germany). These practices have largely failed because they created perverse incentives and caused some law firms to depart from the original mission to protect intellectual property (see further, Torrent Freak, 2012).

CHANGING POWER RELATIONSHIPS

The changes in the business model of creative industries have developed a new set of power relationships that ultimately favour the artists – musicians, visual artists, actors, writers, performers. In so doing, the shift in power threatens the main income streams of producers, labels and distributors, who wielded most control over the exploitation of the product of the creators' labours.

So, how exactly have the power relationships changed in the new business model of the creative arts? Firstly, there has been a decline in the power of pre-network technology record labels. In the case of the much larger labels, investment in new acts was almost a form of venture capitalism. Roles were defined hierarchically in terms of record label, producer and artist, as was the distribution of royalties and profits. The producers, distributors and labels once possessed a royalty share and also distribution rights of the artists' works which they obtained in exchange for paying an advance on the anticipated royalties. Networked technologies (see later) have blurred those lines of demarcation and new alignments have emerged between, say producers, who are often participants in the creation of the artist's brand, if not part of their substantive creative work. Producers may also be the label owners and also involved in promotions and sales in the digital age. Thus, changes in the business model of the industry are understandably threatening to their income streams, income that is, effectively, a return on their investment.

Secondly, there has been a change in the role and power of the publishing houses which collect royalties. Royalties on the performance of music, published works or educational photocopying, on behalf of authors and others to whom rights have been assigned, have changed (certainly in the UK) in the artist's favour since the late twentieth century (Hull, 2004). Previously, the major labels had progressively bought out the independent music publishing companies and created a situation where artists' publishing revenues were used to 'recoup' advances when recording royalties were insufficient, which was the situation in most cases because of the low rate of royalties. The relationship between the labels and publishing has largely been disrupted (see further, Hull, 2004).[8] In the UK, for example, the PRS (Performing Rights Society), ALCS (Authors Licensing and Collecting Service) and MCPS (Mechanical-Copyright Protection Society) all operate online services, which means that artists can collect their own royalties in ways that they could not do so previously. Payments that used to take years to reach the artist can now take weeks or months. As a consequence of digitization and networking, the means of distribution and also the power balance have changed. In three distinct ways digitization has reshaped the delivery of copyrighted material and changed the relationships between authors, producers, collecting societies and public.

Change #1: The Shift Away from Traditional Forms of Music Management

Established artists, whose interests the music industry associations seek to protect, are beginning to leave their labels and explore alternatives which include taking copy controls into their own hands (Geist, 2007). Some (though not all) also feel alienated by the industry bodies (Bylund, 2007; Fine, 2007). A number of established US artists are assisted in this transition by the invocation of 'termination rights' after 35 years which frees their rights to their songs (Rohter, 2011, 2013). Furthermore, there is some anger with the deals that major labels have made with world-wide-web-based distributors, such as Spotify, which pay relatively small royalty rates (an average of £.004 per play) (BBC, 2013a), but also favour companies with massive back catalogues rather than emerging artists (Ingham, 2013). Thom Yorke from Radiohead and producer Nigel Godrich have argued 'that the online streaming service may be good for its investors, but it was bad for artists' bottom lines' (Cherkis and Stenovec, 2013). In many ways such exploitation is nothing new, but what is being transformed here is the ability of major labels to negotiate such deals in the future. Artists are abandoning labels to form creator's coalitions instead, such as the Featured Artists Coalition[9] which represent their interests and oppose copy control and legal actions against their fans (Youngs, 2009).

Change #2: Alternative Business Models Are Appearing

Following on from change #1, established artists are taking matters into their own hands by turning to alternative business models and alternative means to protect their interests and sustain income and innovation (see Rothman, 2013). Michael Starita (quoted by Rothman, 2013) believes that: '[l]abels have backed away, and that's created a complete DIY [do-it-yourself] environment ... a lot of artists now, on top of being an artist, have to wear tons of hats, from being a manager to a booking agent to a graphic artist to a producer'. Below are five examples of this change. Firstly, there are *pay-as-you-like systems.* In 2007, Radiohead released their album 'In Rainbows' and allowed their fans to freely download it and then pay the band what they thought it was worth. Many commentators were highly critical of Radiohead's tactic and argued that 60–70% of downloaders did not pay anything (see NME, 2012). Analytics agency ComScore found that 1.2 million people downloaded the album during the first 29 days of release and 38%, or 456,000, voluntarily paid $6 to download it (Comscore, 2007). Other research suggests that over the first 24 days there had been upwards of 2.3 million downloads from BitTorrent, paying smaller amounts of money (NME, 2012). A rough estimate suggests that the pay-as-you-like approach generated about £1.2m in income, the album later went to no. 1 in the charts after hard copy release. This money went straight into the band's account to be used to support its ventures; money that would otherwise have taken months if not years to reach them; and then minus deductions by the various organizations who had a stake in the band's business.[10] There are arguments that this model only works with bands who have achieved a substantial market share, but there are other models to sustain those who have not (see later).

Secondly, is the *thank you to fans/protest against industry*. Coldplay gave copies of their live album LeftRightLeftRightLeft to fans as 'a thank you to our fans – the people who give us a reason to do it and make it happen' (BBC, 2009a). It gave the band much needed publicity. Trent Reznor (Nine Inch Nails) released the album 'The Slip' free to fans as a '[t]hank you for your continued and loyal support over the years – this one's on me'[11] (Thornton, 2009). In addition to being a thank you, 'The Slip' free download was also a protest against the traditional music process. Reznor released it under the Creative Commons 'attribution non-commercial share-alike'[12] licence (also see Barron in this collection). By releasing the album in this 'direct-approach-to-fans', Reznor also encouraged fans to prosume it: '… to remix it, share it with your friends, post it on your blog, play it on your podcast, give it to strangers, etc.' (Thornton, 2009). It excited fan interest and also attracted new markets through people-sourcing and prosumption (see earlier, Tapscott and Williams, 2007). Marillion, in an early attempt to engage with their crowd-base, distributed 'Happiness is the Road' free to fans via peer-to-peer networks in exchange for their email address (Anti Music, 2009). Marillion later moved towards a crowd-funding business model (Masters, 2013).

Thirdly, is *the loss leader to gain a new market* approach. As mentioned earlier as an example of the way the basic business model of the creative arts has changed, the artist formerly known as Prince released his album free in the *Daily Mirror* to promote his live shows and merchandising.

Fourthly, are *direct to fan music sales*. Artists such as David Bowie,[13] Peter Gabriel[14] and others sell their music directly to their fans. Bowie and Gabriel are well-known performers and have established fan bases, however at the starter end of the market exist www sites such as BandZoogle,[15] also MySpace, which is now old but retains some popularity.

Fifthly are *exclusive retail deals*. Artists such as the Eagles, Carrie Underwood, and David Cook (the American Idol winner), and others have entered into exclusive deals with Wal-Mart, the US's major music retailer. 'In some ways, the arrangements that Wal-Mart has made with Journey and the Eagles represent the mainstream equivalent of the path that artists like Radiohead and Nine Inch Nails have taken by releasing albums on the Internet without a traditional label' (Levine, 2008) or by creating their own labels and distribution companies (see Simply Red or Enter Shikari).

Change #3: Industry Middlemen Replaced by Artist-facing Brokers That Facilitate Music

There have also been seven 'people sourced' broker systems that enable musicians to directly engage with the services they require online, and also their audiences (see Van Buskirk, 2012). The first relates to *ticketing*. CrowdSurge appeared on the scene to provide an alternative to Ticketmaster, which had merged with Live Nation: '[i]t's a white-label service that charges nothing at a basic level – a thin middleman that lets bands (and venues and promoters) essentially run their own mini-Ticketmaster' (Van Buskirk, 2012). The second relates to sales of *music and merchandise*. Bandcamp is an alternative to mass distributors like Amazon because it helps redirect bands' business from Facebook, YouTube, Vimeo, Twitter, MySpace towards Bandcamp where fans can buy merchandise. The third relates to *funding*. Kickstarter is an alternative to banks because it links bands with the money they need to complete their works. 'Bands that can put together a compelling video and have a decent-size fan base on the Internet can use Kickstarter to rack up serious funding in weeks, all without answering to any sort of overlord' (Van Buskirk, 2012). The fourth relates to *tour funding*. GigFunder is an alternative to the promoter in that it helps make the gigs happen and is based upon a true market. Fans simply pledge money to see the band and if there are no pledges in a particular location, the band doesn't play. GigFunder charges 7% (including a 3% PayPal fee). The fifth relates to *subscription sales*. Distro Fm gets fans to directly subscribe to a band in order to help fund them and the bands upload information onto Distro.fm's space. The sixth is Van Buskirk's own idea; to develop artist music stations, say, on Pandora (in the US), where the artists pick the music and play it – a sort of musical tweeting in real time (see Van Buskirk, 2011, 2012). The seventh are online alternatives to traditional forms of copyright control which artists can use. Mentioned earlier was Creative Commons,[16] which provides control over both the moral and financial rights and also enables the free distribution of copyrighted works when the author or artist wants people to have the right to share, to use and also to develop the work they have created. There is a flexibility in the licence, for example, to only allow non-commercial uses, but it also protects people who use or redistribute the work. Copyleft[17] is another form of licensing that can be used to enable individuals to use and modify copyrighted works such as computer software, documents and art (GNU, 2008) (see Lee in this collection).

THE 'BUSINESS' CASE AGAINST FILE-SHARING

At this point it is important to explore the argument justifying IP ownership and look at what it is that is being protected. What are intellectual property rights and what is their purpose? In answer to these questions: '[i]ntellectual property refers to creations of the mind: inventions, literary and artistic works, and symbols, names, images, and designs used in commerce' (WIPO, 2001, 2011). Intellectual property falls into two basic categories 'industrial' and 'literary and artistic' properties. The first is *industrial property*, which is not discussed in this chapter, but: 'includes inventions (patents), trademarks, industrial designs, and geographic indications of source'. The second is *literary and artistic work*, which underlies the discussion in this chapter and is mainly about copyright

> such as novels, poems and plays, films, musical works, artistic works such as drawings, paintings, photographs and sculptures, and architectural designs. But also rights related to copyright include those of performing artists in their performances, producers of phonograms in their recordings, and those of broadcasters in their radio and television programs. (WIPO, 2001, 2011)

The question here is whether this approach is justifiable or not in the information age.

The justification for exclusive rights of control over intellectual property is one of the orthodox arguments underpinning IP regimes. The orthodox claim for establishing and maintaining exclusive rights is mostly based upon a combination of utilitarian and natural rights arguments which combine three principles, the concept of property as the natural right of the creator, the Lockean principle of rewarding mental labour and the cultural need to encourage and promote creativity and produce quality (see Fisher, 2001; also see contributions by Ghosh and Phythian-Adams in this collection). It is a commonsense view based, as outlined earlier, upon property ownership, and IP laws exist to support this view and grant intellectual property rights.

Silbey (2008; also in this collection) argues that despite the dominance of these theories the economic analysis of law tends to undervalue the humanistic element of intellectual property. She observes that US (and many UK) copyright and trademark regimes are based around and legitimized by what she refers to as 'central origin myths', the 'stories that glorify and valorise enchanted moments of creation, discovery or identity' (Silbey, 2008: 320). In these myths, property (including intellectual property) is presented as a natural right and a reward for labour (Locke). By rewarding labour, creativity is encouraged. But, Silbey's research findings contradict this view of the rational and self-interested economic human (*homo economicus*) upon which the intellectual creation myth is based. Yet, she found that the origin stories continue to serve both ontological and epistemological functions: '[t]hey infuse everyday life and relations with significance by explaining why things are as they are and by providing guidance for how things should evolve based on what we already understand about our world' (Silbey, 2008: 320). In contradiction to the concept of *homo faber* (man as essentially a creative being), the central origin myths effectively construct an ideology of intellectual property dominance which becomes the basis for effecting a range of legal, social, economic and technological means of regulation.

Taking this notion of the central origin myths further: in maintaining the principles upon which these labour rights are maintained, the rational actor myth of the selfish creator (*homo economicus)* becomes conveniently or deliberately confused with the rational actor model of the selfish criminal (*homo criminalis*).[18] This confusion can be seen, for example, in many anti-counterfeiting campaigns. As a consequence, the rhetorical force of the traditional (Peelian)[19] view of criminal behaviour is frequently invoked; namely that a 'responsible authority' should prevent theft. In other words, it becomes rational to see the Hobbesian state regarding those who appropriate intellectual property as selfish criminals to be regulated. But, the very concept of intellectual property theft is extremely limited by the abstract nature of the materials, especially online, and also their reproducibility as simulacra[20] rather than physically as individual items. It is certainly not sustained by the law on theft whereby: '[a] person is guilty of theft, if he dishonestly appropriates property belonging to another with the intention of permanently depriving the other of it' (s.1 Theft Act 1968, UK).

Despite the shifts in the business model of creative industries and the many opportunities for developing additional income streams, it is nevertheless quite understandable that some representatives of the creative industries will seek to protect their traditional copyright income. Indeed, some of the artists have been in support of those actions. For example, Metallica, Lilly Allen, Gary Barlow, James Blunt and other acts have strongly criticized file-sharers (BBC, 2009b). Prince, who gave away his album to promote his London shows, tried to sue his fans who sold downloads of his music because he wanted to supply the materials to them himself (BBC, 2014). Prince subsequently dropped the legal actions because the cases were seen as him effectively 'going to war with his own fan base' and they reacted angrily – which he subsequently denied (BBC, 2014). Similarly, other artists retracted their statements or modified them in the light of their fans' reactions; which illustrates the strength of the shift in the business model in terms of point of sale and also in terms of the artists. Yet, the representatives of the creative industries continue to unreflectively feel that their income streams are being threatened.

THE USE OF LEGAL PROCESS TO PROTECT REVENUE STREAMS

If networked technologies have transformed the business model of creative industries, they have also transformed the regulatory process. One of the main means by which music and later movie industry representatives have sought to control copyright revenue streams has been to combine electronic information gathering of mass file-sharing with court enforced disclosure of bulk information about file-sharers and the use of law firms to obtain settlements from those who infringe copyright. In the UK, Internet Service Providers (ISPs) reluctantly complied with court orders in the face of legal threats from the creative industry and also government on behalf of those industries. The 2009 *Digital Britain Report* (BIS, 2009) proposed plans for a graduated response, which is basically three warning letters then legal action (three strikes). It was to be enshrined in a mandatory code which sets out standards of evidence for Internet Service Providers to comply with. This 'graduated response' approach became part of the UK Digital Economy Act 2010, although implementation has been delayed a number of times, and most recently until 2015 (BBC, 2013c). It will, however, emphasize education over enforcement. Once it has been implemented, the UK will join France, New Zealand and South Korea who currently have similar laws (see Giblin, 2014). By comparison, a number of countries have voluntary graduated response practices. The US is currently operating a six warnings (strikes) approach (see Siebens, 2011; BBC, 2013b). US ISPs are still resistant to revealing data on infringers, though the third party data collection of infringers' IP addresses (as elsewhere) initially helped to strengthen the case to obtain court orders to release the downloaders' identity and personal contact information. Ireland has sought to implement a graduated response but is experiencing court proceedings.

There are two fundamental problems with the legal process approach. The first is the inconclusive evidence obtained about wrongdoing and the problem of false positives when identifying infringers (see Hargreaves, 2011).[21] This is because the data collection process for p2p evidence of infringement is digitally based and typically comprises an IP address, a downloaded file name (e.g. music or film or other media) and the time and date it was downloaded – usually by deep-searching Bit Torrent. The initial infringement information is typically collected by intellectual property security firms upon the instructions of a representative of the creative industries. It is then used by a law firm instructed by the creative industries to obtain a court order to get an ISP to release the names and details of the owner of the IP address. The law firm then sends out cease and desist letters/letters before action to file-sharers and/or invoices for any costs incurred. But, not only does having just the name of the shared file lack any proof of content,[22] but the IP addresses of file-sharers are also not conclusive evidence of wrongdoing. This is because many different people may have legitimately used a single IP address, thus many innocent individuals could get caught up in the 'prosecution' process including deceased individuals, elderly grandparents, very young people, homeless people, displaced people and individuals with a copyright licence for the materials (Brainz, 2010):

> knowing the IP address used for an illegal download is different than knowing who did it. The computer may also be on a shared network, it may be a shared computer in somebody's house, or it may be shared by roommates. (Boudett, quoted by McLean, 2013)

Another complication is that the act of file-sharing (downloading and uploading) in p2p networks is primarily a social, rather than financially driven, activity. As mentioned earlier, there is a growing argument that even if the act of file-sharing can be proved, then prosecution may be counter-productive in protecting copyright because it generates so much bad publicity. There is also little evidence that copyright infringement actually restricts income, because of the changing business model. Yet, the courts seem to have, until very recent years, accepted the logic of the argument in favour of the plaintiff.

This brings us to the second problem, which is that there has been a mission creep in the use of legal process to protect copyrights. Under most legal professional rules within different jurisdictions, clients are supposed to avoid conflicts of interests, but what has happened is that lawyers have proactively sought clients after they have sought alleged infringers to whom they have sent speculative invoices loosely veiled as 'cease and desist letters' (US) or 'letters before action' (UK) seeking settlement. The alleged infringers have tended to pay the invoice rather than face the threatened legal action or embarrassment or humiliation. Not only is embarrassment a key driver in getting downloaders to settle financially, but when invoices are not paid, the courts often decided in favour of the complainant; that is until ACS:Law (see later). It was the public outcry over unfairness and poor lawyering in speculative invoice cases that changed client prosecution policies and court decisions in the UK and US to favour defendants (Masnick, 2012). In this context, 'speculative invoicing', as this process became known, not only contradicts the Legal Professions code, but it also quickly becomes 'copyright trolling' and a form of harassment, even extortion, which is a long way from the intended aim of regulating copyright infringement.

WHEN SPECULATIVE INVOICING TURNS INTO COPYRIGHT TROLLING

A useful critique of the practice of speculative invoicing can be found in *The Speculative Invoicing Handbook* (Torrent Freak, 2012).

> The people running this scheme don't write music, they don't create games, they don't even produce pornography. They go out and they talk to people that do – the 'original rights holders'. They encourage them to sign over the distribution rights to their products. It is with these 'distribution rights', along with some harvested IP address data that the companies running the scheme apply for their court order to get your name and address. Some of these rights holders, in the early stages of the scheme, may not have known what they were getting involved with. The scheme has now been operating for several years. A very quick search on the law firms involved makes very clear that this is a nasty business. Any rights holder in on the scheme now can safely be considered as a willing participant in the operation. (Torrent Freak, 2012)

The ACS:Law case was perhaps the most significant and revealing of all the UK file-sharing cases[23] and illustrates the mechanisms of speculative invoicing and also its impact upon the legal profession. In May 2009, ACS:Law made claims on behalf of MediaCAT against suspected copyright infringement through peer-to-peer file-sharing. By November 2009, a further 25,000 claims against downloaders were made. In the first two weeks of January 2010, 10,000 more letters were sent out to alleged infringers based upon information obtained from ISPs (*HCJ Order 67/ 2009*). ACS:Law obtained *Norwich Pharmacal*[24] court orders based upon bit-torrent data (IP addresses of downloaders) to release personal contact details of individual IP address holder from the ISPs. ACS:Law then contacted the IP address holder to accuse them of illegally downloading movies and songs and demanded payments of £495 to avoid court action. ACS:Law claimed that most people opted to settle (outside of court) rather than fight the claims. Very few cases appear have gone to court and ACS:Law's capacity to take them to court remains unclear.

The use of lawyers by music industry representative bodies to protect copyright holders and generate income has ultimately had a perverse and unintended impact upon IP protection. Not only were the creative industries sometimes unaware of what they were getting involved with because some of the 'supermarket law firms' who practised speculative invoicing informed them after they had received monies from alleged infringers. But, the bad publicity generated after bulk speculative invoices were received by non-infringers actually created some public sympathy for downloaders and file-sharers. This led music industry representatives to largely abandon this practice, except against those who uploaded copyrighted materials for profit (Holpuch, 2012). It was at this point when the returns from speculative invoicing caused it to take on a life of its own, independent of the creative industries. The practice of speculative invoicing has had a corrosive and corruptive effect upon the section of the legal professions that deals with bulk cases. That this is the case is not surprising because, as stated earlier, digital network technologies helped facilitate the bulk processing of cases in volumes not previously anticipated.

Speculative invoicing has incentivized law firms to be creative and generate their own business by proactively commissioning their own clients with the lure of fees obtained, thus shifting away from the professional principle of taking instructions from clients and avoiding conflict of interests (SRA, 2013). See, for example, Judge Birss' comments on the relationship between ACS:Law and MediaCAT in the UK: '[w]hilst MediaCAT is the plaintiff, there were rumblings in the court to suggest that ACS: Law was so closely involved in receiving money, that the judge may be made to make a cost order against ACS: Law' (BBC, 2011b). Furthermore, Judge Birss also noted that MediaCAT was not the actual rights holder of the works in question and that a copyright case can only be brought by the rights holder (Birss, 2011; Doctorow, 2010).

The ability of UK law firms to obtain *Norwich Pharmacal* orders to compel Internet Service Providers (ISPs) to release details of alleged 'infringers' had the effect of unleashing a monster. The simple maths highlights the potential for income generation. In the ACS:Law case it was claimed that only 15–40% (about 20% on average) of people receiving the letters ended up paying, but according to Andrew Crossley (head of ACS:Law), ACS:Law had recovered almost £1 million from suspected copyright infringers by April 2010.[25] Crossley took 65% of the money recovered, with 35% going to copyright holders (Birss, 2011).

> Once the names and addresses of the alleged infringers became known, MediaCAT solicitors (ACS: Law) sent around 10,000 letters threatening legal action and asking for £495 in settlement. The judge considers that, following the receipt of those letters, 20% of the addressees have likely agreed to settle and that approximately £1M was collected (with 65% of that sum going to ACS:Law in accordance with their agreement with MediaCAT). (Liotta, 2011)

One suggestion in the ACS: Law case was to remedy unjust enrichment by getting the court to charge £350 for each set of personal contact details rather than multiple numbers. Another suggestion, made by the court in the *Goldeneye et al.* case[26] was fee limiting; to limit the proposed settlement fee to a reasonable and realistic amount (see Masnick, 2012). Such reforms would not stop speculative invoicing, but they would drastically reduce the amount of speculation involved by affecting the overall yield and roll back the mission creep that has taken place as the result of technology.

Where speculative invoicing parted company from conventional legal practice is that many of the so-called prosecutions for non-compliance with speculative invoices were brought without any intention of ever going to court and thus they were kept from judicial oversight. As the ACS:Law study illustrates, from the creative industry point of view, the intention was to frighten individuals into complying and thus create a chilling effect that made them comply with their wishes to not download. But from a law firm business perspective, the intention was to use the chilling effect to get alleged file-sharers to settle. The UK Patent Courts under Judge Birss decided against ACS:Law and effectively caused it to (voluntarily) cease trading (to avoid further action), and the key lawyers involved were disciplined by the legal profession (Law Society). By July 2010, the Solicitors Regulation Authority (SRA) had received a record 418 official complaints and in August 2010, the SRA brought a disciplinary charge against Crossley in response to his actions against suspected copyright infringers.[27] Crossley was also found guilty of 'conduct unbefitting a solicitor'. The firm (and MediaCAT) ceased trading on 31 January 2011, days before the court decision over whether defendants could claim damages against it (Arthur, 2011).

In a further twist of fate, on 21 September 2010, ACS:Law became the victim of a DDOS attack by Anonymous (the hacker group) as part of their Operation Payback in support of The Pirate Bay (Williams, 2010a). When the website was subsequently restored, the back-up file containing the addresses of 12,000 people that ACS:Law had accused was observable to all. This breach of the Data Protection Act was then investigated by the Information Commissioner. Crossley sought to cease trading to get out of prosecution, but the presiding Judge did not allow it. They, ACS:Law, then dropped cases against 26 suspected illegal file-sharers. In May 2011, ACS:Law was fined £1,000 for the privacy breach (BBC, 2011a). Upon reflection the only cases that ACS:Law won in court were by default because the defendants did not attend the hearing. No cases where defendants rejected the allegations appear to have been fought, which strengthens the accusation that the aim of the exercise was to get the accused to settle the invoice.

As speculative invoicing declined in the UK during 2010, the concept and practice travelled to the US where it quickly intensified. Figure 32.1, based upon data from *Infojustice*, illustrates the exponential growth in cases from almost zero in January 2010 to 200,000 some 18 months later.

US 'pay-up-or-else' lawsuits became 'extortion-like mass automated copyright' lawsuits (Masnick, 2010a). As in the UK, the focus of the speculative actions in the US shifted quickly from the music to the

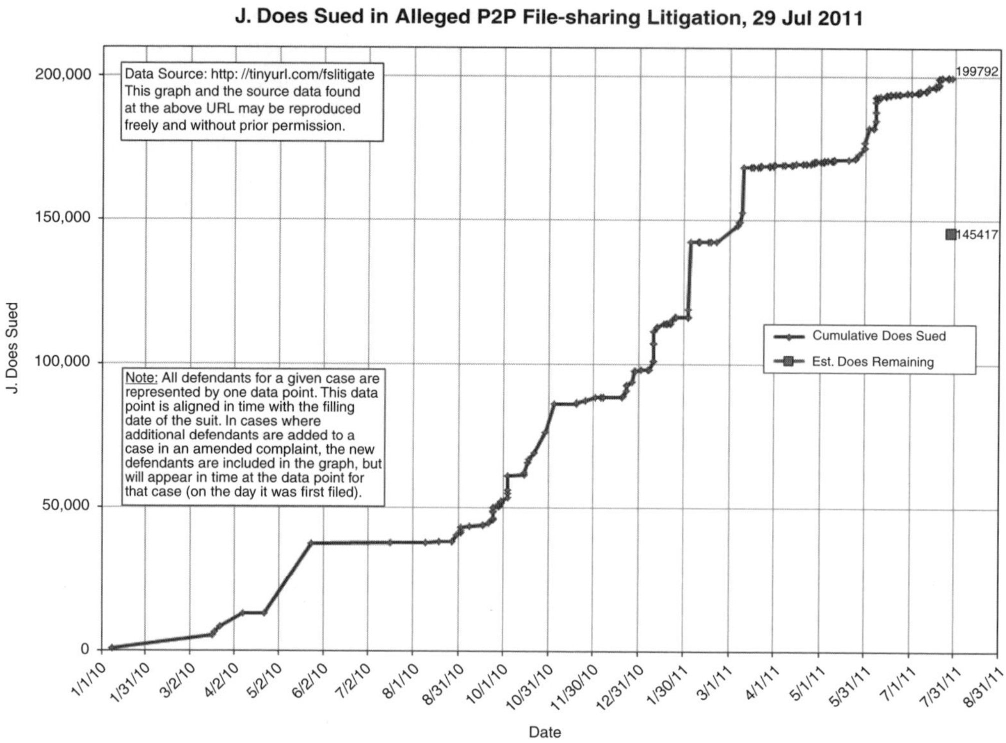

Figure 32.1 John Does sued for alleged file-sharing
Source: Infojustice (www.infojustice.org/wp-content/uploads/2011/08/graph-DoesSued-current.png). Permission to reproduce is given on the graph.

film industry, and specifically the part of the film industry specializing in pornography (Williams, 2012). The 'US Copyright Group', allegedly sought information on 50,000 file-sharers, suggesting that copyright infringement was now regarded as a revenue stream and 'monetizing the equivalent of an alternative distribution channel' (see further Masnick, 2010a). But many of the same problems emerged in the US as they did in Europe. Internet service providers (ISPs), in particular, fought hard against multiple requests for data because they challenged the Group's independence and, importantly, consumer trust was sapped while it cost them money to deliver the requested data. As in the UK, the invoicing practice damaged the cause it sought to protect by bringing the rights owners bad publicity. It was also bad business and short sighted because it threatened the smart new business models of independent filmmakers: models which involved building up a loyal fan base and giving them a real reason to buy into the product. The practice of trolling kills both the artist's and the consumer's good will. Furthermore, not only has speculative invoicing led to a proliferation of lawyers and also proxy copyright holders searching the web, but it has also spawned professional IP loggers who monitor the web for file-sharing information which they share with or sell to lawyers who then operate a no-win, no-fee system for the rights holders. The emergent copyright 'policing industry' has specialized into firms that track p2p downloaders (such as NG3 Systems Limited), firms who say they represent the copyright holders (such as MediaCAT) and specialist law firms (such as ACS:Law) who applied to the courts for court orders to get ISPs to disclose information about downloaders and then sent out the cease and desist requests, letters before action, and invoices (Enigmax, 2010; Espiner, 2010). Recent experience suggests a blurring of these specialized functions, for example, in the US Prenda Law case (see further Mullin, 2013a; 2013b, and later).

The US courts are, however, now clearly acting against speculative invoicers to reduce unjust enrichment and their ability to ply unfair trade, especially after the number of cases escalated exponentially in one year from hundreds to hundreds of thousands (see Figure 32.1) See, for example, cases in the State courts, such as *IN RE: Bittorrent Adult Film Copyright Infringement Cases* involving K-Beech, Malibu Media LLC, Patrick Collins (K-Beech et al., 2012) and explained in Raul and SJD (2012). The US Prenda Law case[28] illustrated new patterns of copyright trolling by creating honeypots[29] to entrap victims, but the US courts have reacted sharply against such practices (Mullin, 2013a, 2013b; Suddath, 2013). Yet, whilst copyright trolling seems now to be declining in the US because of court action, though there have been counter-claims and appeals, the concept and practice has now travelled to Canada (as it once travelled from the UK to the US). The copyright trolls (speculative invoicers) keep bouncing back and seeking out new copyright markets. Canipre (Canadian Intellectual Property Rights Enforcement), a copyright monitoring firm based in Montreal, arguably took 'speculative invoicing' into Canada (McLean, 2013).

> The idea is that Canipre uses its monitoring network to track IP addresses used to download movies illegally. Copyright owners then sue the users of those IP addresses as 'John Does'. Courts can compel Internet service providers to identify their customers, who then receive letters demanding thousands of dollars to settle infringement claims. (McLean, 2013)

Canipre joined forces with Voltage Pictures, a Los Angeles studio that used speculative invoicing extensively in the US (Geist, 2013; *Huffington Post*, 2012, 2013; McLean, 2013). Voltage Pictures, makers of *The Hurt Locker* and other blockbusters, went to court in Canada to request that TekSavvy (an independent ISP) disclose names associated with 1,100 IP addresses suspected of downloading pirate copies of the film. Geist argues that '[t]he Federal Court may think twice before ordering the disclosure of personal information of thousands of subscribers in support of what is now acknowledged to be a speculative invoicing scheme' (*Huffington Post*, 2013). The argument seems to rest on the fact that the 'names' requested are not conclusive evidence of wrongdoing, but also that speculative invoicing is unethical and inappropriate. The courts ordered TekSavvy to reveal the names and addresses of about 2,000 customers in February 2014; however, David Fewer of The Canadian Internet Policy and Public Interest Clinic, which had an 'intervenor' status in the case, believed that 'the court would not be eager to assign penalties at the higher range of what the Copyright Act allows'.

> If Voltage is asking for figures in excess of ($100 CDN) I think the court is going to shut them down pretty darn quickly … [a]nd if that's the case I think Voltage is done because this is no longer a viable business model. And that's what the whole copyright troll thing is about, it's about using the court process to get settlements that are in excess of what you could get for (actual) damages to scare people into settling. (Fewer, quoted in Oliveira, 2014)

Before continuing, it is important to note the different legal position of speculative invoicing in Germany where the law actually permits the practice. *Abmahnungen* (Schmitz and Ries, 2012) is a German legal term, similar to a cease and desist request between private parties when a legal violation has taken place (*einstweilige Verfügung*). What makes it different to US, UK or Canadian law, however, is that *Abmahnungen* not only allows payment of legal costs associated with sending the letter, but it can also be sent to an infringer by a lawyer without his having been hired by a client. It has consequently led to a proliferation of lawyers and also copyright holders trawling the Internet to seek out minor and often unintended violations of copyright law (see Solmecke and

Dierking, 2009). *Abmahnungen* has become a profitable legal tool as it gives legal access to information about IP address owners and the files downloaded, including the time and date. One of the reasons for the survival of *Abmahnungen* is that the German legal system is not based upon common law principles, like the US, UK or Canada, so the courts cannot shape the development of law. Having said that, Germany is still actively prosecuting downloaders in principle, but not so much in practice because of the public backlash.

DISCUSSION AND CONCLUSION

In drawing some lessons from the UK, US and Canadian cases, there has clearly been negative impact upon file-sharing behaviour, but only by creating fear, uncertainty and doubt amongst file-sharing communities along with a distrust and reluctance to participate in file-sharing and other online practices. Whilst this can be seen as a positive step by the representatives of the creative industries, these are, in effect, lost customers. The broader lessons from these cases are more serious in that copyright trolling has created a perverse and corrupting economy. This is because, being purely speculative, speculative invoicing has established the bulk 'pay-up-or-else' legal practice, described by some as 'creative lawyering' and 'unprofessional' by others, in fact most. The practice preyed upon the 'low hanging fruit', the vulnerable; those who either could not defend themselves financially, or were not in a position to defend themselves fairly because of the negative impact in terms of public reputation that defending the case would create.

The bulk speculative invoicing model relied upon settlement and there appears to be no intention to take these cases to court, unless defendants did not contest the case so that firms like ACS:Law won by default. Though not explicit, or illegal, speculative invoicing was therefore a disguised form of extortion or blackmail. ACS:Law also used bullying tactics to protect itself; for example, it took action against its critics (Masnick, 2010b). The speculative invoicing model is largely based upon untruths, as it was alleged (without any conclusive evidence) that the requested payments were damages calculated upon loss of sales. It also established the practice of outsourcing litigation and perversely incentivized (and corrupted) the lawyers involved. Moreover, is it also another worrying example of the reversals of the burden of proof, like speed cameras and possession of illegal imagery. The act (in this case file-sharing) is enough and the individual therefore has to prove their own innocence where not guilty. It also exploits administrative legal procedures to gain default judgments: 'working real injustice'[30], because it is administrative and not judicial, and an unjust procedure, there is no judicial oversight (Davey, 2010; Enigmax, 2010; Harris, 2011).

Finally, as stated earlier, the practice has damaged the cause it sought to protect. Although the 'clients' were initially happy because they received a percentage of the payments made – money they would not have otherwise seen – speculative invoicing eventually drove away clients (representatives of the music industry) because of the damage to their reputation from the negative publicity. The music industry representatives (BPI, in the UK and RIAA/MPAA in the US) became critical of the practice following negative publicity and also because the law is meant for the worst offenders, and not to catch the low-hanging fruit (Holpuch, 2012). Ironically, the adult sex film (porn) industry became the new clients for speculative invoicing and this drift can be seen in the US lawsuits (Williams, 2012).

To conclude, the reason why speculative invoicing persists is simply because the digital technologies enable law firms to generate a large amount of money in a relatively short timeframe and there has been little restriction to date upon that practice. Such pickings have clearly encouraged some law firms and professionals to cross the line from professional to unprofessional behaviour. The technical nature of information gathering and the large number of cases has also clearly caught courts unaware. So court orders have been used to force ISPs to supply personal data about file-sharers, which, as outlined earlier, is inconclusive evidence of wrong-doing, yet law firms have used that data, in some cases, to send out letters to wrongly harass individuals and extort money from them. The courts have, however, fought back by restricting payments and also restricting the activities of the invoicers. The solutions to speculative invoicing therefore seem to fall somewhere between the 'rock' of science and the 'hard place' of law. Since it is based upon a business model, then market solutions such as restricting the amount of information that can be gathered from one court order and the amount of money that can be asked from infringers can quickly reduce the attractiveness of the practice. But, speculative invoicing is only a symptom of a larger transformation in the creative arts.

In the broader picture, new technologies have disrupted the traditional power relationships between the creative industries, the artists and their fan base, particularly in music and film. There has been a shift towards the live event as the artist's prime income generator, increasing the power of the crowd and its involvement in the business model of creation. There is also evidence of a shift in power away from the traditional forms of control to alternative forms of organization and alternative business models. To protect themselves, the creative industries initially attempted to criminalize the virtual space in which information is shared. Litigation was effectively outsourced, automated and perversely incentivized. When this form of 'policing' failed, the law firms involved either discontinued their practice in the area or moved their practice from music to adult films. The main critique of speculative invoicing is that it is administrative and not judicial, and therefore an unjust procedure. Furthermore, copyright trolling can kill the creativity it seeks to protect. But, ironically, it may have partly achieved the industry's original goal to regulate copyright by disrupting the practice of file-sharing by 'policing under the shadow of law', but not by the due process which gives law its legitimacy. In contrast to its shadow, the full gaze of law has largely tended to encourage networking by expanding the distribution of networks. One result of that disruption under the shadow of law has clearly been to shift the consumption patterns of many file-sharers towards streaming, which is another story.

The twist to the argument is that a balance has to be struck. The orthodox arguments for IP rights emphasize the need to control intellectual property rights, but largely undervalue the creative part played by consumers in the creation and consumption of intellectual property. They become subject to the paradox of circulation and control (Wall, 2003).[31] They downplay the humanistic aspects of intellectual properties and in so doing reinvent cultural properties as intellectual property. But for the purposes of discussion, the concept of intellectual property has become embedded in popular parlance and remains a dominant concept. Intellectual property law binds popular signs and symbols to a source of meaning (property) and functions as if it were the only possible source (Gaines, 1992). The value of an intellectual property lies in its social or cultural meaning, which can only be accrued by circulating it and allowing consumers to adopt it creatively. The processes of circulation and control are paradoxical. Too much circulation of an IP leads to the development of secondary or even generic meaning that not only threatens the holder's exclusive rights over the property, but also can demean, debase or even destroy the overall integrity of the property. Too much restriction through over-zealous control through the application of legal, economic or moral tactics such as copyright trolling effectively strangles the IP by killing off public sensibilities of emotional ownership, affiliation and resonance (see Whiteman and also Kirton in this collection). In some intellectual property regimes the democratization of intellectual property – allowing it to be freely circulated – can increase both the cultural and financial value of the property by allowing the exchange of symbols and signs.

ACKNOWLEDGEMENTS

This article draws upon a combination of academic literature, contemporary events and the author's experience in the music industry over 40 years. Before presentation at the 2013 Durham IP Conference, an earlier version was presented to the Innovations in Intellectual Property Research conference, Golden Gate University, San Francisco (4 November 2011). Many thanks to Debora Halbert and also Bill Gallagher, but especially to my colleague Matthew David for his incisive comments on an earlier draft.

NOTES

1 Although quite robustly rejected. See Creative Lawyering or Copyright 'Trolling' – a Copyright Society Event at Suffolk Law, 26 March 2013: www.dmlp.org/blog/2013/creative-lawyering-or-copyright-trolling-copyright-society-event-suffolk-law
2 Copyright trolling is to be distinguished from 'Patent trolling', though the practices are sometimes similar. It is also different to Internet trolling which tends to describe a more personal attack on an individual with the specific aim to upset them – a term which is synonymous with 'cyberbullying', which is 'gradually chipping away young people's self-esteem' (Wakefield, 2014).
3 Please note that the terminology of p2p is used loosely here. Bit Torrent is actually peers (plural) to peer, Napster was not fully peer to peer, and Kazaa became fully peer to peer.
4 The business model has actually changed in favour of the artists, even if the artists themselves do not always agree with the shift.
5 Also see O'Brien in this collection on the problematic concept of 'creative industries' and the role of intellectual property in their fabrication.
6 Knock off Nigel was an antipiracy campaign in the UK which sought to tell viewers of counterfeit CDs that their actions were illegal and that they were losers. In the advertisement Nigel was humiliated by his friends for buying a copied CD and was left feeling lonely and despised by friends. The irony is that this featured on original and legitimately purchased CDs.
7 The link with organized crime is often made in debates and commentaries but not evidenced.
8 My thanks to the editors for bringing this point to my attention.
9 Featured Artists Coalition: http://thefac.org/
10 In my personal capacity as a former artist, I received 25% of 75% of 85% – only 16% of the gross pre-tax income, and still do! Each layer of involvement takes their share of the income. I felt that some of these shares were justified (co-writers, producer), others arguably less so (agents, management, publishers etc.).
11 See further Nine Inch Nails, The Slip, http://dl.nin.com/theslip/signup
12 Attribution-NonCommercial-ShareAlike 2.5 Generic licence: www.creativecommons.org/licenses/by-nc-sa/2.5/
13 David Bowie: www.davidbowie.com/
14 Peter Gabriel: www.petergabriel.com/
15 BandZoogle: www.bandzoogle.com/
16 Creative Commons: http://creativecommons.org/
17 Copyleft: www.gnu.org/copyleft/
18 See Beirne (1993) for the rise of *homo criminalis*.
19 Robert Peel was the founder of the UK police.
20 Simulacra is a copy without an original (see Baudrillard, 1994).
21 The Independent Hargreaves Report on Digital Intellectual Property and Growth found that the UK Digital Economy Act was an example of 'the distortion of public policy by questionable evidence' paras, 10.10 and 10.11 (See commentary on Hargreaves by the Open Rights Group at https://www.openrightsgroup.org/issues/deact).
22 If there is proof of content because the company supplied it then it is entrapment.
23 In the UK the main firms involved in speculative invoicing to varying degrees were ACS:Law, but also Davenport Lyons (Williams, 2010b), Gallant Macmillan, Tilly Baily Irvine, and DigiProtect (Masnick, 2012). In the US, Righthaven (news articles) and Prenda law were the firms in some of the key cases (Suddath, 2013).
24 *Norwich Pharmacal Co. v Commissioners of Customs & Excise* [1974] AC 133.
25 In the UK for example, a fee of, say, £350 for a court order could release up to 10,000 informational records of file-sharers.
26 [2012] EWHC 723 (Ch) Case No: HC11C03290.
27 See further 'Crossley, Andrew Jonathan – 150435: Decisions': (a) prosecution, 18 August 2010; (b) control of practice, 5 February, Solicitors Regulation Authority, www.sra.org.uk/consumers/solicitor-check/150435.article. It will be seen in the SRA's control of practice statement of 5 February 2014, that Crossley was allowed to practise again under certain conditions.

28 The Prenda Law Case is long and complicated and not dealt with in full here. See further the information in *Prenda Law, Plaintiff, v. Paul Godfread, Alan Cooper, and John Does 1–10, Defendants*, Case No. 13-cv-4341, Judge John W. Darrah, http://law.justia.com/cases/federal/district-courts/illinois/ilndce/1:2013cv04341/284511/60
29 Honeypots are software devices that are designed to lure and entrap offenders. Their use may garner intelligence of offending, but that intelligence is usually not regarded as evidence of wrongdoing that would stand up in court.
30 Judge Birss in *Media C.A.T. Ltd. v A [2010] EWPCC 17 (01 December 2010)* (para. 47), http://www.bailii.org/ew/cases/EWPCC/2010/17.html.
31 Developed from Gaines 'double movement of circulation and restriction' (Gaines, 1992: 5).

REFERENCES

Anti Music (2009) 'Marillion use P2P for album release', *Anti Music*, 9 November, www.antimusic.com/news/08/sep/11Marillion_Use_P2P_for_Album_Release.shtml

Arthur, C. (2011) 'ACS:Law and MediaCAT close their doors, ending filesharing claims', *The Guardian*, Technology Blog, 4 February, www.theguardian.com/technology/blog/2011/feb/04/acs-law-media-cat-close-filesharing

Baudrillard, J. (1994) *Simulacra and Simulation*, Ann Arbor: University of Michigan Press.

BBC (2006) 'Microsoft to remove Sony CD code', *BBC News Online*, 14 November, http://news.bbc.co.uk/1/hi/technology/4434852.stm

BBC (2009a) 'Coldplay to give away free album', *BBC News Online*, 1 May, http://news.bbc.co.uk/1/hi/entertainment/8028478.stm

BBC (2009b) 'Lily rallies stars against piracy: Lily Allen says piracy is "having a dangerous effect on British music"', *BBC News online*, 21 September, http://news.bbc.co.uk/1/hi/entertainment/8266287.stm

BBC (2010) 'Prince in second free album deal with newspapers', *BBC News Online*, 1 July, www.bbc.co.uk/news/10459020

BBC (2011a) 'ACS:Law fined over data breach', *BBC News Online*, 11 May, www.bbc.co.uk/news/technology-13358896

BBC (2011b) 'Firm stops pursuing net pirates', *BBC News Online*, 4 February, www.bbc.co.uk/news/technology-12366747

BBC (2013a) 'Spotify reveals artists earn $0.007 per stream', *BBC News Online*, 4 December, www.bbc.co.uk/news/entertainment-arts-25217353

BBC (2013b) 'US internet "six strikes" anti-piracy campaign begins', *BBC News Online*, 26 February, www.bbc.co.uk/news/technology-21591696

BBC (2013c) 'UK piracy warning letters delayed until 2015', *BBC News Online*, 6 June, www.bbc.co.uk/news/technology-22796723

BBC (2014) 'Prince drops $22m pirate action against fans', *BBC News Online*, 30 January, http://www.bbc.co.uk/news/technology-25960300

Beirne, P. (1993) *Inventing Criminology: Essays on the Rise of 'Homo Criminalis'*, New York: SUNY Press.

Birss (2011) Judgment of His Honour Judge Birss in *Media C.A.T. Limited Claimant - and - Malcolm Adams and others*, 17th, 24th January 2011, www.bailii.org/cgi-bin/markup.cgi?doc=/ew/cases/EWPCC/2011/6.html&query=Media+and+CAT&method=boolean

BIS (2009) *Digital Britain: Final Report*, Department for Culture, Media and Sport and Department for Business Innovation and Skills, Cm 7650, 16 June. http://webarchive.nationalarchives.gov.uk/20121126075826/http://www.bis.gov.uk/assets/BISCore/corporate/docs/D/Digital-Britain-Final-Report.pdf

Borland, J. (2001) 'Customers put kibosh on anti-copy CD', *cnet*, 19 November, http://news.cnet.com/2100-1023-276036.html

Brainz (2010) 'The 14 Most ridiculous lawsuits filed by the RIAA and the MPAA', *Brainz*, www.brainz.org/14-most-ridiculous-lawsuits-filed-riaa-and-mpaa/

Bryant, T. (2010) 'Prince will give new album 20TEN away free to Daily Mirror readers', *Daily Mirror*, 3 July, www.mirror.co.uk/3am/celebrity-news/prince-give-new-album-20ten-232881

Bylund, A. (2007) 'Record label defections by major acts a troubling sign for recording industry', *ars technica*, 9 October.

Campbell, T. (2001) 'Internet trolls', *Internet Archive*, http://archive.today/UFv0W

Carey, M. and Wall, D.S. (2001) 'MP3: more beats to the byte', *International Review of Law, Computers and Technology*, 15(1): 35–58.

Cellan-Jones, R. (2009) 'Goodbye "Knock-off Nigel"', *BBC News Online* (.dot life blog), 2 April, www.bbc.co.uk/blogs/technology/2009/04/goodbye_knock_off_nigel.html

Cherkis, J. and Stenovec, T. (2013) 'Indie record labels would support Spotify boycotts by their artists', *The Huffington Post*, 26 July, www.huffingtonpost.

com/2013/07/26/spotify-indie-labels_n_3659833.html?ncid=edlinkusaolp00000003

Davey, F. (2010) 'ACS:Law come unstuck', *Francis Davey Blog*, 8 December, www.francisdavey.co.uk/2010/12/acslaw-come-unstuck.html

David, M. (2010) *Peer to Peer and the Music Industry: The Criminalization of Sharing*, London: Sage.

Doctorow, C. (2010) 'Judge to copyright troll: Get lost', *boingboing*, 9 December, www.boingboing.net/2010/12/09/judge-to-copyright-t.html

Enigmax (2010) 'ACS:Law Take alleged file-sharers to court – but fail on a grand scale', *TorrentFreak*, 9 December, www.torrentfreak.com/acslaw-take-alleged-file-sharers-to-court-but-fail-on-a-grand-scale-101209/

Espiner, T. (2010) 'ACS:Law fails in default judgement attempt', *zdnet*, 10 December, www.zdnet.com/acslaw-fails-in-default-judgement-attempt-4010021288/

Fine, J. (2007) 'Leaving record labels behind', *Bloomberg Business Week*, 28 October, www.businessweek.com/stories/2007-10-28/leaving-record-labels-behind

Fisher, W. (2001) 'Theories of intellectual property', in S. Munzer (ed.) *New Essays in the Legal and Political Theory of Property*, Cambridge: Cambridge University Press.

Gaines, J. (1992) *Contested Cultures: The Image, the Voice, and the Law*, London: British Film Institute.

Geist, M. (2007) 'Why popstars are going it alone', *BBC News Online*, 18 October, http://news.bbc.co.uk/1/hi/technology/7047723.stm

Geist, M. (2013) 'Canipre admits it's behind Voltage-TekSavvy file sharing lawsuits with speculative invoicing scheme', *Michael Geist Blog*, 12 March, www.michaelgeist.ca/content/view/6805/125/

Giblin, R. (2014) 'Evaluating graduated response', *Columbia Journal of Law & the Arts*, 37: 147–209.

GNU (2008) 'What is copyleft?', *GNU Operating System*, www.gnu.org/copyleft/

Hargreaves, I. (2011) *Digital Opportunity: A Review of Intellectual Property and Growth*, Intellectual Property Office, www.ipo.gov.uk/ipreview-finalreport.pdf

Harris, J. (2011) 'Judge Birss hits out as porn costs mount', *The Lawyer*, 27 April, www.thelawyer.com/judge-birss-hits-out-as-porn-costs-mount/1007751.article

Holpuch, A. (2012) 'Minnesota woman to pay $220,000 fine for 24 illegally downloaded songs: Recording Industry Association of America has largely adjusted its anti-piracy strategy to stop suing individual downloaders', *The Guardian*, 11 September, www.theguardian.com/technology/2012/sep/11/minnesota-woman-songs-illegally-downloaded

Huffington Post (2012) 'File-sharing lawsuits come to Canada: Canipre identifies 1 million unauthorized file-sharers', *The Huffington Post Canada*, 28 November, www.huffingtonpost.ca/2012/11/28/file-sharing-lawsuit-canada-canipre_n_2203809.html

Huffington Post (2013) 'TekSavvy File-sharing lawsuit looking more and more like "copyright trolling"', *The Huffington Post Canada*, 3 December, www.huffingtonpost.ca/2013/03/12/teksavvy-lawsuit-copyright-trolling-distributel_n_2862029.html

Hull, G. (2004) *The Recording Industry*, London: Taylor & Francis.

Ingham, T. (2013) 'Nigel Godrich: Major labels did "secret deals with Spotify", leaving small labels with "pittance"', *Music Week*, 15 July, www.musicweek.com/news/read/nigel-godrich-major-labels-did-secret-deals-with-spotify-giving-small-labels-pittance/055395

K-Beech et al. (2012) *IN RE: Bittorrent Adult Film Copyright Infringement Cases (K-Beech, Malibu Media LLC, Patrick Collins v John Does)* Case 211-cv-03995-DRH-GRB Document 39 Filed 05/01/12, www.scribd.com/doc/92100289/K-Beech-Order-amp-Report-amp-Recommendation-Ordered-5-1-12

Levine, R. (2008) 'For some music, it has to be Wal-Mart and nowhere else', *The New York Times*, 9 June, www.nytimes.com/2008/06/09/business/media/09walmart.html?pagewanted=all&_r=0

Liotta, A. (2011) 'Media CAT vs Adams: a new hurdle to the DEA implementation?', *Media Laws*, 29 March, www.medialaws.eu/media-cat-vs-adams-a-new-hurdle-to-the-dea-implementation/

Lobato, R. and Thomas, J. (2012) 'The business of anti-piracy: New zones of enterprise in the copyright wars', *International Journal of Communication*, 6: 606–625.

Masnick, M. (2010a) 'Extortion-like mass automated copyright lawsuits come to the US: 20,000 filed, 30,000 more on the way', *techdirt*, 30 March, www.techdirt.com/articles/20100330/1132478790.shtml

Masnick, M. (2010b) 'ACS:Law now using dubious legal theories to threaten Slyck.com', *techdirt*, 22 May, www.techdirt.com/articles/20100321/2136068650.shtml

Masnick, M. (2012) 'UK court wants to limit copyright trolling ... but not enough to stop it entirely', *techdirt*, 28 March, www.techdirt.com/articles/20120327/05074118257/uk-court-wants-to-limit-copyright-trolling-not-enough-to-stop-it-entirely.shtml

Masters, T. (2013) 'Marillion "understood where the internet was going early on"', *BBC News Online*, 1 September, www.bbc.co.uk/news/entertainment-arts-23881382

McLean, M. (2013) 'Battling Bit Torrent: Can the movie studios beat online piracy?', *Canadian Business*, 8 March, www.canadianbusiness.com/technology-news/battling-bit-torrent/

Mullin, J. (2013a) 'Judge "came in like a tornado" at Prenda Law lawyers', *ars technica*, 11 March, www.arstechnica.com/tech-policy/2013/03/judge-came-in-like-a-tornado-at-prenda-law-lawyers/

Mullin, J. (2013b) 'At long last, "porn troll" Prenda Law begins to pay up', *ars technica*, 6 December, www.arstechnica.com/tech-policy/2013/12/at-long-last-porn-troll-prenda-law-begins-to-pay-up/

Nguyen, T. (2006) 'Kazaa to pay $100 million to record labels', *Daily Tech*, 27 July, www.dailytech.com/Kazaa+to+Pay+100+Million+to+Record+Labels/article3535.htm

NME (2012) 'Did Radiohead's "In Rainbows" honesty box actually damage the music industry?', *NME, Blog*, 15 October, www.nme.com/blogs/nme-blogs/did-radioheads-in-rainbows-honesty-box-actually-damage-the-music-industry

Oliveira, M. (2014) 'TekSavvy ordered to identify alleged copyright violators in lawsuit', *The Huffington Post*, 21 February, www.huffingtonpost.ca/2014/02/21/canadian-isp-to-name-subs_n_4831637.html

Pareles, J. (2002) 'David Bowie, 21st-century entrepreneur', *The New York Times*, 9 June, www.nytimes.com/2002/06/09/arts/david-bowie-21st-century-entrepreneur.html?pagewanted=all&src=pm

Raul and SJD (2012) 'New York judge blasts trolls' practices, recommends banning mass bittorent lawsuits in the district', *Fight Copyright Trolls* (Blog), 2 May, www.fightcopyrighttrolls.com/2012/05/02/new-york-judge-blasts-trolls-practices-recommends-banning-mass-bittorent-lawsuits-in-the-district/

Rohter, L. (2011) 'Record industry braces for artists' battles over song rights', *The New York Times*, 15 August, www.nytimes.com/2011/08/16/arts/music/springsteen-and-others-soon-eligible-to-recover-song-rights.html?pagewanted=all

Rohter, L. (2013) 'A copyright victory, 35 years later', *The New York Times*, 10 September, www.nytimes.com/2013/09/11/arts/music/a-copyright-victory-35-years-later.html

Rothman, L. (2013) 'Can music collectives fill the gap between labels and DIY? A new, old trend may help musicians better navigate the new industry landscape', *Time Magazine*, 12 April, www.entertainment.time.com/2013/04/12/can-music-collectives-fill-the-gap-between-labels-and-diy/

Schmitz, S. and Ries, T. (2012) 'Three songs and you are disconnected from Cyberspace? No in Germany where the industry may turn "piracy into profit"', *European Journal of Law and Technology*, 3(1): 1–14.

Siebens, C. (2011) 'Divergent approaches to file-sharing enforcement in the United States and Japan', *Virginia Journal of International Law*, 52(1): 155–192.

Silbey, S. (2008) 'The mythical beginnings of intellectual property', *George Mason Law Review*, 15: 319–379.

Solmecke, C. and Dierking, L. (2009) 'Die Rechtsmissbräuchlichkeit von Abmahnungen', *Multimedia und Recht*, 11: 727–731.

SRA (2013) *SRA Code of Conduct 2011, Version 8*, Solicitors Regulation Authority, 1 October, www.sra.org.uk/solicitors/handbook/code/

Suddath, C. (2013) 'Prenda Law, the porn copyright trolls', *Bloomberg Business Week*, 30 May, www.businessweek.com/articles/2013-05-30/prenda-law-the-porn-copyright-trolls

Tapscott, D. and Williams, A. (2007) *Wikinomics: How Mass Collaboration Changes Everything*, London: Atlantic Books.

The O_2 (2007) 'Prince announces final six nights of record breaking UK Appearances at The O2', *The O_2*, 11 June, http://archive.today/TiajT

Thornton, D. (2009) 'Passion is why Nine Inch Nails and vinyl are succeeding', *The Way Of The Web*, 7 January, http://www.thewayoftheweb.net/tag/nine-inch-nails/

Torrent Freak (2012) *The Speculative Invoicing Handbook, Second Edition, Scribd.*, www.scribd.com/doc/115443516/The-Speculative-Invoicing-Handbook-Second-Edition

Van Buskirk, E. (2011) 'Pandora redesign emphasizes social sharing, removes listening limit', *evolver.fm*, 21 September, www.evolver.fm/2011/09/21/pandora-rolls-out-big-redesign-emphasizes-social-sharing/

Van Buskirk, E. (2012) '5 powerful music apps that should make middlemen nervous', *WIRED*, 16 May, www.wired.com/underwire/2012/05/5-music-apps-scaremiddlemen/

Wakefield, J. (2014) 'Cyberbullies: How best to tackle online abuse?' *BBC News Online*, 11 February, www.bbc.co.uk/news/technology-26121199

Wall, D.S. (2003) 'Policing Elvis: Legal action and the shaping of post-mortem celebrity culture as contested space', *Entertainment Law*, 2(3): 35–69.

Williams, C. (2010a) 'Police probe British Anonymous activists', *The Register*, 16 December, www.theregister.co.uk/2010/12/16/met_anonymous/

Williams, C. (2010b) 'Anti-piracy lawyers "knowingly targeted the innocent", says law body', *The Register*, 19 November, www.theregister.co.uk/2010/11/19/davenport_lyons_sra/

Williams, C. (2012) 'O2 forced to expose "porn downloaders"', *The Telegraph*, 27 March, www.telegraph.co.uk/technology/broadband/9168016/O2-forced-to-expose-porn-downloaders.html

WIPO (2001) *WIPO Intellectual Property Handbook: Policy, Law and Use*, WIPO (World Intellectual Property Organization) publication no. 489(E). Geneva: WIPO.

WIPO (2011) 'What is intellectual property?', WIPO (World Intellectual Property Organization), www.wipo.int/freepublications/en/intproperty/450/wipo_pub_450.pdf

Youngs, I. (2009) 'Bands "better because of piracy"', *BBC News Online*, 12 June, http://news.bbc.co.uk/1/hi/8097324.stm

PART X

Parameters of Patent

Matthew David and Debora Halbert

Patents are designed to provide intellectual property rights over 'inventions'. This collection does not offer a single meaning of 'invention' in the sense that more detailed textbooks on IP law, and patent in particular, seek to do. However, the notion that a patent should be granted tends to follow a number of basic principles: that the supposed invention be original, non-obvious, useful and have a demonstrable mechanism. If these things were themselves obvious and without need for interpretation, this section would be much shorter than it is. A brief history of the development of patents introduces Susanna Leong's chapter in this section. What each chapter in this section addresses are disputes in relation to both the parameters of patent itself, and in the interpretation of such terms as invention, non-obviousness, originality and the demonstration of how something actually works. What the chapters in this section demonstrate is that disputes over these questions of interpretation place the scope and legitimacy of patent rights into question on a number of fronts.

Colin Darch's focus on patent law in South Africa highlights a range of issues that parallel those developed in Part II (on IP and development), in particular the question of whether the development of a stronger patent system fosters or hinders economic and social development in countries of the Global South. Darch notes that three-quarters of the most important technical innovations of the late twentieth century were not themselves patented, and gives the South African example of the 'dolos' (a 20-ton geometric concrete 'block' used to construct underwater barriers that assist in creating sea defences for ports, and which has been essential in the development of safe and affordable trade infrastructure in developing countries and beyond). More controversial has been the long-standing conflict between the South African government and Western pharmaceutical companies over the state's decision to buy cheaper derivative HIV inhibiting medication from countries like India (see Thomas in this collection on India and US IP watch lists). This raises the question of the relationship between IPRs and development rights, and in particular the right to accessible healthcare). Darch charts the failure to have IPRs in South Africa defined as a part of basic 'human rights', even whilst critics of the status quo argue that current government provision of health care does not go far enough in meeting citizens' human right to life itself.

Despite being placed on the United States Section 301 watch list of countries where US IP has not been 'sufficiently' enforced (in the view of the US Department of Trade), Darch points out that as a part of South Africa's attempts to integrate itself within the global economic and legal regulative system (post-apartheid isolation) the country ranks very high in various listings of enforcement strength. In fact, in relation to the creation of patent oriented technology transfer units, and in the related attempt to turn university research into private property, South Africa has outpaced even the United States, whose Bayh-Dole legislation first allowed patents to be filed on research outcomes that had been originally funded from federal sources within academic laboratories.

Graham Dutfield addresses the question of the relationship between Western science and conceptions of 'invention' that might fit within such a model of knowledge production and utility, and forms of 'traditional knowledge'. In this regard, his work links to those chapters in Part III of this collection, which focus upon geographical indicators and farmers' rights, and which are strongly linked to the notion of 'traditional knowledge', as well as Darch's discussion of traditional knowledge in Part IV. However, Dutfield's focus is in questioning the strength and limitations of the notion of 'biopiracy', a term that developed to decry the practice of patenting processes that had initially been identified in 'traditional knowledge' systems within the Global South. As such, this chapter's exploration of the relationship between 'traditional knowledge' and the Western patent system makes it appropriate to locate it in this section of the collection. In particular, the chapter addresses a number of questions relating to whether what gets patented can be deemed 'novel' if some parallel understanding within a traditional world view already existed. It also links to the question of who should have rights over a process that already exists in nature, even if in order to market it, that process has undergone extensive synthesis by 'patentable' techniques. This question of whether existing biological processes may be open to patent is something that is dealt with again in the following chapter by Susanna Leong.

Dutfield wishes to move away from the good versus evil language that has tended to accompany discourse on 'biopiracy', in which the Global South is presented as the victim of piratical corporations intent on simply stealing traditional knowledge and the flora that such knowledge was said to be able to unlock the secrets of. Whilst Dutfield acknowledges and seeks to highlight how such inequitable practice has gone on, he also wants to show how much more complex relationships between pharmaceutical science, traditional knowledge and indigenous flora really are. First of all, much of what is counted as 'indigenous flora' had migrated between the countries of the Global South along with the very colonial system that sought to exploit such land, people and nature. Colonialism did not just take what if found. It was also party to putting it there in the first place.

Dutfield gives the example of the rosy periwinkle in this regard. Geographical 'origin' is also complicated by the mismatch between political states, communities and the sites where products can be located. It is rarely the case that one voice can be said to speak for all those whose tradition can be linked to the use of a particular product. When something is 'common knowledge' to more than one community, which, if any, should have rights to control/profit from the use of such knowledge by others? It is also true that the link between traditional knowledge and the synthesizing of marketable products is not a simple one. As such, 'benefit sharing' schemes have struggled to create effective channels by which origin, development and application can be reversed into rewards back down the chain.

The attempt to commercialize the appetite suppressant properties of 'Hoodia', a product long known about and used by the geographically dispersed San peoples of Southern Africa, is taken to illustrate such difficulties. Whilst Dutfield supports the development of a new language by which 'traditional knowledge' can engage with the patent processes of 'Modern'/'Western' pharmaceutical sciences, the outcomes to date of the Nagoya Protocol, and in particular the weakness of its framing of 'benefit sharing', and the rather toothless requirement to 'take into consideration' traditional knowledge, lead him to suggest the scope of such mechanisms for translating TK into patent IP remains limited.

Susanna Leong takes up the question of what can be legitimately 'owned' under patent law, in particular the question of when and where it is possible to own living organisms. These might be genetically modified organisms that can, at least in part, be said to have been created or invented, rather than just having been discovered in nature. In relation to such modifications, Leong highlights how the distinction between micro-organisms (which many jurisdictions do allow patent applications on) and marco-organisms (where such applications do not hold), is problematic to define. This is because there is no objective point of transition between the two, and the more subjective criteria by which a micro-organism is defined as one that is not observable with the naked eye is both unclear and has no particular warrant beyond simply being intuitive. Alternatively, biological objects that are not themselves 'organisms', and in particular specific genes whose variant types are either predictors or causes of disease, have also become targets for patent applications.

Leong highlights that different countries and even the same countries at different times have taken different views as to whether or not it is legal to take a patent out on a biological entity that in some sense has been discovered rather than created. Of particular interest has been the case of Myriad Genetics, whose application for patents on genes linked to breast cancer were initially granted in the United States and then revoked, whilst other jurisdictions have taken different views as to whether Myriad's creation of the means by which to identify particular gene mutations should give it the right to claim 'ownership' (by patent) over the gene itself and its potential future uses as a marker and predictor. Whether the artificiality of holding genetic material outside of a host organism again constitutes an 'inventive' step worthy of patent rights in the material so extracted is another thorny issue that has divided legal opinion worldwide. Whilst the extraction and storage clearly require inventive steps, what has been extracted may or may not be said to be 'new'.

Leong also goes on to discuss the question of patent in relation to computer software and business methods/processes. The extent to which these can be described as inventions has led to disputes concerning both the creative/functional distinction that is said to separate what is copyrightable and what is patentable (something touched upon in the chapters in Part VIII), and others over attributions of novelty and non-obviousness. Different legal jurisdictions have sought to develop and apply different criteria by which to deliberate in such matters, but in a global IT and business world, such criteria increasingly run up against one another in practice and in court.

33

Politics, Law and Discourse: Patents and Innovation in Post-Apartheid South Africa

Colin Darch

INTRODUCTION: SOUTH AFRICAN IP LAW AND POLICY

This chapter, when read together with 'The Political Economy of Traditional Knowledge, Trademarks and Copyright in South Africa', also published in this Handbook, is intended to present a broad overview of developments in the various aspects of intellectual property (IP) law and policy in South Africa since the end of the apartheid regime in 1994. Nevertheless, it can also be read in isolation as a discussion of national patent law and practice, together with innovation policy, referring occasionally to exemplary cases from South African jurisprudence. Like its companion text, it links current South African policy and law to developments in the international IP and trade environment, and aims to uncover and examine the discursive narratives that underlie accounts of IP both at macro and micro levels and which often help to determine political and judicial outcomes.

South Africa is a country with an ethnically and linguistically diverse population; the Constitution recognizes 11 official languages, although English, which ranks fifth in terms of the number of speakers, remains the language of prestige in politics, business and education. Since the end of the racially-oppressive *apartheid* system in the early 1990s, the country has been a parliamentary constitutional democracy with a market-oriented economy. South Africa has the 25th largest land area in the world, the 24th largest population and the 28th largest economy. The country occupies a strategically important position on the southern sea routes between the Indian and Atlantic oceans (Kornegay, 2012: 42), and possesses a sophisticated economic, legal and technological infrastructure, while at the same time struggling with many of the problems of poverty that characterize other developing or 'Third World' countries.

With a nominal GDP of US$376 billion, the economy is by far the largest in Africa, nearly twice the size of the next-largest Nigerian or Egyptian economies, although several African states perform better than South Africa when GDP is measured *per capita*. Although the informal sector is relatively small in relation to the economy as a whole in comparison with most African countries, unemployment and underemployment are high, and only around 40 per cent of adults have formal jobs. Such indicators show that economic and social inequalities are extreme, and South Africa's Gini coefficient is, unsurprisingly, one of the world's worst (World Bank, 2009). As a consequence of this juxtaposition of sophisticated infrastructure with chronic social deprivation, unlike most of the rest of the continent, South Africa can be accurately characterized as a 'two-world' economy (Rooks and Oerlemans, 2005: 1224). Despite the high levels of inequality, South Africa is ranked as upper-middle income by the World Bank (2013), and is a member of the BRICS grouping which joins it with Brazil, Russia, India and China, together the largest emerging economies in the world. As a BRICS member, South Africa exercises significant international political and economic influence. In the last ten years, official economic policy has focused especially on industrial development, while continuing to recognize the short-term need to assist the poorest of the poor, partly through welfare programmes. As we shall see, these broader realities are reflected in a wide range of differing attitudes and behaviours by government, business, academics, lawyers and civil society organizations towards the specific area of IP policy and intellectual property rights (IPRs).

In a process that is still ongoing, the South African legal system has emerged from the mixing of several distinctive – and sometimes incompatible – judicial systems. These include Dutch civil law, British common law and several African customary law traditions, as well as a constitutional tradition that is in the process of being constructed on the basis of existing local, foreign and international norms. These often fail to merge happily, as for example when traditional leaders in rural areas assert patriarchal practices regarding land ownership, polygamy or inheritance in ways that disadvantage women and violate the emerging constitutional norms already mentioned (Walker, 2013: 78).

Within this hybrid legal framework, South African IP law is made up of a complex matrix of legislation and amendments, rules and regulations, obligations under international treaties and WIPO agreements, and regional and bilateral commitments. These various responsibilities cover patents, trademarks, and copyright, as well as other aspects of IP, such as the protection of traditional knowledge. The country has ratified ten of the 15 international IP treaties (Teljeur, 2003: 52), and participated in the diplomatic conference that led to the Marrakesh Treaty on copyright exceptions in mid-2013. Much of the primary legislation is out-of-date, and does not deal adequately with the technological changes of recent decades. At the time of writing, in order for South African IP law to achieve domestic and international coherence, 'a process of almost continuous law reform [would be] required' (Teljeur, 2003: 51) and this appears unlikely to happen soon.

The South African judicial system includes some specialist tribunals dealing with particular fields of law such as labour, land claims, or competition issues. There are two nominally specialist courts for patents and trademarks, but many IP matters are in practice dealt with in magistrates' courts, and the absence of specialist knowledge among the judiciary has been the subject of criticism (Harms and Dean, 2012: 104–113). The cohort of about 160 specialist IP lawyers and law firms is organized into the influential South African Institute of IP Law (SAIIPL), established in 1952. Most SAIIPL members focus on patent and trademark litigation. The group is engaged, describing itself as 'the custodian of South Africa's intellectual property rights' and as representing 'the majority of national and international businesses who have built their businesses [sic] on brands, innovation and technology, and who protect their interests through our country's intellectual property laws'. The SAIIPL is active in WIPO and other forums (SAIIPL, n.d.)

IP law is recognized in South Africa as an area of specialization in legal education and research (Klopper at al., 2011). Not all universities approach the subject from the same perspective, however. The University of the Witwatersrand, the University of Cape Town and the University of South Africa (UNISA) all offer conventional LL.M. degrees with a specialization in IP law, and UNISA runs a diploma course jointly with the WIPO Worldwide Academy. This focuses 'on the special circumstances prevailing in developing countries' (UNISA, 2013). Stellenbosch University has an endowed professorship, the Anton Mostert Chair of IP Law, and offers an LL.M. degree in IP law, which the faculty describes as 'the only fully accredited Master of Laws with a focus on Intellectual Property Law as a legal discipline' and as 'designed to train super-specialised academics and equip students … to practice effectively in this field of law and occupy the position of experts' (Stellenbosch University, 2013).

By contrast, the University of Cape Town's IP Law and Policy Unit investigates broader theoretical issues, such as the relationship between IPRs and development, or IPRs and nanotechnology. The Unit 'specialises in patent law and policy, primarily in relation to development issues for new technologies in the area of health, biotechnology, genetics, nanotechnology, synthetic biology, electronic media and business methods' (UCT, 2013). It is also involved in the African Copyright and Access to Knowledge (ACA2K) Project, and is the institutional base for Creative Commons South Africa. It has links to government and works 'with the Department of Science and Technology (DST) on IP issues, and as [a] representative of the DST for meetings in Geneva' (UCT, 2013).

Post-apartheid governments have not done much to reform the inherited legal framework for IP. Indeed, until September 2013, when it finally published a draft IP policy, the government had not developed a coherent developmental policy for IP, but had rather attempted 'ad hoc reforms' in response to immediate practical problems (Davies interview, 2013). IP policy is primarily the responsibility of the Department [i.e. Ministry] of Trade and Industry (DTI), which is counselled by a Standing Advisory Committee on IP (SACIP) established under the 1978 Copyright Act. It is claimed that this body has been sidelined since 1996, when Alec Erwin became minister in the DTI (Dean, 2010: 17). The Department of Science and Technology is heavily involved in initiatives aimed at increasing the protection of innovation, and the Department of Arts and Culture has also played an occasional role in IP issues. Both the broad approach and some ad hoc reforms – for example, the attempt to protect indigenous knowledge – have attracted criticism from civil society and from opposition parties.

For much of the period after 1994, it has been hard to identify the elements for a coherent national IP strategy and policy, despite intermittent attempts to develop one, and despite pressure on the DTI by civil society organizations such as the Treatment Action Campaign (see below). In mid-2011, for example, the DTI organized a meeting at the Council for Scientific and Industrial Research (CSIR) in Pretoria to discuss a policy document that was described as 'an important instrument needed to encourage innovation, technology transfer and research and development' (Hancock, 2011). This meeting did not result in the immediate publication of a policy document, however, and it was only in September 2013 that the important 'Draft National Policy on Intellectual Property (IP) of South Africa: A Policy Framework', was released, together with an invitation for public comment (DTI, 2013).

The DTI recognizes that in an increasingly restrictive global trade environment South Africa must develop a coherent overall IP policy which acknowledges international and treaty obligations, but takes advantage of opportunities to develop strategies that impact on industrial development (Davies interview, 2013). The new draft policy is an expression of that strategic approach. The DTI believes in coordinating such work within the BRICS grouping and WIPO, and points to debates on, for example, the patent system that are already taking place in WIPO and elsewhere (see e.g. WHO et al., 2012).

South African IP policy is developing within a global environment that leaves less and less room for independent national initiatives. The United States exerts constant pressure worldwide to enforce strict protection of its own IPRs, typically although not exclusively through bilateral free trade agreements (FTAs) and TRIPS mechanisms. The five-nation Southern African Customs Union (SACU), in which South Africa is the heavyweight member, has not signed an FTA with the United States and negotiations between SACU and the US have been stalled since 2006, at least partly because of SACU's objections to US demands regarding IP. Trade between South Africa and the United States is regulated within other frameworks such as AGOA (the African Growth and Opportunity Act) and a Trade and Investment Framework Agreement (TIFA) signed in 1999 and renewed in 2012.

DOMINANT AND SUBALTERN IP DISCOURSES IN SOUTH AFRICA

IP practices are embedded in South Africa's legal and economic systems, and much of the literature recognizes the reality of this embeddedness and takes it as the starting point for practical analysis. Indeed, the acceptance of IP as a 'given' form of property, as ontological rather than socially constructed, has contributed to its success both in South Africa and as a worldwide system. It is represented as a 'natural right' in Locke's terms, as the logical way of rewarding artists, musicians, writers, and inventors for their creativity, rather than as the complex historico-legal outcome of centuries of technological development and capitalist political economy. The dominant and largely inherited discourse of IP in South Africa, as in other parts of the world, is thus constituted on the basis of pragmatism and positivism. IP research becomes primarily an exercise in making sense of the way things actually are.

But such an approach masks a deeper reality, which is that the global IP system is expanding rapidly and changing in fundamental ways. Despite the conceptual incoherence of IP and its shallow historical roots, IPRs have increased in economic and political importance in the last few decades. IP issues have entered public consciousness in new ways, while the balance of forces has shifted to favour large commercial interests rather than either creators or consumers. US and EU policy, in defence of industry and commerce, supports the strict worldwide enforcement of IPRs through TRIPS and bilateral FTAs. To some critics, this is not a welcome development:

> The dramatic expansion of intellectual property rights ... threatens to make virtually everything bad about capitalism even worse. Stronger intellectual property rights will reinforce class differences, undermine science and technology, speed up the corporatization of the university, inundate society in legal disputes, and reduce personal freedoms. (Perelman, 2003: 29)

Nevertheless, the positivist discourse presents IP expansion – especially in patent and copyright law – as the extension of the existing system under pressure from technological innovation, and the perception of IP as a common-sense system is reinforced. But expansion has also taken place in other, less obvious ways, including a push for the recognition of IPRs as human rights, a claim that rests on Locke's idea that a person has a right to the fruits of his or her labour (Locke, 1689: 216–217) – the 'labour theory' justification for copyright (e.g. Hughes, 2012: 1221–1222). In modern times, the human rights claim has depended on article 27(2) of the Universal Declaration of Human Rights, adopted in 1948, and more compellingly on article 15(1) of the binding International Covenant on Economic, Social and Cultural Rights of 1966, which South Africa signed in 1994; the government announced its decision to ratify the Covenant only in October 2012 (Petherbridge, 2012). Article 15(1) reads in full:

1. The States Parties to the present Covenant recognize the right of everyone:
   (a) To take part in cultural life;
   (b) To enjoy the benefits of scientific progress and its applications;
   (c) To benefit from the protection of the moral and material interests resulting

> from any scientific, literary or artistic production of which he is the author.

The question is whether article 15(1)(c) really recognizes IP as a human right. The UN's Committee on Economic, Social and Cultural Rights, a subordinate body of the Economic and Social Council, has considered the question. In a discussion paper submitted in 2000, it was argued that the IPRs of natural persons should indeed be recognized:

> The development of a global economy in which intellectual property plays a central role underscores the need for the human rights community to claim the rights of the author, creator and inventor, whether an individual, a group, or a community, as a human right. (Chapman, 2000: 3)

Part of the rationale for this position was the need to create 'an effective intellectual and organizational counterweight to economic interests'; in other words to protect creators against corporations (Chapman, 2000: 3).

Whether recognition would act as a counterweight remains an open question, but it would certainly have other effects. Leaving aside critiques of human rights discourse *per se*, we can acknowledge that human rights derive from the dignity of the human person, and thus have a claim to represent universal and non-culturally-specific values, independent of nationality, race, gender, age, and so on. If this claim to universality is valid, then by implication human rights are also supra-ideological. But the claim is not only that rights are universal; it is that they are also individual and permanent.

To recognize IPRs as a category of human rights is to transform what were originally short-term state grants of monopoly into something qualitatively different – and perpetual. Recognition would consolidate the process of 'propertization' – already well under way – through which the metaphor implicit in the rhetoric of intellectual 'property' has come to be understood literally (Rose, 2002; Carrier, 2004; Hughes, 2006; Loughlan, 2006; Reyman, 2009). Ideas and fixed expression would become forms of property that could be owned in perpetuity. Recognition would facilitate the further criminalization of IPR infringements – again, a process already well under way – as forms of human rights violation, with all the moral overtones that the latter expression bears. It would impose a correlative duty on the state to respect, protect and fulfil IPRs, because 'far from merely being vague statements of aspiration, internationally recognized human rights have the status of international law' (Chapman, 2002: 863).

However, recognition remains problematic. First of all there is the non-trivial difficulty of patent, trademark and copyright terms, which lapse after a defined period:

> the rhetoric of natural rights … is often invoked to argue *for strengthened protection of intellectual property… It is hard to imagine a natural right that miraculously disappears after 20 or 25 years!* (Trebilcock and Howse, 1995: 296, emphasis added)

General Comment no.17 of the UN's Committee on Economic, Social and Cultural Rights (CESCR) makes this same point even more forcefully:

> In contrast to human rights, intellectual property rights are generally of a temporary nature, and can be revoked, licensed or assigned to someone else … intellectual property rights, often with the exception of moral rights, may be allocated, limited in time and scope, traded, amended and even forfeited [but] human rights are timeless expressions of fundamental entitlements of the human person. (CESCR, 2006: 2)

The General Comment is even clearer when it states that it is 'important not to equate intellectual property rights with the human right recognized in article 15, paragraph 1 (c)' (CECSR, 2006: 3).

An additional objection is that the three subsections of Article 15 are written to be read together. Subsection (c) should not and cannot be privileged or treated separately:

> there is a direct relationship between the three sub-sections, the interpretation given to Article 15(1)(c) by definition constrains and probably restricts the interpretation that will be given to the other two sub-sections … The relationship

> between the three sub-sections is in fact of great importance … sections (a), (b), and (c), in principle, each have the same weight. (Cullet, 2007: 424)

South African jurisprudence, in parallel with developments in India (Cullet, 2007: 411) has played a role in slowing down, if not halting altogether, the move towards recognition. In the process of certification of the new Constitution in 1996 (described in detail in Rickard, 2001), the Constitutional Court heard objections that the 'new text' did not recognize IPRs in the bill of rights. The Court rejected the objection, reasoning that:

> the objection was based on the proposition that the right advocated is a 'universally accepted fundamental right, freedom and civil liberty'. Although it is true that many international conventions recognise a right to intellectual property, it is much more rarely recognised in regional conventions protecting human rights and in the constitutions of acknowledged democracies … [it] cannot be characterised as a trend which is universally accepted. In the circumstances, the objection cannot be sustained. (Constitutional Court, 1996: 48–49)

This decision was not universally welcomed in South Africa. In a comment in the *Handbook of South African Copyright Law*, Dean maintained that 'it can be argued that the right to hold intellectual property rights, and more particularly copyright, is a universally accepted fundamental right', and further, that the Constitutional Court decision 'is open to serious question' (Dean, 2012: 1.3). Nevertheless, at the time of writing, the demand for explicit constitutional recognition of IPRs seems to have largely fallen away, since most specialists

> agree that the constitutional property clause has scope to include intellectual property rights. Even Dean, who previously argued that intellectual property should be protected under a separate constitutional property clause … now agrees that intellectual property rights may be included under the constitutional property concept. It would be a logical error to exclude categories of property not explicitly mentioned in the property clause, since the property clause does not specify any particular category of property rights or interests explicitly. (Du Bois, 2012: 192)

Let us now turn to an examination of the rhetoric of IP as it appears in the South African context. The economic interests in play have encouraged some scholars to interrogate local IP narratives in the context of a critique of political economy, and not simply as component parts of a self-contained thought system. Haupt, for example, has attempted precisely this kind of epistemological critique (see e.g., 2008, 2012; Ovesen and Haupt, 2011). Such scholars look behind surface reality in order to ask not only 'how does IP function in South Africa?' but also 'why does it work the way it does?' and 'who benefits?' The last of these questions is clearly important in a developmental state characterized by high levels of social and economic inequality. In the meantime, however, foreign commercial interests, with some support from government, have partially succeeded in dominating the debates about IP in South Africa. The voice of the pro-enforcement, anti-piracy lobby is heard almost to the exclusion of others; in one comparative research project:

> [the] South Africa team documented some eight hundred [industry-inspired] print and broadcast stories over a four-year period in a country with just three major media markets. (Karaganis, 2011: 33)

Consequently, it is hard to avoid the conclusion that the 'evidentiary discourse is … one-sided. Industry reports remain the primary – and in some cases the only – documents in the South African conversation on IP policy and enforcement' (Primo and Lloyd, 2011: 104).

A fundamental claim of the dominant 'discourse of property stewardship' (Reyman, 2009: 14), made both in and about South Africa, is that massive economic damage, assessed at millions of dollars, can be attributed to 'piracy' – that is to say, to IPR infringements. For example, in 2007, the International IP Alliance (IIPA), a monitoring group funded by the US entertainment industry, claimed total 'trade losses' in South Africa of US$122 million (R891 million) for 2006 in the two categories of business software and books alone.

The IIPA is a coalition of associations of content producers, including both the Motion Picture Association of America (MPAA) and the Recording Industry Association of America (RIAA). Its main local ally is the Southern African Federation against Copyright Theft (SAFACT), set up in 1999 to represent the local interests of the MPAA (*The Star*, 2007: 7). These organizations are all interested parties, and their pronouncements require careful assessment. The IIPA works closely with US government agencies, especially the Office of the US Trade Representative (USTR), which produces annual 'Section 301' reports on 'countries who aren't doing enough to meet Hollywood and the pharma industry's definitions of what intellectual property laws should look like' (Masnick, 2012).

Despite the government's conventional – indeed maximalist – official stance regarding IP, South Africa was for several years on the receiving end of a sustained and hostile campaign led by the IIPA:

> anti-piracy efforts in South Africa remain, in key respects, a US-directed enterprise, only partially taken up by local networks of cultural producers and law enforcement agencies ... Although there has been some mobilization on the part of South African musicians, and although US-industry proxies, like SAFACT [Southern African Federation against Copyright Theft], also represent South African film studios and publishers, enforcement discourse and policy at a national level continue to be driven by US- and multinational-funded industry associations. (Primo and Lloyd, 2011: 104)

Between 1998 and 1999 South Africa was on a US government 'watch list' for insufficiently stringent IP enforcement, mainly because of a dispute with pharmaceutical companies about parallel imports of medicine (Love, 1999). In 2003, the IIPA reported that:

> perhaps no country in the world has had a greater increase in audiovisual piracy levels ... Imports of pirated copies of motion picture DVDs ... flood the South African market. Devotion of adequate resources to fight piracy remains lacking ... corruption exists within South African Customs. (IIPA, 2003: 271)

The most recent Section 301 report to focus specifically on South Africa was published in 2007. It featured strong language about domestic piracy and lamented the failure to shift public opinion against piracy:

> Industry reports that piracy levels are getting worse largely as a result of the perception amongst consumers that piracy is a victimless crime. The impact of piracy in South Africa is devastating for legitimate right holders, legitimate distributors, and retail businesses ... Legitimate distributors have reduced employment levels ... many rental outlets have actually closed. (IIPA, 2007: 520)

The attention of both the USTR and the IIPA has now turned elsewhere. But the discourse remains the same; most recently, the South African DTI-sponsored Farlam report on collecting societies repeated similar claims of large-scale losses of revenue (by entertainment conglomerates), also quoting industry rather than independent sources:

> A RiSA report ... on digital music statistics estimates that approximately 3.6 million songs are illegally downloaded in South Africa on a monthly basis, translating into monetary losses of R36 million monthly and R432 million annually. A PricewaterhouseCoopers report ... estimates that if the current trend continues, by 2014 the potential revenue loss due to copyright infringement will be in excess of R500 million per year. (CRC, 2011: 34)

Independent research indicates that it is close to impossible to calculate the economic impact of IP-infringing activity in a robust way whether by sector or nationally. In addition, industry reports invariably discount the effects of commercial piracy as an *economic activity*, momentarily putting aside questions of its morality or legality. The US General Accounting Office has cautiously acknowledged that such effects exist and that 'certain stakeholders may experience some positive effects from counterfeits and piracy, though there is little information available' (GAO, 2010: 9). An OECD report that attempted to test data and methodologies on economic harm concluded that:

> the overall degree to which products are being counterfeited and pirated is unknown and there

> do not appear to be any methodologies that could be employed to develop an acceptable overall estimate … [the] information has significant limitations … and *falls far short of what is needed to develop a robust overall estimate*. (OECD, 2008: 71, emphasis added)

Even in specific areas such as public health there were major obstacles: 'precise measurement of counterfeiting related public health effects is … *virtually impossible* (OECD, 2008: 149, emphasis added).

At the time of writing, the struggle to dominate and control the debate on IP's utility and benefits continues. In one incident, a conference – 'Africa Intellectual Property Forum: Intellectual Property, Regional Integration and Economic Growth in Africa' – was to have taken place in Cape Town in April 2012. The organizers were the US Department of Commerce and WIPO, with heavy industry sponsorship and involvement. The proposed conference aroused a storm of protest from civil society organizations and others when it turned out to be a thinly-disguised enforcement and anti-piracy event, which was described by one over-excited commentator as a 'chilling example of US duplicity and conflict of interest at its worst' (New, 2012). The forum was quietly abandoned, although a similar meeting did take place in Tanzania with WIPO and Japanese sponsorship a year later (WIPO, 2013).

PATENTS, ECONOMIC DEVELOPMENT AND HUMAN RIGHTS

Does IP, especially patenting, promote economic development, even in 'surprising' ways (Brewster, 2011) or is it irredeemably a tool for the aggressive exploitation of poor countries by rich ones (Story et al., 2006)? Serious attention has begun to be paid to this question as it applies to the South African case in research by, for example, Teljeur (2003), Kaplan et al. (2009) and Pouris and Pouris (2011), among others. But even if IPRs do help development, what is an appropriate response when IPRs clash with economic and social human rights, such as the right of access to medical treatment (Martin et al., 2007)? This last battle is still being fought between civil society, the private sector and government, as we shall see below.

The patent system is governed by the Patent Act (no.57 of 1978). Since 2011 it has been managed by the Companies and IP Commission (CIPC), as mandated by the Companies Act (no. 71 of 2008). The CIPC is an autonomous statutory body, and merges two previous entities – the Office of Companies and IP Enforcement (OCIPE) and the Companies and IP Registration Office (CIPRO) – as well as expanding their functions.

South Africa requires an 'inventive step' before a patent can be granted, and the concept must not have been previously published. However, South Africa differs from other jurisdictions in several minor ways, and in some significant ones. The minor ways include the tests for the inventive step, which are similar but not identical to those in other countries. There is no mechanism for third-party objections. Additionally, only qualified patent attorneys can draft and file final applications, although short-term or provisional applications, which protect products or processes still under development, may be filed by inventors themselves.

The South African system is depository or 'non-examining': 'the responsibility for ensuring that the patent is valid rests with the applicant … [the Commission] does not investigate the novelty or inventive merit of the invention' (Pouris and Pouris 2011: 28). It should be noted that the government's draft IP policy of September 2013 proposes establishing a substantive search and examination system with the possibility of both pre- and post-grant opposition, and patent flexibilities, as allowed by TRIPS (DTI, 2013: 9–10). This would bring South African practice into line with other jurisdictions where patent examiners search for 'prior art', meaning relevant information published before a specified date. In South Africa at present the responsibility for validating a patent rests with applicants, who must conduct local and international searches at their own expense. The CIPC validates the documentation, not the substance, with the outcome that invalid patents are often registered. Local searching is not easy; there is no complete online database of local patents, and searches have to be 'carried out by hand ... at the Patent Office through a card-based system' (Pouris and Pouris, 2011: 32). In addition to this failing, there is another major weakness:

> WIPO's International Patent Classification system (IPC) is followed, but only to a limited extent: South Africa classifies up to the level of subclasses (of which there are 628 at present) but not up to the level of groups and subgroups (of which there are approximately 69,000). This crude classification *inevitably leads to excessively broad scope of patents granted.* (Teljeur 2003: 54, emphasis added)

The most hotly-disputed sector in South Africa as far as the social role of patents is concerned is health, and in the popular narrative around access to medicine, the pharmaceutical companies ('big pharma') are the undisputed villains. Worldwide, tens of billions of US dollars are spent on health research every year, of which 10 per cent is spent on the diseases of the global south (affecting 90 per cent of the world's population). The other 90 per cent of the money goes towards finding cures for the lucrative ailments of the wealthy ten per cent of people in the developed north. This anomaly is known as the 10/90 disequilibrium, an expression coined by the Global Forum for Health Research in the late 1990s (GFHR, 1999: 7). It is understandable, though regrettable, that commercial companies, whose first duty is to their shareholders, try to maximize profit; but the disequilibrium applies in the public sector too.

The big pharma companies rely heavily on patent enforcement for profitability, although the effectiveness of their research and development programmes is disputed, as even UN specialized agencies admit:

> the pharmaceutical sector stands out in terms of its dependence on patents to capture returns to R&D, *but its role in innovation and how to enhance its effectiveness are matters of continuing debate.* (WHO et al. 2012: 13, emphasis added)

Big pharma plays the system to maintain control of world markets by 'evergreening' and by fighting measures based on TRIPS and Doha exceptions. These permit the use or importation of cheaper generic versions of branded drugs. Big pharma also muddies the waters by conflating counterfeits and generics. For example, in imposing stringent IP enforcement even when no public health concerns exist, the Anti-Counterfeiting Trade Agreement (ACTA) blurs the distinction between trademark infringement and trademark counterfeiting, and between counterfeit and generic drugs (MSF, 2012: 2–3). It is in this broad context that the ongoing activism of South Africa's Treatment Action Campaign (TAC) can be understood.

TAC was founded in 1998 as a broad-based pressure group organized around access to medicine and specifically the 'availability, affordability and use of HIV treatments' (Friedman and Mottiar, 2005: 513). The South African HIV/AIDS crisis has been described, without exaggeration, as being of 'catastrophic proportions' (De Vos, 2003: 83): an estimated 5.6 million South Africans were living with HIV in 2011 (NDH, 2011: iii). During the two-term presidency of Thabo Mbeki, from June 1999 to September 2008, official policy was strongly influenced, with disastrous consequences, by Mbeki's personal suspicion of the scientific consensus around AIDS and its causality.

TAC recognized that access to medicine is inseparable from human rights and social justice concerns. The campaign was committed to a multi-faceted programme of street action, education and litigation. Its first action – 'intended to be tangible, understandable, emotive, and lifesaving' (Heywood, 2009: 20) – was to demand that the government establish a programme to provide AZT treatment to pregnant women in order to reduce mother-to-child transmission (MTCT) of HIV. The government had run some pilot projects, but they had been closed down. This brought TAC face to face with patent law; the government's reaction to their demands was to cite the high price of patented AZT as an obstacle to its wider use. The patent holder responsible for the high price was GlaxoSmithKline, a British company and one of the biggest of the 'big pharmas'. The subsequent litigation (*Treatment Action Campaign v. Minister of Health*) turned on the question of whether the establishment of pilot sites constituted compliance with section 27(2) of the constitution, which guarantees access to health care (Budlender, 2001: 129–131). When judgment went against the government in the Pretoria High Court, the case was appealed to the Constitutional Court, where most of the High Court's determinations were upheld: socio-economic rights, such as access to health care were indeed justiciable, and the courts had the power to grant relief, including forcing policy changes.

The MTCT case introduced TAC to the moralizing discourse of IP enforcement, and forced the campaign to offer an alternative to it. As Halbert has argued, big pharma had developed an effective rhetorical strategy in which the drug companies presented themselves as the victims of morally bankrupt behaviour by countries behaving like pirates and thieves by appropriating IP (2005: 91). TAC – and its allies overseas – successfully counter-posed 'a contrary image of a greedy and aggressive industry that placed profits ahead of human life' (2005: 107). The defining moment came in February 1998, when the Pharmaceutical Manufacturers' Association (PMA) went to court to challenge the constitutionality of the Medicines Act (1997), which permitted the parallel importation of cheap generics under broadly-defined circumstances. This was viewed by the PMA as IP infringement, and aggressive lobbying succeeded in getting South Africa placed on the USTR watch list (Heywood 2001: 139). TAC intervened in the PMA case as *amicus curiae* on the government's side, and organized public demonstrations against the drug companies. Subsequently, TAC's counter-narrative began to be reproduced in reports in the international press:

> The case is an attempt to block South Africa from importing cheap medicines. The drug companies have spent three years and millions of pounds preparing the case. They have retained virtually every patent lawyer in South Africa ... their [lawyers] will try to stop the South African government from buying the medicines its people so badly need from countries where the prices are lowest, on the grounds that it is infringing world trade agreements ... a tide of outrage is swelling among local activists and international aid organisations who see medicines denied to the sick in the name of commerce. (Boseley, 2001)

After some years, the PMA dropped the case, partly because of the negative publicity, but the government still refused to implement a broad antiretroviral drug (ARV) programme. After further campaigning, TAC finally succeeded in winning a 'much greater victory, the August 2003 decision by the national Cabinet to sanction the distribution of ARVs to people living with HIV/AIDS rather than purely to mothers' (Friedman and Mottiar, 2005: 514).

TAC campaigning against the use of IPRs to deny poor people access to health care continues. At the time of writing, TAC and Médecins Sans Frontières were running a 'Fix the Patent Laws' drive to pressure the government into writing TRIPS and Doha flexibilities regarding generics into national legislation. They argued that the state was still obliged by section 27 of the constitution, guaranteeing access to health care, to make such changes. But the issue of the impact of patent enforcement on such access remains extremely polarized, with almost no common ground between the pharmaceutical industry and either government or activist organizations. The leaking in January 2014 of an industry plan (Public Affairs Engagement, 2014) intended to 'prevent damage to innovation from the ... Draft National IP Policy in South Africa', apparently by clandestine means, provoked a fierce reaction from the country's Minister of Health, Aaron

Motsoaledi. Public Affairs Engagement is a lobbying company based in the US, and was hired by the Innovative Pharmaceutical Association of South Africa (IPASA) to plan a campaign to block reform of the patent system. The Minister accused the companies of conspiring against the state, and described the document as amounting in effect to an attempted genocide in a conspiracy that he described as 'Satanic'. Motsoaledi added that he was 'not using strong words [but] appropriate words' (De Wet, 2014). It seems likely, then, that South Africa's political battles in this area are far from over, and will probably impact significantly on the wider struggles over patents in the global south generally.

PATENTS, INNOVATION POLICY AND HIGHER EDUCATION

A primary objective of government economic policy is to encourage industrial innovation – the ongoing development of new technologies with commercial application. A key policy instrument in pursuit of this objective is patent maximization. Government practice follows international trends by aiming to develop 'institutional structures that facilitate technology development and its progression into national and international markets' (DST, 2012: 18). While local firms 'are innovating at a level that is comparable to that of European business firms' they are hampered by weak institutions, including 'insufficient information/knowledge about technologies … an insufficient amount of venture capital … an insufficient amount of human capital, and … restrictive governmental regulations' (Rooks and Oerlemans, 2005: 1224).

The world of patents is ruled by a discourse in which the causal link between innovation and the granting of monopoly rights via patents is taken as a given. There are two classes of objection to this position, first that patents are often *unnecessary* for innovation; second that they *actually harm* it. There is some historical evidence that the expectation of future profit has indeed helped to drive innovation worldwide (Moser, 2005) – but it is also true that such profits may be available *without* patents. It turns out that more than three-quarters of the most successful global innovations from 1963 to the present have not been patented, although there is some variation across industrial sectors:

> a large share of inventions … are not protected by means of patents, casting serious doubts on the critical role of patents for generating technological breakthroughs. (Fontana et al., 2009: 26)

A South African example of this principle is the *dolos*, a 20-ton geometric concrete device for protecting harbours from oceanic erosion. It was devised in East London in 1963 by engineers working for South African Railways and Harbours (now Transnet) and was never patented, for reasons that have been hotly disputed (Bowen, 1999). Nevertheless, millions of *dolosse* are in use all over the world, and the invention can clearly be considered successful. There is also a growing body of research that supports the second objection, that patent rights do not encourage innovation, but rather inhibit it (Boldrin and Levine, 2008; Stiglitz, 2008).

Despite the accumulated evidence that patents may not serve the purpose of encouraging innovation, they have expanded into new areas, especially since the 1980s. It is now possible to patent algorithms, diagnostic procedures, software, business methods, genetically-modified organisms, and even scientific principles. In the United States, this situation has arisen largely because of the close relationship between the US Patent Office and the Court of Appeals for the Federal Circuit, where patent litigation is decided (Masur, 2011). In South Africa, where the number of patents granted is much smaller, the breadth of patentability can probably be attributed to the country's depositary, non-examining regime.

There are diverging assessments of the value of the South African regime. As we shall see, some commentators believe that it is ineffective, and even that it is in crisis.

They argue that there is no evidence that it stimulates innovation or benefits local industrial development, and indeed suggest that it has the opposite effect: the current regime is detrimental to the country's developmental efforts' (Pouris and Pouris, 2011: 32). Others maintain that the system causes active harm, particularly to public health:

> South Africa's current patent laws puts [sic] the rights of patent-holders before the rights of patients. Our law includes all the worst parts from the TRIPS agreement, but does not include the parts that we can use to make medicines more affordable. (TAC, 2012: 4)

By contrast, in terms of the country's treaty obligations, the number of patents granted, and the measurable 'strength' of the system, South Africa holds

> a particularly advanced formal position in international patent protection, and is a member of, *inter alia*, the Paris Convention, the PCT [Patent Cooperation Treaty], the Budapest Treaty and TRIPS, which ensure national treatment and grant priority to first application for intellectual property protection filed in one member country in respect of corresponding applications filed in other member countries. (Teljeur, 2003: 52)

Other purely formal assessments also rank South Africa highly: the country places 20th in the world on general IP protection, out of 144 countries evaluated, according to the current *Global Competitiveness Report* for 2012–2013 (Schwab, 2012: 325); and a decade earlier was classified 13th in a world index for patent protection devised by Park and Wagh. The index measured 'strength' according to five criteria, namely: coverage, duration, enforcement, treaty membership and limitations on patent rights (2002: 33, 39).

A key legislative instrument for the implementation of innovation policy is the Intellectual Property Rights from Publicly Financed Research and Development Act (No. 51 of 2008, hereafter IPR-PFRD), which came into force in August 2010. The legislation was seen as a highly conventional IP-oriented response to the problem:

> … when the policy documents lapse back into … more familiar territory … they turn to proprietary models of intellectual property protection … underpinned by a market view of higher education. This means that patents and copyrights become the predominant measures for research success, rather than social and developmental impact. (Gray, 2008: 9–10)

New institutional structures were put in place, including the Technology Innovation Agency (TIA) and the National IP Management Office (NIPMO). TIA has subsequently been criticized for ineffectiveness and for a 'flawed understanding of innovation' (Wild, 2012: 4). NIPMO, which was set up in early 2011, has assisted universities and research councils to set up technology transfer offices (TTOs), and holds courses under the rubric 'IP Wise'. Two cooperative TTOs, serving groups of non-research-intensive institutions, have been established regionally, in the Eastern Cape and KwaZulu-Natal, and TIA has also set up regional offices in different provinces to support 'technopreneurs' (DST, 2012: 18). The assumption is that comprehensive IP protection is 'the only valid way of achieving benefit for the country from publicly funded research' (Gray, 2009: 7). Nonetheless, there is some recognition that pay-offs may still be some way away: 'we should not expect to see … benefits for up to 20 years or longer. The question is whether the investment necessary to sustain this process through to success is tolerable' (quoted by Dell, 2010).

There have been some success stories. For example, Stellenbosch University set up InnovUS Technology Transfer as a technology transfer company in 1999 to encourage patenting, licensing and the formation of spin-off companies; InnovUS has reportedly been especially successful with wine biotechnology-related patents. In general, the TTOs are the gate-keepers of patentable research outcomes and require researchers to keep their research secret so that it may, if possible, be patented. Critics argue that the IPR-PFRD

> appears to see open innovation, open source and open access as aberrations that need to be controlled through a bureaucratic process of

> government scrutiny ... the IPR Act and its draconian draft regulations could well block the ability of the government to implement ... open innovation requirements. (Gray, 2009: 7)

The IPR-PFRD follows the 'Bayh-Dole model', named after the US legislation (35 USC §200–212) passed in 1980 that allowed universities, for the first time, to file patents deriving from government-funded research. The model has spread around the world as other countries have tried to 'replicate the high technology-led economic development [in the United States] that Bayh-Dole is generally credited with having helped create' (Stevens, 2004: 93). From the late 1970s, university-held patents in the US have doubled roughly every five years; by 2000 nearly every US university had a technology transfer office (TTO); and licensing revenues also increased rapidly, as did the number of spin-off companies (Nelson, 2001: 13). The widely held assumption is that these developments are primarily outcomes of Bayh-Dole.

However, this assumption and others associated with it are problematic. These assumptions are: first, that the growth in the number of university patents in the US results directly from the Bayh-Dole legislation; second, that the acquisition of patents by universities has a significant financial benefit for them or for the economy in general; and last, that the model is easily applicable in the South African context. An important factor in the immediately pre- as well as post-Bayh-Dole growth of university patents in the US may have been the expansion of patentability, particularly in biotechnology and information technology, which coincided with the rapid growth of those research areas. The legislation magnified an effect that was already present (Mowery et al., 2001; Nelson, 2001). In addition, the marketability of specific patents is hard to predict, and the process is a lottery; not all inventors are George Rieveschl and not all inventions are Benadryl:

> An important finding of empirical innovation research is that the returns to innovation are extremely skewed; most inventions are commercial failures, and the private and social returns are reaped from the few extremely successful and important innovations. (Georghiou et al., 2003: 35)

Data are available for the financial outcomes of TTO activity in US universities in a series of annual reports by the Association of University Technology Managers (AUTM). Revenues are growing, but slowly. In 1995, the income generated by licensing university inventions was 1.7 per cent of total research expenditure; by 2004 this had increased to 2.9 per cent. According to the most recent figures in the AUTM's *US Licensing Activity Survey* for FY2010, total sponsored research expenditure in the surveyed universities was US$59.1 billion, and total licence income was US$2.4 billion, or just over 4 per cent. Most US universities – 130 out of 155 surveyed in research published in 2013 – do not generate enough licensing revenue even to pay the operating costs of their TTOs (Valdivia, 2013: 9). In South Africa, where this type of innovation strategy is still in its infancy, it seems likely that a purely regulatory approach, as typified by the IPR-PFRD, will be unable to 'achieve the developmental intentions of the Act, as it would not sufficiently engage universities and their inventors in the task of considering how best to transfer knowledge generated by public funds to industry and to society' (Ncube et al., 2013: 311).

But financial outcomes may not be the only relevant evaluative measure of the benefits of university research, or indeed of TTOs:

> Although being one of the worlds' [sic] largest economies there is only scarce evidence about how TTO are organized in Germany, how they perform and how performance is shaped by institutional and regional factors. (Hülsbeck et al., 2013: 200)

Indeed, it may be that a TTO's success or failure should not be measured only in economic or crude financial terms. Sorensen and Chambers have suggested a 'knowledge access metric' as a way of evaluating technology transfer (2008), and in South Africa the University of Cape Town has taken the opportunity to expand the concept of 'commercialization' to mean

> the process by which any Intellectual Property emanating from research and development by UCT's employees, students and visitors is or may be adapted or used *for any purpose that may provide any benefit* and 'commercialise' shall have a corresponding meaning. (UCT, 2011: 4, emphasis added)

This has enabled the university to place IP in the public domain when appropriate, while meeting the requirements of IPR-PFRD. Surprisingly, other institutions do not seem to have followed suit.

Last, it appears from research conducted in South Africa even before the passing of the IPR-PFRD, that not only may the assumptions about the impact of Bayh-Dole in the US be unsupported, but that the ease with which it can be replicated has likely also been overestimated. Wolson cites the AUTM surveys to the effect that investment in technology transfer needs to be 'substantial', that there is a 'significant time-lag' before benefits are realized, and that even then the distribution of benefits is uneven (2007: 357). She adds:

> in South Africa, it remains a fairly common perception that the main motivation for a university to undertake technology transfer activities is for the purpose of generating income. This is at least partly attributable to a few well-publicised 'blockbuster technologies' which were very successfully commercialised by certain US universities to generate substantial income streams for the institutions and inventors concerned. These cases have created the perception that university technology transfer activities can provide a substantial new source of income for universities. However … it has become clear that 'big hits' are few and far between, and typical returns, although not trivial, are nonetheless far lower than many had expected. Furthermore, it appears that a number of TTOs do not even recover their full running costs out of income they generate. (Wolson, 2007: 357–358)

The evidence that start-ups or spin-offs (companies set up by academic inventors) are a source of large returns is also ambiguous. A recent Swedish study concluded that 'academic entrepreneurs on average do not make less than they would if staying employed at their university. However, they do take on substantially more risk' (Åstebro et al., 2013: 283).

Huebner has argued that innovation is in decline globally because there are economic and intellectual limits to the human capacity for innovation, and we are 'closer to a technological limit than many people realize'. Consequently, innovation may be slowing down worldwide (2005: 980). In South Africa there has been concern about declining research productivity since the 1980s, and it is only recently that there has been a slight upturn (Pouris, 2012). If the research-to-innovation process is a pipeline, with funding, knowledge and institutional support in at one end, and inventions and new processes coming out at the other end, then the future success of IPR-PFRD depends on keeping the tap open, i.e. the generous funding of basic research. A decade ago, South Africa was fast losing ground: 'the overall picture of South African science … is one of deterioration and decline' (Pouris, 2003: 426). In a 2012 survey, the picture had improved somewhat, with the 'world share of publications … on the verge of reaching its highest contribution in history' (Pouris 2012: 4). Whether this improvement is sufficient and what it means for innovation, as only a part of what has been called a much broader and more complex 'knowledge and innovation ecosystem' remains to be seen (Ncube et al., 2013: 311).

CONCLUSION

For several reasons, South Africa is of interest as a case study in the analysis of ongoing struggles over IPRs and their contested relationship to such issues as economic and social development, or human rights and the state's duty to respect, protect and fulfil those rights, as well as the disputed efficiency and effectiveness of IP as a set of legal, political and economic mechanisms. These reasons include the fact that its complex judicial system is sophisticated enough to produce significant jurisprudence around IP questions; its government is committed to the development – however slowly – of a new kind of IP policy that will, hopefully, serve the interests of the country and its poor rather than only the interests of corporations; and the size of its economy means that advances or defeats in South Africa are noticed and have repercussions in other parts of Africa and the global south. More worrying, however, is the increasing polarization of positions regarding such matters as drug patents, with accusations of 'dirty tricks' being made even by government ministers, as we have seen. Whether it is possible to arrive at compromises that protect both the business interests of large corporations *and* the economic and social rights of disadvantaged populations with regard to access to health and education remains to be seen, but at the time of writing it must be said that the prospects for such compromise do not seem likely.

ACKNOWLEDGEMENTS

I gratefully acknowledge the assistance of Dilshaad Bray, Matthew David, Adam Haupt, Judith Head, Caroline Ncube, Chris Oxtoby and Tobias Schönwetter in the preparation of this chapter. An earlier version was presented at the 'Sage Handbook of Intellectual Property' Symposium, University of Durham, 29–30 June 2013, and in the seminar series of the IP Unit, Faculty of Law, University of Cape Town, 11 November 2013, and I am grateful to participants in those meetings for their supportive criticism and feedback. Full responsibility for any errors of fact or interpretation is mine alone.

REFERENCES

Blogs about South African IP

Afro-IP – www.afro-ip.blogspot.com/

Anton Mostert Chair of Intellectual Property (Owen Dean) – http://blogs.sun.ac.za/iplaw/news-3/from-ipstell/

Caroline Ncube – www.carolinebncube.wordpress.com/

Denise Nicolson – www.africanlii.org/blogs/denise/

Interviews

Rob Davies (Minister of Trade and Industry), Cape Town, 25 April 2013.

Moosa Ebrahim (Chief of Staff, Ministry; DTI), Cape Town, 25 April 2013.

Published Sources

Åstebro, Thomas et al. (2013) 'Does academic entrepreneurship pay?', *Industrial and Corporate Change* 22(1): 281–311.

Boldrin, Michele and David K. Levine (2008) *Against Intellectual Monopoly.* Cambridge: Cambridge University Press.

Boseley, Sarah (2001) 'At the mercy of drug giants', *The Guardian*, 12 February.

Bowen, David (1999) Letter to the editor. *Daily Dispatch* [East London], 9 July.

Brewster, Rachel (2011) 'The surprising benefits to developing countries of linking international trade and intellectual property', *Chicago Journal of International Law* 12(1): 1–54.

Budlender, Geoff (2001) 'South African court rules on the state's obligation to prevent mother-to-child transmission of HIV', *Law, Democracy and Development* 5(2): 129–131.

Carrier, Michael A. (2004) 'Cabining intellectual property through a property paradigm', *Duke Law Journal* 54(1) October: 1–145.

CESCR (2006) *General Comment no.17.* New York: UN Committee on Economic, Social and Cultural Rights. (Document no. E/C.12/GC/17, 12 January).

Chapman, Audrey (2000) 'Approaching intellectual property as a human right: obligations related to Article 15(1)(c)', New York: United Nations, Economic and Social Council (Document E/C.12/2000/12, 3 October).

Chapman, Audrey (2002) 'The human rights implications of intellectual property protection', *Journal of International Economic Law* 5(4) December: 861–882.

Constitutional Court (1996) Certification of the Constitution of the Republic of South Africa, 1996 (CCT 23/96) [1996] ZACC 26; 1996 (4) SA 744 (CC); 1996 (10) BCLR 1253 (CC) (6 September).

CRC (2011) *Copyright Review Commission Report.* Pretoria: Department of Trade and Industry.

Cullet, Philippe (2007) 'Human rights and intellectual property in the TRIPS era', *Human Rights Quarterly* 29: 403–430.

Dean, Owen (2010) 'Why South Africa can't get copy right', *The Times*, 8 April: 17.

Dean, Owen (2012) *Handbook of South African Copyright Law* [Service 14]. Cape Town: Juta.

Dell, Sharon (2010) 'South Africa: jury out on intellectual property laws', *University World News* 62: 19 September (www.universityworldnews.com/article.php?story=20100918075117541).

De Vos, Pierre (2003) 'So much to do. So little done: the right of access to anti-retroviral drugs post-Grootboom', *Law, Democracy and Development* 7(1): 83–112.

De Wet, Phillip (2014) 'Motsoaledi: big pharma's satanic plot is genocide', *Mail and Guardian* 17 January (www.mg.co.za/article/2014-01-16-motsoaledi-big-pharmas-satanic-plot-is-genocide).

DST (2012) *Annual Report 2011/2012*. Pretoria: Department of Science and Technology.

DTI (2013) 'Draft National Policy on Intellectual Property (IP) of South Africa: A Policy Framework', *Government Gazette* 36816 (4 September): 3–43.

Du Bois, Mikhalien (2012) 'Intellectual property as a constitutional property right: the South African approach', *South African Mercantile Law Journal* 24: 177–193.

Fontana, Roberto et al. (2009) *The Nature of Inventive Activities: Evidence from a Data-set of R&D Awards*. Tokyo: Institute of Innovation Research, Hitotsubashi University (IIR Working Paper WP-090-09).

Friedman, Steven and Shauna Mottiar (2005) 'A rewarding engagement? The Treatment Action Campaign and the politics of HIV/AIDS', *Politics and Society* 33(4): 511–565.

GAO (2010) *Intellectual Property: Observations on Efforts to Quantify the Economic Effects of Counterfeit and Pirated Goods*. Washington DC: United States Government Accounting Office.

Georghiou, Luke et al. (2003) *Evaluation of the Finnish Innovation System*. Helsinki: Ministry of Trade and Industry (Publications; no.5/2003).

GFHR (1999) *The 10/90 Report on Health Research 1999*. Geneva: Global Forum for Health Research.

Gray, Eve (2008) *A Critique of Research Dissemination Policy in South Africa, with Recommendations for Policy Reform*. Budapest: International Policy Fellowship Program, Open Society Institute.

Gray, Eve (2009) 'Intellectual property: clash gets to heart of how to build a better life for all', *Business Day* 13 July: 7.

Halbert, Deborah (2005) *Resisting Intellectual Property*. London: Routledge.

Hancock, Tracy (2011) 'South Africa moves to enhance its intellectual property policy,' *Engineering News* (19 August) (www.engineeringnews.co.za/article/indaba-intended-to-enrich-ip-policy-development-2011-08-19).

Harms, Louis and Owen Dean (2012) 'South Africa's specialized intellectual property courts regime', in: *Study on Specialized Intellectual Property Courts*. Washington DC: International Intellectual Property Institute; US Patent and Trademark Office.

Haupt, Adam (2008) *Stealing Empire: P2P, Intellectual Property and Hip-Hop Subversion*. Cape Town: HSRC Press.

Haupt, Adam (2012) *Static: Race and Representation in Post-apartheid Music, Media and Film*. Cape Town: HSRC Press.

Heywood, Mark (2001) 'Debunking conglomo-talk: a case study of the amicus curiae as an instrument for advocacy, investigation and mobilisation', *Law, Democracy and Development* 5(2): 133–162.

Heywood, Mark (2009) 'South Africa's Treatment Action Campaign: combining law and social mobilization to realize the right to health', *Journal of Human Rights Practice* 1(1): 14–36.

Huebner, Jonathan (2005) 'A possible declining trend for worldwide innovation', *Technological Forecasting and Social Change* 72: 980–986.

Hughes, Justin (2006) 'Copyright and incomplete historiographies: of piracy, propertization and Thomas Jefferson', *Southern California Law Review* 79: 993–1084.

Hughes, Justin (2012) 'Traditional knowledge, cultural expression, and the siren's call of property', *San Diego Law Review* 49: 1215–1266.

Hülsbeck, Marcel, Erik E. Lehmann and Alexander Starnecker (2013) 'Performance of technology transfer offices in Germany', *Journal of Technology Transfer* 38(3): 199–215.

IIPA (2003) 'South Africa', in: *International Intellectual Property Alliance 2003 Special 301 Report*. Washington DC: IIPA, 271–287.

IIPA (2007) 'Special mention: South Africa', in: *International Intellectual Property Alliance 2007 Special 301 Report*. Washington DC: IIPA, 520–526.

Kaplan, David et al. (2009) *The Economics of Intellectual Property in South Africa*. Geneva: WIPO.

Karaganis, Joe (ed.) (2011) *Media Piracy in Developing Economies*. New York: Social Science Research Council.

Klopper, Hennie et al. (2011) *Law of Intellectual Property in South Africa*. Durban: LexisNexis.

Kornegay, Francis (2012) 'South Africa takes its place on the world stage among global powers', in: *BRICS New Delhi Summit 2012*, edited by Marina Larionova and John Kirton. London: Newsdesk Communications, 42–43.

Locke, John (1689) *Two Treatises of Government*, 6th edn. London: Millar and others.

Loughlan, Patricia (2006) 'Pirates, parasites, reapers, sowers, fruits, foxes: the metaphors of intellectual property', *Sydney Law Review* 28: 211–226.

Love, James (1999) 'Annotated USTR 301 Report against South Africa', *IP-Health List*, 7 May (http://www.essentialdrugs.org/edrug/archive/199905/msg00015.php).

Martin, Greg et al. (2007) 'Balancing intellectual property monopoly privileges and the need for essential medicines', *Globalization and Health* 3(4) (www.globalizationandhealth.com/content/3/1/4).

Masnick, Mike (2012) 'Could the Special 301 Report be useful? Proposed law would broaden it to condemn Internet censorship', *Techdirt* (18 July) (www.techdirt.com/articles/20120717/01572419723/could-special-301-report-be-useful-proposed-law-would-broaden-it-to-condemn-internet-censorship.shtml).

Masur, Jonathan (2011) 'Patent inflation', *Yale Law Journal* 121: 470–532.

Moser, Petra (2005) 'How do patent laws influence innovation? Evidence from nineteenth-century World's Fairs', *American Economic Review* 95(4) (September): 1214–1236.

Mowery, David C. et al. (2001) 'The growth of patenting and licensing by US universities: as assessment of the effects of the Bayh-Dole act of 1980', *Research Policy* 30: 99–119.

MSF (2012) *A Blank Cheque for Abuse: the Anti-Counterfeiting Trade Agreement (ACTA) and its Impact on Access to Medicines*, February. Geneva: Médecins Sans Frontières.

Ncube, Caroline, Lucienne Abrahams and Titilayo Akinsanmi (2013) 'Effects of the South African IP regime on generating value from publicly-funded research: an exploratory study of two universities', in: *Innovation and Intellectual Property: Collaborative Dynamics in Africa*, edited by J. de Beer et al. Cape Town: University of Cape Town Press, 282–315.

NDH (2011) *The National Antenatal Sentinel HIV and Syphilis Prevalence Survey 2011*. Pretoria: National Department of Health.

Nelson, Richard R. (2001) 'Observations on the post-Bayh-Dole rise of patenting at American universities', *Journal of Technology Transfer* 26: 13–19.

New, William (2012) 'US, WIPO training programme on IP rights in Africa comes under fire', *Intellectual Property Watch* (12 February) (www.ip-watch.org/2012/02/12/us-wipo-training-programme-on-ip-rights-in-africa-comes-under-fire/).

OECD (2008) *The Economic Impact of Counterfeiting and Piracy*. Paris: Organisation for Economic Cooperation and Development.

Ovesen, Håvard and Adam Haupt (2011) 'Vindicating capital: heroes and villains in A Lion's Trail', *Ilha do Desterro* 61 (July–December): 73–107.

Park, Walter G. and Smita Wagh (2002) 'Index of patent rights', in: *Economic Freedom of the World: 2002 Annual Report*, edited by James Gwartney and Robert Lawson. Vancouver: Fraser Institute, 33–41.

Perelman, Michael (2003) 'The political economy of intellectual property', *Monthly Review* 54(8) January: 29–37.

Petherbridge, Demichelle (2012) *South Africa's Pending Ratification of the International Covenant on Economic, Social and Cultural Rights: What Are the Implications?* Stellenbosch: Socio-Economic Rights and Administrative Justice Research Project, Stellenbosch University.

Pouris, Anastassios (2003) 'South Africa's research publication record: the last ten years', *South African Journal of Science*, 99: 425–428.

Pouris, Anastassios (2012) 'Science in South Africa: the dawn of a renaissance?', *South African Journal of Science* 108(7/8): 1–6.

Pouris, Anthipi and Anastassios Pouris (2011) 'Patents and economic development in South Africa: managing intellectual property rights', *South African Journal of Science* 107(11/12): 24–33.

Primo, Natasha and Libby Lloyd (2011) 'South Africa', in: *Media Piracy in Developing Economies* edited by Joe Karaganis. New York: Social Science Research Council, 99–147.

Public Affairs Engagement (2014) 'A proposal prepared for PhRMA and IPASA: campaign to prevent damage to innovation from the proposed draft National IP Policy in South Africa' (http://cdn.mg.co.za/content/documents/2014/01/16/skmbt36314011511040.pdf).

Reyman, Jessica (2009) 'Property, theft, piracy: rhetoric and regulation in MGM Studios v Grokster', in: *Composition and Copyright: Perspectives on Teaching, Text-making and Fair Use*, edited by Steve Westbrook. Albany NY: State University of New York Press, 9–30.

Rickard, Carmel (2001) 'The certification of the constitution of South Africa', in: *The Post-apartheid Constitutions: Perspectives on South Africa's Basic Law*, edited by Penelope Andrews and Stephen Ellman. Johannesburg: Witwatersrand University Press.

Rooks, Gerrit and Leon Oerlemans (2005) 'South Africa: a rising star? Assessing the x-effectiveness of South Africa's national system of innovation', *European Planning Studies* 13(8) December: 1205–1226.

Rose, Mark (2002) 'Copyright and its metaphors', *UCLA Law Review* 50: 1–15.

SAIIPL (n.d.) About Us (www.saiipl.org.za/about-us).

Schwab, Klaus (2012) *Global Competitiveness Report 2012–2013*. Geneva: World Economic Forum.

Sorensen, Jill Ann Tarzian and Donald A. Chambers (2008) 'Evaluating academic technology transfer performance by how well access to knowledge is facilitated: defining an access metric,' *Journal of Technology Transfer* 33: 534–547.

The Star (2007) 'SAFACT: protecting intellectual property rights', *The Star* 12 July: 7.

Stellenbosch University (2013) *Master of Laws (LLM) (Intellectual Property Law)* (www.blogs.sun.ac.za/iplaw/programmes/llm-ip-law/).

Stevens, Ashley J. (2004) 'The enactment of Bayh-Dole', *Journal of Technology Transfer* 29: 93–99.

Stiglitz, Joseph E. (2008) 'Economic foundations of intellectual property rights', *Duke Law Journal* 57: 1693–1724.

Story, Alan et al. (2006) *The Copy/South Dossier: Issues in the Economics, Politics and Ideology of Copyright in the Global South.* Canterbury: Copy/South Research Group.

TAC (2012) *Fix the Patent Laws!* Cape Town: Treatment Action Campaign; Médecins Sans Frontières (www.fixthepatentlaws.org/brochure/Fix%20the%20patents%20web.pdf).

Teljeur, Ethèl (2003) *Intellectual Property Rights in South Africa: An Economic Review of Policy and Impact.* Braamfontein: The Edge Institute.

Trebilcock, Michael J. and Robert Howse (1995) *The Regulation of International Trade*, 2nd edn. London: Routledge.

UCT (2011) Intellectual Property Policy, 27 July. Cape Town: University of Cape Town.

UCT (2013) Intellectual Property Unit: Current Projects. Cape Town: University of Cape Town, Intellectual Property Unit. (http://www.law.uct.ac.za/law/research/groups/intellectual/projects)

UNISA (2013) UNISA-WIPO Intellectual Property Law Specialization Programme (www.unisa.ac.za/default.asp?Cmd=ViewContent&ContentID=16822).

Valdivia, Walter D. (2013) *University start-ups: critical for improving technology transfer* (Washington DC: Brookings Institution).

Walker, Cheryl (2013) 'Uneasy relations: women, gender equality and tradition', *Thesis Eleven* 115(1) April: 77–94.

WHO et al. (2012) Promoting access to medical technologies and innovation: intersections between public health, intellectual property and trade (Geneva: WHO, WTO and WIPO).

Wild, Sarah (2012) 'Technology Innovation Agency to be put under the spotlight: agency puts money before innovation', *Business Day*, 26 October: 4.

WIPO (2013) 'African ministers discuss innovation and IP at WIPO conference', *WIPO News and Events* (www.wipo.int/pressroom/en/articles/2013/article_0004.html).

Wolson, Rosemary A. (2007) 'The role of technology transfer offices in building the South African biotechnology sector: an assessment of policies, practices and impact', *Journal of Technology Transfer* 32: 343–365.

World Bank (2009) *GINI Index* (http://data.worldbank.org/indicator/SI.POV.GINI).

World Bank (2013) *Data: South Africa* (http://data.worldbank.org/country/south-africa).

34

Traditional Knowledge, Intellectual Property and Pharmaceutical Innovation: What's Left to Discuss?

Graham Dutfield

INTRODUCTION: WHY DO DIPLOMATS AND NGOS TALK ABOUT TRADITIONAL KNOWLEDGE? AND SHOULD THEY?

There are numerous international legal instruments on intellectual property (IP) protecting inventions, marks and literary and artistic works, as well as things like designs and plant varieties. There is no specific treaty on geographical indications *per se*[1] but they are provided under the World Trade Organization's rules concerning intellectual property and are well protected throughout Europe among numerous other jurisdictions.

But despite years of lobbying and negotiating there is still no international instrument on traditional knowledge. It is possible that there will be one soon. The World Intellectual Property Organization (WIPO) member states are, at the time of writing, working on the texts of instruments on traditional knowledge, traditional cultural expressions and genetic resources. But a legally binding treaty is far from being a foregone conclusion.

Initial demands for legal responses to the misappropriation of traditional knowledge were made over two decades ago. Prominent early voices include Darrell Posey, Vandana Shiva and Pat Mooney. In 1988, the Society of Ethnobiology, which Posey helped to create, proclaimed the Declaration of Belém at its first conference which took place in Amazonian Brazil. The Declaration recognized 'that native peoples have been stewards of 99% of the world's genetic resources', and urged that 'procedures be developed to compensate native peoples for the utilization of their knowledge and their biological resources'. In due course such calls for compensation led to much wider demands for legal protection regimes. For Posey (1990), an entomologist turned ethno-ecologist, it was a matter of honouring indigenous peoples instead of exploiting them and of responding to large-scale environmental destruction. The way forward was to defend and promote their often highly sophisticated, albeit unappreciated and misunderstood, ecosystems management systems. Posey argued that large areas of the Amazon rainforest are in fact best characterized as anthropogenic cultural landscapes. This differed markedly from the conventional view that they are 'wild' ecosystems to which humans have had to adapt themselves in order to survive. The new perspective implied that the indigenous inhabitants held immense practical knowledge of their local biota and how to manage it in order to serve their subsistence needs. Indigenous peoples for such campaigners meant those groups recognized under the 1989 International Labour Organization Convention 169 Concerning Indigenous and Tribal Peoples in Independent Countries.[2]

For Shiva (1997), this issue was part of a wider campaign to reverse global power structures destructive to human lives, food production systems and the biosphere in favour of the poor and the environment. Accordingly, for her as for like-minded activists, the powerful patent-holding life science corporate sector – typically hailing from the United States and including seed, agrochemical and drug producers – and the World Trade Organization comprised global public enemy numbers one and two, the latter for its pro-business mandate of promoting intellectual property regulation and international trade *de*-regulation (Drahos, 2000). As for indigenous peoples, she, like many others in Asia and Africa, had little use for the term as a category of people whose cultures, circumstances and political needs and interests are distinct from the rural poor more generally.[3] This was at times a cause of friction (Posey, 1996a).

Mooney first made his name internationally by drawing the world's attention to genetic erosion and its causes. He and his then colleague Cary Fowler implicated the seed industries, the institutional norms and practices of the international agricultural research system, and intellectual property rights (Mooney, 1979; Fowler and Mooney, 1990; Fowler, 1994). Fowler coined the term 'farmers' rights' as a counter-concept to breeders' rights as provided by the International Convention for the Protection of New Varieties of Plants (UPOV).[4]

In the same spirit of terminological creativity, Mooney, whose opposition to corporate agricultural monopolies began to take in the life science industries more generally, coined the word 'biopiracy' (Mooney, 2000):[5] a counter-concept to the intellectual property 'piracy' that the emerging economies were being condemned for, principally by the United States government and corporations based there. In a short time, others adopted the word. *Biopiracy* is now an essential part of the discourse.

To be branded a biopirate was damning indeed, as it still is. For example, much of the rhetoric from India when the story broke in the 1990s that preparations of neem tree extracts had been patented by a US company called W.R. Grace assumed that Indian farmer-users of neem extracts to protect their crops had had their knowledge and resources stolen, and indeed that they would no longer even be allowed to use the tree. Given the large proportion of that nation's population still working the land, it followed, as the argument went, that the country itself was a victim of the heinous offence of biopiracy. It was as if the traditional knowledge, even the tree itself, was owned permanently by the Indian nation and had to be defended against usurper corporations using the full force of patent law supported by the World Trade Organization, whose Agreement on Trade-Related Aspects of Intellectual Property Rights (TRIPS) had proved to be so controversial.

Shiva herself was wont to adopt highly inflammatory rhetoric, rather luridly (and in my view regrettably), equating biopiracy to 'intellectual and cultural rape', and describing it also as 'the slavery of the new millennium'. This rather exaggerated, if not offensive, rhetoric, especially given recent publicity concerning the common and often brutal ill-treatment of women in India, was repeated in a number of her short articles during the 1990s. In a more recent one, published in 2001, she also stated that '[a]nything short of stopping biopiracy through reforming TRIPs is participation in a crime against nature and the poor' (Shiva, 2001). To pour further petrol onto the fire, she even claimed that biopiracy is 'worse than the slave trade'.[6]

Biopiracy has since attained the legitimacy of an entry in the *Oxford English Dictionary*. Its online version[7] defines biopiracy as: '[t]he practice of obtaining commercially valuable genetic material, biochemicals, etc., from plant or animal species without fairly rewarding the country or community of origin, esp. by obtaining patents that restrict future use'. This is in fact inaccurate. My own definition (Dutfield, 2005), which in my view better reflects the way the word has been used from the start, is: '(i) the theft, misappropriation of, or unfair free-riding on, genetic resources and/or traditional knowledge through the patent system; and (ii) the unauthorized and uncompensated collection for commercial ends of genetic resources and/or traditional knowledge'. Arguably, this definition might be extended to embrace unfair appropriation through copyright law. Obviously, a lot of journal articles and books document traditional medicinal knowledge, and copyright on these works will be owned by the authors or the publishers. Traditional knowledge holders may not necessarily object. Where they might, the offensive act will either be the documentation itself (where the disclosed traditional knowledge was not intended for wider dissemination), or the acquisition of copyright. Copyright is of course a property right. The originality requirement in copyright law is far less demanding than the novelty criterion of patent law. Assertion of this right would likely be perceived by traditional knowledge holders as an unjust legal claim to knowledge belonging to them which allows them even fewer opportunities to challenge legally.

In the last two decades, a vast amount of academic and other literature, much of it highly critical and rightly so, has been produced on traditional knowledge, its relationship to the formal intellectual property regime, and on IP-related and alternative modes of protection. The 1992 Convention on Biological Diversity paid attention to the issue in the context of conservation, sustainable use, and fair and equitable benefit sharing, albeit in a vague, noncommittal manner. The 2010 Nagoya Protocol to the Convention inched the matter a bit further forward with some nice language, including on customary law and prior informed consent. But again, the feel-good language is qualified by strategic vagueness, frustrating those looking for unequivocal, firm and legally binding obligations on states and businesses (see below). Meanwhile, just a handful of countries provide positive protection[8] of traditional knowledge in their national laws, Peru and Panama being rare examples.

In a 2005 article, Duke University law professor, David Lange (2005), set out a case for benign neglect of traditional knowledge. On the face of it, given the lack of progress, such a call sounds quite rational. Is it not best to cut our losses and let the matter drop before more time, money, effort and goodwill are needlessly expended? Indigenous peoples and other communities 'embodying traditional lifestyles'[9] probably have more pressing concerns anyway, such as getting title to their ancestral lands, defending their rights to live as they choose *whatever they might decide*, and resolving social and economic crises affecting their societies. Besides, for those populations with relatively secure communal rights to land and a sufficient degree of self-determination, there may not be a pressing need to wait for international solutions to take independent action. They already have a lot of freedom to act in their best interests. For example, the Potato Park, an organization representing five Quechua communities in the highlands of Peru, is already using its own trademark to obtain good prices for the communities' products in local markets (Argumedo, 2013). In this chapter, I argue that now is *not* the time for benign neglect. But it *is* high time for a strategic re-think.

THE DARK SIDE VERSUS THE FORCE

Why is so much diplomatic effort *still* being expended on finding a solution to traditional knowledge protection? Is it motivated by a sense of justice for the downtrodden, respect for human rights or other altruistic sentiments, as is mostly the case for the NGOs? Is it the irresistible force of diplomatic momentum: we've started, we've invested time and effort, we've cajoled, we've bargained and we've sacrificed other issues; we've sunk too much into this issue and cannot just stop now. Or is it motivated by plain economic thinking: traditional knowledge has pharmaceutical value which developing countries are not capturing enough of? There is unlikely to be a single reason. Unwillingness or inability to reverse the diplomatic tide is almost certainly a factor. But the persisting perception that traditional knowledge is valuable, primarily for its contribution to pharmaceutical research and development, seems still to loom very large. This is probably the best explanation for the considerable diplomatic efforts, only partially successful as it turned out, to close the genetic resources access and benefit sharing issue at the international level by means of the 2010 Nagoya Protocol to the Convention on Biological Diversity.[10] As mentioned, the Protocol has a number of provisions on traditional knowledge associated with genetic resources which on their face appear to represent genuine breakthroughs in advancing indigenous peoples' rights.

Who are the stakeholders? And who are the intended beneficiaries? For indigenous peoples in Latin America and Australasia, among other parts of the world, they are the knowledge-holding groups meant to gain most of the benefits. However, the tendency elsewhere – admittedly often justifiably – is to treat traditional knowledge as belonging not to specific communities or other populations within a country but to the whole nation. Accordingly, governments in these countries do not advocate and negotiate for the benefit of one or a few population groups but for the whole citizenry. In some cases they are willing to invest quite heavily in measures to resolve the problem as they see it. Thus, the Indian government has a Traditional Knowledge Digital Library comprising published information about uses of plants in the country's mainstream traditional health systems: Ayurveda, Unani and Siddha. (The responsible government agency wisely chose not to include the often undocumented knowledge of localized populations.) Peru now has a National Commission for the Protection of Access to Peruvian Biological Diversity and to the Collective Knowledge of the Indigenous Peoples ('the National Anti-Biopiracy Commission').

Some of the rhetoric has more than a whiff of bio-nationalism, which ignores the reality that many if not most countries' economically valuable genetic resources came originally from somewhere else and can only be improved or modified by accessing material that must still be imported. No country, including those that are most biologically diverse, is self-sufficient. All are at least to some extent reliant on continued introductions of genetic material from other places. This interdependence has several causes. One is what Alfred Crosby called ecological imperialism (Crosby, 1986). By this term he meant that large swathes of colonial lands were turned into offshore Europes. These contained crops and livestock introduced by immigrants (along, sadly, with their diseases) from that continent or else supplied for them by Europeans. Rather like golf courses, essentially miniature coastal Fifeshires recreated in very un-Scottish places from Azerbaijan to Zambia albeit on a much bigger scale with overseas territories treated as biogeographical palimpsests, the exotic naturally-occurring ecosystems were over-written' by those of rural Spain, France and England. Plants and animals (and diseases, albeit not so many) went the other way, too. The Columbian Exchange saw the movement of plants like maize, potatoes and tomatoes from the New World to the Old (Crosby, 1972).

Another cause is that many colonies were used to cultivate crops having distant origins, such as tea and coffee grown in what is now

Kenya, and rubber in Malaysia. Such trends continue: soybean fields cover vast tracts of Brazil, the world's most biologically diverse country. The cultivation of the crop there began with introduced germplasm from the United States. Soybean's centre of origin, though, is China. However, the main reason is that for most of human history plants and plant material have moved freely around the world, whether by people or by the elements. We may say that coffee *originally* comes from Ethiopia or Southern Arabia, not Brazil or Colombia. Rubber originates from Brazil, not Malaysia. However, these facts of historical biogeography should surely have no direct bearing on today's laws and policies.

Thankfully, the international law of genetic resources for food and agriculture explicitly acknowledges this interdependency by virtue of the International Treaty on Plant Genetic Resources for Food and Agriculture. But when it comes to biological resources with medicinal properties, 'hyperownership' (Safrin, 2004) prevails and the rhetoric can still be quite Manichean: evil patent-owning corporations ('the Dark Side') pitted again the underdog governments and indigenous peoples ('the Force') as if the latter two are the natural allies, which they very much are not.

WHAT DOES TRADITIONAL MEDICINE HAVE TO DO WITH PHARMACEUTICALS? ANYTHING AT ALL?

It would be fair to say that the heat of the rhetoric is several degrees lower than it used to be. Nonetheless, the conviction that traditional knowledge and biodiversity contain high realized *and* unrealized pharmaceutical value appears to be the conventional wisdom among a great many developing country government representatives; which implies that they can profitably trade access for benefits subject to supportive regulations and on the basis of shared and agreed international norms.

When one stops to reflect, it is actually quite a counterintuitive view. In the developed world, traditional knowledge has largely been discredited and has mostly been replaced by modern pharmaceutical science which emerged in Europe in the nineteenth century, later spread around the world, and now enjoys justifiably high prestige almost everywhere. That era heralded a shift from knowledge about *material medica* to what became known as pharmacology (Porter, 1997: 448). Physiology, immunology, bacteriology and synthetic chemistry emerged as scientific and professional disciplines and then became dominant. The following medicinal innovations came to the fore: (a) the identification and isolation of single plant-based active ingredients, such as alkaloids, and their preparation in purified form (Magendie, 1821; Burgen, 1996); (b) the production of antitoxins and vaccines to treat or prevent specific infectious diseases (Porter, 1997: 431–48; Gradmann, 2009); (c) the laboratory synthesis of therapeutic chemicals, both copies of ones known to exist in nature, and those that were not (Dutfield, 2009); and (d) the modification and optimization of these molecules and their industrial mass production in standardized tablet and other forms of patient delivery. The science has evolved tremendously since then with a massively expanded array of cellular drug targets and the comparatively recent addition of protein drugs (biopharmaceuticals) produced through genetic technologies (Rasmussen, 2014). But the above categories of innovation do not look obsolete today: new pharmaceutical products continue almost by definition to be synthetic chemicals, which are either completely *de novo* or are modelled on earlier ones and those found in plants and plant products among other natural sources. Some pharmaceuticals are still extracted directly from plants, not necessarily medicinal ones. Nowadays, as we all know, these are provided for a price by a large and highly profitable global industry.

The traditional medicinal antecedents of these products, to the extent that such antecedents exist, are completely different.

The same goes for the traditional medicines used today. Typically, they are processed or unprocessed single or mixed natural products of plant, animal or mineral origin. Whole plants may be used, or else plant or animal parts or their products. Unlike today's pharmaceuticals they are not single chemicals obtained through industrial processes. The notion of the 'active principle', that is, the compound having the therapeutic effect, was, and remains, alien to traditional healers whose treatments are inherently 'impure', allowing for the possibility of synergisms between the various ingredients. Further, their usage is justified on the basis of theories of health, sickness, well-being and efficacy, as well as cultural and spiritual values, which modern practitioners generally do not accept as valid (see Tallis, 2004: 132–9).

Traditional knowledge has of course not gone away. Traditional remedies continue to be popular with many affluent urban people, as do alternative and complementary medicinal preparations that may not be 'traditional' as such, like homeopathic remedies. Neither does the field remain unchanged (Hsu, 2001). Experimentation is not the sole preserve of the white-coated laboratory scientists. Many traditional healers (and farmers) do it too. A much cited figure from the World Health Organization is 80 per cent for the proportion of the developing country population that relies on traditional medicine to meet its primary healthcare needs. Chinese traditional medicine remains highly popular as do the classical Indian health systems like Ayurveda. These are well documented and the systems themselves are officially sanctioned with their own recognized training facilities and registered practitioners. Isolated indigenous peoples in places like the Amazon deploy their localized knowledge of flora and ecosystems to meet many of their healthcare concerns as they have done for millennia. Before the nineteenth century the only healthcare available anywhere in the world was 'traditional'. Much of European medicine at the time was worthless if not positively dangerous. Any innovations were likely to be quack medicines. The same is likely to have been true for many other parts of the world. But some of it has proven efficacy not attributable merely to placebo effects (e.g. Moerman, 1979).[11] Currently, such treatments as sold in the West form a small, but not insignificant, part of the market in medical treatments.

Despite efforts made in some countries to integrate traditional and modern healthcare systems, such as China, it is hardly a straightforward task to reconcile them when they are so different in theory and practice. As we have seen, traditional medicines and modern industrial ones are quite different things chemically. But socially, culturally and epistemologically these systems are fundamentally different to an even greater degree. In which case, the proposition that the modern commercial pharmaceutical sector preys significantly and systematically on knowledge that belongs to traditional healers, their communities or to countries as a whole seems rather doubtful. These conceptual doubts were rejected in a claim made in 1994 by the influential Pat Mooney-headed Rural Advancement Foundation International (RAFI; now ETC Group), who even put a figure on the extent of the exploitation and on what it would cost to pay fair compensation: 'if royalty payments were paid to developing countries on the one quarter of pharmaceutical sales based on products derived from medicinal plants, the royalties due to the South would amount to approximately $5,097 million' (RAFI, 1994: 24). But the assumptions on which this figure was based do not bear any serious critical examination.

However, we must not be too dismissive. The extreme differences do not mean there is a perfect traditional and modern divide marking out two quite separate worlds. First, the Chinese integration policy seems to be quite successful, at least in terms of practices (Goh, 2012). Second, and more relevant to the present theme, one must distinguish between traditional remedies and traditional knowledge-*derived* treatments, the latter being traditional–modern hybrids.

For example, Crofelemer is a US Food and Drug Administration (FDA)-approved botanical medicine for AIDS-related diarrhoea. It is a laboratory-produced substance containing active compounds isolated from the latex of the sangre de grado (*Croton lechleri*) tree which was used by indigenous peoples in South America as a treatment for various ailments including diarrhoea. Building upon the traditional knowledge to develop Crofelemer required the contributions of formally trained scientists and the availability of well-equipped laboratory facilities. Indeed, some modern pharmacologists have persuasively advocated the re-investigation of old herbal medicines no longer in use to seek new therapeutically active ingredients (Adams et al, 2009). The very existence of the discipline of ethnopharmacology with its own journal, founded in 1979, underlines the argument being made here.[12]

Modern pharmacopoeias do contain drugs initially sourced from traditional medicinal or food plants. Recent additions include Artemesinin and Nicosan (or Hemoxin). Artemesinin's antimalarial activity was documented in fourth-century China. In the 1960s, the Chinese military conducted research into medicinal plants, and in 1972 found a substance called Artemesinin in the leaves of the *Artemisia annua* (wormwood) plant. Structurally modified Artemesinin, used in combination with other products, is now the most effective antimalarial available. Nicosan is a sickle-cell disorder treatment from Nigeria, the plant-based 'recipe' for which was disclosed by a Nigerian traditional healer, the Rev. P.R. Ogunyale, who is actually named as a co-inventor on the more than 40 patents on Nicosan granted worldwide.[13] Nicosan has orphan drug investigational status in the United States and Europe.

One can argue that policymaking would be far easier if RAFI's estimate was accurate. Industry might concede quite a lot to be able to access such demonstrably valuable knowledge and resources. But how would they know what to look for and where to find it? Arguably, the most valuable knowledge of health relevance will either be that which is already in wide circulation, or that which is held by just a few people. Knowledge that's valuable is worth spreading around. It's also worth keeping secret. Wide circulation of knowledge is no guarantee of its usefulness but one might reasonably consider knowledge to be more worth investigating scientifically where there is widespread trust in the efficacy of its application. However, being well distributed increases the possibility of its already being disclosed in print or otherwise freely available, making it hard for knowledge holders to capture its value, even less when there are so many such people and they are widely distributed geographically. Why talk to the shaman if you can read the scientific article about his or her drug in, say, the *Journal of Ethnobiology*? As for undisclosed knowledge, making efforts to keep knowledge secret through the generations implies it may be valuable in some way or another. However, the very fact of its being secret makes it unavailable unless reverse engineering is possible. Further, financial offers to disclose it may not be successful: the value to the holder may be of a cultural or spiritual nature that cannot simply be converted into a pecuniary one. Indeed, disclosure may be prohibited or else strictly restricted under customary law.

To avoid being too hypothetical, let us consider a real drug based on undisclosed information that the healer concerned *was* willing to reveal: Nicosan. According to David Newman and Gordon Cragg of the United States National Cancer Institute, Nicosan is 'a mix of plants that came from native healer information and thus can be classified as a "true ethnobotanical preparation"' (2007: 474). In this case, the drug comprises a specific mixture of plant extracts of known origin. The individual in question, a traditional healer, but one with a higher degree from a United States university, was the only one with the knowledge, and he gave his consent to its further development, testing and commercialization (Ogbonna, 2013). The prior informed consent obligation in this situation was hardly a practical difficulty; indeed a memorandum of understanding was agreed upon between Ogunyale and the medical research institute which developed the drug (Wambebe, 2007). However, it is likely that by the time Nicosan has been approved for sale in the United States and Europe, the patents will have expired, and the information disclosed in them will be in the public domain. It is unclear whether the ingredients are endemic to Nigeria *and* available only in that country. If so, the country may have some leverage in terms of getting a share of the benefits for access to the resources. As for the knowledge, this will surely be more difficult. You cannot 'undisclose' what has been revealed, especially once it has been fixed in published form, such as in a journal article or patent specification.

It may be concluded at this point that pharmaceutical scientists *can* learn from shamans and healers. Further, biopiracy is not some kind of urban myth. Instances of unfair appropriation have been well documented (Robinson, 2010). However, despite the existence of scientific value and the evidence of misappropriation, regulating access to traditional knowledge for a share of the benefits from its commercial exploitation is likely either to be futile or to incur costs exceeding the scale of any ensuing benefits. Creating markets for pharmaceutically valuable traditional knowledge is extremely difficult to do. As for the associated genetic resources, regulating access may be feasible but unless they are endemic to the region there may be few practical advantages in doing so. Forming some kind of OPEC-like cartel for traditional knowledge (TK) rather than petroleum might superficially look a promising option, especially for widely held (but not *too* widely held and documented) knowledge. For the associated genetic resources, the possibility may be more feasible. But there are massive practical obstacles which Iran, Iraq, Kuwait, Saudi Arabia and Venezuela certainly did not have to contend with when they founded that organization in 1960. The economic value of petroleum is proven and quantifiable in ways that TK can never be. TK is intangible, meaning that once it is disclosed control is lost and users need not return to the source. 'Raw' genetic material becomes worthless once the section of the DNA molecule of industrial interest has been identified, sequenced and entered into an electronic database for others to access in coded form. Admittedly, with metabolites and other compounds not containing DNA, continuous access may be necessary for scientific investigation and even for commercial exploitation, especially if the plant sources are not widely circulated and the molecule of interest is complex, making it difficult or expensive to synthesize. So there are reasonable possibilities for mutually beneficial transactions in these specific cases. Nonetheless, recent experiences suggest that transacting may only be workable in case-specific contexts and in *ad hoc* ways requiring direct and in most cases painstaking negotiations between indigenous peoples, individual healers if appropriate, and businesses. But even then, things can still go wrong. We will look at an illustrative example below. Suffice it to say here that the idea of the international community being able, through a convention, or a protocol to a convention, to create this market for worldwide adoption, as has been done with plant genetic resources for food and agriculture, is not realistic for health treatments.[14] Traditional knowledge does have pharmaceutical option value, to borrow a term popular in environmental economics. While the magnitude of this option value cannot readily be ascertained, it is surely significant: there is enough evidence to demonstrate that loss of traditional knowledge means cutting off access to a potentially huge and priceless stock of complex biological substances with information about their use that scientists are unlikely to be able to stumble across elsewhere or invent *de novo* in the laboratory. Consequently, there are sound economic grounds for investing in TK protection by supporting the ethno-ecological systems which conserve this knowledge through everyday use and generate further knowledge. The (rhetorical) question is: who is willing to pay?

Industry is not going to be the one to do it, and neither is government. As for indigenous peoples, this is the wrong way to look at it. Keeping traditional knowledge in use is not a matter of simple economics: give them money and they will agree to hand it down to the next generation. Societies enjoying self-determination, secure title to land, and respect for their customary laws may well decide that the wisdom of their elders and healers is worth maintaining. But they may decide they no longer need it, and abandon many of their traditions. That is their right. All the rest of us can do is respect their collective rights and let them make their own decisions as to what traditions they wish to keep.

THE NAGOYA PROTOCOL: TOWARDS A MARKET IN TRADITIONAL KNOWLEDGE AND ASSOCIATED GENETIC RESOURCES?

In 2010, contracting parties to the Convention on Biological Diversity adopted the Nagoya Protocol on Access and Benefit Sharing and the Fair and Equitable Sharing of Benefits arising from their Utilization to the Convention on Biological Diversity ('the Nagoya Protocol'). It is fair to say that the Protocol has been welcomed by many advocates of the rights of indigenous peoples. For our purposes, the most significant articles are 7 and 12, which deal with traditional knowledge and associated genetic resources, and 10 and 11 on global benefit-sharing and transboundary issues respectively. Article 7 explicitly extends the right of prior informed consent in the context of access from governments to indigenous and local communities:

> In accordance with domestic law, each Party shall take measures, as appropriate, with the aim of ensuring that traditional knowledge associated with genetic resources that is held by indigenous and local communities is accessed with the prior and informed consent or approval and involvement of these indigenous and local communities, and that mutually agreed terms have been established.

Article 12 ('Traditional knowledge associated with genetic resources') states in its first paragraph that:

> In implementing their obligations under this Protocol, Parties shall in accordance with domestic law take into consideration indigenous and local communities' customary laws, community protocols and procedures, as applicable, with respect to traditional knowledge associated with genetic resources.

On its face, 'take into consideration' hardly implies a meaningful commitment on anybody to do anything, besides which it only directly binds contracting parties. Businesses' legal obligations are dependent on the existence of a domestic law containing the necessary provisions. Nonetheless, the reference to customary laws and protocols goes some way towards meeting concerns about the unreciprocated imposition of culturally inappropriate external legal norms, rules and procedures governing knowledge and resource transactions such as patents and business contracts. Tobin's view is that the obligation may be more expansive than 'take into consideration' might suggest:

> In order to comply with art. 12, states will need to ensure consideration of customary law not only in the development of national implementing legislation, but also in relevant administrative, judicial and alternative dispute resolution proceedings. The Protocol has placed customary law firmly at the centre of national and global governance of traditional knowledge and associated genetic resources. (Tobin, 2014: 126)

This may well be a correct interpretation, especially for those 22 countries[15] that are also parties to the aforementioned ILO Convention 169. This latter instrument affirms that 'In applying national laws and regulations to the peoples concerned, due regard shall be had to their customs or customary laws'.[16] The fact remains, however, that the transfer of well-defined and legally certain obligations onto corporations to observe customary law is not a given. It may be imposed by means of a court decision, a statute, a constitutional provision, or through administrative processes (WIPO, 2013). Without political will, though, such obligations may never become binding.

There is a major lacuna which the Protocol does at least acknowledge even if it offers no solution for the time being. Article 10 ('Global multilateral benefit-sharing mechanism') requires parties to

> consider the need for and modalities of a global multilateral benefit sharing mechanism to address the fair and equitable sharing of benefits derived from the utilization of genetic resources and traditional knowledge associated with genetic resources that occur in transboundary situations or for which it is not possible to grant or obtain prior informed consent.

Two questions arise. First, how much of the existing stock of genetic resources and traditional knowledge associated with them *does* occur in transboundary situations? Second, under what circumstances might their use occur without the grant or acquisition of prior informed consent being possible?

Whilst it is difficult to say what proportion of genetic resources and TK is cross-boundary, the overall extent of transboundaryness is likely to be very high. Political boundaries are artificial and many ethnic groups' territories straddle borders. The chances are that this situation is frequently going to complicate negotiating between users and providers and thereby increase transaction costs to a potentially prohibitive scale. Another potential negative outcome is that the existence of other countries with overlapping resources and knowledge endowments will undermine providers' bargaining power. Article 10 acknowledges that the Protocol cannot yet resolve this, at least until a *workable* multilateral mechanism is in place to deal with this specific issue, *assuming that such a mechanism is politically or practically attainable*.

Consider the example of Hoodia, a Southern African succulent consumed by the San people for various purposes including warding off hunger pangs. The San people live in Botswana, Namibia, South Africa, Angola, Zimbabwe and Zambia. It is not certain that Hoodia is known about or used by all San communities in these six countries. Furthermore, evidence suggests that other non-San peoples have also used Hoodia. Despite Hoodia's highly scattered distribution, and without helpful legislation in any of these countries, and with the above uncertainties, workable benefit sharing schemes were put into place involving various state and non-state organizations including pharmaceutical businesses.[17]

In the late 1990s, patents were filed in numerous countries on the active compounds of Hoodia and several were subsequently granted. Two major companies, Pfizer and Unilever, and a small British start-up, Phytopharm, became involved in efforts to develop Hoodia-based pharmaceuticals, natural health products, and food supplements. Despite this, and after many years of scientific investigation and deal-making, Hoodia still has *no proven pharmaceutical value.* Some clinical studies were encouraging (Maharaj, 2011), whereas one produced rather disappointing results on both efficacy and safety grounds (Blom et al., 2011). So there is both commercial potential and risk. Unfortunately, Phytopharm, Pfizer and Unilever for a number of different reasons withdrew from the Hoodia scene. It is now highly unlikely that Hoodia will be the long-hoped-for first African blockbuster drug. There may be sufficient benefits to help improve the lives of some San people, but one must doubt that they will ever be substantial.

Hoodia provides a few lessons, both positive and negative. On the one hand, it shows that implementing formal benefit sharing arrangements concerning trans-boundary resources and knowledge can be done with neither the multilateral mechanism envisaged in article 10 of Nagoya, nor even a national TK protection law. The fact that the people, knowledge and resources were spread over more than one country certainly added complications, including additional transaction costs. But the concern about bargaining power mentioned above seems irrelevant here. In this case, Hoodia was known about and patented before commercial partners were sought and the benefit sharing negotiations were initiated. The patents were all held by one entity, the South African government's Council for Scientific and Industrial Research (CSIR). Those seeking to use the active ingredients of the plant for commercial ends had no choice but to approach CSIR first.

This does not make the diminished bargaining position issue irrelevant though. What about the situation where a foreign company wishes to visit a country with access and benefit sharing regulations in place in order to search for genetic resources and TK, with limited published information in patent documents or scientific publications to go on? If the country's neighbours are similarly biologically and culturally diverse but have no access and benefit sharing regulations or ones that are less strict, the likelihood arises that driving a hard bargain will encourage the company to try those other nations.

In article 11, the Nagoya Protocol itself urges cooperation rather than competition where the same genetic resources and TK straddle national boundaries. Where blocs of neighbouring countries adopt common access and benefit sharing regulations, as does the Andean Community,[18] this appears to be a workable approach. However, in most cases individual countries will have their own rules. Accordingly, opportunities to cooperate meaningfully are in most cases rather limited. For countries that welcome users on the basis of mutually agreed terms of access and benefit sharing, competitiveness is bound to creep in. Like the rest of us, companies respond to carrots as well as sticks. In the market economy, frequently multiple suppliers exist for identical but similar goods, yet some are better at attracting customers than others, despite starting off with similar endowments. Companies don't want to waste time and money rummaging around blindly. They want direction. If there are lots of capable and easily contactable people and institutions in one country, such as taxonomists and other plant scientists, knowledgeable indigenous peoples and good universities, who can all direct them to what might be valuable, but fewer of them in another, that might influence their choice of where to go, even if such useful partners insist that rigorous access and benefit sharing rules be properly observed. In such situations, companies prefer legal and regulatory certainty. Scientific capacity building is key here. This is so whether we are talking of university-trained scientists or indigenous people with sophisticated knowledge about local resources and ecosystems. South African scientists had the expertise, equipment and financial resources to identify the active Hoodia compounds and file patent applications.

There is another rather vital lesson from the Hoodia case study: being able to turn something promising enough to attract serious business interest into a successful commercial product of the kind that can generate substantial benefits is probably a very rare feat indeed. Most benefits will be modest and the more ways the share has to be divided among knowledge holders and resource owners, the less that any interested party will end up getting.

Turning to the second question, that of what circumstances would make granting or obtaining prior informed consent impossible, one influential legal guide to the Protocol has this to say:

> it would not be possible to obtain PIC for the utilization of genetic resources obtained from a country that has decided not to establish access requirements. Another possible instance would be in cases in which there is utilization of genetic resources from *ex-situ* collections with no information on country or countries of origin. Although *ex-situ* collections, such as gene banks and other repositories of biological or genetic material, increasingly maintain information about where and when a sample was collected, such information does not always allow identification of the country of origin of the genetic material utilized or the pertinent PIC to be obtained. In these circumstances, a global multilateral benefit-sharing mechanism would nevertheless allow discharge of benefit-sharing requirements. (Greiber et al, 2012: 129)

The authors also observe that:

> An international instrument does not apply retroactively – that is, it cannot be binding to acts that took place before or situations that ceased to exist

> prior to its entry into force. Nevertheless, new benefits arising from prior or ongoing uses could be considered as new situations for benefit-sharing requirements – though access requirements would not apply retroactively. A global multilateral benefit-sharing mechanism could potentially cover these cases. (2012: 129)

What are we to make of this? First, genetic resources and traditional knowledge that are in general circulation may no longer have traceable origins or else have known origins that may go back a long time, possibly centuries. The sources of the genetic resources and the knowledge may be completely different. A good example is the rosy periwinkle (*Catharanthus roseus*), the source of the valuable anti-cancer vinca alkaloids, Vincristine and Vinblastine, which entered the market in the 1960s and have generated very large revenues for Eli Lilly over the decades. The plant originally comes from Madagascar but now grows throughout the tropics and has grown in the Caribbean long enough to be considered as a native plant there. This frequently used to be presented as the classic biopiracy case, with Madagascar and its people the unfortunate victims (Stone, 1992). In fact, it is many years since the company relied on Madagascar for supplies of the plant, and most now come from plantations in Texas. The Eli Lilly researchers who discovered and patented[19] Vincristine and its anti-cancer properties decided to study the plant when a literature search uncovered its use by rural populations in the Philippines. Those at the University of Western Ontario who discovered and patented[20] Vinblastine received plant samples from Jamaica that were considered worth testing, again, because people used the plant for therapeutic purposes there. In both countries the plant was used by rural communities not to treat cancer but diabetes.[21] Neither of the research teams made any secret in their publications of the fact that they were inspired by TK. On the other hand, only the University of Western Ontario team was reliant upon both overseas sources of plant material and unpublished ethnobotanical information when it began research on the periwinkle. Since then two further vinca compounds have come on the market: GlaxoSmithKline's Vinorelbine and Eli Lilly's Vindesine.

The rosy periwinkle case exemplifies the fact that portraying pharmaceutical development as a linear process taking place over a relatively short period is grossly inaccurate with many if not most drugs (Dutfield, 2010). It also suggests that in many cases a prior informed consent requirement is not practicable or applicable. Madagascar has no compelling legal or moral claims to a share of the billions of dollars generated since these drugs came onto the market half a century ago and at no point did a bioprospecting trip to that country ever need to be undertaken. The information on use of the rosy periwinkle was already in the public domain, and while this should not in itself make benefit sharing inapplicable, it would require a very strict legal regime of broad geographical scope for prior informed consent to be mandatory in such circumstances. There was no necessity at any point for the scientists to have visited the Philippines once the proverbial cat was out of the bag and the plant grew in various other countries anyway. It was only with Vinblastine that ethnobiological information and plant samples were directly acquired from local people. In that case a prior informed consent requirement could have benefited the local healers and their communities.

Such situations are likely to be common and bring to mind current debates concerning orphan works in the ambit of copyright. These are artistic and literary works whose authors are unknown and quite possibly long deceased. The fact that these are now so common, especially since the term of copyright was extended in many countries recently, raises some tricky legal and policy challenges in terms of public interest, property rights, user rights, remuneration and the conflicting interests of the different stakeholders: authors, collecting societies, publishers and cultural institutions, etc. These challenges are likewise yet to be satisfactorily resolved, despite recent adoption of a European Directive.[22]

WHAT IS TO BE DONE? IS *ANYTHING* TO BE DONE?

The conviction that traditional knowledge has enabled the industry to generate huge profits has proved to be persistent. Indeed, much of the international law regulating access to genetic resources and benefit sharing has been shaped around this belief. I have tried in this chapter to show that whilst TK is worth protecting and actually should be protected on both human rights and utilitarian grounds, the political strategy that we have been following for the past 20 years needs to be seriously reconsidered. The results have generally been uninspiring.

In terms of legal norm-setting, this strategy has been a two-pronged one. The first is the access and benefit sharing path via the Convention on Biological Diversity and its Nagoya Protocol. The second is based on intellectual property law and comprises: (i) reforms aimed to reduce misappropriation of genetic resources and traditional knowledge such as by enhancing patent prior art searching, restricting the scope of biological, biochemical and genetic subject matter claims in patent law, and requiring patent applicants to disclose the origin of genetic resources and TK that was useful or essential to an invention; and (ii) the adoption of *sui generis* TK protection laws based in part on existing forms of intellectual property rights but with some novel features.

It is difficult to avoid the conclusion that we have been far too reductionist: focusing on a part when we should have been looking at the whole. What use is ecological knowledge without land rights? How can traditional medicinal knowledge stay in use if the lands where the plants grew have been ploughed over? Why do decisions affecting indigenous peoples continue to be made by urban educated elites, well-meaning as they so often are? We need to provide, actually to cede, political space to allow indigenous peoples themselves to establish the rules of engagement. The 2007 United Nations Declaration on the Rights of Indigenous Peoples affirms territorial rights and self-determination and these need to be essential aspects of strategies, activities, laws and regulations. As Darrell Posey used to say: 'rights first, access later'.[23] He did not mean rights in TK per se, but the full range of rights – what he called 'Traditional Resource Rights', covering every issue affecting indigenous peoples' daily lives and long-term futures for which quite separate legal norms may already be available (Posey, 1996b). The legal philosopher Stephen Munzer, in a refreshingly humble article in which he skilfully advocates (cautiously) for corrective justice in the specific context of TK, expresses the inherent weaknesses of all such approaches:

> If I put myself in an imaginary conversation with an indigenous leader who has just seen his or her group conferred, as a matter of corrective justice, with IP rights in TK, he or she might say, 'I have huge problems involving a place for my people to live, access to timber and water, and the prevention of disease – and you have brought me some "rights" which I don't quite understand and seem to be of modest worth!' To some my argument of corrective justice might seem puny in its attempt to support IP rights in TK when indigenous peoples have so many other problems demanding their attention. (Munzer, 2012: 86)

Legally speaking, there needs to be a shift from imposing *our* legal 'solutions' to accepting *theirs:* their own customary practices, norms and laws. It is now time to turn this conceptual reorientation into practical and effective responses to the manifold threats to indigenous people's own intensely knowledge- and genetic-resource-based economies.

NOTES

1 Although there is one on appellations of origin, a subset of geographical indications: the 1958 Lisbon Agreement for the Protection of Appellations of Origin and their International Protection.

2 ILO 169, Art. 1.1(b): '(b) peoples in independent countries who are regarded as indigenous on

account of their descent from the populations which inhabited the country, or a geographical region to which the country belongs, at the time of conquest or colonisation or the establishment of present state boundaries and who, irrespective of their legal status, retain some or all of their own social, economic, cultural and political institutions'.

3 It is noteworthy that of the 22 parties to ILO Convention 169, 15 are in the Western hemisphere. The only African and Asian parties are Central African Republic and Nepal.

4 Personal communication with author, Athens (USA), May 2004.

5 Personal communication with Jean Christie, former RAFI colleague of Mooney's, Ottawa, June 1996.

6 Undated interview with Scott London: www.scottlondon.com/interviews/shiva.html (visited 7 Sept. 2013). To be fair she appears to have moderated the tone of her rhetoric in recent years.

7 Visited 13 September 2013.

8 I use positive protection in the sense used by WIPO; that is, on the basis of a new type of legal right vested in knowledge holders and/or their communities. This may be contrasted with defensive protection, which includes reforms to existing norms to mitigate misappropriation of traditional knowledge. A typical example is the requirement introduced by several countries that the origin of genetic material and traditional knowledge forming an important element of an invention be disclosed in a patent application.

9 In the terminology of the Convention on Biological Diversity, especially Art. 8(j).

10 For the food and agricultural sectors a resolution was found in 2001 with the adoption of the International Treaty on Plant Genetic Resources for Food and Agriculture of the Food and Agriculture Organization of the United Nations (FAO). This sets up a multilateral system of facilitated access to genetic resources for food and agriculture, and provides for benefit sharing and farmers' rights.

11 The author firmly concludes from his research that 'native American medical ethnobotany was not "only placebo medicine"'.

12 An editorial in the very first issue of the journal defines ethnopharmacology as: 'a multidisciplinary area of research, concerned with the observation, description, and experimental investigation of indigenous drugs and their biological activities' (Rivier and Bruhn, 1979).

13 For example, United States Patent No. 5,800,819: 'Piper guineense, pterocarpus osun, eugenia caryophyllata, and sorghum bicolor extracts for treating sickle cell disease'. Like the other Nicosan patents, this was assigned to the National Institute for Pharmaceutical Research and Development of the Nigerian Federal Ministry of Science and Technology.

14 For an intriguing but probably over-optimistic proposal, see Drahos (2000).

15 As of 1 October 2013.

16 Article 8.1.

17 For definitive literature presenting and analysing the San-Hoodia agreements, including by those involved in negotiating them, see Wynberg et al. (2009).

18 This is by virtue of Andean Community Decision 391: Common system on access to genetic resources.

19 See US Patent No. 3,205,220 (issued September 7, 1965) ('Leursidine and Leurocristine and their production').

20 See US Patent No. 3,097,137 (issued July 9, 1963) ('Vincaleukoblastine'). The patent was assigned by the inventors, Beer, Cutts and Noble, to Canadian Patents and Development Ltd., who made a deal with Eli Lilly allowing the latter company to commercially exploit the invention.

21 As expressed by three medical researchers at the University of Western Ontario (Noble et al., 1958: 882), 'the disease of cancer was certainly far from our thoughts when we learned of a tea made from the leaves of a West Indian shrub that was supposedly useful in the control of diabetes mellitus'.

22 Directive 2012/28/EU of the European Parliament and of the Council of 25 October 2012 on certain permitted uses of orphan works.

23 Various personal communications, 1993–1996.

REFERENCES

Adams, M., C. Berset, M. Kessler and M. Hamburger (2009) 'Medicinal herbs for the treatment of rheumatic disorders – a survey of European herbals from the 16th and 17th century'. *Journal of Ethnopharmacology* 121: 343–59.

Argumedo, A. (2013) *'Collective Trademarks and Biocultural Heritage: Towards New Indications of Distinction for Indigenous Peoples in the Potato Park, Peru'*. London: International Institute for Environment and Development.

Blom, W.A.M., S.L. Abrahamse, R. Bradford, G.S.M.J.E. Duchateau, W. Theis, A. Orsi, C.L. Ward and D.J. Mela (2011) 'Effects of 15-d repeated consumption of *Hoodia gordonii* purified extract on safety, ad libitum energy intake, and body weight in healthy, overweight women: a randomized controlled trial'. *American Journal of Clinical Nutrition* 94: 1171–81.

Burgen, A. (1996) 'François Magendie and the new science of drugs'. *European Review* 4: 165–72.

Crosby, A.W. (1972) *The Columbian Exchange: Biological and Cultural Consequences of 1492.* Westport: Greenwood Press.

Crosby, A.W. (1986) *Ecological Imperialism: The Biological Expansion of Europe, 900–1900.* Cambridge: Cambridge University Press.

Drahos, P. (2000) 'Indigenous knowledge, intellectual property and biopiracy: Is a global bio-collecting society the answer?' *European Intellectual Property Review* 22: 245–50.

Drahos, P. with J. Braithwaite (2002) *Information Feudalism: Who Owns the Knowledge Economy?* London: Earthscan.

Dutfield, G. (2005) 'What is biopiracy?', in M. Bellot-Rojas and S. Bernier (eds), *International Expert Workshop on Access to Genetic Resources and Benefit Sharing: Record of Discussion, Cuernavaca, Mexico, 24–27 October, 2004.* Mexico City: CONABIO/Environment Canada. pp. 89–92. http://conabio.gob.mx/institucion/cooperacion_internacional/doctos/version_ingles.pdf (visited 13 September 2013).

Dutfield, G. (2009) *Intellectual Property Rights and the Life Science Industries: Past, Present and Future.* Singapore: World Scientific.

Dutfield, G. (2010) 'Why traditional knowledge is important in drug discovery'. *Future Medicinal Chemistry* 2(9): 1405–9.

Fowler, C. (1994) *Unnatural Selection: Technology, Politics, and Plant Evolution.* Yverdon: Gordon and Breach.

Fowler, C. and P. Mooney (1990) *Shattering: Food, Politics and the Loss of Genetic Diversity.* Tucson: University of Arizona Press.

Goh, C.S. (2012) 'Regulation of the practice of traditional medicine in China, India, and Malaysia'. PhD thesis, University of Leeds.

Gradmann, C. (2009) *Laboratory Disease: Robert Koch's Medical Bacteriology.* Baltimore: Johns Hopkins University Press.

Greiber, T., S. Peña Moreno, M. Åhrén, J. Nieto Carrasco, E. Chege Kamau, J. Cabrera Medaglia, M.J. Oliva and F. Perron-Welch in cooperation with N. Ali and C. Williams (2012) *An Explanatory Guide to the Nagoya Protocol on Access and Benefit.* Gland: IUCN.

Hsu, E. (ed.) (2001) *Innovation in Chinese Medicine.* Cambridge: Cambridge University Press.

Lange, D.L. (2005) 'Comment: Traditional knowledge, folklore and the case for benign neglect', in K.E. Maskus and J. Reichman (eds), *International Public Goods and Transfer of Technology under a Globalized Intellectual Property Regime.* Cambridge: Cambridge University Press. pp. 595–8.

Magendie, F. (1821) *Formulaire pour la Préparation et l'Emploi de Plusieurs Nouveaux Médicamens, tels que la Noix Vomique, la Morphine, l'Acide Prussique, la Strychnine, la Vératrine, les Alcalis des Quinquinas, l'Iode.* Paris: Méquignon-Marvis.

Maharaj, V.J. (2011) 'Summary reports for key Hoodia clinical studies'. Council for Scientific and Industrial Research, http://researchspace.csir.co.za/dspace/handle/10204/5375 (visited 1 October 2013).

Moerman, D.E. (1979) 'Symbols and selectivity: A statistical analysis of native American medical ethnobotany'. *Journal of Ethnopharmacology* 1: 111–19.

Mooney, P.R. (1979) *Seeds of the Earth: Private or Public Resource?* Ottawa: Canadian Council for International Cooperation and International Coalition for Development Action.

Mooney, P.R. (2000) 'Why we call it biopiracy', in H. Svarstad and S.S. Dhillion (eds), *Responding to Bioprospecting: From Biodiversity in the South to Medicines in the North.* Oslo: Spartacus Forlag.

Munzer, S.R. (2012) 'Corrective justice and intellectual property rights in traditional knolwedge', in A. Lever (ed.), *New Frontiers in the Philosophy of Intellectual Property.* Cambridge: Cambridge University Press. pp. 58–87.

Newman, D.J. and G.M. Cragg (2007) 'Natural products as sources of new drugs over the last 25 years'. *Journal of Natural Products* 70: 461–77.

Noble, R.L., C.T. Beer and J.H. Cutts (1958) 'Role of chance observation in chemotherapy: Vinca rosea'. *Annals of the New York Academy of Sciences* 76: 882–94.

Ogbonna, N. (2013) 'What role should customary law play in the protection of traditional medicinal knowledge in Nigeria?' PhD thesis, University of Leeds.

Porter, R. (1997) *The Greatest Benefit to Mankind: A Medical History of Humanity from Antiquity to the Present.* London: HarperCollins.

Posey, D.A. (1990) 'Intellectual property rights and just compensation for indigenous peoples'. *Anthropology Today* 6(4): 13–16.

Posey, D.A. (1996a) 'Shiva fragments'. *Bulletin of the Working Group on Traditional Resource Rights* 3.

Posey, D.A. with contributions by G. Dutfield, K. Plenderleith, E. da Costa e Silva and A. Argumedo (1996b) *Traditional Resource Rights: International Instruments for Protection and Compensation for Indigenous Peoples and Local Communities.* Gland: IUCN.

Rasmussen, N. (2014) *Gene Jockeys: Life Science and the Rise of Biotech.* Baltimore: Johns Hopkins Press.

Rivier, L. and J.G. Bruhn (1979) 'Editorial'. *Journal of Ethnopharmacology* 1: 1.

Robinson, D.F. (2010) *Confronting Biopiracy: Challenges, Cases and International Debates.* London: Earthscan Books.

Rural Advancement Foundation International (RAFI) (1994) *Conserving Indigenous Knowledge: Integrating Two Systems of Innovation. An Independent Study by the Rural Advancement Foundation International.* New York: United Nations Development Programme.

Safrin, S. (2004) 'Hyperownership in a time of biotechnological promise: The international conflict to control the building blocks of life'. *American Journal of International Law,* 98.

Shiva, V. (1997) *Biopiracy: The Plunder of Nature and Knowledge.* Boston: South End Press.

Shiva, V. (2001) 'North-South conflicts in intellectual property rights'. *Synthesis/Regeneration* 25. www.greens.org/s-r/25/25-14.html (visited 7 September 2013).

Stone, R. (1992) 'The Biodiversity Treaty: Pandora's box or fair treaty?' *Science* 256: 1624.

Tallis, R. (2004) *Hippocratic Oaths: Medicine and its Discontents.* London: Atlantic Books.

Tobin, B. (2014) 'Biopiracy by law: European Union draft law threatens indigenous peoples' rights over their traditional knowledge and genetic resources'. *European Intellectual Property Review* 2: 124–36.

Wambebe, C. (2007) 'NIPRISAN case, Nigeria. A report for GenBenefit'. www.uclan.ac.uk/genbenefit (visited 16 September 2013).

World Intellectual Property Organization (WIPO) (2013) *Customary Law, Traditional Knowledge and Intellectual Property: An Outline of the Issues.* Geneva: WIPO.

Wynberg, R., D. Schroeder and R. Chennells (eds) (2009) *Indigenous Peoples, Consent and Benefit Sharing: Lessons from the San-Hoodia Case.* Dordrecht: Springer.

35

Patentable Subject Matter: A Comparative Jurisdictional Analysis of the Discovery/ Invention Dichotomy

Susanna H.S. Leong

INTRODUCTION

Article 27(1) of the Agreement on Trade-Related aspects of Intellectual Property Rights 1994 (TRIPS) sets out the minimum standards of patent protection that member countries must apply – that patents shall be available for *inventions in all fields of technology*, provided they are new, inventive and capable of industrial application. To this general principle, there are exceptions wherein an invention may be excluded from patent protection: (a) inventions the commercial exploitation of which are against *ordre public* or morality; (b) diagnostic, therapeutic and surgical methods for the treatment of humans or animals; and (c) plants and animals other than micro-organisms, and biological processes for the production of plants and animals.

Thus, it may be said that the concept of *an invention* is central to the patent system, as it is generally accepted that the main justification for the patent system is to encourage the progress of science and the production of useful arts through an incentive scheme under which inventors are given an exclusive right by the State to exploit their inventions. In exchange for this exclusive right to exploit their inventions, inventors must disclose the details of their inventions to the public. This allows the public to build on the knowledge of the inventions to further create new knowledge which will be beneficial to society as a whole. The concept of *an invention* is also inextricably linked to the issue of what constitutes 'patentable subject matter' (*Diamond v Chakrabarty* (1980) 447 US 303, 100 S Ct 2204, *per* Burger CJ at 2208), given that under almost all modern patent laws, a patent can only be granted to *an invention* on the condition that it is new, involves an inventive step and is capable of industrial application. However, TRIPS does not provide guidance as to what constitutes *an invention*. Although the Paris Convention 1883 refers to 'patentable inventions', it does not elaborate on what this term actually refers to.

Whilst the patent system is designed to benefit society by promoting innovation and commercializing new technology for ultimate public consumption, it also imposes numerous costs on society. As a result of the exclusive nature of patent rights, access to new inventions by the public is restricted and prices of inventions are kept artificially high. Another cost is the restriction of access by competitors. The proliferation of patents in key industries, such as semiconductors, computer software, and business methods in the internet and biotechnology sectors has created an overlapping set of patent rights requiring all those who seek to commercialize or develop new technology to obtain licences from multiple patentees. There is a growing concern within the intellectual property community about the negative effects of an overly monopolistic patent policy on creation and innovation. Advocates of this school of thought call for the preservation of the public domain and the grant of greater access to the essential building blocks for innovation and creation (Heller, 1998; Heller & Eisenberg, 1998; Lange, 1981; Litman, 1990; Samuelson, 2003; Shapiro, 2001). Countries have seen the need to strike a balance between the interests of different stakeholders and they have taken different approaches to delimit the field of patentable subject matter. Implicit in this is the recognition of the importance of accessibility of knowledge within the patent protection framework so as to promote future innovation. In particular, courts across jurisdictions have consistently embarked on the exercise of distinguishing between inventions (applied knowledge and thus patentable) and discoveries or abstract ideas (esoteric knowledge and thus not patentable). For ease of discussion, we shall refer to this conceptual distinction between a discovery and an invention as 'the discovery/invention dichotomy'.

This chapter examines the international framework of patentable subject matter as set out in TRIPS and the Paris Convention 1883. Against this background, the paper surveys the different approaches adopted by countries such as the United Kingdom, other members in the European Union, the United States of America, Australia and Singapore to deal with the issue of patentable subject matter, paying attention to the interplay of the discovery/invention dichotomy particularly in controversial subject matters such as genetic materials, computer software and business methods. The paper concludes with the general principles which may be gleaned from the cases across different jurisdictions in the assessment of what constitutes an invention deserving of patent protection.

PATENTABLE SUBJECT MATTER AND THE CONCEPT OF 'AN INVENTION'

The Statute of Monopolies 1623

The patent system has a long history. In ancient Europe, letters patent, a type of legal instrument in the form of a published written order, was used by the State to grant certain privileges to a person or corporation. Very often a patent privilege in the form of a monopoly or exclusive right was granted to a person or corporation to attract new and valuable foreign technology so as to boost economic activities within the country. Over time, this system of granting a particular type of letters patent evolved into the modern patent system that we are familiar with today. However, as these privileges in the form of letters patent were granted on the basis of prerogative powers, this resulted in criticisms of the State for creating harmful and arbitrary monopolies which offered little or no benefits to society, except to further enrich the rich and powerful. The Statute of Monopolies 1623 was enacted, in England and Wales, in response to such criticisms and pressures to curb the creation of harmful monopolies.

Section 1 of the Statute of Monopolies 1623 declared, in part, that:

> *all Monopolies, and all Commissioners, Grants, Licences, Charters and Letters of Patents* heretofore made or granted, or hereafter to be made or granted, to any Person or Persons, Bodies Politik or Corporate whatsoever, of or the sole Buying,

> Selling, Making, Working or Using of any Thing within this Realm, or the Dominion of Wales, ... or of any other Monopolies, or of Power, Liberty or Faculty, to dispense with any others, or to give Licence or Toleration to do, use or exercise any Thing against the Tenor of Purport of any Law or Statute ... and all Proclamations, Inhibitions, Restraints, Warrants of Assistants, and all other Matters and Things whatsoever, any way tending to the Instituting, Erecting, Strengthening, Furthering or Countenancing of the same or any of them ... are altogether contrary to the Laws of this Realm, and so are and *shall be utterly void and of none Effect*, and in no wise to be put in Use or Execution. [emphasis added]

However, section 6 of the Statute of Monopolies 1623 states that the above declaration does not extend to:

> any letters patent and grants of privilege for the term of 14 years or under, hereafter to be made, of the sole working or making of *any manner of new manufactures within this Realm*, to the true and first inventor of such manufacture which others at the time of making such letters patent and grants shall not use. [emphasis added]

The concept of 'an invention' in form of 'any manner of new manufactures' may thus be traced to the Statute of Monopolies 1623 in 17th-century England.

Although the dictionary meaning of the word 'manufacture' is to make or produce goods and materials, it was generally settled law (as early as 1842) that the word 'manufacture' as used in the Statute of Monopolies 1623 extended to cover both a process and a product (*Crane v Price* (1842) 1 WPC 393, 4 Man & G 580, 134 ER 239). A method or process is a manner of manufacture if 'it (a) results in the production of some vendible product or (b) improves or restores to its former condition a vendible product or (c) has the effect of preserving from deterioration some vendible product to which it is applied' (*Re GEC's Application* (1942) 60 RPC 1 at 4).

The term 'any manner of new manufactures' underpinned the definition of an 'invention' in the 19th- and 20th-century patent laws of the UK until the enactment of the Patents Act 1977 (UK) in which an 'invention' was not explicitly defined. Elsewhere, such as in Australia, this term 'any manner of new manufactures' remains a key element in the definition of an 'invention' even in post-TRIPS patent legislation. An 'invention' is defined in Sch. 1 Patents Act 1990 (Aust) (Act No 83 of 1990) to mean 'any manner of new manufacture the subject of letters patent and grant of privilege with s 6 of the Statute of Monopolies, and includes an alleged invention'.

The Paris Convention 1883; The Patents Cooperation Treaty; TRIPS

The concept of 'an invention' is not explicitly defined in most modern patent legislation and conventions.

One important international convention is the Paris Convention for the Protection of Industrial Property which was concluded in 1883 (Paris Convention 1883). The Paris Convention 1883 applies to industrial property of a wide range, including patents, trade marks, industrial designs, utility models, service marks, trade names, geographical indications and the practice of unfair competition. Although the Paris Convention 1883 refers to 'patentable inventions', it does not elaborate on what this term actually refers to.

Another important international convention is the Patents Cooperation Treaty (PCT), which was concluded in 1970. Under the PCT, an applicant who is a national or a resident of a PCT Contracting State is able to seek patent protection for an invention in all the countries which are PCT Contracting States by filing an 'international' patent application. The application may be filed with the national patent office of the Contracting State of which the applicant is a national or resident or directly with the International Bureau of WIPO. No definition of an invention is provided in the PCT but excluded subject matter includes scientific and mathematical theories, plant and animal varieties, schemes, rules or methods of doing business, methods for treatment of human or animal bodies, mere presentation of information and computer programs (PCT, Art. 17(2)(a)(i) and PCT, Rule 39).

In TRIPS, article 27(1) states:

> [P]atents shall be available for any inventions, whether products or processes, in all fields of technology, *provided* that they are new, involve an inventive step and are capable of industrial application ... [P]atents shall be available and patent rights enjoyable without discrimination as to the place of invention, the field of technology and whether products are imported or locally produced.

Accordingly, the concept of 'an invention' in TRIPS is a very wide one which includes both product inventions as well as process inventions and it is not limited to any particular field of technology. A patent shall be granted for any subject matter within this category of inventions provided it is new, inventive and is capable of industrial application. There is no specified list of subject matter in TRIPS which is considered not to be an invention and thus not patentable. However, member countries may exclude the following inventions from patentability: (a) inventions the commercial exploitation of which are against *ordre public* or morality; (b) diagnostic, therapeutic and surgical methods for the treatment of humans or animals; and (c) plants and animals other than microorganisms, and biological processes for the production of plants and animals.

DIFFERENT LEGISLATIVE APPROACHES TO PATENTABILITY OF AN INVENTION

The European Patent Convention 1973 and the Patents Act 1977 (c 37) (UK)

The successful conclusion of the European Patent Convention (EPC) in Munich in 1973 marked the establishment of a new modern law of patents. Notably, the EPC does not contain a definition of 'an invention'. Article 52(1) of the EPC states:

> European patents shall be granted for any inventions, *in all fields of technology*, provided that they are new, involve an inventive step and are susceptible of industrial application. [emphasis added]

The reference to 'all fields of technology' was inserted into the EPC in 2007, signifying the adoption of an expanded concept of 'an invention' within the EPC Contracting States.

The UK ratified the EPC in March 1977 and shortly thereafter Parliament enacted the Patents Act 1977 (c 37) (UK). Taking its cue from the EPC, the Patents Act 1977 also does not contain a definition of 'an invention'. This is unlike the position under its predecessor the Patents Act 1949 (c 87) (UK). Section 101 of the Patents Act 1949 (c 87) (UK) states that: 'Invention' means:

> any manner of new manufacture the subject of letters patent and grant of privilege with s 6 of the Statute of Monopolies and any new method or process of testing applicable to the improvement or control of manufacture, and includes an alleged invention.

Section 1(1) of the Patents Act 1977 (c 37) (UK) states that:

> a patent may be granted only for an invention in respect of which the following conditions are satisfied, that is to say:
>
> (a) the invention is new;
> (b) it involves and inventive step;
> (c) it is capable of industrial application;
> (d) the grant of a patent for it is not excluded by subsections (2) and (3) below;
>
> and references in this Act to a patentable invention shall be construed accordingly.

The reasons for not having an explicit definition of 'an invention' in the EPC and in the Patents Act 1977 may be manifold: the inability to reach a consensus on the meaning of 'an invention' amongst the drafters; the recognition that any present attempt at defining 'an invention' may be futile as technological advances could very quickly render such a definition obsolete; that from a policy point of view any attempt to settle on a definition of 'an invention' may be undesirable as it could fetter future technological developments.

The UK House of Lords in *Biogen Inc v Medeva* [1997] RPC 1, a case involving the validity of a patent for products of genetic engineering or recombinant DNA technology, explained the implications of not having an explicit definition of 'an invention' in the Patents Act 1977. Lord Hoffmann explained as follows ([1997] RPC 1, at [41]):

> The Act does not define the concept of an invention. Section 1(1) was intended to reflect, 'as nearly as practicable', Article 52 of the European Patent Convention ('EPC') ... and Article 52 also has no definition of an invention. It seems that the parties to the EPC were unable to agree upon one ... *But the reason why the parties were content to do without a definition was that they recognised that the question would almost invariably be academic. The four conditions in section 1(1) do a great deal more than restrict the class of 'inventions' which may be patented. They probably also contain every element of the concept of an invention in ordinary speech.* I say probably, because in the absence of a definition one cannot say with certainty that one might not come across something which satisfied all the conditions but could not be described as an invention. But the draftsmen of the Convention and the Act, as well as counsel at the bar, were unable to think of any examples. Just in case one should appear, section 1(5) gives the Secretary of State power to vary the list of matters excluded by paragraph (d) 'for the purpose of maintaining them in conformity with developments in science and technology'. [emphasis added]

It may be inferred from Lord Hoffmann's argument that, in practice, the lack of an explicit definition of 'an invention' in the patent legislation may cause few problems given the fact that the basic criteria of patentability namely, novelty, inventiveness and industrial application (provided for in the statute and interpreted by the courts) effectively circumscribe the concept of an invention in most cases.

Although the Patents Act 1977 (c 37) (UK) does not contain an explicit definition of 'an invention', it does however contain a list of things which are declared *not* 'an invention'. It follows that subject matters which fall within this list of things that are declared not 'an invention' are accordingly not patentable.

The list of matters or things that are declared as not inventions under section 1(2) of the Patents Act 1977 include:

> (a) a discovery, scientific theory or mathematical method;
> (b) a literary, dramatic, musical or artistic work or any other aesthetic creation whatsoever;
> (c) a scheme, rule or method for performing a mental act, playing a game or doing business, or a program for a computer; or
> (d) the presentation of information;
>
> but the foregoing provision shall prevent anything from being treated as an invention for the purposes of this Act only to the extent that a patent or application for a patent relates to that thing *as such*. [emphasis added]

Section 1(2) of the Patents Act 1977 implements article 52(2) of the EPC. A number of observations may be made about this list of 'things' which are declared not to be inventions. Firstly, the list is not meant to be exhaustive (*Gale's Application* [1991] RPC 305 at 324, *per* Nicholls LJ and *Lux Traffic Controls Ltd v Pike Signals Ltd* [1993] RPC 107 at 138, *per* Aldous LJ). Secondly, the list consists of four categories, (a)–(d), seemingly connected to one another but on closer examination, one may conclude that 'there is no evident underlying purpose lying behind the provisions as a group' (*Aerotel Ltd v Telco Holdings Ltd* [2007] RPC 7 at [9], *per* Jacob LJ). In fact, it is the opinion of Lord Justice Jacobs that the categories in section 1(2) of the Patents Act 1977 'form a disparate group' and 'one cannot form an overall approach to the categories' (*Aerotel Ltd v Telco Holdings Ltd* [2007] RPC 7 at [9], *per* Jacob LJ).

The subject matter referred to in category (a) is abstract and naturally occurring. In contrast, the subject matter referred to in categories (b), (c) and (d) is not naturally occurring as they all have human authors. Some of the subject matter in certain categories such as literary and other aesthetic creations in (b) and computer programs in (c) are granted protection under other intellectual property laws, namely, copyright. Finally, it should be noted that anything referred to in the four categories from (a)–(d) is not treated as an invention for the purposes of the Patent Act 1977 *only to the extent* that a patent or application for a patent relates to that thing '*as such*'. Implicit in the 'as such' *proviso* is the requirement that something more must be done to the subject matter before it can be regarded as an invention for the purposes of obtaining a patent. However, the precise meaning of the 'as such' *proviso* is far from clear and there has been considerable debate about it over the years. The courts, in considering the 'as such' *proviso*, have looked for some form of technical contribution or technical effect brought forth by the subject matter in question. Another way of looking at this issue of technical contribution or technical effect is to ascertain whether the thing or subject matter in question results in an artificially created altered state of affairs in the physical environment. If there is no change whatsoever in the physical environment as a result of the introduction of the thing or subject matter, it is not an invention. Yet another way of understanding this requirement of a technical contribution or a technical effect is to consider whether, in economic terms, any *value-added element* may be found in the subject matter that concerns an invention. There is now a sizeable case law in this area in the UK and the European Patent Office (EPO), but the cases adopt different approaches in answering the question whether the patent application relates to an excluded subject matter *as such* under the *proviso* and is therefore not capable of being granted a patent.

Discoveries and Scientific Theories

Category (a) of section 1(2) of the Patents Act 1977 (c 37) (UK) is concerned with things that are generally within the realms of science which are naturally occurring in our physical world. The word 'discovery' in (a) is broad enough to include, amongst other things, 'products of nature' whether flora or fauna and all naturally occurring phenomena. It has been said that, 'at the heart of many inventions is a discovery which is an excluded matter' but 'what can be patented is the incorporation of that discovery into technology' (*Lux Traffic Controls Ltd v Pike Signals Ltd* [1993] RPC 107 at 139, *per* Aldous LJ).

This is consistent with the basic principle that a naturally occurring thing or phenomenon without the input of man cannot constitute an invention. Inventions are, in the ordinary understanding, 'man-made' things. Thus, in category (a), the discovery of a thing or phenomenon, without more being done to it, remains a mere discovery which is not considered an invention. In the English case of *Gale's Application* [1991] RPC 303 at 323, Nicholls LJ made the distinction between an idea or an invention on the one hand and the *practical application* of an idea or discovery on the other. The former is not patentable whilst the latter is. In other words, the practical application of an idea or discovery should lead to an altered state of affairs in the physical world. Besides discoveries, scientific theories and mathematical methods are also not regarded as inventions under category (a). According to Lord Justice Jacob in *Aerotel Ltd v Telco Holdings Ltd*, 'a patent after all is a legal monopoly over some commercial activity carried out by human beings' and 'a scientific theory is not activity at all'. Thus, 'it simply is not the sort of thing which could be made the subject of a legal monopoly'([2007] RPC 7 at [9]).

Literary, Dramatic, Musical, Artistic or Other Aesthetic Creations

In category (b) of section 1(2) of the Patents Act 1977 (c 37) (UK), the subject matter referred to is products of fine arts and includes literary, dramatic, musical, artistic works or other aesthetic creations. These are products of aesthetic and cultural expression borne out of the human intellect and they belong to the domain of copyright laws. However, it should be noted that if the aesthetic creation is produced by a technical innovation, for example, a new printing technique for a book which results in a particular layout with aesthetic effect, this new technique may well be patentable (para 2.3.4 Chapter IV (Patentability) of the Guidelines for Examination in the European Patent Office 2010).

Schemes, Rules, Playing Games, Methods of Performing a Mental Act, Methods of Doing Business, Computer Programs

In category (c) of section 1(2) of the Patents Act 1977 (c 37) (UK), things like schemes, rules, playing games, methods of performing a mental act, doing business or a computer program, *as such*, are not considered 'inventions'. The Guidelines for Examination in the European Patent Office 2010 gave examples of the things excluded in category (c): 'a scheme for learning a language, a method of solving crossword puzzles, a game (as an abstract entity defined by its rules) or a scheme for organising a commercial operation' (para 2.3.5 Chapter IV (Patentability) of the Guidelines for Examination in the European Patent Office 2010).

Presentation of Information

Finally, in category (d) of section 1(2) of the Patents Act 1977 (c 37) (UK), the presentation of information *as such* is not considered an invention. Thus, the selection, compilation and arrangement of information in the form of databases is not an invention.

As we have seen in the above discussion, the Patents Act 1977 (c 37) (UK) and the European Patent Convention set out explicit categories of things which are regarded as *not* inventions. This may be seen as being unduly restrictive as an approach towards the patentability of certain subject matter such as computer programs and business methods. However, it may also be said that access to knowledge under such an approach is preserved by legislative articulation of an explicit list of subject matters that are *not* patentable.

The Australian Patents Act 1990 (Act No 83 of 1990 as amended by Act No 35 of 2012)

The criteria for patentability are set out in section 18 of the Australian Patents Act 1990 which provides:

> (1) ... an invention is a patentable invention for the purposes of a standard patent if the invention, so far as claimed in any claim:
>
> (a) is a manner of manufacture within the meaning of section 6 of the Statute of Monopolies; and
>
> (b) when compared with the prior art base as it existed before the priority date of that claim:
>
> (i) is novel; and
>
> (ii) involves an inventive step; and
>
> (c) is useful; and
>
> (d) was not secretly used in the patent area before the priority date of that claim by, or on behalf of, or with the authority of, the patentee or nominated person or the patentee's or nominated person's predecessor in title to the invention.

Furthermore, the term 'invention' is defined in Schedule 1 of the Australian Patents Act 1990 to mean 'any manner of new manufacture the subject of letters patent and grant of privilege within section 6 of the Statute of Monopolies, and includes an alleged invention'.

As for the term 'any manner of new manufacture' in section 6 of the Statute of Monopolies 1623, the Australian High Court in *Re NRDC* [1961] RPC 135 adopted an extended meaning of the term and concluded that 'manufacture' was not confined to physical material things in the sense of an article but was wide enough to include 'any physical phenomenon' in which the new and useful effect may be observed (the key requirement being that it was an artificially created state of affairs and that it belonged to a useful art as distinct from a fine art) and that it possessed practical utility 'in that its value to the country is in the field of economic endeavour' ([1961] RPC 135 at 275). In fact, the Australian High Court went further to explain that the 'physical phenomenon' may include 'a building, a tract or stratum of land, an explosion, an electrical oscillation' ([1961] RPC 135 at 276). As such, the Australian High Court held that agricultural or horticultural processes, such as the process with which the court was concerned in the present case – eradicating weeds without damaging crops by applying selective herbicides – were within the limits of patentable inventions and thus granted the patent application.

In *Cancer Voices Australia* v *Myriad Genetics Inc* [2013] FCA 65, the Federal Court of Australia had to consider whether a valid patent may be granted for a claim that covers naturally occurring nucleic acid – either deoxyribonucleic acid (DNA) or ribonucleic acid (RNA) – that has been 'isolated'. Essentially the act of isolation means removing naturally occurring nucleic acid found in the cells of the human body (either DNA or RNA) from the cellular environment in which it naturally exists and separating it from other cellular components. More specifically, the patent in suit related to a human breast and ovarian cancer disposing gene (BRCA1) and the invention is the successful identification and isolation of this gene. In his judgment upholding the validity of the patent in suit, Nicholas J cited at length the decision of the Australian High Court in *Re NRDC* and reiterated the important principle that the question whether a particular subject matter is patentable under section 18(1)(a) of the Australian Patents Act 1990 involves 'a conceptual inquiry as opposed to a consideration of the etymology of the expression "manner of manufacture"'. In turn, the concept of manner of manufacture has a 'broad sweep' and is intended to cover developments which may be unpredictable.

Sections 18(2)–(4) of the Australian Patents Act 1990 further provide that the following are not patentable:

> (2) Human beings, and the biological processes for their generation, are not patentable inventions.
>
> (3) For the purposes of an innovation patent, plants and animals, and the biological processes for the generation of plants and animals, are not patentable inventions.
>
> (4) Subsection (3) does not apply if the invention is a microbiological process or a product of such a process.

The United States Patents Act (35 USC (US) §1 et seq (2007 Rev Ed))

Section 101 of the United States Patent Act defines patentable subject matter and it states:

> Whoever invents or discovers any new and useful process, machine, manufacture, or composition of matter, or any new and useful improvement thereof, may obtain a patent therefor, subject to the conditions and requirements of this title.

The term 'invention' means 'invention or discovery' (see United States Patent Act §100 (a)) whilst 'process' means 'process, art, or method, and includes a new use of a known process, machine, manufacture, composition of matter, or material' (see United States Patent Act § 100 (b)). The patentability of an invention or discovery is dependent on the satisfaction of specified conditions for novelty and non-obviousness. Besides the conditions of novelty and non-obviousness, there do not appear to be any pre-determined bars to the patentability of any particular subject matter within the United States Patents Act (United States Patent Act §101; 102; 103).

In *Diamond v Chakrabarty* (1980) 447 US 303, 100 S Ct 2204, the United States Supreme Court was presented with the issue of whether a live, human-made micro-organism constitutes a 'manufacture' or 'composition of matter' within section 101 of the United States Patents Act and, consequently, constituted a patentable subject matter under United States patent laws. By a five to four vote, the Supreme Court held that the language in section 101 was wide enough to cover an invention of a living, genetically engineered micro-organism. The majority's judgment, delivered by Burger CJ, confirmed that Congress intended the statutory language in section 101 of the United States Patents Act to be construed widely and he said:

> In choosing such expansive terms [in s 101 the United States Patents Act 35 USC] as 'manufacture' and 'composition of matter' modified by the comprehensive 'any', Congress plainly contemplated that the patent laws would be given wide scope.

> The relevant legislative history also supports a broad construction. The Patents Act of 1793, authored by Thomas Jefferson, defined statutory subject matter as 'any new and useful art, machine, manufacture, or composition of matter, or any new or useful improvement [thereof] … In 1952, when the patent laws were recodified, Congress replaced the word 'art' with 'process', but otherwise left Jefferson's language intact. The Committee Report accompanying the 1952 Act informs us that Congress intended statutory subject matter to '*include anything under the sun that is made by man.*'
>
> This is not to suggest that §101 has no limits or that it embraces every discovery. The laws of nature, physical phenomenon, and abstract ideas have been held not patentable … Thus a new mineral discovered in the earth or a new plant found in the wild is not patentable subject matter. Likewise, Einstein could not patent his celebrated law that $E = mc^2$ nor could Newton have patented the law of gravity. Such discoveries are 'manifestations of … nature, free to all men and reserved exclusively to none. [emphasis added]

The phrase 'anything under the sun that is made by man' has been relied upon by subsequent cases as supporting an expansive interpretation of the scope of section 101of the United States Patents Act (see *Diamond v Diehr* 450 US 175 (1981); *State St Bank & Trust v Signature Financial Group* 149 F 3d 1368 (Fed Cir 1998); *JEM Ag Supply v Pioneer Hi-Bred* 534 US 124 (2001)). It may be said that the US Supreme Court has consistently construed section 101 broadly as 'Congress plainly contemplated that the patent laws would be given wide scope' (*Diamond v Chakrabarty* (1980) 447 US 303, 100 S Ct 2204, at 308). Nevertheless, the patentability of an invention under US patent laws is limited by three judicially created exceptions to section 101: 'Laws of nature, natural phenomena, and abstract ideas' (*Diamond v Diehr* 450 US 175 (1981), at 185). The US Courts have also ruled that mental processes (*Gottschalk v Benson* 409 US 63 (1972), at 67) and products of nature (*Diamond v Chakrabarty* (1980) 447 US 303, 100 S Ct 2204, at 313) are included in the aforementioned three categories of exceptions to patent eligibility.

Until recently, as evidenced in *In Re Bilski* 130 S Ct 3218 (2010) ('*Bilski*') and *Mayo Collaborative Services v Prometheus, Inc.* ('*Mayo*') 132 S Ct 1289 (2012), US courts were generally considered as having taken an expansionary path vis-à-vis patentable subject matter, which prompted the following observation from a leading commentator (Cooper Dreyfuss, 2006):

> A quarter century ago it was unclear whether the subject matter boundaries of the patent system were expansive enough to embrace biotechnology and information technology. Today, it is not clear whether the patent system has *any* subject matter boundaries at all. [emphasis added]

An expansionary approach towards patentability by the courts particularly in the area of methods or process inventions certainly heightens the concerns that the grant of such patents limits access to knowledge and increases the costs of future innovation resulting in an overall decrease in welfare for society as a whole. As we shall see in the discussions below on the patentability of methods or process inventions, there appears a greater resolve by the courts in the United States in recent cases to reverse the expansionary trend on patent eligibility of methods or process inventions.

The Singapore Patents Act 1995

Section 13(1) of the Singapore Patents Act states:

> Subject to subsections (2) and (3), a *patentable invention* is one that satisfies the following conditions:
>
> (a) the invention is *new*;
> (b) it involves *an inventive step*; and
> (c) it is capable *of industrial application*.
>
> [emphasis added]

Section 13(2) of the Patents Act further states:

> An invention the publication or exploitation of which would be generally expected to encourage

> offensive, immoral or anti-social behaviour is not a patentable invention.

Section 13(3) of the Patents Act states:

> For the purposes of subsection (2), behaviour shall not be regarded as offensive, immoral or anti-social only because it is prohibited by any law in force in Singapore.

Like the Patents Act 1977 (c 37) (UK), upon which the Singapore Patents Act (Cap 221) is closely modelled, the statute does not contain an explicit definition of 'an invention', except that in section 113(1) it provides that an invention for a patent:

> shall, unless the context otherwise requires, be taken to be specified in a claim of the specification of the application or patent, as the case may be, as interpreted by the description and any drawings contained in that specification, and the extent of the protection conferred by a patent or application for a patent shall be determined accordingly.

However, it should be noted that when the Singapore Patents Act was first enacted in 1995, it contained, in section 13(2), a list of subject matter that was declared not to be an invention. Section 13(2), on exclusions to patentability, was modelled on section 1(2) of the Patents Act 1977 (c 37) (UK). The categories of things declared not as inventions have been discussed above.

Shortly after the passing of the Singapore Patents Act in 1995, the Patents (Amendment) Act 1995 (Act 40 of 1995) came into effect and section 13(2) was deleted. The then Parliamentary Secretary to the Minister for Law, Associate Professor Ho Peng Kee explained to members of parliament the reasons for deleting section 13(2) (Singapore Parliament Reports (Hansard), Parliament No. 8, Session No. 2, Volume No. 65, Sitting Date 01-11-1995):

> Section 13(2) is a short and non-exhaustive listing of subjects, which are considered non-patentable *eg*, a discovery or mathematical model. The deletion of section 13(2) is intended to conform to Article 27(3) of TRIPS, which does not provide for such a listing. Consequential amendments are also made to section 13(5) and section 30(3)(*b*).
>
> Sir, this deletion will not limit our flexibility in rejecting any subject matter, which is non-patentable under section 13(1). The existing provisions are sufficient to enable Singapore to keep up with advances and changes in science and technology.

Since the Patents (Amendment) Act 1995 (Act 40 of 1995), there is no prescribed list of non-patentable subject matter in the Singapore Patents Act and the only bars to patentability which remain relate to any invention which is 'offensive, immoral or anti-social'. Another category of subject matter which is non-patentable is an invention of a method of treatment (whether by surgery or therapy or of diagnosis) practised on a human or animal body because it shall not be taken to be capable of industrial application (S 16(2) Singapore Patents Act).

Reactions to the deletion of section 13(2) by the Patents (Amendment) Act 1995 (Act 40 of 1995) were divided. Some were of the view that the removal of the list meant that discoveries and mathematical methods could be considered as inventions and, in turn, it would open the floodgates to what 'things' could be granted a patent in Singapore. Others viewed the deletion of section 13(2) as merely a removal of a list of examples. This did not, however, mean that things which were formerly explicitly declared not to be considered inventions were now *de facto* considered inventions and so patentable. The criteria for granting a patent under the Singapore Patents Act remained unchanged. In each case, the courts must be satisfied that that subject matter is within the concept of 'an invention' and that means the requirements of novelty, inventiveness and industrial application must be met.

It has been almost 20 years since the passing of the Patents (Amendment) Act 1995 (Act 40 of 1995) and prophesies of floodgates opening as a result of the deletion of section 13(2) have not been fulfilled in Singapore. It is interesting to note that the Singapore Patents Act, in its present form, is silent on both:

(a) the *positive* aspect of the concept of invention: i.e., a concrete definition of 'an invention'; and
(b) the *negative* aspect of the concept of invention: i.e., the list of things which are declared not inventions (although this list was once part of Singapore laws).

In assessing the validity of a patent which hinges on the issue of patent eligibility, the approach taken by the Singapore courts has been to consider whether the application in issue has fulfilled the requisite criteria of novelty, inventiveness and industrial application. This is evident in the judgments of the Singapore Court of Appeal in *FE Global Electronics Pte Ltd v Trek Technology (Singapore) Pte Ltd* [2006] 1 SLR(R) 874; *First Currency Choice Pte Ltd v Main-Line Corporate Holdings Ltd* [2008] 1 SLR(R) 335 and in *Muhlbauer AG v Manufacturing Integration Technology Ltd* [2010] 2 SLR 724. In general, it may be said that Singapore courts do not consider the concept of an invention as a separate and independent requirement for the grant of a patent. Perhaps in the majority of the Singapore cases to date, the courts did not consider it necessary or meaningful to conduct a separate inquiry as to whether the subject matter disclosed in the patent was an invention or not. Presumably, they were satisfied that careful deliberations over issues of novelty, inventive step and industrial application in those cases adequately and fully addressed the issue of whether the subject matter was a patentable invention or not.

From the above discussions, we see that under the broad umbrella principle enunciated in Article 27(1) of TRIPS, countries have adopted different legislative approaches towards the issue of a patentable invention. Under the EPC, the approach involves not giving a positive definition to 'invention' but sets out a list of subject matters not considered patentable inventions as such. In Australia, the concept of 'any new manufactures' remains a key element in the definition of an invention. In the United States, besides the conditions of novelty and non-obviousness, there do not appear to be any pre-determined bars to the patentability of any particular subject matter within the United States Patents Act. Whereas, in Singapore, the Patents Act 1995 does not contain a definition of an invention or a list of things not considered an invention as such. International harmonization of patents law remains a long-term objective of governments, but despite the divergences in legislative approaches, there is evidence that courts across these jurisdictions do converge towards the view that a distinction must be made between inventions (applied knowledge and thus patentable) and discoveries or abstract ideas (esoteric knowledge and thus not patentable). The 'discovery/invention dichotomy' is a conceptual tool commonly utilized by the courts, particularly in the areas of patentability of biological inventions, genetic materials, computer programs and business/process methods, and it is to this issue which we shall now turn.

PATENTABILITY OF BIOLOGICAL INVENTIONS, GENETIC MATERIALS, COMPUTER PROGRAMS AND BUSINESS/PROCESS METHODS – A COMPARATIVE ANALYSIS ACROSS JURISDICTIONS

Biological Inventions and Genetic Materials

Developments in the field of biotechnology and genetic engineering have raised controversial issues – including the patentability of living organisms. Strong policy reasons, such as the sanctity of life and environmental and ecological concerns, have been put forward to bar the patentability of life forms.

Different countries have different views on the extent of patentability of living organisms.

The European Union Biotechnology Directive 98/44, which came into force on 6 July 1998, provided guidance on the patenting of genes, plants and animals, and the following are not patentable (Cornish et al., 2010: 931–932):

1. Processes for cloning humans;
2. Processes for modifying in humans their germ-line genetic identity;
3. Uses of human embryos for industrial or commercial purposes;
4. Processes for modifying the genetic identity of animals which are likely to cause them suffering without any substantial medical benefit to man or animal, and also animals resulting from such processes.

In Australia, the bar is drawn at the highest level of human beings and the related biological processes for their generation. Section 18(2) Patents Act (Aust) (Act No 83 of 1990) states: 'Human beings, and the biological processes for their generation, are not patentable inventions'. Any other life forms in the lower levels are therefore *prima facie* patentable. However, in light of the recent case of *Cancer Voices Australia v Myriad Genetics Inc*, wherein the Federal Court of Australia has granted patent protection for the identification and isolation techniques for human breast and ovarian cancer disposing genes, it is questionable whether this has the effect of a lowering of the bar. It is interesting to note that the Federal Court of Australia in *Cancer Voices Australia v Myriad Genetics Inc* did not think it necessary to address the exclusion in section 18(2) Patents Act (Aust) (Act No 83 of 1990) and whether an invention relating to human gene identification and isolation comes within the exclusion. Singapore has taken a liberal position with respect to the patentability of life forms. There are no specific bars to the patentability of living organisms. It may be argued that under the Singapore Patents Act life forms including animal clones are potentially patentable inventions provided they satisfy the criteria of novelty, inventiveness and are capable of industrial application. However, the cloning of human beings in Singapore is expressly banned under the Human Cloning and Other Prohibited Practices Act 2004. Under the Human Cloning and Other Prohibited Practices Act (Cap 131B, 2005 Rev Ed), the following acts, *inter alia*, are prohibited:

(a) placing a human embryo clone in the body of a human or animal;
(b) developing any human embryo, that is created by a process other than the fertilization of a human egg by human sperm, for a period of more than 14 days;
(c) developing any human embryo outside the body of a woman for a period of more than 14 days;
(d) collecting a viable human embryo from the body of a woman;
(e) placing any human embryo in an animal;
(f) placing any human embryo in the body of a human, other than in a woman's reproductive tract;
(g) placing any animal embryo in the body of a human for any period of gestation;
(h) placing any embryo in the body of a woman knowing that, or reckless as to whether, the embryo is a prohibited embryo;
(i) importing and exporting of prohibited embryos;
(j) trading in human eggs, human sperm and human embryos.

Therefore, human clones are not patentable subject matter in Singapore.

Against the background of diverse approaches adopted by different jurisdictions in dealing with the issue of patentability, it is, however, clear that patent laws in general protect 'invention' which is to be distinguished from 'discovery, scientific theory or mathematical method' as stated in the EPC, or 'laws of nature, natural phenomena, and abstract ideas' (*Diamond v Diehr* 450 US 175 (1981), at 185) under US patent law, or 'product of nature' as expressed in the Australian case of *Re NRDC*, or 'a mere discovery' as in the Singapore decision of *Merck & Co Inc v Pharmaforte Singapore Pte Ltd* [2000] 2 SLR(R) 708.

Recently, courts in Australia and the United States have been called upon to consider the distinction between a discovery and an invention in the context of patentability of genes or genes sequencing.

In *Cancer Voices Australia v Myriad Genetics Inc* [2013] FCA 65, the Federal Court of Australia held that naturally occurring DNA and RNA which has been extracted from a human breast and ovarian cancer disposing gene and purged of other biological materials with which they are associated is a 'manner of manufacture' within the meaning of an invention under section 18 of the Australian Patents Act 1990 and is thus patentable. Applying the principles enunciated by *Re NDRC*, that a composition of matter may constitute patentable subject matter if it consists of 'an artificial state of affairs, that has some discernible effect, and that is of utility in a field of economic endeavour' ([2013] FCA 65 at [101]), Nicholas J ruled that in assessing the patentability of the isolated nucleic acids referred to in the disputed claims three important factors must be considered. First, the concept of manner of manufacture as one which involves the creation of an artificial state of affairs in *Re NDRC* is a very broad one and in the context of biological material, such an artificial state of affairs may manifest in different ways, for example changes in physical properties of the naturally occurring material when it is isolated. Second, it is clear that naturally occurring nucleic acid exists out of the cell of a human body only as a result of human intervention. Extraction of nucleic acid as well as the purification of extracted nucleic acid both requires human intervention. Finally, an immense amount of research and intellectual effort has been expended in the creation of isolated DNA and RNA which is practically useful as well as economically significant. These factors led the judge in *Cancer Voices Australia v Myriad Genetics Inc.* to conclude that an isolated nucleic acid constitutes an artificial state of affairs within the concept of a manner of manufacture in the definition of an invention under Australian patent law.

It is interesting to point out that over in the United States, litigation was also convened with regards to a US patent that is closely related to the patent at issue in the Australian case of *Cancer Voices Australia v Myriad Genetics Inc*. In the matter of *The Association for Molecular Pathology v Myriad Genetics Inc* 653 F3d 1329 (2011), Myriad Genetics were granted a number of patents after discovering the precise location and sequence of human breast and ovarian cancer disposing genes BRCA1 and BRCA2, the mutations of which can dramatically increase the risk of breast and ovarian cancer. This knowledge has allowed Myriad Genetics to develop medical tests useful for detecting mutations in these genes with a view to assessing a patient's cancer risk. If Myriad Genetics' patents are valid, this would confer on Myriad Genetics the exclusive right to isolate a patient's BRCA1 and BRCA2 genes. The petitioners filed a suit to seek a declaration that Myriad Genetics' patents are invalid under 35 USC §101. The majority of the United States Court of Appeal upheld the validity of the patent claims to isolated DNA sequences (*Association for Molecular Pathology et al. v Myriad Genetics Inc.*, United States Court of Appeals for the Federal Court, 2010–1406, decided August 16, 2012). On appeal, the Supreme Court of the United States unanimously held that a naturally occurring DNA segment is a product of nature and is not patentable merely on the ground that it has been isolated (*Association for Molecular Pathology et al. v Myriad Genetics Inc.*, Supreme Court of the United States, No 12-398, Decided June 13, 2013). In its patent-eligibility inquiry, the Supreme Court referred to *Diamond v Chakrabarty* (1980) 447 US 303, 100 S Ct 2204, and asked whether Myriad Genetics' inventions were new 'with markedly different characteristics from any found in nature'. The Supreme Court concluded that Myriad Genetics did not create or alter either the genetic information encoded in the BCRA1 and BCRA2 genes or the genetic structure of the DNA. What Myriad Genetics did in its inventions was to *discover* the precise location and sequence of the BRCA1 and BRCA2 cancer disposing genes, but a groundbreaking, innovative or even brilliant *discovery* does not by itself satisfy the patent-eligibility criteria under 35 USC §101. In other words, the discovery of the location of BRCA1 and BRCA2 genes did not render the genes 'new … composition[s] of matter' under 35 USC §101 and the act of separating these genes from their surrounding genetic material is not an act of invention. Myriad

Genetics' inventions must be contrasted with the modified bacterium in *Diamond v Chakrabarty* (1980) 447 US 303, 100 S Ct 2204, which was new (as four plasmids were added to the bacterium) and as a result was capable of breaking down various components of crude oil. The modified bacterium in *Diamond v Chakrabarty* was therefore patentable. It is therefore clear that a discovery of what is naturally occurring in nature cannot be a subject of a patent under US patent laws. Underpinning this analysis is the requirement of human intervention in the act of invention so as to create a patentable subject matter. Accordingly, the Supreme Court further held that when gene sequences are refined by synthetic processes to create molecules that do not occur naturally, such as when introns are removed from a DNA sequence to make composite DNA ('cDNA'), something new is created which is patentable.

The judgment of the United States Supreme Court on the validity of the patent claims in relation to isolated DNA sequences is significant for the biotechnology industry as the practice of isolating DNA molecules had given rise to exceedingly valuable property rights. Although the Australian and the US courts have arrived at different conclusions on the issue of the patentability of isolated DNA sequences, both courts embarked on a similar inquiry of what constitutes an invention and, in this regard, the 'discovery/invention dichotomy' remains a useful conceptual tool to assist the courts in making the distinction between what should receive patent protection and what should not. It is clear that in the overall analysis, the factor of human intervention is undoubtedly an important one and few will have issues as to its inclusion in the overall assessment of the distinction between a discovery and an invention. However, difficulty remains with regard to the extent or degree of human intervention that is required to effectively convert a subject matter that is naturally occurring into an artificial state of affairs deserving of a patent protection. In this regard, a bright-line standard may prove to be an elusive objective as the courts' interpretations of the factual matrix in each particular case will undoubtedly impact as to where this distinguishing line is to be drawn, as we have seen in the differing conclusions of *Cancer Voices Australia v Myriad Genetics Inc.* and *The Association for Molecular Pathology v Myriad Genetics Inc.*

Computer Programs and Business Methods/Process Inventions

Different jurisdictions have taken different approaches in assessing the patentability of computer programs and business methods/process inventions. An example of a business method invention is found in *State St Bank & Trust v Signature Financial Group* 149 F 3d 1368 (Fed Cir 1998). The invention in that case for which a patent was sought involved a data processing system for implementing an investment structure for the administration and accounting of mutual funds.

With respect to the patentability of computer software and business methods inventions, the UK Courts and the European Patent Office (EPO) have adopted a whole range of approaches over the years (see *Aerotel Ltd v Telco Holdings Ltd* [2007] RPC 7). These include:

1. 'The contribution approach' (supported by Falconer LJ in *Merrill Lynch's Patent Application* [1988] RPC 1 but rejected by the Court of Appeal in *Merrill Lynch's Patent Application* [1989] RPC 561);
2. 'The technical effect approach' (first adopted by the European Patent Office's Board of Appeals in Decision T208/04 *VICOM SYSTEM INC* [1987] OJ EPO 14, [1987] EPOR 74; Decision T6/83 *IBM CORP/Data Processing Network* [1990] OJ EPOR 5, [1990] EPOR 91; also endorsed by the English Court of Appeal in *Merrill Lynch's Patent Application* [1989] RPC 561; and followed in *Gale's Patent Application* [1991] RPC 305; *Fujitsu Ltd's Patent Application* [1997] RPC 608.); and
3. 'the any hardware approach' (adopted in Decision T931/95 *Pensions Benefit System Partnership* 8 September 2000 EPO; Decision T258/03 *Hitachi* 21 April 2004 EPO; and Decision

T424/03 *Microsoft/Data Transfer* 23 February 2006 EPO; rejected in *Gale's Patent Application* [1991] RPC 305).

Of these, the 'technical effect approach' appears to be most widely applied by the EPO and the courts in the UK, and a computer program or a business method is patentable if the actual contribution of the invention gives rise to a technical effect. In *VICOM/Computer-related Invention* [1987] EPOR 74, the Technical Board of Appeal of the EPO emphasized the technical contribution of the invention for which a patent was sought to determine if it fell within the list of things not considered an invention under article 52(2) and (3) of the EPC. The claims in the patent application were directed at a computer operating in accordance with instructions in a computer programme which resulted in a technical effect, i.e. enhancing digital images on the basis of a mathematical method. The Technical Board of Appeal explained why the invention in this case was not barred from protection by article 52(2) and (3) of the EPC: ([1987] EPOR 74 at 79)

> There can be little doubt that any processing operation on an electric signal can be described in mathematical terms. The characteristic of a filter, for example, can be expressed in terms of a mathematical formula. A basic difference between a mathematical method and a technical process can be seen, however, in the fact that a mathematical method or a mathematical algorithm is carried on numbers (whatever these numbers may represent) and provides a result also in numerical form, the mathematical method or algorithm being only an abstract concept prescribing how to operate numbers. No direct technical result is produced by the method as such. In contrast thereto, if a mathematical method is used in a technical process, that process is carried out on a physical entity (which may be a material object but equally an image stored as an electric signal) by some technical means implementing the method and provides as its result *a certain change in that entity*. The technical means might include a computer comprising suitable hardware or an appropriately programmed general purpose computer. [emphasis added]
>
> ...
>
> The Board, therefore, is of the opinion that even if the idea underlying an invention may be considered to reside in a mathematical method a claim directed to a technical process in which the method is used does not seek protection for the mathematical method *as such*. [emphasis in the original]

On the other hand, in the United States, computer programs and business/process method inventions are not precluded by statute from patentability and therefore are patentable. The test to assess patentability of business process or methods inventions in the United States had been for a considerable time, the 'useful, concrete and tangible result' test applied in *State St Bank & Trust v Signature Financial Group* 149 F 3d 1368 (Fed Cir 1998). In *Diamond v Diehr* 450 US 175, 101 S Ct 1048 (1981), the Supreme Court explained that certain types of mathematical subject matter, on their own, represent nothing more than abstract ideas and will not be capable of being granted a patent until they are reduced to some type of *practical application* such as transforming or reducing an article to a different state or thing. Subsequent United States Court of Appeal cases like *In Re Kuriappan P Alappat* 33 F 3d 1526 (Fed Cir 1994) at 1544, interpreted 'practical application' of an abstract idea to mean the production of 'a useful, concrete and tangible result'. Essentially, if it can be shown that the invention constituted a *practical application* of an abstract idea such as a mathematical algorithm, formula, or calculation such that it produced a 'useful, concrete and tangible result', the invention is patentable. In *In Re Kuriappan P Alappat* 33 F 3d 1526 (Fed Cir 1994) at 1544, the United States Court of Appeals, Federal Circuit held that the data, transformed by a machine through a series of mathematical calculations to produce a smooth waveform display on a rasterizer monitor, constituted a *practical application* of an abstract idea (a mathematical algorithm, formula or calculation), because it produced 'a useful, concrete and tangible result', i.e., the smooth waveform. Also in *Arrhythmia Research Technology Inc v Corazonix Corp* 958 F 2d 1053 (Fed Cir 1992), the United States Court of Appeals,

Federal Circuit held that the transformation of electrocardiograph signals from a patient's heartbeat by a machine through a series of mathematical calculations constituted a *practical application* of an abstract idea because it corresponded to 'a useful, concrete or tangible thing', i.e., the condition of a patient's heart.

However, this test was rejected recently by the United States Federal Court of Appeals in *In Re Bilski* 545 F 3d 943 (Fed Cir 2008) ('*In Re Bilski*') in favour of a narrower 'machine-or-transformation' test, i.e., a process or methods invention is patentable if it is tied to a particular machine or apparatus, or if it transforms a particular article into a different state or thing. On appeal to the United States Supreme Court, the majority declined to accept the 'machine-or-transformation' test as the *sole test* for assessing business process or method patent applications.

The patent application in *In Re Bilski* related to a method of hedging commodities transactions which did not include any use of a computer or other machine. At the United States Patent and Trade Mark Office (USPTO), the patent application was rejected on the basis that no physical transformation was involved. The applicant appealed to the United States Court of Appeals for the Federal Circuit (CAFC).

In an *en banc* review of the standards for determining whether a claimed process is patentable subject matter, the CAFC articulated a new test. In place of the wider 'useful, concrete and tangible result' test, the court adopted a narrower 'machine-or-transformation' test which requires that a process:

(a) be 'tied to a particular machine'; or
(b) 'transform a particular article to a different state or thing'.

According to the CAFC, the 'machine-or-transformation' test was the sole test for the patentability of a process under United States Supreme Court case law. Applying the 'machine-or-transformation' test, the CAFC (by a majority of eight to one) rejected the appeal on the basis that the claimed process in *In Re Bilski* did not transform any article to a different state or thing and it was not a patentable subject matter under United States patent law. The applicant appealed to the United States Supreme Court.

The majority's view in the Supreme Court was that, in general, there should be no judicial exclusions from patentability beyond the long-established categories of 'laws of nature, physical phenomena and abstract ideas'. In terms of the standards for determining whether a claimed process is patentable subject matter, the majority held that the 'machine-or-transformation' test, although useful, was not the sole and exclusive test. The majority considered the current ordinary meaning of the terms 'process' and 'methods' and concluded that there was nothing in United States patent laws that precluded the patentability of business methods. However, they held that the invention in *In Re Bilski*, which related to the concept of hedging risk, was an *abstract idea* and could not be the subject of a patent because patenting an abstract idea would have the effect of preventing preemptive use of risk hedging in all fields.

Having arrived at this conclusion, there was no further need for the majority to define further what constituted a patentable 'process' under United States patent law. Nevertheless, the United States Supreme Court was cautious in not laying down rules which could adversely affect other new and developing technologies and warned against taking the decision in *In Re Bilski* as an endorsement by the United States Supreme Court of any other test the CAFC may have adopted in the past, including the wider test in *State St Bank & Trust v Signature Financial Group* 149 F 3d 1368 (Fed Cir 1998) as to whether the invention produced a 'useful, concrete and tangible result'.

More recently, the Supreme Court of the United States in *Mayo Collaborative Services v Prometheus Laboratories Inc* (No 10-1150 (2012)) evaluated the patent eligibility of methods of adjusting doses of thiopurine drugs in patients with autoimmune disease and concluded that they were not patentable.

Justice Breyer ruled that the relationships between concentrations of certain metabolites in the blood and the likelihood that a thiopurine drug dosage will prove ineffective or cause harm is a 'law of nature' and, as such, process claims directed to methods of applying that relationship are not patentable unless they contain additional features that provide practical assurance that the processes are genuine applications of the law. Central to the court's deliberation of the patentability of the process claims is the recognition that patents are a double-edged sword and that although granting patents to those who discovered laws of nature will encourage their discoveries, there is, however, a real danger that the grant of such process patents will inhibit future innovation by foreclosing more future invention than the underlying discovery could reasonably justify. The principle that patents shall not be granted to 'laws of nature' is a bright-line prohibition which does not distinguish among different laws of nature according to whether or not the principles they embody are sufficiently narrow.

Post *In Re Bilski*, it may be said that the prevailing judicial view is that under United States patent law there should be no judicial exclusions from patentability beyond the long-established categories of 'laws of nature, physical phenomena and abstract ideas'. Therefore, the possibility of patenting business methods remains open post *In Re Bilski* although it is far from clear what kinds of business methods can be patented. The United States Patent and Trade Mark Office has issued preliminary guidelines on the patentability of business methods post *In Re Bilski:* the 'machine-or-transformation' test will continue to be used; anything failing the test will be rejected unless it is clearly not an abstract idea.

However, the Supreme Court of the United States in *Mayo Collaborative Services v Prometheus Laboratories Inc.* has made clear that when a patent claim involves reliance on 'laws of nature', the claim must contain 'significantly more' than that natural law alone and excludes what is 'well-understood, routine, conventional activity, previously engaged in by those in the field' (No 10-1150 (2012), Slip Opinion at 4).

Indeed, the US Supreme Court's *In Re Bilski* and *Mayo* decisions have called into questions the validity of business methods patents previously granted by the USPTO. In 2011, the Leahy-Smith America Invents Act ('AIA') (Public Law No 112-129, 125 Stat 284 (2011)) made significant reforms in US patent law. Notably, and amongst other things, the AIA moves the US patent system closer to a first-to-file system. In the area of business methods patents, the reforms under the AIA take the form of a new transitional procedure for challenging the validity of granted business method patents under the standards and procedures of 'post grant review' (Section 18, Public Law No 112-129, 125 Stat at 329). Parties facing possible patent infringement claims by business methods patents granted prior to *In Re Bilski* and *Mayo* may challenge their validity under the AIA.

Turning to Singapore, there is notably no positive definition of what an invention is and no express list of what does not constitute an invention. Thus, the courts have essentially approached the patentability issue by considering whether the patent application at issue has fulfilled the requisite criteria of novelty, inventiveness and industrial application. This appears to be the approach even for cases which involve business method patents as in *First Currency Choice Pte Ltd v Main-Line Corporate Holdings Ltd* [2008] 1 SLR(R) 335. In that case, the patent was for a method and system for dynamic currency conversion for card payment systems. Judge of Appeal VK Rajah did not think it necessary to consider as a preliminary point whether a business method is within the patentable subject matter boundary, or whether there is such a boundary under Singapore laws, and made no mention of this in his judgment. The methods patent in this case was found to involve an inventive step and held valid.

Nevertheless, it is also clear that in a process patent claim, the Singapore Court of Appeal has, at least on one occasion in *Merck & Co Inc. v Pharmaforte Singapore Pte Ltd*

[2000] 2 SLR(R) 708, drawn a conceptual distinction between a mere discovery (not an invention and so not patentable) and an invention (patentable, if it satisfies novelty, inventiveness and industrial application) in Singapore's patent law.

In this case, the Court of Appeal was concerned with the validity of a pharmaceutical related patent which comprised both 'a process for the lactonisation of mevinic acids and analogs thereof' and the product 'Lovastatin with a diametric impurity of less than 0.2%'. Lovastatin was useful as an anti-hypercholesteremic agent in the treatment of artherosclerosis, hyperlimia and similar diseases in humans. The plaintiff, Merck & Co Inc were the proprietors of the patent in dispute. The defendant, Pharmaforte Singapore Pte Ltd, was a Singaporean company which imported a product called 'Apo-Lovastatin' from a Canadian pharmaceutical company, Apotex Inc. The plaintiff contended that 'Apo-Lovastatin' possessed diametric impurity of less than 0.2%. Consequently, the importation of 'Apo-Lovastatin' into Singapore infringed the product and the process claims in their Singapore patent. The defendant counter-claimed that the plaintiff's Singapore patent was invalid for want of novelty and inventive step. In particular, the defendant claimed that there were many ways to produce Lovastatin of diametric impurity levels less than 0.2% and that the process employed by Apotex Inc to produce 'Apo-Lovastatin' differed from the process claimed by the plaintiff to produce Lovastatin. At first instance, the trial court held that the plaintiff's patent was invalid as its product, Lovastatin, lacked both novelty and an inventive step. The court also found that the process employed by Apotex Inc to produce 'Apo-Lovastatin' differed from the process claimed by the plaintiff to produce Lovastatin. The plaintiff appealed. The Court of Appeal, comprising the then Chief Justice Yong Pung How, LP Thean and Chao Hick Tin JJA, held that although the product Lovastatin was not anticipated by any prior art and so was novel, the patent in dispute was nevertheless invalidated as it lacked an inventive step. When considering the issue of whether the invention involved an inventive step, Justice Chao Hick Tin (delivering the judgment on behalf of the court) held that 'the fact that a discovery is made does not mean there is an invention' and that 'the latter does not necessarily follow from the former'. The Court of Appeal found that numerous techniques, such as re-crystallization or activated carbon, were available to reduce the diametric impurity present in the Lovastatin compound claimed in the plaintiff's patent. The critical question of fact before the court was whether a notional skilled worker faced with the problem of impurities in the compound would use these 'myriad of processes' available to reduce the impurities. If the answer to this question was yes, the plaintiff's process claims in the patent were obvious and lacked an inventive step. The Court of Appeal held that the notional skilled worker would naturally use those techniques to reduce the impurities and 'what the appellants have achieved in the alleged patent is a *discovery. It does not amount to an invention*' [emphasis added].

Justice Chao Hick Tin made reference to the discovery/invention dichotomy, not as a separate independent requirement for patentability, but as a point of consideration within the concept of inventiveness, the second patentability criterion under section 13(1) of the Singapore Patents Act. An invention without an inventive step cannot be regarded as an invention. It appears that a pre-determined threshold of what constitutes a patentable invention does exist in the form of a conceptual distinction between esoteric knowledge (discoveries) and applied knowledge (inventions) in Singapore patent laws. Thus, esoteric knowledge, without more, i.e., an inventive step, cannot be the subject matter of patentable inventions under Singapore laws. Subject matter which cannot be the subject of patents will be weeded out through careful consideration of the criterion of an inventive step. Beyond this criterion, the provision in the Singapore Patent Act does not set out any categories which are deemed non-inventions and thus, as a matter of policy, most subject matter ought to be patentable if it is novel, inventive and capable of industrial application in Singapore, including methods patents.

CONCLUSION

It is undisputed that modern patent law gives protection to inventions in all fields of human endeavour but, as we have seen from the foregoing discussions, countries have adopted different legislative approaches to the issue of what constitutes a patentable invention. Even more fundamental is the question of whether there is value in conducting an independent inquiry of whether the subject matter to be patented constitutes an invention under the law, over and above the criteria of novelty, inventive step and industrial application. Again, divergences on this question are to be expected given the different legislative approaches adopted across countries.

However, it should be noted that traditional patents law is in the process of adapting itself to new technologies far beyond the contemplations of legislatures responsible for laying down the foundations upon which the law was first enacted. Thus, it is submitted that the conceptual inquiry of whether the subject matter to be patented constitutes an invention is not without its merits, and categories of inventions in which such an inquiry should be conducted include biological inventions, genetic materials, computer programs and business/process methods. We have seen that on this issue there appears to be agreement in the courts across jurisdictions that a distinction must be made between inventions (applied knowledge and thus patentable) and discoveries or abstract ideas (esoteric knowledge and thus not patentable). This conceptual distinction, which is termed 'the discovery/invention dichotomy' in this chapter, sets the important baseline that separates patentable inventions from things which are not, or should not be, tied-up in proprietary bundles. Courts across jurisdictions have attempted to draw this important line of distinction with reference to conceptual tools such as 'naturally occurring thing or phenomenon'; 'an altered state of affairs'; 'transformation to a different state or thing'; 'technical effects'; 'human intervention'; or 'genuine application of the laws of nature', etc. It is, however, accepted that a clear and consistent elucidation of where this line is, across all subject matters, may be difficult to achieve as the nature of subject matter and the factual matrix all play a role in influencing the final outcome.

The discovery/invention dichotomy, whilst not explicitly stated in Article 27 of TRIPS, is a well-accepted basis for drawing up exceptions to patentability by courts across various jurisdictions and will continue to be an important conceptual tool relied upon by the courts in their assessments of patentable inventions. In light of the breakneck speed at which scientific discoveries are made especially in the fields of biotechnology and genetic engineering, it is to be expected that discoveries in these areas may challenge accepted notions of what constitutes an invention for the purpose of a patent grant. Nevertheless, the principles enunciated by the courts in these cases, particularly on 'the discovery/invention dichotomy', will continue to inform decisions about what constitutes patentable subject matter.

REFERENCES

Cooper Dreyfuss, Rochelle (2006), 'The Story of Diamond v Chakrabarty: Technological Change and the Subject Matter Boundaries of the Patent System', in Jane Ginsburg and Rochelle Cooper Dreyfuss (eds), *Intellectual Property Stories*, New York, Foundation Press. pp 327–357.

Cooper Dreyfuss, Rochelle (2012), 'The Leahy-Smith America Invents Act – A New Paradigm for International Harmonisation?', *Singapore Academy of Law Journal Special Issue (Intellectual Property Law)*, 24, pp 669–697.

Cornish, William, Llewelyn, David and Aplin, Tanya (2010), *Intellectual Property: Patents, Copyright, Trade Marks and Allied Rights*, 7th edition, London, Sweet & Maxwell.

Heller, Michael A (1998), 'The Tragedy of the Anticommons: Property in the Transition from Marx to Markets', *Harv L Rev*, 111, pp 621–688.

Heller, Michael, A. and Eisenberg, Rebecca, S. (1998), 'Can Patents Deter Innovation? The Anticommons in Biomedical Research', *Science*, 280 (5364), pp 698–701.

Lange, David (1981), 'Recognising the Public Domain', *Law & Contemp Probs*, 44, pp 147–178.

Litman, Jessica (1990), 'The Public Domain', *Emory Law Journal*, 4, pp 965–1024.

Samuelson, Pamela (2003), 'Mapping the Public Domain: Threats and Opportunities', *Law & Contemp Probs*, 66, pp 147–172.

Shapiro, Carl (2001), 'Navigating the Patent Thicket: Cross Licenses, Patent Pools and Standard Setting', in Adam B Jaffe, Josh Lerner and Scott Stern (eds), *Innovation Policy and the Economy*, Boston, MA: The MIT Press. pp 119–150.

PART XI

Patenting the Future

Matthew David and Debora Halbert

From one point of view, all IPRs are simply property rights like any other (see Phythian-Adams and Ghosh in Part I for accounts of such philosophical positions). From this point of view IPRs are granted as a simply (or 'natural') extension of prior possession or effort. However, in all jurisdictions and at all times (though in varying forms) IPRs have been time limited quasi-property rights conferred for the advancement they are assumed to encourage in terms of both future innovation and general welfare. As such, IPRs are always in this sense future oriented and justified in terms of future 'progress' (see Silbey in Part VIII). Time limitedness is meant to strike the balance between reward for past creativity, incentive and scope for future development, as well as for the dissemination of affordable benefits to the general population. Today's rights are legitimized on the basis that they will make tomorrow better. Whilst innovation can simply mean difference in the domains of copyright, trademark and related indicators, brands and trade secrets, in the domain of patents the term innovation implies some kind of improvement relative to what has gone before, whether this is in terms of utility, functionality, efficacy or efficiency.

The chapters in Part XI, however, deal with patents (and other IPRs as well) relative to whole new domains of life and living. The chapters by Jake Dunagan, William Kramer and Matthew Rimmer address new controversies that arise because of human scientific and technical development. In the futures they discuss, human 'progress' has created scope to: (1) manipulate, read and externalize processes once 'black-boxed' within a romantic conception of the 'mind'

(Dunagan); (2) explore space and potentially discover new forms of alien life (Kramer); and (3) address the past consequences of our own effects upon the climate of our own planet. In each case, whole new areas open up for potential patenting; whilst in each case the danger of enclosure by dominant actors needs to be counterbalanced. Just as recent debates over the ownership of living organisms (see Leong in Part X and Oguamanam in Part III in particular) highlight the dangers of IPR enclosure, so debates over the IPR control of neuroscience (Dunagan), space exploration (Kramer) and in relation to climate change limiting technologies (Rimmer) allow us to identify the key interests, benefits and dangers at stake in decisions to award or deny exclusive rights to control our own futures.

Whilst Jake Dunagan notes that the scientific exploration of the human mind has been central to the modern age right back to the seventeenth century, it is only in the last generation that 'neurosciences' have really taken off in terms of effective mapping and manipulation of the human brain. The potential consequences of neuromodification, cognitive enhancement and 'mind reading' are enormous, and the question of who could or should own and control such techniques that might develop in the future becomes central to any neuropolitics that might, and will need to, develop in the future to address the potential of such technologies. The 'romantic' myth of the sui generis creative individual, the unique mind, may have been a convenient fiction in the industrial age. However, in an age of increasingly smart machines, and distributed cognition, cloud innovation, crowd sourcing, and an array of other 'extensions of man' in the domain of thought and expression, this lonely genius is losing its authority. With patents being granted on biological processes within the human body, and with the mind/body distinction being ever further eroded by neuroscience, how best might it be possible to, firstly, conceptualize the human creative process, and secondly, balance the claims to origin between an array of intersecting sources of technical, social and individual innovation?

When researchers at the University of California at San Diego successfully patented a process of electrical brain stimulation that (it is claimed) generates 'flashes of inspiration', what then become the parameters of their rights over such 'flashes'? Dunagan highlights a range of neuroscientific domains in which potential exists for IPR extension. These include language, memory, and thought itself. In response to this threat Dunagan offers a gift from the future – what he describes as a (hopefully) self-defeating prophecy: 'Mindwriter™' from an equally fictional 'Neuroogle+™'. With the tag line 'Record and protect your thought – as you think', this fictional thought recorder, designed to ensure that all your thoughts are recorded for IPR purposes, this 'gift from the future' (fabricated as part of the Institute for the Future 2012 Ten Year Forecast), should make us stop and think how we wish the future to unfold. Stumbling into a shrink wrapped proprietary future, just as we tend to blindly click the digital 'terms of service' buttons on our computer screens every day, is something Dunagan seeks to help us avoid. Whilst the neuroscientific age creates a whole new array of potential manipulations by grasping the mechanisms and processes through which our individual and collective mental apparatus 'work', Dunagan seeks to make us conscious of our need to make choices, and so to be the authors of our own collective future.

William Kramer sees outer space as an opportunity for humankind to rethink the value, scope and dangers of patenting life. Exploring how intellectual property rights might best be extended over, or not extended over, as yet undiscovered alien life provides an opportunity to carry out a valuable thought experiment; one that can investigate the pros and cons of IP extension to living things whilst at the same time setting aside an array of already invested interests and national/territorial systems and differences. Kramer also looks at a number of existing treaties that seek to place international regulations over bioprospecting in spaces currently not defined as the territories of established states (where such practices might constitute a form of biopiracy). Such treaties include the Deep Sea treaty, The Antarctic Treaty, the Moon Treaty and the Deep Space Treaty, as well as the United Nations Convention on the Law of the Sea. Seeking to cut through the 'thicket of often conflicting intellectual property protocols and regulations' that currently exist, Kramer's thought experiment about the tension between extending international IPRs and extending the international commons to space offers a range of valuable insights and proposals regarding life patents. In particular, Kramer highlights how any future discovery of alien life might very well throw into question existing classifications of life that are currently used to warrant the distinction between what can and can't be patented (see Leong in Part X). Treaties covering areas not currently inhabited by humans on earth contain reference to protecting the 'common heritage of (Hu)Mankind'. However, such protection, and the requirement to return some part of whatever profit might be derived from any successful bioprospecting in such regions, remains vague at best. Extrapolating to the prospects of discovering valuable resources in space reminds us of the need to clarify what and whose common heritage needs to be protected here on earth, and begs the question of how this might best be achieved.

Kramer recommends that convenient but arbitrary taxonomies regarding life be avoided in defining what can and can't be patented, and that applications for patents on alien life should be withheld for a considerable time at the very least. Also, patent terms for any alien life discovered (where the claim to invention can only lie in the means by which they were found) should remain highly limited if granted at all. Such limits should be placed on both the duration of patents and over the exclusivity of use during the patent's term. Access should also be enabled for those countries not currently able to pursue space exploration itself. Specimen depositing schemes should widen access for research, patent pooling should be encouraged to prevent undue restrictions on development, and developing countries should be given scope to participate in the space exploration programmes of wealthier nations. Kramer suggests that not only can we learn from the mistakes of the past, but also from thinking through in advance about the future we want rather than the future we will end up with if we carry on with business as usual.

Matthew Rimmer starts from just such a future stored up for us by a combination of past innovation and lack of suitable regulation/direction. He suggests that many of the technologies that have contributed most over the last 200 years to man-made climate change have been encouraged by IPR protection and, in particular, patents. The benefits were privatized, even whilst the costs have been left to future generations to take up. He therefore suggests that one means by which climate change can now be confronted is through addressing the relationship between technology and patent protection. Whilst many older technologies that have increased man-made impacts upon the earth's climate are now outside of patent protection, many innovative technologies that would help reduce the impact of human industrial activity on the planet are protected, mainly because these are more recent developments. This creates a paradoxical situation for developing countries, faced with the choice between highly polluting but free to access technologies, and more environmentally friendly technologies that IPRs make prohibitively expensive to adopt. Rimmer seeks to document attempts within the United Nations to broker forms of technology transfer to developing countries that would suspend or limit patent protection so as to enable developing countries to develop in a more environmentally friendly fashion.

Patent holders, mainly in developed countries, tend to express reservations about having their patents suspended or limited, and lobby actively through their governments and through non-governmental industry bodies, at UN and WIPO events at which such matters are debated. Rimmer notes one key strategy is to lobby to have IPR issues referred to the WTO, and to have them excluded from climate change related discussions. Developing countries and civil society NGOs have sought to bring the two things together, with some limited success. Conflict exists between WIPO, which seeks to create 'exchange' arrangements whereby patent holders can offer to engage with developing counties over green technology transfer; and a number of developing countries (led by Venezuela, Ecuador and the Philippines) who argue for a more robust (perhaps compulsory) requirement to make such technologies available. Suggestions for a 'green technology commons' challenge the suggestion that robust IPRs promote green technology transfer. Developed states claim that strong IPR protection promotes the development of clean technologies, whilst developing states suggest that more limited IPR protection would facilitate take up of such technologies and hence produce a greater overall benefit for humanity (in reducing man-made climate change whilst promoting development). To the extent that representatives of developed states in international forums have tended to give too much voice to the concerns of their own countries' corporate lobbies, when suggesting that patent relaxation for technology transfer would radically harm their interests, and to the extent that rampant climate change does require radical action if development needs and climate control are to be reconciled, Rimmer concludes that the future of humanity will best be served with a move away from the kinds of strong IPR protectionism that got us to where we are now.

36

Who Owns the Extended Mind? The Neuropolitics of Intellectual Property Law

Jake Dunagan

INTRODUCTION

The container of the mind is undergoing a long rupture. Human knowledge of the inner workings of the brain is advancing rapidly, while at the same time people are extending their minds outward, outsourcing more and more cognitive functions to the artifacts and devices populating our environment. The brain sciences are being deployed to explain fundamental aspects of the way we perceive the world, how we think, and how the complex interplay of biology and environment influences our behaviors. And the domains of inquiry and application are expanding: everything from law to love is being explained through a neurocentric lens (Lynch, 2009).

According to science writer Carl Zimmer, we live in the neurocentric age – an age that actually began around the time Thomas Willis and his 17th-century scientific revolutionaries uncovered the mysteries and importance of brain as the seat of consciousness and the soul (Zimmer, 2004). But only in the last generation or so has the transformative power of the brain sciences come into fuller view. This 21st-century neurocentric age is simultaneously alluring and threatening. No knowledge is neutral, and the 'seductive allure of neuroscience' is exerting a strong influence on how we understand our world and ourselves (Dumit, 2004; Weisberg et al. 2008).

Neuropolitics is a recently articulated approach within the social sciences that allows for the re-imagining of culture, power and political subjectivity in light of the increasing understanding of the brain and extended mind. Johns Hopkins political theorist William Connolly defines neuropolitics as 'the politics through which cultural life mixes into the composition of brain/body processes. And vice-versa' (2002: xii). Neuropolitics is an acknowledgement and a response to the new dynamics of power emerging from the brain-driven theory and practice of the neurocentric age.

Neuromodulation, cognitive enhancement and 'mind reading' technologies are being aggressively developed and rapidly deployed. The early, but so far mostly provisional, implementation of these techniques in courtrooms, airports and other contexts has generated strong, negative, visceral reactions in many observers (Karp and Meckler, 2006; Saini, 2009; Madrigal, 2010). These critics fear the personal invasions and potential for abuse that might occur when governments and other entities gain access to these powerful tools for surveillance and/or modulation of individual minds (Moreno, 2006; Shachtman, 2010; Dunagan, 2011).

The subject of this chapter, however – the neuropolitics of intellectual property law – may not elicit the same strong feelings of invasion and repulsion as mental surveillance, but the issue surrounding the 'ownership of the extended mind' is every bit as important to personal freedom, social justice and the practice of democracy.

The idea of a battle within the mental commons is not here intended to be metaphorical. The mental or cognitive commons is the shared pool (or pools) of language, knowledge, arts, habits, and other ideas, that provide context and scaffolding for human thought and expression. If we 'create our cognitive powers by creating the environments in which they exercise those powers' as anthropologist Edwin Hutchins argues (1996: xvi), then the way intellectual property law governs the public domain, as a shared cognitive ecology, is a critical political issue to explore. The mind might be less and less inside the head, but it is moving more and more into a world of control – a world of mental pastures enclosed by property fences, thickets of proprietary technologies, libraries of owned expressions, highways of mental toll booths and labyrinths of requisite permissions.

This chapter identifies domains where intellectual property law is being used as a tool of governance over the scaffolding of our minds and the cognitive commons, and analyzes the dynamics of power and politics within these domains. It makes the case that common property controls, such as end-user licensing agreements and trademarked expressions, are as politically and ethically relevant in the emerging neurocentric age as mental surveillance or cognitive enhancement. It is about novel mechanisms of control and new threats to cognitive liberty, i.e. the capacity and freedom to think certain thoughts and share ideas, expressions and inventions. It is not about the practicalities of patenting new neural technologies[1] or how neuroscientists might navigate through patent thickets – except as this relates to cognitive liberty and the sharing of scientific knowledge.

The chapter is divided into three sections. The first section examines the changing nature of authoring, and how notions of distributed cognition and collaborative creation disrupt the default assumptions of individual authorship. The second section looks at how IP influences and governs creativity and invention. And finally, the third section looks at the shifting boundaries of regulated and unregulated expression, and the political stakes of the privatization of the cognitive commons. Collectively, these three sections combine to begin to orient us to a world in which the extended mind has the potential to be enclosed in property law, and, therefore, a world in which the ability to freely express ourselves is being foreclosed.

AUTHORSHIP AND THE MIND

Because they deal with the organ that defines our humanity, the brain sciences impact everything humans *are* and more importantly, everything humans *think they are*. There are profound implications for IP law stemming from insights into the way the mind works, and especially into the way the mind creates. However, given this transformative potential, the application of cognitive and social neuroscience to the foundations and practice of IP law has been rare (cf. Greely 2004: 148–155; Goodenough and Decker, 2006).

The understanding of human cognition and agency as a distributed process of brains, bodies and techno-culture presents a stark challenge to the romantic authorship model that stands as the foundation of our Western systems of intellectual property rights and policies (Rose 1993). In this section, some of the more destabilizing aspects of this new understanding of the mind for IP are explored within the context of analog ambiguities arising from other non-conforming ways people create and share content.

Authoring the Mind

> The two of us wrote Anti-Oedipus together. Since each of us was several, there was already quite a crowd. (Deleuze and Guattari, 2004: 3)

The idea of a bounded, isolated individual who creates an original work through solitary labor and genius has been the backbone of the 'romantic authorship' model of copyright and patent (Rose, 1993). The figure of the solitary individual author, however, misrepresents the creative process as it generally occurs. Authors and inventors create not from a transcendent void of individual genius, but rather from the chaos of life and crucible of personal experience (Lethem, 2007). Moreover, irrespective of the question of whether the mind's productions *deserve* property protection, the romantic author archetype and legal fiction reflect a deep misunderstanding of how the mind works.

A significant and growing body of research from distinct fields is showing that cognition and creation are highly promiscuous processes involving the coordination of functions among individual regions housed within a brain and body, utilizing technologies and the surrounding environment, and often in concert with other living minds A wide collection of cognitive neuroscientists, anthropologists, philosophers, and social psychologists have developed theories of mind and cognition showing that thinking is a process that does not start and end only with electro-chemical processes inside our grey matter. To proponents of this model, thinking and feeling is a system of coordinated functions within a larger system – an ecology of mind (Bateson, 1972; Clark, 1996; Hutchins, 1996; Chemero, 2009; Malafouris, 2010).

Distributed cognition and theories of the extended mind call into question the notion of bounded, individual authorship. Understanding these related theories of mind is essential to thinking more critically about the processes of creation and how to govern, share and reward those creations. Given this perspective, even the basic concept of a single, coherent mind within an individual is difficult to justify. Our common way of conceiving the mind, as Steven Johnson observes, is to focus on the psychology rather than the sociology of the mind. In this individualistic approach, we miss the fact that 'the mind is more like an orchestra than a soloist' (2004: 6).

'Thinking' as Nietzsche put it, 'is an arbitrary fiction, arrived at by selecting one element from the process and eliminating all the rest' (quoted in Connolly, 2002: 67). The conscious narrator we call a mind, or often a self, represents but a fraction of the total processing that occurs in the brain and within an extended system of thought. In fact, the very feeling of free will – a core tenet of the modern concept of self – may be an illusion created by this internal narrator and sense-maker (Gazzaniga and LeDoux, 1978; Norretranders, 1999; Eagleman, 2012). Some cognitive research has even shown that humans become aware of decisions only after they have already been made – as the mental narrator then retroactively attributes intention to the decision (Gazzaniga, 2005: 89). This line of research is not fully conclusive yet, but it is clear that new insights from the cognitive sciences have disabused us of the naive acceptance of the bounded individual mind as an unproblematic unit of analysis.

Within the brain, and outward through the extended mind, the boundaries we have taken as natural and that we have legally formalized are beginning to blur. 'As the world becomes smarter and smarter and gets to know us better', writes cognitive philosopher Andy Clark, 'it becomes harder to say where the world stops and the person begins' (2004: 7). Contemporary societies, and much less our legal institutions, do not seem fully comfortable with the idea of blurring the boundaries of the individual human body or mind. As Katherine Hayles notes, most of our habits and models of thought wish to avoid 'the realization that the synaptic noise within mirrors the world's noise without' (1999: 276).

Why, however, should we challenge the isolationist, individualist model of the mind and change institutions built on isolated cognition when society seems to reap the rewards of modern civilization from this model?[2] One answer is that even if we accept the argument that individualist notions of authorship and citizenship have enabled social advancement historically, the model and legal assumption of bounded individualism is largely unequipped to deal with the way that value is created and exchanged in the 21st century. Just because it might have 'worked' in the past, does not mean it will work in the future.

Individualist allocation of rights and property was a strategic solution to the challenge of how to allocate and incentivize intangible intellectual property, but as social and economic processes evolve over time, intellectual property rights, as they are deployed today, begin to look more and more anachronistic, and become harder to justify as fair and socially beneficial.[3] The remainder of this article is an attempt to make that case. Recognizing the fragmentary, collaborative and mutually entailing aspects of thought foregrounds the neuropolitical importance of our social structures, formal processes, technological artifacts, built environments, public language, culture, and physical bodies. These are not only partners, but constitutive agents, in the totality of mind. The environment is literally our extended mind, but legally, it is not yet treated as such.

Who Counts as an Author?

Intellectual property works by creating artificial boundaries around content – enclosing information in order for it to be controlled and to generate a return on 'investment'. Authorship, then, acts itself as a boundary function. In *Authors and Owners*, Mark Rose argues that copyright 'not only makes possible the profitable manufacture and distribution of books, films, and other commodities but also, by endowing it with legal reality, helps to produce and affirm the very identity of the author as author' (1993: 1). Intellectual property law constructs a certain kind of subject (an author) for which it can then regulate and control. Becoming an author is the 'gate through which one must pass in order to acquire intellectual property rights' (Boyle, 1996: 125).

But not all entities have equal rights to pass through this gate, for if forms of creative production fall outside the norms of legitimate authorship, then these forms are ignored, censored, stolen or punished. The epistemological foundations of bounded authorship do not accurately reflect the actual flows of influence and interconnectedness of creativity. Moreover, the default modes of the author function are becoming increasingly anachronistic and counter-productive in the distributed but highly connected world we live in now.

Even aside from science-fiction-like visions of directly linking brains within a co-creative hive mind, there are many forms of what might be called messy, noisy or ambiguous creation that copyright and patent law has had a hard time governing effectively. Indigenous knowledge and cultural heritage have been very difficult to codify, creating opportunities for legal (and often unjust) appropriation of indigenous innovations and expressions by individuals or corporations who are more equipped to navigate the letter of IP law in the West (Shiva, 1997; Marden, 1999; Brown, 2004). Furthermore, the question of cultural authorship for art, poetry and other creative expressions, and what is 'prior art' for ancient medicines or technical inventions, is difficult for intellectual property regimes as they stand today. Within the current paradigm there simply are no easy answers to these questions, no 'comfort of absolutes' as anthropologist Michael Brown concludes in his study of the intersections of intellectual property and indigenous rights (2004: 41).

Control requires a system of management based on a particular form of power-knowledge, and the creation of facts that support that system. For IP law, protections are built upon a regime of knowledge that requires clear authorial attribution and provenance. Indigenous and collective models of creation do not fit neatly into this system, and have been dismissed. But as indigenous invention and art come to have value in Western society, IP regimes are both trying to expand conceptually to include these other forms of authorship, and trying to shoehorn alternative authorship into the sort of 'bounded' models that the system knows how to manage. Ironically, this movement for increased intelligibility (and control) of alternative forms of authorship is being led in many cases by the apotheosis of artificial collective existence, the corporation.

Today, even the ownership of our own biological make-up or of certain organisms is not clear cut (Halbert, 2005). The US Supreme Court case of *Diamond v. Chakrabarty* (1980) established the conditions for legal patenting of life forms. Over the years, more and more biological matter, and even living beings, have been enclosed in a property regime. Some estimate that over 20% of the human genome is now functionally enclosed in patents (Jensen and Murray, 2005).

A sometimes troublesome precedent exists that if adequate 'labor' is added to a biological process or element in the biological public domain, then the novel invention born of that labor can be rewarded with property rights. This labor threshold has often been set very low, thus becoming a source of controversy (Coombe, 1998: 94–100). In the famous case of *John Moore v. the Regents of the University of California* (1991), the Court ruled that Moore's own cancer-fighting t-cells could be patented by someone other than Moore, even against his will. In this case a group of UC Berkeley researchers claimed and were awarded ownership of the cells because of the labor they added to extract this natural resource in order to 'reduce it to practice', and thus turn it into a useful medical product (Wald, 2005).

In addition to indigenous art and biological patents, massively distributed and collaborative authorship also creates intellectual property headaches. Without pre-determined arrangements for ownership, collaborative media can be a confusing terrain for determining rights. Potential solutions vary in effectiveness. Wikipedia, for example, technically gives each of the millions of its contributors the right to their specific contribution.[4] Evernote, a popular software application that allows people to post notes, images, and other bits and pieces of their lives allows the user to retain copyright over the materials they post to their account, but requires the user to issue a license to Evernote 'so that our processing, maintenance, storage, technical reproduction, back-up and distribution, and related handling of your Content doesn't infringe applicable copyright and other laws'.[5] Because almost every digital act creates a digital copy, in order to work at all, software applications such as Evernote must have explicit consent to process and share user-generated content.

Or, even more complex, consider the growing movement of collaborative citizen science – most widely noted in the case of *Foldit*. *Foldit* is a game designed by biochemist David Baker and his colleagues to help solve the puzzles of protein folding patterns. It was designed to harness not the 'idling capacity' of networked home computers, such as the popular *SETI@Home* has done since the late 90s, but to utilize the much more effective and efficient spatial manipulating mechanism – brains of human users themselves. As Baker notes there is 'this incredible amount of human computing power out there that we're starting to capitalize on' (in Hand, 2010: 685).

The game did not just lead to engaged users who were very effective in finding new strategies for uncovering optimal protein folding patterns, it also lead directly to major breakthroughs and scientifically publishable results. And the contribution of those 40,000 home users did not go unrecognized, as the *Nature* article published by Baker also included the *Foldit* players in its list of authors (Cooper et al., 2010). If 40,000 home computer users who each contribute a tiny fraction of work toward the final output can be recognized as authors, it is clear that these are highly disruptive and innovative times for the entire concept of authorship. These innovations may or may not collapse the foundation of copyright as we know it, but they will certainly create unprecedented conditions for rapid evolution of this legal and social technology.

A growing number of platforms are being developed to harness the micro-contributions of users; tapping in to what writer Clay Shirky calls the latent 'cognitive surplus' of the global population (2010). In this world of distributed micro-contributions, intellectual property law is being pushed and pulled into uncomfortable positions. While copyright agreements may be fine for Wikipedia, and pride in participation may suffice for *Foldit* players and citizen scientists for now, what will happen when a billion-dollar pharmacological breakthrough is made with the aid of crowd-sourced micro-contributions? How will 'the crowd' be rewarded or compensated for their now highly valuable contributions?

Property Rights in the Cognisphere

Today, billions of people extend their biological selves with computational machines linked via digital networks (Chorost, 2011). In record number, and with uncommon zeal, users around the world are 'actively composing the soap-opera of their own lives [rather] than zoning out in front of someone else's' (Johnson, 2006: 120). They are using the Internet and all the programmable networks in our environment to create the *cognisphere*, described by cyber-literary theorist Katherine Hayles as 'an interconnected cognitive system in which humans are increasingly embedded' (2006: 161). As people integrate sensory and cognitive functions with new technological platforms, they blur the boundaries of personal agency and external control. The insinuation of property rights into our sensory and cognitive prosthetics is one of the most important political questions humans face, and yet most rarely ask these questions with a full awareness of the stakes involved.

Complicating matters further, mental processes are moving into our surrounding devices, but these devices are moving more functions to the 'cloud' of networked computing and communication technologies. Therefore, the mind is moving into a cognisphere of unseen and complex rules and controls that most might never have accepted back in the non-networked world. For example, many terms of service (ToS) for social networking sites require the user, as a precondition of use, to license the owners of the site to search and even share the user's information (including images) with third parties.[6] Also, most of the digital music we 'buy' comes with rules that we cannot share it with friends, and contains limits on the number of devices that are allowed to play the music.

Imagine the application of these rules in other non-networked domains. For example, as a condition of being listed in the telephone directory, what if that allowed the publisher of the phonebook full access to the content and the participants of your phone calls? What if a camera maker could use your images as a condition of using the (licensed, not purchased) camera? Or, imagine a compact disc that will not play in your rental car because the car's player has not been authorized to play it. Thus, the political and power formations generated through intellectual property discourses will profoundly influence the range of experiences available to people in all aspects of their now ubiquitously networked everyday lives.

The broad question of how to fairly reward ownership of content in a very fractionalized and collaborative creative universe remains key to the future of intellectual property. Things get even more complicated when we also try to recognize the contribution of our cognitive augmentations, or the mental extensions of our networked platforms. Consider this challenge raised by musician and renowned producer Brian Eno:

> I think of producing as the act of creating a sonic and conceptual overview of the record. And this type of creation is a whole new category for which there is no current copyright arrangement. When you're using sophisticated tools with very strong personalities, *is the designer of the tools in some*

> *sense responsible for what finally comes out? Should that designer benefit?* When a new tool or technology comes into existence, and suddenly 50 people at the same time see the same obvious idea, is it right that the one who gets to the publisher or patent office first should get all the material benefits of that idea? If not, how else do we share it? (quoted in Kelly, 1995, emphasis added)

This issue is complex, even within the relatively industrialized world of professional music. Anyone who has seen a producer in action, or seen the results that a good producer with the right equipment can do to improve the final musical product, knows that this contribution is not incidental. Eno calls the collective intelligence and creativity of people, technology and space 'scenius' – as opposed to the singular notion of 'genius' (Eno, 2009). How do we recognize or reward this collective contribution fairly, of both the human in the studio and the designer of the tools, as Eno points out?

On the notion of rewarding the designer of tools, consider the implications of this issue when applied to other ways we create. For example, the University of California at San Diego has a patent for:

> A means and method for inducing a temporary physiological state-of-mind to effect persistent changes to the cognitive-emotive profile of an individual, which is adaptable for neurofeedback and 'mental-state' therapeutic and non-therapeutic interventions. (Pineda and Allison, 2008)

In other words, they have a patent for using magnetic stimulation to improve higher cognitive functions including attention, skill-acquisition and memory. Other researchers have demonstrated that direct electrical current applied to the anterior temporal lobe of the brain can help people solve problems faster, and have 'flashes of insight' (Chi and Snyder, 2011). What then, is the proper incentive structure or 'reward' for the designer of these technologies, when new insights or mental creations are generated in the user? If a direct link between an outside intervention and an original and expressible thought or invention can be made, is it absurd to ask the question of whether the designer or owner of that tool can make a claim to the result? If we can demonstrate, possibly by neural recording a brain before and after the creative moment, that these insights or inventions would not have been made without the technology, what then? Are these questions any more absurd than the intellectual property rights to a man's own lymphocytes being held against his will by a public university? And is it possible that the only reason we might be disturbed by this example is because the stimulation is acting directly on the brain, instead of acting on the scaffolding of our extended minds?

This leaves us with a tricky question of balance. No one creates novel products or original expressions in a vacuum. No one works outside of the direct and indirect influence of myriad external cognitive aids, including other people. Yet, when one sees the governmentality of control by powerful agents who own the 'prosthetics' of distributed cognition, one can't help but fear the power those agents have to lock down creativity, and stretch their grip of control into the previously uncontrolled spaces of the mind.

GOVERNING THE NEW

Intellectual property, through all its evolving permutations in law and policy, is at its essence a technique for governing the new. Almost every concept within IP, from invention to original expression or from derivation to the copy, lies upon the policy rationale of encouraging the creation, sharing, and legal protection of useful and novel contributions to society. And yet, as a form of governance practiced today, many legal and political critics argue that IP is most frequently deployed as a tool for the *old* to control the *new*, rather than conceive and nurture it. Incumbent powers have used IP law to stifle competition, impose artificial scarcity, and to permanently extend monopolies and anti-competitive practices in the marketplace (Coombe, 1998; Drahos, 2002; Lessig, 2004; Vaidhyanathan, 2004; Halbert, 2005; McLeod, 2007).

The mind and its creative acts do not end at the borders of our head. As minds are further distributed into technological and social networks, the abuse of IP signals a major threat to cognitive freedom – one that has the potential to regulate access to the very resources in the environment that aid thinking and feeling. And therefore, it has the potential to stifle the possibility for creating *the new* further and further 'upstream', i.e. into the mind.

With distributed cognitive systems and distributed agency, consisting of networked layers of bodies, brains, technologies and discursive scaffolds, how does the concept and practice of intellectual property mediate relations among these structures? If we think *with* our environment, what are the neuropolitics of thinking within a *copyrighted* environment?

Clearing Rights to Think

In *Bound by Law*, a comic book dramatizing the chilling effects of copyright law produced by Duke University's Center for the Study of the Public Domain, the act of producing a documentary film is compared to walking blindfolded through a minefield – every step laden with the fear that a copyright claim might blow up in your face (Aoki, et al., 2006: 9). And even when common sense might tell you you've reached the safety of the commons, sometimes a stray grenade is thrown your way.

John Else's story, as chronicled in *Bound by Law*, is indicative of this fraught creative minefield. Else, a documentary filmmaker, made a film about the life of stagehands on Broadway. During filming, he caught two stagehands having a sandwich and watching TV in the rafters above a live performance. Recalling a famous scene from *Citizen Kane*, the stage hands' nonchalance about the play happening right below them comically juxtaposed 'high' and 'low' culture – a point driven home by the fact that the stagehands were watching the animated comedy show, *The Simpsons*. When Matt Groening and Fox Television became aware that this 4.5-second clip of their show playing on a small TV was going to be included in the documentary, they did not prohibit Else from using the clip, rather they requested Else to pay a licensing fee of $10,000. This sum is huge for a small-budget documentary film, and although Else might have ultimately won a fair use argument in court, he anticipated that the cost of fighting the case against a team of Fox lawyers would be too great, and decided to cut the scene (Aoki et al., 2006: 15–16). Considering punishment in the United States for copyright infringement, carries a penalty of up to $150,000 for every act,[7] who can blame independent content creators for taking a default position of self-censorship, even before being sent infringement notices by content owners (Lessig, 2004: 95–99).

A filmmaker, writer or producer who intends to use content (be it an image, clip, phrase or other expression) that belongs to someone else must first 'clear rights' before that content can be shown legally. Clearing rights involves tracking down the owner or owners of the copyright of the desired content, and asking for and often paying for permission to use it. This process of clearing rights is often time consuming, frustrating and expensive (Aoki et al., 2006: 5–12).

In US law, at least, there is a strong tradition of 'fair use' rights. Fair use of copyrighted materials includes social commentary, parody, political speech, criticism, or when the material in question is incidental (or of such a short duration) that it does not rise to the level of infringement. A short quotation in an academic article is the quintessential example. But what constitutes fair use is anything but clear in the law, and decades of litigation by content owners has squeezed the borders of fair use down to smaller and more limited uses (Lessig, 2004: 141–143).

Content companies, media carriers, artist rights' groups, and other organizations and individuals have been sent into a state of paranoia over the flood of 'pirates' and 'thieves', who they perceive to be eroding their profit margins by illegally distributing copyrighted materials. These organizations have spent millions lobbying to increase their ability to monitor and control how content is made, used and shared (Masnick, 2011). Examples abound of seemingly absurd legal actions by the controllers of content. Teenagers who share music files have been sent 'cease and desist' letters and arrested for infringement.[8] ASCAP, the composer's rights organization, sued the Girl Scouts of America for failing to pay royalties to the owners of the songs they sing around the campfire, including 'Happy Birthday'. Songs overheard on car radios, cell phone ring tones, even catch-phrases uttered in conversation by documentary subjects have routinely come with either a massive price tag to include legally in a film, or an ever-higher cost threat of a lawsuit if included without clearance (Lessig, 2004: 18). Teams of production assistants scour the *mise-en-scène* of location film sets to make sure no unlicensed intellectual property is visible, while other teams place products strategically in the scene for paying advertisers. *The mental commons is a battlefield of neuropolitics, and IP law is a powerful weapon of choice.*

But the battle for the mental commons is not just a problem for documentary filmmakers or professional artists. Ubiquitous mobile cameras and live streaming to the Internet has made billions of media-makers potential, and almost certain, copyright infringers. From forwarding emails to uploading home videos, almost every act we perform on the Internet creates a copy that contains someone else's copyrighted content. YouTube's servers trawl the millions of hours of video on its site to automatically take down any video that its copyright surveillance tools indicate contains unlicensed copyrighted material.[9] Networked technologies have turned regular human social practices into, in legal scholar John Tehranian's phrase, 'a nation of infringers' (2007).

Imagine walking down a typical city street and recording your audio-visual experience using your new Google Glass. Now consider the task of tracking down ALL of the owners of the copyrighted materials in the recording (the store signage, advertisements, the designer clothes people wear, the graffiti on buildings) and asking each of the owners for permission to use their content before sharing or streaming your recording. It is a dilemma that is very real already, but often ignored by the millions posting their home videos on YouTube and similar Internet content-sharing sites (Tehranian, 2007), and one that will only be exacerbated by wearable computers and recording devices.

At this size and scale, the political importance of direct and indirect IP controls becomes evident. The choice between self-censorship and a time-consuming and expensive licensing process, or simply to risk ignoring copyright law, is really no choice at all for a free and open society. If the very act of capturing and sharing events from our lives puts us in the direct line of fire for such legal risk, then we must question whether the intent or effect of the law makes any sense from the perspective of the public good.

Critical legal scholar Rosemary Coombe argues that IP laws have put limits on our individual and collective ability to create and share expressions. This method of control has strengthened the mechanisms for reproducing hierarchies of privilege and power. More of the public domain is moving off limits to copy or imitation, being privatized by those whose 'good will' has turned content into property. By 'controlling mimesis', Coombe argues, 'they police alterity' (1998: 181).

As Rosa Luxembourg has said, 'freedom is the freedom to think differently' (in Rancière, 2004: 74). The freedom to use language, images, knowledge, memories and all other forms of our cultural and scientific heritage in new and challenging ways should not be overly inhibited by the dictates of property. The freedom to use the language of the establishment to critique (or outwardly mock) that very establishment is essential to a healthy democracy. 'Who owns the extended mind?' is a question of priorities and values. The answers we collectively give now will determine the kind of mental commons (and thus what kind of society) we will leave for future generations.

A SERIES OF ENCLOSURES

The 'public domain' is the pool of ideas, facts, histories, laws of science, biological heritage, natural resources, and other elements in our world that in some senses belong collectively to all human beings. But the public domain has often been seen and used by some not as a repository of our collected genius and womb of new creation, but as a vast untapped resource that, when enclosed in a property contract, can be turned into a profitable asset for its owners. What then is the 'public domain' of the cognitive ecology?

Intellectual property law is one of the main governing systems of our mental scaffolding. And yet scholars and critics grasp for appropriate metaphors to describe this seeming extension of property control into the cognitive commons. James Boyle calls the series of moves to privatize the cultural commons as the 'second enclosure movement', harking back to the first enclosure movement of late medieval England, when common land was divided and sold to private individuals (2008: 41–53). In response to this move, he proposes a 'cultural environmentalism' akin to ecological environmentalism that seeks prudent and sustainable stewardship of our common resources. Boyle points to the neuropolitical stakes in this second enclosure movement as well, calling it the 'enclosure of the mind' (2008). If this enclosure continues apace, the critical political question of 'who can have a share of what is common to the community' begins to lose its relevance, as less and less of life's commons even exist to divide.

This section explores several of the major strategies, and sites of control, that incumbent powers are implementing in this broad cultural and cognitive enclosure movement. These strategies for the commodification of cognitive content and the privatization of the scaffolds of our extended minds create new sites for neuropolitics. And, for IP scholars and critics, neuropolitics and the concept of the cognitive commons provides a new lens through which to view familiar IP policy debates. Many of the activities that went unregulated for most of human history, especially of the creative sort, are now squarely within the purview of institutional and micro-political regulatory forces tied to the allocation and enforcement of intellectual property rights.

Enclosing Language

In the abstract, censorship of expression inflames the hearts of those who value a free society. In actual practice, however, censorship is commonly allowed and encouraged to take place. Often to appease public anti-censorship values, the dirty work of censorship is offloaded to the private sphere. Metaphorically speaking, the public sphere stays the 'good cop', while the private sphere plays 'bad cop', as messy political issues turn into more 'straightforward' business issues between private entities.

A famous example of linguistic censorship is illustrative of this conversion. When a non-profit from San Francisco tried to organize a 'Gay Olympics' with the goal of combating stereotypes and prejudice against gays and lesbians, the United States Olympic Committee sued the group for infringement, claiming the USOC (and only the USOC), could decide how the word 'Olympic' could be used. The Supreme Court upheld the USOC's claim, citing the Amateur Sports Act passed by Congress in 1978. As James Boyle points out in his analysis of the case, this ruling effectively gave 'a state grant of a monopoly rent on a piece of the linguistic landscape', as it would if it were granting a trademark for 'Kleenex' or 'Hoover' (1996: 145).

Another lesser-known event in the 'Olympics' of censorship occurred in Belgium in 2008. As part of their 'Derf Denken' (Dare to Think) campaign, the University of Ghent hired the advertising firm Saatchi and Saatchi to create a series of advertisements with challenging, or counter-intuitive, concepts to

Figure 36.1 Saatchi and Saatchi ad for University of Ghent 'Derf Denken' campaign
Image credit: Stuart Candy, 2008.

help represent daring thinking. One of these ads, a flag for the 2020 Darfur Olympics (Figure 36.1), caused a minor controversy. Obviously, from the perspective of 2008, an Olympics held in this war-torn region was daring thinking, but that was not what caused the controversy. Rather, the International Olympic Committee (IOC), owners of the trademarks for the word Olympics, and the image of the Olympic rings, were behind it. The IOC had not authorized the use of their trademarks, and consequently asked for the ads to be pulled. As experiential futurist Stuart Candy notes in his analysis of the controversy:

> Patrolling IP in this context is effectively policing thought. Which is insidious enough in any form, but the stakes somehow come out in sharper relief when it comes to curtailing expressions of possible futures. It could be said that the IOC, in exercising its copyright-holders' veto, is literally curtailing the public's ability to imagine a future in which a now-conflicted region turns things around to the extent of becoming Olympics-ready. (2008)

Eventually, and under protest, Saatchi and Saatchi and the University of Ghent succumbed to the threat and pulled the ad. As is painfully clear in this example, and the many others like it,[10] if large chunks of our language are subject to property protections through trademark and copyright, then our collective capacity to express alternative futures is reduced, and 'the future' as a space of shared imagining is constricted.

Free speech issues were elided in these examples because, in the domain of the law, these were matters for the private world of property and contracts. The movement from public to private law opens the door for increased control of certain trademarked words, images, or phrases by private estates of those who, with the right skills and resources, can fight to protect these resources as their own property.

Boyle calls this a 'Homestead Law on the English language' (1996: 146) and further emphasizes what is at stake:

> A free speech discourse that imagines the only threat to vigorous public discourse is direct censorship by the state is blind to the multiple ways that state-granted property rights fence off the public domain, even directly restrain certain kinds of speech. (1996: 148)

This public language is what we use to create and to share sensibilities. Author Jonathan Lethem makes the critical point that 'appropriation, mimicry, quotation, allusion, and sublimated collaboration consists of a kind of *sine qua non* of the creative act, cutting across all forms and genres in the realm of cultural production' (Lethem, 2007: 61). In this production people fashion works for public consumption, but more fundamentally this production is also part of our personal and collective self-fashioning. And finally, when applied to neuropolitics, the availability of a free and open language is essential to individual thought, and social coordination and collaboration (Clark, 1996: 194–201).

Enclosing Memory

Similar to how open access to language is a prime tenet of a free society, open access to the collective, shared history of life, and the ability to reconsolidate memories from a reservoir of available materials is fundamental to a free society. Yet, copyright law often closes off access to (or places a toll booth in front of) the recordings, writings, and other hypomnemata[11] of humanity's recent cultural heritage. When writer Alice Randall wrote a novel based on characters from the *Gone with the Wind* universe, but told from the perspective of the slaves in the story, the estate of Margaret Mitchell, the original work's author, sued Houghton Mifflin, Randall's publisher. After an immediate lower court injunction stopped publication, an act later called an 'extraordinary and drastic' violation of the First Amendment by the 11th Circuit Court of Appeals in Atlanta, the case became a lightning rod both for critics of the expanding scope of copyright and for those who sought some clarity on the boundaries of 'fair use'. Houghton Mifflin eventually settled the lawsuit with the Mitchell estate by agreeing to make a financial contribution to Morehouse College, and the book was later adorned with the phrase 'an unauthorized parody' (Kirkpatrick, 2002).

Stories of enclosure of our shared public history foreground the politics of 'who decides' how cultural history is shared. If we take Andy Clark, Edwin Hutchins and the other proponents of cognitive parallelism literally, then the bits of mind and life offloaded to Facebook, Google and other platforms that store data 'in the cloud', on servers owned by these companies, are not metaphorical but literal traces of one's extended memory. When a person reviews the images, status updates, and links she has saved on these sites, she is firing up a functioning cognitive system.

These digital cognitive extensions create novel power dynamics. In the analog world, when a person accessed written diaries and photo albums she was also booting up an extended mind. But, control of the 'data' in these books remained with the user exclusively. Moleskin notebooks don't come with a terms of service agreement, yet. But now, in exchange for access to new applications that capture, organize and share our lives, people are handing over the rights to large chunks of their extended minds to Facebook and Google programmers, managers and lawyers.

When Andy Clark tells the story of the time he lost his laptop, he compares it to having temporary brain damage, noting, 'I was left dazed, confused, and visibly enfeebled – the victim of a cyborg equivalent of a mild stroke' (2004: 10). The potential for large segments of the population to share in Clark's experience is increased by the fact that not only are people offloading more and more cognitive functions to their machines, but now the machines themselves are offloading more and more of their (and thus our) functions to other machines – networked 'cloud' servers scattered all around the world and predominantly owned by private corporations. Some of these corporations have capricious CEOs with their own vision for how user data will be 'protected' and traded. Other companies will seek to sell-off or shut-down underperforming sites, relegating gigabytes of user history to the digital scrap heap, as when Yahoo! threatened to shut down delicious.com, a popular bookmarking site (Ha, 2010). And potentially even more concerning are the viruses and 'bot' networks that are controlled by anonymous groups of hackers. As many technology observers have noted, the Conficker Worm now controls the world's largest cloud computing network (De, 2010).

The capacity and legal right to arbitrarily shut down a site or block a user's access to his or her own content certainly demonstrates a kind of neuropower that is unprecedented in history, and massive in its potential effect.[12] Although it may seem slightly sensationalist to say so, but the argument is reasonable, Internet and software companies, as well as skilled and motivated hackers, have the power to wipe memories and cause 'strokes' amongst their users.

Enclosing Ownership

When lawsuits threatening punitive damages, cease and desist letters, strategically biased international treaties and other devices from the public sphere of law are inadequate for the task of complete dominion over content, then some companies and artist groups are not reluctant to seek out other means. Taking patent and copyright from the public sphere of law, and moving it into the private sphere, is accomplished by several tactics. The most common way is the move from selling products to renting or licensing products. In this arrangement, the full rights of ownership remain with the licensor.

These private contracts, in the form of 'shrink-wrap' – packaging that when opened seals the contractual agreement between the user and the licensor – or through End User License Agreements (EULA) – the ubiquitous 'do you agree' forms that are generally ignored by users before clicking 'yes', put legal limits on what a user can or cannot do with the products that they have paid for. Digital surveillance tools included in the software ('spyware') have also often become part of the bargain, as companies seek ways to ensure that they know if and when any contract terms have been violated, and if a termination of the license (by means of deleting the software from the user's computer) is necessary. Sony's infamous 'rootkit', a Digital Rights Management tool included (unbeknownst to users) in music CDs the company sold, caused operating issues and opened up a 'back door' for other malicious software to infect a user's computer.[13]

Almost all of the software and much of the digital content consumers 'purchase' for their computers and mobile devices is, in reality, only licensed to individual users. Generally, in the case of software, licenses prohibit users from copying, sharing, loaning or 'reverse engineering' the product (Halbert, 1999: 61–64). These are actions consumers are used to doing with other products they buy, especially with material goods, like books or lawnmowers. The net effect of this is to constrain experimentation, and thus to constrain freedom, extending more control of the suppliers over the users.

Sharing and tinkering with products are not only easier in the digital world, but most people consider them harmless. Copying or loaning of software, or the trading of music files, does not affect the original copy – it is an inexhaustible resource. Of course, content and software producers see these activities as harmful to their potential sales, an argument that makes sense abstractly, but is backed by ambiguous, incomplete, or occasionally falsified data (Parrish, 2010).

Convincing the public to use software and content in the manner permitted by the content owners has been difficult. While we may be facing 'the most significant regulation of culture that our free society has ever known'

(Lessig, 2004: 170), no amount of money spent on PR, or Boy Scout badges, or punitive lawsuits has been able to significantly change the way humans create and share information, including digital content. The nature of digital content and information, and the way we interact with it, has caused the 'gap between copyright law and [cultural] norms to only grow wider in recent years' (Tehranian, 2007: 546). Becoming a nation of constant infringers turns regular people doing regular activities into criminals, and undermines the trust and confidence citizens have in the logic of the laws they are to follow.

There have been, however, several innovations in recent years that attempt to bridge the gap between cultural norms and IP law, especially those that use the adhesion of licenses for the cause of open access and user freedom. The progenitor of these user-empowering licenses is the General Public License (GPL) that came out of the 'Free Software' movement. This movement is based on four basic freedoms:

- the freedom to use the software for any purpose
- the freedom to change the software to suit your needs
- the freedom to share the software with your friends and neighbors
- the freedom to share the changes you make.[14]

The General Public License codifies these freedoms and binds signatories to abide by these rules.

Another user-empowering licensing regime comes from Creative Commons, a non-profit organization that supports the creation of 'legal and technical infrastructure that maximizes digital creativity, sharing, and innovation'.[15] Creative Commons licenses provide turnkey ways for users to balance certain kinds of activities, like open sharing of content but with some protections, like stipulating only non-commercial uses are allowed. Since their release in 2002, Creative Commons licenses have become extremely popular, with hundreds of millions of users relying on Creative Commons licenses to protect, legalize and generally clarify the kinds of uses that are allowed for the content they produce.[16] As these alternative property and licensing regimes become more mainstream, one-size-fits-all policies, like the ACM 'work for hire' policy, might become harder to justify and harder to deploy without resistance.

Enclosing Enforcement

As this chapter has argued, licenses, lawsuits and other mechanisms for legal enforcement of intellectual property are both complicated and often ineffective. Tracking the activities of millions or billions of users and stopping the flow of information across global digital networks on a case-by-case basis, as most legal interventions require, also makes this kind of enforcement difficult to implement. So, content producers and providers seeking to move closer to the goal of perfect control have begun to take matters into their own hand by directly locking out users from their products. Tactics like Digital Rights Management (DRM) software and Content Scramble Systems (CSS), even with their history of functional and public relations failure, manifest the dissatisfaction of content owners with messy legal and policy processes. The use of technological lockdowns and lockouts reflect a desire for an increased 'level of control for proprietary culture' where 'permissions will no longer be policed by the courts or the law but rather by software codes' (Lessig, 2004: 279–280).

The push to use technological means to embed control both into the platforms and the devices they operate represents another extension of control over our mental ecology, one that transfers power, yet again, from the public to the private domain. It seizes agency from users, or from legal oversight and wholly integrates a control mechanism directly into our cognitive built environment. Tarleton Gillespie, an expert on the tools content providers use to 'wire shut' devices, has criticized the move to 'effectively frustrate' consumers, making devices impenetrable to the tinkering hands of users (2006). Besides usage compliance being directly embedded into technologies, he notes, there is also a growing mandate for anti-circumvention and 'robustness rules'. These rules, included in 'anti-piracy' bills that have been proposed and circulated in the US Congress, would 'obligate manufactures to build devices such that they prevent tinkering – not only must the technology regulate its users, it must be inscrutable to them' (2006: 652).

Intellectual property law needs tools such as fair use and non-commercial use in order for experimentation, innovation and creativity to take place. Indeed these IP gray areas are necessary to promote the progress of arts and science, and are rendered irrelevant if the individual agency necessary to test these boundaries is technologically pre-empted and forestalled. These techniques threaten to create a world of 'user-subjugating software' as Free Software advocate Richard Stallman warns (1999). Siva Vaidhyanathan also fears this enclosure of freedom, where 'home computers would be governed by remote control' (2004: 76). Are people willing to accept the remote governance of their extended minds?

Mindwriter™: An Artifact from the Future

One method for helping people bridge the gap between the lived experience of the present and the abstract landscape of possible futures is to create an 'artifact from the future'. Just as an archaeologist analyzes artifacts and images from past cultures in order to uncover their behaviors, beliefs and ways of living, artifacts from 'the future' are intended to manifest aspects of possible worlds in engaging and often provocative ways. These artifacts help condense forecasts and insights into a tangible form to increase engagement and aid understanding. They are not necessarily predictions of new technologies or behaviors to come, but allow us to think through some implications of change, and the values driving this change.

Often, one uses a familiar genre or medium, such as an advertisement, or street signage, and 'smuggles in' more provocative futures content. Many of the more abstract arguments and ideas expressed in this chapter are embedded in just such an artifact from the future, included in the Institute for the Future's 2012 Ten-Year Forecast.[17]

This 'future product', the Mindwriter™ (Figure 36.2), is built upon technologies that allow for the representation of electro-chemical signals from the brain in machine-readable formats.[18] These technological advances help us to imagine a future when people might directly upload their thoughts to a digital platform (Neuroogle™). They will do this to capture a 'document' of their thinking, but also to put these thoughts into a tangible mode of expression – therefore gaining automatic copyright protection for those expressions. In a knowledge-based, creative economy, securing protection for these expressions could be financially significant and rewarding. Another feature adds an additional layer to the artifact scenario – the idea of cognitive shrink-wrap. This product will not work unless the end-user license agreement can be 'read' in the user's short-term memory.

Artifacts from the future are meant to be provocations, but they also draw upon trends and signals of change that exist today. They show us a possible end result of certain technological, economic and legal trajectories of enclosure. And like any good scenario, we can see both the positive and negative implications of this future. We can all see the benefit of being able to more quickly and thoroughly document our creative thoughts. An explosion of new ideas, connections and inventions might be born. But if this comes at the cost of ownership of these creations, or if the Mindwriter™ becomes a vector for tighter policing of IP, then we might shudder at this Faustian bargain.

We have to pay attention to this artifact because it could potentially come to pass, given a plausible combination of visible trends. The science behind neural interfaces and mind-reading technologies is immature,

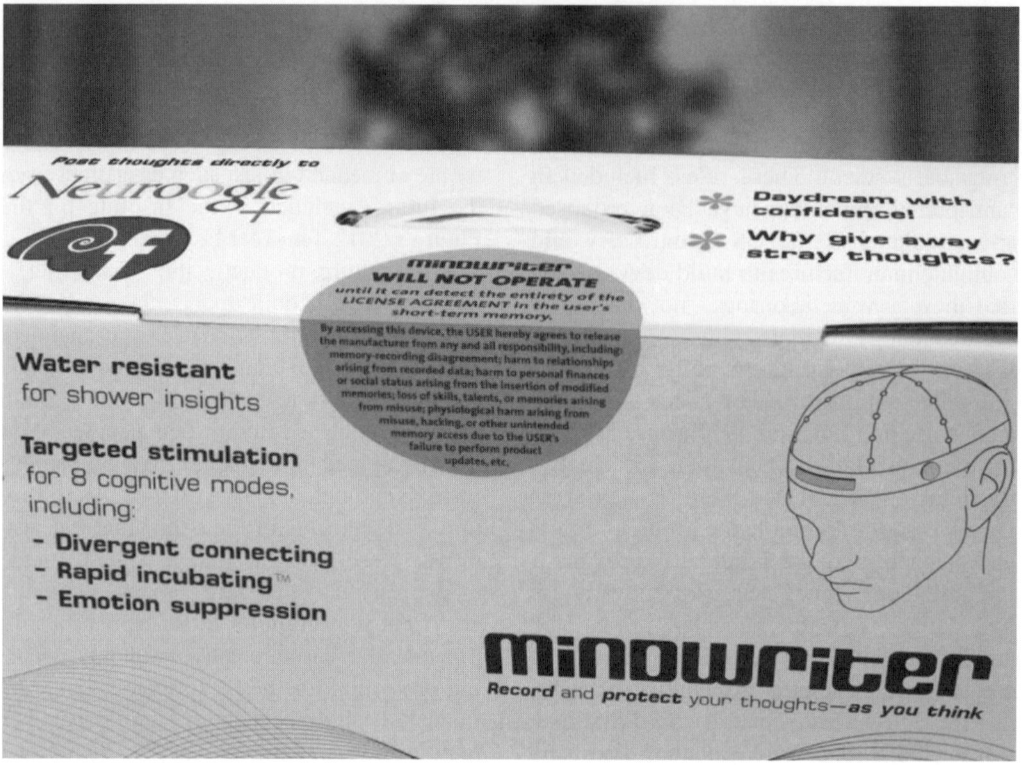

Figure 36.2 IFTF's artiefact portrays a future technology that can automatically record and copyright thoughts

but has already shown promise in translating brain activity into digital information (Kellis et al., 2010; Geere, 2011). The economic incentives for 'getting there first' with phrases, images and creative expression is strong in the knowledge and experience economy. And, in the US, we have wide-reaching copyright protection policy that requires only that an original expression be made in a tangible medium. These conditions make Mindwriter™ a possible, but not necessarily preferable, future product. Sometimes generating a self-defeating prophecy is a gift to the future.

CONCLUSION: ENCLOSING THE FUTURE?

This chapter examined the role of intellectual property in the governance of the extended mind and the private ownership of the scaffolding of cognition. Intellectual property law, we might say, governs the 'adjacent possible' (Johnson, 2010). Complexity theorist Stuart Kauffman first developed this theory of evolutionary change. It explains how, at each level of complexity for a living being, there is a finite, but novel, set of possible directions that are opened up (Kauffman, 2000). A single-celled organism cannot jump up and walk on two feet, but as new adjacent spaces are opened up by millions of years of genetic mutation and natural selection, possibilities expand – eventually ones that include the possibility for legs and feet, and the ability to walk upright on two of them. Some adjacent possibilities that exist are not chosen or are not viable in the long term, and other seemingly modest changes open up entire new possibilities that could not have been predicted from the characteristics of prior forms.

Johnson uses the image of walking into a four-sided room with a door on each of the three new walls. Choosing a door opens you up into a new room with three new doors, each leading into different possibility spaces, and on and on. In terms of creativity and innovation, modern humans have had a good measure of choice about which doors they'd like to open. But if we now imagine this room as our cognitive ecology in a world of heavy intellectual property protections, we can imagine a guard at each of the doors. Much like in Kafka's parable of the man 'Before the Law'[19] who dies after waiting his whole life for the guard to let him through the door of the law, each of the doors of the cognitive adjacent possible are closed before us. The first door is locked behind legal walls; the second door is technologically wired shut; and the third door is blocked by the invisible and insipid force-field of self-censorship.

New sensibilities and new creative opportunities exist behind those doors, and people need the freedom and the capacity to be able to open them. Allowing legacy powers to keep people locked in this small room will crush the creative spirit that is necessary to push humans beyond their narrow view of life, and will thwart the exploration into new ways of being. We might not have been able to choose our biological brains, but we must be able to re-design our extended minds. A fair, open, and future-oriented intellectual property regime will aid in that process; a repressive control-oriented one will not.

NOTES

1 For a useful summary of IP issues in regards to the research and clinical practice of neuroscience, see Ergenzinger et al. (2004).
2 A challenge pointed out by Andy Clark, interview with the author, June 2010.
3 For an argument on how radically individualist models of IP distribution could be a viable solution for the future of IP, see Tim Wu (2008).
4 'The text of Wikipedia is copyrighted (automatically, under the Berne Convention) by Wikipedia editors and contributors and is formally licensed to the public under one or several liberal licenses'. See: http://en.wikipedia.org/wiki/Wikipedia:Copyrights
5 www.evernote.com/about/tos/
6 See Facebook's terms of service: www.facebook.com/terms.php
7 www.copyright.gov/title17/92chap5.html. Section 504, c. 2.
8 See other examples at www.chillingeffects.org
9 https://support.google.com/youtube/topic/2778544?hl=en&ref_topic=2676339
10 See examples at www.chillingeffects.org
11 This Greek term was brought into the wider philosophical lexicon by Michel Foucault, who defined it as the 'notes on the reading, conversations, and reflections that one hears or engages in oneself; keeping kinds of notebooks on important subjects (what the Greeks call "hypomnemata"), which must be reread from time to time so as to reactualize their contents', http://en.wikipedia.org/wiki/Hypomnema.
12 It is not surprising that the embattled dictators of Middle Eastern countries shut down access to the Internet during the uprisings.
13 http://en.wikipedia.org/wiki/Sony_BMG_copy_protection_rootkit_scandal
14 www.gnu.org/licenses/quick-guide-gplv3.html
15 www.creativecommons.org/
16 www.creativecommons.org/about/history/; http://wiki.creativecommons.org/Metrics/License_statistics
17 www.iftf.org/our-work/global-landscape/ten-year-forecast/2012-ten-year-forecast/
18 See the work at Berkeley's Gallant Lab for one of many examples of this quickly developing technological capacity: http://gallantlab.org/
19 http://www.kafka-online.info/before-the-law.html

REFERENCES

Aoki, Keith, James Boyle and Jennifer Jenkins. (2006) *Bound by Law.* Duke Center for the Study of the Public Domain. Accessed March 1, 2011 from www.law.duke.edu/cspd/comics/

Bateson, Gregory. (1972) *Steps to an Ecology of Mind: Collected Essays in Anthropology, Psychiatry, Evolution, and Epistemology.* Chicago: University of Chicago Press.

Boyle, James. (1996) *Shamans, Software, and Spleens: Law and the Construction of the Information Society.* Cambridge, MA: Harvard University Press.

Boyle, James. (2008) *The Public Domain: Enclosing the Commons of the Mind.* New Haven and London: Yale University Press.

Brown, Michael. (2004) *Who Owns Native Culture?* Cambridge, MA: Harvard University Press.

Candy, Stuart. (2008) 'The Darfur Olympics'. *The Sceptical Futuryst* March 15. Accessed March 2, 2011 from www.futuryst.blogspot.com/2008/03/darfur-olympics.html

Chemero, Antonio. (2009) *Radical Embodied Cognitive Science.* Cambridge, MA: MIT Press.

Chi, R. and A. Snyder. (2011) 'Facilitate Insight by Non-Invasive Brain Stimulation'. *PLoS ONE* 6(2) DOI: 10.1371/journal.pone.0016655.

Chorost, Michael. (2011) *World Wide Mind: The Coming Integration of Humanity, Machines, and the Internet.* New York: Free Press.

Clark, Andy. (1996) *Being There: Putting Brain, Body, and World Together Again.* Cambridge, MA: MIT Press.

Clark, Andy. (2004) *Natural Born Cyborgs: Minds, Technologies, and the Future of Human Intelligence.* Oxford: Oxford University Press.

Connolly, William E. (2002) *Neuropolitics: Thinking, Culture, Speed.* Minneapolis and London: University of Minnesota Press.

Coombe, Rosemary. (1998) *The Cultural Life of Intellectual Properties: Authorship, Appropriation, and the Law.* Durham: Duke University Press.

Cooper, Seth, Firas Khatib et al. (2010) 'Predicting Protein Structures with a Multiplayer Online Game'. *Nature* 466(5 August): 756–760.

De, Pallab. (2010) 'Conficker Worms Owns the World's Largest Cloud Network.' *Techie Buzz.* Accessed March 1, 2011 from www.techie-buzz.com/online-security/conficker-worm-worlds-largest-cloud.html

Deleuze, Gilles and Felix Guattari. (2004) *A Thousand Plateaus: Capitalism and Schizophrenia.* London: Continuum Books.

Diamond v. Chakrabarty, 447 U.S. 303 (1980).

Drahos, Peter, with John Braithwaite. (2002) *Information Feudalism: Who Owns the Knowledge Economy?* London: Earthscan Publishers.

Dumit, Joseph. (2004) *Picturing Personhood: Brain Scans and Biomedical Identity.* Princeton: Princeton University Press.

Dunagan, Jake. (2011) 'Politics for the Neurocentric Age'. Doctoral Dissertation.

Eagleman, David. (2012) *Incognito: The Secret Lives of the Brain.* New York: Pantheon Books.

Eno, Brian. (2009) 'Brian Eno on Genius and "Scenius"'. *Synthtopia* July 9. Accessed April 1, 2011 from www.synthtopia.com/content/2009/07/09/brian-eno-on-genius-and-scenius/

Ergenzinger, Edward, Michelle Cunningham, Philip Webber and W. Murray Spruill. (2004) 'Patenting Neuroscience: Challenges and Opportunities in an Interdisciplinary Field'. *Nature Reviews Neuroscience* 5: 657–661.

Gazzaniga, Michael. (2005) *The Ethical Brain.* New York and Washington, DC: Dana Press.

Gazzaniga, Michael and Joseph LeDoux. (1978) *The Integrated Mind.* Springer Publishers.

Geere, Duncan. (2011) 'Brain Scanner Can Recreate Movie Scenes You've Watched'. *Wired UK.* Available at www.wired.co.uk/news/archive/2011-09/23/reconstructingvision

Gillespie, Tarleton. (2006) 'Designed to "Effectively Frustrate": Copyright, Technology and the Agency of Users'. *New Media and Society* 8(4): 651–669.

Goodenough, Oliver and Gregory Decker. (2006) 'Why Do Good People Steal Intellectual Property?' *The Gruter Institute Working Papers on Law, Economics, and Evolutionary Biology* 4(1), Article 3.

Greely, Henry T. (2004) 'Prediction, Litigation, Privacy, and Property: Some Possible Legal and Social Implications of Advances in Neuroscience'. In Brent Garland, ed. *Neuroscience and the Law: Brain, Mind, and the Scales of Justice.* New York and Washington DC: Dana Press.

Ha, Anthony. (2010) 'Is Yahoo about to kill Delicious?' *VentureBeat* December 16. Accessed March 1, 2010 from www.venturebeat.com/2010/12/16/yahoo-sunset-delicious/

Halbert, Debora. (1999) *Intellectual Property in the Information Age: The Politics of Expanding Ownership Rights.* Westport, CT: Quorum Books.

Halbert, Debora. (2005) *Resisting Intellectual Property Law.* RIPE Studies in Global Political Economy. Abingdon: Routledge.

Hand, Eric. (2010) 'People Power'. *Nature* 466(5 August): 685–687.

Hayles, N. Katherine. (1999) *How We Became Posthuman: Virtual Bodies in Cybernetics, Literature, and Informatics.* Chicago: University of Chicago Press.

Hayles, N. Katherine. (2006) 'Unfinished Work: From Cyborg to Cognisphere'. *Theory, Culture, and Society* 23(7–8): 159–166.

Hutchins, Edwin. (1996) *Cognition in the Wild.* Cambridge, MA: MIT Press.

Jensen, Kyle and Fiona Murray. (2005) 'The Intellectual Property Landscape of the Human Genome'. *Science* 310(14 October): 239–240.

Johnson, Steven B. (2004) *Mind Wide Open: Your Brain and the Neuroscience of Everyday Life.* New York: Scribner.

Johnson, Steven B. (2006) *Everything Bad is Good for You: How Today's Popular Culture is Actually Making Us Smarter.* New York: Penguin Press.

Johnson, Steven B. (2010) *Where Good Ideas Come From: The Natural History of Innovation.* New York: Riverhead.

Karp, Jonathan and Laura Meckler. (2006) 'Which Travelers Have "Hostile Intent"? Biometric Device May Have the Answer'. *Wall Street Journal Online.* Available at http://online.wsj.com/news/articles/SB115551793796934752

Kauffman, Stuart. (2000) *Investigations.* Oxford: Oxford University Press.

Kellis, Spencer, Kai Miller, et al. (2010) 'Decoding Spoken Words Using Local Field Potential Recorded from the Cortical Surface'. *Journal of Neural Engineering* 7(5).

Kelly, Kevin. (1995) 'Gossip is Philosophy'. *Wired* 3(5). Accessed July 1, 2010 from www.wired.com/wired/archive/3.05/eno.html

Kirkpatrick, David. (2002) 'Mitchell Estate Settles "Gone with the Wind" Suit'. *New York Times Online.* Accessed May 1, 2011 from www.nytimes.com/2002/05/10/business/mitchell-estate-settles-gone-with-the-wind-suit.html

Lessig, Lawrence. (2004) *Free Culture: How Big Media Uses Technology and the Law to Lock Down Culture and Control Creativity.* New York: Penguin Press.

Lethem, Jonathan. (2007) 'The Ecstasy of Influence: A Plagiarism'. *Harper's Magazine* February: 59–71.

Lynch, Zack. (2009) *The Neuro Revolution: How Brain Science is Changing Our World.* New York: St Martin's Press.

Madrigal, Alexis. (2010) 'Brain Scan Lie-Detection Deemed Far from Ready for Courtroom'. *Wired.* Accessed July 17, 2010 from www.wired.com/wiredscience/2010/06/fmri-lie-detection-in-court/

Malafouris, Lambros. (2010) 'The Brain–Artefact Interface (BAI): A Challenge for Archaeology and Cultural Neuroscience'. *Social Cognitive and Affective Neuroscience* 5(2–3): 264–273.

Marden, Emily. (1999) 'The Neem Tree Patent: International Conflict over the Commodification of Life'. *Boston College International and Comparative Law Review* 22 (Spring): 288.

Masnick, Mike. (2011) 'RIAA Spent $90 Million in Lobbying the US in the Past Decade'. *TechDirt.* Accessed March 20, 2011 from www.techdirt.com/articles/20110106/15414312556/riaa-spent-90-million-lobbying-us-past-decade.shtml

McLeod, Kembrew. (2007) *Freedom of Expression: Resistance and Repression in the Age of Intellectual Property.* Minneapolis: University of Minnesota Press.

Moore v. Regents of the University of California, 51 Cal. 3d 120, 271 Cal. Rptr. 146, 793 P.2d 479, cert. denied 499 U.S. 936 (1991).

Moreno, Jonathan. (2006) *Mind Wars: Brain Research and National Defense.* New York and Washington, DC: Dana Press.

Norretranders, Tor. (1999) *The User Illusion: Cutting Consciousness Down to Size.* New York: Penguin.

Parrish, Kevin. (2010) 'Experts: Losses Due to Piracy are Exaggerated'. *Tom's Guide* June 17. Accessed March 1, 2011 from www.tomsguide.com/us/Piracy-China-USITC-RIAA-MPAA,news-7120.html

Pineda, Jaime A. and Brendon Z. Allison. (2008) 'Method and System for a Real Time Adaptive System for Effecting Changes in Cognitive-Emotive Profiles'. US Patent 7,460,903; filed September 12, 2003 and issued December 2, 2008.

Rancière, Jacques. (2004) *The Politics of Aesthetics.* London and New York: Continuum.

Rose, Mark. (1993) *Authors and Owners: The Invention of Copyright.* Cambridge, MA: Harvard University Press.

Saini, Angela. (2009) 'The Brain Police: Judging Murder with an MRI'. *Wired UK.* Accessed July 17, 2010 from www.wired.co.uk/wired-magazine/archive/2009/05/features/guilty.aspx?page=all

Shachtman, Noah. (2010) 'Air Force Wants Neuroweapons to Overwhelm Enemy Minds'. *Wired.* Accessed March 2, 2011 from www.wired.com/dangerroom/2010/11/air-force-looks-to-artificially-overwhelm-enemy-cognitive-capabilities/

Shirky, Clay. (2010) *Cognitive Surplus: Creativity and Generosity in a Connected Age.* New York: Penguin Press.

Shiva, Vandana. (1997) *Biopiracy: The Plunder of Nature and Knowledge.* Cambridge, MA: South End Press.

Stallman, Richard. (1999) 'The GNU Operating System & the Free Software Movement'. In C. DiBona, S. Ockman and M. Stone (eds) *Open Sources.* Sebastopol, CA: O'Reilly. 53–70.

Tehranian, John. (2007) 'Infringement Nation: Copyright Reform and the Law/Norm Gap'. *Utah Law Review* 3: 537–548.

Vaidhyanathan, Siva. (2004) *Anarchist in the Library: How the Clash between Freedom and Control is Hacking the Real World and Crashing the System.* New York: Basic Books.

Wald, Priscilla. (2005) 'What's in a Cell? John Moore's Spleen and the Language of Bioslavery'. *New Literary History* 36(2): 205–225.

Weisberg, Deena Skolnick, Frank C. Keil, Joshua Goodstein, Elizabeth Rawson and Jeremy R. Gray. (2008) 'The Seductive Allure of Neuroscience Explanations'. *Journal of Cognitive Neuroscience* 20(3): 470–477.

Wu, Tim. (2008) 'On Copyright's Authorship Policy'. *University of Chicago Legal Forum*: 335.

Zimmer, Carl. (2004) *Soul Made Flesh: The Discovery of the Brain – and How it Changed the World.* New York: Free Press.

37

Outer Space, Alien Life and Intellectual Property Protocols: An Opportunity to Rethink Life Patents

William R. Kramer

INTRODUCTION

Intellectual property (IP) policies associated with patenting organisms, their products and processes often conflict and generate a range of economic, political and social issues. Current life-seeking missions in outer space provide an opportunity to reconsider those issues relatively free of special interests that have made IP complex and uneven. Because extraterrestrial life has yet to be discovered, it has no current economic value, cultural significance or territorial connection, allowing for more equitable IP treatment. But from the moment of discovery forward there are predictable political and social pressures that would likely fragment attempts at implementing uniform policy regarding extraterrestrial discoveries. This chapter reviews standards and practices for life patents and international agreements regarding bioprospecting in global commons. The deep seabed, Antarctica and outer space are discussed as applicable models framing the concept of the Common Heritage of Humankind as expressed in the International Law of the Sea and the Outer Space Treaty. Who owns extraterrestrial life, and are the concepts of common heritage appropriate? In conclusion, the chapter offers recommendations for structuring IP regarding extraterrestrial life with the goal of generating interest and debate among the international IP and outer space exploration communities.

Legal and customary rights to the ownership of life have existed for millennia. During the last century, however, debates regarding questions of policies related to patenting living organisms, their parts, products and processes have dramatically intensified in parallel with advances in the technologies facilitating their discovery and use. Globalization of research, commercial production and marketing have increasingly shifted life patenting from a predominantly Western perspective to an international one. Disputes rooted in conflicting bioethical interpretations and cultural traditions of ownership and exploitation of life have exacerbated an already complex process. As the rate of new scientific and engineering discoveries in biology and biotechnology continues to accelerate, the number of life patent applications worldwide will predictably increase. The range of what bioscience and related fields may contribute to medical practice and pharmaceuticals, agriculture, robotics, information technologies, industrial processes, military applications and other areas over coming decades may be well beyond any capacity for prediction (Thieman and Palladino, 2004; Kurzweil, 2005). These elements combine to create a thicket of often conflicting intellectual property protocols and regulations.

Resolving such complex issues can be aided by creating thought experiments. These are hypothetical situations stripped of complexity to clarify analyses without the confusion and inconsistencies that often accompany lengthy histories of special cases and precedents. While the first formal documentation of the process of thought experimentation in the West comes from the early nineteenth century, the technique has likely existed in all cultures since humans gained the capacity of using language to speculate (Mach and Hiebert, 1997). In more modern use, such experiments generally follow the scientific method of proposing and then testing a hypothesis under an array of potential conditions. But whereas scientific hypothesis testing generally involves physical or mathematical testing, thought experiments are tested through reason, conjecture, deduction and, often, dialogue with others. As such, the experiments are primarily mental exercises and no physical manipulations are required. Most frequently, such experiments are impossible to actually perform outside of thought, and implementation is neither intended nor required for them to be beneficial in exploring potential consequences and benefits and evaluating possible outcomes and solutions. When successful, insights gained through the process can be imported from the hypothetical to the actual.

The 1967 Treaty on the Principles Governing the Activities of States in the Exploration and Use of Outer Space, Including the Moon and Other Celestial Bodies (the Outer Space Treaty, or OST) does not address intellectual property rights derived from any living system that may be encountered. There is no commonly accepted protocol for how to assign 'ownership' to any biological resource found in the ultimate commons, outer space.

Considering issues related to how life patents might be addressed in an extraterrestrial context may help in clarifying more mundane applications on Earth. Should extraterrestrial life be discovered on Mars, how might we structure a more efficient, equitable and consistent system for patenting that life and its potential products and processes? Such a circumstance may be less hypothetical than generally believed. Research regarding the potential for extraterrestrial life is a priority among NASA's missions (Bertka et al., 2007). The Viking investigations on Mars in the 1970s and the 2012 Mars Science Laboratory have both contributed to the search for life on that planet, and the Kepler telescope's planet-finding mission is assessing and cataloging planets in our galaxy that may have temperatures favorable for life as we know it. Other government-sponsored space organizations (such as the European Space Agency) share the search for life along with a growing number of private commercial ventures (such as Virgin Galactic and Odyssey Moon). Imagining the discovery of life on Mars provides a scenario that is especially applicable to a discussion of IP.

Should extraterrestrial life (defined throughout this chapter to exclude sapient life, those organisms such as humans and great apes that are capable of self-reflection) be discovered, many argue that existing IP restrictions and liberties regulating Earth's life are sufficient; life and its derivative products and processes will be patentable if other requirements for patenting are met, such as novelty (that the invention has not been patented previously), lack of obviousness to others, and utility. That assumption may be reassuring to some, but begs the question, '*which* IP restrictions and liberties?' There are many national and international regulatory protocols, and many conflict. Regardless, the issue remains largely unaddressed, as evidenced by the paucity of publications addressing IP in this context. Either it has not yet been identified or it has been recognized but not considered a foreseeable regulatory problem. Given the potential range of contentious questions that would evolve from someone's filing an extraterrestrial life patent application, the issue may become ensnarled for years awaiting resolution.

The search for extraterrestrial life provides an excellent opportunity to redefine IP practices related to life patents through thought experimentation. First, outer space offers a venue relatively free of the biases and traditions that have made such patents and the patenting process uneven and, at times, both unjust and counterproductive to invention. Second, while the existence of such life is currently hypothetical, it is possible and, arguably, probable (Bennett and Shostak, 2007). Finally, the OST is clear that outer space represents a commons. There are existing models of regulations and agreements regarding IP derived from commons areas here on Earth (such as the deep ocean floor and Antarctica) that provide starting points for crafting regulations for extraterrestrial IP. The successes and failures of such agreements as the Law of the Sea and the Antarctic Treaty System in addressing IP issues provide valuable lessons guiding future protocols for space. If issues of life patents can be resolved to any degree regarding space life, solutions may be applicable to the problems faced in regulating IP back here on Earth.

This chapter: (1) describes a few of the more pervasive problems with the current regulation of life patents; (2) summarizes several international agreements and regulations that address issues of regulating life patents, especially in international commons; and (3) proposes that the ongoing search for extraterrestrial life provides an opportunity for a thought experiment that may aid in structuring new approaches to the ownership of life, its products and processes. The chapter concludes with recommendations for regulating the exploitation of extraterrestrial life.

PROBLEMS AND INCONSISTENCIES IN LIFE PATENTS

The legal and regulatory mechanism for intellectual property ownership has become increasingly complex over the past century. Like policies regulating taxation, it can be influenced by special-interest politics and used as a tool to benefit some to the disadvantage of others. When IP is related to living organisms, regulatory biases and inconsistencies may be amplified by conflicting cultural traditions and even theological perspectives. This section briefly describes three problem areas in regulating life patents: the nature of biotechnological research and application, the lack of globally uniform and consistent law and application, and issues of indigenous claims of prior knowledge and commonly-held resources, such as those of the global commons.

Issues Regarding the Nature of Patenting Biotechnological Research

As with many other regulatory sectors, policies governing IP related to life must constantly strive to adapt to the novelty of the biotechnology that drives it, making consistent and predictable policy challenging. IP can be especially problematic when applied to rapidly evolving biotechnologies such as genomics and transgenetics, nanomedicine and sub-cellular chemistry and metabolism. Here, where the science is both new and complex, reliance on IP precedents becomes especially difficult. It may fall to the courts to not only interpret policy but to make policy. For example, in the US, patenting unaltered segments of human DNA was generally allowable until reversed by the US Supreme Court in June 2013. In that case, the Court disallowed Myriad Genetics' existing patents for isolated human genes associated with breast cancer (mutations of BRCA1 and BRCA2) by concluding that the genes were a product of nature and thus ineligible for patenting (DeVogue, 2013; US Supreme Court, 2013). However, some have speculated that the highly complex nature of the technology involved may be beyond the technical knowledge of the judges (Koerth-Baker, 2013). This points to an emerging problem that whereas biologists with the US Patent and Trademark Office (USPTO) are scientifically qualified to vet the technical quality of patent applications, the regulatory policies and legal precedents that rule their decisions are frequently outdated and difficult to apply to emerging technologies. The courts, however, while likely experts in policy, regulation and precedent, may lack the scientific expertise to adequately appreciate the technological implications of their decisions, especially as they apply to rapidly evolving fields. The resulting instability and uncertainty decrease the ability for industries to plan efficiently and generate frustration among the affected public.

The patenting process may also be counterproductive by promoting secrecy among competing researchers rather than facilitating the free exchange of information. This retards productivity and inhibits the creative benefit of collaboration. As provided in Albright (2004: 25), the *Journal of the American Medical Association* reported in 1997 that one-third of life science researchers surveyed had been denied access to research results from organizations and facilities other than their own. In 2002, the fraction had risen to nearly one half. This lack of access to data inhibits the ability to confirm the validity of published research. Publications can be held back awaiting patent filing, slowing the overall flow of information. This is problematic in a very competitive industry that measures progress in terms of a few months or even weeks. While there are arguments demonstrating the adverse impacts of patenting on creativity, many maintain that life patents encourage research cooperation (Bugos and Kevles, 1992). As with most such issues, a balance between the two is likely preferable.

Issues Regarding Conflicting Protocols and Regulations in Life Patents

The first US patent for a biological product was issued to Louis Pasteur in 1873 for his culture of yeast that was free of contamination. The yeast was not modified biologically in any way. Rather, Pasteur's invested work was purification, separating the desired yeast organism from its natural environment of contaminating bacteria and other non-target yeast strains. A later case that reinforced judicial opinion regarding the classes of living and life-produced products as patentable was adrenaline. Although a US patent was issued for the compound, the decision was challenged in court in 1911 on the grounds that adrenaline was discovered, not invented. The court upheld the patent and explained:

> Takamine (the patent holder) was the first to make (adrenaline) available for any use by removing it from the other gland-tissue in which it was found, and, while it is of course possible logically to call this a purification of the principle, it became for every practical purpose a new thing commercially and therapeutically. (Dutfield, 2003: 115)

Precedent was set that an extracted, naturally occurring compound could be patentable if it was purified and had the requisite utility and novelty.

The scope of life patents expanded greatly in 1980 with the landmark *Diamond v. Chakrabarty* decision. Here, the US Supreme Court upheld a patent on a genetically modified bacterium designed to break down the chemical structure of hydrocarbons found in petroleum oils through the bacterium's altered metabolic processes. The Court ruled that the resulting bacterium was not a 'product of nature' and was, therefore, an invention and thus patentable. In the majority decision, Chief Justice Warren E. Berger wrote, 'We have cautioned that courts should not read into the patent laws limitations and conditions which the legislature has not expressed', and that 'in choosing such expansive terms as "manufacture" and "composition of matter", modified by the comprehensive "any", Congress plainly contemplated that the patent laws would be given wide scope' (Justia, 1980). Dissenting Justices, however, opined that Congressional intent was clear in not permitting the patenting of bacteria, citing the 1930 Plant Patent Act (the first American protection for new varieties of plants, essentially those created through cuttings and grafts rather than through selective sexual breeding) and the 1970 Plant Variety Protection Act (7 USC §§ 2321–2582), which provides patent protection for the seeds of hybridized plants (Lumelsky, 2004). Congress, whatever its intent, did not expressly forbid patents for living organisms of any kind.

The USPTO maintains that while a patent on a gene covers the isolated and purified gene it does not apply to the gene as it occurs in nature. As such, for example, naturally occurring genes in the human could not be patented *in vivo*, inside the human. However, if extracted and purified or biochemically altered in such a way as to make that gene useful to some other purpose, say, disease research, it could be patented. It follows that the altered gene could be re-inserted back into the original donor who would then contain a mix of both patented and unpatented genes that originated from their body. 'By examining these legal precedents, it becomes clear that the difference between a discovery and an invention is a difference in degree rather than in kind, and when the human and material resources inserted in research reach a certain level, the product of such research is protected under patent law' (Mathur and Dua, 2005: pages unnumbered).

In stating its defense in the *Diamond* case, the US government cautioned the Court that allowing Diamond to patent a bacterium would open the door to patenting genetically engineered human life, a 'prospect sounding dangerously close to slavery' (Banner, 2011: 253). The Court was clear that humans were excluded from any patenting, but parts of humans such as genome segments were patentable. However, any organism other than humans may generally be patentable if it does not occur in nature and if it meets other patenting criteria (such as novelty and utility). In this context, 'organism' includes bacteria, plants, animals and other forms of life. However, hybrid humans are not addressed. For example, insertion of a human gene into a fish is allowable. The question avoided, however, was at what point does the percentage of human genes employed in such a creation violate prohibitions on patenting humans? While a mouse might be engineered through the addition of less than one-tenth of 1 percent of a human genome (as was done with the human Foxp2 gene for speech), would the same rules allowing patenting be permitted if 10 percent of a human genome were engineered and inserted to form a transgenetic chimpanzee egg (Enard et al., 2009)? Eighty percent? Although a US patent application filed by Jeremy Rifkin and Stuart Newman in 1997 for a human-chimpanzee chimera was rejected (they wished to secure a patent on the process of creating a chimpanzee that was genetically up to 50 per cent human to block others from pursuing such transgenic research), these kinds of questions will have to be left to future courts or a legislature bold enough to tackle them (Magnani 1999). But they demonstrate that IP law is open to broad interpretation when technology progresses at a quicker pace than regulation.

The US is certainly not alone in adapting IP policy to emerging biotechnology. India's Patents Act of 1970, section 3(j), stipulates that 'plants and animals in whole or in part thereof other than microorganisms but including seeds, varieties and species and essentially biological processes for production or propagation of plants and animals' are not patentable. India's patent law is in accord with the Agreement on Trade-Related Aspects of Intellectual Property Rights (TRIPS) at 27(3)(b) which sets a minimum standard by stating that members may exclude from patentability all species of plants and animals except microorganisms. This creates a continuing source of confusion, however, for neither the Patent Act and its subsequent iterations nor TRIPS clearly defines 'microorganism'. The definition of microorganism is vague in other nations' statutes as well. In the vernacular, microorganism simply means any uni- or multicellular living thing that is small enough that it is not easily seen without the aid of magnification. While all bacteria are too small to be seen with the unaided eye, under favorable conditions many microorganisms, such as larger protozoans, can easily be seen without technological assistance. Most existing laws are clear that any genetically modified microorganism (for example, a modified bacterium) is patentable, but the regulatory reliance on size alone to determine what may be patented (whether genetically modified or not) may be entirely irrelevant should an application for patenting microscopic extraterrestrial life be filed. As addressed later in this chapter, such Earth-centric concepts as size may have little to do with the nature or complexity of any life discovered.

Significant confusion results from differing patenting regulations between states. The Indian position, for example, agrees with the USPTO regarding microorganisms, that plants and non-human animals are patentable if removed from their wild condition and genetically modified. However, in opposition to the USPTO, India maintains that any process for the medicinal, surgical, curative, prophylactic, diagnostic, therapeutic or other treatment of human beings or similar such process for treatment in animals are not patentable. For example, a technique for growing a replacement human organ *in vitro* would generally be patentable in the US but not in India (Gabriel, 2012). The European Patent Office adds additional ethical caveats to patenting living organisms. Applications for patenting genetically-engineered animals there are denied where the animal would suffer as a result of such engineering in excess of the potential benefit of its use for humans. The European standard arose as a result of the 1985 application to patent the 'Harvard Mouse', genetically engineered to develop cancers to assist cancer researchers. While the application was originally rejected as immoral in Europe because of trauma to the mouse, it was granted 18 years later after further consideration of the degree of suffering in comparison to its potential research and human health benefits. The mouse was granted a patent in the US in 1988, representing the first higher form of life to be patented. In the US, genetically modified organisms are generally patentable because they do not exist in nature (so are novel creations), are certainly not obvious and, where the patent is goal oriented, have credible utility. The variations between the US, India and Europe represent a small sample of the unresolved issues over the kinds of life that can and cannot be patented, conflicting intra- and international jurisdictions, cultural and ethical perspectives and related questions.

Issues Regarding Indigenous Claims and Benefit-Sharing

Bioprospecting, the practice of purposefully collecting natural biological materials in foreign areas and then transporting them back to one's home, 'is as old a concept as medicine itself' (Shankar, 2008: 1). In the modern context, however, and seen in its most favorable light, bioprospecting is the process of: (1) searching for, collecting, and subsequently analyzing naturally occurring biological organisms and/or their products to determine their agricultural or biochemical properties for either direct use by humans or synthesizing and mass-producing target compounds; and/or (2) gathering indigenous knowledge or practices regarding the processes that enable the target organism, its processes or products to be used or enhanced (Pan, 2006: iv). Most often, products are subsequently used as pharmaceuticals or cosmetics, as crops and crop-related agricultural materials and in industrial and manufacturing processes. Frequently, bioprospecting is initiated by industrialized or otherwise technologically advanced nations in countries that have little or none of the technology required to fully capitalize on this process.

Here, the term bioprospecting is generally limited to the two actions listed above where the goal is securing a patent. Generally excluded are expeditions and similar activities that sample the biological environment and organisms for educational or purely scientific purposes, for vouchering, determining environmental components, tracking environmental trends and similar actions.

Regardless of motive, however, the process of bioprospecting may culminate in patenting a compound and/or process in the home nation of the prospector or employer, whether commercial, academic, research or other.

While there is no country that permits patents for a naturally occurring higher organism (whether it has been previously described or not), in the US and many other countries patents on specific chemicals isolated or purified from organisms regardless of taxonomic status can be awarded where such uses or processes are novel (for example, the isolation of insulin from dogs in 1922). In most cases, even though the effects of a biological source (such as chewing willow bark to relieve a headache), methods to increase efficacy and extraction methods may have been known by indigenous peoples for centuries, the metabolic pathways, enzymatic activities and biochemical properties of such compounds are not part of that knowledge. As such, those are generally patentable. The willow bark compound used by many cultures for centuries was patented as aspirin by Bayer in 1900.

Issues Regarding Colonizing Perspectives and Biopiracy

The concept of *terra nullius* (unclaimed land – land belonging to no one) is a fixture in Western law dating from Roman times. Until the mid-20th century, however, it was liberally applied not only to clearly uninhabited and unclaimed lands, such as Antarctica, but also to lands inhabited by those determined by Western colonizers as not having sovereign status. For example, Australia was determined by Britain to be *terra nullius* in the 19th century even though it was clearly populated by indigenous peoples. The 1835 proclamation by Governor Bourke legally established that the land belonged to no one prior to the arrival of the British (Fry, 1946). Aboriginal populations were entirely discounted. A fuller definition of the term *terra nullius*, therefore, would continue that the land is not owned or claimed by any sovereign as territory and that the definition of the legitimacy of such a sovereign is to be determined by the potential settler or colonizer.

A similar concept is also applied to knowledge that is held by non-Westerners, knowledge that may not be recognized as real or legitimate until blessed with a Western patent or other form of cultural possession. This, then, provides justification (and a legal remedy) for market control, a *fait accompli* in favor of Western commercial and political interests. Prior to the September 2012 effective date of pertinent portions of the America Invents Act of 2011 (AIA), language demonstrating the colonizing aspects of US patent law was provided in the US Patent Act of 1952, 35 United States Code Section 102, regarding the definition of prior art in the US and in foreign publications:

> A Person shall be entitled to a patent unless: A. The invention was known or used by others in this country or patented or described in a publication in this or a foreign country before the invention thereof by the applicant for patent, or; B. The invention was patented or described in a trade publication in this or a foreign country or in public use or on sale in this country more than one year prior to the date of the application for patent in the United States.

Enactment of the AIA modified that portion of the Patent Act to read:

> A person shall be entitled to a patent unless, (1) the claimed invention was patented, described in a printed publication, *or in public use, on sale, or otherwise available to the public* before the effective filing date of the claimed invention; or (2) the claimed invention was described in a patent issued under section 151, or in an application for patent published or deemed published under section 122(b), in which the patent or application, as the case may be, names another inventor and was effectively filed before the effective filing date of the claimed invention. (emphasis added)

Prior to these modifications, it followed that if prior knowledge was held in another country but not published, it would generally have been patentable, able to be claimed as property by the patent applicant. Traditional knowledge (TK) that was not published and not known in the US was analogous to the aboriginal peoples of Australia under British rule; they do not exist for consideration in a legal framework that would compete with colonization. Patent law clearly provided a tool for colonization of information similar to the way that subjugation of indigenous populations is a tool for territorial colonization. US policy is not immune to this potentially paternalistic and condescending perspective. In 2011, the USPTO's Copyright and Intellectual Property Services' Copyright and IP Officer, Kathy Moore, defended IP and challenged the accusation that it was a form of theft.

> Just because products and technologies based on TK have been collectively held for a long time, does not mean they cannot be treated as an IP. The publication of illustrated, traditional folk stories is a simple example which is always popular with children. If indigenous people don't find some way of protecting their cultural heritage, it could disappear altogether. (*Fiji Times* 2011: online)

Unethical bioprospecting has fostered the concept of biopiracy, '(i) the theft, misappropriation of, or unfair free-riding on, genetic resources and/or traditional knowledge through the patent system; and (ii) the unauthorized and uncompensated collection for commercial ends of genetic resources and/or traditional knowledge' (Dutfield, 2004: 2). 'Biopiracy rejects the legitimacy of bioprospecting in its entirety. (In) its extreme it holds that all knowledge is public and free' (Pan, 2006: 3). Also included in the derogatory context of the term is patenting without respect to novelty demonstrated by previous use and TK (Smith, 2004). Combining bioprospecting and biopiracy as one and the same, some claim that both are representative of 'an initiative of the North to globalize the control, management, and biological diversity of resources which lie primarily in the Third World' and represents, therefore, an extension of the inertia of colonialism (Shiva, 1997, as quoted in Pan, 2006: 3). Further, Shiva states:

> The IPR (intellectual property rights) regimes in a digital age carry the mask of earlier times, when patents were licenses to plunder and pirate. The primary difference between patents in a digital age and patents in the gunboat age is that the new technologies can colonize life itself, while the older technologies could only colonize land. But patents and IPRs in the digital age share the earlier history of patents as instruments of conquest, which deny prior rights and erase prior histories of cultures. (Shiva, 2000: 501)

The discussion of bioprospecting brings us back to how we might move forward into outer space. As space becomes accessible to mainly Western countries, how might extraterrestrial life be approached in an equitable manner, given the history of commercial colonization through IP?

Issues Regarding Taking from the Global Commons

Garrett Hardin's remarkable 1968 paper 'The tragedy of the commons' commented on the futility of attempts to avoid the problems associated with human overpopulation. He noted 27 years later that the debate had generally shifted from population to economics and the environment, but that the core of his original conclusion still held – any consumptive use of the resources of the commons must be regulated if they are to be maintained (Hardin, 1995). However, the answer to the question he posed in 1968, 'How do you legislate temperance?' in taking from a commons remains as elusive as ever.

Humans have been able to significantly affect ecosystems and the life they support for millennia. It has only been with the advent of more modern technologies, however, that dramatic impacts on global commons areas such as the oceans have been realized (Kurlansky, 1997). As a result, international agreements and similar protocols regulating the conservation and exploitation of biological and mineral resources in these areas have been implemented.

The Convention on Biological Diversity (CBD) was a product of the world conference convened in Rio de Janeiro in 1992 (the 'Earth

Summit') to address, in part, the widely recognized need for international cooperation to foster the conservation of biological diversity as stated in the Preamble of the Convention (Convention on Biological Diversity, 1992). As part of the United Nations Environment Programme (UNEP), the CBD pledges that maintaining such diversity is a common human concern and an integral part of the development process that is of interest to the UNEP and other UN programs. To accomplish that objective, it strives to implement policy to conserve biological diversity, sustain the function of ecosystem components (through principles of multiple and sustained use) and foster the fair and equitable sharing of benefits arising from genetic resources. This final goal is most pertinent to the regulation of bioprospecting and profiting though extraction of global (and perhaps extraterrestrial) commons' resources.

While the CBD addresses bioprospecting within a state's political jurisdiction, it does not provide guidance related to actions within global commons. The International Union for the Conservation of Nature (IUCN) defines the global commons as 'those parts of the Earth's surface beyond national jurisdictions – notably the open ocean and the living resources found there – or held in common – notably the atmosphere. The only landmass that may be regarded as part of the global commons is Antarctica' (IUCN, 1980: Chapter 18–1, pages unnumbered). In the modern sense, global commons areas generally were not claimed either because they were inaccessible or because they offered no tangible asset worth the effort and cost of settlement or exploitation. International waters and their floors (managed under the UN Law of the Sea Treaty and the International Seabed Authority) as well as Antarctica (governed under the Antarctic Treaty System) provide two significant examples of how international treaties have been charged to manage biological resources and bioprospecting within these international commons. They provide useful models for crafting policies regarding bioprospecting in outer space, the ultimate commons.

Still, the basic tenets of the Convention are not new. The concept had been proposed by the IUCN a decade earlier and other aspects of the CBD had their origins in other UN agreements and protocols. The Convention was unique among previous conservation-goaled documents in that it was legally binding on signatories; parties were obliged to implement its provisions. As of 2013, the CBD had been ratified by all countries in the world except for the US (which has signed, but not ratified), Andorra, and the Holy See. It is likely the US withheld support due to concerns within its own borders regarding perceived over-extension of federal control of private lands rather than as a reaction against maintenance of biodiversity (Sovereignty International, 1998). The US supports the CBD's emphasis on programmatic ecosystem approaches to integrated management, conservation and sustainable use (Blaustein, 2006).

Recognizing the economic potential of bioprospecting to unfairly exploit the resources of the commons, Article 1 of the CBD urges the promotion of 'fair and equitable sharing of benefits arising out of the utilization of genetic resources, including by appropriate access to genetic resources' (CBD, 1992: 3). While statements incorporated in the various documents imposed obligations on signatories regarding access to biological materials and directed that countries address the benefits of profit sharing through royalties and other instruments, few states have implemented the protocols. However, as described by Laird et al. (2007), where CBD-negotiated benefits packages are designed they typically include monetary benefits based on a per sample basis, periodic milestone payments, and royalties on net sales and licensing agreements in addition to non-monetary benefits such as training, capacity-building, research exchanges, equipment, technology transfer and joint publications.

> Groups with the most experience in benefit-sharing generally emphasize the importance of non-monetary benefits and 'front-loading' benefit-sharing packages. Front-loading benefit-sharing packages ensures that provider countries receive a stream of benefits through the discovery and development phases, given the small odds of any one partnership yielding a commercial product and

> the fact that all products will not necessarily be billion-dollar 'blockbusters' generating large royalties, or that in most industries products rarely, if ever, achieve this status. (Laird et al., 2007: 118)

International discussions on the protection of TK, access and benefit-sharing in relation to genetic resources continue, with work being conducted by the World Intellectual Property Organization (WIPO) and the World Trade Organization (WTO) in the context of the 1994 TRIPS and Article 10 of the 2001 International Treaty on Plant Genetic Resources for Food and Agriculture. As their mission statement provides, WIPO was created by the UN to 'promote innovation and creativity for the economic, social and cultural development of all countries, through a balanced and effective international intellectual property system' among their 185 Member States (WIPO, 2012). WIPO generally supports both defensive and positive protection approaches to aid in directing derived benefits to TK holders, thus avoiding having them diverted elsewhere within government.

CBD protocols also have the potential to hinder scientific research and resulting publications. For example, should a researcher enter an area to study a plant and subsequently publish notes regarding the location, ecology, biochemical details, ethnobotanical uses or other data regarding that species, there may be no immediate or traceable financial IP-related profit from that publication. However, where subsequent development of patentable products is enabled in whole or part by the publication of that research, no mechanism exists for garnering royalties. 'But as indigenous peoples' groups, governments, and others seek greater control over their knowledge and resources, there is increasing pressure to limit or restrict publication of certain types of data, or at the very least [to require] informed consent before doing so' (Blaustein, 2006: 563, quoting Sarah Laird of 'People and Plants International'). CBD protocols are insufficient to resolve this conflict between the researcher's desire to publish scientific information and the potential for that publication to lead to future profit-generating IP. Once published, access to and use of research data are outside most researchers' control, and such control is counter to the purpose of publication, where the widest possible dissemination is sought. To require a researcher to gain the consent of indigenous populations prior to publication of findings would likely be unmanageable in addition to slowing subsequent research.

Most pertinent to bioprospecting and property rights, however, is that CBD aids in securing rights to control access to *genetic* resources for the countries in which those resources are located. This allows less developed countries to better benefit from their resources and TK. Where genetic resources are at issue, CBD stipulates that bioprospectors must obtain informed consent from the destination's government prior to gaining access and must share the products of their work with that country. However, CBD has no legal enforcement capacity. That is left to the legislatures of individual national and local governments.

There are weaknesses in IP related to biological resources both within and outside global commons. Existing patenting regulations conflict and the various treaties and agreements that have attempted to implement fair use have generally failed:

- categorization of life into patentable and unpatentable entities based on factors such as size and perceived ethical or moral status are flawed;
- protocols differ from one state to another, making uniform application under current patenting regimes very difficult;
- indigenous claims of ownership are difficult to document and may retard research; and
- the relationship between life patents and the biological resources of the Earth's global commons is unclear.

SEEKING SOLUTIONS – OUTER SPACE AS AN INTELLECTUAL PROPERTY THOUGHT EXPERIMENT

The Outer Space Treaty does not address intellectual property rights derived from any extraterrestrial living organism that may be encountered and there is no commonly accepted protocol for how to assign 'ownership' to any biological resources that might be discovered in this ultimate commons. It has been argued that should such life be discovered, legal treatments available for their exploitation will seamlessly mirror the restrictions and liberties found on Earth, and that derivative products and processes will be patentable if other requirements are met. But as previously described, the regulation of patents regarding biological resources here on Earth is strongly associated with several of the most significant problems faced by IP:

- how can regulations governing life patents adapt to the rapidly emerging issues of biotechnology and the uniqueness of their potentials?
- how can the inefficiencies of multiple, overlapping IP jurisdictions be resolved?
- how might resources of the global commons (here, expanded to include the extraterrestrial commons) be more equitably addressed under a concept of 'common heritage of humankind'?

The Biological Nature of Extraterrestrial Life

Whilst it is possible that any extraterrestrial life may share some of the same biochemical and structural properties as life on Earth, given the significantly different environments of Mars or any other known place in our solar system it is unlikely that any organism discovered will be identical to anything found on Earth. Whatever may be discovered will represent a new organism. As a result, it may be extremely difficult to taxonomically classify potential life within any existing phylogenetic system. The specific IP definitions of what kinds of organisms can generally be patented (for example, a purified strain of yeast) and those that cannot (unaltered 'higher' organisms) will, therefore, not likely apply.

What remains is that current IP statutes generally hold that 'microbes' can be considered for patenting where other qualifying criteria are met. Taken at its obvious meaning, microbes are organisms that either cannot generally be seen without technological enhancement, such as a microscope, or can be seen when concentrated in great numbers, such as in a bacterial colony. 'Microbe' is not a taxonomic classification and has little scientific meaning. It follows, then, that what can be patentable and what cannot is a matter of size. On Earth, size is important in describing our ethical and evolutionary relationship to other organisms; in space, it may be totally irrelevant. An organism's size is an evolutionary adaptation responding to varied environments and is undoubtedly influenced by gravity unless it is aquatic or otherwise suspended. The qualifier 'microbe' loses its IP rationale in the extraterrestrial context.

Similarly, as evidenced by the European reluctance to patent the 'Harvard Mouse', patentability is influenced by the perceived ability of the organism in question to be sentient, to experience physical pain or emotional distress as part of the process of making it a commodity. As with size and microbes, our perception of sentience is a product of our experience with Earth's organisms. Ethical sentiments vary widely, changing with culture and time. Like size, assessing degrees of sentience would not be applicable for extraterrestrial IP.

Considering the challenges that will emerge upon encountering extraterrestrial organisms provides an opportunity to redefine life in the context of IP and reconsider the conflicting restrictions and allowances we apply on Earth. As a result, we may have a broader but more consistent and permanent definition, less encumbered by taxonomic and cultural histories and biases.

Prior Discovery, Traditional Knowledge and Utility

Extraterrestrial life's place within the context of our cultures has not been established, so there is no possibility of conflicting issues of prior discovery or TK. We share no history with extraterrestrial lifeforms; they are neither heroes nor villains in our cultures, not even in the context of a bacterial pathogen.

Value

Any extraterrestrial life will have evolved to adapt to an environment where temperatures, radiation type and intensity, gravity, pressure, atmospheric composition and other factors may imbue it with structural, genetic or biochemical properties of considerable commercial potential. Especially for private space ventures, there would be an expectation of financial profit from such a find, given the considerable expense and liability of successfully launching a vessel, finding life and capitalizing on that find. But there is no guarantee of commercial success. This provides a unique situation for our hypothetical thought experiment. Although concerted efforts are underway to find it, the property in question does not currently exist and may never exist; if found, it may have considerable commercial value or almost none. There is also the chance that it may pose a liability to other activities. These unknowns foster the crafting of policies that may be more equitable in the sharing of profits, risks and liabilities.

Territorial Real Property Claims

In developing the hypothetical scenario, issues of life as IP must consider ownership or control of real property, as well. Generally, the entity that claims the land owns the resources it contains, whether living or mineral. Presently, spacefaring nations concur that outer space and the planets, moons and asteroids it contains represent a form of commons similar to the Antarctic or the seabeds in international waters. As stated in Article II of the 1967 OST, 'Outer space, including the moon and other celestial bodies, is not subject to national appropriation by claim of sovereignty, by means of use or occupation, or by any other means'. However, others interpret the Treaty as silent regarding private ownership of real property and argue that it specifically prohibits sovereign claims only; private acquisition is not blocked (Hearsey, 2008; Reynolds, 2008; Wasser and Jobes, 2008; Pop 2009). A third position is that it permits 'functional' real property distinguishable from deeded real property. Here, a sovereign may control, but does not own, the land on which it builds or lands within a defined occupied and used compound. This would not infer territorial sovereignty in any form in that no title would be provided, but would allow for management of the land (Dalton, 2010). As we move from state-sponsored to private space ventures and commercialization, resolution of property issues becomes critical. Ownership of personal property, such as mined ores, is of great concern to private industries looking to space and the costs and liabilities it incurs. Legal and policy ambiguities can certainly be a disincentive to private investment (Cooper, 2003; Hertzfeld and von der Dunk, 2005). A fourth perspective is that extraterrestrial real property be placed within trusteeships that exist apart from government or private control.

Compounding the issue of real property is the second of the two overarching international space treaties, the 1979 Agreement Governing the Activities of States on the Moon and Other Celestial Bodies (the Moon Treaty). It applies not only to Earth's Moon but to all bodies in our Solar System except the Earth itself. Set in its final form a decade after humans first landed on the Moon, Article 11 of the Moon Treaty closely mirrors the OST in stating: 'The Moon is not subject to national appropriation by any claim of sovereignty, by means of use or occupation, or by any other means'. But it continues: 'Neither the surface nor the subsurface of the Moon, nor any part thereof or natural resources in place, shall become property of any State, international intergovernmental or non-governmental organization, national organization or non-governmental entity or of any natural person'. The intent here is clear, that the land itself shall not become property. Inclusion of the phrase regarding natural resources 'in place' may be open to legal interpretation. Once removed from 'place,' however, the status of the resources (ostensibly including living resources) becomes less clear. But while OST was ratified by 100 nations, including all spacefaring nations, the Moon Treaty has been ratified by only 17, none of which are spacefaring, making it less consequential from a regulatory standpoint. It is considered by many to be a failed international law that will have little relevance to space activities until tested in court by an attempt at a property claim (Listner, 2012).

Both treaties are clear that extraterrestrial real estate cannot be claimed as sovereign property by any nation. However, whether outer space belongs to *no one* or *everyone* is another issue.

Common Heritage of Humankind

Where novel biological resources are discovered in uninhabited regions of the global commons (such as Antarctica or deep seabeds under international waters), questions of TK and novelty are generally unchallengeable and patenting may be nearly guaranteed. In such circumstances and where supported by regulation, a portion of the profits generated by the resulting patent may be required to be used for conserving that environment based on benefit-sharing or royalty formulas. Although such arrangements have not been overwhelmingly successful due to conflicting bureaucracies, similar financial arrangements may be appropriate for extraterrestrial finds. Existing protocols governing bioprospecting in the global commons may provide insights for extraterrestrial application.

Concepts pertaining specifically to the 'Common Heritage of Mankind' (CHM) (synonymous with the more recent and gender neutral 'common heritage of humankind') in relation to exploitation of resources within commons are present in the 1967 OST. They were strengthened when drafted into the 1979 Moon Treaty and the subsequent 1982 United Nations Convention on the Law of the Sea (LOS) regarding seabed resources. However, its definition remains vague and somewhat contentious. The term is not defined in a legal context and was likely inserted to represent aspirations for future policies and legislation (Viikari, 2002: 21). When applied to redistribution of wealth, CHM tends to be highly politicized, as evident in Jennifer Frakes' assessment that 'the manner in which the CHM principle will be used will depend on differing perceptions of reality' (2003: 409).

In general, developed states hold that areas where CHM applies are available for common use within the context of traditional freedom of the high seas and that conservation and management may be required to guarantee the continued availability of renewable resources for future generations. Less developed states (typically those without the access, technology or means to exploit Earth's CHM resources to a significant degree) understandably prefer that CHM be applied in a way that prevents exploiters from monopolizing resources. In general, they wish the option to actively participate in management and ensure that they benefit from any profits earned by exploited resources through benefit-sharing (Viikari, 2002; Frakes, 2003).There is little question as to why there are conflicting interpretations of CHM considering non-treaty states', treaty parties', interest groups' and others' (as Frakes states) differing perceptions of reality.

A significant commonality among both developed and developing states is that they ultimately wish to see a degree of exploitation. Without exploitation, neither benefit; with exploitation, developed states likely will benefit and developing states may. It is the disposition of exploitation's profits and the nature of its sharing that are largely in dispute. While all interpretations hold that CHM requires common management to ensure resource conservation for the use and benefit of future generations and non-appropriation as real property or territory, if or how CHM is to be applied in the context of outer-space-derived

IP remains vague. What is clear, however, is that although access to the sea floor resources is limited only by possession of a floating dredge affordable to most of the poorest of states, commercial access to Mars is well beyond their means. When the commons of outer space is only accessible to a very few, it is more difficult to regulate as a commons.

Notably, the common heritage principle regarding resources was first formally introduced to the UN in 1967 (the same year as the OST) regarding ocean resources in UN Document A/6695 (Payoyo, 1997). It was presented as a request to the UN General Assembly, 22nd Session, on 18 August of that year to add as an agenda item: 'Declaration and treaty concerning the reservation exclusively for peaceful purposes of the sea-bed and the ocean floor, underlying the seas beyond the limits of present national jurisdiction, and the use of their resources in the interests of mankind'. When similar common heritage language was added to the OST regarding extraterrestrial resources its only support initially came from a small number of nations (including the United Kingdom and the US). It was recognized, however, that it would be extremely difficult to determine profits in consideration of the diverse sources of expenses and liabilities incurred in identifying, extracting, transporting and refining the resource. In addition, designation of a depository for royalties to be paid by those reaping commercial profits from space exploitation and methods for disbursement has never been determined. It may have seemed premature to focus on addressing these OST details in 1967 because of the likely perception that commercial exploitation may be many decades away, well beyond practical political horizons. With the Apollo Moon landing only two years later in 1969, the possibility of space exploitation may have seemed more of a near-future reality. The more stringent and restrictive language of the 1979 Moon Treaty may have been viewed as a significant threat impeding space development and so was largely avoided by potential signatories (Christol, 1999). Politically, it is more palatable to agree to broad concepts such as CHM when details of the consequences, such as those of benefit-sharing, are decades away. When greater detail was provided in the Moon Treaty and especially LOS, the consequences were more palpable and immediate.

Although the Antarctic Treaty (AT) does not mention CHM specifically, it does include language reflecting its spirit that may be applicable to outer space IP:

- sovereign states and private actors are blocked from establishing territories or otherwise procuring real property;
- there is freedom of scientific investigation that is not geographically confined by sovereign boundaries;
- information flow is encouraged both within and outside the scientific community that contributes to achieving a degree of benefit-sharing;
- mineral extraction for any but scientific purposes is prohibited;
- conservation requirements serve to acknowledge preservation of Antarctic resources for future generations.

Inclusion of these requirements, prohibitions and intents has not prevented developing states from having additional CHM concerns. Many still view the AT as the government and management of a globally-shared resource by a minority of mostly developed states (Frakes 2003).

Despite its often conflicting definitions and applications, however, CHM's intent is clear: the benefits provided to some through exploitation of the resources of the commons, whether from seabeds, Antarctica or potentially Mars, should be shared with non-participating states. Methods include disbursing monetary royalties collected from profits or providing other forms of assistance, such as access, technical expertise, equipment or training.

In the context of IP and extraterrestrial discoveries, the vagueness of CHM allows for creativity in drafting details for its implementation. As with other factors addressed in this chapter, these details should be addressed prior to any discovery, before valuation of the find or knowledge of what state or corporation is sponsoring the discovery. This allows for a greater degree of justice less affected by special interest influences.

Patent Pools

Limited physical access to outer space may create a patenting environment prone to monopolization of resources. The problem may be exacerbated by the nature of the new technologies of space exploration and may contribute to the anticommons effect of repressing, rather than stimulating, invention. But past problems of access to emerging technologies have been successfully mitigated and provide options that may help in the outer space context.

When the US entered the First World War they had fewer than 100 aircraft; France had over 2,000 and Germany had 1,000. Although the Wrights had patented a mechanism for controlling pitch, roll and yaw in 1906, the following decade was fraught with patent infringement suits brought against those who attempted to use 'their' designs (Albright, 2004: 145). Their patent served to impede, not stimulate, the advancement of both the technology and industry (Porter, 2012). The US government broke the logjam with the creation of the Manufacturers Aircraft Association (MAA), creating a patent 'pool' (Dykman, 1964). Aircraft manufacturers paid royalties into the pool and shared patents, a critical compromise enabling the development of American air power. However, this also resulted in the creation of a quasi-monopoly and blocked non-members from experimenting with aircraft of their own design that employed patented technology. The problem was remedied, in part, by placing the MAA under the US Department of Commerce. Although now regulated, information was more easily shared among a wider user group. Federalizing also facilitated substantial federal funding for the industry, and the federal government was by far the industry's primary customer. Lastly, as aircraft tend to fail in dramatic ways, liabilities were shared, in part, by the federal government. The MAA provided a model for similar developments in space exploration in the 1950s with the creation of NASA. This model of shared patents and liabilities provides some guidance for approaching the problem of patenting extraterrestrial life.

RECOMMENDATIONS FOR INTELLECTUAL PROPERTY REGARDING EXTRATERRESTRIAL LIFE

Given the limitations of current national and international regulations in equitably and efficiently addressing foreseeable patenting issues related to the discovery of extraterrestrial life, how might these problems be addressed and resolved? The novelty and hypothetical nature of the situation lends itself well to creative solutions.

Leave Taxonomy Out of IP Regulation

Taxonomic classifications are impermanent, and even for well-described species with millennia-old relationships with humans, hierarchies are constantly challenged. As the ability to detect and recognize novel life forms is improved by advancing technology and as our reach to new environments expands not only to remote areas of the Earth but to Mars and beyond, regulations, treaties and similar instruments should remain as adaptive as possible to the biological novelty we may discover. Any IP or similar policy should not attempt to classify new life for differential treatment. Terms such as microbial or even sentient, for example, may be meaningless in an extraterrestrial legal context.

Withhold Applications for Patents for Alien Life (At Least Initially)

On Earth, patents have been awarded for products resulting from exploitation of deep seabed organisms. Concerns have been expressed to and by CBD that unrestricted use will decrease biodiversity and, importantly, result in unequal sharing of benefits derived from a common resource. Such patents may have a significant anticommons effect on innovation and research. 'Some resources are too important, in terms of the present and future public benefit, to be subject to strong intellectual property protection' (Oldham and South, 2004: 39). While many in the space development industry do not question their ability to patent any life they may discover as they would microbes on Earth, these are assumptions. Prohibiting the patenting of extraterrestrial life outright, at least initially, is worthy of strong consideration.

The first organism discovered will be extremely rare regardless of whether it represents the only one of its kind in the universe or shares its world with trillions of identical others. If the latter, at first recognition we would not know of its numbers or distribution. Regardless, the first will be of immense potential worth. As diverse as life on Earth is, all forms here have basic biochemical processes in common. For example, all life employs DNA and RNA, all are carbon-based, use only five of over 20 nucleotides in DNA and RNA and follow the same base-pairing rules. It is very possible that new life discovered may employ novel metabolic pathways, enzymatic processes, energy storage mechanisms or other biological functions never described previously. To allow the patenting of any of these from that initial find may confer a *de facto* patent on those similar processes exhibited by all other life on that planet. The incredible power of such a patent would be counterproductive to subsequent research.

Hence, the argument runs, prohibit any immediate patenting of discoveries. Later, after the natural status of the organism has been determined, prohibitions could be reconsidered and, if warranted, modified. But the initial collection should not be eligible for patenting.

Place Restrictions on any Patents Granted

Should patents be granted, limit their scope or duration. For example, consider patents that allow some commercial exploitation but free access to the organism by any qualified party for scientific research. Or, limit the kinds of commercial uses that would be protected by the patent. For example, permit the patenting of a metabolic process that allows an organism to rapidly repair cellular damage done by radiation, but disallow patenting of the gene sequence (assuming the organism has genes!) that allows that metabolic process. Make basic physiological and biochemical data derived from the find, such as a DNA sequence, widely and freely available.

Require Specimen Vouchering with Broad Accessibility

The 1977 Budapest Treaty on the International Recognition of the Deposit of Microorganisms for the Purposes of Patent Procedure established a system of International Depositary Authorities (IDAs) for vouchering. Prior to applying for a patent for an organism such as a bacterium, a voucher specimen may be sent to IDA. However, the collection is not a public facility. Specimens generally remain under the legal control of the depositor, and others wishing to use the specimen must have their permission. This favors the patent seeker by aiding in establishing that they were the first to record the find, but it also sequesters the find. While it may be argued that the extraordinary effort required for, say, a private enterprise to venture into space, collect the specimen and return it to Earth justifies singular control of the specimen, it can also be argued that decades of public sponsorship of space research enabled the private investor's accomplishment.

As developed by the WIPO's Intergovernmental Committee on Intellectual Property and Genetic Resources, Traditional Knowledge and Folklore, any living entity or biological material collected is required to be publicly vouchered and deposited in a public institution, such as a museum collection or public research facility. This does not imply free public access, but does require that the specimen or material be available for bona fide scientific research as opposed to sequestration at a private facility. This seems an efficient, equitable, and totally appropriate requirement for extraterrestrial materials as well.

Grant International Patents Only

While most models of intellectual property rights applied to Earth's global commons appear to be fraught with contradictions and lack clarity, the burden of hundreds of years of conflicting geopolitical approaches need not be perpetuated. The issue of overlapping and conflicting legal systems may be avoided if there is one over-arching international administrative system. Such a system would be aided by existing prohibitions in the OST on establishing territorial claims. Limiting the number of regulatory bodies seems essential to uniformity and efficiency (Scuderi, 1989; Balsano, 1995). An international umbrella, such as the OST or its equivalent, should maintain a position of dominance in a hierarchy of other specialized agreements, similar to the Antarctic Treaty's tiered relationship to the Antarctic Treaty System. Should calls for the harmonization of laws, procedures and guiding regulations for space-related IP prove successful, they could be applied to terrestrial issues as well.

Patent Pools

Consider the creation of international patent pools as a remedy for potential monopolization of extraterrestrial life IP.

Expand the Definition of Common Heritage of Mankind

When applied to outer space resources, expand the concept of Common Heritage of Mankind to include extraterrestrial life. As with CHM on Earth where portions of profits made from certain patents are used for the conservation of affected species and their habitats, portions of profits derived from extraterrestrial life patents could be placed in trust for the conservation of extraterrestrial habitats for the benefit of native organisms.

Provide for Developing Countries' Participation in Space Exploration and Exploitation

The International Space Station includes crew from non-spacefaring states. Protocols for providing access to extraterrestrial resources to less developed nations and subsidizing their participation should be considered in the spirit of a shared commons.

CONCLUSION

It is likely that issues of ownership, private profits and intellectual property regarding discovery of extraterrestrial life are not currently of great administrative concern to those in national and international policy positions because there is little anticipation that such discoveries will be made. It may seem so remote that it is not worth the political capital to negotiate compromises. However, that would change rapidly should, for example, the Mars Space Laboratory report signs of endemic life there. At that moment, a clamor for international protocols for ownership and plans for the disbursement of potential profits will predictably move the issue to the top of political, research and commercial agendas.

Every problem we have ever faced did not exist at one time. The earlier potential problems can be identified, the more opportunities there are for avoiding them or mitigating unwanted outcomes. For now, issues of applying IP to extraterrestrial life are hypothetical, but the situation could change tomorrow. To prepare for a potential discovery, it may be extremely productive if representatives of spacefaring nations, involved private industry sectors, academic institutions with research interests, the UN Office of Outer Space Affairs, developing states without direct involvement in space exploration and others formally approached questions of IP and extraterrestrial life in the context of a thought experiment. What protocols might they negotiate that would best address the concerns of all involved? How might such discussions contribute to more uniform and equitable IP practices here on Earth? The chances for crafting such an outcome are optimal now, prior to discovery of extraterrestrial life.

REFERENCES

Albright, M. (2004) *Profits Pending: How Life Patents Represent the Biggest Swindle of the 21st Century.* Monroe, ME, Common Courage Press.

Balsano, A. (1995) 'Intellectual property rights and space activities', *Space Policy*, 11(3): 204–209.

Banner, S. (2011) *American Property – A History of How, Why, and What We Own.* Cambridge, MA, Harvard University Press.

Bennett, J. and Shostak, S. (2007) *Life in the Universe.* San Francisco, CA, Pearson Education, Inc.

Bertka, C., Roth, N. and Shindell, M. (2007) *Workshop Report: Philosophical, Ethical, and Theological Implications of Astrobiology.* Washington, DC, American Association for the Advancement of Science.

Blaustein, R. (2006) 'Genetic resources and the Convention on Biological Diversity', *BioScience*, 56(7): 560–563.

Bugos, G.E. and Kevles, D.J. (1992) 'Plants as intellectual property: American practice, law, and policy in world context', *Osiris*, 7: 74–104.

Christol, C.Q. (1999) 'The 1979 Moon Agreement: Where is it today?' *Journal of Space Law*, 27(1): 1–35.

Convention on Biological Diversity (1992) text at: https://www.cbd.int/doc/legal/cbd-en.pdf

Convention on Biological Diversity (1992) https://www.cbd.int/doc/legal/cbd-en.pdf

Cooper, L.A. (2003) 'Encouraging space exploration through a new application of space property rights', *Space Policy*, 19(2): 111–118.

Dalton, T.R. (2010) *Developing the Final Frontier: Defining Private Property Rights on Celestial Bodies for the Benefit of All Mankind*, Cornell University Law School.

Des Marais, D. et al. (2003) 'The NASA astrobiology roadmap', *Astrobiology*, 3(2): 219–235.

DeVogue, A. (2013) 'Supreme court strikes down BRCA gene patent', *ABC News*, 13 June.

Dutfield, G. (2003) *Intellectual Property Rights and the Life Science Industries: a Twentieth Century History.* New York, NY, Ashgate.

Dutfield, G. (2004) What is Biopiracy? International Expert Workshop on Acccess to Genetic Resources and Benefit Sharing, Record of Discussion: 89–92.

Dykman, H.T. (1964) 'Patent licensing within the Manufacturer's Aircraft Association (MAA)', *Journal of the Patent Office Society*, 46: 646.

Enard, W., Gehre, S. et al. (2009) 'A humanized version of Foxp2 affects cortico-basal ganglia circuits in mice', *Cell*, 137(5): 961–971.

Fiji Times (2011) 'Economic value of traditional knowledge', *Fiji Times*, 28 March, www.fijitimes.com/story.aspx?id=169405

Frakes, J. (2003) 'The common heritage of mankind principle and deep seabed, outer space, and Antarctica: Will developed and developing nations reach a compromise?', *Wisconsin International Law Journal*, 21: 409.

Fry, T. (1946) 'Land tenures in Australian law', *Res Judicatae*, 3: 158.

Gabriel, D.C. (2012) *Patentable and Non-Patentable Biotech Inventions*, K&S Partners, Gurgaon, India.

Hardin, G. (1968) 'The tragedy of the commons', *Science*, 162(3859): 1243–1248.

Hardin, G. (1995) *Living Within Limits: Ecology, Economics, and Population Taboos*, Oxford, Oxford University Press.

Hearsey, C. (2008) *A Review of Challenges to Corporate Expansion into Outer Space.* Conference Report, 9–11 September 2008, American Insitutue of Aeronautics and Astronautics, San Diego, CA.

Hertzfeld, H.R. and von der Dunk, F.G. (2005) 'Bringing space law into the commercial world: Property rights without sovereignty', *Chicago Journal of International Law*, 6: 81.

IUCN (1980) *World Conservation Strategy – Living Resource Conservation for Sustainable Development.* World Conservation Union, United Nations Environment Programme, Word Wide Fund for Nature, Gland, Switzerland. https://portals.iucn.org/library/sites/library/files/documents/WCS-004.pdf

Justia (1980) *Diamond v Chakrabarti*, 447 U.S. 303 (1980). USS Court. Washington, DC, www.supreme.justia.com/cases/federal/us/447/303/case.html

Koerth-Baker, M. (2013) 'Patent life: How the Supreme Court fell short', *BoingBoing*, www.boingboing.net/2013/07/31/patent-life-how-the-supreme-c.html 2013

Kurlansky, M. (1997) *Cod: A Biography of the Fish that Changed the World.* New York, NY, Penguin Books.

Kurzweil, R. (2005) *The Singularity is Near.* New York, NY, Viking Press.

Laird, S. et al. (2007) 'Recent trends in biological prospecting'. Antarctic Treaty Consultative Meeting.

Listner, M. (2012) 'US rebuffs current draft of EU Code of Conduct: is there something waiting in the wings?', *The Space Review*, 16 January, www.thespacereview.com/article/2006/1

Lumelsky, A.E. (2004) 'Diamond v. Chakrabarty: Gauging Congress' Response to Dynamic Statutory Interpretation by the Supreme Court', *Bepress Legal Series*, 288.

Mach, E. and Hiebert, E. (1997) *Knowledge and Error – Sketches on the Psychology of Enquiry.* Boston, MA, D. Reidel Publishing Company.

Magnani, T. (1999) 'The patentability of human-animal chimeras', *Berkeley Technology Law Journal*, 14: 443, Berkeley, CA, www.heinonline.org/HOL/LandingPage?collection=journals&handle=hein.journals/berktech14&div=30&id=&page=

Mathur, A. and Dua, K. (2005) 'A comparative study of DNA sequence patenting in the USA, Europe and Japan, and suggestions for the course of action for India', University of Washington School of Law, *Center for Advanced Study and Research on Intellectual Property Newsletter*, 12(2).

Oldham, P and South, C. (2004) 'Global status and trends in intellectual property claims: Genomics, proteomics and biotechnology', United Nations – Executive Secretary of the Convention on Biological Diversity, ESRC Centre for Economic and Social Aspects of Genomics.

Pan, P. (2006) *Bioprospecting: Issues and Policy Considerations.* Honolulu, HI, Legislative Reference Bureau, State of Hawaii.

Payoyo, P.B. (1997) *Cries of the Sea – World Inequality, Sustainable Development and the Common Heritage of Mankind.* The Hague, The Netherlands, Kluwer Law International.

Pop, V. (2009) *Who Owns the Moon? Extraterrestrial Aspects of Land and Mineral Resources Ownership*, New York, NY, Springer Verlag.

Porter, E. (2012) 'Tech suits endanger innovation', *New York Times*, 19 May, http://nytimes.com/2012/05/30/business/economy/tech-lawsuits-endanger-innovation.html?_r=0

Reynolds, G. and Merges, R. (1998) *Outer Space: Problems of Law and Policy.* Boulder, CO, Westview Press.

Reynolds, G. (2008) 'Who owns the Moon? The case for lunar property rights', *Popular Mechanics* (online), June 2008, http://www.popularmechanics.com/science/space/moon-mars/4264325

Scuderi, E. (1989) 'Space and the law of intellectual property', *Law Institute Journal*, 492–494.

Shankar, U. (2008) 'Bioprospecting – a quest for natural solutions', http://expresspharmaonline.com/20080115/research01.shtml

Shiva, V. (2000) 'North-south conflicts in intellectual property rights', *Peace Review*, 12(4): 501–508.

Smith, S. (2004) Access to Genetic Resources and Intellectual Property Rights: What Is Biopiracy? International Expert Workshop on Access to Genetic Resources and Benefit Sharing, Cuernavaca, Mexico.

Sovereignty International (1998) 'How the Convention on Biodiversity was defeated', (http://sovereigntyonline.org/p/land/biotreatystop.htm)

Thieman, W.J. and Palladino, M.A. (2004) *Introduction to Biotechnology.* San Francisco, CA, Pearson/Benjamin Cummings.

US Supreme Court (2013) *Association for Molecular Pathology et al. v. Myriad Genetics, Inc., et al.*, US Supreme Court, June 13, 2013.

Viikari, L. (2002) *From Manganese Nodules to Lunar Regolith: A Comparative Legal Study of the Utilization of Natural Resources in the Deep Seabed and Outer Space.* Rovanieme, University of Lapland.

Wasser, A. and Jobes, D. (2008) 'Space settlements, property rights, and international law: Could a lunar settlement claim the lunar real estate it needs to survive?', *Journal of Air Law and Commerce*, 73(1): 37–78.

WIPO (2009) 'What is intellectual property?', http://wipo.int/about-ip/en/

WIPO (2012) 'About WIPO', http://www.wipo.int/about-wipo/en/

38

Intellectual Property and Global Warming: Fossil Fuels and Climate Justice

Matthew Rimmer

INTRODUCTION

Intellectual property law has a dirty history. As a legal institution refined in the industrial revolution, intellectual property law has provided incentives for research and development into fossil fuels and polluting technologies. In a provocative 2008 piece, Professor Estelle Derclaye (2008: 264) from the University of Nottingham wondered whether intellectual property law had played a role in encouraging the development of carbon-polluting technologies:

> The question then arises: could intellectual property rights be the cause of global warming? After all, the greatest inventions of the two last centuries include the car, the plane and with them the use of oil and coal to generate energy. They are some of the causes that contribute the most to the increase of levels of CO_2 on the planet. The academic community has given very little attention, if any, to this increasingly important issue.

Recently, there has been increased debate as to whether intellectual property law should be reformed and revised to deal with the environment and climate change. There has been a growing movement of environmentalism and climate activism in the field of intellectual property law – both among civil society organizations, such as 350.org, and countries vulnerable to climate change – a new manifestation of Debora Halbert's theory about intellectual property resistance (Halbert, 2005).

Internationally, there has been much debate over whether international law should address the topic of intellectual property and climate change, particularly focusing upon patent law and technology transfer. There has been forum-shifting on the topic between international climate summits, the World Intellectual Property Organization (WIPO), the World Trade Organization, and regional trade agreements such as the *Trans-Pacific Partnership*.

In the area of patent law, there has been enthusiasm for fast-track mechanisms for the examination of green patent technologies, and patents for humanity (Dechezlepretre, 2013; Lane, 2011, 2012; Rimmer, 2012d). There has been patent litigation in respect of clean technologies, and concerns about the rise of patent trolls (Hamilton, 2013: 75–81; Lane, 2011: 87–147; Rimmer, 2011a: 197–235). There has also been much discussion about the use of access mechanisms – such as compulsory licensing, patent pools, public sector licensing, and open innovation – in respect of clean technologies (Brown, 2013; Chien, 2012; Sarnoff, 2014; Sommer, 2013).

Other areas of intellectual property have also raised questions about biodiversity, environmental protection, and climate change. In the area of trademark law, there has been both a creative development of green trade marks, certification marks, and ecolabels – as well as problems with deceptive and misleading branding. Culture-jammers have often sought to engage in the parody and satire of trade marks of rogue fossil fuel companies (Rimmer, 2013). Consumer regulators – such as the Federal Trade Commission, the Australian Competition and Consumer Commission and the United Kingdom Advertising Standards Board – have taken action against greenwashing (Chon, 2009; Hutchens, 2009; Lane, 2011). In copyright law, there has been debate over access to environmental data (Derclaye, 2014). Trade secrets have also been contested – with clean technology companies raising concerns about the 'theft' of trade secrets. Plant breeders' rights and patents have been deployed to deal with climate-ready crops (Rimmer, 2012a: 320–60; 2012c: 361–91). Access to genetic resources raises questions about the relationship between intellectual property, biodiversity, traditional knowledge, and climate change (Lawson, 2012). The work of the Mary Robinson Foundation for Climate Justice (2013) highlights the intersections between food security, hunger and climate justice.

In addition to intellectual property, there has been experimentation in relation to alternative schemes – such as prizes, grants and open innovation. The UNFCCC Climate Technology Centre and Network – hosted by the United Nations Environment Programme – offers a new model of innovation to facilitate collaboration on the research, development and dissemination of clean technologies. It remains to be seen whether this technology mechanism will encourage a co-operative approach to intellectual property ownership and benefit-sharing.

There has been much debate about ethics in a world of global warming (Broome, 2012; Gardiner et al., 2010; McKibben, 2013a; Posner and Weisbach, 2010). Intellectual property and climate change raises larger theoretical questions about law, justice and ethics. Eric Knight (2013: 5) noted that 'climate change has quickly become the quintessential wicked problem of politics today'. He lamented: 'We struggle because we apply the wrong terms of analysis, using shortcuts that add to the public confusion'. Stephen Gardiner's book, *A Perfect Moral Storm: The Ethical Tragedy of Climate Change*, provides a thoughtful exploration of the ethics of climate change. He maintained that dominant theories are inadequate in dealing with the problem of climate change because they do not account for the problem of intergenerational justice. Gardiner (2011: 41) commented: 'We are extremely ill-equipped to deal with many problems characteristic of the long-term future'. He observed: 'Even our best moral and political theories face fundamental and often severe difficulties addressing basic issues such as intergenerational equity, international justice, scientific uncertainty, contingent persons, and the human relationship to animals and nature more generally'. In particular, Gardiner argued that a number of theories were inadequate for accounting for climate change policy – including cost-benefit analysis, game theory, the free-rider theory, and theories of the commons. He argued that such doctrines failed to properly account for intergenerational equity and justice. Gardiner (2011: 28) is concerned about 'shadow solutions' – which 'may indeed constitute significant action, but without actually responding to the true nature of the problem'.

Engaging in a close analysis of legal and political discourse, this chapter considers conflicts over intellectual property and climate change in three key arenas: climate law; trade law; and intellectual property law. In this chapter, it is argued that there is a need to overcome the political stalemates and deadlocks over intellectual property and climate change. It is essential that intellectual property law engage in a substantive fashion with the matrix of issues surrounding fossil fuels, clean technologies and climate change at an international level. First, this chapter examines the debate over intellectual property and climate change under the auspices of the *United Nations Framework Convention on Climate Change* 1992, and the establishment of the UNFCCC Climate Technology Centre and Network. It recommends that the technology mechanism should address and deal with matters of intellectual property management and policy. Second, the piece examines the discussion of global issues in the World Intellectual Property Organization, WIPO GREEN. It supports the proposal for a Global Green Patent Highway to allow for the fast-tracking of intellectual property applications in respect of green technologies. Third, the chapter investigates the dispute in the TRIPS Council at the World Trade Organization over intellectual property, climate change and development. This section focuses upon the *TRIPS Agreement* 1994. This chapter calls for a Joint Declaration on Intellectual Property and Climate Change from the UNFCCC, WIPO and the WTO.

The paper concludes that intellectual property should be reformed as part of a larger effort to promote climate justice. Rather than adopt a fragmented, piecemeal approach in various international institutions, there is a need for a co-ordinated and cohesive response to intellectual property in an age of runaway, global climate change. Patent law should be fossil fuel free. Intellectual property should encourage research, development and diffusion of renewable energy and clean technologies. It is submitted that intellectual property law reform should promote climate justice in line with Mary Robinson's *Declaration on Climate Justice* 2013.

INTERNATIONAL CLIMATE LAW

The *United Nations Framework Convention on Climate Change* 1992 and the *Kyoto Protocol* 1997 call for technology transfer. There has been much inconclusive debate over intellectual property, technology transfer and climate change at international climate summits over the years (Rimmer, 2011a: 39–82; 2011b; Rimmer, 2012b). Elisa Morgera and Kati Kulosevi (2013: 129) observed:

> The *UN Framework Convention on Climate Change* 1992 and its *Kyoto Protocol* 1997 are central in the international legal framework governing climate technologies and both include commitments concerning technology cooperation. It is, however, commonly accepted that international cooperation must be strengthened to effectively respond to the climate change challenge. Accordingly, technology has been identified as one of the key building blocks in the ongoing negotiations for a future climate regime under the UNFCCC.

Nonetheless, there has been a lack of consensus in terms of options in respect of intellectual property and clean technologies. There were stalemates between competing nation states on the topic of intellectual property rights in the *Copenhagen Accord* 2009, the *Cancún Agreements* 2010, the *Durban Decisions* 2011, the *Doha Climate Gateway* 2012 and the *Warsaw Opportunity* 2013.

During the 2012 meetings, there was, once again, a contentious debate over intellectual property – this time in relation to clean technologies. Disappointingly, the 2012 Doha Climate talks resulted in no declaration or agreement on intellectual property and clean technologies. Indeed, there was a deadlock on the subject of intellectual property. There was instead a cluster of decisions known as the *Doha Climate Gateway* 2012. While such decisions did not address intellectual property or open innovation, the *Doha Climate Gateway* selected the United Nations Environment Programme to host the UNFCCC Climate Technology Centre.

The Executive Secretary of the United Nations Framework Convention on Climate Change, Christiana Figueres, observed optimistically:

> The UN Climate Change negotiations must now focus on the concrete ways and means to accelerate action and ambition. The world has the money and technology to stay below two degrees. After Doha, it is a matter of scale, speed, determination

> and sticking to the timetable. (United Nations Environment Programme, 2012b)

In some quarters, the decision was portrayed as a 'lifeline' for the *Kyoto Protocol* 1997 (Doherty and Lewis, 2012). European Climate Commissioner Connie Hedegaard said that the agreement was a modest achievement. However, Bill McKibben of 350.org, as well as Nnimmo Bassey and Pablo Solon (2012) lamented that the Doha climate talks lacked ambition for meaningful action on climate change: 'There's no longer time for diplomatic delays'. The Friends of the Earth (2012) dubbed the *Doha Climate Gateway* 2012 a 'Qatar-strophe'.

Intellectual Property and Clean Technologies

There has been long-standing debate about access to essential medicines (Abbott and Dukes, 2009; Ho, 2011; Matthews, 2011; Pogge et al., 2010). In November 2001, Doha was the host of tense trade talks over intellectual property and public health. The discussions resulted in the landmark *Doha Declaration on the TRIPS Agreement and Public Health* 2001. The *Doha Declaration* 2001 recognized 'the gravity of the public health problems afflicting many developing and least-developed countries, especially those resulting from HIV/AIDS, tuberculosis, malaria and other epidemics'. The *Doha Declaration* 2001 recognized 'that the *TRIPS Agreement* does not and should not prevent members from taking measures to protect public health'. The topic of access to essential medicines is related to the debate over global warming, because there has been concern about the impact of climate change upon public health (Epstein and Ferber, 2011).

In the 2013 debate over the Doha climate talks, there was a fierce debate over whether there should be text in respect of intellectual property and clean technologies. The Climate Action Network International (2012) argued that there should be a Declaration on Intellectual Property and Climate Change:

> The adoption of a COP Decision for a declaration on climate change and intellectual property that existing international flexibilities on patents, plant varieties, and copyrights especially relating to competition law, compulsory licensing, exceptions and limitations must be interpreted in ways conducive to enabling rapid and efficient uptake of technologies to address mitigation and adaptation.

Such a statement would be a companion to the *Doha Declaration on the TRIPS Agreement and Public Health* 2001.

China observed at the Doha climate talks: 'We're not going to request technology transfer free of charge. We certainly respect intellectual property rights' (Morales, 2012).

South Africa argued that the Doha climate talks should address 'questions of equitable access to sustainable development, intellectual property rights and unilateral trade measures' (SANews.Gov.Za, 2012).

The Philippines (2012) maintained that 'Intellectual Property Rights as a critical issue that needs to be addressed in technology transfer, development and deployment'. The delegation also maintained that developing countries needed assistance to evaluate 'the potential impacts of new and emerging technologies presented as environmentally-sound technologies, before they are developed, transferred and deployed'. The country was particularly concerned about the need to address climate catastrophes, emergencies and disasters. The Philippines delegate, Naderev Saño, made an emotional plea to the Doha climate conference for there to be no further delays in taking international action on climate change (Vidal, 2012).

Egypt complained about the refusal to discuss finance, technology transfer and intellectual property at the Doha climate talks (Parnell, 2012). Its climate change negotiator Ambassador Ahmed Ihab Gamaleldin observed: 'First we had an agreement about technology transfer, and now they told us to rely on the private sector … the private sector will never be willing to finance adaptation measures'. He lamented: 'There is a complete refusal to talk about intellectual property rights'.

The Progressive Latin Americans – such as Venezuela – mooted text on a wide range of co-operative measures on intellectual property and climate change. Venezuela (2012) called on the Conference of the Parties to affirm that 'the flexibilities of the international regime of intellectual property rights as articulated by the [*TRIPS Agreement* 1994] may be used to the fullest extent by developing country parties to address adaptation to climate change and/or mitigation of greenhouse gas emissions, in order to enable them to create a sound and viable technological base'. Venezuela stressed:

> Parties shall ensure that intellectual property rights and agreements shall not be interpreted or implemented in a manner that limits or prevents any Party from taking any measures to promote adaptation or mitigation to climate change, including the improvement of their cost-effectiveness.

It is worth considering the proposals of Venezuela in detail.

Venezuela called for the adoption of a range of intellectual property measures to provide flexible access to clean technologies. First, in its view, the conference should 'create a global pool of goods and technologies to promote mitigation and adaptation to climate change; in which intellectual property right owners of climate technologies are required to make their intellectual property as well as know-how available to developing countries'.

Second, countries should be free to make 'use of full flexibilities contained in the [*TRIPS Agreement* 1994], including compulsory licensing'.

Third, Venezuela supported the use of 'differential pricing on patented technologies for developing countries in order to lower the cost of technology acquisition for developing countries'.

Fourth, the country asked for a review of 'all existing relevant intellectual property rights regulations in order to provide significant information to remove the barriers and constraints affecting environmentally sound technologies'.

Fifth, Venezuela called for the promotion of 'innovative intellectual property rights sharing arrangements for joint development of environmentally sound technologies'.

Sixth, Venezuela asked for a reduction of the term of protection for patents on climate-friendly technologies.

Furthermore, Venezuela maintained that 'developed country parties shall take all practicable steps to ensure that intellectual property rights are interpreted and applied in a manner that promotes, and ensures the cost-effectiveness, of adaptation and mitigation actions'.

Finally, Venezuela suggested that there was a need to 'identify, suggest and promote actions in all relevant forums to exclude intellectual property rights protection and revoke existing intellectual property protection in developing countries and least developed countries on environmentally sound technologies to adapt to and mitigate climate change, including those developed through funding by governments or international agencies'.

Martin Khor (2012) of the South Centre has articulated a number of concerns over developing countries in respect of intellectual property, technology transfer and climate change. He observed:

> Intellectual property should not be treated as something sacred that has to be upheld at all costs. That would send a signal that climate change is not a serious threat, as commercial profits from monopoly would be seen as being on a higher scale of values and priorities than are the human lives that are at stake due to global warming. Technology transfer to developing countries to enable them to combat climate change should be the far higher priority. (Khor, 2012: 19–20)

Khor summarized the variety of proposals put forward by developing countries in respect of intellectual property and climate change. He contended that 'The UNFCCC process should therefore adopt the principle that developing countries can exempt climate-friendly technologies from patents'. Moreover, he said that this position 'should be supplemented with global measures to enable the sharing of trade secrets'.

The International Centre for Trade and Sustainable Development has called for compromises between nation states on options dealing with intellectual property and climate change (Latif et al., 2011). The Centre acknowledged that 'the role of intellectual property rights has remained a particularly divisive issue'. The Centre observed: 'Not only has no agreement been reached in this area, but even the path to a constructive and meaningful discussion seems elusive'. The Centre called for the incremental development of policy options on intellectual property and clean technologies. Such an approach would first involve a consideration of practical and technical measures to build trust such as improving patent information, facilitating access to public domain technology, encouraging public sector licensing, and fast tracking green patent applications. A second stage could address more substantive issues – such as open innovation in green technologies, patent pools based on voluntary licensing and other sharing arrangements, creative uses of existing flexibilities in international instruments, and consideration of alternative intellectual property regimes.

Open Innovation: A Green Intellectual Property Exchange

There was also significant discussion at the Doha talks of co-operative models for facilitating open access to clean technologies.

In their book *MacroWikinomics*, Don Tapscott and Anthony Williams (2010: 96–99) have called for the establishment of a green technology commons. The pair recognized: 'It is quickly becoming clear that climate change will be the biggest issue that human civilisation has ever had to deal with' (2010: 99). Tapscott and Williams were concerned about the limitations of existing responses to the problem of climate change. The writers promoted open and collaborative responses to climate change: 'Tackling climate change will not only require unprecedented transformations in our systems of commerce and industry, it will also require fundamental changes to our way of life' (2010: 99). The pair concluded: 'We need to take the sum of mankind's knowledge about sustainable technologies and industries, and share it for the sake of the planet and the future generations that will inhabit it' (2010: 97).

There have been a number of examples of open innovation projects in respect of the environment, clean technologies and climate change. The Creative Commons established the GreenXChange. The GreenXChange has been promoted as a model for intellectual property exchange. Professor Jonathan Zittrain (2010) was hopeful that the GreenXChange would promote an open and networked approach to clean technology innovation. The Eco-Patent Commons is a somewhat more corporate imagining of a commons. The Eco-Patent Commons was launched by IBM, Nokia, Pitney, Bowes and Sony to share patents which would help enable people to protect the environment. The Global Innovation Commons is a repository of public domain innovations – including in respect of clean technologies. The Global Innovation Commons (2014) 'enables the immediate "open source" generic production of most technologies – even those considered most cutting edge – in markets where patent holders failed to seek or gain protection'.

In 2014, Elon Musk of Tesla Motors announced that his company would allow for open source licensing in respect of its patent portfolio for electric vehicles and related technologies. In June 2013, President Barack Obama made a policy statement at Georgetown University on climate change. He emphasized the need to promote open access to climate data to stimulate innovation in clean technologies, as well as climate change mitigation and adaptation. Obama noted: 'We'll also open our climate data and NASA climate imagery to the public, to make sure that cities and states assess risk under different climate scenarios, so that we don't waste money building structures that don't withstand the next storm'.

In *Green Governance*, Burns Weston and David Bollier (2013) consider the rise of the commons movement globally – with specific reference to eco-commons. Weston and

Bollier provided a fascinating case study of the Global Innovation Commons:

> The idea behind the project is to let entrepreneurs and national governments query the database on a country-by-country basis to identify useful technologies that are in the public domain. When identified, these technologies for energy, water, and agriculture are prime candidates for being developed at lower costs than patented technologies. (Weston and Bollier, 2013: 166–7)

Weston and Bollier champion such initiatives: 'Despite inevitable resistance, eco-digital commons will surge ahead because, consistent with human rights values, they empower people to take responsibility to achieve better, more responsive, and more flexible solutions in the face of costly and deteriorating performance by large-scale State and Market institutions' (Weston and Bollier, 2013: 167).

The Climate Action Network (2012) has proposed building on such models, and establishing an intellectual property exchange: 'Such an exchange would enable secure, efficient and transparent arms-length transactions for intellectual property licensing at a one-stop shop, with a range of standard licenses that can be pre-designated by rights-holders'.

India has been a vocal participant in debates over intellectual property and clean technologies. At the Durban debate, India (2011) emphasized: 'Given the serious energy poverty and developmental challenges many developing countries face and are compelled to prioritize, access to critical mitigation and adaptation technologies is central to their ability to address climate change'. India further commented:

> Many of the technologies that can help India and other developing countries achieve a lower carbon growth are out of their reach due to intellectual property rights and prohibitive costs. India firmly supports a facilitative intellectual property rights regime that balances rewards for the innovators with the common good of humankind and thereby enables developing countries to take early and effective mitigation and adaptation actions at the national level. In the absence of such a facilitative intellectual property rights regime the objective of advancing nationally appropriate mitigation and adaptation actions at the scale and speed warranted by the Convention will not be achievable.

The Indian delegate observed: 'The Prime Minister of India recently noted that climate justice in India's view means "a fair, equitable and transparent global regime for technology transfers"'.

At Doha, India put forward compromise text on intellectual property and climate change. India's lead negotiator, Mira Mehrishi, called for the creation of a fund to enable access to clean technologies with intellectual property rights (Chipman, 2012). Mehrishi commented: 'If we don't get cheap technology we will never be able to adapt to climate change'. She also observed 'We understand that the person who holds the patent doesn't want to give it away for free, but why can't everybody think positively and come up with a solution?'

However, developed countries – including the United States, members of the European Union, Japan, Canada and New Zealand – rebuffed such compromises (Sethi, 2012).

Intellectual Property, Piracy and Climate Change

In a provocative op-ed, Michael Mazengarb (2012) considered whether piracy was a solution for climate change. He observed: 'The issue of pirating clean technologies is contentious as negotiations are underway in Doha, Qatar'. Mazengarb contended: 'It's time to make clean technology affordable and accessible for developing countries'.

Developed countries took the view that there should be strong enforcement of intellectual property, in order to encourage investment in clean technologies. The United States and the European Union insisted that the Doha Climate Gateway should be silent on intellectual property. Other developed countries argued that other forums – such as the World Trade Organization and the World Intellectual Property Organization – would be better placed to address intellectual property and climate change.

It is striking that, while intellectual property was a taboo subject in the Doha Climate talks, the United States simultaneously pressed for expansionist chapters on intellectual property in the *Trans-Pacific Partnership* and the *Transatlantic Trade and Investment Partnership*.

The Edison Electric Institute (2012) – which represented United States energy companies – argued that the multilateral climate talks should not address intellectual property. The Institute contended: 'Intellectual Property Rights is not a barrier to such development and transfer, but rather a significant tool to innovation'. The Institute wanted to block discussion of intellectual property and climate change within this forum: 'We do not see a basis in the UNFCCC for initiating discussions or actions regarding intellectual property rights issues'. The Institute maintained: 'Unlike WIPO and the WTO, it would seem that the UNFCCC lacks competence for undertaking such discussions or actions'. The Institute contended that 'Opening up intellectual property rights issues within the UNFCCC process could well result in a restriction on trade'. The Edison Electric Institute indeed promoted the controversial regional agreement of the *Trans-Pacific Partnership* as a model where 'global innovation is maximized' and 'intellectual property rights are adequately protected'. There are concerns, though, whether the *Trans-Pacific Partnership* would serve to undermine the protection of the environment, biodiversity and the climate (Environmental Investigation Agency et al., 2013; Rimmer, 2012e; The Sierra Club, 2012).

The position of the Edison Electric Institute highlighted the forum-shifting by stakeholders in the debate over intellectual property, clean technologies and climate change.

The UNFCCC Climate Technology Centre and Network

The *United Nations Framework Convention on Climate Change* 1992 features aspirational language in respect of technology transfer. Alexander Zahar, Jacqueline Peel and Lee Godden (2013: 259) outline the philosophy of the existing regime on finance and technology transfer: 'The Convention, in keeping with its North/South view of the world, calls on developed countries, and in particular OECD countries, to assist developing countries through finance and technology transfer'. The *Copenhagen Accord* 2009, the *Cancun Decisions* 2010, and the *Durban Platform* 2011 have established the foundations of a Technology Mechanism – the UNFCCC Climate Technology Centre and Network.

In the lead up to the Doha negotiations, the Technology Executive Committee asked for greater clarity in respect of the role of the Climate Technology Centre regarding matters of intellectual property (International Centre for Trade and Sustainable Development, 2012). The Committee noted: 'Intellectual property rights were identified as an area for which more clarity would be needed on their role in the development and transfer of climate technologies, based upon evidence on a case-by-case basis'.

There was discussion of the topic during the climate talks in Durban. Draft text on 7 December 2012 alluded to intellectual property, suggesting that the Technology Executive Committee should be 'examining effective mechanisms that promote access to affordable environmentally sound technologies, reward innovators and increase the dynamic of global innovation' and 'analysing and recommending further activities to expand technologies in the public domain and promote research and further independent innovation by developing countries'. However, even such euphemistic language was erased in the end.

One of the key positive decisions of the Doha climate talks was the selection of the United Nations Environment Programme (UNEP) to host the UNFCCC Climate Technology Centre for an initial term of five years. The United Nations decided that the Centre would be located in Copenhagen, Denmark (Ministry of Foreign Affairs of Denmark, 2013).

The United Nations Environment Programme (UNEP) (2012b) had put together a collaborative bid. The United Nations Industrial Development Organization (UNIDO) will be a co-manager. The partners of the consortium included research and scientific organizations in Thailand, India, Argentina, Costa Rica, Kenya, Germany, the Netherlands, Denmark and the United States. India will play a key role with The Energy and Research Institute. The United States partner is the magnificent National Renewable Energy Laboratory – an innovator on a wide range of clean technologies. The UNEP emphasized in its bid: 'We will be driven by country needs, recognizing as well that weak institutions are often a barrier to the transfer of technologies and that developing the capabilities of developing countries is critical' (UNEP, 2012b).

It remains to be seen whether the UNFCCC Climate Technology Centre and Network will be successful in encouraging research, development and deployment of clean technologies for the purposes of climate mitigation and adaptation. Dr Rajendra Pachauri, the Director General of The Energy and Resource Institute (TERI), one of the members of the consortium, has discussed the role of the UNFCCC Climate Technology Centre and Network (Mazengarb, 2013). He hoped that TERI can take a leading role in helping to propagate climate-friendly technologies in developing countries through leading by example:

> We ourselves are developing a number of technologies. Just to give you a few examples, we are working with the Australian CSIRO in developing cooling technologies that would use renewable energy technologies on a decentralised basis. This could be a game changer, in a number of developing countries, farmers either have to sell their produce at existing prices, which may not be the very best they can get, or they have to let a lot of their produce to perish because there is no cold chains or cold storage. This would bring about a substantial increase in the income for farmers and it would also prevent a lot of wastage that also takes place, particularly with fruits and vegetables that you really can't store.

Dr Pachauri noted that technology transfer was a complicated process: 'I think that [technology transfer as a one-way process] can be a very misleading view, because you know you really can't paradrop technologies from the developed world into developing countries'. He noted: 'Even if the essential technology has been developed in a developed country, it would need to be customised to conditions, and that can only be done if you have a full partnership with local organisations'. Ideally, Dr Pauchauri envisaged 'an equal involvement on the part of organisations in the developing countries'.

There has been discussion of financial support for the UNFCCC Climate Technology Centre and Network (Raman, 2013). Mark Radka of the United Nations Environment Programme observed that the Climate Technology Centre would be located in a new United Nations building in Copenhagen, with costs covered by the Danish Government. Funding for the start-up period of the Climate Technology Centre came from the European Commission, Denmark, Canada, Japan and the United States. Mark Radka emphasized that there was a need for a financial mechanism to ensure that the Climate Technology Centre received sufficient, sustained and predictable resources. The institution will have an uncertain future without dependable financial support.

There has been debate about the role and function of the UNFCCC Climate Technology Centre and Network. There has been a discussion as to the future work-plan of the Centre in respect of enabling environments, barriers to technology development and transfer, and intellectual property rights. The representative of Japan, Kunihiko Shimada, emphasized that the Centre should focus upon economic barriers to technology development and transfer, and capacity-building in developing countries (Raman, 2013). Wang Can from China maintained that there was agreement to address the issue of intellectual property rights. Representatives from Iran and Kazakhstan also supported the need to address the matter of intellectual property rights. In response, Griffin Thompson from the United States argued against the cherry-picking of issues and topics related to the environment for technology development and transfer.

The Climate Action Network (CAN) (2012) has argued that the Climate Technology Centre should tackle the intellectual property elements of an enabling environment for technology transfer. CAN observed: 'There are cases where intellectual property has been and *can* be a barrier and some parties are concerned that it will be a barrier to the transfer of key climate technologies to help mitigate their emissions and enhance their adaptive capacities'. They further stated:

> By providing appropriate guidelines on the use of existing tools and a platform to facilitate various forms of information sharing on intellectual property solutions among other initiatives, the UNFCCC has the opportunity to proactively prevent Intellectual Property Rights from becoming a widespread barrier while building confidence in the Technology Mechanism among both demanders and suppliers of climate technologies.

CAN recommended:

> the adoption of a COP Decision for a declaration on climate change and intellectual property that existing international flexibilities on patents, plant varieties, and copyrights especially relating to competition law, compulsory licensing, exceptions and limitations must be interpreted in ways conducive to enabling rapid and efficient uptake of technologies to address mitigation and adaptation.

There has also been wrangling about the operation of the UNFCCC Climate Technology Centre and Network (Raman, 2013). There was concern from China and Sudan that observer organizations from developing countries – such as the South Centre and the Third World Network – were not considered for outside collaboration.

The South Centre has undertaken considerable work on intellectual property and clean technologies. Professor Carlos Correa (2012) has written for the South Centre on 'Mechanisms for International Cooperation in Research and Development: Lessons for the Context of Climate Change'. He observed: 'Technology is crucial to face the effects of climate change'. Correa also noted 'The unprecedented challenge posed by climate change finds the developing countries in a phase of expansion of their R&D capacity, but with growing differences among them'. He also contended: 'Since the adoption of the UNFCCC, technological cooperation has been on the agenda, but little action has been taken'. Correa observed: 'There seems to be, however, an increasing recognition, at least by developing countries, that such cooperation must be effectively implemented'. He maintained that 'there are useful experiences and many options open for policy makers to put in practice what has so far remained a mere aspiration'.

There has also been discussion about the relationship between intellectual property, technology transfer, and finance (Sarnoff, 2013).

The UNFCCC Climate Technology Centre and Network needs to play an active role in both debates about intellectual property policy and management.

Reform

In 2013, the Warsaw talks saw further inconclusive discussions about intellectual property and climate change. Making comparisons to Lord Voldemort, the villain of the Harry Potter series, the Egyptian lead negotiator, speaking for the Like Minded Developing Countries, observed:

> Like the Harry Potter series character, in Doha, IPR was the 'word which should not be named'. But we live in the real world not in a fictional world. In this real world we live in, we need to address this issue of IPRs in a pragmatic manner, not run away from this issue. (Sethi, 2013)

The negotiator said: 'To begin with, we can use the financial mechanisms under the Convention to fund the IPR costs to ensure that climate-friendly technology is available to developing countries easily' (Sethi, 2013). The negotiator emphasized 'A dedicated window under the Green Climate Fund for technology transfer and IPR issues should be established' (2013). India's negotiator, T.S.

Tirumurti, commented that 'There is need to be pragmatic and not run way from the issue. The delegate called for the "word" to be named' (Sethi, 2013). The *Warsaw Opportunity* 2013 text failed to resolve the Doha deadlocks over the controversial matters over intellectual property and climate change. Arguably, though, there remains a need for the UNFCCC to address matters of intellectual property policy and practice, both in terms of policy guidelines, and its technology mechanism.

INTERNATIONAL INTELLECTUAL PROPERTY LAW

The World Intellectual Property Organization (WIPO) has emphasized that the question of intellectual property and climate change is a significant global issue within its jurisdiction.

In 2009, the Director-General of WIPO, Dr Francis Gurry, was active on the issue of intellectual property and climate change. He promoted 'green innovation' in his rhetoric on how WIPO could play a significant role in intellectual property and climate change:

> Human activity, including decades of technological development, has damaged our planet. Widespread pollution and spiraling consumption of the world's mineral and biological reserves have put unprecedented stress on the environment. Climate change is one of the greatest threats ever faced by society: glaciers are disappearing; desertification is increasing; in Africa alone, between 75 and 250 million people will face increased water shortages by 2020. As human activity caused the problem, so too can human activity find the solutions. Green innovation – the development and diffusion of technological means to tackle climate change – is key to halting the depletion of the earth's resources. The race is on to develop accessible alternative sources of energy, as we work to harness the wind and tides, capture the power of the sun, and tap the geothermal energy underground. New plant varieties are being developed to withstand drought and flooding. New environmentally friendly materials will help us construct a more sustainable world. (Gurry, 2009)

Gurry highlighted 'the contribution of a balanced intellectual property system to stimulating the creation, diffusion and application of clean technologies; to promoting green design, aimed at creating products that are eco-friendly from conception to disposal; to green branding, helping consumers make informed choices and giving companies a competitive edge'. He stressed that 'the power of human ingenuity is our best hope for restoring the delicate balance between ourselves and our environment' and 'enabling us to move forward from the carbon-based, grey technologies of the past to the carbon-neutral, green innovation of the future'.

WIPO GREEN

The World Intellectual Property Organization (WIPO) has been reluctant to deal with contentious, substantive policy issues relating to intellectual property and climate change – such as patentability, open innovation, public sector licensing, patent pools, compulsory licensing and government use. Instead WIPO has focused upon questions of intellectual property management from a technocratic perspective.

As part of its response to global issues, WIPO has established WIPO GREEN – 'a matchmaking platform designed to accelerate the development and dissemination of green technologies to combat environmental challenges'. Anja von der Ropp (2012), a Legal Officer of the Global Challenges Division of WIPO, has sought to articulate the mission of WIPO GREEN:

> Climate change is one of the defining challenges of our time. Extending the use of environmentally sound technologies is a key component in mitigating and adapting to climate change. WIPO, along with industry partners, recently launched the pilot version of a new platform known as WIPO GREEN, which seeks to accelerate the adaptation, adoption and deployment of green technologies. WIPO GREEN is a sustainable technology exchange that promises to help facilitate the adaptation, adoption and deployment of climate-friendly technologies, particularly in developing countries and emerging economies.

Von der Ropp identified a number of challenges in the field of intellectual property and clean technologies: 'Access to Environmentally Sound Technologies is a priority for many countries confronting the challenges of climate change'. The legal officer stressed that: 'Efforts to promote the diffusion of these technologies, however, are often hindered by a country's capacity to absorb them'. Von der Ropp maintained that barriers to technology diffusion included 'a country's openness to trade and foreign direct investment, or they may result from an inadequate regulatory framework in relation to environmental or intellectual property policy'. There does not seem to be recognition in this vision that intellectual property itself could be a barrier to the diffusion and dissemination of clean technologies. Von der Ropp insisted: 'IP rights play a key role in terms of attracting investors, facilitating entry into new markets and enabling effective collaborations'.

WIPO GREEN has two components: a free Database and a Network. Users can access the WIPO GREEN Database to: 'make available their green technologies for licensing or partnership agreements, enter their technology needs, and search for technologies and needs' (Von der Ropp, 2012). The WIPO GREEN Network offered to 'obtain advice and services to assist transactions' and 'connect with experts worldwide from industry, universities, governments, IGOs and NGOs'.

Presenting WIPO GREEN, Anja von der Ropp (2012) emphasized that the facility would encourage licensing of intellectual property in respect of clean technologies:

> WIPO GREEN is designed to improve knowledge of and access to existing environmentally sound technologies and to help in the search for solutions to specific climate change-related technology challenges on the one hand, and to provide additional marketing and partnership opportunities on the other hand. It achieves this by matching the available technologies, know-how and expertise of 'technology providers' with the expressed needs of 'technology seekers'. It is, in sum, a hub that makes it easier for would-be partners to connect with each other.

Von der Ropp credits the idea for establishing WIPO GREEN to the Japan Intellectual Property Association (JIPA). She observed: 'Industry plays a pivotal role in bringing about green innovation and fostering its broad diffusion and is, therefore, a natural partner in this endeavor'. However, the venture seems to lack a clear focus upon development. WIPO GREEN notes: 'While the mechanism is designed to facilitate the exchange and diffusion of environmentally sound technologies, its role does not extend to establishing specific agreements for technology transfer' (Von der Ropp, 2012). The organization observed: 'Any transactions that take place will be the subject of individually negotiated agreements between the parties concerned, allowing for greater flexibility in business decisions'. As such, it seems that WIPO GREEN will play a relatively limited role in respect of challenging existing business priorities and dominance in defining intellectual property and its relationship to accessing clean technologies.

Von der Ropp maintains that WIPO GREEN is unique because it makes it 'possible to offer packaged technological solutions that include complementary elements, such as the know-how and technical expertise crucial to the effective configuration of a licensed technology for a specific operating context'. She also insists that 'WIPO GREEN will be a valuable tool in supporting the work of this mechanism'.

In September 2013, WIPO promoted WIPO GREEN at the New York Leaders' Summit for the United Nations Global Compact (2013). The two-hour event featured panellists from WIPO, International Finance Cooperation (IFC), General Electric Company, Honda Motor Co. Ltd and Inovent Innovative Ventures. The panellists discussed the role of intellectual property in the transfer of green technologies; technology-driven start-ups; and the role of WIPO GREEN in green growth and technology transfer.

In November 2013, the Director-General of WIPO, Francis Gurry, launched WIPO GREEN (World Intellectual Property Organization, 2013). He emphasized that the site would serve as a commercial marketplace:

> Innovative green technologies have an important role to play in addressing climate change. Our objective is for WIPO GREEN to become a go-to

> platform for green technologies, thanks to our growing network of partners and innovative collaborations with major global technology databases.

WIPO GREEN involved a number of former partners. Takeshi Ueno, President of the Japan Intellectual Property Association emphasized: 'Japan is a leading innovator of green technologies, and WIPO GREEN provides a vital opportunity for Japanese companies to be at the forefront of global efforts to address climate change' (WIPO, 2013). Sean Flanigan, President of the Association of University Technology Managers, said: 'Through the work of WIPO GREEN and the AUTM Global Technology Portal I am confident that thousands of green technologies originating at Universities will become available for license, development or sharing and will make a significant contribution to the economies of developing countries and to global climate change efforts alike' (WIPO, 2013). Klaus Helmrich, a board member of Siemens said: 'WIPO Green is a promising multiplier for the transfer of sustainable technologies' (WIPO, 2013).

Mark Radka, of the United Nations Environment Program and Interim Director of the UNFCCCC Climate Technology Centre and Network said:

> WIPO GREEN can provide developing countries with critical information on green technology products and services that they need to reduce both emissions of greenhouse gases and to deal with the impacts of climate change. WIPO GREEN also acts as a gateway to the various WIPO intellectual property services, which are excellent assets in the fight against climate change. (WIPO, 2013)

However, the role of WIPO GREEN seems somewhat uncertain, given the establishment of the UNFCCC Climate Technology Centre and Network.

A Global Green Patent Highway?

Arguably, though, WIPO could do much more in respect of intellectual property and clean technologies. Rather than persist with its match-making role with WIPO GREEN, WIPO could be better off, working to establish a global patent fast-track.

A number of industrialized countries – including the United States, Australia, the United Kingdom, China and Korea – have introduced fast-tracks for green patent applications. Antoine Dechezlepretre (2013) has undertaken an empirical study on the extent to which the programmes impact upon the diffusion of green technologies. He formed a number of conclusions:

> First, despite a low participation in the programmes, which reflects the strong incentive for patent applicants to keep their patents in the examination process for as long as possible, there is a clear demand for fast-tracking procedures, in particular from small but fast-growing start-up companies in the green technology sector. Second, climate change-related technologies (in particular renewable energy technologies) represent the vast majority of patents in the fast-tracking programmes. Third, the time from application to grant has been effectively reduced by up to 75% for patents entering the accelerated procedure. Fourth, fast-track patents are of higher commercial value than other green patents that were filed at the same time but did not request accelerated examination. Finally, the analysis of patent citation data shows that fast-tracking programmes have accelerated the diffusion of knowledge in green technologies in the short run (during the first years following the publication of the patents), but whether this effect will be the same in the long run remains an open question.

Dechezlepretre (2013) further maintained: 'Given the urgency of addressing environmental challenges, including climate change, the effects of fast-tracking programmes appear encouraging, particularly with regard to accelerating technology diffusion in the short run, though, as it has been mentioned, further research is needed to understand the longer-term effects and licensing practices'.

San Diego professor and patent attorney, Eric Lane (2012: 1170), has called for the establishment of a 'Global Green Patent Highway'. He observed that: 'Patents play a critical role in green innovation by providing incentives to invest in R&D and facilitating implementation and international diffusion of green technologies'. Lane noted that 'several national intellectual property offices offer accelerated examination procedures for patent applications directed to green technologies so clean tech innovators can obtain patents more quickly'. However, he laments that there is a lack of uniformity in terms of the rules and requirements of the disparate fast track programmes: 'Because of these disparities, it can be costly and time consuming for applicants and their patent attorneys to participate in multiple fast track programs'. Lane further commented: 'Harmonization of the disparate green patent fast track programs into a uniform system with a single set of rules and requirements would greatly streamline the process for green patent applicants and boost participation'. He observed that 'the proposed Global Green Patent Highway would be a powerful mechanism for fostering green innovation and should be employed as a tool in the battle to combat climate change'.

Obviously, such a plan would require international co-ordination, as it would involve the harmonization of a range of national patent systems. The WIPO could play a role in the development of a Global Green Patent Highway under the *Patent Co-operation Treaty* 1970.

Reform

In 2013, Francis Gurry was low-key about the topic of intellectual property and clean technologies. In a speech, 'Re-Thinking the Role of Intellectual Property', Gurry (2013) mentioned access to clean technologies only briefly in a larger overview of global trends in intellectual property law. He commented:

> What intellectual property does is to make access a saleable commodity. While this enables technology markets, it also creates social tension over the price of access and over the lack of access. We have seen this tension played out in relation to access to medicines and biomedical technologies, content on the Internet and climate change technologies, although the last area is more a theoretical debate than a full-scale political engagement that has seized the public's attention. (Gurry, 2013: 22–3)

The depiction of the debate over intellectual property and climate change technologies as merely a theoretical question is curious in 2013. The battle between AMSC, the United States Department of Justice and Sinovel (discussed below) over trade secret theft in respect of clean technologies would suggest that the disputes over intellectual property and clean technologies are quite concrete and tangible – and not merely matters of philosophical or theoretical debate (United States Department of Justice, 2013). It is striking, in this account, that the WIPO does not perceive climate change and global warming as a major global trend impacting upon intellectual property law and policy. There is a need for WIPO to address substantive matters in respect of intellectual property and climate change, along with the UNFCCC and WTO.

INTERNATIONAL TRADE LAW

In the absence of agreement in the climate discussions on intellectual property and climate change, there has been a significant amount of debate in the World Trade Organization over intellectual property, clean technologies, and climate change (Rimmer, 2011a: 83–119).

The Intellectual Property Division of the WTO has provided a practical overview for climate change policy-makers (Taubman and Watal, 2010). The Division commented: 'A spectrum of views has been expressed as to whether intellectual property rights present a barrier to technology development, diffusion and transfer in developing countries, whether the intellectual property system is an essential mechanism for technology development and diffusion'. Taubman and Watal noted: 'Some proposals have been made that would lead to significant adjustments to the intellectual property system, particularly concerning the grant and exercise of patents on green technologies'. The Division stressed: 'More generally, discussions are posing questions about the scope of existing standards, and the options that can be exercised within the framework of those standards, both in terms of national legislation and in terms of innovative structures for managing and sharing intellectual property rights'. Taubman and Watal (2010) also stated that: 'Several forms of intellectual property are potentially relevant to climate change mitigation and adaptation initiatives: patents, trademarks, especially certification marks, trade secrets/know-how, plant variety rights, and the suppression of unfair competition'. However, 'the climate change discussions touching on the intellectual property system have principally concerned patents.'

In his book, *A Practical Guide to Working with TRIPS*, Antony Taubman (2011: 191) identified a number of positions to patent law reform in the field of clean technologies and climate change. Taubman observed that 'amidst a dynamic debate over TRIPS and climate change, three general sets of proposals can be identified'. One position is to 'keep the status quo, but implement it more effectively, such as through improved flow of information about patented technologies and licensing opportunities'. A second position is to 'adopt initiatives akin to the access to medicines process, [and] establish specific measures to remove barriers to using TRIPS flexibilities, on the model of TRIPS 31bis'. A third position is to 'implement more fundamental changes to rules on patents, such as revocation or refusal of patents on technologies needed for climate change adaptation or mitigation, and specific carve-outs for least developed countries and other countries vulnerable to climate change impacts'.

On 11–12 June 2013, there was a debate in the WTO TRIPS Council on Intellectual Property, Climate Change and Development, at the request of Ecuador (Saez, 2013). There was a significant debate over intellectual property and clean technologies between members of the WTO. Ecuador (2013) made a lengthy submission. The Latin American country received support from Cuba, Indonesia, China, Bolivia, India, Bangladesh, Nepal, Rwanda and Brazil (Saez, 2013). However, a number of developed countries argued that intellectual property rights promoted the development of environmentally sound technologies, at accessible prices, and technology transfer. These countries included Japan, the EU, Canada, Switzerland, Australia and New Zealand. Oil-rich Saudi Arabia did not want the TRIPS Council to debate intellectual property and climate change. Saudi Arabia maintained that climate change should instead be discussed in organizations such as the United Nations Environment Programme and in the Trade and Environment Committee of the WTO (Saez, 2013).

Ecuador

In the World Trade Organization, Ecuador's submission to the TRIPS Council was entitled, 'Contribution of Intellectual Property to Facilitating the Transfer of Environmentally Rational Technology' (2013). Ecuador focused upon environmentally sound technologies: 'The issue of technology and its transfer is a fundamental aspect of the fight against climate change and adaptation to and mitigation of its harmful effects'. The Latin American country observed: 'The issue of intellectual property rights and the debate over technological co-operation is becoming a fundamental aspect of how best to adapt to and combat the harmful effects of climate change, particularly for developing countries'.

Ecuador was concerned that intellectual property rights can create 'a monopolistic situation characterised by high prices and a restriction of the dissemination of knowledge for adaptation and use of environmentally-sound technology'. To support its argument, Ecuador cited World Bank and OECD data about the costs of royalties and licences for the use of intellectual property rights. Ecuador maintained that 'the question of intellectual property rights should also be included in the discussions on mechanisms for the transfer of environmentally sound technologies'.

Ecuador maintained: 'It is therefore essential to reorient the world intellectual property regime in the context of adaptation and/or mitigation of the harmful effects of climate change, assuming that there is a real intention to support the efforts of the most vulnerable developing countries to adapt and to mitigate those effects'. Noting the linkages between public health and climate change, Ecuador cited the *Doha Declaration on the TRIPS Agreement and Public Health*, which states that the *TRIPS Agreement* 1994 'does not and should not prevent Members from taking measures to protect public health'.

Ecuador emphasized: 'The evaluation and possible revision of the framework for the protection of intellectual property rights for technological applications would be one of the most important options for developing countries with regard to climate change'. In terms of specific options, Ecuador mooted a number of options that could be considered with regard to intellectual property rights and climate change in the context of the international trading system.

First, Ecuador called for a 'reaffirmation of the existing flexibilities in the *TRIPS Agreement* 1994 so that Members use them in connection with environmentally sound technologies, for example through a declaration addressing flexibilities in the *TRIPS Agreement* 1994, climate change and access to environmentally sound technologies'.

Second, the country asked for an

> initiation of a review of Article 31 of the *TRIPS Agreement* 1994 to determine which of its provisions may excessively restrict access to and dissemination of environmentally sound technologies, and particularly its paragraph (f) and the need to include provisions on, as the case may be, the transfer of expertise or know-how to implement compulsory licences.

Third, Ecuador asked for an 'evaluation of the regulation of voluntary licensing and the conditions thereof from the standpoint of the most pressing needs of the most vulnerable developing countries in relation to adaptation to and mitigation of climate change'.

Fourth, the country called for the 'adoption of a provision authorizing exemption from patentability, on a case-by-case basis, for inventions whose exploitation is vital for the diffusion of environmentally sound technologies needed for adaptation and/or mitigation of climate change'.

Fifth, Ecuador asked for an evaluation of patent term reductions under Article 33 of the *TRIPS Agreement* 1994 'in order to facilitate free access to specific patented environmentally sound technologies for adaptation and/or mitigation of the effects of climate change because of urgent need in the public interest'.

Finally, Ecuador called for an 'inclusion of a mechanism in the *TRIPS Agreement* 1994 to promote open and adaptable technology licensing for results obtained from research into climate change and environmentally sound technologies financed through public funds'.

In relation to these options, Ecuador observed that 'the application of new flexibilities included in the *TRIPS Agreement* 1994 would be understood to be only in favour of the vulnerable developing countries and least developed countries'.

In conclusion, Ecuador called for an overarching declaration on intellectual property and climate change:

> We could consider adopting at the Bali Ministerial Conference a declaration in which Members would enshrine the principle that nothing in the *TRIPS Agreement* 1994 can minimize or impair the flexibilities provided for in that Agreement, nor prevent or limit Members taking measures they consider necessary to protect their population from the effects of climate change and to make use of 'environmentally sound technologies'.

India

In response to the contribution of Ecuador, India delivered a statement on intellectual property, climate change and development. India (2013) maintained: 'Although technological innovation is only part of the overall solution to climate change, it in fact an essential aspect of it'. India insisted: 'For moving towards a green economy and to serve the objective of restricting global warming, it is necessary to overcome the dilemma between the need for widespread and rapid diffusion of knowledge and climate technologies to developing countries; and the need for incentives for technological developments and innovations'.

India (2013) emphasized that: 'although the *TRIPS Agreement* 1994 provides a good framework for protecting innovation including environmentally sound technologies, they do create monopolies resulting in the high prices for the green technologies and act as barrier to their diffusion in the developing countries'. India has called for the reduction of patent duration for clean technologies. The country has also asked for a reconsideration of the provisions of Article 31 of the *TRIPS Agreement* 1994 so it does not become a barrier to issuing compulsory licenses in exceptional cases. India also discussed 'innovative mechanisms like *Doha Declaration on Public Health* or co-operative research and development to delink the cost of R&D so that there are no barriers in diffusion of these technologies'.

India's delegate observed that 'on any principle of equity, the industrialized countries have to bear a large share of the burden'. India maintained that developed countries should have a greater responsibility to address climate change, because they are 'historically responsible for the bulk of the accumulated greenhouse gas emissions' and 'they also have high per capita incomes which give them the highest capacity to bear the burden'. India also maintained that developed countries are 'technically the most advanced, and to that extent best placed to provide environmentally sound technology to the developing countries at fair and favourable terms and conditions'. India concluded that 'it's high time that the global efforts towards a cleaner world do not get hindered because of the barriers posed by multilateral agreements like the *TRIPS Agreement* 1994 or by efforts be [sic] some Members to protect narrow commercial interests'.

India has put such a policy stance into practice in terms of patent administration. On 5 July 2013, India's Intellectual Property Appellate Board rejected a patent application by Monsanto in respect of climate-ready crops. In the case of *Monsanto Technology LLC v. The Controller of Patents and Designs*, the Hon. Smt. Justice Prabha Sridevan considered an appeal against a decision of the Controller of Patents and Designs relating to a patent application for 'a method of producing a transgenic plant with increased heat tolerance, salt tolerance, or drug tolerance.'

The Controller of Patents and Designs refused to grant patent as she found the subject matter of the claims lacked an inventive step relative to prior art. Second, the Controller held that the claims do not define any invention under section 2(1)(ja) of the *Patents Acts* 1970 (India), as the structure and function of cold shock protein was already known in cited prior art and it is obvious to persons skilled in making transgenic plants. Third, given 'it is mere application of already known cold shock protein in producing cold stress tolerant plant and tolerant to heat, salt and drought conditions, [the] claims fall within the scope of Section 3(d) of *The Patents Act* 1970 (India)'. Fourth, she also found that the Monsanto application was not patentable under 3(j) of the *The Patents Act* 1970 (India) as the claims also included essential biological processes of regeneration and selection, which included growing plants in specific stress conditions.

In a commentary on the ruling, Vandana Shiva (2013) of the Research Foundation for Science, Technology, and Ecology emphasized: 'This decision will have [a] far reaching impact on India's biodiversity, farmers' rights and food security'.

The European Union

In response to Ecuador's intervention on the contribution of intellectual property to facilitating the transfer of environmentally rational technology, the European Union (2013) provided a sharp rejoinder. The European Union maintained that 'intellectual property may not play as important a role as some seem to think in the transfer of technology in the climate change alleviation context'.

The European Union argued that there was a need to take into account other factors, 'especially as Ecuador refers to Least Developed Countries and the most vulnerable developing countries'. The European Union maintained:

> In Least Developed Countries, patents are not protected because they are not filed in these countries (no obligation to do so via TRIPS) and there is small market value for private business which is the proprietor of the technology. Therefore, companies are free to use these inventions in these countries.

There was an extension of the transition period for least developed countries under Article 66 of the *TRIPS Agreement* 1994 at the World Trade Organization (2013).

Moreover, the European Union (2013) maintained that 'a considerable quantity of key technology is already in the public domain'. The European Union insisted that a 'lack of financial resources, high investment costs, subsidies and tariffs are considered greater barriers to accessing technology than intellectual property protection'. The European Union was unwilling to concede or admit that intellectual property rights could block access to clean technologies.

The European Union (2013) was resistant to policy changes in respect of intellectual property and climate change – particularly in respect of patentability and compulsory licensing:

> We do not believe that a change to the Intellectual Property Rights system is required such as exclusions from patentability or systematic compulsory licensing. The *TRIPS Agreement* 1994 provides for flexibilities that offer possibilities to the countries seeking to use technology. The EU and its Member States spend huge amounts of money in projects entailing cooperation and elements of technology transfer to Least Developed Countries and developing countries as can be seen in its annual reports to this forum.

The European Union maintained: 'Therefore, instead of considering changes in intellectual property legislation, it is far more useful to focus efforts on more operational initiatives, aiming for instance at facilitating technology transfer, disseminating information on relevant (off-patent) technologies, developing mechanisms such as patent pools (to be operated on a voluntary basis), etc.'.

To support its position, the European Union cited an array of research on intellectual property and clean technologies (Abbott, 2009; CERNA, 2008; Climate Group, 2008; Copenhagen Economics, 2009; Johnson and Lybecker, 2009; Karachalios et al., 2010). The European Union maintained that this literature review supported its position that intellectual property rights were not necessarily a barrier to the transfer of climate change technology. Overall, the European Union was rather partial and selective in its literature review of empirical analysis on intellectual property and clean technologies. Frederick Abbott (2009) actually argues that there could be a joint declaration on intellectual property and climate change between the *United Nations Framework Convention on Climate Change* 1992, the World Intellectual Property Organization, and the World Trade Organization.

Moreover, it should be noted that there are different perspectives on intellectual property and climate change, even within the European Union. The European Greens and the European Free Alliance (2012) have issued a Green Position Paper on 'Climate Change, Technology Transfer, and Intellectual Property'. The Parliamentary Grouping commented:

> The role of intellectual property rights in the diffusion of climate technology is disputed. While the US/EU frame them as essential pre-requisites for innovation, technology development and transfer, developing countries claim that they represent a barrier to the actual transfer of climate technologies.

The European Greens and the European Free Alliance supported a flexible approach to intellectual property, and stated that 'such a strategy does not imply the weakening of international standards of protection'. Rather, they stressed that such a strategy 'imposes resorting to a better use of existing flexibilities of the intellectual property system' in order to 'speedily generate and spread innovation'.

The United States

For its part, the United States has argued for the need for strong protection of intellectual property rights in clean technologies. In its *Special 301 Report*, the United States Trade Representative (2013) argued:

> In the field of environmental technologies, strong intellectual property rights protection can provide incentives for the voluntary transfer of critical green goods and services, and can promote economic growth and create jobs, particularly in developing and least-developed countries that need these benefits most. Without such technologies, inventors and consumers alike would be deprived of critical advances with respect to key environmental challenges, including the mitigation of, and adaptation to, climate change. In addition, firms are likely reluctant to enter into technology transfer arrangements in countries with weak intellectual property enforcement regimes.

The United States insisted: 'Intellectual property rights are thus a key driver of private sector investment'. The country enunciated a credo of intellectual property maximalism: 'The United States continues to work internationally to ensure robust intellectual property rights protection and enforcement, which gives inventors and creators the confidence to invest in the production, adoption, and delivery of goods and services without fear of misappropriation, or outright theft, of their intellectual property rights'.

The concern of the United States is not a theoretical one. The United States Department of Justice has taken action against the Chinese company Sinovel in respect of trade secret theft from the wind power, clean technology company, American Superconductor Inc.

In June 2013, the United States Department of Justice (2013) announced that it had charged the Sinovel Corporation, two of its employees, and a former employee of AMSC with conspiracy to commit trade secret theft, theft of trade secrets and wire fraud. A federal grand jury in the Western District of Wisconsin returned an indictment. Acting Assistant Attorney General Mythili Raman of the Justice Department's Criminal Division commented on the action against the Sinovel Corporation: 'Stamping out intellectual property theft is a top priority for this administration, and we will continue to work with our IP Task Force partners to ensure that American ingenuity is protected' (United States Department of Justice, 2013).

This action against the Sinovel Corporation was very much represented as a matter of criminal law – with intellectual property infringement equated with theft and stealing. US Attorney Vaudreuil emphasized: 'The allegations in this indictment describe a well-planned attack on an American business by international defendants – nothing short of attempted corporate homicide'. FBI Executive Assistant Director Richard McFeely stated: 'The Sinovel case is a classic example of the growing insider threat facing our nation's corporations and their intellectual property'. He suggested that the case was a matter of economic espionage: 'We are actively working with our private sector and government partners to disrupt and impact those who have made it their mission to steal U.S. military and corporate secrets' (United States Department of Justice, 2013).

The matter has the potential to escalate into a trade dispute between the United States and China under the international trade agreements of the World Trade Organization – including the *TRIPS Agreement* 1994.

In addition to matters of intellectual property, there is also the potential for trade disputes over clean technologies within the World Trade Organization (Epps and Green, 2010; Gervais, 2012; Wold et al., 2011). There has been concern amongst fair trade and environmental groups such as Public

Citizen and The Sierra Club (2013) about the adverse impact of international trade rules on a clean energy future.

Reform

Ecuador's intervention in the TRIPS Council should provide impetus for further discussion about intellectual property and clean technologies, and the development of a Declaration on Intellectual Property and Climate Change. Such a Declaration should be a joint statement, harmonizing and unifying the approach of the UNFCCC, the WIPO, and the WTO. The Declaration should address matters of intellectual property flexibilities, such as those raised by Ecuador and India. The Declaration should engage with questions about intellectual property licensing, and technology transfer, as advised by the European Union. The Declaration should also include matters of intellectual property enforcement, as recommended by the US.

CONCLUSION

In an age of runaway global climate change, there is a need to reform intellectual property law so that it can support the development and diffusion of clean technologies.

This chapter has made three recommendations to break the deadlock over intellectual property and climate change. First, it has argued that the institutional mechanism of the UNFCCC Climate Technology Centre and Network needs to address matters of intellectual property policy and management. Second, it has called for administrative reforms – such as a Global Green Patent Highway. Third, it has maintained that there should be a Joint Declaration on Intellectual Property and Climate Change, including the UNFCCC, WIPO and the WTO. Such reform in respect of intellectual property and climate change should not be an isolated endeavour. There is a need to ensure that reforms in respect of intellectual property are a part of a larger effort to achieve climate justice.

In his book, *The Future*, Al Gore (2013) reflected that global warming was a key driver of global change:

> The emergent power and accelerating momentum of Earth Inc., the rapid growth of destructive resource-consumption patterns, the absence of global leadership, and the dysfunctional governance in the community of nations have all combined to produce flows of pollution that are seriously damaging the integrity of the planetary climate balance that is essential to the survival of civilization. (Gore, 2013: 280)

He remained hopeful that legislative action could achieve a positive outcome:

> The good news is that we do have the capacity to begin solving the climate crisis – if we awaken to the reality of our circumstances and decide that saving the future of human civilization is a priority. That means recognizing not only the danger but also the opportunity inherent in this crisis. It means abandoning the illusion that there may be some clever technological quick fix for a planetary emergency that requires a multipronged global strategy to convert our energy systems – particularly electricity generation – manufacturing, agriculture, forestry, building technologies, transportation, mining, and other sectors of the world's economy to a low-carbon, highly efficient pattern. (Gore, 2013: 281–2)

Gore maintained: 'The remaining question that is crucial to our future is whether the requisite force of truth necessary to bring about a shift in consciousness powerful enough to change the current course of civilization will emerge in time' (Gore, 2013: 359).

In his book *Overheated: The Human Cost of Climate Change*, Professor Andrew Guzman (2013) from the University of California Berkeley observed that there was a need for substantive political and legal action in respect of global warming:

> We cannot wish away climate change, and we should not pin our hopes on a miracle to save us. What we must do is recognize the seriousness of this challenge and decide what is necessary to halt the warming of the globe. There should be no mistaking the fact that this will involve some economic sacrifice. Our lives are easier because energy

> is plentiful and inexpensive, but we can no longer ignore the impact of our energy use on the climate. We must raise the price of carbon sufficiently to keep the planet from overheating. If we don't, we will trigger human tragedy on a scale the world has never seen. (Guzman, 2013: 230)

Similarly, Bill McKibben (2013b: 745) has commented that 'we don't need to imagine the future of climate change because it is already here'. He observed: 'We know the carbon budget we must abide by to avoid dangerous climate change and we are already seeing the reality of extreme weather events unimaginable even a decade ago'. McKibben warned: 'We know how climate change ends; we now need to try and rewrite this future'.

The United Nations (2013) released the high-level report, *A New Global Partnership: Eradicate Poverty and Transform Economies through Sustainable Development*, which also addressed climate change. The report noted that 'there is one trend – climate change – which will determine whether or not we can deliver on our ambitions' in respect of poverty and development. The report stressed that: 'Scientific evidence of the direct threat from climate change has mounted'. The United Nations emphasized that there was a need to address the question of intellectual property and clean technologies:

> It is crucial that technologies and innovations be widely shared. Low- and middle-income countries have the chance to leapfrog the old model of development and choose more sustainable growth. But they face two significant constraints: technology and finance. Cleaner and more efficient technologies are often patented by private corporations. Finance is also a problem: the benefits of more efficient technologies come from future savings, while the costs are concentrated at the beginning. If developed countries take the lead in applying these technologies, costs will fall and the technologies will become more accessible to developing countries. (United Nations, 2013: 45)

The report recommended: 'To overcome these constraints, governments can use a mix of taxes, subsidies, regulations and partnerships to encourage clean-energy innovation'. The report advised that: 'Partnering countries can use open-innovation forums to accelerate the development of clean-energy technologies and rapidly bring them to scale'. The report was also enthusiastic about open innovation: 'These open-source forums should be linked to real public-works projects that can offer financing, and the chance for rapid adoption and broad deployment'. The report also recommended that there was a need to reduce fossil fuel subsidies.

The report called for 'a new global partnership as the basic framework for a single, universal post-2015 agenda that will deliver this vision for the sake of humanity'. The report noted: 'We have a choice to make: to muddle through as we have done, making progress on some fronts but suffering setbacks elsewhere'. The report observed: 'Or we can be bold and set our eyes on a higher target, where the end of many aspects of poverty is in sight in all countries and where we have transformed our economies and societies to blend social progress, equitable growth and environmental management.'

The Mary Robinson Foundation for Climate Justice (2013) has also taken a strong interest in the relationship between climate change and development. The Foundation hosted a major conference on *Hunger – Nutrition – Climate Justice* in 2013. Mary Robinson (2013) considered the impact of climate change upon law, justice and human rights:

> Climate change arguably poses the 21st century's starkest challenge to human rights – including the rights to life, shelter and an adequate standard of living. This is particularly the case for many people in the developing world who have contributed the least to causing climate change but are disproportionately suffering the impacts each and every day. The poorest people and parts of the world emit negligible amounts of carbon into the atmosphere – while the wealthiest places and people emit the most and have the capacity and resources to adapt and build resilience to climate impacts.

In September 2013, the Mary Robinson Foundation for Climate Justice and the World Resources Institute released a *Declaration on Climate Justice* 2013, with a range of prominent signatories. The Declaration insisted that there should be transformative leadership in respect of climate change. The priority pathways included: giving voice; a new way to grow; investing in the future; commitment and accountability; and rule of law. The Declaration expressed the hope: 'Our vision acknowledges the injustices caused by climate change and the responsibility of those who have caused it'. It called for the building of 'a common future based on justice for those who are most vulnerable to the impacts of climate change and a just transition to a safe and secure society and planet for everyone'.

REFERENCES

Abbott, Frederick (2009) 'Innovation and Technology Transfer to Address Climate Change: Lessons from the Global Debate on Intellectual Property and Public Health', ICTSD Programme on Intellectual Property Rights and Sustainable Development, Issue Paper No. 24, 2009, http://papers.ssrn.com/sol3/papers.cfm?abstract_id=1433579

Abbott, Frederick and Dukes, Graham (2009) *Global Pharmaceutical Policy: Ensuring Medicines for Tomorrow's World*, Cheltenham (UK) and Northampton (Mass.): Edward Elgar.

Broome, John (2012) *Climate Matters: Ethics in a Global Warming*, New York and London.

Brown, Abbe (ed.) (2013) *Environmental Technologies, Intellectual Property and Climate Change: Accessing, Obtaining and Protecting*, Cheltenham (UK) and Northampton (Mass.): Edward Elgar.

CERNA (2008) 'Invention and Transfer of Climate Change Mitigation Technologies on a Global Scale: A Study Drawing on Patent Data', www.cerna.ensmp.fr/images/stories/file/Poznan/final_report_090112.pdf

Chien, Colleen (2012) 'Subpatentable, Unpatentable, and other Overlooked Problems in Access to Clean Technologies', *Santa Clara Law Digital Commons*, www.digitalcommons.law.scu.edu/facpubs/592/

Chipman, Kim (2012) 'India Pushing Intellectual Property Rights at UN Climate Talks', *Bloomberg News*, 6 December, www.businessweek.com/news/2012-12-06/india-pushing-intellectual-property-rights-at-un-climate-talks

Chon, Margaret, (2009) 'Marks of Rectitude', *Fordham Law Review*, 77: 101–41.

Climate Action Network International (2012) 'Tackling the Intellectual Property Elements of an Enabling Environment for Technology Transfer', CAN Submission to the Technology Executive Committee Meeting, Bangkok, Thailand, 6–8 September, http://unfccc.int/ttclear/sunsetcms/storage/contents/stored-file-20130422151253058/CAN_EE.pdf

Climate Group (2008) 'Intellectual Property Rights: The Catalyst to Deliver Low Carbon Technologies', http://www.theclimategroup.org/_assets/files/Intellectual-Property-Rights.pdf

Copenhagen Economics A/S and the IPR Company APS (2009) 'Are Intellectual Property Rights a Barrier to the Transfer of Climate Change Technology?', 19 January, http://trade.ec.europa.eu/doclib/docs/2009/february/tradoc_142371.pdf

Correa, Carlos (2012) 'Mechanisms for International Cooperation in Research and Development: Lessons for the Context of Climate Change', South Centre, Research Paper 43, March, www.southcentre.org/index.php?option=com_content&view=article&id=1675%3Amechanisms-for-international-cooperation-in-research-and-development-lessons-for-the-context-of-climate-change&lang=en

Dechezlepretre, Antoine (2013) 'Fast-Tracking Green Patent Applications: An Empirical Analysis', International Centre for Trade and Sustainable Development, Issues Paper No. 37, February, http://ictsd.org/downloads/2013/02/fast-tracking-green-patent-applications-an-empirical-analysis.pdf

Derclaye, Estelle (2008) 'Intellectual Property and Global Warming', *Marquette Intellectual Property Law Review*, 12: 263–97.

Derclaye, Estelle (2014) 'The Role of Copyright in the Protection of the Environment and the Fight Against Climate Change: Is the Current Copyright System Adequate?', in Joshua Sarnoff (ed.), *Research Handbook on Intellectual Property and Climate Change*, Cheltenham (UK) and Northampton (Mass.): Edward Elgar, forthcoming, http://papers.ssrn.com/sol3/papers.cfm?abstract_id=1961268

Doherty, Regan and Lewis, Barbara (2012) 'Doha Climate Talks Throw Lifeline to Kyoto Protocol', *Reuters*, 8 December, www.reuters.com/article/2012/12/08/us-climate-talks-idUSBRE8B60QU20121208

The Eco-Patent Commons, www.wbcsd.org/work-program/capacity-building/eco-patent-commons.aspx

Ecuador (2013) 'Contribution of Intellectual Property to Facilitating the Transfer of Environmentally Rational Technology', TRIPS Council, World Trade Organization, 27 February, www.wtocenter.org.tw/SmartKMS/fileviewer?id=131645

Edison Electric Institute (2012) 'Views on a Framework for Various Approaches, Including Use of Markets to

Enhance Cost-Effectiveness of, and Promote, Mitigation Actions as Contained in Decision 2/CP.17 on "Outcome of the Work of the Ad Hoc Working Group on Long-Term Cooperative Action under the Convention"', 5 October, www.unfccc.int/resource/docs/2012/smsn/ngo/273.pdf

EnviroMedia Social Marketing and the University of Oregon, *Greenwashing Index*, www.greenwashingindex.com/

Environmental Investigation Agency, Friends of the Earth, Humane Society International, International Fund for Animal Welfare, Oceana, Sierra Club, World Society for the Protection of Animals, and World Wildlife Fund (2013), 'Letter to Ambassador Froman on the Environmental Chapter of the Trans-Pacific Partnership', 11 July, www.sierraclub.org/trade/downloads/NGO-Letter-Ambassador-Kirk-TPP.pdf

Epps, Tracey and Green, Andrew (2010) *Reconciling Trade and Climate: How the WTO Can Help Address Climate Change*, Cheltenham (UK) and Northampton (Mass.): Edward Elgar.

Epstein, Paul and Ferber, Dan (2011) *Changing Planet, Changing Health: How the Climate Crisis Threatens Our Health and What We Can Do About It*, Berkeley and Los Angeles: The University of California Press.

The European Greens and the European Free Alliance (2012) 'Climate Change, Technology Transfer, and Intellectual Property: 13 Key Measures to Promote Innovation and Fight Climate Change', European Parliament, 9 March, www.greens-efa.eu/climate-change-technology-transfer-and-intellectual-property-5484.html

European Union (2013) 'TRIPS Agenda Point On Intellectual Property, Climate Change and Development', TRIPS Council, World Trade Organization, 11 June.

Friends of the Earth (2012) 'Qatar-Strophe: Climate Talks End Without Meaningful Action', Press Release, 8 December, www.foe.co.uk/news/qatarstrophe_climate_talks_end_08122012.html

Gardiner, Stephen (2011) *A Perfect Moral Storm: The Ethical Tragedy of Climate Change*, Oxford: Oxford University Press.

Gardiner, Stephen, Caney, Simon, Jamieson, Dale and Shue, Henry (ed.) (2010) *Climate Ethics: Essential Readings*, Oxford: Oxford University Press.

Gervais, Daniel (2012) 'Climate Change, the International Intellectual Property Regime, and Disputes under the TRIPS Agreement', *Vanderbilt Public Law Research Paper*, 13–16, 19 March, http://papers.ssrn.com/sol3/papers.cfm?abstract_id=2235775

The Global Innovation Commons (2014) www.globalinnovationcommons.org/content/about

Gore, Al (2013) *The Future: Six Drivers of Global Change*, New York: Random House.

The Green XChange, www.greenxchange.cc/

Gurry, Francis (2009) 'World Intellectual Property Day – Promoting Green Innovation', Geneva: World Intellectual Property Organization, Press Release, 21 April, www.wipo.int/pressroom/en/articles/2009/article_0010.html

Gurry, Francis (2013) 'Re-Thinking the Role of Intellectual Property', Speech, Melbourne, Australia, www.wipo.int/export/sites/www/about-wipo/en/dgo/speeches/pdf/dg_speech_melbourne_2013.pdf

Guzman, Andrew (2013) *Overheated: The Human Cost of Climate Change*, Oxford: Oxford University Press.

Halbert, Debora (2005) *Resisting Intellectual Property*, Milton Park (Oxford) and New York: Routledge.

Hamilton, Clive (2013) *Earth Masters: Playing God with the Climate*, Sydney: Allen and Unwin.

Ho, Cynthia (2011) *Access to Medicine in the Global Economy: International Agreements on Patents and Related Rights*, Oxford: Oxford University Press.

Hutchens, Anna (2009) *Changing Big Business: The Globalisation of the Fair Trade Movement*, Cheltenham (UK) and Northampton (Mass.): Edward Elgar.

India (2011) 'Proposals by India for Inclusion of Additional Agenda Items in the Provisional Agenda of the Seventeenth Session of the Conference of the Parties', FCCC/CP/2011/Inf. 2/ Add. 1, 7 October, www.unfccc.int/resource/docs/2011/cop17/eng/inf02a01.pdf

India (2013) 'Intellectual Property, Climate Change, and Development', TRIPS Council, World Trade Organization, 11 June, www.keionline.org/node/1743

International Centre for Trade and Sustainable Development (2012) 'UNFCCC Technology Executive Seeks More "Clarity" on Intellectual Property Rights', *Bridges Trade BioRes Review* 6(4), www.ictsd.org/i/news/bioresreview/150554/

Johnson, Daniel and Lybecker, Kristina (2009) 'Challenges to Technology Transfer: A Literature Review of the Constraints on Environmental Technology Dissemination', Colorado, http://papers.ssrn.com/sol3/papers.cfm?abstract_id=1456222

Karachalios, Konstantinos, Thumm, Nikolaus, Latif, Ahmed Abdel, Roffe, Pedro, Simmons, Benjamin and Amin, Tahir (2010) 'Patents and Clean Energy: Bridging the Gap Between Evidence and Policy', Geneva: the United Nations Environment Programme, the European Patent Office, and the International Centre for Trade and Sustainable Development, 30 September, http://www.epo.org/news-issues/issues/clean-energy.html

Khor, Martin (2012) 'Climate Change, Technology and Intellectual Property Rights: Context and Recent Negotiations', Research Paper 45, April, www.southcentre.org/index.php?option=com_content&view=article&id=1734%3Aclimate-change-technology-and-intellectual-property-rights-context-and-recent-negotiations&lang=en

Knight, Eric (2012) *Reframe: How to Solve the World's Trickiest Problems*, Melbourne: Black Inc.

Knight, Eric (2013) *Why We Argue About Climate Change*, Melbourne: Redback.

Lane, Eric (2011) *Clean Tech Intellectual Property: Eco-Marks, Green Patents, and Green Innovation*, Oxford: Oxford University Press.

Lane, Eric (2012) 'Building the Global Green Patent Highway: A Proposal for International Harmonization of Green Technology Fast Track Programs', *Berkeley Technology Law Journal*, 27: 1119–70.

Latif, Ahmed Abdel, Maskus, Keith, Okediji, Ruth, Reichman, Jerome and Roffe, Pedro (2011) 'Overcoming the Impasse on Intellectual Property and Climate Change at the UNFCCC: A Way Forward', International Centre for Trade and Sustainable Development, Policy Brief 11, November, www.ictsd.org/i/publications/120254/

Lawson, Charles (2012) *Regulating Genetic Resources*, Cheltenham (UK) and Northampton (Mass.): Edward Elgar.

Mary Robinson Foundation on Climate Justice (2013) *Hunger – Nutrition – Climate Justice*, Conference Report, www.mrfcj.org/pdf/2013-06-07_HNCJ-Conference-Report.pdf

Matthews, Duncan (2011) *Intellectual Property, Human Rights and Development*, Cheltenham (UK) and Northampton (Mass.): Edward Elgar.

Mazengarb, Michael (2012) 'Piracy to Solve Climate Change?', *The Verb*, 3 December, www.theverb.org/piracy-to-solve-climate-change/

Mazengarb, Michael (2013) 'Intellectual Property Rights with Pachauri', *The Verb*, 12 November, www.theverb.org/intellectual-property-rights-with-pachauri/

McKibben, Bill (ed.) (2011) *The Global Warming Reader: A Century of Writing about Climate Change*, London: Penguin Books.

McKibben, Bill (2013a) *Oil and Honey: The Education of an Unlikely Activist*, Melbourne: Black Inc. Books.

McKibben, Bill (2013b) 'Don't Imagine the Future – It's Already Here', *Organization*, 20: 745.

McKibben, Bill, Bassey, Nnimmo and Solon, Pablo (2012) 'Letter to COP Negotiators at the Doha Climate Talks', 28 November, www.dailykos.com/story/2012/11/28/1165340/-Doha-Day-2-McKibben-pens-letter-to-COP-Negotiators

McKinnon, Catriona (2012) *Climate Change and Future Justice: Precaution, Compensation, and Triage*, Abingdon (Oxon) and New York: Routledge.

Medicines Patent Pool, www.medicinespatentpool.org/

Ministry of Foreign Affairs of Denmark (2013) 'United Nations has Chosen Denmark as the Location for the New Climate and Technology Centre Network', 28 May, www.um.dk/en/news/newsdisplaypage?newsid=84089de5-ebb0-4cc5-8b4b-67ec67e7c4dc

Morales, Alex (2012) 'Climate Gridlock Frustrating Envoys at UN Talks in Doha', Bloomberg, 1 December, www.bloomberg.com/news/2012-11-30/climate-effort-lacking-ambition-frustrates-envoys-at-un-talks.html

Morgera, Elisa, and Kulovesi, Kati, (2013) 'Public-Private Partnerships for Wider and Equitable Access to Climate Technologies', in Abbe Brown (ed.), *Environmental Technologies, Intellectual Property and Climate Change: Accessing, Obtaining and Protecting*, Cheltenham (UK) and Northampton (Mass.): Edward Elgar, 128–51.

Obama, Barack (2013) 'We Need to Act on Climate Change', Speech, 25 June, www.bloomberg.com/news/2013-06-25/-we-need-to-act-transcript-of-obama-s-climate-change-speech.html

Parnell, John (2012) 'US Considers Shifting Climate Talks to New Forum Outside UN Process', Responding to Climate Change (RTCC), 16 November, www.rtcc.org/2012/11/16/us-considers-shifting-climate-talks-to-new-forum-outside-un-process/

Pearse, Guy (2012) *Greenwash: Big Brands and Carbon Scams*, Melbourne: Black Inc.

Pearse, Guy, McKnight, David and Burton, Bob (2013) *Big Coal: Australia's Dirtiest Habit*, Sydney: NewSouth.

Philippines (2012) 'Submission on Enhanced Action to Technology Development and Transfer to Support Action on Mitigation and Adaptation', FCCC/AWG:CA/2012/CPR.6, 28 November, www.unfccc.int/resource/docs/2012/awglca15/eng/crp06.pdf

Pierre-Louis, Kendra (2012) *Why We Can't Buy Our Way to a Green Planet*, New York: Ig Publishing.

Pogge, Thomas, Rimmer, Matthew and Rubenstein, Kim (ed.) (2010) *Incentives for Global Public Health: Patent Law and Access to Medicines*, Cambridge: Cambridge University Press.

Posner, Eric and Weisbach, David (2010) *Climate Change Justice*, Princeton (NJ): Princeton University Press.

Public Citizen and The Sierra Club (2013) 'Public Citizen and Sierra Club Denounce World Trade Organization Attack on Successful Clean Energy Program', Press Release, 7 May, www.citizen.typepad.com/

eyesontrade/2013/05/public-citizen-and-sierra-club-denounce-world-trade-organization-attack-on-successful-clean-energy-p.html

Raman, Meena (2013) 'UNFCCC Technology Committee Discusses Key Issues on Technology Transfer', *Third World Network*, 1 April, www.twnside.org.sg/title2/climate/info.service/2013/climate130401.htm

Rimmer, Matthew (2011a) *Intellectual Property and Climate Change: Inventing Clean Technologies*, Cheltenham (UK) and Northampton (Mass.): Edward Elgar.

Rimmer, Matthew (2011b) 'Climate Justice for Intellectual Property at Durban', *The Conversation*, 8 December, www.theconversation.com/climate-justice-for-intellectual-property-at-durban-4572

Rimmer, Matthew (2012a) 'Climate-Ready Crops: Intellectual Property, Agriculture, and Climate Change', in Matthew Rimmer and Alison McLennan (ed.), *Intellectual Property and Emerging Technologies: The New Biology*, Cheltenham (UK) and Northampton (Mass.): Edward Elgar, 320–60.

Rimmer, Matthew (2012b) 'The Doha Deadlock: Intellectual Property and Climate Change', *The Conversation*, 11 December, www.theconversation.com/the-doha-deadlock-intellectual-property-and-climate-change-11244

Rimmer, Matthew (2012c) 'The Doomsday Vault: Seed Banks, Food Security, and Climate Change', in Matthew Rimmer and Alison McLennan (ed.), *Intellectual Property and Emerging Technologies: The New Biology*, Cheltenham (UK) and Northampton (Mass.): Edward Elgar, 361–91.

Rimmer, Matthew (2012d) 'Patents for Humanity', *The World Intellectual Property Organization Journal*, 3(2): 196–221.

Rimmer, Matthew (2012e) 'The Trans-Pacific Partnership, the Environment, and Climate Change', *East Asia Forum*, 22 September, www.eastasiaforum.org/2012/09/22/the-trans-pacific-partnership-the-environment-and-climate-change/

Rimmer, Matthew (2013) 'Coal in Court: Whitehaven, Climate Change and Civil Disobedience', *The Conversation*, 19 July, www.theconversation.com/coal-in-court-whitehaven-climate-change-and-civil-disobedience-15991

Robinson, Mary (2013) 'What Makes us Human?', BBC Radio 2, 11 June, www.mrfcj.org/news/2013/what-makes-us-human.htmlSaez, Catherine (2013), 'WTO Members Agree On Draft Extension of TRIPS Transition For LDCs', *Intellectual Property Watch*, 7 June 2013, www.ip-watch.org/2013/06/07/wto-members-agree-on-draft-extension-of-trips-transition-for-ldcs/#sthash.kkwlYJcK.dpuf

Saez, C. (2013) 'WTO TRIPS Council: Discussion Of Innovation Shows Divergent Views; Tobacco Back On Agenda', *Intellectual Property Watch*, 13 June, http://www.ip-watch.org/2013/06/13/wto-trips-council-discussion-of-innovation-shows-divergent-views-tobacco-back-on-agenda/

SANews.Gov.Za (2012) 'Africa: Molewa Delivers South Africa's Position at COP18', SANews.Gov.Za, 6 December, www.allafrica.com/stories/201212070382.html?viewall=1

Sarnoff, Joshua (2013) 'Government Choices in Innovation Funding (with Reference to Climate Change)', *Emory Law Journal*, 62: 1087–157.

Sarnoff, Joshua (ed.) (2014) *Research Handbook on Intellectual Property and Climate Change*, Cheltenham (UK) and Northampton (Mass.): Edward Elgar, (forthcoming).

Sethi, Nitin (2012) 'Doha Climate Talks: Rich Nations Reject India's Offer on Intellectual Property Concerns', *The Times of India*, 6 December, http://timesofindia.indiatimes.com/home/environment/developmental-issues/Doha-climate-talks-Rich-nations-reject-Indias-offer-on-intellectual-property-concerns/articleshow/17510668.cms

Sethi, Nitin (2013) 'Developing Countries Call for Easing IPR Costs of Clean Technologies', *The Hindu*, 15 November 2013, www.thehindu.com/sci-tech/energy-and-environment/developing-countries-revive-ghosts-of-doha-at-warsaw/article5355065.ece

Shiva, Vandana (2013) 'Monsanto's Climate Resilient Plant Patent Rejected by India's Patent Office, Rejection Upheld by the Intellectual Property Appellate Board', 6 July, www.navdanya.org/news/360-monsantos-climate-resilient-plant-patent-rejected-by-indias-patent-office-rejection-upheld-by-the-intellectual-property-appellate-board

The Sierra Club (2012) 'The Trans-Pacific Partnership: What It Could Mean for the Environment', http://action.sierraclub.org/site/DocServer/TPP_Fact_Sheet_Final4-Leave_Behind.pdf?docID=14001

Sommer, Tine (2013) *Can Law Make Life (Too) Simple? From Gene Patents to the Patenting of Environmentally Sound Technologies*, Copenhagen: DJOF Publishing.

Sullivan, Colin (2012) 'Fights Over Technology Transfer, Green Development Funds Cloud Rio+20 Talks', *Climate Wire*, 15 June, www.eenews.net/public/climatewire/2012/06/15/2

Tapscott, Don and Williams, Anthony (2010) *MacroWikinomics: New Solutions for a Connected Planet*, London: Atlantic Books.

Taubman, Antony (2011) *A Practical Guide to Working with TRIPS*, Oxford: Oxford University Press.

Taubman, Antony and Watal, Jayashree (2010) 'The WTO TRIPS Agreement – A Practical Overview for Climate Change Policymakers', Intellectual Property Division, the World Trade Organization, www.wto.org/english/tratop_e/trips_e/ta_docs_e/8_3_overviewclimatechange_e.pdf

UNFCCC Climate Technology Centre and Network, www.unfccc.int/ttclear/templates/render_cms_page?TEM_tcn and www.unep.org/climatechange/ctcn/

United Nations (2013) *A New Global Partnership: Eradicate Poverty and Transform Economies through Sustainable Development: The Report of the High-Level Panel of Eminent Persons on the Post-2015 Development Agenda*, New York: United Nations, www.un.org/sg/management/pdf/HLP_P2015_Report.pdf

United Nations Environment Programme (2012a) 'Proposal to Host the Climate Technology Centre', Prepared for the United Nations Framework Convention on Climate Change Executive Secretary, 16 March, www.unfccc.int/files/cooperation_and_support/technology/application/pdf/main_proposal_unep.pdf

United Nations Environment Programme (2012b) 'Doha Climate Conference Opens Gateway to Greater Ambition and Action on Climate Change', Press Release, 8 December, www.unep.org/Documents.Multilingual/Default.asp?DocumentID=2700&ArticleID=9353&l=en&t=long

United Nations Framework Convention on Climate Change, 'Selection of the Host of the UNFCCC Climate Technology Centre', www.unfccc.int/cooperation_and_support/technology/items/6602.php

United Nations Global Compact (2013) 'Architects of a Better World', United Nations Global Compact Leaders Summit 2013, New York, United States, 2013, www.leaderssummit2013.org/side-events

United States Department of Justice (2013) 'Sinovel Corporation and Three Individuals Charged in Wisconsin with Theft of AMSC Trade Secrets: Theft of Trade Secrets Allegedly Cheated AMSC of More than $800 million', Press Release, 27 June, www.justice.gov/opa/pr/2013/June/13-crm-730.html

United States Trade Representative, (2013) *Special 301 Report*, May 2013 www.ustr.gov/sites/default/files/05012013%202013%20Special%20301%20Report.pdf

Venezuela (2012) 'Submission by the Bolivarian Republic of Venezuela on the Draft Decision Text on Technology Transfer and Intellectual Property Rights', United Nations Framework Convention on Climate Change, 4 September, www.unfccc.int/files/bodies/application/pdf/venezuela_tt_ipr_040912.pdf

Vidal, John (2012) 'Will Philippines Negotiator's Tears Change Our Course on Climate Change?', *The Guardian*, 6 December, www.theguardian.com/global-development/poverty-matters/2012/dec/06/philippines-delegator-tears-climate-change

Von der Ropp, Anja (2012) 'WIPO GREEN: Facilitating Dissemination of Green Technology', *WIPO Magazine*, June, www.wipo.int/wipo_magazine/en/2012/03/article_0006.html

Weston, Burns and Bollier, David (2013) *Green Governance: Ecological Survival, Human Rights, and the Law of the Commons*, Cambridge: Cambridge University Press.

WIPO GREEN, www3.wipo.int/wipogreen/en/about/

Wold, Chris, Gaines, Sanford Gaines and Block, Greg (2011) *Trade and the Environment: Law and Policy*, Second Edition, Durham (NC): Carolina Academic Press.

World Indigenous Network, www.worldindigenousnetwork.net/

World Intellectual Property Organization (2013) 'WIPO GREEN: New Online Marketplace Seeks Environmentally Sustainable Solutions for Climate Change', Geneva, 28 November, www.wipo.int/pressroom/en/articles/2013/article_0025.html

World Trade Organization (2013) 'Responding to Least Developed Countries' Special Needs with Regard to Intellectual Property', 21 August, www.wto.org/english/tratop_e/trips_e/ldc_e.htm

WWF (2012) 'Rio+20 Negotiating Text is Colossal Failure of Leadership and Vision', Press Release, 19 June, wwf.panda.org/wwf_news/?205290

Zahar, Alexander, Peel, Jacqueline and Godden, Lee (2013) *Australian Climate Law in Global Context*, Cambridge: Cambridge University Press.

Zittrain, Jonathan (2010) 'Speech at the Launch of the GreenXChange', Hub Pavilion Davos, 30 January, www.youtube.com/watch?v=zWrP6qBNHVw

Litigation

Monsanto Technology LLC v. The Controller of Patents and Designs (2013) http://www.ipab.tn.nic.in/146-2013.htm

United States Department of Justice v. Sinovel and others (2013) http://www.justice.gov/opa/pr/2013/June/13-crm-730.html

International Treaties

Cancún Agreements 2010 *Outcome of the Work of the Ad Hoc Working Group on Long-Term Cooperative*

Action Under the Convention, CP.16, www.unfccc.int/files/meetings/cop_16/application/pdf/cop16_lca.pdf and *Outcome of the Work of the Ad Hoc Working Group on Further Commitments for Annex I Parties under the Kyoto Protocol at its Fifteenth Session, -/CMP.6* www.unfccc.int/files/meetings/cop_16/application/pdf/cop16_kp.pdf

Copenhagen Accord 2009, UN Doc. FCCC/KP/CMP/2009/L.9 (December 18, 2009).

Declaration on Climate Justice 2013, www.mrfcj.org/media/pdf/Declaration-on-Climate-Justice.pdf

Doha Climate Gateway 2012, COP. 18/CM 18, www.unfccc.int/key_steps/doha_climate_gateway/items/7389.php

Doha Declaration on the TRIPS Agreement and Public Health: Adopted on 14 November 2001, WTO Doc WT/MIN(01)/DEC/2 (2001) ('the *Doha Declaration* 2001').

Durban Decisions 2011, CP.17, www.unfccc.int/meetings/durban_nov_2011/meeting/6245/php/view/decisions.php

Kyoto Protocol to the United Nations Framework Convention on Climate Change 1997, Opened for signature 16 March 1998, 2303 UNTS 148 (entered into force 16 February 2005) ('*Kyoto Protocol*').

Marrakesh Agreement Establishing the World Trade Organization, opened for signature 15 April 1994, 1867 UNTS 3 (entered into force 1 January 1995) annex 1C (*'Agreement on Trade-Related Aspects of Intellectual Property Rights' – TRIPS Agreement 1994*).

Patent Co-operation Treaty 1970, opened for signature 19 June 1970, 1160 UNTS 231 (signed and entered into force on 24 January 1978).

United Nations Framework Convention on Climate Change 1992, Opened for signature 9 May 1992, 1771 UNTS 107 (entered into force 21 March 1994).

Warsaw Opportunity 2013, CP. 19, www.unfccc.int/meetings/warsaw_nov_2013/meeting/7649.php

Author Index

Subject Index